"Michael J. Green's magisterial stuthe deep and long-standing ties bet\
the complex interplay between our
values, a dynamic which has shaped ....u u uan centuries. It
is an indispensable point of reference for students and policy makers seeking
to understand a critical region where history casts a long shadow, notwithstanding the extraordinary changes of recent years."
—James Steinberg, Syracuse University and
former deputy secretary of state

"With impeccable research and lucid prose, Michael J. Green provides a first-rate
account of the deep historical roots of American grand strategy toward Asia. It is
essential for understanding American policy toward a crucial region."
—Joseph S. Nye Jr., Distinguished Service Professor at
Harvard University and author of *Is the American Century Over?*

"Already a renowned Japan expert, Green combines his regional knowledge
with a capacious strategic mind and historical sensibility. This is one of the most
impressive books I have ever read. It is consistently original, providing on every
page fresh insights immersed in a compelling narrative arc, and it is destined to
be a lodestar among scholarship on history, strategy, and statecraft."
—William Inboden, chair of the Clements Center for
National Security at the University of Texas at Austin

"With rich historical records and insightful analysis, this is a fascinating,
most useful reference for students and scholars of U.S.-Asia relations and
American foreign policy."   —*Choice*

"*By More Than Providence* provides the greatest value in illustrating how the
draw of the Asia-Pacific has been an enduring influence in the United States for
nearly two and a half centuries."   —Matthew T. Brundage,
Journal of American–East Asian Relations

"Green brings scholarly and policymaking credentials to this *tour
d'horizon*."   —*Imperial & Global Forum*

"A brilliant and highly readable history of America's evolving grand strategy toward Asia and the Pacific since 1783." —*Asian Review of Books*

"*By More Than Providence* is a gold mine of richly documented historical detail, informed by international relations theory and enlivened by the hands-on policymaker's nose for bureaucratic turf battles, clashing personalities, and Washington intrigue. . . . The Asia-Pacific has long loomed large in American strategic thinking and today its centrality is unparalleled. *By More Than Providence* provides a sweep, power, and coherence that anchors that centrality historically." —T.J. Pempel, *Journal of East Asian Studies*

NANCY BERNKOPF TUCKER
and WARREN I. COHEN
Books on American-East Asian Relations

Edited by
Thomas J. Christensen
Mark Philip Bradley
Rosemary Foote

Nancy Bernkopf Tucker was a historian of American diplomacy whose work focused on American–East Asian relations. She published seven books, including the prize-winning *Uncertain Friendships: Taiwan, Hong Kong, and the United States, 1945–1992*. Her articles and essays appeared in countless journals and anthologies, including the *American Historical Review, Diplomatic History, Foreign Affairs*, and the *Journal of American History*. In addition to teaching at Colgate and Georgetown (where she was the first woman to be awarded tenure in the School of Foreign Service), she served on the China desk of the Department of State and in the American embassy in Beijing. When the Office of the Director of National Intelligence was created, she was chosen to serve as the first Assistant Deputy Director of National Intelligence for Analytic Integrity and Standards and Ombudsman, and she was awarded the National Intelligence Medal of Achievement in 2007. To honor her, in 2012 the Woodrow Wilson International Center for Scholars established an annual Nancy Bernkopf Tucker Memorial Lecture on U.S.–East Asian Relations.

Warren I. Cohen is University Distinguished Professor Emeritus at Michigan State University and the University of Maryland, Baltimore County, and a senior scholar in the Asia Program of the Woodrow Wilson Center. He has written thirteen books and edited seven others. He served as a line officer in the U.S. Pacific Fleet, editor of *Diplomatic History*, president of the Society for Historians of American Foreign Relations, and chairman of the Department of State Advisory Committee on Historical Diplomatic Documentation. In addition to scholarly publications, he has written for the *Atlantic*, the *Baltimore Sun*, the *Christian Science Monitor, Dissent, Foreign Affairs*, the *International Herald Tribune*, the *Los Angeles Times, The Nation*, the *New York Times*, the *Times Literary Supplement*, and the *Washington Post*. He has also been a consultant on Chinese affairs to various government organizations.

MICHAEL J. GREEN

BY MORE THAN PROVIDENCE

Grand Strategy and American Power

in the Asia Pacific Since 1783

COLUMBIA UNIVERSITY PRESS   *New York*

Columbia University Press
Publishers Since 1893
New York   Chichester, West Sussex
cup.columbia.edu

Copyright © 2017 Columbia University Press
Paperback edition, 2019
All rights reserved

Library of Congress Cataloging-in-Publication Data

Names: Green, Michael J., author.
Title: By more than providence : grand strategy and American power in the
Asia Pacific since 1783 / Michael J. Green.
Description: New York : Columbia University Press, [2017] |
Includes bibliographical references and index.
Identifiers: LCCN 2016039620 | ISBN 9780231180429 (cloth) |
ISBN 978-0-231-18043-6 (pbk.) | ISBN 9780231542722 (e-book) Subjects:
LCSH: United States—Foreign relations—Pacific Area. |
Pacific Area— Foreign relations—United States.
Classification: LCC DU30 .G73 2017 | DDC 327.7305—dc23
LC record available at https://lccn.loc.gov/2016039620

Cover Image: Raymond Massey, *The Empress of China Arriving at Whampoa*

For the problem of Asia is a world problem, which has come upon the world in an age when, through the rapidity of communication, it is wide awake and sensible as never before, and by electrical touch, to every stirring in its members, and to the tendency thereof . . .

—Alfred Thayer Mahan, "The Problem of Asia: Its Effect on International Politics," *Harpers New Monthly Magazine*, March 1900.

CONTENTS

Note on Korean, Chinese, and Japanese Terms   xiii
Acknowledgments   xv

Introduction   1

PART ONE
THE RISE OF THE UNITED STATES

1. "A Theatre for the Exercise of the Most Ambitious Intellect":
Seeds of Strategy, 1784–1860   19

2. "How Sublime the Pacific Part Assigned to Us":
Precursors to Expansion, 1861–1898   56

3. "I Wish to See the United States the Dominant Power
on the Shores of the Pacific":
Grand Strategy in the Era of Theodore Roosevelt   78

PART TWO
THE RISE OF JAPAN

4. "Leave the Door Open, Rehabilitate China, and Satisfy Japan":
Defining the Open Door, 1909–1927   115

5. "Between Non-resistance and Coercion":
The Open Door Closes, 1928–1941   151

6. "We Have Got to Dominate the Pacific":
Grand Strategy and the War Against Japan   188

PART THREE
THE RISE OF THE SOVIETS

7. "The Overall Effect Is to Enlarge Our Strategic Frontier":
Defining Containment in the Pacific, 1945–1960   245

8. "Anyone Who Isn't Confused Really Doesn't
Understand the Situation":
Asia Strategy and Escalation in Vietnam, 1961–1968   297

9. "An Even Balance":
Nixon and Kissinger's Redefinition of Containment in Asia,
1969–1975   323

10. "The President Cannot Make Any Weak Moves":
Jimmy Carter and the Return of the China Card, 1977–1980   363

11. "To Contain and Over Time Reverse":
Ronald Reagan, 1980–1989   387

PART FOUR
THE RISE OF CHINA

12. "The Key to Our Security and Our Prosperity Lies
in the Vitality of Those Relationships":
George H. W. Bush and the Unipolar Moment, 1989–1992   429

13. "Engage and Balance":
Bill Clinton and the Unexpected Return of Great-Power Politics   453

14. "A Balance of Power That Favors Freedom":
Strategic Surprise and the Asia Policy of George W. Bush   482

15. "The Pivot":
Barack Obama and the Struggle to Rebalance to Asia   518

Conclusion:
The Historical Case for Asia Strategy   541

Notes   *549*
Index   *689*

NOTE ON KOREAN, CHINESE, AND JAPANESE TERMS

For all Korean, Chinese, and Japanese personal names, in the text I generally follow the custom of putting the family name first. People such as Syngman Rhee and others whose names have traditionally appeared in English with their family name last are exceptions. In the notes, names appear in the form in which they appeared in the original publication.

The accepted systems of spelling for Asian-language names in English have undergone a number of changes over the years. With that in mind, I have chosen to abide by the following guidelines.

I use the Hepburn system for Japanese names and terms.

I use the McCune-Reischauer system for the romanization of Korean names and terms from before 1945, but without diacritical marks. I show contemporary spellings of McCune-Reischauer romanizations in parentheses at the first mention. I spell contemporary Korean names as they are commonly used in South Korea and North Korea.

For the romanization of Chinese, I generally use the pinyin system, which was created after the establishment of the People's Republic of China in 1949. Pinyin displaced the Wade-Giles system, though Wade-Giles is still in use in Taiwan. For this reason, I give the Pinyin spelling in parentheses at the first mention of a term that was originally romanized using the Wade-Giles system. Moreover, I use Wade-Giles for terms like Kuomintang, as they are written in Taiwan, and for phrases in use before 1945, such as the Treaty of Wanghia (now Wangxia). There are some exceptions, such as Canton, that I spell in the form in which they are most familiar.

ACKNOWLEDGMENTS

A fter five years on the National Security Council (NSC) staff, I returned to academia in 2006, intending to teach courses that covered the theory, history, and practice of American statecraft toward Asia. For use as textbooks, I found many volumes on contemporary international relations in Asia and excellent histories of U.S. bilateral relationships. To my surprise, however, I could not find a comprehensive historical study of American statecraft toward Asia as a whole that was more recent than Tyler Dennett's 1922 *Americans in Eastern Asia*.

On reflection, it occurred to me that this same gap in knowledge existed for policymakers. When asked at the NSC to produce strategic planning documents on Asia, I always tried to understand why we define U.S. interests in the region the way we do and also to account for our past successes and failures. As special assistant to the president and senior director for Asia, I could call up detailed briefings on issues ranging from leadership dynamics in Pakistan to North Korea's inventory of ballistic missiles. However, the intelligence community does not analyze the roots of American strategy or policy. The official historians at the State Department or the Joint Chiefs of Staff are second to none as archivists of American diplomatic and military practice, but they too were not responsible for tracing the effects of policy ideas over time. Usually, I had to reconstruct the roots of our strategy myself by calling on former senior directors from previous administrations or by sending my long-suffering staff to work with the little-known but invaluable NSC library. The best work we did for the president and the principals was informed by this historical knowledge.

With that as background, I decided after a few years of separation from government that I would write my own history of American strategic thought on Asia. What I quickly realized, however, was that not all ideas about strategy or policy are created equal. I could compare different schools of thought or ideologies, but in order to reconstruct the evolution of actual American strategy over time, I would also have to account for what happened to foreign policy concepts on the unforgiving front lines of diplomacy and war. I also recognized that this was not a narrative that should begin in 1945, as most do, but rather in the cradle of the republic and the first American encounters with the vast Pacific Ocean and the Far East. This would be a far more daunting task, but one that I found incredibly alluring.

One of the first people I turned to for advice on the project was my Georgetown University colleague Nancy Bernkopf Tucker, an inspiring historian who appreciated the importance of policymakers' perspectives on events. Nancy was characteristically enthusiastic and supportive from that moment until she was lost to us in late 2012. I could not be more proud to have this volume be the first in the new series of Nancy Bernkopf Tucker and Warren I. Cohen Books on American–East Asian Relations that Columbia University Press established in her memory.

Many other scholars, colleagues, and students also contributed to this effort. Gabe Scheinmann was my principal research assistant for the first part of the book and was backed by Austin Dean, Kiyoto Tsuji, and Andrew Scott. For the second half of the book, Samuel Gerstle took the lead, with help from Yingxian Long and Will Colson. Gabe and Sam were incredible: prodding, questioning, and challenging me (in the most respectful way) as I pulled together the strands of this story. Other students at Georgetown also provided constant insights as they re-created the thinking of figures like John Quincy Adams or John Foster Dulles in classroom exercises and research papers.

I also benefited enormously from senior scholars who generously read all or most of the manuscript and gave detailed suggestions, particularly Melvin Leffler, William Inboden, Chen Jian, and Andrew Shearer. Many other colleagues participated in book conferences and roundtable discussions based on first drafts of the chapters, notably:

- A Center for Strategic and International Studies (CSIS) roundtable in 2010 covering chapter 1, with lead commentator Thomas Wright and invaluable input from Commodore Richard Wright, Richard Bush, Henry Nau, and Warren Cohen, among others.
- The 2011 Lone Star National Security Forum at the University of Texas–Austin, covering chapters 2 and 3, which was organized by Eugene Gholtz, with Chen Jian as the fair but tough-minded reader of my draft.
- A 2011 Foreign Policy Research Institute dinner presentation on the overall themes of the book, which prompted encouragement from Walter MacDougall, perhaps my favorite American diplomatic historian.
- A 2012 Mortara Center Book Lab at Georgetown University, covering chapters 4 through 6, organized by Kathleen McNamara, with David Painter, Edward Luttwak, John Keuhn, Paul Heer, Victor Cha, and Kenneth Pollack as readers.
- A 2015 presentation at the CSIS Brzezinski Institute, organized by John Hamre, with fascinating commentary by Zbigniew Brzezinski.
- A 2015 presentation at the Australian National University, organized by Michael Wesley, Peter Dean, and Brendan Taylor.
- A 2015 presentation at the Council on Foreign Relations, organized by Robert Blackwill and Kurt Campbell.

Colleagues who offered additional ideas on original sources from their own research included Paul S. Giarra (on the 1980s maritime strategy), Charles Adel (on John Quincy Adams), David Adesnik (on Ronald Reagan's democracy policy), Taylor Fravel (on Chinese assessments of U.S. Asia strategy), and Ashley Tellis (on the origins of U.S. India policy). I am also indebted to Dr. Evelyn Cherpak and Dr. John B. Hattendorf at the Naval War College Historical Collection, Kelly Barton at the Ronald Reagan Library, and the curators of the Marshall Family Papers at the Filson Historical Society in Louisville, Kentucky. I interviewed many participants in the making of American policy toward Asia, including those who worked alongside me in the Pentagon and White House, just to make sure I captured decision-making as accurately as possible, even for events where I was present. Some of these interviews were with the most senior policymakers—like George Shultz, Zbigniew Brzezinski, Stephen Hadley, and Harold Brown—whereas others were with more junior action officers. Henry Kissinger tolerated my frequent requests to talk about the roots of American

Asia strategy on the margins of CSIS board meetings. I am honored by the trust they all showed in me and by their interest in the subject. At a time in American politics when patriots like these are denigrated as part of the Washington establishment, I can only say that the country has been fortunate indeed to have such stewards in so many turbulent times.

Writing a book like this took time and resources. John Hamre, my mentor and boss at CSIS, could not have been more supportive, and the deans and faculty chairs at Georgetown were equally understanding and encouraging. This work was supported by an Academy of Korean Studies (Korean Studies Promotion Service) grant funded by the Korean government (Ministry of Education) (AKS-2010-DZZ-2102), which allowed me to buy back a semester and to hire research assistants. Victor Cha helped me to secure that grant and was a most collegial wingman as he wrote his own first-rate history on the origins of U.S. alliances in Asia. I also benefited from a prompt but careful security review of relevant portions of the manuscript by the NSC Records Office.

Anne Routon, my three-time editor at Columbia University Press, was—as always—the model of serene learnedness. Profound thanks are due also to Tom Christensen and the other distinguished editors of this new series on American relations with East Asia.

Finally, I have to thank the home team. We lost my Mom and Dad as I wrote this manuscript, but they are forever in our hearts for their patriotism, service to others, and loving impact on us all. My son, Xander, and daughter, Virginia, were in diapers when I started this book. In the interim, they have gone from asking for Elmo to quizzing me about the Battle of Midway and the causes of the Cold War. I could not have two more rambunctious and delightful little historians. As I was busy writing about American strategies toward Asia in bygone eras, my wife, Eileen, was dedicating her professional life to helping the women and girls of Asia today. She constantly humbles me with her compassion and excites me about the region we have both embraced. Asia, wrote one of our earliest commissioners to China, "is a theater for the exercise of the most ambitious intellect." I hope this book kindles just such ambitions in the generation that will write the next chapters of American statecraft.

Bethesda, Maryland/ January 27, 2016.

INTRODUCTION

As China reasserts its power, and as smaller states in Asia bristle and hedge, Americans are engaging in a lively debate about America's grand strategy toward Asia. Some evoke containment of the Soviet Union or the logic of Carl von Clausewitz to propose new competitive strategies toward Beijing.[1] Others draw on the analogies of the First World War or the "Thucydidean trap" of the Peloponnesian Wars to argue for greater accommodation of a rising China.[2] These European models of strategy offer important insights, but entirely missing from the debate is the more important consideration of America's *own* history of statecraft toward Asia and the Pacific. How did the United States become a Pacific power? What are the roots of our strategy today? And why do we have a stake in Asia's future? These are the questions that must be answered if we are to construct an enduring *American* grand strategy for the Asian Century and the rise of China.

For over two centuries, Americans have been tied to the Pacific by commerce, faith, geography, and self-defense. Over that time, Americans have overcome bids for regional hegemony in Asia from the European powers, imperial Japan, and Soviet communism. Modern America's pre-eminence in the Pacific was no accidental by-product of victory in the

Second World War, as many cursory histories suggest. It has intellectual roots going back to the handful of New Englanders who first carried Bibles, ginseng, and visions of Pacific empire to the Far East.

Yet, surprisingly, there has not been a comprehensive treatment of American statecraft toward Asia as a region since Tyler Dennett's 1922 study *Americans in Eastern Asia*.[3] To be sure, there have been compelling histories of U.S. bilateral relations with China, Japan, and India.[4] There have also been revisionist histories that have attempted to recast American diplomacy in the region around the themes of racism and economic imperialism or to place American encounters with Asia in a larger cultural context.[5] However, the roots of modern American strategic thought on the Pacific have remained largely untouched for generations.[6] In a way, this gap in strategic history is understandable. Modern historians tend to eschew human agency, which is strongly implied in any study of strategic intent. Indeed, there has long been skepticism about the ability of the United States to formulate or implement a grand strategy of any kind.

A grand strategy, after all, requires the deliberate assessment of threats and opportunities, and the measured application of ways and means to achieve national objectives in reference to those threats and opportunities. In contrast to military strategy, grand strategy must incorporate diplomatic, informational, military, and economic tools in a comprehensive approach in times of both peace and war. Then, of course, the strategy has to be implemented. Effective grand strategy requires discipline. There must be clear prioritization of strategic objectives, long-term goals must be distinguished from short-term goals, and vital interests must be differentiated from secondary interests.[7] The distribution of power must be well understood, and flexibility must be preserved as the strategy encounters unforeseen challenges.[8] National will and resources must be harnessed to a single purpose.

These are heavy demands on a democratic society. As Richard Betts points out, "The logic of strategy depends on clarity of preferences, explicitness of calculation, and consistency of choice. Democratic competition and consensus building work against all of these."[9]

The American constitutional system of government creates enormous strengths for the United States in the international system: legitimizing government at home and abroad; regenerating national dynamism; attracting foreign talent and admiration; and binding other powers through the reassuring transparency and accessibility of our political process. But the Founders created a system that was designed to prevent precisely the kind of centralization of decision-making imagined by Thucydides, Clausewitz, and other classical strategic thinkers. The word "strategy" itself is derived from the Greek *strategos*—meaning "from the commander." Yet American presidents do not always care for foreign policy strategies, and when they do, their visions may clash with those of career bureaucracies "focused on their own interests, habits, and urges,"[10] secretaries of state who are skeptical of abstract theories,[11] or a Congress jealous of its own prerogatives to approve treaties and declare war.[12] Presidents' racial or social prejudices, susceptibility to "groupthink," or just plain incompetence can also distort the formulation and implementation of grand strategies.[13]

It is therefore no surprise that history is replete with observations about the futility of discovering or designing an American way of strategy. In *Democracy in America*, Alexis de Tocqueville observed: "A democracy can only with great difficulty regulate the details of an important undertaking, persevere in a fixed design, and work out its execution in spite of serious obstacles. It cannot combine its measures with secrecy or await their consequences with patience."[14]

Alfred Thayer Mahan also lamented America's "policy of isolation"[15] at the end of the nineteenth century, and in 1943 Walter Lippmann criticized his fellow Americans' "idealistic objections" to serious strategic thinking in his own time.[16] In the 1950s, Robert Osgood complained of the historic American obsession with the "glimpse of Utopia," and after the Vietnam War, Henry Kissinger warned that foreign policy intellectuals had "retreated from the field of strategy."[17] Many contemporary foreign policy scholars have echoed Les Gelb's admonition in *Power Rules* (2009) that "there is nothing more central to the exercise of power than a good strategy, and the United States does not now have one."[18]

All of this leads diplomatic historian Walter McDougall to ask whether "grand strategy can be said to move a nation even when that nation's fluctuating roster of mostly incompetent leaders are unsure as to why they do anything." His answer is yes: "The historical record would seem to indicate, first, that the United States can and has embraced grand strategies (even during the eras once scorned as isolationist), second, that strategies based on realist premises have been mostly fruitful, and third, that strategies based on idealist premises have been mostly abortive."[19]

"All countries have grand strategies, whether they know it or not," explains Edward Luttwak in *The Grand Strategy of the Byzantine Empire*. He adds: "That is inevitable because grand strategy is simply the level at which knowledge and persuasion, or in modern terms intelligence and diplomacy, interact with military strength to determine outcomes in a world of other states with their own 'grand strategies.'"[20] Or as Leon Trotsky is sometimes reputed to have said, "You may not be interested in strategy, but strategy is interested in *you*."

American grand strategy has always flowed organically from the republic's values and geographic circumstances. It may at times reside in the minds of a close-knit group of elites, such as those around John Quincy Adams, Theodore Roosevelt, or Richard Nixon, but never be clearly articulated as such. It may, in other periods, involve "linking and bringing together a series of processes and decisions spanning years," as Paul Bracken argues, and not "for someone in Washington to posit a grand strategy and then recruit experts to execute it."[21] Ultimately, as Betts concedes, American strategy may be a "metaprocess that links ends and means effectively but not efficiently."[22]

The metaprocess Betts describes becomes clearer in a historical survey that traces concepts chronologically—"thinking in time" rather than focusing on individual case studies that inevitably bring human foibles to the fore.[23] A history of any nation's grand strategy must also be more than just an intellectual history. Statecraft, war, and trade are where the wheat and chaff of strategic debates are sorted out over time. Concepts are contested and tested, and they submerge and reemerge. Over time, some principles become more enduring than others do. These come to define a nation's strategic culture.

Over the course of two hundred years, the United States has in fact developed a distinctive strategic approach toward Asia and the Pacific. There have been numerous instances of hypocrisy, inconsistency, and insufficient harnessing of national will and means. There have been strategic miscalculations—particularly before Pearl Harbor, on the Yalu River, and in Vietnam. In the aggregate, however, the United States has emerged as the preeminent power in the Pacific not by providence alone but through the effective (if not always efficient) application of military, diplomatic, economic, and ideational tools of national power to the problems of Asia.

Of course, the terms of American engagement with Asia have been transformed with the technological revolutions that replaced sail with steam, steam with internal combustion, and then internal combustion with jets, ballistic missiles, and eventually cyberspace. The political, social, and economic revolutions of the past two centuries, particularly nationalism, communism, and globalization, have also created an American relationship with Asia and the Pacific that would have been unrecognizable to the early architects of American engagement with the region.

Yet Asia also has presented a consistent set of geostrategic challenges that have shaped an American way of strategizing toward the region. Asia has always been a region defined by hierarchy; by the waxing and waning of the Sinocentric order; by a geography that surrounds China with smaller peripheral states and offshore island chains and separates the Asian continent from the West Coast of the United States with a vast ocean spanning 7,000 miles; where sources of political legitimacy have constantly been contested as empires have collapsed and arisen; and where economic development has always been diverse and uneven. As military historian Williamson Murray notes, these are the kinds of factors that become the building blocks of a nation's strategic culture: "Geography helps determine whether a given polity will find itself relatively free from threat or surrounded by potential adversaries. Historical experience creates preconceptions about the nature of war and politics and may generate irresistible strategic imperatives. And ideology and culture shape the course of decision-makers and their societies in both conscious and unconscious ways."[24]

If there is one central theme in American strategic culture as it has applied to the Far East over time, it is that the United States will not tolerate any other power establishing exclusive hegemonic control over Asia or the Pacific. Put another way, for over two centuries, the national interest of the United States has been identified by key leaders as ensuring that the Pacific Ocean remains a conduit for American ideas and goods to flow westward, and not for threats to flow eastward toward the homeland.

Early examples of this strategic impulse include Thomas Jefferson's and then John Quincy Adams's assertion of American primacy in the Pacific Northwest as America's gateway to the Pacific; President John Tyler's subsequent extension of the Monroe Doctrine to include Hawaii; and William McKinley's decisions to annex Hawaii and to remain in the Philippines after European powers sought to exploit the vacuum left by Spain's defeat. In more recent history, challenges to U.S. preeminence in the region have prompted external balancing, using the China card to check Soviet expansion, or the Japan and India cards to maintain a favorable strategic equilibrium vis-à-vis China's rise. When the United States has been attacked, as John Lewis Gaddis argues in *Surprise, Security, and the American Experience* (2003), the U.S. response has been to seek safety by "expanding and not contracting its sphere of responsibilities."[25] This is what happened after Pearl Harbor and after the North Korean attack on South Korea in 1950. Scholars have sometimes cast these various periods of expansion as either economic imperialism or offensive realism—and to be sure there were economic interests at stake and chauvinism at play—but the organizing strategic concepts in each case ultimately reflected *defensive* realism, which is to say that they were first and foremost responses to threats to American access and security in the region.[26]

Yet, if the United States has repeatedly embraced strategies to block hegemons and ensure access across the Pacific, it has also struggled to identify the ways and means of those strategies. The enduring geographic challenges of the region and the idiosyncrasies of American political ideology have created five tensions in the American strategic approach toward Asia that reappear with striking predictability.

Europe Versus Asia. America's strategy toward Asia derives from global priorities, and for most of American history, it was Europe rather than Asia that remained the region of greatest importance to the nation's elite. After independence, European powers threatened to isolate and contain the new republic on the eastern seaboard, while the Royal Navy dominated the Atlantic. Then, in the first half of the twentieth century, American leaders came to see the preservation of British power in Europe as the sine qua non for an open liberal order as America rose to global prominence. That pattern repeated during the Cold War, when the Fulda Gap became the central front against Soviet expansion and drew the greatest diplomatic and military resources, even as most of the actual fighting against Communist forces took place in the Far East.

None of this is to say, however, that the American people are more isolationist toward Asia than toward other regions of the world. In fact, the opposite is more often true: polls in 1941 showed that Americans were willing to risk war with Japan but not Germany, and more recent polls show that Americans are far more willing to fight to defend Japan or South Korea than they are to intervene in Syria or go back into Iraq or Afghanistan.[27] From the first encounter with Chinese merchants in Canton in 1784, Americans developed a pride of place in the Far East that they would never have in the Old Country, despite their stronger hereditary ties across the Atlantic. After all, it was Europe, not the Pacific or the Caribbean, that was the focus of George Washington's famous admonition to "avoid foreign entanglements." For Americans, the Pacific has been the theater of future aspirations; as Japan scholar Edwin O. Reischauer wrote in 1968, "We have a great stake in the future of Asia—a far greater stake than the Asia of today."[28] The same might have been said a century earlier by William Henry Seward. When American leaders have retained a disciplined focus on those long-term interests, Asia strategy has flowed logically from global strategy. When Asia strategy has been an afterthought to exigencies in Europe or the Middle East, American policy in the region has proven deeply flawed.

Continental Versus Maritime/China Versus Japan. At the turn of the nineteenth century, Englishman Sir Halford Mackinder argued that the nation that controlled the Eurasian heartland would achieve eventual hegemony in the international system, whereas American strategist Alfred Thayer Mahan posited that security and hegemony depended on control of the seas.[29] As a maritime power in the Pacific, it has always been natural for the United States to anchor its engagement of the region on Japan, as the earliest U.S. naval officers active in the region argued back to Washington. Yet, historically, Asian regional order has been centered on China and the continent. How then does a maritime power shape strategic events on the continent from offshore? As Athens found in confronting Sparta, and the United States learned in Vietnam, challenging continental powers on their own turf from offshore can be disastrous.[30] On the other hand, pursuit of a geostrategic condominium with continental China risks undercutting the offshore island bastion offered by Japan, since China would seek to subvert Japan and the island chain under its historic hegemony.

This fundamental tension between the Mackinder and Mahan views of geography has been exacerbated in American statecraft by the tendency of certain leaders to find greater affinity with either Japan or China. Commodore Matthew Perry, Mahan, and Theodore Roosevelt all saw Japan as the modernizing example that would help tame the quasi-medieval Slavs and Chinese on the continent. Postwar veterans of the maritime services such as George Shultz and Richard Armitage also looked to Japan as the geographic and ideational anchor for America in Asia. In contrast, continentalists such as Humphrey Marshall (more on him later), the American commissioner to China in the 1850s, or Henry Kissinger and Zbigniew Brzezinski in the modern era, have tended to see China as a more natural partner for realizing a favorable balance of power in the Mackinder tradition. China has also evoked great romance for Americans, including Franklin Delano Roosevelt, whose own family was in the China trade for over a century, like many American elites in the Northeast. From the earliest decades of American engagement across the Pacific, the swings between Japan and China have vexed attempts to execute a consistent American strategy.

Defining the Forward Defense Line. Closely related to the continental/maritime tension and the pressures of Eurocentrism has been the question of where to draw the American defensive line against potential hegemonic aspirants in Asia. In the 1820s, the United States drew that line in the Pacific Northwest, and in the 1840s, at Hawaii, though the U.S. Navy was in no position to enforce either defense line at the time. By the middle of the nineteenth century, the goal became establishment of coaling stations running laterally across the Pacific to the China coast. After the United States finally achieved that goal with the annexation of Hawaii, the Philippines, and Guam at the turn of the twentieth century, Theodore Roosevelt discovered a new vulnerability, since Japan would now be in a position to attack U.S. forces in the Philippines from home bases nearby as the U.S. Navy was forced to rush across the vast Pacific to their defense. From 1907 to 1941, U.S. naval strategists struggled with this problem as they drafted and redrafted War Plan Orange, ultimately defeating Japan in a costly island-hopping campaign across the Central and Southwest Pacific.

After the war, the Truman administration drew the American defensive line very deliberately between the offshore island chain and the continent, including Japan but excluding South Korea—which the North then promptly attacked. In response, the United States moved the defensive line to the demilitarized zone (DMZ) on the Korean Peninsula while creeping forward onto continental Southeast Asia until the costs of escalation in Vietnam prompted Nixon in 1969 to announce a new "Guam Doctrine," which caused the U.S. line to recede again. When the U.S. offshore island position was threatened by a massive Soviet military buildup in the Far East a decade later, Ronald Reagan responded with an aggressive maritime strategy that pushed the Soviet fleet back into the Sea of Okhotsk from bases in Japan. Today, the American forward presence in the Western Pacific is again being challenged by China's military buildup and coercive claims to territories within the First Island Chain—and American strategists are debating whether the United States should be risking war over "rocks" in the South China Sea, as one administration official put it in 2012.

Over the course of this history, Americans have learned that the Pacific Ocean does not provide sanctuary against threats emanating from the Eurasian heartland if the United States itself is not holding the line at the Western Pacific. But defining the location of the forward defense line always entails costs and risks that each president has calculated differently—and at times unadvisedly.

Self-Determination Versus Universal Values. It is common for proponents of grand strategy who are steeped in the neorealist traditions of international relations theory to dismiss ideational dimensions of foreign policy as a distraction from vital interests.[31] The fact is, however, that promotion of democratic norms has always been a central element in American foreign policy strategy, not simply because of egoism or idealism but because of the clear strategic advantages of maintaining a favorable ideational balance of power in which like-minded states reinforce American influence, access, and security. This has been particularly true in Asia, where questions of political legitimacy and national identity were critical determinants of what kind of regional order would replace the Qing (then known as the Ching) empire and then the European and Japanese empires. From the moment Thomas Jefferson cast his gaze toward the Pacific Northwest and argued for the establishment of a like-minded republic to prevent European encroachment, expanding the democratic space has been essential to American strategy across the Pacific.

In practice, however, longer-term support for democratic norms often conflicts with immediate demands for commercial access or national defense. Moreover, there is an inherent tension in two key principles embodied in the American Revolution with respect to democracy: self-determination and universality. At times, American diplomacy in Asia has been premised on self-determination, as American diplomats championed their anti-imperialism and their support for the principle of non-interference in the internal affairs of other states (a staple of American declaratory policy in the region until the Carter administration). At other times, American diplomacy has expressed the universalist vision of Thomas Paine, who foresaw that the American Revolution would bring "harbingers of a new world order, creating forms of governance and commerce that would appeal to peoples everywhere and change the course of human history."[32]

These two visions of how to expand the democratic space have collided throughout the history of American statecraft in Asia. During the

1839–1842 Opium Wars, for example, prominent American statesmen debated whether the national interest lay with China's attempt to resist European imperialism or Britain's attempt to impose universal "Christian" values of governance and commerce on a backward China. In the early years of the Second World War, Franklin Delano Roosevelt so feared Japan's appeal as a champion of anti-imperialism in Asia that he sent proxies across the region to call for an end to European colonialism after the war, to Winston Churchill's great annoyance. During the Cold War, American governments tolerated authoritarianism in Korea, the Philippines, and Taiwan in order to block communist expansion in Asia. Jimmy Carter tried to reverse this policy but quickly retreated in the face of renewed Soviet expansion. Reagan then returned to a policy of supporting authoritarian anticommunist regimes, but he soon became an advocate for democratic transitions in all three countries when it became apparent that poor governance and illegitimacy opened them to even greater communist advances.

The real strategic tension, in other words, is not between "interests" and "idealism" but between the United States' two foundational norms of self-determination and universality. Over time, the democratic space in Asia has expanded dramatically, which is a testament to the importance that leaders from Jefferson to Reagan placed on the issue in American approaches to the Pacific and the powerful example of individual liberty. In the immediacy of great-power competition in Asia, however, consistency has proven difficult—and inconsistency has confused friends and adversaries alike.

Protectionism Versus Free Trade. Since the profitable voyage of the *Empress of China* from New York to Canton (Guangzhou) in 1784, trade has dominated American strategic thought toward Asia. Yet here also one finds an inherent tension in American statecraft. The word "protectionism" today carries strong negative connotations, but for the first 150 years of the Unites States, those in the Northeast most actively promoting trade with Asia were also strong advocates of a high tariff at home to protect native industries against British competition. Americans were initially drawn to Asia not to support universal *free* trade but instead to promote their *right to trade* in a world otherwise dominated by British imperial preferences.[33] Toward the end of the century, American strategists noticed that reciprocal tariff reduction agreements with Hawaii signed in 1875 had bound the islands to the United States economically and strategically. Mahan began to argue that American leadership in the region would increasingly depend on the further reduction of tariffs with other nations so as to bind them to the United States as well—a notion that put him at odds with his friend Theodore Roosevelt, a good Republican and passionate advocate of the tariff.

After the disastrous consequences of the 1930 Smoot-Hawley tariffs and prewar protectionism, Americans constructed a postwar global order that embodied the principle of universal free trade in the agreements at Bretton Woods.[34] There was at that point little tension between the principles of free trade and the right to trade. In contemporary theoretical terms, Americans were able to reinforce the *hegemonic stability* identified by Mahan as other states were drawn to the open U.S. market but simultaneously pursue *relative gains* over competitors in Europe and Japan by opening erstwhile colonies and trading blocks to American companies invigorated by wartime production.[35] By the 1960s, however, Japan had begun to outcompete American textile firms, and voices of protectionism reemerged in the U.S. Congress. The battle lines between protectionism and free trade have been drawn and redrawn in American domestic politics ever since—from textiles to consumer electronics, autos, and aerospace. Protectionists have never regained the upper hand, because successive administrations have repeatedly negotiated new bilateral, regional, and global trade agreements that simultaneously reinforce hegemonic stability and Americans' right to trade. However, when new administrations have failed to make the expansion of trade a central pillar of their strategic approach to Asia, they have invariably lost ground in terms of both economic and security interests in the region.

Over the course of more than two centuries of engaging Asia, American statesmen have struggled to find the right balance between each of these five tensions. American strategy has been most successful when applying *all* the instruments of national power, since these reflect foundational American interests and values: protecting the nation and its citizens against harm, expanding economic access and opportunity, and promoting democratic values. As Reischauer put it succinctly in 1955:

> The military and economic arms of policy are in a sense purely subsidiary to the ideological. Through the military arm we can defend some selected spots, but this does us more harm than good if the people in those areas do not elect to use the time bought by our blood to work toward development of a healthy democracy. Through economic aid

we can give the people of an Asian country a better fighting chance to develop democratic institutions, but our economic aid, if they so decide, could be used with equal effectiveness to lay the foundations of a totalitarian regime. Without the support of the military and economic arms, our ideological efforts might prove entirely ineffective, but without the ideological side the other two become almost meaningless.[36]

Of course, the United States has not consistently applied the military, economic, and ideological arms of policy over the course of history, but from those failings, there are valuable lessons for the present.

Organization of the Book

This book begins by tracing the evolution of American strategy toward Asia and the Pacific at the birth of the republic, when merchants, explorers, and missionaries discovered the core truths of the region and from that early stage began to define how the United States could someday establish a maritime and commercial position of preeminence. The book then explains the growth of those early "seeds of strategy" over four systemic challenges to the preservation of a trans-Pacific order linking Asia to the United States: (1) *the rise of the United States* in the nineteenth century amid growing imperial competition from the European powers and the collapse of Sinocentrism; (2) *the rise of Japan* as European power collapsed, and the United States stood almost alone against a new hegemonic challenger in the region; (3) *the rise of the Soviets* as victory over Japan gave way to a new contest for supremacy; and (4) *the rise of China*, as Sinocentric visions of regional order have returned in a new collision with the rules-based order established by the United States.

Each of these four periods is divided into separate chapters that examine the consolidation of strategic concepts in response to changing distributions of power.[37]

Part 1, The Rise of the United States, begins in chapter 1 ("A Theatre for the Exercise of the Most Ambitious Intellect") with the first engagement with the Far East and the consolidation of the North American continent to the West Coast. Chapter 2 ("How Sublime the Pacific Part Assigned to Us") describes how the United States developed the conceptual, diplomatic, military, and economic tools for expansion into the Pacific in the second half of the nineteenth century. Chapter 3 ("I Wish to See the

United States the Dominant Power on the Shores of the Pacific") unbundles the consolidation of American grand strategy in the Pacific in the era of Theodore Roosevelt.

Part 2, The Rise of Japan, begins in chapter 4 ("Leave the Door Open, Rehabilitate China, and Satisfy Japan") with American efforts to sustain regional stability through the Open Door policy with China, culminating in the multilateral "Washington Naval Treaties" of the 1920s. Chapter 5 ("Between Non-resistance and Coercion") explores the panicked strategic debate that emerged as that same treaty system collapsed in the 1930s. Chapter 6 ("We Have Got to Dominate the Pacific") demonstrates how the lessons of the first half of the twentieth century shaped the grand strategy of the Pacific war and set the stage for the contest for regional supremacy that would follow.

Part 3, The Rise of the Soviets, begins in chapter 7 ("The Overall Effect Is to Enlarge Our Strategic Frontier") as the United States adjusted to the Cold War by establishing a network of bilateral alliances and a forward military presence in the Western Pacific. Chapter 8 ("Anyone Who Isn't Confused Really Doesn't Understand the Situation") explains how that expanded network of alliances and forward presence generally stopped communist expansion but then stumbled in Vietnam. Chapter 9 ("An Even Balance") covers Nixon's effort to restore a favorable strategic equilibrium in the region through opening up to China. Chapter 10 ("The President Cannot Make Any Weak Moves") dissects Carter's effort to reverse Nixon's strategies and then his desperate but consequential return to the China card as the Soviets resumed their expansion in Asia. Chapter 11 ("To Contain and Over Time Reverse") concludes the Cold War strategies by examining how Reagan integrated military, economic, and ideational tools to undercut the pillars of Soviet power in the Far East and prepare the way for victory in the Cold War.

Part 4, The Rise of China, begins with chapter 12 ("The Key to Our Security and Our Prosperity Lies in the Vitality of Those Relationships"), as George H. W. Bush sought to maintain the pillars of American strategic preeminence in the Pacific at a time of uncertainty about the very purpose of American power after the Cold War. Chapter 13 ("Engage and Balance") describes Bill Clinton's exploration of new strategic concepts and his eventual return to an alliance-centered strategy of engaging and balancing a suddenly unpredictable China in Asia. Chapter 14 ("A Balance of Power That Favors Freedom") explains how George W. Bush attempted to solidify and expand that framework while simultaneously contending with the military and diplomatic challenges of the War on Terror. Chapter 15 ("The Pivot") ends the chronology by reviewing the promise and pitfalls of Barack Obama's pledge to make the Asia-Pacific region the centerpiece of American foreign policy going forward.

As a whole, the chapters form a continuous evolution of strategic thought as concepts are tested, recede from national debate, and then re-emerge and recombine in times of peril to form the core of a new strategic consensus. Much of the time, there is drift and confusion, even as the core elements of a new strategic approach are quietly taking root. The five tensions discussed earlier are recurring themes, but at key moments the United States has overcome these tensions to develop and execute an effective strategy in the Pacific. And with the exception of the interwar years and perhaps Vietnam, this is a story of successful outcomes. The book concludes with a brief consideration of how policymakers can apply these lessons to the formulation of a grand strategy going forward.

One final definition is important, though close to impossible to explain: What is Asia? There was no concept of "Asia" before the Europeans created one, only the Chinese empire and those states on the periphery. Even today, the question is difficult to answer. For Chinese strategists, the United States, Australia, and India are considered extraregional powers. In Delhi, there is increasing reference to the Indo-Pacific region, whereas Canberra and Washington refer to their membership in the Asia-Pacific region. In Tokyo, the definition of Asia shifts depending on whether the government in power seeks to expand U.S.-Japan alliance cooperation in the region or empower Japanese diplomacy free of dependence on the United States. No two foreign ministries in Asia structure their regional bureaus exactly the same way. In short, the definition of Asia usually reflects the identity and national interest of the government in question.

And so the geographic scope of Asia in this book will reflect the evolving American definitions of interests and national identity. At the beginning of the United States, Asia was called the East Indies, and the locus of interest was Canton, with the Pacific Northwest the anchor on the American continent. Northeast Asia remained thereafter the fulcrum of American geographic definitions of the region. Even after the United States annexed the Philippines, the strategic focus remained on Japan and China, not Southeast Asia, which was largely under European colonial control (and managed in the European Affairs offices of the State Department). In the Second World War, the region was defined by where the Allies fought against the outer reaches of the Japanese empire, and commands were divided into the Pacific Ocean Area (under Admiral Chester Nimitz), the Southwest Pacific Area (under General Douglas MacArthur), the China/Burma/India Theater (under General Joseph Stilwell), and later the British-led Southeast Asia Command (under Lord Louis Mountbatten). In the Cold War, Southeast Asia and the Korean Peninsula became more prominent in the strategies of containment as communist aggression spread. Today, most American strategists refer to the Asia-Pacific broadly but also consider India a critical part of the region's future in terms of balancing China's impact.

Does the United States have a grand strategy for Asia? The evidence often lies in how Americans have defined the region geographically—beginning with the first encounters of merchants, missionaries, and naval officers at the beginning of the republic.

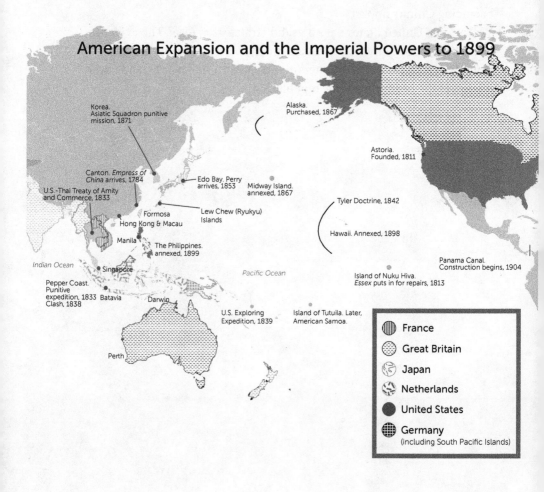

American Expansion and the Imperial Powers to 1899

Korea.
Asiatic Squadron punitive
mission, 1871

Alaska.
Purchased, 1867

Astoria.
Founded, 1811

Canton. *Empress of
China* arrives, 1784

Edo Bay. Perry
arrives, 1853

Midway Island.
annexed, 1867

U.S.-Thai Treaty of Amity
and Commerce, 1833

Tyler Doctrine, 1842

Formosa

Lew Chew (Ryukyu)
Islands

Hong Kong & Macau

Hawaii. Annexed, 1898

Manila

The Philippines.
annexed, 1899

Panama Canal.
Construction begins, 1904

Indian Ocean

Singapore

Pacific Ocean

Island of Nuku Hiva.
Essex puts in for repairs, 1813

Pepper Coast.
Punitive
expedition, 1833
Clash, 1838

Batavia

Darwin

U.S. Exploring
Expedition, 1839

Island of Tutuila. Later,
American Samoa.

Perth

	France
	Great Britain
	Japan
	Netherlands
	United States
	Germany (including South Pacific Islands)

PART ONE

THE RISE OF THE UNITED STATES

In January 1813, the thirty-two-gun frigate *Essex* under the command of Captain David Porter was cruising the South Atlantic in search of British merchant vessels to raid. The first year of America's war with Britain—the "Second Revolution"—had been going badly on land, but the intrepid U.S. Navy had bested British frigates and schooners in single-ship combat across the Atlantic Ocean. The crew of the *Essex* was hungry for its share of glory. The problem for Captain Porter was that he had lost touch with the rest of the navy and could not get past the seventy-four-gun British men-of-war blockading the eastern seaboard to return home for orders. Trapped at sea, Porter called his officers together in the wardroom to inform them of his audacious decision. Instead of returning north to Boston, he would take the *Essex* around the Horn of South America and enter the Pacific Ocean, which was entirely under the control of Britain and lacking any friendly harbor or ally for the young United States. Porter told his officers that the Pacific was fat with British merchant ships and whalers, and the blow to British pocketbooks and prestige would be well worth the risk. The assembled lieutenants and midshipmen, including thirteen-year-old David Glasgow Farragut—later famous for proclaiming "damn the torpedoes, full speed ahead" while in command during the Battle of Mobile Bay in the American Civil War—enthusiastically assented.

The *Essex* would be the first American warship in history to enter the Pacific Ocean, signaling to the world that the young republic would not be intimidated, even by the greatest power at sea, and that, under threat, America would expand rather than retreat.

Writing about Porter's exploits in his history of the U.S. Navy in the War of 1812 a half century later, Harvard senior Theodore Roosevelt noted that until the *Essex* entered the Pacific, American merchant ships and whalers had been forced to keep themselves well armed to beat off British raiders, "Malay proas," and "Chinese junks." But for a moment in 1813, the Americans plied the waters of the Pacific with confidence and pride: "Captain Porter had saved all our ships in those waters, had not cost the government a dollar, living purely on the enemy, and had taken from him nearly 4,000 tons of shipping and 400 men, completely breaking up his whaling trade in the South Pacific."[1]

By the end of the century, President Theodore Roosevelt would ensure that no ancient civilization or modern empire could ignore American power or prestige in the Pacific. The United States would rise to command the West Coast, Alaska, Hawaii, and island outposts offshore from China.

But the arrival of an American empire of commerce and liberty in the Pacific was envisioned long before Roosevelt's own rise to power—or even before Porter and the *Essex* rounded the Horn.

1. "A THEATRE FOR THE EXERCISE OF THE MOST AMBITIOUS INTELLECT"
SEEDS OF STRATEGY, 1784–1860

The next three chapters trace the evolution of American statecraft in Asia from the first encounters with China in the 1780s to the emergence of the United States as a major Pacific power a little over a century later. At the turn of the twentieth century, Theodore Roosevelt and his expansionist allies developed a thoroughly American grand strategy toward the Pacific that combined robust trade, a powerful navy, and pursuit of a maritime balance of power designed to keep the Pacific secure. Most historians begin the story of American statecraft in Asia and the Pacific from this point, but, in reality, the seeds of strategic thinking harvested by men such as Roosevelt, Alfred Thayer Mahan, and John Hay had been planted much earlier.

Even when the new American nation comprised only thirteen states nestled along the eastern seaboard and only a handful of its citizens had ever traveled west of the Missouri River—let alone to the Far East— prominent statesmen and merchants were thinking about how to lay the foundations for what the Founding Fathers foresaw as an "empire of liberty" stretching across the American continent, with influence beyond.[1] These men knew of the potential for profitable trade with China, of the sea otter pelts that could be harvested along the Columbia River in the

Pacific Northwest, and of the Chinese Hong merchants' passion for sandalwood from the Sandwich Islands. Barred by the British from trade
with the West Indies and much of Europe, Yankee merchants and whalers
soon began to rival the British commercial presence across the Pacific
Rim. At the same time, the national government stood toe-to-toe with the
British and Russians, asserting the United States' right to the Pacific
Northwest—hundreds of miles beyond where any but the hardiest Americans had yet settled. By the 1820s, American missionaries and regular
U.S. Navy schooners were following the merchants into the Pacific.
When pirates in Southeast Asia threatened American property in the
1830s, the navy launched punitive expeditions. When European powers
encroached on American interests and missionary activities closer to
home in Hawaii, the national government extended the Monroe Doctrine
to the center of the Pacific.

Initially, Americans were concerned only with expanding trade and
protecting their fellow citizens, but when the Qing Empire was dealt a
devastating blow in the Opium Wars (1839–1842) and Asian regional
order began to collapse from within, Americans were forced to consider their republic's role in the larger transformation beginning in the
Far East. Did the United States stand for anti-imperialism and self-
determination for China or for the forceful opening of China to international trade by the British? As Russia, Britain, and France began to seize
territory from the wounded Qing at midcentury, U.S. naval officers and
diplomats began to call for their own forward outposts in the Western
Pacific and debated whether the republic's core interests lay in preserving China's integrity against the other imperial powers or securing America's maritime position around Japan and the offshore island chain. The
elements of an early American grand strategy for the Pacific were coming into place, while its proponents were discovering the trade-offs and
tensions inherent in great-power politics across a vast ocean. In Washington, however, few members of Congress or the administration were
listening anymore. The republic was heading toward civil war, and the
ambitions of a few Yankee merchant houses, naval officers, and diplomats
in the Far East were of little consequence for a nation on the verge of
self-immolation.

Chapter 1 concludes at this high-water mark of American ambition in
the Pacific. Chapter 2 then traces the continued expansion of America's
presence and interests in Asia in the more restrained postbellum years of
the second half of the nineteenth century. Finally, chapter 3 brings us

back to Roosevelt and the architects of America's Pacific empire at
century's end—bold expansionists who turned instinctively to the definitions of national interest and the instruments of power proposed a half
century earlier. And so—whether they have realized it or not—have most
of those responsible for America's Asia policy since.

"The Adventurous Pursuits of Commerce": Early Canton Trade and the Imaginings of Power and Profit in the East Indies

When America secured its independence from Britain with the Paris
Peace Treaty of 1783, the new nation consisted of only four million souls,
heavily concentrated along the eastern seaboard. The British still held
a string of forts running from the St. Lawrence River across the Great
Lakes; American merchants had lost the protection of the Royal Navy
and were unable to trade in the British imperial system; the nation was
saddled with debt; and the Articles of Confederation provided only the
weakest framework for national policy-making. European powers, even
the colonists' erstwhile ally France, were not eager to see the new nation
expand in North America or transplant its revolutionary ideology in the
Old Country. The geography, values, and commerce for which the revolution had been fought were all in jeopardy.[2]

Yet, despite these uncertainties, there was also a profound conviction
among the Founding Fathers that the new republic would have a major
impact on the international system. The Pacific became an important if
distant part of that vision. Before the revolution, Americans had called
Asia the "East Indies" and knew the region only as a source of tea and fine
porcelain for the best homes of New York, Philadelphia, and Williamsburg. George Washington himself thought that China was populated by
white people until he was informed otherwise after becoming president.[3]
Some colonists had crewed with British ships, including John Ledyard of
Connecticut and John Gore of Virginia, who had sailed as Royal Marines
with Captain Cook's expedition to the Pacific and brought back tales of
fur skins purchased in the Pacific Northwest for sixpence and sold in
Canton for $100.[4] The colonists had fought the revolution in large part
in order to break free of the shackles of Britain's mercantilist Navigation
Acts, but after independence, Congress was unable to settle on terms for
tariffs, and British merchants flooded the former colonies with cheap

goods, causing an economic depression worsened by the massive debt accumulated during the war. Breaking into the East India trade would demonstrate America's new commercial independence to the world and help to restore economic prosperity at home. To the young republic, the Pacific represented an opportunity to trade, and trade would henceforth define the American approach to Asia.

As the War of Independence drew to a close, Philadelphia merchant Robert Morris began to search for markets that would allow him to recover the enormous losses he had incurred as the lead banker for George Washington's Continental army. On November 27, 1783, he wrote to Secretary of State John Jay to apprise him of his plans to initiate a new trading relationship with China: "We are dismissing the remains of our army and getting rid of expense, so that I may hope to see the end of my engagements before next May. . . . I am sending some ships to China, in order to encourage others in the adventurous pursuits of commerce, and I wish to see a foundation laid for an American navy."[5]

Morris's ship, the *Empress of China*, set sail from New York for Canton on February 22, 1784, carrying a cargo of forty tons of ginseng found in the Appalachian Mountains and one Major Samuel Shaw of Boston as supercargo. The expedition was an enormous success, turning a 400 percent profit. When the ship returned to New York the following May, there was a great sensation.[6] Morris reported to Jay: "Our ship from China does tolerably well for the concerned; she has opened new objects to all America. A mandarin signs a passport for all European ships, directed to the commanders of two of the emperor's forts on the river of Canton, nearly in the following words: 'Permit this barbarian boat to pass; she has guns and men, consequently can do the emperor no harm.'"[7]

Undeterred by the Chinese refusal to grant him consular status, Major Shaw reported himself "peculiarly honoured" to represent American friendship to the Chinese and predicted that within a few years Americans would be "engaging in commerce with the subjects of that empire under advantages equal, if not superior, to those enjoyed by any other nation whatever.[8] There was suddenly "everywhere a Rage for East India Voyages," wrote Senator Henry Lee of Virginia to his friend James Madison, adding, "I fear our countrymen will overdo this."[9] Nine voyages were made to the Far East from New York alone before the end of 1787, and by 1790 Americans had sent twenty-eight ships to Canton.[10] The China traders lobbied for and received protective duties from Pennsylvania and New York in 1791 and also enjoyed a two-year delay in the payment of tea duties.[11] They also found liberal credits for trade, and profitable markets in continental Europe for reexport of tea from the United States. By the onset of the Napoleonic Wars, American vessels were second only to Britain's in the tea trade with China.

Merchants and whalers fanned out across the rest of the Pacific Rim as well. In 1787, the *Columbia* and the *Lady Washington* out of Boston were the first American ships to sail directly to the North Pacific around Cape Horn on their way to China, picking up sea otter pelts to be sold in Canton. In 1790, American merchant ships began stopping to procure sandalwood in the Sandwich Islands (modern Hawaii), which proved a popular item for Canton's Hong merchants, who burned it as incense and used it for scented fans.[12] By 1800, American whalers were also stopping in New South Wales and New Zealand, and a few years later, American merchants were trading with the Japanese under the Dutch flag in the only open Japanese port, at Dejima, near Nagasaki (as proxies for the Dutch while Napoleon occupied the Low Countries in Europe).[13] Salem merchants also began to import pepper from the northwest coast of Sumatra (the "Pepper Coast"), which they sold for enormous profits to the housewives of New England. Trade extended to the Indian Ocean as well. Under the 1794 Treaty of Amity, Commerce and Navigation between the United States and Great Britain (the "Jay Treaty"), American merchants retained rights of trade to and from India—important for tea trade— though not with any other British colony. Ironically, this exception was granted by Governor General Lord Cornwallis, the British officer who had surrendered to the colonists at the Battle of Yorktown in 1781.

Ultimately, however, American merchants found themselves seeking commercial advantage in a world that was still dominated by European powers.[14] En route from Boston or Baltimore to Canton, there was not a single seaport beyond Charleston where American ships could lay anchor without the permission of a European power. Usually, that power was Britain. Once in China, the Americans found the port at Canton dominated by the British East India Company. Backed by the guns of the Royal Navy, the British merchants pressed their demands for extraterritoriality and trading rights on the Chinese, while the unprotected Americans had to curry favor with the Qing officials by emphasizing their own spirited anticolonialism and good intentions, in contrast to the British.[15] At other times, the Americans were forced to free ride on British power in order to overcome Chinese intransigence. It was no wonder that the British East India Company accused the Americans of "Jackal Diplomacy"—eager to feed but never to join the kill. Meanwhile, the American merchants lived in a constant state of anxiety that their seamen would be impressed into the Royal Navy or that America's westward expansion toward the Pacific might be blocked by British Canada. "As long as the Americans had reason to fear the English as something more than commercial competitors in a perfectly free field," noted historian Tyler Dennett, "there was little friendliness between the Americans and the English in China."[16]

The Founders understood well that with this new trade in the Pacific, the American merchants would eventually excite the jealousy of the established powers. As John Jay wrote in Federalist Papers No. 4 in 1787 under the pseudonym Publius: "In the trade to China and India, we interfere with more than one nation, inasmuch as it enables us to partake in advantages which they had in a manner monopolized and as we thereby supply ourselves with commodities which we used to purchase from them."

The East Indies trade would expand, Jay predicted, as "the cheapness and excellence of our productions, added to the circumstance of vicinity, and the enterprise and address of our merchants and navigators, will give us a greater share in the advantages which those territories afford, than consists with the wishes or policy of their respective sovereigns." And to defend and expand that trade and deter other powers from seeking to exclude the new republic by force, the American people would require Federalism, as Jay concluded in his Publius essay: "Wisely, therefore, do they consider union and a good national government as necessary to put and keep them in **SUCH A SITUATION** [emphasis in original] as, instead of **INVITING** [emphasis in original] war, will tend to repress and discourage it. That situation consists in the best possible state of defense, and necessarily depends on the government, the arms, and the resources of the country."

Jay wrote specifically of the future of American trade in the Pacific, yet that trade would only be as secure as the homeland of the republic itself. Independence had been sparked in part by the combination of British trade restrictions and London's decision to seal off the colonies east of the Appalachian Mountains under agreements signed with allied Indians in the peace settlement to the French and Indian War.[17] In its infancy, the independent republic was again being squeezed by Britain, France, and Spain on the Continent. The Founders' vision of an Empire of Liberty from coast to coast became intertwined with the more distant dream of a commercial empire in the Pacific. The new republic would have to secure its own point of access to the markets of Asia on the continent of North America itself.

"A Foothold of American Commerce and Empire on the Shores of the Pacific"

In late April 1792, Captain Robert Gray of the American merchant ship *Columbia* encountered British explorer George Vancouver and the HMS *Discovery* off the coast of the Pacific Northwest. Vancouver had already claimed discovery of a great river there, but Gray was the first to pass over the treacherous sandbar at its mouth, naming the river for his ship. The next year, former New York Loyalist Sir Alexander Mackenzie led an expedition west across Canada in search of an exclusive British overland passage to the same territory. Mackenzie reported back to London that with British control of the fur trade around the forty-eighth parallel, American adventurers "who had hitherto enjoyed the traffic along the northwest coast" would "instantly disappear."[18] A clash for control of the Pacific Northwest was now under way, prompting the first of a series of American efforts to assert its forward line on—and then across—the Pacific. The leading champions of that cause were three men who had never been west of the Alleghenies yet understood European power politics and the immeasurable potential of trade with the East Indies. They were Thomas Jefferson, John Jacob Astor, and John Quincy Adams.

Like the other Founding Fathers, Thomas Jefferson had an abiding faith that the new republic would create an empire based not on war and the corruption of men but instead on commerce and the "confidence of a free and virtuous people that would secure ends based on the natural and universal rights of man."[19] Jefferson was keenly aware of British designs on the far-off Pacific coast, writing to the Revolutionary War hero George Rogers Clark from the Congress in Annapolis in December 1783 with word that the British were raising funds for exploring and likely "colonising the lands from Missisipi [*sic*] to California" and asking whether Clark might someday lead an American overland expedition to the same territory.[20] While serving as minister to France in 1786, Jefferson dined with John Ledyard, the veteran of Captain Cook's voyage almost three decades earlier. Ledyard, a colorful adventurer who had dropped out of Dartmouth and paddled down the Connecticut River in a dugout canoe to join Cook's flagship, regaled the future president of the United States with stories of the Sandwich Islands, the death of Cook, and the profitable sea otter fur trade. He implored the American minister to support his proposal for an expedition across Europe in search of passages to the Pacific Northwest via Siberia, Kamchatka, and the Russian territories in North America. With Jefferson's enthusiastic support, Ledyard set off for the Bering Strait, thousands of miles to the east. Two hundred miles short of the Kamchatka Peninsula, the Russians arrested him for spying.[21]

The next opportunity to stake an American claim to the Pacific Coast came seven years later when President Jefferson purchased the Louisiana Territory from France, opening the West to American expansion. Jefferson recruited George Rogers Clark's younger brother William and Captain Meriwether Lewis to charter a Corps of Discovery that would report on the vast western lands gained from the French and to determine whether the Missouri River might flow to the Columbia and allow navigation to the Pacific.[22] After more than two years of arduous travel on bateau, foot, and horse, Lewis and Clark returned to St. Louis in the fall of 1806 with detailed maps, trade agreements with Native American tribes they encountered, but also the news that there was no navigable passageway to the Columbia River explored by Captain Gray fourteen years earlier. Still, Jefferson had another idea for who might gain purchase on the Pacific Northwest—New York fur trader John Jacob Astor.

Astor, said Jefferson, would one day be viewed alongside "Columbus and Raleigh" as the "founder of such an empire which will arise from commerce."[23] A German immigrant who had made his fortune trading furs with Native Americans in upstate New York, Astor followed the profitable example of the *Empress of China* and outfitted half a dozen of his own ships in 1800 to sail from New York to trade furs from the Pacific Northwest with the Hong merchants in Canton.[24] So taken was Jefferson with Astor's pursuit of a Pacific commercial empire that he gave the New Yorker special dispensation to continue trading with China even after all other U.S. trade was suspended under the 1807 Embargo Act.[25]

By 1809, the Embargo Act had been repealed and Astor's trade with Canton picked up, particularly trade in furs. He now sought to establish a permanent station for the American fur trade in the Pacific Northwest, but the field was crowded with competitors: the British championed both the Hudson Bay Company and its Montreal-based competitor the Northwest Company, while the Spanish laid claim to the fur trade from Vancouver Island and the Russians traded through the Russian-American Company based in Alaska. In the midst of this multination, multifirm struggle for dominance over the region, the Russians suddenly provided Astor with the opportunity he had been seeking. In September 1809, the Russian consul in Philadelphia asked Astor whether he might ship furs to China on behalf of the Russian-American Company, which had poor relations with the Chinese and worried about losing the market to the British. Astor leaped at the offer and secured support from Jefferson to establish the Pacific Fur Trading Company in 1810 and to build a fort near the spot where Lewis and Clark had first sighted the Pacific from the Columbia River five years earlier. In March 1811, the schooner *Tonquin* arrived at the Columbia River, and Astor's agents raised the American flag over the first permanent American settlement on the West Coast, naming it Astoria. For Jefferson, the new settlement represented the prospect of an "independent nation on the Pacific Coast, bound to the United States by ties of blood, language and friendship."[26] It would be not a colony but someday a fellow republic—an important precedent for American expansionists later in the century who sought ways to establish outposts in the Western Pacific without stooping to the base imperialism of the Old World.

When war broke out with Britain in 1812, however, Astoria suddenly became an exposed and undefendable outpost at the mercy of the Royal Navy. With little prospect of mobilizing a U.S. force adequate to protect their investment, in 1813 the Pacific Fur Trading Company sold Astoria to the British, who promptly raised the Union Jack over the settlement and renamed it Fort George. President James Madison was sympathetic to Astor's argument that the settlement had strategic value and should be retaken, but other than Captain Porter's frigate *Essex*, there were no U.S. Navy ships in the Pacific, and Porter was unaware of Astoria's fate. Madison would not abandon Astoria, though, instructing the American delegation to the peace negotiations with the British at Ghent in 1814 to secure the return of the settlement. This the American delegation did, pushed by their fellow commissioner John Quincy Adams, the son of the second president of the United States.[27]

John Quincy Adams stands above all other American statesmen in the early nineteenth century. He was the nation's first notable grand strategist. Between 1794 and 1843, Adams served as ambassador to half a dozen European courts, a U.S. senator, secretary of state, president of the United States, and representative to the U.S. Congress from Massachusetts. He had a deep and abiding faith in American exceptionalism and commercial expansion, but he also had unparalleled instincts for the cynical world of European diplomacy and the limits of American power.[28] As the first U.S. minister to Russia in 1809, he had seen the Russian-American Company spread south along the Pacific Coast, while as a delegate to the Ghent negotiations and then minister to the Court of St. James, he sat opposite the most adroit imperialists of his age. In a world in which European alignments shifted unpredictably and America chose to stand alone, Adams came to understand the importance of asserting American prerogatives where he could and harnessing or accommodating European, and especially British, power when he must.[29]

Adams returned from London to Washington in 1817 to become President James Monroe's secretary of state. At Astor's request, Monroe had already dispatched the sixteen-gun sloop *Ontario* to retake Astoria from the reluctant British occupants shortly before Adams assumed his new post. When the British minister angrily confronted the new secretary of state about the aggressive U.S. move, Adams replied coolly that "it would hardly be worth the while of Great Britain to have any differences with the United States on account of the occupation of so remote a territory."[30] Implicit in Adams's reply was the message that the United States *was* prepared to have a difference with the British. Eager to avoid a third war with America, the Royal Navy was instructed to "obviate" any possible confrontation with the American sloop of war.[31] However, the British would not cede the territory itself, rebuffing Adams's demands to extend the U.S.-Canada border to the Pacific Coast (the 1818 Anglo-American Convention only extended the border as far west as the Rockies). Adams had more success with Spain, which did agree to relinquish its claims to the Pacific Northwest under the 1819 Adams-Onis Treaty.[32]

That left the Russians, who proved to be a far more significant problem than Adams had anticipated. The *Ontario* reported back to the secretary of state that during the war with Britain, the Russians had expanded their own settlements as far south as San Francisco and were establishing outposts in the Sandwich Islands. These reports also went to the U.S. Congress, where expansionists like Virginia senator John Floyd and Missouri senator Thomas Hart Benton warned that Russian aggression against Turkey, Persia, Japan, and China demonstrated the threat Moscow posed to the Pacific Northwest and America's overall position in the region.[33] That vulnerability became evident in September 1821, when Czar Alexander I issued an edict, or *ukase*, excluding foreign vessels from anywhere in the Pacific Northwest above 51° longitude—hundreds of miles farther south than the original 1799 Russian claim of 55° longitude. In the *ukase*, which was probably arranged by Russian commercial interests worried about the Americans' return to the Pacific Northwest, the czar also threatened to capture any foreign ships coming within 115 miles of Russian claims.[34]

Monroe and Adams were outraged, telling the Russian minister in Washington that "the United States would contest the right of Russia to any territorial establishment on the American continent, and that they would distinctly assume the principle that the American continents are no longer subjects for any new European colonial establishments."[35] Adams also put the British minister, Lord Canning, on notice that it was "not imaginable that, in the present condition of the world, *any* European nation should entertain the project of settling a *colony* on the Northwest Coast of America."[36] When in 1823 Lord Canning proposed an Anglo-American alignment to prevent European interference in the wars for independence spreading across Spanish America, Monroe determined to put forth his own definitive statement regarding interference anywhere on the continent. With Adams as the lead drafter, the president declared before Congress on January 2, 1823, that the United States would view as hostile actions any efforts by European powers to further colonize the Western Hemisphere but that the United States would not interfere with the internal affairs of European powers confronting the new forces of national self-liberation.[37] The Monroe Doctrine's explicit rejection of further European colonization of North America was not disputed by the British, nor lost on the Russians, who had sparked the overall crisis in the Far Northwest two years earlier.[38] Czar Alexander retreated, agreeing in treaties signed in 1824 and 1825 to divide the U.S. and Russian possessions at 54°40′.[39]

Adams had judged exactly the right timing and level of bluster needed to push back first the British, then the Spanish, and finally the Russians. One of Adams's greatest admirers, future secretary of state William Henry Seward, would later write that Adams was fully prepared to use force to protect American claims, and rightly so.[40] That may not have been true, given the remoteness of the Pacific Northwest and the intervening strength of the Royal Navy. Yet the European powers could not be certain of American restraint, nor how their rivals would exploit a conflict with the Americans to their own advantage in the larger concert of power that characterized diplomacy in the Old World at the time. In that sense, Adams played the Europeans' vulnerabilities perfectly.

For his part, Astor had already abandoned his commercial empire in the Pacific—sandalwood was denuded in the Sandwich Islands, and the

German entrepreneur was distracted by managing his finances in New York.[41] The Columbia River would also prove a disappointment as America's port on the Pacific, until the advent of steamships in the 1830s allowed reliably safe passage over the sandbar and through the currents where the waters met the Pacific. Meanwhile, the western border demarcation between Canada and the United States would not be settled until waves of American settlers created the momentum for permanent borders in the Oregon Treaty of 1846.

Nevertheless, John Quincy Adams had ensured through his tenacious diplomacy that the United States would retain its toehold on the Pacific Coast, exactly as his father's political rival Thomas Jefferson had envisioned three decades earlier. The young republic had secured its forward defense line—a line that would expand thousands of miles across the ocean in the decades to come.

COMMERCE, THE NAVY, AND GOD: EXPANDING RELATIONS WITH THE PACIFIC DURING THE ERA OF MANIFEST DESTINY

By the time John Quincy Adams was elected the sixth president of the United States, in 1824, Americans were entering the Pacific with unprecedented confidence—underpinned by continental expansion, growing commerce, a stronger navy, and missionaries carrying the word of God. By midcentury, the citizens once called the "new people" by the Hong merchants in Canton were everywhere. The exotic "East India" trade was now being more commonly referred to as the "Canton trade," as powerful American merchant firms based in Boston and New York expanded the export of cotton, opium, and specie to the Hong merchants.[42] Trade in sea otter pelts and sandalwood ebbed, as did trade with India after cotton tariffs were imposed in 1816, but entrepreneurial Yankees soon expanded India trade again by packing ice in sawdust to sell in Calcutta, often returning with opium for China. New consulates were established in Batavia (Jakarta today), and Americans began to trade with the Kingdom of Siam in 1821, signing the first U.S. treaty of commerce and friendship in the Pacific with the kingdom in 1833.[43] By 1846, there were 200 American vessels and 5,000 seamen engaged in the carry trade in the Pacific, and over 200 American whalers were operating in the Pacific after overharvesting in the Atlantic.[44] When Samuel Cunard of Canada

initiated trans-Atlantic steamship service in 1840, he anticipated a similar revolution in trade across the Pacific.[45]

The fleet followed commerce. In the flurry of nationalism and naval
pride after the War of 1812, in 1816 Congress passed "An Act for the Gradual Increase of the Navy of the United States" and approved the first
permanent deployment of a warship in the Pacific the next year. In 1821,
the U.S. Navy established a permanent Pacific Squadron. In its early years,
the squadron consisted of a frigate and a few sloops and schooners, often
operating along the West Coast of North America, with occasional runs
to Hawaii.[46] As president, Adams proposed in his 1825 State of the Union
address an even stronger naval presence in the region because the "flour-
ishing of commerce and fishery extending to the islands of the Pacific and
to China still require that the protecting power of the Union should be
displayed under its flag upon the ocean as upon the land."[47] In 1835, the
navy established an East Asia Squadron in order to maintain a more enduring presence on both sides of the Pacific Ocean.[48] And in 1838, Captain Charles Wilkes and the United States Exploring Expedition fulfilled
a goal of Monroe and Adams by exploring all the Pacific islands that
would later figure centrally in American military and diplomatic history,
including Wake Island, the Philippines, the Sulu Archipelago, Borneo,
Singapore, and Polynesia.[49]

With real firepower at sea, Americans no longer needed to rely entirely
on the goodwill of the Chinese or the British to protect their lives, property, or interests in the Far East.[50] In 1826, President Adams ordered a U.S.
Navy squadron to Hawaii to protect U.S. commerce against pirates and
to show the flag to other powers coveting the islands.[51] In 1833, President
Andrew Jackson dispatched the frigate *Potomac* under Captain John
Downes to the Pepper Coast to demand the restitution of property and
the punishment of Sumatrans who had taken the merchant ship *Friendship* and murdered members of its crew.[52] The overzealous Downes (who
had served under Porter on the *Essex*) landed marines and sailors to
destroy the local Raja's fortresses without warning. Congress was scan-
dalized, and on the next punitive raid in 1838, Captain John Read of the
frigate *Columbia* was careful to parlay *before* opening fire and burning
the local village to the ground.[53]

Then, in perhaps the most consequential assertion of American rights
in the Pacific in the period, President John Tyler responded to French
machinations on behalf of the Catholic Church in Hawaii by announcing that the United States would consider any interference in those

islands' affairs to be a hostile act—deliberately extending the Monroe Doctrine thousands of miles to the west.[54] Backed by a stronger navy and facing new competition from the European imperial powers, the U.S. government had begun to push its declared defense line from Oregon into the Central Pacific before the West Coast was even part of the union.

As the religious controversy at the center of the Tyler Doctrine demonstrated, the merchants, diplomats, and naval officers in the Pacific were now also being joined by influential American missionaries carrying the word of God and the values of the republic. "Originating primarily in the seaport communities and often backed by leading merchants," the missionaries "saw religion, patriotism, and commerce working hand in hand."[55] The American Board of Commissioners of Foreign Missions sent their first mission to British India in 1812. Americans also sponsored early British Protestant missionaries in Canton, including Dr. Robert Morrison, who carried a letter of passage from Secretary of State James Madison in order to avoid expulsion by the British East India Company, which generally preferred to keep the locals uneducated and docile.[56] With expanding American trade, the New England missionaries were certain they too would spread their activities across the Pacific, in the words of Reverend Timothy Dwight (later the president of Yale):

> By heaven design'd
> The' example bright, to renovate mankind.
> Soon shall they sons across the mainland roman;
> And claim, on the far pacific shores, their home.
> Their rule, religion, manners, arts convey,
> And spread their freedom to the Asian sea.[57]

The first American missionaries arrived in Canton in 1830, where they learned Chinese and produced a Chinese-language history of the United States.[58] Fed by religious revivals in the United States in the 1830s and 1840s, the missionaries' ranks swelled. By 1850, there were eighty-eight American missionaries proselytizing in China, compared with sixty-two Protestant missionaries from all other nations combined.[59] By the 1840s, Hawaii had turned into a "Pacific New England" because of the schools, churches, and institutions established by the Congregationalists. Over the coming centuries, American missionaries would contribute a uniquely American source of scholarship and diplomacy on the Far East, exerting far more influence on policy than did their counterparts in other

Western countries. American diplomats negotiating the opening of China, Japan, and Korea to commerce and normal relations would all rely on missionaries to be their interpreters.[60] In subsequent years, the children and grandchildren of missionaries would populate the Far East offices of the Department of State.

This expansion of commercial, naval, and missionary activism in the Pacific happened organically as much as it did from any policy design. Indeed, it needs to be put in fuller perspective given the orientation of most American elites at the time. Politically, there was broad consensus in Congress regarding American commercial interests in the Pacific, but trade with China was far more important to Whigs and New Englanders like John Quincy Adams and Daniel Webster than it was to agrarian Democrats, who by midcentury tended to prioritize expansion into areas that would introduce and support slavery.[61] Moreover, although trade with the Pacific was expanding, it never rose above 10 percent of overall U.S. trade, which increased from $13,004,000 in 1821 to $64,022,000 in 1856.[62] The United States also suffered from institutional deficiencies in the execution of foreign policy. The State Department under John Quincy Adams had four clerks in total. The number expanded only slightly over the next few decades, with none of them experienced in Pacific affairs.[63] American consuls abroad were political appointees, often without diplomatic training and with uncertain prospects of promotion to higher diplomatic posts or even remuneration for services rendered. Though the navy produced outstanding officers in the Pacific and Far East Squadrons, including Matthew Maury and Matthew Calbraith Perry, the Department of the Navy itself was usually plagued with weak leadership, and the Mediterranean and Caribbean Squadrons were typically better outfitted and officered. The Pacific, in short, remained a secondary theater of American interest behind the Atlantic and sometimes the Caribbean.

More to the point, the national government still had not extended control of the North American continent to the Pacific Coast. From 1800 to 1840, the number of states and the U.S. population more than doubled, but none of the new states or territories was on the West Coast, despite expanding American settlements in California and Oregon.[64] In 1842, President John Tyler tried to secure Northern California within the union in a tripartite deal that would have given Britain the Pacific Northwest as far south as the Columbia River in exchange for Britain paying Mexico for transferring Northern California and Texas to the United States.[65] There was a logic to Tyler's complex negotiation, since the port of San

Francisco would have been a more reliable point of access to the Pacific than the Columbia River, but American settlers in Oregon wanted the entire territory, and the deal fell apart.[66]

Eventually, Tyler's successor, James Polk, would secure not only Oregon but also all of California as an American outpost on the Pacific. A southerner, Polk was more concerned with expanding territory for American agrarian interests, including slavery, than he was in commerce with the Far East. Indeed, John Quincy Adams and many others who had set their gaze on Asia opposed his 1846 war with Mexico. Yet Polk's controversial successes made possible the new wave of expansionist thinking toward the Pacific that would emerge over the next decade. He began by whipping up a war scare with Britain over the Oregon Territory, forcing London to accept a border well north of the Columbia, along the forty-ninth parallel, and to retreat from any ambitions over California.[67] Polk then turned his attention to Mexico, declaring war over Texas in May and dispatching the USS *Savannah* and two sloops of war of the Pacific Squadron to capture Monterey and claim California as territory of the United States. Almost overnight, Polk had taken a broad swath of territory from Texas to California, gains the humiliated Mexican government acceded to in the Treaty of Guadalupe-Hidalgo in 1848. As Polk's ebullient treasury secretary, Robert Walker, declared, "Asia has suddenly become our neighbor, with a placid intervening ocean inviting our steamships upon the trade of commerce greater than all of Europe combined."[68]

With consolidation of the North American continent, leading Americans now saw themselves as holding an irreversible stake in the future of the Pacific. What that meant beyond commerce, religious proselytizing, protecting American citizens, and ensuring preeminence in the Pacific Northwest and Hawaii was uncertain—until the Sinocentric order encountered by the first Americans in the Far East began to collapse.

"In Honorable Contrast with the Outrageous Misconduct of the English": American Values and the Beginning of the Demise of the Qing

The American merchants who traded at Canton had done so from the beginning with the attitude that China was an independent country on whose good offices they must rely. They had neither the naval power nor the imperializing tradition to do otherwise. Thus, when an American merchant sailor named Francis Terranova was mistakenly accused of murdering a Chinese woman in 1821 and Qing officials threatened to embargo all trade with American ships unless he was turned over, the poor lad was reluctantly sent ashore, to be garroted within sight of his own crew. In the subsequent decade, the new U.S. Far East Squadron would provide somewhat better protection for American merchants in Canton, but so would the European navies for their merchants. Americans accustomed to a powerful and obstreperous Qing court now witnessed China's growing humiliation at the hands of powerful British and French forces. This rapidly shifting balance of power would force Americans to consider not only their mercantile interests but also their nation's stake in the collapsing Sinocentric order in the Far East.

The substance that drove European avarice and poisoned the Qing was opium. The 1834 revocation by Parliament of the East India Company's monopoly had spurred an intense commercial competition to export Indian opium to China and then use Chinese silver to pay for Indian exports of tea to Britain. It was clear that either Britain or China would eventually face a balance-of-payments crisis for lack of silver specie. The Qing moved first, in 1839, by expelling the British from Canton and announcing a plan to eradicate the opium trade altogether. Then the British fought back, crushing China's anachronistic army and forcing the Qing to pay reparations and open the country to greater trade in the first of the infamous unequal treaties, the Treaty of Nanking (Nanjing), which was signed on board the HMS *Cornwallis* on August 29, 1842.[69]

Throughout the mounting crisis, the Americans in Canton had been left "entirely without instructions from the government of the United States."[70] In May 1839, the American merchant houses in Canton decided it was time to take the initiative themselves and sent a memorial (petition) to the U.S. Congress proposing that the United States "act in concert with the governments of Great Britain, France and Holland or either of them in their endeavors to establish commercial relations with this empire upon a safe and honorable footing." They urged the State Department to send envoys to press the Qing for fixed tariff rates and access to other ports in China, as the Europeans were doing. The American merchants also asked for the dispatch of a suitable U.S. naval force to increase American negotiating leverage and protect American lives and property in the midst of the ongoing crisis.[71]

The memorial prompted considerable debate in Congress. On the one hand, there was broad support for negotiating a commercial treaty with

China, which served the economic interests of New England and New York and the ideals of Jeffersonians who still believed that commerce would allow the republic to transform international relations without resorting to the wars and machinations of the Old World. On the other hand, missionaries had reported on the evils of the opium trade, and many Americans remained both anti-British and anti-imperialist. The merchants in Canton had merely sought a remedy for their plight, but their memorial raised fundamental questions about how the United States would apply its republican values to the changing Far East.

The immediate question was how closely the United States should align with Britain's attempt to force open China to international commerce and diplomacy. Two Massachusetts congressmen squared off to present the opposing positions. The first was Caleb Cushing, a Harvard man representing the Third District of Massachusetts, who declared before the House of Representatives on March 16, 1840, that Americans alone in Canton "had manifested a proper respect for the laws and public rights of the Chinese Empire, in honorable contrast with the outrageous misconduct of the English there," and thus had a "favorable opportunity to endeavor to put the American trade with China on a just and stable footing for the future." "But," he continued, "God forbid that I should entertain the idea of cooperating with the British Government in the purpose, if purpose it has, of upholding the base cupidity and violence and high-handed infraction of all law, human and divine, which have characterized the operation of the British, individually and collectively, in the seas of China."[72]

Divine law was *not* with the Chinese, argued a different Harvard graduate, and a representative of Massachusetts's Twelfth District. Like Cushing, former president and now representative John Quincy Adams favored a commercial treaty that would protect the rights and safety of his fellow citizens. But after commissioning detailed Foreign Relations Committee studies on the China problem and poring over the American and British records, he concluded that Britain's war with China served American interests in securing an open and moral international order. As he put it to the Massachusetts Historical Society in December 1841, there is a "law of nations" that is "recognized by the constitution of the United States as obligatory upon them in their intercourse with European states and colonies." However, "The Chinese recognize no such laws. Their government is a hereditary patriarchal despotism, and their own exclusive interest is the measure of all their relations with the rest of mankind.

Their own government is founded upon the principle that as a nation they are superior to the rest of mankind. They believe themselves and their country especially privileged over all others."[73]

In short, any support for Chinese self-determination was trumped by the despotic character of the Qing government and their defiance of most favored nation status and the rule of nations and of God. In stark contrast to Cushing, Adams could "therefore not forebear to express the hope" that Britain "would extend her liberating arm to the furthest bound of Asia, and at the close of the present contest insist upon concluding peace upon terms of perfect equality with the Chinese empire."[74] In the arguments of Cushing and Adams are found one of the fundamental and enduring tensions in American statecraft toward the Pacific: whether the experience of the American Revolution dictated a policy of anti-imperialism or one of spreading universal republican values and ending despotism.

With Britain's crushing defeat of the Qing forces, however, neither Cushing nor Adams would see the realization of their ideal Sino-American relationship. The 1842 Treaty of Nanking was not in fact one of "perfect equality with the Chinese empire" as Adams had hoped. Nor was Cushing able to ignore the fact that the British had now secured trading access that the Americans must also negotiate for themselves on the back of Britain's "base cupidity and violence." The defeat of the Qing forced the Americans to apply their republican principles in ways that reflected their commercial interests and the shifting power dynamics in the Far East—and not for the last time. That responsibility would fall on Cushing, who was appointed the U.S. envoy to China in 1843 as a consolation prize after failing in his bid to become President Tyler's secretary of the treasury.

Cushing arrived in Macau in June 1844 carrying instructions from the State Department to distinguish the United States from Britain. He was specifically to remind representatives of the Celestial Court that the United States had thrown off English subjugation and "now meets England upon equal terms upon the ocean and upon the land," posing no threat to China comparable to the "dissatisfaction" and "alarm" the Celestial Empire must have toward the "immense power of England in India."[75] At the same time, he faced pressure from American merchants for equal access to Chinese markets after the British had forced the Qing to pay the costs of the war, reduce tariffs, accept consuls, open five ports to trade, and lease Hong Kong.

Cushing proved to be a skilled negotiator when the Qing delegation arrived in Macau in June 1844. Twelve days later, in the Treaty of Wanghia (Wangxia), he secured access to the same treaty ports as Britain, with improvements in tariffs and extraterritoriality, and inclusion of a clause allowing Protestant missionaries to learn the Chinese language and erect churches.[76] As diplomat and historian Claude Buss put it, "England shook the tree and the United States helped to pick up the fruit."[77] In exchange for the more generous Chinese concessions, Cushing agreed to an article in the treaty outlawing opium (which American merchants had also traded) and promising to turn over smugglers as a gesture of goodwill. The British had negotiated their treaty on board the HMS *Cornwallis*, whose guns were trained on Nanjing, ready to shell the city if the Manchu (Mantsu) negotiators balked. Cushing, in contrast, explained to his counterparts that the forty-four-gun frigate *Brandywine* had escorted him merely as a friendly gesture to his Chinese hosts. With the ratification of the treaty in the U.S. Senate the next January and the formal establishment of diplomatic relations, Cushing became the first officially recognized American envoy to China.

Yet any satisfaction with the Treaty of Wanghia was relatively short-lived. Cushing's assumptions had been that the attractiveness of American political, commercial, and moral ideals would allow the United States to match European influence; that the Qing would be capable of and willing to abide by the treaty's terms; and that the United States would not require naval bases or occupied territory like Hong Kong in order to enforce the treaty and counterbalance the imperial powers. In the decade following Cushing's mission, all of those assumptions proved wrong. Britain dominated the major new treaty port of Shanghai and appeared hungry to expand its Asian empire from India and Hong Kong to Japan, Korea, or Formosa. The Russians consolidated their positions in Siberia and Petropavlovsk on the Kamchatka Peninsula and began to advance down the Amur River. And the French alarmed American missionaries by negotiating their own guarantees for the protection of Catholic missionaries and their Chinese converts.[78] The Qing Empire, meanwhile, suffered ever-greater convulsions with the bloody Taiping Rebellion (1850–1864) and defeat at the hands of Britain and France in the Second Opium War (1856–1860). A more active American strategy to keep pace seemed inevitable.

THE SOLDIER, THE MISSIONARY, AND THE SAILOR: THREE STRATEGIC VISIONS FOR PACIFIC EMPIRE AT MIDCENTURY

The call for a more active strategy toward Asia in the 1850s emanated "not so much in Washington officialdom as among American representatives in East Asia."[79] These commissioners and consuls were an uneven lot. They had little diplomatic training and spent much of their time dealing with the crimes, kidnappings, and scandals that occurred when ambitious and sometimes desperate Yankees interacted with often xenophobic or equally desperate Chinese. Before the transcontinental telegraph was completed in 1861, their communication with Washington could take months. Grand strategy was the last thing most of them had the training, time, or connections to influence. Naval officers sent to the Far East Squadron were more inclined than their civilian counterparts to think in terms of power and prestige and not just commercial interests, but they often lacked the backing of strong secretaries of the navy, while facing constant suspicion from politicians representing southern and western agrarian states who thought the navy an unnecessary extravagance.[80]

However, there were exceptions in both the diplomatic and naval leaderships in the Far East. Kentuckian Humphrey Marshall watched the collapsing power of the Qing as U.S. commissioner to China and proposed an active Eurasian continental grand strategy designed to restore China as the bulwark against European imperial expansion in the Far East. Missionary Peter Parker served as Cushing's interpreter in Macau in 1844 but later concluded as commissioner himself that the United States needed a strategy of cooperation with Britain and France to pry China open, establishing American offshore island bases as the British had in Hong Kong after the Opium War. Commodore Matthew Calbraith Perry commanded the navy's Far East Squadron and urged a maritime strategy that would secure American interests through naval power, offshore bases, and eventual alignment with Japan. None of these men would fully succeed in convincing the distracted U.S. government in Washington to adopt their strategies. Yet each would anticipate the strategies promoted and implemented by expansionists at the end of the century.

Humphrey Marshall was the first of the three men to advocate a more activist U.S. approach toward the international affairs of East Asia. A graduate of the United States Military Academy, a lawyer, and a former congressman who had commanded the Second Kentucky Cavalry in the Mexican-American War (he later commanded a Kentucky brigade for the Confederate States in the Civil War), he was a rare southerner and army officer representing America in a region of the world dominated by Yankees and naval officers. It was perhaps for that reason that he wrote to a friend after being appointed commissioner in 1852 that he found Asia "a theater for the exercise of the most ambitious intellect."[81]

Marshall presented his credentials to the Qing on the auspicious date of July 4, 1853, and recognized almost immediately that his instructions from Washington were based on an assessment of China that no longer existed in reality. It was now obvious to him that the Europeans were using the Taiping Rebellion's erosion of Qing authority to expand their own power and influence. The British government had been urging the State Department in Washington to work together to take advantage of the Qing's weak position to demand direct diplomatic representation in the capital of Peking (Beijing) and greater access for international commerce. The secretary of state, William Marcy, was an avowed Jeffersonian and declined, ordering Marshall to sustain "cordial relations" and "conference" with the British but to remain strictly neutral in China's civil war.[82] Marshall found this far too passive and asserted his own strategy. The United States would not work with the other powers, but neither would it stand by and accept the dismemberment of China. Marshall had some sympathy for the "Christian king" who led the Taiping rebels, but his main concern was preventing the expansion of European imperialism in Asia at America's expense. To maintain a favorable balance of power in China and thus Asia as a whole, he would back the imperial court.

Marshall's assessment was not without merit. The British were looking to the Taiping rebels to help secure the Yangtze River for British steamboat navigation and linkages to Burma. The Russians were shifting their support to the imperial court to counterbalance the British but were also ready to swallow Manchuria and northern China if the Qing collapsed, using arms sales to the imperial forces to make them dependent on Moscow. In a worst-case scenario, Marshall observed, China would be divided into a pro-Russian state in the north and a pro-British state in the south. Indeed, the Russians had already seized the Amur River in order to gain access to a warm-water port on the Pacific.[83] Marshall asserted an American interest in Asia that would henceforth become almost immutable—in order to preserve a favorable balance of power and American access across the Pacific, there must be *one* China.

As he wrote to Secretary of State Marcy shortly after presenting his credentials to the Qing:

> It is my opinion that the highest interests of the United States are in-volved in sustaining China—maintaining order here, and gradually engrafting on this worn-out stock the healthy principles which give life and health to governments, rather than to see China become the theatre of widespread anarchy, and ultimately the prey of European ambition.
>
> I think that almost any sacrifice should be made by the United States to keep Russia from spreading her Pacific boundary and to avoid her coming directly to interference in Chinese domestic affairs; for China is like a lamb before the shearers, as easy a conquest as were the provinces of India. Whenever the avarice or ambition of Russia or Great Britain shall tempt them to take the prizes, the fate of Asia will be sealed and the future of China's relations with the United States may be considered as closed for the Ages, unless the United States shall foil the untoward result by adopting a sound policy.[84]

When the Taiping rebels took Shanghai on September 7, 1853, the American and European merchants argued that duties were no longer owed to the imperial government. The British chose to collect the duties in the form of banknotes held by the Foreign Office in London, but Marshall ordered the American merchants to provide cash, which would be held by the American consulate in Shanghai until the imperial government had restored order and was prepared to collect. The decision put American political and strategic interests ahead of American mercantile inter-ests for the first time in the Far East.[85]

However, Marshall's geostrategic instincts, bluster, and disobedience quickly put him at odds with the American merchants, the State Depart-ment, the navy, and even the Qing, despite his more benign stance on handling duties. The American merchants had the ear of Secretary of State Marcy, who hailed from Massachusetts and had been governor of New York. Commodore Perry, the commander of the navy's Far East Squadron, had his own vision of a maritime strategy, centered on coaling stations in Japan and the other islands across the Pacific, and considered the Kentucky cavalryman's continental strategy a misapplication of American naval power. He rebuffed Marshall's request for a U.S. naval squadron to take him to parlay with the Qing and instead prepared to get under way for his own mission to open Japan—not the first time State-Navy relations would break down. "Outmaneuvered by the British, neglected by his own people, ignored by the Chinese, and finally distrusted by his government at home, Marshall's efforts in sustaining China were bound to have a tragic ending. Informed of his removal through a newspaper item, Marshall left China for home on January 27, 1854."[86]

Most historians have dismissed Marshall's significance because he failed to change American policy at midcentury.[87] British historian W. C. Costin was even less kind, dismissing Marshall in 1937 as a "suspicious and jealous" backwoodsman.[88] However, whereas Cushing and other American commissioners in China had limited themselves to mercantile interests and occasionally the republican values of anti-imperialism, Marshall took the American debate about China policy to the level of geopolitics—as Dennett noted in the 1920s—discovering "the truth that the weakness, or dissolution, of China, was a matter of national concern to the United States."[89] In this, Marshall anticipated what would become the first comprehensive American strategy toward China at the beginning of the next century—John Hay's "Open Door"—and eventually the China policies of George Marshall and Richard Nixon a half century after that.

Humphrey Marshall's successor, Robert McLane of Maryland, was instructed by the State Department to stick with the neutrality and narrower commercial objectives that characterized the Cushing mission. McLane sought a revision of the Treaty of Wanghia to address the Qing empire's failure to implement terms, but he warned Marcy that this would not be possible "unless Great Britain and the United States shall concur in the policy of exerting a more decided influence on the destiny of China than is compatible with our present neutrality."[90] Unwilling to align with the British or to exert unilateral American power to obtain "commercial intercourse by virtue of treaty stipulations," Washington equivocated.[91] Three months later, as his short term approached its conclusion, McLane politely repeated the need for a clearer policy: "Two alternatives have been presented for the consideration of the President: to maintain the neutrality we now profess between the imperial government and the insurgent forces that are assailing it, awaiting the restoration of order and tranquility in the enjoyment of such commercial rights and privileges as we are able to retain, or, by a positive demonstration of the power of western nations to enforce existing rights, and by extending them, obtain security for the same in the future."[92]

McLane left China without an answer from President James Buchanan or the State Department, but his successor, Peter Parker, already knew what U.S. policy should be: application of American power not only for the purpose of renegotiating the Treaty of Wanghia but also for establishing a powerful U.S. military, diplomatic, and commercial presence across the Pacific.

Parker was born in Framingham, Massachusetts, on June 18, 1804. As a senior at Yale, he read the memoirs of Levi Parsons, who wrote of his experiences learning the Chinese language and traveling to the Orient and the "missionary field of the first importance."[93] The deeply religious Parker determined to make his life as a missionary in China, noting in a June 14, 1833, entry in his diary that the pomp and circumstance of President Andrew Jackson's visit to New Haven had convinced him that he would rather "be a humble missionary in China, though unknown but to the heathen, than to be President of the United States of America with all the attention bestowed by men whose breath is in their nostrils, and who are alike frail and perishable."[94]

Parker first arrived in Canton on October 26, 1834, and after further exploration of Singapore and Malacca, he returned to Canton to open his ophthalmic hospital in November 1835 and later a second hospital in Macau. "China," he wrote in his diary at the time, "contains three hundred thirty three millions of idolaters, but the land is yet to be possessed by Christ." He expressed his certainty that "the barriers will all be taken away and civilization will scatter its blessings through the land, traversing her territory with roads—railroads probably; her harbors and rivers will be navigated by steamboats; her laws will be modified by the foundation of all laws, the Bible."[95]

Parker's passion for saving souls quickly morphed into an interest in diplomacy. In 1837, he made an unsuccessful effort to convince officials of the Tokugawa Shōgunate to take back seven shipwrecked Japanese sailors. During the Opium Wars, Parker quit Canton and returned to the United States, where he shared his vision of America's role in China with President Martin Van Buren and future secretary of state Daniel Webster, among others, arguing that "the American nation probably stands higher in the confidence of the Chinese than any other nation" because America is "not a colonizing nation" and was officially opposed to the opium trade.[96] Already recognized as America's foremost expert on China, Parker was appointed deputy and "Chinese Secretary" to Cushing for the negotiation of the Treaty of Wanghia.

Parker's thinking about American policy toward China initially mirrored Cushing's. As he wrote after participating in the treaty negotiations in 1844:

> Nearly everything that America could ask, or China consistently concede, has been secured. Among the important objects gained is the article which provides for the erection of Hospitals and temples of worship at each of the ports of Canton, Amoy, Foochow, Ninpo & Shanghai. In a political point of view, the channel of direct communication between ... Washington ... and ... Peking ... is a desideratum of great moment ... important commercial advantages [have been] obtained over & above those secured by the English Treaty.... I am convinced that a *real* bond of friendship now binds these two great nations of the East & West. [Emphasis in original.][97]

But as the situation in China deteriorated and the Europeans flexed more muscle, Parker's views began to move from the optimistic and idealistic American exceptionalism of Cushing toward the hard-power logic of Britain and the European powers that John Quincy Adams had urged America to follow during the Opium War. As he wrote to his sister in 1839 after failing to repatriate the shipwrecked Japanese sailors to their homeland, "nothing could be more unfortunate than that all foreign intercourse should thus be forbidden and that China should be placed in a position similar to that occupied by Japan."[98]

While continuing his duties as deputy for McLane, Parker watched with dismay as the Qing treated the Americans with disdain and steadily rolled back promises made in the Treaty of Wanghia. In an early missive to his boss, Commissioner McLane, Parker bordered on discourteous in demanding action to defend American interests and honor:

> Excuse, dear sir, the liberty I take in *respectfully* offering such *suggestions* as occur to my own mind on this unexpected occasion. Two courses suggest themselves, viz: to go on submitting to the discourteous treatment of Chinese officials, or to say to them in unambiguous terms that it can and will be borne no longer.... If the latter is adopted, (and it must be, sooner or later, and when better than now the United States have an unprecedented and imposing naval force in the East?) then inform his excellency that the courtesies between two great and friendly nations can be pretermitted no longer, and that if within a

given time the interview is not granted, his excellency alone must be responsible for the consequences. [Emphasis in original.][99]

Parker returned to the United States in frustration the next year, but in a meeting with President Franklin Pierce, he was asked to return to China as the new American commissioner. He presented his credentials to the Qing on July 15, 1856, but his early idealism about U.S.-China solidarity was now submerged under righteous indignation at how the Treaty of Wanghia had been ignored. Before meeting the Qing representatives to present his credentials and with no instructions from Washington authorizing a change in U.S. policy, Parker inquired with the British and French envoys whether they would be prepared to join in a tripartite naval task force to press for renegotiation of the earlier treaties with the Qing. The French and British were undoubtedly surprised at this return to activism by the American mission, and they demurred. When Chinese authorities seized the British ship *Arrow* and tolerated the murder of a French priest three months later, the British and French attacked the Qing without revisiting American interests with Parker.

Washington was determined to maintain American neutrality during this Second Opium War (also known as the Arrow War) but also gave the U.S. Navy permission to protect American lives and property. In the confusion of a multidirectional conflict involving the British, French, Qing, and Taiping, the U.S. sloop of war *Levant* came under Chinese fire in November 1856. In response, Commander Andrew Foote assaulted and destroyed four Qing forts on the Pearl River, killing 160 Chinese inside. Rather than regretting the loss of life and the use of force against the same Chinese people with whom he had expected "a *real* bond of friendship" after the Treaty of Wanghia, Parker wrote enthusiastically to Washington to applaud the U.S. Navy's action: "This is the first blow that has ever been struck by our navy in China, and it has been done in a manner calculated to secure it an important prestige in the mind of this haughty government."[100] No longer negotiating the opening of hospitals or missions, Parker now saw divine purpose in his diplomatic mission, one that now went beyond protecting American commercial interests to civilizing the Chinese and preparing the way for an American empire in the Pacific.

From Parker's perspective, the next step was obvious. Relations with China were now governed by treaty, and the Chinese were failing to abide by that treaty. Other European powers were enhancing their military presence to ensure that their treaty rights were maintained (and, of course, expanded). In Parker's view, national honor required both an American show of force and alignment with the Europeans as equals. He proposed to Washington that it was time to punish the Qing and to establish a permanent U.S. strategic presence comparable to that of the British in Hong Kong. In a dispatch sent on December 12, 1856, he suggested that a joint Anglo-French-U.S. demarche should be presented to the Qing, demanding full treaty revision, and that noncompliance should be met "as a last resort" with the French occupying Korea, the British Zhoushan (Chusan), an important trading post off the coast of Zhejiang (Chekiang) province, and the United States the island of Formosa, which was discovered to have coal deposits useful for the navy's new steamships.[101] As he explained to the State Department: "Great Britain has her St. Helena in the Atlantic, her Gilbralter [sic] and Malta in the Mediterrenean [sic], her Aden in the Red Sea, Mauritius, Ceylon, Penang and Singapore in the Indian Ocean, and Hong Kong in the China seas. If the United States is so disposed, and can arrange for the possession of Formosa, England certainly cannot object."[102]

Parker was the most influential American voice on China policy at the time, and his message was clear: China policy and Asia strategy could no longer just be a matter of commerce—or the flag following trade. Now trade would have to follow the flag. And like the Europeans, the United States should use its power in the region to uphold American power and prestige. It would require two things that politicians in Washington had repeatedly rejected: a cooperative policy with the Europeans and American overseas possessions.

Parker had support from officers in the navy and from merchants in the Far East, but Secretary of State Marcy continued to adhere to the more neutral and accommodating stance urged over a decade earlier by Cushing. Parker's instructions had been to negotiate a revision of the Treaty of Wanghia to maximize American commercial interests—that was all. The secretary of state acknowledged that the Taiping Rebellion could render the process "difficult and embarrassing" for the envoys, but he cautioned that American policy would be to follow the outcome of the rebellion without interfering, even if that meant the breakup of China into different governments and likely European spheres of influence:

Should the revolutionary movement now in progress in China be successful, and the political power of the country pass into other hands, you will, at your discretion, reorganize the government *de facto*, and treat with it as the existing government of the country. If that vast and populous empire should be divided, and several governments be organized within its present limits, promising stability, you will present yourself to each as the diplomatic representative of the United States, and enter into such treaties with them respectively, as you may deem advisable.[103]

Washington wanted nothing to do with any European war with China, nor to put U.S. interests at risk by obstructing the dismemberment of the Celestial Empire.[104] Presidents Pierce and Buchanan stood by Marcy's vision of an American foreign policy empowered by virtuous commerce, using force only in self-defense and avoiding entrapments in European intrigues and imperialism. Parker resigned as commissioner in 1857 and returned once again to the United States, leaving his successor, William B. Reed, to negotiate the 1858 Treaty of Tientsin (Tianjin) once the British and French had again vanquished the Qing and set the terms for expanded extraterritoriality and commercial access the Americans would follow.[105]

The United States did not want for naval power in this period, of course, but the senior military officer in the Pacific, Matthew Perry, had his eyes on maritime Asia and advocated a policy of "masterful inactivity" in China.[106] Perry, however, was anything but passive. He shared Parker's conviction that the United States should expand its presence and influence in Asia—not in cooperation with the Europeans, as Parker had proposed, but through unilateral application of American naval power—especially with Japan.

The navy had long nurtured ambitions to open Japan. American ships had been temporarily permitted to trade at Dejima, near Nagasaki, after the Dutch fell to Napoleon between 1811 and 1814. Captain Porter of the *Essex* had written to the secretary of the navy in 1815 proposing he lead a U.S. expedition to open Japan, arguing: "We, sir, are a great and rising nation . . . we border on Russia, on Japan, on China."[107] President Monroe expressed interest in following Porter's advice but never sent him.[108] In 1845, Congress passed a resolution calling for the United States to open relations with Japan, and Commodore James Biddle was dispatched to parlay with the Tokugawa Shōgunate for that purpose. Biddle's mission ended with no compromises from the Japanese and considerable embarrassment after Biddle was pushed down on the deck of a Japanese ship by one of its crew and then his two ships, *Columbus* and *Vincennes*, had to be towed out of Edo Bay because of poor winds.[109] Whaling interests in New England continued to clamor for Congress to secure safe harbor for their ships in Japan. In 1853, Secretary of the Navy John P. Kennedy pointed to another strategic rationale, recommending exploration of a string of coaling stations across the Pacific to support a new fleet of American commercial and naval steamships.[110] Then, in late 1853, President Pierce, in his first State of the Union address, stated his intention to expand commerce not only with China but with other Asiatic nations as well.[111] He would send another expedition to open Japan.

Perry had already been lobbying to lead that expedition for years. Though they clashed on maritime versus continental strategy, Perry shared Marshall's view that the Far East was a theater for the most ambitious intellect—an arena for fair competition with the Europeans and an opportunity to shape the future of ancient empires. Whaling interests were of only marginal importance to Perry. His ultimate vision was of a maritime empire of American coaling stations and friendly republics stretching across the Pacific.[112] As he put it to Secretary of State Edward Everett before his 1853 expedition to Japan, "It is idle to suppose that because the policy of the United States has hitherto been to avoid by all means possible any coalition, or even connection with the political acts of other nations, we can always escape the responsibilities which our growing wealth and power must inevitably fasten upon us. . . . [I]n the development of the future, the destinies of our nation must assume conspicuous attitudes; we cannot expect to be free from the ambitious longings of increased power, which are the natural concomitants of national success.[113] Britain, he noted to the secretary, currently dominated the region with important posts from India to China, but "the Japanese and many other islands of the Pacific are still left untouched by this unconscionable government and some of them lay in a route of a great commerce which is destined to become of great importance to the United States."[114] Commander Glynn of the Far East Squadron had predicted shortly before Perry took command that "Japan could be converted into a liberal republic in a short time" and thus become more aligned with the United States than Britain, a sentiment Perry shared.[115] Like Parker, Perry also saw the potential for controlling the coal-rich island of Formosa, as well as the Lew Chew (Ryukyu) and Bonin Islands, eventually connecting these to a Chinese port comparable to Hong Kong in one direction and an American-controlled Hawaii in the other.[116] In this, noted Dennett,

"Perry appears to have been the first American in official position to view not merely the commercial but also the political problems of Asia and the Pacific as a unity."[117]

Perry had a comparatively free hand in Japan. There were no established European powers or U.S. interests to protect, and American power was enhanced not only by the U.S. Navy's growing presence but also by the distraction of Britain, France, and Russia in the Crimean War. Perry drafted his own instructions, which the State Department reviewed (although it is not known whether they revised them). The final instructions stated that:

> Recent events—the navigation of the ocean by steam, the acquisition and rapid settlement of this country of a vast territory on the Pacific, the discovery of gold in that region, the rapid communication established across the Isthmus which separates the two oceans—have practically brought the countries of the east in closer proximity to our own; although the consequences of these events have scarcely begun to be felt, the intercourse between them has already greatly increased and no limits can be assigned to its future extension.[118]

Perry arrived in Edo Bay in July 1853 with an imposing force intended to show that the United States was not to be trifled with but also instructions to emphasize there would be no interference with religion and that the United States was in no way connected with the more predatory European powers.[119] He then refitted in Hong Kong and returned to Japan with twice as many ships in February 1854, concerned that Russian or French fleets would arrive in the interim to forestall the American negotiations or offer to assist the Shōgun against the U.S. Navy.[120] Instead, he found that the Shōgunate was ready to accede to almost all of President Pierce's original demands, confirming them in the March 1854 Treaty of Peace and Amity (the Kanagawa Convention), which paved the way for the United States' first consul general in Japan, Townsend Harris, who negotiated full diplomatic relations in 1858. Ironically, the diplomatic success of Perry's second mission to Japan in 1854 robbed him of the support he would have needed from Washington to seize the Ryukyus and other islands around Japan for the U.S. Navy. Secretary Marcy wrote Perry in May 1854 that "the President is disinclined without the authority of Congress to take and retain possession of an island in that distant country."[121] Pierce had fretted all along that "if, in the future, resistance should be offered and threatened, it would also be mortifying to surrender the island, if once seized, and rather inconvenient and expensive to maintain a force there to retain it."[122]

Perry nevertheless returned to the United States to make the case for a republican maritime empire in the Pacific. Speaking before the American Geographical and Statistical Society in New York on March 6, 1856, he argued that although commerce with Asia was still much smaller than with Europe, the volume of trade with China would "easily be doubled by the establishment of more frequent and more rapid communications," and "the disparity between the value of exports and imports to and from China would be materially lessened by a demand for larger supplies of the products of our country." America would have an advantage over Europe, he told his audience, because "we should receive, by the way of California, intelligence from Canton from six to eight days, and from Shanghai from eleven to fourteen days earlier than by the way of England: and when the Pacific Railroad shall be completed, even England will receive her earliest intelligence from China by the Western route, the Americans having all the advantages of priority and information." Moreover, the establishment of ocean steamers and clipper ships could be brought into "useful and immediate service, in being hastily armed and sent to sea" if threatened by England or France, "the only two nations in the world of sufficient naval strength and experience to contend with us in the Ocean."

If America did not act, Perry warned, America would see "the Saxon race [Britain] upon the eastern shores of Asia," and "eastward and southward will her great rival in future aggrandizement [Russia] stretch further her power to the coasts of China and Siam: Will it be in friendship? I fear not! The antagonistic exponents of freedom and absolutism must thus meet at last, and then will be fought that mighty battle on which the world will look with breathless interest: for on its issue will depend the freedom or slavery of the world—despotism or rational liberty must be the fate of civilized man."

In short, the fate of American trade, security, and republican values was irrevocably intertwined with the fate of Asia and the Pacific. Yet the United States would bring great virtue to the struggle: "advantages of commerce," and the work of "enlightening heathenism, and imparting a knowledge of that revealed truth of God, which I fully believe advances man's progress here and gives him his only safe ground of hope for hereafter." But, he was quick to emphasize, this was not the case with the Japanese, a "rational people" who would be "more open to conviction than their neighbors the Chinese, over whom, in almost every essential, they hold a vast superiority." For the Japanese, the United States would establish "honorable and friendly" relations and not undertake the "appearance of the Christian teacher." Britain, too, would accommodate American naval power, he predicted, bringing a day when "whether the time honored cross of St. George, or the more youthful emblem, the stars and stripes of our own country" one could expect "an equally kind and generous welcome."[123] The final piece would be American outposts and coaling stations in the offshore island chains south of Japan. Like Jefferson's vision of an independent but friendly republic in the Pacific Northwest, Perry foresaw "Christian settlements upon those remote islands, where communities of those who may find themselves crowded out of the more populous parts of the world, can rear up new homes and hold out to the wanderers of the ocean." The United States would not engage in imperialism, though the indigenous inhabitants, he concluded, would ultimately be "doomed to mingle with or give way to some other race" in the same "melancholy fate of our own red brothers."

Perry's vision of a maritime strategy built on a strong navy, island bases, robust commerce, and alignment with civilized and democratic Japan and Britain would return. In fact, it would be reproduced in larger form by Captain Alfred Thayer Mahan and subsequent maritime strategists on the Pacific in the twentieth and twenty-first centuries, from Kennan to George Shultz. If not for the American Civil War, Perry's strategy may have taken root even sooner. As it was, he proved deeply prescient.

ASSESSING EARLY AMERICAN STRATEGIC THINKING ON ASIA

The evolution of American strategic thought on Asia from 1784 to 1860 naturally followed the consolidation of American independence, westward continental expansion, and the growing interaction of Americans with the Far East. From Jefferson's interest in a fellow republic securing the Pacific Northwest to John Quincy Adams's use of diplomacy and the implicit threat of force to keep open the "window on the Pacific," early American strategists understood the future importance that East Asia would play in the nation's destiny. With the transformation of American power in the three decades before the Civil War, the United States developed the tools of national power to play a far more active role in shaping

Asia's own future. By midcentury, the Asia-Pacific, unlike Europe or South America (southern expansion was a political nonstarter because it entailed the addition of slave states), was ripe for commercial expansion and competition with European powers.[124] The initiative in strategic thinking shifted across the Pacific to men like Marshall, Parker, and Perry, who recognized the changing balance of power in the region and sought a more activist U.S. strategy to safeguard longer-term American interests.

However, with continental expansion and industrialization, the American political leadership in Washington was also increasingly distracted and divided by the issue of slavery. By midcentury, the balance of power that mattered most was that between North and South. Asia was a remote region not yet central to the new republic's survival. Successive governments became ever less ambitious abroad as friction grew at home. Thus, as Dennett concludes: "There were fits and starts; brilliant efforts and then lapses. Continuity was lacking. It would even appear as though the Americans, while well equipped to initiate things effectively in Asia, were either by temperament or by the constitutional structure of their government, incapable of seeing things through."[125]

Of course, Dennett was writing in the interwar years and held a particular affection for the Open Door and a policy of cooperation with Britain. It is therefore worth making a fresh assessment of these early Americans' approach to Asia from the broader perspective of grand strategy, the study of which has advanced considerably since the 1920s. Specifically, it is worth asking whether these early American strategists effectively applied the means and ways of national power to achieve the vision and objectives for the nation conceived at that time.

If the measure of effective grand strategy is the application of limited national power in order to achieve desired ends in terms of trade, security, and values, without overextending or engaging in unnecessary conflict, then there is a case to be made that the early American policies toward Asia did produce impressive results, despite the poor report card from distinguished historians of the era such as Dennett. As Warren Cohen has remarked in qualified defense of American policies toward China during the first half of the nineteenth century:

> This was preindustrial America, a nation with vast unoccupied territories, a domestic market yet to be fully exploited, ample investment opportunities for anyone with capital. This was an age in which the

locus of power rested in Europe, in which the Orient mattered little in the world balance of power, and in which the state of technology had yet to put forth challenges to the security Americans could enjoy on their side of the great oceans. The United States was a weak and underdeveloped power which, even had it had the will to exercise political or military authority in East Asia, had not the means. Given its status among the powers, given its limited interests in China or elsewhere in the area, the American practice of trailing British power and utilizing the most-favored-nation clause to further these interests could not easily have been improved upon. Although this tactic, which several historians have labeled "jackal diplomacy," permitted no claim of moral superiority over the procedures employed by Europeans, it was nonetheless a most realistic and satisfactory policy for the United States.[126]

Americans were not just lucky, though. Over the course of the first six decades of American interaction with Asia, decisions were made to apply even limited power to preserve American equities. Americans were not afraid to use coercive tools where necessary and possible—with Japan or along the Pepper Coast, for example. In other cases, U.S. strategy involved the judicious insinuation of the use of force, as with John Quincy Adams's strong stand on the Pacific Northwest after Czar Alexander's *ukase* or Daniel Webster's implicit threat of force under the Tyler Doctrine to defend Hawaii from French encroachments. Overall, the United States projected significantly less power than Marshall, Parker, or Perry wanted, but enough to protect American lives and property and to ensure open points of access to the Pacific.

It is also striking how the European powers became increasingly solicitous of American alignment, opinion, and participation in collective action as the first half of the century proceeded and American power accrued. Washington may have played hard to get, in spite of the ardor of diplomats on the ground such as Parker. Yet the European powers rarely made a direct challenge to clearly articulated American interests, and eventually they backed away rather than test American resolve, as was evident in their responses to American assertions of a national stake in the Oregon Territory, Hawaii, and Japan. The Europeans' approach to the Americans stemmed not from respect but rather from a desire to avoid pushing the new republic into alignment with a rival power in a region that also was still peripheral to the core European strategic contests and required comparatively limited military assets. In a similar way, the Japanese also saw in 1858 the advantages of negotiating with Townsend Harris of the United States because they worried about Russian designs to the north. In that sense, U.S. strategy benefited from European balance-of-power logic even if most Americans eschewed it.

Americans in this period developed a great aversion to any single European power establishing a dominant role in the Pacific Northwest or Asia that would constrain future American expansion (on the continent) or trade (in the Far East). The American view of Britain was most complex. Some Americans, such as Cushing, were determined to pursue a policy that was distinct from Britain's and that reaffirmed America's republican identity, yet they were also unwilling to challenge British power directly or forgo its benefits. Others, such as John Quincy Adams or Perry, kept a careful eye on British power but came to recognize its advantages in terms of bringing stability and a relatively more open order to the region. It is worth remembering that both Adams and Perry had experienced war with Britain—Adams as a diplomat and Perry as a young midshipman in the War of 1812—and that the boundary with Canada was not settled until 1848. It would not be until the beginning of the next century that Anglo-American strategic cooperation in the Pacific really took any substantive form. In the meantime, British power and ambitions were a major consideration in American strategy. France's power was also a driver, particularly because of the rivalry between French Catholic and American Protestant missionaries. Russia was viewed as the most nefarious threat, yet there were moments when Russian and American interests aligned against Britain—in the early American trade from Oregon to China, for example, or later during the American Civil War, when Russia leaned toward the Union and Britain toward the Confederacy. China itself was initially seen as a power to be courted and then alternately as an obstructionist artifact to be pried open or a vulnerable state that must be protected against European expansion.

To the extent that the young United States applied its limited power to the Pacific, it did so primarily in response to threats to American access to the Far East or the prospects of foreign dominance over the Pacific Coast and Hawaii. Notably, when the United States chose not to take action in the Far East, there were rarely long-lasting consequences to American interests. Moreover, in the cases where there were setbacks because of insufficient application of power—for example, with Biddle's expedition to Japan or the Terranova incident—subsequent efforts were

more muscular. Americans understood that power mattered, even
republic was constrained in its application.

One of the hypotheticals of history that one could pose woul
whether the ambitious strategies of Marshall, Parker, or Perry might have
had more currency if American access to China and the Pacific ultimately
had been blocked by European expansion or greater Japanese or Chinese
intransigence. If Japan had refused to accept Perry back in 1854, for example, would the United States actually have seized the Ryukyu Islands?
Would further Chinese intransigence during the Taiping Rebellion have
led Washington to embrace Parker's proposal to occupy Formosa as an
American version of Hong Kong? Would aggressive expansion by one
European power in China have led the United States to align itself
even militarily with other powers or with China itself—as Marshall
proposed—in order to maintain open access to China? Ultimately, none
of these choices was forced on Washington, yet all were plausible, and
the arguments for action were already in place.

It can be said at least that the strategic thinkers of this era were strik-
ingly prescient in identifying the tools necessary for expansionism once
external threats and internal capabilities warranted action. They anticipated the requirement for coaling stations, Japan's potential to stand alone
as a modern nation and potential friend, the eventual need for American
leadership in establishing an "open door" with China, the possibility for
partnerships with like-minded states anchoring American influence and
stability in the region, and the ultimate if tragically violent return of Asia
to the center of world affairs.

Yet these strategists also exhibited all of the tensions in American
statecraft toward Asia that would plague future generations: the secondary importance placed on the region that Porter of the *Essex* and Peter
Parker tried to change; the tension between maritime and continental
strategies captured by Humphrey Marshall's and Commodore Perry's contrasting visions of China and Japan; and the early debates about the role
of American values embodied in Cushing's and Adams's reactions to the
Opium War.

Nonetheless, in fits and starts, with brilliant efforts and then lapses,
Americans were planting the seeds of strategic thinking on Asia that
would blossom as the new republic became a hemispheric and then global
power. Men such as Jefferson, Adams, Marshall, Parker, and Perry—for
all their flaws—deserve renewed respect for anticipating and trying to
shape a future era of American leadership in the Pacific.

2. "HOW SUBLIME THE PACIFIC PART ASSIGNED TO US"
PRECURSORS TO EXPANSION, 1861–1898

The Americans calling for a more robust presence in the Western Pacific at midcentury were not without allies in Washington. One was Senator William Henry Seward of New York, who was primed to establish the United States as a leading Pacific power when he became Abraham Lincoln's secretary of state in 1861. The Civil War would stunt all those ambitions, however, except for the postbellum purchase of Alaska and the annexation of Midway. As the nation entered the Gilded Age of the 1870s and 1880s, the republic turned inward to focus on reconstruction, financial boom and bust, and integration of the West. External threats were removed with the establishment of the Dominion of Canada and the defeat of France's proxy Emperor Maximilian in Mexico in 1867, while foreign trade decreased in importance to the country, never topping 5 percent of gross domestic product in the 1870s and 1880s. Seward had a grand strategic vision for Asia and the Pacific, but for decades afterward no American statesman would follow his lead.

Yet Asia itself continued to undergo a profound transformation. The end of the Concert of Europe and the irreversible decline of the Qing dynasty caused European power politics to spill over to the region, the effect being magnified by steamships, railroads, and the imperialist ideologies of new aspirants such as Germany and Japan. In response, Americans remained moderately active: opening Korea, offering "good offices" to resolve diplomatic disputes, and asserting the republic's paramount interests in Hawaii, Samoa, and the stepping stones across the Pacific. Over the same period, American economic power, national ideology, and political institutions began to burst at the seams. The steel barons of the Gilded Age made possible a modern oceangoing navy. The pressures of industrialization inspired a new national ideology that emphasized expansion abroad as the balm for the republic's growth pains at home. Civil service reforms and reconsolidation of executive power in the presidency allowed strategic thinkers to organize the government to connect ends, ways, and means.

The seeds of strategy were planted with the republic's earliest engagement of the Pacific, but it was in the seemingly fallow years between Seward and Roosevelt that the roots quietly spread.

"Empire Rises Where the Sun Descends": The Strategic Moment of William Henry Seward

William Henry Seward might have become the United States' first real "Pacific" president had Abraham Lincoln not bested him in the Republican primary. As it was, he hoped to fulfill American ambitions in the Pacific as secretary of state, but even that mission was curtailed by the events at Fort Sumter in April 1861. Nevertheless, Seward merits greater appreciation by historians for sustaining a vision of American commercial empire in the Pacific through the cauldron of civil war and thus enabling the grand strategies of the republic forty years later.

Born to the son of a Revolutionary War veteran in Warwick, New York, in 1801, Seward graduated from Union College and entered law and politics. His hero was John Quincy Adams, whose vision of an American commercial republic spreading democratic principles abroad became his own.[1] Elected to the U.S. Senate from New York in 1849, Seward called for a new international activism based on military strength, trade, and republican values. Speaking in the Senate chambers in 1850, he declared that the navy would "command the empire of the seas, which alone is real empire," while trade would convey American republicanism abroad and ultimately transform international norms in ways that would preserve

American preeminence.[2] Seward's greatest interest was the Pacific, which he called "the Far West" and the "new theatre of human activity."[3] He warned his Senate colleagues in 1853 that the United States must "baffle" the designs of Russia, France, and England in the Pacific and then "multiply ships, and send them forth to the East," for "the nation that draws most materials and provisions from the earth, and fabricates the most, and sells the most of productions and fabrics to foreign nations, must be, and will be, the great power of the earth."[4]

Seward believed that American engagement with Asia would be transformational. In terms that are jarringly patronizing by today's standards, he argued that "no one expects the nations of Asia to be awakened by any other influences than our own from the lethargy into which they sunk nearly three thousand years ago, under the spells of superstition and caste."[5] Speaking to the Phi Beta Kappa Society at Yale University in July 1854, he noted that American commerce had already affected the "regeneration of the natives" while the growth of new political institutions in Hawaii had "opened the ports of Japan and secured an intercourse of commerce and friendship with its extraordinary people," and sparked a revolution in China (the Taiping Rebellion—which was initially viewed with sympathy in the United States because of the Christian trappings of the rebels) that might bring "three hundred millions into the society of Western nations." "How sublime the pacific part assigned to us," he told his Yale audience, before concluding in a crescendo finale:

> The eastern nations sink, their glory ends,
> And empire rises where the sun descends![6]

Behind Seward's romantic nationalism lay a shrewd calculation of the power politics of Asia and the sinews of American engagement with the region. While in the Senate, Seward voted for California to join the union in 1850. Statehood for California was packaged as part of the broader Missouri Compromise that included the Fugitive Slave Act and expansion of slavery elsewhere—moves he strongly opposed—but California was America's newest gateway to the Pacific, a prize too important to delay.[7] While in the Senate, Seward also championed Chinese immigration to California, the transcontinental railroad, mail steamers, and the proposal to build a telegraph line through Alaska.[8] All of these were the deliberate building blocks for a future of American power in the Pacific.

On March 5, 1861, Seward was confirmed as Abraham Lincoln's secretary of state, but he was soon forced to harness all of his talents as a
strategist toward defeating the Confederacy and preventing permanent
secession. This meant putting on hold plans for expansion in the Pacific
and avoiding any antagonism of Britain and France, lest those powers
intervene on behalf of the rebellious states. When it came to American
vital interests, the priority was Europe first. Thus, although Americans
had taken the initiative in opening Japan in the 1850s, Seward ordered
his commissioner there in 1861 "to preserve friendly and intimate relations with the representatives of other western powers in Japan" and "to
leave behind" all "jealousies" of the Europeans.[9] Similar instructions went
to the commissioners in China and Siam and to the consuls general in
Batavia and India.

This self-restraint cannot have come easily to the ambitious and often
vainglorious Seward. Yet, although he ceded the initiative to the Europeans in Asia, he did so in a way that would preserve American equities for
the future. Looking back at the debates among Parker, Marshall, Perry,
and Cushing, Seward had seen three strategic options in Asia: (1) cooperate with Europeans to maintain the balance of power and to increase
pressure on China to open up to international trade and norms; (2) build
up China as a regional counterweight *against* European encroachment;
or (3) build up Japan as an example for China, a counterweight to the
Europeans, and a bastion for offshore balancing. Rather than surrender
America's position in Asia entirely, by necessity Seward shifted to the first
of these strategic options, but he never entirely abandoned the other
approaches. He was particularly careful to aim for outcomes that would
lay the foundations for a more independent and self-governed China
and Japan in the future. In 1861, for example, he proposed a joint U.S.-
French-British-Russian-Prussian assault on Japan to enforce prior treaty
obligations and punish the Tokugawa government. This would have had
the advantage of aligning the United States with the European powers
but also that of aiding the more modernizing and liberal Meiji forces in
Japan.[10] Seward's proposal did not come to fruition, but it revealed his
longer-term plans for shaping the regional order in Asia once the United
States emerged from the trials of preserving the union at home.

After the Civil War, Seward also returned to more direct American
support for Chinese territorial sovereignty and integrity. His instrument
was Anson Burlingame of Massachusetts, one of the most remarkable

Americans in the history of U.S.-China relations. An ardent free-state Republican, Burlingame had accepted a duel with southerner Preston Brooks after the South Carolinian beat Charles Sumner unconscious on the floor of the House in May 1856, but Brooks backed down. When Burlingame lost reelection in 1860, Seward offered him a post in Vienna, but the Hapsburgs refused him because of the Massachusetts man's support for Hungarian independence. So, Seward instead sent him to the Qing court.[11] In 1865, Seward instructed Burlingame not "to be technical or exacting in . . . intercourse with the Chinese government, but . . . deal with it with entire frankness, cordiality and friendship."[12] Burlingame explained that this approach sought "an agreement upon the part of the representatives of the Western powers that they would not interfere in the internal affairs of China; would give to the treaties a fair and Christian construction; that they would abandon the so-called concession doctrine, and that they never would menace the territorial integrity of China"[13] or, as he put it elsewhere, to put an end to "British officers who look upon China as a kind of English preserve."[14]

In negotiations to amend the 1858 Treaty of Tientsin, Burlingame convinced the Qing to abide by their treaty obligations in exchange for reciprocal most favored nation status (MFN) with the United States. When Burlingame stepped down in 1867, the Chinese then asked him to negotiate on their behalf with the U.S. government. Welcomed by Seward to Washington, the former U.S. envoy and the secretary of state signed China's first "equal" treaty with a Western power on July 28, 1868. It consisted of eight articles, guaranteeing Chinese sovereignty over its territories, control of inland waterways, and MFN rights in the United States.[15] Some of Seward's generous terms, particularly his welcoming attitude toward Chinese immigration, would later be reversed, but the Burlingame Treaty of 1868 would propel the concept of the "Open Door" from Humphrey Marshall to John Hay and reinforce the enduring if sometimes inconsistent principle in American foreign policy that China must be recognized as a sovereign power in its own right.[16]

Seward's successor, Hamilton Fish, summed up his predecessor's strategy toward China succinctly in 1870:

The present relations between the United States and China are unusually amicable. The policy inaugurated by Mr. Burlingame and Mr. Seward at Washington, whereby the Chinese Empire was placed on the footing of civilized states of the west, and recognized as an organized central power, was essentially an American policy in its inception, and is so regarded in the Chinese mind. From the best information which this Department can obtain, this policy is calculated to increase American influence and interests in China. It meets with the opposition of the British merchants and traders in China, who look upon it as a restraint upon their commerce and legitimate influence.[17]

Seward was highly attentive to the European balance of power in Asia, reflecting both his previous study of the region and his experience manipulating European rivalries to help prevent external intervention on behalf of the Confederacy during the Civil War. He saw Russia as the most benign of the European states at that point, in part because the United States and Russia had avoided conflict as each expanded in the Pacific in the 1830s and 1840s, but also because of a combination of mutual antipathy toward Britain and a brief Yankee fascination with Russian abolitionist movements for their own serfs in the 1850s. As Seward wrote to Ambassador Cassius Clay in Moscow at the beginning of the Civil War on May 6, 1861, ever thinking of eventual expansionism even in the midst of war at home:

> Russia, like the United States, is an improving and expanding empire. Its track is eastward, while that of the United States is westward. The two nations, therefore, never come into rivalry or conflict. Each carries civilization to the new regions it enters, and each finds itself occasionally resisted by states jealous of prosperity, or alarmed by its aggrandizement. Russia and the United States will remain good friends until, each having made a circuit of half the globe in opposite directions, they shall meet and greet each other in the region where civilization first began, and where, after so many ages, it has become lethargic and helpless.[18]

It was these mutual interests in the Pacific that opened the door for Seward to later purchase Alaska. Before the war, Captain Matthew Maury had concluded from his cartographical expeditions that Mercator projections from flat maps had underestimated how close to China the Aleutian Islands actually were.[19] A Virginian, Maury resigned his commission in 1861 to help the Confederate Navy purchase ships for raids against Yankee whalers in the Northern Pacific, further drawing Seward's eye to the value of the Aleutians, which he concluded would allow the United States to "extend a friendly hand to Asia."[20] American possession of Alaska would also block British expansion to the Pacific Coast while deepening friendly relations with Russia as a counterbalance to British power in China. The Russians, for their part, had developed complementary interests, as they were unable to defend Alaska against an increasingly populated British Columbia and were short on finances after losing to Britain and France in the Crimean War. The czar first broached the sale of Alaska in 1859, and then he reopened talks in Washington in early 1867 once the union was restored. At 4:00 A.M. on March 30, Seward and Baron Eduard de Stoeckl, the Russian minister in Washington, agreed on the price of $7.2 million—$2 million more than Seward wanted to pay but a remarkable bargain in retrospect.[21] Initially ridiculed as "Seward's folly" and an American "icebox," the new territory provided a windfall to the republic when gold, oil, and gas were discovered years later.

From Alaska, Seward pushed to secure American ports of influence elsewhere across the Pacific, agreeing with Commissioner Clay on "the necessity of our now having some formidable stand-point in the seas bordering Japan and China, where our armies and navies may rest secure."[22] On August 28, 1867, Captain William Reynolds of the sloop of war *Lackawanna* formally took possession of the Midway Atoll under the 1856 "Guano Law" allowing acquisition of uninhabited Pacific islands in order to utilize the guano (bat and bird droppings) deposited there. To the disappointment of the U.S. Navy, Midway proved unsuitable as a deepwater port, though the atoll would play a central strategic role in the Pacific war with Japan once airpower became a factor. On September 12, 1867, Seward wrote to the U.S. representative in Honolulu, arguing that it was also an opportune time for annexation of Hawaii, provided there was "consent of the people on the Sandwich Islands."[23] There was not yet consent in Hawaii or in the U.S. Congress, and the issue lay dormant. Seward and the U.S. Navy eyed Korea in strategic terms as well, dispatching the steam sloop of war *Wachusett* to the "Hermit Kingdom" in 1867 to investigate the destruction of the American merchant ship *General Sherman* by Korean forces the year before.[24] Seward's goal was not annexation or territorial expansion in Korea, as it had been in Hawaii and Alaska, but he did want America to take the lead in establishing a commercial treaty that would ensure most favored nation status and prevent European (especially French) designs on the peninsula.

Yet, despite this clear articulation of U.S. interests in the Pacific and the concrete plans he took to advance them once the American Civil War was over, Seward retired in 1868, having accomplished only a few of his objectives: the purchase of Alaska, the annexation of Midway, and negotiation of an equal treaty with China. Contrary to his expectations, the American people were not ready for expansion after the Civil War. In material terms, America was powerful, possessing the largest army in the world, a navy with 671 ships, a major industrial base, and an endless flow of immigrants from Europe.[25] But, as Robert Kagan points out, "it was not surprising that American foreign policy in the decade following the Civil War had an erratic quality."[26] The war had been traumatic and exhausting to the American people and their institutions of government. Relations between the administration and Congress were particularly damaged. Lincoln's successor, Andrew Johnson, was suspected by radical Republicans of Southern sympathies, and Congress clipped his powers at every turn, blocking his diplomatic treaties, with the rare exception of the Alaska Treaty.[27] Even when Civil War hero Ulysses S. Grant succeeded Johnson as president in 1869, the radical Republican chairman of the Senate Foreign Relations Committee, Charles Sumner, continued to block the administration's foreign policy initiatives, most notably Grant's treaty to annex Santo Domingo. Postwar Republicans were particularly opposed to overseas expansionism because they still associated it with the South's foreign policy strategy for spreading slavery. To the Republicans now dominant in Congress, America's mission in the world was first to perfect the union at home so that it would stand as a shining example— not to engage in Southern-style filibustering and expansion abroad. Even expansionists like Seward were war-weary and emphasized that their aim was for America to expand "not by force of arms, but by attraction."[28]

Though Seward fell short of his expansionist vision for the United States in Asia and the Pacific, his legacy in terms of regional strategy was still important. He came into office knowing far more about Asia than had any of his predecessors and was therefore better able to gauge and shape strategy from Washington. The completion of the transcontinental telegraph in 1861 meant that he could communicate with his envoys in the Far East in a matter of weeks, significantly shortening communication channels that had relied on wind and sail and that had left the initiative for policy largely in the hands of underresourced diplomats and sailors on the scene. Seward instilled in the State and Navy Departments the longer-term goal of seeking forward presence in the Pacific, and those departments continued to build momentum where they could absent congressional support. He put U.S.-China relations on a new footing. His vision of a transformational American influence on Asia surpassed that of even his hero John Quincy Adams. Despite his failures in implementation, Seward stood unrivaled as a strategist on the region for a generation.

"MAINTAINING A PROPITIOUS ENVIRONMENT": GREAT-POWER POLITICS AND AMERICAN GOOD OFFICES

In the decades after Seward left office, there was little innovation in American statecraft toward the Pacific. As Dennett records, "Every item of policy was, in principle, on record before 1870. After that date came only sifting, integration, elaboration, and the application to specific situations."[29] Yet even as the parameters of statecraft remained largely set, American policymakers did not remain idle. As Walter LaFeber argues, "Important continuities marked the years from 1865 to 1898. . . . [F]rom Seward through William Evarts, James G. Blaine, Gresham, and McKinley, U.S. policymakers were pushed and pulled not by public opinion or Congress but by their own sophisticated worldviews."[30] While the American people were still not inclined toward expansionism, diplomats took increasing note of the expansionist aims of the other powers.

Ironically, it was Russia, considered America's warmest European friend during the Civil War, that seemed to undergo the earliest and most menacing transformation. Thwarted in his expansionist aims to the south by defeat in Crimea and freed from expensive and indefensible supply lines to North America by the sale of Alaska, Czar Alexander III shifted his gaze to the Far East. In 1860, Russia had purchased Sakhalin and the Maritime Province from China and had established Vladivostok. The year after selling Alaska to the United States, Russia consolidated its control in Eurasia by forcibly removing Chinese from the new territories and probing northern China, the Korean Peninsula, and Hokkaidō for weakness. The shift in Russian strategy alarmed Clay, who wrote from Moscow in April 1868 that Russia had suddenly commenced "an aggressive or defensive war along the whole of Asia . . . colonizing northern China and the isles of Japan, thus making 'points d'appui' for future movements."[31] Then, in the 1870s, American public opinion turned sharply against Russia's growing persecution of Jews, prompting Seward's otherwise cautious successor, Hamilton Fish, to condemn the czar for his "egregious" actions.[32] Seward himself had not anticipated the possible turn in Russian strategy or the way that the Alaska purchase might channel Russian expansionist energies in these new directions. The aura of common cause with Russia against Britain and the Confederacy that had eased Seward's purchase of Alaska was quickly fading.

Germany also became an ambitious new entrant in the Asian theater after the defeat of France in 1871 and the subsequent establishment of the German empire under Chancellor Otto von Bismarck. The Franco-Prussian War, the fall of France, and the rise of Germany were initially viewed by other European powers and the United States as positive developments, since Bismarck was seen as a more reliable stakeholder in the international system than the fiery and ambitious Napoleon III of France (who among other things had menaced the United States from Mexico). It soon became evident, however, that the rise of Germany as a nationalistic state had changed the fundamental power balance in Europe and sparked a new power competition abroad, resulting in a scramble for colonies in Africa and the Pacific.[33] The new Imperial German Navy began its acquisitions in the Pacific by seizing "German New Guinea" in 1884 and then rapidly colonizing a series of South Pacific islands covering what today are the Marshall, Solomon, and Mariana Islands. To Americans who had mused about the necessity of coaling stations in the Pacific to link the West Coast to China, Germany was now actively seizing some of the best real estate in the South Pacific. Worse, Bismarck deliberately encouraged the French and Russians to pursue similar imperialist expansion in Asia since it would let rivalry play out far from the European continent while the German chancellor secured "peace and Austro-German predominance in the center and peninsulas of Europe."[34]

Though French expansionism had been set back by defeat in the Franco-Prussian War, the new Third Republic (1870–1940) returned to Asia with exactly the gusto Bismarck had anticipated, culminating in the defeat of China in the Sino-French War of 1884–1885 and the establishment of the *Union Indochinoise* under France in 1887, encompassing what is today Vietnam, Laos, and Cambodia. Americans had to that point viewed French policy in the Far East with a mixture of wariness and opportunism, countering French efforts to expand Catholicism in China and Hawaii in the 1840s and 1850s but also proposing French control of Korea in exchange for American control of Formosa in 1856 (Peter Parker's thwarted concept) and joint expeditions to open Korea in 1867 (proposed by Seward but rejected by the French because of contemporaneous military disasters in Mexico). American interests in Southeast Asia were more limited than in the North Pacific, but the French imperial designs on Indochina reinforced the scramble for mercantile colonies that was exploding across the Pacific.

Britain in many respects was a status quo power in the Pacific by this point, and increasingly the Royal Navy served as the major deterrent preventing the French, Germans, and Russians from even more aggressive expansion in the region. Despite lingering geostrategic rivalry between Washington and London, the two navies had long since established an affinity, captured in American commodore Josiah Tattnall's declaration that "blood is thicker than water," as he violated American neutrality on June 25, 1859, by sending American sailors to help serve the guns of a hard-pressed British squadron under fire from the Taku Forts at the entrance to the Pei Ho River in China.[35] After the Civil War, anti-British sentiment remained high in the United States, but attitudes began to change after British expansionist ambitions in North America ended with the establishment of the Dominion of Canada and Seward's purchase of Alaska. The shifting strategic views of Britain and Russia were reflected in the relationships of the three countries' envoys on the ground in China. In 1857, American commissioner William Reed had worked closely with Russian count Putyatin in preparation for the Treaty of Tientsin in order to counterbalance the influence of Lord Elgin, the British envoy.[36] But, in 1867, Burlingame worked more closely with his British counterpart as they negotiated a revision to the Treaty of Tientsin with the Qing court; it was now the Russian envoy who was on the outside. Throughout the 1870s and 1880s, the British role in Asia would increasingly be seen in a more favorable light by those Americans focused on stability and access in the Pacific, particularly in contrast to the more rapacious expansionism of the other European powers. Importantly, Whitehall would also begin to view American power in the region as a useful way to reinforce a favorable strategic equilibrium for British interests.

Meanwhile, Asian states themselves began to engage in more proactive statecraft, often looking to the United States as a card to play against their rivals. Americans from Perry to Mahan tended to view Japan as progressive and the Asian state most likely to follow the American example of republican government. Perry had given the United States a privileged position in Japan. Seward had of necessity ceded that position to the

British and French during the Civil War, but by the 1870s the United States had resumed efforts to establish its special relationship with Japan. In 1878, for example, the United States preempted European commercial negotiations with Japan by unilaterally granting the Meiji government large measures of tariff autonomy.[37] Despite such American overtures, however, the Meiji government was increasingly turning to Britain to build its navy and to Germany for principal guidance in modernizing its army and many of its political institutions. Empire was more attractive to the Meiji leaders than republican virtues, it seemed. Nevertheless, successive American governments in the late nineteenth century continued to see Japan as the best power within Asia to check European expansion and help open China, until Japan began to manifest its own imperial ambitions.

China also sought to draw out American power in this period. The Chinese themselves had set a precedent by inserting in the 1858 Treaty of Tientsin a clause in Article I in which the United States agreed to "exert their good offices" should other powers act "unjustly or oppressively."[38] This clause existed in no other treaty signed by China with European powers. As president, Ulysses S. Grant had stated that he wanted Asia to view the United States as "the most friendly of the powers," and many did, recognizing that American strategy, though not always effective, was generally centered around maintaining a strategic equilibrium through strengthening Asian states, whereas the Europeans often intended to expand their power by *weakening* Asian states.[39] Between 1879 and 1895, China's viceroy and superintendent of trade, Li Hongzhang (Li Hung-chang), made repeated efforts to trigger the "good offices" clause in the Treaty of Tientsin in an effort to bring the United States to its side in different disputes with other powers.[40]

The promise of "good offices" consequently became a new tool in the kit of American statecraft in this period. Americans interceded in an effort to broker peace on four occasions: (1) in 1874, to protect China from Japanese action against Formosa; (2) in 1879, when during his tour of Asia, former president Grant intervened to prevent a Sino-Japanese war over the Lew Chew Islands; (3) in 1883, in an unsuccessful effort to prevent a French war with China; and (4) in 1895, in fulfillment of treaty commitments to both China and Korea, when the United States helped broker the conclusion of the Sino-Japanese War.[41] In its treaties with China, Americans continued to rely heavily on the "good offices" clause as a tool of statecraft into the 1930s, by which time the approach was proving useless as a check against Japanese expansionism. Nevertheless, in the 1870s, 1880s, and 1890s, it represented a significant new source of American engagement in the Asian strategic landscape. Former president Grant returned from his own diplomatic role in Japan and China in the summer of 1877 flush with excitement about the modernity of Japan, the goodwill of the Chinese toward Americans, and the role the United States might play in sustaining progress in the region.[42]

American engagement in Asia during the Gilded Age did not rest on the provision of "good offices" alone. Despite congressional constraints put on Seward's vision of expansion, Grant and his Republican successors retained an interest in opening new markets in Asia—particularly Korea. In 1866, the armed American merchant steamer *General Sherman* was contracted by a British firm to attempt trade with the Hermit Kingdom of the Korean king Kojong (Gojong). The exact circumstances of what happened are still debated by American and Korean scholars, but the expedition ended with the *General Sherman* in flames and its crew executed. Inquiries with the Korean kingdom yielded neither explanations nor apologies, and in 1871 an expedition of five U.S. warships of the Asiatic Squadron under Rear Admiral John Rodgers landed marines and sailors to level Korean forts on the Han River, killing over 200 of the defenders within. Throughout the 1870s, European naval expeditions had also begun to probe Korea's coastal defenses, and Russian ground forces were positioned on the Yalu River along the border between China and Korea.[43] In 1880, the administration of Rutherford B. Hayes decided to undertake a more concerted political/military expedition to finally open Korea to trade and Western civilization before the peninsula fell to one of the other powers.

The man trusted with the task was Commodore Robert N. Shufeldt, a New York native, veteran of Civil War blockade duty, and advocate of American trade with Africa and the Pacific, who had commanded the *Wachusett* in the unsuccessful first attempt to communicate with the Korean king after the *General Sherman* incident. Shufeldt returned to the Western Pacific on the steamship *Ticonderoga* in the spring of 1880 in an attempt to open direct negotiations with the Korean king through Japan. Frustrated with the Japanese refusal to open Korea to other commercial competitors, Shufeldt steamed to Shanghai in June 1881, where Viceroy Li Hongzhang was eager to supplant the Japanese as an intermediary with the Korean king and to garner technical and diplomatic support from the Americans.[44] After a year of intrigue and maneuvering, the

Chinese route proved fruitful, and on May 22, 1882—in sight of uninvited Japanese and Chinese warships—Shufeldt and representatives of King Kojong signed a treaty opening bilateral diplomatic relations and granting extraterritoriality and most favored nation status for Americans in Korea. Korea, it is worth noting, did not receive the reciprocity inherent in the Burlingame Treaty and the 1878 agreement with Meiji Japan—in part because of the influence of Chinese and Japanese patronizing views of the peninsula and in part because the Hermit Kingdom itself was further behind in accepting the West.

Nevertheless, Shufeldt had paralleled Perry's success in opening Japan, and like Perry before him saw the accomplishment as part of a larger strategic design in which "the acquisition of Alaska and the Aleutian Islands, the treaties with Japan, Sandwich Islands and Samoa, are only corollaries to the proposition that the Pacific Ocean is to become at no distant day the commercial domain of America."[45] Yet, as Shufeldt discovered while negotiating within sight of Japanese and Chinese warships off Incheon (Inch'ŏn), East Asian diplomacy was no longer a matter of the West versus the East. Within Asia, Japan's rapid modernization and China's decline were leading to a clash over which country would have preeminence on the Korean Peninsula and ultimately within Asia itself.

The competition came to a head when an insurrection broke out in Korea in the spring of 1894 and China informed Japan that it would be sending troops to quell the disturbance, in accordance with the Tientsin Convention of 1885. The Japanese government replied that it also would send troops, given the grave nature of the threat to Japanese interests. By the next April, Japan's forces had handily crushed the Chinese, using superior seamanship and rapid-fire guns at sea and advanced logistics and maneuvers on land.[46] As one recent historian notes, "such a seismic reversal in the traditional power balance fractured the previous international harmony within the Confucian world and left an aftershock of enduring territorial and political fault lines."[47] Defeated yet again, the Qing agreed to humiliating terms in the Treaty of Shimonoseki, which weakened Chinese suzerainty over Korea, transferred ownership of Formosa to Japan, and opened new Chinese ports to Japanese access. Japan now asserted its rights in China as an equal to the strongest European powers.[48] Alarmed at this sudden expansion, Russia and its ally France, joined by a German government concerned about its status in the Far East, forced Japan to retreat from those terms in the Triple Intervention, which only paved the way for war less than a decade later between Japan and Russia.[49] The United States again offered its "good offices" to help bring Japan and China together in the negotiations leading to the Treaty of Shimonoseki and refused to join the Europeans in the Triple Intervention after its conclusion.[50] The United States "never interfered in the disputes of others except as animated by a general desire for social tranquility," Japanese foreign minister Mutsu Munemitsu admiringly wrote at the time.[51]

By 1895, the Americans were indeed seen as the friendliest of the powers, as Grant had hoped—and "such it is hoped will always be our aim," wrote Secretary of the Navy Hilary A. Herbert in *The North American Review* in the summer of 1895. "But," he added in light of Japan's unexpected triumph, "let us bear in mind that we can never be assured of our ability to command the peace unless we are prepared for emergencies," adding that "Americans must remember too that only the waters of one ocean, a wide one no doubt, but easily traversed by navies, separate their country from Asia."[52]

"PROTECTION OF THE GREAT GOVERNMENT OF THE UNITED STATES": SECURING STEPPING STONES ACROSS THE PACIFIC

Seward's vision of an extended American presence across the islands of the Pacific had been checked by a Congress loath to grant imperial powers to the presidency or to contradict the noninterventionist, anticolonial republican virtues for which the Civil War had been fought. Yet, at the same time, the American interest in consolidating control over Hawaii and key South Pacific islands such as Samoa and Guam intensified with the completion of the transcontinental railroad in 1869 and new plans for a canal across the isthmus separating the Atlantic and Pacific Oceans. With the overspill of European imperial competition into Asia, Germany and other powers were already coveting many of the critical Pacific island stations on that highway. The Pacific was not only ripe for American stepping stones to the Far East, argued Admiral David Porter in 1887, but could also now become a "highway upon which, unseen until close upon us, an enemy can marshal his hosts and attack us in fifty vulnerable points at once."[53]

Since President Tyler declared an extension of the Monroe Doctrine to Hawaii in 1842, Americans had seen the mid-Pacific islands as an indispensable pillar in the American sphere of influence in the region. Other major powers did not necessarily concur, however. In 1843, the British and French proposed a tripartite pact with the United States under which all three powers would vow never to take the islands, a proposal Tyler rejected.[54] Yet Congress could not bring itself to move beyond the anticolonial impulses of the revolution and actually annex Hawaii directly. Consideration of annexation also faltered in 1854 over the question of whether the island should receive statehood, and if so whether it would be free or slave. Seward's preference was also annexation, but failing that, he attempted to bind the islands more tightly to the United States through a reciprocity treaty (reducing mutual tariffs), an effort that did not pass in the Senate until 1875.[55] As a result, however, Hawaii had developed almost total trade dependence on the U.S. market by the early 1880s.

In 1881, Secretary of State James G. Blaine (an admirer of Seward's and a fellow student of John Quincy Adams's strategic thought) wrote to President James Garfield that there were only three places overseas "of value enough to be taken"—Cuba, Puerto Rico, and Hawaii.[56] Of course, Congress was not interested in "taking" Hawaii at that point, and Blaine reiterated in correspondence with members that the United States remained committed to the independence of the islands. At the same time, he cautioned Congress about the danger that European powers would use "diplomatic finesse or legal technicality" to influence or alter Hawaiian political institutions to draw the islands away from the United States. Ultimately, he explained, "It is too obvious for argument that the possession of these islands by a great maritime power would not only be a dangerous diminution of the just and necessary influence of the United States in the waters of the Pacific, but in case of international difficulty it would be a positive threat to interests too large and important to be lightly risked."[57] As long as possible, he concluded, the United States would endeavor to draw "intimate ties between us and the Hawaiian Islands so as to make them practically a part of the American system without derogation of their absolute independence."[58]

Grover Cleveland, elected in 1885 as the first Democratic president since before the Civil War, was an opponent of expansionism and annexation but differed little from his Republican predecessors on the strategic importance of Hawaii. Arguing that there was "a natural interdependency and mutuality of interest"[59] between the United States and these "stepping stones to the Pacific," he gave support in 1887 to a Senate bill permitting the U.S. Navy to lease Pearl Harbor.[60] Yet Hawaii was also becoming a cauldron of contradictions for American political leaders by the 1880s. American sugar interests—dominant on the islands since Northerners had turned to Hawaii's fertile soil and warm climate to replace lost sugar production from the South during the Civil War—were increasingly engaged in intrigues to force annexation, particularly after the McKinley Act of 1890 raised tariffs on all imported sugar. In 1893, Sanford Dole and the other plantation owners on the island orchestrated a coup against Queen Liliuokalani.[61] The plantation owners' Southern-style filibustering did not sit well with Cleveland, who upon returning to office for a second term in 1893 immediately withdrew from the Senate an annexation treaty that Republican president Benjamin Harrison had negotiated with Hawaii the year before.

Yet, at the same time, the intrigue and instability in Hawaiian politics also reflected the islands' continued strategic vulnerability. Proof of that vulnerability was evident when Japanese and British warships appeared off the Hawaiian coast in response to the 1893 coup against Queen Liliuokalani—just as Cleveland was withdrawing the annexation treaty from the Senate. Japan's victory over China in 1895, and the huge influx of Japanese laborers to Hawaii, who already formed the largest single ethnic group there by 1895, only increased uncertainty about the future of American strategic control over the islands. Viewed in the context of the three decades that led up to annexation in August 1898, it becomes clear that the islands were not just tossed into the imperialist grab bag as an afterthought to the Battle of Manila Bay. Throughout the 1880s and 1890s, American policymakers were finding it increasingly difficult to sustain Blaine's plan to keep Hawaii "practically a part of the American system without derogation of their absolute independence."[62]

Samoa, in contrast, was never part of the "American system," but sitting 5,000 miles from continental Asia and 2,600 miles from Hawaii, the islands attracted increased attention as an important link in the series of American stepping stones across the Pacific. American missionaries had been active in Samoa since the 1830s, and the *Vincennes* had surveyed the island's harbor of Pago Pago in October 1839 as part of the U.S. Exploring Expedition. Captain Wilkes and his officers had concluded that southeastern trade winds would make the harbor too treacherous to exit, but in the era of steam power, the winds were no longer an obstacle to turning the harbor into a forward base.[63] In 1872, Commander Richard W. Meade of the *Narragansett* took it on himself to lease land at Pago

Pago Harbor from the Samoans in exchange for "friendship and protection of the great government of the United States."[64] This generous
security guarantee had no standing at all in the U.S. Congress, but the
Samoan chief honored the lease, knowing no better. A new treaty was
negotiated in 1878, which replaced the earlier security guarantee with the
now more standard "good offices" clause used in the Treaty of Tientsin in
exchange for Samoan guarantees that the U.S. Navy would have access
to Pago Pago.

The problem for the Americans in Samoa was that the British, and
more troubling the Germans, were already there. Germany had begun
commercial activities on the islands as early as the 1850s, and the new
Imperial German Navy now coveted them as a coaling station no less
than the U.S. Navy did. In 1885, German naval officers declared their intention to take all of Samoa, prompting a counterclaim from the U.S. consul that the island should retain its independence under the protection of
the United States. Subsequent British efforts to negotiate tripartite administration of the island broke down over American insistence that Samoa deserved an independent government.[65] More to the point, as Blaine
explained to the other parties in 1889, the United States had preeminent
strategic interests in the island: "The interests of the United States require
the possession of a naval station in these remote parts of the Pacific, and
by a treaty with the lawful authorities of Samoa they have been put in
control of the harbor of Pago Pago for these purposes. We cannot consent to the institution of any form of government in Samoa subject directly or indirectly to influences which in the contingencies of the future
might check or control the use or the development of this American
right."[66]

Surprised by the assertive American stance over the remote islands
and eager to avoid sparking Anglo-American alignment against Germany, Bismarck ordered his negotiators to back down and agreed to tripartite supervision of an independent Samoa in negotiations in Berlin in
1890. The crippling of most of the German and U.S. fleet in Samoa by a
massive typhoon in 1889 also helped defuse the crisis. The Germans were
checkmated, and Samoa was open to the Americans, who would annex
the island formally in 1904.[67]

From Alaska to Hawaii and Samoa, the United States had safeguarded
stepping stones across the Pacific, though none were yet American in
name. It was an era of quiet power politics, if not outright expansion.

Prerequisites for Expansion: Naval Power, National Ideology, and a Fiscal Military State

The mounting pressures on the United States to craft a more proactive and comprehensive grand strategy for the Pacific were emanating not only from developments in the region. Within the republic itself, the Gilded Age had yielded three critical prerequisites for expansion, despite the restrained American attitude toward foreign affairs at the time. These prerequisites were industrialization and the building of a modern navy, the emergence of a new national ideology, and the establishment of a more centralized fiscal military state.

A strong navy had been recognized as indispensable to American power in the Pacific by every statesman who thought about the region from John Quincy Adams through William Henry Seward. In the decades after the Civil War, the United States actually enjoyed the cheap immigrant labor, industrial infrastructure, and advances in metallurgy necessary to sustain a world-class fleet. Yet over the same period, successive governments preoccupied with republican virtue and continental expansion at home allowed the fleet to dwindle to little more than a handful of mothballed ironclads and outdated steamers. The American fleet was so pathetic during the Gilded Age that it became a punch line in Oscar Wilde's satirical 1887 treatment of American life, *The Canterville Ghost*. When the lead American character in Wilde's story laments that her nation has no "ruins and no curiosities," the titular English Ghost replies sarcastically, "No ruins!? No curiosities!? . . . you have your navy and your manners."[68]

The sarcasm rang painfully true. In 1881, the Republic of Chile had humiliated the United States by threatening to sink the American Pacific Squadron if the State Department continued to give diplomatic backing to rival Peru in the War of the Pacific (also known as the Guano War because it was fought over the nitrates produced by bird droppings). The fact was that Chile *could* have followed through on that threat since the U.S. Pacific Squadron at the time consisted only of aged wooden cruisers—no match for the Chileans' British-built armored battle cruisers.[69] Even Shufeldt's *Ticonderoga* was a Civil War era wooden sloop of war that had been recommissioned for his diplomatic cruise.

When Chester Arthur assumed office in 1881, he declared that the United States would be the "chief Pacific power,"[70] and he commissioned the construction of four new steam-powered steel cruisers and gunboats. He also established the Naval War College in Newport, Rhode Island, and the Office of Naval Intelligence in Washington, DC, two institutions that would play critical roles in crafting America's Asia strategy in the decades ahead.[71] Congress resisted any further shipbuilding programs until 1889, when Benjamin Harrison's activist secretary of the navy, Benjamin Tracy, echoed the strategic arguments of a still relatively obscure scholar named Mahan at the Naval War College to win funding for rapid-fire guns, heavy armor, and torpedoes.[72] In his second term, Democrat Grover Cleveland also expanded shipbuilding to provide economic stimulus during the Panic of 1893, warning Congress that the U.S. Navy had slipped to the seventh-ranked navy in the world.[73] The United States was now the second-leading industrial nation in the world in terms of steel and coal output, and if Congress wanted a navy, it could have one. By the time Admiral George Dewey engaged the Spanish Fleet at Manila Bay in 1898, the U.S. Navy had become the sixth-largest fleet in the world, transforming itself from a mostly wood-hulled coastal defense force into a modern battle fleet capable of decisive engagements against other major fleets on the high seas.[74]

The second critical transformation behind expansion toward the end of the nineteenth century was in national ideology. By the 1880s and early 1890s, leading American intellectuals and publicists like Frederick Jackson Turner, Brooks Adams, and Josiah Strong grew anxious that American republicanism would atrophy and collapse with the completion of westward expansion. Boom-and-bust financial cycles culminating in an economic depression from 1893 to 1897, and deadly labor confrontations like the Homestead Strike of 1892 and the Pullman Strike of 1895, only reinforced this angst about where to channel American energy.[75] The answer seemed obvious: America must secure new overseas markets.[76] Whereas political leaders in the decades immediately after the Civil War had seen America's purpose as healing and perfecting the republic at home, Turner, Adams, and Strong led a new intellectual movement that argued the republican form of government could only be saved by expansionism abroad.[77]

Their pessimism about internal decay was offset by a confidence in American superiority abroad reinforced by social Darwinism and a new fascination with "Anglo-Saxonism," the concept that the Anglo-Saxon people had emerged from a process of political natural selection as the most capable of bringing civilization, commerce, and peaceful interdependence to the world. Popularized in Strong's 1885 best seller *Our*

Country and taught with faux intellectual rigor in the leading Ivy League schools and to the emerging captains of industry, the Church, and the navy, Anglo-Saxonism provided a justification not only for American expansion but also for Anglo-American alignment to maintain the international order against the ambitions of less benign aspiring hegemons such as "Slavic" Russia.[78]

The third major transformation was in the structure of the U.S. government. By the 1880s, it was not only the navy that was in bad shape; American political institutions were too small, too weak, and too unprofessional to manage a great power's interests abroad. As Fareed Zakaria notes, Congress had repeatedly thwarted the foreign policy aims of the presidents and had hobbled administrative branch efforts at military and civil service reform in the Gilded Age. Meanwhile, the debt assumed from the Civil War had created a spendthrift culture in Congress that had denied the administrative branch the tools it needed to pursue foreign policy. By the late 1880s, however, all of that began to change.[79] Civil service and military reform passed, Civil War debts were repaid, and the stronger economy created both the resources and the requirement for a professional bureaucracy. By the time of the Battle of Manila Bay, the United States had developed the administrative authority, civil service reform, and tax policies of a "fiscal military state."[80] As Zakaria sums it up, Americans for the first time had both wealth and the political institutions necessary to turn that wealth into power.[81]

STRATEGIC LESSONS FROM THE GILDED AGE

Modern political scientists debate whether expansionism derives from offensive realism (the ability to expand) or defensive realism (the perceived need to expand because of expansion by others).[82] Historians, meanwhile, have often been drawn to the arguments of William Appleman Williams and the "Wisconsin School" that American expansion was driven by economic imperialism and the narrow interest of corporations.[83] To American strategic thinkers in the final decade of the nineteenth century, these would probably have been differences without a distinction. Threats, commerce, and capacity all went into the soup that became the American strategy for expansion into the Pacific.

While the ends of American expansion consolidated around preservation of the Pacific as a highway of commerce and democracy westward and the prevention of threats coming from the East, the ways and means of American statecraft also quietly evolved in the Gilded Age. A steel-hulled oceangoing navy required coaling stations, but the Jeffersonian policy of supporting friendly independent republics on the islands of Hawaii and Samoa no longer appeared sufficient to the task. Annexation of these stepping stones as the U.S. Navy had done at Midway would prove more reliable, particularly as other powers developed the ability to threaten the West Coast of the United States from the same outposts. In terms of the major powers in the Far East, however, the United States took steps to more actively reinforce self-determination for these islands and give them equal status with the West. The Burlingame Treaty and the tariff agreements with Japan encouraged China and Japan to seek similar arrangements with the Europeans, blunting imperial expansion and demonstrating American republican virtues. "Here, I learned to denounce that pride of race which denies the brotherhood of man," Burlingame declared from China, linking his support for "four hundred million Chinese" to his opposition to slavery in the United States.[84]

Other tools of statecraft evolved. The emergence of American "good offices" as a diplomatic tool was premised on absolute American neutrality in this period. As American power in the Pacific grew over the first decades of the twentieth century, the United States would use this same tool to intervene in conflicts or affect outcomes in more deliberate pursuit of its national interest. Thinking on the role of trade also began to shift. Seward had anticipated that commerce would bind the Pacific to the United States, but like all Republicans, his frame of reference was that American competitiveness vis-à-vis European powers depended on a high tariff. Yet, the reciprocity treaty with Hawaii demonstrated that lowering barriers to trade could have an even more powerful binding effect with states in the region. Protectionism would remain the Republican Party's policy—even toward Hawaii, with the McKinley Act of 1890—but strategists and protectionists began to part ways for the first time.[85]

On the whole, the Gilded Age represented a period of inward focus and strategic drift in American foreign policy. Yet, beneath the surface and often without explicit congressional support, tools of American power were being refined and lessons were being learned about the new geopolitical dynamics of the region. These underground currents accelerated, bursting to the surface at the end of the century in the words and actions of the men who presided over America's arrival as a full Pacific power.

3. "I WISH TO SEE THE UNITED STATES THE DOMINANT POWER ON THE SHORES OF THE PACIFIC"
GRAND STRATEGY IN THE ERA OF THEODORE ROOSEVELT

In his book *First Great Triumph*, diplomat and historian Warren Zimmerman describes his subjects—John Hay, Alfred Thayer Mahan, Elihu Root, Henry Cabot Lodge, and Theodore Roosevelt—as men who were "more than simple agents of history." They had "grown up in a period of weak presidents, an exploding economy, growing military power, rising expectations and disappointing performance." With the Spanish-American War in 1898, Zimmerman argues, "the time for action had come, and they seized it."[1] These men were not, however, just hyperactive "war lovers," as one recent popular history suggests.[2] As president, Theodore Roosevelt exhibited a masterful skill at bending regional events to U.S. interests without risk of war: restraining American expansion after victory over Spain; holding the Open Door policy in place for China; intervening to end the Russo-Japanese War on terms that would maintain a favorable balance of power; and reassuring a rising Japan while undertaking the largest peacetime buildup of the navy seen up to that point to maintain a strong deterrent. His grand strategy would have impressed Castlereagh or Bismarck, and clearly impressed Henry Kissinger, who considered it one of the most effectively conceived, articulated, and executed strategies in American history.[3]

Yet, as leader of a peer power projecting interests into the Western Pacific, Roosevelt also discovered the confounding downsides of geography: the vulnerability of forward defense lines across a huge ocean; the temptations and risks of entrapment on the continent of Asia; and the difficulty of aligning democratic values abroad with growing anti-immigration and anti-imperialist sentiments at home. Roosevelt developed answers to all of these tensions—answers that his immediate successors forgot, much to the detriment of U.S. interests. Roosevelt's grand strategy therefore merits careful study not only because it marked a significant turning point in the United States' engagement with Asia and the Pacific but also because it offers lessons for the challenges facing U.S. foreign policy in the region today.

But first, as Robert Osgood argued, "everyone who examines America's adjustment to the status of a world power must reckon with Mahan."[4]

"The Greatest Danger to Our Proximate Interests": Alfred Thayer Mahan and the Problem of Asia

Alfred Thayer Mahan had an unusual career. Though he reached the rank of captain in the U.S. Navy, including service in the Pacific on the *Iroquois* and later as captain of the *Wachusett*, he was not considered a terribly proficient sailor. And although he wrote over one hundred books and articles on history, his historiography was not considered terribly original. His strategic concepts were also derivative. He drew on Henri Jomini's concepts of land warfare to emphasize the importance of strategic locations at sea (choke points, canals, and coaling stations); Sir John Knox Laughton, his contemporary and friend in Britain, introduced him to naval historiography; Sir Julian Stafford Corbett taught him the principles of sea control and maneuvering; and Stephen Luce preceded him at the Naval War College, where he began the instruction of naval strategy and history to officers for which Mahan would become famous.[5] Nor was Mahan the lead architect of either the fleet or the tactics that allowed the U.S. Navy to defeat Spain at sea in 1898.[6] That credit must go to President James Garfield and his secretary of the navy, William Hunt, for their modernization of the fleet in the early 1880s; to President Benjamin Harrison's secretary of the navy, Benjamin Tracy, for his mobilization of Congress; to senators like Eugene Hale and Henry Cabot Lodge for

turning Mahan's annual reports into legislative action; and to Secretary
Hilary Herbert for turning Mahan's theories into strategy and policy in
the late 1890s.[7]

Yet it was Mahan who ultimately exerted the greatest influence on the
foreign policies of both Theodore and Franklin D. Roosevelt (not to mention the war-fighting strategies of the Imperial Japanese Navy). This was
in part because Mahan combined his knowledge of history and the sea
in terms Americans had not seen before, but he was more than an apostle
for naval power. His was the first comprehensive grand strategic concept
for the United States in the Pacific—harnessing diplomatic, ideational,
military, and economic tools in pursuit of national interests at a level of
detail and realism not met by Adams, Perry, or Seward.

Mahan began with careful elucidation of the national interest.[8] His
views were shaped by Anglo-Saxonism, his own Presbyterianism, and the
social Darwinian premise that conflict and competition are constant,
whereas visions of institutionalizing an enduring peace are a dangerous
illusion. In ways far more concrete than those of his predecessors, he
identified permanent American interests in key geographic areas of
the globe in terms of geography, spatial factors, and the distribution of
power.[9] Two regions preoccupied him: the Caribbean and Asia. And although he expressed confidence that the United States would steadily assert dominance over the Caribbean, he warned that Asia would remain
contested (or, as he put it, "debated and debatable") and thus much more
likely to impact the global balance of power. As he wrote to Roosevelt in
1897, it was developments in Asia, not in Europe or the Caribbean, that
represented "the greatest danger to our proximate interest."[10]

Mahan's assessment of the geostrategic significance of Asia to American security flowed from the concept of "physical conformation" he developed in his classic text *The Influence of Sea Power Upon History* (1890).[11]
The U.S. coastlines, he argued, actually made the United States highly
vulnerable compared with other major powers in the world. Although
the harbors and port cities dispersed along the American coasts might
be sources of enormous commercial advantage in peacetime, they created an indefensible line of targets in wartime, as the British had demonstrated with their raids during the War of 1812 and Mahan himself had
seen while serving on blockade duty during the Civil War.[12] The American coastline was particularly vulnerable on the Pacific side, with its
widely separated and underfortified coastal cities. The United States
would gain little benefit from internal lines in such a setting, whereas a

strong maritime adversary operating from island bases in the Pacific would be free to strike along the coast at will. Plans for a canal across the Isthmus of Panama compounded the challenge of physical conformation even further, since it would mean that enemy domination of the vulnerable West Coast would open the Gulf Coast and Atlantic seaboard to attack.

As Mahan explained in "Hawaii and Our Future Sea Power" (1893), this geostrategic reality meant that control of Hawaii was now indispensable for the defense of the United States.[13] With U.S. control of the isthmian canal and Hawaii, the U.S. Navy would have flexible internal lines to shift its fleets from one flank to the other for decisive engagements against enemy fleets. In contrast, control of Hawaii by a hostile power would provide a secure coaling station from which to mount attacks on American trade routes to Asia, the vulnerable West Coast, and the canal route to the Gulf Coast and East Coast. As naval officers had begun to appreciate in the Gilded Age, the combination of geography and technology (steam power and steel) meant that forward presence in the Pacific was necessary not only for access to China but now also for defense of the homeland.

The prospect of a hostile power taking control of Hawaii was hardly fanciful at the time Mahan was writing "Hawaii and Our Future Sea Power." That same year, as was noted, British and Japanese warships appeared off the coast in the wake of the coup attempt against Queen Liliuokalani, and Japanese warships again were dispatched to the islands in June 1897 in a dispute over restrictions on Japanese immigration. The European powers had already been scrambling for control of other islands in the South Pacific, and, as Mahan cautioned, the "German commercial and colonial push" was leading to "conflict between German control and American interests in the islands of the western Pacific."[14]

Mahan also noted the geostrategic implications of the longer-term rise of Asian powers themselves, warning that Asia posed a potential threat to the West not only "Westward by land, but also Eastward by sea."[15] Perry had warned of the Slavs, but Mahan was one of the first strategic thinkers to identify America's realpolitik interest in preventing the rise of *any* rival hegemonic power from within continental Asia. Mahan's focus in 1893 was primarily on China, which he predicted would once again become a "great, civilized, maritime power" (a good century or two prematurely). After Japan's crushing victory over China in 1895, however, Mahan shifted his focus to Japan.

Mahan's attitude toward Japan reflected the views of other senior naval officers posted to the Asiatic Squadron in the nineteenth century. As a young executive officer aboard the 200-foot corvette *Iroquois*, Mahan had seen a Japanese beheading and participated in multinational gunboat diplomacy to open Kobe and Osaka. He had no illusions about the insularity and violence inherent in Japan's political culture, but, like Perry before him, he believed that Japan's rapid modernization and adoption of Western institutions meant that the Japanese could be incorporated as part of a broader alignment of modern maritime states that might sustain a healthy balance of power in the Pacific. Indeed, Mahan argued that skillful alignment of U.S. interests with a rising Japan would be the critical first step toward forestalling a larger collision between East and West that he saw as inevitable as China and then India threw off the imperial yoke and asserted their place in the international system.[16] The Sino-Japanese War was taken by Mahan not as a sign of Japanese expansionism but rather of Japan's readiness to open China's vast markets and end "the folly of [China's] exclusive and conservative policy."[17]

However, Mahan also recognized that American alignment with Japan would require the United States to take out of play the most acute source of strategic competition with the Japanese at that point: the Hawaiian Islands. As Mahan explained to Roosevelt in correspondence on May 2, 1897, "Are we going to allow her [Japan] to dominate the future of those most important islands because of our lethargy? It may well happen if we shut our eyes. . . . Do nothing unrighteous; but as regards the problem, take them first and solve afterwards."[18] Roosevelt in his response completely agreed: "With Hawaii once in our hands, most of the danger of friction with Japan would disappear."[19]

Mahan's disciplined approach to geopolitics reflected his military training. As he put it once: "Political problems into which the element of geography enters have much in common with military strategy. There will be found in both a center of interest—an objective; the positions of the parties concerned, which are the bases of their strength and operations . . . and there is the ability to project their power to the center of interest, which answers to the communications that play so leading a part in military art."[20]

It was from this same perspective of projecting power and communications that Mahan viewed trade and values as critical parts of an American grand strategy. In terms of trade, Mahan associated himself with the general argument advanced by Brooks Adams and others in the 1880s and 1890s that without overseas markets, America's expanding industrial and agricultural capacity would lead to further strife and rot at home. But whereas most of these economic nationalists held the view that American commercial competition abroad required high tariffs at home, Mahan viewed the tradition of tariffs as anachronistically "defensive," and he favored instead a lowering of tariffs in order to expand American influence overseas. For that reason, he had been an enthusiastic supporter of the reciprocity treaty with Hawaii and saw it not only as a defensive bonding with Hawaii but possibly also as the beginning of broader trade liberalization to extend American influence to other parts of the region.[21] Tariffs, he wrote in 1890, were like "a modern ironclad . . . with heavy armor, but inferior engines and guns: mighty for defense; weak for offense."[22] History demonstrated, he argued, that Napoleon's empire had been destroyed not only by a lack of naval power but also by the heavy defensive armor represented by the protectionist "Continental System," which had caused the "empire itself to crash beneath the weight." America did not have to succumb to such a fate, Mahan was certain, for "it is safe to predict that, when the opportunities for gain abroad are understood, the course of American enterprise will cleave a channel by which to reach them."[23] In this, he was prescient, though less influential with his friends in the Republican Party, who supported a high tariff at the time.

Values constituted the final note for Mahan—far less extensive than his writings on material factors such as naval power, geography, and trade—but were indispensable to his geostrategic worldview nonetheless. Empire would not bring security, he held, if it was based on mercantilist exclusionism and exploitation rather than the advancement of individual liberty. America, he argued, must have both commercial and *moral* influence in the Far East:[24] "The United States owes to mankind her due contribution: for in it is one of the greatest hopes—in our own national opinion the very greatest hope—of humanity."[25] Osgood dismisses this aspect of Mahan, whom he clearly admires, as a mere rationalization of "national egoism," but there was realism behind Mahan's focus on values. He was not a humanitarian interventionist or an advocate of aggressive regime change. Indeed, he advised that "coincident with the growth of American power" it might be necessary to consider "retrenchment" of the Monroe Doctrine's support for democracies in South America—so that U.S. power could be applied "more effectively" to the crucial regions of the Caribbean and the Pacific. It was precisely this focus on choosing priorities in the application of America's "moral influence" that revealed how important he considered values and norms to be in the overall strategic equilibrium of a reawakening Asia.

The great-power realism behind Mahan's view of values was particularly evident in his assessment of Japan's impact on the emerging system in Asia. If one focused only on Japan's "obvious material improvements," he held, "little but apprehension could be exacted by the aptitudes she has displayed." He added, "But in that she shows herself open as well to influence by the ideals, intellectual and moral, which by gradual evolution have possessed us, there is the better hope," for in Japan there was evidence of "the Asiatic welcoming European culture," in which is to be found the most conducive condition for happiness and stability, "personal liberty, in due combination with restraints of law sufficient to, but not in excess of, the requirements of the general welfare."[26] Mahan's view of the application of republican values in Asia, like Perry's, was evolutionary—using America's "moral influence" to encourage gradual political liberalization and the development of indigenous political institutions that would help to maintain a favorable ideational balance in the region as material power steadily shifted to the civilizations that "surrounded and outnumbered" the West—"the civilizations at the head of which stand China, India and Japan."[27] His view echoed Jefferson's call for friendly republics in the Pacific Northwest and Perry's hope for similarly aligned republics in the Pacific islands, but Mahan was now arguing for an American strategy to support the gradual democratic transformation of the ancient civilizations of the Far East itself. Many decades later, the Chinese Communist Party would attack this approach as a nefarious strategy for "peaceful evolution"—and they would not be entirely wrong.

In the mind of Mahan—and increasing numbers of his contemporaries—American interests in a favorable balance of material power, free trade, and the spread of liberal norms led logically to strategic convergence with Britain. Mahan was an Anglophile and a follower of Anglo-Saxonism to be sure, but he also saw that the United States had a realpolitik interest in upholding the British-led neoliberal order. Only the United States and Britain combined "freedom and self-government consistent with orderly progress"; "liberty and law; not the one or the other but both," he argued.[28] His study of history had also demonstrated that American access to the Western Pacific had long depended on the preeminence of the Royal Navy—despite the menace it also presented—and that there would have been no Monroe Doctrine or American access to the China market if British naval power had not kept other European powers at bay in the

Atlantic. "In the Pacific we are natural allies," he wrote to British naval historian James R. Thursfield in 1897, the same year that the Salisbury government decided not to contest American supremacy in the Western Hemisphere in the Venezuelan crisis.[29] Mahan had planned for war against the Royal Navy earlier in his career on the navy staff, but by the end of the century, he was a forceful advocate of the Anglo-American imperium evoked in Rudyard Kipling's 1899 ode to American victory over Spain:

> Take up the White Man's burden, have done with childish days
> The lightly proferred laurel, the easy, ungrudged praise
> Comes now, to search your manhood, through all the thankless years
> Cold, edged with dear-bought wisdom, the judgment of your peers![30]

Historians generally agree that Mahan's comprehensive geostrategic view of American interests in Asia was a driving and unifying force among other expansionists of his day, most notably Theodore Roosevelt.[31] The two became friends and intellectual companions after Mahan read a copy of Roosevelt's stunningly detailed history of the U.S. Navy in the War of 1812. Both men were avid students of history, passionate proponents of naval power, and careful observers of geostrategic developments, particularly in the Pacific.

Roosevelt and Mahan did not align on all issues. Roosevelt had joined the Cleveland administration's jingoistic calls for confrontation with Britain in order to uphold the Monroe Doctrine during the Venezuelan crisis at a time when Mahan was calling for Anglo-American entente.[32] Roosevelt also initially saw Russia in a more benign light than Mahan did.[33] Eventually, British restraint and Russian expansionism brought Roosevelt around to Mahan's point of view on both nations. On trade, Mahan was for reducing barriers in order to increase U.S. influence. Roosevelt remained the politician, and a Republican politician always supported the high tariff. "Thank God I am not a free-trader," Roosevelt declared in 1895, adding, "In this country pernicious indulgence in the doctrine of free trade seems inevitably to produce fatty degeneration of the moral fiber!"[34]

On the core issues of grand strategy, however, Roosevelt and Mahan started in the same place. Both viewed a strong navy, trade, and republican self-government as indispensable for the promotion of justice and world order, and both devised strategies for the United States to shape the emerging dynamics in the Far East—with a preference for a maritime strategy centered on the offshore island chain.[35] The two corresponded regularly on developments in the region. When Roosevelt was appointed assistant secretary of the navy in 1897, Mahan gave him early advice. "Your best admiral," he wrote, "needs to be in the Pacific."[36]

WAR WITH SPAIN AND THE GRAND STRATEGY OF A PACIFIC POWER

As tensions rose with Spain over Cuba that summer, Roosevelt prepared a comprehensive war-fighting strategy for President William McKinley on behalf of the Department of the Navy. It was highly derivative of Mahan's thinking, particularly about the Pacific.[37] The memo proposed preparation of orders for the Asiatic Squadron to blockade and if possible seize Manila in the event of hostilities with Spain over Cuba and then for the United States to fill the vacuum left in the Pacific by Spain's defeat. The president and the other departments countermanded most of Roosevelt's recommendations with respect to war planning in the Caribbean—but not his core operational concepts for the Far East.

Ten days after the USS *Maine* was sunk on February 15, 1898—by the Spanish according to William Randoph Hearst's *Morning Journal*—Roosevelt took advantage of Secretary of the Navy John D. Long's absence from Washington to cable Commodore George Dewey, ordering preparations for an attack on the Spanish fleet in the Pacific. Dewey gathered his Asiatic Squadron in Hong Kong to refuel and refit. On April 24, he received orders from the secretary of the navy: "War has commenced between the United States and Spain. Proceed at once to Philippine Islands. Commence operations particularly against the Spanish fleet. You must capture vessels or destroy. Use utmost endeavor."[38]

The next day, Dewey received orders from the British governor-general in Honk Kong to leave the port under British neutrality provisions. Dewey's was the only Western naval force in the Pacific without a home base or reliable source of coal in wartime. As Royal Navy officers saw him off, one was heard to say, "Fine fellows . . . too bad we shall never see them again."

One week later, Dewey's U.S. Asiatic Squadron encountered Admiral Montojo's Spanish fleet at Manila Bay. As Dewey's sailors shoveled coal into the steam engines below decks while singing "We'll Have a Hot Time in the Old Town Tonight" and his anxious officers withstood the initial Spanish bombardment without returning fire, Dewey calmly turned to the captain of his flagship, *Olympia*, and said: "You may fire when you are ready, Gridley." Within minutes, the Spanish fleet was sunk, and within days the navy had secured the surrender of the unsuspecting Philippine garrison at Guam.

With the collapse of Spanish imperial power in the Far East, the United States was suddenly poised to be a Pacific power on a par with France, Germany, Russia, Japan, and someday even Great Britain. America's strategy in the transition from war to peace in 1898 and in the decade that followed was essentially the strategy of a newly established status quo power. American expansion beyond Spain's possessions would have exacerbated great-power rivalry and put the new American island outposts at risk. McKinley—and especially Roosevelt—therefore acted like Bismarck after the Franco-Prussian War, using *self-restraint* to great strategic advantage. Rather than being revisionist war lovers or aggressive proponents of radical democratization, the U.S. government prioritized three key areas: (1) securing the new insular acquisitions or "stepping stones" across the Pacific; (2) ensuring Chinese administrative integrity and most favored nation status for the United States in China; and (3) using diplomacy to sustain a favorable balance of power and ensure that no rival power took a step as bold as the one the United States had just taken.

MAKING THE STEPPING STONES AMERICAN

Insular acquisitions had already been a core element of strategic thinking about America's role in the Pacific for over half a century, punctuated by Tyler's expansion of the Monroe Doctrine to Hawaii in 1842 and the push by Parker, Perry, Seward, and Blaine for further coaling stations in the 1850s. In the summer of 1898, the "stepping stones" across the Pacific were now within easy reach for the McKinley administration. But there were also new complications. Could coaling stations be secured if the larger island chain or archipelago around them was not? Should the United States become a de facto colonial power if it were to take

responsibility for these larger possessions? How would island possessions thousands of miles from the West Coast be defended against rising
powers in the region, especially Germany and Japan? The increasingly
voracious appetite of other major powers for island possessions and large
chunks of China added urgency to these questions.

The easiest strategic call to make was with respect to Hawaii. The
McKinley administration had negotiated a new annexation treaty with
Sanford Dole's Republic of Hawaii government shortly after coming into
office in 1897, but congressional leaders asked him to wait until the grow-
ing tensions over Cuba were resolved first. In the meantime, in March 1898,
Republican senator Cushman Davis of Minnesota submitted a report on
Hawaii to the Senate, laying out the strategic rationale for annexation in
Mahanian terms:

> The chief reason for the annexation of Hawaii is to secure a vantage
> ground for the protection of what the United States already owns. It is
> not primarily to secure new territory, promote shipping, and increase
> commerce, but it is a measure of precaution to prevent the acquisition
> by a foreign, and, perhaps in the future hostile, power of an acknowl-
> edged military stronghold. . . . The main reason why Hawaii is a
> strategical point of value is that the Pacific is so wide that battle ships
> cannot cross it from any foreign naval station to the Pacific coast
> without recoaling, and there is no place to recoal except Hawaii. Ex-
> clusion of foreign countries from Hawaii will therefore practically pro-
> tect the Pacific coast from trans-Pacific attack.[39]

Or, as the former commander of the Asiatic Squadron, Admiral George
Belknap, put it to Congress at the time: "The planting of our flag at
Hawaii will serve notice to the Powers now invading the Orient that thus
far mayest thou go and no farther!"[40] Of course, Hawaii was important
not only to the defense of the continental United States. Each of the three
resupply fleets that arrived in Manila to support Dewey after his victory
over Montojo had stopped to recoal in Hawaii and would have been unable to complete their missions without the stop.[41] For both offensive and
defensive reasons, the war with Spain had highlighted the critical strategic importance of Hawaii. A majority of native Hawaiians submitted pe-
titions to Congress protesting annexation, but Congress fast-tracked the
decision through a joint resolution (avoiding the two-thirds majority

normally used for annexation), and on July 7, 1898, President McKinley formally annexed Hawaii as a U.S. territory.

Even as Hawaiian annexation was being debated in Congress, the navy was quietly acquiring the stepping stones that lay between Hawaii and the Philippines. As part of Roosevelt's broader prewar planning for the region, the navy had been ordered to seize the Spanish possession of Guam in the Mariana Islands in the event of an outbreak of hostilities. Three U.S. warships arrived on June 21, 1898, to inform the isolated and surprised Spanish garrison that the two nations were at war and they were now prisoners of war. Spain formally ceded the islands to the United States in the Treaty of Paris later that year. In January 1899, the navy also seized Wake Island, which the Naval Board had hoped would serve as a cable relay station between the new possessions. Like Midway, Wake proved disappointing for this purpose, though the tiny atoll's strategic worth would eventually be borne out when the U.S. military began to station aircraft in the Pacific decades later.

Meanwhile, ongoing Anglo-German discussions on the Samoa problem had yielded a consensus to divide control of the island between the United States and Germany (Britain gave its piece to Germany in exchange for concessions elsewhere in the Pacific and Africa). Secretary of State John Hay formally agreed to this arrangement in December 1899 and, on February 19, 1900, McKinley signed an executive order instructing the navy to establish a coaling station under its control on the island of Tutuila in what is today American Samoa.[42] With relatively little interference or debate in Congress, the navy's stepping stones between Hawaii and the Philippines were finally secured. In the case of the smaller islands of Guam and Samoa, any consideration of establishing self-governing friendly republics was set aside in the rush to make the stepping stones available to the navy after the defeat of Spain. Self-government would be sorted out later.

The Philippines presented a different problem. There was no navy plan to take the entire archipelago after the defeat of Spain. The Naval Board, on which Mahan sat, argued that the United States needed only "the City and bay of Manila, or Subic Bay."[43] Hay also wanted to limit the U.S. acquisitions to Manila and instructed his peace negotiators to proceed along those lines, agreeing with the Spanish on August 12, 1898, that "The United States will occupy and hold the city, bay and harbor of Manila, pending the conclusion of a treaty of peace which shall determine the control, disposition and government of the Philippines."[44] At first, it appeared that the United States might be able to secure its string of coaling stations from San Francisco to Hawaii, Guam, and then eventually China without colonies or complex military occupations.

However, with the collapse of Spanish imperial power, the Philippine archipelago became anything but a neat and tidy setting for a U.S. naval base. Within days of defeating the Spanish fleet at Manila Bay, Dewey asked for 5,000 additional troops just to help secure Manila, and the McKinley administration responded with a call for volunteers to serve in the Philippines, anticipating that the force would more likely number 20,000. Meanwhile, a German "squadron of observation" under Vice Admiral Otto von Diederichs arrived on the scene around May 1 like a preying vulture. Diederichs outgunned Dewey, and the German fleet's actions were particularly suspect in the wake of recent German encroachment in Manchuria and the Shandong (Shantung) Peninsula, regions that absorbed nearly two-thirds of America's exports to China.[45] The U.S. embassies in Berlin and Paris sent detailed reports giving specific credibility to German ambitions in the Philippine archipelago, and British sources also fed Hay and Roosevelt a steady stream of intelligence on German naval activities in Manchuria and around the Philippine archipelago.[46] By October 1898, Hay had changed his instructions to the peace commissioners. Spain would have to cede all of the Philippines, not just Manila, since "the latter is wholly inadmissible, and the former must therefore be required."[47] Spain was in no position to refuse, and it formally turned over control of the Philippines to the United States on December 10, 1898, under the terms of the Treaty of Paris.

What followed was the first national debate in the United States about the relationship between American values and American strategic interests in the Pacific—a debate that would be repeated in many respects six decades later over Vietnam. On one side were the members of the Anti-Imperialist League, formed on November 19, 1898, by prominent political leaders, including Carl Schurz, George Frisbie Hoar, and Edward Atkinson, and propagated by the scathing critiques of humorist Mark Twain. This group of "goo-goos" viewed big business and immigrants with deep suspicion and saw annexation of the Philippines as the next dangerous chapter in the demise of America's virtue.[48] Some of the anti-imperialists were motivated by racism, warning, as Senator G. G. Vest did in January 1899, that after annexation statehood would come next for the "half-civilized, piratical" inhabitants "seven thousand miles distant, in another hemisphere."[49] Others, such as industrialist Andrew Carnegie, made geostrategic arguments. Carnegie, who shared the Mahanian pre-disposition for annexation of Hawaii and alignment with Britain, warned nevertheless that colonization in the Far East would be "fraught with nothing but disaster to the Republic."[50] He elaborated: "There is seldom a week which does not bring alarming reports of threatened hostilities, or of new alliances, or of changes of alliances, between the powers arming for the coming struggle. It is chiefly this Far Eastern question which keeps every shipyard, gunyard, and armor yard in the world busy day and night, Sunday and Saturday, forging engines of destruction. It is in that region the thunderbolt is expected; it is there the storm is to burst."[51]

On the other side of the argument were the imperialists. These "jingo-ists" also tended to cast their case in moral and sometimes racist terms, most famously when President McKinley allegedly told supporters that America had no choice but to "uplift and civilize and Christianize" the people of the Philippines.[52] At the core of the imperialists' argument was a realpolitik concern that the United States had to secure its position in the Philippines—precisely because of the "alarming reports" of "powers arming for the coming struggle" highlighted by Carnegie.

McKinley and the imperialists eventually prevailed in a vote in the Senate on February 6, 1899, on annexing the Philippines, in what Republican senator Henry Cabot Lodge characterized as "a very near run thing."[53] Politically, however, annexation was something of a pyrrhic victory for the pro-annexation group. Moral arguments about Christianizing and up-lifting the Philippines soon gave way to an ugly counterinsurgency that lasted until 1913 and eventually took the lives of more than 4,000 Americans and tens of thousands of Filipinos.[54] The U.S. Army ultimately prevailed, using some of the same tactics employed to pacify the Plains Indians, but the American people became disillusioned with the odor of death and suffering that characterized empire. In January 1900, a U.S. presidential commission under Cornell University president Jacob Gould Schurman recommended that the United States prepare the Philippines for self-rule by establishing a bicameral legislature, local autonomy, and public schools.[55] William Howard Taft, the first civilian governor-general, appointed in 1901, put those recommendations into effect. This paved the way for the Jones Act in 1916, committing the United States to granting independence. The navy's forward base was secured, and Congress returned to the Jeffersonian concept of building American expansion in the Pacific around friendly self-governing republics.

One question that American strategists had not fully answered up to this point was how far forward the U.S. military presence should be—to the island chains off the Chinese coast or to China itself? On August 8, 1898, Mahan wrote to Secretary Long, summarizing the Naval Board's view that the United States would require coaling stations and ports in Hawaii, Samoa, the Philippines, Guam, and somewhere in mainland China, if possible. As Mahan put it, "the Board is impressed with the advisability of acquiring a coaling station nearer to central China than is Manila, and for this purpose recommends one of the harbors . . . among the Islands of the Chusan Tau harbor or that of Tai Shei Shan."[56] The U.S. minister to China, Edwin Conger, also pushed in the summer of 1898 for the United States to acquire territory in China in order to compete with the other European powers, which were doing the same. "Next to controlling a desirable port and commodious harbor in China, the permanent ownership or possession of Manila and vicinity would be most invaluable to us in securing and holding our share of influence and trade in . . . this country," he explained to Hay.[57]

For Hay, however, an American Hong Kong on the coast of China was one stepping stone too far. When the Boxer Rebellion broke out in China in 1900, the navy renewed its request for an outpost on the China coast, noting that all the other major powers had coal deposits somewhere in Northeast Asia. The navy's preference was to seize the Zhoushan Islands, just south of the mouth of the Yangtze River, arguing that "it is possible that the islands desired can be obtained by our government as one of the results of the present circumstances in China, and it is suggested that negotiations for the acquisition be entered at the proper time."[58] Hay, who had just circulated the Open Door notes pledging no territorial aggrandizement at China's expense, held his ground. The United States would influence its continental interests from the First Island Chain (including the Philippines) and no closer.

The other question that immediately occurred to naval strategists was how the United States would defend these new island acquisitions. The German fleet had helped prompt the decision to occupy and then annex the Philippines, but it was increasingly Japan's growing naval power that was of greatest long-term concern. In 1900, the Naval War College reported on the need to defend and fortify forward bases to hold Japan at the Western Pacific rather than fight the Japanese near Hawaii or the West Coast:

It seems imperative, then, for the United States, in the event of war with Japan, to immediately improve its decided strategic advantages of outpost frontier by using all possible military and naval effort to make Honolulu and some well-chosen harbor in the Philippines impregnable; to keep the principal harbors in the Aleutian Islands under surveillance of fast cruisers; and to force the fighting home to Japan from the Philippines. In this connection, the seizure of the Bonin Islands would be of considerable advantage. . . . We cannot shut our eyes to the rising of this new sea power in the Pacific, nor to the certainty that it must seek expansion in that ocean.[59]

Unable to convince either Congress or top administration officials to secure a naval base on the Asian mainland, the navy instead shifted its focus to defending the Philippines and building a collier fleet that could resupply ships at sea.[60] By 1906, the General Naval Board had finally given up on its request for a base on the Chinese coast.[61] Defending the Philippines, Guam, and Hawaii against an increasingly capable Japanese fleet would be challenge enough.

"INTERNATIONAL MORAL FORCE IS MERE FLAPDOODLE": HAY AND THE OPEN DOOR

With the insular acquisitions of Hawaii, Guam, Wake Island, Samoa, and now the Philippines secure, the United States had in place the long-elusive stepping stones to China. But to what end? As Herring notes, "the U.S. government had shown little interest in China during the Gilded Age."[62] This was equally true of McKinley, Mahan, and Roosevelt, who were far more concerned about the larger strategic balance of power in the Pacific than about action on the continent itself.[63] Mahan had characteristically described Manchuria and China's internal politics as a "hornet's hive" to be avoided by the United States if at all possible.[64]

However, Japan's victory in 1895 had unleashed new entropic forces within the Qing Empire that increasingly powerful American constituencies would not ignore. American missionaries—and there were over a thousand in China at the end of the century—were increasingly the target of xenophobic attacks and demanded protection. In New York, U.S. business leaders formed the American Asiatic Association in 1898 to lobby for commercial access to China. Within the State Department, a new brand of "China hands," such as William Woodville Rockhill, a veteran of the French foreign legion and a scholar of Tibetan studies, who would become the department's chief advisor on the Far East, urged greater action from Washington to prevent China from being carved up by the other powers. The British also pressed for a larger American role, proposing in March 1898 that the United States and the United Kingdom jointly promote a doctrine of open access to China, aimed primarily at blocking further Russian expansion.[65] As the *Atlantic Monthly* summarized the growing pressure for action on China in August 1899: "Surely, no American administration would seriously contemplate the establishment of a dependency or protectorate on the mainland of China, while our interests there may be safeguarded by international control and reciprocity; but it is difficult to see how these securities can be obtained without more definite engagements on the part of our State Department."[66]

It fell to Secretary of State Hay to find an answer that would satisfy these powerful new lobbies for China. Hay, once the class poet at Brown University, had a long and illustrious career before his pivotal role in shaping U.S. strategy in the Far East. At the age of twenty-two, he served as Lincoln's assistant private secretary, later coauthoring a ten-volume biography of the sixteenth president. Far from being an Asianist, his subsequent diplomatic career took him to assignments in Paris, Madrid, and Vienna before he was named by McKinley as ambassador to the United Kingdom in 1897. Hay's mark of genius was levelheaded pragmatism, not visionary grand strategy. He followed Humphrey Marshall's precedent in defining China's territorial integrity as a major U.S. interest in the Far East, but, unlike Marshall, he was not prepared to risk conflict with the other powers in order to keep China open.

Hay's formula for demonstrating American leadership on China without risking war was to send a circular to the other major powers on September 6, 1899—the first of the "Open Door notes"—demanding most favored nation treatment in the other powers' spheres of influence and leased areas. He sought two outcomes: (1) American commercial, rail, and navigational access to Chinese markets; and (2) consensus on the principle that Chinese administrative integrity should be respected as a buffer against intensifying rivalry, conflict, and dismemberment.[67] The British, who had conceived of this approach in the first place, were favorably inclined toward Hay's effort. However, the other powers were ambivalent about making concessions on Chinese administrative integrity or agreeing to collective principles and therefore gave Hay no clear response to his circular in writing. Undiscouraged, Hay nevertheless announced in March 1900 that he had received "final and definitive acceptances" from all the powers.[68]

The tenuous international status of the principles articulated in the first Open Door note became evident as China entered further chaos with the outbreak of the Boxer Rebellion the next year.[69] The well-armed and xenophobic Boxers (a shorthand version of the society's title of "the Righteous and Harmonious Fists") had besieged the foreign legation area of Beijing and, with backing from within the Qing imperial court, had vowed to drive all foreigners from Chinese soil. As Britain, Japan, Russia, and the other Western powers began to mount a joint military expedition to relieve the besieged legation, Hay sent a second circular on July 3, calling for the preservation of Chinese territorial and administrative integrity. This time the other powers did not respond at all. Wary of domestic public opinion after the outbreak of the Philippine insurrection, McKinley reluctantly agreed to send 6,000 U.S. soldiers and marines from the Philippines to join the British-led multinational relief force. Their military mission was to help rescue the besieged Americans and other foreigners in Beijing, but their strategic purpose was to give the United States leverage against other powers, such as Japan and Russia, that would almost certainly jockey for position to carve up China after the conflict ended. Facing pressures to bring the boys home in the lead-up to the November 1900 election, McKinley ordered the U.S. forces withdrawn after the conclusion of hostilities. The Japanese and Russians meanwhile left large numbers of troops on the ground.[70] When war broke out between Russia and Japan in 1904, Hay sent notes to the warring parties and China urging respect for the "administrative entity" of China. He was again ignored.[71]

Was Hay dangerously naïve when he claimed to have international support for his position? Asked by a cabinet member about how he intended to enforce the Open Door, Hay replied, "Armies and navies; international moral force is mere flapdoodle."[72] Yet Hay knew that the United States was not willing to commit U.S. forces or form an alliance with Britain to enforce the Open Door in any meaningful way. As he summed up the problem, "we do not want to rob China ourselves, and our public opinion will not permit us to interfere with an army to prevent others from robbing her."[73] Nevertheless, the Open Door policy would become a central pillar of American policy in the Far East over the next three decades. It was a skillful articulation of U.S. interests and probably slowed imperial expansion within China to some extent, but it was never connected to ways or means that made it enforceable. As Theodore Roosevelt later wrote of it to President Taft in a foreboding prediction of what would unfold: "The Open Door policy in China was an excellent thing, and I hope it will be a good thing in the future, so far as it can be maintained by general diplomatic agreement; but, as has been proved by the whole history of Manchuria, alike under Russia and under Japan, the 'Open Door' policy, as a matter of fact, completely disappears as soon as a powerful nation determines to disregard it, and is willing to run the risk of war rather than forego its intention."[74]

ROOSEVELT AND GREAT-POWER DIPLOMACY AFTER VICTORY

When forty-three-year-old Theodore Roosevelt was vaulted from the vice presidency to replace the assassinated McKinley in September 1901, he knew that the Open Door would not hold unless it was backed by real power. He also worried that even though America's insular acquisitions gave the United States greater leverage in the Far East, these outposts were also exposed and vulnerable. Moreover, he sensed that the American public was reaching the limits of what resources it would expend in defense of American interests in Asia, while he had domestic reform priorities that were more important to his reelection in 1904. On the whole, he wanted to shape a regional equilibrium that would increase American influence and reduce the risk of further conflict.

All of these factors thrust Roosevelt enthusiastically into an unprecedented role for the United States—that of regional power broker. Drawing on the "good offices" precedent of Gilded Age diplomacy and his own idealistic view that "equilibrium among nations also had an ethical dimension," Roosevelt engaged in eight years of strenuous diplomacy aimed at creating a stable regional order.[75] As Henry Kissinger notes in *Diplomacy* (1994), only Richard Nixon would even come close to matching Roosevelt's instinct for the great game of international power politics.[76]

Roosevelt's recognition of the need for a more stable strategic equilibrium was again reinforced by Mahan. Now an international celebrity among foreign policy elites, Mahan had participated in the 1899 Hague Peace Conference, which was called by Russian czar Nicholas II in an attempt to limit armaments and create arbitration mechanisms for inter-national disputes. Mahan returned from the experience profoundly alarmed at both the misguided utopianism and the cynical ploy by Europe to constrain America's new power through arms control treaties. He realized that Hay's newly articulated Open Door policy toward China had no prospect of being upheld based on such idealistic multilateral conventions. What was required was greater attention to the underlying power dynamics in the region. Ever the publicist and eager to alert the American government about the need for a new strategic approach to stabilizing Asia, Mahan outlined his views in a collection of essays he published in 1900 under the title *The Problem of Asia*.

In *The Problem of Asia*, Mahan explained that the United States lacked the preponderance of naval power in the Pacific it would need to defend its new Hawaiian and Philippine bases. The newly planned isthmian ca-nal and an Anglo-American entente in the Atlantic would allow the navy to swing some of its fleet from the Caribbean to the Pacific in contingen-cies, but in general, U.S. naval power in the Pacific would have to be em-ployed judiciously. Mahan's primary concern at this point was not Japan but Russia, the host of the Hague Peace Conference. He worried that British power was no longer enough to counter the growing threat pre-sented by Russia's irredentism in Manchuria, northern China, and Cen-tral Asia (the British obviously agreed, forming an alliance with Japan in 1902). Mahan argued that a new maritime alignment of the United States, Britain, Japan, and Germany was necessary to counter this Eurasian threat and create "a condition of political equilibrium between the ex-ternal powers, whereby the equality of opposing forces, resting each on stable foundations, should prevent the undue preponderance of any one state."[77]

When Japan went to war with Russia in 1904 in a contest over Manchuria, northern China, and Korea, Mahan saw an advantage for the United States. Roosevelt was elated. "Japan is playing our game," he famously wrote.[78] However, Japan's string of victories over Russian naval and ground forces around Port Arthur began to worry American observ-ers. Roosevelt became increasingly concerned that the elimination of Russian power in Asia might "make Japan by itself a formidable power in the Orient, because all the other powers having interests there will have divided interests, divided cares, double burdens, whereas Japan will have but one care, one interest, one burden. If . . . Japan seriously starts . . . to reorganize China and makes any headway, there will result a real shifting of the center of equilibrium as far as the white races are concerned."[79]

Fortunately, from Roosevelt's perspective, Japanese forces had exhausted themselves in the bloody victory over Russia at Mukden (now known as Shenyang) in February 1905. More to the point, Japan was going bankrupt paying for the war. Roosevelt told the French ambassador to Washington, Jules Jusserand, that he "would like to see the war ending with Russia and Japan locked in a clinch, counterweighing one another, and both kept weak by the effort."[80]

When the Russians and Japanese agreed to attend peace negotiations hosted by Roosevelt in Portsmouth, New Hampshire, in the summer of 1905, Roosevelt was presented with a unique opportunity to make the United States the "arbiter of the Pacific balance of power."[81] He articulated America's role in terms of the recent Hague convention (which allowed neutral parties to arbitrate conflicts) and the earlier "good offices" clauses of U.S. treaties in Asia. But privately he saw the negotiations as a way to reestablish an advantageous strategic equilibrium for the United States in the region. He wrote to Lodge of his worry that continued fighting would see Russia "driven completely off the Pacific Coast . . . and yet something like this will surely happen if she refuses to make peace."[82] Faced with Russian obstreperousness, Roosevelt intervened with the Japanese delegation, successfully convincing them to forgo indemnity payments and allow Russia to retain control over the northern half of Sakhalin in order to reach an agreement. When the Treaty of Portsmouth was signed on September 5, 1905, the Japanese delegation's compromises prompted riots in Japan and eventually the downfall of the government of Prime Minister Katsura Tarō.[83]

In fact, the compromises orchestrated by Roosevelt were not enough to restore a balance of power between the two adversaries. Far from being "locked in a clinch, counterweighing each other," Russia was done as an expansionist power in Asia for a generation, whereas Japan was unmistakably on the ascent. Roosevelt had a new problem in Asia. "Fully alive to the danger from Japan,"[84] and unable to count on either a Russian counterweight or Britain, which had signed a security treaty with Japan in 1902 (to the intense irritation of Mahan), Roosevelt developed a comprehensive strategy to manage the rise of Japan that combined restraint, co-optation, and hedging.

The restraint element of Roosevelt's strategy was prompted primarily by concerns about the vulnerability of America's new insular acquisitions in the face of a freshly victorious Japan. As Roosevelt explained to Taft, his secretary of war at the time of the Portsmouth negotiations, "the Philippines form our Achilles; they are all that makes the present situation with Japan dangerous."[85] Roosevelt sought to send reassuring signals to Tokyo, dispatching Taft in 1905, as the Portsmouth negotiations were getting under way, to convey to Japanese prime minister Katsura that American administration of the Philippines would prevent other hostile powers from taking the islands and threatening Japan. Katsura countered that similar logic should apply to a Japanese protectorate over Korea, since it would eliminate one source of strategic competition among the major powers in the region and help to forestall a second war with Russia. Taft acknowledged the point, prompting later scholars in Korea to argue that he had betrayed them to Japan.[86]

In fact, there is no evidence that Taft made any explicit or binding diplomatic agreement along these lines.[87] In acknowledging Katsura's point, Taft was making no concession, since the future of Korea was now beyond U.S. strategic reach. As Roosevelt had explained to Hay on January 25, 1905, "We cannot possibly interfere for the Koreans against the Japanese. They couldn't strike one blow in their own defense."[88] At the same time, Roosevelt repeated to Taft and other audiences that there would be no quid pro quo in American diplomacy with Japan, since that would suggest weakness: "We neither ask nor give any favor to anyone as a reward for not meddling with any American territory. We are entirely competent to prevent such meddling, and require no guarantee of assistance to preserve our territorial integrity."[89]

Three years later, Roosevelt's second secretary of state, Elihu Root, repeated a tacit acknowledgment of Japanese control over Korea and northern China in a more formal agreement reached with the Japanese ambassador in Washington, Takahira Kogorō, on November 30, 1908. With growing war rumors, fueled by British and German observers, Roosevelt needed to demonstrate American and Japanese support for the status quo in Asia. Specifically, Root won agreement from Japan to respect the independence and integrity of China and to maintain equal commercial access for the United States in Japanese leased territories. The two parties also agreed to respect the other's dominant positions—Japan in northeastern China and the United States in the Philippines and Hawaii. The agreement left significant ambiguities in terms of defining Chinese integrity or access for U.S. firms, which would later become sources of friction with Japan. The agreement also reinforced international acceptance of Japan's control over Korea (London had also reached a similar agreement with Tokyo). Strategically, however, the Root-Takahira agreement succeeded in deflating dangerous expectations of a conflict between the United States and Japan and maintaining the prospects for a more stable concert of major powers in the Pacific.[90]

Underlying Roosevelt's careful restraint vis-à-vis Japan was a conviction, shared with Mahan, that skillful management of U.S.-Japan relations would help to avoid not only a bilateral collision but also a larger civilizational clash between the West and a rising Asia in the future. Roosevelt expressed concern that the Japanese would not easily shed their "mistrust of the white race," but he also believed that democratic values could transcend race. He made much of the fact that Japan's political system was closer to that of the United States than to Russia's "crushing despotism," even though Japan was "non-white and non-Christian."[91] Roosevelt felt that Japan would be "a valuable factor in the civilization of the future,"[92] and he intended to treat Japan with respect and equality in order to encourage further convergence with Western norms.

The problem for Roosevelt was that the American public and local politicians in California did not share his conviction about values trumping race or his concern about wounding Japanese pride. When San Francisco segregated the Japanese and other Asian immigrants into "Oriental" schools in 1906, Roosevelt declared the decision "wicked," and Mahan reported to the chairman of the Senate Naval Affairs Committee that it might "possibly bring about war with Japan."[93] Ultimately, Roosevelt bullied the San Francisco School Board and placated the Japanese government into accepting the February 1907 "Gentleman's Agreement" in which Japan would voluntarily curtail further emigration and the United States would not impose restrictions on Japanese immigration or students. Roosevelt extended his open views on immigration to China, which still smarted under the 1882 Chinese Exclusion Act and had none of the leverage of Japan. He nevertheless argued that the United States should welcome more Chinese immigrants, particularly students not of the "cooly class," "so that the vast and populous Empire of China may gradually adapt itself to modern conditions."[94] When he failed to convince Congress to change the exclusion laws, Roosevelt remitted the indemnity imposed after the Boxer Rebellion to "palliate the justifiably righteous indignation of the Chinese."[95] Maintaining a policy of respect for the rising powers of Asia was critical to Roosevelt's strategy of reassurance. His successors would not recognize the wisdom of his approach.

At his core, though, Roosevelt was a realist, and he knew that the best tool to shape Japan's rising power was military preparedness. As he explained to Lodge in 1907, "we should treat her [Japan] courteously, generously and justly, but we should keep our navy up and make it evident that we are not influenced by fear."[96] Roosevelt calculated that the United States had time to shape Japanese thinking before the threat to the maritime domain reemerged. The Japanese were broke and exhausted after war with Russia and would "not look toward the Philippines until affairs are settled on the mainland of Asia in connection with China." Meanwhile, Roosevelt intended to see that the navy was "maintained at the highest point of efficiency, for it is the real keeper of the peace."[97] By November 1907, the navy had built or was building twenty-nine vessels of 10,000 tons or more, in contrast to thirteen ships of comparable tonnage built or under construction by Japan (achieving something slightly better than parity given the U.S. Navy's Caribbean and Atlantic responsibilities). The navy also fortified Guam, Pearl Harbor, and Subic Bay (which had replaced Manila Bay in light of the Spanish Navy's difficulty defending it nine years earlier) and built a new dry dock in San Francisco. But the boldest move Roosevelt made was to order the navy on a worldwide cruise in order to reassure skittish Californians, impress the Japanese, and "get our whole battle fleet on a practice voyage to the Pacific."[98] As Roosevelt explained his objective:

> I concluded that it was imperative that we should send the fleet on what practically would be a practice voyage. I do not intend to keep it in the Pacific for any length of time; but I want all failures, blunders and shortcomings to be made apparent in time of peace and not in time of war. Moreover, I think that before matters become more strained we had better make it evident that when it comes to visiting our own coasts on the Pacific or Atlantic and assembling the fleet in our own waters, we cannot submit to any outside protests or interference.[99]

Roosevelt's "Great White Fleet" sailed in 1907–1908 to California, the Philippines, Australia, and Japan before returning to Hampton Roads, Virginia, via the Suez Canal. In Tokyo, the fleet was met in October 1908 by children waving American flags and singing "The Star-Spangled Banner."

When Roosevelt left office the next year, he was "convinced that he would leave to his successor a heritage of friendship with Japan."[100] But he also wrote to President Taft's incoming secretary of state, Philander Knox, that there was "no more important continuing feature of our foreign policy than this in reference to our dealing with Japan":

> I do not believe that there will be war, but there is always the chance that war will come; and if it did come, the calamity would be very great. And while I believe we would win, there is at least a chance of disaster. We should therefore do everything in our power to guard against the possibility of war by preventing the occurrence of conditions which would invite war and by keeping our Navy so strong that war may not come or that we may be successful if it does come.[101]

However, Knox was also receiving advice from two diplomats within the State Department who had chafed under Roosevelt's dual strategy of deterrence and reassurance toward Japan. In Mukden, the ambitious young consul general, Willard Straight, had sent warnings of Japan's expanding control over Manchuria. Within the State Department in Washington, Third Assistant Secretary Francis M. Huntington Wilson prepared a brief for the next administration on the Open Door policy in the spring of 1908 that claimed all the Western powers had agreed to the Open Door except Japan, making the case for direct U.S. diplomatic and economic steps to stop Japanese expansion on the ground in Manchuria. When Huntington Wilson's draft report went to Secretary Root, he struck out the long indictment of Japan.[102] Huntington Wilson and Straight were furious, but the two ambitious diplomats would soon get a second hearing for their advocacy of a policy of continental intervention and support for China over Japan. Straight had already made his case directly to Taft while escorting him from Vladivostok to Harbin in 1906. Huntington Wilson, meanwhile, had earned promotion to the post of first assistant secretary of state and chief advisor on Far Eastern affairs on the eve of Root's departure as secretary. The grand strategy of Theodore Roosevelt was about to be undone.

Assessing American Grand Strategy at the Dawn of the Pacific Century

Historians examining how the United States thrust itself into a forward position in the Western Pacific at the end of the nineteenth century have given short shrift to the geostrategic factors that shaped elite decision-making. Postwar scholarship has been heavily influenced by revisionist arguments that economic imperialism drove the Open Door and annexation of the Philippines.[103] Clearly, American business had big ambitions for the China market, and this helped to establish important intellectual and political underpinnings for expansionism in the 1890s. Yet economic determinants alone only begin to explain the strategic priorities of U.S. policy in Asia at the time. After all, "at no time during the late nineteenth century did exports constitute more than 7.2% of GNP or was there more than a 2% surplus of exports over imports."[104] The fabled China market itself accounted for only 0.3 percent of American exports in 1890. Nor is there evidence that Roosevelt and the others most responsible for conceiving and implementing Asia strategy were calculating the direct gains for American exports. In fact, they were remarkably ambivalent about specific U.S. commercial interests in China.

Other scholars have focused on the ethnocentrism, religious zeal, and racism behind American expansion in the Pacific.[105] The problem with focusing on ethnocentrism, Christianity, or racism, however, is that both expansionists and anti-imperialists cast their arguments in those same terms. Carl Schurz, for example, was an idealist who had fought for democracy in Europe in 1848 and for the Union in 1861, but he opposed American expansionism at the end of the century because he thought Asians were incapable of democratic government and were a potential poison for America's own democracy at home.[106] In contrast, Theodore Roosevelt supported expansion, arguing that "all men could eventually become civilized."[107] The fact is that all foreign policy arguments at the time were painted in racist hues, but that did not necessarily determine the strategy that resulted.[108]

Ultimately, while the architects of America's Pacific power at the end of the nineteenth century were surely motivated by the economic opportunities they saw and were shaped by the racial attitudes of their day, their primary focus was on *power*—specifically the distribution of power among their potential adversaries, the power of geography, and the instruments and limits of *American power* in the Pacific.

George Herring for one acknowledges this. His single-volume history of American foreign policy is unsparing in its criticism of presidents who were poor at foreign policy and raps Roosevelt for his heavy-handed and ineffective approach to Latin America. But overall, notes Herring, Roosevelt "began to modernize instruments of U.S. power. He recognized

that the combination of 'practical efficiency' and idealism was both necessary and rare. . . . [H]e recognized the limited U.S. interests in China
and Korea and the vulnerability of the Philippines and even Hawaii, [and]
he was the consummate pragmatist in East Asia, refusing to take on
commitments he could not uphold."[109] Henry Kissinger, as we have noted,
rated Roosevelt as the greatest geostrategic president, rivaled only by
Nixon.[110]

Roosevelt's grand strategy deserves these accolades, and his administration merits a central place—perhaps *the* central place—in establishing
the core tenets that guide American strategy toward Asia today. Seward
was the first to try to connect the distinct elements of a coherent Asian
strategy. These included a strong navy, a forward presence in the Western Pacific through insular acquisitions, expanded American influence
through trade with and support for well-governed independent Asian
states, and participation in European-style power politics. After Seward
left office, elements of his toolkit of national power were tested piecemeal
through the Gilded Age. Mahan then pulled these distinct elements
of national power into a coherent concept of grand strategy in Asia, and
Roosevelt, Hay, and Root translated that concept into effective national
policy.

First and foremost, Roosevelt's grand strategy was based on an adept
assessment of the implications that power dynamics within Asia would
have for the global system and American security itself. The title of
Mahan's 1900 book, *The Problem of Asia*, says it all. Before Mahan and
Roosevelt, American interests in Asia had been described primarily
in opportunistic terms. Even John Quincy Adams's forceful defense of
American interests in the Pacific Northwest and John Tyler's extension
of the Monroe Doctrine over Hawaii were ultimately aimed at preventing European powers from containing American continental expansion
and access to Asian markets, whereas Seward's priority on Asia reflected
the opportunities he saw rather than the dangers. In contrast, Mahan
and Roosevelt saw both the opportunities and the dangers to the United
States itself, not only in terms of the direct defense of the West Coast and
the isthmian canal but also in terms of the impact of Asian power dynamics on the stability of the global system as a whole. Asia for Mahan
and Roosevelt was not a secondary theater but rather one linked to other
regions of the world. Their view reflected the reality of great-power competition in the region after the collapse of the Concert of Europe and the
rise of Japan, and accurately anticipated the eventual emergence of China

and India as major strategic players. Their focus was thus on shaping the regional strategic environment and not just exploiting it for mercantile purposes.

The clarity of Roosevelt and Mahan's definition of ends was matched with an accurate assessment of the instruments of power available to the United States—the ways and means of grand strategy. When Roosevelt was assistant secretary of the navy, he orchestrated the most pronounced and effective application of American hard power in Asia in the nineteenth century, defeating the weakest of the European powers—Spain—without provoking counterbalancing by more powerful states like Britain, France, Germany, or Japan against the United States. As president, he then focused on consolidating the U.S. position by building up the navy and fortifying the new island acquisitions while seeking a stable strategic equilibrium through the Open Door and the diplomacy to end the Russo-Japanese War. He exhibited restraint on issues in northern China and Korea that were secondary to American interests or beyond American power to shape, and he conserved American influence for the core issues of securing a forward defense for the American West Coast, ensuring reasonable commercial access in China, and maintaining a stable strategic equilibrium in the region. Roosevelt, Mahan, Hay, and Root sought a concert of power among the major states, standing firm where they had to but accommodating other powers when they could. Above all, they aligned these various instruments of national power so that they were mutually reinforcing. Instead of suffering from the tension between maritime and continental strategies, Roosevelt and his cohort managed to find the right fulcrum between each of these instruments of power and to strike a reasonably successful balance.

Values were also clearly an important dimension of Roosevelt's grand strategy. He recognized that longer-term regional stability and American influence in Asia rested on the establishment of well-governed, independent Asian states that would discourage great-power expansionism and align more easily with the United States. His view in this regard was appropriately *evolutionary* and not revolutionary. He and Mahan saw Japan's continuing prospects for establishing a moderately liberal political order that would stand as an example for the rest of Asia, and they treated Japan with careful respect as a result. Roosevelt appreciated that the United States would not be able to govern the Philippines as a colony and supported the early transition to civilian administration, paving the way for eventual independence decades later. He supported Hay's Open Door

policy and the goal of maintaining Chinese administrative and territorial integrity while remaining realistic about the tools of power the United
States possessed to enforce the policy on the ground. Ultimately, Roosevelt achieved an effective balance of realism and idealism, viewing the
establishment of a stable regional order in moral terms but recognizing
that its underpinnings rested on power.

Yet, while Roosevelt and the architects of Pacific power at the turn of
the century anticipated that independent republics in Asia would ultimately reinforce both stability and American influence, there was also
blatant hypocrisy. The McKinley administration ignored the majority of
native Hawaiians, who petitioned against annexation; Guam and Samoa
went decades without achieving self-government. The image of Americans fighting a war against Filipinos seeking independence also blotted
the purity of the republican virtues that Seward and others assumed
would naturally attract Asian states to American power. Indeed, although
the U.S. Army prevailed in the Philippines, the conflict revealed that the
anti-imperialist tradition in American political culture created a vulnerable center of gravity that could be targeted by insurgents—as Ho Chi
Minh did to great effect six decades later. The majority of Asian states
today enjoy democratic self-government, which despite the enormous
courage and vision demonstrated by the citizens of those nations would
not have been possible without the long-term American commitment
to supporting democratic norms in the region. But expansionism and
American values did not always go hand-in-hand at the dawn of America's Pacific Century. The era unleashed the internal contradictions between the American impulses of anti-imperialism on the one hand and
the spread of republican norms on the other.

Roosevelt and Mahan also failed to anticipate the degree to which securing insular outposts in the Western Pacific would in fact create a new
strategic vulnerability. The Philippines are 6,000 miles from the West
Coast of the United States and only about 1,000 miles from Japan. This is
not to say that leaving the Philippines would have been a better course,
since the resulting vacuum would have invited Japanese or German competition for control of the archipelago and increased the potential threat
to Hawaii without any improvement in American purchase on the problem of China. But Mahan had forewarned in his *Influence of Sea Power
Upon History* that insular outposts "should be able to hold out, independent of the fleet, for a length of time dependent upon its importance, both
to the general defence system and its intrinsic value."[111] Roosevelt was

forced to make some accommodation with Japan and to modernize the navy in order to protect the Philippines. Over the coming decades, the task of defending this exposed position against an increasingly powerful Imperial Japanese Navy would preoccupy military planners and limit the leverage the United States could bring to enforcing the Open Door. Roosevelt was the first great strategist on Asia in the White House and the first to discover the complexities of defining a realistic line of defense in the Western Pacific.

Roosevelt's greatest blind spot, though understandable in the political context of his time, was the utility of free trade in American strategy. Mahan clearly articulated why free trade would increase American strategic influence. Even McKinley, the leading apostle of protectionism in the Republican Party, came, in the final year of his presidency, to support reciprocity treaties that would lower barriers to trade as America began to move from domestic consumption to international markets.[112] For their part, Democrats like Cleveland opposed the tariff because it hurt their political base in the farm belt. But Roosevelt remained an old-fashioned Republican, committed to a high tariff like the stodgy politicians in the Grand Old Party, in contrast to whom he had promised new reform and vitality.

Finally, there was the dilemma left by the Open Door. Hay's two diplomatic circulars constituted America's first coherent "doctrine" on Asia and stand second only to the Monroe Doctrine as guideposts for American foreign policy before the Second World War. The Open Door was intended to protect Chinese territorial integrity and with it American most favored nation status (commercial access). Diminished great-power competition in China would in turn dampen rivalry for the Pacific as a whole. As Mahan noted years later, the Open Door was only a statement of policy and depended primarily on "the opposition of interests, in relation to her [China], of other states; those of Europe, the United States, and Japan."[113] Mahan knew that these power dynamics were highly changeable, and he reminded audiences in and out of government that in addition to an underlying balance among the powers coveting China, "it remains obvious that the policy of the Open Door requires naval power."[114] By 1902, the U.S. Navy had forty-eight ships in the Asiatic Squadron, including a battleship. That was sufficient to maintain a favorable balance of power in the Pacific but not enough to prevent China's collapse internally. For his part, Mahan was prepared to take part of China if that happened rather than fight to prevent a collapse.[115] In contrast, the new China hands in the State Department, such as Huntington Wilson and Straight, echoed Humphrey Marshall fifty years earlier in arguing that the United States' entire position in the Pacific depended on preventing the breakup of China. Their voices would grow after Roosevelt left the White House.

In retrospect, the only enduring tool that might have mustered sufficient power to enforce the Open Door in China as well as the proper balance between maritime and continental priorities would have been a more formal alliance with Great Britain, perhaps embedded within a maritime concert of powers that included Japan. The instinctive attraction of such an alliance to Mahan, Roosevelt, and Hay was evident, but American political and strategic culture at the end of the nineteenth century was still too deeply wedded to nonalignment and noninterference in European power politics to allow more than informal entente with Great Britain. As a result, Roosevelt played the balance-of-power game as well as anyone could absent formal alliances, though that game proved to be beyond the mastery of his successors.

On the whole, however, Roosevelt left the United States in a more secure and influential position in Asia. The coherence of his strategic approach to Asia, and the deftness of his military and diplomatic practice, continue to have important lessons today and have been matched by few other American presidents since.

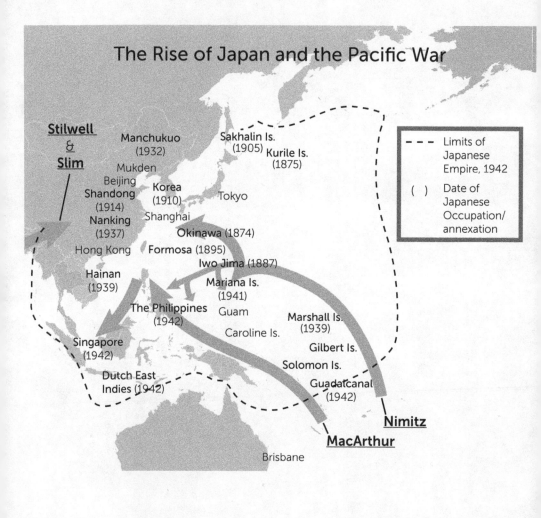

The Rise of Japan and the Pacific War

Stilwell & Slim

Manchukuo (1932)

Mukden

Beijing

Shandong (1914)

Korea (1910)

Nanking (1937)

Shanghai

Hong Kong

Hainan (1939)

Formosa (1895)

Sakhalin Is. (1905)

Kurile Is. (1875)

Tokyo

Okinawa (1874)

Iwo Jima (1887)

Mariana Is. (1941)

The Philippines (1942)

Guam

Caroline Is.

Marshall Is. (1939)

Singapore (1942)

Gilbert Is.

Solomon Is.

Dutch East Indies (1942)

Guadalcanal (1942)

Nimitz

MacArthur

Brisbane

- - - Limits of Japanese Empire, 1942

( ) Date of Japanese Occupation/ annexation

PART TWO

THE RISE OF JAPAN

On the evening of July 26, 1941, President Franklin Delano Roosevelt retired to his study, "the Oval Parlor," in the East Wing of the White House. Earlier that day, he had issued Executive Order 08832, freezing all Japanese assets in the United States, in response to Japan's occupation of French Indochina the week before. He had also reached an agreement with Manila to place all forces in the Philippines under U.S. command and had ordered a squadron of B-17s to the Philippines while ordering the two U.S. carriers on exercises in the Pacific to remain at Pearl Harbor.

Roosevelt did not want war with Japan, at least not yet, with half of Europe under Hitler's heel and Britain standing alone. The navy was also anxious, since new shipbuilding programs would not begin to put them on a par with the Imperial Japanese Navy until mid-1942 at the earliest. Stanley Hornbeck of the State Department's Far East Division had assured them all that Japan was so dependent on foreign trade that Tokyo must back down under the new sanctions. Perhaps . . . but even if Mr. Hornbeck were proven wrong, the United States could not condone the latest Japanese expansion with the whole world in flames.

Behind Roosevelt's desk were shelves full of naval objects and a large collection of books and articles written by Alfred Thayer Mahan. One book stood out from the others—a well-read and finger-worn edition of Mahan's *Influence of Sea Power on History*, given to young Franklin as a Christmas gift in 1897. Franklin had first devoured the book in 1893, when he was only eleven years old. His mother swore that he read it so many times that he must have memorized it. When Franklin was chosen to argue in the school debate at Groton in January 1898 that the United States should not annex Hawaii, he had turned to Mahan to make his arguments. He still had his handwritten notes from the debate: "Mr. Peabody says that if we do not take the islands, some other power will," he had written, "[yet] Captain Mahan himself says it is nonsense to think of annexation unless we decide to spend an enormous sum for fortification": "Why should we soil our hands with colonies? . . . Why can we not leave Hawaii alone, or establish a sound Republic? I appeal to your American common sense: that common sense that has never yet made a mistake and which pray never will."[1]

In fact, young Franklin had been an outspoken imperialist at Groton, inspired by his larger-than-life cousin Theodore, who was then assistant secretary of the navy. On his honeymoon cruise to Europe in 1905, Franklin had perplexed his young bride, Eleanor, by taking up with a group of Japanese officers in order to glean useful intelligence for the Navy Department. Two years later, he followed enthusiastically as the Great White Fleet crossed the Pacific on a mission of strength and goodwill. Then, in 1913, he proudly took the post of assistant secretary of the navy just as Cousin Theodore had done fifteen years earlier.

Yet, in that post, he saw how the influence of Mahan and his cousin had begun to wane. President Taft had decided to go after the Japanese in Manchuria, ignoring Mahan's warning to leave that "hive" alone. As assistant secretary, Franklin had urged Woodrow Wilson to keep the bulk of the fleet in the Pacific to watch the Japanese during the First World War, on the advice of Cousin Theodore and Mahan, but Wilson disagreed and Japan used its free hand to consolidate gains in China. After the war, Congress and the American people were tired of funding a large navy, and the Harding administration negotiated naval limitations with the other powers and reached multilateral agreement on the Open Door in China. Mahan would not have approved of such wishful arms control, but for a time it seemed that war in the Pacific might be obsolete.

Franklin was eventually caught up in that same national mood himself. He abandoned lifelong plans to publish a new edition of Mahan's work and instead turned his attention to more useful political issues in the pursuit of higher office in New York. He began to criticize imperialism and expansion in foreign affairs articles and speeches. When he won the presidency in 1932, he prioritized domestic economic issues above all else, giving only passing reference to foreign policy in his first inaugural address and rebuffing his secretary of state's efforts to curb global protectionism. He was only convinced to increase defense spending after Congressman Carl Vinson promoted new naval shipbuilding legislation in 1933 as a jobs program. With the country in a deep economic depression, he saw his mission as president as restoring confidence in the economy rather than pursuing the ambitious foreign policy in the Pacific that he had once enthusiastically learned from Mahan and Cousin Theodore.[2]

And yet, here he was, sitting in his study beneath the combined works of Mahan, having drawn a line to stop Japan that would surely risk war. He knew that Theodore would not have backed down. His cousin had always understood what was at stake in the Pacific. And at the end of the day, so did he. As FDR would put it to the country in a radio address in November, "We are thinking about something even more important, and that is the possible extension of control by aggression into the whole of the Pacific area."[3] That Franklin Delano Roosevelt would not tolerate.

4. "LEAVE THE DOOR OPEN, REHABILITATE CHINA, AND SATISFY JAPAN"
DEFINING THE OPEN DOOR, 1909–1927

Part 2 of this volume covers the American response to the rise of Japan from the end of Theodore Roosevelt's administration in 1909 through the presidency of his cousin Franklin and the ultimate American victory over Japan in August 1945. That victory has been considered one of the greatest in military history—and the statecraft that preceded it the worst in the history of American grand strategy. Yet it would be a mistake to dismiss the decades between the two Roosevelts as entirely bereft of strategic thought. Americans did not retire from the world in a spate of isolationism, idealism, and what Robert Osgood called the "glimpse of Utopia" before coming back to their senses on December 7, 1941.[1] Nor did victory over Japan resolve the geostrategic challenges the United States faced across the Pacific. As the three chapters in this part demonstrate, American statecraft and military strategy grew in sophistication in many respects before the war, and the prosecution of the war left an unintended legacy of Soviet expansion and communist revolution that vexed postwar strategists. The Pacific war, in other words, may have finally dealt with the challenge of Japan, but it turned out to be just one more chapter in the longer-term American effort to secure the Pacific against rival powers.

Theodore Roosevelt left office in 1909 having crafted a grand strategy toward Asia that left his successors struggling to maintain a formula—as Colonel Edward House put it to Woodrow Wilson—"which will leave the door open, rehabilitate China, and satisfy Japan."[2] President Taft diverged from Roosevelt's maritime-centered grand strategy by pushing for aggressive American investment in Manchuria and northern China to counter Japan, but in the end American industry would not follow and he was forced to retreat sheepishly to a cooperative policy with the other powers, including Japan. Woodrow Wilson then lurched in the opposite direction, antagonizing the Europeans in 1913 by making the United States the first power to recognize the Republic of China, then antagonizing China by giving in to Japanese arrangements with Britain and France to receive German territories after the war, and finally antagonizing Japan by rejecting the antiracism clause in the League of Nations.[3]

Yet, despite the poor reading of Asia's balance of power and the woeful inconsistencies in policy toward Japan and China, self-determination, and trade in the decade after Theodore Roosevelt, the United States nevertheless emerged from the First World War in a position of material and moral prominence in the Pacific. What followed in the 1920s has been obscured by the shadow of the Pacific war, but in fact it represented deliberate diplomatic, military, and economic strategies to sustain a favorable equilibrium and limit Japanese expansion. Through the Washington Treaties negotiated in 1921 and 1922, the State Department capped naval armament and reached an international modus vivendi on China. Meanwhile, through continued revisions to War Plan Orange, the U.S. Navy accurately assessed Japanese and American strengths and vulnerabilities and anticipated the island-hopping strategy that would eventually defeat Japan when war came. In the same period, financiers such as Thomas Lamont of J. P. Morgan crafted loans designed to increase Japanese dependence on the international system and encourage cooperative policies from Tokyo. An exponentially larger number of American diplomats, businessmen, and missionaries were living in Asia, were fluent in Asian languages, and understood events on the ground. By the end of the 1920s, the American approach to Asia and the Pacific appeared to most observers at the time to have been a success.

This chapter ends with that high-water mark of the Open Door policy but also anticipates the failures in American grand strategy that would be revealed over the next decade and in the subsequent chapter, for beneath the veneer of international finance and multilateral diplomatic agree-ments, Asia's regional order was collapsing with a velocity that outpaced the sophistication of American statecraft and the nascent internationalism of the American people. Japanese expansionism, lingering nightmares from the First World War, the chaos of the Chinese Civil War, the collapse of Czarist Russia, the emergence of Bolshevism, the decline of British power, and the crash of the global financial system all combined to over-whelm the United States' ability to formulate an effective grand strategy toward Asia. When that happened, the State Department had no alterna-tive to the gentlemen's agreements of the Open Door, the navy had fallen behind Japan in tonnage and armaments, and protectionism had undone the financial interdependence promoted in the 1920s. After Japan de-clared itself the preeminent power in the Pacific in 1934, American poli-cymakers were forced to reconsider the most fundamental question in grand strategy: Was the Pacific really worth fighting for?

No president between Theodore and Franklin Roosevelt had seriously considered that question. Five presidents in a row assumed that Ameri-ca's position in the Far East could be maintained with minimal effort and risk, failing to understand the underlying geopolitics as the Roose-velts had.

"An Instrument for the Promotion of the Welfare of China": Taft and the Illusion of Dollar Diplomacy

William Howard Taft came to power in March 1909 after riding to vic-tory on Theodore Roosevelt's popularity. As secretary of war, Taft had loyally implemented Roosevelt's Asia strategy between 1904 and 1908, including a trip to the region in 1905 to show U.S. support for the Phil-ippines and to reassure Japan of America's peaceful intentions. Before that, he had served Roosevelt as the first civilian governor-general in the Philippines. Like most understudies, however, Taft intended to make his own mark as president, including on Asia policy, where he thought he brought particular experience. Fat, lawyerly, and trusting of big busi-ness, he bore a much greater physical and philosophical resemblance to the old postbellum Republican Party than had the progressive, imperial-istic, and dynamic Theodore Roosevelt. For the average American, Taft was most famous at the time for introducing baseball's seventh-inning stretch, when, attending a game in Washington in 1910, he rose to stretch his legs after the top of the seventh inning. Taft, at six feet two inches tall and 300 pounds, was visible to all, and the crowd also rose, assuming that he was leaving, until he visibly sat down again.[4]

In Asia, Taft had come to doubt the wisdom of Roosevelt's careful approach to Japan, warning after he became president that "a Jap is first of all a Jap."[5] In a speech to Japanese businessmen in Tokyo in September 1907 while visiting as secretary of war, Taft had declared that "war between Japan and the United States would be a crime against modern civilization. It would be as wicked as it would be insane."[6] As president, however, he put in place a foreign policy team that would take a tack different from Theodore Roosevelt's more accommodating approach toward Tokyo and his caution toward mainland intrigues. For secretary of state, he chose Philander Chase Knox, a corporate lawyer who promised to "smoke out" the Japanese in Manchuria and northern China.[7] Knox's distaste for Japan was not met by a passion for China; he later quipped that he would "never let anything so unimportant as China" interrupt his golf game.[8] Nevertheless, the China hands who had tried unsuccessfully to reverse Roosevelt's strategy the year before were now well positioned, with Francis Huntington Wilson having been promoted to first assistant secretary of state and Willard Straight running the Far Eastern Division.

The larger framework for Taft's approach to China was his doctrine of "dollar diplomacy." Coined originally by Roosevelt as a corollary to the Monroe Doctrine, its intent was to ensure that European investments in Latin America did not weaken the political independence of any republic in the Western Hemisphere. However, whereas Roosevelt saw economic instruments as one component of a geostrategic approach, Taft and Knox made dollar diplomacy the centerpiece of their foreign policy—"substituting dollars for bullets" and returning to what they saw as more enduring Republican Party principles of peace and commerce with all nations.[9] The first proving ground for dollar diplomacy was Latin America, where the result was "few agreements, little stability and numerous military interventions" with America's southern neighbors— all the opposite of what was intended.[10] In 1909, however, the strategy still seemed sound, particularly in China and Manchuria, where U.S. diplomats like Straight had watched Japan and Russia use strategic investments in railroads to carve out special zones of influence at the expense of Chinese sovereignty and potential American business.[11] As Taft wrote to the Chinese prince regent in July 1909, "I have an intense personal interest in making the use of American capital in the development of China an instrument for the promotion of the welfare of China, and an increase in her material prosperity without entanglements or creating embarrassment affecting the growth of her independent political power, and the preservation of her territorial integrity."[12]

Backed by the new "China lobby" of aspiring U.S. businesses, returned missionaries, and a small cadre of Mandarin speakers in the Far Eastern Division, Huntington Wilson and Straight crafted a plan designed to stop Japan from using economic concessions as cover for spreading political control over Manchuria as Tokyo had in Korea.[13] As Huntington Wilson explained to Secretary Knox, "Japan's present policy in Manchuria, if continued, must result in grave impairment to America's policy for the preservation of the territorial integrity of China, and in serious detriment to the accepted principle of the 'open door' and equality of opportunity in Manchuria."[14] The strategic goal of this new approach was worthy, as Robert Osgood later acknowledged, since it aimed to "reduce the dangers of foreign intervention in a strategic area by stabilizing the political situation."[15] Implementation would prove another matter, however.

Much of the implementation fell to the larger-than-life Willard Straight. Straight was a towering blonde giant who drew attention wherever he went. Born in 1880 to a modest missionary family in Oswego, New York, he moved with his parents to Japan and then China, achieving fluency in the languages of both countries. After his parents died in China, he studied at Cornell University and then returned to China to work first for the Imperial Chinese Customs Service and then as a war correspondent for Reuters and the Associated Press during the Russo-Japanese War. While covering the war, he befriended the U.S. ambassador in Moscow, who helped him secure a position as vice consul in Seoul and then as consul in Mukden in 1908, where he earned international renown and notoriety for pulling his pistol on a group of Japanese officials who had roughed up the consulate's coolie guard. The *New York Times* described him in a 1911 profile as being "ever of aggressive mind" and seeming "to possess an inborn acquaintance for the heart of womenkind, for two of the richest and most sought-after heiresses in the United States have been willing to share with this poor young man their enormous fortunes."[16] The first of these was Mary Harriman, the daughter of railroad and shipping magnate E. H. Harriman (and sister of future diplomat Averell Harriman), whom Straight met when her father turned to the consul general in the summer of 1908 to help set up a bank in Manchuria to fund his vision of a Far Eastern railroad that would connect the world. As the elder Harriman put it, "it is important to save the commercial interests of the United States from being entirely wiped from the Pacific Ocean in the future," and "the way to find out what is best to be done is to start something." Straight's "ever aggressive mind" appealed to Harriman, and Harriman's beautiful daughter Mary appealed to Straight. They set about pursuing their respective passions.[17]

In 1909, Straight left the State Department with the blessing of Huntington Wilson and Secretary Knox to become the representative of the American Banking Group in China. The group consisted of J. P. Morgan & Company, Kuhn, Loeb, First National Bank, and National City Bank, and was formed with State Department backing to help fund Harriman's railroad visions and to implement dollar diplomacy in China. The plan was for the group to arrange loans for China to buy back the Chinese Eastern Railroad from Russia and the Southern Manchurian Railroad from Japan. Meanwhile, U.S. bankers would provide loans to help build a new railroad line directly under the Chinese government. Had it worked, the new American-orchestrated consortium would have created a buffer between Japan and Russia and given China the tools to reclaim sovereignty and open greater investment opportunities for American corporations.[18] And it would have made Straight a rich man.

But it did not work at all. Japan and Russia had no reason to sell their railroad assets and every reason to be suspicious of American intentions.[19] In response to the American Banking Group's ploy, Moscow and Tokyo signed an agreement on July 4, 1910, dividing Manchuria into separate zones of influence and vowing to block future outside interventions in their spheres of influence. Huntington Wilson was unapologetic, explaining to Knox in the wake of the Russo-Japanese pact that backing away from the scheme would mean "a horrible loss of prestige" and "complete admissions that the open door is a dead letter in northern China."[20] However, the Russo-Japanese entente now moved events beyond the State Department's control, opening the way for the Japanese annexation of Korea in August 1910. Stunned by this setback, Knox and Huntington Wilson turned to the Europeans for help, but Britain was allied with Japan, France was allied with Russia, and neither was willing to help the Americans out of their self-induced dilemma. Indeed, they found the whole American scheme daft and Huntington Wilson, as one British diplomat described him, to be a "pestulant beast."[21] In June 1912, the State Department retreated again, agreeing under British and French pressure to admit Japan and Russia into the railroad consortium they were launching.[22]

In the meantime, China itself was undergoing a fundamental transformation as the Qing dynasty finally collapsed in February 1912 and Yuan Shikai (Yuan Shih-kai) became provisional president of the Republic of China. In a different era, the American government would have quickly recognized the new republic, but Taft's State Department instead prioritized the preservation of most favored nation status for foreign investors. The banking consortium became their principal vehicle, and the imperial powers their principal allies.[23] In other words, in three years, Taft's Asia strategy had gone from unilateral balance of power against the other imperial powers in northern China, to a concert of power with the Europeans that was aimed at Japan and Russia, to a concert that included Japan and Russia, and finally to abandonment of the principle of Chinese sovereignty that had animated Taft's strategy in the first place.

Knox, Huntington Wilson, and Straight had made three errors of judgment. First, they misunderstood the balance of financial power and business interests in Manchuria. The reality was that the China market was simply not as salient to the American business community as it was to Japan—not even close. Trade with China accounted for only 1 percent of U.S. exports in 1910, whereas Japan's trade with China had doubled over the previous decade, surpassing U.S. trade with China by $16 million.[24] Meanwhile, it was not China but Japan that was becoming the major importer of American goods and capital. Second, the three men badly misread the strategic interests of the other major powers, ineptly prompting a Russo-Japanese entente to further carve up China, announced on the anniversary of American independence. And third, Knox, Huntington Wilson, and Straight misread and overinterpreted the intent of the Open Door policy itself. The ambiguities inherent in the Open Door reflected the expediency with which John Hay had originally conceived and implemented the policy a decade earlier. Huntington Wilson had been pushing a revisionist and expansionist interpretation of the Open Door notes since Root was secretary of state, insisting that the Open Door meant not only equality of *opportunity* but also equality of *investment* in China.[25] Nothing in Hay's original circulars would have prepared the other powers to endorse this specific definition of the Open Door—most of the powers barely endorsed the broad principle of Hay's circular as it was. The misreading of economic interests—ironic for a pro-business Republican administration—and of the great powers' interests and the Open Door itself, left the Taft administration without a policy for influencing the balance of power within China or vis-à-vis a rising Japan.

Nevertheless, Taft did have some successes in Asia. In 1911, his administration signed the Treaty of Commerce and Navigation, establishing most favored nation status with Japan, for example, and his wife championed the planting of the Japanese cherry blossoms along the Tidal Basin that today attract millions of tourists to Washington, DC, every year.[26] However, the centerpiece of his Asia strategy—dollar diplomacy in China—had failed utterly.

In the end, poor Straight would find thwarted not only his plans for wresting control of the Manchurian railroads from Japan but also his amorous designs on Mary Harriman. Frustrated with the turn of events in China and unimpressed with Straight's modest background, Harriman forbade his daughter to accept Straight's proposals for marriage.[27] Undeterred in love, if not finance, Straight set his sights on the second-wealthiest debutante in New York, the beautiful Mary Dorothy Whitney, whom he married in 1911. He would continue to defend dollar diplomacy and the consortia, arguing in articles and academic papers that there had been "no middle course"—that an "alliance of diplomacy, with industry, commerce and finance" was necessary to secure national interests in China in an era of rivalry.[28]

All of this (the strategy, not the love story as far as we know) was too much for another powerful New Yorker to take. Frustrated with the dismantlement of his maritime-focused Asia strategy, Theodore Roosevelt wrote to Taft on December 22, 1910, arguing that U.S. "interests in Manchuria are really unimportant, and not such that the American people would be content to run the slightest risk of collision about them."[29] Taft had violated all of the principles behind Roosevelt's grand strategy: over-investing American power and prestige in continental Asia, needlessly antagonizing Japan, and losing control of the larger strategic equilibrium in the region. It was one of a number of betrayals by Taft that prompted an infuriated Roosevelt to run against him for president in 1912 at the head of the Bull Moose Party, dooming Taft and opening the way for the first Democratic administration in sixteen years.

"A Door of Friendship and Advantage": Woodrow Wilson's Idealistic but Eurocentric Asia Policy

Woodrow Wilson came to office in 1913 convinced, like Taft before him, that he understood the core of American interests in China and Asia better than his predecessor had. In actuality, he had come to office with solid political science credentials on domestic U.S. politics but little understanding of foreign affairs.[30] He campaigned in 1912 against the Republicans' reliance on moneyed trusts, imperialism, and gunboat diplomacy. He argued that America's purpose was to educate the world about democracy. Sympathetic with the revolutions in Mexico and China, within weeks of taking office he moved to withdraw from the international bankers' consortium, end support for the American Banking Group, and recognize Yuan Shikai's Republic of China.[31] The Open Door, the new president declared, would now be "a door of friendship and advantage" for China.[32] As he explained to his cabinet after the series of decisions he characteristically made based on only minimal consultation with them, if the United States acted like the other predatory powers, "we would have got nothing but mere influence in China and lost the proud position which America secured when Secretary Hay stood for the open door in China after the Boxer Uprising."[33] He also declared that America's position would be stronger not in partnership with other countries but by standing independently with China, and thus he would be able to say, "to Russia 'what are your designs on Manchuria,' and to Japan, 'What are your wishes on this part of China,' and to England, Germany or any other country, 'What are your designs,' and being free, the country could help China and restore the relationship which this country occupied toward that country and the world when Mr. Hay was Secretary of State."[34]

A mortified Huntington Wilson immediately resigned, arguing in an open letter to the press that only "the financial force" of the United States could maintain the Open Door.[35] However, J. P. Morgan and his private sector colleagues were all too ready to withdraw from the troublesome railroad banking scheme. The great men of Wall Street were not interested enough in Manchuria or even China to bring the full "financial force" of the United States to bear on the issue, absent the full support of the U.S. government. It was clear that dollar diplomacy was finished.[36]

However, if dollar diplomacy was being revealed as a paper tiger, where were the teeth behind Wilson's new policy of embracing self-determination and democracy in China? There was much to admire about Wilson's initial support for free and independent republics in Asia. He reached outside of the State Department and appointed the progressive University of Wisconsin political scientist and China scholar Paul S. Reinsch as U.S. commissioner to China to ensure deeper understanding of the country, and Reinsch would be the first in a series of scholar-diplomats to shape Asia policy. In the Philippines, Wilson expanded self-rule and eventually, in 1916, won passage of the Jones Act, which committed the United States to granting full independence to the Philippines as soon as a stable government was established in Manila. It was the first case of decolonization in history and echoed Jefferson, Perry, and Mahan's vision of a future Asia dominated by free republics aligned through common values with the United States.

Yet, while Wilson built on and anticipated a tradition of American support for democracy and self-determination in Asia, he also demonstrated the perils of pursuing that goal without regard to the state of democracy and tolerance within the United States itself. Like Roosevelt before him, Wilson soon found his Asia policy confounded by domestic political pressure on Chinese and Japanese immigration. Unlike Roosevelt, however, Wilson made only passing efforts to curb this threat to his foreign policy. He had campaigned in 1912 in support of excluding Asian immigrants from California, and as president he dispatched Secretary of State William Jennings Bryan to California to see if legislation could be passed that would keep his campaign promises in a way that would not "offend the susceptibilities of a friendly nation."[37] It could not. In 1913, California passed the Alien Land Act, constricting Japanese and Chinese immigrants' ability to purchase land.[38] The result was a new source of tension with Tokyo, and ammunition for opponents of liberalism within Japan.[39]

Wilson's open-ended embrace of democracy and self-determination also melted in the face of realpolitik demands with the outbreak of war in Europe in August 1914. Though strictly neutral and heavily influenced by German and Irish Americans, the United States nevertheless had a clear interest in Britain prevailing, since German victory would have opened the Western Hemisphere to a new imperial contest. When Britain turned to its ally Japan to attack German forces in the Far East and to provide warships to support British operations in the Mediterranean, the

Wilson administration remained passive—splitting the American fleet to keep an eye on both the Germans and the Japanese but not checking Japanese expansion in the Pacific as Wilson's assistant secretary of the navy, Franklin Delano Roosevelt, had wanted. In the first three months of the war, Japanese troops took the German lease territory of Shandong, including the 240-mile Qingdao-Tian (Tsingtao-Tien) Railway, and occupied German possessions in the Mariana, Caroline, and Marshall Islands, which had figured so prominently in American strategy in the last century and would become central to the American war effort less than three decades later.

When in January 1915 an emboldened Japanese government delivered to Yuan Shikai's republic a set of twenty-one demands, "watermarked with dreadnoughts and machine guns,"[40] and intended to create a virtual Japanese protectorate had the Chinese accepted,[41] Wilson's response was to inform the Japanese government that the United States "cannot recognize any agreement or undertaking which has been entered into or which may be entered into between the Government of Japan and China, impairing the treaty rights of the United States and its citizens in China, the political or territorial integrity of the Republic of China, or the international policy relative to China commonly known as the open door policy."[42] This first application of what would later come to be known as the "non-recognition doctrine" represented, more than anything, nonaction. It was a self-gratifying retreat to principle that revealed the limits of American will, if not American power. It also set a dangerous precedent for legalistic nonaction as Japanese aggression became more acute in later years.[43]

China hands like Reinsch urged Wilson to stand by his earlier support for Chinese territorial integrity and self-determination in responding to the Twenty-One Demands,[44] but Wilson argued it would be better for China that the United States not "provoke the jealousy and excite the hostility of Japan, which would first be manifested against China herself."[45] Instead, the president proposed "trying to play the part of prudent friend by making sure that the representatives of Great Britain realized the gravity of the situation and just what was being attempted."[46] The British, of course, knew exactly what was happening, but both their latitude to affect issues in the Far East and their long-term power were being hemorrhaged on the killing fields of Flanders. London would be of little help. Wilson continued to argue the rightness of the United States' principled position, but his advisor Colonel House was more candid in his own journal. "Trouble may grow out of this and I advised great caution," he wrote on January 25, 1915, "we are not at present in a position to war with Japan over the 'open door' in China."[47] Nor, he might have added, was the United States prepared to undermine Britain—which House considered the "gyroscope" of world affairs—by confronting its major ally in Asia.[48]

Mahan might have approved of this focus on Anglo-American entente, preservation of the Monroe Doctrine, and caution about fighting a land war in China. But in prioritizing European balance-of-power concerns, Wilson also cast Asia as a secondary theater where short-term temporizing produced longer-term complications for American interests. One example of this poor statecraft was the Lansing-Ishii agreement of May 1917. Robert Lansing was a distinguished attorney, a veteran of international treaties and arbitration relating to the emerging laws of the sea, and a firm believer in freedom of navigation and Anglo-American alignment.[49] He had also once worked in Elihu Root's law firm and approached Asia with Root's same concern about managing rather than confronting Japan's growing power. As counselor at the State Department at the beginning of the Wilson administration, he worried about the diplomatic impact of the California Alien Land Act and saw utility in encouraging Japanese emigration to Manchuria instead.[50] Promoted to secretary of state in June 1915 after pacifist William Jennings Bryan resigned in the wake of Wilson's firm response to the sinking of the RMS *Lusitania* by a German U-boat, Lansing set about trying to reach a longer-term modus vivendi with Tokyo that would preserve U.S. interests in the region. Britain, France, and Russia had already essentially accommodated Tokyo's demand that the former German concession at Shandong would remain under Japanese control after the war.[51] With the U.S. entry into the war in April 1917, the United States now had to clarify its own position on the issue. Unprepared to follow the Europeans' endorsement of Japanese imperialism, Lansing instead reached agreement with Japanese viscount Ishii Kikujirō in Washington in November 1917 that the United States would only recognize Japan's "special interests" in the former German concessions in exchange for reconfirmation of Japan's support for the principle of the Open Door.[52]

President Wilson and Lansing considered this an enormous diplomatic coup, particularly Ishii's endorsement of the Open Door.[53] However, the vague language regarding Japanese interests in China came back to haunt the United States. Lansing had insisted privately to Ishii that acknowledgment of Japanese "special interests" was not endorsement of Japanese control. However, in the first of many cases where subtle diplomatic language was interpreted differently in Tokyo than in Washington, the Japanese side successfully portrayed the Lansing-Ishii notes to the other powers as evidence of American acquiescence in Japan's claim to "paramount" interests in the former German concessions (acquiescence that the European powers, unconstrained by America's republican virtues, had already made). Japan's position would only harden in the months and years ahead, rendering more difficult a lasting solution to the China question in peace negotiations after the war.[54] What had seemed like a smart strategic play for the United States given the exigencies of the war in Europe became a tactical blunder with longer-term implications for U.S. strategy in the region.

The confusion about ends, ways, and means in the Far East during the Great War was also evident in the American intervention in Siberia in 1918. Three crises confronted the Wilson administration in Siberia that year: the Bolsheviks' steady advance toward the Russian Far East, the fate of the 50,000 man Czech Legion, which had fought its way eastward to rejoin the fight against the kaiser after the Bolsheviks had signed a separate peace with Germany, and the danger that Japan might take advantage of the strategic vacuum created by the Russian Civil War. Wilson's War Department was skeptical that military intervention would solve any of these three problems or be worth the diversion of troops from the war effort in Europe, but the president was hostile to Bolshevism and sympathetic to the spirited Czechs, and the British and French were going in with the hope that this would maintain pressure on the Germans, so he overruled his advisors.[55] When U.S. Army major general William S. Graves arrived in Vladivostok to take command of the advance elements of the 8,000 man U.S. expeditionary force on September 1, 1918, he had orders to protect American property and to prevent war materiel from falling into the enemy's hands, while remaining strictly neutral.[56] But instead of the 7,000 Japanese troops he had been told would be deployed as part of the combined expedition with Britain and France, he found over 60,000 Japanese troops taking control of key locations across Siberia. Unable to stop the Japanese troops or the advancing Bolsheviks, the confused American contingent was withdrawn in January 1920.[57]

The Siberian intervention was symptomatic of how far American strategic thinking on Asia had drifted since Roosevelt and how little prepared American statesmen were for the new complexities of the Far

East. It had been difficult enough, as House warned Wilson, to simulta-neously satisfy Japan, keep the "door open," and press for most favored nation status in China. Now the United States was playing a complicated three- (or even four-) dimensional chess game in Asia that also had to ac-count for American interests in the European war and the new threat of Bolshevism. Observing the confused American strategy in Siberia, Wil-son's advisor on Russia at Versailles, journalist and future ambassador to Moscow William Bullitt, warned him that the lax American attitude toward Japan's intervention was "permitting without protest the creation of another great obstacle to a more decent international order."[58] Bullitt had a point. The United States had formulated a grand strategy for pre-vailing in the Great War, and a critical element was keeping Japan on the allies' side. With victory, Wilson was certain the United States would be positioned to establish a new world order and lasting peace. That, Wilson assumed, would then allow a settlement of the Far Eastern problems on terms more favorable to the United States and would put Japan back in the box. But this mind-set also led Wilson to temporize on Asia policy—settling for short-term ambiguity and accommodation of Japan on Shan-dong, Siberia, and other fronts that only emboldened Tokyo and put the United States in a weaker position for settling the peace. This pattern of viewing European challenges as immediate and urgent and Asia prob-lems as longer-term problems would repeat itself in the Second World War and the Cold War.

Wilson discovered just how difficult his temporizing on Asia would make postwar peace negotiations when he arrived in Paris in January 1919. Most of the world, including many Asian nationalists, had been inspired by Wilson's articulation of American war aims in the famous "Fourteen Points" delivered to Congress on January 8, 1918. The president had highlighted freedom of navigation, the removal of economic barri-ers, and self-determination as a principle for the settlement of all colo-nial claims.[59] In Paris, he was received as a triumphant hero and besieged by solicitous delegates from around the world who expected him to use America's new power and prestige to solve their various territorial prob-lems. Those from the Far East, such as Ho Chi Minh of French Indo-china, should have paid attention to the fact that all of the references to self-determination in the Fourteen Points referred to Europe and none to Asia. Wilson's moral standing on Far Eastern questions was further eroded when he allowed the rejection of Japan's proposal for an antira-cism clause that would have stopped the restrictive immigration policies of California, Canada, Australia, and New Zealand—states and dominions whose support he needed to complete the treaty and create the League of Nations. Outraged but well positioned, the Japanese delegation then blackmailed Wilson by threatening to walk out of the talks (as Italy had) if Japanese territorial claims in the Far East were not accepted. Wilson worried that if Japan walked out, Britain might follow. Boxed in, he essentially surrendered on the Far Eastern questions. In order to keep the major powers in the League of Nations, he accepted Japan's continued occupation of the German concessions at Shandong and granted Japan control over German Micronesia, receiving only a verbal commitment from the Japanese delegation to eventually return Shandong.[60]

Parts of the American delegation were deeply apprehensive about these concessions to Japan.[61] Naval advisors did not want their southern flank threatened by a new Japanese military presence in the former German colonies in the South Pacific.[62] Lansing, despite his Rooseveltian approach to Japan overall, thought it was better to call Japan's bluff and move to form the League without making concessions on Shandong and the former German territories and concessions. Japan, he figured, could then be managed collectively as an outlaw state if Tokyo continued to balk at membership. Reinsch thought the entire arrangement was a betrayal of America's solemn commitment to China's territorial integrity and Wilson's own idealism. He resigned in disgust.

Wilson overruled them all, justifying the concessions to Japan with the argument that any compromises made to bring the peace treaty and the new League of Nations into existence could be fixed later in a cooperative approach by all the major powers.[63] As he summarized the situation:

> The whole future relationship between the two countries [Japan and China] falls at once under the guarantee of the League of Nations or territorial integrity and political independence. I find a general disposition to look with favor upon the proposal that at an early date through mediation of the League of Nations all extraordinary foreign rights in China and all spheres of influence should be abrogated by the common consent of all nations concerned. I regard the assurances given by Japan as very satisfactory in view of these complicated circumstances.[64]

When the Open Door was conceived two decades earlier, the goal had been to prevent multiple encroachments on China by managing the balance of interests and power from offshore. After the First World War, the field of players in Asia was reduced primarily to the United States and Japan—a very ambitious Japan that filled the vacuum left by the Europeans' bloody fight on the other side of the globe. Wilson was not willing to use American power at the end of the war to formulate a new strategic equilibrium to preserve the Open Door, nor was he willing to intervene directly within China itself. Instead, he pegged his hopes on a new global collective security system under the League of Nations. Wilson would never see that day come. By the end of the Versailles talks, the president was becoming ill. After returning to the United States, he collapsed while giving stump speeches for the League. On March 17, 1920, the U.S. Senate rebuffed Wilson and rejected the League, dealing it a final blow in votes on November 19 of that year.

Did Wilson leave an enduring strategic path for the United States in Asia? Historian Whitney Griswold, assessing Wilson in the late 1930s, argued that there was a Wilsonian Asia strategy:

> First, the effort to bind Japanese capital investment in China to the cooperative ordinances of the new four-power consortium; second, participation in the Allied military intervention in Siberia in order to prevent Japan from detaching the maritime provinces from Russian rule; third, the insistence on the restoration of Shantung to China, and fourth, codification in treaty form of the principles of the Far Eastern policy of the United States together with the Wilsonian principles of non-aggression and collective security as applied to the Pacific Ocean and the region of Eastern Asia.[65]

Subsequent historians have been less kind. Writing in the 1960s, Roy Watson Curry argued in his study of Wilson's Asia policy that "from the earliest days of his administration Wilson was forced to deal with Far Eastern problems. Each situation brought its individual response in action. There never was any master strategy beyond support for historic policies pursued in relation to the area."[66]

Curry is certainly correct about the inconsistency of Wilson's Asia strategy. Wilson began with a unilateralist emphasis on America's democratic values and self-determination and then ended up cynically rejecting Japan's nonracism clause in pursuit of a Europe-centered collective security system. He acquiesced in the Japanese takeover of Shandong and strategic Micronesian islands, but he was then willing to intervene in Siberia in part to prevent Japan from filling the vacuum left by the Bolshevik Revolution. He pulled out of the international banking consortium in China in 1913, but by 1917 he was again negotiating American participation for fear that China would become too dependent on Japan for loans.

These wide swings in U.S. diplomacy suggest that the twenty-eighth president had no clear plan for shaping the regional order but rather had a vision of an international order that he expected would ultimately protect American interests in the Pacific. At Versailles, Wilson's leading China hand, Reinsch, and the architect of his Japan policy, Lansing, both thought he had put U.S. interests in the Pacific in too much jeopardy in his search for a global collective security system.

Yet, if one focuses on results and not just process, it must be acknowledged that the United States was probably in a stronger aggregate position in Asia in 1920 than it had been in 1909, despite Wilson's lack of a coherent strategy for the region. This had less to do with skillful statecraft and more to do with the implosion of Europe and the acceleration of American military and economic might. A young and vibrant United States paid only limited costs for the flaws in the government's strategic concepts. This would not be the case a decade hence.

Meanwhile, as Taft was searching for economic instruments to secure American interests in Asia and Wilson imagined a new global collective security order to do the same, the U.S. Navy was planning for the future—and hedging against the increasing threat posed by a rising Japan.

"Storm Proof Must Be the Structure, or the Structure Will Not Endure": The Hedge: War Plan Orange

Theodore Roosevelt recognized that his entire approach to Asia, including the Open Door, rested on the credibility and power of the U.S. Navy: the "big stick." Though he did not expect war with Japan, he knew that planning would be an essential element of dissuading Japan from unchecked imperial ambition. In 1900, the General Board of the Navy (hereafter referred to as the Navy Board) was established under the leadership of Admiral George Dewey, the hero of Manila, to continually update force requirements and war-fighting plans to defend America's expanded presence in the Pacific and Caribbean (replacing the somewhat sleepier

Naval General Board).[67] The planners gave a series of color codes to potential enemies, with the most likely—Japan—designated as "Orange" in 1904. When anti-immigration riots broke out in California and jingoistic war talk spread in Tokyo in 1907, Roosevelt asked the General Board to get to work on a plan to defeat Orange. The board would spend the next three decades continually revisiting the problem of how to define American war aims in the Pacific and how to defeat an increasingly powerful Imperial Japanese Navy with a decreasingly resourced U.S. force and exposed forward presence. Their innovative efforts would lay the intellectual groundwork for the military strategy that won the Pacific war.[68]

Preparations for what would come to be known as War Plan Orange proved challenging from the beginning. The planners on the General Board and at the Naval War College in Newport, Rhode Island, agreed on the operational concept that the U.S. Navy would have to defeat the Imperial Japanese Navy in a Mahanian decisive battle somewhere in the Western Pacific. The planners also knew that Japan's "center of gravity" was its heavily populated and poorly resourced home islands, which could be blockaded after a decisive win at sea. However, they were stumped by an inherent contradiction in the larger U.S. strategic approach to Asia. Their planning assumption was that war with Japan would be over preservation of the Open Door in China, which was then becoming the central pillar of America's strategic approach to the region and the major point of geopolitical friction with Tokyo. But how could the United States as a maritime power defeat a large Japanese army in continental Asia in defense of China's territorial integrity?

In theory, the Philippines had provided the United States with a strategic stepping stone to shape developments in China, but when Secretary of State Hay rejected the General Board's proposal for a permanent coaling station on the China coast during peace negotiations with Spain in 1900, the navy was reduced essentially to port calls and gunboat diplomacy to show the flag on Chinese inland waterways. In preparing War Plan Orange, the General Board expressed the hope that this would at least supply "evidence of naval power" to the "people of the East,"[69] but it was clearly insufficient to compel Japan to desist from expansionism in China. Recognizing this weakness, navy planners began to scope out options for aligning with Britain or France in order to take the fight to Japan on the continent in the event of war. This was smart strategic thinking—recognizing a dangerous gap between ends and means and seeking effective ways to remedy the deficiencies through external balancing. However, in early twentieth-century America it was bad politics. George Washington's admonition to avoid foreign entanglements still rolled convincingly off politicians' tongues. When the secretary of the navy caught wind of his staff's musings about grand strategy, he ordered them to cease meddling in diplomatic affairs and to stick to their mission of sea fighting.[70]

The planners then stumbled over another problem as they gamed out scenarios for a Blue versus Orange conflict (Blue being the color code for the United States). The precedent of Japan's attack on Port Arthur at the beginning of the Russo-Japanese War in 1904 and the disparity in U.S. and Japanese naval forces in the Western Pacific suggested that Orange would initiate hostilities with a sudden attack on American forces in the Philippines and Guam. Consequently, Blue would be forced on the defensive while waiting for reinforcements to arrive from the Atlantic. If Blue then rushed more battleships to the Western Pacific and they were badly defeated—as Japan had defeated Russia's fleet at Tsushima—then there would not be sufficient forces to defend Hawaii, the vulnerable Western coastline, or the Panama Canal. As Commander J. H. Oliver wrote to the president of the Naval War College after studying the problem in 1907, the United States would have no choice, given the state of unpreparedness, but to "regard our overseas Pacific possessions temporarily lost, and proceed resolutely to their reconquest . . . through advance across the Pacific upon a broad strategic front."[71] The navy planners concluded by 1909 that Blue would be better positioned by retreating from the Western Pacific to consolidate surviving forces for the defense of Hawaii, the West Coast, and the Panama Canal until the Atlantic Squadron arrived to strike back.[72]

However, the army was understandably resistant to any notion of surrendering its garrisons in the Philippines, Guam, and Samoa, and it insisted in its own 1909 Report on the Defense of the Philippines that the islands could be held if the navy did its part and if the army built one large fortified base near Luzon. According to the army's assessment, "The easiest and most practicable defense from foreign aggression can be made by a strong battle fleet capable of securing and maintaining the command of the sea. Any attempt to hold the islands by land forces alone would involve an enormous army, and require a self-sustaining base in the Philippines. . . . Assuming that the proper defense of the Philippines can be best made by the battle fleet, the selection of a suitable base in these waters becomes essential to the maintenance of any consistent policy in the Orient."[73]

Army chief of staff Leonard Wood convinced his fellow Rough Rider Theodore Roosevelt to stand by the troops, and the Army-Navy Joint Board agreed to choose Corregidor Island off the coast of Luzon, at the mouth of Manila Bay, to be their new Pacific Gibraltar. For now, the navy would put its trust in fortifications, concluding that:

> In the early stages of the war we would be on the defensive. We accept the fact that we cannot make a stand against a determined attack by a large force on anything in that ocean except Corregidor and possibly the island of Oahu. These points we would hope to hold and the dictates of good strategy would probably keep our west coast safe from serious attack. Our power for bringing the enemy to terms is concentrated in our battle fleet and the vital part of the campaign would be the transfer of the fleet to the scene of action properly equipped and ready for battle. After their arrival the plan of action must first be unrelenting and undiverted effort to bring the enemy's fleet to action. To crush their naval force and to drive their vessels off the sea.[74]

The iconoclastic J. H. Oliver at the War College lined up behind the new fortification strategy as well, telling an audience of fellow officers in Newport in June 1910 that with time and expense an impenetrable shield could probably be built in Hawaii and the Aleutians that would protect the West Coast and the Panama Canal. But, he warned, "to advance that shield still further westward so as to include Guam, and even the Philippines themselves, will demand an effort truly gigantic and a money expenditure very, very great. . . . *Storm proof must be the structure, or the structure will not endure*" [emphasis added].[75]

Could the structure endure? Japan's occupation of the Shandong Peninsula and German possessions in the Marianas led planners to revise their assumptions about War Plan Orange in January 1917. The board now authorized planners to prepare for operations against a Japanese initial offensive that was expected to take control of the Pacific as far east as the Guam-Midway line, if not Oahu. The board also concluded that Japan's new geostrategic position would require doubling the size of the U.S. Pacific Fleet and further upgrading fortifications for Corregidor so that it could be defended after being cut off by the Imperial Japanese

Navy.[76] In 1919, the Joint Army and Navy Board concluded that War Plan Orange would probably also require an advance up the Carolines and Marshalls in preparation for counterattacking the Imperial Japanese Fleet and taking Japan's home islands under blockade.[77] This new dimension to U.S. planning was made possible by the advent since 1911 of oil-powered ships, which could be refueled by oceangoing oilers that accompanied the fleet. The navy now looked at islands for building logistical hubs and not as fixed coaling stations. The essence of the insular strategy remained the same, but now with greater flexibility.[78]

Yet even as the army and navy reached consensus on a military strategy to hunker down in the Philippines and await the fleet, both services were steadily diverging from the State Department's diplomatic strategy. The original planning assumption for War Plan Orange had been that the national objective was defense of the Open Door, yet as naval historian Edward S. Miller notes, "In less than a decade, U.S. strategists had retreated from seeing their nation as the firm guarantor of China to a nebulous restraining force that Japan would assail someday to unblock its ambitions. Though never handed down by higher political authority, this perception by naval officers of the roots of a Pacific war never varied after 1914. It was, in the end, correct. The United States never fought for Manchuria in 1931 or China in 1937 or 1941. It fought when Japan attacked it to remove the main impediment to conquest in East Asia."[79]

The navy and the State Department were on different strategic tracks, whether they knew it or not. The fact that no president between the Roosevelts appears to have been briefed on War Plan Orange meant that the divergence endured. Still, the reduction of War Plan Orange to the defense of fortified points in the maritime sphere provided the basis for a realistic hedge should peace collapse, and perhaps a tool of dissuasion against Japanese aggressive expansion if properly resourced. Coming off a massive buildup in the First World War, the navy was now confident that it could fulfill that redefined mission, as long as it had two things: continued parity with the Imperial Japanese Navy in the Pacific and fortification of America's island outposts. As Captain Reginald Belknap warned in a review of the plan he prepared at the Naval War College in November 1921, "Neglect to complete the half-measure of defense already made in the PHILIPPINES and GUAM, would not only encourage a more aggressive course by ORANGE, enough to make war almost certain, but on our part would throw away an invaluable military advantage—of considerable outlay already—and would instead involve us in great pro-longation of war, maximum expenditure, and uncertainty of outcome."[80] Yet throw away that "invaluable military advantage" was precisely what the United States was about to do.

"More Ships than All the Admirals of the World Have Sunk": The Washington Treaty System

In the 1920s, American grand strategy toward Asia centered on a series of multilateral treaties negotiated in 1921 and 1922, known collectively as the "Washington Treaty System." Because that system broke down in the next decade, catapulting the United States into war with Japan, the era is often dismissed as an isolationist backwater during which America re-treated from the world. Yet, as Herring notes, the "era of the 1920s defies simple explanation."[81] This, after all, was the decade when the Council on Foreign Relations was established in New York to chart American engagement with the world, when the professional Foreign Service was established (in 1924) by amalgamating disparate diplomatic and consular services, and when Georgetown University created the first of the nation's graduate schools of international affairs (to be followed by Fletcher and Johns Hopkins University, among others).[82] The United States entered the decade as the leading Western power in Asia, counterpoised against Japan as one of only two states to emerge from the First World War with their military and economic power enhanced. Rather than shirk respon-sibilities or leave the future regional order to others, American leaders attempted to place a bold new stamp on Asian affairs. They acted not in ignorance of the power dynamics in the region but in an attempt to con-trol and tame them. And initially, they had some success. The treaties signed in 1921 and 1922 in Washington at least temporarily solved a series of strategic problems that had bedeviled the United States since Theodore Roosevelt left office. They were followed quickly by efforts to bind the re-gion, and particularly Japan, more closely to the United States through international financial understandings. The result—at least initially—was a better alignment of American power to American interests in the Pa-cific and the establishment of a more stable regional order.

The collapse of the Washington Treaty System is usually attributed to fatal flaws in the treaties themselves—particularly the lack of any monitoring or sanctions mechanisms and the inclusion of the infamous non-fortification clause. However, these flaws only partially explain the paralysis in American statecraft as the regional order collapsed under the combined weight of Chinese nationalism, economic entropy, and rising Japanese militarism over the next decade. The larger problem was that American leaders came to assume that the strategic environment had been permanently changed by the treaties, that international norms were now more effective instruments of deterrence than military power, alliances, or economic sanctions. As international politics spun out of control, American political leaders clung to the belief that the Washington Treaties would provide the moral suasion necessary to deter Japan. They failed to appreciate that the treaties were but one instrument of American statecraft, and that they were useless without American power to back them up. Indeed, they would never have been possible in the first place had Japan and the other powers not been concerned with the preponderance of American economic and naval power after the First World War.

This predisposition to hope that the region's geopolitical problems would be permanently solved by the treaties was a powerful element in American strategic culture at the end of the First World War. Americans were war-weary and deeply suspicious of entangling alliances and overseas obligations after the blood and toil in France. For its part, the navy had plans to build up to a total of twenty-eight battleships after the war. This massive U.S. fleet would have resourced War Plan Orange and the other color-coded plans but also would have elevated the U.S. Navy from a peer of the Royal Navy to the dominant naval power in the world. At Versailles, the British told President Wilson they would not accept this outcome, knowing that he needed British support for the League of Nations. The president's first response was to put off the British by arguing that an Anglo-American accord would be meaningless without a way to cap Japan and others from building their fleets as well. Still, the idea of capping the navy's budget stuck in his head. Campaigning for the establishment of the League of Nations after returning from France in early 1919, Wilson essentially used the navy as a foil, arguing that failure to pass the League would condemn the United States to an endless arms race against the other powers.[83] It was an early sign that the navy's plans for resourcing and implementing War Plan Orange might hit trouble.

Ironically, the era of Republican dominance in the 1920s did not bode well for the navy either. Like their predecessors in the 1870s, Republicans of the 1920s were eager to decrease the size of the federal budget after a major war, including spending on armaments. The real focus of these Republican governments was business (as Calvin Coolidge would famously say, "the chief business of the American people is business!"). By 1929, the United States was the world's largest exporter, driven by private sector innovation in the manufacturing sector and aided by congressional legislation that relaxed antitrust laws.[84] This might have laid the political groundwork for building a strong navy as the handmaiden of commerce. Yet throughout the decade, the expanding size of the domestic market meant that the United States was actually far less dependent on trade than was Japan, the major rival for preeminence in the Pacific.[85] Only a few years after the end of the First World War, the U.S. Navy suddenly found itself with only a handful of committed supporters in Congress.[86] Indeed, antinavalism was stronger in the United States than in any of the other major powers. Many newspapers took up the cause, and the big-navy men encountered a veritable cyclone of opposition in Congress.[87]

When Republican peace progressive William E. Borah of Idaho won international acclaim for presenting a Senate resolution in December 1920, a version of which passed into law the following July, calling on the United States, Japan, and Britain to reduce their navies by 50 percent in five years, incoming president Warren G. Harding decided it was time to turn lemons into lemonade.[88] He instructed his secretary of state, Charles Evans Hughes, to use America's new leadership position to convene an international disarmament conference in Washington, DC. The primary focus would be Asia.

The Washington Conference fit perfectly with Harding's political requirements and with the oratorical and negotiating skills of Charles Evans Hughes. Like Seward, Hughes was a former Republican governor of New York with a belief that economic instruments of power would in the end guarantee American preeminence in Asia if an arms race could be averted. According to one early biographer, Hughes was "phenomenally clear-headed, single-minded, and inconceivably industrious, absolutely fearless, to be sure; but humanly approachable and friendly, good natured, reasonable, jovial—and on the level with his job."[89] Hughes was not just captured in the disarmament and small government spirit of his party and his times; he also recognized that other nations, including Japan, were overextended after the war. His approach to disarmament was based on a realistic assessment of what was possible in terms of both the domestic and international balance of power.[90]

The Navy General Board advised Hughes of fleet requirements going into the disarmament conference. The board declared that the United States would require a fleet equal to that of the British and double that of the Japanese to deal with both threats in the Atlantic and Pacific separately. However, if the Anglo-Japanese alliance held, the General Board stated that it would require a fleet equal to the combined fleets of *both* Britain and Japan.[91] American planners were obsessed with the Anglo-Japanese alliance in a way that seems odd to modern readers who know that Britain and America themselves would form one of history's greatest alliances within a generation. Aware of American concerns, the British had revised the Anglo-Japanese treaty in 1911 to include an article stating that neither party would be obligated to go to war with any third party that had a Treaty of General Arbitration, which Britain had negotiated with the United States.[92] This made little impression on U.S. planners, however, for whom the lessons of the recent war were clear: smaller conflicts triggered alliances and thus became world wars. The Anglo-Japanese alliance also stuck in the craw of the State Department, since it had clearly constrained Britain's ability to cooperate with the United States in checking Japanese ambitions in northern China and Manchuria over the previous two decades. For Hughes, ending the Anglo-Japanese alliance was therefore a high priority at the Washington Conference.

A second goal was to remove the inconsistency and ambiguity surrounding the Open Door policy in China and to achieve the kind of explicit international agreement that Hay had prematurely claimed two decades earlier. An international concert with respect to China would also remove a major source of rivalry with Japan and reduce the threat to the Philippines, which in turn would ensure that the naval tonnage cap stayed in place. Going into the conference, the British had made it clear to Hughes that the Open Door no longer had currency as a basis for international understanding on China, since it had "now become so complicated as to be valuable to either side who cares to use it: in other words, like statistics which can prove either a surplus or a deficit if deftly handled by experts." London recommended instead "a general agreement between the participating Powers guaranteeing the commercial and territorial integrity of China." Hughes concurred.[93]

With these objectives in his mind, Hughes stood before the convention in the elegant marble Continental Memorial Hall on Seventeenth Street in northwest Washington, DC, on November 12, 1921. The delegates of the major powers sat around an enormous U-shaped table covered with green cloth. An additional 1,200 people—including graduate students who had lined up to secure tickets since early in the morning—sat in galleries behind them.[94] Hughes welcomed the delegates and outlined his goals for the conference. Nervous naval officers listened as the Americans' ambitions became clear.[95] Building to a dramatic crescendo, Hughes called for scratching plans to build sixty-six U.S., British, and Japanese capital ships. The naval arms race "must stop!!" he declared, and the room exploded with applause.[96] One journalist wrote that "Hughes sank in thirty-five minutes more ships than all of the admirals of the world have sunk in a cycle of centuries."[97]

Over the next three months, working groups were held in private in the Pan-American building next door, as U.S. Marines guarded the doors with fixed bayonets to keep out the curious press and even more curious graduate students. By early 1922, these intense negotiations had yielded a series of agreements. The most important were:

- *The Four Power Treaty*, signed by the United States, Japan, Britain, and France, which took the place of the Anglo-Japanese alliance. In the treaty, the Four Powers agreed to respect each other's possessions in the Pacific and consult each other in case of conflict.
- *The Five Power Treaty*, which established a 5:5:3 ratio in battleship tonnage for the United States, Britain, and Japan and a 1.67 ratio each for France and Italy. As part of the treaty, the American side also agreed to a nonfortification clause (Article XIX).[98]
- *The Nine Power Treaty*, through which the United States attempted to stabilize great-power competition in China by institutionalizing the Open Door as a binding commitment of the major powers in Asia.
- *The Shantung (Shandong) Treaty*, in which Japan agreed to withdraw troops from Shandong and restore all former interests in Qingdao (Tsingtao) and the railway at Jinan (Tsinan) to China.[99]

These treaties solved, at least temporarily, a range of strategic problems that had vexed U.S. policy toward China over the previous two decades. "The traditional method of promoting American security has been to maintain a balance of power," journalist Walter Lippmann would argue retrospectively in 1935, adding, "The Washington Treaties sought to stabilize this policy under the form of a collective system."[100] The Four Power Treaty now meant that the Anglo-Japanese alliance would no longer menace U.S. war planning or diplomacy in China. Japan had also agreed to withdraw from Shandong and Siberia (though Japan continued to control the railroads and thus maintain de facto hegemony in Shandong). In addition, with the timely intervention of former secretary of state Elihu Root, Japan was convinced to sign an exchange of notes stating that the Lansing-Ishii agreement was now superseded by the Nine Power Treaty and clarifying that Japan had "special" and not "paramount" interests in Manchuria.[101] Finally, Japan and the other powers agreed in Article III of the Nine Power Treaty to codify the pillars of the Open Door notes; namely, that those powers with concessions in China would maintain most favored nation status for the other parties within those concessions.

The arms control agreements in the Five Power Treaty also achieved important American military objectives. The U.S. Navy officers in the delegation were not entirely displeased with the outcome. They already had growing doubts about whether the Harding administration and Congress would support a continued naval building campaign, and the Five Power Treaty froze in place ratios that confirmed the U.S. Navy as co-equal with the Royal Navy and superior in capital ships to the Imperial Japanese Navy.[102] The Japanese delegation was initially instructed to accept nothing less than a 10:7 ratio unless there was a nonfortification clause, in which case they could accept the 10:6 ratio. The British and Americans went into the talks with no intention of discussing a ban on fortifications but in the end agreed to the Japanese demand in order to achieve the 10:6 ratio.[103] Given the Japanese concessions in the Four and Nine Power Treaties, which mitigated the major points of contention for possible wars over the Open Door, the compromise seemed reasonable enough, particularly if the United States built up to its treaty limits.[104]

The Washington Treaties were met with great enthusiasm around the world, but there were also many dissenting voices at the time focused on the nonfortification clause in the Five Power Treaty. Raymond Leslie Buell in *The Washington Conference* (1922), Captain D. W. Knox in *The Eclipse of American Sea Power* (1922), and Hector Bywater in *Sea Power in the Pacific* (1921) all condemned the clause as contrary to the fundamental Mahanian logic that forward fortifications were, together with commerce, the handmaidens of naval power. Commander Chester Nimitz, who would later command the fleets that defeated Japan, wrote in his 1923 Naval War College thesis that "at no time in our history has the BLUE naval tactician been confronted with a problem as difficult as that imposed by the restrictions of the Treaties."[105] Marine lieutenant colonel

Earl H. Ellis, who had begun work on a new doctrine of U.S. amphibious operations during the negotiations, claimed that the U.S. delegates who had agreed to Japan's demand for nonfortification had "cast their votes for the next war," putting himself in hot water with the civilian leadership at the Navy Department.[106] This strategic criticism cascaded through the decades.[107] Historian Tyler Dennett argued in 1933 that with nonfortification "the American Government took a step which rendered a policy of intervention in Asia impossible for fifteen years, and very difficult thereafter."[108] Years later, Secretary of State Dean Acheson would write that "the Washington Conference of 1921 was a disaster."[109] The leading historian of U.S. Navy operations in the Second World War, Samuel Eliot Morison, established another generation of negative interpretation of the clause with his 1963 history arguing that the treaty limitations put the United States at a severe disadvantage when war broke out in December 1941.[110]

Yet, more recent historiography has challenged whether the nonfortification clause was as disastrous for U.S. military planning as navy planners thought at the time or many naval historians argued after the war. At least three elements in the navy and marine corps successes in the Pacific between 1942 and 1945 were prompted by the limitations imposed by the Washington Treaties. First, as John Kuehn notes in *Agents of Innovation*, the limitations on fortifications forced the Navy General Board to create a "fleet second to none" that took advantage of seagoing dry docks, oil replenishment at sea, and other technological alternatives to fixed forward bases.[111] In the summer of 1925, the navy tested this proposition by sending a fleet of fifty-six ships, including twelve battleships, on a long cruise from Hawaii to Australia and New Zealand to demonstrate the ability of the navy to "range for thousands of miles and apply sea power in the absence of preexisting overseas bases"—the basic design criteria that allowed the fleet to defeat the Imperial Japanese Navy two decades later even after losing almost all of its battleships at Pearl Harbor.[112] Second, the limitation on battleship tonnage pushed the navy to convert two battle cruisers—the *Lexington* and *Saratoga*—into carriers and to explore the role of airpower in fleet exercises. And third, the lack of reliable forward fortifications prompted the U.S. Marine Corps to push for a new role in amphibious operations under War Plan Orange. In 1921, the iconoclastic Pete Ellis had proposed a three-phase plan in the Pacific: reduction of the Marshalls; seizing the Carolines as far as Yap; and then taking the remainder of the Carolines, including the Palaus.[113] The alcoholic Ellis was found dead in Japanese-occupied Palau in May

1923 with two empty bottles of whiskey by his bed—"gifts" of local Japanese authorities—but when the Joint Army and Navy Board concluded in August 1924 that War Plan Orange would have to begin with seizing Japanese-held islands as forward operating bases, marine corps commandant John Lejeune convinced his counterparts to give the amphibious assault mission to his marines.[114] In 1935, the Joint Army and Navy Board approved a shift from the "through ticket" line of assault straight from Hawaii to the Philippines to an oblique island chain assault up the Marshalls that would take advantage of fleet mobility and emerging amphibious capabilities.[115]

That assault would be costly, though, because of the decision at Versailles and Washington to allow the Japanese to keep the former German possessions in the South Pacific: modern-day Palau, the northern Mariana Islands, the Federated States of Micronesia, and the Marshall Islands. The naval advisors to President Wilson at Versailles had been deeply disturbed that he let Japan keep these stepping stones toward the Hawaiian Islands, though Wilson himself left the negotiations unhappy only about Shandong.[116] Two years later, Hughes entered the Washington negotiations concerned about the threat of the Japanese-held islands to America's southern flank in the Pacific, but he satisfied himself that the threat could be alleviated through side agreements with Japan giving the United States access to the cable juncture on the island of Yap, ensuring freedom of communication, navigation, and commerce.[117] The shortsightedness of the decision to leave the former German territories with Japan would become apparent to the marines, soldiers, and sailors who had to retake those Pacific islands against fanatical Japanese resistance twelve years later.[118]

Yet even with that threat to America's southern flank in the Pacific, the Washington Treaties still might have provided a basis for maintaining a stable strategic equilibrium in Asia had the Harding and Coolidge administrations remained vigilant about the underlying power dynamics in Asia. They did not. Instead, they began to assume that the treaties had transformed those dynamics and that America could now maintain the peace without greater commitments. As Harding told the Senate when appealing for the treaties' ratification in February 1922, "For more than a half century we have had a part in influencing the affairs of the Pacific, and our present proposed commitments are not materially different in character, nor materially greater in extent, though fraught with vastly less danger, than our undertakings in the past."[119]

The Senate was convinced and approved the treaties on March 27 by a vote of 67 to 27 after adding for good measure text reaffirming that "the United States understands that in the statement in the preamble or under the terms of this treaty there is no commitment to armed force, no alliance, no obligation to join in any defense."[120] Hughes was triumphant, claiming in 1923 that "we are seeking to establish a *Pax Americana* maintained not by arms but by mutual respect and good will."[121]

Respect and goodwill soon proved to be in short supply, however. In 1924, Congress passed the Alien Exclusion Act, which unilaterally abrogated the 1907 gentleman's agreement on Japanese immigration to the United States, sparking public protests in Japan.[122] Vexed by the Chinese Civil War, the United States also failed to follow through on the Nine Power Treaty's agreement with respect to tariff autonomy and abolition of extraterritoriality in China.[123] Nor, as Hughes confessed, was the new *Pax Americana* to be maintained by arms. President Calvin Coolidge, who came to office after the death of Harding in August 1923, initiated the greatest downsizing of government and taxes the country would know; sound economic policy perhaps, but devastating for the U.S. Navy.[124] Coolidge declined to build the navy up to its cap under the Five Power Treaty even after it became evident that the other powers would build around the limitations on battleships with more cruisers. Instead, in 1928, Coolidge's secretary of state, Frank Kellogg, negotiated the Pact of Paris (also known as the Kellogg-Briand Treaty), which outlawed war. The agreement won Kellogg a Nobel Peace Prize the next year but had no material impact on Japanese fleet modernization.

The Washington Treaty negotiations began, as Lippmann noted, as an effort to achieve a favorable balance of power through collective action. Within months of ratification, the treaties were being used to assert that balance of power no longer mattered. This proved to be a dangerous supposition.

"WE SHALL SEE NO WARS OVER JAPANESE INTERESTS ON THE MAINLAND": THOMAS LAMONT AND THE STRATEGY OF ECONOMIC BINDING

Underlying American confidence in the durability of the Washington Treaty System was an assumption that America's enormous financial and industrial power at the end of the First World War would increase both

Chinese and Japanese dependence on American capitalism. Though flawed in some respects, this assumption was not entirely wrong. The United States did have new economic instruments to shape the strategic equilibrium in Asia, as well as business and government leaders who understood the strength of these tools. As Joan Hoff Wilson explains in her history of U.S. business diplomacy in the decade of the 1920s:

> The dominant business creed that had emerged by 1920 contained a basic assumption about the economic and moral leadership of the United States. This assumption was based in part on optimistic expectations of a prosperous and essentially antinormal postwar world—a world in which businessmen envisaged general improvements in the human condition and significant changes in socioeconomic, political, and diplomatic relationships. Although their economic views, in particular, were usually not adequate to cope with altered postwar conditions, tremendous potential existed for the creation of an American-led world industrial community and for the coordination, under business-oriented politicians like Hoover, of the political and economic foreign policies of the United States. *That neither potential was realized between 1920 and 1933 should not obscure the historical importance of the policies pursued* [emphasis added].[125]

The Republican administrations of the 1920s were uniquely willing to outsource major diplomatic tasks to leading industrialists and bankers.[126] The most influential architect of their strategy of binding Japan and China to American economic power was Thomas W. Lamont, the chief executive of the J. P. Morgan Bank. Few bankers before or since have wielded more influence over American foreign policy or over foreign governments than Lamont.

Born in 1870 in Claverack, a town of six hundred on the east bank of the Hudson River, Lamont followed his father, a Methodist minister, to postings in small towns around the Catskill Mountains until being enrolled in the Phillips Exeter Academy in New Hampshire. After graduating from Harvard, Lamont dabbled in journalism and then found his true calling in business, where he caught the attention of John Pierpont Morgan, who stunned the forty-year-old Lamont in October 1910 by offering him a full partnership in the powerful J. P. Morgan Bank. Within a decade, Lamont was acting chief executive of J. P. Morgan and was using his new bully pulpit and Methodist outlook to preach the gospel of transforming the international order through American financial power. Woodrow Wilson was so impressed that he decided to invite Lamont, a lifelong Republican, to join his delegation to the Paris peace talks as a financial advisor, and Lamont later reciprocated by using his ownership of the *New York Evening Post* to champion the League of Nations and to counter the prairie state Republicans' growing isolationism.

The Wilson administration also turned to Lamont in 1919 to help rescue its China policy, specifically to reconstitute the now defunct American banking consortium in China. The State Department had never fully given up on the international banking consortium, even after Woodrow Wilson disavowed dollar diplomacy and withdrew the United States from the consortium in 1913.[127] With America's entry into the First World War, State Department officials saw a useful excuse to reengage the Europeans on the consortium. Third Assistant Secretary of State Breckenridge Long, a protégé of Huntington Wilson, was particularly adamant that the United States must once again use its financial power to blunt Japanese expansionism. As Long confided in his diary in December 1918, Japan's "insulting little ways" and militarist government "must sooner or later lead us into conflict in the Pacific."[128]

Long cornered Lamont on July 9, 1919, after the banker returned home from Paris on the president's ship, and urged him to take leadership of the new consortium the State Department had proposed to the Europeans, Japan, and Wall Street. Lamont agreed, to the delight of Long, who wrote in his diary that night that the banker "feels about it as I do—that is formations will prevent war between us and Japan in the end; that the Japs, will join, and recede from their position of 'reservations' as to Manchuria and Mongolia; that they should be treated very firmly; and that we should start without them if necessary. I have been living for the opportunity, to kick over the Lansing-Ishii agreement."[129]

In fact, Lamont and Long did not fully agree. Whereas Long and the State Department saw American financial power as a blunt instrument to stop Japan in Manchuria, Lamont saw banking as the means to bind Japan to the United States through mutual interdependence. Long was repeating Huntington Wilson and Willard Straight's mistaken mercantilism. This gap between Wall Street and the State Department soon became evident when Lamont agreed to Long's suggestion that he travel to Japan to seal an agreement on Japanese participation in an open multinational consortium to make loans to Manchuria.

Lamont and his party arrived in Yokohama from Vancouver on board the *Empress of Russia* in late February 1920. He spent a month at the elegant Imperial Hotel in Tokyo and was feted by the leading corporate families of Japan, including the Mitsuis and the Iwasakis, who owned the Mitsubishi conglomerate. Lamont also grew close to the brilliant young governor of the Bank of Japan, Inouye Junosuke, with whom he shared a common vision of closer U.S.-Japan ties based on financial cooperation. Before 1916, virtually all of Japan's international trade had been calculated in sterling and settled in London, but the war had caused London's intermediary role to break down in December 1916. After that, the United States emerged as the world's largest creditor nation, and a substantial dollar-yen trade began, led by J. P. Morgan because the larger U.S. financial system was not developed enough to replace London. Inouye recognized that New York was now the safest place to deposit gold and settle trade accounts, and that J. P. Morgan Bank and Lamont would be a critical partner. Based on his visit and his exchanges with Inouye, Lamont left Tokyo convinced that this new international financial architecture was the best hope for checking militarism within Japan.[130]

Upon his return, Lamont provided a comprehensive assessment to Secretary of State Hughes as background for the opening negotiations of the naval treaties in Washington. Japan, he explained, was financially stretched after the war and was now heavily dependent on the United States both for trade and for the deposit of Japanese foreign reserves.[131] Lamont did the State Department's bidding, reaching initial agreement on Japanese participation in the new banking consortium in May, which prompted an elated Long to note it in his diary as "the most important accomplishment of my life so far—the one outstanding achievement of importance and means to our government and the peace in the Far East."[132] Lamont, however, confided to his fellow bankers that he had gone along with State on the consortium "only to be good fellows."[133] The real prize for Lamont was Japan itself. Japan, he explained in an address to the annual meeting of the Academy of Political Science in September 1920, "must become a strong industrial nation and one exporting manufactured goods. To reach that point of attainment, she greatly desires American capital, materials, and cooperation."[134]

The hard numbers over the next decade proved Lamont's premise far more prescient than Long's. The international banking consortium in China made a grand total of one loan. Meanwhile, Japan came to account for 38 percent of foreign direct investment (FDI) into China by 1932, compared with an American share of only 7 percent (over 90 percent of that going to places other than Manchuria, and most of the American investment in Manchuria going to the relatively stable areas controlled by Japan).[135] Moreover, investment in China came to represent fully 80 percent of Japan's total outward FDI, compared with a meager 1 percent share of U.S. FDI abroad. In the interim, Japan surged ahead to become the fourth-largest purchaser of U.S. goods, doing more than three times the volume of American trade with China. As Joan Hoff Wilson concludes, "the pattern of commercial interdependence which emerged by the end of the decade revealed the United States as the best customer of Japan, while Japan rather than America was China's best customer."[136] It was exactly as Lamont had anticipated at the beginning of the decade. The U.S. government was simply inept at mercantilism. The disconnect between the State Department and Wall Street on Asia strategy was now as great as the divergence that emerged between State and the U.S. Navy over the same period.

Lamont continued working to deepen American financial ties to Japan throughout the decade. After the September 1923 Great Kantō earthquake struck Japan, killing over 100,000 people, Lamont helped to arrange a $125 million loan for the Bank of Japan.[137] He continued to urge the U.S. government to consider loans to Japanese projects within Manchuria, including the South Manchuria Railroad, as a gesture of goodwill. He even received a guarantee from Inouye that American most favored nation status would be preserved in northern China if there were U.S. investment. However, public opinion in the United States steadily turned against Japan, particularly after 5,000 Japanese troops were sent back into the Shandong Peninsula to "protect" Japanese property in 1925. Lamont nevertheless believed that his strategy was working. American financial ties to Japan were increasing. Confident that these trend lines would ultimately allow the United States to shape a stable regional order and concert with Japan, he declared to the Institute for Pacific Relations on December 13, 1927, that the United States "shall see no wars over Japanese interests on the mainland of Asia."[138]

In the end, he was wrong, of course, but not because he had misjudged the efficacy of international finance as a new instrument of American statecraft in Asia. Under Lamont's guidance, American banking power had indeed become an internationally recognized force, as Japan's own central banker came to understand. Wielded in isolation from other instruments of power and without sufficient institutional foundations at home and abroad, however, finance proved insufficient to buttress American interests against the growing anarchy that was pulling apart the Washington Treaty System and international order in Asia. Lamont's binding strategy with Japan depended on open markets, yet as early as 1922, the U.S. Congress passed the Fordney-McCumber tariff, which raised import duties on foreign goods to 38.5 percent in an effort to sustain agricultural and manufacturing profits after demand dropped with peace and the resumption of European production.[139] Fordney-McCumber would be matched at the end of the decade by the even more damaging Smoot-Hawley tariffs, which sent Japanese exports down by 50 percent. Lamont's binding strategy also depended on Japan's convergence with a robust international financial system, a vision Inouye shared. Yet Britain's traditional ability to underpin the gold standard and the international financial system Japan would join was collapsing, and private banks like J. P. Morgan—not to mention the newly created U.S. Federal Reserve Bank—would prove incapable of picking up the burden as British financial power imploded in 1931. Impoverished by the policies of the West, Japan's young militarists would condemn Inouye and the internationalists and turn against the United States and Britain—the exact opposite effect of that envisioned by Lamont.

STRATEGIC LEGACIES OF THE WASHINGTON TREATY SYSTEM

In the end, the Washington Treaty System collapsed, Japan made a grab for hegemony in Asia, and a decade of bloody war on land and sea ensued. Yet the failure of the American grand strategy in the prewar years should not obscure the innovative diplomatic, military, and financial tools developed in the 1920s. With the Washington Treaties, Hughes took the first steps "to incorporate American Far Eastern policy into international treaties."[140] Whereas Hay had unilaterally declared a consensus on the Open Door, Hughes forced a treaty on the other powers, anticipating the leading role the United States would play in developing regional institutions decades later. Military strategy was also characterized by open debate and innovative operational planning. The legend of the battleship admirals being hidebound until their big ships went down at Pearl Harbor was never quite right. Nor was Lamont's innovative use of banking

to bind a rising Japan to the United States forgotten when war broke out—
as the Bretton Woods negotiations and postwar international financial
institutions demonstrate. All of these evolutions in American statecraft
in the Pacific would form important foundations in the postwar era.

But first Americans would have to relearn a fundamental truth about
power and competition in Asia that they had forgotten in the years since
Theodore Roosevelt.

5. "BETWEEN NON-RESISTANCE AND COERCION"
THE OPEN DOOR CLOSES, 1928–1941

At the time Lamont declared war to be obsolete in the Pacific in December 1927, the Washington Treaty System still seemed to be an enormous success. Japan was converging with the Anglo-American–centered global financial system. Most of the great powers were generally respecting the Nine Power Treaty and the Open Door in China. American economic power was growing by leaps and bounds, with the United States producing more manufacturing goods than the next six powers combined.[1] A new *Pax Americana* maintained "not by arms but by mutual respect and good will" seemed quite feasible to most internationalists in the United States.

Yet beneath these deceptively positive trend lines, the underlying structure of international relations remained precarious. The Washington Treaty System had essentially resuscitated a nineteenth-century European concert of power at a time when Europe's actual ability to shape events in Asia had already been sapped by war and debt. Meanwhile, Europe's calamitous war had awakened Asians to the twin ideologies of nationalism and communism. Mahan had anticipated two decades earlier that Asia's great civilizations would throw off the yoke of the West, and that moment was rapidly approaching in both China and Japan.

The first blow to the system thus came not from battleships at sea or great-power competition, as the negotiators of the Five Power and Nine Power Treaties had once feared, but instead from within China itself. Anti-foreign riots, prompted by a bloody clash between a Chinese mob and British police in Shanghai on May 30, 1925, had led to a consolidation of power around Chiang Kai-shek (Jiang Jieshi) who demanded tariff autonomy, launched an expedition to control the north of China, and massacred his erstwhile communist allies in Shanghai in 1927.

Initially, the American commissioner sided with the other powers to protect the foreign legations and restore commercial rights, but Secretary of State Kellogg and his director for the Far Eastern Division, Nelson T. Johnson, were progressive believers in the anti-imperialist tradition of American foreign policy and reached agreement with Chiang's government on tariff autonomy while rebuffing British demands for punitive measures against the Chinese nationalists.[2] However, Chiang's consolidation of power pushed Japan in a more menacing direction. In Tokyo, Tanaka Giichi's *Seiyūkai* party formed a new hard-line government and prepared for interventionist ("positive") policies to preserve Japan's position in northern China and Manchuria. When radical Kwantung Army officers moved on their own to assassinate northern warlord Zhang Zuolin (Chang Tso-lin) on June 4, 1928, Tanaka's cabinet was forced to resign.[3] The pendulum then swung back to the noninterventionists in Tokyo, who agreed in London to new Five Power limitations on cruiser and submarine construction (neither of which had been covered in the original Five Power Treaty). American confidence in the Washington Treaty System was briefly restored. As U.S. undersecretary of state William Castle, Jr., explained during the London negotiations, "we buy nearly $400,000,000 a year from Japan; and we sell to Japan something over one-half of that amount. . . . [T]rade will never induce Japan to declare war on the United States. . . . [A]bove all else, Japan is not stupid."[4]

Japan was not stupid, but the London Treaty was deeply unpopular in Japan, and the legitimacy of the noninterventionists in Tokyo was highly contingent on the status of Japan's position in Manchuria and the fate of Japan's convergence with the international economy. Both were drifting toward disaster. In China, Chiang's steady advance north and Soviet moves south continued to threaten Japanese control over Manchuria, which Tokyo relied on for 40 percent of its trade, raw materials, and as a buffer against the traditional Russian enemy. Alarmed at the growing strength of the Chinese Nationalists and the Soviets, influential officers in the Kwantung Army around Lieutenant Colonel Ishiwara Kanji became increasingly vocal in their demands for aggressive steps to secure Japan's "breathing space" in Manchuria before it was too late.

At the same time, Lamont's friend Inouye, now finance minister, announced on January 10, 1930, that Japan would join the international gold standard. The October 1929 New York stock market crash had caused international trade to contract massively—from $5.3 billion in January 1929 to $1.8 billion four years later—but Inouye still thought the international financial system was sound. What he did not anticipate was that bank failures across Europe and North America in the summer of 1931 would cause a massive exodus of gold from Britain, forcing Britain itself to abandon the gold standard on September 18, 1931.[5] Within hours of the Bank of England's decision, the Kwantung Army struck its own blow on the other side of the world, staging a fake attack on a portion of the South Manchurian Railway line near Mukden as a pretext for invading Manchuria. In a single day, the positive forces of economic convergence and strategic accommodation that had underpinned the Washington Treaty System evaporated into thin air.[6]

In Washington, the State Department was caught almost completely off guard by Japan's onslaught. Secretary of State Henry L. Stimson had assumed that the civilian leadership was ascendant again in Tokyo and had the Imperial Japanese Army under control. He thought he understood Japan, based on previous stints as secretary of war (1911–1913), governor-general of the Philippines (1927–1929), and as a protégé of Elihu Root, whose Wall Street firm he had joined after graduating from Harvard Law School in 1890. Like Root, Stimson believed in both the Washington Treaty System and the utility of reaching accommodation with Japan on continental Asia in order to preserve U.S. interests in the Western Pacific and Philippines.[7] His first instinct was therefore to avoid condemning Japan and instead seek to "let the Japanese know we are watching them and at the same time to do it in such a way that will help Shidehara [Japan's Quaker foreign minister], who is on the right side, and not play into the hands of the nationalist agitators on the other."[8] His attitude changed in October 1931, however, after he learned that Japanese forces were bombing Jinzhou (Chinchow), far to the south of the railroad zones. It now appeared that Japan was not merely in a dispute with China over treaty rights but was intent on taking Manchuria—an assault on the

Open Door policy and the Washington Treaty System itself. Stimson intended to work the problem diplomatically, but he began to argue that the United States would also have to consider an international trade embargo to enforce the Nine Power Treaty if Japan did not relent.[9]

Stimson immediately ran into resistance to sanctions from President Herbert Hoover. In many respects, Hoover reflected the prevailing Republican view that trade and good offices served as the principal instruments of American power rather than sanctions or war. Hoover also brought with him a complex view of China, having been trapped by the Boxers in the siege of Tianjin in 1899, where he had been unsuccessfully trying to wrest control of the massive Kaiping coal mines from Chinese authorities for his British employers when the Boxers attacked.[10] After months under siege, Hoover and the rest of the legation were saved as British and U.S. troops broke through the Boxer lines, with their bands playing "It'll Be a Hot Time in the Old Town Tonight" (also played by Dewey's band during the Battle of Manila Bay—a recurring anthem for American adventures in the Far East at the time). Hoover carried with him a traumatic aversion to entanglements within China, which found fertile ground in his own Quaker upbringing.[11]

The world economic crises only compounded Hoover's resistance to overseas adventures. In June 1930, he had made the disastrous decision, against the advice of his economic and foreign policy advisors, to sign the self-destructive Smoot-Hawley Tariff Act, which only worsened the effects of the original stock market crash and shattered the pillars of interdependence with Japan. In the wake of the tariff, U.S.-Japan trade dropped from a total of $672 million in 1928 to $269 million in 1932, a 60 percent collapse.[12] Whatever reputation for internationalism Hoover had brought to office based on his good work leading the American Relief Commission in Europe after the First World War was now behind him. Overwhelmed by the financial crisis at home, he wanted no trouble with Japan. "It would be folly to go to war with Japan over Manchuria," he declared, warning that sanctions would be like "sticking pins in tigers."[13] Instead, Hoover focused on a speech calling for a massive reduction in global armaments in anticipation of that summer's Global Disarmament Conference in Geneva.

Without any real coercive tools at his disposal, Stimson drew on the precedent of the American response to Japan's 1915 Twenty-One Demands by declaring on January 7, 1932, that the United States would not recognize the legality of any action by Japan or China that violated the Open Door or the Kellogg-Briand Treaty—the famous and ineffective "nonrecognition doctrine."[14] Stimson also dispatched U.S. major general Frank Ross McCoy to join a League of Nations–mandated investigation of the Manchurian situation under the direction of V. A. G. Bulwer-Lytton of Britain, reinforcing the fragile international cooperation on the crisis. Finally, Stimson pursued a strategy of external balancing by engaging his British counterpart, Sir John Simon, in a series of long transatlantic telephone conversations in February 1932. The British card ultimately went nowhere, however, since London did not trust American resolve to confront Japan and still retained some sympathy for Japan's efforts to civilize China, not to mention residual nostalgia from the Anglo-Japanese alliance.[15] The nonrecognition doctrine was a weak enough reed as it was, and Britain's decision not to endorse Stimson's approach only highlighted the fragility of the American position.

As Walter Lippmann put it several years later, "When the collective system was tested in 1931–1932, it worked precisely as Americans feared it would work. Relying upon it, the United States took a position in Asia which left it exposed, without support, and embarrassed. Britain and France held back in Asia just as the United States would hold back in Europe when faced with a similar aggression against the collective system."[16]

The Japanese were unimpressed with American statements of principle. On January 28, Japanese carrier-based aircraft attacked Chinese forces and civilians in Shanghai in retaliation for anti-Japanese boycotts and protests, and by mid-February, 90,000 Japanese troops were battling the German-trained forces of Chiang's Fifth Army in the streets of China's most international city. Hoover reluctantly sent 3,000 marines to safeguard American citizens and, under British pressure, Japan finally agreed in March to sign a cease-fire, rendering Shanghai a demilitarized city.[17] In Manchuria, however, the Japanese completed their conquest and dug in for the long haul. In May 1932, ultranationalists in Tokyo assassinated *Seiyūkai* prime minister Inukai Tsuyoshi, sending the internationalists into full retreat and giving room for the militarists to announce the establishment of the puppet Manchukuo regime in September 1932. When the Lytton Report was finally taken up by the League of Nations in February 1933, after a year of investigation, Japanese foreign minister Matsuoka Yōsuke defiantly walked out with his entire delegation.

The next month, Japan officially notified the other powers it was quitting the League for good.[18]

When Franklin Delano Roosevelt became president in March 1933, he proved to be almost as inwardly focused in his first year as Hoover had been in his last. In his March 4, 1933, inaugural address, the new Democratic president announced he would "favor as practical policy the putting of first things first," and focused exclusively on domestic programs, with only one vague sentence dedicated to foreign affairs.[19] That summer, he undercut Secretary of State Cordell Hull's efforts to negotiate currency stabilization with the British and French by ostentatiously firing off a cable on the Fourth of July from the USS *Indianapolis* rejecting the entire arrangement and dismissing the utility of negotiating with a "Britisher."[20] Famous for his first hundred days of domestic economic legislation, Roosevelt initially made a hash of foreign policy. The Roosevelt administration did briefly throw Japan off balance and prompted new diplomatic overtures from Tokyo by normalizing relations with the Soviet Union in November 1933, but, like Roosevelt, Stalin was motivated by the need to focus on internal crises (in Moscow's case, a new round of purges). Japanese leaders quickly recognized that the Americans and Soviets were engaging in buckpassing, and the Russia card proved fruitless for Washington.[21]

Sensing the weakness and division among the other major powers and with Tokyo itself internally divided, Japan's military upped the ante. On April 17, 1934, the Japanese Foreign Ministry spokesman announced what would become known as the "Amau Doctrine," declaring that Japan would "act alone to keep peace and order in East Asia" and "oppose such projects" by foreign powers aimed at assisting China by military or financial means.[22] It was an explicit rejection of the Nine Power Treaty and the Open Door. Ambassador Joseph Grew in Tokyo tried to explain that the doctrine might be more bluster than policy, but he concluded that, "If the policy as therein outlined is adhered to and carried out strictly, it will constitute an element in international affairs as important as, if not more important than, the Monroe Doctrine of the United States. It goes much further than the Monroe Doctrine and places China in a state of tutelage under Japan."[23]

Tokyo had thrown down a challenge that could not be ignored: Just how vital were American interests in China and in Asia? Were they truly less vital than Japan's? And were they really worth fighting for?

Hornbeck, Grew, MacMurray, and the Reassessment of American Interests in the Pacific

Effective grand strategy requires an understanding of fundamental shifts in the distribution of power as they occur. In military strategy, this principle is known simply as "flexibility," the recognition that there will inevitably be a "change in purposes, policies, plans and procedures," if only because one's adversary adjusts to the original strategy.[24] In his study of leadership, *The Powers to Lead* (2008), Harvard's Joseph Nye identifies this same principle as being essential to statesmanship, calling it "contextual intelligence," or the ability to recognize when certain assumptions about the world are no longer valid.[25] Strategic concepts need to evolve as circumstances change. As Robert Dorff argues in the principal text on grand strategy for the Army War College, there are inflection points, during which:

> We must examine a newly emerging system with an eye toward identifying factors and forces that fall into four basic categories: 1) that which is "old" but still relevant; 2) that which is "old" and no longer relevant; 3) that which is "new" and relevant; and 4) that which is "new" but not relevant. Adapting effectively to the new circumstances while simultaneously balancing against the lingering circumstances from the older system is the central challenge. If we jettison too quickly parts of the old framework, we may find ourselves ill prepared to deal with some of the traditional challenges that have endured from one period to the next. If we fail to identify and respond quickly enough to the new characteristics, we will find that we have outdated and only marginally useful instruments for dealing with the new challenges.[26]

By the mid-1930s, American statesmen faced just such an inflection point. American policy between 1927 and 1934 had been reactive and tactical, based on the assumption that the most effective instruments of American power in the region remained economic interdependence and moral suasion. The flaws in that assumption were now laid bare. The emerging system of international relations in Asia had visibly begun to implode, yet there was no new system or concept to replace it other than Japan's bid for domination. For the first time in decades, the leading architects of American statecraft in Asia were forced to question not only the sources of American power but also whether U.S. objectives were really worth a fight. Although they arrived at no clear answers to these questions—taking refuge again in the vague principles of the nonrecognition doctrine—their brief reconsideration of American strategy began to anticipate the answer that the American people would give when the United States was attacked by Japan on December 7, 1941: that even if the Open Door was not worth fighting for, a stable and nonthreatening Asian regional order was.

Although Franklin Delano Roosevelt, Secretary of State Cordell Hull, and Secretary of War Henry Stimson would ultimately have to make these calls, their strategic options were framed by a handful of veteran Asia hands within the Department of State. The most influential of these was Stanley Hornbeck, director of the Far East Division. Hornbeck remained wedded to the legalism of the Open Door and the Washington Treaty System, and grasped desperately for politically acceptable economic, diplomatic, and military tools to sustain the regional order he had helped build. He clashed frequently with Joseph Grew, the U.S. ambassador to Japan, who saw opportunities to preserve the essence of the Washington Treaty System through partial accommodation of Japan's aspirations and deft diplomatic shaping of Japanese domestic politics. Unsatisfied, Hornbeck turned to the most seasoned Asia hand in the department, John Van Antwerp MacMurray, for ways out of America's strategic dilemma in the Far East. MacMurray's 1935 memorandum to the department surprised Hornbeck by not only accepting the demise of the Washington Treaty System but also advocating that the United States withdraw completely from the Western Pacific and cede the area to Japan.

Each of these men was experienced and patriotic in his own way—the first class of truly professional Asia experts in the State Department. They had dedicated their entire careers to American diplomacy in Asia, but when forced to choose how vital American interests were in the Pacific, they diverged in their answers. The attack on Pearl Harbor would galvanize the American public to fight Japan, but it was the collapse of the Washington Treaty System in the mid-1930s that triggered the first strategic debate among the professionals. The arguments of Hornbeck, Grew, and MacMurray shed particular light on that moment.

HORNBECK: "OUR POLICY CONNOTES PRINCIPLES"

Of these three Asia hands, Stanley Hornbeck struggled the hardest to pre-serve the core elements of the Washington Treaty System and the Open Door. The earnest and self-righteous son of a Methodist missionary, he had begun his career as an academic, completing a Rhodes scholarship at Oxford in 1904 before studying under Paul Reinsch at the University of Wisconsin, where he completed a doctoral dissertation in 1909 on the most favored nation clause in international commerce. In those days, the University of Wisconsin had created only the second political science de-partment in the country after Harvard's, and Reinsch instilled in gradu-ate students like Hornbeck a midwestern progressive view of the Open Door as the harbinger of a new system of international relations that would be based on the rule of law and moral suasion.[27] After teaching in China and at the University of Wisconsin, and spending two years at the Carnegie Endowment for International Peace from 1914 to 1916, where he wrote two influential books on Asia (*Contemporary Politics in the Far East* and *The Open Door Policy and China*), Hornbeck was appointed by the Wilson administration to the U.S. Tariff Commission and then to the American Peace Commission in support of the U.S. delegation to the Paris Peace Conference.

After Versailles, Hornbeck moved to China to advise the new U.S. en-voy there, progressive banker Charles R. Crane, who had replaced Horn-beck's mentor Reinsch after the latter resigned in protest over Wilson's treatment of China's interests during the peace negotiations. Hornbeck relished this hands-on diplomacy and decided to "burrow into" the State Department bureaucracy by becoming a professional diplomat in the Far East Division after Republicans retook the government in 1921 and dis-missed Crane from service in China. The young Hornbeck proved a natu-ral at bureaucratic politics, with a survivor's instinct for working with both Democrats and Republicans and a steely unwillingness to resign when crossed by his political masters the way Reinsch and Huntington Wilson had before him (and as MacMurray would as well). From the time he took the helm at the Far East Division in 1928 until he was assigned to be U.S. ambassador to the Netherlands in 1944, he dominated U.S. Asia policy, first as director of the division and then as advisor on political affairs from 1937 to 1944.

When Hornbeck led the Far East Division, the office was at the height of its power. The practice of diplomacy still had strong linkages to the nineteenth century, with quaint French phraseology and polite young men enduring the Washington summers in their tailored, three-piece suits, starched collars, and wing-tipped shoes from Church's of London. But the State Department also now had a well-established if small core of substantive experts on the Far East and through radio the technological means to closely monitor developments in the field and to deliver instructions to post. Hornbeck was assisted in the division by five officers, two of whom were raised in China and one of whom lived most of his life in Japan and spoke fluent Japanese (by 1931, the office would expand to eight officials).[28] Moreover, he faced no serious competition from functional bureaus that would later proliferate across the State Department, from other federal agencies, or from the White House, where it was still considered proper for the secretary of state to conduct foreign policy. And on Asia those secretaries of state—Hughes, Kellogg, Stimson, and Hull—usually turned to Hornbeck. He was, in that sense, the most powerful Asianist in the State Department in the first half of the twentieth century.

Hornbeck's contemporaries and subsequent historians have disagreed over whether his policies were pro-China or anti-China. Grew considered Hornbeck naïvely pro-Chinese and hostile to Japan. That is also the perspective of postwar historians such as Arthur Waldron and K. Marlin Friedrich.[29] On the other hand, many of Hornbeck's contemporaries in the China field considered him hostile to Chinese sovereignty. Typical of Hornbeck's attitude was an article he penned in *Foreign Affairs* in July 1927—even as the State Department was negotiating tariff autonomy with the Nationalists—complaining that "there exists in China no governing authority which can guarantee to foreigners in certain areas either protection, in situ, or conduct to places of security in China or to points of departure from China."[30] Roosevelt's secretary of the treasury, Henry Morgenthau, would later also think Hornbeck was anti-China after Hornbeck mounted opposition to Treasury's plan to organize a rescue loan for China to prevent hemorrhaging of the Nanjing government's currency reserves (mostly silver) in the wake of the U.S. "Silver Purchase Act" of 1934. Morgenthau's aim was strategic—to prevent Japan from predatory moves against a fiscally weakened Nationalist government—but Hornbeck felt no obligation to help the Chinese government and warned that any U.S. loans would only provoke Japanese counteraction.[31]

Hornbeck's stance on Japan and China appears in retrospect to be a jumble of contradictions.

In fact, however, there was a consistent leitmotif in all of these seemingly contradictory moves throughout Hornbeck's influential career. Ultimately, his interest was not defined by U.S. relations with Japan or China or even Asia per se. Indeed, he demonstrated none of the sentimentality toward China of his mentor Reinsch, or toward his colleagues on both sides of the Pacific, who invariably described him as "the most undiplomatic diplomat," a "reactionary," and "hard shelled and dyspeptic."[32] Rather, the unifying theme for Hornbeck's professional career in government was the same one he first explored in his dissertation at the University of Wisconsin: to create an orderly international system based on codification and protection of most favored nation status. Asia was merely his proving ground. In the 840-page study he produced at Carnegie on the Open Door, for example, he described John Hay's contribution not as a modus vivendi to deal with the China problem of the day but rather as "an enduring statement of the traditional and fundamental principles of American Foreign policy."[33] As an advisor at the Paris Peace Conference, he pushed without success for institutionalization of the Open Door through a global multilateral treaty, an idea picked up by Hughes in the Nine Power Treaty in 1922. That same year, he wrote in one of a series of articles in *Foreign Affairs* that "the United States has had a perfectly clear and consistent China policy, insofar as policy connotes principles"; specifically, respect for legal and moral rights of other states, equal opportunity in commerce, no alliances or aggression, and persuasion rather than coercion.[34] Throughout his writings on East Asia policy, Hornbeck repeatedly stressed "that the so-called Far Eastern policy of the United States is not a separate and peculiar policy."[35] He was not interested in the "great game" of geopolitics in the region but almost exclusively and tenaciously focused on consistency with regard to the larger principles of international law and most favored nation status that he held as sacrosanct in American foreign policy.

Thus, as Japanese troops poured into Manchuria in 1931, Hornbeck took a legalistic rather than geostrategic stance. From his perspective, the principles being violated by Japan had to be weighed against the violations of extraterritoriality, the Open Door, and the Nine Power Treaty being perpetrated by the Chinese Nationalists. In a memo to Secretary of State Stimson on October 3, 1931, he warned that the United States should stay out of "the jungle of this Chinese-Japan-Manchurian mix-up," which is "full of hidden explosives, dense underbrush, and quicksand" (an even more colorful warning than Mahan's earlier description of Manchuria as a "hornets' hive").[36] Hornbeck judged that Stimson's nonrecognition doctrine provided the right level of flexibility and the surest way to avoid "war or sanctions."[37] Ultimately, concludes Warren Cohen in assessing the period, Hornbeck was prepared to accept Japanese domination of Manchuria rather than fight.[38] But Hornbeck also remained fixated on the principle of the Open Door, failing to eye the newly emerging system with an understanding of that which was old and no longer relevant.

As Japan completed its conquest of Manchuria and then assaulted Shanghai in early 1932, Hornbeck began to share Stimson's alarm that the liberals in Tokyo had lost control. He also proved remarkably sensitive to academic criticism of his policies within the United States, and particularly to a movement led by Harvard president Lawrence A. Lowell to embargo Japan after the aerial bombing of civilians in Shanghai.[39] Hornbeck grew open to considering sanctions but also recognized the futility of pursuing them under Hoover—and then under Roosevelt as well. Grasping for other tools to dissuade Japan and buttress the Open Door and the Nine Power Treaty, Hornbeck placed his hope in the British and Soviet cards. But, as we know, Stimson's transatlantic telephone coordination with Sir John Simon and Roosevelt's normalization of relations with Moscow failed to yield collective action or effective deterrence against Japanese expansion. Hornbeck also began to call for a naval buildup to the levels of the 1922 treaties, since "the soundest course for us lies on the line of possessing naval strength such that the Japanese will not dare to take the risk of resorting to force against us," but here also he received little support.[40]

With the 1934 Amau Doctrine, Hornbeck began to warn that any powerful nation "possessed of acquisitive and combative proclivities organized as a dictatorship and governed by a resolutely aggressive autocrat (or oligarchy) is bound to be a malefactor state. . . . The existence anywhere of a malefactor state 'on the make' is a matter of legitimate and practical concern to this country."[41] Moreover, he noted, Japan's attempt to pursue its own Monroe Doctrine was "aggressive and is apparently aimed at strengthening and extending Japan's political influence, military position and economic privileges in Eastern Asia, by the use, if necessary, of the same forceable methods which she has employed in obtaining these ends in Korea and Manchuria."[42]

And yet Hornbeck was still not willing to risk war. Having recognized that not only the Open Door and the Nine Power Treaty but also the stability of the Pacific as a whole was now in the balance, he essentially froze. Until then, the instruments of American power had seemed entirely compatible to him: commerce created peace, most favored nation status and international law created commerce, and American moral suasion backed by naval limitation treaties had created the conditions for international law. Suddenly, the entire elegant arrangement was coming apart. Unable to forge new instruments such as sanctions or balance of power to maintain American interests in Asia, and unwilling to either fight for or redefine those interests, Hornbeck essentially called for a time-out. Thus, as his most authoritative biographer, Shizhang Hu, explains, between 1934 and 1937, he advocated a "hands-off" policy on Japan and China. It was in this context that Hornbeck opposed Morgenthau's plan for financial assistance or loans to China in 1935 and discouraged pursuit of any of the American commercial rights he had long championed in China, not to mention the use of economic sanctions, which he had proposed only the year before.[43]

Not until Japan's attack on China in 1937 did Hornbeck begin to reconsider his "hands-off approach," suddenly shifting in favor of sanctions to stop Japan. Even then, he did not expect America would have to fight. When a young officer on the Japan Desk warned that sanctions imposed on Japan in the summer of 1941 might provoke an attack, Hornbeck dismissed him tersely with the words, "no nation ever went to war over sanctions." The master of Asia policy from 1927 to 1941, Hornbeck never fully caught up with the reality unfolding before him.

GREW: SEEK "CONSTRUCTIVE CONCILIATION" OF JAPAN

Hornbeck's main antagonist throughout the mid-1930s and in the years leading up to the war was U.S. ambassador to Japan Joseph Grew. A high-church Boston Brahmin and graduate of Groton and Harvard, Grew could not have provided more of a counterpoint to the progressivism of the earnest midwestern Methodist Stanley Hornbeck. The two shared the basic view that U.S. policy must derive from principles of international law, but in contrast to the abrasive Hornbeck, Grew relished the practice of diplomacy almost as an end in itself. He had traveled across Asia after graduating from Harvard in 1902 and wrote of his experiences in *Sport and Travel in the Far East* (1904)—a favorite of voracious reader Theodore Roosevelt.[44] While recovering from malaria in India during his post-collegiate travels, he befriended the American consul and abandoned his early plans to follow his father into banking, choosing instead a career in the State Department. A diplomat must act "for love of the daily service itself" rather than "grand visions or self-promotion," he later argued, and he put that into practice in postings in Berlin, Denmark, Switzerland, and Turkey before arriving in Tokyo as ambassador in 1932. (Grew also oversaw the establishment of the modern Foreign Service, a further testament to his commitment to professional diplomacy.) In Japan, he saw his mission as tempering Japanese assertiveness through "constructive conciliation" and the day-to-day business of steering bilateral relations in a more positive direction.[45]

Grew's transactional focus on understanding and shaping the Japanese mind drove Hornbeck to distraction. For his part, Grew found Hornbeck's "messianic" and legalistic approach to Asia policy dangerously naïve.[46] The two men despised each other, and their warring cables and memoranda defined the day-to-day U.S. policy reaction to Japan's expansionism throughout most of the 1930s. It was primarily a clash over tactics, but to the extent that Grew was advancing a strategy, it was an effort to return to the proper demonstration of power and respect toward Japan that had been advanced by other patrician practitioners of diplomacy such as Root and Lansing and flowed from maritime strategists such as Perry and Mahan. Grew highlighted agreements reached with the Foreign Ministry in the mid-1930s to show that there were no issues that could not be solved diplomatically between Tokyo and Washington. He certainly did not think China or Manchuria was worth going to war with Japan. At the same time, however, he warned in a series of cables between 1934 and 1936 that war could still occur, and he urged an increase in naval spending and preparations.[47] In that, he had common cause with Hornbeck. And although Grew did not think Manchuria or even the Open Door was worth war with Japan, he did inherit the determination of Root and Lansing to protect American equities in the Pacific even at the risk of war. When he decided that the militarists had permanently gained the upper hand in Tokyo and were intent on seeking domination in Asia, he finally sent his famous "green light" cable in September 1940, calling for Washington to shift to sanctions and pressure to deter Japan.[48]

Although Grew appears to history as more of a transactional diplomat and Hornbeck as more wedded to principle and rule of law, Grew probably had the better understanding of geopolitics in the region. This same instinct would lead him to challenge conventional wisdom at the height of the Pacific war and call for retention of the Japanese emperor and a nonpunitive strategy for establishing a peaceful role for Japan in Asia after the war. But before that point, Grew would be forced to watch dark and dangerous clouds gather and a brutal racial war with the nation he had hoped would be a partner for peace.

MacMurray: "It Cannot Be Anything but a Hostage to Japan"

Battling with Grew and at a loss for how to respond to Japan after the Amau Doctrine, Hornbeck turned for perspective to his predecessor as director of the Far East Division in the Department of State and one of the most experienced veterans of the Washington Treaty negotiations and diplomacy in Asia, John Van Antwerp MacMurray. MacMurray had resigned as minister to China in 1929 in frustration at Kellogg's accommodating stance toward the Nationalists and was biding his time at Johns Hopkins University and then as U.S. minister to the Baltic States. He leapt at the opportunity provided by Hornbeck to play a leading role in East Asia policy again. In the summer of 1935, Hornbeck commissioned him to prepare a comprehensive memorandum on the next steps in U.S. policy toward the Far East. The two men shared similar worldviews with respect to the primacy of international law and the Washington Treaty System, and Hornbeck no doubt expected his seasoned superior to give useful guidance on how to return to those first principles in the current entropic environment.

Instead, to Hornbeck's surprise, MacMurray submitted a brilliantly argued work of realpolitik to the department on November 1, 1935, that argued for withdrawal from the Western Pacific. Like Hornbeck, MacMurray had spent his career crafting an order in Asia based on rule of law and the Open Door. But with fresh eyes on the problem, he concluded that such an order was gone, Japan would dominate, and the United States must retreat. In effect, he concluded that Amau was right, that the United States did not have interests in the region as vital as Japan's.

The seeds for MacMurray's journey to this pessimistic conclusion were planted early in his career, despite the similarities between his outlook and Hornbeck's. Born in 1881 in Schenectady, New York, to a career soldier and Civil War veteran, MacMurray excelled at Lawrenceville Academy and then Princeton, where the university's president, Woodrow Wilson, encouraged him to pursue a career in academia. He would earn a master's degree in Elizabethan literature from Princeton and a degree at Columbia University Law School, but he chose diplomacy instead, accepting his first posting in Bangkok in 1907, with subsequent service in Moscow, Peking, and Tokyo before becoming chief of the Far Eastern Division back in the State Department from 1919 to 1922.[49] These broad diplomatic and academic experiences fused into a worldview that would set MacMurray on a collision course with the senior leadership in Washington and ultimately prepare him to write a far more intellectually honest, if strategically flawed, assessment of American power and purpose in Asia than his successor Stanley Hornbeck could muster. From Woodrow Wilson, MacMurray imbibed an early idealism about America's purpose in the world; from his mentor at Columbia Law School, Frank J. Goodnow (whose daughter Lois he would marry in 1916), he derived the conviction that U.S. foreign policy must be firmly rooted in the rule of law (he would take a sabbatical at the Carnegie Endowment after Hornbeck and publish a masterful two-volume history of U.S. treaties with China);[50] from the U.S. minister to Moscow, W. W. Rockhill, he learned the origins of the Open Door policy and the link between most favored nation status in China and overall stability in East Asia; from his tours across the region, he came to appreciate that U.S. interests should not fall into a myopic bilateral focus on China alone; and finally, from his Irish father, Junius W. MacMurray, who had defied his slave-owning family in Missouri by recruiting and leading a Union artillery battery to fight for the Union, he inherited a stubborn persistence that would cut short his career at the pinnacle of success.

That collision came in May 1925 as MacMurray sailed to assume the position of U.S. minister in Beijing just as China itself was being shaken by the May 30 Movement. MacMurray arrived in China with a deeply embedded belief that order had to be established in China before the unequal treaties and symbols of imperialism could be dropped.[51] In the perennial tension between universal norms and self-determination, MacMurray, like John Quincy Adams, chose universal norms, for, in his

words, "to go beyond the letter and spirit of the Washington Treaty obligations in recognizing hypothetical sovereignty of that [Nationalist] government is not only to exceed what I recall as the purposes of the Washington
Conference but also to encourage a spirit of irresponsibility."[52] This immediately and irrevocably set him at odds with his boss, Secretary of
State Frank Kellogg, who had already chosen China's right of self-
determination over the principle of universal rule of law. Responding to
MacMurray's case for favoring the Treaty System over Chinese sovereignty, Kellogg tersely explained to the new minister in Peking that
abandonment of Chinese sovereignty would be even more certain to
doom the Washington Treaty System and "would not be understood in
the United States and meet quite likely with disfavor."[53] MacMurray continued to urge Washington to take collective action with Britain and
Japan as the Nationalists asserted tariff autonomy in 1926 and tolerated
attacks on foreigners in 1927, but Kellogg rejected a cooperative approach
with the imperial powers and ordered completion of a bilateral U.S.-China
tariff agreement.[54] After an unsuccessful bid to convince Stimson to reverse Kellogg's approach at the beginning of the Hoover administration,
MacMurray resigned from the State Department and his post in China
in October 1929.[55]

One can understand how Hornbeck, who shared MacMurray's commitment to the Washington Treaty System and skepticism about the cohesion of the Nationalist government, might have expected a supportive
strategic memo on Asia policy from his colleague. But MacMurray's
failure to muster American willpower to lead in preserving the Treaty
System left a lasting scar and a deep pessimism about the geostrategic
underpinnings of great-power competition in the Far East. When Mac-
Murray submitted his memorandum to Hornbeck in November 1935, he
explained that during his own tenure in China, the Washington Treaty
System had been allowed to "fall into desuetude," leading to the rise of
militarism and "Japan's determination to make herself dominant in the
Far East."[56] MacMurray could offer no strategy to resurrect the system.
In fact, he asserted, the treaty system had "ceased in practical fact to be
available as a means of accommodating such strains as may arise from
the changes of equilibrium that lately have taken place in the Far East,"[57]
and thus American policy must be made based on the reality that "China
is under the shadow of Japanese domination; and China herself is helpless against it."[58]

With this as the starting point, MacMurray posited three options for U.S. policy in Asia:

(1)   "To oppose the Japanese domination of China and actively take all available means and occasions to frustrate it and assert the contrary position";

(2)   "To acquiesce in it approvingly, and indeed to participate in it, publicly and whole-heartedly withdrawing all objections or reservations and qualifications";

(3)   "To take a passive attitude, conceding nothing from the liberal principles that have traditionally underlain our policy not only in the Far East but throughout the world, but avoiding positive action, or even the appearance of active concern, at least so long as the occasion is unpropitious."[59]

The first option MacMurray rejected out of hand, noting that geography would be entirely on Japan's side. Without a defendable base west of Pearl Harbor, and with the U.S. Navy construction program having fallen behind even the ratios allowed by the Washington and London Naval Treaties, he noted, "even our present spurt to rectify the deficiency gives almost the impression of a challenge."[60] Moreover, war with Japan would be difficult to win, and even victory would create a vacuum that new adversaries such as the Soviet Union would quickly fill (a prescient observation in retrospect). Thus, he concluded, "the avoidance of such a war must itself be a major objective."[61] The Open Door was no longer worth a fight, for "China is for us no longer the primary factor in the Far East. Although it may still be a land of opportunity, we must reconcile ourselves to the realization that very little of that opportunity is likely to be available to us. . . . [I]n contrast, Japan has come to be one of paramount interest to us in the Far East."[62]

On the other hand, MacMurray was unwilling to propose the second option of formally negotiating a concert of power with Japan, since accommodation would "buy us no reconciliation with Japanese, gain us no respect, and ease none of our difficulties; rather it would stimulate them to press home their attack."[63] For MacMurray, that would realistically leave only one option—for the United States to discretely and unilaterally remove U.S. ground forces from China and remove the Asiatic Fleet from the Western Pacific "ship by ship, kept more and more away from Chinese waters and perhaps, indeed (now that the Philippines are entering upon a phase of qualified independence) withdrawn practically *in toto* from the Far East, where it cannot be anything but a hostage to Japan."

Rhetorically, the United States would sustain the Open Door policy, while abandoning it de facto, so that we are "faithful to the principles and ideals of conduct that we profess, and that others, even while dissenting, respect us for maintaining with dignity."[64]

In one tightly argued document, MacMurray essentially sought to resolve the tensions that had challenged American foreign policy strategy in Asia for a century: on the tension in relations with Japan versus China, he chose Japan; on forward presence, he called for retreat; on trade, he implicitly chose protection and retrenchment over reciprocal market opening; and on values, he favored support for international rule of law over self-determination, but not to the point of backing principle with force. It was as if MacMurray was trying to turn the clock back to an earlier and simpler period in American foreign policy—to the era before Theodore Roosevelt and Mahan or even before Seward. In so doing, he surpassed the ability of both Hornbeck and Grew to assess the geostrategic realities in Asia and the looming mismatch between ends and means in American policy. But he also ignored the fundamental lesson Mahan had imparted and that Hornbeck and Grew implicitly came to understand: that there will never be any security for Americans if the Pacific approaches to the United States are dominated by a hostile hegemonic power from within Eurasia. In choosing the ways to redress the mismatch between ends and means, MacMurray chose retrenchment—but his answer was far too simple, too elegant, and too contrary to the strategic character of the American people.

Historians are not exactly sure what Hornbeck did when he received MacMurray's bombshell. It appears that the memorandum went straight to the bottom of his safe (one can picture it wedged under piles of heavy documents related to the Open Door). Eventually, however, the memorandum got out, perhaps because MacMurray made sure his colleagues in the State Department knew about it. As such, it was resurrected by people like Grew before the war and George Kennan afterward as a model of honest realpolitik analysis.[65] In that sense, MacMurray's memorandum serves as something of an intellectual bridge between the prewar and postwar years, a comprehensive piece of grand strategy that defined the problem expertly but chose a cheap and unsustainable solution.

A Historian Judges the Strategic Debate

As Hornbeck, Grew, and MacMurray grappled with the collapse of the Open Door and the death throes of the Washington Treaty System in the mid-1930s, the nation's leading historian of American Asian policy presciently offered his own answer to the question of what was at stake for the United States. Professor Tyler Dennett of Princeton University had published the only comprehensive account of American statecraft in the region in 1922 and had won the Pulitzer Prize for his biography of John Hay in 1934.[66] He wrote in an era when social science was not yet hampered by impenetrable theories and methods or obscure postmodernist critique but instead sought to unveil the patterns of history and contemporary events in ways that would provide usable insights for policy. In the mid-1930s, Dennett saw the unfolding forces of history in ways that Hornbeck, Grew, and MacMurray could not. Even today, his clear thinking demonstrates the utility of historical inquiry to the formulation of grand strategy.

The subtext of much of Dennett's scholarship leading up to his 1922 tome *Americans in Eastern Asia* was that the United States needed to overcome its historic resistance to a "cooperative" policy with the other major powers in Asia, particularly Great Britain. As the book went to print, Charles Evans Hughes was in Constitution Hall negotiating the same grand strategy Dennett had urged. But Dennett was crestfallen by the nonfortification clause, "a step," he argued in the *Annals of the American Academy of Political and Social Science* in 1933, "which rendered a policy of intervention in Asia impossible for fifteen years, and very difficult thereafter," adding, "The motive appears to have been that American interests in the Far East, while considerable, were not worth fighting for. If they could be conserved by agreement, well and good; if not, at least they were not worth the cost of preparedness to defend them."[67]

MacMurray, who had spent his career implementing those very agreements, could not have put it more concisely in his own 1935 memorandum. Yet Dennett was not satisfied with that answer. "Do not forget," he reminded his readers in the 1933 article, "that in 1898–1902 we played for a bigger stake than now." The Open Door and now Stimson's nonrecognition policy "while apparently as pacific and humanitarian as the Sermon on the Mount, are in fact no more so than the Bill of Rights and the Declaration of Independence, for both of which much blood had to be spilt."[68]

After Japan's invasion of China in the summer of 1937 and its subsequent aerial bombing of the gunship USS *Panay* in the Yangtze River as it evacuated American citizens from the Japanese assault on Nanjing (killing three and wounding forty-eight), the hollowness of Hornbeck's hands-off approach and Stimson's nonrecognition policy echoed even more loudly for Dennett. Things seemed to change when President Roosevelt gave a muscular speech in Chicago in October 1937 declaring that "the epidemic of world lawlessness is spreading" and calling for an international "quarantine against the patient." It sounded tough, but nobody knew exactly what it meant, and the administration did not follow up with specific policies.[69] Hornbeck's new hard line failed to gain traction in the White House. American strategy toward the Pacific continued to run on inertia, even as the Amau Doctrine of 1934 was followed with further violence and expansionism by Japan.

Dennett finally called the administration's strategic drift for what it was in a *Foreign Affairs* article in 1938. Likely aware of the MacMurray memo from the tight-knit world of Asia experts he inhabited, Dennett began his *Foreign Affairs* piece by reviewing the same basic choices for strategy that MacMurray had posited, but boiling them down to two:

> The broad choice before the United States in the Far East is between non-resistance and coercion. The American Government, in the face of continued Japanese encroachment upon American rights, make protests; appeal to reason, honor, fair dealing and respect for treaties; and "reserve its rights." It may even withdraw from the Orient entirely. Or it may adopt any of several forms of coercion, beginning with threats and widening out through naval demonstrations and economic measures (of which there are many) to military action. The action, of whatever nature, could be independent, or it could be cooperative with other Powers, concurrent, concerted or associated or allied. Whatever the measures adopted, whatever the objective—whether narrowly to protect American lives and property, to preserve American interests, to avoid war at any cost, or more broadly to promote orderly international relations—the alternatives are essentially the same.[70]

The choice was that stark, in Dennett's view. The Stimson Doctrine was not a real strategy. The United States could not maintain its presence in China or the Western Pacific with half measures, just as MacMurray had warned. "There could be no second thoughts, no change of mind, about

American withdrawal from the Philippines," wrote Dennett, "the United States would have to withdraw lock, stock and barrel."[71]

But, argued Dennett, pacifist withdrawal from Asia—what he reminded his readers Theodore Roosevelt had once called a "scuttle and run policy"—would come with enormous costs. These costs would not come in terms of commercial interests, which would be affected only negligibly, but rather in the stability of America's Pacific flank. Thus, he argued, "If the United States is to undertake a strong policy against Japan it must shape it not as intervention in the Sino-Japanese war but rather as a defense of orderly processes of international government in the Pacific, and it must confine its efforts severely to that declared purpose."

It was probable, though not certain, he warned, that "the employment of military measures short of war in the present juncture would suffice to cause Japan to pause." Americans were clearly not ready for war, he acknowledged, but they would have to understand that a coercive strategy would require preparedness not only for war but also for what would follow victory, since the United States "would be left with continuing obligations in the Pacific and the Far East which would make the retention of the Philippines in 1899 look by comparison like kindergarten children playing one of Shakespeare's tragedies."[72] In this, too, he was as prescient as MacMurray about what American postwar responsibilities in Asia would look like after the defeat of Japan.

Either way, Americans must choose, he argued, since "all that can be said for the moment is that both Japan and the United States are living dangerously, the one by a policy of ruthlessness, the other by indecision." And the dangerous consequence of this indecision was that "the Japanese assume that under no circumstances will Americans fight."

In this, concluded Dennett, "the Japanese are mistaken."[73]

"Control by Aggression Into the Whole of the Pacific Area": Waking to the Gathering Storm

Indeed, the Japanese were mistaken. But by the mid-1930s, the navy and army had fallen to a miserable state of readiness. The Asiatic Squadron had been struggling since the previous decade to maintain a presence in the Yangtze and Pearl River deltas with aged First World War–era flush deck destroyers, gunboats, submarines, and a few tender-based seaplanes.[74] An anxious Navy Department had accepted the 10:10:7 ratios negotiated for the United States, Great Britain, and Japan in a new round of talks in London in 1930 on the condition that the U.S. Navy would build up "in sufficient strength to support the national policies and commerce, and to guard the continental and overseas positions of the United States."[75] However, President Hoover did just the opposite, cutting the army and navy budgets by 5.6 percent each and refusing to authorize the construction of a single ship between 1929 and 1933.[76] Meanwhile, Republican senators led by Gerald P. Nye and William Edgar Borah conducted a series of hearings on the role of munitions manufacturers in causing the previous war—all in an attempt to keep the pressure on Hoover to disarm, and eventually leading Congress to pass the 1935 Neutrality Acts, which constrained the ability of the Roosevelt administration to provide arms to those nations threatened by growing Japanese and German militarism.[77]

In March 1933, the Naval War College had completed another of its more than 100 extensive reviews of War Plan Orange. The report, authored by Captain R. A. Koch, anticipated with stunning clarity how Japan would take advantage of American weakness to secure its own "Monroe Doctrine" in the Pacific. Koch's team, playing ORANGE (Japan), concluded that the enemy would seek to "terminate BLUE's influence and potential power in the Western Pacific" by attacking and destroying the Asiatic Squadron without warning in late winter or early spring (the ideal time for amphibious landing operations in the Philippines and Guam) and then successfully cut up BLUE's fleet as it crossed the Pacific, before concluding the conflict by declaring peaceful intentions to guarantee self-determination for the peoples of Asia (an insightful merging of the military and ideational dimensions of the coming struggle with Japan).[78] Koch recommended that the secretary of the navy either build up to the treaty limits or withdraw completely from the Western Pacific, but not assume that current strategic objectives could be met without more resources. All those who understood the geopolitics of Asia were now echoing the same theme: prepare to fight, or prepare to withdraw.

The voices calling for a stronger navy at this point were few and far between. Hornbeck and Grew were among them by now, despite their other disagreements. So was Stimson, but with the election of Franklin D. Roosevelt he stepped down to resume the practice of law on Wall Street. There was hope that Roosevelt, a former assistant secretary of the navy, amateur yachtsman, and collector of model warships, might become a new champion of the fleet, but one of his first moves as president was to cut defense spending by $125 million for fiscal year 1933–34.[79]

Ironically, the most effective champion of a strong navy in these years was a southern Democratic congressman from a landlocked district in Georgia, Carl Vinson. Sworn in as the youngest member of Congress at age thirty in 1914, Vinson represented Baldwin County until 1965 (he had no children but is survived today by his grandnephew, former Georgia senator and former CSIS chairman Sam Nunn, and his namesake, the supercarrier USS *Carl Vinson*). From the beginning, he worked on behalf of the navy, unsuccessfully introducing legislation in 1916 for the "largest building program ever undertaken by any government at one time in the history of the world for strengthening a navy."[80] He was also a voice in the wilderness warning about the dangers of the nonfortification clause and other limitations contained in the 1922 Washington Naval Treaties. Few listened to him at first, but in 1931 he became chairman of the House Naval Affairs Committee after the Democrats' victory in the House in the 1930 midterm elections. Then, in 1932, he had a fellow Democrat elected to the White House.

Vinson wrote to President-elect Roosevelt in December 1932, warning that since 1922 the navy had provided for only 40 ships, compared to 148 ships built by Britain, 164 by Japan, 196 by France, and 144 by Italy.[81] Despite Roosevelt's initial disinclination to use his political capital on defense spending, Vinson worked with the administration to pass a bill in June 1933 authorizing a modest $238 million for new naval construction, cleverly attaching it to the National Industrial Recovery Act, which convinced Roosevelt and assured its passage as a jobs program. The next year, Vinson and Senator Park Trammell of Florida pushed through the first of a series of "Vinson Acts" (the two others were in 1938 and 1940) designed to build the navy back up to the treaty limits by 1942. As the chief of naval operations, Admiral William D. Leahy, would later put it, by 1940 Vinson had "contributed more to the national defense than any other single person in the country except the President himself."[82]

With a floor under the navy's budget, and the prospect of recapitalizing ships by 1942, the navy planners could begin reviewing War Plan Orange with slightly more confidence than they had felt before Vinson's intervention. Still, they recognized that with Japan's large head start, any campaign in the Pacific would be longer and bloodier than they had once anticipated. In 1934, the Navy General Board approved a new variant of War Plan Orange called "Royal Road," which anticipated a sustained campaign across the Marshalls and eastern Carolines, middle Carolines, Truk, the southern Philippines, and the western Carolines and Pelews, culminating in a decisive fleet engagement and blockade of Japan.[83] That same year, the marine corps drew on the early amphibious concepts of Lieutenant Colonel Earl Ellis and published *The Tentative Manual for Landing Operations*.[84] Marines were still jumping out of the side of open boats and were years away from developing the famous amphibious tractors of the Second World War, but they occupied a central role (approved by the Joint Army and Navy Board in 1929) in "Royal Road." The army, in contrast, began to recognize that its mobilization plans were wildly unrealistic and, despite protests from officers in the Philippines, began to consider a narrower plan aimed at defending only the entrance of Manila Bay rather than all of Luzon.[85]

The navy watched nervously as delegates headed off to London for a third naval conference in December 1935, urging the State Department to seek "maintenance of parity with Great Britain, and maintenance (or betterment) of ratio with Japan," but they did not have to worry since the Japanese walked out of the talks anyway—dooming on paper the Washington Treaty System years after it was doomed in reality.[86] Still, the Japanese walkout foreshadowed a further burst of military spending and expansion by Japan, and the army and navy staffs were growing anxious about their ability to execute their new plan. The United States had a 10:8 ratio with Japan in 1936, but that ratio steadily worsened in subsequent years because of the delay between budgeting and the laying of keels, not to mention the two-ocean responsibilities of the navy as the situation deteriorated in Europe.[87]

Reflecting this situation, in May 1935 the Navy General Board and then in 1936 the Joint Board amended War Plan Orange so that they would only try to hold Corregidor and the Bataan Peninsula in the Philippines.[88] (The new plan was approved by army chief of staff Douglas MacArthur, who would violate his own planning directive six years later by unsuccessfully attempting to stop the Japanese at the beaches across Luzon.) With Japan's early successes in the war against China following the July 7, 1937, Marco Polo Bridge Incident and the growing cloud of conflict in Europe, the army staff began to worry that a prolonged Pacific campaign to retake the Philippines would not only be difficult but also incredibly resource-consuming, stripping the United States of necessary forces in the Atlantic. The army staff also had serious doubts about the wherewithal of the American people to sustain that campaign, not anticipating, of course, how Pearl Harbor would rally the public. As a result, the army began to consider a more restricted defensive plan, securing the Alaska-Hawaii-Panama line and virtually abandoning anything west of that.[89] As General Stanley Embick, the chief of army war planning and a former base commander at Corregidor, put it to his colleagues on the Joint Board, the intent to defend the Philippines in War Plan Orange was "an act of madness."[90]

The navy did not entirely disagree with the army's flip-flop, but it wanted to maintain the offensive element in the plan. Confronted with a mismatch of ends and means, they again looked to align with Britain against Japan. On August 24, 1937, Chief of Naval Operations (CNO) Admiral William D. Leahy wrote in his diary, "if it were possible to obtain an equitable agreement with Great Britain to share the effort and the expense, this appears to be a wonderful opportunity to force Japan to observe Treaty agreements and to depart from the mainland of Asia, which would insure western trade supremacy in the Orient for another century."[91] President Roosevelt, however, would not sign on to external alignment at this point. A new Neutrality Act had passed Congress in 1937, and he knew the American public was not yet ready for alliance with Britain or confrontation with Japan. It would take further aggression from Japan before domestic American politics caught up with the strategic realities in Asia. Thus, on November 27, Roosevelt instructed the State Department to reject a proposal from the British foreign secretary that the United States and Britain make an "overwhelming display of naval force with the Royal Navy providing eight to nine battleships" for a joint deployment to the Far East.[92] It was an enormous lost opportunity.

Left without an ally to maintain the strategic balance in the Pacific, the Joint Army and Navy Board instructed their Joint Planning Committee to amend War Plan Orange to ensure that the United States could hold an initial "position of readiness" from Alaska to Hawaii to Panama.[93] The resulting 1938 Orange Plan split the difference, incorporating the army's preference for a strong defensive perimeter as well as the navy's desire for offensive operational planning. But shortly afterward, events in Europe, particularly Hitler's annexation of Czechoslovakia in March 1939, led planners to rethink their initial assumption that there would be a Blue versus Orange conflict unrelated to events elsewhere in the world. After six months of intensive study, the Joint Board planners concluded that the Philippines could not be held. Without Britain being able to send forces to Asia, the planners grew concerned that it would be difficult enough for the U.S. Navy to hold Hawaii and protect the West Coast. They advised the president not to focus on holding the Philippines at the risk of the Atlantic and Pacific Coasts.[94] A concerned Roosevelt ordered the Joint Army and Navy Planning Board to prepare a series of plans in preparation for scenarios ranging from regional to multifront global warfare. The admirals and generals started working on five Rainbow Plans: Rainbow Two incorporated War Plan Orange and was premised on an American-only counteroffensive against Japan in the Pacific, but Rainbow Five, which assumed a global war in alliance with Britain and France, formed the starting point for the grand strategy of the war one year later.[95]

While the army and navy scrambled to adjust their plans to changing strategic realities, Grew and other American diplomats clung to the hope that diplomacy could still prevent conflict with Japan. When Japan's affable ambassador to the United States, Saitō Hiroshi, died in 1939, the Roosevelt administration had his ashes returned to Yokohama with honors aboard the USS *Astoria*. The Japanese public was briefly touched, as Grew reported in April from Tokyo . . . but only briefly.[96] Japan's assault on China continued. In 1939, Stanley Hornbeck recommended to Secretary of State Hull—this time in concert with Secretary of the Treasury Morgenthau—that the 1911 Treaty of Commerce and Navigation with Japan be abrogated. Japan imported 80 percent of its oil, 75 percent of its scrap iron, and 60 percent of its machine tools from the United States, and Hornbeck was certain that this dependency would cause Japan to yield to a negotiated settlement to end the war with China.

The navy, however, was not certain that it had the fleet needed to back up a suddenly more muscular diplomatic stance. As Commander of the U.S. Asiatic Fleet Admiral Thomas C. Hart warned Washington in a report from the front, sanctions might seem effective, but

> for every note written, there should be some increase in the United States armed forces in the Far East. When dealing with a nation whose policies are determined by a ruthless military clique which worships the sword and understands nothing but force, such a procedure may have merit. For our own future safety, we cannot permit a nation imbued with such ideals to acquire the power resultant from domination over the people and resources of China, and eventually, the Far East. A free, stable, democratic government in China is essential to the peace

of Eastern Asia and our own welfare, and every effort should be made
to support such a government, and our own rights in the Far East, even
if it results as a last resort by armed intervention.[97]

Hart's warning notwithstanding, on July 26 President Roosevelt announced the United States' intention to abrogate the 1911 Treaty of Commerce and Navigation, giving Japan six months until a full embargo on
trade and oil would come into effect.[98]

With Germany's blitzkrieg victories over Poland and France between
September 1939 and June 1940, and the signing of the Axis Pact among
Japan, Germany, and Italy on September 27, 1940, Roosevelt began to prepare the reluctant American people to understand the need for alignment with Britain and the other democracies as the totalitarian threats
in Europe and Asia metastasized. In a December 29, 1940, fireside chat
listened to by 75 percent of Americans, the president explained that "if
Great Britain goes down, the Axis powers will control the continents
of Europe, Asia, Africa, Australia, and the high seas—and they will be in
a position to bring enormous military and naval resources against this
hemisphere."[99]

Roosevelt backed the Third Vinson Act that year, authorizing the construction of 250 warships, nearly double the number of vessels approved
in the first six years of his term.[100] Whereas, only weeks before, Congress
had been hesitant to spend $2 billion on overall defense modernization,
the fall of France prompted the members to approve a $10.5 billion defense
bill.[101] The president also called Republican Henry L. Stimson—now an
outspoken advocate of military preparedness—back from his Wall Street
law firm to return to service as secretary of war, one of the great bipartisan national security gestures in history. In addition, the president recruited Republican Frank Knox as secretary of the navy. In order to
demonstrate his seriousness of purpose to the peoples of Asia, Roosevelt
also recalled General Douglas MacArthur to active duty as commanding
general of the United States Army Forces in the Far East (USAFFE) to
take command of the 22,000 U.S. troops in Manila and to accelerate
training of the 110,000 Philippine troops nominally under arms. He also
ordered the bulk of the U.S. West Coast Fleet to remain in Hawaii after
annual exercises.[102]

However, the president was not ready for war. As Akira Iriye explains
it, in the summer of 1940:

President Roosevelt did not want Japanese penetration of South-East Asia, but he was not ready to involve American force actively in the region which would surely result in a war with Japan. Such a war would be premature and divert resources from the Atlantic. The best strategy, he reasoned, was therefore to do something to prevent Japan's southward expansion. In the spring of 1940 the most obvious means open to him was to keep the bulk of the United States fleet in Hawaiian waters. The ships, the majority of which were normally kept on the west coast, had completed their annual exercises in the vicinity of Hawaii, but instead of sending them to their home bases, Roosevelt decided to keep them in the central Pacific. That, he thought, would give the Japanese a signal of American determination to prevent their rash action in Asia. Beyond this, however, he was not ready to go.[103]

The president's real focus was on keeping Britain in the war. On March 11, 1941, he convinced Congress to pass the Lend-Lease Act as a way around the earlier Neutrality Act, since there were no "sales" to the belligerents. The bill, given the symbolic number of H.R. 1776,[104] also extended aid to Chiang's Nationalist forces fighting the Japanese.[105] After decades of reluctance to align with Britain, Roosevelt had also authorized Anglo-American staff talks in early 1941, which led to agreement that in the event of America's entry into the war, Europe would be the vital theater and Germany and Italy would have to be defeated first, essentially confirming Rainbow Five.[106] In order to maintain a strong defense in the Pacific, the British wanted American naval power deployed to Singapore to deter a Japanese attack and to protect Australia and New Zealand, but the American side had no desire to help protect British colonies at this point. Indeed, implicit in the decision not to reinforce Singapore or the Far East was an understanding by the navy and army staffs that all U.S. forces in the region could end up being swallowed and destroyed in the initial Japanese attacks. At Britain's request, however, beginning in February 1941, the United States did warn Japan that the United States would intervene if Japan moved against British or Dutch colonial possessions in Southeast Asia.[107]

These moves helped better prepare the Allies for eventual war but did little to slow Japan's advances. With the Netherlands and France under German control and Britain fighting for survival, Japan began to put pressure on French Indochina and the Dutch East Indies. On July 23, 1941, a desperate Vichy government in French Indochina gave up on appeals for help to the United States and Britain and signed an agreement allowing Japanese troops to enter their territory.[108] Japanese forces were now poised to strike at British and Dutch colonies in Southeast Asia. On July 26, President Roosevelt signed Executive Order 08832 freezing all Japanese and Chinese assets in the United States.[109] Then, on September 12, Grew sent his famous "green light" cable from Tokyo, shifting his view on sanctions and calling for more pressure on Japan in order to convince the militarists that "their hand is being overplayed."[110] The president also agreed with Philippine president Manuel Quezon to place all forces in the Philippines under the command of General MacArthur.[111]

Whether Roosevelt intended it or not, the order freezing Japanese assets led to the rejection of all export licenses for oil and other commodities to Japan.[112] In Tokyo, the government of Prince Konoe Fumimaro decided that they now faced two choices: either humiliating retreat in China or seizing oil-rich Indonesia and Southeast Asia and expanding the war to America, Britain, and the Netherlands. Foreign Minister Matsuoka convinced the cabinet that Hitler would prevail in Europe, and the weak American position in Asia convinced General Tojo Hideki, who replaced Konoe in October 1941, to prepare for the second option—war with the United States.[113] The chief of naval operations, Admiral Harold R. Stark, had warned Roosevelt that an oil embargo would tempt Japan to invade the oil-rich Dutch East Indies before the U.S. Navy was ready to fight.[114] Like Hornbeck, however, the president believed Japan was so dependent on trade with the United States that Tokyo would bend.[115] Stark was right. Rather than serving as a deterrent, the American embargo intensified and accelerated Japanese planning for war against the United States.[116] Later, during the war, the Joint Chiefs would refer to the Pacific war as "Mr. Hornbeck's War" because they did not feel the State Department had given them time to get ready.[117]

As historian David Reynolds has indicated, there was enormous irony to these developments. The American public still was not willing to go to war to save Britain. However, as "isolationists" and "interventionists" debated how far to go in supporting Britain in Europe and conjured up visions of the bloodied battlefields of the First World War and whether the Atlantic was a wall of security, there was relatively little public debate or opposition to the increasing buildup of the U.S. Navy or the economic sanctions against Japan.[118] In Gallup polls in July 1941, 79 percent of respondents said that the United States should "stay out" of the war against Germany and Italy.[119] However, when asked in September 1941 whether the United States should "take steps to keep Japan from becoming more powerful, *even if it meant risking a war* [italics mine]," 70 percent answered "yes."[120] Lippmann was absolutely right when he wrote several years earlier that the United States was never "isolationist" with respect to the Pacific.

Yet, in October 1941, as war was clearly approaching, the Navy General Board expressed doubt that it could actually execute War Plan Orange and Rainbow Five without a long and costly war in the Pacific. Despite the crash building program sponsored by Vinson, in 1941 Japan had parity with all the other Allied naval forces combined in the Pacific, with a ratio of 10:11 in battleships, 10:3 in carriers, 36:36 in cruisers, 113:100 in destroyers, and 63:69 in submarines.[121] Echoing the themes of MacMurray in 1935, the board sent a stunning memo to the secretary of the navy on October 18 recommending that the United States consider abandoning both the Open Door and the Philippines:

> It appears that the making of an offensive war in the Pacific is so difficult considering the distances and inferior bases available . . . that it might be well to accept the policy that the United States will not adopt an imperialistic view towards the Philippine islands or any other territory in the Far East: that the United States will not enforce the doctrine of the Open Door in China by force of arms in the Western Pacific; primarily because it is not enforceable; that the United States will not attempt to dictate policies in the Far East, but will use other means in negotiation. . . . It appears sound that the strategic military frontiers are at present approximately determined by the line from the Aleutian Islands through the outlying islands of the Hawaiian Group to Samoa.[122]

The navy, which had been so prescient in recognizing the geostrategic and precise military threat that would emanate from Japan, was suddenly questioning the objectives of U.S. policy two months before the war, largely because they recognized the stark shortcomings in their means to achieve those objectives. The next month, on November 23, Roosevelt approved a rigid ten-point response to Japan's diplomatic proposal, since he knew that the Japanese Army was moving troops into Vietnam despite the Foreign Ministry's ongoing negotiations. The president decided not to inform the Navy General Board.[123]

For his part, Roosevelt appeared to have now decided what was at stake. His intention had been and would remain preventing Nazi domination in Europe, but he knew that Japan's effort at domination in the Pacific was now closely related to events in Europe because of the 1940 Axis Pact. The issue was not just American control of the Philippines or even the Open Door in China but the security of the entire Pacific region itself, as Dennett had warned in his writings. Roosevelt was still the avid student of Mahan. As he put it to the people in a press conference on November 28, 1941—just one week before Pearl Harbor:

> We are of course thinking not only about the American flag in the Philippines, not only about certain vital defense needs which come from that open end of the horseshoe, but we are thinking about something even more important, and that is the possible extension of control by aggression into the whole of the Pacific area. And we are thinking about what it would mean to this country if that policy were to be used against us in the whole Pacific area. I don't think that anything more can be said at this time.[124]

He could only say one thing beyond that: "We are waiting."

LESSONS AND LEGACIES FROM THE JAPANESE CHALLENGE

Was war with Japan avoidable? The prewar years are a Rorschach test for international relations theories. Structural realists argue that the collapse of British power and the rise of Japan into that vacuum created the conditions for near certain conflict. Neorealists argue that the war could have been avoided with policies to maintain the balance of power. Liberal institutionalists point to the collapse of the international economic order and the weakness of international institutions as the root cause, in addition to a failure to accommodate Japan's legitimate aspirations as a rising power.

The leading historian of U.S.-Japan relations in the interwar years, Akira Iriye, believes that "war across the Pacific was not inevitable. At least as of June 1941, both Tokyo and Washington were intent upon avoiding such an eventuality." But by then, he notes, the United States was rushing to rearm and reinvigorate Britain and China while Japan was rushing to consolidate its position in Southeast Asia. He added: "Under these circumstances, only a break-up of that [U.S.-led] partnership or Japan's reversal of southern expansionism could have prevented a Pacific war."[125] The problem was that reversal of Japan's southern expansionism would not have happened *without* concerted Anglo-American-Chinese action, and breaking up that coalition would only have opened the way for *further* expansion by Japan. The lesson, in other words, is that great powers should never be put in the position where they are "rushing to rearm."

Put another way, the conditions for war between the United States and Japan were set over the course of decades and were the result, in part, of poor strategic conceptualization by American leaders many years before Pearl Harbor. Theodore Roosevelt and Hay embraced the Open Door as supplemental to their geopolitically focused maritime strategy—the Open Door was one means to an end but not the most important means (compared with the fleet and an effective balance of power), and certainly not a vital end in itself. Roosevelt's real interest was in establishing a favorable strategic equilibrium in the Pacific, measured in terms of power and not international law or agreements. Subsequent American statesmen generally lost that underlying geopolitical basis for defining how the Open Door fit in American strategy. Taft made the Open Door the objective of U.S. strategy in the Pacific with dollar diplomacy, and Wilson used it as a rhetorical flourish as he pursued global institutions. Navy planners struggled to understand how they would fight a naval war with Japan over conflicts on the Manchurian plain, whereas financiers like Lamont focused on economic interdependence and binding with Japan in contradiction of the Open Door. Though briefly fused in the Washington Naval Treaties, the diplomatic, informational, military, and economic instruments of American power worked at cross purposes for much of the interwar period.

No president between the two Roosevelts thought that the Open Door was worth war with Japan—and it probably was not. Harding, Coolidge, and Hoover all used the Washington Treaty System as an excuse to cut military expenditures because they could not see the China problem leading to war, particularly given their faith in multilateral agreements. What they failed to see was that even if equal investment or opportunity in China and Manchuria were not vital to the United States, the security of the Pacific was. The second Roosevelt recognized that domination of Asia by a rival power was no more acceptable than domination of

Western Europe by a rival power. Had the statesmen in between understood the ends of American strategy, they would have better resourced
and aligned the ways and means. They also would have avoided the
wild inconsistencies in how the United States defined maritime versus
continental interests, the forward defense line, and the role of trade and
values.

In fact, the contradictions between maritime and continental interests
did not have to be so stark, as Mahan understood at the beginning of the
century. A strong maritime position, underwritten by naval power built
to the treaty limit and backed by alignment with Britain—as Mahan had
urged—would have given the United States far more purchase on the
problems in China. Japan, after all, was also a maritime power with vital
interests in the Pacific approaches to its homeland, which were as important as preserving a buffer in Manchuria and Korea. An American offshore balancing strategy that utilized this leverage might have dissuaded
unilateral Japanese action in Manchuria and facilitated cooperation
with the other powers to press for both improved governance and greater
autonomy for the new Chinese republic. One can imagine the strength of
the American position had Franklin D. Roosevelt agreed to the British
proposal to make a massive display of Anglo-American naval power in
the Pacific in 1937 or if the United States had initiated such strategic cooperation earlier in the decade. Maritime powers could not easily have
solved the problems within China but could have better deterred another
maritime power from taking advantage of them.

By not pursuing a stronger navy and closer maritime alignments,
the U.S. strategy exacerbated the vulnerability of forward American bases
in the Western Pacific. It is stunning how quickly planners would redefine the necessary American defensive line, in large part reflecting uncertainty about the definition of American interests. Once the Open Door
was no longer the objective, for example, the navy retrenched. Yet the
advocates of retracting the defensive line to Hawaii and the mid-Pacific
did not recognize the implications of abandoning the Philippines-Guam
line—which would have put imperial Japan in an even stronger position
to mount a sustained attack and even invasion of Hawaii. On the other
hand, if the United States had built to the treaty limits and strengthened
its air capabilities earlier, this would have significantly complicated Japanese planning by putting Formosa and Kyushū at risk and raising the
prospect of rapid relief of the Philippines. As it was, it was the United
States that was caught off balance.

That said, military power alone would not have solved the American strategic problems in Asia. Economic instruments were at least as important. An understanding of this reality was evident in the original formulation of the Open Door. Republican administrations put a particularly high priority on economic instruments in Asia policy in the first part of the twentieth century. Yet, all too often, fickle protectionist lobbying and misunderstanding of markets undercut the strategic impact of the United States' growing economic weight in Asia, as Taft's failed dollar diplomacy indicated. Roosevelt eventually began to reverse the protectionist trends with the 1934 Reciprocal Trade Agreements Act, which shifted trade negotiation power away from Congress and eventually ushered in a reduction of U.S. duties from 46 percent in 1934 to 12 percent in 1962.[126] However, the major strategic impact of trade liberalization would not be felt until after the war was over. By 1934, Japan was already decoupling from the international economy and rejecting convergence in the wake of the collapse of the international financial system and the protectionism of Smoot-Hawley.[127]

American values mattered as well. For postwar purveyors of a neorealist grand strategy such as Robert Osgood, the greatest shortcoming in interwar statecraft was Wilsonian idealism.[128] This charge is not entirely fair. Wilson was on the right side of history when he recognized the Republic of China in 1913 and later when he set the Philippines on the course to full independence in 1916. His decisions were not only consistent with American ideals but also positioned the United States for the emerging ideational contest with a rising Japan that sought preeminence through pan-Asian nationalism. (It is worth remembering that in contrast to other colonies that were supposedly "liberated" by Japan, many of the Philippine military forces stayed loyal to the United States even under Japanese occupation.) However, Wilson's policy-making style undercut the power and influence his principled stance might have accrued. He made decisions like the recognition of the Republic of China in a unilateral and disruptive manner, he cynically allowed anti-Asian racist attitudes to prevail in domestic U.S. politics and at Versailles, and he articulated a vision of universal self-determination that he had no intention of realizing in Asia.[129] As a result, a generation of Asian leaders, ranging from Yoshida Shigeru to Ho Chi Minh, who witnessed Wilson's hypocrisy, became disillusioned by the hollowness of American moral leadership (Yoshida because he was an imperialist and Ho because he was for national liberation). The difficulty in sustaining a consistent policy on democracy and self-determination was not Wilson's alone, of course. The clash between Secretary of State Kellogg and his Far East Division over extending tariff autonomy to China in 1927 reflected the same tension that had led Caleb Cushing to condemn the British and John Quincy Adams to praise them during the Opium War a century earlier. They all struggled with the same tension: was America's democratic example about self-determination or universal norms and rule of law? With Japan seeming to champion self-determination against "Western" universal norms, this tension became acute.

None of this is to say that the American instinct to support democratic values and self-determination was antithetical to good grand strategy in the first half of the twentieth century. The ideational balance of power mattered enormously to America's ability to influence regional order in Asia, as Franklin D. Roosevelt came to appreciate more than his immediate predecessors had. Roosevelt, notes Reynolds, "insisted with growing fervor that, in the age of urban warfare, the world could and did threaten America, and that American values could and should transform the world. The two themes were interconnected, for the president argued that only in a world in which American values reigned supreme could the United States feel secure. This global perspective on international events was distinctly Rooseveltian."[130]

In many respects, Franklin Delano Roosevelt returned to the strategic trajectory his cousin Theodore had started before it was interrupted by Taft, Wilson, and their successors. It was under Theodore Roosevelt that the United States became a Pacific power, introduced the Open Door, and first confronted a rising Japan. By the time of the younger Roosevelt's second term, the Open Door was dead, Japan was pursuing autarkic hegemony in East Asia, and America's Pacific power was in jeopardy.

It is illustrative to consider how TR would have evaluated America's strategic performance in the Pacific in the decades between his term and the mounting crises of the 1930s that confronted his cousin. We know that he was openly critical of Taft's effort to confront Japan in Manchuria with dollar diplomacy. Theodore Roosevelt understood that the Open Door was a means and not necessarily an end in itself. He would therefore have been surprised and frustrated at the State Department's legalistic obsession with the Open Door and its failure to understand that it meant nothing without naval power to maintain the strategic balance in Asia more broadly. This is not to say that Roosevelt would have necessarily opposed the Washington Treaties, which were supported by Elihu Root, among other former Rooseveltians (and Roosevelt himself won the Nobel Peace Prize for negotiating the Treaty of Portsmouth, after all), but he would have made certain that the United States built up to the treaty limits, and he would have listened more attentively to the navy's concerns on questions such as the disposition of the former German possessions in the South Pacific.

One can also imagine that Theodore Roosevelt would have used alignment and counterbalancing more effectively to impose a cost on Japan for expansion in Manchuria and northern China. He might have agreed to the nonrecognition doctrine, but not without using Russian, British, or even Chinese Nationalist cards more effectively to isolate and bleed Japan. He appreciated during the Russo-Japanese War, for example, that while the United States did not have a vital enough stake in continental Asia to risk major war, there was sufficient interest in the balance of power within the continent to pursue active offshore balancing strategies, which he did in part through the Portsmouth negotiations when he was president. At the same time, Roosevelt would have been careful to avoid gratuitous confrontations with Tokyo over immigration or other racially charged issues. Perhaps the one area where Theodore might not have understood his cousin Franklin's foresight was in the latter's support for trade liberalization, though that would have been a reflection of the different political parties the two men inhabited as much as anything.

Ultimately, Theodore and Franklin were joined across the decades by their recognition that the United States did have vital interests in the Pacific that were worth fighting for. They understood that American security, economic prosperity, and values would be fundamentally put at risk if a rival hegemonic power dominated the Pacific. For Theodore, it was hypothetical. For Franklin, it became real. And he was willing to fight.

6. "WE HAVE GOT TO DOMINATE THE PACIFIC"
GRAND STRATEGY AND THE WAR AGAINST JAPAN

In war, "to win is not enough," Napoleon warned, "it is necessary to profit from success." Decades later, Otto von Bismarck explained in his memoirs that, "The task of the commanders of the army is to annihilate the hostile forces; the object of war is to conquer peace under conditions which are conformable to the policy pursued by the state. To fix and limit the objects to be attained by war, and to advise the monarch in respect to them, is and remains during the war just as before it a political function, and the manner in which these questions are solved cannot be without influence on the method of conducting the war."[1] Thus, as the preeminent naval historian of the Pacific war, Admiral Samuel Eliot Morison, wrote, "Whilst political consideration should have no place in military strategy . . . political considerations should have a more important weight in higher or grand strategy."[2]

The political aims of American grand strategy for the Second World War were articulated at a summit between President Roosevelt and Prime Minister Winston Churchill on board the heavy cruiser USS *Augusta* in Placentia Bay, Newfoundland, on August 9, 1941—four months before Japan attacked Pearl Harbor. Before that meeting, Roosevelt had met Churchill only once, in London in 1918, where he remembered that the future prime minister had "acted like a complete stinker."[3] On board the *Augusta*, however, Churchill desperately needed to convince Roosevelt to bring America into the war. Not fully comprehending the significance of what he had done, Churchill agreed to a joint declaration that committed the nascent Western alliance to the elimination of threats from aggressor states, the preservation of freedom of the seas, free trade, and self-determination and social progress.[4] These were the essential elements of the global and regional order the United States had been pursuing for decades. Later, the assembled diplomats, political advisors, and staff officers joined together on the deck of the HMS *Prince of Wales* for a common church service at which they sang "Onward Christian Soldiers," accents of British public school graduates, lowland Scots officers, Yankee politicians, and Southern VMI grads blending and drifting across the bay. Back in London, however, Churchill's friend Lord Beaverbrook warned that the American-drafted document was so sweeping that it would put the British Empire itself at risk.[5]

The United States pursued victory in the Pacific from 1941 to 1945 with an eye toward achieving the peace articulated in the Atlantic Charter, which twenty-four more nations signed as members of the new United Nations in January 1942. To a significant degree, the objectives of the charter were achieved. However, the exigencies of military strategy and some faulty assumptions about the sources of international order also shaped geopolitical considerations in ways that would leave the United States with certain postwar conditions that were—as Bismarck might have said—"less conformable to the policy pursued by the state," for as Morison wrote anxiously from the early Cold War, during the Pacific war the United States "lost sight of the old principle that our enemies of today may be wanted as allies of tomorrow."[6]

This chapter focuses on how American strategic thinking toward Asia and the Pacific evolved over the course of the campaign against Japan. Over 100,000 books have been written in English about the war, mostly on military tactics and strategy. Our concern is the geostrategic debate, including not only how international alignments were applied to the defeat of Japan but also how assumptions about postwar order shaped military, diplomatic, and economic planning—and how the lessons of fighting in the Pacific informed strategy for the rest of the century. The central argument of this book has been that American grand strategy toward Asia has deep historical roots and did not simply appear out of whole cloth with the Second World War. Indeed, the debates and tensions in American strategic culture traced throughout this book replayed themselves with a fury in the depths of the Pacific war. Yet, at the same time, the war was undeniably transformational in its impact on American strategic culture—giving birth to a permanent national security establishment and cementing American preeminence in the Pacific. It is impossible to understand contemporary American strategy in Asia without taking into account these sources of continuity and change in the prosecution of the war against Japan from December 8, 1941, to August 15, 1945.

The chapter begins with a brief examination of the national security strategy-making apparatus and style that emerged with total war, and it then examines the evolution of strategic thinking toward the Pacific along the five tensions that defined American statecraft before the war and have since: (1) the consequences of a Europe-first strategy on the Pacific theater; (2) the redrawn definition of forward defense lines as the American forces fought across the Central and Southwestern Pacific; (3) the confused geopolitics of relations with China, Russia, and Japan as the Americans fought a maritime war alongside continental allies; (4) the complications of fighting a war for democratic values and self-determination alongside European imperial allies; and (5) the transition from pursuing relative gains in trade to creation of universal free trade.

Between 1941 and 1945, the formulation of American grand strategy graduated from the eras of John Quincy Adams or Theodore Roosevelt, when strategic concepts flowed from the innovation of a small handful of men. The stakes were higher than ever before. Japan had tried to push the United States out of the Pacific. In response, the American people harnessed all the material and ideological force at their disposal to push their way back in and to make certain they would never be pushed out again.

PRESIDENTIAL COMMAND

Effective grand strategy in wartime requires the integration of all instruments of national power, something the United States had done only in the Civil War and never toward the Pacific. To the extent that diplomatic, informational, military, and economic factors were effectively brought together with respect to Asia before 1941, it was in the minds of rare men such as John Quincy Adams or Theodore Roosevelt. After December 1941, the crafting of grand strategy again fell essentially to one man— Franklin Delano Roosevelt—but the president also organized his government to manage the enormous geopolitical complexities of alliance relations, mobilization at home, and execution of military operations across vast distances. These personalities and institutions at the center of this effort left their stamp on the campaigns that won the war and on the statecraft that emerged after victory.

Roosevelt enhanced his own role as grand strategist and commander in chief with three innovations. First, he established a group of personal advisors and emissaries to bypass the large and slow-moving federal bureaucracies, particularly the State Department. These advisors were men tied to Roosevelt by breeding, domestic politics, or blood, including his closest advisor, Harry Hopkins, Undersecretary of State Sumner Welles, Assistant Secretary of State for Economic Affairs Averell Harriman, and former Supreme Court justice Jimmy Byrnes, who led the Office of War Mobilization and later became secretary of state.[7] Second, Roosevelt imposed his control over grand strategy through the series of summit meetings he held with Churchill and other Allied leaders throughout the war, most notably at Casablanca, Cairo, Tehran, and Yalta. At these conferences, Roosevelt resolved disagreements between different services or commanding officers; established priorities, timing, and resources for major offensives; and discussed the most sensitive political issues with his counterparts. Finally, Roosevelt brought to the prosecution of the war a clear and consistent "world point of view" that was grounded in a sustainable interpretation of the beliefs of the American people, the potential of the Wilsonian vision after the last war, and the need to temper that vision with balance-of-power realism.[8]

At the same time, however, the centralization of grand strategy in the mind of Roosevelt was also cause for confusion, conflict, and imprecision in execution by his advisors, cabinet members, and war captains. Roosevelt's hybrid of idealism and realism gave birth to widely divergent views within his cabinet about what assumptions should underpin planning for a postwar world order. At one extreme were his cohorts from the New Deal, such as Vice President Henry A. Wallace, a quasi-socialist who wanted to expand the New Deal abroad, or Wilsonian idealists such as Secretary of State Cordell Hull, who abhorred balance-of-power logic.[9] On the other end of the spectrum were hard-power realists, including Secretary of the Navy James Forrestal and Secretary of War Henry Stimson, who were deeply suspicious of liberal internationalism and Roosevelt's concepts of collective security under the United Nations, and subscribed to Walter Lippmann's thesis in *U.S. Foreign Policy: Shield of the Republic* (1943) that idealism had been overplayed before the war and that balance of power was now the key to an enduring peace.[10] Roosevelt's decision early on that he would defer all major postwar political decisions with Churchill and Stalin until after victory also confused long-term geostrategic planning, though it obviously reduced friction among the Allies as the war was prosecuted.[11]

The main casualty of Roosevelt's command style was the State Department, which should have played a central role in helping the president determine geostrategic issues. Secretary Hull's constant feuding with Roosevelt's close advisors, and his insistence that diplomacy and war fighting be kept on separate tracks, only compounded the problem.[12] There were exceptions in the field, such as Foreign Service officer John Paton Davies, who worked with General "Vinegar" Joe Stilwell in the China-Burma-India theater, or Grew, who shaped postwar planning on Japan, but they were the exception rather than the rule among diplomats. Hull thus abdicated his influence on planning beyond the two issues he cared about most—decolonization and free trade—where he did keep the president focused on elements of the Atlantic Charter that were not always embraced by Churchill or Stalin.[13]

The U.S. military, in contrast, organized itself to ensure comprehensive control over geostrategic planning. In January 1942, the Joint Army and Navy Board was replaced by the Joint Chiefs of Staff (JCS) in order to coordinate military strategy with Britain through a new U.S.-U.K. Combined Chiefs of Staff (CCS). With centuries of imperial strategy behind them, the British were initially far more prepared than the Americans were to think through the implications of global war, so the JCS began to hold their own sessions in July 1942 under Roosevelt's chief of staff and liaison to the JCS, Admiral William Leahy.[14] Once an ensign on board the USS *Olympia* at the Battle of Manila Bay, Leahy's subsequent experience was primarily in politics and diplomacy. By the end of the war, he had emerged as Roosevelt's "alter ego" and then Truman's closest advisor, though he was a convener and consensus builder rather than the designer of grand strategy himself.[15] The army chief of staff and first among equals was General George C. Marshall, a protégé of General John Pershing and the finest organizational strategist in American military history.[16] After March 1942, the navy was led by Chief of Naval Operations Fleet Admiral Ernest King, an Anglophobic (oddly after serving on British vessels in the First World War), hard-drinking, foul-mouthed disciplinarian whom the president said was so tough he "cut his toenails with a torpedo net cutter" (yet never failing to appear in neatly pressed Brooks Brothers uniform complete with silk pocket handkerchief).[17] Among the chiefs, King would become the champion of the Pacific theater, constantly pressing for resources to go to the war against Japan and meeting almost daily with Roosevelt to discuss operations.[18]

The JCS did not accept the artificial distinction between statecraft and war asserted by Hull and by the prewar army and navy boards, embracing a geopolitical approach that eclipsed all civilian leaders outside of the White House. Historian Mark Stoler has noted that "no individual, save Harry Hopkins, was closer to and more influential with FDR than the Joint Chiefs."[19] They were men who had once served in the Philippines on horseback and at sea aboard coal-fueled battle cruisers, but over the course of their subsequent careers they mastered naval aviation, mechanized warfare, and (in the case of Army Air Corps Chief of Staff "Hap" Arnold) bomber operations. They also became masters of grand strategy. When Truman began meetings with the JCS in May 1945, he quipped that "if the South had had staff organization like that, the Confederates would have won the Civil War."[20]

In order to ensure a comprehensive geostrategic framework for planning, Marshall established the JSSC (Joint Strategic Survey Committee) in November 1942 to provide overall strategic guidance for military planning and to liaise between the State Department and the services, though clearly with State in the back seat.[21] Nominally, FDR gave authority over policy toward liberated areas to the State Department at the same time, but it only really began to play a significant role with changes in cabinet positions in 1944.[22] When James Forrestal became secretary of the navy upon the death of Frank Knox in April of that year, he began to push for more effective cross-governmental coordination and strategic planning to make up for the inefficiencies caused by the president's imprecise planning guidance.[23] Then, in November, an aging and dispirited Cordell Hull was replaced by Edward Stettinius, a former General Motors and Lend-Lease executive, who worked with Forrestal and Secretary of War Stimson to establish a new State-War-Navy Coordinating Committee (SWNCC) in December 1944 to plan political and military policy for the occupation of liberated areas, particularly Germany and Japan.[24] The committee represented the first effective effort to integrate diplomatic, military, and academic expertise for postwar planning, and by 1945 it was drafting memoranda directly for the president.[25] Indeed, the success of SWNCC led Forrestal to recommend it to President Truman as a model for the new National Security Council, which was established by law in 1947.[26]

The one remaining giant in the grand strategy mix was Treasury Secretary Morgenthau, who played a dominant role in plans for a punitive occupation policy for Germany but was then contained by SWNCC with respect to postwar planning for Japan and the Pacific. Still, his influence on the postwar global trading and financial system negotiated at the Bretton Woods meetings in the summer of 1944 was considerable.[27]

These men, operating under Roosevelt's giant shadow, would debate and conduct grand strategy from 1941 to 1945 with an organizational efficiency and focus that the country had never known before. Yet the core strength and weakness in the decision-making process resided with the president himself. Roosevelt mobilized the American people and held together a diverse alliance of democracies and dictatorships. On the other hand, although he gave clear directions on major aspects of war-fighting strategy, he kept his geopolitical plans vague—relying on his own instincts about how postwar order would be maintained. Consequently, for all its organizational innovation and planning, the Roosevelt administration ultimately lacked a decision-making system on the most important long-term geostrategic questions of the war.[28] When the president died suddenly on April 12, 1945, Truman was thrust into the position of deciding major unresolved political questions in the final months of the war, without the benefits of his predecessor's intent and often with lasting consequences for future U.S. strategy in Asia.

EUROPE VERSUS THE PACIFIC

In the years before the war, the American people were psychologically more prepared to fight in the Pacific than the Atlantic, but Roosevelt was focused, as the American elite had been for over a century, on Europe. Rainbow Five set the objective of defeating Hitler first in the event of global conflict, and the Joint Board confirmed this prioritization in the first secret "ABC" staff talks with the British, in March 1941.[29] Collapse of the British core of the liberal international order was as unacceptable to Roosevelt as it had been to Wilson in the last war. As the Joint Board reported to the president in September 1941, "The security of the United Kingdom is essential to the prosecution in the Eastern Hemisphere of military operations against Germany and Japan. Its safety is also highly important to the defense of the Western Hemisphere."[30]

Ultimately, however, the real question was one of resources. The long gap in shipbuilding in the interwar years meant that the fleet would not have enough ships to fulfill missions in both the Atlantic and the Pacific until mid-1943.[31] That tension became apparent almost immediately after the ABC-1 talks in March 1941, when the British requested that American ships be transferred from the Pacific Fleet to help fight the U-boat menace in the Atlantic. Stimson, Knox, and Admiral Harold B. Stark (King's immediate predecessor as CNO, and an Atlanticist by inclination) agreed, but Hull objected that this would remove pressure on Japan at a critical diplomatic juncture, and so Roosevelt compromised by sending some, but not all, of the ships requested by the British.[32] It was an early sign that balancing the demands of the European and Pacific theaters of operation would be challenging.

After the Japanese attack on Pearl Harbor, a vengeful navy leadership and American public wanted to drop the "Europe first" strategy and immediately take the war to Japan. In preparation for a meeting between Roosevelt, Churchill, and their staffs in Washington in late December 1941, the Joint Board prepared a memorandum warning that Japan enjoyed air and naval superiority in the Pacific and demanding immediate U.S. attention.[33] Roosevelt, however, stuck with "Europe first." The attack on Pearl Harbor had not changed the strategic logic behind the ABC-1 agreement or his own commitment to Churchill.[34] As the president reminded his military leaders, Germany was the sole threat agreed on by all three major powers (the United States, Britain, and the Soviet Union, which had been invaded by the Nazis in June); Germany was the stronger of the two major adversaries, meaning that a defeat of Germany could lead to a rapid defeat of Japan, whereas the reverse was not necessarily true; and Germany posed a greater threat to the two other allies, since Hitler already controlled half of continental Eurasia and was only miles from Moscow. Defeat of either Britain or the Soviets would have made total victory nearly impossible for the United States. Japan, in contrast, was poised to seize most of East Asia but not to knock any one of the big three Allies out of the war. The Americans could counterattack Japan from Hawaii or the West Coast but needed Britain to survive in order to eject Hitler from Europe. As Andrew Roberts concludes in his history of the war, "the collapse of Japan within four months of Hitler's death was a powerful vindication of the Germany First policy adopted by the Allies after Pearl Harbor."[35]

That said, JCS support for "Europe first" was premised on an early cross-channel invasion of the Continent, and the JCS were keen to launch that offensive as early as 1943. The British Imperial Staff—and particularly Churchill—had too many memories of the slaughter in Flanders and too many doubts about the fighting abilities of the untrained American soldiers, and pushed instead for an indirect attack on the Axis powers in the Mediterranean.[36] This view only raised suspicions within the JCS, who considered the opening of a Mediterranean front to be a distant third-place priority behind the Pacific and an excuse to conduct peripheral attacks that preserved the British Empire with American lives.

When the Pacific-oriented King replaced the more European-oriented Stark as the lead navy representative on the JCS in March 1942, with the titles of both commander in chief United States Fleet and chief of naval operations (CNO), the momentum among the chiefs swung toward emphasizing a near-term counteroffensive in the Pacific. King had a compelling case for going on the offensive in the Pacific, reinforced by the relative autonomy the JCS had established through agreement in the CCS that the Americans would take the lead in the Pacific and the British in the Indian Ocean.[37] In February 1942, 80,000 British and Commonwealth troops had surrendered to the Japanese at Singapore in the worst defeat in British military history. On May 6, Lieutenant General Jonathan Wainwright had surrendered the surviving American garrison on Corregidor in the Philippines after desperate fighting to the entrance of Malinta Tunnel itself. Meanwhile, the prime ministers of Australia and New Zealand were demanding that their forces be returned from the Middle East to defend their homelands, and Chiang Kai-shek was warning that China would collapse without more aid in the wake of successful Japanese offensives that same spring. If Japan cut off Australia or the Nationalists in China, the Americans would be in no position to begin a counteroffensive or prevent a linkup between Japanese and German forces in the Indian Ocean. For its part, the U.S. Navy never had more than four aircraft carriers in the Pacific before late 1943. If they were sunk and the Japanese took Midway or the Aleutian Islands, then Hawaii itself would have been under constant enemy air assault.[38] King enjoyed support for his focus on the Pacific from General MacArthur, who was in Australia, eager to counterattack and liberate the Philippines.[39]

Even after the Japanese thrust south toward Australia was stopped at the Battle of the Coral Sea in early May and the Japanese thrust east across the Central Pacific was blunted at Midway in June 1942, King still insisted that it was time to seize the initiative and go on the offensive to defeat the main Japanese battle fleet in the spirit of Mahan and War Plan Orange.[40] Marshall and the army leadership stateside also now began to swing in King's direction as they saw Churchill and the British Imperial Staff dig in their heels against an early invasion of Europe.[41] Even Dwight D. Eisenhower, Marshall's top planner and the future commander of the Normandy invasion, argued, "We must turn our *backs* upon the Eastern Atlantic and go, full out, as quickly as possible, against Japan!" [emphasis in original].[42] By the summer of 1942, the Joint Chiefs were in agreement: if there was no option for a cross-channel invasion in the next twelve months, a major offensive in the Pacific would be the priority.[43]

Roosevelt was concerned about the Pacific and wanted an offensive somewhere in 1942 before midterm elections, but he still was not prepared to shift major resources to the Pacific at the expense of the European theater. His political and strategic instincts were astute; Gallup polling in late June showed that 50 percent of the American public identified Germany as the "number one enemy in the war," compared with 25 percent who said Japan and 23 percent who said "both."[44] This was a considerable shift in opinion compared with the months before and just after Pearl Harbor. Meanwhile, the Germans had taken Tobruk in North Africa on June 20 and were advancing south toward the Caucasus from Russia, threatening to link up with Japanese forces advancing west from Burma. Churchill and Stalin were desperately insisting on a second front against Hitler to relieve pressure on their beleaguered forces. Convinced that a knockout blow against the Germans could still mean "the defeat of Japan, probably without firing a shot or losing a life,"[45] Roosevelt pledged to Churchill in July 1942 that the Americans were in for an invasion of North Africa. Operation Torch, the Allied invasion of North Africa, was set in motion for November 8 of that year.[46]

The "Pacific first" advocates backed off, but not for long. In presenting war strategy to Roosevelt and Churchill at the Casablanca Conference in January 1943, King acknowledged the "Europe first" decision but proposed doing a 70:30 resource split between the Atlantic and Pacific—a significant shift, since King estimated the split in resources was about 85:15 at the time.[47] The Joint Chiefs of Staff were working up plans for a strategic offensive against Japan, having secured the sea lanes to Australia and

New Zealand with the victories at the Battle of the Coral Sea, the Kokoda Track, and Guadalcanal between May 1942 and January 1943, and having secured the Central Pacific with the victory at Midway. The British, however, continued to make the case for a strategy to contain Japan so that the Allies could focus maximum resources on Germany first.[48] General Alan Brooke, the chief of the British Imperial Staff, so infuriated the Americans at one point that King accused the British of viewing the entire Pacific strategy "as meaning that anything which was done in the Pacific interfered with the earliest possible defeat of Germany and that the Pacific theater should therefore remain totally inactive."[49]

In subsequent CCS talks in March 1943, the JCS pressed their case again, arguing that the Allied invasion of Sicily should be dropped in order to proceed with plans for a British land invasion of Burma from India and a U.S.-led amphibious invasion via the Andaman Islands, which the Americans had codenamed "BUCCANEER."[50] The British objected, again advocating the establishment of a strong defensive line in the Pacific and letting the Japanese bog themselves down across multiple fronts from China to the South Pacific. The Americans responded that rather than being bogged down, the Japanese forces would entrench their positions, making it harder and bloodier to extract them. Subsequent events proved the Americans partly correct.

By the time Churchill, Roosevelt, and their commanders met in Washington, DC, for the TRIDENT Conference on May 12–27, 1943, the Allies had finally reached a workable consensus: they would go on the offensive in the Pacific to prevent Japanese forces from strengthening their positions, but they would only use the available resources planned for the region to accomplish that aim.[51] They put off plans for an invasion of Burma after Churchill convinced the president how "distasteful" jungle warfare would be at that point, but they did agree to build up the China-Burma-India theater by intensifying air operations against the Japanese and increasing the flow of air forces and airborne supplies to China.[52] It helped reduce the tension between theaters that U.S. war production was now in full swing, meaning that by the time of TRIDENT, nine of seventeen U.S. Army divisions and nineteen of the sixty-six U.S. air groups that were overseas were already in the Pacific—an even better ratio than the 70:30 proposed by King in Casablanca.[53] After two years of playing second fiddle to Europe, the Pacific had begun to receive the resources needed to pursue a multipronged counteroffensive against Japan. But the regional commanders—particularly MacArthur—would continue to clamor for resources from Washington throughout the war, prompting an exasperated Marshall to complain that all his top commanders seemed to own square globes with only their theater on top. He called it "Theateritis," and no amount of resources would fully provide a cure.[54]

Meanwhile, even with the growth in resources, the United States had yet to decide on the best route to Tokyo and victory.

The Island-Hopping Campaign and the Antecedents of the Modern Defense Line

From Captain David Porter of the *Essex* to the Naval War College officers working on War Plan Orange in the interwar years, Americans had debated for more than a century over which islands had to be secured to protect the maritime approaches to the United States and to ensure access to the Western Pacific. With the loss of the Philippines and Guam by May 1942, the JCS were forced to choose between a series of imposing routes through Japan's "spiderweb" of island defenses in order to take back lost outposts and strike at the enemy's home islands. As Admiral Raymond Spruance recounted to an audience after the war, "the early loss of the Philippines left us with no base west of Pearl Harbor. The war in the Pacific became largely a matter of the seizure of advance bases and their subsequent development for the support of fleet, air and ground forces."[55] It was a bloody validation of the vision of Ellis and the other prewar planners—and a lesson in the value of forward presence in the Pacific that would not be forgotten by the U.S. military after the war.

The Rainbow Five plan had assumed that the U.S. Pacific Fleet would surge from Pearl Harbor to the Marshall and Caroline Islands and then reinforce the Philippines, Singapore, or Indonesia as needed. By May, all of those islands were in Japanese hands, and the Pacific Fleet was mauled and in need of refitting and replacements. The new JCS therefore scrapped Rainbow Five. Nevertheless, the strategic problem anticipated by the War Plan Orange planners remained: Tokyo was 3,400 miles from Pearl Harbor and 3,600 miles from Brisbane. The war had to be taken to the Japanese islands, but how and through what route?

In a February 1942 letter, Roosevelt outlined to Churchill the routes from which he thought the counteroffensive would likely take place.[56] What Roosevelt called the "left flank" approach would have been to attack eastward from India and Burma with British land and naval forces in the lead, but the British did not have the resources or the Pacific-first mentality to make that option realistic until much later in the war. That left the Americans with three routes to Tokyo on what Roosevelt called the "right flank"—all of which had earlier been the subject of intensive studies at the Naval War College in the interwar years.[57] The shortest route would have been through the Aleutian Islands, but the weather was considered too large a problem, and the fighting there stopped after a fierce but limited engagement on Attu and an unopposed U.S.-Canadian landing to clear remaining Japanese forces thought to be on Kiska in May 1943. The second route was for General MacArthur to swing north from his base in Australia to New Guinea and then Mindanao, with the U.S. Pacific Fleet operating in support of the U.S. Army. The third route was for the navy to advance through the Central Pacific, taking the Gilbert, Marshall, and Caroline Islands and then the Marianas and—it was expected—Formosa. This third route represented the essence of navy thinking in War Plan Orange.[58] In the end, the JCS really only had these last two prongs as realistic options in 1942–1943: a haymaker punch straight through the Central Pacific or an uppercut from New Guinea to the Philippines.

The New Guinea to Mindanao route was championed by MacArthur. Already the most controversial and iconic American military leader of his generation, MacArthur had won public admiration and a Congressional Medal of Honor for his defense of the Philippines (though he also won countless detractors in the navy and marine corps, whom he blamed for Japan's victory despite the superior preparedness and performance of those maritime services on Luzon).[59] His publicity machine was unrelenting, claiming fantastically over the course of the fighting in the Philippines that the Japanese had lost 150,000–200,000 men and the Americans only 120, but it worked politically, and polls showed he was the most popular American figure of 1942.[60] MacArthur believed he had a unique understanding of the "oriental mind," having served in the Philippines in the 1920s and 1930s and most recently as commander of U.S. Army Forces in the Far East. He was certain that liberation of the Philippines was now indispensable to demonstrate to the entire region the futility of Japan's Greater East Asian Co-prosperity Sphere. His staff also attacked the logic of a Central Pacific offensive, noting that "spider webs" of islands and atolls the navy wanted to take in the Central Pacific were too close together and too heavily fortified, which would allow Japan to impose a heavy cost with each landing and to reinforce one island or atoll from

Japanese air forces in surrounding islands. Ironically, as army chief of staff in 1935, MacArthur had signed off on War Plan Orange, which featured a Central Pacific counteroffensive to rescue U.S. forces in the Philippines. Now that Japanese forces were in Manila, however, he wanted the army and navy to strike back directly from the south to evict them. This was his holy grail. When asked by President Manuel Quezon if he could liberate the Philippines, MacArthur answered without hesitation: "I intend to do just that. And when I stand at the gates of Manila, I want the President of the Commonwealth at my right hand and the Prime Minister of Australia at my left."[61]

The Central Pacific route was championed by King and the new commander of the Pacific Fleet, Chester Nimitz, a soft-spoken Texan who had formally taken command on board a submarine in Pearl Harbor in late December 1941 because there were no longer any U.S. battleships afloat on which to hold the ceremony.[62] King and Nimitz did not oppose working in tandem with MacArthur's strategy, but they insisted on a two-pronged offensive lest MacArthur's forces be exposed to continuous flank attacks by Japanese air and naval forces based on the spiderweb of South Pacific island chains MacArthur's staff had already warned were a threat. MacArthur had the Republicans in Congress on his side, but he irritated Marshall and worried the Democratic president. Nimitz enjoyed strong support from King and thus easy indirect access to the president.

In May 1943, in time for the TRIDENT Conference in Washington, the JCS compromised by agreeing to attack along both routes—essentially endorsing Nimitz's vision of Pacific theater strategy but satisfying MacArthur.[63] Nimitz would have all forces in the Central Pacific and MacArthur would have all those in the Southwest Pacific, including his own navy—the Seventh Fleet. It was an artful political and bureaucratic compromise but arguably suboptimal as military strategy. By violating Mahanian principles and dividing the fleet between two offensives that were out of aircraft range for mutual support, the United States ran considerable risk that the Imperial Japanese Navy, which still enjoyed near parity in forces throughout 1943, could focus its own power on defeating each of the American fleets decisively. That would have left the rest of the naval and ground forces vulnerable to Japanese air attack. Fortunately for Nimitz and MacArthur, the Japanese fleet commanders became tactically aggressive but strategically intimidated after Midway, sending their naval forces out in near suicidal but isolated sorties. And by the end of 1943, U.S. *Essex*-class carriers were surging into the Pacific at such a rate (one carrier with its fully trained aircrew a month) that multiple-pronged offensives were possible without strategic risk.[64]

In the TRIDENT Conference, the JCS also proposed an eventual attack from the "Western" flank in China and Burma to support the Nimitz and MacArthur fronts. However, the planned Chinese offensive was blunted by furious Japanese assaults, and British offensives did not materialize in a serious way in Burma until 1944 because of resource limitations and an attempted Japanese invasion of India. This meant that, for much of the war, Nimitz and MacArthur would largely be on their own.

Even with the temporary agreement of May 1943 to support both Nimitz and MacArthur, the JCS still did not have a clear strategic picture of where the South and Central Pacific offensives would ultimately take them and how they would finally force Japan to capitulate. There would be two thrusts, but would they end with an invasion of Kyushū and Honshū? The liberation of the Philippines? An assault from Formosa? Strategic bombing from the Central Pacific islands? The JCS had difficulty answering these problems because the United States was still largely on the defensive in the Pacific, with only two operational carriers available in the first half of 1943—*Enterprise* and *Saratoga* (*Lexington* had been lost at the Coral Sea, *Yorktown* at Midway, and *Hornet* and *Wasp* in the Solomons). Thus, argues historian Tsuyoshi Hasegawa, "Despite turning the tide of the war since Midway and Guadalcanal, the United States was [still] fighting in the Pacific without a coherent, long-term strategy."[65]

American forces nevertheless began the first phase of the two-pronged counteroffensive in June 1943. MacArthur took Papua with support from the Seventh Fleet and Australian forces while Nimitz sent Admiral William "Bull" Halsey to capture the Munda airfield in the central Solomons, from which he could bomb the main forward Japanese air base at Rabaul (which Japan had seized from Australian forces in early 1942). The successful advances by Nimitz and MacArthur suggested why the nonfortification clause in the 1922 Washington Naval Treaty might not have been so deleterious after all. Rather than assaulting bases the Japanese had fortified, the Allies "island-hopped" past them, leaving 100,000 Japanese soldiers marooned on Rabaul and tens of thousands stranded on other islands. The navy was able to effect this more flexible strategy precisely because of replenishment capabilities that were developed to get around the nonfortification clause. U.S. ships in the Pacific were "long-legged," meaning that they could roam for months without putting into port, in contrast to the Royal Navy, for example, which still needed to send its ships into port every few weeks.[66] Nimitz and MacArthur used these technological and doctrinal advantages to demonstrated admirable strategic and tactical flexibility, but their success clearly was also built on innovation and planning in the interwar years.[67]

Despite the strategic successes, however, the island-hopping campaign proved brutal and bloody at the tactical level. Nimitz chose to begin his Central Pacific assault on the Gilbert Islands so that he would have airfields from which to soften up the harder Japanese positions in the Marshalls. The key atoll in the Gilberts was Tarawa, where the Second Marine Division lost over 1,000 dead and 2,000 wounded when their landing craft ground to a halt on a coral shelf, forcing them to wade ashore under heavy enemy fire. MacArthur seized on these logistical challenges and evidence of fierce Japanese resistance to reiterate his call for shifting resources to the Southwest Pacific,[68] but at the Cairo Conference in December 1943, the JCS and the CCS confirmed that the counteroffensive would continue along both prongs. MacArthur would advance from New Guinea to the Philippines, while Nimitz would capture the Carolines and Marianas to begin a strategic bombing campaign on Japan itself from the islands of Guam, Tinian, and Saipan.

The next phase of the strategy proved to be an enormous success. First, Nimitz used the Marshall Islands as a base to pound Japan's main forward anchorage at Truk in the Carolines—isolating and neutralizing Japan's "Pearl Harbor" in the Central Pacific, the tough nut that prewar planners once thought they would have to take at great cost. Then Nimitz swung northwest to the Mariana Islands, which the Japanese high command rightly considered to be a critical link in the outer air and naval defenses of the home islands. When U.S. forces attacked Japan's major base in the Mariana chain at Saipan in June 1944, the Imperial Japanese Navy surged its combined fleet and local fighter aircraft to seek a decisive Mahanian engagement with their enemy. The resulting "Great Marianas Turkey Shoot" was disastrous for Japan, which lost over 600 aircraft and 3 carriers to the Americans' superior numbers, pilot experience, antiaircraft doctrine, and submarine screen. By July 1944, Nimitz held Saipan, Guam, and Tinian, and Japan's major base at Truk was out of action.

Meanwhile, MacArthur had advanced to within 300 nautical miles of Mindanao, and his long-range bombers were already attacking Japanese forces in the Philippines. He sought authorization to plan for an assault on Mindanao. Nimitz and King argued that the next move should have been to take Formosa, from which U.S. Army Air Force (USAAF) bombers could better reach Japan and navy submarines could choke off Japan's oil supplies from Southeast Asia. MacArthur and Nimitz explained their respective positions to President Roosevelt in a meeting at Pearl Harbor in July 1944, and the president seemed swayed by MacArthur.[69] Beginning with that discussion, the JCS, worried about the manpower needed to take an island Japan had held since 1895, began to rethink the Formosa option. Meanwhile, evidence mounted that Japanese forces in the Philippines were becoming less confident and aggressive. In September 1944, the JCS proposed and the CCS concurred on a strategy to forgo invasions of both Mindanao and Formosa in favor of direct landings on Luzon in the Philippines.[70] A delighted MacArthur landed the U.S. Sixth Army at Leyte the next month, luring the Imperial Japanese Navy out to its final destruction at the hands of the U.S. Third and Seventh Fleets—but not before Japan unleashed the Kamikaze for the first time—a sure signal that resistance would become even more fanatical as the fight approached the home islands.

In fact, with each new strategic success in the Pacific, the costs continued to rise at the tactical level. The JCS began to imagine with horror the butcher's bill of an opposed landing on the Japanese home islands. King and Arnold still believed that a naval blockade and aerial bombardment could force Japan to surrender without an invasion, consistent with pre-war assumptions behind War Plan Orange. However, MacArthur was convinced from the ferocious resistance he encountered in New Guinea that Japan would force the Allies to fight on the home islands. He wrote to Marshall, arguing that the United States "must not invade Japan proper unless the Russian army is previously committed to action in Manchuria" to keep Japanese ground forces pinned down on the continent.[71] However, coordinating military planning with Stalin was impossible, and Marshall had to assume that Japan would force the Allies to fight for every inch taken in Kyushū even if the Soviets did attack from the other flank. Preparing for the worst, the JCS began to plan the transfer of army units from Europe to the Pacific for the eventual invasion of Kyushū.[72]

So prominent was Mahan's doctrine of the decisive fleet engagement—which he assumed would lead to blockade and surrender—that War Plan Orange had never grappled with the enormity of possible ground and air operations in Japan. The landings at Iwo Jima in February 1945 and the bloody slog through Okinawa from April through June of that year foreshadowed what the fight would have been like. In June 1945, U.S. signals intelligence inaccurately assessed that 300,000 Japanese troops would oppose the Allies on Kyushū, which led to estimates by the Joint War Plans Committee that U.S. forces would suffer somewhere around 200,000 casualties while invading the Japanese home islands. On August 2, however, MacArthur's staff revised those estimates, admitting that Japanese forces were twice as large as originally thought and were rapidly being reinforced. American invasion forces would now be in a 1:1 ratio with the defenders on the Japanese home islands, a far worse situation than in Okinawa or Iwo Jima, with dreadful implications for the likely casualty figures.[73] In the end, Japan surrendered before the butcher's toll would be collected for an invasion of Kyushū. The long-sought Soviet attack on Japanese forces in Manchuria with only weeks left in the war helped, but it was ultimately the use of the atomic bomb that compelled Japan to surrender—a technology unimaginable to the prewar planners and inescapable for those who followed.[74]

Meanwhile, the lessons from the campaigns across the Central Pacific and from Australia to the Philippines left a deep and bloody mark on American strategic thinking about forward presence in the Pacific. The navy and marine corps were determined never again to be put in a position where they would have to claw their way across those islands to the Western Pacific. For its part, the new U.S. Army Air Force also discovered its own corollary to the Mahanian dictum of forward basing. Their bombers had brought down Japan from the islands of the Central Pacific. Retaining air dominance over those "unsinkable aircraft carriers" became a central tenet of USAAF postwar planning and exercises. Moreover, the Pacific air campaign demonstrated that potential opponents without major fleets, including the Soviets, could, in the future, use island-based airpower to approach and threaten the United States. The USAAF now demanded a leading role in the navy's historic theater.[75]

Roosevelt had known all along that control over the Pacific islands would be critical after the war, and early in the war he had described to Leahy the need for a global string of maritime air and naval bases centered on the Pacific and the Bonin Islands, the Kuriles, Truk, and the Solomons.[76] Still a Wilsonian in part, the president wanted those bases under the new United Nations and wanted the islands to be UN trusteeships.[77] From Roosevelt's perspective, the main purpose of the bases was for the victorious powers to keep an eye on Japan, which the allies had failed to do to contain Germany after the last war. The JCS, in contrast, were thinking about the future and not the past. Leahy told the president that it was critical for the United States to hold all the islands taken in the Pacific as permanent bases and not to turn them over to the United Nations.[78] The generals and admirals were uncomfortable with Roosevelt's inchoate trusteeship scheme. Too much blood had been spilled retaking islands that had been cavalierly dispensed with by diplomats and idealists in the peace that followed the last war. The JCS were content to have Britain and Russia also police Europe, but they saw no alternative to U.S. strategic preeminence in the Pacific and in the Western Hemisphere. Secretary Knox therefore asked the General Board in early 1943 to prepare plans on which U.S. bases should be retained in the Western Pacific.[79] By April 1943, the JCS were focusing on plans for long-term control of the former German territories in the South Pacific, where Nimitz and MacArthur were then fighting.[80] As King told the press on background on July 24, 1943, "After this war, whether we are criticized for imperialism or not, we have got to take and run the Mandated Islands, and perhaps even the Solomons. We have got to dominate the Pacific."[81]

Roosevelt, however, stuck with the idea of trusteeship. The Atlantic Charter made it clear that this was a war to protect democracy and self-determination: if the United States insisted on annexing conquered territory, how could Roosevelt argue that France or Britain should allow the independence of former colonies and the protection of Pacific island territories under UN trusteeship? The president was confident that the United States would be able to retain de facto strategic control without contradicting the principles of the Atlantic Charter and a new global and regional order favorable to American values.[82] His key advisor, Harry Hopkins, had confided to General Stilwell that, after the war, the United States must have strong bases in Formosa, the Philippines, "and anywhere we damn please."[83] But the optics would not allow a new form of imperialism.

Nevertheless, throughout the war, the State and Interior Departments would struggle with the JCS on the status of the Mandated Islands, anticipating longer-running fights about the U.S. military presence in Southeast Asia, Okinawa, and Korea after the war. As we will see, the JCS were also concerned about Roosevelt's pledge to turn over Japan's Kurile Islands to the Soviet Union after the war. The strategic stakes were high. As secretary of the navy, Forrestal explained in testimony before a joint session of the Senate and House Committees on Naval Affairs in July 1945, the United States had to seek naval superiority in pivotal areas, including "the waters contiguous to Japan and to the Philippines."[84]

Eventually, the JCS would win unhindered access to key military ports and airfields in the South Pacific. What they did not anticipate was a long-term military presence in Japan, let alone on the Korean Peninsula. The Potsdam Proclamation in July 1945 stated only that "The occupying forces of the Allies shall be withdrawn from Japan as soon as [the Potsdam Proclamation's] objectives have been accomplished and there has been established in accordance with the freely expressed will of the Japanese people a peacefully inclined and responsible government."[85] Even MacArthur, who was ordered by the JCS in July 1945 to be prepared to lead those forces, was apparently giving little thought to how long a U.S. military presence in Japan would be necessary after the war.[86] The strategic instinct was to hold the "stepping stones" across the Pacific. The strategic need for a long-term military presence in Japan and Korea would not be forced into the American consciousness until the onset of the Cold War.

By 1945, however, the American strategic concept of islands in the Western Pacific had rotated ninety degrees to starboard. For a century, strategists from Perry to the planners of War Plan Orange had been looking at the stepping stones that would sustain American engagement laterally across the vast Pacific. With the lesson that the defensive line had to be drawn forward and the anticipation that threats would emanate from the Eurasian continent in the future, strategic thinking shifted to control of the islands stretching longitudinally from north to south along the Western Pacific: the First Island Chain, from Japan through Taiwan and the Philippines, and the Second Island Chain, stretching from Japan to Guam and the Southwest Pacific. These island features would consume postwar planners in the same way that Hawaii, Midway, Wake, Guam, and the Philippines had consumed planners in the prewar era.

CONTINENTAL AND MARITIME GEOPOLITICS AND THE PRECURSORS OF POSTWAR ORDER

Despite Bismarck's maxim that the objects in war must be fixed and limited with an eye toward conquering the peace, the reality is that the statesman's geopolitical toolkit often changes significantly once hostilities have commenced and the nation is fixated on military victory over a hated foe. In peacetime, there was room for considering longer-term strategies aimed at maintaining a stable balance of power in the region. After Pearl Harbor, however, the focus was on harnessing American and

Allied military might to crush Japan and achieve the objective of unconditional surrender articulated at the Casablanca Conference in January 1943 and reaffirmed at Potsdam in the summer of 1945. Other peacetime strategic considerations, such as whether to emphasize maritime or
continental access and influence, were similarly bound by logistical realities in wartime: the United States would support China and encourage the Soviets to attack Japan's one million soldiers on the continent so
that U.S. military power could be applied to defeating Japan on the maritime flank. Winning quickly, totally, and with minimal U.S. casualties
was the principal driver for geostrategic thinking.

Yet even though the pursuit of unconditional surrender narrowed the
geostrategic toolkit in wartime, Roosevelt also entered the war with some
assumptions about postwar order that shaped his government's interaction with the Allies throughout the war. As was noted, the president
foresaw a world in which the United Nations would maintain peace and
stability with support from a global police force, backed by regional balances of power underpinned by Britain and Russia in Europe and a unified China in Asia. His cabinet and the JCS struggled to understand how
this vision would be put into effect and how U.S. interests would be protected. It was a hybrid of realism and liberal internationalism that left
numerous seams.

From the start of the war, a small group of foreign policy intellectuals
began to pull at those seams, urging a strategy that prioritized balance of
power and maritime dominance over the prevailing national sentiment
for a concert of power with the continental powers in Asia. In an article
in *Foreign Affairs* in July 1943, for example, Sir Halford Mackinder revived
his theory that the nation controlling the Eurasian "heartland" would be
positioned to dominate world affairs. With the elimination of German
military power, he explained, the Soviets would be left largely in control of the heartland from Belarus to Siberia. Mackinder steered clear of
onerous thoughts of yet another world struggle with a totalitarian state—
concluding hopefully that China's rise would allow the "ordering of the
Outer World" and a counterbalance to traditional Russian ambitions—but
the geostrategic implications of his argument were unmistakable.[87]

Less optimistic and eventually more influential on postwar American
foreign policy and international relations theory was the Dutch-born Yale
University professor Nicholas John Spykman. In *America's Strategy in
World Politics* (1942), Spykman warned against Pollyannaish expectations
of a new collective security order after the war and reminded his readers

that American security had always depended on a stable strategic equilibrium in Asia: "The concern of the United States with the balance of power in Asia antedates the threat of the emergence of a great naval empire across the Pacific. It was originally inspired not by any worry about our position in the Western Hemisphere but by anxiety about our position as an Asiatic power."[88]

Spykman blended Mackinder's heartland theory with Mahan's focus on sea lanes, urging a focus on controlling the maritime "rimland" around Eurasia. He did not believe a rising China would serve as a friendly counterweight to Russia, believing instead that it might seek the day when the Pacific would be controlled "not by British, American or Japanese sea power, but by Chinese." He warned that with the end of European colonialism, American access to Asia would be perpetually challenged by one or another rising power within the region.[89] Japan was only the first aspirant of hegemony in Asia, he argued, and just as the United States was now using China to counter Japan, in the future Japan might be the critical American counterweight to a rising China. The United States had twice intervened in European wars to preserve British power, he explained in *America's Strategy*, and thus, "If the balance of power in the Far East is to be preserved in the future as well as in the present, the United States will have to adopt a similar protective policy toward Japan."[90]

Reviewers of Spykman's prominent book were stunned. "What were those eminent scholars at Yale thinking?" wrote one critic at the time.[91] The United States had only just entered the war, and China was an ally against the despised Japanese. Roosevelt had established the prevailing view that the war should give way to a collective security regime, and the president remained fairly consistent in his vision of the respective roles of China, Russia, and Japan throughout the war. But Mackinder and Spykman were reawakening American intellectuals and strategists to the stubborn influence of both power and geography in international affairs. Even as the president spoke of collective security, the balance-of-power realists' arguments began to resonate with many of Roosevelt's senior commanders and diplomats as American forces battled across the Pacific, for as the war progressed, Americans found that China disappointed, Stalin proved untrustworthy, and Japan was leaving a detritus of former possessions from Korea to Burma that would have to fit into the new regional order without the stabilizing gravitational pull of Japanese power. These hard realities shook many of the assumptions about postwar regional order that Americans brought to the fight in 1941—and anticipated the

maritime and containment strategies that would emerge with the Cold
War a decade later.

CHINA

China's weakness had long been a magnet for great-power competition
in Asia and thus a threat to U.S. interests in the Pacific. Roosevelt was
therefore determined to ensure that after the war China would be strong
enough to resist foreign pressures and friendly enough to stay closely
aligned with the United States for generations to come.[92] Americans had
deep sympathy for China and felt moral outrage at its subjugation. *The
Good Earth*, Pearl Buck's novel about the tribulations of a contemporary
Chinese village, won a Pulitzer Prize in 1932 and became a hit movie in
1937, and Chiang Kai-shek made repeated appearances on the cover of
Time magazine before and during the war. Roosevelt certainly also had
his own personal and family connections to China, though as his biographer Robert Dallek notes, the president "had a good general grasp of
Chinese realities, a clear conception of how he hoped to use China during
and after the war, and a healthy appreciation of his limited powers to influence events there."[93] Roosevelt knew that the Soviets might be tempted to
fill the vacuum left by Japan's defeat and believed that "in any serious conflict of policy with Russia, [China] would undoubtedly line up on our side,"
as he put it once to Britain's foreign minister Anthony Eden.[94]

   The immediate strategic imperative in 1941 and 1942 was therefore to
keep China in the war. The collapse of China would be a "loss of face by
the United Nations among the peoples of Asia," King warned,[95] and Roosevelt told his son Elliott that "the job in China can be boiled down to one
essential—China must be kept in the war tying up Japanese soldiers."[96]
Lend-Lease supplies had been flowing to Chinese forces since 1941, and
immediately after Pearl Harbor, Roosevelt appointed General Stilwell to
serve as Chiang's chief of staff at the generalissimo's request. That same
month, Claire Chennault's American Volunteer Group (AVG)—the legendary "Flying Tigers"—went into combat for the first time, intercepting
a squadron of Japanese Kawasaki KI-48 "Lily" bombers heading for an
attack on Kunming and downing three of the enemy aircraft. (Before being incorporated into the USAAF in 1942, Chennault's American pilots
would down 294 more Japanese planes while losing only 10 of their own
P-40 fighters.)[97] Further promises were made to provide fighter aircraft

and bombers to the China Air Force (CAF) and to fly supplies over the Himalayan "hump" to compensate for the loss of land corridors cut off by Japanese ground forces.

Initially, the president and the JCS determined that if China held, then it could be used as a base from which to bomb Japan and turn the tide of the war.[98] With the shift from defense to offense in late 1942, however, American confidence in Chiang began to flag. Stilwell wanted an all-out assault against Japanese forces in Burma but watched in frustration as Chiang marshaled his U.S. military supplies for a future fight with the Communists at home. Stilwell then clashed with Chennault, who tried to follow up on earlier commitments to Chiang by providing the China Air Force with one hundred new P-47s and thirty new B-25s.[99] The key to keeping China in the war, Stilwell argued to the JCS, was to maintain pressure on Chiang to send his forces into action against the Japanese, not to give him unconditional aid. With USAAF requirements for North Africa increasing, Stilwell succeeded in ensuring that the CAF received only twenty upgraded P-40s by the end of 1942—only 1 percent of the aircraft Lend-Lease program for Britain at that time and less than 10 percent of the program for the Soviets.[100]

While Lend-Lease fell short of initial U.S. pledges, Roosevelt nevertheless took other steps to demonstrate confidence in the centrality of China to the war effort and postwar regional order. In May 1943, he ordered Chennault to do what was necessary to begin an air offensive from China. Marshall objected to the idea, arguing that Japan was still well positioned to launch ground offensives against the USAAF and CAF air bases, but the president considered the bombing campaign essential to show support for Chiang and to elevate Chinese morale.[101] Besides, the president told reporters in February 1943, "If we took one island [in the Pacific] in the advance from the south, once a month . . . it would take about fifty years before we got to Japan."[102] An offensive from China still seemed more promising. In November 1943, the president approved Operation Matterhorn, a program to bomb Japan with B-29s based in Chengdu (Chengtu).[103]

Roosevelt also took steps to elevate Chiang's status in the Allies' war councils. He continually reminded Churchill and Stalin of the central importance of China to both war fighting and the postwar international order. He pushed the Allies to agree to appoint Chiang as the Supreme Commander of the United Powers in China, Thailand, and Indochina— though he confessed privately that the generalissimo was not "getting much of a command."[104] In January 1943, Roosevelt also began to restore Chinese sovereignty, renouncing U.S. extraterritoriality, including century-old rights in the International Settlements at Shanghai and Amoy (modern-day Xiamen) and the control of diplomatic quarters in Peking.[105] All of these steps appeared to correct previous undercommitment to China's sovereignty in the interwar period, which Roosevelt hoped would promise to secure a more stable China at the center of Asia after the war.

Roosevelt's support for China's international status probably reached the high-water mark at the first Cairo Conference on November 23–26, 1943, where Chiang received commitments from the president and Churchill that territories "stolen" from China would be returned (specifically, Formosa, Manchuria, and the Pescadores) and that Korea would be granted independence.[106] Roosevelt also told Chiang about his plans to support China with a major offensive against Burma.[107] As the president explained to General Stilwell at the conference, his personal commitment to China was based on a determination that U.S. policy would never again favor Japan over China.[108]

Yet Chiang's success at Cairo had much to do with the fact that Stalin had skipped the meeting for fear his appearance alongside the Chinese leader would provoke the Japanese, with whom the Soviets were not yet at war. When the leaders gathered again in Tehran a week later, Stalin showed up and Chiang was disinvited at the Soviets' insistence. The results for China were devastating. Stalin confirmed a pledge he had first floated to Hull in October in Moscow that the Soviet Union would attack Japan once Germany fell,[109] and Churchill—always skeptical of Roosevelt's assessment of China's importance—seized on the Soviet pledge to urge the president to shift away from his China-centered strategy in the Far East and to drop plans for an invasion of Burma, despite the promise to Chiang only days earlier.[110] The JCS reinforced this shift by noting that American advances in the Gilbert and Marshall Islands were already obviating the need for bombing campaigns from mainland China. Absent from the summit and eclipsed in strategic relevance by the Soviets, Chiang was effectively "demoted from the ranks of the Big Four."[111]

By now, Roosevelt was also paying increased attention to the observations of diplomats in the field, particularly Stilwell's political advisor in the China-Burma-India (CBI) theater, John Paton Davies, who described in detail the poor morale and defections in Chiang's armies. Davies was one of the most prescient yet ill-treated American diplomats in Asia of the mid-twentieth century. His skeptical views of Chiang during the war would later lead to three years of anticommunist loyalty investigations and eventually force his resignation from the Foreign Service in 1954. Yet Davies was anything but a communist sympathizer: he was a hard-headed realist, whom George Kennan would tap to help design postwar Asia strategy for the State Department Policy Planning staff. Davies brought to his assignment as Stilwell's political advisor two important cards. First, he knew the military well, thanks to prewar service at the U.S. embassy in Beijing with then colonel Joseph Stilwell, the military attaché, and Colonel A. A. Vandegrift, future commandant of the U.S. Marine Corps, who led the security detachment at the embassy. This experience helped Davies buck the overall trend in the State Department under Hull and to think in terms of integrated military and diplomatic strategies. Second, for all his knowledge of Asia (he was the son of missionaries in China), Davies suffered from none of the sentimentality that infected the president, the State Department leadership, and the public with respect to China. He was a careful guardian of American strategic interests and was more likely than not to agree with Mahan's characterization of internal Chinese politics as a "hornet's nest." This earned him the ire of Hornbeck, among others, who accused him of being a "poor salesman" for China with the president.[112]

Davies worried that U.S. military strategy in the Pacific was subordinating longer-term political considerations. As he cautioned Stilwell in a memo in September 1943, while U.S. military leaders "want the job accomplished as soon as possible, with minimum of fuss over international political and economic issues . . . to our allies the conduct of the war is a function of overall political and economic policy."[113] To his wife, he confided that he did not "know which is more important at this juncture— ensuring the victory or planning for what we are going to do with the victory. I am inclined to think the latter is more important."[114] Davies did not believe the assumption that China was indispensable for either the defeat of Japan or a stable postwar order. At one point in 1943, he confided to his British counterpart that the Allies might need Japan after the war as a counterweight to China and the Soviet Union and would not necessarily benefit from the "extermination" of Japan.[115] Ultimately, Davies saw that Chiang needed the United States more than the United States needed China, and he urged Washington to condition aid to the generalissimo on his willingness to fight the Japanese rather than horde weapons for the coming confrontation with the Communists.

Davies was swimming against the tide of U.S. politics and public opinion. Congress remained sympathetic to the Chinese Nationalists' cause (Chiang's wife, Soong May-ling, had received a standing ovation when she addressed a joint session in February 1943),[116] and polls showed that a majority of Americans wanted a formal military alliance with China after the war.[117] However, much of the JCS was already beginning to sour on China as a strategic partner, and Roosevelt's own doubts began to show as well. When Chiang requested $1 billion in new economic aid—an enormous sum at the time, given rampant corruption and mismanagement in the Chinese economy, China hands like Davies aligned with Morgenthau at Treasury to convince Roosevelt to reject Chiang's loan request in January 1944.[118] After Japanese forces smashed Chiang's armies in the Ichi-go offensive that spring and summer in Hunan, Henan (Ho-nan), and Guangxi (Kuang-hsi) provinces (confirming Marshall's suspicion that Operation Matterhorn would provoke a Japanese counterattack), Roosevelt again sided with Chiang's critics and agreed to support Stilwell's request to take overall command of Chinese forces. A wily and justifiably outraged Chiang preempted the move by firing Stilwell, but the episode further eroded goodwill toward the generalissimo at senior levels in Washington.

All of this forced the president to begin to rethink the American relationship with Mao Zedong's (Mao Tse-tung) Chinese Communist Party (CCP) forces based around Yenan. Roosevelt had been loath to approach the Communists, for fear it would complicate a coalition with the Nationalists, prompt Chiang to stop fighting the Japanese entirely, provoke a civil war—or all three.[119] The reports from the field began to have an impact, however, and one particularly cogent memo sent by Davies in January 1944 caught the president's attention by warning that too close an alignment with Chiang risked entanglement "not only in a civil war in China" but also in a "conflict with the Soviet Union." Mao's deputy, Zhou Enlai, had issued a standing invitation to send American observers to the CCP headquarters at Yenan, and Davies urged Washington to respond.[120] Exasperated with Chiang and eager to forestall a broader civil war within China, Roosevelt approved the dispatch of the U.S. Army Observation Group (AOG, the "Dixie Mission") to Yenan in July 1944, where the Americans were serenaded by cadres singing "My Old Kentucky Home" and wooed by Mao's call for a CCP-U.S. alignment to prevent Soviet domination of the continent. The State Department representative on the AOG, John Service, was enraptured, and sent over fifty-one reports describing the high morale and "religious summer conference" atmosphere of the Communists.[121] He would pay for his naïve enthusiasm in the McCarthy-era anticommunist purges a decade later.

With the channel open, Roosevelt saw an opportunity to shift the fight back to Japan and restore stability within China by brokering an agreement between the Nationalists and the CCP. He first tried to do so by dispatching to Yenan his envoy to China, former Oklahoma oil tycoon and Republican secretary of war Patrick Hurley. Hurley emerged from his plane at Yenan on November 7, 1944, whooping his signature Indian war call, to the confusion of the Chinese and the dismay of the American diplomats on the ground. After squabbling with his own delegation and clashing with the CCP leadership, he left Yenan empty-handed. Most historians have pointed to Hurley's conservative anticommunism, his clashes with the Foreign Service, his uncouth mannerisms, and the nickname "clown" he earned from the Communist leadership as evidence he was the wrong man for the job.[122] For their part, Grew (at that point acting secretary of state) and the president praised Hurley's efforts.[123] In the end, there may not have been any diplomat who could have brokered the irreconcilable Nationalist and Communist camps. Out of options on the ground in China, the president turned to the Soviets for help.[124]

When the Big Three met at Yalta in February 1945, Roosevelt extracted from Stalin a statement of "readiness to conclude with the National Government of China a pact of friendship and alliance between the U.S.S.R. and China in order to render assistance to China with its armed forces for the purpose of liberating China from the Japanese yoke."[125] This appeared to be a significant move, giving Chiang potential leverage vis-à-vis both the Japanese and the Communists. However, the price in terms of Chinese sovereignty was high: in language eerily similar to the concessions given to Japan in the Lansing-Ishii agreement in 1916, Roosevelt agreed secretly at Yalta that the Soviet Union historically enjoyed "preeminent interests" in Port Arthur and the Chinese Eastern and South Manchurian Railroads, and he pledged that Mongolia would be made independent of China.[126] Stalin agreed that those terms would "require concurrence of Generalissimo Chiang Kai-shek" but also made it clear that they were the conditions for his entry into the war against Japan, which he knew was a high priority for Roosevelt. Stalin also insisted that the agreement be kept from Chiang for reasons of secrecy (relating to the Soviet attack on Japan), which it was until June, when Hurley finally convinced Washington to let him tell Chiang about the U.S.-Soviet condominium and to seek Chinese negotiations with Moscow on the particulars. Hurley was instructed to tell Chiang pointedly that the United States is "definitely committed to the agreements reached . . . and that these were Stalin's conditions for entering the war against Japan."[127] Chiang bristled in particular at the language about "pre-eminent interests" and the lease of Dalian, and he continued to resist agreement with Stalin on the Yalta terms until the Soviet invasion of Manchuria finally forced his government to accept it as a fait accompli.[128]

After the war, some historians argued that this betrayal of Chinese sovereignty had to be understood "against the background of U.S. objectives in China and President Roosevelt's attempt to construct a 'large policy' that would enable the United States, with Soviet compliance, to promote a strong, non-communist, postwar China."[129] Stalin, however, had little interest in supporting a strong anticommunist China under Chiang. Indeed, Stimson, Harriman, and the veteran China hand John Carter Vincent at the State Department all urged Roosevelt not to undercut China by forcing the Yalta concessions on Chiang.[130] Though he may have been focused on the "large policy," Roosevelt had traded concrete concessions on Chinese sovereignty to Stalin in exchange for broad statements of solidarity with the Nationalists that had little meaning in fact. American China policy was hanging on weak hooks.

Despite all the frustrations and disappointments with internal Chinese politics, however, Roosevelt never entirely gave up on his vision of a strong China as the cornerstone of a regional balance of power within Asia. He told Secretary of State Stettinius in January 1945, before Yalta, that U.S. policy was still based on the belief "that despite the temporary weakness of China and the possibility of revolutions and civil war, 450,000,000 Chinese would someday become united and modernized and would be the most important factor in the whole Far East."[131] SWNCC concluded in its April 1945 long-term planning document for China that U.S. policy was "based on the need to have China as a principal stabilizing factor in the Far East as a fundamental condition for peace and security," and it noted the need to continue supporting the National Government while remaining "realistically alert" to the widespread dissatisfaction with the KMT in the country over corruption and the lack of basic freedoms.[132] Over the next month, SWNCC's confidence in Chiang and the Kuomintang (KMT) eroded, leading to a new set of recommendations on May 28 that "no commitments should be made until internal unity and stability are achieved, the Chinese government is supported by the Chinese people, and the Chinese economy has been sufficiently developed to support a modern army and air force."[133] Despite this recommendation, there remained considerable momentum behind the original assumptions about China's role. The tonnage of supplies flying to China over "the hump" continued to increase from 10,000 tons per month in December 1943 to 20,000 tons per month in July 1944, eventually peaking at over 70,000 tons per month by war's end.[134] These aid shipments were made not in the hope that they might spur Chiang to action against the Japanese but instead as a deliberate down payment on a postwar Sino-U.S. relationship aimed at maintaining a stable balance of power in Asia.[135]

In sum, then, U.S. policy at the end of the war was based on the vague assumption that China could form the future core of stability in Asia (just as it had once been the greatest source of instability and conflict); that reconciliation between Communists and Nationalists could be achieved; and that massive material aid would ensure those positive outcomes. Yet events on the ground were throwing all of these assumptions into doubt. As historian Michael Schaller concludes, these "unresolved questions of basic policy could only contribute to eventual disaster."[136]

But what could have been done? Many postwar scholars claimed that a clean break with Chiang and a full embrace of the Communists might have averted later confrontation, since the CCP "had a sincere feeling of friendship toward America" and "were still willing to join in a viable coalition sponsored by the United States."[137] Yet subsequent events suggest that Chiang's instincts about the CCP were right—that the two ideologies were locked in a death struggle from which only one would emerge victorious.[138] And in the context of the postwar contest for supremacy between Moscow and Washington, and the communist threat to every U.S. ally and partner in the region, the CCP's ideology under Mao would have been inimical to U.S. interests. Even Davies, who urged outreach to the CCP to forestall Soviet dominance of China during the war, later acknowledged that his plans were based on an "underestimation of the Communists' commitment to ideology."[139]

Recent scholarship suggests that the alternative—embracing Chiang more fully—might have done considerable damage to the Japanese and perhaps better positioned the KMT for the coming conflict with the CCP. For years, the prevailing view of Chiang was set by Barbara Tuchman's hagiography of the generalissimo's nemesis, Stilwell, but new research has offered a corrective to that Vietnam-era dismissal of the KMT's fighting prowess.[140] As China historian Rana Mitter puts it in his reassessment of

Chiang's war, "during the war against Japan, Chiang had played an appallingly bad hand much better than might have been expected."[141]

Ultimately, Davies was right. The United States had limited ability to determine outcomes within China. Earlier engagement of the CCP might have reduced later enmity toward the United States after Chiang fell. Earlier provision of airpower might have weakened Japanese forces and helped to forestall later Communist advances. Neither would have achieved the postwar outcome sought by Roosevelt in China, which was a complete nation that assured a stable balance of power within Asia. China was indeed a "hornet's nest."

In retrospect, the U.S. focus during the war should have been on how developments in China would both accelerate the defeat of Japan *and* affect the larger strategic equilibrium in the region after the war. The United States had some tools to shape internal developments but was better positioned to influence the relations among the major powers. For this reason, the Soviet dimension of the China problem was critical. The lack of U.S. engagement with the CCP is not what drove the Communists into the Soviets' arms. That was caused by Stalin's dominant position in Manchuria after his attack on Japanese forces in August 1945—and the United States had begun to set the stage for that disruptive Soviet presence in Manchuria and the Far East at Yalta.[142] As George Kennan warned from Moscow in April 1945, "It would be tragic if our natural anxiety for the support of the Soviet Union at this juncture, coupled with Stalin's use of words which mean all things to all people, and his cautious affability, were to lead us into an undue reliance on Soviet aid or even Soviet acquiescence in the achievement of our long-term objectives in China."[143] That was just what the United States had done, however.

RUSSIA

Twice in the hundred years before Pearl Harbor, the United States had attempted to wield the "Russia card" in order to restore imbalances in the strategic equilibrium in Asia. The United States had been disappointed twice. First, in the 1850s and 1860s, spurred by common suspicion of British hegemony, Americans and Russians had aligned in Canton and then agreed on a price for the purchase of Alaska by the United States. Russian-American amity was cut short, however, by subsequent anti-Jewish pogroms and menacing Russian moves south against northern China in the decade after the American Civil War. The second time was in 1933, when Roosevelt hoped that normalization with the Soviet Union would serve as a check against Japan after the invasion of Manchuria. Instead, Stalin reciprocated normalization by reaching accommodation with Japan on Manchuria. Even after pitched battles with Japanese forces at Nomonhan on the Mongolia-Manchuria border in 1939, Stalin chose to avoid further confrontation and eventually negotiated a nonaggression pact with Japan in April 1941. That pact—while it saved Stalin from a two-front war when Hitler invaded from the west two months later—also cleared the way for Japanese forces to move against Southeast Asia and eventually Pearl Harbor, Guam, and the Philippines. It therefore followed that a central tenet of U.S. grand strategy from the beginning of the war would be to encourage the earliest possible Soviet offensive against Japan. More than ever before, American planners thought they needed to wield the Russia card in Asia.

Within twenty-four hours of the attack on Pearl Harbor, Roosevelt and Hull approached the Soviet ambassador in Washington about joining the fight against Japan.[144] Three days later, with his air force in tatters and most of the Asiatic Squadron's surface combatants sunk or retreating to the Dutch East Indies, MacArthur radioed Marshall from Manila, urging Washington to bring the Soviet hammer down on Japan from the north: "The mass of enemy air and naval strength committed in the theater from Singapore to the Philippines and eastward establishes his weakness in Japan proper and definite information available here shows that entry of Russia is enemy's greatest fear. Most favorable opportunity now exists and immediate attack on Japan from north would not only inflict heavy punishment but would at once relieve pressure from objectives of Japan drive southward."[145]

Stalin, however, was in no position to help. At the time that Mac-Arthur sent his desperate radio message to Washington, German infantry units were within fifteen miles of the Kremlin, and Soviet reserves were almost completely depleted. Even Roosevelt's proposal to let the Americans do the fighting by opening Siberian air bases from which USAAF planes could strike the Japanese homeland and shuttle bombers between Manila and Vladivostok proved too risky for Stalin, who could not afford another front with Japan.[146] When Roosevelt asked again for the use of air bases in the Russian Far East in June 1942, Stalin said no a second time.[147]

By mid-1943, the Soviet victory at Kursk and the Allies' invasion of Italy had begun to relieve the pressure on Stalin, and it was in this context

that the Soviet leader explained to Hull in October in Moscow his decision to attack Japan once Germany was defeated. By that point, the
American island-hopping campaign in the Pacific had demonstrated
that Japan could eventually be bombed into submission from the Pacific
side, but it was also increasingly evident that Japanese resistance would
be fanatical on the home islands, that the Kwantung Army would still be
intact, and that Chiang's forces were of limited offensive utility.[148] Moreover, the JCS were still uncertain whether Stalin would actually follow
up on his pledge to attack Japan.[149] Eager to avoid heavy casualties in land
battles on the Japanese homeland, the JCS believed they needed a Soviet
attack. This view was particularly strong in the army, which would have
borne the brunt of the casualties. In preparation for the Yalta meetings
in February 1945, Marshall prepared a memorandum for Roosevelt urging him to convince Stalin to commit to attacking Japan. Soviet offensive
operations were "necessary to provide maximum assistance to our Pacific
operations," the JCS memo emphasized, the objectives of a Soviet attack
being "the defeat of the Japanese forces in Manchuria, air operations
against Japan proper in collaboration with United States air forces based
in eastern Siberia, and maximum interference with Japanese sea traffic
between Japan and the mainland of Asia."[150]

Soviet participation in the war against Japan was also important to
Roosevelt's vision of a postwar collective security order among the victorious Allies. The president had high confidence in Stalin, famously stating in August 1943, "I think that if I give him everything I possibly can and
ask for nothing from him in return, *noblesse oblige*, he won't try to annex
anything and will work with me for a world of democracy and peace."[151]
Roosevelt explained to Congress on March 1, 1945, that the Yalta agreement spelled "the end of the system of unilateral action, the exclusive alliances, the spheres of influence, the balances of power, and all the other
expedients that have been tried for centuries—and have always failed."[152]
Apparently, the fact that he had just secured the agreement by honoring
Soviet "spheres of influence" in Manchuria, China, and Eastern Europe
did not strike him as contradictory or ironic.

Yalta has passed into the history books as a betrayal of Eastern Europe
and China. After the war, the president's admirers would reject these
criticisms as 20/20 hindsight, claiming that at the time Roosevelt acted
out of pragmatism and not idealism. As future national security advisor
McGeorge Bundy argued in *Foreign Affairs* in 1949, "Critics of Yalta have
never shown that Mr. Roosevelt or Mr. Churchill granted anything that

they were in a position to withhold (except perhaps the Kurile Islands). The object of the western statesmen at Yalta was to persuade Stalin that the common interest required genuine cooperation on the basis of self-restraint by the Great Powers. It seemed for a moment that he was persuaded. In the event, we have seen that he was not."[153] Or as Dallek concludes in his more recent biography of Roosevelt, "the suggestion that Roosevelt could have restrained this Soviet expansion [in East Asia and Central Europe] through greater realism or a tougher approach to Stalin is unpersuasive."[154]

Yet, by the time of Yalta, increasing numbers of Roosevelt's lieutenants and advisors did think the president was running a serious risk by trying to satisfy Stalin's geostrategic ambitions. Mackinder and Spykman had already made the intellectual case that certain geostrategic realities would persist after the war, and Walter Lippmann warned in his influential 1943 treatise on U.S. grand strategy *U.S. Foreign Policy: Shield of the Republic* that the United States and the Soviets could easily fall into rivalry if left standing without common enemies.[155] Roosevelt's first ambassador to Moscow, William Bullitt, wrote the president throughout 1943, arguing that "to win the peace at the close of this war will be at least as difficult as to win the war" and urging the United States to work with Britain to leverage their temporary economic influence over Moscow to seek a "balance of power" to prevent Soviet domination of Eurasia after the war.[156] Averell Harriman, who was serving as ambassador in Moscow during the war (1943–1946), intensified the embassy's warnings that the Soviets' "totalitarian" outlook and increasing noncooperation presaged future troubles.[157] Harriman tried, without success, to convince the president that the Soviets would attack Japan because it was in their interest, not because of Lend-Lease or U.S. concessions in China.[158]

Roosevelt's decision to hand the Kuriles to the Soviets became a source of particular concern for key officials in the State Department who were planning postwar foreign policy for Asia. As Grew and others in the department pointed out, the transfer of the Kuriles to Russia violated the Atlantic Charter pledge that the Allies were not fighting for territorial aggrandizement. Nor were the Kuriles immaterial to JCS planners, who had studied taking the islands to bomb Japan and recognized the Kuriles as "the obvious springboard of the most possible route of attack on us" by Soviet forces after the war.[159] Roosevelt, however, considered the development of a concert of power with Russia in Europe and Asia as ultimately more important than maintaining a postwar balance of power, and to the extent that he was worried about balance of power in the region, it was primarily vis-à-vis postwar Japan. As Cold War historian Marc Gallicchio notes, "FDR planned to preserve the peace by surrounding the defeated Axis powers with military bases. In Asia, this meant depriving Japan of the Kuriles."[160] Roosevelt never really consulted the JCS on his decision, and Marshall and the chiefs were not inclined to reopen the issue despite expressions of concern from their staffs.[161]

After Roosevelt died in April 1945, Forrestal, Harriman, and Grew tried to make the case for renegotiation of Yalta in the wake of blatant Soviet noncompliance in Poland and Eastern Europe.[162] They had sympathy from the JCS, several of whom were never comfortable with Roosevelt's efforts to "sweeten" the deal for a Soviet attack on Japan, but the chiefs kept their opposition silent (until the Cold War, when King and others retrospectively explained their reservations to Congress).[163] In May 1945, Grew wrote to the secretary of war, recommending that commitments on the Far East made at Yalta only be maintained once Moscow agreed to the "unequivocal" return of Manchuria to China and landing rights on the Kurile Islands, among other conditions.[164] Further, Grew wanted to know from the JCS just how crucial Soviet entry into the war really was. Leahy had already made it clear to his colleagues that he did not think the Soviet entry into the war was necessary at this point, or worth the geopolitical cost.[165] Around the same period, Stimson also began to talk to the JCS about contingency planning to deal with Soviet expansion.[166]

By now, however, the war was rapidly coming to a close, and there was far too much momentum behind Roosevelt's original commitments to Stalin and Stalin's own planning for an attack on Japan. For his part, Truman was not inclined to reverse agreements made by his predecessor.[167] As Marshall explained to Stimson on July 23 after the secretary of war expressed concern at Stalin's moves in Eastern Europe and intentions in the Far East, "even if we went ahead in the war without the Russians, and compelled the Japanese to surrender, that would not prevent the Russians from marching into Manchuria anyhow and striking, thus permitting them to get virtually what they wanted in the surrender terms."[168] The army still wanted the Soviets in, and Marshall felt that the Russian attack would probably help shorten the war and save American lives. Stimson, though he thought the bomb might yet obviate the need for a Soviet move into Manchuria, did not object.[169] Neither he nor the president could tell the army it could not have diplomatic policies that the generals thought might significantly reduce American casualties.

Truman was clearly more suspicious of Stalin than Roosevelt had been. He also knew at the time of his first meeting with Stalin at Potsdam on July 16, 1945, that the atomic bomb was ready to use against Japan. The military requirement for Soviet entry into the war had significantly diminished, and Truman hoped that use of the bomb would make the increasingly uncooperative Soviets more "manageable."[170] Yet Truman also realized the truth of what Marshall had pointed out—that a Soviet attack on Japan was already a fait accompli. Indeed, Stalin accelerated his timetable for the invasion of Manchuria after learning of the atomic bomb from Truman during the conference.[171] Initially evasive about the U.S. commitment to turn over the Kuriles to the Soviets, Truman tried proposing that the United States continue to have access to air bases on the islands after the war.[172] In the end, Truman concluded he had no choice but to honor Roosevelt's commitment to Stalin on China, Manchuria, and the Kuriles, but he ensured that Soviet forces would not enter Japan's northern island of Hokkaidō or play a role in the occupation of Japan the way they had in Germany.

On August 9, 1945, Soviet airborne and mechanized forces launched a massive attack on Japan's exhausted Kwantung Army in Manchuria. Within weeks, Soviet forces were in control of Manchuria, the northern part of Korea, and all four of the Kurile Islands. From Manchuria, they would eventually back Mao's armies in northern China; in northern Korea, they would later install Kim Il-sung; and from the Kuriles they would threaten American and Japanese sea lanes in the Pacific during the Cold War and eventually build a fortified bastion for their ballistic missile nuclear submarines in the Sea of Okhotsk.

None of these Cold War developments were foreseen by Roosevelt or even Truman, who continued to call for Roosevelt's vision of a new UN-centered collective security system with the Soviets despite his growing suspicion of Stalin.[173] Yet, in the final weeks of the war, the American public sensed that a new menace was arising in Eurasia, with 71 percent of respondents telling Gallup they disapproved of Russia's international behavior and 60 percent expressing concern that Russia "wanted to take over the world."[174]

Over the course of the war, the United States had pursued the Russia card relentlessly, motivated both by the exigencies of the war and the hope for a more stable postwar order. By the time the Soviets were actually ready to attack in the Far East, the United States was in less urgent need of help, since the atomic bombings proved decisive in compelling Japan's surrender.[175] Roosevelt and the JCS could not have anticipated the decisive importance of the atomic bomb in 1942—or even in early 1945. His defenders are therefore partly right in arguing that the president was driven more by pragmatism than idealism in dealing with Stalin (nor was Truman in a good position to reverse Roosevelt's commitments by the time he came to office, as was noted). Yet even without knowing about the transformational strategic impact of the atomic bomb, Roosevelt could still have anticipated the implications of a stronger Soviet position in the Far East, particularly as it became evident that China would be neither whole nor strong. The Soviet attack may have been a fait accompli in the summer of 1945—but that was not the case in 1943 or even in the spring of 1945. Stalin invaded Manchuria not because of sweeteners from Roosevelt, as Harriman had foretold, but because it was in the Soviets' strategic interest. At Tehran and Yalta, Roosevelt had gone too far in empowering the Soviets in the Far East at the expense of China and even Japan.

Roosevelt was driven by the lessons of the last war—that Russians had to stay in the fight to reduce Western casualties and that a collective security order must emerge from the ruins of war in order to keep down the former foes and prevent another cataclysmic fight. He might have done better studying how his Cousin Theodore looked at the Russo-Japanese War, however. The elder Roosevelt understood that a lopsided victory by one power on the continent of Asia would have positioned that power to challenge the United States for control of the Pacific. His intervention in 1905 to stop the war and preserve a more stable balance on the continent was brilliant statecraft. With millions of Americans engaged in a global war against totalitarianism, FDR faced very different circumstances, of course, but he should have known that the realities of power politics and geography were still immutable . . . particularly since he was an avid student of Mahan.

JAPAN

Roosevelt and Churchill declared at the Casablanca Conference in January 1943 that their goal was nothing less than the unconditional surrender of Japan and Germany. The leaders clearly intended to avoid the mistakes made after the First World War, when Germany was allowed to nurse its wounds and eventually rearm. Beyond that, however, the only prior definition of "unconditional surrender" in the American experience was the Civil War. The term implied destruction of war-making potential, military occupation, and some form of reconstruction, but that left much room for interpretation. As far as the U.S. Congress and public were concerned, "unconditional surrender" meant simply revenge. Roosevelt and Hull also spoke of a punitive peace, though the president never gave precise guidance on Japan's future. In late 1941 and early 1942, this was entirely understandable. As the war progressed, however, more deliberate thinking emerged about Japan's postwar role.

Though Spykman foreshadowed the strategic logic for postwar alignment with Japan in his "rimland" concept, the first Americans to make the case for a nonpunitive peace were those scholars and diplomats who knew Japan and the Far East best. Most prominent among the scholars was Hugh Borton, a historian at Columbia University before the war, who chose to join the State Department in 1942 because his pacifist convictions as a Quaker would not let him enter the army. It was through the Quaker American Friends Service Committee that Borton first traveled to Japan in the 1920s, eventually studying at Tokyo Imperial University and publishing authoritative histories of the Tokugawa period and Japan's modern social and political development before the war cut short his research.[176] At the State Department, Borton recommended as early as 1943 that the emperor of Japan should be retained after the war in order to provide stability for a society where cultural and political traditions would make the implantation of democracy a challenge.[177] Implicit in his recommendation was an appreciation that the United States would need a stable Japan after the war in order to avoid chaos in Asia. Borton's recommendations resonated with other Japan experts consulted by State, including Professor George Blakeslee of the Fletcher School of Law and Diplomacy, and the Far East Department's senior advisor, Joseph Ballantine, as well as China hands like Davies. By late 1943, Joseph Grew had taken it on himself to explain in speeches around the country and in testimony before Congress that Shintōism and the emperor might be used to pacify the Japanese people once the militarists were eliminated.[178] Grew's arguments influenced Leahy and Stimson, the latter of whom had inherited from his mentor Elihu Root an appreciation of the need for some alignment with Japan to keep the continental powers at bay.[179]

When Forrestal pushed for more deliberate postwar planning and convinced Roosevelt to authorize the establishment of the SWNCC in December 1944, the arguments for retaining the emperor fused with broader assertions that the United States needed to control postwar Allied policy toward the Pacific as a whole. Initially, Treasury Secretary Morgenthau dominated postwar economic planning for both Germany and Japan and sought a highly punitive approach, but with the death of Roosevelt, Morgenthau lost his personal connection to the White House, and Stimson, Forrestal, Leahy, and SWNCC seized back the momentum for Japan planning that they had partly lost in the case of Germany.[180] In preparation for the invasion of Japan, SWNCC prepared a memorandum in April 1945 determining that postwar goals in Japan would be (1) "to insure that Japan will not become a menace to the United States or to the peace and security of the world" through disarmament of Japan's armed forces; (2) "to bring about the eventual establishment of a peaceful and responsible government" in Japan; (3) to prevent the imposition of "any form of government not supported by the freely expressed will of the people"; and (4) to allow "an economy which will permit the peacetime requirements of the population to be met."[181] The proposal made enormous sense to Forrestal, who had argued that it would be a mistake "to ignore the existence of 75 or 80 millions of vigorous and industrious people, or to assume they will not join with Russia if no other outlet is afforded them."[182] That same month, SWNCC began planning for the establishment of a Pacific–Far Eastern High Commission, comparable to the Allied coordinating body for postwar Europe—the European Advisory Committee—but with tensions rising with the Soviets over Eastern Europe, the Navy and War Departments pushed for the eventual establishment of an Allied "Advisory Committee" for the Pacific in lieu of a more integrated "High" commission for the region. To reinforce the message of American control, the first meeting of the new Advisory Committee was held in Washington rather than in Asia.[183]

The arguments of Grew and Borton about the future role of the emperor also gained traction. Marshall, Stimson, John J. McCloy (the War Department's cochair of SWNCC), and Forrestal all agreed on the need to signal to the Japanese that the emperor could be retained in some form. They saw the advantage in terms of postwar stability and easing the surrender of Japanese troops across the Western Pacific. However, Undersecretary of State Dean Acheson and other New Dealers were opposed to this and wanted the emperor system completely eradicated.[184] Polls demonstrated that in 1945 a majority of Americans still wanted Emperor Hirohito executed or tried as a war criminal.[185] In the end, Truman took the advice of his politically savvy secretary of state, Jimmy Byrnes, and went into Potsdam in July 1945 only with the position that "from the moment of surrender the authority of the Emperor and the Japanese Government to rule the state shall be subject to the Supreme Commander of the Allied Powers [SCAP] who will take such steps as he deems proper to effectuate the surrender terms."[186] Douglas MacArthur as SCAP would ultimately recommend that the imperial system be retained.[187] The Soviets pushed back, but Truman made it clear that there would be no Soviet occupation zone in Japan as there had been in Germany and that the United States alone would determine the future of the imperial system.[188]

Despite deep American animosity toward Japan throughout the war, American planners demonstrated remarkable foresight, discipline, and quiet influence with respect to postwar Japan policy. This was a contrast to the wishful thinking and inconsistency in planning for postwar policy toward China and Russia. The instincts of Perry and Mahan in favor of alignment with maritime powers like Japan proved to be deeply engrained in the American strategic DNA, even at the height of total war against the empire of Japan.

Yet it must also be recognized that none of the strategic assessments of Japan's postwar role went further than recommending that the United States fill the vacuum created by Japan's defeat. The wartime debates over forward bases concerned primarily the island stepping stones that strategic planners had been eyeing for a century and had fought for from 1942 to 1945; no conclusions were reached about what sort of U.S. military presence might be desirable in Japan beyond a transitional occupation period. The notion of a security treaty or alliance with Japan remained obscure at best. For its part, SWNCC was focused on a basic transformation of Japanese society, not the active use of Japan's geography or economy to proactively shape the regional balance of power. As the July 19, 1945, SWNCC directive on occupation policy for Japan instructed: "It is desirable, as a part of the function of military government in Japan, to undertake a program of reeducation and reorientation of the Japanese, designed to bring about a Japan which will cease to be a menace to international security."[189]

It would take the Korean War to shift American strategic thought toward making Japan the linchpin for regional containment. At the end of the Pacific war, it was perhaps bold enough that planners were seeking ways to keep Japan aligned with the United States and to prevent the resurgence of militarism and the opening of a strategic vacuum in the Pacific. The strategy certainly fit the circumstances known at the time.

Democratic Values and the Former Imperial Space

As impressive as U.S. planning was for Japan itself, the United States was caught almost completely unprepared to manage the former imperial space vacated by Japanese forces after Tokyo's surrender on August 15, 1945. Key decisions, such as the partition of the Korean Peninsula at the thirty-eighth parallel, were made in all-night sessions on August 10 and 11, in the last moments of the war, as U.S. military officers and State Department officials consulted small maps from *National Geographic* and raced to establish some "operable American occupation zones" before the Soviets swept too far south and the war came to an end.[190] A similar rushed and ill-informed decision-making process would characterize the decision to divide Vietnam at the sixteenth parallel, with Japanese forces north of that line surrendering to Chiang and those south of the line surrendering to British forces. The later results of this lack of planning in both Korea and Vietnam would be tragic.

One major problem for U.S. policy with respect to postwar planning was insufficient logistics and manpower. Even though 40 percent of all U.S. war materiel was going to the Pacific by 1945, much of that was used for shipping limited ground forces over vast distances, and there were far too few Allied soldiers and marines to replace every former Japanese imperial policeman and soldier in Asia.[191] As the war drew to an end, U.S. and Allied ground forces had only advanced as far as Okinawa and Burma, leaving huge expanses in between. At the end of the war, the United States was still a maritime power—dominant in the Pacific but with only weak purchase on the continent. It is doubtful that more U.S. resources to the Burma campaign or the landing of a few divisions in northern China would have changed that basic fact, even if it had been sound military strategy. Not surprisingly, the early Cold War tensions in Asia erupted in precisely this vast continental expanse from India to Manchuria.

Managing Japan's vacated imperial space also raised fundamental questions about American democratic values and the purpose of the war. The American public was not willing to defeat Japanese imperialism only to restore British, French, and Dutch imperialism in the areas recently occupied by Japan. Roosevelt thought he had sent this signal loud and clear in the Atlantic Charter in the summer of 1941. Had Churchill studied his counterpart more carefully, he would have understood that despite being an earlier advocate of paternalistic and quasi-imperialist policies over the Philippines while serving as assistant secretary of the navy (and as a student at Groton and Harvard), Roosevelt had undergone a conversion in the 1920s. In a July 1928 article in *Foreign Affairs*, for example, the future president repudiated imperialism and reminded his readers that Americans were "exceedingly jealous of our own sovereignty and it is only right we should respect similar feeling among other nations."[192] As president, Roosevelt had overseen the passage of the Tydings-McDuffie Act, granting full independence to the Philippines, and then stood proudly with President Manuel L. Quezon in November 1935 when his nation established itself as a constitutional democracy. Roosevelt believed that this Philippine precedent was the model that European states should follow in order to grant their former colonies self-rule after the war.[193] As Sumner Welles put it in a speech in May 1942, the war meant that "the era of imperialism is over."[194] Recognizing that he had misread the Atlantic Charter, Churchill tried to reassure Parliament that of course its call for self-determination would not apply to possessions of the Crown.[195] Not so, replied Roosevelt in a press conference in October 1942: "We have already made it perfectly clear that we believed that the Atlantic Charter applied to all humanity. I think that is a matter of record."[196]

Roosevelt was particularly adamant about extending the principles of the Atlantic Charter to Asia. This was a matter of grand strategy and not simply domestic politics or superficial morality. The United States was now engaged in an ideological war with Japan over what path of decolonization Asian states should pursue: one based on Japan's anti-Western East Asian Co-prosperity Sphere or one based on the kind of transition to democratic self-governance demonstrated in the Philippines. These issues had always been important to American statecraft toward Asia. In the nineteenth century, the ideational contrast with British imperialism had served American diplomacy well, and the vision of a community of self-governed republican states in the Pacific had appealed to Pacific-looking statesmen from Jefferson to Wilson. In Asia, however, Wilson had never followed through on the principle of self-determination promised in his Fourteen Points—in large part because the Germans had never posed an ideational threat to U.S. power in that region, and the other imperial powers in Asia, including Japan, were allies. In the Pacific war, however, the Japanese vision of pan-Asian solidarity against the West did resonate across parts of Asia, despite Japanese brutality, and therefore posed a real threat both to the war effort and to longer-term American leadership in Asia.

This threat was identified early in the war by American planners. When Roosevelt dispatched his personal advisor, Lauchlin Currie, to take the pulse in Asia, Currie reported back in alarm in August 1942 that in Asian eyes the United States was becoming identified with British imperialism.[197] Roosevelt subsequently asked his former rival for the presidency, Wendell Willkie, to tour Asia, denouncing imperialism and extolling the virtues of democracy and self-determination. Willkie loyally obliged, declaring in speeches at home and abroad that Asians were no longer willing to be "Eastern slaves for Western profits."[198] The Office of War Information also began to propagandize in Asia about the distinctions between the United States and its European allies with respect to decolonization.[199]

Within the State Department, the Advisory Committee on Post-war Foreign Problems recommended in August 1942 that "the United States should work toward the liberation of the Far East and that some form of international trusteeship should be established" for former European and Japanese colonies.[200] Meanwhile, State Department planners began work on a draft "Pacific Charter" to extend self-determination and democratic governance into Asia.[201] Initially, the JCS shared this view of the Pacific war as an ideological contest. As the JSSC reported to the JCS in May 1943 "an unsuccessful outcome, permitting a coalition under Japan's hegemony of the people of East Asia (about 55% of the world's population), would appear likely to offer, indeed, a greater ultimate threat to the United States than would a similar outcome in Europe."[202] Later, Office of Strategic Services (OSS) field reports from operatives in western Java in 1944 would warn that Japanese propaganda was emphasizing pan-Asian solidarity, nationalism, and "an anti-Western bias that bordered on sheer hatred."[203]

In September 1944, Hull sent a memorandum to Roosevelt arguing that it was time to send a consistent and clear position on the postwar status of the European colonies, with "early, dramatic, and concerted announcements . . . making definite commitments as to the future of the regions of Southeast Asia," including specific dates when independence or complete (dominion) self-rule will be accorded. "Failure of the Western powers to recognize the new conditions and forces in Southeast Asia and an attempt to reestablish pre-war conditions," he warned, "will almost surely lead to serious social and political conflict, and may lead to ultimate unifying of oriental opposition to the West."[204] Roosevelt was sympathetic, of course, but he had also instructed his administration to avoid distracting the Allies from the immediate task of war fighting by focusing too much on specific planning coordination for postwar policies. Instead, Roosevelt took it on himself to nudge Churchill toward decolonization, much to the chagrin of both the imperialist prime minister and the anti-imperialist secretary of state.

India was the earliest target for Roosevelt. Even before Pearl Harbor, the United States had established direct diplomatic representation with the governor-general in Calcutta and had insisted that Lend-Lease equipment be sent directly to the Indian government and not through the Colonial or War Offices in Whitehall.[205] Roosevelt first raised the idea of Indian independence with Churchill in Washington in December 1941, but—as Churchill recalled—"I reacted so strongly and at such length that he never raised it verbally again."[206] Roosevelt did return to the issue in writing, though, passing a letter to Churchill through Hopkins in March 1942, suggesting that India be given autonomy similar to the original U.S. Articles of Confederation.[207] When Churchill replied that the current intransigence of the Indian nationalists made this impossible, Roosevelt again wrote to warn that if Britain failed to grant greater autonomy and "India should subsequently be successfully invaded by Japan with attendant serious military or naval defeats for our side, the prejudicial reaction on American public opinion can hardly be over-estimated."[208] The president also sent career diplomat William Phillips to India in 1943 to meet with Mohandas Gandhi (Davies had already quietly met Gandhi on his way to take up his position with Stilwell in 1942). Phillips was refused access to the iconic independence leader but nevertheless pressed his British hosts to recognize growing Indian nationalism and grant independence.[209] Churchill was unmoved by these repeated entreaties by the Americans. His imperialism was as firmly entrenched as Roosevelt's republicanism. As the president quipped about Churchill's views on India to the press in off-the-record remarks upon his return from Yalta, "Yes, he is mid-Victorian on all things like that. . . . Dear old Winston will never learn on that point. He has made his specialty on that point. This is, of course, off the record."[210] The president would press Churchill until the Anglo-American alliance bent, but he would not let it break over Indian independence.

Indochina was an easier case for Roosevelt. The president had a strong dislike for the French, as did many Americans, because of the Vichy collaboration with the Axis powers and its responsibility for the first American casualties in North Africa.[211] Roosevelt's preference was for trusteeship and eventual independence for French Indochina based on the Philippine model, and he raised this idea frequently with the other wartime leaders.[212] However, even with respect to decolonization in French Indochina, the president refused to give specific guidance to the State and War Departments, prompting Hull's unsuccessful memo of September 1944 pleading for concrete decisions and milestones. By then, the tide had turned on the question of strategy toward the former European empires. Japan was no longer expanding in Asia—now it had to be dislodged, and Roosevelt needed the British to go on the offensive in Burma while the Americans fought in the Pacific. With the establishment of the British-led Southeast Asia Command (SEAC) at the Quebec Conference in September 1943 (dismissed by Americans in the CBI theater as the "Save England's Asian Colonies" command), London retook the initiative and ensured that French and Dutch imperial interests were protected.[213] The British and French also had a trump card in the planning for postwar occupation of Europe. As Hull ruefully noted in his memoirs, "we could not alienate them in the Pacific and expect to work with them in Europe."[214]

Thus, in negotiations over the new UN Charter at Dumbarton Oaks in 1944, the United States agreed that trusteeship would apply to the League of Nations mandates only and not former European colonies. Roosevelt confirmed this arrangement at Yalta, even though the president continued privately to view Indochina as a good candidate for trusteeship until the day he died.[215] As SWNCC concluded in its postwar guidance for policy toward the former colonies in Southeast Asia in May 1945:

> The Government of the United States should neither oppose the restoration of Indo-China to France, with or without a program of international accountability, nor take any action toward French overseas possessions which it is not prepared to take or suggest with regard to the colonial possessions of our other Allies. . . . The Government of the United States should continue to exert its influence with the French in the direction of having them effect a liberalization of their past policy of limited opportunities for native participation in government and administration, as well as a liberalization of restrictive French economic policies formerly pursued in Indo-China.[216]

It was a nonstrategy that would eventually lead to a colossal tragedy.

Japan's original colonies of Korea and Formosa were not to be treated the same as French and British colonies, of course. At Cairo, Roosevelt promised to return Formosa to China, and the island eventually became the refuge for Chiang and the Nationalists after the victory of Mao and the CCP in 1949. Korea, it was generally agreed at Potsdam, would be jointly occupied in anticipation of eventual trusteeship—as promised at Cairo[217]—and presumably (from the American perspective) democratic elections and self-determination. The Soviet invasion of Manchuria forced what then lieutenant colonel and future assistant secretary of state for East Asia Dean Rusk called his "ten-second extemporaneous decision" to divide Korea at the thirty-eighth parallel before notifying the War Department's Joint War Plans Committee.[218] With Soviet forces past the Yalu and Tumen Rivers, the Americans were pleasantly surprised to find that Stalin agreed to halt his occupation at the thirty-eighth parallel. Nevertheless, postwar planning for Korea had taken little account of exactly when or how the Korean people would establish democratic institutions and self-rule. It is revealing that in the vast SWNCC files there are no folders pertaining to Korea. Indeed, it is a remarkable omission given Korea's history as the "cockpit" of Asia and the central role the peninsula would soon play in the Cold War.

The gap between initial rhetoric and eventual policy on democracy and self-determination in Asia has led some historians to decry American hypocrisy during the war. As Herring puts it, "despite the rhetoric of republicanism, U.S. wartime policies actually strengthened dictatorships and heightened oppression in many countries."[219] However, Asia was exceptional in important respects. The United States had set a historic precedent with decolonization in the Philippines and recognized that Japan's pan-Asian ideology was a real ideational threat that had to be countered. The United States did push to implement the freedoms articulated in the Atlantic Charter, and there was considerable friction with Britain, not to mention the other European powers, as a result. Yet, as Davies observed in a strategy memo in late 1943, the United States "more or less committed to certain vague political and economic principles enunciated in the Atlantic Charter and 'Four Freedoms.' But this policy had never appeared to override the purely military strategy of defeating the Axis. One political policy, however, seemed to have prevailed over military strategy and that was maintenance of Britain as a major power."[220]

One hundred years after Caleb Cushing and John Quincy Adams offered clashing visions during the Opium War of an America that stood
by self-determination in Asia versus an America that upheld the British-
led international order, there was still no resolution of the tensions inherent in what Mahan called the "moral influence" of the United States
in the region.

TRADE AND ECONOMIC STRATEGY

The Roosevelt administration entered the Second World War haunted by
memories of the Great Depression and determined to prevent trade barriers and economic blocs from ever undermining international peace
again. The Atlantic Charter had stated that all states "great or small, victor or vanquished" would have "access, on equal terms, to the trade and
the raw materials of the world which are needed for their economic prosperity."[221] Wilson's Fourteen Points had also called for free trade, but had
gone nowhere. In contrast to policies on decolonization, Roosevelt and
his administration were determined not to wait for postwar peace negotiations to begin putting free trade into effect. "Thus," explains economic
historian Alfred Eckes, "six months after the United States became a co-
belligerent, this country had indicated its intention to create a new world
economic order based on the principles of an efficient distribution of
international labor, convertible currencies, and maximum utilization
of human and physical resources."[222]

Conventional historiography states that the United States committed
itself to open multilateral trade during the Second World War in order to
prevent economic blocs from returning the world to a state of conflict. In
contrast, revisionists from the Wisconsin School have argued that multilateral trade and financial institutions established during the war were
the culmination of a strategy of economic imperialism that began with
the Open Door.[223] Ultimately, the strategy of breaking down trade barriers and "unclogging the lifeblood of a free society"—as Roosevelt put it
in 1944 to the Bretton Woods Conference[224]—was desirable from multiple perspectives. As a State Department committee on postwar trade
planning put it in late 1943, restoration of world trade would be essential
"to the attainment of full and effective employment in the United States
and elsewhere, to the preservation of private enterprise, and to the
success of an international security system to prevent future wars."[225]

Dismantlement of preferential trading blocs, in short, brought together Wilsonian idealists, New Dealers concerned with full employment, great-power realists seeking American supremacy, and economic nationalists seeking relative gains for U.S. firms over their heretofore protected European competitors.[226] This convergence of idealism and the interests of the nation, firm, and worker would create in Congress the consensus necessary to overcome generations of protectionist impulses.

As with the emphasis on self-determination, Churchill soon discovered that the open economic liberalism espoused in the Atlantic Charter was aimed in part at the British Empire. In fact, the original draft of the Atlantic Charter included a clause proposed by the American side that pledged nondiscriminatory trading practices by the Commonwealth countries. Churchill objected, and Roosevelt agreed that the charter did not imply "formal and immediate obligation on the part of the British" to abrogate preferential arrangements with the dominions. Yet the Americans subsequently began to demand exactly that.[227] Hull and Morgenthau insisted, for example, that U.S.-led postwar economic stabilization plans be negotiated separately with each of the British dominions as independent countries.[228] The U.S. side also included provisions in the Lend-Lease agreements for the elimination of cartels and commodity arrangements (Article VII), which the British were later told were due as "policy" payment in lieu of interest on the American loans.[229] When several British cabinet members and senior officials (including John Maynard Keynes, who was Acheson's counterpart for the negotiations) balked at ending exclusive arrangements with the dominions, Roosevelt personally lobbied Churchill at Yalta to implement Article VII.[230]

All of this caused great consternation in political quarters in Australia and New Zealand, where the ruling Labor Party had stood for full employment based on precisely the cartels and protectionism the Americans were breaking apart.[231] Americans also began to view India as a market that could be weaned from the British imperial system after the war. As prominent India scholar Kate Mitchell wrote in *Far Eastern Survey* on June 6, 1945, Americans were keen to work with a new breed of industrialists, such as Jehangir Ratanji Dadabhoy Tata, something she warned would not be possible as long as India's "economic development is controlled and suited to fit the needs of British industry and finance exclusively."[232] The United States was now a major economic power in Southeast Asia, presaging a transition in economic primacy from Great Britain across all Asia, to include India, Australia, and New Zealand.[233]

As Hull worked at breaking apart trading blocs and preferential arrangements, Henry Morgenthau and the Treasury Department worked to ensure that the establishment of a new postwar international financial architecture "placed Washington in a position to control exchange rates and the circulating medium."[234] The United States had enormous financial leverage over all the Allies, and Morgenthau sought an approach that would give the British enough liquidity to recover from the war without allowing London to return the pound sterling to its prewar hegemonic status based on the imperial trading preferences the United States was now unraveling. The British were not in a strong position to demand anything more than that of Washington. The future of financial architecture now meant that states in the system would be conducting their trade not in pounds sterling but in dollars.[235]

The debate between the United States and Britain over the future international economic order begun with the Atlantic Charter and the Lend-Lease negotiations climaxed in the summer of 1944 when representatives of forty-four nations gathered at the stunning Mount Washington Resort at Bretton Woods in New Hampshire to establish the International Monetary Fund and the International Bank for Reconstruction and Development (which later expanded to become what is today the World Bank Group). Richard Gardner describes the Anglo-American tensions regarding the future world economic order in this way:

> The British appeared to regard the International Monetary Fund as an automatic source of credit; the Americans seemed to consider it as a conditional provider of financial aid. The British emphasized their freedom to maintain equilibrium by depreciation and exchange control, placing on creditor countries the main burden of adjustment; the Americans looked forward to the early achievement of free and stable exchanges, specifically rejecting the suggestion of any one-sided responsibility on the United States. Most disquieting of all, the British considered their adherence to multilateral principles contingent upon bold new measures of transitional aid; the Americans claimed that the Bretton Woods institutions would meet Britain's post-war needs and that no additional measures would be required. Without a meeting of minds on these matters, it was hard to see how the two institutions could be made to work.[236]

And yet the United States and Britain made certain that these institutions did work. The British did not have enough leverage to achieve the outcomes they wanted, and the United States needed to retain British power too much to force the British economy to the mat. Both saw the longer-term importance in terms of geopolitical stability. The agreements reached at Bretton Woods thus underpinned the greatest boom in trade and investment the world had ever seen. And free trade would prove critical to American strategic preeminence in Asia and the Pacific, precisely as Mahan had foreseen a half-century earlier.

The multilateral economic liberalism of Bretton Woods was perhaps the most prescient and influential piece of statecraft the United States achieved during the war. It was made possible because military *and* economic triumph in the war had submerged the tensions inherent between the pursuit of relative gains and the strategic influence and growth derived from free trade. As economic competition grew from within Asia a generation later, those tensions would reemerge.

Conclusion: The War as Crucible

Faced with the prospect of a hostile new order in the Far East, the United States finally confronted Japan, was attacked, and then prevailed. Victory was due first and foremost to the soldiers, sailors, airmen, marines, and coasties (members of the U.S. Coast Guard) who fought in the air, on sea, on small pillbox-strewn islands, and in rugged jungle terrain—together with the Filipinos, Australian "Diggers," New Zealand "Kiwis," and other Commonwealth forces who fought alongside them. It must also be remembered that Chinese forces and civilians paid an enormous price tying down a million Japanese troops for over eight years, whatever the shortcomings in Chiang's organization and operations.[237]

As commander in chief, Roosevelt excelled in the most important tasks before him: mobilizing the American people and holding together a broad international coalition until the Axis powers were vanquished. At sea, Nimitz innovated and outthought his Japanese counterparts, buying time for the navy and USAAF to rebuild, overwhelm the Japanese fleet, and then choke off their home islands. On land, MacArthur compensated for tactical dereliction in defense of the Philippines by mounting a series of brilliant amphibious assaults up from Australia to liberate the archipelago.

The price paid for prewar mistakes was high, though. Inconsistent swings between Japan and China, self-defeating protectionism, and the failure to build the fleet up to Washington Treaty levels all combined to increase Japanese hostility and weaken deterrence at the same time. The U.S. fleet did not return to parity with Japan until 1943, and then dislodging Japanese forces from the Pacific cost over 60,000 lives, with army and marine units suffering an average of 7.45 casualties (dead, wounded, and missing) per 1,000 combatants committed *per day* compared with 2.16 for the European theater.[238]

A price was also paid in the postwar period for mistakes made in the grand strategy that guided the conduct of the war. By the standards of Bismarck, Liddell Hart, and Morison, the United States won much of the peace it sought to establish through war but also left dangerous legacies. These were generally in the seams that had always perplexed American strategic approaches to the region.

The Europe first strategy caused the United States to midwife a reintroduction of Western imperialism into Southeast Asia that undercut the American ideational victory and opened the area to a new ideological threat from Soviet communism. The American forward defensive line was unalterably defined forward in the Western Pacific but was no more fixed in 1945 than it had been after victory in 1898. Island stepping stones in the Pacific had to be occupied, but that was less clear with respect to Japan itself, let alone Korea or Southeast Asia, until a new Eurasian threat prompted the United States to redefine the defensive line even farther forward onto the continent. China and Japan also remained unfixed in the longer-term strategy. Roosevelt was determined to ensure that in the future U.S. policy would always favor China rather than Japan, yet confidence in China and in the American ability to affect outcomes on the continent waned throughout the war while understanding of Japan's future geopolitical importance grew. With China diminished, Roosevelt's concept of balancing Russia while pursuing collective security arrangements with Moscow made ever less sense; yet he never changed his approach to Stalin, and initially neither could Truman. As the Soviets took advantage of their new perch and China fell to communism, the Europeans proved a weak reed to hold together the twice-liberated (once by the Japanese and once by the Allies) Southeast Asians. Key officials and diplomats such as Forrestal and Davies saw the growing contradictions in Roosevelt's initial strategic concepts and warned of the potential for such developments, but their observations did not change the thrust of U.S. policy.

Despite these inconsistencies, however, the bottom line is that the American people were ultimately willing to fight to ensure that the Pacific remained a conduit for trade and ideas flowing west and not threats flowing east. They harnessed all the instruments of national power to that purpose. Some of these instruments, such as the economic diplomacy of Lend-Lease and Bretton Woods, would underpin longer-term U.S. strategic influence and stability in the region for decades.

In addition, the American people broadened their definition of Asia considerably. During the war, American troops had served everywhere from the Himalayas to the South Pacific. The Indian subcontinent and the Indian Ocean had now entered the American strategic mental map. Southeast Asia and the Korean Peninsula occupied a more prominent if still somewhat ill-defined position. Australia and New Zealand now looked to the United States for security, and U.S. strategic planners in turn saw Australia as an indispensable southern pillar to forward presence and stability in the region.

Moreover, the war introduced a new currency to international security—nuclear weapons. Although the use of the atomic bomb had provided the war-ending strategy that had eluded War Plan Orange and thus spared Japan and the Allies the large-scale horror of an invasion of the home islands (though the horror of the atomic bombings themselves should never be forgotten), it also forced an entirely new template on thinking about strategy toward the region. Nuclear umbrellas, deterrence, nonproliferation, and counterproliferation would henceforth have to be part of the thinking about regional order and stability and would further link regional developments to global security. When asked by a reporter if he thought the atomic bomb would revolutionize warfare, Leahy answered that it would not, since defensive weapons were always designed to counter the latest weapons.[239] He could not have been more wrong.

Finally, for the first time, the war created a class of professional strategists in the United States. Henceforth there would be more cogs in the machine. The days of a handful of men like John Quincy Adams, Mahan, or Lamont defining America's approach to Asia were over. But many of the issues of geography, power, and values that they had wrestled with were not.

The Cold War (1955)

Aleutian Is.
Attu Is.

Sea of Okhotsk

Beijing

US-Japan Treaty of Mutual
Security (September 8, 1951)

Mutual Defense Treaty Between
the United States and
the Republic of Korea
(1953)

Shanghai

Tokyo

Okinawa

Sino-American Mutual Defense Treaty,
(December 2, 1955)

Hong Kong
Hanoi

Taiwan (ROC)

Pacific Ocean

Manila Pact
(1954)

US-Philippine Mutual
Defense Treaty
(August 30, 1951)

Guam

Malaya
Singapore

Jakarta

ANZUS Treaty
(September 1, 1950)

PART THREE

THE RISE OF THE SOVIETS

President Lyndon Baines Johnson sat hunched over in his chair at lunch in the Cabinet Room of the White House surveying the fourteen men arrayed before him. It was noon on March 26, 1968, and these were the "Wise Men"—veteran foreign policymakers of the Roosevelt, Truman, and Kennedy administrations who had first assembled in July 1965, and again in November 1967, to advise Johnson on the war in Vietnam. Sitting across from the president was former secretary of state Dean Acheson, his clipped mustache and Grenadier Guard appearance a stark contrast to the former Texas schoolteacher slouching in the head chair. Under Acheson, in the early 1950s the State Department had designed the architecture of bilateral alliances that ensured postwar American dominance of the Pacific. But it was also on Acheson's watch that China had fallen to communism and that North Korea had attacked the South in the wake of the secretary's famous announcement that the United States would draw a "defense perimeter" to protect Japan and the offshore islands—pointedly leaving out the vulnerable Korean Peninsula. A dignified man who before the war had actively campaigned for intervention in Europe to stop Hitler, Acheson was still wounded by the repeated Republican charges that he had been soft on communism. In part because of that experience, he had been a stalwart on Vietnam and had led the Wise Men in urging Johnson to stay the course when the group assembled in November the year before.

This time, however, Acheson's demeanor was grave. Secretary of State Dean Rusk had already reported to the president that his dinner with the group the night before had not gone well. Two months earlier, the North Vietnamese had violated the Tet New Year cease-fire and struck up and down Vietnam, including the U.S. embassy compound, where the ambassador and his staff had just held a "Light at the End of the Tunnel" party to celebrate progress in the war. Though U.S. forces eventually decimated the attacking Vietcong and regular North Vietnamese Army units in pitched battles that favored American firepower, the American public was nevertheless stunned by the audacity of the North Vietnamese offensive. It now appeared that the war would grind on for five or ten years more, Assistant Secretary of State for East Asia and Pacific Affairs Phil Habib had told the Wise Men at dinner with Rusk. Worse, the group learned from Pentagon briefers that General William Westmoreland had requested over 200,000 additional troops, which would mean calling up the reserves and spending billions of dollars more on the war.

As lunch was served, former national security advisor McGeorge Bundy opened by warning the president that there had been a major shift in the group's view of the war since the last time they met. Then Acheson delivered the bottom line. "Mr. President," he began, "we can no longer do the job we set out to do in the time we have left, and we must begin to take steps to disengage." When General Earle Wheeler, the chairman of the Joint Chiefs, intervened to argue that U.S. objectives should not be measured in terms of military progress, Acheson turned on him and asked in frustration, "Then what in the name of God are five hundred thousand men out there doing—chasing girls?" As the discussion continued, it was clear that only three of the Wise Men stood with Wheeler and the Joint Chiefs; the rest wanted to find a way out of Vietnam.

From where the president sat, he could see rising above his guests a series of painted wall murals depicting great military victories from the American Revolution. The image was incongruous with the depressing debate going on around the table. Just two decades earlier, the United States had achieved the greatest military triumph in its history, emerging from the Second World War unrivalled in the Pacific and promising to lead a new era of democratic peace and open economic prosperity. At that point, Indochina had been a sideshow—a peripheral theater of U.S. interests at best when compared with Japan or Western Europe. Yet here a small revolutionary regime fighting in the name of self-determination had humbled the champion of democracy and the mightiest military and economic power in the world.

How had it come to this? And how would the United States recover its position in Asia?[1]

7. "THE OVERALL EFFECT IS TO ENLARGE OUR STRATEGIC FRONTIER"
DEFINING CONTAINMENT IN THE PACIFIC, 1945–1960

Part 3 of this volume covers the evolution of American strategy toward Asia and the Pacific through the Cold War. In the course of those five decades, the United States suffered its greatest humiliation in Asia with the Vietnam War yet sustained a network of bilateral alliances that eventually helped force the demise of the Soviet empire. This was also the beginning of an era in which the United States for the first time defined preeminence in Asia as a core strategic interest—not as an end in itself but as the only reliable means to ensure that never again would a threatening hegemon emerge in the region. With the exception of Vietnam, American strategy aimed to preserve that preeminence as cheaply as possible. Truman initially relied on the collapsing collective security vision he had inherited from Roosevelt after Yalta, and he subsequently defined the American defensive perimeter safely offshore when China fell to communism. After the North Korean invasion of the South in June 1950, the United States expanded that defensive perimeter forward and negotiated the first of a series of bilateral security treaties to include Japan, Australia/ New Zealand, and the Philippines and later Korea and Taiwan. President Dwight D. Eisenhower then sought to reduce the risk and expense of American commitments in Asia by supplementing those bilateral treaties

with nuclear weapons and with a multilateral security arrangement—
the Southeast Asian Treaty Organization (SEATO)—to contain the
newest threat emerging on the mainland in Indochina.

Chapter 7 ends with U.S. containment strategy in Asia hanging on that
precarious multilateral arrangement. Chapter 8 then accounts for the
American failures in Vietnam—failures that ironically were the result of
poor Asia strategy, despite the fact that the war was ostensibly fought to
save Asia from communism. Chapter 9 assesses Richard Nixon's brilliant
but politically costly restoration of American credibility with the opening to China. Chapter 10 explores Jimmy Carter's desperate attempt to resurrect the China card as Moscow resumed expansion. Finally, Chapter 11
finishes the discussion of Cold War strategies in Asia by examining Ronald Reagan's unrelenting commitment to advancing free trade, democratic values, and a strong navy until Soviet expansion was permanently
reversed in the Pacific.

With each of these evolutions in containment strategy toward the region, the familiar tensions and pendulum swings in American statecraft
emerged. Throughout this period, the preservation of a free Europe remained the highest priority for Washington, and resource allocation to
NATO shaped strategic planning for the Pacific at every turn. Japan constituted the center of U.S. Asia strategy for the first two decades of the
Cold War, succeeded by China as Nixon and Carter sought to counterbalance the Soviets; and then Japan took center stage again as Reagan
instituted a new maritime strategy to roll back Soviet expansion. The
forward defensive line was explicitly drawn offshore after the war, then
extended to Korea and Indochina in response to communist attacks, and
then drawn offshore again (except for Korea) by Nixon in 1969, until finally Reagan used the offshore island chain as a base for pressing the
Soviets' own bastion on the continent. Democratic values also waxed and
waned as a priority. They were a centerpiece of the foreign policy strategies
of John F. Kennedy and Ronald Reagan; were secondary considerations for
Eisenhower and Nixon in the wake of Korea and Vietnam; and were for
Jimmy Carter a wildcard that never fit in with his foreign policy strategy at
all. All these administrations championed free trade but increasingly
found that particular pillar of American internationalism under siege
at home as East Asian economies began to succeed exactly as the early
postwar planners intended.

These same tensions were evident as President Johnson met with the
surviving Wise Men in the White House in March 1968. Enormous dis-

tortions had crept into American policy toward Vietnam: a geostrategi-
cally insignificant state on the continent was absorbing the bulk of American strategic assets and attention; American military escalation was
marginalizing the ability of an already shaky South Vietnamese regime
to stand alone; and American foreign policy appeared to be aligned with
a status quo establishment against forces of change and self-determination.
This was hardly the position the veteran foreign policy hands around the
table expected to find themselves in as they dealt with the chaos and
opportunity in the Pacific after the surrender of Japan twenty-two years
earlier.

The Wise Men and Asia

The architects of American Cold War strategy in Asia emerged from the
Second World War with one foot still planted in the 1930s. In Washington, the State Department was just moving from the Old Executive
Office Building to Foggy Bottom, and the White House Situation Room
did not yet exist. The foreign policy elite frequently saw one another at
the Metropolitan Club or on the newly fashionable Georgetown dinner
circuit.[1] Many were protégés of MacMurray, Hornbeck, Stimson, or Stilwell and were as connected to that world of tweed and khaki as they were
to the national security state that would begin to transform Washington
within a decade. After the cauldron of the Second World War, they were
certain of American righteousness and the indispensability of American
leadership, but the world they would encounter did not conform to the
expectations they had developed during the war.

As the pieces of the Yalta puzzle came undone, the American foreign
policy elite struggled to rebuild the foundations of a new American-led
order in the Pacific. They agreed on certain principles even as the Asian
theater changed before them: that Europe must remain the central front
in the emerging competition with Moscow, since the loss of the industrialized Old World would leave the United States perpetually vulnerable;
that, in the Pacific, the highest priority would be securing Japan and the
offshore island chain; and that although every effort must be made to keep
China whole, the United States would not risk a land war on the continent.
On these points, there was little dissent. However, on the specific nature of
the Soviet threat and on the questions of whether to embrace or confront
a communist China, how far to rehabilitate Japan, how quickly to get out

of Korea, and whether to support decolonization in Southeast Asia, there were profound disagreements.

The commander in chief, Harry S. Truman, was not the cosmopolitan intellectual that Roosevelt had been, particularly with respect to understanding of the Pacific. Whereas Roosevelt had devoured the collected works of Mahan before graduating from high school, Harry Truman had summarized his worldview in Missouri at the age of twenty-seven by saying, "one man is just as good as another, so long as he's honest and decent and not a nigger or a Chinaman."[2] Yet historians have been wrong when they attributed the postwar confrontation with Moscow to the difference between Truman's homespun and racially tinged realism and his predecessor's neo-Wilsonian idealism. Like Roosevelt, Truman believed in collective security, proposing in 1946 that the United Nations become the custodian of U.S. nuclear weapons and taking North Korean aggression first to the United Nations in June 1950.[3] Truman's personal qualities favoring firmness, clarity, and confrontation, explains historian Waldo Heinrichs, only "reinforced the Rooseveltian inclination toward containment."[4] They did not represent a significant departure.

Truman both constrained and empowered those who made his foreign policy in dealing with the challenges in Asia and the Pacific. Despite his firmness with Moscow, he pushed for dramatic cuts in defense spending, insisting on a balanced budget (hard to believe today) and a shift of resources to his domestic agenda. On the other hand, he did not seek to manage foreign policy himself. Excluded from FDR's foreign policy decision-making as vice president and suspicious of his predecessor's use of personal envoys, Truman returned the management of diplomacy to the State Department. Even the landmark 1947 National Security Act, which created a cabinet-level civilian secretary of defense, institutionalized the wartime JCS, and established the National Security Council (NSC) and the Central Intelligence Agency (CIA), initially had the effect of further empowering Truman's secretaries of state as the postwar vicars of American foreign policy.[5]

Truman's secretaries of state brought strong worldviews, though not particularly on Asia. His first secretary, South Carolinian Jimmy Byrnes, never formed a coherent foreign policy strategy to compete with the powerful Joint Chiefs. That changed in 1947 with the appointment of iconic former army chief of staff George C. Marshall. Marshall's most important legacy, however, was the reconstruction plan for Europe that bears his name. He had served briefly as Truman's special envoy on

China, an experience that soured him on entanglements on the Asian continent and reinforced his view that controlling the Western Pacific was sufficient to protect vital American interests.[6]

Marshall's undersecretary and successor (in 1949), Dean Acheson, was the progeny of Canadian immigrants who flew the Union Jack and celebrated Queen Victoria's birthday in his childhood. He combined a deep belief in the order provided by the British Empire before the war and the liberal values the United States offered to sustain that order as British power declined after the war.[7] He began as a defender of Yalta while undersecretary, but with the mounting crisis in Europe in 1947–1948, he embraced a more assertive defense of the free world against communist expansion. However, Acheson had no firsthand experience with Asia, and despite his abstract belief in the principles of democracy and self-determination, he instinctively sided with the Europeans on the tough questions of decolonization in Asia in the early postwar years, to the exasperation of the State Department Asia hands. As Warren Cohen notes, "He allowed them only symbolic acts, shows of concern—nothing that required major commitment of American resources or power."[8] With the Korean War, he would begin to impart real "purpose, direction and meaning" to Truman's Asia policy, but before that he sought, like Marshall, to maintain control over the Pacific and keep the focus on Europe rather than continental Asia.[9]

Inevitably, the secretaries and the president depended heavily on their directors (after 1949, "assistant secretaries") for Far Eastern affairs. When Acheson assumed the post of undersecretary in August 1945, he pushed out the conservatives who had dominated Asia policy under his predecessor, Joseph Grew (a man Acheson dismissed as the "Prince of Appeasers" for his prewar views of Japan),[10] and replaced them with New Deal Wilsonian reformers from the China service like John Carter Vincent. Vincent was a firm believer in decolonization, reform, and neutralization of Japan, and disengagement from Chiang's forces in China—positions that put him at odds with the European Affairs office (which still controlled much of U.S. policy toward Southeast Asia) and the conservative anticommunists who wanted to support Chiang and rearm Japan.[11] Eventually, Acheson's own liberal, Yalta-based views gave way to a sterner anticommunism, and the soft-spoken Southerner became a political liability. Playing it safe, Acheson replaced Vincent in September 1949 with the Europeanist and Marshall protégé W. William Butterworth, whose greatest asset was that he had no track record on Asia policy that would draw congressional criticism. Butterworth's short tenure ended just before the Korean War, when conservative pressures from Congress in the wake of the loss of China led Acheson to appoint Dean Rusk as assistant secretary. Rusk, the colonel who had arbitrarily drawn the line at the thirty-eighth parallel on the Korean Peninsula before Potsdam, was a rags-to-riches Georgian who believed in America's mission to help the defenseless and hold the line against communism in Asia.[12] His reliably consistent Manichean worldview would align perfectly with Truman and Acheson, and later with Kennedy and Johnson, whom he served as secretary of state.

In the early postwar years, Marshall and Acheson also turned to George Frost Kennan, director of the new Office of Policy Planning at the State Department from 1947 through 1949, and the author of the famous February 1946 "long telegram" from Moscow and July 1946 "Mr. X" article describing Soviet behavior in Foreign Affairs.[13] Kennan had "a knack for seeing relationships between objectives and capabilities, aspirations and interests, long-term and short-term priorities," as Gaddis put it, and he steadily imposed that same discipline on strategic thinking about Asia and the Pacific.[14] A realist who focused on scaling American ambitions to American means, Kennan never accepted Truman's rhetorical commitment before Congress in March 1947 to "support free people wherever freedom was under attack," arguing in Asia that the United States should dispense with the idea of democratization in Japan and the island world generally.[15] For Kennan, the focus of U.S. strategy should be defending the strong points—what he called the "workshops"—of industrialized Western Europe and Japan. Everything else flowed from that objective.[16]

Kennan's combination of minimalism and offshore balancing drew on two contradictory traditions in American strategic thinking toward Asia and the Pacific. On the one hand, he took inspiration from MacMurray's 1935 memorandum advocating a withdrawal from the Western Pacific rather than risk war with Japan. A generation behind MacMurray in the Foreign Service, Kennan wrote to the aging diplomat in December 1950 that he knew of "no document on record in our government with respect to foreign policy which is more penetrating and thoughtful and prescient. . . . It has done a great deal to clarify my own thinking on Far Eastern problems."[17] On the other hand, Kennan's focus on denial of the offshore island chain and control of sea lanes was quintessentially Mahanian, and he was not about to advocate abandoning the Western Pacific as MacMurray once had.

Kennan's instincts for realism, minimizing risk on the continent, and ensuring maritime dominance were further reinforced by his top Asia advisor on the Policy Planning staff, John Paton Davies, who had come with him from Moscow to Policy Planning. Kennan attributed "whatever insight I was able to muster in those years into the nature of Soviet policies toward the Far East" to Davies, who in many ways was the "shadow warrior" of strategic thinking toward the region in the Truman years.[18] Davies coined for Kennan a rhetorical question that Acheson would repeat: "Strategically, is China a springboard or a morass?"[19] The influence of Kennan and Davies on overall U.S. foreign policy strategy waned under Acheson, who favored a more muscular response to the Soviets in Europe, but on Asia the two realists would exert a considerable influence through the first part of the Korean War.

At the other end of the spectrum from liberal New Dealers like Vincent, but notably more willing to accept risk in the defense of U.S. interests in Asia than Kennan, was Truman's secretary of the navy and then first secretary of defense, the scrappy, pug-nosed Irishman from New York, James Vincent Forrestal. Forrestal had been a "Pacific-Firster" during the war and an early convert to Grew's strategy of working with Japan after the war in order to maintain a favorable balance of power against the Soviet Union. In contrast to Acheson, Kennan, Vincent, and most in the State Department, Forrestal believed that Moscow's expansion was driven primarily by relentless ideology, which had to be stopped, rather than by great-power politics, which had to be managed.[20] He also disagreed with the assumption that dominance of continental Asia by communist forces would pose no threat to the American maritime position.[21] Consequently, in his view, stronger defense budgets, support for Nationalists in China, and the rehabilitation of Japan were keys to balancing against the Soviets in the region. Though a skilled bureaucratic operative (he bested Admiral King in 1942 for control of ship production), and despite general support from the JCS, Forrestal lost almost every one of these postwar debates before leaving office in March 1949. Nevertheless, his views resonated with conservative Republicans in Congress and with incoming policy planners such as Paul H. Nitze, who would lend a harder edge to containment strategy after Korea—not to mention with his own son Michael Forrestal, who would become a key player on the NSC staff during the Vietnam War.

The intellectual influence of the Wise Men was enormous, but the debates about containment in Asia destroyed many of them. After battling in vain for stronger defense budgets and a more active deterrence in Asia, Forrestal was fired in 1949 for colluding with Republicans to stay in power if Truman lost reelection. He then leapt to his death from the sixteenth floor of Bethesda Naval Hospital, where he was convalescing from intense mental stress.[22] On the other side of the debate, Vincent and Davies were marginalized within the State Department for alleged sympathies toward Mao and were eventually purged in the McCarthy Red Scares of the early 1950s. Davies, the finest strategic thinker on Asia produced by the Foreign Service up to that point, would spend the critical years before Vietnam selling furniture in Peru (despite having powerful friends like Dean Rusk and Averell Harriman, his name was not formally cleared until the end of the Johnson administration). Kennan would retire to a prestigious post at Princeton University and win accolades in academia (and two more ambassadorships), but he ended his career appalled at the continued U.S. military presence in Japan and the escalation in Vietnam, distortions of the lower-risk containment strategy he had tried to leave as his legacy. Acheson would remain an icon in Democratic Party ranks, the dean of the Wise Men, but be personally scarred by the McCarthy era and the loss of China.[23]

A young Harvard professor named Henry Kissinger wrote in 1955 that "the United States could ill afford another decade of poor statecraft like that since 1945."[24] Yet it was amid the ashes and uncertainty of postwar Asia that these same men built the institutions and alliances that have in fact preserved American preeminence for over seven decades.

It just did not seem that way as orderly plans for Asia gave way to chaos in the years after Japan surrendered.

THE SEARCH FOR STRATEGY BEFORE THE COLD WAR TURNED HOT, 1945–1950

On August 15, 1945, the United States stood supreme. The three totalitarian foes, Germany, Italy, and Japan, had surrendered unconditionally; the American economy was larger than the rest of the world's economies combined; the American homeland was virtually unscathed; and the United States alone had the atomic bomb.

In Asia, General Douglas A. MacArthur would have a free hand running the occupation of Japan, and the United States would secure its dominant maritime position through a combination of bases on the off-shore island chains and the denial of island bases or power projection to potential adversaries. Building on understandings at Yalta and Potsdam, U.S. leaders expected that a unified China would fill the vacuum that had drawn in great-power competition in Asia for a century and that China would thus serve as a regional counterweight to Soviet power in the Far East. The former European and Japanese imperial spaces were supposed to ease toward self-determination under United Nations trusteeships, with transitional security provided by the European powers in Southeast Asia—and by the United States in the southern half of the Korean Peninsula and the Philippines. Japan's pursuit of an autarkic trading bloc and European imperial preferences were both finished, and the European colonies and dominions would now be folded into the new open trading system agreed to at Bretton Woods. Despite troubling developments in Soviet behavior in Eastern Europe, a new collective security order through the United Nations still seemed possible. "America must dominate the Pacific," Admiral King had declared during the war, and so it seemed that America would. Superficially, the conditions appeared ripe for headlong demobilization, and U.S. forces were reduced from 12 million troops to 3 million in July 1946 and then to 1.6 million in 1947.[25]

In fact, however, a stable order in the Far East proved far more elusive than postwar planners had anticipated. As historian Ronald Spector explains, "On the mainland of Asia, in the vast arc of countries and territories stretching from Manchuria to Burma, peace was at best a brief interlude."[26] Russia now enjoyed an unprecedented position in the region thanks to concessions made at Yalta and the collapse of traditional foe Japan. Rather than serving as a centerpiece for stability, China went from civil war to unification under a hostile communist force aligned with Moscow. Deprived of raw materials from its former colonies and shaken by revolution on the mainland, Japan, and with it the entire off-shore island chain, appeared vulnerable to intimidation from the communist camp. In contrast to Europe, where the confrontation between Stalin and the West would come primarily at the seams of both sides' respective zones of influence and competition, continental Asia—from India to Indochina—offered vast territories and a billion people to the victors in the new struggle between democracy and communism. A strategy premised on a stable and unified China, collective security, a neutralized Japan, and limited offshore balancing would not hold.

"Who Are We Neutral Against?":
The "Loss of China"

In August 1945, Roosevelt's vision of shifting China from being the locus
of Asian rivalry into a net exporter of security still seemed vaguely promising to many Americans. Stalin maintained his commitment to recognize Chiang's Nationalist government and did not object (though Foreign
Minister Molotov expressed concern) when U.S. Marines of the Third
Amphibious Corps landed at Tianjin and Qingdao to expedite the surrender of Japanese forces to the Nationalists. Undercut by U.S.-Soviet cooperation, a bewildered Mao Zedong concluded that he had little choice
in the near term except to fly to Chongqing (formerly Chungking) for
talks with Chiang Kai-shek that same month.[27] The possibility of a
brokered peace between Communist and Nationalist forces seemed at
hand, and with that the stability in the heart of continental Asia sought
by Americans since the time of Humphrey Marshall in the mid-nineteenth
century.

However, these superficially promising trends did not hold up under
closer scrutiny. On August 20, 1945, Truman's personal representative over-
seeing U.S. aid to China, Edwin Locke, Jr., sent a memorandum to Washington warning that despite Stalin's nominal support of the Nationalist
government, a civil war was looming in which Moscow would support
Mao and the United States could be drawn into direct conflict with the
Soviet Union because of its support for Chiang. Better, cautioned Locke,
to cut all Lend-Lease aid to the Nationalists now and avoid that combus-
tible scenario.[28] At the State Department, John Carter Vincent grabbed
Locke's recommendation and succeeded in cutting the size of the proposed U.S. military assistance group for Chiang's forces from 4,000 to
900 personnel and in limiting the marines' rules of engagement to
strict neutrality between Nationalist and Communist forces, prompting one irreverent marine officer under Communist sniper fire to ask
sarcastically, "Who are we neutral against?" Vincent also pressed for a
termination of aid for Chiang's forces.[29] Forrestal and his colleagues in
the Pentagon countered that neutrality was tantamount to retreat, and
they warned that only Chiang could forestall Soviet expansion and the
emergence of a new threat to U.S. interests in the Western Pacific.[30]
Truman's political problem was compounded in November 1945 by

Patrick Hurley's angry resignation in protest of the administration's "betrayal" of Chiang.[31] In the succeeding months, Roosevelt's vision of China's leading role in Asian order quickly began to dissipate.

Desperate to restore credibility to his China policy and to take the issue off the front pages, President Truman prevailed on George C. Marshall to become his personal envoy to China in December 1945. Marshall had commanded the Fifteenth Infantry Regiment in China for three years after the First World War, where he had become personally close to Stilwell, a fact that made Chiang and some Republicans nervous.[32] But, in his opening moves, the former army chief of staff split the difference between the opposing camps on China policy by promising Forrestal and the JCS that for the time being the marines would stay and the United States would continue to transport Nationalist forces into Manchuria and northern China to demobilize the remaining Japanese, but he also committed to Vincent and the State Department that he would directly engage Mao's Communist Party.[33] Meanwhile, as Truman put it in a December 15 statement announcing Marshall's appointment, the administration would remain focused on achieving a "strong, united, and democratic China."[34] That was the one thing Locke had warned could *not* be achieved.

Through the force of his personality, Marshall did manage to keep peace talks going at first, but he was defying the entropic physics on the ground. Moscow was facilitating the entry of Mao's forces into Manchuria as Soviet troops withdrew, and by the spring of 1946, the Communist forces easily ejected the rag-tag Nationalist garrison from Changchun, the former Japanese capital of Manchuria.[35] Chiang then launched his own offensive into Manchuria in 1946, effectively dooming any remaining prospect for a peaceful U.S.-brokered unification of China. Furious at Chiang and still hoping for a brokered outcome, Truman and Marshall came down on Vincent's side of the China policy debate and imposed a devastating arms embargo on the Nationalists that lasted until the next summer.[36]

Forrestal warned that the arms embargo would lead to Communist victory, Soviet domination of Manchuria's rich resources, and an unacceptable risk to Japan and the U.S. offshore island position.[37] As the JCS framed the strategic choices in a ten-page memo, military aid to the Nationalists would buy time and space for "proper political action to be applied to the Chinese National Government." On the other hand, warned the chiefs:

The United States can choose to withdraw entirely from China and permit conditions in that country to drift further into chaos and disunity with the probable result that the Soviets will gain complete control over Manchuria and will sweep over the remainder of China. If this should occur, the United States must be prepared to accept eventual Soviet hegemony over Asia. . . . It is the opinion of the Joint Chiefs of Staff, however, that the military security of the United States will be threatened if there is any further spread of Soviet influence and power in the Far East. Early countermeasures are called for if this danger of Soviet expansion is to be halted. With a disarmed and occupied Japan, the only Asiatic government at present capable of even a show of resistance to Soviet expansion in Asia is the Chinese National Government.[38]

Vincent responded to these points by arguing that the Soviet Union was focused on Eastern Europe and internal rebuilding and would not likely assume a forward position in China.[39] And if the Soviets did move forward into China, he wrote to Marshall, the United States could respond appropriately—though how that would be possible in the wake of a Communist victory he did not elaborate. In any case, stressed Vincent, the core U.S. objective was not sentimentality or missionary work—nor at this point even the stated U.S. goal of achieving a unified China—which itself was only the means to a larger end. That larger end, he asserted to Marshall, was "to prevent China from becoming a major irritant in our international relations." From that perspective, he noted, even a stalemate between the opposing forces in China could be a desirable outcome.[40] Marshall forwarded Vincent's memo to the president. It was an argument for realism and flexibility evocative of Hornbeck or MacMurray, which appealed to Marshall's own strategic instincts, and for strategic detachment, which appealed to Truman's budget priorities.[41]

Despite their skepticism of Chiang, however, Truman and Marshall were not willing to abandon the Nationalists completely, as Vincent and others in the State Department were urging.[42] Domestic American politics and events in Europe weighed heavily on the president's thinking. He had announced the "Truman Doctrine" of supplanting Britain to stop communism in Greece and Turkey in March, and in June Marshall had proposed his plan for large-scale reconstruction of Europe. With pro-Chiang Republicans in control of both houses of Congress after the 1946 midterm elections, Truman realized that he had to show some support for the Nationalists in order to secure congressional backing for the Marshall Plan in Europe.[43] On the other hand, Marshall worried that *too much* U.S. military support for Chiang risked provoking a Soviet counterintervention in China and opening an unwelcome second front that would be equally risky for the administration's strategy for Europe.[44] Truman continued to search for a middle ground that would neutralize the China problem as an irritant in domestic U.S. politics.

On July 11, 1947, the administration announced that the former commander of U.S. forces in China, Lieutenant General Albert C. Wedemeyer, would "proceed to China without delay for the purpose of making an appraisal of the political, economic, psychological and military situation—current and projected."[45] Wedemeyer had helped Chiang's forces win one of their largest victories against the Japanese at the Battle of West Hunan on June 7, 1945, and stated only weeks before his appointment as Truman's envoy that the administration would not be able to justify its decision to "send four hundred million dollars to Turkey and Greece for the definite purpose of blocking the spread of communism and then fail to send similar assistance to China where the spread of communism is just as dangerous and even more advanced."[46] In that sense, his appointment was politically useful with Republicans in Congress but likely to undercut Truman's own arguments. Wedemeyer faithfully conveyed the president's message urging Chiang to undertake reforms but recommended upon his return that the president increase military aid and dispatch U.S. military advisors down to the battalion level of the Nationalist forces. This was the same approach that had reversed the Communist insurgency in Greece.[47] Marshall urged Wedemeyer to keep the report classified, which he did, but the contents quickly leaked.[48]

Recognizing that Truman had to respond to the Wedemeyer recommendations, and surprised at how quickly Nationalist morale was collapsing in China, Vincent and Kennan agreed within the State Department to a policy of increasing aid to China but worked to channel most of the aid to the economy while blocking Wedemeyer's proposal for an increase in U.S. military advisors.[49] Truman submitted that plan to Congress in February 1948.[50] The resulting China Aid Act of April 1948 proved to be enough to save the Marshall Plan in Europe among Republicans, but for Chiang it was too little, too late. In late 1948, CCP general Lin Piao (Lin Biao) launched the Pingjin campaign in northern China, backed by Soviet and captured Japanese heavy weapons and hundreds of thousands of additional troops integrated from defecting Nationalists, former warlord armies, and North Korea.[51] The Nationalists fought hard, inflicting over one million casualties on the enemy, but their rigid command-and-control structure and shaky morale quickly collapsed across the entire country.[52] On October 1, 1949, Mao proclaimed the establishment of the People's Republic of China (PRC), and Chiang and the Nationalists' leadership fled to Formosa.

The Nationalists' demise was not a surprise to the U.S. administration. American intelligence estimates had already concluded back in the summer of 1948 that Chiang's forces could collapse,[53] and Marshall had informed the State Department that the U.S. goal should now be "to preserve a maximum freedom of action" and avoid further antagonizing Mao's forces with any increase in support to the collapsing Nationalist government.[54] Butterworth and the newly renamed Bureau of Far Eastern Affairs began to focus on quiet ways to prevent Communist China from becoming "an adjunct of Soviet power."[55] By January 1949, the administration had concluded in NSC 34/1 that U.S. policy would be to maintain readiness to "exploit opportunities" for splitting China from the USSR while avoiding direct intervention in China.[56]

To win congressional support for this new approach in anticipation of an imminent Communist victory, Acheson convinced Truman to issue a white paper on China explaining why the United States had never had much ability to affect the outcome of the Chinese Civil War and need not fear expansion from a monolithic Sino-Soviet empire in Asia.[57] Kennan, who had originally proposed the idea of the white paper, read the draft from his hospital bed while recovering from recurring ulcers and proclaimed it "the greatest state document ever produced by the American government."[58] When the white paper (officially, *United States Relations with China with Special Reference to the Period 1944–1949*) came out in August 1949, however, it proved to be a political disaster. In addition to implying that the administration had not tried to stop Mao's victory, the report was followed by the Soviets' first atomic bomb test and then a month later Mao's declaration of the founding of the PRC. Republicans chafing from Truman's surprise victory over the moderate Thomas Dewey in November 1948 were ready to go on the offensive on foreign policy and now had the perfect target. Rather than closing the debate on China policy, the white paper provided grist for an ugly debate on communism and Asia that would affect a generation of policymakers.

It is worth briefly reflecting on the polarized debate on China and Asia that resulted from the "loss of China" and how it affected strategic thinking thereafter. The anti-Red purges of Senator Joseph McCarthy were among the ugliest chapters in American history. They silenced China experts and former New Dealers who, despite occasional naïvete about the Chinese Communist Party, understood nationalism and anticolonialism in Asia in ways that would have proven invaluable during the lead-up to the Vietnam War. At the same time, it is worth noting that the most vocal supporters of Chiang and the Nationalists in Congress also had deep ties and a rich understanding of China as well. Congressman Walter Judd of Minnesota, who became the most active critic of Chinese communism in Congress, had spent ten years in China as a medical missionary before being elected to Congress in 1943 and probably understood the country as well as any of the advocates of accommodation to the CCP in the State Department.[59] Neither side had a monopoly on truth in the debate, even if much historiography of the period is understandably more sympathetic to the victims of McCarthyism such as Vincent and Davis.

Precisely because the white paper was used as evidence of communist sympathy in the McCarthyite witch hunts of the early 1950s, the report's findings were accepted as honest and correct by many mainstream scholars in subsequent decades. However, the white paper's three main propositions merit further scrutiny: (1) that Chiang's defeat was certain; (2) that accommodation with Communist China was possible; and (3) that even without accommodation, Communist China could not threaten U.S. interests elsewhere in Asia.

On the inevitability of Chiang's defeat, it is useful to define *victory* more precisely. Since a unified China had been the objective of U.S. policy for a century, the Truman administration implicitly defined victory as unification—an objective that probably was well beyond the capabilities of Chiang, particularly after his forces had exhausted themselves in more than a decade of war with Japan and had squandered opportunities for land reform and popular mobilization.[60] Yet, as Vincent explained to Marshall in a moment of unintended insight, the unification of China was a *means* to an end, not necessarily an end in itself. Ultimately, the larger U.S. interest was the containment of hegemonic threats to the U.S. position in the Pacific. That objective could arguably have been met if Chiang fought the Communists to a standstill—a much more achievable aim than unification of China.

For one thing, as historian Steven Levine concludes in his study of the fight in Manchuria, Communist victory on that front was "far from secure, and its margin of victory in the civil war was thinner than it might

ar to have been."[61] The 1946 U.S. arms embargo left Chiang short
mmunition he needed to fight in the north (even after the partial
resumption of assistance in 1947–1948), and the combination of proper
equipment and American advisors at the battalion level may well have
been enough to tip the balance in the pitched conventional battles in
Manchuria and the north and ended the war in a stalemate and the blunting of communist expansion. A divided continental Asian nation with a
corrupt partner in the south is essentially where the United States ended
the Korean War four years later, and where the Johnson administration
unsuccessfully sought to end the Vietnam War two decades hence. Had
the outcome of the Chinese Civil War been a divided China on the continent, Chiang's forces would have served as a buffer against communist
support for North Korea and later Vietnam. Arguably, the United States
committed hundreds of thousands of troops to Korea and Vietnam and
lost tens of thousands of men because it was unwilling to commit a few
thousand advisors and a few hundred million dollars in additional aid to
Chiang in 1947.

The counter to this logic was offered in the 1949 white paper itself,
which maintained that "to have supported the Government's military
operations in China to the same comparative degree as those in Greece
were supported would have required an advisory group of many thousands, unpredictably large amounts of equipment, and the involvement
of United States advisers in the direction of modern large-scale war, *and
rather than representing a calculated risk it would have represented an
incalculable risk*" [emphasis added].[62] A core U.S. objective was to avoid
a land war in Asia against the Soviets and Chinese Communists that would
have put Western Europe at peril. From that perspective, the decision not
to side with Chiang more forcefully may have protected larger U.S. strategic equities beyond China and could be considered a prudent management
of risks in the Far East.

However, that global risk-management strategy still required mitiga-
tion of the threats posed to the U.S. position in Asia by a Chinese Communist victory. The second proposition in the white paper, made explicit
in NSC 34/1, was that collateral risk to Asia of a Communist victory could
be managed by coaxing China away from Moscow following Tito's example in Yugoslavia in 1948. This strategy seems obvious with the hindsight of normalized U.S.-China relations and was the mainstream view
of historians for decades. However, more recent historiography has rein-

forced what many in the administration understood at the time—that there was no real prospect of orchestrating a Sino-Soviet split. Both former Soviet and Chinese archives now demonstrate that the CCP had far deeper ties to Moscow in this period than was previously appreciated.[63] Unlike Tito, Mao was a committed world revolutionary driven primarily by the need to consolidate internal power rather than the kind of foreign policy realpolitik that would have made accommodation with the United States a useful tool to counter Soviet power (as it would become several decades later).[64] Even pure realpolitik logic would not have pointed to a Chinese strategy of countering the Soviets in 1945–1950, since the Soviets' twelve divisions in the Far East were a minor threat compared with the combined air and naval power of the United States in the Pacific.[65]

Key U.S. officials and analysts at the time pointed out precisely these factors. Before being tasked with finding ways to accelerate a Sino-Soviet split, for example, Kennan had predicted as early as 1946 that Mao would not have many choices other than close alignment with Moscow.[66] And in the summer of 1949, as the white paper was coming out, the intelligence community assessed that in reality "the CCP's present anti-Americanism is primarily dictated by the opposite CCP and U.S. positions regarding the USSR and world Communism. . . . At present, there is little chance of orienting the CCP away from the USSR."[67]

As Davies himself would later acknowledge with characteristic candor in a 1962 interview with *Look* magazine, he and his colleagues had mistaken the relative popularity of the Chinese Communist Party for democratic instincts, which never actually materialized.[68]

In the end, as Gaddis notes, it was easier for the Truman administration to "accept the argument that a victory for communism in China would pose no overwhelming threat to American interests" and that Mao would not bow "blindly to Moscow's wishes"[69]—even with the lack of evidence of any Sino-Soviet fissures and the discouraging news of the Sino-Soviet alliance in February 1950.

If the Sino-Soviet split was still a chimera, one must finally judge the Truman administration's risk management strategy against the actual threat posed to U.S. interests in the region from a *hostile* communist regime in Beijing. Again, despite the positive spin of the white paper, intelligence estimates in 1949 made little effort to hide the disastrous impact of Mao's victory on continental Asia. As a major estimate in the summer of 1949 stressed:

In Korea, the CCP's successes have contributed greatly to the confidence of the North Korean regime and to the feeling of defeatism in the Republic of Korea. Through its relationship with North Korean political leaders, the CCP is capable of providing significant military and economic aid to North Korea. The opportunity of South Korean leaders to offset the development of such an adverse trend had largely passed and it now appears that South Korea can do little to forestall such a development. . . . The CCP will probably not employ military force to gain its objectives in Southeast Asia and it has no significant economic resources with which to maneuver. Its success in China, however, will permit strong and unremitting political pressure on Southeast Asia.[70]

Even beyond its impact on continental Asia, Acheson and the State Department were surprisingly complacent about the significance of a Communist victory for the offshore island chain. The island of Formosa sat directly in Japan's sea lanes, and yet Acheson was prepared to let the island go to the Communists if necessary to avoid confrontation with the new regime in Beijing. Dean Rusk, General MacArthur, Secretary of Defense Louis Johnson, JCS Chairman General Omar Bradley, Pacific Fleet Commander Admiral Arthur W. Radford, and John Foster Dulles (then working on the peace treaty with Japan) all argued that "under no contingency should [the U.S.] permit Formosa to fall into Communist hands."[71] Kennan actually urged seizing Formosa as a U.S. forward base, with "sufficient resolution, speed, ruthlessness and self-assurance—the way Theodore Roosevelt might have done it."[72] But Acheson would have none of it. A few weeks after the establishment of the PRC, Acheson called in a group of China scholars to talk with Truman about the next steps, including their recommendation that the administration stay neutral on Formosa so as not to jeopardize negotiations with Beijing.[73] The next month, NSC 37/7 rejected interventionism in Formosa in favor of "calculated inactivity." In a telling line, the NSC concluded that U.S. military occupation of Formosa was out of the question because of "the present disparity between our military strength and our global obligations . . . a disparity that may well increase as a result of our budgetary limitations and the commitments implicit in the North Atlantic Treaty."[74] To summarize, then, the Truman administration's decision to limit the risk of major land war with the Soviet-led bloc in China by backing away from Chiang may ultimately have been a prudent grand strategy—consistent with offshore maritime instincts—but that strategy was undercut by the extent to which the focus on Europe drove wishful thinking about a Sino-Soviet split and woeful inattention to the defense of core interests in the Western Pacific against a newly empowered communist bloc. As the intelligence community predicted, that impact would be felt most heavily in Korea and Indochina.

At the time, though, the administration's major focus outside of China remained Japan.

THE REVERSE COURSE: JAPAN

When General MacArthur led his unarmed staff off the plane at Atsugi Air Base on August 30, 1945, he was gambling that Japanese authorities would submit to the U.S. occupation in an orderly manner. And they did.[75] In Washington, the Far Eastern subcommittee of SWNCC, chaired by Vincent, began to modify the planning objectives for the occupation of Japan to focus on the transition from disarmament to the longer-term goal of helping Japan "conform as closely as may be to the principles of democratic self-government."[76] "I can tell you this," Vincent said on NBC News, "the occupation will continue until demobilization and demilitarization are completed. And it will continue until there is assurance that Japan is well along the path of liberal reform."[77]

Implicit in the liberal reformers' vision was that Japan would be liberal but neutral, a concept anathema to those focused on maintaining a balance of power in the Pacific. Outgoing Japan hands like Grew "scoffed at the idea of turning hordes of inexperienced New Dealers loose on Japan."[78] Kennan, then serving in Moscow, argued that the pursuit of a liberalized and neutral Japan would be foolhardy, and Davies sent a memorandum to Washington on Kennan's behalf claiming it was a "delusion to assume that Japan can be reconstructed as a neutral, self-sufficient nation, enjoying friendly relations with both the United States and Soviet Union."[79] Worried that economic recovery had to be a higher priority than democratic liberalization, Grew's protégé Robert Fearey warned from Tokyo that "even a confirmedly democratic-capitalistic Japan would be likely to forego the friendship of the United States to align itself with a potential enemy of the United States . . . if it believed it might thereby overcome the [economic] difficulties facing it."[80] Forrestal had been of that same view since the spring of 1945, worrying that the elimination of Japan might mean Soviet domination of Asia as well as Europe.[81]

Nevertheless, domestic liberalization and international neutralization remained the thrust of U.S. policy toward Japan in the first years after the war, popularized in op-eds by Walter Lippmann and embraced by Vincent's colleagues in the State Department, such as Japan Affairs director John K. Emmerson, who responded to the critics by emphasizing that, "Our acts in Japan should not be conditioned by a fear of Communism so strong that we lean toward the very elements we have set out to destroy. We shall assure ourselves of a 'favored position' in Japan if we succeed in effecting lasting reforms, in giving impetus to a genuine liberal movement, and in starting the process of democratization in Japanese education. Then, perhaps, will Japan become neither a 'place d'armes' for the Soviet Union nor a 'place d'armes' for the United States."[82]

Thus began the multidecade battle between the State Department's "Chrysanthemum Club," who wanted Japan remade in shades of Wilsonian internationalism and New Deal reform, and the Mahanian Cold Warriors, who saw Japan's inherent power as a critical asset in the struggle with the Soviet Union.[83] Under Vincent's influence, this first round went to the Chrysanthemum Club, but by 1947, U.S. priorities had begun to shift. Crises were mounting with the Soviets in Europe, Japan was beset by labor unrest, and communist insurgencies were gaining momentum across Japan's former empire. In Washington, Acheson began his transition from liberal New Dealer to Cold Warrior after the Greek Crisis, and Kennan and Davies were using their new perch at Policy Planning to proselytize their maritime strategy for the Pacific.

The shift to a new Japan strategy was punctuated in July 1947 in revised SWNCC recommendations on "The Revival of the Japanese Economy." The future priority, argued the committee, must be to revive Japan as the engine of Asian growth and to promote Japanese economic expansion into Southeast Asia to fill the vacuum left by the collapse of the former Japanese and European empires.[84] Kennan and Davies also ensured that draft peace treaties with Japan working their way through the department avoided "drastic disarmament and democratization" and instead supported the U.S. objective of "a stable Japan, integrated into the Pacific economy, friendly to the U.S. and, in case of need, a ready and dependable ally of the U.S."[85] Purges of wartime Japanese bureaucratic and political leaders ebbed, and in November 1948, the president approved a new economic strategy for Asia based on greater centralization of Asian trade through Japan, facilitated by most favored nation status for Japan and backed by a four-year, $1.3 billion aid package to Tokyo.[86] Banker Joseph Dodge, appointed to oversee Japanese recovery efforts, called his new charge the "border area in the worldwide clash between Communism and democracy."[87] His ideological frame was different but echoed the arguments of Perry and Mahan.

Yet Japan's dependence on its former imperial spaces in Korea and Southeast Asia also exposed the vulnerability of the offshore island chain to developments on the continent. As the JCS noted presciently in January 1950: "The security interest of the United States in the Far East, short of military action, hinges upon finding and securing an area to complement Japan as did Manchuria and Korea prior to World War II. Accepting Communist control of China for the foreseeable future and realizing that a Japanese economy depending largely on resources from China and Korea could draw Japan into the communist orbit; or that a Japanese economy depending for the foreseeable future upon financial assistance and resources from the U.S. is unacceptable; the urgency strategically of an arrangement with Southeast Asia stands strongly."[88] Japan, in short, was not just a bulwark against communist expansion on the continent of Asia. Its *own* security and that of the offshore island chain ultimately did depend on finding solutions to the growing chaos in Korea and Southeast Asia.

"OUR POLICY SHOULD BE TO CUT OUR LOSSES AND GET OUT OF THERE": KOREA

In the early postwar years, otherwise historically literate American strategists demonstrated abysmally poor understanding of the geostrategic importance of the Korean Peninsula in the history of international relations in East Asia. Korea had always been the "cockpit" of Asia, the place where Japanese, Chinese, and Russian armies collided and were destroyed. China's Ming Court concluded in 1599 that control of Korea would give the Japanese the manpower and position to cleave China in two, as indeed it eventually did, and three centuries later Japan's great modernizer and strategist of the Meiji era, Yamagata Aritomo, famously called Korea "a dagger aimed at the heart of Japan" and determined that hostile control of the peninsula by China or Russia was unacceptable to Japanese security.[89]

None of these historic dynamics surfaced in the American postwar planning for Korea. SWNCC guidance for the occupation of Korea in November 1945 cited the Atlantic Charter as the guiding principle for U.S. occupation and recommended elimination of the separate U.S. and Soviet occupation zones in return for a temporary trusteeship and early independence.[90] Secretary Byrnes instructed the department that "our sole objective in Korea is the development of democratic self-govt. and the establishment of an independent Korea which we might reasonably expect to maintain amicable relations not only with the USSR and the US but also with other United Nations."[91]

Since Stalin wanted first and foremost to deny the peninsula to the United States and Japan, he agreed on its divided occupation at the thirty-eighth parallel until full independence could be granted to all Koreans five years later. But the Korean people on both sides of the parallel were desperate for self-rule after decades of subjugation under Japan. In the South, Lieutenant General John R. Hodge and his exhausted Twenty-Fourth Corps veterans from the battlefields of Okinawa tried to make sense of the squabbling factions that declared themselves a provisional independent government. Hodge's civil affairs officers had all been trained in Japanese and turned inevitably to the former Japanese police and their Korean proxies to maintain civil order, eventually deciding that the seventy-five-year-old U.S.-educated Syngman Rhee represented the best prospect for a cohesive government. In the more industrialized North, the Soviet Twenty-Fifth Army began to dismantle and cart off Japanese-built factories, while young Korean women dressed as men to avoid rape at the hands of marauding bands of Soviet soldiers.[92] The Soviet occupiers also began to purge local political leaders such as popular Christian nationalist Cho Man-sik, firmly installing one of their own former partisan officers, Kim Il-sung. Meanwhile, Koreans agitated for faster independence and land reform, with violent protests spreading across the South.[93]

The clear strategic consensus in Washington was that despite these trends, Korea did not have to be held. As Vincent told a public audience in 1947, the goal was only to "neutralize" Korea as an irritant in U.S. foreign policy.[94] The JCS argued that it needed the two divisions then stationed in Korea to cover defense commitments in Europe after the defense budget was slashed from $81.6 billion in 1945 to $13.1 billion in 1947.[95] SWNCC recognized in August 1947 that trusteeship would likely fail in Korea without U.S. military support but nevertheless concluded,

"Every effort should be made . . . to liquidate or reduce the U.S. commitment of men and money in Korea as soon as possible without abandoning Korea to Soviet domination."[96] Even Forrestal, always ready to stand against Soviet expansion, agreed that any future U.S. counteroffensive in the Far East would bypass Korea as it had in the Second World War, and efforts to defend Korea would leave U.S. air and naval bases vulnerable to Soviet conquest by land. The U.S. military therefore had no business remaining on the peninsula, in his view.[97] Kennan, the architect of a limited offshore strategy, agreed that "our policy should be to cut our losses and get out of there as gracefully but promptly as possible."[98]

At the same time, all the advocates of withdrawal from Korea were aware of Forrestal's caveat that "precipitate withdrawal . . . would lower the military prestige of the United States."[99] Acheson himself followed the March 13, 1947, Truman Doctrine speech by testifying before Congress that "there are other places [besides Greece, the focus of Truman's speech] where we can be effective. One of them is Korea, and I think that is another place where the line is clearly drawn between the Russians and ourselves."[100] Here the administration struggled with ways to maintain American "prestige" and influence on the peninsula without becoming— as NSC 8 put it in April 1948—"so irrevocably involved in the Korean situation that any action by any faction in Korea or by any other power in Korea could be considered a *casus belli* for the U.S."[101]

The administration tried three tools to remove Korea as a draw on U.S. diplomatic and military resources. First, in November 1947, Truman pushed a UN resolution, over the Soviets' boycott, that called for free elections, the withdrawal of foreign troops, and establishment of a UN commission for Korea. In 1948, Syngman Rhee won election in the Republic of Korea (ROK) in the South, and the Soviets put Kim Il-sung in charge of the Democratic People's Republic of Korea (DPRK) in the North. Though the U.S. goal was not a divided peninsula, the formation of the ROK nevertheless established the "line between the Russians and ourselves" that Acheson had described to Congress. Second, pursuant to NSC 8, the United States began to train and equip a lightly armed South Korean military to replace the U.S. occupation forces as they withdrew. Finally, the administration offered a package of economic assistance to the new Korean government, though it was only about half the amount then being provided to Greece.[102]

None of these tools proved to be effective in the way Acheson had promised Congress. The new South Korean government struggled for stability and legitimacy. The South Korean military was trained and equipped to manage domestic insurrection but not the massive mechanized units being formed in the North. And despite Truman's call to help the Koreans increase their standard of living so as to "stand as a beacon to the people of northern Asia in resisting the control of the communist forces,"[103] Congress defeated, diluted, and delayed economic aid bills until only a few months before the North would invade.[104] U.S. troop withdrawals from the South were essentially completed in 1949, and while the ROK government turned the tide of rebellion in the South, the Soviets continued to provide heavy artillery and tanks to the North Korean soldiers, many of them battle-hardened veterans of the Chinese Civil War.

In the end, none of this mattered, Kennan explained to Acheson in mid-1949, since the collapse of the South would have no major impact on overall U.S. strategic interests in the region.[105] The more important problem, he and his colleagues argued, was finding a secure source of raw materials on the continent so that Japan would not be seduced into the communist bloc. And, at the time, Southeast Asia seemed a more viable candidate for that purpose than the turbulent and vulnerable Korean Peninsula.

"Plain Fact Is That Western Democratic System Is on Defensive": Southeast Asia

American strategic thinking about Southeast Asia had been a jumble of contradictions during the Second World War. On the one hand, the Roosevelt administration recognized that the United States was engaged in a crucial ideational battle with Japan over competing models of self-determination in Asia and therefore initially pressed Britain, France, and Holland to liberate their Southeast Asian colonies under the principles of the Atlantic Charter. On the other hand, Roosevelt's Europe-first strategy left little room for friction with the Allies or U.S.-led ground operations on the continent of Asia, prompting Roosevelt eventually to deemphasize decolonization and turn over the Southeast Asia Command to the British.

The Yalta agreement, had it held, would have left time to resolve these contradictions. With American dominance in the maritime sphere and a unified China to hold the entire regional equilibrium together, Soviet influence would have been far removed from Southeast Asia, leaving time for the United States to gradually wean the Europeans of their colonies as a new open political and trading order took hold, anchored on Bretton Woods and a recovering Japan. However, Communist victory in the Chinese Civil War opened Southeast Asia to contiguous borders with a hostile revolutionary state, a situation that the weakened European powers could not counter in terms of either military power or ideology. Time simply would not be on the Americans' side.

The signs of chaos came early. Lord Louis Mountbatten of the British-led Southeast Asia Command tried for the first year after the war to maintain stability in an area stretching from India to Indochina while nervously watching as the new Labor government in London precipitously demobilized his Commonwealth Forces. The British granted independence to Burma and India in 1947, and both new governments were almost immediately involved in civil wars (domestic insurgencies would delay British independence for Malaysia and Singapore another decade). In the Dutch East Indies, Mountbatten's Indian troops—sometimes aided by Japanese units that remained under arms to protect their own civilians—fought pitched battles with Indonesia's new independent army before withdrawing in 1946.[106] The Dutch held out another three years until they granted Indonesia independence in 1949. In Indochina, Ho Chi Minh stepped forward in August 1945 to declare an independent Democratic Republic of Vietnam, appealing for recognition by the United States based on the Atlantic Charter and an impassioned appeal to the principles of the American Founding Fathers.[107] The Americans refused to fly in French troops to restore their former colony, but Mountbatten, with tacit American support, flew Indian troops into Hanoi in September 1945, and the former French colonial administrators emerged from Japanese jail cells to reclaim control from the "Anamese." After the humiliation of May 1940, France would not give up its colonies so easily.

By 1947, Secretary of State Marshall knew exactly the dilemma the United States faced in the region.[108] As he explained in a cable to the embassy in Paris in May:

Plain fact is that Western democratic system is on defensive in almost all emergent nations southern Asia and, because identified by peoples these nations with what they have considered former denial their rights, is particularly vulnerable to attacks by demagogic leaders political movements of either ultra-nationalist or Communist nature which promise redress and revenge past so-called wrongs and inequalities. . . .

We fear continuation conflict may jeopardize position all Western democratic powers in southern Asia and lead to very eventualities of which we most apprehensive.[109]

Kennan and Davies, despite their neorealist rejection of democratization, explained to Marshall that European imperialism was bankrupt and that the United States would have to prepare for a postcolonial Southeast Asia where the United States would be "confronted with the problem of assisting the non-communist nationalist leaders to retain their supremacy over the communists."[110] The administration could point to the successful example of the Philippines' independence in March 1947 (caveated though it was by assurances that the United States could continue operating out of Clark Air Field and Subic Bay under a ninety-nine-year lease signed in March 1947[111] and later CIA help defeating the Marxist Hukbalahap insurgents).[112] Kennan and Davies also focused on the decolonization of Indonesia, since the Dutch were unlikely to hold power and the archipelago could serve "as the anchor in that chain of islands stretching from Hokkaidō to Sumatra which we should develop as a politico-economic counter-force to communism on the Asiatic land-mass and as base areas from which, in case of necessity, we could with our air and sea power dominate continental East Asia and South Asia."[113] Marshall and Acheson agreed, since expending depleted Dutch resources in Southeast Asia would only make the Netherlands more vulnerable in Europe. And Truman, who had none of Roosevelt's ethnic ties to the old country or distaste for the French, pressed the Dutch to let Indonesia go.[114]

On Indochina, however, the Asia hands split with the Atlanticists. Both Vincent and General Wedemeyer, in opposite camps on China policy, united in urging immediate trusteeship for Indochina.[115] Acheson, Kennan, and the Atlanticist leadership of the State Department took the opposite view. The Dutch were too weak to hold the East Indies and not important enough in Europe to garner American deference, but France was now seen as strategically pivotal in Europe, and French control over its former colonies was deemed essential to the restoration of the French economy and anticommunist political leadership in Paris.[116] Moreover, the French appeared to have more fight in them than the Dutch.

After failing to win U.S. support for his provisional government, Ho Chi Minh tried negotiations with the returning French, but Paris peeled off the more accommodating members of the Viet Nam Doc Lap Dong Minh Hoi ("League for Vietnamese Independence"—or "Viet Minh"), and the communists ruthlessly suppressed the remaining elements to seize control of the movement and continue fighting for independence under arms. When Ho secured recognition and critical military support from Moscow and Beijing in January 1950, the United States responded by providing diplomatic recognition and military aid to the French-backed governments in Vietnam, Cambodia, and Laos the next month. The conflict in Vietnam was now a major front in the Cold War, and the State Department instructed its embassies worldwide that French success in Indochina was critical for stability in Europe and to prevent "Chinese imperialism" in Asia.[117]

In hindsight, it became clear that the Asia hands were right—support for Vietnamese trusteeship and independence may have been a viable strategy in 1945–1946, as Vincent and Wedemeyer had proposed. Reflecting on American mistakes in 1999, former defense secretary Robert McNamara concluded that the United States missed a critical opportunity to avoid the later Vietnam War in 1945–1946 because of a fundamental misunderstanding of the origins of Ho Chi Minh's nationalism.[118] More recent scholarship by Fredrik Logevall provides further evidence, including Stalin's own suspicion of Ho's Titoist inclinations, that a U.S. strategy based on the principles of self-determination and the Atlantic Charter might well have succeeded in Indochina as it had in Yugoslavia (in contrast to China, where Mao's revolutionary motives were an insurmountable obstacle). Ultimately, however, U.S. policy was derivative of an overall strategy aimed at Europe. As Clark Clifford, a White House aide to Truman between 1945 and 1950, later explained, he could "not ever recall having had to focus on Southeast Asia" in its own right: "Indochina, as it was then universally known, was regarded by our government as a French problem. President Truman was prompted from time-to-time by the State Department to approve statements that seemed to me to be little more than reiterations of the long-standing American attitude against 'colonialism.'"[119]

The French, however, would be out of Indochina in less than a decade and out of NATO's integrated military structures the decade after that. Meanwhile, Americans would still be dying in Indochina during the decade after that. Europe was undoubtedly the central front in the new contest with Moscow, but the question still remains whether France's colonies were so important to that European mission that the United States had to put itself at such an ideological disadvantage as scores of new nation-states rose from the ashes of empire in Asia. It is yet another of the "what if" questions lost to history, for after Mao's victory in China and the Korean War, it would be too late to revisit that question in the same way again.

Kennan and the Asian Defense Perimeter

Overall, it was not turning out to be the Asia that most Americans had anticipated at the end of the Second World War. The American people were eager to reduce their commitments to security abroad, and American policy toward Asia was becoming reactive as the assumptions behind Yalta unraveled with no clear organizing principle to replace them. The administration had embarked on a clear strategy for collective security in Europe, but as Kennan explained to Marshall in a long letter from Manila in March 1948, the United States was "operating without an overall strategic concept for the entire Western Pacific."[120]

Kennan knew that the JCS and the navy had been working on their own strategic plans for the Pacific since 1946 in an effort to tackle the same problem that had bedeviled them in War Plan Orange before the war: how to shape events in continental Asia from an offshore position. The JCS had concluded in the October 1946 "Strategic Concept and Plan for the Employment of United States Armed Forces" that in Asia the United States should seek to hold "a prospective enemy at the maximum possible distance, and conversely to project our own advance bases into areas well removed from the United States. . . . [T]he overall effect *is to enlarge our strategic frontier*" [emphasis added].[121] Then, in 1947, the navy staff detailed in Naval Planning Study (NPS) 3 how this extended strategic frontier in the Pacific would allow the United States to attack the Soviet Union from offshore using airpower operating from carriers in the Yellow Sea and Sea of Japan and from land-based bombers in the First Island Chain.[122] By June 1947, the JCS had agreed on a military strategy toward China that would emphasize an American defensive line offshore in the Western Pacific.[123]

Kennan drew on these studies and consulted broadly with American diplomats and military commanders in the region during travels in early 1948. In his cable to Marshall in March, he spelled out what he thought should be a new grand strategy for offshore maritime control of the Pacific—one with minimal risk on the continent of Asia and therefore to the U.S. position in Western Europe. As he explained to Marshall:

Okinawa would be made the center of our offensive striking power in the western Pacific area. It would constitute the central and most advanced point of a U-shaped U.S. security zone embracing the Aleutians, Ryukus [sic], the former Japanese mandated islands, and of course Guam. We would then rely on Okinawa-based air power, plus our advanced naval power, to prevent the assembling and launching of any amphibious force from any mainland port in the east-central or northeast Asia. . . . Japan and the Philippines would remain outside this security area, and we would not attempt to keep bases or forces on their territory, *provided* that they remained entirely demilitarized and that no other power made any effort to obtain strategic facilities on them.[124]

[margin note: Okinawa based airpwr naval pwr.]

From this maritime bastion, Kennan emphasized, the United States could "endeavor to influence events on the mainland of Asia in ways favorable to our security, but would not regard any mainland areas as vital to us."[125]

Kennan's formulation elegantly drew together military and diplomatic instruments of American power in the Pacific in a way no senior strategic thinker had in peacetime since Theodore Roosevelt. However, in its elegance and simplicity, the Kennan strategy had three weaknesses. The first, as discussed, was failing to see that some continental areas, such as Korea, were vital to Japan's security, even if those same continental areas were not in and of themselves directly vital to U.S. interests. As historian and intelligence officer scholar Paul Heer notes, "In Indochina as in Korea, Kennan was never able to enunciate a policy that would have reconciled his desire to eliminate US commitments on the mainland of Asia with his belief that US prestige should not be compromised there."[126] The second weakness was Kennan's assumption that in a competitive theater like the Western Pacific, the United States could keep Okinawa without a Japanese backlash and hope that Japan itself would remain unarmed and unintimidated by the Soviets without a security relationship with the United States.

[margin note: Korea vital]

These were problems of *ways*. The third problem in Kennan's integrated strategy was one of *means*. The Soviet threat in the Pacific clearly did not require the U.S. Navy to maintain anything close to the nearly one hundred carriers it had deployed in August 1945.[127] Nevertheless, in order to execute the offshore military strategy behind Kennan's defensive line, the navy staff calculated that it would need at least three carriers in the Pacific (and another three in the Atlantic).[128] Secretary of Defense

Louis Johnson was put in office by Truman in March 1949 for one major purpose, however, and that was to accelerate already deep cuts in defense spending that Forrestal had resisted.[129] Johnson canceled the navy's major supercarrier program and targeted the marine corps for elimination, prompting the resignation of the secretary of the navy and the sacking of the chief of naval operations after the public "revolt of the admirals" in 1949.[130] Acheson, who was a stronger supporter of defense spending than Kennan was, put up futile resistance until being outflanked by the budget hawks in the White House.[131] The ongoing cuts left the U.S. Navy with only one carrier in the Pacific in 1950, backed by two destroyer divisions, three submarines, and a pair of auxiliary ships.[132] Cuts to the army were just as severe. This depletion of *means* only exacerbated the problem of *ways* in Kennan's vision for an offshore shaping strategy.

Nevertheless, the *ways* of Kennan's proposed strategy received broad acceptance from both the U.S. military and Secretary Acheson. In Japan, MacArthur told the press in March 1949 that U.S. strategy in the Pacific would henceforth be to form a defensive line running from the Philippines, through the Ryukyus, to Japan and the Aleutians. He pointedly left out Korea.[133] Then, on January 12, 1950, Secretary of State Acheson inserted the same definition of the Asian defense perimeter in a speech before the National Press Club, highlighting on a map of the region that Korea was not included.[134]

In North Korea, Kim Il-sung, who had been pressing Moscow and Beijing to support an invasion to "liberate" the South, began to find his patrons more compliant.[135]

THE COLD WAR TURNS HOT: KOREA AND THE FORMATION OF AMERICAN FORWARD ALLIANCES IN THE PACIFIC

At dawn on June 25, 1950, the thirty-eighth parallel erupted with the thunder of North Korean heavy artillery fire and the roar of Soviet-built T-38 tanks crossing into the South.[136] Acheson had been gardening at his quiet Maryland farmhouse when the call came in from State reporting the attack. He immediately concluded that this was a Soviet-backed challenge "aimed at the entire position of the independent nations in the Pacific."[137] The president agreed, telling the nation on June 27, "in these circumstances, the occupation of Formosa by Communist forces would be a direct threat to the security of the Pacific area and to United States forces performing their lawful and necessary functions in that area."[138] That same day, the United States took advantage of the Soviets' ongoing boycott of the United Nations Security Council to pass Resolution 82, authorizing the use of force to defend the Republic of Korea. At Acheson's recommendation and with JCS concurrence, the president also ordered the Seventh Fleet to prevent any attack on Formosa, called on Chiang to cease all military operations against the mainland, and ordered the strengthening of U.S. forces in the Philippines and increased military assistance to that government and to the French in Indochina.[139] The administration was nearly unanimous in determining that the security of the island chain could not be divorced from events on the mainland after all.

Kennan was the outlier. Recalled from Princeton to help formulate the U.S. diplomatic response to the North Korean attack, he reiterated in NSC 73 on July 1 that the vital interests at stake remained America's maritime position in Asia and military prestige globally. Rather than be drawn into what he saw as a Soviet probe of American resolve, he characteristically argued for limiting and prioritizing U.S. objectives. Tibet, the Nationalist-held islands of Quemoy and Matsu off the Chinese coast, and Portuguese-owned Macau were probably expendable, he noted, but Hong Kong was British and therefore was not. As for Korea, Kennan argued that blunting the North Korean attack and returning to the status quo ante bellum would be sufficient, since the Korean Peninsula held no inherent strategic value.[140] Above all, Kennan argued to his colleagues, the United States should avoid a risky counterinvasion of the North.[141]

Kennan's respect and influence were at an all-time high because of his framing of U.S. interests at the outset of the Korean War and his assessment of Soviet and Chinese intentions, but on the issue of limiting the UN police action to a restoration of the status quo ante bellum, Kennan was isolated.[142] His minimalist realism could not contend with a concept as elastic and unquantifiable as "national prestige"—one he himself had embraced. Other more dominant voices called for broader war aims. These voices would increasingly define the next phase of American strategy in the Pacific as a whole.

One of the first to criticize Kennan's minimalism was John Foster Dulles. Though a staunch Republican, Dulles had been chosen by Acheson to prepare for peace negotiations with Japan in May 1950[143] as part of a bipartisan outreach to Republicans in Congress that also saw the more conservative Dean Rusk take over as assistant secretary of state for Far

Eastern Affairs and former Wall Street banker and Forrestal protégé
Paul H. Nitze succeed Kennan at Policy Planning.[144] On July 24, 1950,
Dulles wrote to Nitze, complaining that "the 38th Parallel was never intended to be, and never ought to be, a political line. . . . I believe strongly
that we should not now tie our hands by a public statement precluding the
possibility of our forces, if victorious, being used to forge a new Korea
which would include at least most of the area north of the 38th parallel."[145]
Rusk also worried that reestablishing the status quo ante bellum would
leave the South and Japan vulnerable. He and his deputies argued for the
destruction of Kim Il-sung's forces and for the unification of the peninsula if the opportunity presented itself.[146] He convinced Acheson, who
agreed with Nitze's assessment that there was "no arbitrary prohibition
against crossing the parallel" and accepted MacArthur's assessment that
the deed could be done with minimal risk of war with China.[147] America's most recent experience with warfare had ended with total victory
over a totalitarian foe. Dulles, Nitze, and Acheson concluded that it was
appropriate to demonstrate that communist adventurism would end with
a similarly decisive setback for the enemy.

Kennan continued to argue that the United States should not invest its
power in uncontrollable events on the Asian mainland, particularly in
Korea. "It is beyond our capabilities to keep Korea permanently out of the
Soviet orbit," he wrote to Acheson on August 21, 1950. "The Koreans cannot really maintain their own independence in the face of both Russian
and Japanese pressures."[148] The best solution, he continued, would be to
seek a comprehensive settlement with the Soviet Union that would terminate hostilities in Korea and reduce American military capabilities in
the region to a "mixed combat force, commanded and operated as a unit,
capable of dealing a sharp blow on a limited front almost anywhere in the
world on short notice."[149]

But Kennan's influence was now rapidly waning. On September 9,
1950, the president authorized UN forces to move north of the thirty-
eighth parallel to topple Kim Il-sung, provided Soviet or Chinese
Communist intervention had not taken place or been threatened.[150]
Meanwhile, Kennan's original definitions of containment and of the defense perimeter in Asia were being revised and expanded. Nitze had begun the process when he was tasked earlier in the year by Acheson and
the NSC to review containment strategy in the wake of the loss of China
and the Soviets' development of the atomic bomb. As the new director
of Policy Planning, Nitze consulted with his predecessor but eventually

NSC 68 : from Kennan's
departure limited strong pt. defense [277]

drafted NSC 68 as a departure from Kennan's limited strong-point defense, arguing instead for a forward perimeter defense based on the assumption that "a defeat of free institutions anywhere is a defeat everywhere."[151] Nitze and his fellow authors of NSC 68 decided that "frustrating the Kremlin's design" should be "an end in itself, not a means to a larger end."[152] This outlook reduced the geographic and hard-power constraints behind Kennan's strategy to secondary importance. Put another way, it expanded the geographic scope of American vital interests in the Pacific from the Mahanian focus on sea lanes, strong points, and island chains to something more akin to Spykman's Rimland concept from 1942, which involved the envelopment of continental Eurasia to contain threats to the maritime sphere. Eventually, this objective of "frustrating the Kremlin's design" would lead to a forward line against communism on the continent of Asia itself.

Nitze was a brilliant and persistent foreign policy intellectual. He was of German heritage and, while traveling to his father's homeland as a child, had witnessed the enthusiastic crowds welcoming war in Hamburg in August 1914. He later made a fortune on Wall Street and used his independent wealth to pursue graduate studies in philosophy and international law at Harvard, joining Forrestal's staff at the Navy Department in 1942, founding the School of Advanced International Studies (SAIS) with Christian Herter in 1943, and then leading the Strategic Bombing Survey for Truman after the war. He would emerge as one of the chief architects of strategy toward the Soviet Union from Truman through Reagan—at each stage shaping the broader context for Asia policy—beginning with NSC 68.[153]

When Nitze's draft first came across Truman's desk in April 1950, the president responded by asking for a program for implementation and budgeting. His priority at the time was on domestic spending, and the new strategy sounded very expensive. The bureaucracy proved incapable of producing an answer without further guidance on whether the White House would actually be willing to expand defense and foreign assistance spending.[154] It was a political chicken-and-egg problem. When Kim Il-sung attacked South Korea that June, however, NSC 68 came off the shelf and became the centerpiece of U.S. strategic planning going forward.[155] Nitze had written relatively little about Asia in NSC 68, but events in the Far East now turned his controversial draft into a document of historic consequence.

In Korea, the UN forces' successes on the battlefield seemed to augur well for Truman's expanded war aims. After sending North Korean forces into headlong retreat with his flanking amphibious landing at Inch'ŏn in mid-September 1950, MacArthur promised the president that the war would be won by Christmas. He should have tempered his enthusiasm after waves of bugle-blowing Chinese troops bore into the U.S. First Cavalry Division fifty miles from the Yalu River in early November 1950, but the Chinese attacks subsided a week later and U.S. troops settled in for what they assumed would be the last Thanksgiving of the war. Then, on November 25, renewed Chinese attacks sent UN forces into a bloody retreat south, crushing the hopes for total victory and early unification of the peninsula.[156]

With this setback, Truman returned to the status quo ante bellum as his objective. Chinese intervention with Soviet air support had changed the equation for the president. The United States could not let a major ground war with China and the Soviet Union in Korea drain U.S. military power at the expense of Europe, where the JCS planned to deploy six divisions of U.S. troops to the new NATO defense force in spite of the ongoing fight in Korea.[157] Acheson told the president that the key now was to draw a line in Korea and show the allies U.S. resolve, "So that we can get results in our European defense plans."[158]

This Europe-first approach once again put Truman and Acheson at odds with the Asia-first Republicans in Congress—to whom MacArthur appealed for support. When the Republican minority leader in the House of Representatives read on the House floor a letter from MacArthur criticizing this new limited war strategy, Truman summoned the JCS and secretary of defense and with their support relieved MacArthur of command. The UN "police action" would continue in Korea for two and a half more years until the final armistice in July 1953 under President Eisenhower. It was, said General Omar Bradley, as far as the United States could go, for to expand the fight to Red China would have been "the wrong war, at the wrong place, at the wrong time, and with the wrong enemy."[159] But even as a limited war, the Korea conflict would force a redefinition of American grand strategy in Asia that continues to shape the region to this day.

JOHN FOSTER DULLES AND THE SAN FRANCISCO SYSTEM

With the conflict in Korea, U.S. strategy had gone in five short years from the collective security vision of Yalta, to an offshore maritime defense perimeter, to major combat on the continent of Asia. As Gaddis observed after the attack on 9/11, when faced with strategic surprise, the United States tends to expand rather than contract its security commitments abroad.[160] So it was after the Korean War. Between 1951 and 1954, the United States would establish a "hub and spokes" system of American alliances, in contrast to the collective security approach of NATO in Europe. The Truman administration would begin with Japan, the Philippines, and Australia/New Zealand in the "San Francisco System." With a hardening of competition against the Soviets and China in Asia, the Eisenhower administration would complete the architecture with a second wave of alliances covering Korea, Taiwan, and Southeast Asia. The principal architect of the strategy for both presidents Truman and Eisenhower was John Foster Dulles.

Born in Washington, DC, in 1888 and a graduate of Princeton and George Washington Universities, Dulles was no stranger to the American traditions of expansionism, exceptionalism, and anticolonialism in Asia and the Pacific. His maternal grandfather was Secretary of State John Watson Foster, who had supported the annexation of Hawaii before its time in 1893. Dulles's paternal grandfather, John Macy Dulles, had served as a missionary in Madras, India, and represented China at the Hague Convention in 1907, accompanied at the time by young Dulles himself, then a junior at Princeton. Dulles would later advise his uncle Robert Lansing at Versailles in 1919, participating actively and effectively in negotiations over war reparations with the allies.

Raised on a daily dose of cold baths and Bible studies by his father, a Presbyterian reverend, Dulles brought to American foreign policy a vision that combined hardheaded realism and moral progressivism.[161] After returning from Versailles, he contributed regularly to the Council on Foreign Relations' journal *Foreign Affairs* and then encapsulated his theory of international relations in *War, Peace, and Change*, published in 1939.[162] In the book, Dulles explained the inevitable cycles of war and peace in world history and the need to break that cycle with a new collective security order based on Wilsonian idealism and a recognition that balance of power matters. Roosevelt met Dulles that year, declared the book "splendid," and expressed his intention to pick up the same theme himself when appropriate, which is, of course, precisely what he did.[163]

Dulles, however, was a Republican and rose in prominence as the principal foreign policy advisor to Roosevelt's opponent for the 1944 presidential election, Governor Thomas E. Dewey of New York. Dewey represented the more moderate East Coast wing of the Republican Party, which was badly divided against midwestern nationalists who had opposed intervention in Europe before the war and generally favored an Asia-first approach during and after it. When Dewey asked Michigan senator Arthur Vandenberg to negotiate a foreign policy platform that would bridge both wings of the party in early 1944, Dulles emerged as one of the principal drafters, helping to produce a document that reaffirmed internationalism while reiterating the party's commitment to American sovereignty. Dulles now had standing with both wings of the Republican Party as well as credibility within the Democratic administration as a moderating force against isolationism on the right.

It was this reputation that in the spring of 1950 led Truman to recruit Dulles to lead negotiations on a peace treaty and a bilateral security pact with Japan. Though Acheson despised Dulles's pious demeanor and rigid ideological views, he stepped aside knowing that Dulles would have a better chance of convincing Congress to support new treaties committing the United States to the security of key maritime democracies in the Pacific, and Acheson preferred to keep his own focus on Europe.[164] Before the North Korean attack, the administration had been divided on key aspects of the treaty negotiations with Japan. The JCS had been opposed to an early peace treaty, whereas State viewed it as essential to keeping Japanese support in the intensifying conflict with the Soviet Union and China. The JCS wanted greater latitude to use its military position in Japan, whereas State saw an end to the U.S. military presence (except for the Ryukyus) as a diplomatic necessity to keep Japan friendly. With the outbreak of the Korean War, Dulles helped to forge a new consensus between State and Defense that an early peace treaty was necessary but so was a longer-term U.S. military presence on the main islands of Japan.[165] In September 1950, the JCS and State agreed on ten common goals for the treaty negotiations, including denial of the Japanese archipelago to the Soviets; exclusive U.S. control of the Ryukyus and strategic trusteeship over the Marianas, Caroline, and Marshall Islands; the right through bilateral agreement with Japan to station military forces in key bases in Japan; recognition of Japan's right of self-defense under the UN Charter; and the possibility that U.S. forces could assist the Japanese government with domestic disturbances.[166] These points formed the basis for U.S. negotiations and the essential elements of the peace and security treaties completed with Japan in September of the next year.[167]

With Japan as the linchpin of American alliances in the Pacific, the question remained how the U.S.-Japan accommodation would relate to the rest of the Asia-Pacific security architecture. In his second major treatise on international relations, *War or Peace* (1950), Dulles had proposed "an association of the free nations of Asia and the Pacific."[168] The idea of a "Pacific Pact" had also resonated with Kennan's Policy Planning staff and Wilsonian idealists in Congress, but when Dulles tested the idea with Canberra, Wellington, and Tokyo on a trip to the region that began in January 1951, he found strong resistance.[169] Japanese prime minister Yoshida Shigeru was concerned about Japan's economic recovery and the fragile domestic consensus supporting the U.S.-Japan alliance and did not want to put those more important goals at risk by signing on to an open-ended collective security arrangement.[170] Meanwhile, Australia, New Zealand, and the Philippines still bore too much animosity toward Japan to contemplate any kind of collective security arrangement that might encourage Japanese rearmament.[171] What the Australians wanted, and Australian foreign minister Sir Percy Spender demanded of Dulles, was a security commitment from the United States as the quid pro quo for Australia signing a nonpunitive peace treaty with Japan and agreeing to end the American occupation there.[172] "Those who bore the brunt of the struggle against Japan must also be the architects of any peace treaty," Spender wrote in the Australian paper *The Age*, "It will take more than assurances from Washington, no matter how successful the occupation of Japan has proven."[173]

By the spring of 1951, Dulles concluded and Acheson concurred that the United States should drop its collective security plan and instead sign separate treaties with Japan, the Philippines, and Australia/New Zealand—all of which were to come into effect in parallel with a peace treaty with Japan formally ending the war and the American occupation of Japan.[174] The Philippines signed the Mutual Defense Treaty in Washington on August 30, and on September 1 Australia and New Zealand signed the ANZUS Treaty in San Francisco. Most of the Allied powers then gathered in San Francisco to sign a peace treaty with Japan on September 8, and the United States and Japan completed the set with the bilateral Treaty of Mutual Security that same day.[175]

Though wrapped in the language of the United Nations and Wilsonian idealism, there was no mistaking the fact that this new San Francisco System aimed to establish a bipolar order in Asia that was designed to contain the expansion of Soviet and Chinese communism and to secure the offshore island chain. As Dulles put it in a 1952 *Foreign Affairs* article describing the treaties:

> From our standpoint, the arrangements which we have been consider-
> ing add up to a determination—with the concurrence and help of the
> peoples concerned—to make safe the offshore island chain which
> swings south through Japan, the Ryukus [*sic*], the Philippines, Austra-
> lia, and New Zealand. In addition, the President has declared that the
> United States will not permit the status of Formosa, now the seat of
> the National Government of China, to be changed by force, and the
> Pacific Fleet has been instructed accordingly. That sum total is an im-
> pressive development of United States policy and a formidable deter-
> rent to the domination of the Pacific by Communist imperialism.[176]

The Soviets, though present in San Francisco, protested the peace treaty and did not sign, and the PRC, ROC, and the two Koreas were not invited because of divisions over the ongoing Korean War. India objected to the West's imposition on Japanese sovereignty and signed a separate agree-ment, and Japan's former Southeast Asian colonies eventually signed after limited reparations agreements were reached—all indications that the re-gion was not quite as bipolar as the drama at San Francisco suggested.[177] On the margins of the treaty negotiations with Japan, Dulles also secured commitments from Yoshida not to trade with Communist China, despite the Japanese leader's belief that China trade would become indispensable to Japanese autonomy.[178] Dulles further protected the integrity of the off-shore island chain by refusing to stipulate in the peace treaty which boundaries of maritime territories Japan would renounce and by success-fully including language clarifying that rights, titles, and benefits with respect to such territories would not be conferred to any country that re-fused to sign the treaty. Dulles thus skillfully (if cynically) left the future disposition of Formosa and Japan's former South Pacific mandates under de facto American control and preserved Japanese claims on the North-ern Territories (then under Soviet occupation per the Yalta agreement) as a wedge issue between Tokyo and Moscow for the future.[179]

At the same time that Dulles locked *in* Japan and kept *out* the Soviets, he ensured that the San Francisco treaties did not overexpose the United States to security commitments beyond Japan. As he explained in his 1952 *Foreign Affairs* article, "The United States should not assume formal commitments which overstrain its present capabilities and give rise to military expectations we could not fulfill, particularly in terms of land forces. The security treaties now made involve only islands, where security is strongly influenced by sea and air power."[180] The United States retained forces in both Japan and the Philippines, for example, but whereas the U.S.-Japan treaty stipulated that those forces were in Japan for "the security of Japan against armed attack," the U.S.-Philippines Mutual Defense Treaty stated more loosely that "the Parties separately and jointly by self-help and mutual aid will maintain and develop their individual and collective capacity to resist armed attack."[181] In the case of the ANZUS Treaty, the JCS successfully argued against establishing any NATO-style joint planning or staff functions that would divert U.S. forces or focus from Northeast Asia (despite Acheson's appeals to provide greater commitments, given that Diggers and Kiwis were then fighting side by side with U.S. forces in Korea).[182] The ANZUS Treaty would feature all the formal trappings of NATO but not joint and combined planning arrangements or stationing of U.S. forces in Australia or New Zealand.[183]

Overall, Dulles's achievement at San Francisco was remarkable. The United States embarked on the unprecedented expansion of security commitments to states in the Far East but did so with maritime democracies considered most vital to the offshore island chain and with limited draw on the resources needed to protect Japan and Western Europe. It was a formula that began with Kennan's 1948 offshore maritime strategy but fortified the First Island Chain based on prior JCS planning and Nitze's expanded definition of containment in NSC 68.

Yet the Rimland defensive line was still incomplete. The San Francisco System had secured the offshore island chain but still left open the question of how to manage communist expansion on the continent of Asia. As Melvin Leffler explains:

> Neither Taiwan nor Korea nor Indochina was part of the [Acheson] defense perimeter, but they had to be protected nonetheless. The defense perimeter was a wartime concept; it defined the areas that were deemed vital to waging a hot war. But U.S. officials were struggling to win the cold war. And unless the United States could demonstrate the credibility of U.S. commitments in peripheral areas, and unless they could preserve essential Third World markets and raw materials, vital countries like Japan, Germany, France, Holland, and the United Kingdom might be maneuvered out of the American orbit.[184]

Acheson and Truman left office with the longer-term architecture for these boiling parts of Asia unresolved. Dulles, however, would return to power to tackle them the next year.

THE NEW LOOK AND THE EXPANSION
OF ALLIANCES TO THE FRONTLINE STATES

Dwight D. Eisenhower won the presidency in November 1952 with a combination of hard-core anticommunism and the reassuring promises that he would bring the fighting in Korea "to an early and honorable end."[185] Dulles lent the president ballast on the right and helped secure his own selection as secretary of state by drafting a plank in the 1952 Republican foreign policy platform that pledged an Eisenhower administration would "end the neglect of the Far East" and "isolate, encircle, and bring about the collapse of the Peking government."[186] Eisenhower shared his secretary of state's blunt views of Chinese communism. And as the negotiations at San Francisco would suggest, Dulles also shared Eisenhower's pragmatic views on limiting the application of American power abroad, despite the ambitious rhetoric of the Republican platform.[187]

Eisenhower brought to the presidency an unprecedented discipline with respect to the formulation of American national security strategy and the alignment of ends, ways, and means.[188] Concerned that NSC 68 gave no limit to either ends or means and with the U.S. defense budget exceeding $85 billion and 12 percent of GDP when he came into office (from a base of 3 percent in 1950), the new president launched a major review of containment strategy in the summer of 1953 called the Solarium Project. Under Solarium, task forces were established to consider three alternate explanations of Soviet behavior and corresponding U.S. levels of effort necessary to manage the threat. The first task force, led by Kennan, argued for the continuation of Truman's containment strategy, while the two others focused on "deterrence" and "liberation," respectively.[189] The three papers were then debated and synthesized into a comprehensive strategy in NSC 162/2 in October 1953 that brought back Kennan's long-term view of the Soviet threat—thus reducing the requirement for heavy investment in military capabilities—while at the same time searching for ways to put asymmetrical pressure on the Soviet Union and China in the spirit of Nitze's NSC 68.[190]

The Solarium exercise and the corresponding NSC memoranda had important implications for U.S. strategy toward Asia and the Pacific. Consistent with Kennan's long view of containment, the administration narrowed its initial objective of rolling back communism in China, shifting instead to a strategy outlined in NSC 166/1 in November 1953 that aimed to encourage a Sino-Soviet split but using pressure rather than inducements to impose a cost on Moscow's junior partner.[191] The theory was that allowing Communist China to "stew in its own juices" would over time force Mao to confront the same "overwhelming economic and social problems which contributed so largely to the downfall of the National Government" and force Beijing to give up revisionist confrontation in search of Western assistance.[192]

At the same time, consistent with Nitze's view that frustrating Soviet expansionism was in itself a vital interest, the Eisenhower administration elevated the importance of denying the frontline states of Korea, Formosa, and Indochina to the enemy (and other such states in other regions of the world). In order to achieve this latter objective with minimal cost and risk, Eisenhower and Dulles developed a broader concept, known as the "New Look," that highlighted the importance of alliances and nuclear weapons as comparatively cheap multipliers for American power abroad.[193] Alliances would provide forward bases for U.S. air and naval power, increase the manpower available to the United States, and keep the threat far from American shores. The threat of massive nuclear retaliation would backstop those alliances, reduce the need for overall manpower, and deter attack on the United States.[194] Or, as Dulles put it, "We need allies and collective security. Our purpose is to make these relations more effective, less costly. This can be done by placing more reliance on deterrent power and less dependence on local defensive power."[195]

But if alliances were cost-effective in terms of reducing requirements for American manpower to respond to Soviet expansion, they also carried risks in terms of entrapment in conflicts with the Soviet bloc on the mainland of Asia. Thus, in Korea and Taiwan, as former NSC staffer and Asia scholar Victor Cha notes in his history of alliance formation in Asia, the administration sought arrangements "not only to defend against communism, but also to inhibit the highly unpredictable leaders of both countries from provoking conflicts with North Korea and mainland China that might embroil the United States in a larger war on the Asian mainland."[196]

In the case of Korea, the Truman NSC had already concluded that any bilateral alliance should in part be formed in order to "avoid the extension of hostilities beyond Korea to Communist China."[197] Immediately after the U.S. presidential election in November 1953, Eisenhower sent Vice President Richard Nixon to Seoul to inform South Korean president Syngman Rhee that there would be no U.S.-ROK Treaty of Mutual Security absent a separate guarantee that the Seoul government would refrain from using force against the North without U.S. approval.[198] Given the North Korean threat, Rhee's government had little choice but to agree, and it signed a supplemental side agreement spelling out the constraints on offensive action against the North in parallel with the October 1, 1953, U.S.-ROK Treaty of Mutual Security.[199]

The administration was even more wary of Chiang's Nationalists. Despite Eisenhower's threat in his first State of the Union address in February 1953 that the Seventh Fleet would no longer shield China from Nationalist forces on Formosa, there was considerable debate within the administration about whether to extend a security commitment to Chiang at all.[200] The issue was forced in September 1954, when the Peoples Liberation Army (PLA) began shelling the islands of Quemoy and Matsu (Jinmen and Mazu)—small and militarily insignificant outposts off the Chinese coast that were garrisoned by Nationalist troops. Mao's intention was to send a signal of resolve toward the United States in opposition to U.S.-ROC security ties, but the effect was the opposite.[201] With the Korean experience fresh in their memory, Eisenhower and Dulles concluded that Mao intended to take back Formosa, a move that would have split the island chain and posed a significant setback for the United States.[202] Aiming to stabilize the cross-Strait situation rather than open a new front against Beijing that would drain American military resources, Dulles offered a mutual security treaty to ROC foreign minister George Yeh on the condition that he also sign a side agreement committing to joint agreement on any use of force against the mainland.[203] After eight grueling rounds of negotiations, Yeh finally agreed. The result, Dulles explained to Eisenhower, "stakes out unqualifiedly our interests in Formosa and the Pescadores and does so in a way that will not allow the Chinese nationalists to involve us in a war with Communist China."[204]

The third piece of the new post–San Francisco architecture of alliances on the front line in Asia was in many ways the most complicated. There the problem was not belligerent allies but uncertain lines of defense. The United States had long planned on defending the Philippines and restoring U.S. forward bases there after the war, but Truman steadfastly refused to consider extending American security commitments beyond the archipelago to the rest of Southeast Asia, telling Churchill in December 1951 that he would not commit ground forces and that "paper security agreements not backed by commitments of forces are worse than none at all."[205]

By the time of the Eisenhower administration, however, the situation in Indochina had deteriorated to the point that a hands-off approach to Southeast Asia was no longer considered feasible. In an early draft document on Southeast Asia policy in April 1953, Eisenhower's NSC stressed that Southeast Asia was key to securing the "off-shore defense positions (Japan, Ryukyus, Formosa, Philippines, Australia, and New Zealand), *even at the grave risk of general war*" [emphasis added].[206] And Dulles told the Senate Foreign Relations Committee when introducing the U.S.-ROK treaty in 1954, "The offshore island chain has, in essence, two land bases: at the north, the Korean mainland, and in the south, we would hope in Indochina."[207] In fact, Eisenhower had already told his advisors that he considered Indochina to be an even higher priority than Korea.[208] As an NSC memo noted in early 1954:

> In the event all of Southeast Asia falls under communism, an alignment with communism of India, and in the longer term, of the Middle East (with the probable exceptions of at least Pakistan and Turkey) could follow progressively. Such widespread alignment would seriously endanger the stability and security of Europe. . . . Communist control of all of Southeast Asia and Indonesia would threaten the U.S. position in the Pacific offshore island chain and would seriously jeopardize fundamental U.S. security interests in the Far East. . . . The loss of Southeast Asia, especially of Malaya and Indonesia, could result in such economic and political pressures in Japan as to make it extremely difficult to prevent Japan's eventual accommodation to communism.[209]

domino theory in SE Asia [handwritten marginal note]

This was, in effect, the strategic implication of what Eisenhower would publicly announce in April 1954 as the "domino theory" of communist expansion in Southeast Asia.[210]

Yet despite the elevated importance of holding Indochina, "even at risk of general war," Eisenhower and Dulles continued to try to limit that risk. They understood precisely the dilemma they faced. First, there was a clear asymmetry of effort between the West and the Soviet Union in both the Korean and the Indochina theaters, since the communist forces had the continental home field advantage, and the United States and Western allies were being forced to divert considerably more forces from the European front than was Moscow.[211] Second, although European military forces were the most effective in battling the communist enemy, their presence only reinforced the imperialist image of the United States and made political victory more elusive.[212] And third, the French were flagging faster than indigenous governments were building the capacity to stand on their own.

Eisenhower and Dulles thought they had an example of success that the French could follow. In the Philippines, a combination of national independence, democratic reforms, and aggressive mobile tactics was breaking the back of the Hukbalahap communist insurgency. Eisenhower and Dulles offered further aid to Paris in exchange for a comparable promise of Vietnamese independence and more aggressive counterinsurgency tactics on the ground. France responded by taking its $400 million in new aid and launching a major offensive into northwest Vietnam, where General Henri Navarre deployed eighteen battalions of his Far Eastern Expeditionary Force for a final decisive battle against the elusive Vietminh in the fortified village of Dienbienphu. Vietnam, alas, was not the Philippines. Enjoying contiguous borders with the PRC, General Ngo Vien Giap's Vietminh forces cut off the French command at Dienbienphu and slowly shelled and starved it into submission with the help of Chinese-supplied advisors and heavy weapons. Eisenhower authorized American-contracted air transport and sent the French forty bombers and two hundred U.S. Air Force mechanics for support, but he was not willing to commit U.S. forces without backing from the U.S. Congress and Britain—or at least Australia—and London and Canberra both said no.[213]

On May 7, the Vietminh overran all but one of the remaining French positions, and with a final cry of "Vive la France," Dienbienphu's radio operator went off the air. It was over for the French—and indeed for residual European power in East Asia. In June, a center-left government under Pierre Mendès-France came to power in Paris, pledging peace in Indochina. At ongoing peace talks sponsored by London and Moscow in Geneva, it was obvious that most U.S. allies were prepared to live with a divided Indochina in order to reduce tensions with Beijing. Losing diplomatic and military momentum, the Eisenhower administration relented to a final agreement that would denote a "provisional military demarcation line" between North and South.[214] Dulles, unhappy about the Geneva conference and frustrated with the allies' perfidious behavior, mused throughout that it might be best to let the French get out of Indochina and then try to rebuild from the foundations.[215] He would get his wish.

As Dienbienphu was falling, the JCS explained that there were now two broad military options to stop communist expansion after the setback in Indochina: either a "static defense" like Korea, which would require years to build up U.S., French, and British forces and would ultimately intensify anti-Western sentiments, or a more immediate and decisive "offensive to attack the source of Communist military power being applied to Southeast Asia" (namely China), which the aggressive chairman of the JCS, Admiral Arthur Radford, favored.[216] However, Eisenhower had already told the NSC how anxious he was about U.S. ground intervention, which he said "would absorb our troops by divisions,"[217] and Army Chief of Staff Matthew Ridgway provided the president with huge projections on troop requirements, which reinforced his reluctance.[218]

With Dienbienphu falling and Eisenhower unwilling to commit ground forces, the United States turned instead to a collective security framework that might stop communist expansion in Southeast Asia without U.S. boots on the ground. The problem was that Southeast Asia was still an untidy collection of current and former European colonies, with limited resilience and capacity for self-defense and a confused mix of dependence and resentment toward the former imperial overlords. The Far East Division at the State Department argued that it would be better to go for a broad and inclusive pact "that would bring in India, Burma and Indonesia, along with the Philippines and Thailand," and allow Asians to bond in anticommunism *without* their European protectors, since "a chain with links of moderate strength is much more useful than a chain with some strong links and some missing links."[219] However, Burma, India, and Indonesia were not interested, and Vietnam, Cambodia, and Laos were prohibited by the Paris Agreement from joining any formal military alliance.[220] In the end, only two Southeast Asian countries were prepared to join a new U.S.-led organization: the Philippines and Thailand. Meanwhile, Dulles concluded that he needed France, Britain, Australia, and New Zealand in the organization to provide some muscle, if not ideational glue (Pakistan would join as well, in a bid to outflank its nonaligned rival India).

Though imperfect, the polyglot grouping of European and Asian allies would be enough for Dulles, who explained to the NSC on July 24, 1954, that the new Southeast Asian Treaty Organization would give the

[margin annotation: anti alliance]

president the discretionary authority to use force in the event of Chinese aggression against Southeast Asia, which he currently did not have, while guaranteeing the support of those nations in the event of any U.S. action. The point was to reinforce deterrence without the risk of entrapment in a major land war or heavy U.S. military presence on the ground. It was imperfect, but as Dulles put it, "drawing the line was more important than what was inside the line."[221]

Yet, what was inside the line mattered. Dulles confided to his staff the week after selling SEATO to the NSC that the United States might be "tying itself down to people who wouldn't fight,"[222] and he confessed to the president that the treaty "involved committing the prestige of the United States in an area where we had little control and where the situation was by no means promising."[223] He tried to limit the risks of larger war by ensuring that there would be no standing military command structure like NATO or deployment of U.S. forces that might lead to unwanted entrapment in conflict on the ground in Southeast Asia. The Australians warned the State Department in August that this would lead to a "treaty without teeth of any kind, or to a treaty into which it would be very difficult to put any teeth subsequently."[224] General James Van Fleet, who returned that same month from a mission to assess U.S. military assistance programs in Asia, also warned that SEATO would be a hollow organization. Van Fleet recommended that instead the administration follow the NATO model in Europe and integrate the U.S.-ROK, U.S.-ROC, U.S.-Philippines, and U.S.-Japan alliances into a new collective security organization that would truly deter Communist China.[225] The NSC concurred that in time the U.S. goal should be "a Western Pacific collective defense arrangement, including the Philippines, Japan, the Republic of China, and the Republic of Korea, eventually linked with the Southeast Asia security structure and ANZUS," but the administration was not prepared to empower Chiang and Rhee in such a collective arrangement, and Yoshida would not bring in Japan.[226] Nor did Dulles and the president want any arrangement that might trigger U.S. military action in Southeast Asia against their will.

Thus, SEATO was as far as the administration was willing to go.[227] On September 8, 1954, the United States, France, Great Britain, New Zealand, Australia, the Philippines, Thailand, and Pakistan signed the Southeast Asian Collective Defense Treaty ("Manila Pact"), with Vietnam, Cambodia, and Laos to participate as observers.[228] In the end, this organization provided only marginal help in deterring communist aggression in

Indochina or reducing the potential burden on the United States itself. The red lines against aggression were deliberately vague, and the collective security commitments and planning were deliberately limited.[229] The one clear advantage that emerged was the necessary collective security pretext for U.S. military action. Based on additional protocols to the Manila Pact extending security provisions to Vietnam, the secretary of defense authorized the JCS to begin long-range planning to support the establishment of an independent Vietnamese army.[230] Beyond that initial investment, the NSC concluded that a request from within SEATO would be sufficient for the U.S. government to provide all overt and covert support available within executive branch authority and at once consider requesting congressional support for military action to "reduce the power of communist China in Asia at the risk of, but without deliberately provoking war."[231] However, limited military strikes against China that made sense in 1954 became far less palatable after Beijing's first nuclear weapons test, in 1964. Ultimately, that would leave only the alternative of static defense, a strategy that the JCS warned in its May 1954 memo to the NSC would require 900,000 troops, of whom 650,000 would be ground forces.[232] That was a fairly accurate if unanticipated description of where the United States would find itself fifteen years hence.

EISENHOWER'S LEGACY IN ASIA STRATEGY

After the creation of SEATO, there was relatively little strategic innovation by the Eisenhower administration on Asia. In December 1954, the administration codified its established plan for applying the New Look to the region in NSC 5429 and basically stuck with that approach until leaving office at the end of the decade. On the whole, Eisenhower's strategy met the carefully delineated U.S. national security objectives of holding the line against communist expansion while reducing the resources and risk required. Between 1955 and 1960, only North Vietnam was lost to the communist bloc in Asia, while the overall number of U.S. ground forces in the region decreased and U.S. defense spending dropped from 13.1 percent to 9.4 percent of GDP.[233]

Was this wisdom or inertia? Historians have often charged that it was the latter, which raises the question of what else Eisenhower might have done to shore up the U.S. position in Asia and perhaps avoid later tragedy in Vietnam.

One path not taken would have been to follow up on Acheson and Kennan's strategy of drawing China away from the Soviet Union. Eisenhower and Dulles were certainly aware of the growing fissures between Moscow and Beijing, particularly after Khrushchev assumed power, but the president never wavered from his assessment that conflicts of interest of both partners with the noncommunist world were more powerful than the communist camp's internal divisions.[234] In this, Eisenhower probably read Mao's intentions and the larger strategic dynamics accurately. Ideologically, Mao's revolutionary confrontation with the West only intensified with the social upheaval he wrought at home, culminating in the tragedy of the Great Leap Forward. Structurally, there was still no balance-of-power logic for Beijing to pursue Sino-U.S. rapprochement to counter the Soviets, since American air, naval, and nuclear capabilities continued to pose an overwhelming threat to China in the Pacific compared with the fifteen weak divisions the Soviets maintained in the Far East.[235] All of that would change in a decade, but there was no sign of that transformation of the strategic landscape in the final years of the Eisenhower administration. Dulles probably did not need to be as rigid as he was with respect to outreach toward Beijing, but it was not the case that he lost a strategic opening. Even in 1958, the CIA estimated that "Communist China will almost certainly remain firmly aligned with the USSR. Peiping [Beijing] will continue to acknowledge Moscow as the leader of world Communism, but as Communist China grows in strength and stature, it will probably play an increasingly important role in the formulation of general Bloc policy. Although there will almost certainly be some frictions, these are unlikely to impair Sino-Soviet cooperation during the period of this estimate."[236]

Although Eisenhower and Dulles probably did not misread the Sino-Soviet bloc in this period, they certainly did miss the trends in nationalism in Asia, to the detriment of U.S. prestige and influence. When nonaligned nations agreed to meet in Bandung, Indonesia, in April 1955, Dulles immediately viewed the gathering as a profound threat to the Western camp. At first, he considered trying to block the meeting, but then he concluded that a more effective approach would be to blunt Chinese influence by organizing friendly states behind the scenes.[237] However, this "with us or against us" approach to nationalism in postcolonial Asia only pushed neutral states relatively closer to Beijing and reinforced the narrative that the United States was "not really interested in the attainment of full sovereign positions in world affairs by the new south and southeast Asian countries," as the American ambassador in Indonesia warned.[238] The U.S. dilemma was compounded by the decision to build SEATO around the former colonial powers, which only sharpened the racial contrasts to Bandung's apparent pan-Asian solidarity—an impression reinforced by Japan's decision to accept an invitation to the conference as a sign of its own reacceptance in the region.[239]

Eisenhower recognized that Dulles's tactical response to Bandung and nonalignment was not solving this larger strategic problem. As he lamented to the NSC, the Communists had been able to identify themselves and their purposes with the widespread growth of nationalism, while the United States "had failed to utilize this new spirit of nationalism in its own interests."[240] For the president, "the standing of the United States as the most powerful of the anticolonial powers is an asset of incalculable value to the Free World," and it was being squandered in Asia.[241] After Bandung, Dulles tried to enlist British support for a "Bandung in reverse," in which the leading powers would all pledge to end colonialism by a date certain, but the conservative government of Anthony Eden soured on the idea, and the conference never materialized.[242] In the greatest ideational competition in South and Southeast Asia since 1941, the administration found itself stymied and reduced to reactive and ineffective statecraft.[243] Or, as Hans Morgenthau put it in a 1956 critique of America's "Immature Asia Policy" in the *New Republic*, American misunderstanding of the power of nationalism and anticolonialism caused a failure to align political objectives with psychological, military, and economic tools.[244] Insistence on pro-American positions by newly independent states turned Jefferson's logic on its head. The point of independent republics had to be their independence.

In other areas, Eisenhower and Dulles showed somewhat better appreciation of how emerging nationalism in Asia influenced U.S. strategy, particularly vis-à-vis Japan. The conservatives in Tokyo had emerged from San Francisco generally united in their support for alignment with the United States but in search of different ways to reduce their relative dependence on Washington. Yoshida's answer had been to use Article 9 (the Peace Clause) in the postwar Japanese Constitution to avoid entrapment in a U.S. Cold War confrontation with the communist bloc. In 1955, his successor, Hatoyama Ichirō, chose a more confrontational path with Washington, calling for revision of the U.S.-Japan Security Treaty, scrapping Article 9, and establishing trade and diplomatic relations with China and the Soviet Union.[245]

Alarmed at the possible defection of America's most important ally in the Pacific, Dulles drew a hard line. He supported Japanese negotiations with Moscow for the return of Japanese POWs still languishing in Siberia, which had broad public sympathy in Japan, but he threatened to separate the Ryukyus from Japan permanently if Tokyo accepted Soviet demands for two of the Kurile Islands as a condition for signing a bilateral peace treaty.[246] Dulles also rebuffed Japanese requests for a revision of the Security Treaty.

This hard-line response to Hatoyama has generally elicited criticism from historians (not unlike the scholarly criticism aimed at the Obama administration when it drew a hard line with Hatoyama's grandson Yukio under similar circumstances in 2009). In fact, Dulles and the State Department read internal Japanese politics astutely and recognized that the majority of conservative Liberal Democratic Party (LDP) opinion was not with the prime minister's public tilt toward Moscow. When Hatoyama's beleaguered cabinet fell in 1956 and a year later was replaced by the solidly anticommunist Kishi Nobusuke, Dulles softened the U.S. stance to harness a form of Japanese nationalism Washington could live with. He supported the opening of Sino-Japanese trade offices and agreed to a revision of the U.S.-Japan Security Treaty to make the arrangement more equitable.[247] The new security treaty, signed in Washington in January 1960 by Secretary of State Christian Herter (who had replaced the ailing Dulles in April of the previous year), ended the U.S. role in Japan's domestic security and committed Japan to providing U.S. bases in Japan "for the security of Japan and the maintenance of international peace and security in the Far East."[248] This explicit alignment with U.S. security objectives in the Far East sparked protests in Tokyo and would remain contested in the Japanese Diet for decades to come, but it formulated the basis for eventual American victory in the Cold War in Asia and remains the pillar of U.S.-Japan security relations and regional stability to this day.[249]

Meanwhile, the thinking of Eisenhower and Dulles with respect to the role of nuclear weapons in American Asia strategy did evolve, even if the policy of the New Look appeared fixed. They began determined to use nuclear weapons as a way to minimize the need for forward conventional military forces that would increase the risk of entrapment in major war on the continent of Asia. Eisenhower and Dulles never formally abandoned this idea but were forced by a series of crises along the First Island Chain to question whether massive nuclear retaliation was too blunt an instrument to deter aggression against the newly expanded Asian defense perimeter.

The first of these crises hit when 10,000 PLA forces overwhelmed Kuomintang (KMT) troops on the small island of Yijiangshan in January 1955 and began firing on the nearby Dachen Islands. Eisenhower declared publicly that he was prepared to use a nuclear weapon "like a bullet or anything else" to defend American interests in securing the offshore island chain.[250] The president and Dulles believed the threat worked, but in fact they did not have Congress, the British, or the Japanese on board for engaging in nuclear war over small islands near the Chinese coast. Indeed, Eisenhower's proposal that Chiang abandon the islands in exchange for U.S. naval protection in the Straits suggests how much the president actually recognized the risk of relying on nuclear weapons for deterrence in murky tactical situations.

When the Taiwan Straits crisis resumed in August 1958 with new PLA artillery attacks, Eisenhower authorized the JCS to be prepared to use nuclear weapons to support Nationalist forces in the event of a major PLA assault and simultaneously deployed B-47 bombers with nuclear weapons capability to Guam to back up six carrier battle groups sent to the region as a show of force.[251] Historians still disagree on how ready Eisenhower really was to actually use nuclear weapons in that second crisis.[252] Nevertheless, his doubts must have been mounting, for he ordered Dulles and the Department of Defense to review the strategy of massive nuclear retaliation after the crisis abated.[253]

A few years earlier, the threat of nuclear retaliation had seemed an elegant alternative to stationing static conventional forces along the front lines in Asia, but the Taiwan crises exposed the limitations of that instrument of national power. Nuclear weapons were not the "paper tiger" Mao claimed, but Eisenhower did come to recognize that the threshold for nuclear retaliation in Asia was too high for the weapons to have utility in the fluid and ambiguous confrontations over small islands and remote jungles that constituted the front lines of the Cold War in that part of the world. With Khrushchev's decision to provide Beijing with technical support on nuclear and missile development in 1957, the U.S. nuclear card would be further limited. Ironically, nuclear weapons would force the United States back to reliance on massive conventional forces for limited war aims in Southeast Asia—a complete reversal of the logic of the New Look.[254]

In short, while the New Look generally held the line in Asia during Eisenhower's tenure, its weaknesses were also exposed. The falling utility of nuclear weapons, the inability to harness Asian nationalism, and the hollowness of SEATO would all soon emerge as major liabilities in U.S. strategy and limit the options for responding to communist success in Indochina. Lippmann had anticipated precisely this Achilles heel in U.S. strategy in a column he wrote in 1954, warning that:

failing unity or nuclear weapons (handwritten margin note)

> America can hold an island like Okinawa by herself. America can keep Formosa out of the control of Peking . . . but on the mainland of Asia she has not the power to defend large territory with a massive population unless she is inside a coalition which includes at least some of the countries of Asia. . . . American military power, which is on the sea and in the air . . . cannot occupy, it cannot pacify, it cannot control the mainland, even in the coastal areas, much less in the hinterland. Any American who commits American power in violation of this principle is taking an uncalculated and incalculable risk.[255]

Meanwhile, in Vietnam, the floor was falling out from underneath American plans for a "third force" between colonialism and communism that would obviate the need for massive military intervention. South Vietnamese president Ngo Dinh Diem rejected a national referendum in 1956 as called for under the Paris Agreement and instead consolidated his control with particularly brutal effect against the communist Vietcong. In January 1959, Hanoi decided to arm the Vietcong and prepare for the overthrow of the government in Saigon.

American containment on the continent of Asia would be tested once again.

8. "ANYONE WHO ISN'T CONFUSED REALLY DOESN'T UNDERSTAND THE SITUATION"
ASIA STRATEGY AND ESCALATION IN VIETNAM, 1961–1968

[handwritten marginalia: confused / self-determination w/ communist revolution]

The American defeat in Vietnam was a humiliating failure of grand strategy. In the numerous studies done of the war, there have been two dominant explanations for that failure. The first has been that the American leadership did not understand the Vietnamese on their own terms and that it confused national self-determination with communist revolution.[1] The second common explanation has been that the United States did not design a military strategy that aligned ends, ways, and means to strike at the enemy's Clausewitzian "center of gravity," whether that was winning the hearts and minds of South Vietnamese, protecting strategic hamlets, or hitting North Vietnam itself.[2] Both lines of criticism have merit and will be explored further, but there is a third explanation for the American failure in Vietnam that is particularly important in the context of this book: the lack of a coherent *regional* strategy to guide decision-making on the war.

[handwritten marginalia: not targeting center of gravity]

In the immediate aftermath of the Second World War, Kennan, Mac-Arthur, and Acheson had all agreed on an offshore maritime strategy centered on the First Island Chain. The United States was then pulled onto the continent in response to the North Korean invasion of the South in 1950. In Southeast Asia, however, the Truman and Eisenhower

no regional collective security worked

administrations continued to seek ways to avoid a continentally based defensive line, turning instead to SEATO's loose collective security, nuclear weapons, military assistance, and covert means to maintain a buffer against communist expansion. None worked in Indochina. When the United States escalated its ground presence in South Vietnam and its air attacks against North Vietnam in response to the Gulf of Tonkin crisis in 1965, these blunt military instruments bought time for vulnerable states such as Indonesia, Malaysia, Singapore, and Thailand to begin to develop economies and militaries that were more resilient. Meanwhile, in Northeast Asia, U.S. diplomacy helped push forward Japan-Korea normalization and a more enduring connection among the bilateral spokes of the 1951 San Francisco System. A snapshot of U.S. Asia strategy in 1966 would therefore have looked promising. Indeed, without American military escalation at that point, the entire subregion would have been at considerably greater risk.

no definition of regional strategy

Over the next three years, however, the Johnson administration continued to increase military commitments without evolving its regional strategy in any way or moving beyond a narrow definition of success measured by enemy soldiers killed. As several historians and eyewitnesses to the policy have pointed out, at no point did the administration define the importance of Vietnam to U.S. national interests in a regional or global context.[3] After the danger of dominos falling elsewhere in Asia subsided, the administration was trapped in its own arguments about the need to preserve national "prestige"—primarily with reference to Europe and domestic politics, rather than Asia, the theater supposed to be most threatened. The administration became fearful of either withdrawal or taking the fight into North Vietnam, losing its perspective on how Vietnam mattered to regional and global grand strategy at that point. The U.S. military never lost a pitched battle, but after years of tactical escalation being met by counterescalation, the North Vietnamese finally broke Johnson's will to fight with the unexpected and brazen Tet Offensive in 1968.

Richard Nixon would restore a more favorable balance of regional and global power to cover American withdrawal from Vietnam after 1969. By the presidency of Ronald Reagan, the United States would be rolling back Soviet expansion in Asia. Both presidents looked at Asia as a regional strategic problem. The Vietnam War might have ended differently, or at least done less damage to U.S. interests, had Johnson done the same.

This chapter introduces the "best and brightest" who managed Asia policy for Kennedy and Johnson, explains the path to escalation of U.S.

involvement there, and then reviews the strategic dynamics within the region and the options rejected or never considered that might have embedded the Indochina problem in a more durable regional strategy.

"The Best and the Brightest": Kennedy and Johnson's Asia Hands

John Fitzgerald Kennedy ascended to the top of the Democratic Party and the presidency of the United States in 1960, promising to transform America's role in the world, particularly in the Third World. He criticized Eisenhower and Dulles for oversimplifying the communist threat and for their rigid and dangerous overreliance on nuclear weapons under the New Look. Now the United States would counter the threat of communist expansion at its source by developing capabilities to operate all along the spectrum of national power. Under this new concept of "flexible response," which Kennedy previewed in his March 1961 State of the Union message to Congress, the administration would revive conventional military capabilities and invest in the emerging arts of counterinsurgency and special operations while increasing the roles of development assistance, cultural exchange, and other nonmilitary tools to strengthen vulnerable states on the front lines of freedom.[4]

Central to Kennedy's new approach was a rejection of Dulles's inflexible opposition to neutralism in the Third World. Kennedy had traveled to Southeast Asia as a congressman and senator beginning in 1951 and saw the power of nationalism in Asia. In the Senate debate over intervention in Indochina on April 6, 1954, he had warned that U.S. intervention could not succeed "without participation of the armed forces of other Asian nations [and] without the support of the great masses of people of Indo-China"—support the United States would never garner "if the French persist in their refusal to grant . . . legitimate independence and freedom."[5] Campaigning in 1960, he publicly echoed Eisenhower's private despair that the United States had become the protector of the status quo and had "allowed the Communists to evict us from our rightful estate": the defense of a better way of life.[6] Instead of the black-and-white world portrayed by Dulles, Kennedy spoke in Wilsonian tones of a world safe for "diversity" in which the nonaligned developing world would resist communism but not necessarily have to ally with the West.[7] With programs like "food for peace" and the Peace Corps, he would support the independence of nations so that "neither Russia nor China could control Europe and Asia."[8] Or, as Forrestal's son Michael described it in a planning memo he prepared while he worked on Southeast Asia in the Kennedy NSC, "If the impression is conveyed that the changes within the Communist bloc require corresponding flexibility in our own attempts to deal with each local situation, the range of choices available to the President may hopefully be increased."[9] It was meant to be a flexible strategy of denial rather than control, realigning the United States with the goals of self-determination inherent in American Asia policy from the beginning of the republic.

To reinforce the image of American respect for Asian diversity, Kennedy appointed ambassadors such as Harvard's preeminent Japan scholar Edwin O. Reischauer to Tokyo and that university's leading Keynesian institutional economist, John Kenneth Galbraith, to India—very much in the tradition of Wilson's appointment of University of Wisconsin professor Paul Reinsch to China in 1913. In Delhi, Galbraith told Prime Minister Jawaharlal Nehru that the United States itself was traditionally a neutralist nation, supportive of sovereignty and self-determination, even under communist-leaning governments, as long as it is not "merely a stage which precedes a communist takeover."[10] The administration entreated Nehru to consider a different balance-of-power logic, which would end direct East-West confrontation.[11] Kennedy also invited Indonesian president Sukarno to Washington and leaned closer to Jakarta in its dispute with the Netherlands over control of West Irian/West Papua. His game was to harness Indonesian nationalism and help it triumph over communism.[12] It was, in the words of Kennedy, a "New Frontier," and the youth and vigor of the president seemed to inspire a new alignment of American ideals with the emerging Asian power dynamics.

Yet, despite the promise of newness and flexibility in the application of diplomatic, economic, and military means to counter communism in Asia, Kennedy and his team never wavered from or reexamined the identification of *ends* it inherited from the Truman and Eisenhower administrations. The guiding principle remained essentially the same as that stated in NSC 68: that a loss of freedom anywhere set back the cause of freedom everywhere. "No son of mine is going to be soft on Communism," the president's acerbic father, Joe, declared to supporters in 1960.[13] Hailing from an Irish-Catholic constituency in the era of Joe McCarthy, John F. Kennedy had carefully protected and brandished his anticommunist credentials, declaring before the American Friends of Vietnam in 1956 that

Vietnam "represents the cornerstone of the Free World in Southeast Asia, the keystone to the arch, the finger in the dike."[14] This hard-line definition of ends was only reinforced when the new president heard of Soviet premier Nikita Khrushchev's January 6, 1961, speech in Moscow promising Soviet support for indigenous revolutions against fascists and capitalists so that "wars of national liberation" would yield the inevitable socialist world. The Kennedy administration promised to be flexible on ways and means but came into office determined to stop Khrushchev's wars of revolution on the front lines.

After almost two decades of State Department leadership in the formulation of foreign policy strategy, Kennedy shifted the initiative back to the White House. His management style, which favored ad hoc task forces over Eisenhower's structured NSC meetings, enhanced the power of the people close to the Oval Office and replicated aspects of FDR's approach to policy formation.[15] The president's brother, Robert, inserted himself periodically in almost all aspects of foreign policy and made several trips to Asia while serving as attorney general. At the NSC, as assistant to the president for national security affairs, former Harvard dean McGeorge Bundy presided over a staff that grew in size, function, and influence.[16] Bundy's father had been a clerk for Justice Oliver Wendell Holmes and an aide to Henry L. Stimson, who chose young "Mac" Bundy to help him write his memoirs, *On Active Service in Peace and War*.[17] Bundy was by dint of breeding, experience, and mentoring one of his generation's leading denizens of foreign policy realism.

Bundy was not, however, a foreign policy intellectual in the tradition of Kennan, Nitze, or even Dulles. That role fell to his first deputy and later national security advisor under Johnson, Walt Whitman Rostow. An economic historian from MIT, born in New York to fervently patriotic immigrants, and educated at Yale and in Britain with a Rhodes scholarship, Rostow was given a mandate to develop policy for Asia and the Third World while Bundy focused on management of the Atlantic Alliance and Europe. Rostow had already established an academic reputation for his theories on the linkage between economic and political development and argued that these same elements together with counterinsurgency could defeat communism in the Third World, particularly if backed by American airpower, a lesson he derived from service as a targeter for the U.S. Army Air Corps during the Second World War.[18] His supreme confidence that social science theory could be parsimoniously applied to cultures as diverse as those in Asia made his academic colleagues nervous. Lucian Pye, a leading Asianist at MIT, lamented to his seminar class after hearing of Rostow's appointment, "You know, you don't sleep quite so well anymore when you know some of the people going to Washington."[19] Nevertheless, Rostow stood out among Kennedy's senior political appointees for his efforts to establish an intellectual framework for flexible response that would be something other than reactive to events.

Beginning in the spring of 1961, at the NSC and then through inter-agency working groups as the lead from Policy Planning, Rostow worked multiple drafts of a Basic National Security Policy (BNSP) document that would chart an affirmative path toward a more sustainable foreign policy. The BNSP was a global strategic document, but with respect to Asia it noted that the immediate objective was to reduce tensions with Beijing (or Peking, as it was still known), through a combination of "sticks" de-terring aggression and "carrots" encouraging longer-term rapprochement, while yielding no ground to communist expansion. Seeking ways to re-duce American risk on the continent, the BNSP suggested gradual mili-tary disengagement from both Korea and Indochina, with the "United Nations or other neutral peace force . . . empowered to occupy a neutral-ized belt between North and South Korea and another between North and South Vietnam."[20] The line would then be held against communist expansion in those areas with a combination of economic and political development tools championed by Rostow in academia, backed by American air and naval power. While ambitious and optimistic in terms of where it drew the lines against communist expansion in Asia, the BNSP bore strong resemblance to the offshore strategic concepts Kennan had urged fifteen years earlier (though Rostow was willing to abandon Tai-wan in ways Kennan was not).[21]

Bundy and the president were skeptical, though. The national security advisor shared drafts of the BNSP with the president in February and March 1962 but chose not to have the NSC approve the document. In its breadth of activity, he wrote to Rostow, the strategy lacked "a clear sense of limits, and of priorities."[22] The same sentiment was echoed by Rostow's replacement as deputy national security advisor, Carl Kaysen, who worried that the strategy would not allow distinction between "vital and periph-eral" interests.[23] The Kennedy team's preference was for case-by-case decision-making as events unfolded. Rostow retained his faith in the in-struments of American power, particularly economic development and airpower, but he fell in line with the incremental view of decision-making that dominated the Kennedy and the Johnson administrations thereafter.[24] Ironically, that path would result in even greater confusion about which interests were truly vital as North Vietnam defied calibrated application of flexible response.

With the White House focused on calibrated and tactical response, the State Department was not well positioned to produce a new strategic framework either. Although Secretary of State Dean Rusk was the first real Asia expert to lead the department and signaled the region's importance by making Asia (Thailand) his first official destination as secretary (a first, and one not replicated until Hillary Clinton's visit to Japan on her first trip as secretary, in 2009), he was never part of Kennedy's inner circle or the vicar of foreign policy that Dulles, Marshall, and Acheson had been. Rusk was hired as everyone's "number-two choice"—likable, competent, and credible on anticommunism, but not sparkling with brilliance or insightful on the changes occurring even within his own region of expertise.[25] Though his influence would grow when fellow southerner and Camelot outsider Lyndon Baines Johnson became president in November 1963, he was rarely the innovator of ideas or a check on the president's own instincts. His views on the developments in Southeast Asia could be summarized by an observation he made early in the administration: "[I]f you don't pay attention to the periphery, the periphery changes. And the first thing you know the periphery is the center . . . what happens in one place cannot help but affect what happens in another."[26] He let events come to him rather than trying to shape them in advance, and thus the periphery did become the center.

Capable men serving under Rusk did bring a more strategic appreciation of the dynamics within Asia and skepticism about the enterprise in Vietnam, either by dint of long service in the region or relevant experience elsewhere. However, most of them did not last, or they expended their energy fighting over ways and means rather than the objectives of policy. Rusk's first deputy (still referred to then as undersecretary) was former ad executive, Connecticut governor, and ambassador to India Chester Bowles. Early on, Bowles urged Rusk and the president to adopt a comprehensive strategy for Asia and the Pacific rather than impose a global Cold War approach to a dynamic and changing region, but he quickly fell out with Rusk and the White House over his open advocacy of negotiated "neutralization" for Vietnam and his leaks opposing the Bay of Pigs operation in Cuba. After less than a year on the job, he was sent back to India for a second tour as ambassador.[27]

Averell Harriman also stood out as a grand veteran of the Democratic Party's foreign policy establishment and an advocate of a more restrained application of containment in Asia. Though already a former ambassador and cabinet secretary, and not an Asia expert per se, he was put in charge of the Far East Division at State from December 1961 to April 1963, where he tried to inject new energy into the badly beaten and risk-averse division. It was a remarkable feat for a man already seventy years old, but he had confidence as the scion of one of America's wealthiest families and credibility as one of the early Jeremiahs on Stalin during the war. In the end, he had too much confidence, though. As he moved up to be undersecretary for political affairs in 1963, he set his sights on the top job in the department, incurring the quiet wrath of Rusk. He then lobbied Johnson directly for a central role managing Vietnam policy, but instead he was sent on a series of unsuccessful diplomatic missions to win Soviet support for mediation with Hanoi. Harriman remained loyal to the stated objectives of stopping communist victory over South Vietnam, and Johnson remained loyal to Harriman but never let him into the innermost circle of decision-making.[28] He ended his career in policy trying to finalize a peace agreement with the Vietnamese in Paris before the Nixon administration came to power in 1969 but failed—he believed—because Republicans did not yet want peace.[29]

Harriman's successor as assistant secretary in 1963 was Roger Hilsman, a brash veteran of Merrill's Marauders and OSS service with Burmese guerrillas, and an unabashed advocate of the new doctrine of counterinsurgency. Kennedy warmed to his fellow Pacific War veteran quickly, but as the U.S. Army moved from counterinsurgency doctrine to more traditional search-and-destroy missions in Vietnam, Hilsman grew increasingly strident in his opposition and resigned in March 1964 to teach at Columbia University.[30] His replacement, Bill Bundy (in the newly renamed Bureau of East Asia and Pacific Affairs), was the brother of the national security advisor and was a former CIA officer with experience in Southeast Asia. His name "would probably be on more pieces of paper dealing with Vietnam over a seven-year period than anyone else's," and yet, notes David Halberstam in his classic study *The Best and the Brightest*, "he was the man about whom the least was known."[31] Bundy expressed accurate views of the situation in Vietnam and Southeast Asia, but ultimately he supported the use of force and was not going to oppose the White House or the administration consensus. At one point, he proposed neutralism for South Vietnam backed by intensive bombing to cover U.S.

ASIA STRATEGY AND ESCALATION IN VIETNAM, 1961–1968

prestige as Saigon fell, but Rusk rejected the notion and, as far as we know, Bundy never raised the idea again.[32]

Johnson agreed to continue hearing opposition views on the war from Bowles's successor as undersecretary of State, George Ball, but by the time of Johnson's presidency, the general trend line in the State Department under Rusk was set. The president was open to hearing about *options* to achieve the objective of a noncommunist Vietnam but not a reformulation of policy goals.

In time, the most important dissent on Vietnam strategy would come from Secretary of Defense Robert S. McNamara. Initially, McNamara turned over Asia policy to his deputy so that he could focus on modernizing Pentagon systems and procurement practices the way he had turned around Ford Motor Company as CEO during the years before Kennedy recruited him. As the situation in Vietnam deteriorated, McNamara became the point man on the war, using the same statistical analysis in applying American military power that had made him a star at Harvard Business School, the Army Air Corps, and Ford. By 1967, those statistics no longer allowed the data-driven secretary to pretend that success as defined by the administration was possible in Vietnam. By then, however, the prestige of the United States had been committed to such an extent that options were greatly reduced.

These men were brilliant in their own ways, but as Halberstam stresses, they were mostly "functional, operational, *tactical* men, not really intellectuals, and tactical men think in terms of options, while intellectuals less so; intellectuals might think in terms of the sweep of history and might believe that twelve months would make little difference in Vietnam, that if the sweep of history was bad in 1964, it would probably, if anything, be a good deal worse in 1965."[33]

The Kennedy and Johnson national security teams applied their experience as statisticians, targeters, and social scientists to improve the efficiency and flexibility of the instruments of American power—but they did so in reaction to events and without reexamining the precise interests that they were trying to defend. They were the protégés of Marshall, Acheson, and Forrestal and had a charge to keep, despite the transformational veneer of flexible response. The problem was *not* that the new team either embraced an illogical new grand strategy or operated without strategic concepts. The problem was that strategic concepts were inherited without the kind of contextual reappraisal that is so essential to the strategic art. As Les Gelb summarizes in describing what went wrong with

Vietnam: "Each post-war President inherited previous commitments. Each extended those commitments."[34]

"To Take All Necessary Steps": Escalation

The first test of flexible response was actually not in Vietnam but in tiny neighboring Laos. When Kennedy came to office, the French-established government in this landlocked nation was teetering on the edge of collapse under pressure from the Pathet Lao—anti-French insurgents now backed by Hanoi. During the transition, Eisenhower had urged Kennedy to make Laos his highest foreign policy priority in Asia, since a communist victory there would have flanked South Vietnam and caused further dominos to fall.[35] Kennedy's more hawkish advisors, including Rostow, believed that as many as 60,000 U.S. troops would have to be inserted in Laos and neighboring Thailand and Vietnam, and the Joint Chiefs—still operating under the assumptions of the New Look—argued for consideration of tactical nuclear weapons if North Vietnam or China counterintervened.[36] Kennedy was inclined to be tough after the loss of U.S. credibility in the Bay of Pigs that April, but he was also more wary of the hawkish voices in the Pentagon because of that fiasco. With encouragement from Harriman, he rejected military intervention and opted for a negotiated settlement in Geneva and neutralism for Laos. Some, like Hilsman, thought it was a precedent for how Kennedy might have handled Vietnam.[37] More likely, it reflected the president's lack of confidence in the fighting mettle of the Laotians, whose army Kennedy dismissed as a "bunch of homosexuals" compared with the Vietnamese.[38] If anything, neutralism in Laos put a greater political and strategic premium for the president on holding the line in South Vietnam.

In Vietnam, the situation was deteriorating. The number of assassinations of pro-government South Vietnamese by the Vietcong had quadrupled to over 4,000 between 1959 and 1961, and the North was sending tens of thousands of newly trained insurgents to the South each month.[39] Vice President Johnson returned from a trip to the region in May 1961 with dire warnings that the neutralization strategy in Laos had "drastically weakened the ability to maintain any strongly pro-US orientation" elsewhere in Southeast Asia.[40] In October, Rostow and General Maxwell Taylor, the president's military advisor, upon returning from their own visit to Vietnam, recommended the deployment of 8,000 U.S. troops to reverse the tide.[41] Reviewing the Rostow-Taylor recommendations, as well as dissenting views from Galbraith (whom the president had asked to visit Vietnam on a return trip from India) and Ball, Kennedy chose calibrated escalation.[42] A November 1961 NSC Action Memorandum spelled out the U.S. strategy going forward: "U.S. objectives and concept of operations [are] to prevent communist domination of South Vietnam; to create in that country a viable and increasingly democratic society, and to initiate, on an accelerated basis, a series of mutually supporting actions of a military, political, economic, psychological, and covert character designed to achieve this objective."[43]

While Galbraith, Ball, Hilsman, and others were warning that South Vietnamese president Ngo Dinh Diem's incompetence and repression in the South were a large part of the problem, Kennedy chose not to press Saigon for reforms while the South Vietnamese government was under pressure from the North. In December, the president approved an increase in the number of U.S. advisors, as Diem had requested. When Kennedy made the decision, there were just 1,000 U.S. military personnel on the ground. A year later, there would be 11,000.

Over the next eighteen months, Vietnam fell to the back burner as the Berlin and Cuban missile crises beset the White House, and administration officials read inflated accounts of Diem's successful control over "strategic hamlets" from General Paul Harkins and the willfully deceptive U.S. Military Assistance Command in Vietnam (MACV). When South Vietnamese Army units attacked Buddhist pagodas, and an elderly priest seized world headlines by immolating himself in protest in downtown Saigon in the summer of 1963, Washington was gripped with crisis over Vietnam once again.[44] The Joint Chiefs backed the MACV and wanted to stand by Diem, whereas Harriman, Hilsman, and Forrestal on the NSC staff wanted to be rid of the problematic South Vietnamese leader. Worried that intervention against Diem would make the United States look like colonial overlords, the White House approved a vague effort to encourage agitated South Vietnamese military officers to replace him. To Kennedy and Johnson's horror, the United States lost control of the coup, and Diem and his brother were pulled from a Catholic church and murdered in the back of an armored personnel carrier on November 2.[45] The administration now faced only greater uncertainty, repeated coups, and an increase in South Vietnamese dependence on American power and decision-making. Three weeks later, Kennedy himself was assassinated in Dallas.

Lyndon Baines Johnson came to power preoccupied with Kennedy's domestic legislative agenda and committed to Kennedy's advisors' stance on Vietnam. As the new president told McGeorge Bundy, the United States had to stay "very firm" on Vietnam.[46] Some historians argue that Kennedy would not have escalated U.S. involvement in Vietnam had he lived (a parallel to the hopeful and unprovable expectation that FDR might have avoided confrontation with the Soviets two decades earlier had he lived longer). They note that Kennedy ordered plans for a drawdown of the U.S. military presence, without highlighting that these plans were based on the premise of U.S. victory by 1965.[47] They argue, echoing Hilsman, that Kennedy had set a deliberate precedent by choosing neutralism for Laos, ignoring his repeated rejection of the same proposal for Vietnam. The assessment that Kennedy would have backed away from escalation pits one interpretation of his temperament against the intellectual framework he had constructed for Vietnam before being assassinated, a framework loyally implemented by his advisors and Johnson. Robert Kennedy himself later stated on the record that there was no way his brother would have backed down in Vietnam.[48]

Gambling that Johnson would not intervene but prepared for escalation if he did, Hanoi expanded support for direct Vietcong attacks against U.S. facilities in the South. Congress gave Johnson a green light for counterescalation in August 1964 after North Vietnamese patrol boats attacked a U.S. destroyer operating in the Gulf of Tonkin, prompting a congressional resolution on August 10 authorizing the president "to take all necessary steps, including the use of armed force" to "assist Vietnam and SEATO member states."[49] Johnson held onto that resolution until he won reelection against Barry Goldwater and then turned to McNamara for recommendations on the next steps. In January 1965, the defense secretary laid the options on the table: (1) withdraw from Indochina as a whole (in which case the country would fall); (2) engage in a limited air campaign and incrementally increase advisors (continuing a strategy that was not yielding results); or (3) deploy major U.S. ground units and force the North to the negotiating table.[50]

Johnson leaned toward the third option. Bombings of the North began in February 1965 in direct retaliation for a damaging Vietcong attack on the massive U.S. Air Force Base at Pleiku, and then with the broader aim of forcing the North to accept a cease-fire in the South. Far from being cowed, however, the North expanded operations, backed by new pledges from Mao that China would intervene to support the North against increased American attacks. With the U.S. air base at Da Nang now in danger of encirclement by enemy forces, Johnson approved the first deployment of U.S. combat units, and 3,500 marines came ashore to join the 25,000 advisors already on the ground in Vietnam.

In taking each of these steps, the president was not oblivious to the risk of entering a quagmire, as the leaked Pentagon Papers and subsequent historiography have demonstrated.[51] His political advisors kept telling the press, "This President is not about to get involved in a land war in Asia. He is just not going to do it."[52] But as Johnson recalled in his memoirs, he worried more about the impact on the commitment of the American people to internationalism if he allowed Vietnam to fall the way Truman had lost China.[53] And although there were reasons to doubt the prospects for success, there was no precedent to suggest that complete failure was a possible scenario. In the Dominican Republic, the United States had just toppled a communist sympathizer with a token show of force, and the U.S. effort to date in Southeast Asia had been waged by fewer ground forces than Britain still maintained in the region to protect Malaysia. The North Vietnamese were tougher than other foes—that was clear—but in Asia the U.S. military had always blunted if not defeated totalitarian aggression.

And so, in April 1965, Johnson approved a significantly expanded combat role for U.S. forces in Vietnam. His aim was still a negotiated and acceptable stalemate that kept the South free. In a speech at Johns Hopkins University on April 7, he hinted at political dialogue and offered a billion dollars in postwar economic reconstruction aid for the region, but Hanoi scornfully rejected the proposal. In mid-May, he halted the bombing, but the North did not respond. Johnson would not negotiate from weakness. "When we are strong," McGeorge Bundy had reminded him, "then we can face negotiation."[54] In late July, the president gathered his national security team. Rusk, Bundy, and McNamara agreed that the North was engaged in naked aggression and that a further escalation of ground forces was required. McNamara emphasized that "a gigantic arc from SV [South Vietnam] to Iran and the Middle East" hung in the balance.[55] Ball warned in a last-ditch memorandum that the North's will would not be broken by bombing or more ground forces, but although Johnson tolerated and appreciated the undersecretary's dissent, he saw him as an Atlanticist and an expert on the international economy, with "no more than a thimble of expertise on Asia."[56] The president approved the dispatch of 50,000 more troops (for a total of 125,000 on the ground), with more in the pipeline. In a press conference held to announce the deployment on July 28, he told the American people, "we did not choose to be the guardians at the gate, but there is no one else."[57]

These initial deployments of U.S. ground forces demonstrated the skill and firepower of the U.S. Army, particularly when a regiment of the First Cavalry Division broke waves of North Vietnamese Army (NVA) assaults at the Battle of Ia Drang Valley in November 1965. But heavy U.S. casualties also revealed how tough the NVA were in a pitched fight, and Hanoi responded to the U.S. escalation by deploying additional NVA regiments to bleed the Americans in the rugged terrain of the central highlands. In February 1966, Westmoreland told the president that it would take more troops to go on the offensive, and the president authorized another increase. By the summer of 1966, there were 429,000 U.S. forces on the ground. With divisions of troops now at his disposal, Westmoreland's search-and-destroy tactics ceased to bear any resemblance to the counterinsurgency doctrine that had so animated the Kennedy administration in 1961—and thus ultimately created even greater distance between the government in Saigon and the Vietnamese people.

At home, opposition to the war grew, but the political establishment held. In November 1967, Johnson organized his first meeting of the "Wise Men"—veterans of the Truman and Kennedy administrations, led by Acheson. They urged the president to stay the course in Vietnam, with only Ball (now out of government) dissenting.[58] Rusk and Rostow were equally resolute. Among Johnson's core advisors, only McNamara began to lose heart. The United States had by now dropped almost as much ordnance on North Vietnam as it had on Japan and Germany combined during the Second World War, and North Vietnamese advances in antiaircraft fire were threatening to cause casualties to U.S. air crews comparable to those in that earlier war.[59] McNamara did the math, and he predicted that the United States would need to send 600,000 U.S. troops to Vietnam to have any chance of success. Anything beyond that, he assessed, would risk general war with China. Anything less would eventually result in the collapse of the South.[60] At his urging, Johnson tried further bombing halts to encourage Vietnamese compromise, but the North now had the strategic initiative and remained defiant.

The breaking point came when the North Vietnamese violated the Tet New Year's truce and attacked across the length of South Vietnam in late January 1968, including in the ancient capital of Hue and the modern capital of Saigon. North Vietnamese forces, exposed on the offensive, were pounded by U.S. airpower and mobile army and marine units, losing all the ground they had gained. Tet was a massive military mistake by Hanoi, but it nevertheless resulted in a brilliant strategic victory. Westmoreland reported that he would now need an additional 206,000 troops at a cost of over $10 billion, with activation of reserve units back in the United States. In Johnson's book, this meant Vietnam would no longer be a limited war. It would now require cutting back his ambitious domestic agenda.

In the final gathering of the Wise Men, on March 26–27, only Supreme Court Justice Abe Fortas, General Maxwell Taylor, and former undersecretary Robert Murphy agreed with the Joint Chiefs that the president should stay the course. "The establishment bastards have bailed out!" cried the president to his aides after the meeting.[61] With inflation, a crisis in the gold standard, and a defeat in the first presidential primary vote in New Hampshire, Johnson then bowed out himself.[62] On March 31, in a solemn TV address to the nation, the president promised a major cutback in bombing and a readiness to undertake peace negotiations. He also declared that he would not seek reelection to the presidency.

For Want of an Asia Strategy

The war in Vietnam would last seven more years, but Tet was the turning point. It proved that the U.S. strategy was fundamentally flawed. The entire purpose of calibrated escalation at each point had been to break the North's will to continue the fight in the South, but with each escalation the North only received more backing from Beijing, deployed more troops across the demilitarized zone, and became more defiant. There were no off-ramps or alternate paths in the U.S. strategy to deal with this defiance—only further escalation. As Johnson aide Bill Moyers lamented in a 1968 interview with *The Atlantic*, "We always seemed to be calculating the short-term consequences of each alternative at every step of the process, but not the long-term consequences."[63] The United States was prepared only for limited war, but the North signaled that it was willing to continue fighting even to the point of total war. Flexible response imposed no upward limits on the means employed—until Tet forced Johnson to consider calling up the reserves, and the administration finally found where that limit was. Tet was check, if not checkmate.

In Vietnam, the United States failed to address the most fundamental element in strategy—the definition of ends. Missing entirely was any consideration of why Indochina mattered to U.S. interests. As Les Gelb notes in his influential study of Vietnam War decision-making, "no systematic or serious examination of Vietnam's importance to the United States was ever undertaken within the government."[64] Townsend Hoopes, former undersecretary of the air force, and a front-row witness to military escalation, wrote in 1968 that there was no comprehensive grand strategy or consistent objective set for Vietnam, only ad hoc meetings, and thus "decisions and actions that marked our large-scale military entry into the Vietnam War in early 1965 reflected the piecemeal consideration of interrelated issues, and this was the natural consequence of a fragmented NSC and a general inattention to long-range policy planning."[65] Indochina was barely a footnote in American foreign policy before the Korean War, but fifteen years later, Rusk's warning had come true—the periphery had become the center.

With ambiguity about the ends of grand strategy, military strategy foundered. In his famous 1981 Army War College thesis, Colonel Harry Summers blamed the U.S. Army for treating Vietnam as a guerrilla war when in fact the main enemy units after 1964 were primarily regular NVA. The army should have fought Vietnam the way they fought Korea, he argued, by leaving the domestic counterinsurgency to indigenous forces and focusing American combat power against North Vietnam— the actual center of gravity in Clausewitzian terms.[66] Yet risking general war with China over Vietnam would have further turned American strategic priorities on their head.[67] If the independence of South Vietnam was not enough to merit increased U.S. ground forces after Tet, the American public would not have supported a war on the continent against China. Increased strategic bombing was a less strategically risky course, but as both Johnson and Nixon found, that blunt instrument could occasionally bend but never break the North Vietnamese will to fight.[68] The U.S. military strategy might also have been more effective at securing South Vietnam had Westmoreland used the deliberate counterinsurgency strategies championed early in the war by Hilsman and President Kennedy.[69] In fact, as Andrew Krepinevich notes, the marines' "combined action platoons" were clearing and holding hamlets without relying on overwhelming firepower and attrition and provided better results than the army's search-and-destroy missions.[70] However, pacification campaigns would still have had to contend with the steady infiltration of NVA units from the North and the weak center in Saigon.[71]

Ultimately, the effectiveness of the U.S. military's operational concepts depended on what the nation's definition of ends was. Without that, the U.S. military lost unity of command, with the theater command in Hawaii focused on the Chinese threat and then three wars in Vietnam itself: (a) the army's conventional ground war of attrition; (b) pacification efforts on the margin by the marines and occasionally by the army; and (c) what Hoopes called the "curiously remote air war against North Vietnam."[72] General Maxwell Taylor famously asked in 1965 if the commander in Vietnam knew his mission objective, and he received no answer. In polls five years later, a majority of general officers in Vietnam said they still could not answer the question.[73]

At the White House, the answer increasingly became that a free and independent Vietnam mattered to U.S. national interests as a matter of prestige. "I am not going to be the President who saw Southeast Asia go the way China went," stormed Johnson on more than one occasion.[74] Some realists, such as Hans Morgenthau, argued that the administration had become too "obsessed with the fear of permanent loss of prestige which we imagine would follow a temporary setback" and thus "oblivious to the much more serious loss of prestige which would ensue, and has already ensued, from the continuation and escalation of a losing enterprise."[75] Yet even skeptics of escalation who agreed that Indochina held no inherent vital interest for the United States were transfixed by the issue of American credibility. George Kennan told a packed Senate Foreign Relations Committee hearing in February 1966 that "*If it were not for the considerations of prestige that arise precisely out of our present involvement* [emphasis added], even a situation in which South Vietnam were controlled exclusively by the Viet Cong, while regrettable, and no doubt morally unwarranted, would not, in my opinion, present dangers great enough to justify our direct military intervention."[76]

Kennan would not advocate a unilateral U.S withdrawal until 1969 for fear that it might embolden China and the Soviets and cause difficulties elsewhere. General Matthew B. Ridgway would similarly resist publicly advocating disengagement until an article in *Foreign Affairs* in 1971, precisely because of his concerns about the impact of retreat on American prestige.[77]

Prestige is undoubtedly an important element in national power, but it can also be a source of vain pride when it is divorced from considerations of the reality of international relations, as Morgenthau warned during the war. Where precisely was American prestige in Vietnam a vital strategic interest in the late 1960s? Historian Frank Ninkovich observes that although officials recognized that Indochina was unimportant in itself, in a global context it "spoke volumes about the degree to which America and Europe adhered to the belief system that was central to the entire project of modern foreign policy."[78] Or, as Robert Kennedy put it while attorney general: "If Americans did not stop communism in South Vietnam, how could people believe that they would stop it in Berlin?"[79] Europe, in other words, continued to define U.S. strategy in Southeast Asia. Yet no European allies sent troops to Vietnam, despite both Eisenhower and Johnson pleading to London for just the pipe band of the storied Black Watch Regiment. Britain decided to pull its own forces out of Malaysia in 1965, and de Gaulle advised Harriman against escalation, having normalized France's relations with China in 1964. To the extent that NATO allies watched the Vietnam War, it was out of concern for a possible degradation of NATO capabilities caused by U.S. escalation on the other side of the world. As Ball warned, "what we might gain by establishing the steadfastness of our commitments we could lose by an erosion of confidence in our judgment."[80] The North Korean attack in June 1950 arguably did matter to the security of Europe, since it was rightly seen as a Soviet-backed conventional invasion aimed in part at testing U.S. resolve. But Europe was far more secure and detached from Asia in 1966 than it was in 1950.

Therefore, in terms of both prestige and geostrategy, Vietnam mattered in one place, and that was in Asia. McGeorge Bundy held afterward that the administration knew this, that Vietnam was "important primarily in the context of that region rather than the context of the worldwide scene."[81] Eisenhower's NSC had identified Indochina as the bookend to Korea that held back a communist takeover of continental Asia, and in November 1961 there was NSC consensus that if Vietnam fell, all of Southeast Asia would collapse.[82] All of this, it was assumed, would put the more vital offshore island chain and Japan in peril. Johnson returned from his own trip in August 1963 warning that the loss of Vietnam would mean the United States would have to pull back to San Francisco and leave "the vast Pacific . . . a Red Sea."[83]

Yet the U.S. escalation in Vietnam was never backed by a strategy focused on securing Asia as a whole. Rostow had tried to formulate a long-term grand strategy, to include Asia, with the BNSP, but he was pushed back to the ad hoc decision-making process that the president and the foreign policy principals preferred. Hilsman also urged formulation of an integrated strategy, complaining in a final memo to Rusk as he left the State Department in March 1964 that

> we have so far failed as a Government to mesh fully the many different instrumentalities of foreign policy and thus to obtain full benefit from mutually reinforcing actions. This is true throughout Southeast Asia, but especially in South Viet-Nam. It applies to all instrumentalities of foreign policy equally, but it can best be summed up by Clausewitz's dictum that war is politics pursued by other means. We must learn better how to tailor our military might, aid, etc., to political purposes and, most important, to orchestrate military power more neatly with diplomacy and politics.[84]

Chester Bowles went furthest in pushing a regional strategy to put Vietnam in context. In a June 1962 memo that evoked Kennan's own March 1948 appeal from Manila for a coherent regional strategy, Bowles wrote:

> The military decisions we have made thus far in Vietnam and Thailand and our contingency planning for Laos have been forced on us by events. . . . However, our step-by-step military response has not been accompanied by a comparable effort to think through our ultimate *political* aims for Southeast Asia as a whole. As long as we lack a political "grand design" for Southeast Asia, the initiative will continue to rest with our adversaries and with our allies and camp followers, whose parochial views often ignore the global forces with which American policy must contend. As matters now stand, we may find ourselves forced to choose between an escalating war or a humiliating retreat in an area where the strategic conditions are disadvantageous to us and where direct U.S. military participation would be roundly denounced by domestic critics as "another Democratic war." If in the meantime we have failed to go beyond Mr. Eisenhower's famous "falling dominoes" analogy to explain our political objectives in Southeast Asia, we may find ourselves increasingly the captive of events with unpredictable results both at home and abroad. [Emphasis in original.][85]

Those political objectives, Bowles argued, should be "guaranteed national independence, more rapid economic development, and maximum freedom of choice within their own cultures and religions." These American principles would provide the "affirmative, understandable, appealing purpose which has been largely lacking since the days of Roosevelt."[86] Bowles, however, was already falling out of favor with the core members of Kennedy's national security team.

In fact, the Eisenhower, Kennedy, and Johnson administrations were correct in identifying the danger to the rest of Asia if Chinese and Soviet-backed communist revolutions succeeded in quickly toppling South Vietnam in the first half of the 1960s. Although the United States and Britain had turned the tide on communist insurgencies in Malaysia, Burma, and the Philippines, Beijing maintained connections to communist parties throughout Southeast Asia and retained plans for renewed fighting in the future.[87] The U.S. ambassador in Bangkok warned in 1961 that Thailand always blew with the wind and was under pressure from Russia to turn neutral in the Cold War because of the deteriorating situation next door in Vietnam, an outcome the ambassador thought likely if Saigon fell.[88] In Malaya (Malaysia after 1962), the government urged Washington throughout the early 1960s to stop a communist takeover in South Vietnam "before it is too late."[89] The Philippine foreign secretary likewise warned the incoming Kennedy administration that if the United States did not do more to stop communist victory in South Vietnam, then America's Asian allies would have to "revise their policies toward the U.S. government."[90] Singapore, the most strategic port between Aden and Hong Kong, lay exposed without an army or government of its own after being ejected from Malaysia by Tunku Abdul Rahman in 1965. Perhaps most important, the Australian government of Prime Minister Robert Menzies continued to push for U.S. military intervention in Vietnam to stem the communist tide.[91]

Indonesia was the most important domino of all in Southeast Asia. The remaining offshore balancers, Kennan and Ball, both shared with the hardliners in the Kennedy and Johnson administrations the view that hostile control of that vast archipelago and its natural resources would threaten vital sea lanes and outflank Malaysia, Thailand, Burma, and the rest of continental Southeast Asia.[92] "What price holding onto continental Asia if we have a hostile Indonesia at its back?" warned a September 1961 NSC memo.[93] In the early Kennedy years, Indonesia seemed a likely candidate for the president's policy of accepting diversity within the neutral camp, since Indonesian nationalism was seen as a counterforce to any ideological alignment with Beijing.[94] Sukarno's April 1963 visit to Washington and his statement to Kennedy that Indonesia and all of Southe Asia "wanted to be free of domination from the outside" certainly seen promising.[95] But then, in 1964, Sukarno suddenly moved closer to Mao in order to align himself politically with Indonesia's three-million-member Communist Party (the PKI) as a counterbalance to the Indonesian military. Sukarno announced a new "Djakarta-Phnom Phen-Hanoi-Peking-P'yongyang axis," promising to work with Beijing to "crush America," while his foreign ministry discussed defense agreements with China in case of imperialist attacks.[96]

In other words, when Johnson chose escalation in 1965, there was a serious communist threat to all of Southeast Asia. Michael Lind has written that the war in Vietnam was necessary to buy these vulnerable states time to fortify their political, economic, and military capabilities—and he is right.[97] After listening to leading scholars condemn Johnson for escalation in Indochina at a Harvard dinner party held in his honor in the autumn of 1968, Singapore's prime minister, Lee Kuan Yew, turned on his hosts angrily and said, "You make me sick," before explaining that countries like his would have fallen without the American stand in Vietnam in 1965.[98] The academics, expecting sympathy for their views from a downtrodden Asian leader, were probably crestfallen.

An American counterpunch was needed in 1965, and as American forces blunted North Vietnamese momentum, the rest of Asia began to recover its footing. In Indonesia, Sukarno's revolutionary vision came to a crashing halt when a countercoup in September 1965 (this time not orchestrated by the CIA) crushed the communists and brought to power a neutral but decidedly anticommunist regime under General Suharto. Most importantly, Japan emerged as the engine of economic growth for the region as a whole. In 1960, the CIA had warned the incoming administration that the Soviets were focused on producing a powerful anti-American movement in Japan, capitalizing on antigovernment protests over the revision of the Security Treaty that would lead to neutralism in Tokyo if unchecked.[99] McNamara and McGeorge Bundy continued to warn Kennedy and Johnson that retreat in Vietnam would almost certainly push Japan over the edge to neutralism.[100] They completely missed what was really happening. Japan's dominant conservatives recognized that their cohesion against the Left and their country's prosperity depended on the protective umbrella provided by the Security Treaty with the United States. Rather than searching to defect from the West after the controversial 1960 treaty revision, Prime Minister Ikeda Hayato and his successors focused the nation on doubling Japan's national income, which the Liberal Democratic Party (LDP) had essentially accomplished by 1965.[101] This economic miracle marginalized the neutralist Left in Japan and energized manufacturing in countries like Malaysia, Singapore, and Thailand, all of which began to develop greater political stability and economic inclusiveness, in sharp contrast to South Vietnam. Japan also provided $500 million in economic aid to Seoul and normalized diplomatic relations with the Republic of Korea in June 1965, a move that helped the South overcome North Korea economically and lock itself more solidly into the Western bloc (and, in that case, a piece of regional statecraft quietly enabled by American diplomats).[102]

In 1962, Japanese economist Kaname Akamatsu predicted with publication of his "flying geese" theory that Japan's model of industrialization would trickle down to the rest of Asia.[103] His work should have been read by Bundy, McNamara, and the CIA. These broader regional developments did not inform the decisions to escalate U.S. involvement in Vietnam after 1965. By then, the administration was trapped in an ad hoc and piecemeal test of wills with Hanoi driven by vague considerations of prestige rather than accurate calculations of U.S. interests in the rest of Asia. This omission stands in contrast to the San Francisco System of alliances negotiated by Dulles to preserve longer-term U.S. interests in the Pacific even in the midst of fighting during the Korean War.

To be sure, there were ideas percolating about a regional approach. Reischauer argued in 1968, for example, that the United States needed a new regional strategy that would "minimize, if not entirely eliminate, our military presence in the less developed countries of Asia," replacing it with increased economic aid, and reinforcing U.S. security guarantees to Japan, Korea, and Taiwan, which were stable and not in danger of internal civil war.[104] Echoing positions Eisenhower and Kennedy had once expressed, he warned that the alternative would be to "run the risk of drifting unconsciously into a position of standing for the *status quo* [emphasis in original] rather than change in a part of the world that needs change desperately and undoubtedly will have it. When we do this, we condemn ourselves to what in the long run must be the losing side."[105]

Senator Mike Mansfield also pleaded for a regional perspective on the Vietnam problem. After deploying as a marine in the Philippines and China in the 1920s (having already served in both the navy and the army), Mansfield wrote a probing graduate thesis on the history of U.S.-Korea relations at the University of Montana and then taught East Asian studies there from 1933 to 1943 before winning a seat in the U.S. Senate.[106] The plainspoken but sophisticated Montanan became a confidant to Roosevelt, Truman, and Eisenhower on Asia and a respected Senate colleague of Kennedy and Johnson. At first, he had convinced then senator Kennedy to stand by Diem, but Mansfield turned against the escalation of U.S. involvement in Vietnam when he realized that the United States had ceased to be on the side of that all-important force in twentieth-century Asia: nationalism and self-determination. Returning to his earlier scholarship, he pointed out that the United States would do best to stand back and let nationalism work for U.S. interests, since Vietnam's historic enmity toward China would eventually turn Vietnam into a counterbalance against Beijing's regional ambitions.[107] Other prominent Asia scholars, such as Robert Scalapino, were more skeptical that nationalism would work for the United States in the short term. Scalapino noted in 1966 that "most Asian Communists, and particularly the young militants of Hanoi, regard China as model, guide, and protector," though he did acknowledge that this could prove a new basis for strategy in the coming years.[108] Standing by American values of self-determination and playing historic intraregional rivalries to ensure a stable balance of power would have been the elements of a coherent long-term Asia strategy evocative of Theodore Roosevelt, but they did not appeal to the White House in 1966 or 1968.

India, too, might have been a closer partner in limiting the reach of Chinese-backed communist revolution, as Kennedy and Galbraith once hoped. If anything, India's 1962 war with China over the Himalayan Mountains opened the potential for even closer U.S.-India cooperation, but that natural alignment between two major democracies was undercut when U.S. ally Pakistan aligned with China first to counter Indian strength.[109] In that case, subregional rivalries worked squarely against U.S. strategic interests, and Washington was not prepared to cede Pakistan any further to Beijing even in the pursuit of a better balance of power closer to East Asia.

An even bigger strategic play—the one that many historians and policymakers argued after the fact should have been pursued in lieu of military escalation—would have been to accelerate the Sino-Soviet split. Divisions between Moscow and Beijing were certainly becoming more pronounced by the mid-1960s. Kennedy's first National Intelligence Estimate on China highlighted the fact that Khrushchev had removed his technical experts and engineers from China and that the Soviets were losing influence over Mao.[110] Rostow and Hilsman both argued at various points that there was merit to testing warmer ties with Beijing.[111] To be sure, the McCarthy-era purges of men such as John Paton Davies had both denuded and chastened the State Department on China policy, and Rusk's first head of Policy Planning discouraged any proposals for changes vis-à-vis Beijing. In March 1963 polls, 47 percent (versus 34 percent) of Americans believed China was a greater threat than the Soviet Union.[112] There is no doubt that these domestic political factors dampened movement toward testing rapprochement with Beijing.

At the same time, however, the early advocates of a new policy toward Beijing in the administration also recognized, as the June 1962 draft BNSP put it, that even successful pursuit of a Sino-Soviet split would still mean that both Moscow and Beijing "will be basically hostile to us though perhaps in different degrees and in different ways."[113] Ironically, U.S. escalation in Vietnam increased Sino-Soviet rancor as both Moscow and Beijing competed for Hanoi's affection and legitimacy as the leader of world socialist revolution.[114] Beijing deployed 250,000 troops into the North after 1965 to deter an American invasion and outdo the Soviets in solidarity with Ho, while Soviet premier Aleksey Kosygin promised in Hanoi in February 1965 that Moscow would give "all-out Soviet aid" if the United States invaded the North, in addition to promising economic aid.[115] On the other hand, unilateral deescalation by the United States would only have emboldened Mao, since it was, as the NSC rightly told Johnson in 1967, the "test case for [China's] vaunted doctrine of 'people's wars' . . . on which Mao's very claim to fame in the Marx-Lenin-Stalin lineage is based."[116]

In subsequent years, Mao would become preoccupied with continuous revolution at home to prevent Soviet-style reactionary trends, coupled with support for revolutions abroad through what Evelyn Goh calls "aggression by seepage" (providing logistical and ideological support but not direct combat).[117] As historian Chen Jian explains, Mao's fear of the revolutionary energies released by the Cultural Revolution led him to introduce stabilizing "structural changes" to the Maoist state. At the same time, he worked to shift the target of Maoist anti-imperialism from the Western "Old World" to the increasingly hostile Soviet Union and thereby allow for greater openness with noncommunist countries.[118] But these more favorable conditions did not exist before 1969. Up to that point, the net effect of the Sino-Soviet split was a more aggressive PRC. A truly prescient U.S. strategy might have anticipated Beijing's later interest in removing troops from the Vietnamese border in order to deal with the Soviet military buildup on the Amur River, but here as well, the Soviet forces in the Far East were only just beginning to increase, and major Sino-Soviet clashes would not occur until 1969.[119]

In short, a U.S. rapprochement with Beijing before 1969 may have yielded some insights into possible future trends and served as a down payment for what came later, as well as possibly reducing the risks of general war, but there was insufficient evidence at the time to indicate that the collapse of Saigon would have led to anything other than emboldened moves elsewhere in Southeast Asia by Beijing and Hanoi.

Nevertheless, the elements of a coherent regional strategy were evident had Johnson and the Wise Men chosen to look for them. Neutralism in 1965 would have been disastrous for the rest of Asia, but after 1965, the frontline states beyond Indochina were increasingly secure and offered the baseline for a stronger forward defense line. This clearly would not have been through a collective security organization, though. SEATO had already failed in that regard, with the Europeans using the treaty to constrain American action, and the Thais under political pressure for joining a European collective in the first place.[120] A broader pact dominated by Asians would have given the United States an ideational advantage over the communist bloc, but McGeorge Bundy rejected the proposal when it surfaced through Rostow because he did not want to dilute the defense capabilities of SEATO—a curious decision given SEATO's poor collective defense capabilities to begin with.[121] Instead, the State Department launched a "New Pacific Community" aimed at mutual help and countering communism among the Pacific Islands and maritime states, but even this modest new collective security initiative soon atrophied because of differences between Washington and Canberra over which nation should lead in the Pacific Islands.[122]

Of course, the San Francisco System had worked well for the participants without being a collective security arrangement, and there was no reason why a new collective arrangement was required in the late 1960s to enhance deterrence. Investing in the security treaties with Thailand and the Philippines in Southeast Asia and Japan, Korea, and Taiwan in Northeast Asia would have imposed a formidable wall of bilateral arrangements to block further expansion of communism. Backed by that wall of security, the United States would have found by the late 1960s that a combination of more counterinsurgency operations in South Vietnam and recapitalized air and naval power was a far cheaper way to stop communist expansion than the huge conventional army formations being sent into Vietnam to fight the NVA and Vietcong.

The problem with this approach from Johnson's perspective was that it smacked too much of Acheson's failed defensive line in January 1950. Nevertheless, a regional strategy would have aligned ways and means toward achieving the real objective of U.S. grand strategy in the Pacific— the prevention of a hostile hegemon from dominating the region. Absent that regional approach, Johnson let the Communist Bloc bleed the United States on a peripheral front of little direct consequence to Soviet or American interests.

Yet Kennedy and Johnson must also be credited for what did *not* happen on their watch: the Soviets made no advances on the European front as the United States dealt with fires in Asia; the offshore island chain in the Pacific remained undamaged, and Japan remained secure; major U.S. alliances were not seriously harmed materially or politically; general war with China or the Soviets on the continent was avoided; and no regional hegemon yet threatened to seriously remove American influence and power from Asia.

It should also be noted how investments in alliances, institutions, and capabilities decades before 1965–1968 allowed these successes, despite huge errors in strategic judgment in Vietnam itself. The United States was able to deploy and sustain thirty-four maneuver battalions in Vietnam against hostile forces and deter counteraggression against the First Island Chain or Korea because of the forward presence and alliances established with Japan, Korea, Taiwan, Thailand, and the Philippines, and the muscle of U.S. air and naval power. A visionary grand strategy established decades earlier compensated for strategic errors of judgment in Indochina in the short term.

The next president would learn from those errors—particularly with respect to the broader Asian canvas for American strategies of containment.

9. "AN EVEN BALANCE"
NIXON AND KISSINGER'S REDEFINITION OF CONTAINMENT IN ASIA, 1969–1975

Richard Nixon came to office at the nadir of American confidence in Asia and took decisive steps to restore a favorable balance of power while realigning American ends with reduced American means. In his first four years, he achieved major successes, including the Paris Peace Accords to end the Vietnam War (though these would look less positive in subsequent years), the historic opening to China, and major arms-control agreements with the Soviets. But he also unnerved American allies with his sudden tilt toward Beijing and with his proposals for reduced U.S. defense commitments, and he lost control of foreign policy as an angry Congress asserted itself after the U.S. invasion of Cambodia. Consumed with lists of political enemies and under siege from the press, his presidency collapsed in 1974 with a shudder that seemed to prove Tocqueville's point that a democracy "cannot combine its measures with secrecy or await their consequences with patience."[1]

Yet it was Nixon's focus on a new balance of power in Asia to which Jimmy Carter would later turn in the face of Soviet expansion, despite having repudiated realism in the first place, and that Ronald Reagan would refine and resource to push the Soviets out of the Pacific. It was not a straight line from Nixon to the collapse of the Soviet threat to Asia, but it was in his presidency that the reversal of fortunes began.

Nixon, Kissinger, and the Pursuit of a New Equilibrium

Nixon respected power. He wallowed in it—and he measured it. He came to office knowing that in relative terms American economic power had declined from one-half to one-quarter of global GDP in the postwar period, and that overextension in Vietnam had put the American people's very commitment to internationalism at risk. He would not brook retreat, but he needed a way to keep the United States in an undisputed leadership position in international affairs in relative if not absolute terms.[2] As his new national security advisor, Henry Kissinger, explained to the press in December 1969:

> For about twenty years after the end of the war, American foreign policy was conducted with the maxims and the inspiration that guided the Marshall Plan, that is, the notion of a predominant United States, as the only stable country, the richest country, the country without whose leadership and physical contribution nothing was possible, and which had to make all the difference for defense and progress everywhere in the world.[3] Now whichever Administration had come into office would have had to face the fact, I believe, that we have run out of that particular vision. Conditions have changed enormously. We are now in a world in which other parties are playing a greater role. They have regained some of their self-confidence. New nations have come into being. Communism is no longer monolithic and we, therefore, face the problem of helping to build international relations on a basis which may be less unilaterally American.[4]

Bipolarity had long served U.S. interests, but whereas earlier Cold Warriors like Dulles had been suspicious of multipolarity, Nixon and Kissinger now saw the advantages to the United States in a more "pluralistic world"—indeed, the inevitability of such a world. As Nixon put it at the beginning of his presidency, "I think it will be a safer world and a better world, if we have a stronger, healthy United States, Europe, Soviet

Union, China, Japan, each balancing the other, not playing one against the other, *an even balance*" [emphasis added].[5]

Kissinger's dissertation topic and major field of scholarship had been the development of the Concert of Europe in the nineteenth century. Like fellow postwar realist and Jewish-German immigrant Hans Morgenthau, he rejected the notion that a Wilsonian perpetual peace was possible. Transforming the world in America's image was folly. At most, the United States could stabilize the global system and maintain a favorable balance of power among the major states.[6] Yet Kissinger understood that even maintenance of a concert of power required constant agility, friction, and maneuvering. The equilibrium could be more stable, but never perfectly stable.[7] This was the essence of statecraft and the achievement of Castlereagh and Metternich, the British and Austrian protagonists in his dissertation.

This process of constant intrigue and manipulation appealed enormously to Nixon's own political instincts and personality. To Nixon, the Quaker grocer's son from Whittier, California, Kissinger's brilliance trumped the East Coast establishment Harvard intellectuals who had surrounded his sparkling nemesis, John F. Kennedy. To Kissinger, the refugee from Hitler's Germany, Nixon was a vehicle for a realist foreign policy that would avoid the history and tragedy he had seen befall the Old World, not to mention the boundless definition of ends seemingly presented to the American people by Truman, Kennedy, and Johnson.[8] Nixon eventually grew jealous of Kissinger's fame, particularly when the two men appeared jointly on *Time* magazine's "Man of the Year" cover in 1972, while Kissinger privately came to dismiss Nixon as a drunkard and a "meatball head," but they found each other indispensable.[9]

Scholars and journalists debate which of the two men was the visionary and which the implementer. With respect to Asia, however, it was clearly Nixon who had the greater experience and imagination at the beginning of the administration.[10] By birthright, scholarship, and experience, Kissinger was a Europeanist. In contrast, Nixon was the first president from the Pacific Coast, with wartime service as a navy logistics officer in the South Pacific and then unprecedented access to NSC decision-making and diplomacy as Eisenhower's vice president, particularly with respect to East Asia. Ideologically, Nixon had anchored Ike on the right because of his leading role as a young senator investigating the Alger Hiss affair and communist influence on U.S. China policy, but he stayed close to the political center by departing from other China lobby Republicans, who backed MacArthur against Truman in 1951. Indeed, during the Eisenhower years, Nixon's views on Asia closely paralleled those of John Foster Dulles, with whom he shared a view that the neutralism of Nehru and Prince Norodom Sihanouk of Cambodia was immoral and that academic talk of abandoning Taiwan for Red China was "naïve wooly-headed thinking."[11]

But Nixon also made the study of Asia a central theme in his years out of power and his later return to the top of the Republican Party establishment. In 1967, he traveled across the region, quizzing ambassadors and regional leaders and gradually formulating a new strategic approach to Asia. He published his views in *Foreign Affairs*, in an article titled "Asia after Viet Nam" in the fall of 1967.[12] In the article, Nixon explained that drawing a line in 1965–1966 had successfully blunted Chinese ambitions against the rest of South and Southeast Asia but that now it was time to conceive of a broader strategy for the region as a whole.[13] He concluded from his travels that "the tide of nationalism was now shifting in U.S. favor"—a trend that meant the United States could be confident in accepting a new multipolarity centered on "India, the world's most populous non-communist nation; Japan, Asia's principal industrial and economic power; China, the world's most populous nation and Asia's most immediate threat; and the United States, the greatest Pacific power."[14] India, he explained, would set a democratic example and sustain a favorable balance of power in the region; Japan, already firmly in the U.S. camp, could contribute more "diplomatically and militarily," including a relaxation of the constraints imposed by Article 9 of the Japanese constitution; and the United States would continue to be the ultimate guarantee against major aggression but would need to count on Asian allies to do more for themselves for collective security. Finally, based on this "marshaling of Asian forces" to deter Chinese aggression or revisionism, Nixon raised eyebrows by arguing that the United States should take "the long view," recognizing that "we simply cannot afford to leave China forever outside the family of nations."[15]

The 1967 *Foreign Affairs* essay was a remarkably coherent tapestry of regional trends and U.S. interests and capabilities, the likes of which the Kennedy and Johnson administrations had never produced. Indeed, the essay still stands as a usable framework for thinking about how multipolarity in Asia plays to American interests. Although he would later stray from his own insights about Japan and India, Nixon nevertheless entered office with the most coherent strategic framework for U.S. foreign policy toward Asia of any new president since Theodore Roosevelt.

Nixon wanted this strategy to flow from the top. He loathed the ad hoc nature of Kennedy's and Johnson's national security decision-making but was also hesitant to empower the cabinet and the State Department in the kind of inclusive and deliberative process that Eisenhower had encouraged. Therefore, in his first days in government, Nixon signed off on National Security Decision Memorandum (NSDM) 2, which gave Kissinger, as national security advisor, the responsibility both for setting the agenda and for chairing all National Security Council meetings. The preexisting Senior Interdepartmental Group, chaired by the undersecretary of state, was abolished, and a new NSC-led Defense Policy Review Committee kept control over the Pentagon.[16] With these bureaucratic coups de grace in place, the Europeanist Kissinger soon became an intimate partner in the formulation of policy toward Asia with the man who considered himself the first Pacific president.

The State Department, which had dominated foreign policy in the Truman and Eisenhower years and then shared power with the White House in the Kennedy and Johnson years, now dropped precipitously to second-tier status. Secretary of State William P. Rogers, a former deputy attorney general and loyal public servant, was the politically weakest secretary of state in a generation. He was allowed to handle secondary foreign policy issues, including in parts of Asia, but never the major Nixon initiatives. Ironically, below Rogers were some of the strongest Asia experts the department had ever put in senior positions. The undersecretary for policy was U. Alexis Johnson, just back from a posting as ambassador to Japan and with previous assignments in Korea, Manchuria, and Thailand. The assistant secretary of state for East Asia was Marshall Green, a former assistant to Ambassador Grew in Tokyo and a protégé of Dulles in the San Francisco treaty negotiations. Green had hosted Nixon in Jakarta while serving as ambassador in 1966, and he impressed the future president with his suggestions for a low military profile and more "modest, mutual, and multilateral" diplomacy in the region, prompting Nixon to nickname him "Low Profile Green."[17] Kissinger was less enamored of the career diplomat, but Green would later acknowledge that despite mistakes that stemmed from Kissinger's failure to draw on the enormous regional expertise at State, the national security advisor was nevertheless a "brilliant" strategist. Setting process aside, Green concluded, there were no differences between State and NSC over Asia strategy, with the exception of Cambodia.[18]

The power of Kissinger's NSC attracted some of the brightest young minds on Asia policy. Several of them, including Tony Lake, Morton Halperin, and Winston Lord, would form the core of Bill Clinton's foreign policy team two decades later, and others, such as Richard Solomon and Peter Rodman, would serve under Ronald Reagan and George H. W. Bush. Lord was particularly close to Kissinger, perhaps because of his Rockefeller Republican credentials as a descendent of the Burlington Textile and Pillsbury Flour Company families and his education at Hotchkiss and Yale. While at the Fletcher School of Diplomacy, Lord met his future wife, Shanghai-born author Bette Bao Lord. The marriage prevented him from joining the Foreign Service but sparked a lifelong interest in China and Asia that he pursued in the Department of Defense and then directly under Kissinger in the NSC.[19] Lord would play a central role in defining the Guam Doctrine and implementing the opening to China, and he later served as ambassador to Beijing under Reagan and George H. W. Bush and then as assistant secretary of state for the region under Clinton.[20]

While Rogers was a weak link at the State Department, other cabinet members expanded their influence over foreign policy toward Asia. Treasury Secretary John Connally was a tough and politically astute former governor of Texas and was Nixon's favorite member of the cabinet. Since Kissinger cared little about the economy and Nixon fancied himself a businessman, Connelly was able to drive a bruising rebalancing of the international economy that had macroeconomic merit but little to recommend it in terms of foreign policy toward U.S. allies, particularly Japan.[21] Melvin Laird, one of the best secretaries of defense in history, focused on preserving the fighting capabilities of the U.S. military even as he managed cuts that he knew as a former congressman were coming with the withdrawal from Vietnam. Finally, Kissinger's deputy Al Haig merits attention—not for his initial imprint on Asia policy overall but because he drove the military dimension of Vietnam War policy and because he would later return as Reagan's first secretary of state and a champion of a Sinocentric strategy in Asia.

In Asia, Nixon, Kissinger, and his foreign policy team attempted to realign ends and means along three specific lines of effort: (1) "Vietnamization" of the war, which would allow an orderly U.S. withdrawal from

Indochina and return to a more sustainable strategy of offshore balancing; (2) shifting more responsibility for defense to Asian allies under the "Guam" or "Nixon" Doctrine, which would compensate for a relative decline in American resources; and (3) opening to China, which would reduce the demands for American security in the region, presumably put more pressure on North Vietnam, and serve as a counterweight to Soviet ambitions. Each line of effort was intended to complement the two others, each evolved as Nixon moved from concept to implementation, all three eventually became disconnected from one another, and yet all three have remained cornerstones of American strategy ever since.

VIETNAMIZATION

After Barry Goldwater's crushing defeat in the 1964 presidential election, Nixon recognized that he had an opening to return as the Republican standard-bearer and that Vietnam would be the defining issue for the next election. Over the next four years, he positioned himself as a prudent hawk, supporting air and naval bombardment in 1965 but expressing caution about escalation on the ground and publicly distancing himself from Eisenhower and Omar Bradley's calls to expand the ground war into Laos and Cambodia and north of the DMZ in November 1967.[22] In his acceptance speech at the Republican convention in Miami in August 1968, Nixon promised an honorable end to the war three times.[23] Ending the war was a political and strategic necessity, but "honor" was more than empty political sloganeering. As Kissinger noted in a *Foreign Affairs* article he penned just before the Nixon administration took office, "however fashionable it is to ridicule the terms 'credibility' or 'prestige,' they are not empty phrases; other nations can gear their actions to ours only if they can count on our steadiness."[24]

An "honorable" end to the war, as Kissinger went on to explain in *Foreign Affairs*, required the United States "(1) to bring about a staged withdrawal of external forces, North Vietnamese and American, [and] (2) thereby to create a maximum incentive for the contending forces in South Viet Nam to work out a political agreement."[25] The dilemma, as Kissinger implicitly acknowledged, was that the American and North Vietnamese people had asymmetrical thresholds for casualties in the conflict, causing U.S. "military operations to have little relationship to our declared political objectives."[26] When Nixon took office, the North

Vietnamese were negotiating with the Americans in Paris not out of desperation resulting from American military pressure but in order to accelerate America's withdrawal and thereby hasten eventual North Vietnamese victory.[27]

Kissinger was also taken with a December 1968 RAND Corporation analysis of the Vietnam problem, which he used as the basis for National Security Study Memorandum (NSSM) 1 to elicit reactions from the bureaucracy over the first three months of 1969. As the answers came in, the White House settled on a strategy that would combine the most hawkish and dovish in a range of options proposed in the original RAND report.[28] The report, prepared by a team led by Daniel Ellsberg, who would later become famous for leaking a top secret Defense Department study of the history of U.S. involvement in Vietnam (the "Pentagon Papers"), among others, presented a range of options. The most hawkish option focused on "military escalation aimed at negotiated victory," to be achieved through "air and ground operations in Cambodia," "unrestricted bombing of North Vietnam including Hanoi," and "mining of Haiphong"— with the goal "to destroy the will and capability of North Vietnam to support insurgency." The most dovish option proposed "substantial reduction in U.S. presence while seeking a compromise settlement" through regular withdrawals combined with Vietnamization.[29] Though the authors of the RAND report saw these two options as mutually exclusive, Nixon and Kissinger perceived them as necessary interlocking components of a strategy that would end the war at maximum advantage to U.S. interests and without lasting damage to U.S. prestige and deterrence.[30]

In theory, it made sense that negotiators in Paris would need military pressure to increase their leverage and that a U.S. retreat covered by increased violence would deter future foes. In practice, the internal contradictions between *predictable* withdrawal and *unpredictable* use of force would later cause Nixon's policy to unravel on the home front as Congress and the American people reacted against what appeared to them to be an escalation of violence overall.

Historians have struggled with the question of whether at this point Nixon and Kissinger intended to save the Saigon regime of Prime Minister Nguyen Van Thieu but were subsequently hamstrung by Congress or whether the intent was only to find a "decent interval" before the inevitable end.[31] Up until his resignation in August 1974, Nixon repeatedly stated his willingness to use unremitting airpower to stop the North Vietnamese from conquering the South, but neither he nor Kissinger were

willing to invest ground forces again the way Johnson had, with the exception of the limited invasion of Cambodia. What can be said is that the
survival of an independent South Vietnam was returned to a secondary
national interest in 1969—important only to the extent that it affected
American prestige and the ability to deter aggression beyond Indochina.
Those ends could be met—at least it seemed—through a combination of
statecraft with the big powers surrounding Vietnam and bloody-minded
bombing to keep the communist forces at bay.

Nixon and Kissinger's Vietnamization strategy thus unfolded over five
distinct but interrelated battlefields: (1) the negotiating table in Paris; (2)
the ground campaign in South Vietnam; (3) the bombing campaign
against North Vietnam; (4) the peripheral struggles in Laos and Cambodia; and (5) the American home front.

In Paris, Nixon resumed talks with the North Vietnamese that Johnson had initiated in May 1968. Some of Johnson's negotiators alleged that
Nixon had sabotaged their efforts by sending conservative stalwart Anna
Chan Chennault (widow of the legendary Flying Tigers commander
Claire Chennault) to convince Thieu not to cooperate until after Nixon
was elected. Other Johnson era officials argued that this would not have
been a major factor in the talks either way.[32] Whatever the impact of
Chennault's intervention in the talks before the election, however, Nixon
decided that the negotiations should continue once he assumed office,
and he assigned Henry Cabot Lodge Jr. to lead the U.S. delegation. Meanwhile, in August 1969, Kissinger began his own, more important, secret
negotiations with the North Vietnamese, brokered by former French diplomat Jean Sainteny.[33]

Nothing was achieved for close to two years. The American (public
and private) position was set forth in Nixon's speech on October 7,
1970—peace required a cease-fire in place linked with a timetable for
complete withdrawals by both the United States and North Vietnam, release of U.S. POWs, and an Indochina peace conference. However, Hanoi
refused to acknowledge that they had forces in the South, and it demanded unconditional withdrawal of U.S. forces as well as Thieu's resignation. The two sides were at an impasse, but each side thought it had
reasons why their negotiating positions would improve.

Nixon and Kissinger hoped that external pressure from Moscow and
Beijing as a quid pro quo for improved relations with the United States
would force Hanoi to compromise. However, the president underestimated
the historic animosity between the Chinese and Vietnamese (masked

by China's material aid to Hanoi), the competition in Indochina between Moscow and Beijing, and therefore the limits of Chinese leverage.[34] The Chinese leaders would do no more than encourage Hanoi to negotiate with the Americans. And in Beijing in 1971, Premier Zhou Enlai told Kissinger his bottom line: "Since you have admitted that withdrawal of your forces is a good thing and beneficial for world peace and peace in the Far East, you should be able to make up your mind and withdraw from Indochina. This would be an honorable withdrawal and a glorious withdrawal."[35]

For their part, the North Vietnamese concluded that Nixon intended to withdraw U.S. forces no matter what transpired on the battlefield.[36] In fact, on March 15, 1969, Nixon had approved a policy of "Vietnamization"—in effect, implementation of the political decision Johnson had made in 1968 to turn over more of the war to the Army of the Republic of Vietnam (ARVN). Secretary of Defense Laird wanted a public timetable for troop withdrawals to prevent Congress from trying to impose one, but Kissinger prevailed on the president to hold off the first announcements in the summer of 1969, arguing that inflexible timetables for withdrawal would hurt the U.S. bargaining position and violate the "cardinal rule" of realism: that "military force and diplomacy must work together."[37] However, politics favored Laird's view, and withdrawal soon took on a tempo as irreversible as escalation had from 1965 to 1968.[38] In September 1969, Nixon authorized the withdrawal of 40,500 troops despite increased activity by the Vietcong. Then, in April 1971, the president announced the withdrawal of a further 100,000 troops by December of that year.[39] Kissinger warned that the lack of flexibility to respond to North Vietnamese attacks or intransigence in Paris made the United States appear like a "reluctant giant" and undermined the goal of sustaining American prestige.[40] But the president's policies on Vietnam were popular. If anything, Nixon argued, the withdrawals were happening *too* slowly.[41] When Kissinger arrived for talks in Paris that May, U.S. troop levels had fallen from 540,000 to 270,000. Recognizing the impact of the troop numbers on his negotiating position, Kissinger secretly offered a deadline for unilateral withdrawal in return for the release of American POWs and a cease-fire— dropping earlier demands for mutual withdrawal.[42] But the North Vietnamese held firm.

However, if Hanoi correctly assessed the inevitability of U.S. ground forces withdrawing, they badly misread Nixon's willingness to cause them pain. In July 1969, Nixon told his staff that he was "ready to use whatever military pressure was necessary" to prevent the North from taking over South Vietnam by force.[43] By September, the NSC was working with the Pentagon to develop Operation Duck Hook—plans for intense bombing of the North and mining of Haiphong Harbor.[44] When the North Vietnamese opened a new offensive into ostensibly neutral Laos in 1970, Nixon authorized B-52 bombing at the request of the Lao prime minister. "Letting the Communists kick over the Geneva accords in Laos," Kissinger warned in a March 1970 NSC Special Action Group Meeting, would remove "North Vietnamese restraint in South Vietnam."[45]

Nixon had always favored airpower over boots on the ground—an inheritance of Eisenhower's "New Look"—and believed the bombing would punish the North without inflaming public opinion at home. The problem was that the American people were now conditioned by Nixon's troop withdrawal announcements to expect only deescalation. Protests at home against the bombings in Laos gave a hint of this dilemma, but it was in Cambodia that the domestic and international pieces of Vietnamization started to really unravel. When Nixon came to office, Sihanouk was still keeping Cambodia neutral under the terms of the 1954 Paris Peace Accords, with U.S. military power nearby as a hedge.[46] However, North Vietnamese forces were also rapidly expanding their operations in Cambodia, building up the Ho Chi Minh trail as well as sanctuaries for arms caches and military hospitals inside the Cambodian side of the border. Nixon authorized secret bombing of these targets in March 1969, but NVA units continued pouring into Cambodia, taking control of at least two provinces of the country by the end of the year.[47] If the Cambodian border became an open wound, the entire western border of South Vietnam would be open to flanking attacks just as the Americans were trying to withdraw.

At this point, the State Department and the White House agreed that Cambodia's neutrality should be upheld. But that consensus changed when Sihanouk was deposed by the Cambodian National Assembly on March 18, 1970, and replaced by General Lon Nol, who immediately called for an end to neutrality and direct military support from the United States. Deputy National Security Advisor Al Haig, JCS Chair Earl Wheeler, General Creighton Abrams in Saigon, and Admiral John McCain in Hawaii all urged the president to intervene militarily in Cambodia to support the new Phnom Penh government.[48] Secretaries Rogers and Laird took the opposite tack, particularly after friendly Republicans on the Senate Foreign Relations Committee warned Marshall Green that military intervention in Cambodia would mean "Republicans wouldn't be able to elect a dog catcher for years after."[49] Key members of Kissinger's NSC staff also urged him to consider alternative approaches: smaller hit-and-run operations, a modus vivendi with Hanoi to limit fighting in Cambodia, or complete reprogramming of resources back to the central fight in South Vietnam.

From Kissinger's perspective, however, none of these alternatives would be enough to stop the deteriorating situation in Cambodia from undermining Vietnamization.[50] He and Nixon concluded that military intervention in Cambodia was necessary to force the North Vietnamese to compromise in Paris and to ensure that the South Vietnamese would not be flanked from the west as U.S. forces withdrew.[51] Nixon believed that the American public would support the invasion, particularly in the wake of his April 20 announcement that another 150,000 U.S. troops would be coming home from Vietnam. Speaking to the nation in a televised address on April 30, pumped up on frequent viewings of George C. Scott in *Patton*, the president declared that it was "time for action" and described his plan to send U.S. forces into Cambodia.[52]

The 32,000 U.S. and 43,000 South Vietnamese troops that crossed the Cambodian border on May 1 scored some initial tactical successes, uncovering large enemy arms caches and driving the Vietcong units into the hills, but it soon became clear that these gains could not be consolidated without a more permanent presence on the ground. At home, the public was divided, but the crisis mounted on college campuses, particularly after Ohio National Guard troops fired on protestors at Kent State University on May 4, 1970, killing four and wounding nine. The turmoil spread to Kissinger's own NSC staff, where several of his best directors resigned in protest, including future national security advisor Tony Lake and Bill Watts, whose argument with Kissinger over Cambodia became so heated that he almost assaulted the national security advisor at his desk before resigning on the spot.[53] NSC Asia staff who had worked on the Cambodia decision and did not resign could hear the chants of protesting students out on the Ellipse, including those of their own college-aged children.[54] More problematic, Congress turned against the war. On June 30, the Senate passed an amendment to the Foreign Military Sales Act that would cut off all military spending on the Cambodia invasion and all support for Cambodian forces. The amendment failed in the House but was resurrected successfully in December and enacted in

January 1971, effectively barring all spending on ground forces in Cambodia. On January 12, Congress repealed the Gulf of Tonkin resolution.[55]

This was only the beginning of a mounting congressional campaign to constrain the administration's prosecution of the war not only in Cambodia but also in Vietnam. Nixon used American airpower to blunt the North's April 1972 Easter Offensive against the South and then again with Operation Linebacker II in December 1972 (the "Christmas Bombings") to force the North to come back to peace talks in Paris after they had broken down the month before. The final January 1973 Paris Peace Accords, which had essentially been in place in October the year before as the North Vietnamese sought to lock in concessions before Nixon was re-elected, provided for a cease-fire during U.S. withdrawal, the return of U.S. POWs, and a process of dialogue between Saigon and the Vietcong with the aim of peaceful unification.[56] But peaceful unification could only really be guaranteed by the threat of American airpower if and when the North broke the agreement and resumed attacks on the South. Nixon soon lost the ability to provide that hedge. When the president ordered bombing in 1973 in a futile effort to stop the Khmer Rouge from taking over the whole of Cambodia, Congress responded in December by banning all funds for future military operations in or over Indochina.[57] The next December, Congress passed further legislation capping U.S. forces in Vietnam at 6,000 by mid-1975 and 4,000 by the end of that year.[58]

As North Vietnamese forces tore across South Vietnam in the spring of 1975, Gerald Ford, Nixon's vice president and his successor in the wake of his Watergate resignation, concluded he could do nothing more than order the evacuation of all remaining U.S. military and diplomatic personnel by helicopter from Saigon. Revelations that Nixon had pledged in a letter to Thieu in late 1972 that there would be "swift and severe retaliatory action" if the North broke the cease-fire only caused outrage in the U.S. media rather than a surge of public support for the collapsing South Vietnamese government.[59] Ford was checkmated. As his assistant secretary of state for East Asia and Pacific affairs, Phil Habib, lamented, "even though Richard Nixon had promised them [South Vietnam] that if the agreement was broken, we'd be back to save them, Gerry Ford never got to keep that agreement."[60]

Nixon and Kissinger had read the strategic situation in Southeast Asia well, but not the political dynamics at home.[61] Had this been a two-player game, then a strategy of escalating violence would have reinforced the policy of Vietnamization. Militarily, the U.S. invasion of Cambodia did prevent the North from a flanking attack in their 1972 Easter Offensive. Diplomatically, the bombing of North Vietnam did force Hanoi to make concessions at the negotiating table in Paris.[62] But from 1969 to 1975, the war in Vietnam was *not* a two-player game—and Nixon's invasion of Cambodia and Christmas bombing lost him the support of a critical third player—the American people. Through Congress, they asserted an inflexible adherence to withdrawal that ironically reinforced the "reluctant giant" impression that Nixon and Kissinger had been so desperate to avoid. It is difficult to disagree with William Bundy's assessment that "had the declared policy (Vietnamization) been followed in straight-line fashion, as urged by William Rogers and Melvin Laird among his closet advisors—there might still have been a case for residual use or threat of U.S. airpower at some point, to permit the withdrawal to be completed in orderly fashion."[63]

Had Vietnamization been the entirety of U.S. strategy, this self-imposed setback would have been devastating for U.S. credibility in Asia, but Nixon painted on a broader canvas. Although he lost control of the process of withdrawal from Indochina, he had other plans to ensure the continuance of America's relative primacy in an increasingly multipolar Asia.

THE GUAM DOCTRINE AND REBALANCING ALLIANCES

The second dimension of Nixon's effort to recalibrate the ends, ways, and means of American foreign policy was to shift a greater burden for self-defense to the successful allies in the Far East. The concept had its lineage in Eisenhower's New Look and Johnson's campaign assurances in 1964 that he was "not about to send American boys 9 or 10,000 miles away from home to do what Asian boys ought to be doing for themselves"—and it flowed logically as an extension of the Vietnamization of the war itself.[64] The policy also echoed the tradition of offshore maritime strategy advocated since the middle of the previous century and represented the first retrenchment of the American defense line in the Western Pacific since the Second World War. Though the approach was dubbed the "Guam Doctrine" when first explained by the president in the summer of 1969 while on a stop in that small Pacific island and subsequently was called the "Nixon Doctrine," historians have debated how much of the approach was truly strategic. Kissinger biographer Walter Isaacson notes, for example, that the Nixon Doctrine was partly a response to a "packaging problem"—or as he puts it: "Nixon did not want the American withdrawals from Vietnam to seem like merely a helpless reaction to a sorry situation. Instead, he wanted to take the idea of Vietnamization and wrap it in the guise of a coherent, purposeful philosophy."[65]

Historian Jeffrey Kimball also argues that Nixon proceeded without an encompassing doctrine, latching onto the press characterization of his policy as the "Nixon Doctrine," which he then implemented inconsistently and without a coherent design.[66] This explanation resonates with Kissinger's own memoirs, which depict the initial rollout of the doctrine in Guam as a complete surprise to Kissinger—as ad hoc presidential observations rather than a coherent strategy.[67]

These portraits of opportunism and ad hoc decision-making all have a grain of truth but should not detract from the central strategic concept behind Nixon's effort to rebalance alliances in the Pacific. Within the administration, there was broad recognition of the shifting terms of power and the need to recalibrate alliance relationships to sustain American preeminence in the Pacific months before Nixon's remarks in Guam. Nixon himself had spent years thinking about how to effect a favorable multipolarity in Asia, as he described it in the pages of *Foreign Affairs* in 1967. Or, as Robert Osgood concluded in an early examination of Nixon's grand strategy, the new approach represented "*military retrenchment without political disengagement*" [emphasis added]:[68] "The simple fact is that President Nixon feels compelled to do what the Eisenhower Administration aspired to do after the Korean war and what any president would try to do after a period of expanding military involvement and expenditures culminating in war—particularly when the war has been peculiarly unpopular and unsuccessful."[69]

Moreover, although Nixon's announcement in Guam in July 1969 surprised Kissinger, in January 1969 the national security advisor had already initiated interagency policy reviews to assess the emerging balance of power in the Pacific, the requirements for U.S. forward military posture, and the options for basing and alliance roles and missions going forward. The conclusion was briefed to the NSC in NSSM 13 on May 28, stating that the United States "shall basically pursue our current relationship with Japan as our major partner in Asia . . . and seek an increasingly larger Japanese role in Asia," including "moderate increases and qualitative improvement in Japan's defense efforts."[70] Over the same period, "Low Profile Green" was providing Nixon with memos updating his discussion in Jakarta on the need to reduce the U.S. military footprint in the region and arguing that the Asian allies are ready to "fend for themselves."[71]

These bureaucratic inputs fused with Nixon's underlying views on Asian balance of power as he spoke to reporters from prepared notes at the Officers' Club in Guam on July 25, 1969, while en route to a wider tour of Asian capitals. He began by acknowledging that Asian leaders had grown worried that the United States might withdraw from the region after Vietnam. That would not happen, he emphasized, since Asia posed both "the greatest threat to the peace of the world" and "the greatest hope for progress in the world." Still, he observed, many of the noncommunist nations had made great strides. As a result, he explained, the United States would henceforth keep all its treaty commitments, provide economic and military assistance, and provide a "shield" if a nuclear power threatened the freedom of an allied nation or a nation whose survival was vital to American security. At the same time, the president emphasized, the United States was "going to encourage and has a right to expect that this problem will be increasingly handled by, and the responsibility for it taken by, the Asian nations themselves."[72]

The U.S. press reacted with great enthusiasm.[73] The response in the region was more anxious, as many mistook the statement as a reduction of U.S. *ends* (and thus commitments to allies), when in fact Nixon was talking about a realignment of *means*.[74] Kissinger was caught uncharacteristically off guard by the Guam statement, but he saw "the kernel of something useful to frame something conceptual."[75] When it became clear that the president intended this to be a centerpiece of his foreign policy, repeating the key elements in a nationally televised address on November 3, the national security advisor tasked NSC staffer Winston Lord with establishing more concrete goals for implementation.[76]

The next January, Lord presented his conclusions to Kissinger, eschewing the notion that the president or any previous U.S. government could construct a grand strategy for Asia and the Pacific. As Lord put it in his memo to Kissinger:

It is useful at the outset to recognize that there is no such thing as a grand strategy for Asia. If we can restrain the natural impulse to package a grand strategy, future discussions of American policy in Asia will be more illuminating than past ones. Most treatment of possible U.S.

post-Vietnam Asian policies has tended to compartmentalize them neatly under strategic labels that describe U.S. base postures and imply U.S. political postures, e.g., "mainland," "offshore," "Pacific outposts." Such treatment is misleading. The strategic headings are oversimplified and just won't hold up under the glare of Asian complexities. It is fruitless to try and draw abstract defense lines which represent "vital interest" boundaries on which we would "fight." And even if we could construct a master plan, we would not adhere rigidly to it for the sake of consistency if events dictated tactical aberrations.[77]

"First class," Kissinger wrote on the margins, and then the administration began to actually implement the new doctrine and design a grand strategy around it. The first public iteration came in the February 1970 Foreign Policy Report to the Congress, which stated that "our interests, our foreign policy objectives, our strategies and our defense budgets are being brought into balance—with each other and with our overall national priorities."[78] The administration then finalized plans for a substantial military retrenchment in Asia and the Pacific. In addition to the troop reductions in Vietnam, the United States would pull 20,000 soldiers (one division) from South Korea; 12,000 from the Japanese home islands, with an additional 5,000 from Okinawa; and 16,000 from Thailand. Globally, the Pentagon shifted its war-fighting readiness from the two-and-a-half-war principle that had prevailed through the 1960s (the Second World War ability to fight in Europe and Asia simultaneously while managing one Third World insurgency) to a new baseline capability necessary to defend against one full-scale communist attack in either Europe or Asia while simultaneously deterring communist enemies on the other side of the world and responding to a minor contingency in a third theater.[79]

Although the Guam Doctrine drew on elements of Nixon's own experience and Eisenhower's New Look—including a reexamination of how nuclear deterrence could backstop more limited conventional military commitments in the Pacific—it also resembled Kennan's original offshore formulation for Asia strategy in 1948.[80] Like Kennan, Nixon was looking to limit American exposure on the continent of Asia, particularly after the bloodletting in Vietnam. Within Asia, Nixon and Kennan both viewed Japan as the most important buttress of regional stability. And globally, Nixon considered Western Europe the central front in the Cold War, as Kennan had. In short, despite Nixon's boast that he would have the first

"Pacific presidency," the Guam Doctrine clearly prioritized the trans-Atlantic alliance over the Pacific. Although Nixon cut forces across Asia and the Pacific, he resisted Senate pressure for troop drawdowns in Europe, vowing to sustain current force levels in NATO indefinitely.[81] Meanwhile, the JCS interpreted the new global requirements as meaning that in the event of communist attacks in both Europe and Asia, "the defense of NATO will take precedence" and thus "US Forces would assist allies in a holding action in the Pacific-Asian area to the extent feasible and consistent with the requirements for the defense of the United States, its territories and possessions, essential US and allied shipping and airlift, and NATO."[82]

In addition, the new doctrine would return Southeast Asia to something closer to its relative importance (or unimportance) under Kennan's original vision of the region two decades earlier. Taiwan, according to the JCS, would now assume increased importance (as Kennan would have had it) because of plans to return Okinawa to Japan and reduce the U.S. military footprint on the main islands.[83] The offshore maritime strategy of pre–Korean War thinking was unmistakable, despite Lord's admonition to Kissinger that such "strategic headings are oversimplified."

In other respects, however, the Guam Doctrine was markedly different from Kennan's approach. Whereas Kennan wanted the United States out of Korea in order to sustain a clearer maritime stance in the region and reduce the dangers of entrapment on the continent, Nixon was unwilling and unable to extricate the United States from the peninsula. South Korean president Park Chung-hee urged Washington to exempt his country from the new doctrine in light of the North Korean threat.[84] Nixon wrote to Kissinger in November 1969 that on the peninsula he envisioned "air and sea presence at whatever level necessary for [the] kind of retaliatory strike we have planned. On other hand, [I] think it is time to cut number of Americans there [in Korea] in half," enough, he explained in a subsequent note, for the "US to provide a trip wire and air and sea support only."[85] To justify the removal of a full division from the South, the JCS noted in its long-term planning document that the defense of South Korea was important insomuch as its loss "would pose a major threat to US security threats by serving as a platform for aggression against the Japanese homelands and other islands to the south."[86] The importance of Korea was still derivative of the security of Japan and the offshore island chain but worth continued investment of forces—even if reduced.

For his part, Kennan was initially attracted to the administration's realism and offshore strategy. He had voted for antiwar candidate Eugene McCarthy but called the president-elect's office to offer his services and advice after the election. Kissinger returned the favor by commenting that the Johnson administration had underutilized Kennan's expertise, but Nixon's staff never responded, and a disgruntled Kennan went off to teach at Oxford.[87] As Nixon increased the bombing campaign over North Vietnam, Kennan finally broke with the administration and publicly called for unconditional withdrawal from Vietnam in November 1969.[88] The former policy planner wanted no intellectual ownership of Nixon's foreign policy. And unlike Eisenhower with the Solarium exercise, Nixon offered none.

As Osgood observed at the time, the essence of the Nixon Doctrine was to reduce the means and not the ends of U.S. foreign policy objectives in Asia. But the *ways* of implementing the strategy posed contradictions and challenges.[89] As former Pentagon official Earl Ravenal warned in *Foreign Affairs* in 1971: "Instead of the classic progression from the definition of foreign policy interests to the formulation of objectives, to the prescription of strategies, to the calculation of forces and their costs, we now see a constrained calculus that proceeds in reverse from limited budgets to trimmed forces to arbitrary strategies."[90]

The biggest challenge would be convincing allies to do more for their own defense while remaining closely aligned with the United States. The last thing Nixon wanted was for a reduced U.S. military presence to cause U.S. allies in the region to defect and pose independent centers of power that would complicate American leadership. That variation of multipolarity was not acceptable. In his own assessment of the Nixon Doctrine at the time, Osgood judged that defections by allies were unlikely as long as the U.S. commitment to treaty obligations continued, but he also noted that this would require deft diplomacy.[91] Kissinger was also acutely aware of the problem and in September 1969 highlighted for the president an independent assessment of the administration's strategy that emphasized the "overwhelming fear" of abandonment by countries across the region and the danger that Japan's own debate could lead either to nuclear weapons or, if the Left defeated rearmament, "accommodation with Red China or the USSR."[92] Nixon was taken by the assessment (which remains anonymous in the declassified State Department files) and returned it to Kissinger with key passages underlined throughout and instructions to send copies to Rogers, Laird, and Attorney General

John Mitchell. Ultimately, as Winston Lord cautioned in his memo to Kissinger in January 1970, the success of the Guam Doctrine would depend on how well the administration could shape "the growing power of Japan and the new U.S.-Japanese partnership whose future health *depends greatly on how the two allies manage China policy*" [emphasis added].[93] This insight was exactly right, but in the end, the United States and Japan could not have managed their respective China policies worse.

Nixon certainly demonstrated great interest in Japan when he began his tenure in office. He knew many Japanese leaders and had confidence that the more robust security role embraced by LDP conservatives like Kishi Nobusuke would help buttress Asia's balance of power as the United States withdrew from Vietnam.[94] Guided by an interagency team led by Marshall Green, Nixon and Kissinger had developed what seemed like a coherent approach to Japan by January 1969. First, the administration would encourage Japan to do more for its own security without taking on direct responsibilities for the defense of other Asian states. Second, Nixon and Kissinger were prepared to make an early promise to return Okinawa to Japan, recognizing that holding onto the islands might lead Tokyo toward "more friendly and wide-ranging relations with its communist neighbors,"[95] whereas reversion would open the way for more generous Japanese financial support for U.S. bases under the bilateral Status of Forces Agreement when the 1960 Security Treaty came up for renewal in 1970.[96] Third, Nixon wanted to rebalance economic relations with Japan, given a U.S. bilateral balance-of-payments deficit with Tokyo that was projected to top $1 billion in FY 1968 and $3 billion by the end of Nixon's first term.[97]

These three elements were not necessarily mutually exclusive, but they required a disciplined approach that the administration proved incapable of sustaining with Japan (in contrast to the discipline behind Nixon's China policy). Nixon, though he trusted Kishi, was not prepared for the free-riding inclinations of Kishi's successors Ikeda Hayato and Sato Eisaku. Meanwhile, Kissinger admitted that Japan was the major power he understood least, and this deficit grew when he allowed the leading Japan expert on the NSC staff, Richard Sneider, to be sent off to Embassy Tokyo after a series of testy encounters with the new White House.[98] The greatest corrupter of Nixon's Japan strategy, however, would be the domestic U.S. politics of trade—an attitude Treasury Secretary John Connally captured early in the administration when he declared, "Foreigners are out to screw us . . . our job is to screw them first."[99] And thus the careful statecraft needed to keep Tokyo closely aligned while reducing Japanese dependence on the United States for security was sacrificed at the altar of xenophobic protectionism.[100]

The core political issue was textile trade, which had plagued U.S.-Japan ties since the 1930s. As vice president, Nixon had resisted protectionist pressures, but over the 1960s the trade deficit with Japan had deteriorated, and Nixon needed South Carolina senator Strom Thurmond and the two million southerners working in the textile trade to turn Dixie Republican under his 1968 "Southern Strategy." As a candidate, Nixon pledged to enact quotas on synthetic fibers, quotas aimed primarily at Japan. The fact that Japanese imports only amounted to 1 percent of all textile manufacturing in the United States was irrelevant; Japan's remarkable economic success had focused American voters on their own vulnerabilities and threatened to erode support for free trade and the Republican Party.[101]

Characteristically, Nixon and Kissinger tried for a complex grand bargain with Japan that combined all three parts of the administration's initial Japan policy. In March 1969, Prime Minister Sato explained to Nixon that he wanted to secure a commitment for the return of a nuclear-free Okinawa. The JCS continued to argue that the risk to U.S. security would be too great, but U.S. ambassador to Japan Douglas MacArthur II promised the Joint Chiefs in a meeting at the Pentagon that the administration would do a "snow job" on the Japanese to expand Tokyo's support for collective security once Okinawa was returned. "You mean like you are doing on us?" replied the cagey Admiral Arleigh Burke, but in the end, the Pentagon agreed to reversion in exchange for arrangements to continue using U.S. bases in Okinawa for the defense of Korea and Taiwan.[102] Meanwhile, the Treasury Department demanded that "U.S. balance of payments and trade goals should be given a high priority in the *quid pro quos* we should seek for concessions on Okinawa."[103] By late May, Nixon agreed, in an NSC session, to accept reversion of Okinawa by 1972 if agreement on terms could be reached in 1969. Kissinger, who saw the trade issues as marginal at best, agreed to cut a secret deal with Prime Minister Sato's aide Wakaizumi Kei that linked voluntary restraints of Japanese textiles with reversion of Okinawa and expanded Japanese collective security responsibilities.[104]

When Nixon and Sato met on November 21 in Washington, they issued a joint communiqué confirming that Okinawa would be returned to Japanese sovereignty by the end of 1972, while Sato acknowledged that "the security of the Republic of Korea was essential to Japan's own security" and "that the maintenance of peace and security in the Taiwan area was also a most important factor for the security of Japan."[105] In a private pull aside, Sato then appeared to agree to voluntary textile export restraints, pursuant to Kissinger's arrangement with Wakaizumi. Nixon and Kissinger thought they had achieved a masterful piece of diplomacy, but Sato's statement on textile exports ("zensho shimasu," or "leave it to me") turned out to be a classic Japanese political term of evasion, while the Japanese prime minister's implicit promise to support U.S. defense commitments to Korea and Taiwan was never implemented by Sato or subsequent Japanese governments until after the Cold War.[106]

The White House had just read Japan wrong, failing to recognize that Sato and Wakaizumi did not actually have the power to prevail over the stubborn trade ministry on the textile issue or over more pacifist members of the LDP on the implicit promise of support for the American commitment to the security of Korea and Taiwan.[107] The next March, Nixon wrote a personal letter to Sato expressing his "disappointment and concerns" on the textile issue, adding the words again in Japanese ("shitsubo to kennen") to emphasize his frustration and his mistrust of Sato's translators.[108] Sato was particularly duplicitous, to be sure, but Nixon and Kissinger were also uncharacteristically trusting . . . and thus vengeful. Sato and the LDP won a landslide election victory the next year thanks to the agreement on Okinawa reversion, but Nixon came away distrustful of Japanese trickery.[109] The experience would contrast with the ease of striking grand bargains with the authoritarian Mao two years later, much to the strategic and political detriment of Sato and Japan.

After discovering a different Japan than he anticipated, Nixon hit Tokyo with a series of "shocks" over subsequent years. His administration placed strict controls on soybean exports to Japan amid a downturn in domestic production in 1973, causing a jump in the cost of one of the staples of the Japanese diet. Using his authority under the Trading with the Enemy Act—a particularly galling symbol for defeated Japan—the president then suspended dollar convertibility to gold and imposed a 10 percent import surcharge, driving up the value of the yen and undercutting Japanese trade competitiveness.[110] Officials in Tokyo told the *New York Times* that the shock would "be bad, very bad. People here just won't forget how this was done."[111] And finally came the greatest of the "Nixon shocks"—the surprise opening to China.

Battered by the suddenness of the Guam Doctrine and then the staccato of the Nixon shocks, Japanese political leaders reeled. Opportunistic nationalists like Defense Minister Nakasone Yasuhiro pushed through plans for a major increase in Japan's defense budget and offensive capabilities, prompting the *Asahi Shimbun* to declare in headlines in 1971 that henceforth it would be "autonomous defense to the fore and alliance to the rear" for Japan.[112] Hedging and decoupling by the United States' key ally in the Pacific were precisely the opposite of what Nixon and Kissinger had hoped to achieve with the Nixon Doctrine, but that was the direction Japan appeared to be heading in response to Nixon's policies.

And yet the U.S.-Japan alliance survived. Once again, the larger strategic designs of the president and his national security advisor changed the regional equilibrium in ways that compensated for the considerable (and lasting) damage done diplomatically to a key ally. The Nakasone plan for autonomous defense was never implemented because the external requirement for security was drastically reduced by the American opening to China and the ensuing détente with the Soviet Union.[113] Japanese industrialists, who had seen growth potential in a new defense spending spree, abandoned Nakasone's plan unceremoniously as they eagerly turned to the vast untapped China market, while those still depending on defense sales within Japan suddenly had to contend with cheaper and more competitive U.S. arms exports as a result of the dollar shock. The entire geostrategic and macroeconomic chessboard flipped, leaving Japan confused, resentful, and hedging, but still aligned with the United States after all the pieces fell into place . . . and watching jealously as China came to the fore in U.S. Asia policy.

"Our Leader Has Taken Leave of Reality": The China Card

Nixon and Kissinger eventually determined that opening to China might allow a realignment of ends and means that would sustain a favorable balance of power and American preeminence, not only in the Pacific but globally. Broadly speaking, rapprochement with Beijing would reduce the demand for U.S. provision of security goods; unsettle the Soviets, who would then hopefully be more amenable to U.S. demands for a less confrontational relationship; and—the president hoped—give the United States more leverage on North Vietnam.

Nixon eventually achieved most of these objectives with his China policy. He reduced the requirement for security goods from the United States in the Pacific, which kept Japan aligned (though bruised) after the

Guam Doctrine and allowed Nixon to refocus military forces on Europe. He propelled the Soviets toward détente by making the Washington-Beijing link stronger than Moscow's connection with either. And though Beijing was not willing to pressure Hanoi to give up on conquering the South, Nixon's opening to China marked what China expert and journalist Jim Mann calls "the true end of the domino theory," since the fall of Indochina would no longer portend further Chinese-backed communist assaults on the neighboring states.[114] In addition to these geostrategic payoffs, the opening to China was important for its sheer audacity. Power in international relations is measured by theorists in terms of material attributes or more abstract ideational factors such as "soft power" or identity, but competence and willpower are themselves critical attributes of a great power. After five years of apparent incompetence and reactive incrementalism in Vietnam, Nixon demonstrated through his visit to China in February 1972 that the United States again had the willpower and the agility to seize the initiative in international affairs.

Despite his being admired for boldness in foreign affairs, though, there is only patchy evidence that Nixon was actually preparing a China card before he became president. As was noted, he once called talk of switching diplomatic relations from Taiwan to the PRC "naïve wooly-headed thinking."[115] More privately, the former vice president, during one of his Asian trips in 1965, did begin to muse with U.S. diplomats about the future of the ROC and the need for a more normal relationship with Beijing.[116] By the time of his 1967 Foreign Affairs article on Asia, Nixon was demonstrating openness to some kind of relationship with both China and Taiwan in the future, but he was clearly not ready to betray the Taiwan lobby and close friends like Anna Chennault. For his part, Kissinger in 1962 had rejected the idea that the United States could promote a split between China and the Soviet Union, advising against "chasing a will-o'-the-wisp of Soviet domestic developments or a split in the Communist bloc."[117]

Indeed, knowing what he knew, it would have been unwise for Nixon to assume before his presidency that there was a China card to play vis-à-vis the Soviets as he took office. When Nixon and Kissinger began work in the White House in January 1969, Mao's China was still an avowedly hostile and unpredictable entity in international affairs. The Cultural Revolution was in its third and most extreme year: all Chinese ambassadors abroad but one had been recalled; attacks on foreign embassies were on the increase; and Chinese military support for Hanoi was at an all-time high. The Defense Department reported to the White House in January 1969, in its first briefing on China, that although Moscow and Beijing suffered from a "divergence of basic interests," there was little chance of a larger Sino-Soviet split. The State Department gave its assessment in February that the "Chinese believe that most of their explicit and implicit policy objectives at this stage in history must be pursued *against* the U.S. rather than in *collaboration* with it" [emphasis original].[118] In March, the administration's first National Intelligence Estimate on China concluded that "Mao will remain an insurmountable obstacle to any accommodation with the USSR, and there is little alternative to continuing hostility toward the US."[119] Leaders across Asia told Marshall Green that spring, during his first tour through the region as assistant secretary of state for East Asia, that China just was not ready for opening.[120] Only a special National Intelligence Estimate prepared by the CIA noted somewhat more optimistically that within Beijing's "fairly rigid strategic framework, there are signs of some great flexibility in tactics" toward the West.[121] Not surprisingly, Nixon came to office expecting the Soviets to be the more logical card to play vis-à-vis Hanoi.

Yet Nixon was clearly interested in exploring what might be possible with China over time despite these near-term hurdles.[122] As early as February 1969, he sent Kissinger a memo instructing him to find a way to reach out to Beijing.[123] Haig recalls Kissinger telling him that "our Leader has taken leave of reality. He has just ordered me to make this flight of fantasy come true."[124] But as Marvin and Bernard Kalb note, Kissinger was "a mere passenger on the Administration's China train. The President was clearly its sole engineer."[125] The national security advisor dutifully directed the NSC and Green's interagency group on Asia to review current U.S. policies toward both Chinas.[126] Meanwhile, the top China hand on the NSC staff, John Holdridge, worked internally on a potential strategy to open dialogue with Beijing.[127]

By the spring of 1969—just after the bureaucracy's skeptical assessments were turned in to the White House—there was new evidence of a fundamental strategic confrontation between Moscow and Beijing as Chinese and Soviet forces clashed along the Ussuri River (which runs north to south from Khabarovsk toward Vladivostok between China and the USSR). This was not the first military clash between the two powers, but it was the first time Beijing responded by publicly attacking the Soviets in propaganda statements. All the other pieces of disconnected evidence quickly began to fall into place: the Soviets' sudden expansion from twenty-four to thirty-nine divisions in the Far East that year and occupation of part of Xinjiang in August; a corresponding military buildup in the north by the Chinese; the intensity of the ideological rift between Moscow and Beijing in the wake of the 1968 Brezhnev Doctrine and Soviet interventions in Czechoslovakia; and the depth of China's innate nationalism and historic fear of foreign empires interfering in Chinese internal affairs.[128]

Green discovered as he traveled with Nixon through Asia that summer that the president was intrigued by the idea that "there was some merit in the Soviet Union being worried about our relations with China."[129] It was the mirror image of Dulles's concept that pressuring China would raise Beijing's costs of alignment with the Soviets and eventually force a split in the communist camp; now the president wanted to raise Moscow's costs of hostility through U.S. rapprochement with China. In July, Kissinger recommended that the United States attempt an improvement in relations with Beijing, for as he put it, "the hostility between China and the Soviet Union served our purposes best if we maintained closer relations with each side than they did with each other."[130]

Nixon began to send indirect signals to Beijing as he traveled from Guam across the region in July and August. When Brezhnev proposed an anti-China front in Asia, Nixon asked Presidents Yahya Khan of Pakistan and Nicolae Ceaucescu of Romania to inform Beijing that he preferred to work with China to counter the Soviets instead.[131] In his toast in Romania and in State Department statements that summer, he referred to the "People's Republic of China" instead of "Communist China." Then, in September, Nixon authorized the U.S. ambassador in Poland to propose talks to his Chinese counterpart, one of the few Chinese diplomats still abroad. This proved far more difficult than expected, with China convulsed in the Cultural Revolution at home, but on December 2, the American finally chased down a startled second secretary from the Chinese embassy (thinking he was the chargé d'affaires) at a diplomatic reception, and on January 8, initial U.S.-China contacts were begun.[132]

In the first four months of 1970, Marshall Green and the State Department worked around the clock to prepare the White House for the new diplomacy with Beijing. Green had always been interested in a transformation in U.S.-China relations, but he was also highly sensitive to the potential damage to American credibility if U.S. allies and partners—particularly Japan—were undercut by rapprochement with Beijing.[133]

Nixon had also begun with a similar instinct for multipolarity in Asia centered on U.S. allies, and Lord had reinforced the necessity of coordinating approaches to China with Japan in his Guam Doctrine memo for Kissinger. Green therefore recommended a conditions-based approach to Beijing that would begin with demands for China's renunciation of force to resolve the cross-Strait problem. He then laid out an iterative process that would be closely calibrated with Tokyo.[134]

By this point, however, Kissinger was no longer interested in strategic or tactical advice from the State Department and was primarily commissioning interagency papers like Green's as a way to distract the bureaucracy from the real diplomacy. An incremental, quid pro quo approach carefully coordinated with allies was hardly the recipe for the secrecy and sudden boldness that the White House saw as essential for domestic politics and grand strategy.[135] Events quickly moved beyond the State Department's purview. After clashes between Soviet and Chinese forces in Xinjiang in which an entire Chinese brigade was annihilated in August, Mao's advisors recommended that China "play the U.S. card"— recalling that China's ancestors had once "counseled negotiating with faraway countries while fighting those that are near."[136]

The first manifestation of China's new approach came in the unlikeliest of venues in April 1971, when—with Mao's approval—the manager of China's table tennis team invited the U.S. team to visit China after a chance encounter between their players at the World Table Tennis Championships in Nagoya, Japan. After the Americans' successful one-week visit to China later that month, Nixon announced reduced trade restrictions on China, and Beijing reciprocated by signaling that it was ready to receive an envoy from the United States. It is not certain that Nixon wanted Kissinger for that role, but on June 3, Pakistan's ambassador in Washington delivered a warmly written invitation from Zhou Enlai personally inviting Kissinger to Beijing that summer.[137] Feigning illness during a visit to Pakistan on July 9, Kissinger left the press corps and State Department officials behind in Islamabad and flew secretly to China to open a new chapter in American strategy in Asia. Recognizing his own place in history, Winston Lord entered the cockpit as the plane entered Chinese airspace so that he could claim to be the first U.S. official since 1949 in the PRC.[138]

In the seventeen hours of secret discussions that followed in Beijing, Kissinger and Zhou each made an unsuccessful pitch for their immediate priorities—Kissinger for Chinese pressure on Hanoi and Zhou for

American abandonment of Taiwan. Yet, despite failing to reach accord on these objectives, both men recognized that they had laid a sufficient foundation to begin planning for a presidential visit.[139] On July 15, 1971, Nixon announced to the world on national television that his national security advisor had been in China and that he himself would go the following year.[140]

As Green had hoped, the Soviets were stunned—accepting within weeks Nixon's secret proposal for a U.S.-Soviet summit, which Moscow had been rebuffing up to that point.[141] But, as Green had feared, America's closest friends in the Pacific were equally shocked. Taipei was given only thirty minutes' warning before Nixon's national address, suffering a humiliating defeat the same day at the United Nations as Beijing's supporters successfully tabled a resolution to expel the ROC from the UN General Assembly.[142] The Japanese ambassador received a comparably more generous grace period of several hours before Nixon publicly disclosed Kissinger's trip, but Japan had already taken a stand in support of Taiwan at the UN that same day and had endured withering criticism from the PRC for the Japanese military buildup encouraged by Nixon's Guam Doctrine. The Sato cabinet was exposed and politically ruined.[143] In Southeast Asia, the Philippine government panicked, Thailand grew anxious, and in Indonesia, where racial views toward the Chinese were still hostile, there was deep resentment of Nixon's move. In Saigon, officials hoped that the announcement might lead to greater Chinese pressure on Hanoi to cease fighting.[144]

Eventually, most of these governments saw advantages to Sino-U.S. rapprochement in terms of regional stability and economic opportunities and took advantage of the new U.S. policy in subsequent years. Nixon and Kissinger realized the damage they had done to Japan, in particular, and Green convinced the president to fly to Alaska on September 26, 1971, to greet the Japanese emperor and empress on their polar flight to Europe, their first outside Japan and their first step on foreign soil in the United States.[145] Sato's successor, Tanaka Kakuei, then took matters into his own hands and rushed to normalize relations with China, to the delight of many in the Japanese business community, in September 1972. All of these steps were a balm to the wound to Japanese pride and confidence in Washington, but the sense of betrayal would not be forgotten in Tokyo for decades afterward. Taipei, meanwhile, was put on a slippery slope toward termination of diplomatic relations at the end of the decade, while

Rapprochement ·

the government in Saigon waited in vain for China to begin pressuring Hanoi to end the war.

At home in the United States, the news was electrifying. Nixon's gamble had been a huge political success, restoring his popularity and prospects for a lasting legacy. The diplomacy nevertheless remained intricate and complex, and the outcome of engagement still uncertain. In Kissinger's second visit to China on October 20, the two sides delicately maneuvered to ensure that their respective publics would think it was the other side that needed rapprochement more. Nixon then headed for his own encounter with Mao in February 1972, still trying to assess his counterpart's intentions. In preparation for the visit, he jotted down a tidy summation of how the two countries' interests stacked up:

WHAT THEY WANT

1. Build up their world credentials
2. Taiwan
3. Get U.S. out of Asia

restrain chinese expansion ·

WHAT WE WANT

1. Indo China(?)
2. Communication—To restrain Chinese expansion in Asia
3. In Future—Reduce threat of confrontation by China Super Power

WHAT WE BOTH WANT

1. Reduce danger of confrontation & conflict
2. A more stable Asia
3. A restraint on U.S.S.R.[146]

Nixon and Mao would make only marginally more progress than Kissinger and Zhou had on the crux of the first two categories—Indochina and Taiwan. Nixon thought that a trade-off between the two issues was inevitable, but there was no deal to be had with Mao, since Nixon had already given away Indochina by announcing Vietnamization and was not yet ready to abandon Taiwan.[147] At best, the two sides could reach a modus vivendi on Taiwan based on Kissinger's agreement with Zhou the previous October that "the United States acknowledges that all Chinese on either side of the Taiwan Strait maintain there is but one China" and would not "challenge that position."[148]

In the third category, however—"what we both want"—Nixon achieved his signature success, for what both nations clearly wanted was to restrain Moscow: the Chinese to contain the Soviets in Asia, and the Americans to pressure the Soviets toward détente.[149] The meeting of minds with respect to Moscow was so deeply rooted that, during his visit to China, the president handed over classified information on Soviet military capabilities in the Far East.[150]

The common front against Moscow also contributed to a broad understanding with respect to Japan, though not in terms the leaders in Tokyo would necessarily have found flattering. Nixon argued in the face of long-standing Chinese criticism of the U.S.-Japan alliance that "if the U.S. is gone from Asia, gone from Japan, our protests, no matter how loud, would be like—to use the Prime Minister's phrase—firing an empty cannon; we would have no rallying effect because fifteen thousand miles away is just too far to be heard."[151]

From Mao's perspective, Nixon's shoddy treatment of the Japanese government in his opening to China probably fueled expectations that Tokyo's privileged position in U.S. strategic thinking toward Asia was likely to decline in the future. But Mao also saw Japan as a useful buttress against the Soviets and subsequently conveyed to Nixon his concern—perhaps with a hint of mischief—that the United States had begun to neglect Tokyo *too* much.[152] Double containment of both Moscow and Tokyo cemented Nixon and Mao's agreement on the utility of the U.S.-Japan alliance, despite historic Chinese misgivings about Japan.

Capturing these views in a joint statement for the world was no small endeavor. Zhou had rejected Kissinger's initial draft in October because Mao thought it foolish to pretend the United States and China had common views of the world. Instead, Zhou proposed a three-part document in which Nixon and Mao would each state their views of the world and then the two leaders would commit jointly to moving toward normalization of bilateral relations. Though initially panicked, the American delegation recognized that it was a brilliant formula.[153] After last-minute negotiating crises as Green pointed out flaws in some of Kissinger's original text with Zhou, the two sides released the "Shanghai Communiqué" on February 27, 1972.[154] The document was a masterful message of convergence on geostrategic interests and the management of significant divergences on regional interests and fundamental values, with each side stating its positions rather than seeking consensus. But as Nixon stated to the world from Shanghai, it was the beginning of the journey, not the end. Indeed, it was the most significant U.S. agreement on Asia since the San Francisco System was launched two decades earlier.

On the issue of Taiwan, the United States stuck with language acknowledging that "all Chinese on either side of the Taiwan Strait maintain there is but one China and that Taiwan is a part of China" while affirming "the ultimate objective of the withdrawal of all U.S. forces and military installations from Taiwan." Critically, the U.S. statement on Taiwan was premised on two caveats that the Chinese side has since sought to downplay: first, that the United States had an "interest in a peaceful settlement of the Taiwan question by the Chinese themselves"; and second, that the progressive reduction of military forces and installations in Taiwan would occur "as tension in the area diminishes."[155] It should have served as an early warning that the Taiwan issue would return with a fury after the Chinese side rejected American language proposing "an equitable and peaceful resolution" to the cross-Straits problem, since "equitable" might imply that the people on Taiwan would get a vote and—more menacingly—since Beijing refused to foreswear the use of force to resolve the Taiwan question. In fact, Zhou mused during the negotiations that if future U.S. administrations failed to honor Chinese expectations with respect to Taiwan, it might lead to "other means" to liberate Taiwan, a rare but unmistakable reference to the use of force.[156] Decades later, Beijing and Washington continue to disagree on exactly what the Shanghai communiqué meant with respect to the security of Taiwan—a downside of the ambiguities and contradictions that were necessary to create the Shanghai Communiqué.

Shanghai communiqué

With respect to U.S. allies, the U.S. side stated that it placed "the highest value on its friendly relations with Japan" and reiterated "close ties with and support for the Republic of Korea." The Chinese side reiterated its opposition to a revival of Japanese militarism and its support for "the Japanese people's desire to build an independent, democratic, peaceful and neutral Japan" as well as Beijing's principle that "all foreign troops should be withdrawn to their own countries." With the common Soviet threat, these differences appeared more ideological than real, but they still remain Chinese longer-term objectives and complications for U.S. policy with respect to Japan.

Expressing the differences on values also proved impossible to do without parallel and largely contradictory statements from the two sides. The U.S. side expressed support for "individual freedom and social progress for all the peoples of the world, free of outside pressure or intervention," while the Chinese side stated that it "firmly supports the

struggles of all the oppressed people and nations for freedom and liberation and that the people of all countries have the right to choose their
social systems according to their own wishes and the right to safeguard
the independence, sovereignty and territorial integrity of their own
countries and oppose foreign aggression, interference, control and sub-
version." For the last time in a diplomatic document, the United States
reaffirmed its commitment to noninterference in the internal affairs of
other countries. To the extent this was even the case after 1945, it proved
impossible to sustain politically after Nixon.

Indeed, the success of the Shanghai Communiqué depended on both
sides' willingness to defer satisfaction on their most fundamental values
and strategic traditions in order to focus on common and immediate geostrategic interests. Yet, implicit for both the Chinese and American leaders
was the assumption that change would favor their own side over time. For
China, this meant a gradual reduction of the U.S. military presence in Taiwan and Asia as Chinese power and self-confidence grew, while for the
United States it meant that engagement would lead gradually to positive
social and political change in China as Beijing opened to the international
community. Whereas China saw material changes accruing to its benefit
over time, the U.S. side saw ideational changes favoring its worldview.
Nixon, Kissinger, Mao, and Zhou were too astute to state that explicitly,
but these were the assumptions that underpinned broad acceptance of
the communiqué among both nations' elites.

Yet despite these unresolved contradictions in U.S.-China relations,
the most important operative phrase in the entire document remained
the guiding principle that "progress toward the normalization of relations
between China and the United States is in the interests of all countries."[157]
This process would take longer than either Nixon or Mao expected, but
it would fundamentally change the balance of power in Asia and the lives
of billions.

NIXON'S LEGACY IN ASIA STRATEGY

The clarity and consistency in Nixon and Kissinger's grand strategy
toward Asia can be compared only with that of Theodore Roosevelt, as
was noted at the outset of this chapter. Neorealists ever since have pined
for the glory days of 1969–1972. The Nixon administration was preoccu-

pied with the structure of international relations, unlike any administration before or since. Given the deterioration of American power and
credibility in Vietnam, that focus was appropriate. At the structural
level, Nixon and Kissinger midwifed a new post-Vietnam era of American strategy that realigned ends and means and shifted the structure of
global geopolitics from bipolarity to a new multipolarity, establishing
a favorable equilibrium that went a significant way toward restoring the
credibility of American power. And despite all the flaws in his approach to
other Asian powers and the unsettled issues in relations with Beijing, it
was Nixon and Kissinger who had the foresight and willpower to set U.S.-
China relations on a trajectory that every president since has generally followed and that has resulted in a wealthier and more stable Asia-Pacific.

Negative assessments of Nixon's foreign policy strategy tend to emphasize the moral consequences of his realist-based approach. In a turbulent
era in international affairs, the United States appeared to accept the inevitability of the Chinese Cultural Revolution, the Soviet gulags, and the
killing fields of Cambodia and East Pakistan. As Gerald Ford's secretary
of state, Kissinger became so concerned about the rising backlash against
this realism that he dedicated a speech in Minneapolis to explaining
"moral foundations of foreign policy" in July 1975.[158] In the cradle of midwestern progressivism, he argued that "Our choice is not between morality and pragmatism. This nation must be true to its own beliefs, or it
will lose its bearings in the world. But, at the same time, it must survive
in a world of sovereign nations and competing wills. We need moral
strength to select among often agonizing choices and a sense of purpose
to navigate between the shoals of difficult decisions. But we need as well
a mature sense of means lest we substitute wishful thinking for the
requirements of survival."

A pragmatic foreign policy, he continued, recognizes that security
must always be the first priority, but "security is a means, not an end,"
since "the purpose of security is to safeguard the values of our free
society." It was evident throughout the speech that the secretary of state
worried about Americans using, as he put it, "moral convictions to escape
reality" instead of "drawing on them as a source of courage and self-
confidence." Eighteen months later, a new president would come to office
determined to reverse the relationship between morality and pragmatism,
ushering in a chaotic foreign policy much as Kissinger had feared. Kissinger's logic in Minneapolis was compelling, but his attention to values

came too late to sustain a political consensus behind the realism he saw as critical for continued American leadership in the world.

In realist terms, Nixon and Kissinger used Asia to achieve their major global objective, which was a reframing of U.S.-Soviet relations. The CIA accurately estimated in April 1972 that Sino-U.S. rapprochement would reduce the chances of Soviet military aggression against China and would "give Moscow an incentive to 'normalize' its relations with the U.S."[159] Stalled negotiations with Moscow on Strategic Arms Limitations Talks (SALT I) were propelled forward to agreement in May 1972 by the opening to China. As Kissinger told the president, "with conscientious attention to both capitals we should be able to continue to have our mao tai and drink our vodka too."[160]

However, the CIA was also prescient in warning that over the coming decade Moscow, in large part because of Sino-American rapprochement and an expanding strategic conflict with China, would take a more active diplomatic and military stance in the Far East. In particular, the CIA accurately predicted that the Soviets would become more intransigent in their support for Hanoi in order to contain what they saw as growing Chinese influence in the Third World.[161] The JCS assessed that Soviet forces were poised to develop the "capability to strike the United States and its Asian allies, to harass US military forces, and to interdict Free World LOCs [lines of communication] in the Pacific-Asian area."[162] Détente would reduce tensions in Europe but also prove to be an interlude while the Soviets expanded their capabilities in Asia (in addition to Africa and the Middle East), both to counter China and to threaten the dominant U.S. maritime position. Stability would prove elusive and require new adjustments—as Kissinger might have predicted from his own study of the history of international affairs.

Thus, while Nixon's strategy was highly effective in transforming the critical U.S.-Soviet relationship and opening a new era in bilateral U.S.-China relations, it was inefficient in terms of other U.S. equities in Asia. To achieve *global multipolarity*, Nixon and Kissinger drifted toward a new Sino-U.S. *bipolarity* in Asia—contradicting precisely the multipolar strategy for the region that Nixon had called for in his 1967 *Foreign Affairs* piece. Over the latter part of the 1970s, it would become evident that improved Sino-U.S. relations would not serve as a sufficient buttress against Soviet expansionism in South and Southeast Asia and against the maritime bastion of Japan. Relationships with Japan, India, and Southeast Asia would have to be rebuilt and the credibility of U.S. commitments restored after the bruising they took in the Nixon years.

The damage to U.S.-Japan relations was highlighted as early as the fall of 1971, in NSSM 122, which warned that U.S.-Japan ties had entered the "most difficult period since the end of World War II," largely because of "[t]he President's intention to visit Peking and our new economic policies, both, however justifiably, announced without prior warning or consultations with the Japanese."[163] Through the Guam Doctrine, the surprise opening to China, and the rebalancing of the dollar, Nixon had restored the credibility of American *power*, but he had also inadvertently raised lasting questions about the credibility of American *commitments*. In the words of Nixon's undersecretary of state for policy, U. Alexis Johnson, while the president and Kissinger "embarked on a period of rapturous enchantment with China," they shoved Japan, "our most important ally in Asia by far," to the "back burner."[164] Or, as Marshall Green recognized, the century-old tension between Japan and China in American foreign policy had reemerged: "There has always been a tendency in the Foreign Service, as in fact in our government, that goes back for at least 100 years, for officials to be either pro-Japanese or pro-Chinese. It seemed we had once again fallen back into that syndrome, with the President favoring China over Japan. He would never say so, but that would seem to have been the case."[165]

Green observed that in summits with Chinese leaders, the attractive female interpreters were trained to laugh at Nixon's jokes before translating so that Mao or Zhou would know to laugh as well. In Japan, stone-faced young men of the foreign ministry translated earnestly and officiously, boring the president and convincing Kissinger that it is "impossible to make conceptual deals with the Japanese."[166]

There may have been more at play in Nixon's mind than just pique at Japan or enchantment with Chinese interpreters, though. There have always been American foreign policy thinkers who worried about a convergence of major powers in Asia against the United States. Nixon justified his own rough treatment of Japan in a memo to Kissinger on March 12, 1973, warning that Japan might eventually "choose China, and that their resources and Chinese intelligence are going to do to us in Asia what the Common Market may do to us in Europe." The United States must make Japan's inability to decide work for U.S. interests, Nixon stressed, and therefore "lean a little bit towards China wherever we can."[167]

Recognizing that this was hardly a sustainable policy, Kissinger began to argue publicly that Japan was an important center of world power in its own right, the third pillar of a new "trilateralism" of the great democracies in North America and Europe, as he put it in a speech in April 1973.[168] Nixon and Kissinger ensured that Japan did not dealign, but there was nevertheless a new element of drift and uncertainty in the U.S.-Japan alliance that would not be corrected until Ronald Reagan and Nakasone Yasuhiro came to office. Indeed, even to this day, the trauma of the "Nixon shocks" continues to surface in the author's meetings with Japanese scholars and officials.

The damage was not only to Japan; American influence receded elsewhere around the periphery of China. Secretary of State William Rogers noted in an internal memorandum on November 8, 1971, that "largely as a result of U.S. initiatives under the Nixon Doctrine and with respect to China policy, the Philippines is moving toward a foreign policy concept of depolarization and de-emphasis of its bilateral relationship with the U.S."[169] The pattern would repeat across Southeast Asia. In part, this was by design as Nixon and Kissinger returned U.S. Southeast Asia policy to the secondary status it had initially held in the Truman and Eisenhower administrations. As a practical matter, the cost to U.S. interests was limited by the more benign Chinese stance toward Southeast Asia and the establishment of the Association of Southeast Asian Nations (ASEAN) in 1967.[170] Still, after Nixon, it would be decades before another American administration would consider engagement of Southeast Asia a high priority.

Relations between the United States and India—an important democratic actor in the Asian multipolarity Nixon envisioned in his 1967 *Foreign Affairs* essay—also suffered with the emergence of a Sinocentric U.S. foreign policy in Asia. Nixon was never favorably disposed toward the Indians, whom he called "no goddam good" and considered less reliable than Pakistan's leadership.[171] When the West Pakistan Alawi League was refused autonomy by Islamabad and India intervened in December 1971, the Nixon administration made that bias transparent. As war broke out between India and Pakistan, Kissinger viewed the conflict primarily through the lens of the new Sino-U.S.-Soviet triangular dynamic. As he told Nixon in a rebuttal to the positions of State, JCS, and the CIA, "We really don't have any choice [but to oppose India]. We can't allow a friend of ours and China's to get screwed in a conflict with a friend of Russia's."[172] Kissinger also worried about maintaining the Pakistan channel to Beijing.[173] As a result, Washington leaned heavily against Delhi. Al Haig told the Chinese ambassador that in the unfolding crisis in South Asia the United States would take "every step in full coordination with you."[174] Nixon ordered a U.S. carrier battle group to the Indian Ocean to pressure India and deter the Soviets, while Kissinger provided the Chinese with detailed satellite images and other intelligence on Indian and Soviet military moves.[175] The White House even pressed China to increase its own military presence on the Indian border.[176]

Yet India's alignment with Moscow was an outward projection of internal South Asian tensions—and not a regional or global alliance that Moscow could easily wield against Beijing. Nixon and Kissinger misread the fierce independence and nonalignment of the Indians and inappropriately cast the U.S. relationship with India in adversarial terms. The result was prolonged estrangement between the oldest democracy in the modern world and the largest democracy in Asia, which lasted until Ronald Reagan and Indira Gandhi warmed to each other a decade later. Flipping India from the Soviet to the U.S. column may not have been possible, but softening the Delhi-Moscow connection was an option cast aside when China became the centerpiece of U.S. strategy.

The irony in the cases of both Japan and India was that Nixon could have used the China card to reshape the global balance of power without doing as much damage as he did to these key relationships in Asia. Indeed, Nixon had originally envisioned in his 1967 *Foreign Affairs* piece that eventual U.S. engagement of China would *require* stronger ties to Japan and India—as indeed it did after the Cold War. India and Japan were never obstacles to improving ties with China. When Nixon's China policy began to falter in 1973–1974, it had nothing to do with U.S.-Japan or U.S.-India relations and everything to do with the president's own domestic political crises, Chinese disappointment at détente with the Soviets, and Mao's attacks on Premier Zhou for his handling of China-U.S. strategic relations in the context of heightened "succession tensions" in the last years of the Chinese chairman's life.[177]

And falter it did. Sino-U.S. relations peaked with Kissinger's February 1973 visit to Beijing, where the two sides agreed to establish liaison offices, but over the course of that year, Nixon's triumphant opening to China gave way to a new mood of fatigue, outrage, and tragedy in American foreign policy toward Asia. In April 1973, U.S. citizens and select Cambodian citizens were evacuated from Phnom Penh by U.S. Marine helicopters. Hundreds of Cambodians declined to be evacuated, including one of the country's few capable leaders, Sirik Matak, who handed a letter to Ambassador John H. Dean refusing transport and concluding poignantly, "I never believed for a moment that you would have this sentiment of abandoning a people which has chosen liberty."[178] Then, as North Vietnamese forces launched their final offensive against the South in March 1975, General Vo Nguyen Giap dropped the veneer of socialist uprising and used regular units to drive through the demoralized ARVN forces and take Saigon in less than two months.[179] Kissinger pushed for airlifts of U.S. allies from South Vietnam but could not do so without congressional approval.[180] President Ford's hands were tied, and Nixon, who had resigned on August 9, 1974, because of the Watergate bugging scandal, could only watch developments on TV in frustration.

Though beset by economic crises and by severe limits placed on his executive power by Congress, Gerald Ford nevertheless took what steps he could to restore U.S. credibility in Asia.[181] Ford had been a member of the isolationist "America First" organization while at Yale, but the Second World War transformed him into a passionate internationalist. He and his advisors worried that the fall of Indochina had confirmed U.S. allies' worst suspicions: that the Guam Doctrine was a declaration of American retreat from Asia. Kissinger was so concerned that he told reporters on background on May 5, 1975, "The United States must carry out some act somewhere in the world which shows its determination to continue to be a world power."[182] That opportunity came a week later, when Khmer Rouge forces seized the U.S. container ship *Mayaguez* in international waters near Cambodia and detained the crew. With little hesitation and strong support from his national security team, Ford sent in a rescue mission led by the Third Marine Expeditionary Force that shot up the Khmer Rouge defenses. Though the United States suffered casualties and the crew had already been released, the coercive arm of American diplomacy nevertheless enjoyed a brief but much needed encore.

Ford was also deeply troubled about the credibility of America's moral mission after the abandonment of Indochina. At a time of retrenchment and national fatigue, the president authorized Operation Babylift on April 3, 1975, evacuating thousands of Vietnamese children just before the fall of Saigon.[183] He then mounted a national campaign to overcome congressional opposition to accepting further refugees from Indochina and successfully secured passage on May 23, 1975, of the Indochina Migration and Refugee Assistance Act.[184] Hundreds of thousands of immigrants followed these first refugees from Vietnam, Laos, and Cambodia—

contributing to the American experience and forming an unbreakable bond with their homelands in the years to come. It may have been Ford's finest moment as president.

More broadly, Ford and his team recognized the need to reframe American strategy toward Asia in ways that would be credible and enduring over the longer term. Japan was still reeling from the Nixon shocks and in need of strategic reassurance (in November 1974, Ford made the first trip to Japan by a sitting president and his first overseas). Thailand and the Philippines were dissolving SEATO and questioning the value of hosting U.S. forces after communist victory in Indochina (U.S. forces would leave Thailand in July 1976, but the Philippines opted to continue hosting bases for the rest of the Cold War).[185] Meanwhile, relations with other important countries such as Malaysia and Indonesia had been sidelined by the Vietnam War but now had potential to expand.[186] At home, conservative forces within the Republican Party and Ford's own cabinet, including Defense Secretary Jim Schlesinger and Chief of Staff (and after 1975 Secretary of Defense) Donald Rumsfeld, were pushing back against détente with the Soviets and inclining Ford toward regional approaches that deemphasized the previous focus on Sino-U.S.-Soviet global tripolarity.[187] The U.S.-China normalization process was already on hold anyway because of Beijing's preoccupation with the reactionary "Gang of Four" and opposition from Ford's pro-Taiwan challenger for the Republican nomination, Governor Ronald Reagan of California. Domestic politics and international pressures all pointed to the need for a new equilibrium in U.S. Asia strategy after Nixon.

A month after the fall of Saigon, the NSC staff prepared a memo for Kissinger (who was now serving as both secretary of state and national security advisor) offering three notional options for rethinking American strategy toward the region: "We could continue the strategy we have been pursuing, sustaining our friends and developing our strategic and diplomatic position; we could go to a more maritime strategy, concentrating on the island nations and perhaps such peninsulas as Korea while abandoning our remaining Asian mainland positions; or we could move toward an emphasis on economic relations and draw down our military presence throughout Asia as a whole."[188]

The administration's preference was clearly the first—continued engagement. But the congressional mood and doubts in the region after the fall of Saigon made the two other options real dangers and not just straw men for drafting purposes. The president and the NSC determined that it would be vital to offer a new affirmative vision for American engagement in the Pacific.

The opportunity came during Ford's visit to the region at the end of 1975. Speaking at the East-West Center in Hawaii on December 7 after visiting China, the Philippines, and Indonesia, Ford announced a "New Pacific Doctrine." The United States, the president emphasized, "is a Pacific nation" whose role in the region rested on six pillars: (1) the United States would stand by its allies but insist on "popular legitimacy and social justice"; (2) the U.S.-Japan alliance "is a pillar of our strategy"; (3) U.S.-PRC rapprochement must continue; (4) the United States had a "continuing stake in stability and security in Southeast Asia"; (5) the United States would stand with the Republic of Korea; and (6) the U.S. commitment to the region was now based on an enduring "structure of economic cooperation," noting that U.S. trade that year had surpassed trade with Europe.[189]

It was a prudent, well-balanced, and credible articulation of U.S. interests in Asia—restoring Japan to a central position, reiterating the importance of American values, and focusing on the expanding economic underpinnings of an enduring American commitment to the region. But within a year, it would not matter, because the turmoil of the Nixon years had opened the way for a new president with a passion for reconstructing American foreign policy.

new affirmative position for Am. engagement in the Pacific

FIGURE 1. Thomas Jefferson in Paris, where he dined with Connecticut Yankee and former Royal Marine John Ledyard and heard his vision of expanded American commerce with Canton, the Sandwich Islands, and the Pacific Northwest. John Trumbull, 1788. *Source*: White House Collection/White House Historical Association.

FIGURE 2. Fort Astoria in 1813. America's first toehold on the Pacific was established by fur trader John Jacob Astor, whom Jefferson said would stand beside "Columbus and Raleigh" as the "founder of such an empire which will arise from commerce." Circa 1813. *Source*: Library of Congress, Washington, DC.

FIGURE 3. John Quincy Adams (center) after signing the Treaty of Ghent ending the War of 1812. Adams vigorously defended American claims to the Pacific Northwest at Ghent and later as secretary of state. *Source*: Sir Amédée Forestier, *The Signing of the Treaty of Ghent, Christmas Eve, 1814*, Smithsonian American Art Museum, Gift of the Sulgrave Institution of the United States and Great Britain.

FIGURES 4, 5, AND 6. The first proponents of an active American strategy for the Far East. (Facing page, left, top) U.S. Commissioner to China Humphrey Marshall, who advocated policies to protect China from European imperialism, foreshadowing the Open Door. *Source*: Courtesy of the National Archives. https://research.archives.gov/id/528271.
(Facing page, right, middle) Peter Parker, who traveled to China in 1834 as a missionary but became the most vocal proponent of imperialist competition with the Europeans as U.S. commissioner from 1855 to 1857. *Source*: Courtesy of the National Archives. https://research.archives.gov/id/528271.
(Facing page, left, bottom) Commodore Matthew Calbraith Perry, pictured here during his 1856 speaking tour in New York, where he regaled audiences with tales of his mission to Japan and advocated a maritime strategy in the Pacific that anticipated Alfred Thayer Mahan's writings at century's end. *Source*: Alexander Beckers and Victor Piard, between 1855 and 1856.

FIGURE 7. Alfred Thayer Mahan published *The Influence of Sea Power Upon History* between stints as president of the Naval War College. He would turn next to the geopolitics of Asia. *Source*: *Alfred Thayer Mahan*, circa 1900. LC-USZ62-3124, Library of Congress Prints and Photographs Division.

FIGURE 8. John Hay—poet, presidential secretary, and pragmatist—two years after he authored the "Open Door Notes" and near the end of a long and illustrious career as an American diplomat (1901). *Source*: LC-USZ62-48334, Library of Congress Prints and Photographs Division.

FIGURE 9. Theodore Roosevelt salutes the freshly painted battleships of the navy's Great White Fleet as they pass in review before departing on a global tour that would take them to Japan and Australia. *Source*: Theodore Roosevelt Collection, Harvard College Library.

FIGURE 10. Charles Evan Hughes at the signing of the Washington Naval Treaty, November 12, 1921, or February 6, 1922. In the wake of the First World War, the naval powers sought to reduce defense expenditures and seek diplomatic solutions to conflicts of interest. The treaties worked for a time before collapsing a decade later with the Japanese invasions of Manchuria and then China. *Source: The Conference on Limitation of Armaments, Washington, D.C.* LC-H27-A-4041, Harris and Ewing Collection, Library of Congress Prints and Photographs Division.

FIGURES 11, 12, AND 13. Three State Department protagonists in the debate about how to respond to Japanese expansion in the 1930s.
(Facing page, left, top) Joseph Grew, who retained a Mahanian focus on the geopolitical importance of Japan to the United States, even during the darkest moments of crisis and war. *Source*: Underwood and Underwood, LC-USZ62-73808, Library of Congress Prints and Photographs Division, May 7, 1924.
(Facing page, right, top) Stanley Hornbeck, who championed the Open Door and resistance to Japan, though he showed little affection for China (public domain). *Source*: Harris and Ewing Collection, LC-H25-56680-DG, Library of Congress Prints and Photographs Division.
(Facing page, bottom) J. V. A. MacMurray, the veteran China hand who ultimately saw competition with Japan for Asia as futile and eventually recommended abandonment of the Open Door and quiet retreat to Hawaii. *Source*: National Photo Company Collection, LC-F8-33280, Library of Congress Prints and Photographs Division.

FIGURE 14. Admiral Chester Nimitz briefs President Franklin D. Roosevelt, General Douglas MacArthur, and Admiral William Leahy on the Pacific campaign in January 1944. He is pointing to Tokyo, but the men in the room still did not have a plan to force Japan's final capitulation, despite the advance of MacArthur's forces up the Southwest Pacific and Nimitz's hard-won string of naval and marine corps victories across the Central Pacific. *Source*: U.S. Navy, September 1944.

FIGURE 15. John Foster Dulles and Secretary of State Dean Acheson (standing, third and fourth from right) watch as Japanese prime minister Shigeru Yoshida signs the 1951 San Francisco Peace Treaty. The subsequent "San Francisco System" of bilateral alliances with Japan, Australia, New Zealand, the Philippines, and later Korea, the Republic of China, and Thailand would serve as the main pillar of American containment strategy during the Cold War. As Acheson's successor, Dulles would struggle to respond to communist advances against continental Southeast Asian nations not included in the system. *Source*: © Bettmann/ CORBIS.

FIGURE 16. President Lyndon Baines Johnson meets with the "Wise Men" for the second time, on March 26, 1968, to discuss Vietnam. At this meeting, he would be told by the majority around the table that the war could not be won. Facing the camera from left to right are Henry Cabot Lodge, Dean Acheson, and President Johnson. *Source*: LBJ Library Photo by Yoichi Okamoto, White House Photo Office, March 26, 1968.

FIGURE 17. President Richard Nixon with (from left) Marshall Green, Henry Kissinger, William Rogers, and U. Alexis Johnson en route to Honolulu and a meeting with Japanese prime minister Kakuei Tanaka. The secretary of state was relegated to second-tier status during the Nixon years despite the policy acumen and regional expertise of Johnson and Green, two of the strongest Asia experts ever to hold senior positions at the State Department. *Source*: © Bettmann/CORBIS.

FIGURE 18. Deng Xiaoping in Washington, DC, on January 28, 1979, flanked on his left by National Security Advisor Zbigniew Brzezinski and on his right by Secretary of State Cyrus Vance. Assistant Secretary of State Richard Holbrooke sits beneath the photo to Vance's right. Brzezinski was enthusiastic about using the China card against the Soviets and Vance was a skeptic, but Brzezinski prevailed. Deng found Carter's overall approach to Asia quixotic, but useful for China. *Source*: White House Staff Photographers, *Zbigniew Brzezinski hosts a dinner for Chinese Vice Premier Deng Xiaoping*, Jimmy Carter Library, 28 January 1979.

FIGURE 19. President Ronald Reagan and Japanese prime minister Yasuhiro Nakasone review a Japanese Self Defense Force honor guard in front of Akasaka Palace in Tokyo, Japan, May 4, 1986. Nakasone pledged to turn Japan into an "unsinkable aircraft carrier," making possible Reagan's maritime strategy and the reversal of Soviet advances in the Far East, though mounting bilateral trade friction vexed both leaders. *Source*: Courtesy Ronald Reagan Library.

FIGURE 20. Secretary of Defense Perry meets with his team on the way to Japan in October 1995. Perry sits at center right, flanked by Assistant Secretary of Defense Joseph Nye on his right and Assistant Secretary of State Winston Lord on his left. Directly across the conference table is NSC Senior Director Stanley Roth, flanked on his left by Deputy Assistant Secretary of Defense Kurt Campbell. Perry's Pentagon helped to reverse the Clinton administration's initial confrontation with Japan over economic issues and to revitalize the U.S.-Japan alliance after several years of drift. Clinton then complemented this balancing strategy against a rising China with greater engagement of Beijing and negotiations for China's entry into the World Trade Organization. *Source*: Courtesy of Joseph Nye.

FIGURE 21. President George W. Bush prepares for meetings with China's Hu Jintao in Beijing in November 2005. The president is speaking with the author, surrounded by (left to right) National Security Advisor Stephen Hadley, Assistant Secretary of State for East Asia and Pacific Affairs Christopher Hill, and U.S. ambassador to China Sandy Randt. *Source*: Author's photo.

FIGURE 22. President Barack Obama speaking to the Australian parliament in the House of Representatives in Canberra, November 17, 2011. Obama announced that even as U.S. defense spending decreased and it drew back from wars in the Middle East, Asia would remain a top defense and economic priority under his "rebalance" toward the region. *Source*: Reuters/ Jason Reed.

10. "THE PRESIDENT CANNOT MAKE ANY WEAK MOVES"
JIMMY CARTER AND THE RETURN OF THE CHINA CARD, 1977–1980

*align fp w/
american morality*

Jimmy Carter came into office in January 1977 rejecting virtually everything Nixon had represented. Whereas Nixon and Kissinger had sought to realign American ends and means, Carter intended to realign American foreign policy with American morality.[1] Carter wanted to cut the costs of containment, emphasize human rights in relations with allies, reach out to foes, and improve America's moral standing in the world.[2] He approached his task with an engineer's obsession with tactics and an evangelical's penchant for sweeping moral pronouncements, but as historian George Herring notes, "he lacked a sense of history and the ability to see how events and issues were connected."[3] He came to office without a holistic view of Asia and did not visit the region until June 1979—his third year in office.

This incoherence was exacerbated by ongoing crises in the national economy, the American military establishment, and congressional relations. The Vietnam War had triggered runaway inflation, compounded by the oil shocks of 1973 and 1979. On the military side, U.S. defense spending shrank from 8.1 percent of GDP in 1970 to 4.9 percent in 1977—the lowest figure since before the Second World War—with over 200,000 deployable troops cut from the U.S. Army and Marine Corps. Over the same period, the Soviets increased defense spending dramatically, reaching parity in surface combatants with the U.S. Navy (except for carriers) and growing the Red Army by over 200,000 troops, which made it more than twice the size of the U.S. Army.[4] Meanwhile, Congress was asserting its prerogatives in foreign policy in ways not seen in a century: tying Ford's hands on Vietnam; requiring a review of all forward military presence (the "Nunn" amendment);[5] and imposing legislation that would deny assistance to any country that engaged "in a consistent pattern of gross violations" of human rights.[6] As a candidate, Carter had benefited from this combination of painful economic stagflation, popular antimilitarism, and congressional restraints on the executive branch. As president, he was almost undone by it.

Carter entered office with the weakest foreign policy resumé of any president since Truman—and arguably with even less, since Truman at least inherited FDR's experienced foreign policy team when he suddenly became chief executive in 1945.[7] In the absence of an overarching national security framework other than reducing military spending and restoring moralism to American foreign policy abroad, the Carter administration broke into warring camps of pragmatic idealists and hard-power realists. In part, this reflected Carter's own desire for debate in the policy-making process, but it also was symptomatic of the schizophrenia in Carter's own worldview.[8]

The idealists were led by Cyrus Vance, secretary of the army under Kennedy and deputy secretary of defense under Johnson. A graduate of Yale Law School, Vance was a public servant and respected attorney in the tradition of Stimson, Acheson, and Elihu Root. In 1976, he was everyone's first or second choice for secretary of state, and he assumed the position in January 1977.[9] Vance was preoccupied with completing the languishing second round of Strategic Arms Limitation Talks (SALT II) with Moscow in order to prevent an arms race, create a permissive environment for reductions in American defense spending, and allow a focus on North-South relations and not just East-West problems of the Cold War.[10] For him, Asia was a secondary or even tertiary concern, compared with the central problem of sustaining détente and easing U.S.-Soviet competition. In a 1978 synopsis of foreign policy issues before the Senate Foreign Relations Committee, for example, Vance mentioned not a word about Asia.[11] Balance of power was even less important as a consideration or, as Vance put it, "practical self-interest" dictated that the United States now prioritize action on such transnational issues as "human rights, economic development, energy, population growth, environmental damage, food, nuclear proliferation, and arms transfers."[12] These transnational themes were taken up with enthusiasm in the State Department by former civil rights activists wholly unschooled in international affairs— including UN Ambassador Andrew Young and Assistant Secretary of State for Humanitarian Affairs Patricia Derian—often to the dismay of the secretary of state himself.[13] Although ideologically Carter felt closest to Vance among all cabinet members, the president's frustration with the State Department mounted over time, and the initiative shifted to the realists, particularly on Asia policy.[14]

The realists were led by Zbigniew Brzezinski, the Polish-born son of aristocrats and diplomats, who had been schooled in Canada and at Harvard and catapulted to influence in Democratic foreign policy circles while teaching at Columbia University. Having witnessed the ravages of Nazism and Stalinism in his native Poland, Brzezinski was a proponent of the primacy of military power and "deplored the moralism of Woodrow Wilson."[15] For Brzezinski, the nature and existence of Soviet power was the major obstacle to the production of a stable world. In his view, détente had not moderated Soviet behavior—it had only provided cover for Moscow to intervene across Southwest Asia and Africa.[16] In the tradition of academic national security advisors like McGeorge Bundy, Walt and Eugene Rostow, and Kissinger, Brzezinski took it on himself to craft a grand strategy for the president, producing what would eventually become the "Carter Doctrine"—a harder-line stance against Soviet expansion than the president had originally intended or Vance found acceptable.[17] Not surprisingly, the left wing of the Democratic Party despised Brzezinski: Clark Clifford told President-elect Carter that instead of national security advisor, Carter would be better off making the Columbia professor "the first American Ambassador to the Bermuda Triangle."[18]

Brzezinski was by heritage and temperament a continentalist like Kissinger—focused on the Eurasian powers rather than the maritime domain and the Pacific. Though normalization with China would become his signature accomplishment as national security advisor, his prior academic writings, like Kissinger's, were infused with caution about overreliance on Beijing. In 1961, he had warned that any Sino-Soviet split would be dangerous, since mutual antagonism in the communist camp would only intensify revolutionary competition in the Third World (he was right about that).[19] He later supported Nixon's opening to China but was highly critical of the distortion in U.S. Asia policy it caused, noting in

1972 in the journal *Foreign Policy* that a trilateral U.S.-China-USSR structure would never be as stable as one based on the democratic camps of
North America, Europe, and Japan.[20] In this same period, he developed
a quiet fascination with Japan and used a Ford Foundation grant to live
in the country for six months in 1971, after which he convinced David
Rockefeller to launch the Trilateral Commission to bring together leading American, European, and Japanese business and intellectual leaders.
The commission served as a recruiting ground for future members of the
Carter cabinet and as a crash course on foreign policy for Carter himself.
Though Brzezinski would surpass even Nixon and Kissinger's zeal for using the China card against the Soviets, he was far more careful than his
predecessors had been to ensure that relations with Japan and Europe
were not harmed in the process.

Brzezinski's realist instincts were backed by Secretary of Defense
Harold Brown, who had served under McNamara at the Defense Department as director of defense research and later as secretary of the air force
and then president of the California Institute of Technology. Brown had
earned his PhD in physics at the age of twenty-one from Columbia and
brought scientific precision to problems of politics and public policy in
Asia, as the author discovered while working as his research assistant in
the early 1990s at Johns Hopkins University. Brown struggled constantly
with a shrinking defense budget and sought to use both alignment with
China and greater defense spending by Japan to compensate for declin-
ing U.S. resources in the Pacific, but his primary concern was the defense
of Western Europe, which he prioritized throughout his tenure.[21] Walter
Mondale was also an important actor in foreign policy decision-making
but was mostly attuned to domestic politics. A Hubert Humphrey protégé, he was inclined at first to the idealistic but cast a vote over time to
help Brzezinski. He had a keen interest in Japan and was sent there for
consultations within the first ten days after the inauguration. Later, he
would become ambassador to Japan.[22]

At the beginning of the Carter administration, the betting was that
Vance would bring foreign policy prerogatives back to the State Department, but Brzezinski proved the more effective bureaucratic player. He
proposed letting Vance run day-to-day foreign policy while he chaired
a Special Coordination Committee (SCC) that handled "cross-cutting issues requiring coordination in the development of options and the implementation of Presidential decisions"—in short, all the administration's
major initiatives.[23] Brzezinski also benefited as Soviet expansionism in

the Third World undercut Vance's case for making SALT and détente the centerpiece of U.S. foreign policy. On Asia, Brzezinski had a powerful weapon on the NSC staff in Michael Oksenberg, a leading Sinologist from the University of Michigan, who was unafraid to throw his weight around in interagency interactions and even with Brzezinski, whom he once chastised in an internal memo for appearing to the Chinese as "vain, perhaps overly confident, and somewhat prone to verbosity."[24] As Brzezinski took control of China policy from Vance, it was Oksenberg who drove for faster and larger results in the relationship with Beijing. "Oksenberg was a great advocate of a special relationship with China," Brzezinski recalled later, "but I took the larger picture into mind."[25]

Vance's assistant secretary of state for East Asia and the Pacific, Richard Holbrooke, was no wilting flower himself. He had joined the Foreign Service two weeks after graduating from Brown University in 1962, and four years later became the youngest member of a special cell on Vietnam policy reporting directly to President Johnson in the White House. Troubled by the Vietnam War, Holbrooke resigned from the State Department in 1972 to edit *Foreign Policy* magazine. He soon became the darling of Democratic internationalists, and later he would serve as the foreign policy coordinator for Carter's presidential campaign. At State, Holbrooke established the East Asia Informal Group with his counterparts from other agencies—a tradition that continues to this day—but on China policy he was frequently and almost gratuitously cut out by the better informed and better connected Oksenberg.[26] The Asia team was rounded out by Deputy Assistant Secretary of Defense Morton Abramowitz, a cerebral Foreign Service officer who made the top Asia position at the Pentagon one of the most powerful in Washington because of his access to Brown and his expertise on Asia, cultivated in the Bureau of Intelligence and Research and as political advisor to the Pacific Command.

Though none of Carter's principals were personally or intellectually invested in Asia, these officials at the assistant secretary level stood out for their expertise on the region. Some, like Abramowitz, had been in government a few years earlier as Indochina fell to communism, fielding desperate phone calls from U.S. ambassadors pleading for more helicopters or more policy support from Washington. All the senior Asia officials worried about the credibility of American staying power, particularly in the wake of Carter's campaign pledge to withdraw troops from Korea and the cavalier attack on alliances by the new human rights lobby within the administration.[27] Despite tactical differences and turf struggles, they sent joint memos up the chain that bordered on insubordination—pleading for a more coherent strategy and firmer demonstrations of American commitment to the region. In the end, they finally scored some important successes in Asia. The two key elements, they agreed from the beginning, would be taking greater advantage of China's opening and shoring up U.S. alliances with Japan and the Republic of Korea.

THE CHINA CARD REDUX

Most foreign policy experts in the Ford years had wanted to get normalization with China back on track after the 1976 election, and Carter himself had supported Nixon's Shanghai Communiqué during the presidential campaign.[28] At the outset of the new administration, Brown, Brzezinski, Oksenberg, and others urged the president to keep up the momentum toward normalization, and Kissinger introduced Vance to his Chinese counterparts to facilitate a resumption of negotiations.[29] However, the new president's mind was elsewhere. Preoccupied with SALT II negotiations with Moscow and the Panama Canal Treaties, Carter gave no major guidance on China during the first part of 1977.[30]

Vance and Brzezinski each continued to press the president to authorize negotiations with the PRC, but with different objectives in mind. For Vance, the focus was on maintaining a stable trilateral equilibrium with the Soviet Union—not using China to ratchet up pressure on Moscow.[31] As he put it to Carter in April 1977, "Right now the United States has a closer relationship with each Communist superpower than either has with the other. We must continue to maintain that fragile equilibrium recognizing always how dangerous it is, but recognizing also that some other relationship between the three nations could be more dangerous."[32]

Brzezinski, in contrast, wanted to pursue normalization with China for exactly the purpose Vance opposed—to put greater pressure on Moscow.[33] From Brzezinski's perspective, Vance's evenhanded approach was too "mechanical" and would "result in rewarding intransigence by one party and ignoring restraint or accommodation by the other."[34] Brown, who took his case directly to Carter in the Oval Office in late March 1977, argued that closer strategic cooperation with China would force the Soviets to take the "China factor" into account vis-à-vis the United States—though Brown saw Vance's point and was willing "to annoy the Soviets, but not *too* much" [emphasis added].[35] Brown's view was that the administration should do what was in America's interest with the PRC "and not let concerns about Soviet reactions be a major constraint."[36]

Carter was initially inclined toward Vance's evenhanded approach, cautioning in May 1978 that with respect to China the administration "should not ass-kiss them the way Nixon and Kissinger did, and also be careful not to antagonize domestic constituencies," including both the conservative Taiwan lobby and the liberal human rights lobby.[37] The president assured Soviet leaders in his first summit, in June 1979, that he would not use China against Soviet interests and would keep Moscow abreast of U.S.-China developments.[38] In June, Holbrooke, Oksenberg, and Abramowitz prepared Policy Review Memorandum (PRM) 24 on China in a way that bridged—for the time being—the competing visions of Vance and Brzezinski. The U.S. goals would be: "(1) to prevent a deterioration in the bilateral relationship [with China] that would harm [U.S.] strategic interests; (2) to keep the Sino-US relationship qualitatively better than Sino-Soviet relations; and (3) to engage the PRC in wider global relations."[39] It was a muddled compromise but preserved some basis for policy toward Beijing. Meanwhile, Vance was given authorization to resume negotiations on normalization with Beijing in an evenhanded manner, meaning—as he saw it—"that policy should carefully move in tandem, granting trade privileges to both [the USSR and China], especially the most-favored-nation privilege, but not engage in a military relationship with either."[40]

Vance's first meeting with the Chinese leadership in Beijing, in August 1977, did not go well. Not only did the Chinese side detect his caution vis-à-vis the Soviets, they were disappointed when he walked away from promises made by Nixon and Ford to work on "something like the Japanese solution"—which meant the United States would cut official ties with Taiwan upon normalization with the PRC.[41] After the trip, Brzezinski immediately worked to change the president's strategy and to take charge of the negotiations himself.[42] Oksenberg, who had accompanied Vance, prepared a memorandum within the NSC titled "China Policy in the Doldrums: Analysis and Measures for Minimizing Risks of Erosion in the Relationship," which warned that the United States must make a more deliberate shift toward Beijing in order to avoid a new PRC-USSR rapprochement.[43] This would be a recurring alarm from Oksenberg, despite the lack of evidence that Beijing sought in any way to actually realign with the Soviets. For his part, Brzezinski was ready to accept China's "three principles" of normalization—cutting diplomatic ties with

Taipei, withdrawing U.S. troops from Taiwan, and ending the U.S.-ROC security pact—as long as he could obtain some form of assurance that Beijing would not use force to reunify with the island.[44] Vance was strongly opposed to letting Brzezinski take over the negotiations, but Carter was swayed by Vice President Mondale and sent Brzezinski to Beijing in May 1978.[45]

As Brzezinski's plane passed over Chinese airspace on May 20, Oksenberg replayed Lord's 1971 rush to the cockpit and declared excitedly to the rest of the delegation, "We're in China! We're in China!"[46] The Chinese officials gave Brzezinski a warm welcome, recognizing his anti-Soviet credentials and his proximity to the president. In meetings with Communist Party chairman Hua Guofeng and Vice Premier Deng Xiaoping (returned from political punishment the year before), Brzezinski repeated Nixon's promise that the United States *would* cut ties with Taiwan as part of normalization and announced that Carter was ready to complete talks within the year—assurances Vance had not been authorized to offer.[47] In exchange, the Chinese leaders made oblique suggestions that they would not absorb Taiwan by force, a sufficient basis for future negotiations though still not a formal renunciation of use of force.[48] For Brzezinski and Oksenberg, the trip was a major step forward, but Carter complained that the national security advisor had been "overwhelmed with the Chinese," and reminded him that relations with the Soviet Union were much more important than those with China "as far as the safety of our country is concerned—the prevention of war—at least for the rest of this century."[49] Nevertheless, the president and Vance both wanted normalization with China, and Carter authorized Leonard Woodcock, the head of the U.S. liaison office in Beijing, to proceed with negotiations along the terms set by Brzezinski with a target date of mid-December.

Whereas Vance was content to proceed carefully toward normalization, it was the White House that now controlled the negotiations with Beijing. Oksenberg was clamoring for faster results in the "special relationship," while Brzezinski saw normalized relations with China as part of a larger counterpunch against growing Soviet adventurism in the Third World.[50] In March, Brzezinski sent Carter a memo warning of a "sense of drift which afflicts the Administration's foreign policy in general, and Asian policy in particular." It was important to launch a more ambitious Asia strategy, he argued, since the United States needed to counter Soviet moves not on terrain favorable to Moscow but rather in ways that would remind the Soviets of "their vulnerabilities in the East"—particularly vis-à-vis China.[51] In a subsequent memo to the president in October, Brzezinski reiterated that the coalescing of Asian countries around shared anti-Soviet sentiment afforded the opportunity for "matching our cooperative relationship with Western Europe by a newly cooperative relationship with the Far Eastern states (notably Japan and China), and by growing ties with the Persian Gulf region."[52] Echoing this theme, the Pentagon argued in its 1978 annual report to Congress on Chinese military power that the Peoples Liberation Army (PLA) no longer represented a direct threat to the United States but rather "a strategic counterweight to the Soviet Union."[53]

Battered by Soviet moves across the global chessboard and eager to avoid a new U.S. military buildup, Carter increasingly embraced Brzezinski's logic on the need for a decisive move with China. After great secrecy—Carter kept Vance in the dark until forty-eight hours before the announcement and then refused the secretary's last-minute request for a delay to finish SALT talks with the Soviets—the White House and the People's Republic of China simultaneously issued a joint communiqué from Washington and Beijing on December 15, 1978, announcing that they would normalize diplomatic relations by January.[54]

The announcement came as a shock to Moscow, particularly given Carter's earlier assurances that he would keep the Soviets abreast of U.S.-China issues. But it also demonstrated a level of strategic initiative that had been entirely lacking in the Carter administration up to that point. Moreover, within one week after the announcement of Sino-American normalization, Deng Xiaoping made his historical call to launch the "reform and opening" project that would transform China's economy and society. The two events were related: stabilization of U.S.-China ties proved to be an indispensable ingredient in Deng's victory over the radical Left in China and in his subsequent economic reforms, which eventually brought half a billion Chinese out of poverty. Despite mounting tensions in U.S.-China relations in later years, the Deng formula established in the winter of 1978 remains the pillar (if shaken) of China's engagement with the world to this day. This was no small legacy for Carter and Brzezinski.

Yet Carter's rush to normalization was also plagued with unintended consequences. Japan was not a problem, as it had been in 1971–1972, since Tokyo had already normalized and softly aligned with China against the Soviets, signing a Peace and Friendship Treaty with the PRC in 1978 that contained an "anti-hegemony" clause clearly aimed at Moscow. Indeed,

Beijing was now urging the Americans to follow the "Japanese model." Taiwan, on the other hand, proved an even larger challenge than it had been for Nixon. Oksenberg argued that Taiwan was too minor an issue to obstruct normalization, and the CIA reinforced this view by predicting that Nationalist military capabilities and international political and economic consequences would deter the PRC from attacking the island even after termination of the U.S.-ROC defense treaty.[55] However, when the Carter administration consulted former president Nixon on normalization with Beijing, Nixon warned against complacency about Taiwan, telling Oksenberg that to "terminate a defense treaty could sow seeds of doubt about us, particularly in Asia," adding that, "The President cannot make any weak moves in the foreseeable future. For whether this move is weak or not, the termination of our relations with Taiwan will be seen as such."[56]

Nixon's warning notwithstanding, the administration thought it could compensate for the severance of diplomatic relations with Taipei by offering legislation to Congress that would establish a new American Institute in Taipei to regulate cultural and economic ties with Taiwan. Termination of the U.S.-ROC defense treaty would be offset by resumption of a modest package of arms, which the State Department argued might "reassure Congress and Taiwan that we continue to have an interest in Taiwan's legitimate defense requirements" and simultaneously be small enough to "elicit no more than a *pro forma* objection from Beijing."[57]

Far from being reassured, however, Congress was outraged that the administration had not consulted with members and had failed to secure credible guarantees that Beijing would renounce the use of force against Taiwan.[58] Barry Goldwater and twenty-four congressional colleagues filed suit in federal court to block termination of the U.S.-ROC Security Treaty, eventually losing in the Supreme Court 7 to 2. Meanwhile, Congress voted by 339 to 50 in the House and 85 to 4 in the Senate to add language to the Taiwan Relations Act declaring "any effort to determine the future of Taiwan by other than peaceful means, including by boycotts or embargoes, a threat to the peace and security of the Western Pacific area and of grave concern to the United States," and ensuring that "the United States will make available to Taiwan such defense articles and defense services in such quantity as may be necessary to enable Taiwan to maintain a sufficient self-defense capability."[59] Despite U.S. private assurances to Deng that military sales would be limited, Carter had no choice but to sign the law on April 10.

Thus, just as Carter deserves credit for locking in place the framework for China's modern relationship with the United States, his administration must take some responsibility for introducing the divisiveness in the formulation of China policy that has complicated overall U.S. relations with Asia ever since. Termination of the U.S.-ROC Security Treaty may have been unavoidable as part of the larger strategic play with Beijing, but considerable damage was done to U.S.-China and U.S.-ROC ties by not establishing a clearer understanding that U.S. support for Taiwan's security would continue to be linked to PRC military threats to the island.

Nevertheless, the administration's trajectory with Beijing was set. As the NSC prepared for Deng's visit to the United States from January 28 to February 5, Brzezinski explained to Carter that the visit afforded an opportunity to move Sino-U.S. relations "from consultation to cooperation and coordination" on regional and global issues and to reassure Beijing of the U.S. objective "to disentangle ourselves from the Chinese civil war and to have the Chinese solve the Taiwan issue by themselves."[60] During his tour of the United States, Deng impressed the American public by donning a ten-gallon hat in Texas. He also alarmed Carter by responding to the president's warning not to invade Vietnam and risk war with Moscow by casually stating that he was ready to take hundreds of millions of Chinese casualties fighting the Soviets if necessary.[61] The Taiwan issues were contentious but did not derail the national excitement about the first-ever visit of a Chinese communist leader. On the whole, it was a historic visit.

Less than two weeks after Deng's departure, Oksenberg was arguing for more, warning in a heated memo to Brzezinski that "the Soviets are feeling their oats and are projecting a mood of almost disdain for the U.S."[62] What was needed, he argued, was "lengthy analysis of *all* the moves available to us—and I do not mean words or trips—for shaping an effective response to the challenge. The moves could be partially military, partially economic, partially adjustments to our human rights or military sales policies. We must also be willing to address the issue in a forthright manner of linkage, and recognize that what we do in one place will affect what happens in another" [emphasis in original].[63] "Time is running out on us," he warned, and he reminded Brzezinski that it was the national security advisor's responsibility for presenting the president with a "coherent strategy" for the next steps.[64]

There were several concrete steps that might have followed normalization. One was extension of most favored nation (MFN) status and

Export-Import (EXIM) credits to China. The Jackson-Vanick amendment to the 1974 Trade Act withheld normal trade relations or credits for
any nonmarket economy that denied its citizens the right to emigrate.
China was certainly one such country, but Carter waved the conditions
on China while imposing them on the Soviet Union, despite Vance's push
to extend trading rights to both communist countries simultaneously.[65]
The other option was to extend military support to Beijing. The NSC and
Department of Defense (DOD) staff had begun exploring that option two
years earlier, and in July 1979 Brzezinski had proposed to Carter consideration of "a limited security arrangement with the Chinese" and suggested
sending Brown to Beijing to negotiate specifics.[66] Vance, however, was
adamantly opposed to militarizing the relationship or sending the secretary of defense. Carter chose instead to send Vice President Mondale
that July, who hinted in Beijing that Brown might visit in the future to
discuss military arrangements.[67] These were significant steps, but Oksenberg urged more, warning Brzezinski the next month of a "chilling" in
Sino-U.S. relations since "the US had so far failed to entirely cut off Taiwan, failed to address claims/assets issues, failed to extend MFN after
signing the Trade Agreement, and had yet to sell dual-purpose [military-
related] technology."[68]

Vance's objections to a military relationship with China were finally
undercut by the Soviet invasion of Afghanistan in December 1979. The
secretary of state was convinced that the U.S. tilt toward China was one
factor behind the Soviet invasion, but he was alone in that conviction, and
Carter concluded that it was now necessary to threaten Moscow with a
new U.S.-China military relationship. Brown was authorized to visit his
counterparts in China the next January.[69] Though supportive of using
a U.S.-China military relationship to put the Soviets on their back
foot, Brown nevertheless approached his mission "gingerly."[70] He was
certain that strategic discussions made sense, but he wanted to approach
the transfer of military technology with greater care, given the potential
threat to regional allies. His Chinese hosts were disappointed and kept
him up past midnight with demands for jet fighter engines and more advanced offensive capabilities, but Brown held the offer to strategic intelligence, some technology transfer, and provision of defensive weapons
such as antitank missiles and antiaircraft systems that could not be used
against maritime allies of the United States.[71] The Chinese side eventually accepted. Separately, the CIA also arranged for China to provide
small arms and ammunition to the mujahideen in Afghanistan for their

fight against the invading Soviet forces.[72] There would be for the first time a modest but unmistakable defense relationship between Washington and Beijing aimed at countering Soviet ambitions within the Eurasian continent.

Meanwhile, the administration's preoccupation with using China to counter Soviet adventurism extended to the turbulent events in Indochina. From the beginning of the administration, Vance and Holbrooke had wanted to normalize relations with Vietnam as part of the healing process after the war and to ensure that the United States could compete with both Moscow and Beijing for influence in the region.[73] Brzezinski, in contrast, worried that U.S. normalization with Hanoi in the wake of the 1978 Soviet-Vietnamese security treaty would obstruct U.S. relations with Beijing. As he told the president in July 1978, "You need to choose: Vietnam or China, and China is incomparably more important to us."[74] The president made his choice and put off normalization with Vietnam. When Vietnam subsequently invaded Cambodia on Christmas Day 1978, the administration again leaned toward China, supporting the ousted pro-Chinese Khmer Rouge government as the representative of Cambodia at the United Nations, despite that regime's genocide against its own people.[75] Then, when China invaded Vietnam a month after Deng's visit to Washington—in large part to demonstrate Moscow's inability to protect its new ally in Hanoi—the president and the NSC focused first on avoiding direct U.S. involvement and second on ensuring that the Soviets did not escalate against China.[76] In each of these cases, U.S. human rights concerns and longer-term U.S. influence within Southeast Asia were subordinated to the goal of maintaining a favorable Chinese balance of power vis-à-vis the Soviets.

The China card was now becoming the answer to almost every strategic challenge the administration faced in the region, including—as we will see—the deficiencies in American military assets. But was the long-term bet on China correct? Oksenberg obviously had little doubt. Brzezinski recalls thinking of the relationship only as a "security relationship of convenience" and for his part "never had expectations" of Sino-U.S. economic convergence and interdependence. As he put it retrospectively, "China seemed backwards and poor . . . they could not accomplish what they wanted against a determined foe. The whole point of the special relationship was to raise the Soviets' level of anxiety."[77] Brown, too, recalled that there was no hint of the power China would become, only concerns about China's weakness relative to the Soviet Union.[78]

Others, like Carter's man in Beijing, Ambassador Leonard Woodcock, questioned whether there might be a longer-term divergence with Beijing. As he explained in a cable to Washington in February 1980, there were still important contradictions in U.S. and Chinese approaches to the rest of Asia. These contradictions, he concluded, "make the PRC uncomfortable in seeming to embrace too warmly a country such as the United States, which is still viewed by much of the Third World as an imperialistic superpower and whose relations with some of Beijing's closest traditional friends (e.g. North Korea and Pakistan) leave much to be desired. Even as Beijing's relationship with the U.S. has become closer and warmer it has still not fully abandoned the ideological baggage of its three world doctrine in which China's natural allies are seen as the Third World."[79]

In short, normalization with China corrected a near-term strategic imbalance vis-à-vis the Soviet Union but did not necessarily constitute a sustainable basis for American preeminence in the Pacific for the longer term. Ultimately, that depended more on the state of American forward military capabilities and the hub and spokes of alliance relationships established with the San Francisco System. On that front, Carter proved to be his own worst enemy.

"Everybody Wanted to Get Out of Asia": Saving Alliances and Forward Presence

Carter came into office in 1977 with little thought to deterrence, war fighting, or alliance management in Asia. Nor is there evidence that either Vance or Holbrooke had a plan for alliances in the region until political issues were thrust on them. Brzezinski had wanted to upgrade the status of Japan as part of trilateralism with Europe and North America but was not focused on the alliance in the immediate context of deterrence in Asia. Oksenberg's preoccupation was clearly the "special relationship" with China rather than alliances. And while Brown took up principal responsibility for modernizing the U.S.-Japan alliance in the absence of other champions in the cabinet, his highest priority was marshaling what resources he could to shore up the army and air force in Europe, which was still considered the central front in the Cold War.[80] At the beginning of the administration, Carter ordered consideration of a range of global war-fighting strategies under PRM 10; tellingly, not *one* of those strategies focused on Asia. To the extent that Asia entered into the planners' calculations at all, it was in the context of hoping China would pin down Soviet forces and free the United States from having to fight a two-front war while defending Western Europe.[81]

Meanwhile, U.S. alliances in the region came under assault from Carter political appointees who had been happy to see the Thieu government in Saigon go and now viewed the allied governments of Park Chung-hee in Seoul, Ferdinand Marcos in Manila, and Chiang Ching-kuo in Taipei in a similar negative light. Carter had specifically proposed to withdraw U.S. troops from the Korean Peninsula in 1975 and then reiterated his pledge on the campaign trail in 1976.[82] Convinced that Congress and the American people would no longer tolerate human rights abuses in Korea or the risk of ground wars in continental Asia—and without fully consulting his advisors or allies in the region—Carter announced on January 26, 1977, that he would go ahead with plans to withdraw all U.S. ground forces from Korea.[83] It was a bombshell not only in Seoul but across Northeast Asia.

In some respects, Carter's decision harkened to the offshore balancing strategy of Kennan, but it was fundamentally a political decision in response to the American experience in Vietnam and the president's own dislike of the South Korean leader. Brzezinski maintained years later that "there was absolutely no strategic rationale regarding forward presence or offshore balancing" behind the announcement, adding that "it was Carter's idea and he stuck to it."[84] After the announcement, the president instructed that all aid to South Korea and the Philippines henceforth be conditioned on human rights reforms.[85] He then dispatched Brown to Japan and Korea in July 1977 to explain that, despite these new policies, Asia would be safer because of improving relations with China and (at that point) the Soviet Union and because American security commitments to allies were undiminished.[86] Predictably, Brown failed to convince the allies of the president's logic.[87] Japan's resistance to the withdrawal plan was particularly unnerving and eventually turned almost everyone in the administration against withdrawal—except for the president himself.[88]

With bureaucratic rivalry melting in the face of potential policy calamity, Holbrooke's East Asia Informal Group went into high gear working on a plan to save U.S. alliances without embarrassing the president.[89] The Pentagon had assumed that either Holbrooke or Abramowitz had proposed Korean troop withdrawal to Carter. In fact, Abramowitz had authored an internal study in 1968 for Undersecretary of State Nicholas Katzenbach that had recommended withdrawal from Korea, but after seeing the crisis in U.S. credibility in the wake of the Vietnam War, Abramowitz became strongly opposed to Carter's Korea plan.[90] Holbrooke may well have authored the idea of withdrawal for Carter during the campaign, but he, too, was now committed to reversing the policy. "Everybody wanted to get out of Asia," Abramowitz recalls, "and Brzezinski called us [Abramowitz, Armacost, and Holbrooke] the 'Three Cassandras' for warning of the consequences of withdrawal." That did not stop the three Asia hands from pushing back against the Korea withdrawal plan even at considerable risk to their own professional careers.[91]

On April 14, 1977, the "Three Cassandras" authored a proposal under PRM 13 that would advance only a "symbolic" withdrawal from Korea, to be followed by a reexamination of the situation on the peninsula.[92] Unconvinced even by this consensus view among his Asia experts, Carter again overruled his advisors, ordering the withdrawal of one brigade (6,000 troops) by 1978, a second brigade and all noncombat support elements by 1979, and complete withdrawal of all remaining headquarters units and nuclear weapons by 1982.[93] Internal resistance against withdrawal only hardened. In June 1977, Brzezinski, who earlier had remained neutral on the issue, began to send memoranda to the president that highlighted the growing hostility of Congress toward withdrawal.[94] One major problem was that congressional embarrassment over "Koreagate" (the bribery of several congressmen by the Korean CIA) made it impossible to vote for the military assistance package needed for the ROK forces to fill the gaps left by the United States.[95] The CIA also began to build an analytical case against withdrawal, chronicling the strong opposition of other allies, particularly Japan.[96] Abramowitz was warning the White House that the JCS would turn against Carter if the withdrawal went ahead.[97] Then, in July, Brown's testimony on the withdrawal plan before Congress elicited unexpected opposition, prompting Brzezinski to finally suggest that the president might be better off stretching out the schedule further or making it conditional on steps by North Korea.[98] Yet still the president remained adamant. Alarmed at the continuing collateral damage to other alliances in the region, Holbrooke, Abramowitz, Armacost, and Oksenberg sent a joint memo to Vance, Brown, and Brzezinski in April 1978 warning that "U.S. prestige in Asia is low" and would become "irretrievable" if the U.S. troop issue was not resolved soon.[99]

The turning point finally came in January 1979, when the CIA increased its estimates of the size of the North Korean Army, corroborating an earlier U.S. Army estimate and prompting the House Armed Services Committee to call on Carter to delay any withdrawal until the committee "can evaluate the full significance and long range implications of this new information for America's national security posture in the Far East."[100] Suspicious that the bureaucracy was trying to box him in, Carter still clung to his earlier campaign pledge, reiterating it to President Park during a visit to Seoul on July 1.[101] However, when the Korea withdrawal plan emerged as an obstacle to moving forward on SALT II in Congress that same summer, the president finally relented, ordering a halt (except for one symbolic Hawk missile battery) and a two-year review of whether the policy should be implemented based on "restoration of the North-South military balance and/or evidence of tangible progress toward a reduction of tensions on the Korean peninsula."[102] Similar efforts to cut off aid to the antidemocratic regime of Ferdinand Marcos in the Philippines were also abandoned as the Pentagon sought to renew the leases for the U.S. Air Force and Navy bases at Clark and Subic Bay.[103] The entire episode, recalls Abramowitz, had been a "disaster from the beginning."[104]

Underlying Carter's about-face on the U.S. alliances with Korea and the Philippines was the same factor that shifted China policy so profoundly in the middle of the administration—the growing threat from the Soviet Union and the relative decline in American conventional military capabilities. At first, the administration's concern had been vulnerabilities in Europe, as the global military strategy review PRM 10 had indicated, but by 1978 it was evident that the Soviets were preparing capabilities to open a second front against the United States in the Far East in the event of general war. Just as the Soviets were expanding naval exercises around Japan and deploying Backfire bombers in the Far East for the purpose of interdicting U.S. and allied sea lanes in the Pacific, the administration was cutting the navy and shifting resources to Europe. Gerald Ford's secretaries of defense, Jim Schlesinger (1973–1975) and Don Rumsfeld (1975–1977), had set the long-term goal for U.S. naval forces at 575 and 600 ships, respectively; under Carter, the goal dropped to 425–500 ships.[105] In January 1978, JCS Chair General George Brown testified that "at current levels of force structure, war in Europe would require the great preponderance of general purpose forces. . . . If this were to occur, control of the seas between the continental United States and

Hawaii could be maintained, as could the sealanes between Alaska and the Lower 48. However, broad sea control beyond those lanes would be a difficult challenge."[106] The United States now had "a one ocean Navy," the chief of Naval Operations told Congress, and his orders were to prioritize the Atlantic and NATO.[107]

With U.S. general-purpose forces slated to swing to Europe in a crisis, the JCS concluded in October 1978 that Japan would have to help deter the Soviets in Asia—but the Joint Chiefs also warned that the Japan Self Defense Forces were not up to the mission.[108] In fact, the U.S.-Japan alliance had been drifting since the Nixon shocks, and there was growing evidence that Tokyo might be hedging for the possibility of a post-American Pacific order. The 1975 Japan Defense Agency White Paper, for example, had concluded that the Soviets were becoming the dominant power in the Far East, and that same year Foreign Minister Miyazawa Kiichi declared that not only Indochina but now also North Korea would be exempt from Article VI (provision of U.S. bases in Japan for the security of the Far East) of the 1960 treaty.[109] In 1976, the left-leaning cabinet of Takeo Miki shifted defense planning from "required defense capabilities" to "basic defense capabilities" and put a cap on defense spending of 1 percent of GDP. At just the time that Soviet capabilities were growing above those of the United States in the Pacific, Japan appeared to be swinging dangerously toward neutralism.[110]

It fell to Brown and the Defense Department to bring Japan back into alignment.[111] Brown was skeptical, as he put it later, that "Japan could be a surrogate for U.S. presence, given views in the region and the tiny fraction of support for such a role in Japan itself—and not from the most savory bunch, either."[112] Instead, he focused on establishing bilateral Guidelines for U.S.-Japan Defense Cooperation that would deepen planning and exercises to increase deterrence against attacks on Japan itself, including, he hoped, the sea lanes closest to the home islands. When the guidelines were completed in November 1978, the role of Japan in the security of Korea and Taiwan—flagged by Nixon in 1969 with Prime Minister Sato—went unmentioned. However, the document helped to confirm that alliance cooperation with the United States would be the basis for Japanese defense-planning assumptions going forward and thus addressed some of the uncertainty about Japanese strategic intentions.[113] Brown also wanted more financial contributions from Tokyo, and he won agreement in 1978 that Japan would provide $33.3 million to cover some yen-denominated costs incurred by U.S. forces stationed in the country.

However, American taxpayers were still spending almost ten times more on defense than their Japanese counterparts were.[114] When yet another Japanese budget was passed in 1980 with defense capped at less than 1 percent of GDP (per the 1976 Japanese cabinet decision), a frustrated Brown declared that it "falls seriously short, whether measured by the security situation, by the discussions held between senior officials of our two governments over the last year, or by considerations of equitable burden-sharing."[115]

American efforts to increase Japanese defense spending met resistance for a number of reasons.[116] One problem was a reluctance to remilitarize Japan among the Carter administration's own liberal idealists. Vance and his successor, Edmund Muskie (appointed in May 1980 after Vance resigned in protest over the failed military mission to rescue U.S. hostages in Iran), had opposed even mentioning the words "burden-sharing" to Tokyo.[117] The Japanese side also resented the adversarial way Washington officials framed the issue around American economic interests and global security responsibilities instead of the common challenges in the Asia-Pacific (though, to be sure, many in Tokyo used that as an excuse to continue free-riding).[118] Simply put, Japanese officials could not discern a clear U.S. military strategy for the region.[119]

In fact, there was none. The prioritization of NATO, the Korean troop question, the NSC preoccupation with China, and the cascading Soviet challenges in other parts of the Third World had all put the administration in a defensive and reactive mode in the Pacific when it came to military planning. There was one important exception, though. On his own initiative—in the tradition of the innovative Naval War College architects of War Plan Orange—Admiral Thomas Bibb Hayward was building the case for a new military strategy in the Pacific that would use the alliance with Japan as the fulcrum to go on the offensive against Soviet expansion. As commander of the Seventh Fleet from 1976 to 1977 and then the Pacific Fleet from 1977 to 1978, Hayward had watched the Soviet military buildup in the Far East with both concern and fascination. Hayward worried that the "swing strategy" would have removed the only credible U.S. threat to the Russian Far East and allowed Soviet forces to steal the march on NATO by shifting forces from east to west before U.S. reinforcements arrived in Europe. In September 1977, as CINCPACFLT (commander in chief of the Pacific Fleet), he ordered overhead satellite imagery that showed the Soviets had built a second trans-Siberian railroad for exactly that purpose, taking advantage of Moscow's shorter internal lines to knock the United States off balance in the Pacific. When Senator Sam Nunn was shown the imagery at CINCPACFLT HQ in Malacapa in January 1978, he was shocked.[120] Convinced that the navy in the Pacific could help offset the deteriorating global balance vis-à-vis Moscow, and concerned that his forces had only planned for defense in the Pacific, Hayward commissioned a series of studies around the concept of "Sea Strike"— direct U.S. attacks on Soviet bases in the Far East in the event of general war in Europe. One major consideration for Hayward was how to ensure through employment of U.S. forces in Japan that in a general war Tokyo would not be inclined toward neutrality.[121]

A decorated fighter pilot with over 140 combat missions in Korea, and a respected strategist, Hayward nevertheless came under criticism for his offense-oriented concept elsewhere in the Pentagon and within the navy staff. As Hayward recalls, "there were plenty of people on our side who thought we were nuts."[122] Undeterred, he brought the concept back to Washington as chief of naval operations in July 1978 and steadily broadened support among navy flag rank officers and in Congress for what would emerge in the Reagan administration as The Maritime Strategy—a deliberate integration of the U.S.-Japan alliance and forward U.S. naval and air capabilities in an offensive strategy aimed at the Soviet Union itself.

That integrated strategy never took shape in the Carter years. Even after the Soviet invasion of Afghanistan propelled the president to announce what would be called the "Carter Doctrine" in the 1980 State of the Union address, the focus of deterrence was on NATO and now the Persian Gulf, with defense spending increasing by only a paltry $6 billion to $303 billion to support the new doctrine. The Pacific theater continued to be starved for resources but—as Hayward demonstrated—not for ideas.

CARTER'S LEGACY IN ASIA STRATEGY

In his comparison of presidential leadership styles in foreign policy, former Kissinger aide Peter Rodman ends his critique of Jimmy Carter's divided and often chaotic process by acknowledging that "the Carter administration had a number of achievements to its credit, amidst a turbulent period in international and American politics."[123] These achievements extended to Asia.

First and foremost, Carter transformed the regional landscape by completing the process of normalization with China, and he did so without upsetting the broader set of American relationships in the region, with the notable exception of Taiwan. In part, this was possible because Japan had already adjusted to the Nixon shocks and had moved closer to China by the time of U.S. normalization with Beijing. However, credit is also due to Brzezinski and Brown, in particular, for remaining focused on Japan and the broader relationships with U.S. allies in Asia and Europe as normalization and security ties with Beijing proceeded. The administration's mishandling of Korean troop withdrawal, and its adversarial approach to "burden-sharing," created counterproductive friction with Tokyo, but at a strategic level, the U.S.-Japan alliance was probably more stable in 1981 than it had been in 1977. Improving relations with China and Japan at the same time—always a challenge in American foreign policy—was an important accomplishment.

However, the Carter administration's China policy was driven by the exigencies of Soviet expansion and the deficit of American power to respond. That led to mistakes. American policymakers searched in vain for evidence that the China card was moderating Soviet behavior the way it had in 1971 and 1972. As the Soviets continued to "feel their oats" (in Oksenberg's words), the administration pushed with increasing desperation for some deterrent effect from U.S.-China alignment. Deng was puzzled by the inconsistencies of Carter's approach. He told party officials in a closed address in March 1979 that the United States had been weak in the face of Soviet expansion, wasting time on SALT talks when real action was needed. Deng also told the cadres that he thought the Americans were far too optimistic that the China card would cause the Soviets to take pressure off Europe, though he explained that China could nevertheless benefit from demonstrating to NATO that "China was a reliable friend against the Soviets." Perhaps most amazing, Deng revealed that even as Carter was personally urging him not to invade Vietnam, other senior U.S. officials were providing intelligence to demonstrate the weakness of Soviet division strength in the Far East in order to *encourage* a Chinese attack.[124] The Chinese could see little willpower, logic, or consistency in the American approach to the Far East. As for the longer-term strategy, as Jim Mann points out, "questions about the long-term implications of these policies—about what might happen to America and China if the anti-Soviet basis of their friendship collapsed—were swept aside."[125]

In retrospect, it is difficult to argue that Carter should *not* have normalized relations with the PRC. Even without immediate moderation
in Soviet behavior, the policy did open China to the world for the longer
term and helped redress Chinese weakness vis-à-vis Moscow to some
extent. However, the geopolitical premise of the policy was flawed, as was
Carter's dismissive approach to Congress on Taiwan. His effort to "disentangle" the United States from China's civil war left a legacy of mistrust
that has hobbled U.S. policymaking ever since.

Elsewhere in Asia, Carter made modest progress. His approach ·to
Southeast Asia veered from a focus on human rights and healing with
Vietnam to a more classical anti-Soviet containment strategy. It is possible that normalization with Vietnam would not have obstructed progress
in Sino-U.S. relations and may even have forestalled the Vietnamese
invasion of Cambodia, as Vance and Holbrooke had hoped, but that
judgment is difficult to make even in hindsight. Either way, the administration's isolation of Vietnam and support for the Khmer Rouge after
the invasion—though morally questionable—generally aligned with
Japan, ASEAN, and other partners in the region. The United States' net
relations in Southeast Asia were therefore slightly better in 1981 than they
were in 1977.

In South Asia, U.S. policy spun in circles but ended up only slightly
worse for wear. Carter's human rights priorities caused him to distance his
administration from Pakistan, only to court Prime Minister Zia al-Huk
with promises of new aid and a visit to Washington after the Soviet invasion of Afghanistan in 1979.[126] Carter took the opposite tack with India,
starting out by courting Prime Minister Morarji Desai and promising to
continue selling India uranium despite the 1978 U.S. nonproliferation
act—only to be frustrated when Desai's successor, Indira Gandhi, welcomed Brezhnev to Delhi in December 1980 in the wake of the Soviet
invasion of Afghanistan.[127] Despite this confusion in relations with the
powers in the region, the Indian Ocean and South Asia did emerge more
prominently in overall U.S. Asia strategy in the late 1970s. At CINCPAC-
FLT HQ, Admiral Hayward prompted the navy and the Pentagon to
think about the Indo-Pacific as one continuous maritime theater. The
importance of the Indian Ocean as a fulcrum between the Persian Gulf
and Pacific theaters was demonstrated by the establishment of a naval
support facility on Diego Garcia in October 1977 and deployment of pre-
position ships and equipment there in 1980.[128] The intent was to prepare
for a swing of Western Pacific–based forces to the Gulf, but the broadening

of CINCPACFLT's focus on the Indian Ocean (always in the area of responsibility but never a priority) was important.

Carter also deserves credit for trying to restore human rights and democracy as U.S. foreign priorities toward Asia. He ultimately failed because he introduced these themes as deliberate counterpoints to the pursuit of geostrategic interests, instead of formulating an integrated strategy that combined values and other instruments of power. He brought in activists from the civil rights movement and turned them loose on the foreign policy establishment, allowing them to bypass the regional bureaus in the State Department and to condition aid to key allies on specific human rights reforms.[129] In the end, the insurgent human rights activists in the administration were cut out of the process by the veteran foreign policy officials, with both sides deeply resentful of the other.[130] In 1977, a perplexed Jessica Tuchman on the NSC staff asked in an internal memo, "*What are we really after*? Is it to change totalitarian systems to democracies? To improve the social and economic welfare of the billions of impoverished people of the world? To increase domestic support for foreign policy in general? To make ourselves feel good?" [Emphasis in original][131]

The Carter administration never really answered that question. Jackson-Vanik conditions linking MFN to human rights performance were placed on the Soviet Union but not on China, the Khmer Rouge genocide was overlooked in the effort to isolate Vietnam, and allies such as the Philippines were put under enormous pressure that suddenly evaporated in the face of compelling geostrategic concerns.

For his part, Brzezinski's definition of human rights "meant not the human rights of individuals as such, though that has to be a dimension of U.S. policy, but rather the oppression of smaller countries by strong totalitarian states."[132] From this perspective, pressure put on smaller U.S. allies such as the Philippines established the administration's credibility but "had no geostrategic consequences" compared with the larger importance of preventing Soviet hegemony.[133] Like his fellow European-born strategist Henry Kissinger, he found that morality in foreign policy resided in the higher domain of preserving order and preventing totalitarian expansion, and thus forbearing Chinese human rights abuses if Soviet power could thereby be contained. But Brzezinski's was only one of the definitions of human rights at play in the administration.

Ultimately, Carter would have been better positioned had he harnessed democratic norms to the purpose of stabilizing regional order and strengthening the internal governance of friends and allies against external threats in the tradition of Jefferson or John Quincy Adams. He should have worked with the regional bureaus in the State Department and with allied leaders, and not against them. Instead, he introduced the radical anti-imperialism of modern-day goo-goos—an understandable instinct for the Democratic Party after Vietnam—but one bound to fail.[134] Yet even with his dysfunctional approach, the elevation of human rights and democracy concerns during Carter's presidency ensured that future administrations would be expected to make progress in their own ways—as Ronald Reagan did when democracy came to Korea, Taiwan, and the Philippines in the 1980s. Never again would American diplomats be instructed to tell foreign governments that their government stood by the principle of noninterference in internal affairs with respect to the treatment of citizens of a foreign land.

Despite these successes, however, none of Carter's Asia policies succeeded in reversing Soviet advances the way Nixon's use of the China card had earlier in the decade. Carter advanced relations with China and searched for ways to elevate Japan's role, but both policies fell short in terms of shaping Soviet behavior because they were premised on a strategy of compensating for American weakness. Much of that institutional, economic, and military weakness Carter inherited, but he only compounded the problems. Ultimately, Carter came to understand the utility of balance-of-power strategies, but he never understood the purpose of American power itself.

The next president came to office determined to redress that shortcoming.

11. "TO CONTAIN AND OVER TIME REVERSE"
RONALD REAGAN, 1980–1989

As Barack Obama acknowledged during the 2008 election campaign, Ronald Reagan was a transformational president. His flaws were legend, of course. He never mastered the details of policy, allowing ideological clashes and maverick initiatives that almost undid his presidency with the Iran-Contra controversy in 1986. His policies in Central America were highly divisive at home, and he had major failings in the Middle East, where intervention in Lebanon was suddenly reversed after the bombing of the U.S. Marine barracks in 1983. Yet despite these scattered foreign policy failures, Reagan personified the confidence and willpower to lead that had been suppressed within the American spirit for over a decade, and in so doing he laid the groundwork for the peaceful collapse of the Soviet Union and the triumph of the West.

The conceptual key to Reagan's success was an explicit recognition of the link among capitalism, liberty, and military strength. He viewed the Nixon, Ford, and Carter responses to Vietnam as failures because those presidents had designed strategies to sustain the status quo with diminished American means. Reagan was not interested in preserving the status quo—he believed that the Cold War could be won because of fundamental Soviet weakness. As he put it in May 1982, "the Soviet dictatorship has forged the largest armed forces in the world. It has done so by pre-empting the human needs of its people, and, in the end, this course will undermine the foundations of the Soviet system."[1] Reagan knew that after Vietnam the American people would be reluctant to "bear any burden," but he believed rightly that they would support renewed military strength, closer alliances, and an asymmetrical forward policy that would put stress on the Soviet system over time.[2] As president, he doubled U.S. defense spending from $155 billion in 1980 to $320 billion in 1988; shifted from defense- to offense-oriented military strategies in Europe and the Pacific; aligned more closely with democratic allies and anticommunist revolutionaries; accelerated democratic transitions; and championed free trade and the primacy of the market.

In April 1985, columnist Charles Krauthammer dubbed this approach "The Reagan Doctrine," but the worldview had been evident as early as Reagan's 1964 nomination speech for Barry Goldwater ("A Time of Choosing"), in which he deplored attempts to "buy our safety from the threat of 'the bomb' by selling into permanent slavery our fellow human beings . . . behind the Iron Curtain" and by telling "them to give up their hope of freedom because we are ready to make a deal with their slave masters."[3] This same theme was also central to Reagan's 1982 National Security Strategy[4] and his 1983 National Security Decision Directive (NSDD) 75, which stated that the goal of U.S. strategy is "to contain and reverse the expansion of Soviet control and military presence throughout the world, and to increase the costs of Soviet support and use of proxy, terrorist and subversive forces."[5] The doctrine was tempered by pragmatism on the whole, but, as Gaddis points out, Reagan was the first president since Johnson to read NSC 68 and the first since Truman to embrace its explicit strategy for defeating Soviet communism.[6]

Was this worldview—this "doctrine"—grand strategy? Writing at the time, Robert Tucker argued that Reagan never reconciled the fundamental mismatch between ends and means that Nixon, Ford, and Carter also struggled with, and harsher critics dismissed Reagan as an unpredictable ideologue.[7] These critiques certainly resonate to some extent, but Reagan's approach still merits the label "grand strategy" because his central concept for winning the Cold War (a) integrated all instruments of American power; (b) was consistently if broadly applied over time and across major agencies; and (c) was agile in implementation (particularly after the emergence of Mikhail Gorbachev as a change agent within the Soviet

Union), reflecting Reagan's own contextual intelligence as a political leader.

Reagan's strategic approach held up particularly well in Asia. His administration initially stumbled over Taiwan policy as the White House tried unsuccessfully to revise the terms of Carter's normalization with Beijing—a reflection of Reagan's own close ties to Taiwan and of Republican resentment over the way normalization had been implemented by Carter. After that first misstep, however, the Reagan administration set in place a sustained forward strategy in the Pacific that resulted in significantly diminished Soviet ambitions; improved ties with all the other major powers—particularly Japan, but also China and India; movement toward an integrated economic vision of an Asia-Pacific community; and democratic transitions in South Korea, the Philippines, and Taiwan.

Reagan's Asia policy also benefited from comparatively strong consensus and consistency within the administration. His national security team fought endless bureaucratic and ideological battles with respect to arms control and the Soviet Union, but they were generally united on Asia, where they shared both deep personal experience and a more uniform commitment to Reagan's worldview. The one exception to this general rule came in the early months of the administration with the appointment of Alexander Haig as secretary of state. Reagan had determined that he wanted to shift power from the White House and NSC back to State and Defense, and Haig assumed this empowered him to follow his mentor Henry Kissinger's dominant role under Nixon and Ford.[8] But whereas Haig saw himself as the "vicar" of foreign policy, other senior political appointees dismissed him as a self-aggrandizing "CINCWORLD" with none of Kissinger's conceptual or bureaucratic genius.[9] Haig also tried to advance a geostrategic perspective that was dissonant with the president, particularly on Asia. His priorities for U.S. foreign policy were Europe (he had commanded NATO) and China, which he argued should be the linchpin of American strategy in Asia—a point he reinforced by making China his first travel destination in the region, without stopping in Japan.[10] This Atlanticist and continentalist worldview led to enormous fights with the White House in the first year of the administration, but as Haig later acknowledged, his instincts were never the same as the president's on Asia.[11] Haig had played a central role in Kissinger's China policy and helped to check some of the more ideological impulses of the new White House toward Beijing, but he was incompatible with Reagan temperamentally and ideologically and resigned in July 1982.

Haig's successor was, in the assessment of the author, the most effective U.S. secretary of state on Asia and the Pacific in the history of the republic. George Shultz began his embrace of Asia as a student at Princeton, where in 1941 he chose to do his senior seminar on U.S. policy in the Pacific. When war was declared, he joined the marine corps so that he could be sure to serve in the Pacific theater. He came out of the war with no animus toward Japan and pursued a PhD in industrial economics at MIT, which led to a distinguished career in academia and government service. When Nixon made him his director of the Office of Management and Budget in 1970, he surprised Shultz by sending him to Japan and Korea. Asia policy was hardly the responsibility of the OMB director, but Nixon told Shultz that as a future leader in the Republican Party he needed to understand Asia. When Shultz was appointed secretary of the treasury in 1972, the president sent him back to Asia for a tutorial with Singaporean leader Lee Kuan Yee to further his strategic education on the region.[12] Shultz took a long-term view of Asia that was cognizant of the region's violent history and its enormous potential for the future. He was fond of comparing foreign policy with gardening, a metaphor for patient and persistent engagement that suited the gradually unfolding layers of Asian international relations.[13]

Like Reagan, Shultz integrated values, economic engagement, and military power in his view of foreign policy. The values of liberty and democracy are not only "the source of our strength, economic as well as moral," he argued in *Foreign Affairs* in the spring of 1985, they are also "more central to the world's future than many have realized."[14] For one thing, as he told Congress that same year, shared values with "Japan, and other democratic friends have an enduring quality precisely because they rest on a moral base, not only a base of strategic interest."[15] For that same reason, Shultz viewed Japan rather than China as the linchpin of U.S. strategy in Asia, because China had aligned with the United States for strategic reasons that could prove transient, or as Shultz put it in his memoir: "In recent decades this fascination [with China] has tended to make U.S. foreign policy in Asia Sinocentric, especially after President Nixon's dramatic opening to China in February 1972. For me, the centerpiece has always been Japan. By far the largest economy in Asia, Japan is a key strategic partner and a dramatic example of successful democratic governance in an area where that is secure."[16]

Shultz was hardly anti-Chinese in his outlook—indeed, cooperation with Beijing expanded considerably under his watch—but unlike the Carter administration, he recognized both the need "to exercise due prudence against the possibility of a different orientation over the long-term" and the reality that "China's future mix of policies will in some degree be influenced by our own."[17] For Shultz, engagement of Beijing backed by unflinching commitment to democratic values and alliances would be the best way to help ensure that China continued "along the pragmatic, moderate, and outward-looking modernization course it has charted."[18] In his focus on the moral dimensions of strategy and achieving a maritime balance of power from the Pacific, Shultz was the first real Mahanian in the cabinet in a generation.

Shultz did not have an easy time as secretary, clashing so often with Secretary of Defense Caspar Weinberger on Soviet policy that he considered resigning until Weinberger finally went first in 1987. On Asia and the Pacific, however, the two secretaries came from similar backgrounds. Whereas Shultz had been a Pacific marine, Weinberger, after attending Harvard, had enlisted in the U.S. Army, serving as an intelligence officer on MacArthur's staff after earning a battlefield commission in the South Pacific, an experience that convinced him he "would much rather defend California or Oregon from New Guinea than from California itself."[19] He had headed the Bechtel Corporation, which inclined him to focus on developments in the Middle East as secretary of defense, but he was sympathetic to Shultz's conviction about the centrality of alliances and American military power in the Pacific. Like Reagan, the two secretaries were not looking to outsource responsibility for balance of power as their predecessors had—their aim was to integrate the democratic allies with renewed American strength to roll back Soviet ambitions everywhere, including in Asia.

Reagan had not intended for his national security advisors to be as strong as Nixon's or Carter's, but proximity to the president inevitably made them central figures on Asia policy.[20] Reagan's first national security advisor, Richard Allen, had honed his foreign policy ideas in the 1960s at the Center for Strategic and International Studies (CSIS), where he worked with former chief of naval operations and CSIS cofounder Arleigh Burke on a strategy paper calling for a "forward strategy" based on a foundation of overwhelming military strength and unrestrained political warfare that would "erode" communism and bring "victory" to the United States and its allies.[21] Whereas Haig valued U.S.-China relations most, Allen had deep ties to conservatives in Japan, Korea, and Taiwan, and the two foreign policy titans clashed repeatedly in the first year of the administration. Allen resigned in 1982 after carelessly leaving an expensive gift from a Japanese contact in his safe without declaring it, and he was replaced by Judge William Clark, who smoothed relations with State on Asia policy, particularly after Haig's departure.[22] In a series of tumultuous changes, Reagan then went through two more national security advisors before Colin Powell took the reins in 1987, but the course of Asia strategy was by then generally set and well understood by the principals.

As with previous administrations, so much of the success or failure of Asia policy rested on the assistant secretaries and their counterparts at NSC and Defense—and Reagan's cabinet officials generally made excellent choices. Allen had brought into the NSC a pair of veteran CIA Asia hands recruited by Vice President George Herbert Walker Bush, who was himself an experienced China hand, having served as the first U.S. Liaison Office director to the PRC for President Nixon. The two CIA experts on the NSC staff, China hand Jim Lilley and Korea hand Don Gregg, were both veterans of the frontline clandestine service in Asia. John Holdridge, the son of a prewar U.S. Army officer in China and himself a West Point graduate and a veteran of Kissinger's NSC, served as assistant secretary of state under Al Haig before becoming U.S. ambassador to Indonesia in 1982. His successor at State from 1982 to 1986 was Paul Wolfowitz, a University of Chicago PhD with strong conceptual skills and a commitment to morality in foreign policy that had been shaped by his family's experience in the Holocaust. Wolfowitz had comparatively little Asia experience—Shultz's chief of staff had to recommend he sit on a fork during meetings in Asia to avoid falling asleep from jet lag—but proved a steady hand when American strategic and moral priorities collided with the democratic crises in the Philippines and Korea.[23]

Perhaps the most respected and influential Asia expert over the course of the Reagan administration was Gaston Sigur—a soft-spoken graduate of Louisiana State University who had trained in Japanese during the war and had worked long stints in Tokyo as a scholar and representative of The Asia Foundation. Sigur's political connections in Tokyo were unsurpassed, and the new administration agreed with his academic and newspaper articles criticizing Carter's approach to normalization but urging continued engagement with China while restoring the U.S.-Japan alliance "as the cornerstone of U.S. policy."[24] Sigur was invited by Clark to serve as senior director for Asia on the NSC staff in 1982 in order to build the link with Japan, later moving over to become assistant secretary of state for East Asia and Pacific affairs in 1986.[25] Reagan warmed to Sigur, who resembled the president in both age and demeanor, and Sigur in turn helped the president forge a close relationship with Japanese prime minister Nakasone Yasuhiro while encouraging the president to adopt a more measured approach to China.

At Defense, the lead on Asia went to Richard Armitage, a bald, barrel-chested former wrestler from the U.S. Naval Academy class of 1967 who had volunteered for multiple combat tours in Vietnam, finally leading a rickety flotilla of some 30,000 Vietnamese sailors and refugees to safety in the Philippines after the fall of Saigon.[26] All combat veterans from Vietnam came away from the war with a powerfully formed worldview, and for the Vietnamese-speaking Armitage, it was the centrality of Asia in American foreign policy and the moral and strategic imperative of standing by allies. As Armitage told Jim Mann in an interview in 2000, cutting and running in Vietnam had been "very akin to getting a lady pregnant and leaving town."[27] And for Armitage and his colleagues, what Carter had done to Korea was just as bad. Armitage's focus on Asia, even after he was promoted to assistant secretary for international security affairs in 1983, prompted one senior British official to tell him in horror, "Young Man, what is all this about Asia—for us it is the far side of the moon!"[28] Over the course of the Reagan administration and his subsequent career, Armitage would engender the deep loyalty not only of the Japanese but also of a new generation of Asia experts in both the Republican and Democratic foreign policy establishments.

At the East Asia Informal Group meetings initiated in the Carter era, Sigur, Armitage, and Wolfowitz (and later Sigur's replacement at NSC, Jim Kelly, and others) would patch up the feuds between their respective bosses and keep a consistent and steady hand on Asia policy for the duration of Reagan's time in office.[29] In terms of regional expertise and bureaucratic muscle, they were not necessarily more qualified than Carter's Asia team, but they had one thing that Holbrooke, Abramowitz, and Oksenberg lacked—a president with a coherent worldview and the skills to lead. They were also unified in their determination to reverse the damage they perceived to American prestige from Carter's Korea troop withdrawal pledge and excessive Sinocentrism.

From 1981 to 1989, Reagan instituted a new maritime strategy centered on Japan, reconceptualized the Asia-Pacific as a region, and advanced democratic transitions in the Philippines, Korea, and Taiwan. Ironically, though, the story has to begin with China—not because Reagan intended his Asia policy to center on China but because a self-induced crisis in China policy at the beginning of the administration forced him to temper his initial ideological instincts toward the region with more pragmatic foreign policy considerations.

CHINA: STUMBLING INTO A SUSTAINABLE FRAMEWORK

The Reagan administration came into office with three criticisms of Carter's China policy that were generally correct. First, the Carter administration had assumed that China wanted a closer strategic association against Moscow than Beijing was in fact prepared to offer. Second, in pursuit of that elusive strategic association, the Carter administration had treated Taipei with unnecessary disrespect. And third, the Carter administration had swept aside differences with Beijing over democratic values. However, the Reagan administration also entered office with its own contradictions on China policy. White House officials like Allen assumed that quasi-official ties could be reestablished with Taipei without a significant backlash from Beijing, whereas Haig assumed that he could return U.S. China policy to its Nixonian roots without significant backlash from the White House. These contradictions within Reagan's own team would have to be resolved before China policy could stabilize.

Allen clearly started out closer to the president's thinking on China and Taiwan than Haig did, particularly given Reagan's personal history with Taipei. In 1971, Reagan had written to Chiang Kai-shek and Madame Chiang to express his sadness at the "immoral" vote by the UN General Assembly to recognize the PRC and then visited Chiang in Taipei in 1972 at Nixon's request to reassure the ROC of U.S. friendship.[30] While running for president, Reagan had hammered Carter on China policy, arguing in December 1978 that the United States had gained "virtually nothing we didn't already have" from normalization. "We simply gave in to Peking's demands," he told an audience listening in on one of his frequent radio broadcasts, suggesting he would establish a U.S. liaison office in Taipei comparable to the one in Beijing before normalization with the PRC.[31] George H. W. Bush, who had headed that office in the PRC, traveled to Beijing as vice presidential candidate in August 1980, along with Allen, to reassure the Chinese leadership that Reagan would not be reckless, and

Reagan issued a statement upon their return that he would continue to build steady relations based on full normalization with Beijing and an extended "hand of friendship to all Chinese"—but he also reiterated that U.S. policy would develop according to the Taiwan Relations Act and pledged to upgrade Taiwan to quasi-official status in Washington.[32]

These internal contradictions began to complicate Reagan's Asia policy as early as the 1981 inaugural ceremonies, where the irrepressible anticommunist Anna Chennault secured prominent positions for representatives from Taiwan, incurring the wrath of the Chinese ambassador. Meanwhile, at the State Department, Haig was going in the other direction, implementing policies to put China at the center of Asia policy as a way to increase pressure on Moscow.[33] When an unnamed senior official at State announced in February 1981 that there would be no official relationship with Taipei and declared patronizingly that "there is a difference between campaigning and governing," an exasperated Richard Allen forwarded the article with a cover memo to Reagan warning that the State Department was sabotaging the president's pledge to prioritize the Taiwan Relations Act over the first two U.S.-China communiqués.[34] The White House then left Haig out to dry in June by declaring it had "no explanation" for a statement the secretary of state made that U.S. relations with China had been "on the decline steadily" for the past three years (including blatantly the first five months of Reagan's term).[35] The press enjoyed the public spats but, as Holdridge recalls, "we always felt we were walking on eggs."[36]

The division between the two camps came to a head over the question of arms sales to both Taipei and Beijing. John Carbaugh, a wily staffer for conservative Republican senator Jesse Helms, had been angling to convince the administration to sell Taiwan the advanced F-5G fighter and to convince the press and Taipei that the sale was a done deal—sending Beijing into high dudgeon and sharpening the debate within the administration.[37] When Allen moved toward consideration of the sale in the spring of 1981, Haig, who worried that it would represent "a symbolic challenge to China's sovereignty and territorial integrity" and "set back U.S. global strategy," orchestrated a Defense Department study of the ROC Air Force requirements to slow things down.[38]

Over the same period, Haig made his own push for arms sales to Beijing, believing—like Carter officials before him—that it would cement an anti-Soviet alignment between the United States and China. Despite the fact that the administration had concluded in a National Security

Decision Memorandum on June 4, 1981, that it was prepared to relax restrictions on arms and technology sales on a case-by-case basis but not yet major weapons sales, Haig unilaterally announced two weeks later in Beijing that the United States was prepared to sell defensive weapons to the PRC.[39] Holdridge, Armitage, and the rest of the U.S. delegation were "absolutely flabbergasted" at this unauthorized announcement and made sure the president ordered Haig to pull back from arms sales to Beijing—just as Haig had put the brakes on Allen's push for sales of the F-5G to Taiwan.[40]

Haig continued to press for arms sales to China, predicting to Reagan that even a modest offer of defense technology to Beijing would silence Chinese criticism of U.S arms sales to Taiwan. In this, however, he completely misread Chinese views of the Taiwan problem. From Beijing's perspective, the administration was trying to return U.S.-China relations to the state of negotiations in mid-1978, and China raised the ante in October 1981 by demanding a concrete timetable for complete cessation of arms sales to Taiwan based on the Chinese interpretation of the previous joint communiqués.[41] Despite differences on overall China policy, nobody in the administration wanted an open rupture with Beijing that would undermine strategy toward the Soviet Union. The administration's contradictory impulses on China had to be resolved.

The hot button issue of the F-5G came to a head when the Pentagon study concluded in November that the advanced fighter did not offer sufficient loiter time to combat Peoples Liberation Army (PLA) Air Force fighters over the Taiwan Strait. Haig seized on the finding to argue that arms sales should be frozen at the current levels of quantity and quality. He was immediately checked by Allen at the White House.[42] After Allen resigned over the Japanese watch incident, Clark brokered a compromise under which Taiwan would develop an indigenous version of the less advanced F-5E, but this did little to ameliorate Beijing's ongoing demand for an end to all arms sales. Thinking he had the upper hand with Allen gone, Haig argued that the administration had to satisfy Beijing's demands, and he proposed that future arms sales be decreased regardless of whether there was "further progress toward a peaceful resolution and to the continued abatement of military tensions in the Taiwan Strait."[43] However, the secretary of state failed to understand that the real defender of Taiwan was not Allen but the president himself. When his last gambit on China policy failed, Haig resigned. As he later noted in his memoirs, "the China question convinced me that Reagan's world view was indeed different from my own."[44]

With the Haig-Allen feud at an end, the administration took steps to restore a united front toward Beijing. Vice President Bush and John Holdridge visited China in May 1982 to reassure Deng that the United States would not let Taiwan arms sales disrupt U.S.-China relations but also to explain that Reagan would not delink arms sales reductions from expectations of peaceful resolution of cross-Strait issues. Bush's old ties to Deng and the Chinese leadership helped enormously.[45] On August 17, the United States and China issued what is now called the "Third Communiqué," the operative sections stating the U.S. intention "gradually to reduce its sale of arms to Taiwan, leading, over a period of time, to a final resolution," but linking that goal to "the Chinese policy of striving for a peaceful resolution of the Taiwan question" and both governments' efforts "to adopt measures and create conditions conducive to the thorough settlement of this issue."[46] Mindful of Carter's mistakes vis-à-vis Taiwan, Gaston Sigur ensured that a simultaneous set of "Six Assurances" was made to Taiwan that committed the United States to honor the Taiwan Relations Act and avoid any direct or indirect pressure on Taipei to accept Beijing's position on cross-Strait issues.[47]

Officials and scholars have debated whether the Third Communiqué was a historic step forward in U.S.-China relations or just an escape from Reagan's self-imposed policy crisis. Critics of the Reagan White House, including Haig, argued that the communiqué merely returned U.S.-China relations to the status quo after an unnecessary ideological fight over Taiwan in the first year of the administration.[48] That is certainly true to a significant extent. On the other hand, little was lost in terms of U.S.-China relations. As Armitage explained to Congress in June 1983, the different tone in U.S.-China relations had actually begun at the end of the Carter years, when China stopped pursuing a strategic relationship toward the United States with the same "vim and vigor" as it had in 1973.[49] Shultz, who was not part of the initial policy fights over China, thought that the Sinocentrism of American policy over the previous decade had to be broken sooner or later. He explained to the president after becoming secretary that he had earlier developed a theory of industrial relations at MIT according to which management's efforts to preserve good relations with workers for relations' sake alone ultimately stifled innovation and created even larger friction down the road. That was the problem with U.S. China policy before 1982, he told the president, and thus a recalibration of Beijing's expectations was overdue.[50]

Moreover, although the ideological fight over China policy was certainly not necessary, the Third Communiqué and the Six Assurances
probably were. The communiqué reestablished the link between arms
sales and the Chinese threat to Taiwan—at least for the American side—
and the Six Assurances put in place a straightforward formula for protecting American interests in the security of Taiwan independent of
developments in U.S.-China relations. The policy worked. China did
not become an issue in the 1982 midterm elections, as some in the administration once feared, and Congress, Taipei, and Beijing all now understood the administration's bottom line. When Chinese premier Zhao
Ziyang later tried to reopen the issue during a visit to the Oval Office
in April 1984, demanding that the Taiwan Relations Act be changed, Reagan
gave him a simple answer: "You're right. We must toughen it up!"[51] From that
point on, the Chinese leadership dropped anything but pro forma protests
on Taiwan with Reagan.

The administration now settled on a formulation of China's role in
U.S. strategy that saw merit in maintaining better ties with Beijing than
Moscow had but without any illusions about the political and systemic
differences between Washington and Beijing or a preoccupation with
preserving the "special relationship" with China for its own sake.[52] The
dynamics in Asia were changing: the U.S. economy and defense budget
were resurgent, and it was Moscow that faced growing internal economic
and social tensions. Beijing, now less fearful of the Soviet military threat,
sought increasing flexibility in its own approaches to Asia independent
of Washington.[53] The president himself set the direction in an NSC
review of China policy on September 20, 1983, when he declared to his
foreign policy team that the long-term U.S. goal must not only be to improve relations with Beijing but also "to continue to do things which will
encourage Chinese efforts to moderate the Communist system and
expand their opening to the West."[54]

By 1983, Reagan's China policy had done more than just return to the
status quo ante bellum. His more sober view of the utility and risks of
viewing China as a "card" against Moscow set more realistic—and ultimately more productive—parameters around cooperation with Beijing.
Reagan approved peaceful nuclear cooperation with China in 1983 and
then made the first trip to China by a U.S. president since Ford in 1984.[55]
It was a trip about symbolism rather than substance but played well at
home in the lead-up to the 1984 U.S. presidential election and satisfied
Deng that relations with the United States were on track.[56] Meanwhile,

after careful coordination with Tokyo and Taipei, the administration approved limited arms sales to China of helicopters, 155 mm artillery rounds, and TOW missiles in June 1984 that would threaten Soviet armored formations but not be able to hit Japan or Taiwan.[57] For the administration's Asia hands, all of these steps were effective precisely because Reagan had "started over on arms sales with China *after* locking in Japan and Taiwan" instead of pursuing arms sales with Beijing in order to lock in a Sinocentric Asia strategy, as Haig had proposed.[58]

There was now less domestic debate about China in the United States and a more general sense of optimism about China's future under Deng.[59] In 1985, *Time* magazine named Deng "Man of the Year" for having "launched the world's most populous nation on an audacious effort to create what amounts to a new form of society."[60] When pro-democracy student demonstrations spread across major cities throughout China in December 1986 and prominent liberals, including General Secretary Hu Yaobang, were purged from the party, Deng quelled international fears by declaring that "China needs further opening" to the outside world, even as he cautioned that the country's mistakes "were due to demanding too much and moving too fast."[61] Economic opening to the West also looked promising. In October 1986, Beijing announced new regulations for foreign investment, further signaling its desire to integrate into the free trade system and demonstrating to the Reagan administration the utility of China's entry into the General Agreement on Tariffs and Trade (GATT).[62] As Shultz told the press while touring an economic reform center in Dalian in March 1987, he was confident that "China is irrevocably launched on a course of modernization" and would not roll back reforms, but privately he conveyed to Chinese counterparts the importance of progress on human rights and democracy.[63] At the Brookings Institution the next month, Sigur reiterated the U.S. goal of continuing to build a "friendly and cooperative relationship with China that will be a stabilizing factor in East Asia and the world." There was now a bipartisan consensus on this point, he explained to the mostly Democratic audience, and this made for an optimistic prognosis for the future of the relationship.[64]

When Shultz made his last visit to China as secretary in 1988, he asked Deng what he thought of Gorbachev's political reforms, which appeared to be working. Deng told Shultz that Gorbachev had it backward and that Perestroika would "blow up in his face." China, he explained, would change its political system more gradually, keeping the Communist Party in constant control. Deng's plans for gradual political reform in China sounded convincing at the time, Shultz acknowledged in an interview in his San Francisco penthouse in 2014, but then he added, after pausing in thought for a moment, "Of course, that has not happened."[65]

AN "UNSINKABLE AIRCRAFT CARRIER": THE MARITIME STRATEGY AND JAPAN

Although China policy consumed the Reagan administration politically in its first year, the president's real intention had been to center U.S. Asia strategy on the alliance with Japan and the revitalization of American air and naval power in the Pacific. As Reagan came to power in 1981, the Soviets were on track to expand their Pacific fleet exponentially from what it had been in Nixon's time, including an increase in nuclear-powered ballistic missile submarines from eleven to twenty-four; nuclear-powered guided submarines from fourteen to twenty; nuclear attack submarines from four to twenty-two; guided-missile cruisers from three to ten; light cruisers from three to four; frigates from thirty-two to fifty; and the addition of ten new guided-missile frigates and an aircraft carrier, which it did not have in 1973.[66] The Soviets had also built up their airpower with bases in the Northern Territories, Vietnam (Da Nang), and the Russian Far East, and had built up their ground forces with the deployment of 500,000 troops in the Soviet Far East and 10,000 troops in the Northern Territories near Japan. Inspired by the examples of Mahan and the Imperial Japanese Navy, Soviet admiral Sergey Gorshkov had led one of the great naval expansions in history, with the aim of contesting American maritime dominance in the Pacific.[67] The Soviet goal was ambitious—the "exclusion of the forward deployment of U.S. military power, a pliant, non-aligned China, and a quiescent Japan."[68]

This was not a problem that was going to be solved by external balancing with China; by major Japanese rearmament, which would necessarily be limited despite Tokyo's growing tension with Moscow; or by a coalition with Southeast Asia or Oceania, which were far removed from the Soviet naval threat.[69] Moreover, as Admiral Hayward had been warning, the Carter administration's strategy to swing forces out of the Pacific to counter Soviet threats against Central Europe or the Persian Gulf put U.S. maritime dominance in the Pacific at even greater risk. Like MacMurray and the planners of War Plan Orange in the mid-1930s, the Reagan administration was presented with the dilemma of conceding to an adversary's expansive offensive capabilities in the Western Pacific or trying to counter them with revitalized American naval power and forward presence. Reagan would double down.

As chief of naval operations at the end of the Carter administration, Hayward had been socializing his offensive maritime strategy with the flag officers in the navy, but he had been stymied by the Carter Defense Department's planning for a short thirty-day war limited primarily to Central Europe, with the navy in a secondary supporting role.[70] Hayward's brain trust at the Naval War College advised him that his offensive naval doctrine would be impossible without a new national strategy. What the navy needed, the professors in Newport argued, was better marketing in Washington.[71] Their salvation came in the person of an impatient thirty-eight-year-old naval reserve aviator named John F. Lehman. Another protégé of Arleigh Burke, for whom he wrote studies in the 1970s on the need for more aircraft carriers, Lehman had inserted the 600-ship navy pledge into the 1980 Republican Party platform and then as Reagan's first secretary of the navy overcame internal Pentagon resistance to make it his personal crusade with the White House and Congress. At first, the brash reservist struck the navy brass as a rank amateur, but they soon came to see him as the most influential secretary of the navy since Forrestal.[72]

Lehman's message was simple and direct: the United States could no longer afford the swing strategy now that the Soviets' largest fleet was in the Pacific and America's own trade interests in that region were set to surpass those in the Atlantic.[73] The only option, Lehman argued, was to deploy in offensive positions forward "so that the United States could quickly take action against the Soviet homeland or its offshore deployments, if necessary." The alternative was not an alternative, as he would later explain to Congress:

> If we were forced to a passive strategy, such as some have advocated, then we would provide the Soviets with the opportunity to prey on our vulnerabilities and fight a war of attrition against our merchant marine. We would start taking losses as we took in World War II because merchant ships don't go any faster today and are, in fact, bigger targets than they were then and the Soviet attack subs are far more effective.

If that ever happens, we cannot replace them; we cannot fight a war of attrition in strategic sealift and that is the surest formula for losing the war that I can think of.[74]

In May 1982, the White House established the broader national strategy the navy had been waiting for in NSDD 32, which anticipated horizontal escalation in the event of a conflict with the Soviets and called for a robust forward presence and enhanced "collective defense arrangements" with allies to contain and reverse Soviet expansionism.[75] NSDD 32 set the context for codification of the new Maritime Strategy within the navy staff the same year and the eventual articulation of the strategy in a special supplement to the January 1986 issue of the U.S. Naval Institute journal *Proceedings* that included articles by Lehman, the new chief of naval operations, Admiral James D. Watkins, and the commandant of the marine corps.[76]

The Maritime Strategy anticipated three phases of world war. First, U.S. forces would deploy antisubmarine warfare assets to push Soviet submarines to defensive positions, assemble carrier battle forces and move them toward the anticipated battle areas, and launch amphibious assaults on key littoral positions. Second, U.S. forces would embark on an offensive campaign, destroying Soviet submarines while carrier task forces seized control of the Norwegian Sea, the Eastern Mediterranean, and the North Pacific. Third, U.S. forces would take action against the base and logistics network that supported the Soviet navy. Contrary to the earlier "swing strategy," which called for a wartime redeployment of Pacific naval forces to the European theater, the Pacific theater would be as important as the Atlantic.[77] Moreover, since the Maritime Strategy specifically targeted Soviet SSBNs (submarines carrying nuclear-armed missiles) in their maritime bastions, the United States sought to prove that in a war it could alter the nuclear balance of power in Washington's favor, which would change Soviet calculations about the correlation of forces and thus reinforce nuclear and overall deterrence.[78]

Given the strategic options of retreating in the face of Soviet threats against the U.S. forward maritime position in the Pacific or turning on the offensive, Reagan chose the bolder and riskier option. "You have to understand something the Navy doesn't want to come clean on," said Princeton University professor and former Council of Foreign Relations Pentagon Fellow Barry Posen in an interview in 1985, "to threaten the Soviet SSBN force is to wage nuclear war. It is very escalatory."[79]

The strategy also could not be done without Japan. In fact, when Hayward had first gathered senior admirals in 1979 to describe the maritime strategy, one major source of skepticism had been the assumption that Japan was ready for or capable of playing anything like the role Hayward envisioned. But that skepticism was based on U.S.-Japan relations as they had unfolded in the 1970s, when the bookstores in Tokyo were full of Soviet-encouraged anti-American titles and Japanese neutralism appeared to be a real danger. Reagan and his secretaries of state and defense envisioned a very different context for U.S.-Japan relations in the 1980s.

George Shultz used to say that with Japan you quickly went from "grand strategy to fruit puree," but the reality of Japanese domestic politics did not deter him or the president from making Japan the centerpiece of their Asia strategy. The 2000 Republican Party platform declared as much, and speeches and NSC documents throughout the Reagan administration consistently began with that theme.[80] As Shultz noted in his memoirs, "President Reagan saw the Asia-Pacific region as a key part of our future and Japan as of central importance in that region."[81]

One of Reagan's first moves on Asia policy was to ask Carter's ambassador to Japan, former Democratic senator Mike Mansfield of Montana, to stay on in Tokyo. The week after the inauguration, Mansfield sent a cable directly to Reagan, making the case for a stronger partnership with Japan. The key, he noted, was to involve Japan more explicitly in the Western decision-making process; encourage a more active and independent Japanese role in Asia; and broaden bilateral networks and mechanisms with the recognition that Japan will increasingly have the option to choose its own way and that the United States will need an effective mechanism for coordination with Japan.[82] Allen strongly endorsed the recommendation in a cover memo, which also coincided with Weinberger's view that "Japan lies in one of the most strategically important geographic locations in the world and in the most vulnerable position vis-a-vis Soviet military power in the Pacific. . . . [I]f the United States and Japan can jointly deter the Soviets from attack or from gaining a dominant influence in the Pacific, the United States will have far more flexibility in using our forces to deter war in the Middle East, Europe and elsewhere."[83]

NSDD 32 had put alliances at the center of U.S. strategy for both the Atlantic and the Pacific, beginning with Japan, which the strategy memo noted should be "encouraged to contribute more to their own and mutual defense efforts."[84] In the focus on Japan, the Reagan NSC was building on Brzezinski's own instincts that the Nixon administration had underplayed Tokyo's role as a key member of the Western camp. There was also a broad continuity from Brown to Weinberger on the need for Japan to do more for its own defense. The difference was that the Reagan administration sought specifically to elevate Japan to NATO levels of decision making and to agree on a division of roles and missions and integration of defense strategies with Japan rather than focusing on the amount of Japanese spending per se.[85] The Reagan administration's aim was a more equal partnership, as Mansfield had proposed, with the emphasis on *partnership* rather than burden sharing. It reflected the fundamental tenet that jointness with allied forces is itself a powerful source of deterrence rather than a simple calculus of "fair" burden sharing that had so grated in Tokyo.

Initially, the Reagan administration hit some of the same political "fruit puree" in Tokyo that had confounded Nixon and Carter. For most of the postwar period, Japanese politics were dominated by the "mainstream" factions of the ruling LDP, which maintained an arm's-length relationship with the United States on defense issues in order to retain greater freedom to focus on economic growth and relations with Asia. Prime Minister Suzuki Zenkō was in that tradition—pro-alliance, but wary of entrapment (*makikomare*) in U.S. containment strategies. Nevertheless, Suzuki was eager to cement an early relationship with the new president and dispatched his foreign minister, Masayoshi Itō, to Washington in March 1981. As Commander James Auer, USN, the Japan Desk director in the Pentagon and one of the architects of the new approach to Japan, recollects, Weinberger pitched to Itō the idea of a new approach to security cooperation based on a division of roles and missions:

Weinberger proposed the U.S. would provide Japan a nuclear umbrella, would keep the aircraft carrier U.S.S. MIDWAY at Yokosuka and would bring in other aircraft carriers if necessary, for example, to strike Vladivostok, and would protect Japan's sea lanes in the Southwest Pacific and the Indian Ocean, significantly beyond the literal commitment of the Security Treaty. If Japan needed the U.S. side's opinion of what Japan should do, the Secretary said he believed Japan should defend its own territory, the sky and sea surrounding Japan and the sea lanes of the Northwest Pacific.[86]

Untrained in military strategy, Itō was not sure how to respond to Wein-berger's proposal, but in his March 21 press conference he referred for the first time to the U.S.-Japan "alliance" (*domei*)—a term still so controversial in Japan that he was forced to resign after he uttered it.[87] Undeterred, Mans-field, Armitage, and Auer worked with younger pro-defense politicians in the LDP and a more ambitious generation of Japanese Foreign Ministry officials to produce a joint communiqué for the prime minister's planned summit with Reagan in Washington on May 8–9.[88] In that communiqué, a slightly bewildered Suzuki agreed to "an appropriate division of roles between Japan and the United States" and "to make even greater efforts for improving [Japan's] defense capabilities in Japanese territories and in its surrounding sea and air space, and for further alleviating the finan-cial burden of U.S. forces in Japan."[89] Then the prime minister explained at the National Press Club what his aides had told him—that Japan can in accordance with national policy defend its own territory, sea lanes up to 1,000 miles.[90]

Armitage and the U.S. side were surprised by Suzuki's public commit-ment but were familiar with the 1,000-mile number, which they had ear-lier floated to Japanese counterparts as the distance from Japan to the Philippines and Guam.[91] Whether Suzuki knew what he was saying was never clear, but alliance managers in both Washington and Tokyo seized on the commitment as a benchmark for Japan to acquire real capability in air defense and antisubmarine warfare in order to bottle up Soviet air and naval forces in the Far East.[92] Japan was poised to form the "shield" as the United States developed the "spear" in the navy's emerging Mari-time Strategy against Soviet forces in the Far East.[93]

In November 1982, Suzuki stepped down (in part because of his con-fused management of relations with the United States) and was replaced by Nakasone Yasuhiro, the same pro-defense, antimainstream political figure who had advocated greater military autonomy from the United States for Japan in the Nixon years. But Nakasone had changed—he was attracted to Reagan's vision of Japan as a fully empowered member of the Western camp, and he knew and trusted senior U.S. officials such as Sigur at the NSC. More importantly, he understood that his vision of a stron-ger Japanese security posture would not fly in Japan or Asia unless it was linked to the alliance with the United States.

The difference from Suzuki was immediately noticeable. In his first visit to Washington in January 1983, Nakasone publicly referred to Japan as America's "unsinkable aircraft carrier." His ministers returned unreservedly to the original 1969 Nixon-Sato formula, calling peace and security on the peninsula a "vital" interest to Japan and providing $4 billion in economic aid to Korea. In 1983, Nakasone relaxed a cabinet ban on arms exports to allow dual-use technology transfers to the United States, and in 1986 he agreed to R&D cooperation with the United States to support President Reagan's anti–ballistic-missile Strategic Defense Initiative (SDI—also known popularly as "Star Wars" at the time). Neither scheme led to significant technology cooperation, but the prospect of a combined U.S. and Japanese industrial and technology base sent a powerful signal to Moscow.[94]

Perhaps even more significant to the Soviets was Nakasone's decision to accept the deployment of U.S. F-16s to Misawa in northern Honshū—in part to counter the deployment of Soviet MiGs in the Russian Far East but also with the intent of signaling that Japan was prepared to support U.S. horizontal escalation strategies because the F-16s were dual-capable and could hypothetically carry nuclear weapons against Soviet targets.[95] Over the same period, Nakasone also committed to paying billions of dollars of yen-based costs for U.S. bases in Japan; broke the cabinet's 1 percent of GDP ceiling on defense spending; extended strategic aid to Pakistan and other frontline states in the Cold War; and approved a new exclusively "defensive" defense doctrine to secure Japan's sea lanes and bottle up Soviet forces where the U.S. Navy could attack them under the Maritime Strategy.[96] Though the public had grown wary of Soviet expansion, only a handful of Japanese politicians and officials really understood the importance of the whole strategy. It was "all about stopping Japanese neutralism," recalls Armitage. And it worked.[97]

Nakasone also benefited in his own ways from this new partnership with the United States. The two leaders publicly referred to each other collegially as "Ron" and "Yasu," and Nakasone made sure to stand by Reagan's side for photographs at G-7 summits of the Western leaders rather than cowering nervously at the end of the line like previous Japanese prime ministers. The Japanese public, though uneasy with some of Nakasone's nationalism, were enthralled. Japan was also elevated to something closer to NATO levels of consultations. When Washington engaged in Intermediate Nuclear Forces (INF) talks with Moscow, for example, NATO allies were prepared to settle for removal of Soviet SS-20s from West to East, but Nakasone prevailed on Reagan to insist publicly on elimination of *all* the missiles rather than depositing the threat in Japan's own neighborhood.[98]

Reagan and his top officials were confident that Tokyo's willingness to stand with the more assertive U.S. containment strategy would complicate Soviet planning in the Pacific and restore overall global deterrence—and they saw immediate results in Soviet behavior.[99] When U.S.-Japan joint naval exercises changed from defensive to offensive scenarios (with Japan as the shield and the U.S. forces as the spear), the Soviets responded by shifting their own maneuvers back to defense again. Most notable was how the Soviet navy halted the practice developed in the 1970s of loitering SSBNs off Hawaii and then making a threatening dash for the West Coast of the continental United States.[100] Nor could Moscow ignore the new capabilities Japan was developing to defend its own sea lanes by the end of the decade: 60 destroyers (three times the number in the U.S. Seventh Fleet), 100 modern P-3 ASW aircraft (five times more than in the Seventh Fleet), and 300 F-15 and F-4 fighters (more than the U.S. Air Force had in Korea, the Philippines, and Japan combined).[101] As the commander of the U.S. Pacific Fleet put it to Congress in 1987, "We count on every one of those allied ships. We have another role to play. If they are not filling those, somebody has to or we are going to sustain greater losses. That is a key element in the maritime strategy."[102] Within five short years, Japan had filled precisely the critical role in U.S. strategy envisioned in NSDD 32.

At the same time, however, the Reagan administration recognized deep vulnerabilities in the newly enhanced security relationship with Japan. Japan's Self Defense Forces still faced significant legal and political constraints against effective joint war-fighting with U.S. forces, particularly Tokyo's continued ban on exercising the right of collective self-defense and strict prohibition against "integration in the use of force" for offensive operations by the United States.[103] This meant that Japanese planning for defense against direct attack on the home islands and U.S. offensive planning for the Maritime Strategy occurred in parallel rather than jointly as they would have with NATO or Korea. Japanese forces were also woefully undertrained and short of actual ammunition. As Auer confessed after the Cold War had safely ended, Japan's new defense commitments with the United States were effective at deterring the Soviets but may not have worked in an actual shooting war.[104] The Reagan administration also encountered anxiety about Japan's new security role in other parts of Asia, with Lee Kuan Yee famously telling the administration that encouraging Japan to rearm was like offering a box of rum chocolates to an alcoholic. All this led Shultz to conclude that although the region supported Japan's having a stronger "strategic relationship with the United States," there was much less support for Japanese rearmament.[105]

But perhaps the biggest threat to the newly enhanced alliance with Japan came from within the United States itself.

"Japan Bashing" and the Protectionist Surge

America's strategy toward Asia since Kennan and the "reverse course" in 1947 had aimed to make Japan the economic hub of a resilient and democratic Western Pacific, rooted in the Bretton Woods system and open economic internationalism. The U.S. Congress supported that approach not only because of the geostrategic lessons of closed markets in the 1930s but also because American exporters enjoyed enormous relative gains as preferential trading systems around the world were opened to competition. By the 1960s, however, American firms began to fall prey to competition from recovering U.S. allies abroad, beginning with Japan. Textile trade alone had nearly crippled Nixon's relationship with Tokyo. In Reagan's first term, the U.S. trade deficit with Japan tripled, from $16 billion to $49.7 billion, and the list of aggrieved U.S. industries expanded to iconic manufacturers of autos and consumer electronics.

Trade friction featured prominently in Mansfield's first cable to the president, in January 1981, and remained a preoccupation in NSC documents and meetings throughout the Reagan administration.[106] In contrast to Nixon, Reagan was unwilling to exploit trade problems with Japan for electoral advantage. Instead, his administration sought to use congressional pressure to encourage change in Japanese economic policies that would in turn preempt the need for protectionist legislation in Congress. In April 1981, the administration convinced Japan to agree to voluntary export restraints of autos, and over the next four years Tokyo was prodded to announce eight separate initiatives to open the Japanese market to foreign goods.[107] To the administration's alarm, however, these "voluntary" Japanese measures barely stemmed the growing protectionist tide on Capitol Hill. The dam burst in 1985, the year, notes trade scholar Mac Destler, that "foreign trade suddenly became what it had not been for half a century: one of the central issues in American politics."[108] There were 300 pieces of protectionist legislation generated in Congress that year. They included a July 1985 proposal by congressional Democrats to place a

25 percent surcharge on Japanese products; a 92 to 0 Senate resolution demanding trade retaliation against Japan, and legislation to curb Japanese textile imports that passed both houses and forced a presidential veto.[109]

Despite this political pressure, Reagan would not abandon his free trade principles, as he put it in August 1985: "I am opposed to protectionism. Protectionism is a two-way street, and you may help some industry with protectionism or some group of employees, and you find that you have done it at the expense of other industries and other employees."[110]

Reagan's economic team generally shared his philosophy, but fissures emerged on how to deal with the political problems caused by growing trade friction with Japan. The president himself was not at risk—he had just won a landslide reelection in 1984—but his internationalist agenda and the alliance with Japan were. In his first term, free traders had been dominant. Shultz, who had been Reagan's chair of the Council of Economic Advisors (CEA), saw the root problem as Japan's higher savings rate, which caused production to exceed demand and lead to an overreliance on exports for economic growth. Although he agreed that Japan had to be convinced to take visible measures for political reasons, he argued that the solution ultimately depended on policies that encouraged U.S. firms to produce more competitive goods and U.S. householders to increase their savings rate.[111] He was backed in this assessment by Martin Feldstein, his successor at the CEA from 1982 to 1984, and by the treasury secretary, former Merrill Lynch chairman and CEO Donald Regan.[112]

However, in the second term, there emerged in Reagan's economic team two new leaders who believed that more drastic surgery was necessary. James Baker, who became treasury secretary in February 1985 after switching jobs with Regan, came to office with few beliefs other than "a Texan's aversion to high interest rates and a politician's indifference to longer-range policy effects."[113] He did not share Shultz's strategic view of the centrality of Japan as an ally or Regan's strict laissez-faire approach to trade and monetary policy.[114] Correcting the investment/savings imbalance may have been the right economic policy answer, but in Baker's view it would do little in the near term for either international economic relations or Reagan's support for free trade.[115] Baker's tougher view on trade aligned with that of the powerful new U.S. trade representative (USTR), Clayton Yeutter, an agricultural economist and Republican Party stalwart from Nebraska, who shared Reagan's negative view of protectionism but was ready to wield a bigger stick against closed foreign markets to ensure Congress did not return to the misguided policies of the 1930s.

The tough-minded Baker quickly took control of economic policy-making, centralizing eight different economic policy groups under a single Economic Policy Council he chaired. The centerpiece of his trade policy would be Section 301 of the Trade Act of 1974, which gave the president "discretionary authority to impose retaliatory measures against any foreign governmental act, policy, or practice that 'burdens or restricts United States commerce' and either violates international obligations or is determined by the President to be 'unjustifiable, unreasonable, or discriminatory.'"[116] Career Treasury Department officials argued against the use of Section 301 by pointing out that Japan had not actually violated any international trade regulations under GATT, and Shultz feared that invoking Section 301 would serve only to exacerbate bilateral tensions with Japan. However, Reagan was convinced by Baker's argument that domestic politics required action against Japan, and he gave the USTR a green light in September 1985 for the first self-initiated Section 301 investigation of Japanese unfair trade practices against U.S. tobacco products.[117] Using Section 301 as the stick, the NSC authorized broader bilateral negotiations for market opening in Japan under the Market Oriented Sector Specific (MOSS) talks.[118]

With the Sturm und Drang of Section 301 to distract Congress and motivate the Japanese government to open markets, Baker initiated steps to bring the macroeconomic picture into faster realignment. Recognizing the traumatic impact of Nixon's unilateral dollar shock in 1971, Baker began a new process of consultation with U.S. industrial allies on macroeconomic and exchange rate issues aimed at *collective* efforts to redress imbalances in the dollar's high value vis-à-vis the yen and the deutsche mark.[119] The idea of target zones to keep U.S. exports competitive against the yen was first proposed in 1982 by scholars at the Institute for International Economics in Washington, DC, but had been ignored by Regan's Treasury Department.[120] In the meantime, however, the dollar had appreciated 50 percent against the yen and other leading currencies as the Federal Reserve kept interest rates high in order to battle the debilitating inflation left from the Carter years, further disadvantaging U.S. exporters and raising the risks of protectionist legislation in Congress. By 1985, Baker was ready to act. Shultz privately urged him not to intervene in currency markets, but as secretary of state he had little say in the matter.[121] In meetings at the Plaza Hotel in New York on September 22, the finance ministers of Britain, France, Germany, and Japan agreed to coordinated intervention (the Plaza Accord) in foreign exchange markets to drive down the value of the dollar.[122] Over the next six months, the dollar value of the yen appreciated from 240 to 150.

With Section 301 and the Plaza Accord, Baker relieved congressional pressure for protectionist legislation and allowed Reagan to stay true to his free trade ideals, but the tension in U.S.-Japan relations barely abated. With the rapid appreciation of the yen, the Japanese economy suddenly appeared to balloon in size, and Japanese investors flooded into the United States looking for bargains under the cheaper dollar. Books with ominous-sounding titles like *Buying into America* became best sellers as Japanese companies bought landmarks from New York City's Rockefeller Plaza to California's Pebble Beach Golf Course. With the Cold War ebbing and Japan looming as a new economic superpower, polls began to show that Americans were more fearful of Japan's economy than of Soviet nuclear-armed missiles.[123] The alliance would stand firm to the end of Reagan's term, but the shifting opinions on Japan were a worrying harbinger of tensions to come.

RESPONDING TO THE RISE OF ASIAN REGIONALISM

It was not just Japan that was outgrowing the postwar framework for U.S. strategy—Asia as a whole was bursting at the seams from economic growth and new patterns of intraregional trade and investment. The two new "Asian tigers," Korea and Taiwan, were following Japan's export-oriented growth model, while Southeast Asian economies like Thailand, Malaysia, and Indonesia were booming with Northeast Asia's success and the decline of communist insurgency threats at home.[124] Even the continuing chaos in neighboring Indochina posed only limited danger because of Sino-U.S. rapprochement and the stabilizing effect of ASEAN.[125] With regional economic interdependence and increased national confidence came a search for new ideas about how Asians might define a regional order on their own. Although that regional vision was now far more likely to approximate Western norms rather than Marxist-Leninist thought, there was also a growing sense in the region that perhaps Asia had finally outgrown the West.

For decades, American governments had been wary of regional groupings in Asia that were not led by Washington. In 1955, Dulles viewed

Bandung as dangerous neutralism. Kennedy tried to embrace pluralism in Asian relations in the early 1960s but ultimately offered little more than the short-lived "New Pacific Community." Nixon saw utility in Asian multipolarity but fiercely opposed any alignment among Asian powers at U.S. expense. There was a simple formula at play: any proposal for regional multilateralism that threatened to weaken the bilateral hub and spokes arrangement of the San Francisco System was a threat to U.S. interests.

By the mid-1980s, however, new proposals for alternative multilateral institutions in Asia were proliferating. The Japanese and Australians were exploring ideas for a Pacific Rim economic grouping; Malaysian prime minister Mahathir Mohamad came to power in 1981 championing a vision of East Asian autonomy from the West; Gorbachev in 1985 proposed a new regional multilateralism devoid of alliances; and calls for zones free of nuclear weapons began to spread from Western Europe to America's Pacific allies.[126] Despite a reputation among historians for being messianic, Reagan in fact demonstrated far greater agility in responding to these myriad proposals than his predecessors had. His administration listened respectfully to proposals for regional economic groupings that might enhance trans-Pacific cooperation but came down like a hammer on schemes that were explicitly aimed at weakening U.S. alliances or forward military presence. In so doing, Reagan helped to midwife the first reemergence of multilateralism in U.S. Asia strategy since the Washington Treaty System collapsed a half-century earlier.

The administration's attention was drawn to the issue after Australia and Japan hosted the first Pacific Economic Cooperation Conference (PECC) summit of business and academic leaders in Canberra in 1980.[127] Though the United States was invited to participate, and similar nongovernmental meetings had occurred in the past, the establishment of the PECC was clearly a harbinger of more significant forums as governments sought ways to capture Asia's new economic growth and interdependence. Washington was supportive, but uncertain how to channel the new regionalism in directions that reinforced the administration's overall strategy to reverse Soviet expansion. In June 1983, the NSC staff proposed that Reagan use an upcoming visit to the region to demonstrate "a watershed in U.S. understanding and response to the shift in the world's center of economic activity in the direction of the Pacific Basin."[128] Specifically, the NSC suggested that Reagan link Asia-Pacific regionalism to the successful G-7 Williamsburg Summit in May, which had demonstrated Western solidarity in defense of free markets and political liberty. Working with the Philippines and Thailand, the NSC hoped to advance an ASEAN-generated proposal to turn the PECC into an Asian version of the Organization for Economic Cooperation and Development (OECD) in Europe.[129] Reagan agreed until the Soviets shot down Korean Airlines flight 007 in August, forcing the NSC staff "to make the political-military dimension of the trip a major, if not the predominant, motif."[130]

Convinced the United States still needed a long-term strategy for Asian regionalism, Shultz asked Ambassador Richard Fairbanks to take the lead in developing recommendations for the White House on the next steps. The affable and respected Fairbanks spent hours on couches in Asian capitals listening patiently to views on the way forward. His final report, in June 1984, reassured the administration that the American position was not in immediate danger and that a steady and patient approach could yield a trans-Pacific framework that would serve U.S. interests. The key lesson, he reported, was that contradictory visions of regionalism prevailed—from the more ambitious Australians and Japanese to the cautiously nonaligned ASEAN states such as Indonesia, where one official told him that Western approaches to institution-building were like kissing in public, which makes Asian girls "embarrassed and angry."[131] Fairbanks recommended a multipronged approach, which Sigur and the East Asia Informal Group embraced: the United States would build on the PECC; participate in the newly established ASEAN Post-ministerial Conference of regional foreign ministers (later to become the ASEAN Regional Forum); and develop the basis for a trans-Pacific summit that included the United States, Canada, and Mexico (what would later become the Asia Pacific Economic Cooperation forum).[132] Rather than repeat Dulles and Eisenhower's mistake of fearing regionalism, Shultz told Congress in January 1985, he saw "enormous encouragement" in that a "sense of Pacific community is emerging."[133]

Not all proposals for regionalism were so benign, however. Soviet general secretary Mikhail Gorbachev embraced regional multilateralism in a speech in Vladivostok on July 28, 1986, in which he declared that the Soviet Union is "a dedicated advocate of disbanding the military groupings, renouncing the possession of military bases in Asia and the Pacific Ocean and withdrawing troops from the territories of other countries." But Soviet power in Asia was ebbing, and Moscow's calls for neutralism mostly fell on deaf ears. The Koreans were still furious at the downing of flight 007, and Japanese prime minister Nakasone was fully invested in

Reagan's Maritime Strategy. In Southeast Asia, the Soviets retained their alliance with Vietnam, their base at Cam Ranh Bay, and their puppet Heng Samrin regime in occupied Cambodia, but Moscow began to lose ground thanks to concerted U.S. and Chinese diplomatic and military pressure on Vietnam to withdraw from Cambodia.[134] By 1989, the Vietnamese politburo had announced a new "diversification" of foreign policy, and Gorbachev acceded to a withdrawal from Cambodia.[135] Three years after the Vladivostok speech, it was Moscow's allies that were all turning neutral.

The Reagan administration also blunted Soviet-backed antinuclear movements that spread from Western Europe to Japan, Australia, and New Zealand after NATO deployed Pershing II missiles to counter the Soviet deployments of SS-20s in the early 1980s.[136] The administration drew the battle line in New Zealand, where the Labor government of David Lange had come to power in July 1984 energized by antinuclear sentiment in the wake of recent French testing in the South Pacific and searching for a new source of national identity after abandoning the party's socialist principles in favor of dramatic market-opening measures.[137] The New Zealand debate had enormous impact on neighboring Australia, where the Labor government of Bob Hawke and Kim Beazley had just stared down their own antinuclear left wing, and on Japan, the centerpiece of Reagan's maritime strategy and home port to the Seventh Fleet. When in 1987 New Zealand's parliament passed an act banning all nuclear-powered ships from entering its ports or territorial waters, Washington had to make an example, suspending all commitments to Wellington under ANZUS (though intelligence sharing quietly continued).[138] It was a sad chapter in relations between two democratic allies who had bled together from Monte Casino to the frozen hills of Korea, but in geostrategic terms Japan and Australia trumped far off New Zealand. The antinuclear wave in Asia subsided.

The common theme across these episodes was that the Reagan administration approached Asia as a distinct region—drawing on global priorities but shaping the balance of power and ideas as it existed across the Pacific. Nowhere was this more evident than in the adminstration's approach to India, where Reagan accepted pluralism among nonallies in order to diminish Soviet influence.

In contrast to his strategy on Japan, Reagan did not come into office with a clear strategy on India. Initially, his pro-Western ideology and support for Pakistan as a frontline state against the Soviets played poorly in

Delhi. By 1982, however, the tone in U.S.-India relations had begun to change. Indian prime minister Indira Gandhi made the first visit by an Indian leader to Washington in thirteen years that July, declaring the United States the world's "beacon of democracy" and developing a warm personal relationship with Reagan.[139] Reagan reciprocated by sending Bush and Shultz to Delhi and granting U.S. approval for India to use French uranium for the Tarapur reactor. By 1984, the NSC concluded in NSDD 147 that India's emerging primacy in South Asia and the Indian Ocean was *in and of itself* in the United States' strategic interest regardless of whether India explicitly aligned or allied with Washington.[140] Though Nixon had offered this insight in his 1967 *Foreign Affairs* article, he did the opposite in office. Now, quiet endorsement of India's emergence as a regional power was official U.S. strategy. That concept would recede in the George H. W. Bush and Clinton administrations but reemerge as a central tenet of George W. Bush's Asia strategy in 2001.

The Reagan administration's approach to regionalism and nonaligned India has never been fully appreciated by scholars, who tend to cast his foreign policy in Asia as a retread of Dulles's ideological opposition to neutralism and multilateralism. What set Reagan apart from Dulles, Nixon, and even Kennedy on these issues, though, was his unbounded faith in the power of democratic values.

DEMOCRATIC CONSOLIDATION AND CONTAINMENT IN ASIA

The Vietnam War had turned the American debate about values in foreign policy into a maelstrom, repeating a pattern that followed the Philippine insurrection, the First World War, and more recently the war in Iraq. Reeling from the effects of Vietnam, Nixon and Kissinger had posed idealism as a self-indulgent distraction from the pursuit of interests. Carter reacted by deliberately creating a policy where idealism might be a disruptive break on the immoral pursuit of interests. Reagan sought a path between the two extremes.

From Reagan's perspective, Carter had violated the highest moral and strategic priority of the twentieth century, which was resisting totalitarian expansion. Influenced by Georgetown University professor Jeane Kirkpatrick's seminal 1979 article "Dictatorships and Double Standards," Reagan campaigned on the principle that the United States must distinguish between authoritarian regimes aligned with the West and totalitarian regimes opposed to it.[141] In her anticommunism, Kirkpatrick—who became Reagan's UN ambassador—had little tolerance for the American ideal that "it is possible to democratize governments, anytime and anywhere, under any circumstances."[142] She would urge Reagan to stand by America's smaller authoritarian allies in pursuit of the higher purpose of defeating totalitarian threats to the international order.

This view stood in stark contrast to that of George Shultz, who put allies at the center of containment strategy but argued:

> We should never lose sight of an ultimate goal for our foreign policy. . . . The goal that the President enunciated is that of a free and democratic world whose states enjoy free elections, free press, free trade unions, free enterprise and other free institutions. . . . If we do not act to support democratic forces, and act with a sense of moral purpose, we cede the field of political action to those who would act to destroy democracy rather than build it; we would remain solely in a defensive position, where the only direction in which we could move is retreat.[143]

These tensions in Reagan's approach to authoritarian allies would never be settled in the counterrevolutionary battlefields of Central Asia or Africa that preoccupied Kirkpatrick—but they would in Asia, where democratic convulsions pushed Reagan solidly toward the worldview of Shultz.

In fact, Reagan was forced to confront the question of dictators and double standards in Asia before even coming to office. No U.S. ally had suffered more strategically from Carter's public campaign on human rights than the Republic of Korea, and Reagan's advisors intended to make the U.S.-ROK alliance an example of the democratic camp's new solidarity against communism. However, a month after Reagan's election victory, Korean president Chun Doo-hwan had sentenced popular democracy activist Kim Dae-jung to death for sedition. The president-elect's choice between allies and democracy would now be put to the test. Allen, Armitage, and Lilley were all in agreement that either a public execution of Kim or a break with Seoul would be unacceptable, and they used their anticommunist credentials and political contacts in Seoul to convince Chun's Blue House advisors to put Kim under house arrest until the opposition leader could eventually travel to the United States. In exchange, Chun was offered the first state visit to Washington of any Asian ally.[144] The quiet diplomacy averted a crisis and showed solidarity against Pyongyang and Moscow as Reagan used the visit to quash Carter's deferred troop withdrawal plan from Korea. In Korea, however, U.S. support for Chun sparked a new wave of street protests that were now aimed more directly at the United States. These would come back to vex the administration later.

The next test came in the Philippines. While the incoming Reagan administration testified to Congress about the importance of promoting reforms in Manila, Haig (solidly in the Nixonian realpolitik camp) emphasized that the Clark and Subic Bay bases were too important to U.S. security interests to allow public derision of Philippine strongman Ferdinand Marcos.[145] When Marcos visited the United States in September 1982, Reagan privately encouraged reforms but publicly called the Philippine president an "old and good" friend and the U.S.-Philippine security relationship part of "the shield behind which the whole region can develop socially and economically."[146] The next August, Marcos crossed the line when popular opposition leader Benigno "Ninoy" Aquino was assassinated while being escorted off the plane in Manila by security forces after his return from exile in the United States.[147] Reagan canceled a trip to the Philippines scheduled for the following November and then delayed military assistance offered to Marcos during the Philippine president's previous visit to Washington. Still, when pressed on the Philippine situation during a presidential debate against Walter Mondale on October 21, 1984, Reagan gave a Kirkpatrick-like answer, arguing that the United States would be "better off trying to retain our friendship [with Marcos] and help them [the Philippine government] right the wrongs we see, rather than throwing them to the wolves and then facing a communist power in the Pacific."[148]

In contrast to the Carter administration, where human rights officials engaged in open battle with the regional assistant secretaries and NSC directors, it was now the Asia experts of the East Asia Informal Group who pushed for a firmer line toward Marcos. As one participant noted in 1985, "Those of us involved in this policy who are Asianists, not politicos or pundits, *knew* what we were doing. The Philippines was going to be a crisis and we recognized it over 2 years ago" [emphasis original].[149] The members of the East Asia Informal Group had watched developments in the Philippines with an eye toward both threats and opportunities, noting that Marcos had underreported the strength of the communist New

People's Army (NPA) but also that the protest movement was now receiving the support of the anticommunist Catholic Church.[150] Shultz had encouraged the search for new sources of stability beyond Marcos—and the Asia hands pursued them.[151]

The priority on democratic transition was clear in Wolfowitz's testimony to Congress in November 1984: "Our interest in the bases and our interest in democratic reform are complementary, not mutually exclusive. We are convinced that democratic reform is essential to thwart a Communist victory that would end at one stroke both our hopes for democracy in the Philippines and our access to these vital facilities."[152] Wolfowitz's view was then echoed in the same hearings by the Pentagon's Armitage: "My appraisal today is unchanged from my testimony in earlier hearings; that is, absent a comprehensive program of economic revitalization, political liberalization, and reinstitution of military professionalism, we can see a situation of strategic stalemate in 3 to 5 years in the Philippines."[153]

Reagan, however, was still reluctant to abandon a friend and ally the way Carter had abandoned the shah of Iran several years earlier.[154] In NSDDs on policy toward the Philippines in January and February of 1985, the principals agreed that "while President Marcos at this stage is part of the problem, he is also necessarily part of the solution," and they approved a strategy "to set the stage for a peaceful and *eventual* [emphasis added] transition to a successor government" by quietly supporting "responsible members of Marcos' party, the businessmen and professionals, the Catholic hierarchy, the military professionals, and responsible members of the democratic opposition."[155] The breaking point then came in February 1986, when Marcos rigged an emergency election against Aquino's widow, Corazon, prompting large-scale "People Power" protests across the country. Shultz finally convinced the president that if the United States did not now drop Marcos, "the extremist opposition to Marcos will take over from Aquino and eventually bring Marcos down. The U.S. will then face a radicalized Philippines. And that could well lead to another Vietnam."[156] On February 25, Shultz announced that the United States would be the first country to recognize Cory Aquino as the president of the Republic of the Philippines, while four U.S. helicopters took Marcos and his family to Clark Air Base for a flight to Guam and exile.

Just at the moment the United States turned the corner in the Philippines, Korea threatened to enter a new round of instability. The previous democratic crisis had been resolved by freeing Kim Dae-jung, but the

Korean military had brutally suppressed large protests in Kwangju in 1980 and kept martial law in place, while resentment against both the military and the United States seethed. In 1986, the fractured opposition forces in the Korean National Assembly finally united under one party and presented Chun's government with a petition for direct elections. Chun initially agreed to talks, but as opponents continued to take to the streets, he suspended all debate on reform in April 1987 and then announced on June 10 that he had chosen former General Roh Tae-woo to be his successor.[157] The streets of Seoul erupted in larger and more violent protests, with radical pro–North Korea agitators targeting American institutions like the Chamber of Commerce.[158] Publicly, administration officials such as Gaston Sigur professed their confidence in Korea's democratization, arguing that "the Koreans on their own can do this. They have got the institutions . . . they simply have to put them to work, and there has got to be the will on the part of both the government and the opposition to do it."[159] Privately, Jim Lilley (now ambassador in Seoul) and other U.S. officials made it clear that if Chun resisted democratic reforms, he could lose American support just as Marcos had.[160] With waning support among the middle class and confronting a credible political threat from friends in the United States—and facing the reputational pressure of hosting the 1988 Summer Olympics—General Roh took matters into his own hands and announced on June 26 that he would support free and direct elections for president the next year. Aided by division in the opposition camp, he won reelection in Korea's first free and fair election and was then replaced in the next two elections by the original leaders of the opposition.

Many factors led to democratization in Korea and the Philippines, including the importance of the middle class in Korea and the Catholic Church in the Philippines; the ability of Aquino, Kim Dae-jung, and others to push their followers toward nonviolent protest; and overreach by the authoritarian leaders in both countries. In addition to these factors, the role of the United States must be considered instrumental. Critics on the left charge that the United States obstructed a more natural path to democratization because of the military presence in both countries, though these critics are unable to point to any direct causality or answer the question of how communist expansion would have been resisted otherwise. Neorealist observers such as Robert Tucker assert that neither Carter nor Reagan cared substantially about democratization, and the 1980s therefore represented only "the triumph of continuity over change and of interest over ideology."[161] That is also wrong. By 1980, Carter had largely abandoned his earlier idealism in the name of security. What Reagan did was to fuse interests and ideals; to focus on strengthening the institutions of freedom rather than just weakening the hold of authoritarian leaders; to ensure that allies were better governed at home so that they would be more resilient against imperialism from abroad; and to stay on the right side of history. Carter's strong credentials on human rights did not sway authoritarian leaders in Asia—Reagan's strong credentials on national security did.

The impact of the Korean and Philippine examples was enormous. In Taiwan, democratic activists illegally formed the Democratic Progressive Party in 1986, and the ruling Kuomintang (KMT) abandoned martial law the next year. The success of Korea's military and economy once the generals removed themselves from politics would later send a powerful signal to other men in uniform running Indonesia and Burma as those countries transitioned toward democracy. As Jefferson, John Quincy Adams, and Mahan argued, "moral" questions did bear on American legitimacy, credibility, and power in the Pacific. Shultz's statement to Congress in January 1985 has stood the test of time: "It is no accident . . . that America's closest and most lasting relationships are its alliances with its fellow democracies."[162]

REAGAN'S LEGACY IN ASIA STRATEGY

Beginning in 1969, Richard Nixon had sought an "even balance" in Asia. Whereas Dulles had been suspicious of multipolarity, Nixon and Kissinger saw opportunity in a more pluralistic world. In an age when the U.S. share of global GDP had sunk from half to one-quarter, Nixon understood that it would be sufficient to sustain American preeminence in *relative* rather than absolute terms. Reagan did not change that, but he did do something that Nixon knew and forgot and Carter never fully understood: he built his Asia strategy around closer integration with maritime allies, a robust forward presence, support for free trade and democratic values, and recognition of China's integrity and security as being important to the overall stability of the region. Surrounded by maritime strategists in the Mahanian tradition, Reagan saw China as one element but not *the* element in a successful approach to the region. In a focused mission to roll back the Soviet communist threat to Asia, Reagan went further toward overcoming the tensions between Europe and Asia, Japan and China, forward defense lines, self-determination and universal values, and free trade and protectionism that had confounded U.S. policies so often before and have since.

After initial strategies of containment were shattered in Tet, Nixon had stemmed the tide of American retreat from Asia, but he had not built a strategy or even imagined one to achieve victory in the Cold War. Carter cemented the most important pillar of Nixon's new equilibrium by normalizing relations with China. But it was Reagan who created a picket fence centered on Japan and extending to the Indian Ocean, with the major democracies better governed and secure and confident in Washington, and Soviet proxies and partners like Vietnam and India defecting from Moscow. Reagan leveraged these maritime and ideational advantages to attack Moscow's center of gravity and greatest weakness—the corrosion of communism on the state, economy, and society. And so a decade that had begun with unprecedented Soviet power projection into Northeast Asia, mad submarine runs at the U.S. West Coast, threatening air and naval bases in Vietnam, and agitprop to encourage neutralism among U.S. allies ended with the pillars of the Soviet empire crumbling. For the second time in history, the United States had prevented a rival hegemon from dominating Asia.

In order to sustain an undisputed American leadership position in relative rather than absolute terms, however, Nixon, Ford, Carter, and Reagan all required powerful states to emerge in Asia that also opposed Soviet expansion. China, Japan, and India all filled that role and were essential parts of the regional geometry that reversed and eventually undermined Soviet expansion. When the Soviet Union collapsed, relative American preeminence became harder to define. Absent the focus of a common Soviet threat, the key question became: American preeminence relative to whom? To a powerful Japan poised to overtake the United States economically? To a China that fundamentally diverged from the United States in terms of neoliberal norms? To an India that still sought greater autonomy and equality vis-à-vis the West?

Over the following decades, American strategy toward Asia would drift—until it became clear precisely how challenging it would be to sustain an open and stable Pacific order for the remainder of the twenty-first century.

Asia's Emerging Multilateral Architecture

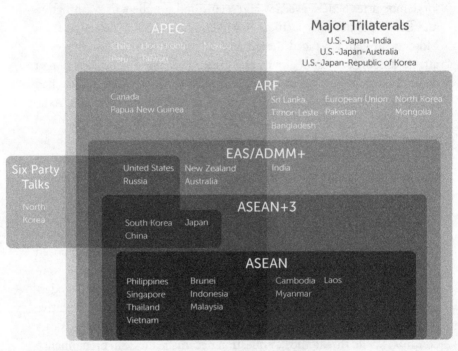

PART FOUR

THE RISE OF CHINA

At 9:00 A.M. on May 30, 2015, U.S. secretary of defense Ashton Carter rose to the podium in the Island Ballroom of Singapore's Shangri-La Hotel to address the hundreds of defense officials, scholars, and journalists gathered for the Fourteenth International Institute for Strategic Studies (IISS) Asia Security Summit. The American secretary of defense is always the most-quoted speaker at the annual dialogue, but this year the delegates were particularly focused on how Carter would explain American strategy in the aftermath of a string of bold Chinese moves that many thought represented a deliberate assault on the American-led postwar order in the Pacific.

Two months earlier, the front page of the *New York Times* had featured overhead imagery from the Center for Strategic and International Studies showing Chinese construction of six military-type facilities on features in the South China Sea that had previously been only small atolls or underwater coral reefs. Officials of the PLA claimed that these peaceful facilities would be made available for common response to humanitarian emergencies, but as Carter arrived in Singapore, new imagery showed artillery on the man-made islands, plus runways long enough to handle any fighter, bomber, or transport aircraft in the Peoples Liberation Army

(PLA) inventory. When the Philippines and other claimants to the atolls protested this military expansion into areas they once controlled, the Chinese Foreign Ministry spokesmen replied that these were sovereign parts of China and warned "smaller countries" not to make "mischief."

For several years, experts in Washington had debated whether China's increasingly coercive behavior in the East China and South China Seas represented a nationalist reaction to provocations by these smaller claimants or whether Beijing was implementing a more deliberate strategy to assert preeminence within the First and Second Island Chains in order to push the U.S. Navy out of the Western Pacific. American and regional officials had called on Beijing to be more transparent about its intentions, and on May 27—just in time for the Shangri-La meeting—China responded by announcing a new military doctrine. "The traditional mentality that land outweighs sea must be abandoned," stated the English translation read by the delegates seated in the ironically named Island Ballroom, "and great importance has to be attached to managing the seas and oceans and protecting maritime rights and interests." In pursuit of that goal, China would "seize the strategic initiative in military struggle, proactively plan for military struggle in all directions and domains, concentrate superior forces, and make integrated use of all operational means and methods." Since Deng Xiaoping's time, China's grand strategy had been guided by the maxim that China should "hide its power and bide its time." That restrained era of Chinese foreign policy was clearly coming to an end.

In welcoming the delegates to the dialogue the night before Carter's address, Singapore's prime minister, Lee Hsien Loong, said what everyone in the hall already understood: "Realistically speaking competition between major powers is unavoidable. The question is what form this competition will take."

The audience now turned to Carter for the answer. He spoke deliberately and with confidence. The United States "would continue to fly, sail and operate wherever international law allows," he asserted, noting that the construction of an artificial island with an airstrip did not confer sovereign rights or permit restrictions on air and maritime transit. He put China on notice that its actions were a cause of concern to many nations represented in the room, reminding Beijing of the expanded defense cooperation almost all of them were now seeking with the United States in response to Chinese coercion. He reiterated his personal commitment to "rebalancing" U.S. forces to the Pacific and pointed to the strong recovery of the U.S. economy.

The speech was well received. The secretary refused to be baited by a PLA colonel who fired a provocative question at him, but also making it clear that Washington took China's rapid militarization of the island disputes seriously and would stand by U.S. allies in the region.

Yet, in the hallways afterward, experts from across the region also began to raise questions. The U.S. Navy was rebalancing to the Asia Pacific, but that meant an increase from the current 58 ships to 64 ships in 2020, while the Chinese were poised to deploy a fleet of over 70 submarines and 170 major surface combat vessels in the same time frame. And although it was true that most countries in the region wanted closer relations with the United States, Chinese money still talked. Despite urging a cautious approach to allies in response to Beijing's proposal for a Chinese-led Asian Infrastructure Investment Bank (AIIB), for example, Britain, South Korea, and Australia had all broken ranks and joined the bank in March. Only Japan and the United States now sat outside the new Chinese institution, uncertain what to do next. The obvious answer was to finish and ratify the Trans-Pacific Partnership (TPP), which would have locked all the region's major economies other than China into a U.S.-Japan–centered trading framework, but the necessary trade legislation was still inching its way through the U.S. Congress because of strong resistance from protectionists in the House.

After a period of drift in the post–Cold War world, American policy-makers had recognized that the rise of China constituted the greatest challenge to an open Asia-Pacific order, and since the mid-1990s there had been a broad bipartisan consensus that the United States could manage this new challenge with a combination of "engaging" and "balancing" China as Beijing's power accrued. That was still the basis for Carter's confidence at Shangri-La, but the margin for error now seemed much narrower indeed.[1]

The Search for Strategy After the Cold War

When the Cold War ended in 1991, virtually no strategic thinkers anticipated that within a decade China would emerge as the central challenge to American preeminence in the Pacific. There was no Spykman predicting that an erstwhile Eurasian ally would become a new strategic competitor after victory, and no Mahan pushing for consolidation of maritime powers to protect the Pacific against the challengers from the continental heartland.[2] Such thoughts were too encumbered by history and power dynamics associated with a different era. History had ended, Francis Fukuyama famously wrote in 1989, asserting, like many other scholars, that the great ideological and major-power clashes that had characterized world affairs since the United States became a republic were over. Even the navy embraced this newest fad in international relations when the Cold War ended, declaring that the "world has changed dramatically" in its September 1992 white paper.[3] Instead, strategists at the outset of the post–Cold War era were distracted by minutiae, in the words of Jeremi Suri, trying to "make a cake from crumbs—to find some coherent unity in a fragmented, incoherent, post–Cold War world."[4]

It was another moment in international relations that required identification, as the Army War College manual on strategy teaches, of that which is "old" but still relevant, that which is "old" and no longer relevant, and that which is "new" and relevant.[5] With the fall of the Berlin Wall in November 1989, the administration of George Herbert Walker Bush focused its grand strategy in Asia and the Pacific on preserving that which was *old but still relevant*. Despite enormous political pressure at home to recast Japan as an economic threat and China as an intolerable suppressor of human rights and moral adversary of the United States, Bush expended considerable political capital sustaining a forward military presence, free trade, cooperative relations with Beijing, and a close U.S.-Japan alliance. He failed to articulate the conceptual framework for these policies, which ultimately contributed to his defeat in the 1992 election (when Ross Perot siphoned off votes around the issues of trade and internationalism), but he preserved the instruments of American power and influence in the Pacific that his successors would need.

Bush's successor, William Jefferson Clinton, focused on what he thought was *new and relevant*. He promised to reconfigure his national security structure to compete with Japan on techno-nationalist grounds and never again "coddle the butchers of Beijing" as Bush had. But then Clinton came to recognize that not all that seemed new was relevant and not all that seemed old was irrelevant. By the mid-1990s, Japan's economy was stuck in neutral and China had surprised the region by bracketing Taiwan with missiles in an unexpected show of strength. Clinton's response, which built on investments made by his predecessors, was characterized best by one of the principal architects of his new strategy, Harvard professor Joseph Nye. The United States would "engage and balance," Nye explained, bringing China into the World Trade Organization but discouraging revisionist behavior on China's part by revitalizing the U.S.-Japan alliance.[6] This yin and yang strategy was supplemented by a fuller embrace of regional multilateralism, including the first region-wide Asia Pacific Economic Cooperation (APEC) summit and new sub-regional groupings to deal with North Korean nuclear proliferation.

Every president since Clinton has essentially followed the same line. George W. Bush centered his Asia policy on Japan and transformed relations with India to sustain a favorable strategic equilibrium in Asia, but he also initiated new strategic and economic dialogues with China. Barack Obama elevated the framework of dialogue with China to include half the U.S. cabinet in an integrated "Strategic and Economic Dialogue" and then announced a "pivot" to Asia that essentially represented a return to balance-of-power diplomacy in Southeast Asia as that region came under increased Chinese pressure. In a contradictory era of increased economic interdependence and growing great-power rivalry, the logic of engaging and balancing remains compelling.

Yet a strategy that combines both reassurance and deterrence is always fraught with challenges. Such a strategy does not lend itself to the clarion call of containment. It requires senior policymakers who know Asia well enough not to be sidetracked by crises in Europe or the Middle East. It requires sustained attention not only to China but to the region as a whole, particularly Japan and Korea, and increasingly India and Southeast Asia. It requires a nuanced understanding of the importance of the offshore island chain and a credible but agile approach to forward military posture and definition of America's forward defense line. It requires a sustained commitment to free trade and a consistent and realistic stance on democracy and human rights. In short, it requires recognition of the need to shape a favorable balance of power as well as the idiosyncrasies that have confounded statecraft in pursuit of that objective throughout American history.

Strategists on Asia should not despair. To be sure, regional strategies cannot be detached from global strategy, and since the Cold War, the United States has flailed from "engagement and enlargement," to "the Global War on Terror," to the amorphous "restoring respect for America." None quite fit for Asia. At the same time, however, a bipartisan consensus has emerged around the broad strategy to engage and balance in order to sustain American primacy in the region over this same period. Moreover, the number of Americans who say Asia is the most important region to U.S. interests vaulted from 21 percent in 1994 to over 50 percent beginning in 2012.[7] Meanwhile, the United States has generally succeeded in strengthening alliances, expanding partnerships, and laying the groundwork for an open and inclusive multilateral diplomatic architecture to link North America and the Pacific. As a result, over the past four decades, there has been an expansion of democratic norms in Asia, and the collapse, contraction, or revision of communist and totalitarian states. This successful outcome explains why historians grade almost every recent U.S. president *highest* on their Asia policy.[8] Despite massive inefficiencies in U.S. policy-making toward Asia, the net result has been effective.

However, strategists on Asia should also be nervous, for as a trans-Pacific community of rules-oriented nations has emerged, so has China's absolute and relative power and Beijing's apparent willingness to use coercion against its neighbors, whatever the regional rules or norms may be. In short, the engage and balance strategy has worked, but it is not certain that it will succeed in the end. As a result, the margin for error in American statecraft toward Asia is narrowing, and the costs of a historical and inconsistent stewardship of U.S policy will rise. Part 4 of this study continues the history of American Asia strategy through the first twenty-five years of the post–Cold War era—from George H. W. Bush, to Clinton, to George W. Bush, to Obama—in anticipation of the concluding chapter and its review of lessons learned in a new era of competition for regional leadership.

12. "THE KEY TO OUR SECURITY AND OUR PROSPERITY LIES IN THE VITALITY OF THOSE RELATIONSHIPS"
GEORGE H. W. BUSH AND THE UNIPOLAR MOMENT, 1989–1992

George Herbert Walker Bush was one of the best-prepared presidents in American history regarding foreign policy (though Dwight Eisenhower and John Quincy Adams could certainly vie for that honor).[1] He brought to office experience as the youngest navy fighter pilot in the Pacific during the Second World War; as a member of the U.S. Congress; as the top U.S. diplomat in China; as head of the CIA; and as vice president to Ronald Reagan. His breeding and survival in combat and politics made him an internationalist but also an "incrementalist" and "pragmatic conservative"—the "guardian of Reagan's legacy" who "wanted to promote democracy, but not at the risk of war."[2] These characteristics served the United States and the world extremely well as the Berlin Wall fell in 1989 and the Bush administration midwifed the unification of Germany, the transformation of Europe, and then the peaceful collapse of the Soviet Union.[3] Bush's deep internationalism and network of personal relationships around the globe also explained his success mobilizing a Democrat-controlled Congress and a coalition of thirty-four nations to reverse Saddam Hussein's invasion of Kuwait in 1990–1991.

In Asia, where the end of the Cold War brought as many complications as it did benefits, Bush focused on conserving U.S. power and preserving U.S.

relationships, alliances, and institutions. His first overseas trip as president was to East Asia, which now accounted for half of U.S. trade. Bush's geopolitical instincts toward Asia were well honed. He knew China but was not the "inveterate China-lover" his opponents sometimes portrayed.[4] As UN ambassador during Nixon's opening to Beijing, Bush had fought hard to retain UN membership for Taiwan (he had not been read into Kissinger's secret negotiations with the PRC). Then, during the 1980 campaign, he had played a key role in reassuring Beijing that the Reagan administration would not reverse the overall terms of normalization, despite the Republican candidate's strong attachment to Taipei.[5] The common denominators in both cases were loyalty and an aversion to rapid shifts in foreign policy.

Bush was probably inclined toward the Nixon/Kissinger view that the United States needed China rather than the Reagan/Shultz view that China needed the United States.[6] He felt no animus toward Japan from his experience in the war, but as one contemporary Asia staffer on the NSC concluded, Bush felt "the Chinese were more like us" than the Japanese were, and he would have looked to advancements in U.S.-China relations as his main legacy in Asia had the Chinese government's use of force against protestors in Tiananmen Square not occurred.[7] Bush certainly did not pursue China relations at the expense of Japan, nor did he envision a bipolar Sino-U.S. condominium in the region. The Bush administration's National Security Strategy documents always opened the Asia section by highlighting, as Reagan had, that Japan was the cornerstone of U.S. strategy in Asia. During his first trip to the region, Bush made a point of stopping in Japan before visiting China. Again, loyalty and preservation of the institutions of American power were of central importance to his worldview.

All of Bush's national security team generally shared these same instincts. At the outset of the administration, former Carter NSC Asia senior director Mike Oksenberg called them the most experienced leadership on China policy in American history.[8] National Security Advisor Brent Scowcroft and Secretary of State James Baker both recall in their memoirs the close and cohesive working relationship at the top of the administration—a deliberate contrast to the disorganization of Reagan's policy-making process and the backbiting and infighting that had characterized the Nixon, Ford, and Carter presidencies.[9] Other historians, however, have dismissed the Bush team as mere "technocrats" compared with previous conceptual strategists such as Kennan or Kissinger.[10]

Like the president, Secretary of State Jim Baker argued that the United States "must work in close concert with its friends and allies," but his real skill was as a tough negotiator, which did not always endear him to America's partners. He began his job at State with only cursory knowledge of China (by his own admission) and a demonstrated disinterest in Japan, which he visited no more often than he visited the capital of Kazakhstan while serving as secretary.[11] Like Kissinger and Haig before him, Baker considered China the centerpiece of U.S. strategy in Asia.[12] However, after the 1989 Tiananmen incident, he chose to leave China policy almost entirely to the White House.[13] His assistant secretary of state for East Asia and Pacific Affairs, Richard Solomon, was a veteran of the Nixon and Ford NSCs and the Policy Planning staff, and a noted China scholar, but he focused most of his attention on crises and opportunities in Southeast Asia and broader regional multilateralism.[14] Among Baker's powerful inner circle on the seventh floor of the State Department, Counselor Robert Zoellick emerged as a leading thinker on Asia's emerging multilateral diplomacy, and Deputy Secretary Lawrence Eagleburger served as the White House China liaison, but the rest focused primarily on Europe and the Middle East. The U.S. ambassador in Beijing, James Lilley, was closest of all to Bush on China policy, with ties going back to Yale, the Skull and Bones secret society (reputedly), and service together in China in the early 1970s.[15]

For his part, Scowcroft could have been the chief strategist on China policy, and he had both the experience under Ford and the expertise on his staff with Senior Director Douglas Paal, a former intelligence officer with a PhD in East Asian languages from Harvard. However, Scowcroft chose to be an honest broker and confidant of the president rather than an activist national security advisor in the tradition of Kissinger or Brzezinski.[16] On Japan, Scowcroft's instincts were generally negative like Baker's, and he confessed in his memoirs that he found Japan "probably the most difficult country" with which he had to work. Ultimately, the president, who knew the leadership in Beijing, relied on his own instincts on China.[17] He treated the Japanese leaders with respect and courtesy but little apparent enthusiasm. Security alliances in Asia were largely managed by the Defense Department, where Secretary Richard Cheney and JCS Chairman Colin Powell focused on preserving American forward presence in the Pacific at a time of momentous changes in Europe. Serious clashes between the Pentagon and State Department over Asia were a rarity.

Despite knowing more than any of his predecessors about the region, Bush never publicly articulated a longer-term vision for Asia and the Pacific. In part, this was a matter of temperament, but it also reflected the rapid changes in the international system that occurred during his presidency. Bush's first National Security Strategy, in 1990, declared the end of containment.[18] But what would come next? As John Lewis Gaddis noted in *Foreign Affairs* in the spring of 1991, "the passing of the Cold War world by no means implies an end to American involvement in whatever world is to follow; it only means that the nature and the extent of that involvement are not yet clear."[19]

Over the four years of Bush's presidency, four different answers to what the new system would look like appeared. In year one, the Cold War was still on but waning; in year two, a "new world order" based on a return to the UN and collective security seemed to have been born with the Gulf War; in year three, the Soviet Union collapsed and American unipolarity emerged; and in year four, a deep and sudden U.S. recession seemed to imply American decline and threw the Bush administration's Asia policy into turmoil. It was an extremely confusing time. Long after the Bush presidency, international relations scholars continued to debate what that era of unipolarity meant to American foreign policy. As a group of leading theorists asked in 2001: "What is the character of domination in a unipolar distribution? If world politics is always a mixture of force and consent, does unipolarity remove restraints and alter the mix in favor of force? Is a unipolar world likely to be built around rules and institutions or based more on the unilateral exercise of unipolar power?"[20]

For its part, the Bush administration eschewed the phrase "unipolarity"—choosing instead to argue in the March 1990 National Security Strategy document that bipolarity would likely be followed by increased "multipolarity and interdependence."[21] Yet, for half a century, U.S. internationalism had been premised on resisting an adversary determined to undermine global order. Recognizing that the Pentagon could not plan in a world without adversaries, JCS Chairman Colin Powell began work on a "base force concept" that would keep the United States ready to deter or defeat regional rogue powers, such as Iraq or North Korea, that were increasingly armed and capable.[22] At the core of the concept would be somewhat reduced forward deployed forces in the Atlantic and Pacific, backed by highly mobile contingency forces in the United States.[23] Bush approved Powell's strategic concept in late June 1990 and outlined the new strategy in a speech at Aspen, Colorado, on August 2—

the day Saddam Hussein invaded Kuwait. The Gulf War validated, at least for the moment, the focus on regional rogues, which also preserved a win-win context for relations with the other *major* powers in the system.[24]

However, the NSC's National Security Strategy and the Pentagon's base force concept did not put to rest the strong impulse to search among the other major powers for potential threats to U.S. unipolarity. This became evident on March 7, 1992, for example, when the *New York Times* leaked sections of the Pentagon's draft biannual Defense Planning Guidance (DPG) with the headline, "U.S. Strategy Plan Calls for Insuring No Rivals Develop."[25] The unfinished draft candidly pointed to the need to hedge not just against regional rogue states but also against the rise of *any regional rivals*—including particularly India, China, and Japan. The DPG was later sanitized in its final form, but it nevertheless revealed deeper conceptual undercurrents in the national security bureaucracy that contradicted the administration's public expression of confidence in a more multipolar international system.

Meanwhile, new academic and political arguments took hold asserting that the United States would lose its primacy if it did not shift to the techno-nationalist definition of national security allegedly being employed by erstwhile allies like Japan. Laura D'Andrea Tyson and the Berkeley Roundtable on the International Economy (BRIE) led the academic charge against the Reagan-Bush era laissez-faire economic policies, pointing to Japan's success at government-led industrial policy as the new definition of geostrategic primacy.[26] These ornate Schumpeterian theories of shifting international power were translated into the popular consciousness by commentators and politicians such as James Fallows, Chalmers Johnson, Paul Tsongas, and Richard Gephardt, all of whom quipped that the Cold War had ended "and the Japanese won."[27]

Bush would not take the bait—from either the national security bureaucracy or the economic nationalists. American post–Cold War strategy would be about building ties with all the major powers, not forming blocs against them or pursuing zero-sum techno-nationalist policies. As Scowcroft put it in a speech in 1992, "the key to our security and our prosperity lies in the vitality of those relationships."[28] Yet, in Asia, the most important relationships were under pressure. In the first two years of his administration, Bush was put on the defensive on China policy because of Tiananmen, and for the last two years, he struggled to preserve U.S.-Japan relations amid a worsening recession. In the end, Bush left a strong legacy on which his successors could rebuild U.S. engagement with Asia,

including workable if bruised relations with China and Japan, a sustainable forward military presence, and the beginnings of a trans-Pacific
trade architecture. At the time, however, his conservative focus on preserving relationships looked defensive and reactive. It stood alone without an overarching conceptual framework for foreign policy, particularly in Asia. "I don't do the vision thing," the president famously said in
1987, and in Asia it hurt him.

"The Time for Reasoned, Careful Action": China Policy and Tiananmen

When Bush took office in January 1989, the U.S.-China bilateral relationship appeared to be on a positive trajectory. Diplomatic, economic, military, and cultural exchanges were all expanding, and the strategy of
gradually enmeshing China into the existing international system looked
promising, with continued economic liberalization and Beijing's preparations to enter the GATT (General Agreement on Tariffs and Trade).[29]
Military-to-military cooperation had reached a high-water mark, with the
United States upgrading Chinese F-8 fighter jets under the "Peace Pearl"
project started in the Reagan years. There were problems to be sure: U.S.
economic sanctions had failed to deter China from selling Silkworm missiles to Iran; U.S. business investors were hitting obstacles in the Chinese
market; and human rights abuses continued. Still, Deng Xiaoping's liberal deputies, Hu Yaobang and Zhao Ziyang, appeared ready to make the
gradual reforms without U.S. pressure. This suited Bush, who as Baker
noted was determined "to end the oscillation between [the] extremes of
confrontation and fascination" that had characterized U.S.-Chinese relations since 1945.[30]

The president made his first visit to China during his swing through
Asia in February 1989, hoping to solidify U.S.-China relations, encourage
reform, and preempt the Sino-Soviet rapprochement expected with
Gorbachev's visit to Beijing that May.[31] On the strategic front, Bush was
largely successful, with Deng reassuring him that there would be no res-
urrection of the old Sino-Soviet alliance and declaring that he wanted to
see U.S.-China economic ties expand.[32] But there were also hints of new
trouble as well. Deng took a hard line on U.S. interference in China's internal affairs, and Chinese authorities then blocked dissident physicist Fang

Lizhi from attending the official U.S. Embassy dinner for the president. Rather than speak out on behalf of democratization in China, the White House instead blamed Ambassador Winston Lord for inviting Fang in the first place.[33] Tellingly, criticism of Bush's apparent disdain for human rights came not only from the traditional defenders of Taiwan on the right but now also the leadership of the Democrat-controlled Congress.

The Fang Lizhi incident was a small harbinger of what followed on June 4, 1989, when Deng and hard-liners in the Communist Party leadership ordered Peoples Liberation Army (PLA) armored and airborne units into Tiananmen Square in Beijing to evict students and other citizens who had been protesting for greater democracy since the death of Hu Yaobang that April. Hundreds were killed when the PLA used live ammunition on the protestors—and the world was left with the indelible image of one defiant man halting an oncoming tank, armed with nothing more powerful than a handful of groceries and a willingness to die for his convictions. The assumptions about China seemed broken, the West was outraged, and a Democrat-controlled Congress now had its cudgel to go after the realpolitik Republican strategies of the Bush administration. Relations between the United States and China entered the greatest crisis since 1971.[34]

The Bush administration was not ignorant of the democratic values at stake: Eastern Europe, Taiwan, Korea, and the Philippines were all in the middle of their own democratic transitions, and congressional views could not be ignored.[35] Nevertheless, the president's instinct was to preserve as much of the U.S.-China relationship as possible, prioritizing geostrategic and personal leadership ties over human rights concerns.[36] At a news conference on June 5, Bush outlined his policy: "This is not the time for an emotional response," he started, "but for a reasoned, careful action."[37] He would later write that, "for this understandably proud, ancient, and inward-looking people, foreign criticism (from peoples they still perceived as 'barbarians' and colonists untutored in Chinese ways) was an affront, and measures taken against them a return to the coercions of the past."[38]

In order to show the Chinese leaders and the U.S. Congress that the United States could not continue with business as usual, but in a way intended not to obstruct the core of U.S.-China relations, on June 29 Bush temporarily stopped all high-level exchanges with China, instituted a number of economic and financial sanctions, and suspended military sales.[39] When Baker appeared to implement a longer-term halt to senior-level diplomatic interaction, the president reacted angrily, and the secretary of state "dropped the China policy account like a hot potato."[40] The president then secretly sent Scowcroft and Eagleburger to Beijing in late July 1989 in order to reopen the lines of communication with China's leaders. Deng scoffed at any notion that China should accommodate democratic demands from the Chinese people or send a positive signal on the issue to the West, but Scowcroft came away from his meetings in Beijing confident that he had conveyed the president's intention to keep the door open to dialogue despite the enormous differences over human rights and democracy.[41]

Nixon and Kissinger also came to the aid of the White House. "No government in the world would have tolerated having the main square of its capital occupied for eight weeks by tens of thousands of demonstrators who blocked authorities from approaching the area in front of the main government building," Kissinger argued in the *Washington Post* in August 1989, acknowledging the brutality of the response but urging a calm consideration of the strategic interests at play in U.S.-China relations.[42] Kissinger's foray into the debate brought further fire from the Democrats in Congress, including the influential chair of the House Asia Subcommittee, Stephen Solarz, who pointed out in the *Washington Post* the next week that China was no longer important to counterbalance the Soviets and needed to be held accountable for its actions.[43] With so much at stake in personal and strategic terms, Nixon and Kissinger then traveled to Beijing in November 1989 and returned with the report that China remained "essential to the balance of power of both Japan and the Soviet Union in Asia" and must be looked to as an ally in the future rather than as an adversary over Tiananmen.[44] At Nixon's urging, Bush sent Scowcroft and Eagleburger on a second trip to Beijing at the end of the year. Again, Deng held firm against the request for some softening of the Chinese attitude to help placate Congress, and responded by demanding American loans and technology to expand economic ties.[45] Worse yet, Scowcroft was photographed toasting Deng at a welcoming banquet, causing a public outcry back in the United States and prompting a *Washington Post* opinion editorial from (now) former ambassador Winston Lord criticizing the administration's feigned indignation and calling for a more "balanced" approach to China.[46]

The White House had called for an unemotional and strategic perspective on Tiananmen. In fact, both Solarz and Lord had provided one—pointing out that the balance-of-power logic that had driven the

Nixon opening to China was no longer salient from eith€
Chinese perspective. It was a mistake to argue—as Nixon c
United States needed China to balance Japan. This was a lev
litik that would not resonate, even with the ongoing U.S.-Japa
ficulties. The Scowcroft trips—although important in terms
a channel open—gave the appearance that the administratio. ...vught
the United States needed the relationship more than China did. The pursuit of strong relations with China absent a larger strategic construct for
Asia led to steps that left the administration politically vulnerable at
home, ultimately putting the relationship at greater risk.

That became apparent in January 1990, when the Democrat-controlled
Congress came back into session flush with indignation at the president's
China policy.[47] The Berlin Wall had come down the previous November,
and by the end of the next year, the Soviet Union itself would collapse.
Both Reagan and Bush had attempted to wean U.S.-China relations from
the original unifying factor of anti-Soviet balancing, but now the consequences of losing that disciplining geostrategic consideration were
becoming apparent. No longer could the White House expect to dictate
China policy without congressional approval. So although Bush held firm
against congressional legislation aimed at China—bucking domestic sentiment to veto a bill sponsored by Congresswoman Nancy Pelosi that
aimed to extend visas for Chinese students in the United States who did
not want to return home (particularly sensitive in Beijing, where students
had led the protests)—he had a much harder time on trade, where the
Constitution gave greater authority to Congress.[48]

At stake was most favored nation (MFN) status for China, which had
to be renewed every year by the president because of the 1975 Jackson-
Vanik Amendment to the 1974 Trade Act with respect to communist
trading partners. The Soviet Union, not China, had been the original target, but now failure to grant a waiver for Beijing would have put high
tariffs on China's $12 billion in exports to the United States and inevi-
tably lead to countermeasures against U.S. companies in China.[49] Declaring that "America must not allow the principle of freedom and
democratic discourse to become a victim of Chinese governmental tyranny," Pelosi led the assault in Congress.[50] Bush vowed to veto any effort
to override his waiver for China and appealed to strategic concerns,
arguing that protectionism would have no positive effect on the human
rights situation and would alienate the United States from key allies in
Asia and on the UN Security Council.[51] He ultimately turned the corner

by appealing to the business community and enlisting pro-trade demo-crats like Senator Max Baucus of Montana. The president renewed MFN status at the last minute, on May 25, 1990, and then only after the Chinese had agreed to buy $2 billion in Boeing airplanes and release Fang Lizhi to the United States.[52] China was also desperate to repair the relationship, as lending to China fell by 40 percent after Tiananmen and foreign direct investment shrank by 22 percent.[53] As Warren Cohen notes, the debate over extending MFN status finally "awakened China's leaders to the terri-ble cost of alienating the United States" in a way that Bush and Scowcroft had failed to do through personal diplomacy.[54]

By 1991, Congress was distracted by the Gulf War, and U.S. investment, student exchanges, and subcabinet-level visits to China returned to pre-Tiananmen levels.[55] China supported economic sanctions in response to Saddam's invasion of Kuwait; the Chinese Foreign Ministry worked in concert with the State Department to end the conflict in Cambodia; and China was flexible about joint entry with Taiwan and Hong Kong into the new Asia Pacific Economic Cooperation (APEC) forum in 1991.[56] But something fundamental had changed. Military cooperation came to a complete halt, and there was no progress on political liberalization after the release of Fang Lizhi, particularly with congressional pressure off and with Europe and Japan rapidly moving past sanctions to new investment and technology deals.[57] President Bush also took steps over Beijing's objec-tions that he might not have made before Tiananmen, including a meeting with the Dalai Lama and a decision to sell F-16 fighters to Taiwan in Sep-tember 1992. Finally, the administration pressured China harder on intel-lectual property rights issues and defied Beijing's wishes by agreeing to Taiwan's entry into the GATT before Beijing's.[58]

Sinologist Harry Harding summed up his history of U.S.-China rela-tions in 1992 by stressing that in the future, "Rather than portraying Sino-American relations as a pure convergence or a complete divergence of interests, as was often the case in the past, it will be wiser to portray them as a mixture of complementary and competitive objectives. Such a relationship will be primarily characterized not by antagonism, nor by harmony, but rather by hard bargaining with complicated trade-offs within and between issues."[59]

This would be precisely the more balanced relationship that Solarz and Lord had called for in the immediate aftermath of Tiananmen, but the Bush administration was forced into it by domestic pressure rather than strategic foresight. The president was right to stop the congressional assault on MFN, for a trade war with Beijing would have done strategic damage not only to U.S.-China relations but also to America's position in Asia as a whole. However, absent a new strategic framework for China policy after the Cold War, the president faced alternative definitions of U.S. interests from new constituencies in Congress, which fueled contentious debates in the 1992 presidential election campaign and led to a dysfunctional China policy in the first years of the Clinton administration.[60] In short, the pursuit of continuity in China policy compounded the problem of discontinuity.

"The Japanese Don't Have Nuclear Missiles Pointed at Us": Protecting the Linchpin of the Maritime Strategy

Bush's first National Security Strategy (NSS), in 1990, declared that the emergence of Japan and Germany as global leaders had been a success for U.S. policy. The subsequent 1991 NSS then included an entire section dedicated to explaining the importance of these two allies' roles in the international system after the Cold War. Japan, these core strategic documents announced, would remain the "centerpiece" of U.S. Asia strategy. Yet officials also worried that America's key alliance in Asia had lost its moorings with the collapse of the Soviet threat. Two developments in particular would undercut the strong success of Reagan's partnership with Japan: the shift from trade friction to techno-nationalist confrontation, and Japan's inability to step up as an ally during the Gulf War.

The reduction of the bilateral U.S.-Japan trade deficit in the late Reagan years had temporarily relieved some political pressure in relations with Tokyo, but at the same time, the rapid appreciation of the yen after the 1985 Plaza Accord had prompted Japanese firms to undertake dramatic expansion of overseas operations, particularly in the United States.[61] The Japanese themselves displayed a new arrogance, with senior trade officials arguing that the revalued Imperial Palace grounds were now worth more than the entire state of California, and economists in Tokyo predicting Japan's GDP would surpass the United States' by 2005.[62] Public opinion surveys in 1990 found that more Americans (64 percent according to a June 1990 survey) saw Japan's economic power as a threat than felt threatened by Soviet military power, and Michael Crichton's 1992 xenophobic murder mystery *Rising Sun*, about a Japanese corporation's dominance of American technology and politics, became a best seller.[63]

Bush was affected politically by these trends, convening a small cell to review Japan policy during the transition, but he did not waver in his fundamental commitment to free trade.[64] In his inaugural address, he equated free trade with free speech, free elections, and "the exercise of free will unhampered by the state."[65] The president had a strong distaste for protectionism. He ended Reagan's voluntary restraints on the Japanese auto, steel, and machine tool industries, and twice he vetoed protectionist legislation aimed at the textile industry.[66] Although he allowed his trade representative, Carla Hills, to wield the threat of "Super 301" sanctions against Japan under the 1988 Omnibus Trade Bill, he hoped that stronger multilateral rules and enforcement mechanisms would allow him to reduce U.S. reliance on resorting to such punitive measures. Indeed, Hills and the rest of the administration were worried that the self-generating sanctions contained in Super 301 legislation might spark a self-destructive trade war.[67] Instead of sanctioning Japan, the Bush administration pursued a handful of symbolic Super 301 cases while seeking other outlets to contain the economic problem with Japan.

The first of these outlets to manage the Japan problem was the ongoing Uruguay Round of the GATT, which the administration hoped would bring Japan more substantially into the maintenance of an international free trade regime that would open agriculture, services, and high-technology products—competitive exports not fully covered by existing multilateral trade rules.[68] Rather than leading in the GATT negotiations, however, Japan proved obstructionist. As the American ambassador in Tokyo, Michael Armacost, recalls, Japan's negotiating tactics "were a logical means of defending their nation's commercial interests, but they provided dispiriting evidence that Japan's leaders were unprepared to incur significant political risks to facilitate an agreement."[69]

The second outlet was the administration's proposal for a bilateral Structural Impediments Initiative (SII). Recognizing that neither the appreciation of the yen nor the threat of Super 301 were addressing the pervasive structural problems in U.S.-Japan economic relations—namely nontariff barriers in Japan and the enormous imbalance between Japanese and American levels of saving and investment—the Treasury Department began to prepare plans for a massive effort to attack the specific distortions in the Japanese, and ostensibly American, economic policies.[70] Carla

Hills and the USTR's office embraced the proposal, since it provided a way to push for market opening without the risky weapon of Super 301.[71] The Japanese government also welcomed the initiative, hoping to bog down U.S. officials in dozens of subdialogues. In fact, the wide-ranging SII talks surprised the Japanese government because the Japanese public sided more often than not with the American proposals once they understood the benefits they would enjoy as consumers from a more open market. The talks helped to spark a broader Japanese economic debate and led to several concrete steps to ease imports, such as passage of a new law governing large retail stores in Japan.[72]

However, neither the GATT nor SII mollified a U.S. Congress increasingly frustrated with Japan's reticence and alarmed at the collapse of manufacturing in the American Midwest's "rust belt." Within the administration, free traders and national security experts split with economic nationalists. "Certainly they're allies and friends," acknowledged Commerce Secretary Robert Mosbacher, "but they have been beating us 50-to-zip as far as trade goes."[73] As higher U.S. interest rates and the shock of Saddam Hussein's invasion of Kuwait in 1990 combined to send the global economy into recession, desperate White House political advisors began to side with the economic nationalists. In December 1991, on the way to fiftieth anniversary commemoration ceremonies at Pearl Harbor on board Air Force One, they handed the president a draft speech that bashed Japan's economic policies and promised to protect American jobs. A frustrated Bush tossed the draft in the trash and handwrote his own speech more fitting to the solemn occasion.[74] Instead of attacking Japan, he praised Prime Minister Miyazawa Kiichi's statement of remorse and evoked the past to warn against a return of isolationism and protectionism after the Cold War.[75]

Still, Bush could not fully stem the tide of protectionism, for the politics of the trade imbalance were being made immeasurably more complex by Japan's apparent dominance over technologies once controlled by the American defense sector. The Pentagon's decision to help Japan build its own indigenous fighter jet for the first time since the war sparked particular outrage "as the Japan threat transformed from the irritants of trade to an apparent challenge to America's military advantage."[76] The 1988 National Defense Authorization Act had required the Pentagon to clear U.S.-Japan defense technology cooperation with the commerce secretary and the U.S. trade representative in order to ensure protection of the American industrial base—and Congress used the amendment to grill the new administration's nominees for key positions about Japan's new FSX jet in 1989.[77] Media pressure also mounted, with *Business Week* asking on its March 27, 1989, cover, "Can the Pentagon Keep Shielding Japan?" and the *New York Times* declaring U.S. policy toward Japan "so confused and uncoordinated that many American officials say they cannot figure out how it is made or why economic concerns are regularly subordinated to military and political objectives."[78] An exasperated Defense Department official tried to convince the *Times* that they were picking the wrong enemy, pointing out that "the Japanese don't have nuclear missiles pointed at us!"[79] Eventually, the administration pressured Japan to transfer phased-array radar and composite technologies back to the United States in exchange for basing the new FSX jet on the American F-16 airframe.[80] Indeed, the FSX turned out to be the high-water mark of Japan's pursuit of an indigenous jet fighter, since the complexity of integrating advanced fighters had outpaced Japan's specific advances in subsystems and components. None of that mattered in the early 1990s, however—Japan's technological dominance appeared unstoppable.

During the Reagan years, the economic threat from Japan had been offset by the contributions Japan made in containing the Soviet Union. Japan's defense budget had increased by 1.6 times during the 1980s (compared with 1.4 times for the United States), and Japan covered 40 percent of the costs to host U.S. troops stationed on Japanese soil. Globally, Japan contributed to U.S. strategy by increasing official development assistance (ODA) from $2.22 billion in 1984 to $8.96 billion in 1989—providing an economic boost to frontline states in the Cold War, such as Pakistan and Turkey.[81] By the time of the Bush administration, Japan was second only to the United States in underwriting global institutions such as the United Nations and the World Bank.

With the collapse of the Soviet Union, however, Japan was no longer a frontline ally, and the ability of the self-defense forces to bottle up the Soviet Navy in the Far East proved largely irrelevant when the next big crisis hit—Saddam Hussein's August 1990 invasion of Kuwait. Used to avoiding explicit commitments of troops for anything other than the direct defense of Japan and to funding development assistance only after careful bureaucratic vetting, the Japanese government was caught flat-footed by the Gulf crisis. A strong leader like Nakasone might have found a way around those obstacles, but instead Japan was led in 1990 by a weak prime minister sitting atop a Liberal Democratic Party that was itself adrift as the end of Cold War ideological divisions and years of corruption eroded its raison d'être. Prime Minister Kaifu Toshiki was thus genuinely stunned when President Bush dismissed his government's prompt action to freeze Iraqi bank accounts after the invasion of Kuwait as insufficient. "My bottom line," Bush told the Japanese prime minister in a phone call several days after the Iraqi invasion, "is that when this chapter of history is written, Japan and the U.S. and a handful of other countries will have stood side-by-side."[82] Kaifu's panicked government responded by hastily cobbling together a new plan to send doctors, transport planes, ships, and other equipment to the Gulf, but most of the pledges fell apart as they met bureaucratic and political resistance in Tokyo. With U.S. pressure mounting and Japan unable to step up, the Japanese Foreign Ministry spokesman reluctantly stated that his nation would pledge "$1 billion; and not a dollar more!"[83] Secretary of State Baker, the master negotiator, then squeezed $13 billion out of Japan in operation "Tin Cup"—a huge sum, but one rendered so reluctantly that Japan was criticized around the world for its risk-averse "checkbook diplomacy."

To be sure, Kaifu's weak leadership was a major factor in Japan's poor performance, but Japanese decision-making also suffered from the absence in Washington of trusted interlocutors from the Reagan years such as Shultz, Weinberger, Armitage, and Sigur.[84] The essence of alliance management, as Shultz liked to say, was like gardening, but few senior officials under Bush had made such investments in the alliance with Japan. Baker was a dealmaker, not a gardener, and he was focused on getting results in the war against Saddam, *not* on shoring up alliances in the Pacific. To squeeze the $13 billion commitment out of Tokyo, he brought with him senior members of Congress who promised protectionist legislation to cover the costs of the war if Japan did not step up and provide funding itself. This blunt instrument proved effective in the short term but was hardly an efficient style of alliance management for the longer term. The president had hoped the Gulf War would showcase the relevance of the U.S.-Japan alliance after the Cold War, but instead it showcased the weaknesses on both sides.[85]

Bush's difficulty settling on a durable post–Cold War vision for the U.S.-Japan alliance became most evident on his last official visit to Tokyo as president, in early January 1992. With its poll numbers collapsing as the recession hit home, the White House had been putting off the trip, but it finally invited twenty-one CEOs of major U.S. corporations, including Detroit's Big Three automakers, to come along. "No longer do you hear him uttering psalms to free trade and the global partnership between the U.S. and Japan," wrote a cynical *Business Week*, quoting the "new Bush" as promising "to be sure that the trade is fair and continuing to get fairer."[86] In Tokyo, the president caught the flu and vomited on Prime Minister Miyazawa before international cameras during the emperor's state dinner in his honor.[87] The image of the president hawking auto goods, noted Thomas Omestad, an associate editor of *Foreign Policy*, "seemed to confirm a loss of international status to the Japanese, who offered their pity but little that was tangible."[88] After twelve years of Republican rule, the largely liberal American press hammered Bush, with cartoons of U.S. autos flying off the deck of an aircraft carrier commanded by the Second World War veteran and splashing harmlessly into the Pacific.[89]

Bush was absolutely right on strategic and economic grounds not to overreact to the protectionist pressures on the U.S.-Japan relationship, but he was caught in the transition to a new era in trade politics. As Richard McCormack, his undersecretary of state for economic affairs, later reflected:

> Because of our primary strategic role in coordinating the global Cold War effort of the free world, trade policy took a distinctly second-tier supportive function during much of that period. We were anxious to see a prosperous world, integrated into an overall global economic system that would be supportive of our beliefs and values. We did not always attempt to wring the last possible concession out of our trading partners during the earlier part of that 25-year period, and by and large we succeeded in spreading prosperity around much of the globe. . . . Because of the vast superiority of the American economy during the earlier part of that period, there were only limited constraints upon American presidents in managing trade policy. But as prosperity spread and the Cold War became history, opposition to dramatic expansions of access to the American market began to build, adding increasingly heavy political burdens in selling the policy to the American people.[90]

The irony was that Japan's economic model had already begun to collapse when the Tokyo Stock Exchange fell 35 percent from January to December 1990—but perceptions took several years to catch up with economic reality. In the interim, Bill Clinton promised to take on the Japanese challenge based on Tokyo's own strategies for targeting high-tech industries.

He would later abandon those ideas, but not before using them to help win the 1992 presidential election.

Preserving Forward Posture After the Cold War

Facing domestic pressure on the China and Japan relationships after the collapse of the Cold War structure, the Bush administration recognized that even more worrisome questions were building about the future of the U.S. forward military presence in the Pacific. The United States had contracted its forward military posture in the immediate aftermath of both the Pacific war and Vietnam War, and it was logical to many members of Congress that the same might be expected after the demise of the Soviet Union. When Democratic senator Alan Dixon of Illinois declared in a hearing on Asia in February 1990 that the U.S. military only kept troops in Korea because it had a "Holy Roman Empire complex," the administration knew it had a problem.[91] Rather than wait for Congress to force cuts, Cheney and his deputy assistant secretary for East Asia, Carl Ford, went to sympathetic members such as Senator John McCain to ask that Congress demand that the administration prepare a strategy for forward presence in the Pacific under the FY 1990 Defense Authorization Act.[92] Instead of reacting, as it had in the cases of China and Japan, the administration took the initiative.

In its official response to Congress in the 1990 East Asia Strategic Report (EASR), the Department of Defense made the case that with the end of superpower confrontation, the "traditional aspect of our military presence in the region—the role of regional balancer, honest broker, and ultimate security guarantor—will assume greater relative importance to stability."[93] This was particularly true, the Pentagon report noted, because U.S. trade across the Pacific was now 50 percent larger than trade across the Atlantic, or as Admiral Huntington Hardesty of CINCPAC put it, "our interdependence is such that regional instability could disrupt growth, alienate allies, and jeopardize our economic vitality."[94]

However, with expectations high for reduced defense expenditures, the Department of Defense had to choose where it could make changes. On the Korean Peninsula, the 1990 EASR promised to "shift U.S. forces from a leading role to a supporting role, and to reduce as possible our force level in Japan while maintaining essential bases which enable us to provide regional stability and deterrence in Northeast Asia."[95] Worried about congressional interest in pulling all remaining U.S. forces out of Korea (and a return to the Carter administration's self-inflicted crisis in Asia policy), the Pentagon and State negotiated an agreement with Seoul in 1991 under which Korea would pay a third of U.S. forces' own base costs.[96] In the Philippines, the report admitted that a reduction of about 2,000 personnel "may be possible" but stressed that Clark and Subic Bay still formed a "cornerstone of our regional basing structure and military presence."[97] Overall, the report called for a careful "phased approach" to force reduction, informed by "caution and innovation" that would allow the United States to respond to "global and regional reactions." In Phase I, over the following three years, the United States would reduce its current force of 135,000 by 14,000–15,000; Phase II (years three through five) would see larger force reductions; and Phase III (years five through ten) would see forces stabilize at a somewhat lower level. By promising conditions-based reductions but underscoring the administration's commitment to forward presence, Cheney and Ford put a floor under domestic pressure and reassured nervous allies overseas.

In 1992, the Defense Department issued its second EASR, this time reflecting a renewed North Korean threat and the breakdown of base negotiations with the Philippines.[98] With respect to Korea, the report announced suspension of planned "Phase Two" ground force withdrawals from the peninsula because of the North's nuclear weapons program and the need to compensate for allied apprehension about the withdrawal of U.S. tactical nuclear weapons from the Pacific (discussed later).[99] The bases in the Philippines, on the other hand, had gone from the "cornerstone" of forward presence to a diplomatic and political liability. Negotiations being led by Armitage on extending the U.S. lease for Clark and Subic Bay were making little headway with the government of Corazon Aquino and her rambunctious young democracy. Clark was returned to the Philippines in November 1991 after damage from a massive volcanic eruption rendered the air force base largely useless (and the government of the Philippines kept insisting on the same price nonetheless). The next month, the Philippine Senate rejected the administration's best offer for extending the naval base at Subic Bay. From the Pentagon's perspective, the bases had lost their strategic importance with the end of the Vietnam War, the collapse of the Soviet Union, and the imperative to preserve forward posture elsewhere as defense budgets decreased.[100] The navy announced that it could replace the lost ship-repair facilities in Japan and pledged to sustain a presence in Southeast Asia thanks to Singapore's offer to provide access to Changi Naval Base for U.S. ship visits in 1990.[101]

Once a critical link in the U.S. strategic concept of an offshore island chain defense, the Philippines now found itself largely alone as the final piece of the disengagement from Southeast Asia that had started with Nixon's Guam Doctrine. Within a decade, however, Manila would again come under pressure from China, and the decade after that the United States would be pivoting back to Southeast Asia in the continuing struggle to define the proper line for forward U.S. presence in the Western Pacific. Nevertheless, for the time being—and in a period of enormous uncertainty about the nature of international order and the role of the United States—Bush had managed to avoid what might have been yet another self-defeating debate about where America should draw its forward defensive line in the Pacific.

Managing the New Dynamics and Unfinished Business of the Cold War in Asia

While Bush focused on preserving forward presence and trying to stabilize ties with the two major Asian powers, he also faced a mix of old and new problems in the region that resulted from the demise of Soviet power. China and the Korean Peninsula were still divided, and Southeast Asia struggled with the aftershocks of Cold War competition, but the collapse of the Soviet Union also allowed states to realign in ways that offered new diplomatic solutions to old problems as well as new movement on broad Asian multilateralism. Though basically conservative in its instincts, the Bush administration generally moved adroitly to seize these new opportunities while reinforcing the commitments that had underpinned American credibility and influence throughout the Cold War—though some of the most dangerous developments, such as North Korea, were passed on to the next president unresolved.

On the Korean Peninsula, the shift from bipolarity to unipolarity highlighted the promise and peril of the emerging system. On the positive side, the ROK and DPRK simultaneously entered the United Nations on September 17, 1991, and the North and South signed a nonaggression pact (called "The Basic Agreement") in December 1991 and then in January 1992 issued a joint agreement banning the acquisition or use of nuclear weapons on the Korean Peninsula.[102] The Bush NSC and State Department had a quiet but critical role in shaping the outcome of all three steps forward.[103] Particularly important was President Bush's announcement on September 27, 1991, that the United States would unilaterally remove all tactical nuclear weapons from surface warships, attack submarines, and tactical aircraft. Though initially prompted by concerns about the large number of U.S. and Soviet tactical nuclear weapons still deployed around the world, the announcement also removed Pyongyang's excuse for refusing safeguards inspections under its 1985 agreement with the International Atomic Energy Agency (IAEA).[104]

Yet at the same time the demise of the Soviet Union drove Pyongyang to pursue overtures to the West to offset increased dependence on China, the systemic changes also had the effect of accelerating Kim Il-sung's quest for autarkic security through nuclear weapons. The Pentagon had concluded at the beginning of the Bush administration that the current balance of overall military forces on the peninsula continued to favor the North.[105] When the IAEA finally conducted inspections of the North's Yongbyon facility in May 1992, it found significant discrepancies in North Korean accounting for plutonium harvested from the reactor.[106] Meanwhile, the North was continuing a crash program in ballistic missiles, including the construction of 450–500 SCUDs. Despite the promise of simultaneous entry of both Koreas into the UN and the North-South agreements, the Bush administration would leave office in 1993 with North Korea on the verge of crisis over proliferation—a crisis that would never be fully resolved. In handing over the State Department to Warren Christopher, Baker raised only one issue of significant concern in Asia— the Bush administration's failure to curb the DPRK nuclear program.[107]

With the end of the Cold War, there also seemed to be some promise for improvement in cross-Strait relations, but it soon became apparent that the strategic equilibrium between Beijing and Taipei was shifting in destabilizing directions. In 1990–1991, China introduced new weapons systems aimed at Taiwan, including ballistic missiles and new fighter aircraft such as the Sukhoi Su-27 from Russia. James Lilley, the U.S. ambassador in Beijing and Bush's closest confidant on China policy, recommended new arms sales to Taipei in response and followed through on that recommendation when he returned to Washington to assume the post of assistant secretary of defense for international security affairs, overcoming objections in the State Department, where the sale was

considered a violation of the Third Communiqué.[108] Bush's announcement on September 2, 1992, at a General Dynamics factory in Fort Worth
that he would approve the sale of 150 F-16 A/B fighters to Taiwan was met
with raucous applause by the workers who made the jet—and deep cyni-
cism by reporters counting electoral votes in Texas—but it was also based
on real concerns about a shifting military balance against Taiwan,
which would become a more serious challenge for the next president.[109]

In Southeast Asia, the democratic wave unleashed in the late Reagan
and early Bush years hit the rocks as Burma's military junta, the State Law
and Order Restoration Council (SLORC), overturned the 1990 election
victory of democratic forces and imprisoned the opposition's leaders, including the iconic Aung San Suu Kyi. In response, the administration took
a harder stance on Burma than it had toward China after Tiananmen—
both because it could do so without strategic risk and because Tiananmen
had made it politically necessary to do so. Secretary Baker condemned the
regime's political brutality, suspended the U.S. textile agreement with
Rangoon, and called (mostly without success) for other states in the region
to take similar steps.[110]

Meanwhile, in Cambodia, Assistant Secretary Solomon was given
broad latitude to pursue a comprehensive peace settlement, via the UN
Security Council, that would end Chinese military assistance to the
Khmer Rouge; establish a political process under then Prince Sihanouk
that would create a new government through UN-supervised elections;
and end Vietnam's ongoing pursuit of regional hegemony. More broadly,
through the Cambodia peace talks, Solomon aimed to build constructive
patterns of cooperation with Beijing and to support ASEAN's efforts to
stabilize the region.[111] Here, the end of the Cold War structure opened
important new possibilities, and Solomon succeeded on every count.
Complex negotiations among eighteen parties began in Paris in the summer of 1989 and yielded an agreement in October 1991 that gave the United
Nations full authority to supervise a cease-fire, disarmament of factional
armies, repatriation of displaced Khmer, and preparations for national
elections. The largely successful effort also opened the door for the United
States and Vietnam to establish a "road map" to normalization, which
resulted in the establishment of diplomatic relations in July 1995.[112]

With India, the Bush administration proved somewhat more resistant
to new thinking after the Cold War. Whereas Reagan's NSC had seen
India's rising power as reinforcing a stable equilibrium in Asia, the Bush
administration's draft DPG had argued for a policy to "discourage Indian

hegemonic aspirations over the other states in South Asia and on the Indian Ocean."[113] There were modest changes that resulted from the end of the Cold War: the ruling Congress Party abandoned its Soviet-oriented socialist economic model and began slowly opening to international investment and trade in order to keep up with China. India also remained neutral during the Gulf War, normalized relations with Israel in 1992, and agreed to regular bilateral U.S.-India "Malabar" naval exercises.[114] However, the undertone of mistrust toward Indian strategic intentions expressed in the 1992 DPG never fully dissipated in Washington. "I can't say that the end of the Cold War brought any greater interest in Washington in India," lamented William Clark, Bush's ambassador to Delhi at the time, "We [still] saw India as the embodiment of Krishna Menon and the Indians saw the U.S. as the embodiment of John Foster Dulles."[115] Though the 1990 NSS had predicted greater "multipolarity and interdependence" rather than unipolarity, the Bush administration's stance toward India indicated the limits of how useful the White House really saw the rise of new poles like India in the international system.

Finally, with the easing of East-West tensions, the rise of the European Union, and the first stirrings of a free trade agreement in North America, calls for a new multilateral regime for Asia intensified in the Bush years. This time, the proposals came not as a way to break U.S. bilateral alliances but instead from America's closest ally in the region. In January 1989, Australian prime minister Bob Hawke proposed the idea of an East Asian free trade organization focused on "open regionalism"—tellingly without mentioning the United States as a member.[116] Whereas the Reagan administration's review of regional debates on multilateralism had concluded that Washington could take an evolutionary approach, Baker and the State Department reacted to Hawke's proposal with noticeable urgency.

With his counselor Bob Zoellick in the lead, Baker prevailed on the Australians to invite the United States to the inaugural ministerial meeting of the new Asia Pacific Economic Cooperation group in Canberra in November 1989 (along with Australia, Japan, Canada, South Korea, New Zealand, Indonesia, Malaysia, the Philippines, Singapore, Thailand, and Brunei). Together these member states accounted for half the world's output and a third of global trade. By 1991, APEC had added Taiwan, China, and Hong Kong, and was building considerable momentum. However, as Baker notes in his memoir, "agitation for an exclusively East Asian trading bloc refused to go away."[117] Malaysian prime minister Mahathir Mohamad continued to promote his anti-Western East Asian Economic Community (EAEC) and drew support from ASEAN member states and trade hawks within Japan and Korea who were tiring of U.S. economic pressure.

Baker recognized that "the U.S.-Japanese partnership was key. If the partnership held, then freer trade and investment through APEC was not only possible but likely. If it fractured, an East Asian trading bloc was a virtual certainty."[118] To be sure, Baker had not invested in alliance maintenance with Japan, but he unleashed all of his considerable negotiating acumen to kill the EAEC, reminding Korean counterparts, for example, "that it was Americans, not Malaysians, who had shed their blood for Korea forty years before."[119] In the end, the EAEC survived, with the last "C" changed from "Community" to "Caucus" by anxious Japanese, Korean, and Singaporean officials eager to avoid an open trans-Pacific rift in the region's emerging multilateral architecture.[120] Intra-Asian and trans-Pacific formulas would continue to compete, but Baker, the cool-handed Texan, took great pride in laying the foundation for APEC and the open trans-Pacific architecture that all of his successors would champion in that contest.[121]

"We should be attentive to the possibilities for multilateral action without locking ourselves into an overly structured approach," Baker noted in *Foreign Affairs* in December 1991 with APEC in mind. But the bottom line was clear: Washington's priority was the hub and spokes of U.S. alliances and forward presence in the region. Baker and Bush were focused more on preserving the old and relevant than on embracing the new and yet untested. As Baker emphasized in his *Foreign Affairs* piece, "What was a secondary aspect of our Cold War–era security presence is becoming the primary rationale for our defense engagement in the region: to provide geopolitical balance, to be an honest broker, to reassure against uncertainty."[122]

GEORGE H. W. BUSH'S LEGACY IN ASIA STRATEGY

It appeared axiomatic for the Bush administration that until the United States understood what was truly new about the international system in the post–Cold War era, the world's greatest power must not let itself become a source of *instability* or *uncertainty* in a region so critical to the global economy. In the end, Bush deserves enormous credit for avoiding passing fads and for leaving in place workable if bruised relations with China and Japan, a sustainable forward military presence, and the early elements of a trans-Pacific economic architecture. Every one of his successors eventually returned to the building blocks he left in place.

However, the historic American role in Asia was not just—as Baker asserted in *Foreign Affairs*—"to be an honest broker" and "to reassure against uncertainty" by remaining a predictable force in the region. Missing from that formulation was a concept of how U.S. policy might actively *shape* the region's future in order to reinforce the liberal, rules-based order so critical to U.S. interests. George H. W. Bush came to office with ambitions for U.S.-China relations but less thought to how alliances might be harnessed or new relationships built with major powers freed from the Cold War, such as India. Perhaps in the political context of the times, sustaining key relationships was accomplishment enough, but it left the president looking defensive and reactive in Asia at a time when he was being given credit for unifying Germany and transforming Europe. Not surprisingly, Bill Clinton and Ross Perot attacked Bush in the 1992 presidential campaign not on Europe policy but on Asia.

13. "ENGAGE AND BALANCE"
BILL CLINTON AND THE UNEXPECTED RETURN
OF GREAT-POWER POLITICS

When he became president, Bill Clinton was already a man steeped in internationalism. He had majored in international relations at Georgetown University and studied at Oxford as a Rhodes Scholar. He had worked for the preeminent internationalist of the U.S. Senate, fellow Arkansan William J. Fulbright. As governor of Arkansas, Clinton had led trade missions to Japan and Taiwan. Yet despite this pedigree, Clinton's internationalism was colored first by his political instincts—and it was clear that the American people were ready for some relief at home after the Cold War. "I refuse to be part of a generation that celebrates the death of communism abroad with the loss of the American Dream at home," he declared when announcing his candidacy in Little Rock on October 3, 1991.[1] Popular bumper stickers that year read "Saddam Hussein still has his job—what about you?"[2] "It's the economy, stupid," Clinton's chief political advisor reminded him throughout the campaign, and by focusing on an activist theme of government intervention to help American workers, he survived dangerous political scandals and secured the presidency with only 43 percent of the vote on November 4, 1992, aided in large measure by the antitrade third-party candidacy of Ross Perot, which siphoned votes away from Bush.

ded much grist for Clinton's rhetorical mill, with conse-
lations across the Pacific to follow. Though not a protec-
rot, Clinton seized the mantle of economic nationalism
promising to establish a National Economic Council (NEC)
mulate Japanese-style industrial policies.[3] He criticized
Bush's nostalgia "for a world of times past, when foreign policy was the
exclusive preserve of a few aristocrats," and he attacked the incumbent for
"coddling tyrants" after Tiananmen.[4] With the Gulf War no longer in the
headlines and Clinton's own Vietnam War–era ambivalence about the
military as background, he implied that the United States could and
would spend less on defense.[5] He waxed eloquently about new cost-saving
opportunities to use multilateral forums like the Asia Pacific Economic
Corporation (APEC) in Asia before perplexed but impressed debate audiences in New Hampshire.[6] Like lite beer commercials that were popular at
the time, his foreign policy promised to be great tasting and less filling.

Clinton displayed impressive contextual intelligence—always an
important ingredient for effective strategic thinking. When power or circumstances changed, he was quick to make adjustments in his approach.
His intellectual eclecticism also made for a more inclusive coalition of
Democratic Party foreign policy visions. Yet that same intellectual agility and inclusiveness meant that he came to office with conflicting priorities in foreign policy and sent confusing signals to friends and foes about
his real bottom line. A telling early statement to Congress on the administration's Asia policy in March 1993 listed ten policy objectives for the
region, ranging from engaging China to settling the Cambodia issue,
but was prefaced with the caveat that the objectives were "not listed in any
order."[7] Clinton had criticized Bush for not having a coherent strategic vision beyond the verities of the Cold War, yet it is even more difficult to
define a coherent and consistent Clinton doctrine. When asked to serve as
secretary of state during the transition in 1992, Colin Powell declined
because he had "no clear idea" where Clinton really stood on foreign policy
or defense issues.[8]

Clinton's national security team reflected the intellectual eclecticism
displayed by the president himself. The *New York Times* described them
collectively as "an ideological peacock made up of every wing of the
Democratic Party."[9] Very few of the top officials came with significant
experience on Asia policy, but they did recognize the centrality of Asia
to much of the new president's economic and foreign policy thesis and
argued he should make the region a priority after Bush's preoccupation

with Europe.[10] In keeping with that theme, Clinton made Japan his first overseas visit, in February 1992.

Broadly speaking, there were three groups of foreign policy experts around Clinton, each reflecting the president's evolving views on the world. Most influential at the outset were the idealists. Clinton's first national security advisor, Tony Lake, had won fame in Democratic Party circles for quitting Nixon's NSC over Cambodia and had spent part of his time in the political wilderness working on human rights issues, "as if to atone"—according to the *National Review*.[11] Lake saw himself as a "pragmatic neo-Wilsonian" and asserted democracy promotion as a central tenet of Clinton's early national security strategies.[12] His former NSC colleague Winston Lord was brought in to be assistant secretary of state for East Asia and Pacific affairs because of his deep experience with the region but also because of his outspoken criticism of Bush's realpolitik approach to China after Tiananmen. Madeleine Albright, appointed first as ambassador to the United Nations with cabinet rank and in 1997 as secretary of state, considered the "most pressing order of business for Clinton's foreign policy in the first term" to be genocide, though her focus was on the Balkans and Africa rather than Asia.[13] The idealists' overarching vision for the post–Cold War era was an expansion of the community of democratic nations and a clearer American voice on human rights.

On the other flank were the economic nationalists. They believed that the Reagan and Bush administrations had been losing the real geostrategic competition to countries such as Germany and Japan because of a doctrinaire Republican unwillingness to retaliate against unfair trade practices or to champion key technologies and industries at home. Leading up to the election, Clinton's first chair of the Council of Economic Advisors, Laura D'Andrea Tyson, published a series of monographs and books with titles like *Who's Bashing Whom?* that argued for a more aggressive American industrial policy.[14] Elsewhere, Brookings scholar Kenneth Flamm had developed policy proposals for the United States to beat Japan at its own game by demanding commercial technology transfers (in flat-panel displays, semiconductors, etc.) in exchange for continued U.S. support for Japan's defense capabilities. Flamm was appointed to a senior post in the Pentagon, where he launched the "Technology-for-Technology" (TfT) Initiative based on his theories.[15] Attorney W. Bowman Cutter was placed in charge of international trade at the NEC and developed bilateral trade negotiating strategies with Japan premised on the assumption that the supposedly statist Japanese government could deliver targeted market shares for U.S. exports the way Tokyo had once appeared to deliver targeted dominance in certain technology sectors.[16] Whereas the idealists saw a spreading community of democracies, the economic nationalists viewed leading democratic allies as major adversaries and the source of American decline.

Clinton himself had free trade instincts and preferred to copy Japan rather than enter into a trade war. Indeed, he disappointed the most hardline "revisionist" critics of Japan by not appointing them to senior positions in the new administration. Nevertheless, cabinet members such as Commerce Secretary Ron Brown and U.S. Trade Representative Mickey Kantor championed the economic nationalists' agenda, and even the erstwhile free trade State Department bent to the economic nationalist winds, as Secretary of State Warren Christopher promised that he would "harness our diplomacy to the needs and opportunities of American industries and workers" and then appointed economic officers to run the Japan Desk in lieu of the traditional political/military experts.[17] For the first few years of the Clinton administration, the U.S. government became a giant laboratory for theories of Japanese economic development and state-driven innovation—until those theories were eventually proven wrong in analysis and practice.

The third group—and ultimately the one to which Clinton's contextual intelligence drove him—were the traditional national security realists. The most senior was Vice President Al Gore, a veteran of the Senate Armed Services Committee and a player in national security decision-making in the Situation Room in the way that Richard Nixon or George Herbert Walker Bush had been as vice presidents.[18] Gore's focus, however, was primarily on Europe and the Western Hemisphere, and in Asia he had a number of missteps when he took the public stage.[19] Samuel "Sandy" Berger, a Yale Law School classmate of the president, was appointed deputy national security advisor to Tony Lake and then national security advisor because of his extensive trade experience with the law firm of Hogan & Hartson. As the administration matured, he became a steady hand on national security policy overall.[20] Lord, though brought in because of his views on human rights, also became an important voice for a more disciplined Asia policy, as one would expect of Henry Kissinger's former aide.

Ultimately, however, the return to strategic realism was led from the Pentagon, where officials were less enamored of faddish theories of international security (though there was briefly an assistant secretary of defense for democratization at the outset of the administration) and more attuned to the health of American alliances and emerging political and military threats abroad. The first secretary of defense, Les Aspin, had been a successful leader on the House Armed Services Committee but proved to be a disastrous manager at the Pentagon. His deputy and successor, William Perry, brought a seasoned understanding of Asia and a team of strategic thinkers that would drive Asia policy overall. Known for his political and bureaucratic savvy and his ability to make quick decisions, Perry quickly filled the role of credible foreign policy spokesman for the Clinton administration in the view of the media.[21] In the Carter years, Perry had led the discussions with China on military-to-military cooperation and had come to see the rise of China as the most important geostrategic development of the coming decades. His intellectual interest in what he later called "preventive defense" led him to combine confidence-building with Beijing and greater security cooperation with America's Asian allies as a hedge—the central construct that would guide U.S. Asia strategy in the years to come.[22]

Perry recruited senior officials to the Pentagon who knew Asia or shared his strategic views. His first assistant secretary for international security affairs (responsible for all policy outside of the former USSR) was Charles Freeman, a leading China hand in the State Department, who ensured continuous military-to-military engagement with the Peoples Liberation Army (PLA) even as U.S.-China relations spun in circles in the first year of the administration. Freeman's successor, Harvard professor Joseph Nye, had coined the term "soft power" in 1990 to argue for a holistic measure of national strength that encompassed military, economic, and reputational aspects of foreign policy strategy.[23] He had long experience with Japan and took a particular interest in the country during his first job under Clinton as head of the National Intelligence Council. When he moved to the Pentagon in 1994, he turned to fellow Harvard professor and national intelligence officer for East Asia Ezra Vogel for advice on how to revitalize the U.S.-Japan alliance. He then named another junior faculty colleague from Harvard, Kurt Campbell, to be his deputy assistant secretary for East Asia. Though Campbell had done his academic work on Russia, Nye selected him because he had demonstrated an aptitude for getting things done in the unruly Clinton White House. And Nye intended to get things done with respect to Asia policy.

Secretary of State Warren Christopher had served in the navy in the Pacific and claimed that his "life and career in California" had led him to believe that "American foreign policy was too Eurocentric," but he was generally seen in Asia as being preoccupied with the Middle East and Europe and brought little innovation or coherence to strategy toward the Pacific.[24] His successor, Madeleine Albright, was more activist but also appeared to Asian counterparts as focused primarily on other regions.

It is difficult to trace a clear strategic "debate" in the Clinton administration—the process resembled more of an unruly scrum as bad ideas were sorted out and the economic and national security realists steadily asserted themselves. Whereas Bush's strategic vision had been modest but implemented with consistency, collegiality, and predictability— Clinton confused Asian governments with bold but constantly changing definitions of U.S. interests that varied based on personalities and domestic U.S. politics. Clinton meandered between protectionism and free trade, Japan and China, defense cuts and robust forward presence, and Europe and Asia. His administration was a parable of the need for coherent conceptualization of strategy. Yet through a process of trial and error, Clinton midwifed a dual strategy of engagement and balancing toward China that defined the subsequent Bush and Obama administrations' overall approach to the Asia-Pacific region. In so doing, he returned to the same principles and foreign policy tools that George H. W. Bush had safeguarded at his own political peril.

THE STRATEGY OF ENLARGEMENT AND ENGAGEMENT

If there was a theme to Clinton's foreign policy at the outset, it was the need to free resources for domestic priorities, and the administration struggled to nest its diverse and contradictory definitions of national security under that single framework. After nine months of internal deliberations, Tony Lake spelled out the logic of the new approach in a speech at the Johns Hopkins University School of Advanced International Studies (SAIS) in September 1993. In the speech, "From Containment to Enlargement," Lake emphasized that although the United States would now prioritize the domestic economy, the administration would lower the overall requirements for security through a new strategy of "engagement, prevention and partnership."[25] "Engagement," he explained, could be expanded as opposing blocs gave way to a more open international system; "prevention" could be achieved through democracy promotion, economic growth, free markets, and respect for human rights; and "partnership" would help to shift to allies more of the burden for their own security. Lake sounded a more traditional note when he reiterated the need for the United States to "avoid the risks" of withdrawal or abandonment of security commitments to allies, but the central theme of his speech was clear: the "primary task" for the United States would now be to strengthen "our society and economy" at home.[26]

The themes of engagement, prevention, and enlargement were elaborated in the Bottom-up-Review (BUR), which was released by the Pentagon the next month. The BUR also flowed from the premise that funding had to be shifted from defense toward domestic priorities. After pushback from outgoing JCS Chair Colin Powell, Aspin proposed in the BUR that U.S. forces be cut by one-third—a larger hit than the one-quarter cut in Bush's base force plan but less than Clinton's political advisors had wanted. In the BUR final report, the Pentagon asserted that even with those larger cuts, the United States could still maintain the ability to deter a foe in one region while responding at the same time to a contingency elsewhere and simultaneously continuing to invest in longer-term capabilities to hedge against the emergence of a major-power foe.[27] This was possible, according to the BUR report, precisely because Cold War–era forward U.S. military bases in Europe, the Middle East, and the Pacific would demonstrate U.S. commitment and provide the infrastructure for rapid responses from a smaller force.[28] The JCS also took some comfort from the fact that many of Aspin's cuts came to missile defense rather than core missions of the services. The most important assumption behind the BUR, however, was that the Pentagon would be able to do more with less because the White House strategy of engagement and enlargement would reduce requirements for the United States to provide security in the first place.[29]

At that point, the White House did not have such a strategy in place. The NSC had initiated a drafting process for a comprehensive National Security Strategy (NSS), but all the major agencies of government had been included, and as a result the White House was still plodding through new drafts each month. The final NSS, "A Strategy of Engagement and Enlargement," was finally published on July 1, 1994, after more than twenty redrafts. Rather than setting priorities, the new NSS simply combined all the contradictory impulses of Clinton's campaign.[30] It would have been better, quipped the principal State Department drafter, Robert Gallucci, to simply call it the "strategy of engorgement." Others in the

State Department quietly referred to the draft as "globalony."[31] Or, as Jeremi Suri observes, the end of the Cold War had given birth to an intellectual conceit that if there was "a messianic new age of American achievement, why should we even think about accepting compromises and lesser evils?"[32] Hard choices in foreign policy were deferred, and domestic politics drove decisions.[33]

Herein lay the fundamental flaw in the administration's concept of engagement and enlargement, for even as Clinton's team asserted that it would reduce the security burden on the United States by enlarging the community of like-minded nations, it was simultaneously launching diplomatic assaults on Japan and China that undercut the prospects for partnerships deemed so essential for the strategy to work in the first place. To some extent, the problems in relations with Japan and China were inherited from the Bush administration. As Sandy Berger recalls, "the administration inherited a bunch of horses that were galloping" with respect to U.S.-Japan and U.S.-China relations.[34] But Clinton was not just reacting to events; he was allowing his national security team to test new theories of political economy, human rights, and security with the major powers in Asia.

The economic nationalists drove the Japan strategy. Their assumptions were based on the revisionist critiques of Japan and U.S. trade policy by academics and journalists in the 1980s.[35] These self-proclaimed revisionists had asserted that Japan's economy operated like a national weapon to weaken other states in the international system and that only Japanese-style industrial policy at home and targeted market opening in Japan would reduce the direct threat posed to U.S. interests.[36] The fact that Japan's economic bubble had burst in 1990 had little impact on their arguments about the invincibility of "Japan, Inc." since the precipitous decline in domestic Japanese demand temporarily fueled the revisionists' logic by ballooning the U.S. bilateral trade deficit with Japan from $41 billion in 1990 to almost $50 billion in 1993.[37]

Pumped up on the rhetoric of the campaign and eager to finally get tough on arrogant Japanese trade officials, the economic nationalists pushed for an approach that was the very antithesis of engagement and enlargement. Though the president himself was more inspired than threatened by Japan, he was intrigued by the revisionists' thesis and held a series of meetings with outside experts who shared their perspective. U.S. Trade Representative Mickey Kantor also began to hold his own "Saturday Group" sessions on Japan with a select group of officials focused on the Japanese economic threat. The expert group included no political or security experts and no Japan experts other than those who already accepted the revisionist thesis.[38] Driven by this unified view, the administration developed a new "results oriented" approach to Japan trade policy, which Clinton explained to visiting Japanese prime minister Kiichi Miyazawa during the two leaders' first summit in Washington, in April 1993.[39] When Clinton paid a reciprocal visit to Tokyo in July for the G-7 summit meeting, he and Miyazawa agreed to initiate a "Framework for New Economic Partnership." Miyazawa assumed that the new bilateral framework would initiate a process that would help Japan avoid U.S. demands for qualitative and quantitative targets for market opening, but Clinton believed the exact opposite: that the framework represented a Japanese commitment to targeted or measurable outcomes.[40] It was a classic case of what Japanese bureaucrats call a *tamamushi-iro*—an insect that looks completely different from opposite angles.

When the Japanese government realized that the new administration intended to demand guaranteed outcomes rather than just a negotiating framework, they balked. The Clinton administration, in turn, made it clear to Tokyo that Japan would not be coddled by national security officials as it had been during the Reagan and Bush years. When Undersecretary of Defense for Acquisition and Technology John Deutch told his Japanese counterparts in Tokyo in October 1993 that joint missile defense development would require targeted technology transfer back to the United States, for example, the Japanese side concluded that defense cooperation had now been subsumed under the economic framework talks.[41] The Americans appeared to be prioritizing jobs over helping Japan defend against nuclear missiles. The bilateral relationship entered a period of friction and mutual antagonism not seen since the Second World War.[42]

The irony of the revisionist framework for demanding targeted results from Japan was that the once powerful Ministry of International Trade and Industry (MITI) no longer had sufficient control over the Japanese economy to deliver the targeted and measurable results promised by Kantor's "Saturday Group." The revisionists had overstated the statist and centralized nature of Japanese economic policy to begin with, and the economic nationalists now missed the significant changes happening within Japan after the collapse of the economic bubble.[43] Rather than acquiesce to an anachronistic if flattering portrayal of its power, MITI fought back, charging the administration with protectionism and appealing to international rules established in the new World Trade Organization (WTO) in

unilateral economic retaliation.[44] The Clinton administration
not only Japan but also the WTO, which had removed Super
heavy artillery from the American unilateral trade arsenal
for liberalization of services and binding arbitration of trade
disputes. Even with the United States threatening stiff punitive tariffs on
automobiles in the spring and summer of 1995, Tokyo held firm, backed by
a sympathetic European Union. The Clinton administration was left with
two choices: a straight-out trade war of sanctions and retaliation, or retreat. On June 28, Kantor and Trade Minister Hashimoto Ryūtarō reached
a last-minute deal that promised only vague compliance and no clear targeted increases for U.S. auto sales in Japan. "Now for the first time," Robert
Uriu concludes in his thoughtful insider's account of the revisionism and
Clinton economic policy, "it was the United States that was forced to give
up on nearly all its demands."[46]

China policy—also a "galloping horse" when Clinton took over—was
similarly beset by domestic politics, poor analysis, and weak foreign policy strategy. As Nancy Tucker points out, China policy had "moved from
a man who personally cared about American relations with China to one
who saw China through the eyes of advisers with competing agendas."[47]
Christopher later acknowledged in his memoirs that Clinton's campaign
rhetoric had left the administration "boxed in" on China.[48]

The core issue was whether to renew most favored nation (MFN) status
for China. After campaigning against Bush on China, Clinton fell in line
with demands from congressional Democrats to link MFN status to
human rights improvements. What followed was a bruising political fight
as different political and policy agendas collided in public. Absolutists
on human rights in the administration and Congress demanded clear criteria for approving MFN that would be driven by human rights, not unlike the measurable trade targets demanded of Japan. Economic advisors, on the other hand, wanted quick approval of MFN as China pulled
out of its Tiananmen hangover and began to grow at double-digit rates.[49]
Lord, who cared about both U.S.-China relations and human rights,
sought ways to measure "overall progress" on specific issues such as emigration from China and reform of prison labor while maintaining "lee-
way" on judgments about whether Beijing had met those conditions.[50]
On May 28, 1993, Clinton temporarily ended the internal policy fight and
took the issue away from Congress by issuing an executive order extending
China's MFN status, with renewal the next year dependent on China's progress on human rights.[51] By July, Lord was leading a State Department re-

view that recommended a policy of "comprehensive engagement" under which other political, security, and economic issues with Beijing would be decoupled from human rights going forward.[52]

Christopher headed to Beijing in March 1994 modestly confident that he could achieve sufficient progress to satisfy Congress before MFN was revisited that summer, but his trip proved to be a setback instead. Unbeknownst to Christopher, Assistant Secretary of State for Humanitarian Affairs John Shattuck had preceded the secretary and had secretly met with prominent dissident Wei Jingsheng in Beijing. Wei then went public about the meeting, and when Christopher himself arrived, the Chinese "blasted the hell out of everybody."[53] Recognizing the disarray within the administration and comforted by the powerful U.S. business voices lobbying in favor of unconditional MFN extension, Beijing stonewalled on emigration, prison labor, and the other human rights issues raised the year before. Allies in Europe and Japan were no help, since they had never signed on to the original U.S. strategy in the first place and were eager to expand their own economic ties with Beijing. In June, Clinton retreated entirely from linking human rights and MFN and authorized a second unconditional extension.[54]

With both Japan and China, then, Clinton turned campaign pledges and untested academic theories into inflexible policies that contradicted his core foreign policy theme of enlargement and engagement. He was right to focus on trade problems with Japan and human rights abuses in China, but his tactics in each case did not fit into a larger strategic concept. Moreover, Clinton misread the most fundamental element of strategy: power. His administration failed to enlist U.S. allies, the business community, or internal Japanese or Chinese political supporters for its agenda, while Tokyo and Beijing each took full advantage of these openings to isolate the trade and human rights hawks in Washington and ultimately force Clinton to back down. The president who had promised to build a bridge to the twenty-first century suddenly found himself back at square one, reacting to events in the region instead of determining outcomes.

On those grounds alone, the first two years of Clinton's Asia policy might be deemed a failure, but in one area Clinton did break significant new ground. From a hint muttered at the New Hampshire primary debate about the importance of APEC, to testimony by Lord in March 1993, and finally in a series of presidential speeches in Tokyo and Seoul that July, Clinton introduced an American vision for trans-Pacific multilateral architecture that changed the debate about future institutionalization of regional economic and security cooperation. Proposing a new "Asia Pacific Community" in Seoul that summer, Clinton offered to host a first leaders' summit for APEC that fall in Seattle, elevating the group to the status of the U.S.-NATO or G-7 summits.[55] In the same speech, Clinton abandoned his predecessors' more rigid adherence to the hub and spoke alliance system and announced that he would embrace a new regional security dialogue being proposed by ASEAN. "Some in the United States have been reluctant to enter into regional security dialogues in Asia," he told his audience in Seoul in a veiled reference to Baker's *Foreign Affairs* article the year before, "but I see this as a way to supplement our alliances and forward military presence, not to supplant them."[56] The next year, the United States would join the new ASEAN Regional Forum (ARF) of Asian foreign ministers as a full member.[57]

Asia policy veterans of the Bush administration were immediately skeptical about Clinton's enthusiasm for multilateralism and predicted that the new ARF would "remain limited in scope and operational significance," while the "Asia Pacific Community" concept would be pulled apart by regional rivalries and economic dynamics beyond the control of the United States.[58] Nevertheless, Clinton deserves credit for channeling regional impulses toward a trans-Pacific rather than intra-Asian framework. Just as important, the commitment to join the annual APEC summits and ARF foreign ministers' meetings (though the latter had been anticipated in the Reagan era) ensured that at least twice a year the Asia hands in subsequent administrations would be able to command the attention of the entire U.S. government as they prepared their principals for the meetings. Whereas Reagan and Bush had tinkered cautiously with multilateralism, Clinton took charge. The contest between the evolving trans-Pacific and intraregional architectures was not over, but the initiative shifted for a time toward Washington.

That said, the administration's new multilateralism was still only one "overlapping plate of armor"—as Clinton put it in Seoul—resting on top of the great-power relationships that continued to define real power and influence in the region. And those relationships were troubled, with a contentious U.S.-Japan alliance, a volatile U.S.-China relationship, and a string of petty fights with Southeast Asia over second-tier issues. Henry Kissinger warned in the *Los Angeles Times* in June 1993 that, on its current course, the administration's disaggregated approach to the region would lead down the road of "splendid isolation" and the growing collision of great powers in Asia at America's expense.[59]

"Malaise," Crises, and Recalibration

On May 5, 1994, national security officials in the Clinton administration awoke to an unwelcome headline in the *Washington Post*. "U.S. Aide Sees Relations with Asia in Peril," it read, exposing an internal memo from Lord to Christopher detailing the perilous state of American standing in Asia. As the *Post* article put it, "Five months after President Clinton proclaimed the birth of a new Pacific community of lucrative trade and shared interests, the State Department's top Asia hand has warned in a letter to Secretary of State Warren Christopher that U.S.-Asia relations are being infected by a 'malaise' of disputes over human rights, trade, and other concerns."

The "malaise" memo, written by Lord based on a volley of anxious cables from U.S. ambassadors in the region and obtained by the *Post*, cited the tug-of-war with China over human rights, trade disputes with Japan, and conflicts in Southeast Asia, including a dispute with Singapore over the caning of an American teenager accused of vandalism. The malaise memo, noted the *Washington Post*, was trying to "prod Christopher and by extension Clinton to do something they frequently are accused of avoiding: set priorities and make a clear choice."[60] Or, as Richard Solomon observed in *Foreign Affairs* at the same time, "if something is clear this far into the Clinton administration, it is that even a 'domestic' president committed to solving economic problems at home cannot do so at the expense of America's relations abroad—and especially with Asia."[61]

The reality was that despite global American unipolarity and Clinton's ambitious moves on regional multilateralism, American sway over Asia and the Pacific was receding in key respects. The share of East Asian exports to the United States fell from 34.1 percent in 1986 to 24.2 percent in 1992, while intra-Asian trade rose to 45 percent of East Asia's total trade. Over this same period, the idea of Asia detaching from the United States gained currency within the region as the Clinton administration turned inward and juggled its conflicting foreign policy agendas. As Japanese journalist Funabashi Yōichi put it in *Foreign Affairs* in his influential article "The Asianization of Asia" in the winter of 1993–1994:

> Asia will no longer put up with being treated simply as a card; it will now demand respect as a player. Its success stories are likely to inspire

and provide voice for original, distinctly Asian ideas on a host of issues. . . .

The question facing the United States is whether it will be able to understand these ideas dispassionately and coexist in harmony with Asian nations.[62]

The divergence of American and Asian zeitgeists highlighted by Funabashi was a problem of identity, political narratives, and soft power, but the administration's challenge was also compounded by the unexpected re-emergence of real material threats to security over the same period. It turned out that those Cold War divisions considered old and no longer relevant by some in the incoming administration were in fact still very relevant.

The most dangerous legacy of the Cold War was on the Korean Penin-sula. Baker had warned Christopher during the transition that the North Korean nuclear problem was not solved, and in February 1993 Pyongyang proved the point by declaring its intention to leave the Nonproliferation Treaty in response to IAEA demands for inspections of the North's nuclear facilities.[63] After stonewalling in talks in New York for another year, the North escalated further in April 1994 by declaring that it would unload the nuclear fuel rods from its five megawatt reactor at Yongbyon, potentially harvesting enough plutonium to produce several nuclear bombs.[64] Clinton now faced his first serious security crisis in East Asia. He responded by declaring on *Meet the Press* in November 1993 that North Korea "cannot be allowed to develop a nuclear bomb."[65] He also ordered the Pentagon to prepare military options ranging from a block-ade to strikes on the Yongbyon reactor, recognizing the possibility that these moves might lead to North Korean retaliation and escalate to full war.[66]

The rest of the administration watched the military preparations with a sense of unreality and angst until former president Jimmy Carter sur-prised them all by traveling to Pyongyang to defuse the crisis with his own unauthorized provisional agreement with Kim Il-sung on June 17, 1994. Lacking any better diplomatic plan themselves, the administration turned the negotiations over to Gallucci, who took the Carter proposal and negotiated what safeguards and verification he could with the North Koreans in Geneva, completing the U.S.-DPRK "Agreed Framework" on October 21, 1994.[67] Under the Agreed Framework, North Korea would freeze its program at Yongbyon and submit to safeguard inspections by the IAEA in exchange for the construction of two light-water reactors and provision of heavy fuel oil (ostensibly to compensate for lost commercial power generation, even though there were no indications the Yongbyon reactor was ever intended for that purpose). Based on the Geneva agreement, the United States and key allies established the Korean Peninsula Energy Development Organization (KEDO) in March 1995 to begin working on the light-water reactors.[68] The core parts of the reactors would be completed only after the IAEA had completed all necessary safeguard inspections in North Korea somewhere later in the process. In the meantime, KEDO began planning for the construction of the light-water reactor, and the IAEA inspectors prepared to go back into Pyongyang to see what the North had done with the plutonium there.

The Agreed Framework temporarily defused the North Korean nuclear crisis but was deeply unpopular with the Republican Congress. The administration argued that the light-water reactors were "proliferation proof" and would not be completed until the North had submitted to full inspections. They also pointed out that Korea and Japan were willing to bear the brunt of the costs. For their part, the North Korean leadership consoled themselves that they would not have to submit to inspections until the core parts of the light-water reactor were ready, and as North Korea's most senior defector, Hwang Jang-yop, told the author in October 2003, "by then we would confront the United States with a new deterrent"—a reference to the regime's still hidden uranium enrichment program.[69] That, of course, is exactly what happened.

While the State Department shifted to implementation of the Agreed Framework, Pentagon planners came away from the crisis deeply disturbed at the increasing North Korean ballistic missile capabilities and the poor state of readiness in the U.S.-Japan and U.S.-ROK alliances revealed by the crisis. Perry initiated joint planning with Seoul for possible collapse or instability in the North, particularly after South Korean president Kim Young-sam promised Seoul was ready to absorb the North on its own after the death of Kim Il-sung.[70] In the case of Japan, it became apparent in the spring 1994 crisis that the Self Defense Forces had virtually no legal or political authority to plan with the United States with respect to interdiction operations, minesweeping, rear area logistical support, or missile defense—all the basic requirements for the United States to operate from Japan in response to a crisis on the peninsula. The Pentagon was further alarmed when the coalition government of Socialist prime minister Murayama Tomiichi published its new midterm defense advisory report (the "Higuchi Report"), which ranked multilateral security cooperation as a higher priority than the U.S.-Japan alliance for Japan's defense policy going forward.[71] The consequences of Clinton's adversarial Japan policy now became fully apparent.

The Higuchi Commission report was particularly disturbing to Joe Nye, who had listened through hours of attacks on Japan in the White House Situation Room as chair of the National Intelligence Council (NIC) and worried about the dangerous drift in the alliance.[72] Anticipating his own move to the Pentagon to take over as assistant secretary for international security affairs, Nye and his Harvard colleague and national intelligence officer for Asia, Ezra Vogel, had been quietly reviewing U.S.-Japan relations since the spring of 1994. When the Higuchi Commission came out, Vogel and Nye recruited the author and Dr. Patrick Cronin of the National Defense University to examine the defense debate in Japan and explore ways to revitalize the alliance. Our public report in November 1994 highlighted the divergence in U.S.-Japan relations and specifically recommended upgrading the bilateral Guidelines for U.S.-Japan Defense Cooperation to prepare the alliance for new security challenges in the region that the crisis with North Korea had exposed.[73]

That same month, Nye assumed his new position as assistant secretary of defense for international security affairs and immediately took steps to stem the hemorrhaging of U.S. credibility in Asia pointed out in Lord's "malaise" memo. Recognizing that U.S. troop drawdowns were driving allies in the region to hedge, he proposed to revive the Bush-era East Asia Strategic Reports to put a clear floor under the U.S. commitment to forward presence in the region. The fight from force planners in the services and the Joint Staff was ferocious at first, but Nye won Perry's support to publish a fourth EASR in February 1995, committing the United States to maintain 100,000 troops forward deployed for the foreseeable future (the Bush EASRs had reduced the number from 135,000 to 100,000).[74] Nye then elaborated on the strategic rationale in *Foreign Affairs* that summer. In a direct attack on the economic nationalists, he rejected the "clichéd" idea that geoeconomics had replaced geopolitics. He then dismissed other strategic alternatives to alliance-based forward presence being bandied about in the academic literature, such as replacement of alliances with multilateralism or an offshore balancing strategy from the Western Hemisphere.[75] The Nye article and the EASR were clear: forward presence was the core of U.S. strategy; Japan was the "linchpin"; and there would be no Carter-like uncertainty about the U.S. commitment to the Republic of Korea, which Nye argued was now essential not only for geopolitical reasons but also as a "vital component in our national objective of supporting and promoting democracy."[76] It was an unvarnished embrace of the principles behind the Reagan/Shultz/Weinberger maritime strategy and was hailed by Richard Armitage and other Republicans watching from the wings.

The economic nationalists outside of government were furious. Chalmers Johnson, the intellectual father of the revisionist school on Japan, dismissed Nye's approach as an "ossified strategy" in the pages of *Foreign Affairs* and argued elsewhere that Japan policy had been "hijacked by a bunch of dilettantes" in reference to Campbell, Cronin, and the author.[77] Within the administration, however, the economic nationalists were losing steam. The successful ratification of the North American Free Trade Agreement (NAFTA), the limitations imposed by a Republican Congress, the new World Trade Organization, and the recognition that Tokyo's economic model was in fact flawed had all led to a changed view of the Japanese economic threat. When two sailors and a marine abducted and raped an underaged girl in Okinawa in September 1995, prompting unprecedented calls in Japan for closing U.S. bases, the Pentagon's alarm at the drift in the alliance reached the level of the president and First Lady Hillary Clinton. Expecting pushback from the White House when he first briefed his plan for revitalizing the U.S.-Japan alliance that fall, Nye was surprised to find support from unlikely allies such as U.S. Trade Representative Mickey Kantor, whose fights with Japan were now over.[78]

It is important to stress that the new strategy for Japan was not initially premised on balancing a rising China but rather on restoring the tools of American influence and engagement necessary to realize the cooperative international dynamics envisioned in the strategy of enlargement and engagement, and after April 1994 by the recognition that the alliance was not ready for crises on the Korean Peninsula. By 1996, however, the China variable loomed much larger.[79] China's defense budget began to grow at nearly 15 percent annually; advanced equipment from former Soviet production lines was modernizing the PLA Air Force and Navy; Beijing had tested new nuclear weapons at its Lop Nor site in Xinjiang; and there were now permanent Chinese military facilities being built on Mischief Island in the South China Sea.[80] The twin Cold War challenges of the Korean Peninsula and Taiwan Strait highlighted in the 1969 Nixon-Sato communiqué were both now moving again to the front burner in alliance relations with Japan.

The acute crisis that focused the administration on China's potential challenge to the status quo began not in Asia but at Cornell University, where the school had invited its distinguished alumnus President Lee Teng-hui of the Republic of China to attend the June 1995 alumni reunion. The visit of any leader in Taipei to the United States was controversial enough after the 1979 normalization with the PRC, but Lee was particularly annoying to Beijing because of his pro-Japan leanings and disinterest in maintaining the traditional Kuomintang (KMT) line that there is "one China" incorporating both the mainland and Taiwan. At first, Christopher told Beijing that President Lee would definitely *not* be given a visa to attend the meeting at Cornell, but then the secretary was forced to retract that promise when his hand was forced by pro-Taiwan sentiment in Congress.[81] Beijing then responded with far greater fury than either Taipei or Washington had anticipated. After initial grumbling by Jiang and the Foreign Ministry, the PLA suddenly bracketed Taiwan with missiles in July and August; conducted major naval exercises in December; built up troops across the strait in February; and conducted further missile tests in March 1996, with some missiles landing within sixty kilometers of the Japanese-inhabited island of Yonakuni. The Pentagon concluded that the possibility of an actual Chinese attack on Taiwan was still less than 5 percent to 10 percent, but Beijing's belligerence demonstrated that the assumptions that had driven China policy since 1972 may have been wrong—that China might well use its growing power to force a change in the status quo with Taiwan.[82]

There was little debate in the administration that a muscular response was now necessary. Strategic surprise, as Gaddis notes, typically leads to expanded American demonstrations of commitment.[83] Perry took the lead by arguing that the administration had to push back in a way that would not lead to direct military confrontation with China. The Yokosuka-based carrier USS *Independence* happened to be nearby in the Philippines, but Pacific commander Admiral Joseph W. Preuher was hesitant to send it directly into the strait between Taiwan and the mainland and convinced Perry to order the carrier and its escort ships just outside the 110-mile-long body of water on March 10 instead.[84] After Beijing announced that there would be extensive PLA amphibious exercises, the administration announced the next day that a second Carrier Battle Group led by the USS *Nimitz* would be sent to the Western Pacific from the Persian Gulf.[85] Christopher called the Chinese exercises "risky and reckless," and Lake announced that there would be "grave consequences" should China use force against Taiwan.[86]

The impact of the 1995–1996 Taiwan crisis on U.S. relations with both Japan and China was profound. In Japan's case, Nye and Campbell had been working with the Defense and Foreign Ministries on a joint statement for Clinton's November 1995 visit to Japan for the APEC summit but ran into resistance from Socialist prime minister Murayama Tomiichi, who rejected any mention of upgrading bilateral Defense Guidelines or the China problem and insisted on including a clause pledging Japan would never be in a war.[87] In the end, Clinton never issued that version of the statement, since he canceled the November visit to focus on a political crisis at home (he would miss two of the APEC summits he initiated).[88] By the time the president arrived in Tokyo for a rescheduled summit in April 1996, Murayama had been replaced by the more hawkish leader of the LDP, Hashimoto Ryūtarō, and China's month-long military exercises off Taiwan had altered the political debate about the alliance in both Tokyo and Washington. In their joint Security Declaration on April 17, 1996, Hashimoto and Clinton called the alliance their mutual "cornerstone for achieving common security objectives," highlighted the importance of China playing a "positive" regional security role, and pledged to revise the 1978 U.S.-Japan Defense Guidelines to deal with regional crises.[89]

When completed the next year, the new Defense Guidelines emphasized that henceforth Japan's scope for defense operations with the United States would be expanded to cover "situations in the area surrounding Japan that have a direct impact on the security of Japan."[90] The 1969 Nixon-Sato communiqué would finally be operationalized as it had not been even with Harold Brown's 1978 U.S.-Japan Defense Guidelines. As international relations scholar Evelyn Goh concludes, "By 1997, the United States–Japan alliance had evolved from being a component of the U.S. Cold War global deterrence strategy to a more regionally focused partnership for crisis management and potential power balancing."[91] Clinton's contextual intelligence mattered. He abandoned the facile assumptions behind the strategy of enlargement and engagement and the faddish theories about Japanese techno-nationalism and returned squarely to the balance-of-power logic he had decried only a few years earlier.

While Clinton reintroduced balancing to U.S. strategy in Asia, however, he did not abandon engagement. As Joe Nye repeatedly told his colleagues, "If you treat China as an enemy, China will become an enemy. It will become a self-fulfilling prophecy."[92] The U.S.-Japan Joint Security Declaration "stressed the interest of both countries in furthering cooperation with China"—signaling clearly that balancing had to be complemented by deeper engagement with Beijing.[93] After stumbling over MFN and human rights for the first few years of the administration, the realists on Clinton's national security team now focused on a mechanism that would reinforce mutual interdependence with China, provide an international context for resolving trade disputes, and counteract the zero-sum competitive dynamic emerging in the security relationship.[94] That mechanism would be Chinese membership in the new WTO. The economic case for China's admission to the WTO also made increasing sense: between 1980 and 1995, Chinese government control of production and trade halved; the state's share of industrial output fell from 80 percent to 47 percent, state-controlled exports fell from 100 percent to 57 percent, and imports fell from 99.8 percent to 44.8 percent.[95] The Reagan administration had first considered bringing China into what was then the General Agreement on Tariffs and Trade (GATT) years earlier, but now the strategic, political, and economic logic for Chinese WTO membership was overwhelming.

Low-key talks on WTO accession had already resumed for the first time since Tiananmen in March 1993, and by November 1995, the new U.S. trade representative, Charlene Barshefsky, had given her Chinese counterparts a draft road map for reaching an accession agreement to the WTO with the United States (the most important negotiation China would face among the member economies). During the 1996 U.S. election campaign, Clinton sent a team of negotiators to Beijing in order to demonstrate his seriousness about resuming higher-level negotiations once reelected.[96] Over the next year, discussions remained largely stalled over China's insistence on being given concessions as a developing country, as well as the heightened security confrontations over Taiwan, but when President Jiang Zemin met Clinton at the APEC summit in Manila in November 1996, the two leaders agreed to an exchange of state visits and accelerated WTO talks the next year.[97] With the talented economic reformer Zhu Rongji driving the process in Beijing, the momentum toward China's accession accelerated.

By the end of 1996, in Lord's view, the United States "had gone from crisis to genuine, major progress" and "relations with China and Japan were both on the right track."[98] The April 1996 U.S.-Japan Joint Security Declaration and the November 1996 Clinton-Jiang summit had put in place the twin pillars of a new strategy to "engage and balance" a rising

China, backed by investment in the longer-term process of building an effective multilateral architecture in Asia through APEC and ARF. In some respects, the Clinton team had combined the successful China policies of Nixon and Carter with the successful Japan and defense policies of Reagan.

It would soon become evident, however, that the strategy was still less than the sum of its parts. Many Clinton political appointees and State Department Asia hands were not comfortable with balance-of-power logic, viewing the Nye Initiative as a necessary but temporary recalibration on the way to a new "strategic partnership" with China. In the White House, the preoccupation was not Asia at all but increasingly Europe and the crises in Serbia and Kosovo. Indeed, in the last few years of the Clinton administration, the size of the Europe office of the NSC ballooned to three times the size of the East Asia office.[99] And finally, the economic officials at USTR and the NEC were still focused on market opening and not the development of regional architecture in Asia and the Pacific per se—pursuing relative gains rather than open and free trade. Despite successes in 1996, Asia policy had no senior steward like George Shultz and steadily lost the intellectual architects of the engage-and-balance strategy, such as Perry, Nye, and Campbell. Political and economic tremors across the Pacific would soon highlight these shortcomings.

THE ASIAN FINANCIAL CRISIS
AND THE LOSS OF STRATEGIC FOCUS

Since at least John Hay's Open Door notes, the United States has sought to lock Asia into a set of rules that would ensure open economic access while resisting regional blocs that operated on alternate rules and limited American influence and trade. In the 1930s, U.S. protectionism spawned exactly the blocs that were inimical to American interests in the Pacific. In 1997, the United States came close to making that same mistake for the second time—not because of protectionism at home but because of the aggressive pursuit of U.S.-centered global economic norms in response to Asia's worst financial crisis since the war.

The Clinton administration's successful launch of the APEC summits and the "Asia Pacific Community" in 1993 had not eliminated aspirations within the region for a narrower East Asian community that would exclude the United States. Indeed, as U.S. ambitions for market liberalization intensified, the calls within Asia for an alternative arrangement also grew. At Blake Island in Seattle in November 1993, Clinton had convinced fellow leaders from the Pacific Rim to release a declaration affirming their commitment to economic openness, partnership, and cooperation; environmental protection; education; infrastructure improvements; and the use of APEC as a forum for future economic issues and enterprises.[100] The agreement was aspirational but not binding—in the spirit of ASEAN multilateralism and Japanese bureaucratic practice.

After Blake Island, however, the administration pushed for more binding agreements to open markets. First, in conjunction with the Blake Island summit, C. Fred Bergsten of the Institute for International Economics and a group of like-minded economists produced a report recommending that APEC be turned into a free trade area adhering to the rules being established within NAFTA.[101] The proposal was "the stuff dreams are made of" declared *The Economist*, which supported the concept but was skeptical that the other Asian economies would agree to it.[102] The next year, at the leaders' meeting in Bogor, Indonesia, the United States led in establishing a commitment by APEC leaders to "complete the achievement of our goal of free and open trade and investment in the Asia-Pacific no later than the year 2020," with the industrialized economies achieving the goal of free and open trade and investment no later than 2010.[103] Meanwhile, Clinton had insisted on including Russia in APEC to compensate for NATO expansion, as well as Mexico, Chile, and Peru from the Western Hemisphere. What had begun in the minds of Asians as a counterbalance to NAFTA and the European Union was now losing its East Asian regional character as Washington took charge and appeared to be reshaping the group on the model of NAFTA.[104]

The objective of reducing trans-Pacific barriers to trade was clearly in U.S. and ultimately regional interests. However, the American mission of creating open rules in Asia had long been in tension with regional aspirations for a postcolonial, anti-Western identity. American diplomats and soldiers had struggled with this tension in the face of Japan's Greater East Asian Co-prosperity Sphere during the Second World War and then again with the emergence of the nonaligned bloc at Bandung in the 1950s. The success of American diplomacy in Asia was often determined at this intersection of global rules and regional identity. By 1997, that intersection was becoming increasingly hostile terrain for the Clinton administration.

The clash between what came to be known as the "Washington Consensus" and "Asian values" erupted in July 1997 when the Thai baht collapsed and Bangkok in desperation turned to the International Monetary Fund (IMF) for a bailout. The contagion then quickly spread to Indonesia, which requested IMF support in October, and South Korea, which turned to the IMF for stabilization funds in November. Over the next five months, American and Asian officials and politicians exchanged emotional charges. Washington argued that the crisis was the result of profligate government spending and the use of easy credit for nonproductive investments by crony capitalists in Southeast Asia—in effect a replication of Japan's own "bubble economy." The demands from the U.S. Treasury Department and the American-dominated IMF were correspondingly austere: reduction of current account surpluses, corporate restructuring, and greater transparency. From the Asian perspective, the crisis was caused by overreliance on the U.S. dollar and the predatory investments of "vulture capitalists" in New York and London who had driven the Thai and other exchange rate markets into dangerous territory in the pursuit of short-term profits.[105]

Asian officials were particularly upset at the administration's unwillingness to provide any funding to Thailand, compared with the robust $20 billion response to the bailout of Mexico in 1993 and the administration's more flexible and generous support for a Russian bailout occurring at the same time.[106] The implication was that the administration did not place the same geostrategic value on Asia as it did other parts of the world. In fact, the Treasury Department and Clinton's newly created National Economic Council were afraid to go to Congress for funding after the Mexican and Russian bailouts, and incorrectly assessed that the crisis could be contained within Thailand.[107] The regional experts in the NSC and State Department were largely outside that decision-making process. By the time Korea became embroiled, however, the NSC had mobilized and had warned the president of broader national security implications—an important intervention but a reflection of Clinton's poor decision to create parallel and often unconnected staffs for economic and national security policy.[108] Overall, the American response appeared demanding, paltry, and slow.

Thus, even as the IMF reached terms for economic stabilization funds with the afflicted economies and stopped the contagion from spreading, Washington diverged with East Asian governments on the lessons of the crisis and the path forward. The Americans turned to APEC. At the Vancouver APEC summit in 1997, the United States, Australia, and Canada won support to proceed with Early Voluntary Sectoral Liberalization

(EVSL) to align APEC more closely with the WTO. The next November in Manila, USTR took control of the negotiating process from State, breaking the consensus-oriented approach in APEC and pressing for specific targeted liberalization commitments, especially in agriculture.[109] The Japanese representatives, under pressure from powerful agricultural interests at home, countered that USTR was replaying its failed approach to earlier U.S.-Japan trade negotiations and organized other Asian powers to resist Washington's initiative. Incensed at Vice President Al Gore's "Reformasi" speech in Kuala Lumpur attacking Malaysian prime minister Mahathir's authoritarian tendencies (Clinton had skipped APEC for a second time), the Southeast Asian members of APEC rallied behind Japan and blocked the USTR initiative. It was an embarrassment for the United States and a pyrrhic victory for Japan, which had just crippled its own multilateral progeny, APEC.

Meanwhile, the Japanese Finance Ministry conspired with other East Asian governments to launch a regional alternative (or at least supplement) to the IMF that would be controlled by Asians themselves. In September 1997, Japan's iconoclastic vice minister for finance, Sakakibara Eisuke— who earlier had written a book declaring that the Japanese economy had "surpassed capitalism"—proposed a new $100 billion Asian Monetary Fund (AMF) at a meeting of East Asian banking and financial officials in Hong Kong.[110] Deputy Treasury Secretary Lawrence Summers caught wind of the proposal and woke Sakakibara in the middle of the morning to vow American opposition. "I thought you were my friend!" he yelled at the slumbering Japanese official.[111] By November, Sakakibara and the Ministry of Finance had buckled under domestic pressure (on the cost of the proposal) and U.S. criticism, agreeing to fold their proposal into the IMF-led bailout plan.[112] Meanwhile, China won kudos in the region in comparison with the United States for agreeing not to devalue the renminbi during the crisis, which helped to counter the deflationary impact of the IMF bailout and further integrate the Chinese and Southeast Asian economies. Finally, in December 1997, ASEAN, Japan, China, and Korea began to hold summit meetings on their own as part of a new "ASEAN Plus Three" dialogue.[113] Although initially short on substance, the East Asian–only dialogue paved the way for the establishment of the Changmai Initiative—an intraregional debt swap arrangement that replicated the AMF and initially threatened to challenge the hegemony of the IMF.

In other words, for want of a comprehensive Asia strategy, the Clinton administration had won the battle over the Asian financial crisis but risked losing the war over regional architecture by legitimizing the very exclusionary East Asia institutions Washington opposed.[114] The United States would pay a significant price in terms of influence in Southeast Asia for years afterward—and ironically, China, not Japan, would fill the void.

The Clinton administration also slipped back into the familiar pattern of caroming between Japan and China. For the engage-and-balance strategy to work, Beijing needed to understand that the U.S.-Japan alliance was the linchpin of security and rules-based order in the region, and the United States and Japan had to be careful not to undermine engagement with China by excluding Beijing from a major role in defining the region's future. This in turn required precisely the consistent and disciplined approach to foreign policy strategy that had always been lacking in the administration. Contextual intelligence without a well-grounded foreign policy concept can result in flip-flops that are self-defeating. The growth of Sino-Japanese strategic competition after the 1996 Taiwan crisis only made the problem harder.

The pendulum swings between Japan and China in U.S. foreign policy resumed as the administration sought ways to reduce tensions in the U.S.-China relationship after the crises in the Taiwan Strait. If there was a concern in 1997–1998 within the White House and State Department and among outside experts who influenced their views, it was that U.S. policy had become on balance *too* provocative toward China.[115] The accelerating WTO accession talks helped but were limited to the economic realm. Meanwhile, the tensions with Sakakibara over the financial crisis further eroded the spirit of the April 1996 Clinton-Hashimoto joint statement and the U.S.-Japan leg of the U.S.-Japan-China triangle. Thus, when Japanese journalists asked in 1996 for clarification that Article V (the defense clause) of the 1960 U.S.-Japan Security Treaty would apply in the event of a crisis with China over the contested Senkaku Islands, Secretary of State Christopher equivocated and urged a peaceful resolution by all sides.[116] This ad-libbed expression of neutrality sent shock waves through Tokyo, prompting the Defense Department to make its own unilateral clarification in November 1996 that Article V had always applied to the Senkakus, whereas State continued its studious neutrality on the question.[117]

Then, in advance of Clinton's October 1997 summit with Jiang Zemin in Washington, the NSC and State Department announced that the United States and China were "working toward a constructive strategic partnership in the Twenty-first Century." As Nancy Tucker noted at the time:

Almost immediately, and unsurprisingly, the detail and nuance disappeared and the infelicitous concept of strategic partnership alone remained. Not only did it fail to describe Sino-American relations accurately, but it also confused and distressed genuine strategic partners in Asia such as South Korea and Japan. Furthermore, it sent an erroneous message to Beijing regarding the level of importance that Washington accorded China, raising false expectations about a U.S. willingness to meet Beijing's demands on sensitive issues such as arms sales to Taiwan.[118]

The slight was compounded in June 1998 when Clinton spent eight days in China without visiting Japan, revisiting the "strategic partnership" with Jiang in their joint press conference and then criticizing Japan's economic policies from the podium with Jiang by his side.[119] The White House thought it had more than checked the Japan box when President Clinton rushed to Tokyo for the funeral of Japanese prime minister Obuchi Keizō earlier in the year, but the Japanese press raised cries of "Japan passing," and coverage of the trip across the United States and Asia warned that Washington was signaling its intention to shift from Japan to China as the core U.S. partner in the region.[120]

The backlash against this apparent new condominium with Beijing back in Washington was as damaging to relations with China as Clinton's new overture to Beijing had been to relations with Japan. A group of conservative defense experts calling themselves the "Blue Team" (after the blue hats traditionally worn by the opposition in Chinese military exercises) led the charge.[121] Backed by Republicans in Congress and officials within the Pentagon, the Blue Team produced assessments of China's growing military capabilities through the Defense Department's Office of Net Assessment and encouraged congressional legislation mandating annual Defense Department reports on PLA capabilities (which were not entirely opposed by equally concerned officials within the Pentagon).[122] As one group of administration officials championed the idea of moving to a new "strategic partnership" with China, another group focused on the growing threat posed by China's military power. Whether he wanted it or not, Clinton now had two contradictory China policies instead of one integrated approach that incorporated both Japan and China.

The administration also overreached in its North Korea policy, raising questions about security commitments to allies and prompting another split with Congress over Asia. Though the administration could not know the full extent of North Korea's clandestine efforts to enrich uranium and weaponize plutonium, it was obvious that Pyongyang was trying to raise the price for cooperation in the Agreed Framework. In June 1998, the North threatened to export ballistic missiles if it was not paid $500 million; in July it was caught constructing an enormous underground complex thought to be related to clandestine nuclear work; and on August 31 it responded to U.S. pressure by launching a prototype Taepodong intercontinental ballistic missile over Japan.[123] Facing enormous pressure from Congress and Tokyo to cease heavy fuel oil shipments to the North under the Agreed Framework, Clinton ordered a review of North Korea policy in November 1998 under Bill Perry, now retired as secretary of defense. Perry recommended a two-track approach that would include U.S. moves toward lifting sanctions and toward normalization in exchange for concrete actions by Pyongyang to move toward a "complete and verifiable" end to the North's nuclear programs.[124] Over initial State Department opposition, he also established the Trilateral Coordination and Oversight Group (TCOG) in April 1999, with Japan and Korea, to ensure that not only South Korean president Kim Dae-jung's accommodating views toward Pyongyang were heard but also the harder-line views of Japan.[125]

With a presidential letter in hand and Japan and Korea in support, Perry traveled to Pyongyang in May 1999 to present his proposal.[126] His delegation heard such a belligerent response that they returned worried that war might occur, but after a year of dialogue, in June 2000 the administration announced the easing of sanctions against North Korea instituted under the Trading with the Enemy Act, the Defense Production Act, and the Export Administration Act. Then, on October 12, North Korean vice marshal Jo Myong-rok appeared in the Oval Office sitting next to President Clinton, bedecked in medals and promising in a joint statement to "make every effort in the future to build a new relationship free from past enmity."[127] Less than two weeks later, Secretary of State Madeleine Albright was sitting side-by-side with North Korean leader Kim Jong-il in a stadium full of regimented and adoring North Korean citizens in Pyongyang.[128] The *New York Times* described for readers the incongruous image as the American champion of human rights "enthusiastically applauded the 90-minute authoritarian display of choreography and chorus."[129]

The U.S. approach toward North Korea had turned from crisis to collaboration with dizzying speed. State Department officials evoked Nixon's opening to China and waxed enthusiastically about establishing a new diplomatic mission in Pyongyang. However, the positive atmosphere and the ambiguous discussions surrounding the North's nuclear and missile programs did little to mask the growing threat from Pyongyang's arsenal. In September 1999, the U.S. intelligence community had concluded that North Korea "will 'most likely' have developed an ICBM capable of delivering a 200-kg warhead to the US mainland by 2015."[130] Nor was there any concrete evidence in the talks with Pyongyang that a verifiable termination of the North's nuclear or missile programs was remotely possible, even if the prospect of a temporary halt to missile exports was. When Albright tabled the next step of a presidential visit to Pyongyang at the end of 2000, Clinton was tempted, but an outside group of Asia experts and the incoming George W. Bush administration urged him not to go.[131] Clinton wisely concurred, but left in his wake anxious allies and a deeply suspicious Republican transition team.

As he left office, Clinton could point to concrete advances in relations with both Japan and China. The U.S.-Japan Defense Guidelines led to new emergency preparedness legislation in Japan and expanded cooperation on missile defense. U.S.-China talks on WTO accession were interrupted several times, particularly after the accidental U.S. bombing of the Chinese embassy in Belgrade in May 1999, but Zhu Rongji and USTR Charlene Barshefsky came to a historic agreement the following November on China's entry into the WTO.[132] The Perry Initiative did not reverse North Korea's march toward nuclear weapons, but it did institutionalize unprecedented U.S.-Japan-ROK cooperation through TCOG. All of these instruments would help to buttress the next administration's Asia policy. At the same time, however, Clinton left office with doubts across the region about the ultimate American disposition toward Japan, China, and North Korea—and resumed movement toward an alternative regional architecture exclusive of the United States. Had Clinton stayed true to the statecraft that emerged in the middle of his administration, he would have had a far stronger finish.

CLINTON'S LEGACY IN ASIA STRATEGY

Two competing narratives emerged at the end of the Clinton administration about the state of U.S. grand strategy. In one, captured by Harvard's Stephen Walt in the March–April 2000 issue of *Foreign Affairs* ("Two Cheers for Clinton's Foreign Policy"), Clinton is credited with "sustaining

American hegemony on the cheap . . . in an era when there was little to gain in foreign policy and much to lose." Clinton, Walt argued, had to contend with a hostile Republican Congress and the lack of an imminent threat that would have lent itself to the creation of an overarching grand strategy. In the end, Clinton abandoned his early idealism and embraced realpolitik, including "an effective combination of engagement and deterrence" vis-à-vis a rising China. "Clinton's handling of the major Asian powers deserves high marks," Walt concluded.[133]

In the counternarrative, presented by Richard Haas of Brookings in the May–June 2000 issue of *Foreign Affairs* ("Squandered Presidency"), Clinton is charged with "symbolism over substance" and "short-term crisis management over long-term strategizing." Clinton's failure to create priorities among the issues of human rights, trade, Taiwan, and Korea, and his lack of attention to great-power diplomacy, meant that China "oscillated from being portrayed as a human rights outcast to a would-be strategic partner." "In the end," concluded Haas, "Clinton forfeited control over the American debate on China and never managed to develop a durable post–Cold War rationale for the relationship."[134]

Both narratives are essentially correct. Through his contextual intelligence and underlying inclination to preserve American primacy, Clinton developed the elements of a new strategy to shape Asia's emerging order to American values and interests that his successors would follow. However, those elements were never embedded in a cohesive and durable theory of the power dynamics in the region or of the region's relative importance. As Haas pointed out, the key relationships with Japan and China were buffeted as crises emerged, assumptions shifted, friends became enemies, and enemies became friends—depending on events and the personalities in charge of policy. Clinton's approach to Asia was therefore defined as much by the historic tensions in American statecraft—the swings between Japan and China, the confusion over prioritizing human rights, the allure of economic nationalism, and the distractions of Europe—than by the innovative new tools he brought to the job.

The next administration would use most of those tools—to Clinton's credit—but attempt to bring greater strategic coherence to Asia policy as a whole.

14. "A BALANCE OF POWER THAT FAVORS FREEDOM"
STRATEGIC SURPRISE AND THE ASIA POLICY OF GEORGE W. BUSH

The academic critique of George W. Bush's Asia policy is often difficult to distinguish from the academic critique of the Iraq War. Resentful of alleged "unilateralism" and "militarism" in Iraq, scholars have often thrown the same charges at the forty-third president's Asia strategy without examining the policies on their respective merits. For example, Bush is accused of "over-reliance on bilateral hubs and spokes" and "neglecting regionalism" in Asia,[1] yet he was the only president to attend every APEC summit, and his administration took the lead in *initiating* more new multilateral forums and institutions in Asia than any of his post–Cold War predecessors or his immediate successor (including, among other new diplomatic initiatives, the Six Party Talks in Northeast Asia; the U.S.-Japan-Australia Trilateral Security Dialogue; the Asia-Pacific Partnership on Clean Climate and Energy; the U.S.-Japan-India-Australia Quad; and the Asia Pacific Democracy Partnership). Critics also charged that Bush engaged in excessive "economic unilateralism" and dropped economic diplomacy in favor of geopolitics,[2] yet his administration completed or initiated more free trade agreements (FTAs) in Asia than the United States had in decades (including the U.S.-Singapore FTA, the U.S.-Australia FTA, the U.S.-Korea FTA, and the multination Trans-Pacific Partnership). According to critics, Bush "explicitly militarized" his Asia policy,[3] yet the tide was turned on terrorism in the region through cooperation with allies and partners rather than through direct U.S. combat operations in the Pacific Command's Area of Responsibility. Ultimately, Senator Barack Obama and a host of like-minded academics charged, Bush lost American respect and influence in Asia.[4] And yet, according to the Chicago Council on Global Affairs survey of regional soft power in Asia in 2008, publics in the region thought the United States had *increased* its soft-power influence over the previous decade by more than any other power, including China.[5]

This is not to say that the Bush Asia strategy was without flaws—indeed, the administration fell into some of the historic pitfalls of American statecraft toward the region that plagued Clinton, particularly in 2007 and 2008, Bush's final two years. Nor was Asia policy immune from the effects of the Iraq War, as will be discussed. Ultimately, however, Asia policy between 2001 and 2008 reflected a different strategic impulse from that of Iraq. Whereas thinking on Southwest Asia was driven by a sense of urgency after the terrorist attacks in the United States on September 11, 2001, Bush's Asia policy was on the whole much more akin to the evolutionary statecraft of George Shultz, who was in fact one of Bush's first mentors on foreign policy when Bush was governor of Texas. And with the exception of North Korea policy—which became a highly contentious derivative of the Iraq debate—there was broad consensus among the principals at the outset of the administration about the geostrategic chess game being played vis-à-vis the major powers in Asia. The Bush administration came to office with a clear strategic concept on Asia, focused on shaping a favorable geopolitical equilibrium in the region, and that generally held through a series of short-term crises and the attacks of 9/11. The fact that Barack Obama did not fundamentally contest or change Bush's Asia strategy in 2009 attests to the overall durability of that approach.

The author held positions on the NSC staff with responsibility for the conceptualization and execution of Asia strategy from 2001 through 2005.[6] The historian thus becomes the inside chronicler, with the advantages of added insight but the pitfalls of subjectivity. As much as possible, however, this section will apply the same critical template used on all administrations that came before.

George W. Bush himself came from a family committed to internationalism and public service. As he rose to become the Republican front-runner, his new foreign policy advisors saw strength in his management skills, decisiveness, and spiritual grounding. His travel to Asia had been limited, though, the most notable experience being a six-week stint in China when his father was U.S. Liaison Office director in 1975.[7] As governor of Texas, he knew Latin America well but needed a centralized team of advisors to help him turn his instincts into strategy with respect to the big powers. George Shultz began that education in a gathering in his San Francisco apartment overlooking San Francisco Bay in late April 1998. Governor Bush also warmed to Condoleezza Rice, a Russia expert and protégé of Brent Scowcroft, who engaged in long foreign policy discussions with the future president in the gym during a weekend retreat at George H. W. Bush's family home in Kennebunkport, Maine.[8] The core group of foreign policy advisors soon expanded to eight friends and colleagues from the Reagan and George H. W. Bush administrations, including four with deep experience working together on Asia: Richard Armitage, Paul Wolfowitz, Bob Zoellick, and former defense secretary Richard Cheney. In a lighthearted moment, the eight advisors named themselves "the Vulcans" after the Roman god of fire and industry.[9]

The prevailing theme for the Vulcans was the need to return to the disciplined management of great-power relations that had characterized the Reagan and Bush foreign policies. In one of the Vulcans' first meetings, Governor Bush told his advisors that China was not a "strategic partner" as senior Clinton administration officials had been suggesting but instead a "strategic competitor" that had to be handled with respect but firmness.[10] His foreign policy would begin by returning U.S. allies to their rightful place as "partners, not satellites," he explained in a speech at The Citadel in September 1999.[11] Two months later, at the Ronald Reagan Library, he expanded on his proposed Asia policy: "The greatest threats to peace come when democratic forces are weak and disunited. Right now, America has many important bilateral alliances in Asia. We should work toward a day when the fellowship of free Pacific nations is as strong and united as our Atlantic Partnership. If I am president, China will find itself respected as a great power, but in a region of strong democratic alliances. It will be unthreatened, but not unchecked."[12]

Bush cited Mackinder in the Ronald Reagan speech, but it was pure Mahan. Japan was put back in the center of U.S. Asia strategy, with Japan experts assigned to key positions, including Jim Kelly as the assistant secretary of state for East Asia and the Pacific and Torkel Patterson as senior director for Asia at the NSC (I joined the NSC Asia office with him). The administration's blueprint for Japan policy followed an October 2000 National Defense University report, authored under the supervision of Armitage and Nye, that argued for a U.S.-Japan alliance that would anchor the United States in Asia the way the U.S.-U.K. special relationship traditionally anchored the United States in Europe.[13] The Nye Initiative toward Japan now became, in effect, a core pillar of Bush's Asia policy.

Bush's casting of China as a "strategic competitor" was not a prescription for containment or even for changing the parameters of U.S.-China joint statements as Reagan had threatened to do during the 1980 campaign. "We do not deny there is one China," Bush stated at the Ronald Reagan Library in November 1999, "but we deny the right of Beijing to impose their rule on a free people."[14] It was a much firmer position than his father had taken but still to the center compared with influential conservative intellectuals at the Project for a New American Century (PNAC) or *The Weekly Standard*, who argued in an editorial in March 1999 that the Republican Party should no longer "love commerce more than it loathes Chinese communism."[15] These more hawkish views toward China would be nested in the Pentagon, where Secretary of Defense Donald Rumsfeld hired key members from among the "Blue Team" that had attacked Clinton's defense policy toward China in the 1990s. The president and the original Vulcans were for the most part more optimistic about U.S.-China relations. "China," said Rice during the campaign, "has its own interests. It's a great power in the traditional sense. You need a broadly based policy, try to encourage economic liberalization, compete where you must on security."[16] In office, the new administration settled on an enduring three-word description of their goal for U.S.-China relations—one that would convey both optimism and principle. The United States, said the president and key cabinet officials, would seek ties with Beijing that are "cooperative, constructive and candid."[17]

The rest of Asia strategy flowed from this central premise that China's rise would best be shaped through a mix of engagement and shoring up a favorable strategic equilibrium centered on the maritime democracies. In the first meeting of the Vulcans, Bush raised India as a high priority. As Rice put it during the campaign, "India is an element in China's calculation, and it should yet be in America's, too."[18] U.S.-India relations were languishing in the wake of Delhi's May 1998 nuclear test and Washington's subsequent imposition of sanctions.[19] Clinton staged a highly successful political visit to India in March 2000 but continued to insist that India join the Non-Proliferation Treaty (NPT) and the Comprehensive

Test Ban Treaty (CTBT) before there could be sanctions relief—positions unacceptable to Delhi.[20] Bush, as Vulcan Robert Blackwill put it, wanted to view India differently: as a "strategic opportunity" and not a "recalcitrant irritant."[21] The administration would no longer approach India policy through the narrow prism of nonproliferation or India-Pakistan tensions, instead pursuing constructive relations with both Islamabad and Delhi that were tailored to U.S. interests and to their differing situations. In discussions with the Vulcans, the president did not expect that India would align with the United States against China or even that this should be a U.S. goal, but he echoed the logic of Nixon's 1967 *Foreign Affairs* article and Reagan's 1984 NSDD 147 that the rise of Indian power in itself was in U.S. geostrategic interests.[22]

Bush therefore entered office with a straightforward but coherent strategic concept for management of great-power relations in Asia—what Rice called "a balance of power that favors freedom."[23] Three of the new deputies—Armitage at State, Wolfowitz at Defense, and Lewis "Scooter" Libby at the Office of the Vice President—had worked closely together on Asia for Reagan.[24] Rice restructured the NSC to give greater focus to Asia, shifting India from the Near East office into the Asia office and ensuring the latter was the same size as the Europe office, which had ballooned under Clinton.[25] Declaratory policy on Japan, China, and India remained consistent, as it had under Reagan and George H. W. Bush.

However, the administration's strategic concepts would be tested. The president, inexperienced in foreign policy, faced crises in relations with both Japan and China in his first months. Ideological divisions would prompt open fights over policy toward North Korea and Taiwan. The new India partnership would grind down in the nonproliferation bureaucracy. Southeast Asia strategy—not a focus of the Vulcans—meandered at times. And relations with every country would change after September 11, 2001.

SUBMARINE AND AIRPLANE COLLISIONS: EARLY TESTS AND RECALIBRATION

Don Rumsfeld famously quipped during the war in Iraq that "you go to war with the army you have, not the army you might want or wish to have at a later time"—and so it was with the major allies positioned at the center of the Bush foreign policy strategy toward Asia.[26] The first challenge was with Japan. Between the issuance of the October 2000 Armitage-Nye

Report and the first months of the Bush administration, U.S.-Japan relations entered potentially troubled waters. Prime Minister Mori Yoshirō, though conservatively aligned with the new U.S. administration, was heading toward single-digit support rates in the polls at home because of Japan's sluggish economy. Worse, a U.S. submarine, the USS *Greeneville*, had collided with a Japanese high school vocational fishing boat near Pearl Harbor on February 9, killing nine Japanese students and crew members. *Time* magazine called it the first major foreign policy challenge for the new administration, and the new national security leadership feared the tragedy might unravel U.S. strategy in the region overall, not an unreasonable concern given the crisis caused by the Okinawa rape in 1995.[27] Understanding the centrality of Japan to the new administration's foreign policy and to its own forward presence in the Pacific, the U.S. Navy handled the incident with great sensitivity. The vice chief of naval operations traveled to the hometown of the sunken Japanese ship and bowed deeply in remorse, and on March 19 Mori used his final summit with Bush to steady the relationship.[28] Crisis was averted, in large part because of a clear understanding of strategic priorities in both Washington and Tokyo.

What came next could not have been more fortuitous for the Vulcans' Asia strategy. On April 24, a desperate ruling LDP in Japan threw caution to the wind and elected as their party president and next prime minister an iconoclastic lion-maned reformer named Koizumi Junichiro. In Washington, the NSC convened Japan experts from across the U.S. government to assess the potential of the new Japanese government (the meetings could have been held in Japanese, so extensive was Japan experience around the table).[29] Koizumi's dramatic attacks on the old guard of his own party were wildly popular with the Japanese public and promising for the Japanese economy, but his stance on the alliance was less clear. The NSC deputies met that May and forwarded the Japan experts' recommendation that the president invite Koizumi to Camp David to chart a shared vision along the lines of the Armitage-Nye Report. Uncertain what to expect, Bush was bemused and then charmed as Koizumi explained his commitment to the alliance the next month at Camp David by crooning from his favorite Elvis Presley song: "I need you, I love you." The two leaders issued a joint "Partnership for Security and Prosperity," charting plans for diplomatic, military, and economic cooperation together.[30] Koizumi would become one of the president's closest friends and confidants among world leaders. For veterans of the Reagan administration such as Assistant Secretary of State for East Asia and Pacific Affairs Jim Kelly, the Bush-Koizumi relationship surpassed even that between Reagan and Nakasone.

Relations with the Republic of Korea also produced surprises, though less fortuitous ones. The Vulcans had told the president that the Agreed Framework with North Korea was deeply flawed and that it bought the North Koreans time to cheat, but also that engagement with Pyongyang based on the accord was important, "so long as it addresses political, economic, and security concerns, is reciprocal, and does not come at the expense of our alliances and relationships," as Powell put it in his confirmation hearings.[31] In contrast to Japan, however, Korean politics were steadily moving to the left, where mistrust of the United States was strong. Within the Bush administration, there were also growing divisions between the regionalists and counterproliferation experts on the North Korean nuclear program—not over the basic nature of the problem but instead over the tactics of how much to stand by allies in confronting the North. Seoul's drift toward accommodation with Pyongyang brought out precisely these divisions.

President Kim Dae-jung of Korea was a strong advocate of the U.S.-ROK alliance but also a crusader for engagement with the North. Warned not to press the new American president too soon, Kim nevertheless requested an early March summit in Washington to make his case for continuing with Clinton's planning for a U.S. summit with the North. Powell tried in his initial meeting with Kim at the State Department to paper over differences between Seoul and Washington, promising to continue engagement with the North. However, the secretary's public comments prompted a *Washington Post* headline stating "Bush to Pick Up Clinton Talks on N. Korean Missiles" and a White House rebuke that sent Powell back in front of the press to confess that he had "leaned too far forward on his skis."[32] Kim then pressed his case directly with the president in the Oval Office. Bush, who had told his NSC before the meeting that he was "through picking up his [Kim Jong-il's] food" after North Korean temper tantrums, was taken aback.[33] He promised to continue the Agreed Framework but asked Kim for more time to review U.S. policy. Three months later, the White House announced that it was ready for broader dialogue with Pyongyang, to include human rights, conventional threats, and missiles—and to honor the Agreed Framework as long as North Korea did.[34] The problem—though the administration did not have concrete evidence yet—was that North Korea was already cheating on the 1995 accord. There would be no easy solution on North Korea.

The Vulcans' proposed approach to China was also tested in the early months of the new administration. On April 1, National Security Advisor Rice received a call at Camp David from the White House Situation Room informing her that a PLA fighter jet had collided with a routine EP-3 surveillance flight, forcing the U.S. Navy pilot to make an emergency landing on Hainan Island, where his aircraft and twenty-four crew members were taken by the Chinese authorities.[35] Rumsfeld wanted to take a hard line with Beijing and taunted Powell's proposal for a diplomatic approach by saying the secretary of state might do better if he said "pretty please."[36] Rumsfeld's deputies were not yet fully in place at the Pentagon, though, and JCS Chair Hugh Shelton had been an army protégé of Powell's. The secretary of defense was left to "kibbitz from the side" as Powell designed and led a diplomatic strategy that eventually resulted in the return of the crew with no U.S. apology on April 11.[37] The fact that it took the president a dozen calls to finally get Chinese leader Jiang Zemin on the phone—catching him in Santiago with the help of the Chilean government—only reinforced for the White House the need for *more* engagement and crisis management protocols with Beijing, particularly at the level of the president.[38]

Importantly, the president's personal commitment to building a relationship with Jiang to avoid future crises did *not* come at the expense of treaty allies or Taiwan. On April 24, he approved sales of submarines, destroyers, and antisubmarine aircraft to Taiwan, though not the expensive and more provocative Aegis missile defense destroyers on Taipei's original shopping list.[39] The next day, on *Good Morning America*, he responded to a hypothetical question about what he would do if China attacked Taiwan by declaring that he would "rise up to defend Taiwan."[40] Returning to the White House afterward, he asked his aides if he had just gone too far. "You just ripped the band aid off our policy of strategic ambiguity" on Taiwan, they told him. "Good," he replied, and Rice and Deputy National Security Advisor Stephen Hadley agreed—it was better to start with a firm stance and reassure rather than do it the other way around.[41] Longtime China watchers predicted there would be difficulties with Beijing, but the next February, Jiang Zemin was serenading Bush with "O Solo Mio" in Beijing, and the two leaders continued a mutually respectful and nonconfrontational relationship that extended to Jiang's successor, Hu Jintao.

Other elements of the Vulcans' Asia strategy moved forward incrementally in the first months of the administration. In Delhi, Ambassador Robert Blackwill publicly vowed that American engagement would be consistent with India's rise as a global power, and Zoellick—now U.S. trade representative—signaled during a visit in August a readiness to lift the remaining sanctions on India.[42] Delhi reciprocated by welcoming the U.S. decision to leave the ABM Treaty and strengthen missile defense, to the surprise of traditional arms-control experts and old school India *wallah* (India hands) who had expected more of an anti-American response from the nonaligned India. However, the bureaucratic reality in Washington proved another matter, and interagency talks on expanded defense and technology cooperation crept forward at a slow pace because of traditional pockets of concern about nonproliferation norms and relations with Pakistan.[43]

Meanwhile, in Southeast Asia, some states watched the firmer U.S. position toward Beijing with initial anxiety but then growing confidence as the administration managed the EP-3 crisis astutely and in close consultation with partners such as Singapore. On the whole, bilateral relations with the ASEAN member states advanced or stalled on their own merits, with new trade agreements launched for Singapore and military exchanges with Malaysia but with concern over political turmoil in Jakarta slowing U.S. engagement in Indonesia. The administration focused on incrementally making up lost ground after the financial crisis, energized by NSC staffer Karen Brooks, who had deep contacts in Jakarta, Manila, and Bangkok.

By the summer of 2001, the Bush administration had largely turned strategic concepts on Asia into policy and had weathered external crises and internal divisions with far more success than any new foreign policy team had since Nixon replaced Johnson. Unilateral decisions to leave the ABM Treaty and the Kyoto Protocol outraged progressives in parts of the world, but as promised, the new administration stabilized and improved relations with all the major powers. For a president narrowly elected by a citizenry where only 4 percent said they made their choice based on foreign affairs, Bush had established a disciplined if not highly consequential pattern of statecraft—until events unimagined by the Vulcans suddenly made national security the defining issue of his presidency.

"The World's Great Powers Find Ourselves on the Same Side": 9/11 and Asia

On September 11, 2001, at 8:50 A.M. I was meeting with a senior official from the Japanese prime minister's office in the Old Executive Office Building to follow up on the June 30 Bush-Koizumi joint statement. A muted television set in the corner of the room began to show repeated images of smoke billowing horizontally from the top of one of the World Trade Center buildings—"a small plane accident," the Asian Affairs staff secretary explained. Another twelve minutes into our discussion, the second tower was hit and the rest of the Asia staff rushed in—"It's an attack!" Moments later, our building was evacuated by the Uniformed Secret Service, except for Asia Senior Director Torkel Patterson, a former navy officer who instinctively rushed for the Situation Room below the Oval Office. Six confused and emotional hours later, Patterson (who had held my job during the Gulf War) called. "You are authorized to inform the Japanese Embassy on behalf of the most senior officials in the White House that the United States is under attack and that other key U.S. allies are preparing to invoke Article V of our security treaties to come to our defense." I had been on the phone with the Japanese and other embassies all day and called the Japanese political minister to convey the message. He was initially taken aback: "But under the U.S.-Japan Security Treaty, Article V only provides for the U.S. defense of Japan," he replied. And then, after a long pause, he gravely responded: "I understand . . . we will inform the Prime Minister immediately." Though the attacks had occurred in New York and the Pentagon—and we would soon learn that the enemy was in Afghanistan—it was already obvious that U.S. policy in Asia would not be the same.

The administration's first public effort to articulate U.S. grand strategy in the wake of 9/11 was the September 2002 *National Security Strategy of the United States* (NSS). Most of the media at the time focused on what they saw as an unprecedented provision for launching preemptive war or asserting primacy through force—what outsiders labeled the "Bush Doctrine."[44] However, one group of experts at the Institute for Defense Analyses (IDA) rightly understood that "over the longer term the NSS may prove far more significant" as it related to great-power politics.[45] As the NSS stated, in the wake of September 11, "the world's great powers find ourselves on the same side—united by common dangers of terrorist

violence and chaos." It then noted with specific reference to China that
"recent developments have encouraged our hope that a truly global consensus about basic principles is slowly taking shape."[46] In that same context, the NSS also highlighted the central role of allies and reiterated the
need for "a new balance of power that favors freedom."[47] The ensuing
Global War on Terror did not alter the Vulcans' fundamental assumptions or objectives with regard to the big powers in Asia, but the play-
book would now change significantly.

The most immediate and far-reaching impact of 9/11 in Asia was on U.S.
alliances, which, as the NSS noted, were "energized" by the attacks. When
the attack occurred, Australian prime minister John Howard was still in
the United States after visiting the president. Returned on U.S. military
aircraft because of the no-fly provision over U.S. airspace, on September 17
Howard convened Parliament in Canberra and gave a speech formally invoking Articles IV and V of the ANZUS alliance.[48] Australian forces
would be in at the "pointy end of the spear" fighting the earliest engagements in Operation Enduring Freedom (OEF) in Afghanistan and then
Operation Iraqi Freedom (OIF).[49] Already closely linked to the United
States through intelligence sharing and almost a century of shared combat operations, the Royal Australian Navy, Army, and Air Force would
reach unprecedented levels of jointness and interoperability with the U.S.
military over the next decade.

Pivoting off the Armitage-Nye Report, the NSS stated that the United
States would "look to Japan to continue forging a leading role in regional
and global affairs based on our common interests, our common values,
and our close defense and diplomatic cooperation."[50] Many senior officials
in Tokyo and Washington were scarred veterans of the poor U.S.-Japan
alliance response to the 1990–1991 Gulf War and moved quickly to avoid a
similar debacle, which would have undermined the overall U.S. standing in Asia. Koizumi was one of the few world leaders to urge the president not just to find the perpetrators of the attack but to *defeat* terrorism.
He sent a short personal note to the president within a week of the attack,
signing it with the words, "I am your friend. I will always be your friend."
On September 19, he announced a seven-point package to assist the
United States, including the first use of the Self Defense Forces abroad
while combat was ongoing.[51]

It was an unprecedented move that many observers predicted would
fall victim to domestic Japanese politics, but Koizumi's determination
was clear when CNN and front-page newspaper stories around the world

carried shots of the carrier USS *Kitty Hawk* being escorted out from Tokyo Bay by two Japanese destroyers—the Stars and Stripes and Rising Sun flags flapping in the breeze. In fact, the Japanese ships were not yet authorized to engage abroad (and the *Kitty Hawk* was only undergoing brief sea trials), but on October 18 Koizumi's proposal convincingly passed the Diet. Japan dispatched refueling ships to the Arabian Sea for OEF, and then a reconstruction battalion to Samawaha in southern Iraq for OIF.[52] Whereas Japanese prime minister Kaifu had reluctantly pledged funds for the Gulf War and received little credit, Koizumi hosted the first major reconstruction conference for Afghanistan and was one of the first world leaders to pledge money for Iraq ($5 billion initially)— volunteering to pressure European and Gulf State leaders who were being less forthcoming.[53] Though credit is due to Koizumi, the robust Japanese response was also possible because the Vulcans and seniormost officials across the U.S. administration saw the 9/11 and Iraq crises as transformational moments in the alliance and invested time and personal credibility to ensure that the relationship came out stronger.[54]

Korea also provided major support to OEF and OIF, but whereas Koizumi used the crises in the Middle East to demonstrate solidarity with Washington, Korea's new president after February 2003, Roh Moo-hyun, was trapped in a narrative of his own making about mistrust of the United States. Roh was almost an accidental president, propelled to office on a wave of social media and candlelight protests after U.S. Army heavy-track vehicles tragically hit two Korean schoolgirls on a rural road in June 2002. In contrast to the U.S. Navy's deft handling of the submarine incident in March 2001, the Pentagon and the U.S. Army initially refused to apologize for the Korean accident before a formal U.S. military investigation was completed. The desperate U.S. ambassador in Seoul, Thomas Hubbard, unilaterally helped to defuse the crisis on November 27 when he waved a cable from the White House in front of the press announcing that he had received "the President's apology" (in fact, the cable expressed the president's "deep regret" at the Pentagon's insistence, but only Hubbard and the drafters at the NSC were any the wiser).[55] Nevertheless, the damage was done, and Korean politics lurched in directions that would complicate U.S. strategy in Asia for the next five years. Although many of the political dynamics in Korea were beyond U.S. influence, the administration paid a price for not initially approaching Korea with the same strategic discipline as it had toward Japan—a recurring lesson of American statecraft that should not be lost.

Eventually, Roh would dispatch the third-largest contingent to Iraq, after the United States and Britain, negotiate a high-level FTA with Washington, and successfully launch a joint plan for realigning U.S. bases in Korea—but he would not abandon his anti-American discourse. The White House and Blue House NSCs developed close ties over those years, in part because those closest to the presidents were best positioned to close their respective leaders' ideological gaps. At one point, I urged my friend Korean NSC secretary general Lee Jeong-seok to work with us to celebrate the accomplishments of our alliance in Afghanistan and Iraq as we had with Japan and Australia. "We can't do that," he replied candidly, "since we told our political base that we were cooperating in order to stop a U.S. attack on North Korea." Of course, Bush never had any intention of attacking North Korea, as he explained publicly and privately to Roh. Yet even as public opinion polls in Korea showed the highest level of support for the U.S.-ROK alliance in history, Roh's political allies among the more radical nongovernmental organizations (NGOs) came out into the streets to protest whenever Bush (or I, on one occasion) visited Seoul.[56] The president handled the situation with amazing patience, while administration Asia hands were left explaining to Congress and the media that the U.S. relationship with Korea was like Mark Twain's comment about the music of Richard Wagner—it really was not as bad as it sounds.

Ultimately, the U.S.-Korea alliance emerged from 9/11 and Iraq far stronger than it had been before those jarring episodes. Over the next two presidential cycles in Korea, no candidate on the left would follow Roh's example of running implicitly or explicitly against the U.S. alliance. The 2002 NSS may have papered over some of the tensions, particularly with Seoul, but it was generally correct in predicting that "America's alliances in Asia not only underpin regional peace and stability, but are flexible and ready to deal with new challenges."[57]

The NSS prediction that 9/11 could reshape great-power relations was perhaps overstated with respect to China. Beijing was never a real partner in the War on Terror, unlike Japan, Australia, or Korea. However, the attack on 9/11 redirected the American national security debate away from the question of whether China was a friend or enemy and allowed room for a more nuanced and consistent policy of engagement toward Beijing than might otherwise have been the case. As a result, U.S.-China relations emerged stronger from the Global War on Terror without the United States conceding any geopolitical interests or moral principles.

Bush set the tone early with Beijing by agreeing to attend the APEC summit in Shanghai only six weeks after the attacks on New York and Washington, and a grateful President Jiang reciprocated by helping negotiate a major statement by the assembled leaders on collaboration against terrorism.[58] Like Theodore Roosevelt with a rising Japan a century earlier, Bush understood that reassurance backed by principled strength would be critical as Chinese power, ambitions, and insecurities grew. He paid constant attention to his Chinese counterparts' "face"—praising Hu Jintao's efforts in response to the 2003 SARS outbreak at a time when many world leaders were condemning his failings; publicly rejecting trade cases against China on labor and the environment in 2004 that might have proven tempting politically;[59] and attending the Beijing Summer Olympics in 2008 over the objections of some of his political advisors.[60]

At the same time, Bush did not compromise on his commitment to U.S. allies and democratic norms in pursuit of better ties with Beijing. On February 18, 2002, he told the National Diet that on his Asia trip that year he stopped first in Japan because "America and Japan have formed one of the great and enduring alliances of modern times."[61] In November 2005, he gave a major speech in Kyoto praising democracies in Asia and arguing that "by meeting the legitimate demands of its citizens for freedom and openness, China's leaders can help their country grow into a modern, prosperous, and confident nation."[62] The press predicted disaster the next day in China, but Hu welcomed Bush warmly.[63] In 2004, Bush met with the spiritual leader of Tibet, the Dalai Lama, over Chinese protests, and in 2008 he attended the conveying of the Congressional Gold Medal to the Tibetan spiritual leader. In summit meetings with his Chinese counterparts, Bush consistently raised religious freedom, rule of law, and freedom of expression as areas that would make China's society stronger in turbulent times.[64] He pressed for the release of prisoners of conscience, with some success (though it became more difficult as time passed), and met with Chinese dissidents at the White House.[65] Over these years, no U.S. ally in Asia suspected that the United States would tilt toward China at their expense or confront China against their own interests.

On Taiwan policy, however, the administration suffered for a time from internal divisions. Bush came into office with the most pro-Taiwan stance of any president since Reagan, but some on the right continued to argue that it was still not strong enough. Frustrated at the lack of

tone toward China after 9/11, they drew new battle
Taiwan's president, Chen Shui-bian, who was antago-
inting that he might take symbolic and even legal steps
ice from the mainland. Columnists in *The Weekly*
ington Times detailed the bureaucratic battles between
and detractors in Washington, while Taipei interpreted the mixed signals coming from the administration as a green
light to begin pushing for a new referendum and constitutional revision
to undercut the One China policy framework in domestic ROC law.[66]

On December 9, 2003, Chen finally did hear from Bush directly at
a press conference in the Rose Garden with visiting Chinese premier
Wen Jiabao. Asked about cross-Strait tensions, the president warned that
"the comments and actions by the leader of Taiwan indicate that he may
be willing to make decisions unilaterally to change the status quo, which
we oppose."[67] Taipei was shocked, and Chen's supporters in Washington
sought a scapegoat to blame for the president's statement. The fact was,
however, that it was President Bush speaking entirely for himself.

The next month, I took over as the senior Asia official on the NSC staff
and was ordered by Rice and the principals to reboot our policy process
on Taiwan. With Deputy Assistant Secretary of State Randy Schriver's
steady guidance on cross-Strait issues and with participants from key
agencies, we established a coordinating cell at the NSC to ensure a single
message while reengaging Chen and his lieutenants on a new bilateral
agenda to reinforce Taiwan's security, economic prosperity, and opportunities to contribute to the international community. When the People's
Political Consultative Congress in Beijing ratified an Anti-secession Law
in March 2005 authorizing the use of force should Taiwan declare independence, Washington and Taipei stayed in lockstep, using Beijing's new
threat to restoke international support for Taiwan and block European
Union momentum to open arms sales to China.[68] Then, in November
2005, in his speech at Sophia University in Tokyo, the president singled
out Taiwan's democracy as an example for the entire region—sending a
clear signal to Beijing that U.S. support for Taiwan was undiminished.
The Washington-Beijing-Taipei triangle stabilized, though the president's
own personal trust toward Taipei never fully returned.[69]

Based on his initial determination to approach China with a "cooperative, constructive and candid" framework, the president had managed
to deepen personal trust with Jiang and then Hu through a series of

potential crises in U.S.-China relations. But the stability in U.S.-China relations was still the result of process rather than longer-term vision. Increasingly confident in Bush's stewardship of the relationship, Chinese officials were urging a return to Clinton's promise of a U.S.-China "strategic partnership." This was a nonstarter, however, given the political realities of U.S.-China relations in the United States and the administration's disciplined anchoring of Asia strategy on democratic allies. After his reelection, the president sent me to Beijing (after stops in Tokyo and Seoul) with a letter I hand-delivered to Hu in the Great Hall of the People on February 2, 2005, proposing to bring U.S.-China relations "to the next level" in President Bush's second term.[70] Hu was visibly pleased to receive the missive from the president, but his staff later asked, "What *is* the next level?"

With Rice's blessing, Zoellick (now deputy secretary of state), began work on a longer-term vision for the relationship that would capture both the opportunities and the fundamental disagreements with China. He explained his concept in a speech in New York on September 21, 2005, which called for China to be not just a taker but a "responsible stakeholder" in international society.[71] In Washington, observers thought he was being too accommodating toward China, while his audience in New York was aghast at what seemed an impossibly high bar for U.S.-China relations to meet. "We have many common interests with China," Zoellick told his audience, "but relationships built only on a coincidence of interests have shallow roots." He was clear that "real trust with China would only be possible when China became a democracy," but "we can cooperate with the emerging China of today, even as we work for the democratic China of tomorrow."[72]

Beijing was initially confused. The next morning, the Chinese ambassador in Washington asked to meet urgently with me to confirm that the White House viewed the "responsible stakeholder" theme as a positive vision for U.S.-China relations. Zoellick subsequently initiated a dialogue with his Chinese counterpart, Executive Vice Foreign Minister Dai Bingguo, to discuss the concept in more detail. Over two days of meetings in Washington and New York in December 2005, Dai explained that "responsible stakeholder" did not translate well into Chinese, and he proposed yet again the label "strategic partnership." Japan or Australia are strategic partners because we share norms, Zoellick explained in response, but different value systems did not mean that China could not also give back to international society by using its power to push for denuclearization on the

Korean Peninsula or better governance in sub-Saharan Africa. That was the best path for U.S.-China relations. Dai then laid out China's view of international affairs, a nineteenth-century realpolitik exposition on the distribution of international power and alignment in Asia that contrasted with Zoellick's twenty-first-century mosaic of regional and global governance and norms. Nevertheless, Dai appeared to come away pleased with the serious strategic discourse and agreed enthusiastically to further discussions in Beijing, which continued under Zoellick's successor, John Negroponte, and his deputy assistant secretary for China, Princeton professor Tom Christensen. Treasury Secretary Hank Paulson then added another girder under U.S.-China relations in 2006 with the establishment of the Strategic Economic Dialogue (SED), designed to cut across obstructions in the Chinese system that had hitherto hindered progress on market access issues and to expand cooperation on bilateral and global economic issues ranging from energy to macroeconomic policy.[73]

A few months after Zoellick's "Responsible Stakeholder" speech, two veteran Asia experts at the National Defense University's Institute for National Strategic Studies, Phillip Saunders and James Pryztup, produced an analysis contrasting the speech with the earlier Armitage-Nye Report. The two visions of regional order seemed in tension, they noted—one Sinocentric and the other anchored on Japan—but ultimately, they concluded, a sound U.S. strategy required the right balance between both approaches.[74] The history of American statecraft certainly supports their conclusion. Nye's original "engage and balance" approach to Asia had taken deeper root in U.S. strategy.

In retrospect, 9/11 and the War on Terror could have completely derailed relations with another major Asian power with which the administration *did* seek a new strategic partnership—India. With Pakistan suddenly a frontline state, Washington might have lowered its ambitions with Islamabad's rival India, whereas traditionally nonaligned India might have recoiled at the new American assertion of preeminence and military preemption. Instead, Delhi and Washington stayed focused on the larger geostrategic opportunity each provided to the other. For Washington, this meant a better strategic equilibrium in Asia, and for Delhi it meant the endorsement of the world's leading power for India's rise. Still, the relationship moved forward incrementally. On December 13, 2001, Islamic extremists attacked the Parliament Building in Delhi, bringing India and Pakistan to the brink of war until mediation by the UN Security Council permanent members and Pakistani president Musharraf's promise to combat internal extremism defused the crisis. Deputy National Security Advisor Stephen Hadley also needed time for his assignment to socialize the bureaucracy in Washington to a more forthcoming partnership with Delhi in the sensitive areas of space, high technology, nuclear power, and missile defense—particularly coming so soon after the 1998 Indian nuclear test. On January 13, 2004, the United States and India finally announced the excruciatingly negotiated "Next Steps in Strategic Partnership (NSSP)"—a process of expanded reciprocal steps to remove the obstacles to cooperation on energy and technology that had kept the world's oldest and largest republics unnaturally divided for so long.[75]

Yet even with the agreement on the NSSP, the lead Indian and American architects of the transformed relationship knew that bolder action was possible. Peaceful nuclear cooperation was the Gordian knot holding back closer strategic alignment between Washington and Delhi and India's own economic development, and leading officials in the Ministry of External Affairs (MEA) began to ask me in early 2005 whether the two leaders might cut this knot themselves. In fact, a small group of energy and nonproliferation experts in the White House had quietly begun work on a new framework for peaceful nuclear cooperation with the developing world as a way to reduce carbon emissions and proliferation dangers.[76] Consultations with key members of Congress and the national security advisors of Britain and France also indicated that there could be broad support for bringing India into the nonproliferation framework even if India did not join the Non-Proliferation Treaty. In March, Secretary of State Rice told Prime Minister Manmohan Singh in Delhi that the administration was ready to discuss cutting the Gordian knot.[77] Singh faced continued resistance from his own nuclear bureaucracy and from nonaligned ideologues in the Ministry of Foreign Affairs, but he was ready to make the announcement when he traveled to Washington that July for a state visit with President Bush.

The specifics were negotiated right up to the last minute, being completed only minutes before the two leaders' press conference at the White House on July 18.[78] When Rice and her Indian counterpart approved the final text in the Roosevelt Room, she handed it to me for delivery to the Executive Secretariat in the basement of the White House. Chased down the hall by a sari-clad diplomat and her colleague from the Indian

Department of Atomic Energy, who were ordered to intercept the document by their own immediate superiors in Delhi, I escaped through a hidden stairway and delivered the document for public release.[79] The Bush-Singh joint statement committed the administration to work for a change in U.S. law to facilitate India's acceptance into the Nuclear Suppliers Group and the international nuclear order. In exchange, India agreed to separate its civil and military nuclear programs, to abide by international nuclear norms (including a moratorium on testing), and to assist the United States in its nonproliferation efforts.[80] The International Atomic Energy Agency, Japan, Britain, France, and eventually even China agreed to the new status for India. Skeptics from the nonproliferation community argued that the deal would encourage other states to leave the NPT, but none have. Ratification in Congress took considerable effort by the president, Rice, and other officials, but they pushed it through successfully, recognizing, as one senior official said, that the United States had an enduring interest in "India becoming a major world power in the 21st century."[81]

When I left the NSC staff in December 2005, the Bush administration was coming under intensified criticism for its involvement in Iraq, but I felt generally confident that we had kept our bearings on strategy toward Asia. Powell and Armitage had been told by their Japanese and Chinese counterparts when they left the year before that both relationships with Washington were the best they had been for years.[82] Relations with India and Pakistan were also strong at the same time for the first time in American history. We had completed an internal review of Asia strategy led by the NSC in 2004 as a draft NSPD (presidential directive) to ensure that our policies were aligned with our original objectives and with the new global requirements imposed by the War on Terror. Overall, the Vulcans' original strategic objectives for allies and major-power relations in Asia conformed to the demands of a post–9/11 world. Clear strategic concepts had imposed a discipline on the policy process even in the face of unforeseen calamities.

That was not true for every part of the region, however. Indeed, the areas where initial strategic thinking had been least focused or coherent were the most affected. The Global War on Terror had made Southeast Asia policy markedly harder, and setbacks in Iraq had consequences for North Korea policy that shook the foundations of the progress made with U.S. allies.

COLLATERAL CHALLENGES: SOUTHEAST ASIA AND NORTH KOREA

In the traditional Mahan-Kennan maritime view, U.S. interests in Southeast Asia have often been derivative of larger power concerns in Northeast Asia, Europe, or globally. In the early postwar years, for example, Washington had viewed the problems of Southeast Asia through a European prism, and the Clinton administration's response to the 1997–1998 Asian financial crisis was driven first by concerns about global norms and financial stability until the crisis hit Korea and triggered the involvement of the national security experts. Therefore, it should not be entirely surprising that, after the trauma of 9/11, the American instinct was to view Southeast Asia through the lens of international terrorism.

This was not without cause. In the weeks and months after 9/11, the region came alive with terrorist threats linked to the terrorist group Jemaah Islamiya (JI). Its operatives were found to have trained in Al Qaeda camps and then deployed to previously undetected branches in Malaysia, the Philippines, Singapore, Thailand, Australia, and Pakistan.[83] In early January 2002, Singaporean authorities were stunned to discover a major domestic JI plot to attack visiting U.S. Navy ships.[84] On October 12, 2002, JI bombed a popular nightclub in Bali, killing 202 tourists, many of them young Australians. In February 2002, JI links to antigovernment insurgents on the southern island of Mindanao prompted Manila to request the deployment of 1,300 U.S. troops to train Philippine Armed Forces on counterinsurgency in Operation Balikatan (shoulder-to-shoulder).[85] Meanwhile, the counterterrorism efforts of Indonesia's Megawati Sukarnoputri could only be described as lackluster after the attacks, as she allowed Abu Bakar Bashir, the spiritual leader of JI, to meet with his followers in Jakarta and then released him for a time on good behavior. Initially, the only reliable counterterrorism force in that country of 212 million people was a cell of a few dozen Balinese police agents supported by Australian and American experts. The general assessment in and out of government after 9/11 was that the next front would be in Southeast Asia. The fight did not start well, and its outcome was hardly certain.[86]

As the United States commenced military operations in Afghanistan and then Iraq, American standing in Southeast Asia came under greater risk. The terrorist threat in the Far East could not be ignored, but a narrative dominated by counterterrorism and wars against Muslims was becoming counterproductive and unsustainable. There was, however, an opportunity to build a new narrative around economic engagement with ASEAN—collectively the third-largest U.S. trading partner in the region, after Japan and China. While Zoellick was still at USTR, he had worked with the NSC's Karen Brooks to launch the Enterprise for ASEAN Initiative (EAI) as an à la carte framework for each of ASEAN's member states to deepen their economic engagement with the United States based on their individual level of economic development, with a range of options from the U.S.-Singapore FTA negotiation to basic Permanent Normal Trading Relations for Laos.[87] The White House also used a state visit in May 2003 to express gratitude to President Gloria Macapagal Arroyo of the Philippines, who early on stood with the United States after 9/11 despite a significant Muslim minority at home and the risk to millions of Philippine citizens working in the Middle East. And, once at State, Zoellick followed up on EAI with a comprehensive agenda for political, security, and economic cooperation under the ASEAN-US Enhanced Partnership in November 2005.[88]

These diplomatic steps helped, but the American image really only turned around when the United States led international relief efforts in the wake of the massive December 26, 2004, Asian tsunami. At first, official Washington did not know the extent of the damage—that scores of communities had been destroyed and hundreds of thousands killed from India to Indonesia. Elements of the U.S. Seventh Fleet happened to be steaming near the epicenter of the tsunami, though, and the task force commander had the foresight to make ready for major humanitarian and relief operations while Washington caught up. As satellite images demonstrating the extent of the destruction came into the White House, the handful of experts still in the office during Christmas break pulled together a proposal to join with Japan, Australia, and India in a "Quad" task force that would spearhead international relief efforts and help NGOs and stricken governments get supplies to isolated communities across the Indian Ocean.[89] The incredible speed, capacity, and goodwill of the United States at this critical juncture were unmistakable. As Singapore's Lee Kuan Yee observed, "Millions of ordinary Indonesians—and especially their political leaders—will remember that the Americans came swiftly to help when they were stricken. It will begin to undo the influence of Arab Islamic fundamentalists who have made tolerant Muslims in Southeast Asia view Muslim grievances, especially America's unqualified support for Israel's government, through Arab spectacles."[90] Indeed it did. In Pew polls taken after the relief operations, 79 percent of Indonesians said that U.S. aid efforts had improved their views of the United States, and favorable views toward the United States more than doubled, from 15 percent at the beginning of the Iraq War to 38 percent. However, that number was still well below the 61 percent of Indonesians who had expressed a favorable and sympathetic view of the United States in Pew polling immediately after 9/11.[91] By the end of the Bush administration, the terror threat in Southeast Asia looked very different than it had in 2001, and the president's personal relationships with almost all his counterparts in the region were strong. Those were important accomplishments considering how dangerous the threat to Southeast Asia had been, but the United States still had a diplomatic deficit to climb out of because of the War on Terror and the ongoing conflict in Iraq.

Meanwhile, the post–9/11 North Korean nuclear problem was best described by *New York Times* columnist Nick Kristoff, who wrote in December 2002 that "all our options regarding North Korea are hideous, and those responsible for making policy on North Korea must have committed mortal sins in previous lives for God to torture them so."[92] We wondered ourselves what our counterparts in other parts of the administration had done in past lives to have themselves thrown at this impossible problem.

Since the visit by Kim Dae-jung to Washington in March 2001, policy formulation toward North Korea had been worked through two parallel and often conflicting groups—one led by Kelly at the State Department and the other by Robert Joseph, the senior director for counterproliferation, at the NSC. When the intelligence community unanimously concluded in the early summer of 2002 that the North had been cheating on the Agreed Framework through a clandestine program to develop a new path to nuclear weapons through highly enriched uranium (HEU), the regional and proliferation experts agreed on what would happen next: Kelly was authorized by the president to explain to the North Koreans in Pyongyang that comprehensive dialogue was possible but only if the North came clean about the clandestine HEU program and returned to compliance with the Agreed Framework.

The counterproliferation experts fully expected the North to deny the existence of the HEU program, but to our surprise (I was among the delegation), North Korean first vice foreign minister Kang Sok-ju acknowledged the program's existence and claimed that North Korea possessed "even more powerful weapons"—presumably a reference to ongoing weaponization of plutonium harvested from the Yongbyon reactor. It was the United States that now had to make concessions and end its "hostile policy," Kang countered, by lifting all economic sanctions, removing the nuclear umbrella over Japan and Korea, and then consummating the new agreement in a Bush-Kim summit.[93] The North had cheated on the Agreed Framework and was now demanding the dismantlement of U.S. security policy in Northeast Asia just to come back to the table. Kelly walked out of the talks rather than listen to further blackmail.

What would happen next was unclear. In Washington, the principals asked for three option papers: Joseph wrote a strategy for "tailored containment" of North Korea, in effect cutting off all aid and diplomacy but not using force; Samantha Ravich in the vice president's office wrote a strategy for toppling Kim Jong-il's regime from within; and I was tasked with writing an "international strategy" that would align U.S. allies and China against the North in a diplomatic process backed by collective pressure.

When I was given this assignment, I remembered that when Kissinger was national security advisor, he used to commission three options to ensure that his option—the reasonable middle—would prevail. Since either regime change or tailored containment would be impossible without regional cooperation, I thought my option had to be that reasonable middle. When the principals convened on November 13, however, they opted for tailored containment, with only elements of my international approach.[94] But when the president was briefed, he chose his own strategy—one that looked much more like the international approach but contained key elements of tailored containment—namely that diplomacy do nothing to enhance the Kim regime's position if it continued pursuing missiles and nuclear weapons.

The NSC Asia and Counterproliferation staffs were then collectively tasked by the president and Rice with putting together a strategy that would establish a multilateral forum to bring about international pressure on the North. In drafting the paper, we recommended establishing a "contact group" of the outside parties much like the one the United States and NATO had used to isolate and then negotiate with Slobodan Milosevic in Serbia in the 1990s. The concept was that the United States, Japan, Korea, and China would negotiate and then present their collective demands to Pyongyang. It had never been tried, but Rice and the president believed it would be far preferable to continued bilateral U.S.-DPRK talks that put all the regional pressure on the United States to defuse crises rather than on North Korea to denuclearize. The key was to keep pressure on China to host the talks and to assume greater responsibility for the outcome. The president approved the memo, and Secretary Powell was authorized to win support in the region.

When Powell pitched the idea of multilateral talks during travel to Tokyo, Seoul, and Beijing in February 2003, the Japanese and Koreans were enthusiastic, but Chinese president Jiang Zemin balked. "China is not associated with the North Korean nuclear program," he said while chuckling dismissively to his assembled staff, "it is a problem for the United States and the DPRK to resolve." Powell explained the president's position—that if this was to be done diplomatically, there would have to be a multilateral approach. After several rounds, Jiang suddenly recognized the coercive subtext of Powell's message: U.S. forces were massing near Iraq, and it would clearly be better for Beijing to work diplomacy with Powell than for Rumsfeld to pursue other courses. "I see," Jiang finally said soberly, and the next day he ordered his Foreign Ministry to get to work organizing the talks. The charge that George W. Bush was "unilateralist" was wrong. What he wanted with North Korea diplomacy was multilateralism.

Beijing nevertheless continued to drag its feet, insisting first on "preparatory" talks in Beijing on April 23–25, 2003, where Chinese officials tried again to broker a U.S.-DPRK bilateral negotiation. The mood shifted, however, as during the talks Chinese officials nervously watched television images of U.S. Marines pulling down Saddam's statue in Baghdad. "Your current course will only bring your country chaos," Madame Fu Ying of the Chinese Foreign Ministry warned the North Koreans. But the North had its own message. After the closing dinner, the head of the North Korean delegation, Li Gun, told Kelly on instructions from Pyongyang that the North had a "nuclear deterrent" and would "demonstrate," "transfer," and "expand" that deterrent if the United States did not end its "hostile policy."[95] The Chinese side claimed not to know about the North's threat (despite likely having the entire grounds under surveillance) but was alarmed enough by developments to agree to host a full six-party session with Korea, Japan, and Russia that August.

The Six Party Talks succeeded in pushing China to the center of the North Korean nuclear problem for the first time, but momentum again stalled after the first round. There were now two problems. First, the State

Department, in its eagerness to move the process forward, had abandoned the original plan of five-on-one talks and agreed instead to Chinese demands that the North Koreans be invited as an equal partner in the diplomacy. That gave Pyongyang the veto power to once again demand concessions merely to show up at talks. The second problem was that the conflict in Iraq shifted from scenes of triumphant marines in Baghdad to violent insurgencies in Fallujah and Mosul. With the coercive element gone, talks about talks dragged on as Chinese diplomats shuttled between Pyongyang and Washington trying to bribe and cajole the North back to the table without ever putting serious pressure on the North Korean regime to reverse its nuclear weapons program.

In order to reestablish a coercive element to American diplomacy and demonstrate that the United States would not tolerate North Korean threats at any level, Armitage ordered the East Asia and Pacific Affairs Bureau to begin organizing a campaign with Treasury, the FBI, and other agencies to go after the North's illegal and illicit trade.[96] The North had been making hundreds of millions of dollars from counterfeiting currencies, cigarettes, and over-the-counter drugs while distributing heroin and meta-amphetamines to neighboring states, including Japan and Australia.[97] On June 29, 2005, the president issued Executive Order 13382 ordering the Treasury Department to freeze assets of three North Korean entities "responsible for WMD and missile programs."[98] Then, on September 15, the Treasury Department designated the Macau-based Banco Delta Asia a "primary money laundering concern" under Section 311 of the USA Patriot Act, freezing about $25 million in North Korean funds.[99] The impact on the overall banking system—including in China—was devastating for Pyongyang. "You really figured out how to hurt us," one North Korean diplomat later confided to the NSC's Victor Cha on the margin of international negotiations.[100]

On September 19, 2005, the Six Party Talks—led on the U.S. side by Kelly's successor Christopher Hill—produced a first joint statement, committing the North to full denuclearization, *after which* the other parties would discuss the North's peaceful nuclear use.[101] It was the biggest step forward on diplomacy with the North in a decade, but within days Pyongyang backtracked, demanding that light-water reactors be provided *before* denuclearization (in blatant contradiction to the agreement and the earlier Agreed Framework). Then the full implications of the new financial sanctions hit Pyongyang, as commercial banks around the world began to reject the North's deposits.[102] On October 9, 2006,

Pyongyang followed through on Li Gun's threat to "demonstrate" the North's deterrent, conducting a first underground nuclear test near the village of P'unggye.[103] In response, the UN Security Council unanimously condemned the test and approved new sanctions against the North under Resolution 1718, while Secretary of State Rice dispatched undersecretaries Nicholas Burns and Robert Joseph to Asia to coordinate on implementation of the new sanctions.[104] The North, through its own brazen defiance, was helping to unify the international community and strengthen the coercive element needed for effective diplomacy.

Then, suddenly, U.S. pressure on the North came to a halt. In early January, Hill had arranged an encounter with North Korean officials at a Berlin conference brokered by Asia Society chairman and Democratic foreign policy advisor Richard Holbrooke.[105] The North, Hill reported, was ready to come back to the table. Consumed with other foreign policy challenges and by increasing friction with a Democrat-controlled Congress, Rice was favorably disposed toward reducing tension in Northeast Asia. Through sanctions, the international community had demonstrated its strong will, she concluded, and now was the time to test diplomacy again.[106] Joseph and the Treasury officials were ordered to stand down, and implementation of new sanctions came to a halt.[107] Hill, who had no demonstrated interest in either Asia policy or counterproliferation, focused on the diplomacy of demonstrating that a deal with Pyongyang was possible. And there were some initial results when the Six Party Talks reopened. The North agreed to incremental steps to decommission its aging Yongbyon reactor, including a freeze, disablement of some facilities (the cooling tower), and another promise of eventual dismantlement.[108] In exchange, Pyongyang would receive an initial shipment of 50,000 tons of heavy fuel oil and an additional $400 million in aid.

But the North had one more demand before moving forward—the return of all $25 million in illicit funds frozen in Banco Delta Asia as a result of U.S. sanctions.[109] Now committed to a renegotiation with the North and unwilling to reopen the crisis, the administration authorized Hill to announce on February 13 that the Banco Delta Asia funds—money earned through counterfeiting and drug deals—would be returned to the North for "humanitarian" purposes.[110]

The decision to retest diplomacy with Pyongyang now became something of a trap. The return of North Korea's $25 million had shattered the international cooperation needed to keep the pressure on the North's illicit money operations.[111] Then work continued on a U.S.-DPRK deal even after it was discovered that North Korea had helped Syria build the al-Kibar nuclear reactor bombed by the Israeli Air Force in September 2007—a dangerous precedent of outward proliferation that demonstrated the North's intention to follow up on Li Gun's 2003 threat that Pyongyang was willing to "transfer" its deterrent.[112] Finally, when Pyongyang demanded that Washington remove the DPRK from the sanctions list of state sponsors of terrorism—despite an explicit U.S. pledge not to do so until there was progress determining the fate of Japanese citizens abducted by the North several years earlier—Hill pushed for the administration to comply over Tokyo's objections, denigrating Japan as a major obstacle to further diplomatic progress and infuriating the government of Shinzo Abe.[113]

The most experienced Asia hands among the Vulcans—Armitage, Zoellick, Libby, and Wolfowitz—were all out of office at this point (as was I). The president himself was instinctively opposed to lifting sanctions, but the NSC principals concluded that derailing diplomacy this late would risk reopening the nuclear crisis with North Korea for the incoming administration.[114] In October 2008, the White House announced that terrorism sanctions on the North would be lifted, pointing out that many other legal and regulatory restrictions on economic activity with the regime were still in place.[115] Pyongyang then refused to produce its end of the bargain—a short verification protocol explaining its plutonium facilities as a notional guide to future inspections. The retesting of North Korean intentions was spent.

When dissecting the decision-making process on North Korea after 2007, it is difficult to discern a clear strategy on Asia or on counterproliferation. Instead, the policy was driven by the desire to avoid the expenditure of limited political and strategic capital on a problem that clearly would not be solved before the next presidency and might explode as the next president took office. There was some broader geostrategic logic to this approach, but the damage to Japan and to counterproliferation tools was also unmistakable and probably unnecessary.[116] North Korea had demonstrated an uncanny ability to muddy U.S. strategy, as it had earlier with Clinton and would yet again with Obama.

It is striking that the problems in Asia strategy after 9/11 emerged not with the major powers—Japan, India, and China—that had been the focus of the Vulcans but instead in Southeast Asia and the Korean Peninsula. These were the same bookends of East Asia that defied Kennan's crafting of a maritime-based strategy sixty years earlier. Neither stood as traditional "strong points" for U.S. foreign policy strategy, as Kennan had defined Japan after the Second World War or as the Vulcans defined Japan and India. Yet history should have suggested that these two subregions would be critical in the next phase of Asian international relations, as the rise of Chinese power reframed the Korean Peninsula and Southeast Asia in geopolitical terms more compelling than just terrorism or proliferation. Some of the Vulcans steeped in Asia policy understood this, but not all.

Korea, for example, did not fit neatly into Secretary of Defense Rumsfeld's longer-term thinking about U.S. military requirements in the region. Under Rumsfeld, the Defense Department initiated a major review of U.S. forward basing, proposing in September 2004 that U.S. ground forces in Korea be consolidated away from the DMZ and south of Seoul, while U.S. naval and air forces would be given more "lilly pads" and other access points to Southeast Asia and the Indian Ocean.[117] This plan reflected the growing missile threat from China to U.S. bases and the historic U.S. preference for a flexible forward posture based in the maritime domain. It also helped to realign U.S. bases in Korea in a more politically and logistically sustainable hub. The entire plan took enormous bureaucratic and diplomatic effort, which Andrew Hoehn, a lead architect of the posture review, recalls that Rumsfeld embraced with far greater passion than he did the ongoing conflict in Iraq.[118]

However, Rumsfeld's goal was a flexible and deployable force, vis-à-vis the emerging challenge from China and the global requirements in the War on Terror, and U.S. forces on the Korean Peninsula were focused entirely on the North Korean threat and therefore not well configured for either of those other challenges. Without waiting for Seoul to catch up to U.S. strategy, in May 2003 the Pentagon ordered the Second Brigade Combat Team (Stryker Brigade) of the Second Infantry Division to stop training to defend South Korea and to prepare for deployment to Iraq in two months, despite earlier Pentagon assurances that U.S. forces in Korea would not be pulled off the peninsula.[119] The stunned Korean government quietly agreed, but the Pentagon then pushed for Seoul's agreement that the remaining U.S. forces on the peninsula would have sufficient "strategic flexibility" to be able to deploy to contingencies elsewhere in the region if needed.[120] Wary of China's reaction to explicit agreements with the United States on strategic flexibility, Roh's government leaked their objections to the plan, and the Korean president took the issue directly to Bush over breakfast in the White House on June 10, 2005. Over Rumsfeld's objections, the president agreed to defer decisions on strategic flexibility for the future rather than force a rupture with Seoul.[121]

The episode was illustrative. On the one hand, the secretary of defense was engaging in prudent planning for contingencies in Asia—plans that the Obama administration largely followed, prompting one scholar to call this the "pivot" before Obama's "pivot."[122] On the other hand, it became evident that pushing Korea too hard to support U.S. contingency planning risked undermining U.S. efforts to show a common front, vis-à-vis a rising China. It was becoming a complicated chessboard where requirements for military planning and diplomatic influence—or shaping and hedging—were coming into conflict with one another.

TRADE, VALUES, AND INSTITUTIONS

The American ability to shape a favorable balance of power in Asia rested on more than contingency planning or diplomacy with the major powers, of course. Trade and support for universal values were also indispensable instruments of power. Increasingly, these issues were intersecting in the debate over Asia's emerging institutional architecture.

Multilateral institution building is not usually thought of as a "Republican" priority, but the first serious attention to regional architecture began under Reagan, and it was the first issue Rice raised with the Asia directorate as my colleagues and I engaged in strategic planning exercises early in the administration. Asia was "under-institutionalized," she argued in Friday night sessions in early 2001, challenging us to think of ways to encourage new regional structures as she had seen emerge in Europe a decade earlier. President Bush was fully committed to the region's largest multilateral forum, APEC, and unlike both his predecessor and successor, he attended every summit meeting of the group, even in the midst of crises at home or elsewhere in the world. However, most of the Bush administration's innovation occurred in functional areas of what might be called "minilateral" cooperation, such as the U.S.-Japan-Australia Trilateral Security Dialogue started in 2001; the Asia-Pacific Partnership on Clean Climate and Energy (Australia, Canada, China, India, Japan, Korea, and the United States) established in 2004 to accelerate the development and deployment of clean-energy technologies; the 2005 "Quad" in response to the Asian Tsunami; and, of course, the Six Party Talks, which were conceived initially as the precursor for a Northeast Asian security forum once denuclearization was on track. One might also include the administration's establishment of the G-20 after the 2008 financial crisis, which had far broader Asian participation (Japan, China, Korea, Australia, Indonesia, India, ASEAN) than previous global forums.

Meanwhile, on the trade side, the administration began building from bilateral to regional and global free trade agreements. At USTR, Zoellick began the process with the U.S.-Australia and U.S.-Singapore agreements, and his successors Rob Portman and Susan Schwab continued with negotiations on KORUS, the U.S.-Korea Free Trade Agreement. Zoellick believed that trade could be best promoted through what he referred to as "competitive liberalization"—or overlapping bilateral, regional, and global trade agreements.[123] In 2006, the U.S. delegation to APEC led in proposing a "Free Trade Area of the Pacific" (FTAAP) that would bond all APEC members in a high-quality trade liberalization process. The next year, Schwab announced that the United States would be joining the Trans-Pacific Partnership (TPP) launched by New Zealand, Singapore, Chile, and Brunei to expand the agreement into a building block toward FTAAP. The other APEC members agreed that some form of trans-Pacific trade architecture would be their common endeavor.

Yet, over the same period, intra-Asian groupings that did not include the United States continued to evolve as well, still fueled by resentment of American indifference over the 1997–1998 financial crisis and the desire for leverage against NAFTA and the European Union. The quality of these discussions had changed markedly, with Japan in particular now arguing for an East Asia Community that would advance democratic norms rather than challenge the West. But Japan's confidence in its ability to manage that process without the heft of the United States was overdone. In mid-2004, a senior colleague in the Japanese Ministry of Economy, Trade, and Industry (METI) explained to me that Japan's plans for a new East Asia Summit (EAS) and associated trade pact might not include the United States but were designed to "build an Asian cage with China inside it." I told him that he would soon be calling back for help once Japan discovered it was stuck in a cage with China. Six months later, he did. When I asked what he was going to do about it, he explained that Japan would invite India, Australia, and New Zealand to join the summit and the new Regional Comprehensive Economic Partnership (RCEP) to restore a favorable balance of influence for Japan, but he also promised to keep in close touch.[124]

Southeast Asian diplomats initially chortled about their new exclusive grouping but then suddenly also grew alarmed in late 2004 when China used Laos and Cambodia as proxies in internal ASEAN meetings to table a proposal that the second East Asia Summit be held in Beijing, with the host nation responsible for determining the agenda and participants. This was a fundamental threat to "ASEAN centrality" and the ability of the association to hold together against great-power interference. Friendly ASEAN states like the Philippines and Singapore became much more solicitous of U.S. views on regional multilateralism and more transparent about ASEAN's own deliberations. In the White House, we organized regular meetings of the like-minded members of APEC to strategize together on how to ensure that APEC, EAS, and the other disparate institution-building processes hewed to our common interest in an open and inclusive Asia-Pacific region. The ambassadors and Deputy Chiefs of Mission from Australia, New Zealand, Canada, and Japan provided good strategic suggestions, while their counterparts from the Philippines, Korea, and Singapore gave early warning of Chinese initiatives to skew the agenda in less favorable directions.

The question then became whether the United States should seek to force its way into the EAS, since it was not technically invited to become a member at that point. The president took personal interest in the question and asked his friends Koizumi and John Howard about their impressions of the first EAS meeting, in 2005. Both said the same thing—that it was poorly organized and boring, and they had been talked into it by their foreign ministries. State was pushing for the president to join the summit, but there were reasons to wait and watch. Bilateral FTAs and FTAAP had real momentum, whereas the RCEP talks were sure to bog down with India and other protected economies in the room. The Australian government, which was set to host the 2007 APEC meeting in Sydney, also worried about the distracting impact of an American push to join the EAS that same year. And for the United States to join the EAS, it would have to sign and ratify the ASEAN Treaty of Amity and Cooperation. Australia and Japan had earlier done so with signing statements declaring that their foreign policies would not be altered because of the pact's reference to "non-interference in internal affairs." The administration studied doing the same, but the Burmese regime's crackdown on nonviolent protestors in the August 2007 Saffron Revolution made the thought of such an agreement with Burma unthinkable for the president. Ultimately, he decided in 2008 that he would not box in his successor, and instead left the choice on participation in the EAS to the next administration.[125]

This was the right decision at the time, but in the eyes of the region, it was conflated with apparent disengagement from one of the more established planks of institution-building in Asia: the ASEAN Regional Forum (ARF). The reality was that the ARF was dreadfully unproductive, with ASEAN insistence on consensus for all documents from a membership that included countries as diverse and uncooperative as China, North Korea, and Pakistan. The most notable outcome of the meetings was the skits, in which foreign ministers dressed in ridiculous costumes for song and dance after the meetings. Faced with the choice of attending her first ARF meeting in 2005 or tending to immediate diplomatic crises in the Middle East, Rice chose to do what Albright and Christopher had previously done and sent her deputy to Southeast Asia. She did allow me to make the case for going to the ARF. It was not exactly the Treaty of Versailles, I acknowledged, but in Southeast Asian diplomacy, Woody Allen's quip was right—80 percent of success is just showing up. In the end, Zoellick performed well, in both the diplomacy and the skit, but Secretary Rice's absence was noted. The next year, Rice took the stage at the ARF with a vengeance, performing the Brahms Violin Sonata no. 3 in D Minor with a noted Malaysian violinist, but the narrative about American disinterest would not dissipate.[126]

Underlying the debate about engagement in the EAS were fundamental questions about how best to advance democratic norms in the region. Had the president cared nothing for human rights in Burma, he could have signed the Treaty of Amity and Cooperation with a regime that had just driven peacefully protesting monks and students off the streets of Rangoon and into political prisons. The fact was, however, that the president cared deeply about human dignity, compelled by his own faith and by supporters from Midland, Texas, who never failed to highlight for him the suffering in North Korea, Darfur, and other dark spots on the globe. In his second inaugural address, in January 2005, Bush committed the United States to ending tyranny, with a promise that his administration "will persistently clarify the choice before every ruler and every nation, the moral choice between oppression, which is always wrong, and freedom, which is eternally right."[127] On the right, conservatives embraced this merger of idealism with realism, whereas critics on the left linked the speech to Iraq and miscast the president's intention as liberating countries at the point of the gun.[128]

The fact was that democracy was making steady progress across the Asia-Pacific region, and it was in the United States' interest to support that trend. After the second inaugural, however, the major thrust of democracy promotion was toward the Arab world, packaged in a new Broader Middle East and North African (BMENA) initiative under the NSC's lead on democracy and the Middle East, Elliott Abrams.[129] I joked with Elliott that over one-half of the world's Muslims lived in my area—South and East Asia—and promised not to exercise my majority voting share as long as we retained an evolutionary approach to democratic development in Asia, which had been working. We agreed that democracy promotion and human dignity would remain central elements in our strategic approach to the region, at least for the NSC. We saw no contradiction between American idealism and self-interest.

The challenge, as always, would be drilling strategic concepts into policy and diplomacy. In Asia, there was much to harness. Japan had been championing democratic norms in regional architecture since Koizumi had come to office, and other states, such as Vietnam, were more willing to bridge ideational gaps with the United States in the wake of China's new assertiveness.[130] India was also moving incrementally away from its nonalignment instincts and engaging the administration in discussions of how we might coordinate our support for democracy promotion even if our approaches differed. ASEAN itself had commissioned an Eminent Persons Group to draft a new charter for the organization, and in their 2006 proposal the group argued that regional peace and stability rested on "the active strengthening of democratic values, good governance, rejection of unconstitutional and undemocratic changes of government, the rule of law, including international humanitarian law, and respect for human rights and fundamental freedoms."[131] The ASEAN bureaucrats would later reinsert the traditional ASEAN principle of "non-interference in internal affairs," but the trend lines were positive.[132]

Crises soon forced decisions. On February 1, 2005—just weeks after the second inaugural address—King Gyanendra of Nepal suddenly declared a state of emergency and dismissed Parliament in the face of a growing Maoist insurgency in the countryside. Although the Maoists had no connection to the current government in Beijing, the Chinese nevertheless saw an opportunity to wean the Himalayan country away from India and make the "yam between two boulders" (as Nepalese called themselves) a proxy to cut off Tibetan exiles and put strategic pressure on India.[133] Beijing offered aid and sent a series of high-level officials to woo Gyanendra in Kathmandu.[134] The "realist" instinct would have been to continue arming the king to counter Chinese influence, but the administration reached agreement with Delhi and London to coordinate a reduction of military aid coupled with joint démarches (representations) to both Kathmandu and Beijing insisting on a restoration of the democratic process. In 2007, the king agreed to restore Parliament, and Beijing stopped short of providing competing military aid, though it continued to exert effective pressure to halt the flow of Tibetan refugees.

In Vietnam, progress toward a historic visit to Washington by Prime Minister Phan Van Khai was interrupted when the State Department Office of Religious Freedom put the country under sanctions watch for closing hundreds of Protestant "house churches" in the Central Highlands and repressing the activities of Catholic priests in urban areas. The Vietnamese urged the administration to ignore the issue in the common effort to counterbalance China, but I was sent to Hanoi just before the Tet (Vietnamese New Year's) celebration to explain that a summit in Washington would not be possible without marked progress on reopening house churches and releasing Catholic priests. Negotiations with Vietnamese officials eagerly awaiting Tet—as the streets outside filled with motor scooters carrying celebratory kumquat trees—went well. Recognizing that this was a pillar in the president's strategy and not just the result of congressional pressure, Hanoi agreed to new commitments in support of religious freedom.[135] When I reported that progress back to the president in the Oval Office immediately after my return, he asked me if the Vietnamese were more afraid of China than of God. It appeared they were.

Burma was perhaps the most egregious case in the region, and the source of greatest tension between the regionalists at State and the White House. China was beginning to dominate the former British colony, and there were strong voices within the region calling for an easing of U.S. sanctions. After the 2007 Saffron Revolution, however, the president and the first lady pushed in the opposite direction, placing greater pressure on the junta with targeted sanctions against the ruling cronies that had been authorized with the JADE Act of 2008.[136] The Obama administration would later claim and deserve partial credit for opening a more productive relationship with Than Shwe's reformist successor, Thein Sein, but it was clear from my meetings with Thein Sein in August 2013 that his motivation was to end his country's isolation and develop the economy in ways that avoided strategic dependency on China. There will always be debate about the efficacy of sanctions in international diplomacy, but it is difficult to see how Thein Sein's government would have made such a bold reform decision had there not been continued and mounting pressure from the United States.

In all three cases—Nepal, Vietnam, and Burma—the president made improvement of democracy and human rights a central pillar of his strategy toward the region. His approach integrated human rights and democracy priorities in ways evocative of George Shultz. He moved not in reaction to congressional pressure but out of personal conviction. As he put it to us at the time, he would be a realist in the short term but remain an idealist for the long term. The historic American tension between supporting the independence of countries and insisting that they be justly governed would not disappear, but in Asia George and Laura Bush demonstrated that these goals need not be incompatible.

BUSH'S LEGACY IN ASIA STRATEGY

On December 26, 2007, American diplomatic historian and foreign policy essayist Walter Russell Mead handed out grades for Bush's foreign policy. "You've got to look at it regionally, and in Asia they haven't done that badly," he concluded:

> We have good relations with China, with Japan, and with India. There seems to be a little bit more cohesion to the democracies in Asia, so all of this strikes me as a good thing. And let's also not forget that many people were worried when Indonesia shifted toward democracy—that we'd see a rise of terrorism and instability. Sometimes we need to take a look at the dogs that don't bark, and Indonesia isn't barking.[137]

For Asia, Meade gave Bush an A– (he is a hard grader).

There was far greater continuity to Bush's Asia strategy than there was divergence from Clinton or George H. W. Bush—particularly when compared with American policy toward the Middle East over the same period. Bush built on the engage-and-balance approach of Clinton but brought far more discipline and consistency to great-power relations than Clinton had. The strategic relationship with India had been transformed, China policy was stable, and the U.S.-Japan alliance had moved significantly toward the vision in the 2000 Armitage-Nye Report, despite the last-minute blow on North Korea. Democracy now registered as a high priority among Asian elites in polling conducted across the region, and the United States had completed a series of trans-Pacific trade agreements and set the stage for the TPP.[138] Although the United States had not joined the East Asia Summit, the option for expanded participation in new aspects of regional architecture was left open. In January 2009, polls showed that American standing was measurably higher in Asia than it had been in 2000.[139]

Tellingly, the Bush administration faced the most trouble where initial foreign policy conceptualization had been weakest—in Southeast Asia and the Korean Peninsula. Both areas were in need of repair, and the next administration made important advances in relations with Southeast Asia, in particular. On the whole, though, George W. Bush had advanced a balance of power that favored freedom, much as the Vulcans had envisioned eight years earlier.

That Barack Obama chose not to run against Bush's Asia policy was itself proof that the overall strategy had been effective in advancing American interests. Instead, Obama ran on Iraq. He cared about Asia, but the strategic lessons he drew from the wars in the Middle East did not fit the Pacific.

15. "THE PIVOT"
BARACK OBAMA AND THE STRUGGLE TO REBALANCE TO ASIA

B y the time Barack Obama became the forty-fourth president of the United States, the broad contours and consensus behind a strategy of engaging and balancing a rising China had taken root. Jeffrey Bader, Obama's principal advisor on Asia during the campaign and later at the White House, told the candidate early on that the Bush administration had managed major-power relations in Asia well but that there was the need for reengagement with Southeast Asia and the lingering problems on the Korean Peninsula.[1] Obama did not campaign on Asia policy, but he did promise a transformational presidency after six years of war in Iraq and the worst financial crisis in a generation. As he put it in his first major foreign policy speech in October 2007 at DePaul University, "I'm not running to join the kind of Washington groupthink that led us to war in Iraq—I'm running to change our politics and our policy so we can leave the world a better place than our generation has found it."[2] As a candidate, he reformulated the broader debate about foreign policy to contrast himself with George W. Bush and with Democratic primary opponents such as Hillary Clinton, who had supported the Iraq War.[3] In his 2007 speech at DePaul, he promised to focus on engagement and downplayed the utility of military force.[4] He never dropped that binary formula, repeating it until his final National Security Strategy, in February 2015, and in his January 2016 State of the Union address, despite the failure of diplomacy alone to deter Russia's Vladimir Putin, Syria's Bashar al-Assad, the Islamic State, or other aggressors in the international system.[5] Obama was determined that his legacy would be ending wars, not risking new ones.

Whereas George W. Bush had turned to Cold Warrior George Shultz as the lodestar for his foreign policy vision, Barack Obama turned to liberal antiwar policy veteran Tony Lake. Obama also drew personnel and policy ideas from "the Phoenix Initiative," a group of progressive foreign policy experts led by Brookings Institution scholar and Lake protégé Susan Rice.[6] The Phoenix Initiative advanced a big idea about foreign policy: "that the great issues of the future, such as climate change, terrorism, and pandemic disease, cannot be solved through traditional means of nation-to-nation military and diplomatic dealings."[7] Some of Obama's advisors reiterated the importance of traditional alliances and great-power politics.[8] However, the new currency of Obama's foreign policy would be to engage unconditionally with authoritarian regimes such as Cuba, Syria, Iran, and North Korea; to emphasize multilateralism; to focus on potential adversaries on common transnational threats; and to restore America's image abroad.

Obama inherently understood the rising importance of Asia. Though not the first "Pacific President" (Taft, Hoover, and Kennedy had all spent at least parts of their professional lives there, and Nixon and Reagan both hailed from the West Coast), his childhood in Indonesia and Hawaii gave him unique perspectives on the region.[9] The members of the Phoenix Initiative called for the Asia-Pacific to be viewed as a "first-order priority of a national security strategy," and the administration recruited the best Asia hands in the Democratic foreign policy establishment, including Bader, Kurt Campbell, and James Steinberg, among others.[10] As president, Obama would declare a "pivot" and then a "rebalance" toward the Pacific, becoming the first president to endorse what was essentially an Asia-first policy.[11]

And yet, Asia was not a region that would suddenly be transformed by engagement with authoritarian regimes, emphasis on transnational challenges such as climate change, or "restoring" America's image abroad. Indeed, as Funabashi Yōichi and observant U.S. journalists in the region noted in 2008, the major Asian powers had been happy with Bush's commitment to free trade, strong alliances, and careful management of

great-power relations. If anything, they worried about the Democratic
Party's tendency toward protectionism and dogmatic views on transnational issues such as climate change and nonproliferation.[12] Kissinger also
warned the next administration against idealistic thinking about new
concepts of interdependence in Asia, noting in the *Washington Post* in
April 2008 that Asia was "a part of the world where nations still possess
the characteristics of traditional European states. The major states of
Asia—China, Japan, India and, in time, possibly Indonesia—view each
other the way participants in the European balance of power did, as inherent competitors even when they occasionally participate in cooperative ventures."[13]

The Iraq-driven framework for foreign policy that Barack Obama
brought to office was initially popular at home and among publics in
Europe and parts of Asia, but a framework premised on the diminution
of the nation-state did not provide a durable conceptual basis for formulating grand strategy in a region still dominated by power politics. Indeed,
many in the Obama White House prided themselves on not adopting
grand strategies in the first place, instead advancing a simple doctrine of
"Don't do stupid stuff."[14] It was perhaps a pithy critique of the previous
administration, but also a guarantee that the new administration would
react to events in Asia far more than it shaped them.

And thus, as Obama pivoted to Asia, U.S. policy pivoted unevenly
between the five tensions that had bedeviled American statecraft so often in the past.

ASIA VERSUS EUROPE

For two centuries, European affairs had trumped the Pacific in American
foreign policy, but the Obama presidency coincided with a series of public opinion surveys from the Chicago Council on Foreign Affairs and
German Marshall Fund showing that for the first time the American
people viewed Asia—not Europe—as the region most important to U.S.
interests.[15] It was thus with impeccable timing and fanfare that Secretary
of State Hillary Clinton chose Asia for her first overseas trip, in February
2009—the first secretary of state to do so since Dean Rusk—declaring, to
the surprise of many in the region who had never seen Bush leave, that
America "was back in Asia."[16] In November 2011, Clinton announced in
the pages of *Foreign Policy* magazine that the United States was under-

taking a "pivot" toward Asia. Over the coming decade, she explained, the United States would "lock in a substantially increased investment— diplomatic, economic, strategic, and otherwise—in the Asia-Pacific region."[17] Clinton's energetic assistant secretary for East Asia and Pacific affairs, Kurt Campbell, put real substance behind the new approach. Clinton attended every ASEAN Regional Forum (ARF) meeting, in contrast to all her predecessors and to the relief of Southeast Asian states looking for support as Beijing sought to exploit divisions within ASEAN's ranks over the South China Sea territorial disputes. Bader, Campbell, and the administration's Asia hands also prevailed over White House skeptics to win the president's commitment to join the East Asia Summit in November 2011 in Bali, convincing the enthusiastic Indonesian hosts to hold the summit back-to-back with APEC's so that the U.S. president would only have to make one trip to the region. Woody Allen's quip that 80 percent of success in life is just showing up resonated with the new Asia team, and the administration was clearly committing to being present at as many venues as possible.

As he headed to the East Asia Summit in Bali, Obama also began to emphasize the military aspects of his Asia policy. Speaking to the Australian parliament on November 16, 2011, he promised that "after a decade in which we fought two wars that cost us dearly, in blood and treasure, the United States is turning our attention to the vast potential of the Asia Pacific region."[18] Six months earlier, he had announced that all U.S. forces would be withdrawn from Afghanistan by the following September—and he now wanted to demonstrate that far from being an isolationist, he was ramping up the U.S. military commitment to a rising Asia. Chinese assertiveness in the East China and South China Seas and North Korean provocations in 2010 had sharpened the requirement for muscular demonstrations of American power, and the announcement played well among allies. From Canberra, Obama traveled to Darwin, in the north of Australia, where he highlighted plans to deploy 3,000 U.S. Marines on a rotational basis.[19] The next January, he went to the Pentagon to personally unveil the results of a new Pentagon Defense Strategic Review under which U.S. forces would "of necessity rebalance toward the Asia-Pacific region."[20] According to the Pentagon's review, the U.S. military would continue to counter terrorism and deter aggression, while developing capabilities for "power projection despite anti-access/area denial challenges" from potential foes such as China and Iran.[21] In June 2012, Defense Secretary Leon Panetta announced in Singapore that the U.S. Navy would shift

,5 Pacific/Atlantic division of ships to 60:40 in the future.[22]

nd majors coming back from multiple deployments to Afghan-
raq began applying to study Chinese, Korean, and Japanese
Urdu and Arabic.

....p.. ot (or "rebalance" as it was now being called by officials) sparked
severe criticism from China's official media and caused Chinese public
opinion toward the United States to plummet.[23] Elsewhere in Asia, however, the administration's pledge to focus on the region was welcomed. In
a 2014 CSIS survey of foreign policy elites in Asia, for example, 77 percent
of Chinese experts disapproved of the pivot, arguing that it was "too
confrontational towards China," but over 80 percent of experts from the
rest of Asia supported the stated intentions of the policy.[24] The problem,
as the 2014 CSIS survey demonstrated, was that a majority of Asian elites
also expressed doubt about the commitment and ability of the Obama
administration to actually follow through on the promises of an Asia-first
policy.[25] In Europe, officials feared that the pivot was real, whereas in Asia
they worried that it was not.

One clear source of doubt was the downward trajectory of the U.S.
defense budget. In his speech to the Australian parliament, the president
stressed that "reductions in U.S. defense spending will not—I repeat, will
not—come at the expense of the Asia Pacific." But 60 percent of a rapidly
shrinking fleet was hardly reassuring. A 2010 congressionally mandated
bipartisan panel under Bill Perry and Stephen Hadley had recommended
a 350-ship navy because of the growing importance of the Pacific.[26] Secretary of Defense Bob Gates proposed a budget for just over 300 ships that
year. The president and Congress then cut close to $500 billion more out
of the defense budget for the coming decade, rendering a fleet of 280 ships
more likely. The same week that President Obama sought to reassure the
Australian parliament that the defense cuts would not affect Asia and the
Pacific, Gates's successor, Leon Panetta, wrote to the leadership of the Senate Armed Services Committee warning that the navy was in danger of
shrinking to its smallest size since 1915.[27] Meanwhile, the Pacific Command's share of spending on foreign military finance (FMF) designed to
assist frontline states with military capabilities never rose above 1 percent
of the total worldwide. By the time President Obama headed to Asia in
April 2014 for summits in Japan, Korea, and China, Assistant Secretary of
Defense for Acquisition Katrina McFarland told the press that, because of
budget pressures, "the pivot is being looked at again, because candidly, it
can't happen."[28] The White House forced McFarland to retract the state-

ment, but the main surprise about her statement was its candor. The resource problem for Asia and the Pacific only became more acute as Iran and the Islamic State both threatened to undermine U.S. allies across the Middle East and as Vladimir Putin seized Crimea and increased military pressure on Ukraine and the Baltic States.

A second source of doubt was about American willpower, a doubt that stemmed from Obama's obvious aversion to using force in international affairs. This concern took on specific meaning in September 2013, when the president drew a red line against the use of chemical weapons by Syria and then reversed himself when Syria defied that red line, suddenly turning over the decision on whether to use force to a vote by Congress.[29] America's allies in Asia had been ambivalent about a bombing campaign in the Middle East but were alarmed that a U.S. president would pull back from a stated commitment to use force and rely instead on the unpredictable U.S. Congress.[30] All administration statements and actions with respect to China and North Korea were now viewed in Tokyo and Seoul through this new troubling prism. As Singapore's Lee Kuan Yee warned, Asian leaders are highly attentive to how the United States upholds security commitments in other parts of the world.[31] The notion that a superpower could compartmentalize judgments of its willpower by region was proven deeply flawed. Ironically, ending wars in the Middle East proved far less reassuring for Asians than the White House expected.

The third source of doubt about the pivot was the lack of a cohesive strategic concept animating the focus on Asia. The president came to office interested in the Pacific, but his policies emerged in a series of speeches and documents reacting to events instead of flowing from a deliberate definition of ends, ways, and means by the National Security Council. The administration's first National Security Strategy, in May 2010, gave no hint of the pivot, simply listing the importance of U.S. alliances in Asia (*after* a section on U.S. alliances in Europe) and spotlighting China and India in a section on "Engagement" in the report.[32] Nor was there any NSC assessment of the nature of power in the region or the efficacy of different instruments of U.S. statecraft.[33] The chief of naval operations suddenly found himself called to the White House to explain what the military dimensions of the policy could be—*after* the speeches and pronouncements declaring the United States had a new strategy.[34] One U.S. ambassador to a key country in the region explained to me that he was sent to his post without any guidance from State or NSC on what the strategy for the pivot would be. Ends, ways, and means were all defined on the fly.

Not surprisingly, the articulation of the strategy therefore varied widely depending on which principal was speaking. The dozen or so speeches on the pivot by the most senior officials under the Obama administration all began with a list of top U.S. priorities—and the list changed almost every time, depending on the speaker. For example, Secretary Clinton's 2011 *Foreign Policy* article listed six priorities, but the next November, in a major speech on Asia, National Security Advisor Thomas Donilon dropped two of them—"forging broad-based military presence" and "advancing human rights and democracy"—while adding a new priority: "pursuing a stable and constructive relationship with China."[35] Then, in 2013, Secretary of State John Kerry criticized the military emphasis of the rebalance and suddenly added "climate change" as one of the administration's top three priorities for Asia.[36] With the exception of the secretaries of defense, no two speeches on Asia by principals listed the same U.S. priorities—a stark contrast to the consistent declaratory policy on Asia by Reagan or the Bushes. The American press took little note, but to observers in Asia the inconsistencies suggested a lack of consensus on the administration's bottom line in the region. That lack of clarity also prompted a competitive scramble by Japan and China to define themselves into the center of the as yet undefined pivot.

JAPAN VERSUS CHINA

On the eve of Clinton's first trip to Asia, in February 2009, the secretary held a small dinner on the eighth floor of the State Department with a group of Asia experts. Other than me, they were mostly associated with the Democratic Party and were primarily experts on China. One after another, they made the case for a new era of bilateral cooperation with Beijing, asserting that a Sino-U.S. condominium centered on common efforts against climate change and the financial crisis would end the risk of confrontation with a rising China and transform Asia. Clinton listened attentively and took notes, but then she cut them off, asking to hear about Japan since—as she put it—our alliances would be the cornerstone of her approach to Asia.[37] It was a telling moment, both about Clinton's strategic instincts and about the broader intellectual forces influencing the administration's pivot toward Asia.

For most of the administration's Asia hands, it was now axiomatic, a decade after the Nye Initiative, that successful Asia strategy required a strong alliance relationship with Japan. Clinton therefore stopped first in Japan on her Asia trip, and Bader made certain that the president's first visit with a head of state was with Japanese prime minister Asō Tarō, on February 29, 2009.[38] When a Chinese fishing boat deliberately rammed a Japanese Coast Guard cutter in September 2010, sparking a major confrontation between Tokyo and Beijing, Clinton was the first to reiterate clearly that Article V of the U.S.-Japan Security Treaty applied to the defense of the Senkaku Islands that both countries claimed—just as Campbell's boss, Secretary of Defense Perry, had been the first to do so when the island dispute erupted in 1996 and Secretary of State Christopher dithered.[39] After China refused to respond to the North Korean sinking of the South Korean corvette *Cheonan* in April 2010 and lethal shelling of civilians on Yeongpyeong Island in November of that year, the Pentagon deployed warships to the area and Clinton stood with the Japanese and Korean foreign ministers in front of the State Department to show solidarity.[40] Campbell came within a hair of successfully negotiating an unprecedented trilateral collective security statement for that meeting (an attack on one is an attack on all) before the South Korean side backed out because of domestic pressures against the pro-U.S. Lee Myung-bak administration and concerns about China's response.[41]

At the same time the Obama administration sustained the balance piece of Asia policy, it also sought to go beyond the level of *engagement* with Beijing established by the Bush administration. On the whole, the Obama administration recognized that Bush had left a stable U.S.-China relationship, not through joint communiqués, "strategic partnerships," or other diplomatic edifices but through personal connections with Jiang and Hu and principled consistency on alliances, democracy, and free trade. But the Obama team clearly worried that this approach was not sustainable in the aftermath of the financial crisis, and it therefore sought new ways to institutionalize what Deputy Secretary of State Jim Steinberg in 2009 called "strategic reassurance" with China.[42] First, the White House reframed the Bush administration's three-word description of how the United States would approach China (cooperative, constructive, and candid), dropping the word "candid" and inserting instead a vision of "*positive*, constructive, and comprehensive" [emphasis added] relations.[43] Obama also elevated Treasury Secretary Hank Paulson's Strategic Economic Dialogue to a much broader Strategic and Economic Dialogue

(S&ED), which included both State and Treasury as equals.[44] Finally, whereas the Bush NSC had eschewed a fourth communiqué with Beijing as a potentially counterproductive regurgitation of Clinton's "strategic partnership," Obama chose to issue a joint statement with Hu in Beijing on November 19, 2009, that included a section on "building and deepening bilateral strategic trust," in which the two sides agreed to respect each other's "core interests."[45]

These overtures were not necessarily intended to mark a deliberate break from the engage-and-balance framework generally followed since the Clinton administration or to reopen a bilateral condominium with China—but they certainly looked that way to the region. India reacted immediately to the Obama-Hu joint statement, rejecting the document's proposal for Sino-U.S. strategic cooperation in South Asia and taking its concern directly to Obama when Prime Minister Singh visited Washington on November 24.[46] Tokyo, Taipei, and Manila also looked askance at the Yalta-like spheres of influence seemingly implied by expressions of support for "core interests"—particularly after senior Chinese officials began to expand the definition of "core interests" beyond Taiwan, Xinjiang, and Tibet (the first areas mentioned in the joint statement) to include the East China and South China Seas, where there were territorial confrontations with U.S. allies.[47] As former Australian prime minister Kevin Rudd and numerous others observed, the United States suddenly faced a "credibility problem" with U.S. allies and partners in Asia.[48] Thus, when Hu Jintao traveled to Washington in January 2011 for a reciprocal summit with Obama, negotiation of a second joint statement passed to Clinton's State Department, where Campbell and China Desk Director David Shear conducted a forty-eight–hour marathon negotiating session to extract references to "core interests" and instead insert language acknowledging that the relationship between the United States and China is both vital and *complex*" [emphasis added].[49]

Then the pendulum swung back. When John Kerry replaced Clinton as secretary of state in 2013, the *People's Daily* welcomed the new secretary with an editorial claiming he was the best person to "reconstruct the mutual trust relationship between China and the United States which have [sic] been damaged during Clinton's tenure."[50] National Security Advisor Tom Donilon, Kerry, and Donilon's successor, Susan Rice, all confirmed in public addresses that president Xi Jinping's proposal for a "new model of great power relations" between the United States and China would be the conceptual framework for bilateral relations going

forward.[51] Even after China provocatively declared an Air Defense Identification Zone over Japanese and Korean controlled islands in December 2013, Vice President Biden reconfirmed Xi's "New Model" formula in
a speech in Beijing (though with an emphasis on the need for China to
build trust).[52]

On instructions from the highest level, the Japanese government asked
the NSC and State Department not to publicly embrace Xi's concept,
under which the United States, China, and Russia were "great" powers but
Japan and other maritime democracies in Asia were relegated to second-
tier status. From the perspective of U.S. allies, the "new model of great
power relations" was simply the latest effort by China to assert a bipolar
condominium, spheres of influence, core interests, and a U.S.-China "strategic partnership" at their expense. Eventually, Secretary of Defense Timothy "Chuck" Hagel found a way to save U.S. alliances from the administration's rhetorical trap in a speech at the Shangri-La defense summit in
Singapore on May 31, 2014, when he expressed the president's commitment to a "new model of relations" with Beijing, without ascribing exclusive *great*-power rank to China at Japan's expense.[53] Nevertheless, the
lack of discipline in declaratory policy continued to alarm Japan and
frustrate China.[54]

To be sure, unexpected changes in Japan and China caught the administration off guard. Early on, Washington had to deal with the demise of
Asō's LDP government and then the first inexperienced, vaguely anti-
American, and generally "loopy" government of Hatoyama Yukio of the
opposition Democratic Party of Japan (DPJ).[55] Xi Jinping proved to be far
more nationalistic and assertive when he came to power in 2013 than most
experts had expected, while ideological liberals in the Obama administration were uncomfortable with the more nationalistic tone of Prime
Minister Shinzo Abe when the LDP returned to power in Japan in 2013.[56]
The growing Sino-Japanese confrontation over the Senkakus also increased the stakes for the United States, since support of Japan under
Article V of the U.S.-Japan Security Treaty would deter China but could
also put the United States at greater risk of entrapment in a Sino-Japanese
confrontation. Senior administration officials appeared to take both sides
of the debate in public. For example, in December 2012, a senior U.S. military commander told the press that the United States was not going to go to
war over "a rock in the middle of the Pacific Ocean," and the commander
of U.S. Pacific Forces asserted repeatedly—much to Tokyo's consternation—
that climate change was the greatest threat to Asian security, never

mentioning China's military pressure on maritime states like Japan.[57] Other officials, such as Clinton and Campbell, were steadfast in expressing support for Japan and the Philippines as China put pressure on disputed islands under their control. Obama himself tried to end the confusion in Tokyo in April 2014, when he declared unequivocally in a joint statement with Abe that Article V of the U.S.-Japan Security Treaty did apply to the Senkaku Islands, but then his staff undercut the effect by delaying publication of the statement in the hope of getting final concessions from Tokyo in trade talks. Japanese senior political figures privy to the negotiations wondered whether the U.S. government really meant to signal that the pork tariff rate was more important than the defense of Japan.[58]

By 2015, the Japan piece of Obama's Asia strategy had finally fallen into place. Prime Minister Abe set a historic precedent during his April 27–28 visit to Washington by making the first speech to a joint session of Congress by a Japanese leader, and he put an exclamation point on the U.S.-Japan alliance by revising the 1998 U.S.-Japan Defense Guidelines, promising to pass legislation that summer allowing Japan to exercise the right of collective self-defense in support of U.S. operations near and beyond the Japanese archipelago.[59] The agreement moved the United States and Japan a significant step closer to the kind of joint and combined command relationships that make NATO and the U.S.-ROK alliance such effective deterrents. It represented an important legacy for Obama's successors to leverage. However, the clarity behind the administration's commitment to Japan at that point had much to do with the increasingly blatant Chinese coercion against other claimants in the South China Sea.[60] American policy was reacting to events, not shaping them. The administration would have been much better positioned had it developed a clear strategic concept of regional order and the relative roles of Japan and China in the years before China's buildup in the South China Sea and Abe's April 2015 visit to Washington.

STRUGGLING TO DEFINE THE FORWARD DEFENSE LINE IN ASIA

When a senior U.S. military commander in the Pacific stated that the United States was not going to fight a war over a "rock," he was inadvertently revealing the challenge of maintaining forward presence in the

Western Pacific against a rising military power in the region. Twice before in its history, the United States had faced this same problem. In the prewar years, officers on the navy staff and at the Naval War College struggled with how to defeat and deter the powerful Imperial Japanese Navy from across the Pacific. The depletion of U.S. naval forces in the Philippines in the interwar years tempted Japanese expansion, but the development of mobile fleet operations and island-hopping eventually led to victory. Then, in the late 1970s, the United States faced the threat of a rapid Soviet military buildup in the Far East. The navy and air force pushed the Soviets back from the Central Pacific, using the geographic advantages of the Japanese archipelago and the new maritime strategy to bottle up Soviet ships and subs in the Sea of Okhotsk.

Now, for the third time, the U.S. position on the offshore island chain was under military pressure. In 2009, as Obama assumed the presidency, a RAND study revised estimates on China's missile capabilities across the Taiwan Strait to argue that "the United States can no longer be confident of winning the battle for the air in the air," which represented "a dramatic change from the first five-plus decades of the China-Taiwan confrontation."[61] Soon analysts were concluding that China was developing the capabilities to overwhelm a handful of U.S. bases in Japan and Guam with ballistic missiles, rendering the entire offshore island chain vulnerable.[62] Under Beijing's 2008 Near Sea Doctrine, the PLA planned for denial of the East China and South China Seas to the United States, coupled with improved power projection toward Guam and the so-called Second Island Chain.[63] The Defense Department began to refer to this new Chinese strategy to deter and defeat U.S. intervention in a conflict in maritime Asia as "Anti-access/area denial" (A2/AD).[64] And as Toshi Yoshihara of the Naval War College warned, the economic, financial, and industrial strength behind China's naval modernization this time was far greater than what the United States faced from Imperial Japan and the Soviet Union in the twentieth century.[65]

The Pentagon's initial response to the A2/AD threat was to promote Air-Sea Battle (ASB), a concept under which the navy and air force would jointly attack and sever the enemy's "kill chain" before they could destroy U.S. carriers and bases with ballistic missiles.[66] The concept was then expanded in January 2012 to include all the services under the Joint Operational Access Concept (JOAC).[67] Technologically, the weapons systems under exploration were feasible, but strategically ASB was fraught with complications. This was evident in the administration's extreme reluctance to focus on military competition with China at a time when "strategic reassurance" was a priority with Beijing. The navy and air force chiefs repeatedly denied that ASB was aimed at China, which made it virtually impossible to promote the concept with Congress or U.S. allies.[68] When the influential Center for Strategic and Budgetary Assessments (CSBA) published a detailed operational proposal for ASB in May 2010 that included suggested targeting of PLA bases within China, there was a backlash not only from Beijing but also in Washington.[69] The *Washington Post*, for example, published an internal assessment prepared by the marine corps commandant that argued "an Air-Sea Battle-focused Navy and Air Force would be preposterously expensive to build in peace time" and would result in "incalculable human and economic destruction" if ever used in a major war with China.[70] Retired marine colonel T. X. Hammes offered an alternative approach that would better suit U.S. capabilities, budgets, and strategy—"offshore control"—reminiscent of War Plan Orange's aim to interdict imperial Japan's sea lanes and blockade its home islands.[71] However, a war-winning strategy based on a longer-term blockade would risk prompting exactly the kind of surprise attack on U.S. bases in the Pacific that Japan tried in December 1941 in order to break the American will for a long fight. The operational problem was complex, and the politics even more so. The administration was having enormous difficulty setting a national strategy to deal with the growing challenge to U.S. allies and forward presence in the Western Pacific.

In 2012, a confused and frustrated Congress commissioned an independent assessment of U.S. forward posture strategy in the Pacific from CSIS. Their first question was "what is our strategy?" One particular concern from the Senate Armed Services Committee was how spending for the Pentagon's plan to disperse marines from Okinawa to Guam, Hawaii, and Australia could be justified, since the dispersal strategy did not fit the war plans the members had seen for high-intensity conflict on the Korean Peninsula or in the Taiwan Strait.[72] In its report back to Congress, *U.S. Force Posture Strategy in the Asia Pacific Region* (2012), CSIS noted that the United States required a broader strategy not only to defeat possible aggression by China or North Korea but also the "right combination of assurance and dissuasion" to "maintain a favorable peace before conflict occurs."[73] In effect, CSIS endorsed the idea of a partial rollback of the Guam Doctrine and reengagement militarily in Southeast Asia. A more distributed U.S. military presence supported through access arrange-

ments and defense cooperation would help to shore up
of vulnerable states around the maritime periphery of (
states could remain resilient against terrorism, natural \
mately external coercion. The CSIS report made the ca:
time "shaping" of the strategic environment would be j
as the war-winning deterrence capabilities being prope
Southeast Asia could not again become a dangerous vacu
tegic dynamics of Asia as it had been in 1941 and 1954.

Ultimately, the Pentagon moved on all the tracks being debated among experts in this period, particularly after Beijing unilaterally declared an Air Defense Identification Zone (ADIZ) over the East China Sea in December 2013, prompting senior officials to be more explicit about U.S. opposition to Chinese coercion.[74] In April 2014, the United States and the Philippines signed an Enhanced Defense Cooperation Agreement (EDCA) giving the United States greater access to facilities in the Philippines, and in October the administration eased the forty-year-old arms ban on Vietnam to provide nonlethal surveillance and patrol equipment to Hanoi.[75] Japan followed suit with a decision to make overseas development assistance available for dual-use civil-military infrastructure development to complement the U.S. approach.[76] Consistent with offshore control strategy and recommendations in the CSIS report, the navy decided to deploy an additional attack sub to Guam and began to work on plans to develop technologies to counter A2/AD under a new "Advanced Capabilities and Deterrence Panel" (ACDP) led by the defense undersecretaries for acquisition and policy, which led to a crash technology program known as the "Third Offset."[77]

The Obama administration was clearly surprised by China's coercive moves against the First Island Chain. As one senior official confessed to the *Washington Post*, "we did not see that coming."[78] Though haltingly at first, the United States responded not by retreating but by expanding its areas of responsibilities as it had so often in the past—expanding security engagement with Southeast Asia in the most significant way since Nixon pulled back in 1969 with the Guam Doctrine. Meanwhile, North Korean provocations against the South prompted President Obama and Korean president Park Geun-hye in October 2014 to delay the planned transition of wartime operational control from the United States to South Korea, reversing a core element in Rumsfeld's vision for a more flexible U.S. commitment on the peninsula. Despite the conceptual weaknesses of the pivot, the strategic impulse when challenged in the Pacific

...o define the American defense line forward. What Andrew Krepin-vich of CSBA termed an "archipelagic defense" was now reemerging as a feature of U.S. military strategy in the Pacific.[79]

However, exercises, engagement, and weapons development all cost money. In the final two years of the Obama administration, Pentagon planners wrestled with how they could sustain legacy assets such as aircraft carriers and simultaneously invest in enhanced engagement and new technologies given the deep cuts to defense begun by the Obama White House—not to mention the renewal of tensions in the Middle East and Russian pressure on Central Europe. Spending barely began to match the rhetoric and promises of the new approach. Equally problematic was that China's construction of interlocking airfields on reclaimed land features across the South China Sea, which had begun in 2014, was shifting the strategic momentum away from Washington. Though easily targeted in a major conflict, the new airfields posed an overwhelming threat to Southeast Asian militaries and a significant complication for American planners, who now had to guard against a flank that only a decade earlier had been a point of counteraccess for U.S. forces. Beijing's commitment to the contest and its tolerance for risk threatened to outpace the United States and its allies.[80]

There was another challenge as well. A strategy aimed at dissuading revisionist assaults on the existing order required more than weapons systems and bases. Since it was spending less on defense, the Obama administration had an even more compelling need to expand trade and the democratic space in Asia.

Self-Determination Versus Universal Values

The strategic inconsistencies in the pivot in part reflected deeper questions about America's role in the world after the war in Iraq. Despite his promise to "restore America's moral standing" during the campaign, Obama struggled with two competing impulses. On the one hand, his advisors called for a new worldwide concert of democracies to overcome obstruction by the authoritarian governments of Russia and China in the UN Security Council.[81] Clinton, in her 2011 article for *Foreign Policy*, also emphasized "steadfast support for democracy and human rights" as one of the pillars of the "strategic turn to the Asia-Pacific."[82] This Wilsonian idealism echoed the views of prominent Democratic Party foreign policy leaders such as Lake and Madeleine Albright, and had strong supporters within the administration such as Anne-Marie Slaughter at Policy Planning and Samantha Power at the NSC and later the United Nations. On the other hand, many in the Obama campaign and administration reacted against the Bush administration's emphasis on democratic values, associating the theme with Iraq, unilateralism, and the use of force.[83] During the 2008 campaign, Democratic defense intellectuals argued that Bush's emphasis on moral authority for the Iraq War had squandered the Republican's previously strong credentials on national security, and they proposed a less sentimental realpolitik "hard power" of their own.[84] As one prominent Democratic critic of Obama put it, this new approach meant that "no longer is the promotion of freedom, liberty, and democracy around the world one of our fundamental principles. Instead, the Obama administration appears to be approaching most situations opportunistically and with a decidedly short-term perspective."[85]

The role of values in the pivot thus swung between these two competing visions—the one emphasizing universality of democratic norms and the other an uncharacteristically neorealist approach that one might associate with Nixon or George Herbert Walker Bush. President Obama contradicted himself constantly. In 2011, he argued in a speech at the State Department that henceforth support for democracy would be a "top priority" "that must be translated into concrete actions, and supported by all of the diplomatic, economic and strategic tools at our disposal." Then, in a major address at the United Nations in September 2013, he listed four other priorities for U.S. foreign policy, noting that although human rights and democracy remained important, "we can rarely achieve these objectives through unilateral American action." Obama, noted Fred Hiatt of the *Washington Post*, had turned "180 degrees . . . in a little more than two years."[86]

Those presidential speeches were primarily about the Middle East, but the inconsistencies were clear in Asia policy as well. Clinton, for example, told the press during her first trip to Beijing that the administration would not allow human rights issues to "interfere" with U.S.-China economic relations.[87] She also raised eyebrows in the human rights community when she implied in her 2011 *Foreign Policy* article that while democracy and human rights would be on the agenda with regimes like Vietnam, Burma, or North Korea, this would deter the administration from plans to "deepen engagement with partners with whom we disagree."[88] President Obama offered a robust statement of support for human rights and political space in China when welcoming the first high-level Chinese delegation for the Strategic and Economic Dialogue in Washington in July 2009 but then declined to meet the Dalai Lama during the Tibetan spiritual leader's visit to Washington in October 2009 out of deference to China, marking the first time a sitting president had skipped a meeting with the Tibetan spiritual leader since 1990. (Obama rescheduled a meeting with the Dalai Lama after his trip to Beijing.)[89] Dissidents such as Uighur leader Rebiya Kadeer, who were welcomed in the Oval Office by Bush, found their access strictly limited under Obama, even at lower levels of the State Department.[90] Obama never met a single dissident leader from Asia in the White House. When the blind activist lawyer Chen Guangcheng fled house arrest and escaped to the U.S. embassy in Beijing in April 2012, the White House remained silent, leaving the resolution and risk to U.S.-China relations to Campbell and the State Department.[91] U.S. government spending to advance democracy internationally fell by 28 percent under Obama, and USAID spending in support of governance and democracy abroad dropped 38 percent between 2009 and 2015.[92] It seemed, wrote Ken Roth of Human Rights Watch in 2010, that Obama was "in thrall to Chinese economic power and barely interested in risking anything to protect the rights of the 1.3 billion Chinese still living under a dictatorship."[93]

None of this is to suggest that the Obama administration ignored human rights. The U.S. embassy in Beijing worked tirelessly to secure the release of three Chinese dissidents in 2009, for example.[94] The administration also strongly supported the establishment of a U.N. Commission of Inquiry on North Korean human rights in March 2013. U.S. diplomats and nongovernmental groups worked across the region to improve governance and protect closing civil society space against new waves of authoritarian controls in China, Cambodia, Sri Lanka, and elsewhere.

The problem was that the administration sent a strong signal to the region that violations of human rights and democratic principles would carry little risk for relations with the United States under Obama. Indeed, his campaign pledge to meet "unconditionally" with some of the world's most authoritarian regimes had signaled as much. By 2016, democracy and civil society space in Asia were closing; Beijing's repression of dissent was the most aggressive since Tiananmen; Thailand's democracy was sliding backward after repeated military coups; and international NGOs were finding it increasingly difficult to operate across the region.

The one area in Asia where the administration could point to the success of its unsentimental view of engagement was Burma/Myanmar, where bilateral relations and the human rights situation both improved. The administration had taken a gamble with the country's new reform-minded president, Thein Sein, easing sanctions on agriculture, telecommunications, and tourism in April 2012 and promising further relief if the government could make visible progress in terms of releasing political prisoners, reaching settlements in conflicts with ethnic minorities, and ensuring free and fair elections for president in 2015.[95] The next logical step would have been to relax the ban on exports of goods from Burmese workers to the United States in order to help the people on the ground, but instead, on May 18, 2012, the White House suddenly lifted the ban on investment in the Myanmar Oil and Gas Enterprise (MOGE), the corrupt and nontransparent source of cash for the Burmese military elite responsible for repressing democracy in the first place.[96] There was no explanation for handing over this last major source of U.S. leverage with the job half done other than advantaging U.S. corporations and consolidating engagement with Burma before the president's visit to the region later that year. Over the coming years, the regime made progress on the release of political prisoners and on elections, which brought Aung San Suu Kyi's National League for Democracy back into power in 2016 but also saw serious setbacks in press freedom and intensifying ethnic disputes in the Rakhine state.[97] Meanwhile, the lifting of the investment ban in 2012 required U.S. industry to provide Responsible Investment Reports that began coming out in 2016. The reports showed clearly that U.S. companies were being ethical and responsible in their own operations, but had no idea how MOGE was using the funds it had received.[98] American leverage and attention to democratic progress—even toward its signature example of engagement—had dissipated.

FREE TRADE VERSUS PROTECTIONISM

Reagan and both Bushes had come to office as unabashed free traders, and Bill Clinton's experimentation with economic nationalism belied a deeper commitment to trade he espoused to his inner circle from the first day of his presidency.[99] Barack Obama was more ambivalent about trade. As the *New York Times* observed during the campaign, he appeared to be "part of the conflicted middle ground within the Democratic Party that is groping for a proper balance between being friendly to free trade agreements, believing they are beneficial to the economy, but also seeking to level the playing field for the United States when it comes to labor and environmental standards and addressing job losses that come with globalization."[100] For opportunistic rather than ideological reasons, Obama campaigned against all the major free trade agreements under negotiation or in effect in 2008, including NAFTA, KORUS, and deals with Colombia and Central America. Meanwhile, he studiously avoided commenting on the Trans-Pacific Partnership (TPP) negotiations opened in Asia by Bush.[101]

As president, Obama initially saw little political merit in pursuing free trade agreements. The financial crisis had caused world output growth measured in GDP to slow significantly, falling 1.7 percent in 2008 after a 3.5 percent decline in 2007, while global trade contracted more than at any time since the 1930s.[102] America's real imports fell by 21.4 percent, and real exports fell by 18.9 percent.[103] These facts suppressed support for free trade at home, with 58 percent of Americans in 2008 responding that globalization was bad for the country, compared with 48 percent who thought so a decade earlier (support for free trade would later bounce back in polls).[104] Therefore, instead of focusing on trade liberalization, Obama worked the G-20 summits begun by Bush in 2008 in order to blunt global protectionism in the wake of the financial crisis. In this, his administration was largely successful, ever mindful of the devastating impact of protectionist Smoot-Hawley legislation in the wake of the Great Depression of 1929.[105]

For almost a year in office, Obama did not pick up the TPP negotiations begun by Bush in 2008 with Singapore, Brunei, Chile, and New Zealand or the KORUS Free Trade Agreement completed with Seoul. Only when Australian prime minister Kevin Rudd and Korean president Lee Myung-bak pleaded with the president to move forward on free trade efforts in the Pacific during his November 2009 visit to the region did he begin to move in a significant way. On December 14, 2009, U.S. Trade Representative Ron Kirk notified Congress that President Obama planned to enter TPP negotiations "with the objective of shaping a high-standard, broad-based regional pact."[106] The president also committed to KORUS, though he forced the Koreans to renegotiate the chapter covering autos before a deal could be reached for the third time, in 2010, and finally passed in Congress in 2011.[107]

By his January 2010 State of the Union address, Obama had warmed to trade enough that he made a pledge to double U.S. exports in five years, though he did not say exactly how he would do it in the Pacific.[108] The Trans-Pacific Partnership offered the best framework in Asia, particularly since competing free trade negotiations such as RCEP did not include the United States.[109] In his January 2013 State of the Union address, Obama moved incrementally forward, referencing his commitment to TPP but still not the Trade Promotion Authority (TPA) necessary to complete the negotiations. The administration's cautious approach to the politics of TPP began to change the next month, when Prime Minister Abe told the president explicitly during his first visit to Washington that Japan wanted to join the TPP negotiations.[110] Instantly, TPP presented an opportunity for market opening in the world's third-largest economy, and the traditional pro-trade constituencies in Congress began to mobilize in support. China, too, began to soften its opposition to TPP, now seeing the agreement as being likely to move faster than RCEP and perhaps provide external momentum for economic reforms as the WTO had done two decades earlier.[111]

One major problem remained. Despite the skillful U.S. negotiating team led by Trade Representative Mike Froman, the president would not ask Congress for Trade Promotion Authority, the traditional legislation granting the administration authority to negotiate an agreement that Congress would then vote on (formerly called "Fast Track"). No previous administration had ever successfully negotiated a trade agreement without TPA or comparable congressional negotiating authority since 1934—precisely because the other side would be hesitant to put its best deal on the table without knowing whether Congress would force a renegotiation.[112] Instead, the administration argued to trading partners that a good deal was the best guarantee of congressional support, an argument few experienced trade experts in Tokyo, Hanoi, or Canberra found fully convincing in the context of their own domestic politics. Without explicit presidential campaigning for TPA, it was difficult to ask the leaders of Japan, Malaysia, Vietnam, or Australia to take a political hit from their own domestic opponents to trade.

The main obstacle to TPA in Congress was not Republicans but rather a Democrat, Senate Majority Leader Harry Reid, an outspoken opponent of trade deals.[113] The White House simply was not willing to jeopardize other legislative priorities or the Democrats' chances in the difficult 2014 midterm elections for the sake of trade. Obama called for TPA in his 2014 State of the Union address but only began working to achieve it after Republicans took the House and Senate in the November 2014 elections.[114]

In the January 2015 State of the Union address, Obama finally gave a full-throttle call for both TPP and TPA, arguing that without it China would write the rules for the world's fastest-growing region. "Why would we let that happen?" he asked skeptics from his own party. "We should write those rules. We should level the playing field. That's why I'm asking both parties to give me trade promotion authority to protect American workers, with strong new trade deals from Asia to Europe that aren't just free, but fair."[115]

With Abe's visit to Washington that April and the outlines of a final deal closer, the Republican-led Congress approved TPA in June 2015. Then, on October 15, negotiators reached agreement in principle on TPP in Atlanta. But it now seemed too late. The administration had focused on environmental and labor issues in the negotiations to satisfy Democratic members who would never have supported TPP in the first place, ignoring issues important to the Republicans that would be needed for passage of the deal. Moreover, whereas George H. W. Bush, Clinton, and George W. Bush had personally lobbied members for their support for trade deals, the Obama White House stood more aloof. When Senate Majority Leader Mitch McConnell declared on December 15 that the deal would not pass the next year, the consequences of the president's reluctant commitment to free trade became apparent.[116]

The stumbles over TPP contrasted with Beijing's ambitious proposal in 2013 for a Chinese-led Asian Infrastructure Investment Bank. On its own merits, the Chinese proposal had pros and cons: (1) Asia needed more infrastructure investment; (2) China would spend money on infrastructure in the region one way or another; and (3) the U.S. Congress would not likely support U.S. funding of a bank dominated by Beijing that lacked the transparency and governance of the numerous other international financial institutions around the world where the United States was spending money. Holding a weak hand, the administration chose to fight the new bank, adamantly urging U.S. allies not to join.[117] It was a weak hand poorly played. By May 2015, all major U.S. allies in Asia and Europe had joined the bank except for Japan.

Obama was not a protectionist, but neither was he a dedicated free trader. His own ambivalence exacerbated a historic tension of great consequence for the U.S. position in Asia. Yet the uncertainties around U.S. trade strategy were not as debilitating as they might have been in another era. The U.S. economy, though struggling to produce higher wages, was recovering from the 2008 financial crisis faster than that of any country in Asia, including China, where growth had begun to slow.[118] Goldman Sachs, which had coined the acronym "BRICS" in 2001 to encourage investment in China and the emerging markets, began to shift its recommendations back to investing in the United States.[119] The real American economy compensated for unsteady economic statecraft, but the contest over Asia's trade architecture would continue. To many in the region, it appeared that the Obama administration had squandered the most important round.

OBAMA'S LEGACY IN ASIA STRATEGY

It will take years to assess the legacy of Obama in Asia, but it is not too soon to begin identifying the character of his strategic thinking and statecraft toward the region. Barack Obama was not the first "Pacific President," but he was the first to declare Asia as the highest priority in U.S. foreign policy. He advanced important U.S. interests, including upgrading U.S.-Japan defense guidelines and aligning the trans-Pacific and intra-Asian institutional architecture by joining the East Asia Summit and convincing Southeast Asians to time the meeting with APEC. He eventually advanced TPP, the greatest trade liberalization effort in Asia since Bretton Woods, though he did so dangerously late. For a time at least, he reversed the Guam Doctrine after three decades of unsteady U.S. interest in Southeast Asia. On the whole, the Obama administration's approach to Asia represented far more continuity than discontinuity. Even otherwise negative critics give Obama credit for scoring some significant successes in Asia with the pivot.[120]

However, the conceptualization and implementation of the pivot were piecemeal, inconsistent, and poorly coordinated. The Obama administration swung between Asia and the Middle East and between China and Japan; struggled to find a consistent response to Chinese coercive moves against the First Island Chain; waxed hot and cold on trade; and confused dissidents and democracy supporters about the administration's stance on freedom. Meanwhile, the administration's signature theme of emphasizing engagement over confrontation with adversaries produced mixed results in Burma and led to dangerous inaction on North Korea, which rebuffed the president's proposals for dialogue with a nuclear test in May 2009 and then defied his subsequent hands-off policy of "strategic patience" when it made its third and fourth nuclear tests in February 2013 and December 2015.[121] By positing a binary choice between dialogue and war in the campaign and in the National Security Strategy documents, the president had left himself vulnerable in the gray area in between. Xi, Putin, and Kim Jong-un all found that point and exploited it to expand their own interests.

The Obama administration prided itself on moving beyond the geo-political old-think of prior administrations but ironically demonstrated why historically informed grand strategies are so crucial to statecraft in a competitive region like Asia.

CONCLUSION
THE HISTORICAL CASE FOR ASIA STRATEGY

I s the United States capable of grand strategy? Two centuries of American engagement with Asia and the Pacific strongly suggest that the answer is yes. American grand strategy has been episodic and inefficient, but in the aggregate it has been effective. The American people have repeatedly mustered the willpower, focus, and resources to prevail when access to an open order in the region has been fundamentally challenged, and they have contributed in the aggregate to a more prosperous and just Asia-Pacific region. It did not matter whether the United States had a preponderance of power at the time. John Quincy Adams and Richard Nixon advanced American interests in Asia at times of limited power in ways that Calvin Coolidge, Harry Truman, or Bill Clinton sometimes did not during times of seemingly abundant national power. The critical difference was the former leaders' clarity of purpose and deliberate identification of ends, ways, and means.

It is also evident in this study that the most effective American strategies have been rooted in a clear understanding of the geopolitics of the region. Asia has changed enormously with technology, war, economic growth, and social revolution, but it is still a region where international relations are defined by hierarchy and competition. It may be fashionable in some corners to argue that nation-states no longer dominate the international relations of Asia—that we now live in an era of epistemic communities, nonpolarity, multilateralism, and shared transnational challenges that diminish the centrality of national power. However, it is a fallacy to believe that multilateralism or transnational challenges will transform the geopolitics of Asia in the foreseeable future, even as we must work on these nonstate challenges on their own merits. When CSIS in a 2009 survey asked hundreds of experts across Asia whether they wanted greater multilateral cooperation, for example, more than 80 percent answered yes. When asked if they would rely on regional institutions in the event of pandemics, terrorism, financial crises, or military confrontations ten years hence, more than 80 percent of respondents answered no—choosing instead their own national capabilities or global institutions like the UN or IMF before putting faith in regionalism.[1] In follow-up surveys in 2014, the confidence in regional collective security and community-building was no higher overall, and among the larger powers, it was markedly lower.[2] Administrations that have thought they could transform regional geopolitics through multilateralism or transnationalism have inevitably found themselves retreating to the balance-of-power strategies that should have been their starting point. As Trotsky would say, you may not be interested in strategy—but strategy is interested in *you*.

Although most successful American strategies have begun with geopolitics, pure realpolitik has never been a sustainable basis for American policy in Asia and the Pacific. A Metternich would not long survive in the pluralistic foreign policy process in Washington (the exception, Henry Kissinger, almost proves the rule, as he rushed to explain the moral dimensions of foreign policy in his closing years as secretary of state lest his strategies be reversed); nor would the United States have achieved the successes it has in Asia over the longer term with a purely Metternichean realpolitik approach. Maintenance of balance-of-power and stable great-power relations are the sine qua non for effective grand strategy, but the United States is much better positioned to protect its interests at a time of shifting power in Asia today precisely because of past investments made to support the spread of democratic norms and more open markets.

It is important to recognize these strengths in American strategic culture at a time when China's own strategic intentions are coming under increasing scrutiny. After years of debate about whether modern leaders in Beijing themselves are capable of grand strategy, there is growing clarity in the era of Xi Jinping that China is putting in place economic, military, and foreign policies to wean Asia from dependence on American leadership and enhance China's own centrality in the region. Though China is attempting to combine attraction and coercion toward neighboring states, the net effect of Chinese policies has thus far been to push most governments closer to the United States. This is because Beijing now evokes fears of hierarchical domination, whereas Washington increasingly stands for the right of smaller states to determine their own political destiny without coercion by larger powers. Nevertheless, most states are also hedging to some extent, knowing that the United States is separated from them by thousands of miles of ocean, whereas China is separated from them by mere rivers, mountains, or inland seas. They are also hedging because China's willingness to leverage its power is becoming more apparent to the entire region. A clear and consistent demonstration of American strategic intent is therefore more important than ever in Asia. Indeed, it is indispensable to stable U.S.-China relations, which have suffered most from inconsistency in Washington.

Improving this situation requires mastering a strategic concept at least as complex as three-dimensional chess. To use that analogy, on the top board, the United States must seek to reinforce a rules-based regional order underpinned by U.S. leadership and backed by strong alliances, partnerships, trade agreements, and multilateral engagement. On the middle board, the United States will have to work toward a stable and productive relationship with China, constantly seeking new areas of cooperation based on a recognition of how much China can potentially contribute to global progress and prosperity. On the bottom board, the United States will have to continue ensuring that it has the military capabilities and posture necessary to defeat any attempts to overturn the current regional order through force.

Moves on each of the three boards impact the other boards, yet without continual play on all three of the boards, imbalance and crisis become more likely. This complex three-dimensional chess game allows ever less margin for error as China evolves its own pieces from pawns and knights to rooks and queens. Meanwhile, there is a parallel game with North Korea that at any time could change the dynamics on the three other boards. And unlike real chess, of course, the players do not know the precise utility or impact of the pieces arrayed on the board, particularly those new pieces in the domains of cyber and outer space.

Steady play in this three-dimensional chess game will require better management of the five tensions that have vexed American statecraft toward the region so often in the past. Of course, there is no absolute choice between Europe and Asia, maritime and continental approaches, forward defense and Pacific depth, self-determination and universality, or free trade and protectionism. Each reflects a conundrum in the geography of Asia and the Pacific or a foundational contradiction in the values of the United States itself. It may be possible, however, to turn these uniquely American tensions into strategic advantages.

Instead of pitting Asia policy against Europe policy by declaring a "pivot" to Asia, for example, the United States would do far better working *with* Europe to reinforce support for a rules-based system within Asia. There will still be a question of prioritizing resources, of course. In the Second World War, the consequences of a "Europe first" strategy for the Pacific theater were eventually overcome with massive wartime production. That will not likely be the case in the current budgetary environment. Moreover, the United States will have to respond to intractable problems in other parts of the world, ranging from Russian bullying to Islamic terrorism and Iranian irredentism. Asia will merit a higher proportion of diplomatic, military, and developmental resources given the return of economic and geopolitical weight to the region, but there will be more immediacy to the violent acts against Americans and American interests in the Middle East. Asia hands will need to recognize that failures of commitment or deterrence in Europe or the Middle East will inevitably reverberate in Asia. However, principals meeting in the Situation Room of the White House to manage a crisis in the Middle East or Central Europe should never again do so without also having a clear picture of U.S. objectives and strategy in Asia to inform their decision-making. Asia, after all, is now affecting the global order after years of being the object of events in the West.

The perennial swings between continental and maritime priorities and thus between China and Japan must also be controlled. China is the independent variable that could most impact regional stability in the future. However, when U.S. administrations declare "strategic partnerships," "respect for core interests," or a "new model of great power relations" in order to stabilize U.S.-China relations, the signal to the entire region is that Washington is accepting a bipolar condominium that elevates China above America's democratic allies. When subsequent friction with China then causes the United States to swing back to its allies to restore the strategic equilibrium, both China and the United States' allies are left uncertain about where American interests really lie. Thus, as Richard Armitage and Joe Nye put it in a 2007 report, the key to a successful

China policy is "getting Asia right."[3] That begins with Japan, a nation now bonded to the United States by common values and common interests in maritime security, but should also include India, Australia, Indonesia, and other aspiring stakeholders in the region. As Nixon recognized after the sapping of American power in Vietnam, multipolarity in Asia often works better for the United States when potential adversaries are on the rise. Whereas Chinese leaders speak of *global* multipolarity vis-à-vis the United States, with the implicit assertion being that China represents the Asian pole, the United States has historically been prepared to embrace the rise of other powers within Asia in order to maintain a favorable strategic equilibrium in that region. It is ultimately in the interest of the United States for states in Asia to be free from coercion, something that cannot be said with confidence in Asian capitals about China.

This is not to say that progress on issues with China should somehow be calibrated to progress with Japan or other allies and partners. Indeed, Japan can benefit when the United States and China reach agreements to reduce greenhouse gas emissions or improve military-to-military transparency and confidence-building, as long as the approach is carefully coordinated with allies. Every administration should seek to expand cooperation and trust with Beijing where possible. China should be treated with respect, as Theodore Roosevelt treated Japan a century ago, but not to the point that it appears the United States is willing to accommodate Chinese interests at allies' expense. Those administrations that have been most consistent on this point have had the most successful China policies because they established clear expectations and avoided surprises. In recent history, the examples of Ronald Reagan and George Shultz come to mind.

The definition of the United States' forward defense line in the Pacific will become increasingly complex as China tries to draw its own defense line forward to the First and Second Island Chains and North Korea develops its missile and nuclear inventories. There is less debate about where that American line should be than there was with the MacMurray Memo or War Plan Orange in the interwar years, let alone the debates of the mid-nineteenth century about coaling stations. The United States has been drawn back into establishing more engagement and presence in Southeast Asia decades after the Guam Doctrine, to recommit to the defense of the Senkaku Islands in the East China Sea, and to continue with wartime operational control on the Korean Peninsula—all because China and North Korea have strategically surprised Washington (an expansion of the American area of responsibility that Gaddis might have predicted).

Nevertheless, as Beijing increasingly backs its own expanding defense line with fortified islands, fighter planes, submarines, surface combatants, and ballistic missiles, there is the possibility of another MacMurray emerging in the halls of the State Department, Pentagon, or NSC to recommend that the defensive line be pulled back to Hawaii.

However, the American people have learned much since 1935 about the importance of keeping threats as far west across the Pacific as possible. Moreover, whereas in the late 1930s Southeast Asia consisted of weakly held colonies ripe for the picking, today the region is made up of successful nation-states. Indeed, Southeast Asia and the Korean Peninsula can no longer be considered strategically important only because they form the front lines against the hegemonic aspirations of America's adversaries. Korea is the world's twelfth-largest economy, and ASEAN as a whole constitutes America's fifth-largest trading partner. These states must today be viewed as essential "strong points" in the same way Kennan saw Germany and Japan in his early concepts of containment.

The United States will have to be resolute in its support of allies but agile enough to recognize that this will be country-by-country retail work and not a simple matter of forming a new collective security system. NATO would have been impossible if Western Europe had been trading as much with the Soviets as U.S. allies do with China today. That does not mean, however, that Asian states are prepared to be coerced by China without seeking the support of larger neighbors such as Japan, Australia, India, or—most of all—the United States. With a steady demonstration of strategic intent and commitment, the United States will find its universe of partnerships and alliances expanding. This is fundamentally a question of balance of power and not of containment, since the strategy is not premised on limiting China's own economic growth or diplomatic relations with other states.

The tension between self-determination and universal values will be equally complex. When democracy is reversed in Thailand or reforms stumble in Burma/Myanmar, should the United States temper expectations of progress lest Beijing fill in the vacuum left by American pressure and disengagement? There is no ready-made answer to this question, but each decision will have to be made with the recognition that the United States will never win a mercantilist/realpolitik contest vis-à-vis a cash-rich/conscience-free Chinese leadership. American statecraft must reflect the values of Congress and the American people if engagement of any government is to be sustained. Moreover, support for civil society and good governance will eventually yield dividends, as it did in every case of democratization in the region over the past half century. That is an advantage authoritarian regimes will never have, even if the dividends take longer to materialize.

Nevertheless, consistency will be vital. If it is understood that the American president will speak openly but respectfully about human dignity, then there will be less backlash when the president is forced to do so by public opinion at home, as the George H. W. Bush administration might have learned after Tiananmen. Senior policymakers will also have to integrate the principles of freedom of religion, women's empowerment, and human rights into their overall grand strategy rather than allow an open fight between regional and functional bureaus, as happened in the Carter and Clinton administrations. That only weakens both arms of American diplomacy as the other governments play the factions in the U.S. government against each other.

The United States can also take great confidence in the fact that citizens in a majority of states in the region now identify with the norms of democracy, human rights, good governance, and rule of law.[4] To be sure, postcolonial democracies such as India and Indonesia continue to guard sovereignty zealously and adhere to the principle of noninterference in other countries' internal affairs. However, there is no alternate regime type that attracts states the way Japanese pan-Asianism or Soviet communism briefly did in an earlier era of imperialism. The right of states to determine their own future free from coercion in Asia is more important to U.S. interests than ever, but it will depend on a combination of both engagement and support for improved governance and democratic institutions, without which these same states will remain vulnerable to coercion over time. The tension between self-determination and universality, in other words, is potentially healthy if policymakers understand both dimensions of the problem.

The losing battle for the Trans-Pacific Partnership in the Obama administration and the opposition of both presidential candidates to TPP in 2016 suggest that the tension between free trade and protectionism is becoming greater as time passes. Yet, in many respects, that close call on trade legislation reflects a failure of strategic vision and leadership as much as it does real divisions among the American people. In 2015, 70 percent of Americans supported free trade, while fewer than 20 percent of the members of unions that opposed it were actually engaged in manufacturing that might be affected by foreign competition.[5] American manufacturing, meanwhile, was on the rise in this period. Nevertheless, trade has become a proxy for other problems with the U.S. economy in terms of stagnating middle-class wages that are more related to globalization and automation than trade agreements. Had President Obama understood the centrality of trade to American internationalism and influence the way Reagan and Bill Clinton did—and made the case for it—then the trade arm of American engagement in Asia and the Pacific would have had more credibility at home and abroad from the beginning.

It is also noteworthy that strategically vulnerable states in the region, including Japan and Vietnam, have been eager to liberalize their economies in order to deepen ties to the United States as China increasingly used its economic leverage to extract geopolitical concessions. American tariff reductions in recent agreements with Australia, Korea, and Japan have been minimal, since the U.S. market is already open. The real progress has always been in the reduction of foreign partners' barriers to trade, particularly in behind-the-border rulemaking. Hegemonic stability is now underpinned by the willingness of other states in the region to bind their economies more closely to the United States for self-defense and economic growth. Trade negotiations touch on sovereignty and are always contentious, but an American grand strategy for Asia and the Pacific that does not continue to build on this advantage and extend it to North America and Europe will be like a stool with only two legs. Or as Mahan said, like shallow-draft ironclads rather than oceangoing battle cruisers. Over time, this broader trade and financial architecture will incentivize reformers within China itself to harmonize regulations, remove barriers, and improve the rule of law and intellectual property rights. In short, the impact of U.S.-led trade agreements within the United States is marginal, but the impact on regional order is enormous.

In conclusion, as Mahan warned, the ability of the United States to shape events within China has always been limited, but a grand strategy that sets the regional stage in terms of deterrence, trade, and values will increase the prospects for peaceful management of the next power transition in Asia. There was nothing inevitable about conflict with Japan, as Theodore Roosevelt knew, or about the invincibility of the Soviet Union, as Ronald Reagan demonstrated. Both presidents made mistakes but successfully evoked the vision of John Quincy Adams, William Henry Seward, and dozens of other strategic thinkers who, over the course of history, understood that the United States would have to secure its position in the Asia Pacific by more than providence.

NOTES

Introduction

1. Robert D. Blackwill and Ashley J. Tellis, *Revising U.S. Grand Strategy Toward China*, Council on Foreign Relations Special Report, April 2015, http://www.cfr.org/china/revising-us-grand-strategy-toward-china/p36371; Thomas G. Mahnken, ed., *Competitive Strategies for the 21st Century: Theory, History, and Practice* (Stanford, CA: Stanford University Press, 2012).

2. Michael D. Swaine, *America's Challenge: Engaging a Rising China in the Twenty-First Century* (Washington, DC: Carnegie Endowment for International Peace, 2011); Michael D. Swaine, "China: The Influence of History," thediplomat.com, January 14, 2015; Graham T. Allison, "Avoiding Thucydides's Trap," *Financial Times* (London), August 22, 2012; Graham T. Allison, "Obama and Xi Must Think Broadly to Avoid a Classic Trap," *New York Times*, June 6, 2013.

3. Tyler Dennett, *Americans in Eastern Asia: A Critical Study of the Policy of the United States with Reference to China, Japan and Korea in the 19th Century* (New York: Macmillan, 1922).

4. Warren I. Cohen, *America's Response to China: A History of Sino-American Relations*, 5th ed. (New York: Columbia University Press, 2013); Walter LaFeber, *The Clash: U.S.-Japanese Relations Throughout History* (New York: Norton, 1997); Raymond E. Vickery, Jr., *The Eagle and the Elephant: Strategic Aspects of US-India Economic Engagement* (Baltimore: Johns Hopkins University Press, 2011). Other books on Asia broadly speaking include John Curtis Perry, *Facing West: Americans and the Opening of the Pacific* (West-

port, CT: Praeger, 1994), which according to its author is concerned with "people and not policy" (p. xix).

5. See, for example, James Bradley, *The Imperial Cruise: A Secret History of Empire and War* (New York: Little, Brown, 2009); Bruce Cumings, *Dominion from Sea to Sea: Pacific Ascendancy and American Power* (New Haven, CT: Yale University Press, 2009).

6. Two other noteworthy exceptions would be Marvin Kalb and Elie Able's book on the historic background to the Vietnam War, *Vietnam: Roots of Involvement: The U.S. and Asia, 1784–1971* (New York: Norton, 1971), which has two concise chapters on the earliest beginnings of American policy toward Asia, and Walter MacDougall's engaging *Let the Sea Make a Noise . . . : A History of the North Pacific from Magellan to MacArthur* (New York: Avon Books, 1994), which has an excellent discussion of American strategic views of the Pacific in the context of a broader history of international relations in the region.

7. John Collins, *Grand Strategy: Principles and Practices* (Annapolis, MD: Naval Institute Press, 1973), 1; Hans Morgenthau, *The Impasse of American Foreign Policy* (Chicago: University of Chicago Press, 1962), 191; Hans Morgenthau, "Another Great Debate: The National Interest of the United States," *American Political Science Review* 46 (1952): 73; Hans Morgenthau, "Alliances in Theory and Practice," in *Alliance Policy in the Cold War*, ed. Arnold Wolfers (Baltimore: Johns Hopkins University Press, 1959), 191. The preceding two works are cited in Michael G. Roskin, "National Interest: From Abstraction to Strategy," in *U.S. Army War College Guide to Strategy*, ed. Joseph R. Cerami and James F. Holcomb (Carlisle, PA: Army War College, 2001), 66.

8. Collins, *Grand Strategy*, 25; Robert H. Dorff, "A Primer in Strategy Development," in Cerami and Holcomb, *U.S. Army War College Guide to Strategy*, 12.

9. Richard K. Betts, "Is Strategy an Illusion?" *International Security* 25, no. 2 (Autumn 2000): 40.

10. Edward Luttwak, *Strategy: The Logic of Peace and War* (Cambridge, MA: Harvard University Press, 1987), 233.

11. Peter Rodman's posthumous study of presidents' relationships with their cabinets suggested that most secretaries of state preferred "pragmatism" to vision. See Peter Rodman, *Presidential Command: Power, Leadership, and the Making of Foreign Policy from Richard Nixon to George W. Bush* (New York: Knopf, 2009), 282–285. Warren Zimmerman also noted that of all the cabal of expansionists around Theodore Roosevelt at the turn of the twentieth century, Secretary of State John Hay was the one man who "lacked conceptual and strategic grasp." See Warren Zimmerman, *First Great Triumph: How Five Americans Made Their Country a World Power* (New York: Farrar, Straus, and Giroux, 2002), 83. There are notable exceptions, of course, including John Quincy Adams, Henry Kissinger, and George Shultz.

12. Ole R. Holsti, *Making American Foreign Policy* (New York: Routledge, 2006), 243.

13. Holsti, *Making American Foreign Policy*, 327–339. Scholarly work on the distorting effects of individual leaders on foreign policy is captured in Torbjorn L. Knutsen, *A History of International Relations Theory*, 2nd ed. (New York: University of Manchester Press, 1997), 245. See also Robert Jervis, *Perception and Misperception in International Politics* (Princeton, NJ: Princeton University Press, 1976); Graham T. Allison, *Essence of Decision* (Boston: Little, Brown, 1971); George Sinkler, *The Racial Attitudes of American Presidents from Abraham Lincoln to Theodore Roosevelt* (Garden City, NY: Doubleday,

1971); Reginald Horsman, *Race and Manifest Destiny* (Cambridge, MA: Harvard University Press, 1981).

14. Alexis de Tocqueville, *Democracy in America* (New York: Vintage, 1945), 240–245, cited in Walter A. MacDougall, "Can the United States Do Grand Strategy?" (presentation, Foreign Policy Research Institute, April 2010).

15. Zimmerman, *First Great Triumph*, 121.

16. Walter Lippmann, *U.S. Foreign Policy: Shield of the Republic* (Boston: Little, Brown, 1943), 49.

17. Robert Endicott Osgood, *Ideals and Self-Interest in America's Foreign Relations* (Chicago: University of Chicago Press, 1953), 264; Henry Kissinger, *Does America Need a Foreign Policy?* (New York: Simon and Schuster, 2001), 29.

18. Les Gelb, *Power Rules* (New York: HarperCollins, 2009), 95. See also Andrew Krepinevich and Barry Watts, "Lost at the NSC," *The National Interest*, January–February 2009; Aaron Friedberg, "Strengthening U.S. Strategic Planning," in *Avoiding Trivia: The Role of Strategic Planning in American Foreign Policy*, ed. Daniel W. Drezner (Washington, DC: Brookings Institution Press, 2010); Michele Flournoy and Shawn Brimley, "Strategic Planning for National Security," *Joint Forces Quarterly* 41 (2nd quarter 2006): 80, quoted in Drezner, *Avoiding Trivia*, 3; Stephen D. Krasner, "An Orienting Principle for Foreign Policy," *Policy Review*, no. 163 (October 1, 2010).

19. MacDougall, "Can the United States Do Grand Strategy?," 5.

20. Edward Luttwak, *The Grand Strategy of the Byzantine Empire* (Cambridge, MA: Belknap Press of Harvard University Press, 2009), 409, cited in Timothy Andrew Sayle, "Defining and Teaching Grand Strategy," *The Telegram: Newsletter of the Hertog Program in Grand Strategy*, no. 4 (January 2011).

21. Paul Bracken, "Scholars and Security," *Perspectives on Politics* 8, no. 4 (December 2010): 1096–1097.

22. Betts, "Is Strategy an Illusion?" 42.

23. Richard Neustadt and Ernest R. May, *Thinking in Time: The Uses of History for Decision Makers* (New York: The Free Press, 1986), 251–252. On the folly of using isolated historical examples ("no more Munichs" or "no more Vietnams") to generalize the lessons of history, see also Yuen Foong Khong, *Analogies at War: Korea, Munich, Dien Bien Phu, and the Vietnam Decisions of 1965* (Princeton, NJ: Princeton University Press, 1992).

24. Williamson Murray, introduction to *The Making of Strategy: Rulers, States, and War*, ed. Williamson Murray, MacGregor Knox, and Alvin Bernstein (New York: Cambridge University Press, 1994), 1–2.

25. John Lewis Gaddis, *Surprise, Security, and the American Experience* (Cambridge, MA: Harvard University Press, 2003), 13.

26. On economic imperialism, see William Appleman Williams, *The Tragedy of American Diplomacy* (New York: Norton, 1959). On offensive realism, see Fareed Zakaria, *From Wealth to Power* (Princeton, NJ: Princeton University Press, 1998). For definitions of defensive realism, see Robert Jervis, "Cooperation Under the Security Dilemma," *World Politics* 30, no. 2 (1978); Kenneth Waltz, *Theory of International Politics* (Columbus, OH: McGraw-Hill, 1979).

27. See, for example, Michael Green, "America Is Not Isolationist in the Pacific," *Foreign Policy*, February 3, 2014, http://foreignpolicy.com/2014/02/03/america-is-not

-isolationist-in-the-pacific/; Dina S. Smeltz and Craig Kafura, "Americans Affirm Ties to Allies in Asia," The Chicago Council on Foreign Affairs, Chicago Council Surveys, October 28, 2014, https://www.thechicagocouncil.org/publication/americans-affirm-ties -allies-asia; Mark Preston, "Poll: Americans Back Airstrikes, but Oppose Use of U.S. Troops in Iraq, Syria," cnn.com, September 29, 2014, http://www.cnn.com/2014/09/29 /politics/poll-americans-back-airstrikes/; Dina Smeltz and Ivo Daalder with Craig Kafura, "Foreign Policy in the Age of Retrenchment: Results of the 2014 Chicago Council Survey of American Public Opinion and US Foreign Policy," The Chicago Council on Global Affairs, September 15, 2014, http://www.thechicagocouncil.org/survey/2014/_resources /ChicagoCouncilSurvey.pdf; Scott Snyder, "American Attitudes Toward Korea: Growing Support for a Solid Relationship," Chicago Council Survey, The Chicago Council on Global Affairs, October 2014, http://www.thechicagocouncil.org/sites/default/files /USSouthKorea_Snyder.pdf; Michael J. Green, "U.S.-Japan Alliance Central to American Views of Asia: Assessment of the 2014 Chicago Council Survey," The Chicago Council on Global Affairs, October 2014, http://www.thechicagocouncil.org/sites/default/files /USJapan2014-Green.pdf.

28. Edwin O. Reischauer, *Beyond Vietnam: The United States and Asia* (New York: Vantage, 1968), 54–56.

29. H. J. Mackinder, "The Geographical Pivot of History," *Geographical Journal* 23, no. 6 (April 1904); H. J. Mackinder, "The Rivalry of Empires," in *Democratic Ideals and Reality: A Study in the Politics of Reconstruction* (1919) (New York: Henry Holt, 1942); A. T. Mahan, *The Influence of Sea Power Upon History, 1660–1783* (1890) (New York: Dover, 1987); Paul Kennedy, "Mahan Versus Mackinder: Two Interpretations of British Sea Power," in *Strategy and Diplomacy, 1870–1945: Eight Studies* (London: George Allen and Unwin, 1983); Brian W. Blouet, *Halford Mackinder: A Biography* (College Station: Texas A&M Press, 1987); Jon Sumida, "Alfred Thayer Mahan, Geopolitician," in "Geopolitics, Geography and Strategy," special issue, *Journal of Strategic Studies* 22, nos. 2–3 (June–September 1999); John B. Hattendorf, ed., *The Influence of History on Mahan: The Proceedings of a Conference Marking the Centenary of Alfred Thayer Mahan's "The Influence of Sea Power Upon History, 1660–1783"* (Newport, RI: Naval War College Press, 1991); Jon Tetsuro Sumida, *Inventing Grand Strategy and Teaching Command: The Classic Works of Alfred Thayer Mahan Reconsidered* (Baltimore: Johns Hopkins University Press, 1997).

30. Jack S. Levy and William R. Thompson, "Balancing on Land and at Sea: Do States Ally Against the Leading Global Power?" *International Security* 35, no. 1 (Summer 2010): 40.

31. See, for example, Osgood, *Ideals and Self-Interest in America's Foreign Relations*, 18; Krepinevich and Watts, "Lost at the NSC."

32. George C. Herring, *From Colony to Superpower: U.S. Foreign Relations Since 1776* (New York: Oxford University Press, 2008), 12.

33. Philip Zelikow, as quoted in Robert Zoellick, "The Currency of Power," *Foreign Policy*, no. 196 (November 2012): 67–73 at 69.

34. The reversal of protectionism began with the Reciprocal Trade Act of 1934.

35. Robert O. Keohane, *After Hegemony: Cooperation and Discord in the World Political Economy* (Princeton, NJ: Princeton University Press, 1984); Michael Mastanduno, "Do

Relative Gains Matter? America's Response to Japanese Industrial Policy," *International Security* 16, no. 1 (Summer 1991): 73–113; Duncan Snidal, "Relative Gains and the Pattern of International Cooperation," *American Political Science Review* 85, no. 3 (September 1991): 701–726; D. Krasner, "An Orienting Principle for Foreign Policy," *Policy Review*, no. 163 (October 1, 2010).

36. Edwin O. Reischauer, *Wanted: An Asian Policy* (New York: Knopf, 1955), 185.

37. This structure draws on John Lewis Gaddis's observation that there were distinct deflection points in the evolution of U.S. containment strategy based on an incoming administration's "geopolitical code," or set of assumptions and worldviews about the ongoing contest with the Soviet Union. See John Lewis Gaddis, *Strategies of Containment* (New York: Oxford University Press, 1982).

Part 1

1. Theodore Roosevelt, *The Naval War of 1812: Or the History of the United States Navy During the Last Great War with Britain* (New York: G. P. Putnam and Sons, 1882), 209.

1. Seeds of Strategy, 1784–1860

1. Albert K. Weinberg, *Manifest Destiny: A Study of Nationalist Expansionism in American History* (Chicago: University of Chicago Press, 1963), 72–81.

2. Robert Kagan, *Dangerous Nation: America's Place in the World from Its Earliest Days to the Dawn of the Twentieth Century* (New York: Knopf, 2006), 52.

3. John Paton Davies, "America and East Asia," *Foreign Affairs* 55, no. 2 (January 1977): 368.

4. Jared Sparks, *Memoirs of the Life and Travels of John Ledyard* (London: Henry Colburn, 1828).

5. Letter from Robert Morris to John Jay, November 27, 1783, in *The Revolutionary Diplomatic Correspondence of the United States*, ed. Francis Wharton (Washington, DC: Government Printing Office, 1889), 4:735.

6. On the *Empress of China* and other early China trade, see Arthur Power Dudden, *The American Pacific: From the Old China Trade to the Present* (New York: Oxford University Press, 1992); Foster Rhea Dulles, *The Old China Trade* (Cambridge, MA: Riverside, 1930); Foster Rhea Dulles, *China and America, the Story of Their Relations Since 1784* (Princeton, NJ: Princeton University Press, 1946), 1–17.

7. Letter from Robert Morris to John Jay, May 19, 1785, in *The Correspondence and Public Papers of John Jay*, ed. Henry P. Johnston (New York: Burt Franklin, 1890), 3:143–144.

8. Letter from Samuel Shaw to John Jay, May 19, 1785, in Johnston, *The Correspondence and Public Papers of John Jay*, 3:149.

9. Letter from Richard Henry Lee to James Madison, May 30, 1785, in *Letters of Delegates to Congress, 1774–1789*, ed. Paul H. Smith, Ronald M. Gephart, and Gerard W. Gawalt, 26 vols. (Washington, DC: Library of Congress, 1976–2000), 22:418.

10. Tyler Dennett, *Americans in Eastern Asia: A Critical Study of the Policy of the United States with Reference to China, Japan, and Korea in the 19th Century* (New York: Macmillan, 1922), 9; Kagan, *Dangerous Nation*, 96.

11. Dennett, *Americans in Eastern Asia*, 27.

12. L. G. Churchward, *Australia & America, 1788–1972: An Alternative History* (Sydney: Alternative Publishing Cooperative, 1979), 5.

13. C. Hartley Grattan, *The United States and the Southwest Pacific* (Cambridge, MA: Harvard University Press, 1961), 71; Churchward, *Australia & America, 1788–1972*, 14; M. P. Lissington, *New Zealand and the United States, 1840–1944* (Wellington: A. R. Shearer, Government Printer, 1972), 5.

14. Sometimes that worked to Americans' advantage, as American ships were able to trade at Dejima after Napoleon conquered the Dutch. See Bob Tadashi Wakabayashi, *Anti-foreignism and Western Learning in Early-Modern Japan: The New Theses of 1825* (Cambridge, MA: Harvard University Asia Center, 1992), 91.

15. Warren I. Cohen, *East Asia at the Center* (New York: Columbia University Press, 2000), 292–294; Dennett, *Americans in Eastern Asia*, 169.

16. Dennett, *Americans in Eastern Asia*, 56; Donald R. Hickey, *The War of 1812: A Forgotten Conflict*, bicentennial ed. (Urbana-Champaign: University of Illinois Press, 2012), chap 1.

17. Robert J. Allison, *The American Revolution* (Oxford: Oxford University Press, 2011), 5–7.

18. Washington Irving, *Astoria, or Anecdotes of an Enterprise Beyond the Rocky Mountains* (Paris: Baudry's European Library, 1836), 16.

19. Robert W. Tucker and David C. Hendrickson, *Empire of Liberty: The Statecraft of Thomas Jefferson* (New York: Oxford University Press, 1990), ix.

20. *Thomas Jefferson to George Rogers Clark*, Annapolis, December 4, 1783; available from the Avalon Project Documents in Law, History, and Diplomacy, Lillian Goldman Law Library, Yale University, http://avalon.law.yale.edu/18th_century/let21.asp.

21. Edward G. Gray, *The Making of John Ledyard: Empire and Ambition in the Life of an Early American Traveler* (New Haven, CT: Yale University Press, 2008), 124–169.

22. James Morton Callahan, *American Relations in the Pacific and the Far East, 1784–1900* (Baltimore: Johns Hopkins University Press, 1901), 14–15. See Stephen E. Ambrose, *Undaunted Courage* (New York: Touchstone, 1996), 476–484.

23. William Earl Weeks, *John Quincy Adams and American Global Empire* (Lexington: University of Kentucky Press, 1992), 49.

24. Kenneth Wiggins Porter, *John Jacob Astor: Business Man* (Cambridge, MA: Harvard University Press, 1931), 1:133.

25. The act had been passed in a self-defeating attempt to remain neutral in the ongoing Napoleonic Wars. See Porter, *John Jacob Astor*, 1:421–422.

26. Peter Stark, *Astoria: Astor and Jefferson's Lost Pacific Empire: A Tale of Ambition and Survival on the Early American Frontier* (New York: HarperCollins, 2014), 24, 692, 910; Porter, *John Jacob Astor*, 1:243.

27. The Treaty of Ghent contained a provision for returning all possessions taken during the war. As Astoria ended the war in British possession, the United States argued that it should be returned. However, the British stated that because the private holders of

Astoria had sold the territory to them, their possession was the result of a commercial transaction, not conquest, and therefore did not fall under the provisions of the treaty. And yet, when the U.S. Navy attempted to reclaim the fort (by using the USS *Ontario*, dispatched in 1817), the British handed it over under the provisions of the Treaty of Ghent. The United States retook possession of Astoria in August 1818 (formal transfer was made in October 1818). See Alfred A. Cleveland, "Social and Economic History of Astoria," *Quarterly of the Oregon Historical Society* 4, no. 2 (June 1903): 130–149.

28. Charles N. Edel, *Nation Builder: John Quincy Adams and the Grand Strategy of the Republic* (London: Cambridge University Press, 2014), 27–28.

29. For John Quincy Adams's prepresidential career, see Samuel Flagg Bemis, *John Quincy Adams and the Foundations of American Foreign Policy* (New York: Knopf, 1949). For an accounting of his entire career as it relates to foreign policy, see James E. Lewis, *John Quincy Adams: Policymaker for the Union* (Wilmington, DE: SR Books, 2001).

30. Edel, *Nation Builder*, 323.

31. Edel, *Nation Builder*, 324.

32. William Earl Weeks, *John Quincy Adams and American Global Empire* (Lexington: University of Kentucky Press, 1992), 139; Bemis, *John Quincy Adams and the Foundations of American Foreign Policy*, 338.

33. Report to the Congress, 45:16-2, January 25, 1821, cited in James Morton Callahan, *American Relations in the Pacific and the Far East, 1784–1900* (Baltimore: Johns Hopkins Press, 1901), 32.

34. George C. Herring, *From Colony to Superpower: U.S. Foreign Relations Since 1776* (New York: Oxford University Press, 2008), 151–152.

35. Foster Rhea Dulles, *America in the Pacific: A Century of Expansion* (Boston: Houghton Mifflin, 1932), 27–28, quoted in Dexter Perkins, "John Quincy Adams," in *The American Secretaries of State and Their Diplomacy*, ed. Samuel Flagg Bemis (New York: Knopf, 1928), 4:95.

36. Letter from Secretary of State John Quincy Adams to Hon. Richard Rush, Envoy Extraordinary and Minister Plenipotentiary of the United States, London, July 22, 1823, in *American State Papers 1: Foreign Relations*, 5:446–448.

37. Albert Bushnell Hart, *The Monroe Doctrine: An Interpretation* (Boston: Little, Brown, 1920), 19–20, 299–316; Bemis, *John Quincy Adams and the Foundations of American Foreign Policy*, chap. 18.

38. Hart, *The Monroe Doctrine*, 282–298; Claude A. Buss, *The Far East: A History of Recent and Contemporary International Relations in East Asia* (New York: MacMillan, 1955), 119.

39. Buss, *The Far East*, 119.

40. William Henry Seward, *Life and Public Services of John Quincy Adams, Sixth President of the United States* (Auburn, NY: Derby, Miller, 1849).

41. John Denis Haeger, *John Jacob Astor: Business and Finance in the Early Republic* (Detroit: Wayne State University Press, 1991), 159.

42. Dennett, *Americans in Eastern Asia*, 69; John Curtis Perry, *Facing West: Americans and the Opening of the Pacific* (Westport, CT: Praeger, 1994), 46.

43. Pensri Duke, *A Century and a Half of Thai-American Relations*, ed. Wiwat Mungkandi and William Warren (Bangkok: Chulalongkorn University Press, 1982), 9; Vimol

Bhongbhibat, ed., *The Eagle and the Elephant: 150 Years of Thai-American Relations* (Bangkok: United Production, 1982), 34–36.

44. Callahan, *American Relations in the Pacific and the Far East, 1784–1900*, 69; John H. Schroeder, *Shaping a Maritime Empire: The Commercial and Diplomatic Role of the American Navy, 1829–1861* (Westport, CT: Greenwood, 1943), 143.

45. Daniel Walker Howe, *What Hath God Wrought: The Transformation of America, 1815–1848* (Oxford: Oxford University Press, 2007), 215.

46. Grattan, *The United States and the Southwest Pacific*, 81.

47. President John Quincy Adams, First Annual Message to Congress, December 6, 1825, The American Presidency Project, http://www.presidency.ucsb.edu/ws/?pid=29467.

48. Schroeder, *Shaping a Maritime Empire*, 1.

49. Nathaniel Philbrick, *Sea of Glory: America's Voyage of Discovery: The U.S. Exploring Expedition, 1838–1842* (New York: Penguin, 2003). For further reading, see William Ragan Stanton, *The Great United States Exploring Expedition of 1838–1842* (Berkeley: University of California Press, 1975); David B. Tyler, *The Wilkes Expedition: The First United States Exploring Expedition (1838–1842)* (Philadelphia: American Philosophical Society, 1968); Charles Henderson, *The Hidden Coasts: A Biography of Admiral Charles Wilkes* (London: Greenwood, 1971); Charles Wilkes, *Narrative of the United States Exploring Expedition During the Years 1838, 1839, 1840, 1841, 1842*, 5 vols. (London: Wiley and Putnam, 1845), https://archive.org/stream/narrativeunited10wilkgoog#page/n11/mode/2up.

50. Schroeder, *Shaping a Maritime Empire*, 44.

51. Churchward, *Australia & America, 1788–1972*, 34.

52. Letter form Levi Woodbury to Commodore John Downes on board the U.S. frigate *Potomac*, August 9, 1831, forwarded by Andrew Jackson to Congress on July 12, 1832, in *American State Papers: Naval Affairs*, 4:153; Jon Meachem, *American Lion: Andrew Jackson in the White House* (New York: Random House, 2008), 213–215; Robert Erwin Johnson, *Far China Station: The U.S. Navy in Asian Waters, 1800–1898* (Annapolis, MD: U.S. Naval Institute Press, 1979), 1–2.

53. Schroeder, *Shaping a Maritime Empire*, 24–28.

54. Edward P. Crapol, "John Tyler and the Pursuit of National Destiny," *Journal of the Early Republic* 17, no. 3 (October 1997): 481–482.

55. Herring, *From Colony to Superpower*, 159.

56. Dennett, *Americans in Eastern Asia*, 84.

57. Annabelle S. Wenzke, *Timothy Dwight* (Lewiston, NY: Edwin Mellen, 1989), 257–258.

58. Foster Rhea Dulles, *China and America*, 41.

59. Dennett, *Americans in Eastern Asia*, 181.

60. Buss, *The Far East*, 119–120.

61. Howe, *What Hath God Wrought*, 707.

62. Isaac Smith Homans, *An Historical and Statistical Account of the Foreign Commerce of the United States* (New York: G. P. Putnam, 1857), 67; Schroeder, *Shaping a Maritime Empire*, 5.

63. Fred Kaplan, *John Quincy Adams: American Visionary* (New York: HarperCollins, 2014), 818.

64. Walter A. MacDougall, *Promised Land, Crusader State: The American Encounter with the World Since 1776* (New York: Houghton Mifflin, 1997), 77.

65. Edward P. Crapol, "John Tyler and the Pursuit of National Destiny," *Journal of the Early Republic* 17, no. 3 (October 1997): 467–491.

66. Nor would the Mexican government have likely agreed.

67. Joseph Schafer, "The British Attitude Toward the Oregon Question, 1815–1846," *American Historical Review* 16, no. 2 (January 1911): 273–299. The British envoy in Mexico wanted to contest control over California, where British citizens had also settled, but London was not looking for new foreign entanglements on the North American continent.

68. Walter LaFeber, *The Clash: A History of U.S.-Japan Relations* (New York: Norton, 1997), 11.

69. John K. Fairbank, *Trade and Diplomacy on the China Coast: The Opening of the Treaty Ports, 1842–1854*, 2 vols. (Cambridge, MA: Harvard University Press, 1953); Peter Ward Fay, *The Opium War, 1840–1842* (Chapel Hill: University of North Carolina Press, 1975); David Scott, *China and the International System, 1840–1849* (New York: State University of New York Press, 2006), 22–24.

70. Dennett, *Americans in Eastern Asia*, 89.

71. House Document 40:26-1, quoted in Dennett, *Americans in Eastern Asia*, 99–100.

72. Dennett, *Americans in Eastern Asia*, 104.

73. Josiah Quincy, *Memoir of the Life of John Quincy Adams* (Boston: Crosby, Nichols, Lee, 1860), 337–339.

74. Quincy, *Memoir of the Life of John Quincy Adams*, 337–339.

75. Dennett, *Americans in Eastern Asia*, 138.

76. Callahan, *American Relations in the Pacific and the Far East, 1784–1900*, 88–90; Dulles, *China and America*, 46; Kuo Ping Chia, "Caleb Cushing and the Treaty of Wanghia, 1844," *Journal of Modern History* 5, no. 1 (March 1933): 34–54; Dennett, *Americans in Eastern Asia*, 138–182.

77. Buss, *The Far East*, 126.

78. H. M. Cole, "Origins of the French Protectorate Over Catholic Missions in China," *American Journal of International Law* 34, no. 3 (July 1940): 473–491.

79. John Paton Davies, "America and East Asia," *Foreign Affairs* 55, no. 2 (January 1977): 372.

80. Samuel P. Huntington, "National Policy and the Transoceanic Navy," (United States Naval Institute) *Proceedings* 80, no. 5 (May 1954): 487–493.

81. Letter from U.S. Commissioner to China Humphrey Marshall to Charles Conrad, September 25, 1852, from the Marshall Family Collection as compiled by William E. McLaughry and provided by the Filson Historical Society, Louisville, KY.

82. See H. Barrett Learned, "William Learned Marcy," in Bemis, *The American Secretaries of State and Their Diplomacy*, 4:153. See also Ivor D. Spencer, *The Victor and the Spoils: A Life of William L. Marcy* (Providence, RI: Brown University Press, 1959), 303–308. For an integrated international and domestic history of the Taiping Rebellion, see Steven R. Platt, *Autumn in the Heavenly Kingdom* (New York: Knopf, 2012); Dennett, *Americans in Eastern Asia*, 214; Te-kong Tong, *United States Diplomacy in China, 1844–1860* (Seattle: University of Washington Press, 1964), 132.

83. Daniel Henderson, *Yankee Ships in China Seas; Adventures of Pioneer Americans in the Troubled Far East* (Freeport, NY: Books for Libraries, 1946), 211–212.

84. Letter from Humphrey Marshall to Secretary Marcy, July 6, 1853, 33rd Congress, 1st session, House Executive Document 123, 203–205.

85. Dennett, *Americans in Eastern Asia*, 216–224.

86. Tong, *United States Diplomacy in China*, 144.

87. See, for example, John King Fairbank, *The United States and China* (Cambridge, MA: Harvard University Press, 1983), 313.

88. William Conrad Costin, *Great Britain and China, 1833–1860* (Oxford: Clarendon, 1937), 182.

89. Dennett, *Americans in Eastern Asia*, 206.

90. Letter from Robert M. McLane to William L. Marcy, August 20, 1854, Message of the President of the United States James Buchanan communicating in compliance with a resolution of the Senate, the correspondence of Messrs. McLane and Parker, late commissioners to China, December 20, 1858, 35th Congress, 2nd session, Executive Document 22, 169.

91. Letter from Robert M. McLane to William L. Marcy, August 20, 1854, Message of the President of the United States James Buchanan communicating in compliance with a resolution of the Senate, the correspondence of Messrs. McLane and Parker, late commissioners to China, December 20, 1858, 35th Congress, 2nd Session, Executive Document 22, 169.

92. Letter from Robert M. McLane to William L. Marcy, November 19, 1854, Message of the President of the United States James Buchanan communicating in compliance with a resolution of the Senate, the correspondence of Messrs. McLane and Parker, late commissioners to China, December 20, 1858, 35th Congress, 2nd session, Executive Document 22, 292.

93. Rev. George B. Stevens and Rev. W. Fisher Markwick, *The Life, Letters and Journals of the Rev. and Hon. Peter Parker, M.D.: Missionary, Physician, and Diplomatist; The Father of Medical Missions and Founder of the Ophthalmic Hospital in Canton* (Boston: Congregational Sunday School and Publishing Society, 1896), 43–44.

94. Stevens and Markwick, *The Life, Letters and Journals of the Rev. and Hon. Peter Parker, M.D.*, 66–67.

95. Stevens and Markwick, *The Life, Letters and Journals of the Rev. and Hon. Peter Parker, M.D.*, 128.

96. Stevens and Markwick, *The Life, Letters and Journals of the Rev. and Hon. Peter Parker, M.D.*, 185–187.

97. Edward V. Gulick, *Peter Parker and the Opening of China* (Cambridge, MA: Harvard University Press, 1973), 124.

98. Stevens and Markwick, *The Life, Letters and Journals of the Rev. and Hon. Peter Parker, M.D.*, 167.

99. Letter from Peter Parker to Robert McLane, April 6, 1854, Message of the President of the United States James Buchanan communicating in compliance with a resolution of the Senate, the correspondence of Messrs. McLane and Parker, late commissioners to China, December 20, 1858, 35th Congress, 2nd session, Executive Document 22, 20.

100. Gulick, *Peter Parker and the Opening of China*, 188–189.

101. Gulick, *Peter Parker and the Opening of China*, 18.

102. Dulles, *America in the Pacific*, 77.

103. Instructions to Minister to China from Secretary of State Marcy to Mr. McLane, November 9, 1853, in Message of the President of the United States to the Senate, 36th Congress, 1st session, Executive Document 39.

104. Schroeder, *Shaping a Maritime Empire*, 170; Gulick, *Peter Parker and the Opening of China*, 190.

105. Callahan, *American Relations in the Pacific and the Far East, 1784–1900*, 160; Schroeder, *Shaping a Maritime Empire*, 170.

106. Schroeder, *Shaping a Maritime Empire*, 174.

107. Perry, *Facing West*, 47.

108. Callahan, *American Relations in the Pacific and the Far East, 1784–1900*, 78; Dennett, *Americans in Eastern Asia*, 244.

109. David Long, *Sailor-Diplomat: A Biography of Commodore James Biddle* (Boston: Northeastern University Press, 1983), 209.

110. Dennett, *Americans in Eastern Asia*, 184.

111. President Pierce's First Annual Message, December 5, 1853.

112. Callahan, *American Relations in the Pacific and the Far East, 1784–1900*, 76.

113. Dennett, *Americans in Eastern Asia*, 272.

114. Dennett, *Americans in Eastern Asia*, 273.

115. Callahan, *American Relations in the Pacific and the Far East, 1784–1900*, 77.

116. Henderson, *Yankee Ships in China Seas*, 224.

117. Dennett, *Americans in Eastern Asia*, 270.

118. Dennett, *Americans in Eastern Asia*, 263.

119. Samuel Eliot Morison, *"Old Bruin" Commodore Matthew Perry* (Boston: Little, Brown, 1967), 266.

120. LaFeber, *The Clash*, 14; Arthur Walwurth, *Black Ships Off Japan* (New York: Knopf, 1946).

121. Dennett, *Americans in Eastern Asia*, 274.

122. William R. Nester, *Power Across the Pacific: A Diplomatic History of American Relations with Japan* (London: Macmillan, 1996), 38–39.

123. Matthew C. Perry, *A Paper by Commodore M.C. Perry, U.S.N.: Read Before the American Geographical and Statistical Society, at a Meeting Held March 6th, 1856* (New York: D. Appleton, 1856).

124. Kagan, *Dangerous Nation*, 252

125. Dennett, *Americans in Eastern Asia*, 185.

126. Warren I. Cohen, *America's Response to China: A History of Sino-American Relations*, 5th ed. (New York: Columbia University Press, 2013), 27.

2. Precursors to Expansion, 1861–1898

1. Warren Cohen, *America's Response to China: A History of Sino-American Relations*, 5th ed. (New York: Columbia University Press, 2010), 29.

2. *Congressional Globe*, March 11, 1850, 262, 31st Congress, 1st session, in Ernest N. Paolino, *Foundations of the American Empire: William Henry Seward and US Foreign Policy* (Ithaca, NY: Cornell University Press, 1973), 27.

3. Paolino, *Foundations of the American Empire*, 28; George C. Herring, *From Colony to Superpower: U.S. Foreign Relations Since 1776* (New York: Oxford University Press, 2008), 256.

4. Frederic Bancroft, *The Life of William H. Seward* (New York: Harper and Brothers, 1900), 1:469.

5. William H. Seward, "The Destiny of America Speech at Capital University, Columbus, Ohio, September 14, 1853" (Albany, NY: Weed, Paesons, 1853).

6. From an address by Seward titled "The Physical, Moral, and Intellectual Development of the American People" before Phi Beta Kappa Society of Yale College: New Haven, July 26, 1854, in *The Works of William H. Seward*, ed. George E. Baker (Boston: Houghton, Mifflin, 1884), 4:165–166.

7. Tyler Dennett, *Americans in Eastern Asia: A Critical Study of the Policy of the United States with Reference to China, Japan, and Korea in the 19th Century* (New York: Macmillan, 1922), 408.

8. Seward got involved in extending telegraph lines to Russia in 1863. See U.S. Department of State, *Foreign Relations of the United States*, http://digicoll.library.wisc.edu /FRUS/Browse.html [hereafter cited as *FRUS*], *1863, Vol. II*, 850–875.

9. Letter from William Henry Seward to Minister Robert Pruyn, November 15, 1861, *FRUS, 1862, Vol. II*, 817–818.

10. Dennett, *Americans in Eastern Asia*, 413–414.

11. Frederick Wells Williams, *Anson Burlingame and the First Chinese Mission to Foreign Powers* (New York: Scribner's, 1912); John Schrecker, "'For the Equality of Men—For the Equality of Nations': Anson Burlingame and China's First Embassy to the United States, 1868," *Journal of American–East Asian Relations* 17 (2010): 9–34.

12. Seward to Williams, August 14, 1865, *FRUS, 1865, Vol. III*, 461.

13. Schrecker, "'For the Equality of Men—For the Equality of Nations,'" 10–11.

14. As quoted in John R. Haddad, *America's First Adventure in China: Trade, Treaties, Opium, and Salvation* (Philadelphia: Temple University Press, 2013), 213.

15. Haddad, *America's First Adventure in China*, 224.

16. As quoted in Haddad, *America's First Adventure in China*, 213. Burlingame's remarkable career is well described in Guoqi Xu, *Chinese and Americans: A Shared History* (Cambridge, MA: Harvard University Press, 2014), chap. 1.

17. Mr. Fish to Mr. Low, *FRUS, 1870–1871*, 322.

18. Seward to Cassius Clay, May 6, 1861. *FRUS, 1861, Vol. I*, 277–281.

19. John Curtis Perry, *Facing West: Americans and the Opening of the Pacific* (Westport, CT: Praeger, 1994), 74.

20. Dennett, *Americans in Eastern Asia*, 416.

21. There continues to be some debate among historians about Seward's rationale for the purchase of Alaska. There are only four documents in the *Foreign Relations of the United States* pertaining to the purchase. Paolino believes that it was a purely commercial rationale, that Alaska would be a useful depot for the Asia trade. Because of the Johnson administration's tenuous relationship with Congress, Seward issued few public statements on Alaska. Of course, for Seward, trading depots were strategic. See Henry W. Temple, "William H. Seward," in *The American Secretaries of State and Their Diplomacy*, ed. Samuel Flagg Bemis (New York: Pageant, 1958), 7:113; Archie W. Shiels, *The Purchase of Alaska* (College: University of Alaska, 1967).

22. Cassius Clay to Seward, April, 17, 1868, *FRUS, 1868, Vol. I*, 470–471.

23. Dennett, *Americans in Eastern Asia*, 416.

24. Dennett, *Americans in Eastern Asia*, 417.

25. James C. Bradford, "You May Fire When Ready, Gridley, 1865–1922," in *The Navy*, ed. W. J. Holland (Washington, DC: Naval Historical Foundation, 2000), 62–69.

26. Robert Kagan, *Dangerous Nation: America's Place in the World from Its Earliest Days to the Dawn of the Twentieth Century* (New York: Knopf, 2006), 273.

27. Fareed Zakaria, *From Wealth to Power: The Unusual Origins of America's World Role* (Princeton, NJ: Princeton University Press, 1998), 67.

28. Kagan, *Dangerous Nation*, 281.

29. Dennett, *Americans in Eastern Asia*, 674.

30. Walter LaFeber, *The New Empire: An Interpretation of American Expansion, 1860–1898*, 35th anniversary ed. (Ithaca, NY: Cornell University Press, 1998), xix.

31. Cassius Clay to William H. Seward, April 17, 1868, *FRUS, 1868, Vol. 1*, 470–471.

32. Mr. Fish to Mr. Curtin, July 22, 1872, *FRUS, 1872–1873*, 493.

33. Frank Ninkovich calls this "the diplomacy of imperialism." See Frank Ninkovich, *Global Dawn: The Cultural Foundation of American Internationalism, 1865–1890* (Cambridge, MA: Harvard University Press, 2009), 280–282.

34. Ninkovich, *Global Dawn*, 282.

35. Dennett, *Americans in Eastern Asia*, 338–340.

36. Dennett, *Americans in Eastern Asia*, 311.

37. LaFeber, *The New Empire*, 45.

38. Dennett, *Americans in Eastern Asia*, 321.

39. Kagan, *Dangerous Nation*, 331.

40. Tyler Dennett, "American 'Good Offices' in Asia," *American Journal of International Law* 16, no. 1 (January 1922): 1–24; Kagan, *Dangerous Nation*, 329.

41. Dennett, "American 'Good Offices' in Asia."

42. Dennett, "American 'Good Offices' in Asia."

43. France led a limited invasion of a Korean island in 1866 in retaliation for the execution of French priests who were proselytizing in the country. It marked the first military encounter between Korea and a Western nation. See Daniel C. Kane, "Bellonet and Roze: Overzealous Servants of Empire and the 1866 French Attack on Korea," *Korean Studies* 23 (1999): 1–23.

44. Charles Oscar Paullin, "The Opening of Korea by Commodore Shufeldt," *Political Science Quarterly* 25, no. 3 (September 1910): 470–499.

45. Paullin, "The Opening of Korea by Commodore Shufeldt," 482–483; James A. Field, Jr., *History of United States Naval Operations: Korea* (Washington, DC: Department of the Navy, Naval Historical Center, 2000), 1. Like Perry, Shufeldt also held the Chinese in some contempt, noting that democracy would be hard for the Chinese to accept and insisting that America would have to continue using force to keep China open to commerce. He was frustrated with the Japanese intransigence in Korea but recognized in Japan a potential strategic partner in the Pacific. See R. W. Shufeldt to A. A. Sargent, "China for the Chinese; Results of Commodore Shufeldt's Observations," originally printed in the *San Francisco Bulletin*, March 30, 1882, Reprinted in the *New York Times*, http://query.nytimes.com/gst/abstract.html?res=9902EEDF173DE533A25753C3A9659C94639FD7CF.

46. U.S. Adjutant-General's Office, Military Information Division, *Notes on the War Between China and Japan* (Washington, DC: Government Printing Office, 1896), 1–34.

47. S. C. M. Paine, *The Sino-Japanese War of 1894–95: Perceptions, Power and Primacy* (New York: Cambridge University Press, 2003), 2.

48. Akira Iriye, "Japan's Drive to Great-Power Status," in *The Cambridge History of Japan*, vol. 5, *The Nineteenth Century*, ed. Marius B. Jansen (Cambridge: Cambridge University Press, 1989), 721–782.

49. Frank W. Ikle, "The Triple Intervention. Japan's Lesson in the Diplomacy of Imperialism," *Monumenta Nipponica* 22, no. 1 (January 1967): 122–130.

50. Lawrence H. Battistini, "The Korea Problem in the Nineteenth Century," *Monumenta Nipponica* 8, nos. 1–2 (1952): 47–66.

51. Mutsu Munemitsu, *Kenkenroku: A Diplomatic Record of the Sino-Japanese War, 1894–1895*, ed. Gordon Mark Berger (Princeton, NJ: Princeton University Press, 1983), 138.

52. Hilary A. Herbert, "Military Lessons of the Chino-Japanese War," *North American Review* 160, no. 463 (June 1895): 685, 698.

53. David D. Porter, Office of the Admiral, *Report of the Admiral of the Navy, July 6, 1887, United States Congress, The Executive Documents of the House of Representatives, for the First Session of the Fiftieth Congress, 1887–88* (Washington, DC: Government Printing Office, 1889), 34.

54. William Michael Morgan, "Strategic Factors in Hawaiian Annexation" (unpublished PhD diss., Claremont Graduate School, 1980), 5–7.

55. Secretary of State Blaine was also concerned about the potential for "coolie immigrants" to draw the islands away from the United States and toward China politically. See James G. Blaine to Mr. Comly, December 1, 1881, *FRUS, 1881–1882*, 636–638. See also Edward Crapol, *James G. Blaine: Architect of Empire* (Wilmington, DE: SR Books, 2000), 183.

56. Alice Felt Tyler, *The Foreign Policy of James G. Blaine* (Minneapolis: University of Minnesota Press, 1927), 208.

57. Letter from Blaine to Comly, November 19, 1881, *United States Department of State Index to the Executive Documents of the House of Representatives for the First Session of the Forty-Seventh Congress, 1880–81*, vol. 1 (1881–1882), Hawaii, 633–635.

58. Letter from Blaine to Comly, November 19, 1881, *United States Department of State, Index to the Executive Documents of the House of Representatives for the First Session of the Forty-Seventh Congress, 1880–81*, vol. 1 (1881–1882), Hawaii, 633–635.

59. Fourth Annual Message (first term) by President Grover Cleveland, December 3, 1988, http://www.presidency.ucsb.edu/ws/index.php?pid=29529&st=hawaii&st1.

60. LaFeber, *The New Empire*, 4.

61. William Adam Russ, *The Hawaiian Republic, 1894–98, and Its Struggle to Win Annexation* (Selinsgrove, PA: Susquehanna University Press, 1961); Thomas J. Osborne, *"Empire Can Wait": American Opposition to Hawaiian Annexation, 1893–1898* (Ann Arbor, MI: University Microfilms International, 1979); William Reynolds Braisted, *The United States Navy in the Pacific, 1897–1909* (New York: Greenwood, 1958); Akira Iriye, *Pacific Estrangement: Japanese and American Expansion, 1897–1911* (Cambridge, MA: Harvard University Press, 1972); Wayne H. Morgan, *America's Road to Empire: The War with Spain and Overseas Expansion* (New York: Wiley, 1965); Sylvester K. Stevens, *American Expan-*

sion in Hawaii, 1842–1898 (Harrisburg, PA: Archives Publishing, 1945); Allan Lee Hamilton, "Military Strategists and the Annexation of Hawaii," *Journal of the West* 15 (1976): 81–91; Hugh B. Hammett, "The Cleveland Administration and Anglo-American Naval Friction in Hawaii, 1893–1894," *Military Affairs* 40 (1976): 27–32; Ernest May, *Imperial Democracy: The Emergence of America as a Great Power* (New York: Harcourt, Brace, and World, 1961); "Hawaiian Islands," *Compilation of Reports of Committees: 1789–1901*, vol. 6. Senate Committee on Foreign Relations, February 26, 1894, 53rd Congress, 2nd session, Senate Report 227, 363–1169.

62. For details, see Morgan, "Strategic Factors in Hawaiian Annexation."

63. Nathaniel Philbrick, *Sea of Glory: America's Voyage of Discovery, the U.S. Exploring Expedition* (New York: Penguin, 2003), 134–138.

64. J. A. C. Gray, *Amerika Samoa: A History of American Samoa and Its United States Naval Administration* (Annapolis, MD: United States Naval Institute, 1960), 58.

65. In December 1878, after the signing of the Samoa Treaty, President Rutherford B. Hayes noted that "while it does not appear desirable to adopt as a whole the scheme of tripartite local government which has been proposed, the common interests of the three great treaty powers require harmony in their relations to the native frame of government, and this may be best secured by a simple diplomatic agreement between them. It would be well if the consular jurisdiction of our representative at Apia were increased in extent and importance so as to guard American interests in the surrounding and outlying islands of Oceanica." Rutherford B. Hayes, Fourth Annual Message, December 6, 1880, posted online by Gerhard Peters and John T. Woolley, The American Presidency Project, http://www.presidency.ucsb.edu/ws/index.php?pid=29521&st=samoa&st1.

66. United States Department of State, *The Executive Documents Printed by Order of the House of Representatives for the First Session of the Fifty-First Congress, 1889–90*, vol. 1 (1889–1890), Germany, 195–204.

67. Herring, *From Colony to Superpower*, 295–296.

68. Oscar Wilde, *The Canterville Ghost: An Amusing Chronicle of the Tribulations of the Ghost of Canterville Chase when His Ancestral Halls Became the Home of the American Minister to the Court of St. James* (Boston: J. W. Luce, 1906), 81. It first appeared in the magazine *The Court and Society Review* in February 1887.

69. Nathan Miller, *The U.S. Navy: A History*, 3rd ed. (Annapolis, MD: Naval Institute Press, 1997).

70. Robert Seager, *Alfred Thayer Mahan: The Man and His Letters* (Annapolis, MD: Naval Institute Press, 1977), 507.

71. Steven Otfinoski, *Presidents and Their Times: Chester Arthur* (Tarrytown, NY: Marshall Cavendish, 2010), 75; Ronald Spector, *Professors of War: The Naval War College and the Development of the Naval Profession* (Newport, RI: Naval War College Press, 1977).

72. LaFeber, *The New Empire*, 122–127.

73. United States Navy Department, *Report of the Secretary of the Navy* (Washington, DC: Government Printing Office, 1893), 13.

74. Kenneth J. Hagan, *This People's Navy: The Making of American Sea Power* (New York: The Free Press, 1991), 208–209.

75. LaFeber, *The New Empire*, 3–10; Edward C. Kirkland, *Industry Comes of Age: Business, Labor, and Public Policy, 1860–1897*, vol. 4, *The Economic History of the United States*

(New York: Holt, Rinehart, and Winston, 1961); John A. Garraty, *The New Commonwealth, 1877–1890* (New York: Harper and Row, 1968).

76. Thomas McCormick, "Insular Imperialism and the Open Door: The China Market and the Spanish-American War," *Pacific Historical Review* 32, no. 2 (1963): 155–169.

77. LaFeber, *The New Empire*, 62–101.

78. Josiah Strong, *Our Country* (Cambridge, MA: Belknap Press of Harvard University, 1963); Warren Zimmerman, *First Great Triumph: How Five Americans Made Their Country a World Power* (New York: Farrar, Straus, and Giroux, 2002), 35–36; Joseph A. Fry, "From Open Door to World Systems: Economic Interpretations of Late Nineteenth Century American Foreign Relations," *Pacific Historical Review* 65, no. 2 (1996): 277–303.

79. Zakaria, *From Wealth to Power*, 92–93.

80. John Brewer, *The Sinews of Power: War, Money, and the English State, 1688–1783* (London: Unwin Hyman, 1989), xvii, cited in Zakaria, *From Wealth to Power*, 93.

81. To make this point, Zakaria relies heavily on Stephen Skowronek, *Building a New American State: The Expansion of National Administrative Capacities, 1877–1920* (Cambridge: Cambridge University Press, 1982).

82. Kenneth Waltz is the most prominent scholar of defensive realism. John J. Mearsheimer is best known for his work on offensive realism. See Kenneth N. Waltz, *Theory of International Politics* (Reading, MA: Addison-Wesley, 1979); John Mearsheimer, *The Tragedy of Great Power Politics* (New York: Norton, 2001).

83. William Appleman Williams, *The Tragedy of American Diplomacy* (New York: World Publishing, 1959).

84. As quoted in Haddad, *America's First Adventure in China*, 224.

85. Joanne Reitan, *The Tariff Question in the Gilded Age: The Great Debate of 1888* (University Park, PA: Pennsylvania State University, 1994).

3. GRAND STRATEGY IN THE ERA OF THEODORE ROOSEVELT

1. Warren Zimmerman, *First Great Triumph: How Five Americans Made Their Country a World Power* (New York: Farrar, Straus, and Giroux, 2002), 30.

2. Evan Thomas, *The War Lovers: Roosevelt, Lodge, Hearst and the Rush to Empire, 1898* (New York: Little, Brown, 2010). Thomas gives a vivid description of the rush to expansion on the eve of the Spanish-American War, but TR's legacy as a strategist must be viewed in the fullness of his restraint and careful diplomacy after victory.

3. "I wish to see the United States the dominant power on the shores of the Pacific": Theodore Roosevelt, 1900; Henry Kissinger, *Diplomacy* (New York: Simon and Schuster, 1994), 38–43.

4. Robert E. Osgood, *Ideals and Self-Interest in America's Foreign Relations: The Great Transformation of the Twentieth Century* (Chicago: University of Chicago Press, 1953), 32.

5. Philip A. Crowl, "Alfred Thayer Mahan: The Naval Historian," in *Makers of Modern Strategy*, ed. Peter Paret, Gordon Alexander Craig, and Felix Gilbert (Princeton, NJ: Princeton University Press, 1986), 456.

6. Crowl, "Alfred Thayer Mahan," 449.

7. Nathan Miller, *The U.S. Navy: A History*, 3rd ed. (Annapolis, MD: Naval Institute Press, 1997), 149; "Report of Policy Board," *Proceedings of the United States Military Institute* 16 (1890): 201–273. See also Walter LaFeber, *The New Empire: An Interpretation of American Expansion, 1860–1898*, 35th anniversary ed. (Ithaca, NY: Cornell University Press, 1998), 80–101.

8. Zimmerman, *First Great Triumph*, 115.

9. Francis P. Sempa, foreword to Alfred Thayer Mahan, *The Problem of Asia: Its Effect Upon International Politics* (New Brunswick, NJ: Transaction, 2003), 6.

10. Robert Seager II and Doris D. Maguire, eds., *The Letters and Papers of Alfred Thayer Mahan* (Annapolis, MD: Naval Institute Press, 1975), 2:509.

11. Alfred Thayer Mahan, *The Influence of Sea Power Upon History, 1660–1783* (Boston: Little, Brown, 1890).

12. Zimmerman, *First Great Triumph*, 97.

13. Alfred T. Mahan, "Hawaii and Our Future Sea Power," in *The Interest of the United States in Sea Power, Present and Future* (Boston: Little, Brown, 1898), 31–58. Originally published in the *New York Times'* "Forum" section in 1893.

14. Alfred T. Mahan, "The United States Looking Outwards," in *The Interest of the United States in Sea Power, Present and Future*, 8. Originally published in the *Atlantic Monthly*, December 1890.

15. Alfred T. Mahan, "Possibilities of an Anglo-American Reunion," in *The Interest of the United States in Sea Power, Present and Future*, 123. Originally published in the *North American Review*, November 1894.

16. Alfred T. Mahan, "A Twentieth-Century Outlook," in *The Interest of the United States in Sea Power, Present and Future*, 243–245. Originally published in *Harper's New Monthly Magazine*, September 1897.

17. John W. Foster to Charles Deny, September 26, 1894, cited in Thomas McCormick, "Insular Imperialism and the Open Door: The China Market and the Spanish-American War," *Pacific Historical Review* 32, no. 2 (May 1963): 156.

18. Seager and Maguire, *The Letters and Papers of Alfred Thayer Mahan*, 2:505, cited in William Michael Morgan, "Strategic Factors in Hawaiian Annexation" (unpublished PhD diss., Claremont Graduate School, 1980), 143–144.

19. Roosevelt to Mahan, May 3, 1897, *The Letters of Theodore Roosevelt*, ed. Elting E. Morison, 8 vols. (Cambridge, MA: Harvard University Press, 1951–1954), 1:607–608, cited in Morgan, "Strategic Factors in Hawaiian Annexation," 145.

20. Alfred Thayer Mahan, *The Problem of Asia and Its Effects Upon International Policies* (Boston: Little, Brown, 1905), 19.

21. LaFeber, *The New Empire*, 86.

22. Mahan, *The Interests of America in Sea Power, Present and Future*, 4.

23. Mahan, *The Interests of America in Sea Power, Present and Future*, 5.

24. Alfred Thayer Mahan, "The Effect of Asiatic Conditions Upon World Policies," *North American Review* 171, no. 528 (November 1900): 609–626.

25. Mahan, "The Effect of Asiatic Conditions Upon World Policies," 624.

26. Mahan, *The Problem of Asia: Its Effect Upon International Politics*, 130.

27. Alfred Thayer Mahan, "A Twentieth-Century Outlook," in *The Interest of the United States in Sea Power, Present and Future*, 243–245, originally published in *Harper's*

New Monthly Magazine, September 1897. Mahan's respect for Japan was enhanced by its maritime status and by its potential as a "Teutonic power." His disdain for China was evident in his comments during the Boxer Rebellion that "as a rule, the Oriental, whether nation or individual, does not change." See also Tyler Dennett, Review: Mahan's "The Problem of Asia," *Foreign Affairs* 13, no. 3 (April 1935): 466.

28. Alfred T. Mahan and Charles Beresford, "Possibilities of an Anglo American Reunion," *North American Review* 159, no. 456 (November 1894): 551–573.

29. Seager and Maguire, *The Letters and Papers of Alfred Thayer Mahan*, 2:529. The question was whether Britain would accept American mediation of the dispute between Britain and Venezuela over the borders of British Guiana.

30. Rudyard Kipling, "The White Man's Burden," *McClure Magazine*, February 1899, 290–291.

31. See, for example, Howard K. Beale, *Theodore Roosevelt and the Rise of America to World Power* (Baltimore: Johns Hopkins University Press, 1956); Richard Turk, *The Ambiguous Relationship: Theodore Roosevelt and Alfred Thayer Mahan* (New York: Greenwood, 1987).

32. Robert Seager, *Alfred Thayer Mahan: The Man and His Letters* (Annapolis, MD: Naval Institute Press, 1977), 335–336.

33. McCormick, "Insular Imperialism and the Open Door," 157.

34. Cited in Douglas A. Irwin, "Goodbye, Free Trade?" *Wall Street Journal*, October 9–10, 2010, http://www.wsj.com/articles/SB10001424052748704696304575538573595009754.

35. Greg Russell, *The Statecraft of Theodore Roosevelt: The Duties of Nations and World Order* (Dordrecht: Republic of the Letters, 2009).

36. Seager and Maguire, *The Letters and Papers of Alfred Thayer Mahan*, 2:506.

37. Edmund Morris, *The Rise of Theodore Roosevelt* (New York: Coward, McCann, and Geoghegan, 1979), 586.

38. Cited in George Dewey, *Autobiography of George Dewey* (New York: Scribner, 1913), 179. See also William Roscoe Thayer, *Theodore Roosevelt: An Intimate Biography* (Boston: Houghton Mifflin, 1919), 121; Robert W. Love, Jr., *History of the U.S. Navy, 1775–1941* (Harrisburg, PA: Stackpole Books, 1992), 407; Nathan Miller, *The U.S. Navy*, 157; Morris, *The Rise of Theodore Roosevelt*.

39. Morgan, "Strategic Factors in Hawaiian Annexation," 196–197.

40. George Belknap, "Address Before the Commercial Club of Boston," February 19, 1898, Belknap Papers, Library of Congress, quoted in Morgan, "Strategic Factors in Hawaiian Annexation," 191.

41. Dirk Bonker, *MIlitarism in a Global Age: Naval Ambitions in Germany and the United States Before World War I* (Ithaca: Cornell University Press, 2012), 40; Derek B. Granger, "Dewey at Manila Bay: Lessons in Operational Art and Operational Leadership from America's First Fleet Admiral," *Naval War College Review* 64, no. 4 (Autumn 2011): 127–141.

42. A. C. Gray, *Amerika Samoa: A History of American Samoa and Its United States Naval Administration* (Annapolis, MD: United States Naval Institute, 1960), 107–108. See also Paul Kennedy, *The Samoan Triangle: A Study in Relations* (New Haven, CT: Yale University Press, 1974); George Herbert Ryden, *The Foreign Policy of the United States in Relation to Samoa* (New Haven, CT: Yale University Press, 1933).

43. Seager, *Alfred Thayer Mahan*, 393.

44. "Protocol of Agreement Between the United States and Spain," August 12, 1898, in U.S. Department of State, *Foreign Relations of the United States*, http://digicoll.library .wisc.edu/FRUS/Browse.html [hereafter cited as *FRUS*], *1898*, 829.

45. Thomas McCormick, *China Market: America's Quest for Informal Empire, 1893–1901* (Chicago: Quadrangle, 1967), 120–125.

46. McCormick, "Insular Imperialism and the Open Door," 157. See also Osgood, *Ideals and Self-Interest in America's Foreign Relations*, 60–63.

47. Mr. Hay to Mr. Day, October 26, 1898, *FRUS, 1898*, 935.

48. Robert Beisner, *Twelve Against Empire: The Anti-imperialists, 1898–1900* (New York: McGraw-Hill, 1968), 98.

49. Senator G. G. Vest, "Objections to Annexing the Philippines," *North American Review* 168, no. 506 (January 1899): 112.

50. Beisner, *Twelve Against Empire*, 85.

51. Andrew Carnegie, "Americanism Versus Imperialism," *North American Review* 168, no. 506 (January 1899), 1.

52. Max Boot, *The Savage Wars of Peace: Small Wars and the Rise of American Power* (New York: Basic Books, 2002), 105; Richard F. Hamilton. *President McKinley, War, and Empire* (New Brunswick, NJ: Transaction, 2006).

53. Beisner, *Twelve Against Empire*, 156; William Widenor, *Henry Cabot Lodge and the Search for an American Foreign Policy* (Berkeley: University of California Press, 1980), 116.

54. Boot, *The Savage Wars of Peace*, 125.

55. Kenneth E. Hendrickson, Jr., "Reluctant Expansionist: Jacob Gould Schurman and the Philippine Question," *Pacific Historical Review* 36, no. 4 (November 1967): 405–421.

56. Mahan to John D. Long, Naval War Board, Washington, DC, August 15–20, 1898, in Seager and Maguire, *Letters and Papers of Alfred Thayer Mahan*, 2:583.

57. Conger to William R. Day, August 26, 1898, quoted in Marilyn B. Young, *The Rhetoric of Empire: America's China Policy, 1895–1901* (Cambridge: Harvard University Press, 1968), 99.

58. John D. Long to John Hay, July 31, 1900, National Archives, Record Group 59, Department of State, Miscellaneous Letters, quoted in Richard D. Challenger, *Admirals, Generals, and American Foreign Policy 1898–1914* (Princeton, NJ: Princeton University Press, 1973), 4.

59. Lieutenant John M. Ellicott, USN, "Sea Power of Japan," Naval War College, Newport, RI, 1900, RG 8, Box 15, Folder 19, pp. 17–22.

60. Challenger, *Admirals, Generals, and American Foreign Policy 1898–1914*, 40.

61. Dewey to Bonaparte, April 12, 1906, RG 80, Office of the Secretary of the Navy File No. 13669, in William Reynolds Braisted, *The United States Navy in the Pacific, 1897–1909* (New York: Greenwood, 1958), 188.

62. George C. Herring, *From Colony to Superpower: U.S. Foreign Relations Since 1776* (New York: Oxford University Press, 2008), 330.

63. Thomas J. McCormick, *"A Fair Field and No Favor": American China Policy During the McKinley Administration, 1897–1901* (PhD diss., University of Wisconsin, 1960); McCormick, "Insular Imperialism and the Open Door"; Young, *The Rhetoric of Empire*.

64. Mahan to J. B. Sterling, December 23, 1898, in Seager and Maguire, *Letters and Papers of Alfred Thayer Mahan*, 2:619.

65. Tyler Dennett, "The Open Door Policy as Intervention," *Annals of the American Academy of Political and Social Science* 168 (July 1933): 78; Tyler Dennett, *John Hay: From Poetry to Politics* (Binghamton, NY: Dodd, Mead, 1933), 403–404. See also Michael Hunt, *The Making of a Special Relationship: The United States and China to 1914* (New York: Columbia University Press, 1983), 153–154.

66. "The Break-up of China, and Our Interest in It," *Atlantic Monthly* 84, no. 502 (August 1899): 276–280.

67. Raymond Esthus, "The Changing Concept of the Open Door, 1899–1910," *Mississippi Valley Historical Review* 46, no. 3 (December 1959): 436.

68. Esthus, "The Changing Concept of the Open Door, 1899–1910," 436; Hunt, *The Making of a Special Relationship*, chap. 6; Warren Cohen, *America's Response to China*, 5th ed. (New York: Columbia University Press, 2010), 42–59; Tyler Dennett, *Americans in Eastern Asia: A Critical Study of the Policy of the United States with Reference to China, Japan, and Korea in the 19th Century* (New York: Macmillan, 1922), chap. 32.

69. Yoneyuki Sugita argues that these principles were quintessentially American and marked the beginning of a new era of international relations in the Asia-Pacific. See Yoneyuki Sugita, "The Rise of an American Principle in China: A Reinterpretation of the First Open Door Notes Toward China," in *Trans-Pacific Relations, America, Europe, and Asia in the Twentieth Century* (Westport, CT: Praeger, 2003), 3–20.

70. Diane Preston, *The Boxer Rebellion* (New York: Berkley Books, 2000), 320–335; Jane Elliot, "Who Seeks the Truth Should Be of No Country: British and American Journalists Report the Boxer Rebellion, June 1900," *American Journalism* 13, no. 3 (1996): 255–285.

71. Thomas A. Bailey, *A Diplomatic History of the American People*, 3rd ed. (New York: E. S. Crofts, 1945), 565.

72. Claude A. Buss, *The Far East: A History of Recent and Contemporary International Relations in East Asia* (New York: MacMillan, 1955), 371.

73. A. L. P. Dennis, *Adventures in American Diplomacy, 1896–1906* (New York: Dutton and Col, 1928), 258, cited in Dennett, "The Open Door Policy as Intervention," 80.

74. Roosevelt to Taft, quoted in Buss, *The Far East*, 379.

75. Russell, *The Statecraft of Theodore Roosevelt*.

76. Kissinger, *Diplomacy*, 41. See also H. W. Brands, "Theodore Roosevelt: America's First Strategic Thinker," in *Artists of Power: Theodore Roosevelt, Woodrow Wilson, and Their Enduring Impact on U.S. Foreign Policy*, ed. William N. Tilchin and Charles E. Neu (Westport, CT: Praeger Security International, 2006), 33–44; H. W. Brands, *TR: The Last Romantic* (New York: Basic Books, 1997); James R. Holmes, *Theodore Roosevelt and World Order: Police Power in International Relations* (Washington, DC: Potomac, 2006); Widenor, *Henry Cabot Lodge and the Search for an American Foreign Policy*.

77. Mahan, *The Problem of Asia and Its Effects Upon International Policies*, 100.

78. Brands, *T.R.*, 529.

79. Morison, *The Letters of Theodore Roosevelt*, 4:760; cited in Russell, *The Statecraft of Theodore Roosevelt*, 7.

80. Edmund Morris, *Theodore Rex* (Westminster: Modern Library, 2002), 356.

81. Walter A. MacDougall, *Let the Sea Make a Noise . . . : A History of the North Pacific from Magellan to MacArthur* (New York: HarperCollins, 1993), 448.

82. Henry Cabot Lodge and Charles F. Redmond, eds., *Selections from the Correspondence of Theodore Roosevelt and Henry Cabot Lodge* (New York: Da Capo, 1971), 155.

83. F. de Martens, "The Portsmouth Peace Conference," *North American Review* 181, no. 588 (November 1905): 641–648; Eugene P. Trani, *The Treaty of Portsmouth: An Adventure in American Diplomacy* (Lexington: University of Kentucky Press, 1969); Frederick W. Marks III and Frederick W. Marks, *Velvet on Iron: The Diplomacy of Theodore Roosevelt* (Lincoln: University of Nebraska Press, 1979); Peter E. Randall, *There Are No Victors Here!: A Local Perspective on the Treaty of Portsmouth* (Portsmouth, NH: Portsmouth Marine Society, 1985); Steven Ericson and Allen Hockley, eds., *The Treaty of Portsmouth and Its Legacies* (Hanover, NH: Dartmouth College Press, published by University Press of New England, 2008); Fredrik Stanton, *Great Negotiations: Agreements That Changed the Modern World* (Yardley, PA: Westholme, 2010).

84. Robert Kagan, *Dangerous Nation: America's Place in the World from Its Earliest Days to the Dawn of the Twentieth Century* (New York: Knopf, 2006), 295.

85. Morison, *The Letters of Theodore Roosevelt*, 5:762.

86. Raymond Esthus's 1959 article was important in shifting general scholarly opinion away from the idea that there was a "secret" agreement between Taft and Katsura in 1905. The idea first arose in 1924 when Tyler Dennett found the "agreed memorandum of conversation" recording Taft and Katsura's conversation and published an article declaring it a "secret" agreement between the United States and Japan (Dennett would later back away from this controversial stance). In this case, the use of "agreed" signified only that the two sides agreed that the memorandum accurately reflected the conversation. Moreover, it was not unusual for such a memorandum to be made. However, Esthus does point out that Roosevelt had made clear to Japan that he favored their takeover of Korea. See Raymond A. Esthus, "The Taft-Katsura Agreement—Reality or Myth?" *Journal of Modern History* 31, no. 1 (March 1959): 46–51. Many Korean scholars continue to see the discussion as a betrayal nonetheless. See, for example, Jongsuk Chay, "The Taft-Katsura Memorandum Reconsidered," *Pacific Historical Review* 37, no. 3 (August 1968): 321–326.

87. See Esthus, "The Taft-Katsura Agreement," 46–51.

88. Morison, *The Letters of Theodore Roosevelt*, 4:1112.

89. Morison, *The Letters of Theodore Roosevelt*, 5:46.

90. For Japanese elite opinion on the Root-Takahira agreement, see Akira Iriye, *Pacific Estrangement: Japanese and American Expansion, 1897–1911* (Cambridge, MA: Harvard University Press, 1972), 134–136. For more background from the American side, see Walter LaFeber, *The Clash: U.S.-Japanese Relations Throughout History* (New York: Norton, 1997), 87–91.

91. Brands, *T.R.*, 529.

92. Joseph Bishop, *Theodore Roosevelt and His Time* (New York: Charles Scribner's Sons, 1920), 1:381.

93. Seager, *Alfred Thayer Mahan*, 477.

94. Seventh Annual Message of President Theodore Roosevelt, December 3, 1907, http://www.presidency.ucsb.edu/ws/index.php?pid=29548&st=china&st1.

95. Herring, *From Colony to Superpower*, 354.

96. Lodge and Redmond, *Selections from the Correspondence of Theodore Roosevelt and Henry Cabot Lodge*, 153.

97. Joseph Bucklin Bishop, ed., *Theodore Roosevelt's Letters to His Children* (New York: Charles Scribner's Sons, 1919), 197.

98. Morison, *The Letters of Theodore Roosevelt*, 5:725. See also Thomas Bailey, *Theodore Roosevelt and the Japanese-American Crises; an Account of the International Complications Arising from the Race Problem on the Pacific Coast* (Stanford, CA: Stanford University Press, 1934), 224.

99. Morison, *The Letters of Theodore Roosevelt*, 6:956, cited in Charles Neu, "Theodore Roosevelt and American Involvement in the Far East, 1901–1909," *Pacific Historical Review* 35, no. 4 (November 1966): 442.

100. Neu, "Theodore Roosevelt and American Involvement in the Far East, 1901–1909," 442.

101. Letter from Theodore Roosevelt to Senator Knox, date unclear, Papers of Theodore Roosevelt, Manuscript Division, Library of Congress, 120–126, http://www.mtholyoke.edu/acad/intrel/trjapan.htm.

102. See Esthus, "The Changing Concept of the Open Door, 1899–1910," 435–454.

103. See, for example, William Appleman Williams, *The Tragedy of American Diplomacy* (New York: World, 1959), 23–44; LaFeber, *The New Empire*.

104. Arthur M. Schlesinger, Jr., *The Cycles of American History* (Boston: Houghton Mifflin Company, 1999), 132–135, quoted in Robert Zevin, "An Interpretation of American Imperialism," *Journal of Economic History*, 32, no. 1 (March 1972): 343–344; Joseph A. Fry, "From Open Door to World Systems: Economic Interpretations of Late Nineteenth Century American Foreign Relations," *Pacific Historical Review* 65, no. 2 (May 1996): 286.

105. See, for example, George Sinkler, *The Racial Attitudes of American Presidents from Abraham Lincoln to Theodore Roosevelt* (Garden City, NY: Doubleday, 1971); Michael H. Hunt, *Ideology and U.S. Foreign Policy* (New Haven, CT: Yale University Press, 1987). Hunt notes that the same rationale used to justify eliminating American Indian opposition to continental expansion was used to justify overseas expansion at the end of the century. See Hunt, *Ideology and U.S. Foreign Policy*, 55. See also Matthew McCullough, *The Cross of War: Christian Nationalism and U.S. Expansion in the Spanish-American War* (Madison: University of Wisconsin Press, 2014).

106. Beisner, *Twelve Against Empire*, 22–24.

107. Kagan, *Dangerous Nation*, 297.

108. For elaboration on this thesis, see Eric Love, *Race Over Empire: Racism & U.S. Imperialism 1865–1900* (Chapel Hill: University of North Carolina Press, 2004).

109. Herring, *From Colony to Superpower*, 377.

110. One recent history that does justice to TR's strategic legacy is Henry J. Hendrix, *Theodore Roosevelt's Naval Diplomacy: The U.S. Navy and the Birth of the American Century* (Annapolis, MD: Naval Institute Press, 2009).

111. Cited in Walter LaFeber, "A Note on the 'Mercantilistic' Imperialism of Alfred Thayer Mahan," *Mississippi Valley Historical Review* 48, no. 4 (March 1962): 681.

112. Quentin R. Scrabek, *William McKinley: Apostle of Protectionism* (New York: Algora, 2008), 7–8.

113. Alfred Thayer Mahan, *The Interest of America in International Conditions* (Boston: Little, Brown, 1910), 178–183.

114. Alfred Thayer Mahan, *Naval Strategy Compared and Contrasted with the Principles and Practice of Military Operations on Land: Lectures Delivered at U.S. Naval War College, Newport, R.I., Between the Years 1887 and 1911* (Boston: Little, Brown, 1911), 110–111.

115. See Dennett, Review of Mahan's "The Problem of Asia," 469.

PART 2

1. FDR's handwritten notes for the debate are included in *F.D.R.: His Personal Letters, Early Years*, ed. Elliott Roosevelt (New York: Duell, Sloan, and Pierce, 1947), 160–164.

2. Taken from Greg Robinson, *By Order of the President: FDR and the Internment of Japanese Americans* (Cambridge, MA: Harvard University Press, 2001), 12; John Lamberton Harper, *American Visions of Europe: Franklin D. Roosevelt, George F. Kennan, and Dean G. Acheson* (Cambridge: Cambridge University Press, 1994), 23; Roosevelt, *F.D.R.: His Personal Letters, Early Years*, 160–164. On the strategic and Mahanian links between the two presidents, see J. Simon Rofe, "'Under the Influence of Mahan': Theodore and Franklin Roosevelt and Their Understanding of American National Interest," *Diplomacy & Statecraft* 19, no. 4 (December 2008): 741; William L. Neumann, "Franklin Delano Roosevelt: A Disciple of Admiral Mahan," (United States Naval Institute) *Proceedings* 78 (July 1952).

3. President Roosevelt, Excerpts from the Press Conference, November 28, 1941, http://www.presidency.ucsb.edu/ws/index.php?pid=16047&st=philippine&st1=#ixzz1KHBh1KF5.

4. Defining the Open Door, 1909–1927

1. Robert E. Osgood, *Ideals and Self-Interest in America's Foreign Relations: The Great Transformation of the Twentieth Century* (Chicago: University of Chicago Press, 1953), 264.

2. Charles Seymour, ed., *The Intimate Papers of Colonel House* (Boston: Houghton Mifflin, 1928), 25.

3. John Milton Cooper, Jr., *The Warrior and the Priest* (Cambridge, MA: Harvard University Press, 1983), 267.

4. Michael Benson, *William H. Taft* (Minneapolis: Lerner, 2005), 7–8.

5. George C. Herring, *From Colony to Superpower: U.S. Foreign Relations Since 1776* (New York: Oxford University Press, 2008), 375. See also Warren I. Cohen, *America's Response to China: An Interpretive History of Sino-American Relations*, 5th ed. (New York: Columbia University Press, 2010), 70.

6. David H. Burton, *William Howard Taft: Confident Peacemaker* (New York: Fordham University Press, 2004), 50.

7. Walter A. MacDougall, *Let the Sea Make a Noise . . . : A History of the North Pacific from Magellan to MacArthur* (New York City: Basic Books, 1993), 488.

8. Herring, *From Colony to Superpower*, 372.

9. William Howard Taft, Fourth Annual Message, December 3, 1912, http://www.presidency.ucsb.edu/ws/index.php?pid=29553&st=dollar&st1=#axzz1aUzQ6J4o.

10. Herring, *From Colony to Superpower*, 373.

11. Walter V. Scholes and Marie Scholes, *The Foreign Policies of the Taft Administration* (Columbia: University of Missouri Press, 1970), 111.

12. Telegram to Prince Chun, the Prince Regent of the Chinese Empire, July 15, 1909, cited in Paolo E. Coletta, *The Presidency of William Howard Taft* (Lawrence: University of Kansas Press, 1973), 194–195.

13. Michael H. Hunt, *The Making of a Special Relationship: The United States and China to 1914* (New York: Columbia University Press, 1983), 208–212. On the role of missionaries, see Andrew Preston, *Sword of Spirit, Shield of Faith: Religion in American War and Diplomacy* (New York: Anchor, 2012), 177.

14. Michael H. Hunt, *Frontier Defense and the Open Door* (New Haven, CT: Yale University Press, 1971), 148.

15. Osgood, *Ideals and Self-Interest*, 103.

16. "Willard Straight Who Is to Marry Dorothy Whitney: A Career That Reads Like a Romance Is That of the Missionary's Son Who Became a Figure in Finance, Politics, and International Affairs, and Who Won the Love of Two Heiresses," *New York Times*, July 30, 1911.

17. Harriman quoted in George Kennan, *E. H. Harriman's Far Eastern Plans* (New York: Country Life, 1917), 4, 26–36.

18. Scholes and Scholes, *The Foreign Policy of the Taft Administration*, 158.

19. The Japanese government objected that Americans were contemplating a "very important departure from the terms of the treaty of Portsmouth." See The Minister of Foreign Affairs to Ambassador O'Brien, January 21, 1910, in U.S. Department of State, *Foreign Relations of the United States*, http://digicoll.library.wisc.edu/FRUS/Browse.html [hereafter cited as *FRUS*], *1910, China*, 251.

20. Huntington Wilson to Philander Knox, July 27, 1910, Philander Knox Papers, Library of Congress, Box 28, July 20–December 9, 1910 Folder.

21. Scholes and Scholes, *The Foreign Policy of the Taft Administration*, 194.

22. Hunt, *The Making of a Special Relationship*, 210; Cohen, *America's Response to China*, 74.

23. Cohen, *America's Response to China*, 74.

24. Cohen, *America's Response to China*, 75.

25. Hunt, *Frontier Defense and the Open Door*, 185.

26. "Treaty of Commerce and Navigation Between the United States and Japan," *American Journal of International Law* 5, no. 2, Supplement: Official Documents (April 1911): 100–106.

27. "Willard Straight, Who Is to Marry Dorothy Whitney," *New York Times*, July 30, 1911.

28. Willard Straight, "China's Loan Negotiations," in *Recent Developments in China*, ed. George H. Blakeslee (New York: G. E. Stechert, 1913), 121.

29. Elting E. Morison, ed., *The Letters of Theodore Roosevelt*, 8 vols. (Cambridge, MA: Harvard University Press, 1951–1954), 7:189–190.

30. John Milton Cooper, Jr., *Woodrow Wilson: A Biography* (New York: Knopf, 2009), 5.

31. Herring, *From Colony to Superpower*, 384.

32. Wilson speech on March 19, 1913, "The Passing of Dollar Diplomacy," *American Journal of International Law* 7, no. 2 (April 1913): 339.

33. Cohen, *America's Response to China*, 79.

34. Woodrow Wilson, *The Papers of Woodrow Wilson*, ed. Arthur S. Link (Princeton, NJ: Princeton University Press, 1966), 27:237.

35. Francis M. Huntington Wilson, *Memoirs of an Ex-Diplomat* (Boston: Bruce Humphries, 1945), 220.

36. Charles Vevier, "The Open Door: An Idea in Action, 1906–1913," *Pacific Historical Review* 24, no. 1 (February 1955): 49–62; "Bryan's Aide Quits; Criticizes President," *New York Times*, March 20, 1913.

37. Cooper, *Woodrow Wilson*, 12.

38. Paola E. Colleta, "The Most Thankless Task: Bryan and the California Alien Land Legislation," *Pacific Historical Review* 36, no. 2 (May 1967): 163–187.

39. Akira Iriye, *Across the Pacific: An Inner History of American–East Asian Relations* (New York: Harcourt, Brace and World, 1967), 131.

40. Russell H. Fifield, *Woodrow Wilson and the Far East: The Diplomacy of the Shandong Question* (Hamden, CT: Archon, 1965), 25.

41. The document included demands that China never seek the restoration of Shandong to Germany; agree to expanded Japanese railroad rights in South Manchuria and Inner Mongolia; pledge never to "cede or lease to any other Power any harbor or bay or any island along the coast of China"; and—most problematic from an American viewpoint—accept Japanese military, political, and financial advisors and armaments.

42. Secretary of State Bryan to Ambassador Guthrie, May 11, 1915, *FRUS, 1915, China*, 145.

43. For a critique of American legalism during the Open Door period, see George F. Kennan, *American Diplomacy*, 60th anniversary exp. ed. (Chicago: University of Chicago Press, 2012), chaps. 2 and 3.

44. Cohen, *America's Response to China*, 86–87.

45. Paul S. Reinsch, *An American Diplomat in China* (Garden City, NY: Doubleday, Page, 1922), 137.

46. Phyllis Marchand and Margaret D. Link, eds., *The Papers of Woodrow Wilson* (Princeton, NJ: Princeton University Press, 1980), 32:197.

47. Noriko Kawamura, *Turbulence in the Pacific: Japanese-U.S. Relations During World War I* (Westport, CT: Praeger, 2000), 37.

48. Walter Russell Mead, *Special Providence: American Foreign Policy and How It Changed the World* (New York: Routledge, 2009), 126.

49. Robert Lansing, *War Memoirs of Robert Lansing, Secretary of State* (Indianapolis: Bobbs-Merrill, 1935); Daniel Malloy Smith, *Robert Lansing and American Neutrality, 1914–1917* (New York: Da Capo, 1958).

50. Cohen, *America's Response to China*, 92.

51. Fifield, *Woodrow Wilson and the Far East*, 54.

52. Burton F. Beers, *Vain Endeavor: Robert Lansing's Attempt to End the American-Japanese Rivalry* (Durham, NC: Duke University Press, 1962).

53. Cohen, *America's Response to China*, 86.

54. B. Anonymous, "The Situation in the Far East," *Foreign Affairs* 1, no. 4 (June 1923): 21. For more on the Lansing-Ishii agreement, see Cohen, *America's Response to China*, 85–86; Carl Walter Young, *Japan's Special Position in Manchuria* (Baltimore: Johns Hopkins Press, 1931); Beers, *Vain Endeavor*.

55. Carl J. Richard, *When the United States Invaded Russia: Woodrow Wilson's Siberian Disaster* (Lanham, MD: Rowman and Littlefield, 2013), 17–54.

56. Betty Miller Unterberger, *America's Siberian Expedition: A Study of National Policy, 1918–1920* (Westport, CT: Greenwood, 1969), 54. See also John Albert White, *The Siberian Intervention* (Princeton, NJ: Princeton University Press, 1950); Betty Miller Unterberger, "President Wilson and the Decision to Send American Troops to Siberia," *Pacific Historical Review* 24, no. 1 (February 1955): 63–74; Christopher Lasch, "American Intervention in Siberia: A Reinterpretation," *Political Science Quarterly* 77, no. 2 (June 1962): 205–223; Eugene P. Trani, "Woodrow Wilson and the Decision to Intervene in Russia: A Reconsideration," *Journal of Modern History* 48, no. 3 (September 1976): 440–461; Richard, *When the United States Invaded Russia*.

57. Meanwhile, 5,000 additional U.S. troops sent to Archangel under the "American North Russia Expeditionary Force" (or "Polar Bear Expedition") engaged in direct combat with the Bolsheviks before withdrawing in April 1919. For more on that expedition, see Leonid Strakhovsky, *The Origins of American Intervention in North Russia* (Princeton, NJ: Princeton University Press, 1937); George Kennan, *The Decision to Intervene* (Princeton, NJ: Princeton University Press, 1958). The Czechs happily were rescued, but only after turning over the hapless Kolchak to his Bolshevik enemies, who executed him.

58. Link, *The Papers of Woodrow Wilson*, 46:512.

59. "President Woodrow Wilson's Fourteen Points," January 8, 1918. For further reading, see Erez Manela, *The Wilsonian Moment: Self-Determination and the International Origins of Anticolonial Nationalism* (New York: Oxford University Press, 2007); David M. Esposito, *Legacy of Woodrow Wilson: America's War Aims in World War I* (Westport, CT: Praeger, 1996); Arthur S. Link, *Wilson the Diplomatist: A Look at His Major Foreign Policies* (Baltimore: Johns Hopkins University Press, 1957); Arno Mayer, *Politics and Diplomacy of Peacemaking: Containment and Counterrevolution at Versailles, 1918–1919* (New York: Knopf, 1967); Georg Schild, *Between Ideology and Realpolitik: Woodrow Wilson and the Russian Revolution, 1917–1921* (Westport, CT: Greenwood, 1995).

60. Cohen, *America's Response to China*, 86–87.

61. MacDougall, *Let the Sea Make a Noise*, 517.

62. Edward S. Miller, *War Plan Orange: The U.S. Strategy to Defeat Japan, 1897–1945* (Annapolis, MD: Naval Institute Press, 1991), 110–116.

63. Shizhang Hu, *Stanley K. Hornbeck and the Open Door Policy, 1919–1937* (Westport, CT: Greenwood, 1995), 43–44.

64. Fifield, *Woodrow Wilson and the Far East*, 284–285.

65. A. Whitney Griswold, *Far Eastern Policy of the United States* (New York: Harcourt, Brace, 1938), 223.

66. Roy Watson Curry, *Woodrow Wilson and Far Eastern Policy, 1913–1921* (New York: Octagon, 1968), 313.

67. John D. Long, "Establishment of the General Board: General Order No. 544," March 13, 1900, http://www.history.navy.mil/research/library/online-reading-room

/title-list-alphabetically/g/general-orders/general-order-no-544-1900-establishment
-general-board.html.

68. Michael Vlahos, "The Naval War College and the Origins of War-Planning Against Japan," *Naval War College Review* 33, no. 4 (July–August 1980): 23–41; Edward S. Miller, *War Plan Orange*.

69. Paper of the General Board of the United States Navy, Letters, Dewey to Meyer, December 30, 1909, quoted in Richard D. Challener, *Admirals, Generals, and American Foreign Policy 1898–1914* (Princeton: Princeton University Press, 1973), 22–23.

70. Miller, *War Plan Orange*, 25.

71. J. H. Oliver, "Memorandum Submitted to the President of the War College," April 20, 1907, RG 8, JNOpP, 1, Naval War College, Newport, RI.

72. Vlahos, "The Naval War College and the Origins of War-Planning Against Japan," 30–32.

73. "Plan of Defense of Manila Bay," Headquarters Philippines Division, Artillery Officer, Manila, P. I. Naval War College, Newport, RI, 1909, RG 8, Box 26, Folder 5.

74. Memorandum on Plans Campaign-Orange by the Navy Department General Board, 1910, Naval War College, Newport, RI, RG 8, Box 48, Folder 9,

75. "Our Situation in the Pacific Ocean," lecture delivered by Commander J. H. Oliver, USN, at the Naval War College, June 3, 1910, Naval War College, Newport, RI, RG 8, Box 48, Folder 8.

76. Strategic Problem, Pacific, by the General Board to the Secretary of the Navy, January 15, 1917, at the Naval War College, Newport, RI, RG 8, Box 49, Folder 5.

77. Strategy of the Pacific, Joint Board No. 325, Serial No. 28-d, to the Secretary of War and Secretary of Navy, December 18, 1919, in Naval War College, Newport, RI, Edward S. Miller Collection Material Relating to War Plan Orange, Box 3, Folder WPO 1919; Memorandum for CNO, Joint Board No. 325, Serial No. 37, December 22, 1919, Naval War College, Newport, RI, Edward S. Miller Collection Material Relating to War Plan Orange, Box 3, Folder WPO 1919; Miller, *War Plan Orange*, 37.

78. John H. Maurer, "Fuel and the Battle Fleet: Coal, Oil, and American Naval Strategy, 1898–1925," *Naval War College Review* 34, no. 6 (November–December 1981): 69–70.

79. Miller, *War Plan Orange*, 25.

80. Lecture by Captain R. R. Belknap for Fleet–War College Sessions on The Blue-Orange Situation, November 1, 1921, p. 4, Naval War College, Newport, RI, RG 8, Box 105, Folder 2.

81. Herring, *From Colony to Superpower*, 436.

82. Warren I. Cohen, *Empire Without Tears: America's Foreign Relations, 1913–1945* (New York: Knopf, 1987), 2, 11; Robert D. Schulzinger, *The Wise Men of Foreign Affairs: The History of the Council on Foreign Relations* (New York: Columbia University Press, 1984), 5–30.

83. MacDougall, *Let the Sea Make a Noise*, 523.

84. Cohen, *Empire Without Tears*, 19, 23–35; Melvyn P. Leffler, "Expansionist Impulses and Domestic Constraints, 1921–1932," in *Economics and World Power: An Assessment of American Diplomacy Since 1789*, ed. William H. Becker and Samuel F. Wells, Jr. (New York: Columbia University Press, 1984), 246.

85. From 1916 to 1931, the share of U.S. exports to China nearly quadrupled, from 1.1 percent of total U.S. exports to 4 percent. Similarly, the share of U.S. exports to Japan also rose, from 3.9 percent to 6.4 percent. (China and Japan combined therefore accounted for over 10 percent of U.S. exports in 1931, compared to 5 percent in 1916.) However, trade continued to comprise about 11 percent of overall U.S. GDP growth in this period, and the role of trade grew from 10 percent to 35 percent of Japan's GDP in the first half of the twentieth century. See U.S. Bureau of the Census, *Historical Statistics of the United States, Colonial Times to 1957* (Washington, DC: Department of Commerce, 1960), 528.

86. Robert W. Love, Jr., *History of the U.S. Navy, 1775–1941* (Harrisburg, PA: Stackpole, 1992), 528.

87. Merlo J. Pusey, *Charles Evan Hughes* (New York: MacMillan, 1951), 2:454.

88. Raymond Leslie Buell, *The Washington Conference* (New York: D. Appleton, 1922), 147.

89. John Palmer Gavit, *Charles Evans Hughes, the Man: Side-Lights Upon the Personality of the Former Governor of New York* (New York: The Nation Press, 1916), 3.

90. Pusey, *Charles Evan Hughes*, 2:445–452, 463.

91. William R. Braisted, "The Evolution of the United States Navy's Strategic Assessments in the Pacific, 1919–31," in *The Washington Conference, 1921–22 Naval Rivalry, East Asian Stability and the Road to Pearl Harbor*, ed. Erik Goldstein and John Maurer (Portland, OR: Frank Cass, 1994), 106.

92. Anonymous, "The Situation in the Far East," 16.

93. John MacMurray to Charles Evans Hughes, October 3, 1921, Charles Evans Hughes Papers, Library of Congress, Reel 124.

94. One of those students, Claude Buss, recounted his experiences at the conference to me several times before his death at age ninety-five in 1998. After witnessing the Washington Treaty negotiations, he went on to serve in the Foreign Service, surrendering Manila to the Japanese in 1942 and teaching generations of American military and diplomatic personnel about the geostrategy of Asia after the war.

95. Quincy Wright, "The Washington Conference," *American Political Science Review* 16, no. 2 (May 1922): 290.

96. Charles Evans Hughes, *Address of Charles E. Hughes, Secretary of State of the United States and American Commissioner to the Conference on Limitation of Armament, on Assuming the Duties of Presiding Officer at the Conference, Washington, D.C., November 12, 1921* (Washington, DC: U.S. Government Printing Office, November 12, 1921), 6.

97. Herring, *From Colony to Superpower*, 454.

98. The clause stipulated that the United States would maintain the status quo in fortifications on "the insular possessions which the United States now holds or may hereafter acquire in the Pacific Ocean, except (a) those adjacent to the coast of the United States, Alaska and the Panama Canal Zone, not including the Aleutian Islands, and (b) the Hawaiian Islands." See "Treaty Between the United States of America, the British Empire, France, Italy, and Japan, Signed at Washington," February 6, 1922, *FRUS, 1922, Vol. I*, 252–253. Britain was similarly limited to the status quo in fortifications in the Pacific, with the exception of Australia, New Zealand, and Canada, and Japan agreed to maintain the status quo on Formosa, Okinawa, the Bonins, Pescadores, and other Pacific islands.

99. The full text of all these treaties can be found in *FRUS, 1922, Vol. I*.

100. Walter Lippmann, "Britain and America: The Prospects of Political Cooperation in the Light of Their Paramount Interests," *Foreign Affairs* 13, no. 3 (April 1935): 370.

101. Anonymous, "The Situation in the Far East," 28.

102. John T. Kuehn, *Agents of Innovation: The General Board and the Design of the Fleet That Defeated the Japanese Navy* (Newport, RI: Naval Institute Press, 2008), 2.

103. Kuehn, *Agents of Innovation*, 26.

104. The U.S. and British delegations did not go into the talks expecting fortifications to be a topic. See "Proposal for a Limitation of Naval Armament, Presented by the Secretary of State at the First Plenary Session of the Conference," November 12, 1921, *FRUS, 1922, Vol. I*, 53–61. When the Japanese delegation raised fortifications, Hughes explained to Britain's foreign minister, Arthur James Balfour, that the U.S. Navy would not accept it. See "Note by the Secretary to the British Empire Delegation of a Conversation Between the Secretary of State and Mr. Balfour, of the British Empire Delegation," December 1, 1921, *FRUS, 1922, Vol. I*, 74–75. When it became clear that the only way to win Japanese support for the 10:6 ratio was to accept a nonfortification clause, Hughes agreed as long as it represented a freeze on new fortifications, except for Hawaii, Australia, and New Zealand. See "Secretary of State to the Ambassador in Japan (Warren)," December 3, 1921, *FRUS, 1922, Vol. I*, 84–86. Once the Japanese delegation received permission for that formula from Tokyo, the fortification issue was put aside early in the conference and the focus for the remainder of the meeting was types of tonnage, ship scrapping, and types of ships. See "Memorandum by the Secretary to the British Empire Delegation of a Conversation at the Department of State," December 12, 1921, *FRUS, 1922, Vol. I*, 90–99.

105. Cited in Williamson Murray, "U.S. Naval Strategy and Japan," in *Successful Strategies: Triumphing in War and Peace from Antiquity to the Present*, ed. Williamson Murray and Richard Hart Sinnreich (London: Cambridge University Press, 2014), 287.

106. P. N. Pierce, "The Unsolved Mystery of Pete Ellis," *Marine Corps Gazette* (February 1962), 36, quoted in William B. Hopkins, *The Pacific War: The Strategy, Politics and Players that Won the War* (Minneapolis: Zenith Press, 2008), 8.

107. For a fuller treatment of the "pros and cons" of the Washington Treaties, see Thomas H. Buckley, "The Icarus Factor: The American Pursuit of Myth in Naval Arms Control, 1921–36," in Goldstein and Maurer, *The Washington Conference*, 134–136.

108. Tyler Dennett, "The Open Door Policy as Intervention," *Annals of the American Academy of Political and Social Science* 168, American Policy in the Pacific (July 1933): 81.

109. Dean Acheson, *This Vast External Realm* (New York: Norton, 1973), quoted in Roger Dingman, *Power in the Pacific: The Origins of Naval Arms Limitation, 1914–1922* (Chicago: University of Chicago Press, 1976), 216.

110. Samuel Eliot Morison, *The Two-Ocean War: A Short History of the United States Navy in the Second World War* (Boston: Little, Brown, 1963).

111. Kuehn, *Agents of Innovation*.

112. Kuehn, *Agents of Innovation*, 25.

113. Dirk Anthony Ballendorf and Merrill L. Bartlett, *Pete Ellis: An Amphibious Warfare Prophet, 1880–1923* (Annapolis, MD: Naval Institute Press, 1997), 119–121; Hopkins, *The Pacific War*, 12; Henry I. Shaw, Jr., Bernard C. Nalty, and Edwin T. Turnbladh, *History of U.S. Marine Corps Operations in World War II*, vol. 3, *Central Pacific Drive* (Washington, DC: Historical Branch, G-3 Division, Headquarters, U.S. Marine Corps, 1966), 5.

114. B. A. Friedman, ed., *21st Century Ellis: Operational Art and Strategic Prophecy for the Modern Era* (Annapolis, MD: Naval Institute Press, 2015), 77, 599.

115. John A. Adams, *If Mahan Ran the Great Pacific War: An Analysis of World War II Naval Strategy* (Bloomington: Indiana University Press, 2008), 29.

116. Cooper, *Woodrow Wilson*, 509.

117. "Statement Issued to the Press by the Department of State," December 12, 1921, *FRUS, 1922, Vol. I*, 31–33. The bilateral agreement on freedom of navigation was signed on February 11, 1922. See Pusey, *Charles Evan Hughes*, 2:445–452.

118. Writing in the *American Political Science Review* at the time, for example, Quincy Wright noted that, "Though China has by no means regained full territorial and administrative integrity, yet substantial steps in this direction have been taken. The United States will have less cause to worry about the Philippines, agreement has been reached on the vexing problems of Yap and the Pacific cables, and the Anglo-Japanese alliance has been superseded." See Wright, "The Washington Conference," 295.

119. "Message of President Harding to the Senate," February 10, 1922, *FRUS, 1922, Vol. I*, 303.

120. Allen Wescott, "Notes on International Affairs from March 5 to April 5," (United States Naval Institute) *Proceedings* 48, no. 1 (January 1922): 851.

121. Herring, *From Colony to Superpower*, 467.

122. Iriye, *Across the Pacific*, 151.

123. Iriye, *Across the Pacific*, 144.

124. Robert H. Ferrell, *The Presidency of Calvin Coolidge*, American Presidency Series (Lawrence: University of Kansas Press, 1998).

125. Joan Hoff Wilson, *American Business & Foreign Policy, 1920–1933* (Lexington: University of Kentucky Press, 1971), 29.

126. Herring, *From Colony to Superpower*, 443.

127. Breckinridge Long Papers, Library of Congress, Box 181, China Loan, February–August 1917 Folder, "Memorandum," June 25, 1917, Reinsch to Lansing; Curry, *Woodrow Wilson and Far Eastern Policy*, 21–24.

128. Breckinridge Long Papers, Library of Congress, Box 1, Diary 6 Folder, 131.

129. Breckinridge Long Papers, Library of Congress, Box 2, Diary 7 Folder, 190.

130. Mark Metzler, *Lever of Empire: The International Gold Standard and the Crisis of Liberalism in Prewar Japan* (Berkeley: University of California Press, 2006), 96–98; Edward M. Lamont, *The Ambassador from Wall Street: The Story of Thomas W. Lamont, J.P. Morgan's Chief Executive* (Lanham, MD: Madison Books, 1994), 155–157.

131. After the war, the end of the U.S. gold embargo meant trade with the United States was the key to Japanese economic growth. See Metzler, *Lever of Empire*, 120–121. On Lamont at the Washington Conference, see "Impressions of the Present Situation in Japan," issued to the American delegates to the Washington Naval Conference, found in "Washington Conference Folder," The Papers of Charles Evans Hughes, Reel 123, cited in David L. Asher, "Convergence and Its Costs: The Failure of Japanese Economic Reform and the Breakdown of the Washington System, 1918–1932" (PhD diss., St. Anthony's College, Oxford University, 2002). The author is indebted to David Asher for over two decades of periodic discussions on the interplay of finance and diplomacy in this period and in the modern era.

132. Breckinridge Long Papers, Library of Congress, Box 2, Diary 8 Folder, 33.

133. Lamont, *The Ambassador from Wall Street*, 194.

134. Thomas W. Lamont, "The Economic Situation in the Orient," in *Inflation and High Prices: Causes and Remedies: A Series of Addresses, Papers Presented at the National Conference Held Under the Auspices of the Academy of Political Science in the City of New York, April 30, 1920*, ed. Henry Rogers Seager (New York: Columbia University, 1922), 69.

135. Herring, *From Colony to Superpower*, 468.

136. Wilson, *American Business & Foreign Policy, 1920–1933*, 210–211.

137. Lamont, *The Ambassador from Wall Street*, 196.

138. Lamont, *The Ambassador from Wall Street*, 237.

139. Edward S. Kaplan, *American Trade Policy 1923–1995* (Westport, CT: Greenwood, 1996), 8–10, 13.

140. Claude A. Buss, *The Far East: A History of Recent and Contemporary International Relations in East Asia* (New York: MacMillan, 1955), 382.

5. The Open Door Closes, 1928–1941

1. George C. Herring, *From Colony to Superpower: U.S. Foreign Relations Since 1776* (New York: Oxford University Press, 2008), 439, 446.

2. Arthur Waldron, "War and the Rise of Nationalism in Twentieth-Century China," *Journal of Military History* 57, no. 5 (October 1993): 87–104.

3. Ikuhiko Hata, "Continental Expansion, 1904–1941," in *The Cambridge History of Japan*, vol. 6, *The Twentieth Century*, ed. Peter Duus (Cambridge: Cambridge University Press, 1989), 285–289.

4. Prepared remarks by William R. Castle Jr., special ambassador to Japan during London Naval Conference, at the Williamstown Institute of Politics, August 13, 1930, cited in T. A. Bisson, "The United States and the Orient: A Survey of the Relations of the United States with China and Japan—June 1, 1929, to September 1, 1930," *Pacific Affairs* 3, no. 12 (December 1930): 1136–1137.

5. Mark Metzler, *Lever of Empire: The International Gold Standard and the Crisis of Liberalism in Prewar Japan* (Berkeley: University of California Press, 2006), 236.

6. U.S. Department of State, *Peace and War: United States Foreign Policy, 1931–1941* (Washington, DC: Government Printing Office, 1943), 2–8.

7. Henry L. Stimson and McGeorge Bundy, *On Active Service in Peace and War* (New York: Harper and Brothers, 1947), 126.

8. Stimson quoted in Richard N. Current, *Secretary Stimson: A Study in Statecraft* (New Brunswick, NJ: Rutgers University Press, 1954), 5–6.

9. Current, *Secretary Stimson*, 83.

10. Walter W. Liggett, *The Rise of Herbert Hoover* (New York: H. K. Fly, 1933), 76–113.

11. William E. Leuchtenburg, *Herbert Hoover: The 31st President, 1929–1933*, The American Presidents Series (New York: Times Books, 2009), 13.

12. Susan B. Carter, ed., *Historical Statistics of the United States*, millennial ed. online (Cambridge: Cambridge University Press, 2006), http://hsus.cambridge.org/HSUSWeb/HSUSEntryServlet.

13. Justus D. Doenecke and John E. Wilz, *From Isolation to War, 1931–1941* (Arlington Heights, IL: Harlan Davidson, 1991), 35.

14. Secretary Stimson to the Consul General at Nanking, January 7, 1932, in U.S. Department of State, *Foreign Relations of the United States*, http://digicoll.library.wisc.edu /FRUS/Browse.html [hereafter cited as *FRUS*], *1932, Vol. III: The Far East*, 7–8.

15. Shizhang Hu, *Stanley Hornbeck and the Open Door Policy, 1919–1937* (Westport, CT: Greenwood, 1995), 144.

16. Walter Lippmann, "Britain and America: The Prospects of Political Cooperation in the Light of Their Paramount Interests," *Foreign Affairs* 13, no. 3 (April 1935): 368.

17. Donald Jordan, *China's Trial by Fire: The Shanghai War of 1932* (Ann Arbor: University of Michigan Press, 2001).

18. Ikuhiko Hata, "Continental Expansion, 1904–1941," in Duus, *The Cambridge History of Japan*, 6:297.

19. Franklin Delano Roosevelt, Inaugural Address, March 4, 1933, posted online by Gerhard Peters and John T. Woolley, The American Presidency Project, http://www .presidency.ucsb.edu/ws/?pid=14473.

20. Charles P. Kindelberger, *The World in Depression, 1929–1939* (Berkeley: University of California Press, 1986), 231.

21. Roosevelt was motivated by the Russian market as well as the possibility of countering Japanese and German threats. See Justus D. Doenecke and Mark A. Stoler, *Debating Franklin D. Roosevelt's Foreign Policies, 1933–1945* (Lanham, MD: Rowman and Littlefield, 2005), 18–19; Mary E. Glantz, *FDR and the Soviet Union: The President's Battles Over Foreign Policy* (Lawrence: University of Kansas Press, 2005), chap. 2.

22. Unofficial Statement by the Japanese Foreign Office, April 17, 1934, in *FRUS, 1931–1941, Japan, Vol. I*, 224–225.

23. Grew to Secretary of State, April 20, 1934, in *FRUS, 1934, Vol. III: The Far East, The Far Eastern Crisis*, 117–121.

24. John M. Collins, *Grand Strategy: Principles and Practices* (Annapolis, MD: Naval Institute Press, 1973), 25.

25. Joseph Nye, *The Powers to Lead* (Oxford: Oxford University Press, 2008).

26. Robert H. Dorff, "A Primer in Strategy Development," in *U.S. Army War College Guide to Strategy*, ed. Joseph R. Cerami and James F. Holcomb (Carlisle, PA: Army War College, 2001), 12–13.

27. Hu, *Stanley Hornbeck and the Open Door Policy, 1919–1937*, 18.

28. Stanley Hornbeck, "Has the United States a China Policy?" *Foreign Affairs* 5, no. 4 (July 1927): 628.

29. Hu, *Stanley Hornbeck and the Open Door Policy, 1919–1937*, 4. Waldron and Friedrich agree. See K. Marlin Friedrich, "In Search of a Far Eastern Policy: Joseph Grew, Stanley Hornbeck, and American-Japanese Relations 1937–1941" (PhD diss., Washington State University, 1974).

30. Hornbeck, "Has the United States a China Policy?" 624. Revealingly, he published this article even as Secretary of State Frank Kellogg had ordered the Far East Division to negotiate a tariff autonomy agreement with the Nationalist government in China.

31. Warren I. Cohen, *America's Response to China: An Interpretive History of Sino-American Relations*, 5th ed. (New York: Columbia University Press, 2010), 115–116.

32. Hu, *Stanley Hornbeck and the Open Door Policy, 1919–1937*, 4–5.

33. Hu, *Stanley Hornbeck and the Open Door Policy, 1919–1937*, 27.

34. Hornbeck, "Principles and Policies in Regard to China," *Foreign Affairs* 1, no. 2 (December 1922): 121–122.

35. Stanley Hornbeck, *The United States and The Far East: Certain Fundamentals of Policy* (Boston: World Peace Foundation, 1942), 3.

36. Hornbeck memo to Secretary of State Stimson, October 3, 1931, cited in Hu, *Stanley Hornbeck and the Open Door Policy, 1919–1937*, 134.

37. Hu, *Stanley Hornbeck and the Open Door Policy, 1919–1937*, 137.

38. Cohen, *America's Response to China*, 106.

39. Hu, *Stanley Hornbeck and the Open Door Policy, 1919–1937*, 143.

40. Hornbeck memo, May 24, 1932, Hornbeck Papers, Box 454, cited in Hu, *Stanley Hornbeck and the Open Door Policy, 1919–1937*, 185.

41. "Principles of American Policy in Relation to the Far East," an address delivered to the Conference on the Cause and Cure of War, January 18, 1934, Hornbeck Papers, Box 484, quoted in Friedrich, "In Search of a Far Eastern Policy," 11–12.

42. Hornbeck quoted in Friedrich, "In Search of a Far Eastern Policy," 40.

43. Hu, *Stanley Hornbeck and the Open Door Policy, 1919–1937*, 171.

44. Joseph Grew, *Sport and Travel in the Far East* (New York: Houghton Mifflin, 1910).

45. Friedrich, "In Search of a Far Eastern Policy," 40.

46. Friedrich, "In Search of a Far Eastern Policy," 9.

47. Joseph Grew, *Turbulent Era: A Diplomatic Record of Forty Years, 1904–1945*, ed. Walter Johnson, assist. Nancy Harvison Hooker, 2 vols. (Boston: Houghton Mifflin Company, 1952).

48. Grew, *Turbulent Era*, 2:1224–1229.

49. From the Mudd Manuscript Library, Princeton University, John Van Antwerp MacMurray Papers, 1715–1988, http://diglib.princeton.edu/ead/getEad?eadid=MC094&kw=.

50. J. V. A. MacMurray, *Treaties and Agreements with and Concerning China* (New York: Carnegie Endowment, 1921).

51. Cohen, *America's Response to China*, 104.

52. MacMurray to Secretary Kellogg, August 1, 1925, *FRUS, 1925, Vol. I*, 809.

53. Dorothy Borg, *American Policy and the Chinese Revolution, 1925–1928* (New York: Macmillan, 1947), 127.

54. MacMurray to the Secretary of State, April 23, 1927, *FRUS, 1927, Vol. II*, 209–210; Secretary Kellogg to Ambassador MacMurray, April 20, 1927, *FRUS, 1927, Vol. II*, 204.

55. J. V. A. MacMurray, *How the Peace Was Lost: The 1935 Memorandum: Developments Affecting American Policy in the Far East*, ed. Arthur Waldron (Stanford, CA: Hoover Institute Press, 1991), 27.

56. MacMurray memorandum in Waldron, *How the Peace Was Lost*, 63.

57. MacMurray memorandum in Waldron, *How the Peace Was Lost*, 61.

58. MacMurray memorandum in Waldron, *How the Peace Was Lost*, 127.

59. MacMurray memorandum in Waldron, *How the Peace Was Lost*, 128.

60. MacMurray memorandum in Waldron, *How the Peace Was Lost*, 128.

61. Waldron, *How the Peace Was Lost*, 130.

62. Waldron, *How the Peace Was Lost*, 132.

63. Waldron, *How the Peace Was Lost*, 131.

64. Waldron, *How the Peace Was Lost*, 136.

65. Waldron, *How the Peace Was Lost*, 29–45.

66. Tyler Dennett, *John Hay: From Poetry to Politics* (New York: Dodd, Mead, 1934).

67. Dennett, "The Open Door as Intervention," *Annals of the American Academy of Political and Social Science* 168 (July 1933): 81.

68. Dennett, "The Open Door as Intervention," 83.

69. Franklin D. Roosevelt, "Quarantine Speech," October 5, 1937, http://millercenter.org/president/speeches/speech-3310.

70. Tyler Dennett, "Alternative American Policies in the Far East," *Foreign Affairs* 16, no. 4 (April 1938): 389.

71. Dennett, "Alternative American Policies in the Far East," 391.

72. Dennett, "Alternative American Policies in the Far East," 397.

73. Dennett, "Alternative American Policies in the Far East," 399.

74. William R. Braisted, *Diplomats in Blue: U.S. Naval Officers in China, 1922–1933* (Gainesville: University Press of Florida, 2009), 3.

75. General Board Report on Disarmament Conference of 1932, October 24, 1931, pp. 4–6, Naval War College, Newport, RI, RG 8, Box 100, Folder 10. See also William R. Braisted, "The Evolution of the United States Navy's Strategic Assessments in the Pacific, 1919–31," in *The Washington Conference, 1921–22: Naval Rivalry, East Asian Stability and the Road to Pearl Harbor*, ed. Erik Goldstein and John Maurer (Portland, OR: Frank Cass, 1994), 106–107.

76. Ronald Spector, *Eagle Against the Sun* (New York: Free Press, 1985), 25; James F. Cook, *Carl Vinson: Patriarch of the Armed Forces* (Macon, GA: Mercer University Press, 2004), 70.

77. Stuart L. Weiss, "American Foreign Policy and Presidential Power: The Neutrality Act of 1935," *Journal of Politics* 30, no. 3 (August 1968).

78. Captain R. A. Koch, USN, Blue-Orange Study, March 31, 1933, Naval War College, Newport, RI, RG 8, Box 49, Folder 7.

79. Jonathan Kirshner, *Appeasing Bankers: Financial Caution on the Road to War* (Princeton, NJ: Princeton University Press, 2007), 108; Julian E. Zelizer, "The Forgotten Legacy of the New Deal: Fiscal Conservatism and the Roosevelt Administration, 1933–1938," *Presidential Studies Quarterly* 30, no. 2 (June 2000): 331–358.

80. Cook, *Carl Vinson*, 49.

81. Carl Vinson to Franklin D. Roosevelt, December 28, 1932, President's Personal File 9501, Roosevelt Library, Hyde Park, NY, quoted in Cook, *Carl Vinson*, 74.

82. William D. Leahy, *I Was There: The Personal Story of the Chief of Staff to Presidents Roosevelt and Truman* (New York: McGraw Hill, 1950), 178, quoted in Cook, Carl Vinson, 178.

83. Plan 0-1 Orange, "The Royal Road," prepared by Commander C. W. Magruder, War Plans Division, 1934, Naval War College, Newport, RI, Edward S. Miller Collection, Material Relating to War Plan Orange, Box 5, Folder WPO 1934: Royal Road.

84. William B. Hopkins, *The Pacific War: The Strategy, Politics, and Players that Won the War* (Minneapolis: Zenith, 2008), 12.

85. Grace Person Hayes, *The History of the Joint Chiefs of Staff in World War II: The War Against Japan* (Annapolis, MD: Naval Institute Press, 1982), 6.

86. Memorandum from Commander J. B. Earle, U.S.N., to Chief of Staff on 1935 Conference for Further Limitation of Naval Armaments, February 8, 1934, Naval War College, Newport, RI, RG 8, Box 101, Folder 1. See also Rough Draft of Letter from President, Naval War College to the General Board on the 1935 Conference for Further Limitation of Naval Armaments (date unclear but sometime after January 26 in 1934), 2, Naval War College, Newport, RI, RG 8, Box 101, Folder 1; Norman H. Davis, "The New Naval Agreement," *Foreign Affairs* 14, no. 4 (July 1936): 578–583.

87. Stephen E. Pelz, *The Failure of the Second London Naval Conference on the Onset of World War II* (Cambridge, MA: Harvard University Press, 1974), 205.

88. Hopkins, *The Pacific War*, 21.

89. Michael K. Doyle, "The U.S. Navy and War Plan Orange, 1933–1940: Making Necessity a Virtue," *Naval War College Review* 33 (May–June 1980): 58.

90. Spector, *Eagle Against the Sun*, 58.

91. Library of Congress, Admiral W. D. Leahy's Papers and Diary, diary entry for August 24, 1937, 104, quoted in Malcolm H. Murfett, *Fool-proof Relations: The Search for Anglo-American Naval Cooperation During the Chamberlain Years, 1937–1940* (Singapore: Singapore University Press, 1984), 46.

92. Memo of conversations with British Ambassador, November 27, 1937, *FRUS, 1937, Vol. III: The Far East*, 111, 724–726, cited in John Mcivkar Haight, Jr., "Franklin D. Roosevelt and a Naval Quarantine of Japan," *Pacific Historical Review* 40, no. 2 (May 1971): 207.

93. Hopkins, *The Pacific War*, 22.

94. John Costello, *The Pacific War 1941–1945* (New York: HarperCollins, 1981), 63.

95. Hopkins, *The Pacific War*, 33; Henry G. Gole, *The Road to Rainbow: Army Planning for Global War, 1934–1940* (Annapolis, MD: Naval Institute Press, 2003), 107.

96. Letter from Joseph C. Grew, Tokyo, to Secretary of State on "Return of Ashes of Ambassador Saitō to Japan by the U.S.S. Astoria," April 26, 1939, Naval War College, Newport, RI, RG 8, Box 71, Folder 5.

97. Report on the Far Eastern Situation by Commander in Chief of the Asiatic Fleet H. E. Yarnell to President of the Naval War College, July 20, 1939, Naval War College, Newport, RI, RG 8, Box 18, Folder 1.

98. Abrogation by the United States of the Treaty of Commerce and Navigation Between the United States and Japan Signed February 21, 1911, Note from Secretary of State Hull to Japanese Ambassador Horinouchi, July 26, 1939, *FRUS, 1939, Vol. III: The Far East, Undeclared War Between Japan and China*, 558–559.

99. Franklin Delano Roosevelt, Fireside Chat 16: On the "Arsenal of Democracy," December 29, 1940, http://millercenter.org/scripps/archive/speeches/detail/3319.

100. Pelz, *The Failure of the Second London Naval Conference on the Onset of World War II*, 210.

101. Spector, *Eagle Against the Sun*, 60.

102. Waldo Heinrichs, "FDR and the Admirals: Strategy and Stagecraft," in *FDR and the U.S. Navy*, ed. Edward J. Marolda (New York: St. Martin's, 1998), 124; Ricardo Trota Jose, *The Philippine Army, 1935–1942* (Manila: Ateneo de Manila University Press, 1992), 190–194.

103. Akira Iriye, *The Origins of the Second World War in Asia and the Pacific* (London: Longman, 1987), 98.

104. Ian Kershaw, *Fateful Choices: Ten Decisions That Changed the World, 1940–1941* (New York: Penguin, 2007), 231.

105. See Conrad Black, *Franklin Delano Roosevelt: Champion of Freedom* (New York: PublicAffairs, 2003), 564.

106. Spector, *Eagle Against the Sun*, 67; Hopkins, *The Pacific War*, 33.

107. Scott D. Sagan, "The Origins of the Pacific War," *Journal of Interdisciplinary History* 18, no. 4, The Origin and Prevention of Major Wars (Spring 1988): 893–922.

108. Iriye, *The Origins of the Second World War in Asia and the Pacific*, 148.

109. President Roosevelt, Executive Order 8832—Freezing Japanese and Chinese Assets in the United States, July 26, 1941, http://www.presidency.ucsb.edu/ws/index.php?pid=16148&st=china&st1=#ixzz1KGGJbrHR.

110. Grew, *Turbulent Era*, 2:1223–1229.

111. National Archives at St. Louis, Military Personnel Records, Philippine Army and Guerilla Records, http://www.archives.gov/st-louis/military-personnel/philippine-army-records.html.

112. Spector, *Eagle Against the Sun*, 68–69.

113. Eri Hotta, *Japan 1941: Countdown to Infamy* (New York: Vintage, 2014), 10–11.

114. Samuel Eliot Morison, *History of United States Naval Operations in World War II*, 15 vols. (Urbana: University of Illinois Press, 2001), 3:58. Originally published 1947–1962.

115. Willard Range, *Franklin D. Roosevelt's World Order* (Athens: University of Georgia Press, 1959), 17.

116. Iriye, *The Origins of the Second World War in Asia and the Pacific*, 159–166.

117. Mark A. Stoler, *Allies and Adversaries: The Joint Chiefs of Staff, the Grand Alliance, and U.S. Strategy in World War II* (Chapel Hill: University of North Carolina Press, 2003), 104.

118. David Reynolds, *From Munich to Pearl Harbor: Roosevelt's America and the Origins of the Second World War* (Chicago: Ivan R. Dee, 2001), 5–6.

119. Conducted October 13, 1941. See Dr. George H. Gallup, *The Gallup Poll: Public Opinion, 1935–1971* (New York: Random House, 1972), 1:245.

120. Gallup, *The Gallup Poll*, 1:297.

121. Pelz, *The Failure of the Second London Naval Conference on the Onset of World War II*, 221.

122. Memorandum, General Board to Secretary of the Navy, October 18, 1941, GB File 422, GB Papers WNY, cited in Michael A. McDevitt, "The United States Navy, the Philippines and the Fight for Appropriations, 1920–1932" (MA thesis, History, Georgetown University, July 1974), 266.

123. Stoler, *Allies and Adversaries*, 61.

124. President Roosevelt, Excerpts from the Press Conference, November 28, 1941, http://www.presidency.ucsb.edu/ws/index.php?pid=16047&st=philippine&st1=#ixzz1KHBh1KF5

125. Iriye, *The Origins of the Second World War in Asia and the Pacific*, 140.

126. Michael A. Bailey, Judith Goldstein, and Barry R. Weingast, "Institutional Roots of American Trade Policy: Politics, Coalitions, and International Trade," *World Politics* 49, no. 3 (April 1997): 309–338.

127. The Reciprocal Tariff Act tied U.S. tariff reductions to reciprocal steps by foreign partners and then required a simple majority rather than a two-thirds majority to pass. This incentivized Congress to lower duties and made it easier to get the treaties through. See Bailey, Goldstein, and Weingast, "Institutional Roots of American Trade Policy," 309–338.

128. Robert E. Osgood, *Ideals and Self-Interest in America's Foreign Relations* (Chicago: University of Chicago Press, 1953), 1–23; Henry A. Kissinger, *Diplomacy* (New York: Simon and Schuster, 1994), chaps. 2 and 15.

129. See Enez Manuela, "Imagining Woodrow Wilson in Asia: Dreams of East-West Harmony and the Revolt Against Empire in 1919," *American Historical Review* 111, no. 5 (December 2006): 1327–1351.

130. Reynolds, *From Munich to Pearl Harbor*, 4.

6. Grand Strategy and the War Against Japan

1. Otto von Bismarck, *Bismarck: The Man and the Statesman; Being the Reflections and Reminiscences of Otto* (New York: Harper, 1898), 2:105.

2. Samuel Eliot Morison, *Strategy and Compromise* (New York: Little, Brown, 1958), 7.

3. Jon Meachem, *Franklin and Winston: An Intimate Portrait of an Epic Friendship* (New York: Random House, 2004), 5; Kenneth S. Davis, *FDR: The War President, 1940–1943* (New York: Random House, 2000), 258–259.

4. First, their countries seek no aggrandizement, territorial or otherwise. Second, they desire to see no territorial changes that do not accord with the freely expressed wishes of the peoples concerned. Third, they respect the right of peoples to choose the form of government under which they will live; and they wish to see sovereign rights and self-government restored to those who have been forcibly deprived of them. Fourth, they will endeavor, with due respect to their existing obligations, to further the enjoyment by all states, great or small, victor or vanquished, of access, on equal terms, to the trade and to the raw materials of the world that are needed for their economic prosperity. Fifth, they desire to bring about the fullest collaboration between all nations in the economic field, with the object of securing for all improved labor standards, economic advancement, and social security. Sixth, after the final destruction of the Nazi tyranny, they hope to see established a peace that will afford to all nations the means of dwelling in safety within their own boundaries and that will afford assurance that all men in all lands may live out their lives in freedom from fear and want. Seventh, such a peace should enable all men to traverse the high seas and oceans without hindrance. Eighth, they believe that all nations of the world for realistic as well as spiritual reasons must come to the abandonment of the use of force.

5. Davis, *FDR*, 273.

6. Morison, *Strategy and Compromise*, 7.

7. Michael Fullilove, *Rendezvous with Destiny: How Franklin D. Roosevelt and Five Extraordinary Men Took America into the War and into the World* (New York: Random House, 2014).

8. George C. Herring, *From Colony to Superpower: U.S. Foreign Relations Since 1776* (New York: Oxford University Press, 2008), 545. As Warren Kimball notes, it was a "canard that Franklin Roosevelt had no foreign policy and merely reacted to day-to-day events."

See Warren Kimball, *The Juggler: Franklin Roosevelt as Wartime Statesman* (Princeton, NJ: Princeton University Press, 1991), 7. For more on FDR as commander in chief, see also James MacGregor Burns, *Roosevelt: The Soldier of Freedom* (New York: Harcourt Brace Jovanovich, 1970); Davis, *FDR*. For perspectives on Roosevelt's balancing of politics and foreign policy, and idealism and realism, see Robert Dallek, *Franklin D. Roosevelt and American Foreign Policy, 1932–1945* (New York: Oxford University Press, 1979); Kimball, *The Juggler*; Davis, *FDR*.

9. Cordell Hull, *The Memoirs of Cordell Hull*, 2 vols. (New York: Macmillan, 1948), 85.

10. Walter Lippmann, *U.S. Foreign Policy: Shield of the Republic* (Boston: Little, Brown, 1943).

11. Roosevelt centralized decision-making by design, not by obsession. See Nigel Hamilton, *The Mantle of Command: FDR at War, 1941–1942* (New York: Houghton Harcourt, 2014), 152.

12. Herring, *From Colony to Superpower*, 541.

13. Hull, *Memoirs*; Arthur W. Schatz, "The Anglo-American Trade Agreement and Cordell Hull's Search for Peace, 1936–1938," *Journal of American History* 57, no. 1 (June 1970): 85–103.

14. Andrew Roberts, *Masters and Commanders: How Four Titans Won the War in the West, 1941–1945* (New York, Harper, 2009), chap. 3.

15. Henry H. Adams, *Witness to Power: The Life of Fleet Admiral William D. Leahy* (Annapolis, MD: Naval Institute Press, 1985).

16. Mark A. Stoler, *George C. Marshall: Soldier-Statesman of the American Century* (Boston: Twayne, 1989).

17. Roberts, *Masters and Commanders*, 98.

18. John A. Adams, *If Mahan Ran the Great Pacific War: An Analysis of World War II Naval Strategy* (Bloomington: Indiana University Press, 2008), 169–218.

19. Mark Stoler, *Allies and Adversaries: The Joint Chiefs of Staff, the Grand Alliance, and U.S. Strategy in World War II* (Chapel Hill: University of North Carolina Press, 2000), x.

20. William D. Leahy, *I Was There: The Personal Story of the Chief of Staff to Presidents Roosevelt and Truman* (New York: McGraw-Hill, 1950), 105.

21. Stoler, *Allies and Adversaries*, 104, 107.

22. Edwin Hayward, "Coordination of Military and Civilian Civil Affairs Planning," *Annals of the Journal of Political Science and Social Science* 257, no. 1 (January 1950): 219.

23. Townsend Hoopes and Douglas Brinkley, *Driven Patriot: The Life and Times of James Forrestal* (New York: Knopf, 1992), 188.

24. Judith Munro-Leighton, "American Policy vs. Asian Revolution: SWNCC Recommendations Regarding Post–World War II China, Korea, and Vietnam" (PhD diss., University of Kentucky, 1994), 15–23.

25. SWNCC Meeting Minutes, Meeting 22, Item 2, cited in Alan Francis Ciamporcero, "The State-War-Navy Coordinating Committee and the Beginning of the Cold War" (PhD diss., State University of New York at Albany, 1980), 37.

26. Alfred Goldberg, ed., *History of the Office of the Secretary of Defense* (Washington, DC: Government Printing Office, 1984), 126.

27. See Henry Morgenthau, Jr., "Bretton Woods and International Cooperation," *Foreign Affairs* 23, no. 2 (January 1945): 182–194; Henry Morgenthau, Jr., *The Morgenthau*

Diaries: World War II and Postwar Planning, 1943-1945 (Bethesda, MD: University Publications of America, 1997); Herbert Levy, *Henry Morgenthau, Jr.: The Remarkable Life of FDR's Secretary of the Treasury* (New York: Skyhorse, 2010).

28. Gaddis Smith, *American Diplomacy During the Second World War* (New York: Knopf, 1985), 91–92.

29. Stoler, *Allies and Adversaries*, 39.

30. Franklin D. Roosevelt, Papers as President: The President's Secretary's File (PSF), 1933–1945, Series 1: Safe File, Box 1, American-British Joint Chiefs of Staff, "Joint Board Estimate of United States Over-All Production Requirements," September 11, 1941, The Joint Board, Washington, DC, 12, http://www.fdrlibrary.marist.edu/_resources/images/psf/ps fa0004.pdf.

31. Roberts, *Masters and Commanders*, 50.

32. Waldo Heinrichs, *Threshold of War: Franklin D. Roosevelt and American Entry into World War II* (New York: Oxford University Press, 1988), 107.

32. Stoler, *Allies and Adversaries*, 42; Roberts, *Masters and Commanders*, 51.

33. Grace P. Hayes, *The History of the Joint Chiefs of Staff in World War II: The War Against Japan* (Annapolis, MD: Naval Institute Press, 1982), 37.

34. Andrew Roberts, *The Storm of War: A New History of the Second World War* (New York: HarperCollins, 2011), 214.

35. Roberts, *Masters and Commanders*, 139.

36. Martin Gilbert, *Churchill: A Life* (New York: Henry Holt, 1991), 722.

37. Ernest Joseph King and Walter Muir Whitehill, *Fleet Admiral King: A Naval Record* (New York: Norton, 1952), 366–369.

38. Roberts, *The Storm of War*, 252.

39. Mark A. Stoler, "The 'Pacific-First' Alternative in American World War II Strategy," *International History Review* 2, no. 3 (July 1980): 434. See also Hayes, *The History of the Joint Chiefs of Staff in World War II*.

40. King and Whitehill, *Fleet Admiral King*, 398.

41. Stoler, "The 'Pacific-First' Alternative in American World War II Strategy," 435.

42. Eisenhower quoted in Stoler, "The 'Pacific-First' Alternative in American World War II Strategy," 436.

43. Stoler, *Allies and Adversaries*, 71–86.

44. Dr. George H. Gallup, *The Gallup Poll: Public Opinion, 1935–1971* (New York: Random House, 1972), 1:339.

45. Roosevelt quoted in Stoler, "The 'Pacific-First' Alternative in American World War II Strategy," 442.

46. Rick Atkinson, *Army At Dawn: The War in North Africa, 1942–1943* (New York: Henry Holt, 2002), 16.

47. Alan F. Wilt, "The Significance of the Casablanca Decisions, January 1943," *Journal of Military History* 55, no. 4 (October 1991): 520.

48. John Miller, Jr., "The Casablanca Conference and Pacific Strategy," *Military Affairs* 13, no. 4 (Winter 1949): 210; Hayes, *The History of the Joint Chiefs of Staff in World War II*, 280–282.

49. King quoted in Wilt, "The Significance of the Casablanca Decisions, January 1943," 520.

50. Stoler, "The 'Pacific-First' Alternative in American World War II Strategy," 449; King and Whitehill, *Fleet Admiral King*, 420.

51. Edward S. Miller, *War Plan Orange: The U.S. Strategy to Defeat Japan, 1897–1945* (Annapolis, MD: Naval Institute Press, 1991), 213–215.

52. Hayes, *The History of the Joint Chiefs of Staff in World War II*, 398–401; Dallek, *Franklin D. Roosevelt and American Foreign Policy, 1932–1945*, 397.

53. Dallek, *Franklin D. Roosevelt and American Foreign Policy, 1932–1945*, 354.

54. Prepared Remarks by John Lewis Gaddis for Karl Von Der Heyden Distinguished Lecture at Duke University, February 26, 2009, http://www.duke.edu/web/agsp/grandstrat egypaper.pdf.

55. Address Delivered to Alumni of Brown University Commencement by Raymond Spruance, June 1946, Naval War College, Newport, RI, Ms. Coll. 12, Series 2, Box 2, Folder 1. See also Morison's take in Samuel Eliot Morison, *The Two-Ocean War: A Short History of the United States Navy in the Second World War* (Boston: Little, Brown, 1963), 77–78.

56. R-106, the Former Naval Person, from the President, Secret and Personal, February 18, 1942, cited in Kimball, *The Juggler*, 363.

57. King and Whitehill, *Fleet Admiral King*, 436.

58. Morison, *Strategy and Compromise*, 83–84; for histories of the Pacific war, see Ronald Spector, *Eagle Against the Sun* (New York: Free Press, 1985); John Costello, *The Pacific War 1941–1945* (New York: HarperCollins, 1981); William M. Leary, ed., *We Shall Return!: MacArthur's Commanders and the Defeat of Japan 1942–1945* (Lexington: University of Kentucky Press, 1988); William B. Hopkins, *The Pacific War: The Strategy, Politics, and Players that Won the War* (Minneapolis: Zenith, 2008); Ian W. Toll, *Pacific Crucible: War at Sea in the Pacific, 1941–1942* (New York: Norton, 2012).

59. See John Gordon, *Fighting for MacArthur: The Navy and Marine Corps' Desperate Defense of the Philippines* (Annapolis, MD: Naval Institute Press, 2011).

60. Michael Schaller, *Douglas MacArthur: The Far Eastern General* (New York: Oxford, 1989), 73.

61. MacArthur quoted in William Manchester, *American Caesar* (New York: Little, Brown, 1978), 287–288.

62. E. B. Potter, *Nimitz* (Annapolis, MD: Naval Institute Press, 1976), 19.

63. Hayes, *The History of the Joint Chiefs of Staff in World War II*, 408–409.

64. Miller, *War Plan Orange*, 353.

65. Tsuyoshi Hasegawa, *Racing the Enemy: Stalin, Truman, and the Surrender of Japan* (Cambridge, MA: Harvard University Press, 2005), 27.

66. On the "long-legged" U.S. Navy, see Morison, *Strategy and Compromise*, 105. See also John T. Kuehn, *Agents of Innovation: The General Board and the Design of the Fleet That Defeated the Japanese Navy* (Annapolis, MD: Naval Institute Press, 2008).

67. Hopkins, *The Pacific War*, 177.

68. Hopkins, *The Pacific War*, 185–194.

69. King and Whitehill, *Fleet Admiral King*, 568.

70. Robert Ross Smith, "Luzon Versus Formosa," in *Command Decisions*, ed. Kent Roberts Greenfield (London: Harcourt Brace, 1960), 360–375; Hopkins, *The Pacific War*, 245; Hayes, *The History of the Joint Chiefs of Staff in World War II*, 603–624.

71. MacArthur quoted in Hasegawa, *Racing the Enemy*, 41.

72. Hasegawa, *Racing the Enemy*, 27–28.

73. Douglas J. MacEachin, *The Final Months of the War with Japan: Signals Intelligence, U.S. Invasion Planning, and the A-bomb Decision*, Central Intelligence Agency (declassification report), December 1998, 9–26.

74. Richard B. Frank, *Downfall: The End of the Japanese Imperial Empire* (New York: Random House, 1999), 293–294. Hasegawa argues that the atomic bombs and Soviet intervention were both critical to the Japanese surrender in August. Hasegawa, *Racing the Enemy*, 295.

75. Hal Friedman, "Arguing Over Empire: American Interservice and Interdepartmental Rivalry Over Micronesia, 1943-1947," *Journal of Pacific History* 29, no. 1 (June 1994): 41–42.

76. Friedman, "Arguing Over Empire," 37.

77. Leahy, *I Was There*, 314.

78. Leahy, *I Was There*, 314.

79. Michael Sherry, *Preparing for the Next War: American Plans for Postwar Defense, 1941–1945* (New Haven, CT: Yale University Press, 1977), 52–54.

80. Stoler, *Allies and Adversaries*, 140–141.

81. Stoler, *Allies and Adversaries*, 144.

82. Leahy, *I Was There*, 314. The internal American debate over the future sovereignty and military utility of Pacific territories was part and parcel of the broader debate among the Allies about the postwar status of European colonial possessions in the Far East, which is discussed later in the chapter.

83. John Paton Davies, *China Hand: An Autobiography* (Philadelphia: University of Pennsylvania Press, 2012), 151.

84. Forrestal testimony quoted in Davis, *FDR*, 159–160.

85. Proclamation Calling for the Surrender of Japan, Approved by the Heads of Government of the United States, China, and the United Kingdom, Potsdam, Germany, July 26, 1945, in U.S. Department of State, *Foreign Relations of the United States*, http://digicoll.library.wisc.edu/FRUS/Browse.html [hereafter cited as *FRUS*], *Diplomatic Papers, the Conference of Berlin (the Potsdam Conference), 1945, Vol. I*, 1474–1476.

86. Schaller, *Douglas MacArthur*, 108–110.

87. Halford J. Mackinder, "The Round World and the Winning of the Peace," *Foreign Affairs* 21, no. 4 (July 1943): 595–605.

88. Nicholas John Spykman, *America's Strategy in World Politics: The United States and the Balance of Power* (New Brunswick, NJ: Transaction, 2007), 155. Originally published by Harcourt, Brace, 1942.

89. Spykman, *America's Strategy in World Politics*, 398.

90. Spykman, *America's Strategy in World Politics*, 469–470.

91. Edgar S. Furniss, Jr., "The Contribution of Nicholas John Spykman to the Study of International Politics," *World Politics* 4, no. 3 (April 1952): 382.

92. Dallek, *Franklin D. Roosevelt and American Foreign Policy, 1932–1945*, 389–390.

93. Dallek, *Franklin D. Roosevelt and American Foreign Policy, 1932–1945*, 535–536.

94. Dallek, *Franklin D. Roosevelt and American Foreign Policy, 1932–1945*, 390.

95. Stoler, *Allies and Adversaries*, 112.

96. Ronald Heiferman, *Flying Tigers: Chennault in China*, reissue ed. (New York: Ballantine, 1978), 81.

97. Quangqiu Xu, "The Issue of U.S. Air Support for China During World War II: 1942–1945," *Journal of Contemporary History* 36, no. 3 (July 2001): 461.

98. John D. Plating, *The Hump: America's Strategy for Keeping China in World War II* (College Station: Texas A&M University Press, 2011), 5. See also Heiferman, *Flying Tigers*, 104.

99. Xu, "The Issue of U.S. Air Support for China During World War II: 1942–1945," 468.

100. Xu, "The Issue of U.S. Air Support for China During World War II: 1942–1945," 476.

101. Hebert Feis, *The China Tangle: The American Effort in China from Pearl Harbor to the Marshall Mission* (Princeton, NJ: Princeton University Press, 1953), 64.

102. Dallek, *Franklin D. Roosevelt and American Foreign Policy, 1932–1945*, 388–389.

103. Michael Schaller, *The U.S. Crusade in China, 1938–1945* (New York: Columbia University Press, 1979), 144.

104. Dallek, *Franklin D. Roosevelt and American Foreign Policy, 1932–1945*, 328–329.

105. Feis, *The China Tangle*, 62.

106. Hugh Borton, "Preparation for the Occupation of Japan," *Journal of Asian Studies* 25, no. 2 (February 1966): 203. For an in-depth look at the U.S. decision to return Taiwan to China, see Richard Bush, "The Wartime Decision to Return Taiwan to China," in *At Cross Purposes: U.S.-Taiwan Relations Since 1942* (London: M. E. Sharpe, 2004). See also "Joint Communique with Churchill and Chiang Kai-shek on the Cairo Conference," December 1, 1943.

107. "The First Cairo Conference: Proceedings of the Conference," *FRUS, The Conferences at Cairo and Tehran, 1943*, 312–315; Stoler, *Allies and Adversaries*, 166–167.

108. Willard Range, *Franklin D. Roosevelt's World Order* (Athens: University of Georgia Press, 1959), 178.

109. Hasegawa, *Racing the Enemy*, 23.

110. Stoler, *Allies and Adversaries*, 165–168; King and Whitehill, *Fleet Admiral King*, 525.

111. Paul D. Mayle, *Eureka Summit: Agreement in Principle and the Big Three at Tehran* (Newark: University of Delaware Press, 1987), 159.

112. Davies, *China Hand*, 151.

113. Davies, *China Hand*, 136.

114. Davies, *China Hand*, 140.

115. Davies, *China Hand*, 141.

116. For contrasting takes on Chiang, see, for example, Feis, *The Chinese Tangle*, versus Chin Tung-liang, *General Stilwell in China, 1942–1945: The Full Story* (New York: St. John's University Press, 1972).

117. In a September 1943 survey, 56 percent of respondents said there should be a "permanent military alliance" with China. See Gallup, *The Gallup Poll*, 1:411.

118. Schaller, *The U.S. Crusade in China, 1938–1945*, 154.

119. Dallek, *Franklin D. Roosevelt and American Foreign Policy, 1932–1945*, 523.

120. Schaller, *The U.S. Crusade in China, 1938–1945*, 140–141.

121. William P. Head, *Yenan!: Colonel Wilbur Peterkin and the American Military Mission to the Chinese Communists, 1944–1945* (Chapel Hill, NC: Documentary Publications, 1987), 101. For more on Service's arguments for moving to the CCP, see John S. Service, *The*

Amerasia Papers (Berkeley: University of California Press, 1971); Joseph W. Esherick, ed., *Lost Chance in China: The World War II Despatches of John S. Service* (New York: Random House, 1974).

122. Russel D. Buhite, *Patrick J. Hurley and American Foreign Policy* (Ithaca, NY: Cornell University Press, 1973), 160–162; Robert Dallek, *The Lost Peace: Leadership in a Time of Horror and Hope, 1945–1953* (New York: HarperCollins, 2010), 144; Schaller, *The U.S. Crusade in China, 1938–1945*, 147–200.

123. See, for example, "The Acting Secretary of State to Ambassador Hurley," January 25, 1945, *FRUS, Diplomatic Papers, 1945, The Far East, China*, 181.

124. Edward R. Stettinius, Jr., *Roosevelt and the Russians: The Yalta Conference* (Garden City, NY: Doubleday, 1949), 87; Dallek, *Franklin D. Roosevelt and American Foreign Policy, 1932–1945*, 501.

125. Communiqué on the Crimea Conference of the Heads of Government of the Soviet Union, the United States and Great Britain, February 11, 1945.

126. Roosevelt had promised this to Stalin in January 1944. See Hasegawa, *Racing the Enemy*, 23.

127. John Lewis Gaddis, *The United States and the Origins of the Cold War* (New York: Columbia University Press, 2000), 214; Dallek, *The Lost Peace*, 93–94; Forrest C. Pogue, "Yalta in Retrospect," in *The Meaning of Yalta: Big Three Diplomacy and the New Balance of Power*, ed. John L. Snell (Baton Rouge: Louisiana State University Press, 1956), 197.

128. Warren I. Cohen, *America's Response to China: An Interpretive History of Sino-American Relations*, 5th ed. (New York: Columbia University Press, 2010), 163; Harry S. Truman, *Memoir*, vol. 1, *Year of Decisions* (Garden City, NY: Doubleday, 1955), 269–270, 315–320.

129. Pogue, "Yalta in Retrospect," 94.

130. Cohen, *America's Response to China*, 163.

131. Dallek, *Franklin D. Roosevelt and American Foreign Policy, 1932–1945*, 501.

132. State-War-Navy Coordinating Committee Memo 83/1, April 3, 1945, *FRUS, Diplomatic Papers, 1945, Relations in the Far East, China*, 74. For the full document, see United States Post-War Military Policies with Respect to China, U.S. State Department, April 3, 1945, NARAII, RG 353, State-War-Navy Coordinating Committee Subcommittee on the Far East, Entry 518, Box 112.

133. SWNCC 83/1, U.S. Policies Toward China, Summary of Actions and Decisions, Part II, May 28, 1945, NARAII, RG 353, State-War-Navy Coordinating Committee General Secretariat Records, Entry 500, Box 3, Part II, p. 164.

134. Plating, *The Hump*, 245–246.

135. James McHugh, U.S. naval attaché in Chongqing, had written a memo on October 5, 1942, predicting that increased assistance over "the hump" would probably not convince Chiang to go on the offensive but arguing that aid was still critical to cement postwar relations with the Chinese. The memo was read by Knox, King, Stimson, Marshall, and the president himself. See Plating, *The Hump*, 91.

136. Schaller, *The U.S. Crusade in China, 1938–1945*, 100.

137. Head, 163.

138. The dominant view among China scholars in the West was that the United States lost an opportunity for nonideological rapprochement with the CCP during the war, but

scholarship over the past decade has trended more in the direction of arguing (based on CCP archives, among other sources) that there was no real "lost opportunity" in China after all. For examples of the argument that although the CCP was sincere in its communist ideology, it was also searching for American support and therefore at least a short-term alignment may have been possible, see Steven Levine, "Chinese Communist Policy Toward the United States: Opportunities and Constraints, 1944–1950," in *Uncertain Years: Chinese-American Relations, 1947–1950,* ed. Dorothy Borg and Waldo Heinrichs (New York: Columbia University Press, 1980), 235–278; Steven Goldstein, "Sino-American Relations, 1948–1950: Lost Chance or No Chance?" in *Sino-American Relations, 1945–1955,* ed. Harry Harding and Yuan Ming (Wilmington, DE: Scholarly Resources, 1989), 119–142. Steven Levine refers to Goldstein's interpretation as the "ideological approach" and Hunt's as the "situational approach." See Borg and Heinrichs, *Uncertain Years,* 179–180. For the argument that once the CCP's victory was assured, Sino-U.S. cooperation was doomed because of ideological differences, see Tang Tsou, *America's Failure in China, 1941–1950* (Chicago: University of Chicago Press, 1963); Anthony Kubek, *How the Far East Was Lost, American Policy and the Creation of Communist China, 1941–1949,* ed. George W. Dearmond (Chicago: Henry Regnery, 1963); Jingbin Wang, "No Lost Chance in China: The False Realism of American Foreign Service Officers, 1943–1945," *Journal of American–East Asian Relations* 17 (2010): 118–145; Michael M. Sheng, "America's Lost Chance in China? A Reappraisal of Chinese Communist Policy Toward the United States Before 1945," *Australian Journal of Chinese Affairs,* no. 29 (January 1993): 135–157; Richard Bernstein, *China 1945: Mao's Revolution and America's Fateful Choice* (New York: Knopf, 2014), 391.

139. Davies, *China Hand,* 232.

140. Barbara W. Tuchman, *Stilwell and the American Experience in China, 1911–1945* (New York: MacMillan, 1971). See also Rana Mitter, *Forgotten Ally: China's World War II, 1937–1945* (New York: Houghton Mifflin Harcourt, 2013); Jay Taylor, *The Generalissimo: Chiang Kai-shek and the Struggle for Modern China* (Cambridge, MA: Belknap, 2011).

141. Mitter, *Forgotten Ally,* 369.

142. This argument is well presented in Bernstein, *China 1945,* 21, 192–193, 396.

143. Kennan to Secretary of State, April 16, 1945, cited in Davies, *China Hand,* 253.

144. Hasegawa, *Racing the Enemy,* 19.

145. John Gordon, *Fighting for MacArthur: The Navy and Marine Corps' Desperate Defense of the Philippines* (Annapolis, MD: Naval Institute Press, 2011), 78.

146. Ernest R. May, "The United States, the Soviet Union, and the Far Eastern War, 1941–1945," *Pacific Historical Review* 24, no. 2 (May 1955): 153–154.

147. May, "The United States, the Soviet Union, and the Far Eastern War, 1941–1945," 158.

148. May, "The United States, the Soviet Union, and the Far Eastern War, 1941–1945," 160.

149. King and Whitehill, *Fleet Admiral King,* 542.

150. Memorandum by the Joint Chiefs of Staff, January 23, 1945, quoted in May, "The United States, the Soviet Union, and the Far Eastern War, 1941–1945," 162.

151. Wilson D. Miscamble, *From Roosevelt to Truman: Potsdam, Hiroshima, and the Cold War* (New York: Cambridge University Press, 2007), 52.

152. Address to Congress on the Yalta Conference by Franklin D. Roosevelt, March 1, 1945, http://www.presidency.ucsb.edu/ws/index.php?pid=16591&st=%5C%22spheres+of +influence%5C%22&st1=#axzz1rBMoIuIu.

153. McGeorge Bundy, "The Test of Yalta," *Foreign Affairs* 27, no. 4 (July 1949): 621.

154. Dallek, *Franklin D. Roosevelt and American Foreign Policy, 1932–1945*, 533.

155. Lippmann, *U.S. Foreign Policy*, 143–146.

156. Kimball, *The Juggler*, 83. See also Gaddis, *The United States and the Origins of the Cold War, 1941–1947*, 63–65.

157. Gaddis, *The United States and the Origins of the Cold War, 1941–1947*, 51, 201.

158. Herring, *From Colony to Superpower*, 591.

159. "U.S. Position with Regard to General Soviet Intentions for Expansion," July 6, 1945, file ABC 092 USSR (15 Nov 44), RG 165, NA, quoted in Marc Gallicchio, "The Kuriles Controversy: U.S. Diplomacy in the Soviet-Japan Border Dispute, 1941–1956," *Pacific Historical Review* 60, no. 1 (February 1991): 80.

160. Gallicchio, "The Kuriles Controversy," 76–77.

161. Roberts, *Masters and Commanders*, 548.

162. Gaddis, *The United States and the Origins of the Cold War, 1941–1947*, 202–203.

163. King and Whitehill, *Fleet Admiral King*, 591.

164. Memorandum from the Acting Secretary of State to the Secretary of War, included in Joseph Grew, *Turbulent Era: A Diplomatic Record of Forty Years, 1904–1945* (Boston: Houghton Mifflin, 1952), 2:1455.

165. Leahy, *I Was There*, 319.

166. Stoler, *Allies and Adversaries*, 259–261.

167. Truman, *Memoir*, 75–76; Gaddis, *The United States and the Origins of the Cold War, 1941–1947*, 215.

168. Sherry, *Preparing for the Next War*, 186.

169. Gaddis, *The United States and the Origins of the Cold War, 1941–1947*, 214.

170. Martin J. Sherwin, *A World Destroyed: The Atomic Bomb and the Grand Alliance* (New York: Knopf, 1977), 224.

171. Hasegawa, *Racing the Enemy*, 154–165.

172. Truman, *Memoir*, 441.

173. See, for example, Address in San Francisco at the Closing Session of the United Nations Conference by Harry S. Truman, June 26, 1945, http://www.presidency.ucsb.edu/ws/index.php?pid=12188&st=united+nations&st1=#axzz1rBMoIuIu.

174. Gallup, *The Gallup Poll*, 1:591.

175. Frank, *Downfall*, 293–294. Hasegawa argues that the Soviet intervention was also critical. See Hasegawa, *Racing the Enemy*, 295.

176. See Hugh Borton, *Japan Since 1931, Its Political and Social Developments* (New York: International Secretariat Institute of Pacific Relations, 1940); Hugh Borton, *Peasant Uprising in Japan of the Tokugawa Period* (New York: Paragon Book Reprint Corporation, 1968).

177. Hugh Borton, "Preparation for the Occupation of Japan," *Journal of Asian Studies* 25, no. 2 (February 1966): 205.

178. Grew, *Turbulent Era*, 2:1406–1417; Rudolph V. A. Jansens, *What Future for Japan? U.S. Wartime Planning for the Post-War Era, 1942–1945* (Amsterdam: Editions Rodopi, 1995), 72–74; Hasegawa, *Racing the Enemy*, 22; Judith Munro-Leighton, "The Tokyo Surrender: A Diplomatic Marathon in Washington, August 10–14, 1945," *Pacific Historical Review* 65, no. 3 (August 1996): 458.

179. Munro-Leighton, "The Tokyo Surrender," 459.

180. Schaller, *Douglas MacArthur*, 111.

181. "Politico-Military Problems in the Far East: United States Initial Post-Defeat Policy Related to Japan," SWNCC 150/4, September 6, 1945, from the Archives of the Diet Library of Japan.

182. Hoopes and Brinkley, *Driven Patriot*, 208.

183. Ciamporcero, "The State-War-Navy Coordinating Committee and the Beginning of the Cold War," 80–82.

184. Michael Schaller, *The American Occupation of Japan: The Origins of the Cold War in Asia* (Oxford: Oxford University Press, 1985), 16.

185. Gallup, *The Gallup Poll*, 1:513.

186. James F. Byrnes, Reply to Japan's First Surrender Offer, August 11, 1945, Japan's Surrender Communiqués, http://en.wikisource.org/wiki/Japan%27s_Surrender_Communiqu%C3%A9s.

187. Leahy, *I Was There*, 435.

188. Schaller, *The U.S. Crusade in China, 1938–1945*, 258–260.

189. State-War-Navy-Coordinating-Committee Directive on Positive Policy for Reorientation of the Japanese, July 19, 1945, NARAII, Record of the War Department General and Special Staffs, Military Intelligence Division, "S-C Intelligence Reference Pubs. ("P" File)," RG 165, Box 2176, ARC ID 1557240, NM-84 Entry 79.

190. Munro-Leighton, "The Tokyo Surrender," 460, 464.

191. Stephen E. Ambrose, *Rise to Globalism: American Foreign Policy, 1936–1980*, 2nd ed. (New York: Penguin, 1980), 76.

192. Franklin D. Roosevelt, "Our Foreign Policy: A Democratic View," *Foreign Affairs* 6, no. 4 (July 1928), 573–586.

193. Range, *Franklin D. Roosevelt's World Order*, 109.

194. *U.S. Department of State Bulletin* 6 (May 30, 1942): 488, quoted in Gary R. Hess, "Franklin Roosevelt and Indochina," *Journal of American History* 59, no. 2 (September 1972): 50.

195. Foster Rhea Dulles and Gerald D. Ridinger, "The Anti-colonial Policies of Franklin D. Roosevelt," *Political Science Quarterly* 70, no. 1 (March 1955): 6.

196. Dulles and Ridinger, "The Anti-colonial Policies of Franklin D. Roosevelt," 8.

197. John J. Sbrega, "'First Catch Your Hare': Anglo-American Perspectives on Indochina During the Second World War," *Journal of Southeast Asian Studies* 14, no. 1 (March 1983): 68.

198. Herring, *From Colony to Superpower*, 571.

199. Kimball, *The Juggler*, 129.

200. Minutes cited in Gerloff D. Horman, "The United States and the Netherlands East Indies: The Evolution of American Anti-colonialism," *Pacific Historical Review* 53, no. 4 (November 1984): 440.

201. Hess, "Franklin Roosevelt and Indochina," 63–65.

202. Stoler, *Allies and Adversaries*, 112.

203. Frances Gouda, *American Visions of the Netherlands/East Indies/Indonesia: U.S. Foreign Policy and Indonesian Nationalism, 1920–1949* (Amsterdam: University of Amsterdam Press, 2002), 110.

204. Hull to Roosevelt, September 8, 1944, quoted in Hess, "Franklin Roosevelt and Indochina," 107–109.

205. Auriol Weigold, *Churchill, Roosevelt and India: Propaganda During World War II* (New York: Routledge, 2010), 27–28.

206. Dallek, *Franklin D. Roosevelt and American Foreign Policy, 1932–1945*, 319.

207. Winston Churchill, *The Hinge of Fate: The Second World War, Vol. IV* (Boston: Houghton Mifflin, 1950), 213–219, cited in Dulles and Ridinger, "The Anti-colonial Policies of Franklin D. Roosevelt," 7.

208. R-132, Roosevelt to Churchill, April 11, 1942, in Kimball, *The Juggler*, 446.

209. Kenton J. Clymer, *Quest for Freedom: The United States and India's Independence* (New York: Columbia University Press, 1995), 128–166.

210. Dulles and Ridinger, "The Anti-colonial Policies of Franklin D. Roosevelt," 16.

211. Christopher Thorne, "Indochina and Anglo-American Relations, 1942–1945," *Pacific Historical Review* 45, no. 1 (February 1976): 79.

212. Hess, "Franklin Roosevelt and Indochina," 72–76.

213. Stoler, *Allies and Adversaries*, 224.

214. Dulles and Ridinger, "The Anti-colonial Policies of Franklin D. Roosevelt," 14.

215. Roosevelt to Hull, January 24, 1944, *FRUS, Cairo and Tehran 1943*, 872–873, quoted in Hess, "Franklin Roosevelt and Indochina," 360.

216. "Suggested Reexamination of American Policy with Respect to Indo-China," SWNCC, May 1, 1945, NARAII, RG 353, State-War-Navy Coordination Committee Subcommittee on the Far East, Entry 518, Box 112.

217. Hakjoon Kim, "The American Military Government in South Korea, 1945–1948: Its Formation, Policies, and Legacies," *Asian Perspective* 12, no. 1 (Spring–Summer 1988): 51–83.

218. Munro-Leighton, "The Tokyo Surrender," 464.

219. Herring, *From Colony to Superpower*, 560.

220. Davies, *China Hand*, 139.

221. The Atlantic Charter, August 14, 1941.

222. Alfred E. Eckes, Jr., *A Search for Solvency: Bretton Woods and the International Monetary System 1941–1971* (Austin: University of Texas Press, 1975), 57.

223. See William Appleman Williams, *The Tragedy of American Diplomacy* (New York: Norton, 1962); Walter LaFeber, *America, Russia and the Cold War, 1945–1966* (New York: Wiley, 1967).

224. Herring, *From Colony to Superpower*, 580.

225. "Summary of the Interim Report of the Special Committee on the Relaxation of Trade Barriers, December 8, 1943," cited in Gaddis, *The United States and the Origins of the Cold War*, 22.

226. G. John Ikenberry, "The Political Origins of Bretton Woods," in *A Retrospective on the Bretton Woods System: Lessons for International Monetary Reform*, ed. Michael D. Bordo and Barry Eichengreen (Chicago: University of Chicago Press, 1993), 170.

227. Roger Bell, "Testing the Open Door Thesis, Australia 1941–1946," *Pacific Historical Review* 51, no. 3 (August 1984): 288–290.

228. "Assistant Secretary of State Berle to Treasury Secretary Morgenthau," March 2, 1943, *FRUS, Diplomatic Papers, 1943, Vol. I*, 1058.

229. Kimball, *The Juggler*, 189.

230. "Discussions Concerning Post-War Trade Policies" (Briefing Book Paper, Yalta Conference), *FRUS, Conferences at Malta and Yalta, 1945*, 325–327. See also Richard N. Gardner, *Sterling-Dollar Diplomacy: Anglo-American Collaboration in the Reconstruction of Multilateral Trade* (London: Oxford University Press, 1956), 23.

231. David Roll, *The Hopkins Touch: Harry Hopkins and the Forging of the Alliance to Defeat Hitler* (Oxford: Oxford University Press, 2013), 144.

232. Kate L. Mitchell, "India and American Prosperity," *Far Eastern Survey* 14, no. 11 (June 6, 1945): 137.

233. Walter LaFeber, "Roosevelt, Churchill, and Indochina: 1942–1945," *American Historical Review* 80, no. 5 (December 1975): 1294.

234. Randall Bennett Woods, *A Changing of the Guard: Anglo-American Relations, 1941–1946* (Chapel Hill: University of North Carolina Press, 1990), 115.

235. For additional reading on the budding U.S.-led postwar financial and economic structure, see Robert A. Pollard, *Economic Security and the Origins of the Cold War, 1945–1950* (New York: Columbia University Press, 1985); Richard N. Gardner, *Sterling-Dollar Diplomacy*; Eckes, *A Search for Solvency*.

236. Gardner, *Sterling-Dollar Diplomacy*, 143.

237. Bernstein, *China 1945*, 21.

238. Frank, *Downfall*, 136.

239. Leahy, *I Was There*, 432.

Part 3

1. Walter Isaacson and Evan Thomas, *The Wise Men: Six Friends and the World They Made: Acheson, Bohlen, Harriman, Kennan, Lovett, McCloy* (London: Faber and Faber, 1986), 698–703; Clark Clifford with Richard Holbrooke, *Counsel to the President* (New York: Random House, 1991), 512–514; Larry Berman, *Lyndon Johnson's War: The Road to Stalemate in Vietnam* (New York: Norton, 1989), 194; George W. Ball, *The Past Has Another Pattern: Memoirs* (New York: Norton, 1982), 408; "Summary of Notes from Meeting with 'Wise Men,'" March 26, 1968, in U.S. Department of State, *Foreign Relations of the United States, 1964–1968, Vol. VI: Vietnam, January–August, 1968*, 471–474, http://digicoll.library.wisc.edu/FRUS/Browse.html.

7. Defining Containment in the Pacific, 1945–1960

1. Townsend Hoopes, *The Devil and John Foster Dulles* (Boston: Little, Brown, 1973).

2. Harry S. Truman, *Dear Bess: The Letters from Harry to Bess Truman, 1910–1959*, ed. Robert H. Ferrell (Columbia: University of Missouri Press, 1998), 39.

3. John Lewis Gaddis, *The Cold War: A New History* (New York: Penguin, 2001), 54.

4. Waldo Heinrichs, "Roosevelt and Truman: The Presidential Perspective," in *Uncertain Years: Chinese-American Relations, 1947–1950*, ed. Dorothy Borg and Waldo Heinrichs (New York: Columbia University Press, 1980), 4.

5. Michael J. Hogan, *A Cross of Iron: Harry S. Truman and the Origins of the National Security State: 1945–1954* (Cambridge: Cambridge University Press, 1998), 5–21.

6. That earlier experience prompted Marshall in January 1947, as he transitioned to the job of secretary, to deliver an impolitic speech condemning both Chiang's Nationalists and Mao's Communists for their intransigence. See "The Situation in China," Statement of General of the Army George C. Marshall, released January 7, 1947, Bulletin, January 19, 1947, 83–85. Marshall's restraint on China was praised by many, though his top commander in China during the war, General Albert Wedemeyer, considered Marshall deficient in his understanding of the geopolitics of the region. See Ed Cray, *General of the Army: George C. Marshall, Soldier and Statesman* (New York: Rowman and Littlefield, 1990), xii.

7. Robert J. McMahon, *Dean Acheson and the Creation of an American World Order* (Washington, DC: Potomac, 2009), 21, 58, 65.

8. Warren I. Cohen, "Acheson, His Advisors, and China, 1949–1950," in Borg and Heinrichs, *Uncertain Years*, 16–17.

9. McMahon, *Dean Acheson*, 129.

10. McMahon, *Dean Acheson*, 39.

11. Vincent outlined his views of Asia in a public speech at Wellesley College in 1947. See John Carter Vincent, "Our Far Eastern Policies in Relation to Our Overall National Objectives," in *America's Future in the Pacific: Lectures Delivered at the Second Quadrennial Institute, Mayling Soong Foundation, Wellesley College* (New Brunswick, NJ: Rutgers University Press, 1947), 5–6. For more on Vincent, see Gary May, *China Scapegoat: The Diplomatic Ordeal of John Carter Vincent* (Washington, DC: New Republic Books, 1979). On the switch from Grew to Acheson, see Marc Gallicchio, *The Scramble for Asia: U.S. Military Power in the Aftermath of the Pacific War* (Lanham, MD: Rowman and Littlefield, 2008), 71–72.

12. Following Rusk's appointment, John Foster Dulles told Wellington Koo on June 2, 1950, "there was recently a better attitude on the part of the State Department toward Formosa" and "there was some possibility of reconsidering the question of military aid." Quoted in Yuan Ming, "The Failure of Perception: America's China Policy, 1949–50," in *Sino-American Relations, 1945–1955: A Joint Reassessment of a Critical Decade*, ed. Harry Harding and Yuan Ming (Wilmington, DE: Scholarly Resources, 1989), 148. See also Thomas W. Zeiler, *Dean Rusk: Defending the American Mission Abroad* (Wilmington, DE: Scholarly Resources, 2000), 1–25; Cohen, "Acheson, His Advisors, and China, 1949–1950," 31.

13. X, "The Sources of Soviet Conduct," *Foreign Affairs* 25, no. 4 (1947): 566–582; John Lewis Gaddis, *Strategies of Containment* (New York: Oxford University Press, 1982), 18–21. Warren Cohen argues that Acheson was not initially taken with Kennan's long telegram from Moscow in 1946 and relied less on the suggestions of Policy Planning Staff (PPS) than Marshall had, although he did listen to Kennan and John P. Davies at key moments. See Cohen, "Acheson, His Advisors, and China, 1949–1950," 15–16.

14. Gaddis, *Strategies of Containment*, 24.

15. John Lewis Gaddis, *George F. Kennan: An American Life*, reprint ed. (New York: Penguin Books, 2012), 299.

16. Gaddis, *Strategies of Containment*, 56.

17. George Kennan to John Van Antwerp MacMurray, December 19, 1950, quoted in Paul James Heer, "George F. Kennan and US Foreign Policy in East Asia" (PhD diss., The George Washington University, 1995), 7–8.

18. George F. Kennan, *Memoirs, 1925–1950* (New York: Pantheon, 1987), 239. Originally published by Atlantic-Little Brown, 1967.

19. In his autobiography, Davies quotes from his own August 1948 draft of a Policy Planning staff position paper: "Until China develops a modern transportation network in its vast hinterland it will, excepting for its coastal fringe, more closely resemble a strategic morass than a strategic springboard." See John Paton Davies Jr., *China Hand: An Autobiography* (Philadelphia: University of Pennsylvania Press, 2012), 303. The draft became Policy Planning staff paper 39 and later NSC 34. A few months later, Acheson used the phrase at a March 18, 1949, executive session of the Senate Foreign Relations Committee: "I doubt very much whether China is a great strategic springboard for the Communists . . . it might 'turn out to be a strategic morass,'" Acheson quoted in McMahon, *Dean Acheson*, 99.

20. McMahon, *Dean Acheson*, 65.

21. Walter Millis, ed., *The Forrestal Diaries* (New York: Viking Press, 1951), 173–180; cited in Melvyn P. Leffler, *A Preponderance of Power: National Security, the Truman Administration, and the Cold War* (Palo Alto, CA: Stanford University Press, 1992), 129.

22. Townsend Hoopes and Douglas Brinkley, *Driven Patriot: The Life and Times of James Forrestal* (Annapolis, MD: Naval Institute Press, 1992), chap. 32.

23. David Halberstam, *The Best and the Brightest* (New York: Modern Library, 2002), 83, 339–340.

24. Henry Kissinger, *The Necessity for Choice* (Westport, CT: Greenwood, 1960), 1.

25. Gaddis, *Strategies of Containment*, 23.

26. Ronald H. Spector, *In the Ruins of Empire: The Japanese Surrender and the Battle for Postwar Asia* (New York: Random House, 2007), xi.

27. Warren Cohen, *America's Response to China*, 5th ed. (New York: Columbia University Press, 2010), 164.

28. Memorandum by Mr. Edwin A. Locke, Jr., Personal Representative of President Truman in Charge of the American Production Mission in China, to President Truman, August 20, 1945, in U.S. Department of State, *Foreign Relations of the United States*, http://digicoll.library.wisc.edu/FRUS/Browse.html [hereafter cited as *FRUS*], *1945, Vol. V: The Far East: China*, 448–451.

29. Marine officer cited in Marc Gallicchio, *The Scramble for Asia*, 89. See also Marc Gallicchio, *The Cold War Begins in Asia: American East Asian Policy and the Fall of the Japanese Empire* (New York: Columbia University Press, 1988), 95–97; May, *China Scapegoat*, 132.

30. Forrestal, *Diaries*, 173–180, cited in Leffler, *A Preponderance of Power*, 129.

31. Cray, *General of the Army*, 555–557.

32. Richard Bernstein, *China 1945: Mao's Revolution and America's Fateful Choice* (New York: Knopf, 2014), 341, 351–352.

33. May, *China Scapegoat*, 141–142; He Di, "The Evolution of the Chinese Communist Party's Policy Toward the United States, 1944–1949," in Harding and Ming, *Sino-American Relations, 1945–1955*, 38; Cohen, *America's Response to China*, 168–169.

34. Statement by President Truman: United States Policy Toward China, December 15, 1945, http://www.presidency.ucsb.edu/ws/index.php?pid=12261&st=china&st1=#axzziz69 GjZkw.

35. Lloyd E. Eastman, *Seeds of Destruction: Nationalist China in War and Revolution* (Stanford, CA: Stanford University Press, 1984), 223–224.

36. Lloyd E. Eastman, *The Nationalist Era in China, 1927–1949* (New York: Cambridge University Press, 1991), 304; Odd Arne Westad, *Decisive Encounters: The Chinese Civil War, 1946–1950* (Stanford, CA: Stanford University Press, 2003), 49.

37. Minutes of Meeting of the Secretaries of State, War, and Navy, Military Aid to China: Chinese Requests for Ammunition and Military Matériel and Equipment; Lifting of Embargo on Arms Shipments to China; Attempts to Speed Flow of Supplies to China, February 12, 1947, *FRUS, 1947, Vol. VII: The Far East: China*, 795–797. See also Hoopes and Brinkley, *Driven Patriot*, 305.

38. Memorandum by the Joint Chiefs of Staff to the State-War-Navy Coordinating Committee, June 9, 1947, *FRUS, 1947, Vol. VII: The Far East: China*, 841–842.

39. Memorandum by the Director of the Office of Far Eastern Affairs (Vincent) to the Secretary of State, February 7, 1947, *FRUS, 1947, Vol. VII: The Far East: China*, 789–793.

40. May, *China Scapegoat*, 154.

41. May, *China Scapegoat*, 154.

42. The Director of Far Eastern Affairs (Vincent) to the Secretary of State, February 7, 1947, in *FRUS, 1947, Vol. VII: The Far East: China*, 789–793.

43. Thomas J. Christensen, *Useful Adversaries: Grand Strategy, Domestic Mobilization, and Sino-American Conflict, 1947–1958* (Princeton, NJ: Princeton University Press, 1996). See also Tang Tsou, *America's Failure in China, 1941–1950* (Chicago: University of Chicago Press, 1963).

44. Leffler, *Preponderance of Power*, 128, 130.

45. Harry S. Truman, Directive to General Wedemeyer, July 9, 1947, *FRUS, 1947, Vol. VII: The Far East: China, Mission to China of Lieutenant General Albert C. Wedemeyer to Appraise the Political, Economic, Psychological, and Military Situation*, 640–641.

46. Wedemeyer, quoted in William Stueck, *The Wedemeyer Mission: American Politics and Foreign Policy During the Cold War* (Athens: The University Press of Georgia, 1984), 17.

47. Albert Wedemeyer, Report to the President, 1947, 19 September 1947; the report to the president is attached as an appendix to Albert C. Wedemeyer, *Wedemeyer Reports!* (New York: Henry Holt, 1958).

48. Vincent summarized the State versus JCS views in his own memo to Marshall in Vincent to Marshall, June 20, 1947, *FRUS, 1947, Vol. VII: The Far East: China*, 849. See also Waldo Heinrichs, "U.S. China Policy and Cold War in Asia," in Borg and Heinrichs, *Uncertain Years*, 288.

49. Cohen, "Acheson, His Advisors, and China, 1949–1950," 15.

50. United States Department of State, *The China White Paper* (Stanford, CA: Stanford University Press, 1967), 269–271.

51. Richard C. Thornton, *China: A Political History, 1917-1980* (Boulder, CO: Westview, 1982), 206; James Reardon-Anderson, *Yenan and the Great Powers: The Origins of Chinese Communist Foreign Policy, 1944-1946* (New York: Columbia University Press, 1980); Stephen Levine, *Anvil of Victory: The Communist Revolution in Manchuria, 1945-1948* (New York: Columbia University Press, 1987).

52. Freda Utley, *The China Story* (Chicago: Henry Regnery, 1951), 35. Utley puts killed and wounded at 1,233,600 between 1946 and 1949.

53. ORE 45-48: The Current Situation in China, July 22, 1948, in John K. Allen, Jr., John Carver, and Tom Elmore, eds., *Tracking the Dragon: National Intelligence Estimates on China During the Era of Mao, 1948-1976* (Washington, DC: National Intelligence Council, 2004), 4-5.

54. Marshall, quoted in Department of State, *The China White Paper*, 280.

55. PPS Memorandum, September 7, 1948, *FRUS, Vol. VIII: The Far East: China*, 146-165.

56. NSC 34/1, "United States Policy Toward China," January 11, 1949, *FRUS, 1949, Vol. IX: The Far East: China*, 475. The strategy was elaborated in NSC 48/2: The Position of the United States with Respect to Asia, December 30, 1949, *FRUS, Vol. VII: The Far East and Australasia, part 2*, 1215.

57. Department of State, *United States Relations with China with Special Reference to the Period 1944-1949*, Department of State Publication 3573, Washington, 1949, cited in Dean Acheson, *Present at the Creation* (New York: Norton, 1969), 302-303. The idea of the white paper, first suggested by Kennan, and proposed by Marshall in November 1948, had been rejected by Truman because he believed "to reveal Chiang's ineptness and the corruption of his regime would be tantamount to the United States delivering the final blow." However, in August 1949, Truman "agreed [with Acheson] that the time had come." Secretary of Defense Louis Johnson and the JCS objected. But the white paper was published anyway, perhaps because of "awareness of the ties between Chiang's lobbyists and Republican critics." See Cohen, "Acheson, His Advisors, and China, 1949-1950," 24-25.

58. Nancy Bernkopf Tucker, *China Confidential: American Diplomats and Sino-American Relations, 1945-1996* (New York: Columbia University Press, 2001), 61-63.

59. William Inboden, *Religion and American Foreign Policy, 1945-1960: The Soul of Containment* (New York: Cambridge University Press, 2009), 157-226; Andrew Preston, *Sword of Spirit, Shield of Faith* (New York: Anchor, 2012), 477.

60. For definitive scholarship on the sources of Chiang's defeat, see Suzanne Pepper, "The KMT-CCP Conflict," in *The Cambridge History of China*, vol. 12, *Republican China 1912-1949, Part 2*, ed. John K. Fairbank and Albert Feuerwerker (Cambridge: Cambridge University Press, 1986), chap. 11, 723-788; Lloyd E. Eastman, "Nationalist China During the Sino-Japanese War 1937-1945," in Fairbank and Feuerwerker, *The Cambridge History of China*, vol. 12, chap. 11, 547-608.

61. Levine, *Anvil of Victory*, 7.

62. Department of State, *The China White Paper*, 351-352.

63. See, for example, Alexander V. Pantsov and Steven I. Levine, *Mao: The Real Story* (New York: Simon and Schuster, 2012). See also Zhu Feng (储峰), "A Review on the Sino-Soviet Military Relation, Party-to-Party Relation and State-to-State Relation in the 1950s (20世纪50年代中苏军事关系与中苏两党两国关系述评)," paper presented at the Second Conference on the History and Reality of Sino-Russia Relations, Beijing, PRC, April

2008; Yang Kuisong (杨奎松), "Soviet Military Assistances in Chinese Civil War (关于解放战争中的苏联军事援助问题——兼谈治学态度并答刘统先生)," *Modern Chinese History Studies* (近代史研究) 23, no. 1 (January 2001): 285–306.

64. See, for example, John W. Garver, "Little Chance," *Diplomatic History* 21, no. 1 (1997): 87–94 at 87; Chen Jian, "The Myth of America's 'Lost Chance' in China: A Chinese Perspective in Light of New Evidence," *Diplomatic History* 21, no. 1 (1997): 77–86 at 77; Douglas Macdonald, "Communist Bloc Expansion in the Early Cold War: Challenging Realism, Refuting Revisionism," *International Security* 20, no. 3 (Winter 1995–1996): 152–188; Doak Barnett, *China and the Major Powers in East Asia* (Washington, DC: Brookings Institution, 1977), 178–179. For the case that accommodation was possible only if the Truman administration had accepted major concessions, see Odd Arne Westad, "Losses, Chances, and Myths: The United States and the Creation of the Sino-Soviet Alliance, 1945–1950," *Diplomatic History* 21, no. 1 (1997): 105–115 at 107.

65. Wooseon Choi, "Structure and Perceptions: Explaining American Policy Toward China (1949–50)," *Security Studies* 16, no. 4 (October–December 2007): 555–582.

66. Kennan to Byrnes, January 10, 1946, *FRUS, 1946, Vol. IX: The Far East: China*, 116–119.

67. ORE 45-49: "Probable Developments in China," June 16, 1949, in Allen, Carver, and Elmore, *Tracking the Dragon*, 50.

68. Leonard Gross, "John Paton Davies, Jr.: Quiet End to a Shabby Era," *Look*, March 4, 1969, 82. In his autobiography, Davies is frank about his false assumptions. "My estimate of the redness of the Chinese Communists was affected by my assumption that belief in a creed is susceptible to withering, decay and perversion. The Chinese Communists were backsliders, I said, and would return to revolutionary ardor only if driven to it by domestic or foreign pressure. In this paper I obviously underestimated the commitment of the Chinese Communist ruling party at that time to ideology and the dexterity with which Mao and company manipulated it." See Davies, *China Hand*, 224. He added that, "In retrospect, the idea of politically capturing the Chinese Communists was unrealistic. It reflected my underestimation of the Communists' commitment to ideology." See Davies, *China Hand*, 232.

69. John Lewis Gaddis, "The American 'Wedge' Strategy, 1949–1955," in Harding and Ming, *Sino-American Relations, 1945–1955*, 159.

70. ORE 45-49: "Probable Developments in China," June 16, 1949, 46–47. A subsequent National Intelligence Estimate concluded that the emergence of a Chinese Communist-controlled regime, under Soviet influence if not under Soviet control, "would result in an extensive loss of US prestige and increased Communist influence throughout the Far East, as well as an intensification of threat to US interests in the Western Pacific area." See ORE 45-48: "The Current Situation in China," July 22, 1948.

71. Senators H. Alexander Smith and William F. Knowland, as quoted in Yuan Ming, "The Failure of Perception: America's China Policy, 1949–50," in Harding and Ming, *Sino-American Relations, 1945–1955*, 148.

72. Kennan Memo on PPS 53, "United States Policy Toward Formosa and Pescadores," July 6, 1949, *FRUS, 1949, Vol. IX: The Far East: China*, 356–359.

73. Choi, "Structure and Perceptions," 574. On arguments for protecting Taiwan, see June M. Grasso, *Truman's Two-China Policy: 1948–1950* (Armonk, NY: M. E. Sharpe, 1987), 89–91.

74. NSC 37/7, quoted in Robert L. Messer, "Roosevelt, Truman, and China: An Overview," in Harding and Ming, *Sino-American Relations, 1945–1955*, 74; NSC 37, "The Strategic Importance of Formosa," December 1, 1948, *FRUS, 1949, The Far East: China, Vol. IX*, 261–262.

75. John W. Dower, *Embracing Defeat: Japan in the Wake of World War II* (New York: Norton, 1999).

76. Basic Directive for Post-Surrender Military Government in Japan Proper by the State-War-Navy Coordinating Committee, NARAII, SCAP, Civilian Property Custodian Policy and Management Group, Policy Branch, Subject File, 1945–1950, RG 331, Stack 290, Row 15, Compartment 14, Shelf 3, Box 3653, Folder 53.

77. Transcript of NBC Program "Our Foreign Policy," focusing on "Our Occupation Policy for Japan" with Maj. Gen. John Hildring, John Carter Vincent, and Capt. R. L. Dennison, SWNCC members, released October 6, 1945, NARAII, RG 353, State-War-Navy Coordinating Committee General Secretariat Records, Entry 507, Box 113.

78. Gallicchio, *The Scramble for Asia*, 71.

79. Memorandum by First Secretary of Embassy in Soviet Union (Davies), August 10, 1946, *FRUS, 1946, Vol. VIII: The Far East*, 285–286.

80. Memorandum by Mr. Robert A. Fearey of the Office of the Political Adviser in Japan, "Reappraisal of United States Security Interests and Policies in Regard to Japan," April 17, 1946, *FRUS, 1946, Vol. VIII: The Far East*, 209–210.

81. Melvin Leffler, *A Preponderance of Power: National Security, the Truman Administration, and the Cold War* (Palo Alto: Stanford University Press, 1992), 86.

82. Memorandum by the Assistant Chief of the Division of Japanese Affairs (Emmerson), October 9, 1946, *FRUS, 1946, Vol. VIII: The Far East*, 338–339.

83. The "Chrysanthemum Club"—named for the seal of the Japanese imperial family—is a moniker given to a range of U.S. scholars and experts on Japan, including the onetime U.S. ambassador to Japan (1961–1966) and Harvard professor Edwin O. Reischauer, who sought to bring a greater depth of understanding to U.S.-Japan relations. See George R. Packard, *Edwin O. Reischauer and the American Discovery of Japan* (New York: Columbia University Press, 2010), 251–255.

84. Study on Revival of the Japanese Economy presented by State Member, SWNCC, July 22, 1947, NARAII, Records of the War Department General and Special Staffs, Civil Affairs Division, General Records, Security-Classified Papers of the Army Member of the Combined Civil Affairs Committee, Jan. 1942–June 1949, RG 165, NM-84, Entry 468, Box 631. The final version is adopted by SWNCC on October 16, 1947, but with the changed condition that includes "to prevent burdens from being imposed on Japan, after she becomes self-supporting, which would prevent her from maintaining that self-supporting status." Revival of the Japanese Economy, a Report by the State-Army-Navy-Air Force Coordinating Subcommittee for the Far East, October 16, 1947, NARAII, Records of the War Department General and Special Staffs, Civil Affairs Division, General Records, Security-Classified Papers of the Army Member of the Combined Civil Affairs Committee, Jan. 1942–June 1949, RG 165, NM-84, Entry 468, Box 631.

85. Memorandum by Mr. John P. Davies, Jr., of the Policy Planning Staff to the Director of Staff (Kennan), August 11, 1947, *FRUS, 1947, Vol. VI: The Far East*, 485–486.

86. Michael Schaller, *The American Occupation of Japan: The Origins of the Cold War in Asia* (New York: Oxford University Press, 1985), 143–144.

87. Schaller, *The American Occupation of Japan*, 146.

88. Report to Joint Chiefs of Staff on "Program for Assistance to the General Area of China," January 16, 1950, File 1721/43, Records of the Joint Chiefs of Staff, RG 218, NARA, quoted in Schaller, *The American Occupation of Japan*, 407.

89. Yamagata Aritomo, founder of the Imperial Japanese Army, as quoted in Alice Miller and Richard Wich, *Becoming Asia: Change and Continuity in Asian International Relations Since World War II* (Stanford, CA: Stanford University Press, 2011), 7.

90. SWNCC Memo on United States Initial Policy to Korea, November 23, 1945, NARAII, RG 43, Records of International Conferences, Commissions, and Expositions, NND 760090, Box 15.

91. Secretary of State Byrnes to the Political Adviser in Korea (Langdon), April 5, 1946, *FRUS, 1946, Vol. VIII: The Far East: China*, 657–658.

92. Spector, *In the Ruins of Empire*, 144–154.

93. William Stueck, *The Korean War: An International History* (Princeton, NJ: Princeton University Press, 1995), 10–46.

94. Vincent, "Our Far Eastern Policies in Relation to Our Overall National Objectives," 5–6.

95. Ronald L. McGlothlen, *Controlling the Wave: Dean Acheson and U.S. Foreign Policy in Asia* (New York: Norton, 1993), 33.

96. SWNCC Decision on United States Policy in Korea, August 4, 1947, NARAII, RG 43, Records of International Conferences, Commissions, and Expositions, NND 760090, Box 15.

97. Memorandum by the Secretary of Defense (Forrestal) to the Secretary of State, *FRUS, 1947, Vol. VI: The Far East*, 817–818.

98. Kennan quoted in Heer, "George F. Kennan and US Foreign Policy in East Asia," 233–234.

99. Memorandum by the Secretary of Defense (Forrestal) to the Secretary of State, *FRUS, 1947, Vol. VI: The Far East*, 817–818.

100. Acheson quoted in McGlothlen, *Controlling the Wave*, 27–28.

101. NSC 8, "Report by the National Security Council on the Position of the United States with Respect to Korea," April 2, 1948, quoted in Heer, "George F. Kennan and US Foreign Policy in East Asia," 237.

102. McGlothlen, *Controlling the Wave*, 40.

103. Special Message to the Congress Recommending Continuation of Economic Assistance to Korea by President Truman, June 7, 1949, http://www.presidency.ucsb.edu /ws/index.php?pid=13202&st=korea&st1=#axzz1yvsAj6Lh.

104. McGlothlen, *Controlling the Wave*, 78–80; Stueck, *The Korean War*, 24–25, 29–30, 35–36.

105. Heer, "George F. Kennan and US Foreign Policy in East Asia," 240.

106. Spector, *In the Ruins of Empire*, 167–179.

107. The Democratic Republic of Vietnam made repeated overtures to Washington between August 1945 and November 1946. See *Report of the Office of the Secretary of Defense Task Force on United States–Vietnam Relations, 1945–1967*, "Section I: The United States and Vietnam, 1945–1950," A-2, C-65–79 (the fully declassified version is available at the United States National Archives, http://media.nara.gov/research/pentagon-papers

/Pentagon-Papers-Part-I.pdf); Fredrik Logevall, *Embers of War: The Fall of an Empire and the Making of America's Vietnam* (New York: Random House, 2012), 92–98.

108. Leffler, *A Preponderance of Power*, 92–93.

109. Secretary of State George Marshall to Embassy in France, May 13, 1947, *FRUS, 1947, Vol. VI: The Far East*, 95–97.

110. PPS 51: "United States Policy Toward Southeast Asia," March 29, 1949, *FRUS, 1949, Vol. VII: The Far East and Australasia, part 2*, 1128–1133.

111. Gallicchio, *The Scramble for Asia*, 14, 147. For details, see Stephen R. Shalom, *The United States and the Philippines: A Study of Neocolonialism* (Philadelphia: Institute for the Study of the Human Race, 1981).

112. Major Lawrence M. Greenberg, *The Hukbalahap Insurrection: A Case Study of a Successful Anti-insurgency Operation in the Philippines, 1946–1955* (Washington, DC: U.S. Army Center of Military History, Analysis Branch, 2005).

113. Kennan to Marshall/Lovett, December 17, 1948, quoted in Heer, "George F. Kennan and US Foreign Policy in East Asia," 310.

114. Robert J. McMahon, *Colonialism and the Cold War: The United States and the Struggle for Indonesian Independence, 1945–1949* (Ithaca, NY: Cornell University Press, 1981).

115. Logevall, *Embers of War*, 88.

116. Leffler, *A Preponderance of Power*, 92.

117. William J. Duiker, *U.S. Containment Policy and the Conflict in Indochina* (Stanford, CA: Stanford University Press, 1994), 45–46.

118. Robert S. McNamara, James G. Blight, and Robert K. Brigham, with Thomas J. Biersteker and Col. Herbert Y. Schandler (U.S. Army, ret.), *Argument Without End: In Search of Answers to the Vietnam Tragedy* (New York: PublicAffairs, 1999), 16–17.

119. Logevall, *Embers of War*; Clark Clifford, "A Vietnam Reappraisal," *Foreign Affairs* 47, no. 4 (July 1969): 603.

120. Kennan to Marshall, March 14, 1948, *FRUS, 1948, Vol. I: General; the United Nations, part 2*, 531–538.

121. Cited in Michael A. Palmer, *Origins of the Maritime Strategy: The Development of American Naval Strategy, 1945–1955* (Annapolis, MD: Naval Institute Press, 1990), 20.

122. Palmer, *Origins of the Maritime Strategy*, 35. Though Truman rejected the JCS proposal to annex Micronesia outright in 1946, he did ensure U.S. military control over the key islands under a form of "strategic trusteeship" nominally supervised by the United Nations, while ensuring continued access to bases in the Philippines and Okinawa. See Hal Friedman, *Creating an American Lake: United States Imperialism and Strategic Security in the Pacific Basin, 1945–47* (Westport, CT: Greenwood, 2001), 72.

123. JCS 1721/5: "United States Policy Toward China," June 9, 1947, cited in John Lewis Gaddis, "Defensive Perimeter Concept," in Borg and Heinrichs, *Uncertain Years*, 70. See also Memorandum by the Secretary of Defense (Forrestal) to the Secretary of State, *FRUS, 1947, Vol. VI: The Far East*, 817–818.

124. Kennan to Marshall, March 14, 1948, *FRUS, 1948, Vol. I: General; the United Nations, part 2*, 531–538. The outline of key island bases conformed with the JCS's own conclusions on ideal basing requirements two years earlier. See JCS Memo to SWNCC on Strategic Areas and Trusteeships in the Pacific, June 28, 1946, NARAII, RG 353, State-War-Navy Coordinating Committee General Secretariat Records, Entry 505, Box 117.

125. Kennan to Marshall, March 14, 1948, *FRUS, 1948, Vol. I: General; the United Nations, part 2,* 531–538.

126. Heer, "George F. Kennan and US Foreign Policy in East Asia," 297.

127. The U.S. Navy had ninety-nine carriers in 1945, including all types ranging from fleet to escort carriers. See Naval History and Heritage Command, U.S. Ship Force Levels: U.S. Navy Active Ship Force Levels, 1945–1950, http://www.history.navy.mil/research /histories/ship-histories/us-ship-force-levels.html#1945.

128. Palmer, *Origins of the Maritime Strategy,* 13.

129. Leffler, *Preponderance of Power,* 271.

130. Jeffrey G. Barlow, *Revolt of the Admirals: The Fight for Naval Aviation, 1945–1950* (Washington, DC: Naval Historical Center, 1994), 183–186.

131. Barlow, *Revolt of the Admirals,* 176.

132. Edward J. Marolda, *Ready Seapower: A History of the U.S. Seventh Fleet* (Washington, DC: Naval History and Heritage Command, 2012), 20.

133. Dennis D. Wainstock, *Truman, MacArthur and the Korean War: June 1950–July 1951* (Westport, CT: Greenwood, 2011), xxvii.

134. "This defensive perimeter runs along the Aleutians to Japan and then goes to the Ryukyus. . . . The defensive perimeter runs from the Ryukyus to the Philippine Islands. . . . So far as the military security of the other areas in the Pacific is concerned, it must be clear that no person can guarantee these areas against military attack. But it must also be clear that such a guarantee is hardly sensible or necessary within the realm of practical relationship. Should such an attack occur—one hesitates to say where such an attack could come from—the initial reliance must be on the people attacked to resist it and then upon the commitments of the entire civilized world under the Charter of the United Nations which so far has not proved a weak reed to lean on by any people who are determined to protect their independence against outside aggression." Remarks by Dean Acheson before the National Press Club, ca. 1950, Harry S. Truman Administration, Elsey Papers, http://www.trumanlibrary.org/whistlestop/study_collections/koreanwar /documents/index.php?documentdate=1950-00-00&documentid=kr-3-13&page number=1.

135. See, for example, William W. Stueck, *Rethinking the Korean War: A New Diplomatic and Strategic History* (Princeton, NJ: Princeton University Press, 2002).

136. Revisionist histories written under the later influence of the Vietnam War attempted to portray the ensuing conflict as a civil war, but more recent historiography based on the opening of Soviet archives leaves little doubt that Kim Il-sung's attack was sanctioned by both Moscow and Beijing, even if initiated by Kim himself. See, for example, Bruce Cumings, *The Origins of the Korean War* (Princeton, NJ: Princeton University Press, 1981), which draws heavily on internal Korean sources, contrasted with more recent studies using Soviet archives and Chinese sources, such as Kathryn Weathersby, "The Soviet Role in the Korean War, the State of Historical Knowledge," in *The Korean War in World History,* ed. William Stueck (Lexington: University of Kentucky Press, 2004), 61–92; Stueck, *Rethinking the Korean War;* John Lewis Gaddis, *We Now Know: Rethinking Cold War History* (Oxford: Oxford University Press, 1997), 71.

137. McMahon, *Dean Acheson,* 125.

138. Robert Dallek, *Harry S. Truman* (New York: Times Books, 2008), 105–106.

139. Statement by the President on the Situation in Korea by President Truman, June 27, 1950, http://www.presidency.ucsb.edu/ws/index.php?pid=13538&st=korea&st1=#axzz1yvsAj6Lh.

140. NSC 73: "The Position and Actions of the United States with Respect to Possible Further Soviet Moves in the Light of the Korean Situation," July 1, 1950, *FRUS, 1950, Vol. I: National Security Affairs; Foreign Economic Policy*, 331–338.

141. Heer, "George F. Kennan and US Foreign Policy in East Asia," 266–267.

142. Gaddis, *George F. Kennan*, 428–429. See Gaddis, "'Defensive Perimeter' Concept," 109–112; Douglas Brinkley, *Dean Acheson: The Cold War Years, 1953–71* (New Haven, CT: Yale University Press, 1994), 76.

143. James Chace, *Acheson: The Secretary of State Who Created the American World* (New York: Simon and Schuster Paperbacks, 1998), 262.

144. Leffler, *A Preponderance of Power*, 344; Cohen, "Acheson, His Advisors, and China," 18–19.

145. Dulles to Nitze, July 14, 1950, quoted in Heer, "George F. Kennan and US Foreign Policy in East Asia," 268.

146. Leffler, *Preponderance of Power*, 374–375.

147. McMahon, *Dean Acheson*, 141.

148. Kennan to Acheson, August 21, 1950, *FRUS, 1950, Vol. VII: Korea*, 623–628.

149. Gaddis, *George F. Kennan*, 401.

150. NSC 81/1: "United States Courses of Action with Respect to Korea," September 9, 1950, *FRUS, 1950, Vol. VII: Korea*, 712–721.

151. NSC 68, April 4, 1950, *FRUS, 1950, Vol. I: National Security Affairs; Foreign Economic Policy*, 237–239.

152. Gaddis, *Strategies of Containment*, 93.

153. Nicholas Thompson, *The Hawk and the Dove: Paul Nitze, George Kennan, and the History of the Cold War* (New York: Henry Holt, 2009).

154. Leffler, *A Preponderance of Power*, 358.

155. Acheson, *Present at the Creation*, 373–381, 420; Stueck, *The Korean War*, 43.

156. Roy E. Appleman, *Disaster in Korea: The Chinese Confront MacArthur* (College Station: Texas A&M University Press, 1989); Mathew B. Ridgway, *The Korean War* (Garden City, NY: Doubleday, 1967), chap. 4; Allen S. Whiting, *China Crosses the Yalu: The Decision to Enter the Korean War* (Stanford, CA: Stanford University Press, 1960), chaps. 6 and 7.

157. Gaddis, *Strategies of Containment*, 112.

158. Notes on NSC meeting, November 28, 1950, *FRUS, 1950, Vol. VII: Korea*, 1246–1247.

159. Testimony Before the Senate Committees on Armed Services and Foreign Relations, May 15, 1951. Military Situation in the Far East, hearings, 82nd Congress, 1st session, part 2, p. 732 (1951).

160. John Lewis Gaddis, *Surprise, Security, and the American Experience* (Cambridge, MA: Harvard University Press, 2004).

161. Richard Immerman, *John Foster Dulles: Piety, Pragmatism and Power in U.S. Foreign Policy* (New York: Rowman and Littlefield, 1999), 2.

162. John Foster Dulles, *War, Peace, and Change* (New York: Doubleday, 1939).

163. Immerman, *John Foster Dulles*, 22.

164. McMahon, *Dean Acheson*, 153.

165. Kennan to Acheson, August 21, 1950, *FRUS, 1950, Vol. VII: Korea*, 623–628; David W. Mabon, "Elusive Agreements: The Pacific Pact Proposals of 1949–1951," *Pacific Historical Review* 57, no. 2 (May 1988): 161; Heer, "George F. Kennan and US Foreign Policy in East Asia," 201; Acheson to Louis Johnson, September 7, 1950, *FRUS, 1950, Vol. VI: East Asia and the Pacific*, 1293–1296; Acheson, *Present at the Creation*, 434–435.

166. The Secretary of State to the Secretary of Defense (Johnson), September 7, 1950, *FRUS, 1950, Vol. VI: East Asia and the Pacific*, 1293–1296, quoted in Ayako Kusunoki, "Specialists in Foreign Policy: 'Japan Hands' and the Formation of U.S. Security Policy Toward Japan, 1945–1951" (PhD diss., University of Southern California, 2002), 109.

167. "Memorandum for the President," Acheson and Marshall to Truman, January 9, 1951, *FRUS, 1951, Vol. VI: East Asia and the Pacific*, 787–789.

168. John Foster Dulles, *War or Peace* (New York: Macmillan, 1950), 229–230.

169. The Secretary of State to the United States Political Adviser to SCAP (Sebald), February 8, 1951, *FRUS, 1951, Vol. VI: East Asia and the Pacific: Multilateral Relations, part 1 (1951)*, 150–151; Memorandum by Robert A. Fearey of the Office of Northeast Asian Affairs, February 14, 1951, *FRUS, 1951, Vol. VI: East Asia and the Pacific: Multilateral Relations, part 1 (1951)*, 155–156; Memorandum by Robert A. Fearey of the Office of Northeast Asian Affairs, February 16, 1951, *FRUS, 1951, Vol. VI: East Asia and the Pacific: Multilateral Relations, part 1 (1951)*, 156–164 (161–162 in particular).

170. John W. Dower, *Empire and Aftermath: Yoshida Shigeru and the Japanese Experience, 1878–1954* (Cambridge, MA: Harvard University Press, 1979); Richard B. Finn, *Winners in Peace: MacArthur, Yoshida, and Postwar Japan* (Berkeley: University of California Press, 1995); Makoto Iokibe, ed., *The Diplomatic History of Postwar Japan*, trans. Robert D. Eldridge (London: Routledge, 2011).

171. "Interest of the United States in a Regional Alliance of East Asian and Pacific Powers; Negotiation of a Mutual Defense Treaty with the Philippines and a Security Treaty with Australia and New Zealand" ["Memorandum by the Special Assistant to the Consultant (Allison) to the Ambassador at Large (Jessup), Subject: Pacific Pact"], August 14, 1950, *FRUS, 1950, Vol. VI: East Asia and the Pacific*, 131–133; Dower, *Empire and Aftermath*, 388–389; Iokibe, *The Diplomatic History of Postwar Japan*.

172. Mabon, "Elusive Agreements," 147–177; H. W. Brands, Jr., "From ANZUS to SEATO: United States Strategic Policy Towards Australia and New Zealand, 1952–1954," *International History Review* 9, no. 2 (May 1987): 251.

173. Percy Spender, "Australia and the Peace Treaty," *The Age*, March 9, 1950.

174. McMahon, *Dean Acheson*, 152.

175. The U.S. military presence was premised on the expectation "that Japan will itself increasingly assume responsibility for its own defense against direct and indirect aggression." Treaty of Peace with Japan, signed at San Francisco, September 8, 1951, http://www.taiwandocuments.org/sanfrancisco01.htm.

176. John Foster Dulles, "Security in the Pacific," *Foreign Affairs* 30, no. 2 (January 1952): 181–182.

177. Aaron Forsberg, *America and the Japanese Miracle: The Cold War Context of Japan's Postwar Economic Revival, 1950–1960* (Chapel Hill: University of North Carolina, 2000), 70–72.

178. On December 24, 1951, Yoshida sent a letter to Dulles supposedly ghostwritten by Dulles himself. After expressing a desire to conclude normal trade relations with the Nationalist government, "As regards to the Chinese Communist regime, that regime stands actually condemned by the United Nations of being an aggressor. In view of these considerations, I can assure you that the Japanese Government has no intention to conclude a bilateral treaty with the Communist regime of China." Yoshida letter, quoted in Qingxin Ken Wang, *Hegemonic Cooperation and Conflict: Postwar Japan's China Policy and the United States* (Westport, CT: Praeger), 123.

179. Kimie Hara, *Cold War Frontiers in the Asia-Pacific: Divided Territories in the San Francisco System* (New York: Routledge, 2007), 9, 12.

180. Dulles, "Security in the Pacific," 184.

181. "Security Treaty Between the United States and Japan," September 8, 1951, Article I, American Foreign Policy 1950–1955, Basic Documents Volumes I and II, Department of State Publication 6446, General Foreign Policy Series 117 (Washington, DC: Government Printing Office, 1957); "Mutual Defense Treaty Between the United States and the Republic of the Philippines," August 30, 1951, Article II, American Foreign Policy 1950–1955, Basic Documents Volumes I and II, Department of State Publication 6446, General Foreign Policy Series 117 (Washington, DC: Government Printing Office, 1957).

182. Secretary of State to the Secretary of Defense (Lovett), April 4, 1952, *FRUS, 1952–1954, Vol. XII: East Asia and the Pacific, part 1*, 75–77; Brands, "From ANZUS to SEATO," 252–253.

183. Brands, "From ANZUS to SEATO," 259–264.

184. Leffler, *A Preponderance of Power*, 382–383.

185. Dwight D. Eisenhower, "'I Shall Go to Korea' Speech," October 25, 1952, http://www.eisenhower.archives.gov/education/bsa/citizenship_merit_badge/speeches_national_historical_importance/i_shall_go_to_korea.pdf.

186. Cohen, *America's Response to China*, 5th ed., 181.

187. Frank Ninkovich, *Modernity and Power: A History of the Domino Theory in the Twentieth Century* (Chicago: University of Chicago Press, 1994), 203–204.

188. Andrew F. Krepinevich and Barry D. Watts, "Lost at the NSC," *The National Interest*, January 6, 2009, http://nationalinterest.org/article/lost-at-the-nsc-2959.

189. "Paper Prepared by the Directing Panel of Project Solarium," June 1, 1953, *FRUS, 1952–1954, Vol. II: National Security Affairs, part 1*, 360–404.

190. Gaddis, *Strategies of Containment*, 145.

191. Eisenhower's aide General Andrew J. Goodpaster and Policy Planning Staff Director Robert Bowie both considered the Solarium Project the death of the "rollback" strategy, particularly vis-à-vis China. See "Project Solarium: A Collective Oral History with Andrew J. Goodpaster, Robert R. Bowie, George F. Kennan," in *George F. Kennan and the Origins of Eisenhower's New Look: An Oral History of Project Solarium*, ed. William B. Pickett (Princeton, NJ: Princeton Institute for International and Regional Studies, 2004), 24, 32. For further details, see Nancy Bernkopf Tucker, *The China Threat: Memories, Myths, and Realities in the 1950s* (New York: Columbia University Press, 2012), 56, 91; NSC 148, "US Policy in the Far East," April 6, 1953, *FRUS, 1952–1954, Vol. XII: East Asia and the Pacific, part 1*, 287; NSC 166/1, "US Policy Towards Communist China," November 6, 1953, *FRUS, 1952–1954, Vol. XIV: China and Japan, part 1*, 281.

192. Taken from a letter from Walter S. Robertson to Philip C. Jessup explaining the China strategy and reproduced in Hearing Before the Committee on Foreign Relations on Nomination of Walter S. Robertson of Virginia to be Assistant Secretary of State, United States Senate, 83rd Congress, March 24, 1953 (Washington, DC: Ward and Paul), 47–48.

193. John Foster Dulles, "Policy for Security and Peace," *Foreign Affairs* 32, no. 3 (April 1954): 357–359.

194. Gaddis, *Strategies of Containment*, 151–153.

195. John Foster Dulles, "The Evolution of Foreign Policy," Before the Council of Foreign Relations, New York, N.Y., Department of State, Press Release No. 81 (January 12, 1954), http://www.nuclearfiles.org/menu/key-issues/nuclear-weapons/history/cold-war/strategy/article-dulles-retaliation_1954-01-12.htm.

196. Victor D. Cha, "Powerplay: Origins of the U.S. Alliance System in Asia," *International Security* 34, no. 3 (Winter 2009–2010): 159. For a fuller treatment, see Cha, *Powerplay: Origins of the American Alliance System in Asia* (Princeton, NJ: Princeton University Press, 2016).

197. NSC 48/5: "United States Objectives, Policies and Courses of Action in Asia," May 17, 1951, *FRUS, 1951, Vol. VI: East Asia and the Pacific*, 49.

198. Letter, Secretary of State to the Vice President, November 4, 1953, *FRUS, 1952–1954, Vol. XV: Korea*, 1590, cited in Cha, "Powerplay," 176.

199. Mutual Defense Treaty Between the United States and the Republic of Korea, October 1, 1953, http://avalon.law.yale.edu/20th_century/kor001.asp. On the side agreement, Dennis Van Vranken Hickey writes, "When ratified by the U.S. Senate, lawmakers insisted on adding an 'understanding' to the document—the United States would consider military action only if the ROK was attacked by an external enemy. It was the Senate's intention that 'the treaty would not require US action if the ROK launches an attack on the DPRK.'" See Dennis Van Vranken Hickey, *The Armies of East Asia: China, Taiwan, Japan, and the Koreas* (Boulder, CO: Lynne Rienner, 2001), 24.

200. Tucker, *The China Threat*, 64.

201. Tucker, *The China Threat*, 71. See also Shu Guang Zhang, *Deterrence and Strategic Culture: Chinese-American Confrontations, 1949–1958* (Ithaca, NY: Cornell University Press, 1992), 189.

202. Forrest C. Pogue, *George C Marshall*, vol. 4, *Statesman, 1945–1959* (New York: Penguin, 1987), 468–469; Tucker, *The China Threat*, 69–75.

203. Cha, "Powerplay," 170.

204. Memorandum by the Secretary of State to the President, November 23, 1954, *FRUS, 1953–1954, Vol. XIV: Japan and China*, 929.

205. Position paper prepared in the Department of State, December 29, 1951, *FRUS, 1952–1954, Vol. XII: East Asia and the Pacific, part 1*, 1–3. Nitze continued to argue from Policy Planning that the "loss of Southeast Asia would present an unacceptable threat to position of U.S., both in Far East and world-wide," but an exasperated Joint Chiefs of Staff responded that they could not plan a military strategy until they knew whether the president believed "the U.S. must hold in this area or go down." With that decision in hand, the JCS would have the necessary directive to figure out the cost and requirements of the necessary military action. See Memorandum by the Director of the Policy Planning Staff (Nitze), March 5, 1952, *FRUS, 1952–1954, Vol. XII: East Asia and the Pacific, part 1*, 68–69. Truman was unwilling to make such a determination.

206. Draft of Statement of Policy Proposed by the National Security Council on United States Policies in the Far East, April 6, 1953, *FRUS, 1952–1954, Vol. XII: East Asia and the Pacific*, 286–289.

207. "Statement of Hon. John Foster Dulles, Secretary of State," Hearings Before the Committee on Foreign Relations on a Mutual Defense Treaty Between the United States of America and the Republic of Korea Signed at Washington on October 1, 1953, United States Senate, 83rd Congress, January 13 and 14, 1954 (Washington, DC: Government Printing Office, 1954), 8–9.

208. "Memorandum of Conversation, by the Secretary of State," March 24, 1953, *FRUS, 1952–1953, Vol. XIII: Indochina, part 1*, 419. See also Logevall, *Embers of War*, 338–339, 346.

209. NSC 5405: "Statement of Policy by the National Security Council on United States Objectives and Courses of Action with Respect to Southeast Asia," January 14, 1954, *FRUS, 1952–1954, Vol. XII: East Asia and the Pacific, part 1*, 366–376.

210. Eisenhower said in a press conference on April 7, "You have a row of dominoes set up, you knock over the first one, and what will happen to the last one is the certainty that it will go over very quickly." See "Editorial Note," *FRUS, 1952–1954, Vol. XIII: Indochina, part 1*, 1281.

211. Draft of Statement of Policy Proposed by the National Security Council on United States Policies in the Far East, April 6, 1953, *FRUS, 1952–1954, Vol. XII: East Asia and the Pacific*, 286–289.

212. As one characteristic Far East Bureau memo warned in July 1954, "the present instance of this self-defeating habit of mind is—or at least must seem to be—a relatively minor matter. Its significance, however, cannot be dismissed—and I fear will not be dismissed by our Asia friends." See Memorandum by the Regional Planning Adviser in the Bureau of Far Eastern Affairs (Ogburn) to the Acting Assistant Secretary of State for Far Eastern Affairs (Drumright), July 23, 1954, *FRUS, 1952–1954, Vol. XII: East Asia and the Pacific*, 662–665.

213. Requirement for United Kingdom or Australia articulated in "The Secretary of State to the Embassy in France," April 5, 1954, *FRUS, 1952–1954, Vol. XIII: Indochina, part 1*, 1242; Recognition London and Canberra would not be forthcoming in "Memorandum of Discussion at the 192d Meeting of the National Security Council," April 6, 1954, *FRUS, 1952–1954, Vol. XIII: Indochina, part 1*, 1253–1254. See also Logevall, *Embers of War*, 366, 377, 389.

214. Dwight D. Eisenhower, *Mandate for Change 1953–1956* (Garden City, NY: Doubleday, 1963), 366. The United States did not sign the agreement, but France, Britain, China, and the Soviet Union did.

215. "Memorandum of Discussion at the 202d Meeting of the National Security Council," June 17, 1954, *FRUS, 1952–1954, Vol. XIII: Indochina, part 2*, 1713–1717.

216. Memorandum by the Joint Chiefs of Staff to the Secretary of Defense (Wilson), May 21, 1954, *FRUS, 1952–1954, Vol. XII: East Asia and the Pacific*, 514–516. JCS repeated its "offensive" option over static defense with the president that summer. See Memorandum of the Substance of Discussions at a Department of State–Joint Chiefs of Staff Meeting, July 23, 1954, *FRUS, 1952–1954, Vol. XII: East Asia and the Pacific*, 653–657.

217. "Memorandum of Discussion at the 179th Meeting of the National Security Council," January 8, 1954, *FRUS, 1952–1954, Vol. XIII: Indochina, part 1*, 949.

218. Mathew B. Ridgway, as told to Harold H. Martin, *Soldier: The Memoirs of Mathew B. Ridgway* (New York: Harper, 1956), 277.

219. Memorandum by the Regional Adviser in the Bureau of Far Eastern Affairs (Ogburn) to the Acting Assistant Secretary of State for Far Eastern Affairs (Drumright), July 23, 1954, *FRUS, 1952–1954, Vol. XII: East Asia and the Pacific, part 1*, 662–665.

220. "Memorandum of Conversation," June 29, 1954, *FRUS, 1952–1954, Vol. XII: East Asia and the Pacific, part 1*, 584. See also Richard Mason, "The Manila Conference, 1954 versus the Bandung Conference, 1955: The United States, the Cold War, and the Challenge of Non-Alignment," *Malaysian Journal of History, Politics, and Strategies Studies* 38, no. 1 (2011): 5–6; Mohammad Hatta, "Indonesia's Foreign Policy," *Foreign Affairs* 31, no. 3 (April 1953): 444–445.

221. Minutes of a Meeting of Southeast Asia, July 24, 1954, *FRUS, 1952–1954, Vol. XII: East Asia and the Pacific, part 1*, 665–671.

222. Memorandum of Telephone Conversation Between Dulles and Merchant, August 30, 1954, *FRUS, 1952–1954, Vol. XII: East Asia and the Pacific, part 1*, 820–822.

223. Memorandum of Conversation with the President, by the Secretary of State, August 17, 1954, *FRUS, 1952–1954, Vol. XII: East Asia and the Pacific, part 1*, 735.

224. The Australian Embassy to the Department of State, August 31, 1954, *FRUS, 1952–1954, Vol. XII: East Asia and the Pacific, part 1*, 824.

225. Memorandum by the Assistant Secretary of State for Far Eastern Affairs (Robertson) to the Secretary of State, October 25, 1954, *FRUS, 1952–1954, Vol. XII: East Asia and the Pacific*, 953–955.

226. The Acting Director of the Office of Northeast Asian Affairs (McClurkin) to the Ambassador in Japan (Allison), September 16, 1954, *FRUS, 1952–1954, Vol. XII: East Asia and the Pacific, part 1*, 911–912.

227. Brands, "From ANZUS to SEATO," 265.

228. The parties issued the "Pacific Pact" the same day, reaffirming their shared commitment to the UN Charter and cooperation in broader fields beyond defense.

229. There was to be no standing military committee or other formal structure for planning in SEATO, and even the name "SEATO" was reconsidered at one point since it implied the collective security arrangements of NATO. See United States position paper prepared for the ANZUS Council Meeting, October 8, 1954, *FRUS, 1952–1954, Vol. XII: East Asia and the Pacific, part 1*, 936.

230. Report of the Office of the Secretary of Defense Vietnam Task Force on United States–Vietnam Relations, 1945–1967, Section IV, U.S. and France's Withdrawal from Vietnam, 1955–1960, iii.

231. NSC 5429/2: "Statement of Policy by the National Security Council on Review of U.S. Policy in the Far East," August 20, 1954, *FRUS, 1952–1954, Vol. XII: East Asia and the Pacific, part 1*, 771–774.

232. Memorandum by the Joint Chiefs of Staff to the Secretary of Defense (Wilson), May 21, 1954, *FRUS, 1952–1954, Vol. XII: East Asia and the Pacific, part 1*, 514–516.

233. Gaddis, *Strategies of Containment*, 162; military adjustments outlined in "Mutual Security Program (Korea)," Hearing of the United States Senate Committee on Foreign Relations, Washington, DC, April 13, 1956, 182–191.

234. Eisenhower and Dulles recognized the longer-term potential for a Sino-Soviet split but rejected it in the near term, noting that "conflicts of interest of both partners with the noncommunist world" were more powerful still than their internal divisions, but saw the potential for a split as China asserted its own independent domination over the Far East. See NSC 166/1: "U.S. Policy Toward Communist China," November 6, 1953, *FRUS, 1952–1954, Vol. XIV: Japan and China, part 1*, 280. See also Gordon H. Chang, *Friends and Enemies: The United States, China, and the Soviet Union, 1948–1972* (Stanford, CA: Stanford University Press, 1990), 3; John Lewis Gaddis, "The American 'Wedge' Strategy, 1949–1955," in Harding and Ming, *Sino-American Relations, 1945–1955*, 157–159. This calculus was based in part on National Security Council studies done in 1953 that argued that the United States could not "expect to split the two Communist giants" on its own: "Soviet behavior toward the Chinese would be more decisive." See Gaddis, *Strategies of Containment*, 194. Nancy Tucker generally concurs with this assessment, but notes that Eisenhower and Dulles did suffer from insufficient information on China and a predilection for assigning Chinese motives to ideology rather than nationalism. See Tucker, *China Threat*, 181–182.

235. Wooseon Choi, "Structural Realism and Dulles' China Policy," *Review of International Studies* 38, no. 1 (January 2012): 124–127.

236. NIE 13-58: "Communist China," May 13, 1958, in Allen, Carver, and Elmore, *Tracking the Dragon*, 124.

237. "Memorandum from the Acting Chief of the Reports and Operations Staff (Gilman) to the Secretary of State," February 8, 1955, *FRUS, 1955–1957, Vol. XXI: East Asian Security; Cambodia; Laos*, 29.

238. U.S. Ambassador to Indonesia Hugh Smith Cumming, quoted in Cary Fraser, "An American Dilemma: Race and Realpolitik in the American Response to the Bandung Conference, 1955," in *Window on Freedom: Race, Civil Rights, and Foreign Affairs, 1945–1988*, ed. Brenda Gayle Plummer (Chapel Hill: University of North Carolina Press, 2003), 118–119.

239. Young quoted in Kweku Ampiah, *The Political and Moral Imperatives of the Bandung Conference of 1955: The Reactions of the US, UK and Japan* (Kent: Global Oriental), 65.

240. Eisenhower quoted in Jason C. Parker, "Small Victory, Missed Chance: The Eisenhower Administration, the Bandung Conference, and the Turning of the Cold War," in *The Eisenhower Administration, the Third World, and the Globalization of the Cold War*, ed. Kathryn C. Statler and Andrew L. Johns (New York: Rowman and Littlefield, 2006), 160.

241. Dwight D. Eisenhower, *Mandate for Change 1953–1956* (Garden City, NY: Doubleday, 1963), 373–374.

242. Jason C. Parker, "Small Victory, Missed Chance," 161–168; Macmillan quoted in H. W. Brands, *The Specter of Neutralism: The United States and the Emergence of the Third World, 1947–1960* (New York: Columbia University Press, 1989), 117.

243. One of the memoranda prepared for Solarium highlighted that "the U.S. finds itself in the anomalous position of being identified in Asia as imperialist and the supporter of Western European colonialism and in Europe as hastening the break-up of colonial relationships." See "Memorandum to the National Security Council by the Executive Sec-

retary (Lay)," July 22, 1953, *FRUS, 1952–1954, Vol. II: National Security Affairs, part 1*, 408. With respect to already independent Indonesia, however, the NSC concluded the next month in a supplement to NSC 124/2 that the United States would "seek to strengthen the non-communist political orientation of the government" through "respect for Indonesia's independence" in foreign policy. See "Memorandum by the Secretary of State and the Acting Secretary of Defense (Anderson) to the Executive Secretary of the National Security (Lay)," August 27, 1953, *FRUS, 1952–1954, Vol. XII: East Asia and the Pacific, part 2*, 377. Ultimately, the administration found itself unable to show what Indonesia considered respect for independence, since allies Australia and Holland still were in a dispute with Jakarta about West Irian. America's credibility was further damaged by unsuccessful CIA efforts to turn the Indonesian elections of 1955 with millions of dollars. More embarrassing was an episode in May 1958 when a CIA-supplied B-24 bomber crashed while trying to resupply a group of Indonesian colonels planning a coup. The Indonesians captured the American pilot, who still had his PX card from Clark Air Force Base in the Philippines. See Evan Thomas, *The Very Best Men: Four Who Dared: The Early Years of the CIA* (New York: Simon and Schuster, 1995), 159.

244. Hans Morgenthau, "The Immaturity of Our Asian Policy," *New Republic*, March 12, 19, 26, and April 16, 1956, reproduced in Hans J. Morgenthau, *The Impasse of American Foreign Policy* (Chicago: University of Chicago Press, 1962), 251–277.

245. Makoto Iokibe, Caroline Rose, Tomaru Junko, and John Weste, eds., *Japanese Diplomacy in the 1950s: From Isolation to Integration*, Routledge Studies in the Modern History of Asia (New York: Routledge, 2007), 4.

246. Kennan had proposed in 1947 that the territorial problem over the Kuriles would serve as a wedge between Moscow and Tokyo, and it did. Dulles's threat to separate the Ryukyus was based on the argument that Japanese territorial concessions to Moscow as a condition for a peace treaty would inevitably force the United States to reconsider territorial demands. The ploy worked, given considerable opposition to Hatoyama's diplomacy within his own party. See Michael Schaller, *Altered States: The United States and Japan Since the Occupation* (New York: Oxford University Press, 1997), 113–126; Tsuyoshi Hasegawa, *The Northern Territories Dispute and Russo-Japanese Relations*, 2 vols. (Berkeley: University of California Press, 1998).

247. Tucker, *The China Threat*, 136–137.

248. Treaty of Mutual Cooperation and Security Between Japan and the United States of America, http://www.mofa.go.jp/region/n-america/us/q&a/ref/1.html.

249. Tadashi Aruga, "The Security Treaty Revision of 1960," in *The United States and Japan in the Postwar World*, ed. Akira Iriye and Warren I. Cohen (Lexington: University of Kentucky Press, 1989), 61–79; Marc Gallicchio, "Occupation, Domination and the Alliance: Japan in American Security Policy, 1945–69," in *Partnership: The United States and Japan, 1951–2001*, ed. Akira Iriye and Robert A. Wampler (New York: Kodansha International, 2001), 115–134 at 124; Walter LaFeber, *The Clash: U.S.-Japanese Relations Throughout History* (New York: Norton, 1997), 319.

250. Dwight D. Eisenhower, "The President's News Conference," March 16, 1955, posted online by Gerhard Peters and John T. Woolley, The American Presidency Project, http://www.presidency.ucsb.edu/ws/?pid=10434#axzz2jJiCyBxN.

251. JCS 947046, August 25, 1958, *FRUS, 1958–1960, Vol. XIX: China*, 76, cited in Tucker, *The China Threat*, 143.

252. Gaddis argues that he was while Nancy Tucker and Robert Accinelli argue that he was not. See Gaddis, *Strategies of Containment*, 169; Tucker, *China Threat*, 145; Robert Accinelli, "A Thorn in the Side of Peace: The Eisenhower Administration and the 1958 Offshore Island Crisis," in Robert S. Ross and Changbin Jiang, eds., *Re-examining the Cold War: U.S.-China Diplomacy, 1954–1973* (Cambridge: Cambridge University Press, 2002), 104.

253. Tucker, *China Threat*, 147; Gordon Chang, "To the Nuclear Brink: Eisenhower, Dulles and the Quemoy-Matsu Crisis," *International Security* 12, no. 4 (Spring 1988): 96–122.

254. H. W. Brands, "The Age of Vulnerability: Eisenhower and the National Insecurity State," *American Historical Review* 94, no. 4 (October 1989): 963–989; Robert R. Bowie and Richard H. Immerman, *Waging Peace: How Eisenhower Shaped an Enduring Cold War Strategy* (Oxford: Oxford University Press, 1998); Samuel R. Williamson, Jr., and Steven L. Rearden, *The Origins of U.S. Nuclear Strategy, 1945–1953* (New York: St. Martin's, 1993), chap. 6; David A. Rosenberg, "The Origins of Overkill: Nuclear Weapons and American Strategy, 1945–1960," *International Security* 7, no. 4 (Spring 1983): 12–21. Note also that Dulles clarified that nuclear retaliation was meant to supplement, not replace, "mobile" conventional forces. It was not the United States' intention "to turn every local war into a general war." See "Statement by Hon. John Foster Dulles, Secretary of State," Hearings Before the Committee on Foreign Relations on Foreign Policy and Its Relation to Military Programs, United States Senate, 83rd Congress, March 19 and April 14, 1954 (Washington, DC: Government Printing Office, 1954), 4. Nevertheless, the expectation that the threat of massive retaliation would reduce the requirement for conventional forces was not met.

255. Walter Lippmann, "Foundations of Strength in Western Alliance," *The Age*, May 7, 1954, http://news.google.com/newspapers?nid=1300&dat=19540507&id=Z7YUAAAAIBAJ &sjid=xMUDAAAAIBAJ&pg=3777,866616. Syndication of original column in *New York Herald Tribune*, May 6, 1954.

8. ASIA STRATEGY AND ESCALATION IN VIETNAM, 1961–1968

1. David Halberstam, *The Best and the Brightest*, 20th anniversary ed. (New York: Random House, 1992); Arthur Schlesinger, *The Bitter Heritage: Vietnam and American Democracy, 1941–1966* (Boston: Houghton Mifflin, 1967); David L. Anderson, "The Vietnam War and Its Enduring Historical Relevance," in *The Columbia History of the Vietnam War*, edited by David L. Anderson (New York: Columbia University Press, 2011), 2–3. See also George C. Herring, *America's Longest War: The United States and Vietnam, 1950–1975*, 4th ed. (Boston: McGraw-Hill, 2002); Robert D. Shulzinger, *A Time for War: The United States and Vietnam, 1941–1975* (New York: Oxford University Press, 1997); Lloyd C. Gardner, "Hall of Mirrors," in *Why the North Won the Vietnam War*, ed. Marc Jason Gilbert (New York: Palgrave, 2002), 235–236; George W. Allen, *None So Blind: A Personal Account of the Intelligence Failure in Vietnam* (Chicago: Ivan R. Dee, 2001), 284.

2. Harry G. Summers, *On Strategy: A Critical Analysis of the Vietnam War* (Novato, CA: Presidio, 1982); Ulysses S. Grant Sharp, *Strategy for Defeat: Vietnam in Retrospect* (Novato, CA: Presidio, 1998); Robert Gallucci, *Neither Peace Nor Honor: The Politics of American Military Policy in Viet-Nam* (Baltimore: Johns Hopkins University Press, 1975), 38–40; William C. Westmoreland, *A Soldier Reports* (Garden City, NY: Doubleday, 1976); Dave Richard Palmer, *Summons of the Trumpet: U.S.-Vietnam in Perspective* (San Rafael, CA: Presidio, 1978).

3. See, for example, Allen, *None So Blind*, 282.

4. Frank Ninkovich, *Modernity and Power: A History of the Domino Theory in the Twentieth Century* (Chicago: University of Chicago Press, 1994), 245–247; Andrew F. Krepinevich Jr., *The Army and Vietnam* (Baltimore: Johns Hopkins University Press, 1986), 27–33.

5. Kennedy quoted in "'United Action?'" *New York Times*, April 11, 1954.

6. Quoted in John Lewis Gaddis, *Strategies of Containment* (New York: Oxford University Press, 1982), 174.

7. "If we cannot end our differences now, at least we can help make the world safe for diversity." John Fitzgerald Kennedy, Speech, June 10, 1963, American University, Washington, D.C., Commencement Address, *Public Papers of the Presidents of the United States: John F. Kennedy, 1963* (Washington, DC: Government Printing Office, 1964).

8. John F. Kennedy, "Pioneers for Peace," September 26, 1963, reprinted in *Department of State Bulletin* 49 (July–December, 1963): 634.

9. Memorandum from Michael V. Forrestal of the National Security Council Staff to the President's Special Assistant for National Security Affairs (Bundy), April 10, 1962, in U.S. Department of State, *Foreign Relations of the United States*, http://digicoll.library.wisc.edu /FRUS/Browse.html [hereafter cited as *FRUS*], *1961–1963, Vol. XXIII: Southeast Asia*, 59–61.

10. Memorandum of a Conversation, The White House, November 7, 1961, *FRUS, 1961–1963, Vol. I: Vietnam*, 544–546.

11. Editorial Note, *FRUS, 1961–1963, Vol. I: Vietnam*, 540–541.

12. Memorandum from Robert W. Komer of the National Security Council Staff to the President's Special Assistant for National Security Affairs (Bundy), March 27, 1961, *FRUS, 1961–1963, Vol. XXIII: Southeast Asia*, 333–334.

13. Quoted in Halberstam, *The Best and the Brightest*, 18.

14. Kennedy quoted in Mark Moyar, *Triumph Forsaken: The Vietnam War, 1954–1965* (Cambridge: Cambridge University Press, 2006), 120.

15. Theodore C. Sorenson, *Kennedy: Decision-Making in the White House* (New York: Harper and Row, 1965), 281–282.

16. David Rothkopf, *Running the World: The Inside Story of the National Security Council and the Architects of American Power* (New York: PublicAffairs, 2004), 84–93; Gaddis, *Strategies of Containment*, 198.

17. Henry L. Stimson and McGeorge Bundy, *On Active Service in War and Peace* (New York: Harper, 1948).

18. Gaddis, *Strategies of Containment*, 222.

19. Quoted in Halberstam, *The Best and the Brightest*, 160.

20. Draft for Basic National Security Policy, March 26, 1962, Papers of John F. Kennedy, Presidential Papers, National Security Files, 27, http://www.jfklibrary.org/Asset-Viewer /Archives/JFKNSF-294-001.aspx#.

21. Rostow argued that the United States' "obsolete and inflexible policy" toward the KMT "divides the anti-communist coalition at its European core, alienates the crucially important uncommitted peoples of Asia, cements the Sino-Soviet alliance and stands as a roadblock to any relaxation of tensions in the Far East." See Draft for Basic National Security Policy, March 26, 1962, Papers of John F. Kennedy, Presidential Papers, National Security Files, 28, http://www.jfklibrary.org/Asset-Viewer/Archives/JFKNSF-294-001.aspx#.

22. Memorandum from the President's Special Assistant for National Security Affairs (Bundy) to the Chairman of the Policy Planning Council and Counselor of the Department of State (Rostow), April 13, 1962, FRUS, 1961–1963, Vol. VIII: National Security Policy, 263.

23. Memorandum from the President's Deputy Special Assistant for National Security Affairs (Kaysen) to the Chairman of the Policy Planning Council and Counselor of the Department of State (Rostow), April 16, 1962, FRUS, 1961–1963, Vol. VIII: National Security Policy, 268–271.

24. Godfrey Hodgson, "Walt Rostow," The Guardian, February 16, 2003, http://www.theguardian.com/news/2003/feb/17/guardianobituaries.usa as of January 8, 2014.

25. Halberstam, The Best and the Brightest, 31.

26. Rusk Press Conference, May 4, 1961, Department of State Bulletin 44 (May 22, 1961): 763, quoted in Gaddis, Strategies of Containment, 201.

27. Howard B. Schaffer, Chester Bowles: New Dealer in the Cold War (Cambridge, MA: Harvard University Press, 1993), 202–231.

28. Walter Isaacson and Evan Thomas, The Wise Men: Six Friends and the World They Made: Acheson, Bohlen, Harriman, Kennan, Lovett, McCloy (New York: Simon and Schuster, 1986), 633–634.

29. "Ex-Governor, Averell Harriman, Advisor to 4 Presidents, Dies," New York Times, July 27, 1980.

30. Roger Hilsman, To Move a Nation: The Politics of Foreign Policy in the Administration of John F. Kennedy (Garden City, NY: Doubleday, 1967), 334–336.

31. Halberstam, Best and the Brightest, 479.

32. Martin, "William P. Bundy, 83, Dies"; Marvin Kalb and Elie Abel, Roots of Involvement: The U.S. in Asia, 1784–1971 (New York: Norton, 1971), 176–177.

33. Halberstam, The Best and the Brightest, 303.

34. Leslie H. Gelb, "Vietnam: The System Worked," Foreign Policy, no. 3 (Summer 1971): 141.

35. President's views recounted in: Telegram from the Chief of the Military Assistance Advisory Group in Viet-Nam (McGarr) to the Commander in Chief, Pacific (Felt), May 10, 1961, FRUS, 1961–1963, Vol. I: Vietnam, 129–131.

36. Gordon M. Goldstein, Lessons in Disaster: McGeorge Bundy and the Path to War in Vietnam (New York: Holt Paperback, Times Books/Henry Holt, 2008), 46–47.

37. Richard Ellison and Roger Hilsman, Vietnam: A Television History, Episode 103, interview with Roger Hilsman, 1981 (Boston: WGBH Boston Video, 1983), http://openvault.wgbh.org/catalog/vietnam-c3d5d3-interview-with-roger-hilsman-1981.

38. As quoted in Seth Jacobs, The Universe Is Unraveling: American Foreign Policy in Cold War Laos (Ithaca, NY: Cornell University Press, 2012), 12.

39. Michael Burleigh, *Small Wars/Far Away Places: Global Insurrection and the Making of the Modern World, 1945–1965* (New York: Viking, 2013), 461.

40. Johnson quoted in Moyar, *Triumph Forsaken*, 131.

41. Gaddis, *Strategies of Containment*, 243.

42. Kalb and Abel, *Roots of Involvement*, 127–132.

43. William Conrad Gibbons, *The U.S. Government and the Vietnam War: Executive and Legislative Roles and Relationships, Part II, 1961–1964, prepared for the Committee on Foreign Relations, U.S. Senate, by the Congressional Research Service, Senate Print 98-185, Pt. 2* (Washington, DC: Government Printing Office, 1985), 40.

44. Ellison and Hilsman, *Vietnam*, interview with Roger Hilsman.

45. Sharp, *Strategy for Defeat*, 20–21.

46. Ellison and Hilsman, *Vietnam*, interview with Roger Hilsman.

47. Michael H. Hunt, *Lyndon Johnson's War: America's Cold War Crusade in Vietnam, 1945–1968* (New York: Hill and Wang, 1996), 68.

48. George F. Will, "The JFK We Had and the Memory That Lives," *Washington Post*, November 20, 2013, http://www.washingtonpost.com/opinions/geoege-f-will-john-f-kennedy-the-conservative/2013/11/20/92be8164-513d-11e3-a7f0-b790929232e1_story.html.

49. There were two alleged attacks on U.S. destroyers in the Gulf of Tonkin, but the second may have been based on mistaken signals intelligence rather than actual actions by the North. Tonkin Gulf Resolution: Public Law 88-408, 88th Congress, August 7, 1964, General Records of the United States Government, Record Group 11, National Archives, http://www.ourdocuments.gov/doc.php?flash=true&doc=98.

50. Kalb and Abel, *Roots of Involvement*, 178–179.

51. See, for example, Phillip E. Catton, "Refighting Vietnam in the History Books: The Historiography of the War," *Organization of American Historians* 18, no. 5 (October 2004): 7–11.

52. Kalb and Abel, *Roots of Involvement*, 185.

53. Lyndon B. Johnson, *The Vantage Point: Perspectives of the Presidency, 1963–1969* (Dumfries: Holt McDougal, 1971), 151–152.

54. Memorandum from the President's Special Assistant for National Security Affairs (Bundy) to the President, January 9, 1964, *FRUS, 1964–1968, Vol. I: Vietnam, 1964*, 8–15.

55. McNamara quoted in Hunt, *Lyndon Johnson's War*, 97.

56. David L. DiLeo, *George Ball, Vietnam, and the Rethinking of Containment* (Chapel Hill: University of North Carolina Press, 1991), 64–66.

57. Statement by President Johnson at White House News Conference on July 28, 1965, "We Will Stand in Viet-Nam," *Department of State Bulletin* 53 (August 16, 1965): 262; *The Pentagon Papers*, Gravel ed. (Boston: Beacon, 1971), 4:632–633.

58. Isaacson and Thomas, *The Wise Men*, 676–681.

59. Figures cited in Stephen E. Ambrose, *Rise to Globalism: American Foreign Policy, 1938–1980*, 2nd ed. (New York: Penguin, 1982), 290.

60. Gaddis, *Strategies of Containment*, 261.

61. Herring, *America's Longest War*, 225–226.

62. "Economic Consequences of War on the U.S. Economy" (Sydney: Institute for Economics and Peace, 2011), 12–13, http://www.thereformedbroker.com/wp-content/uploads

/2012/02/Economic-Consequences-of-War.pdf; Anthony S. Campagna, *The Economic Consequences of the Vietnam War* (New York: Praeger, 1991).

63. Kalb and Abel, *Roots of Involvement*, 192.

64. Gelb, "Vietnam: The System Worked," 146.

65. Hoopes, *The Limits of Intervention*, 61–62.

66. Summers, *On Strategy*, chap. 9.

67. Hunt, *Lyndon Johnson's War*, 106.

68. Gallucci, *Neither Peace Nor Honor*, 38–40; Westmoreland, *A Soldier Reports*; Sharp, *Strategy for Defeat*; Palmer, *Summons of the Trumpet*.

69. Hilsman, *To Move a Nation*; Andrew Preston, *The War Council: McGeorge Bundy, the NSC, and Vietnam* (Cambridge, MA: Harvard University Press, 2006), 106–107.

70. Krepinevich, *The Army and Vietnam*, 6.

71. Jeff Record, *The Wrong War: Why We Lost in Vietnam* (Annapolis, MD: Naval Institute Press, 1998), 100–105.

72. Summers, *On Strategy*, 148.

73. In a 1974 survey of army generals who had commanded in Vietnam, "almost 70 percent of the Army generals who managed the war were uncertain of its objectives." See Douglas Kinnard, *The War Managers* (Hanover, NH: University Press of New England, 1977), 25, cited in Summers, *On Strategy*, 105.

74. Robert Dallek, *Flawed Giant: Lyndon Johnson and His Times, 1961–1973* (New York: Oxford University Press, 1998), 99.

75. Hans J. Morgenthau, "Shadow and Substance of Power," reproduced in Hans J. Morgenthau, *Vietnam and the United States* (Washington, DC: PublicAffairs, 1965), 9–20 at 12.

76. "Kennan on Vietnam," *New Republic*, February 26, 1966, 20, quoted in Paul James Heer, "George F. Kennan and US Foreign Policy in East Asia" (PhD diss., The George Washington University, 1995), 340.

77. Matthew B. Ridgway, "Indochina: Disengaging," *Foreign Affairs* 49, no. 4 (July 1971): 583–592.

78. Ninkovich, *Modernity and Power*, 219–221.

79. Robert Kennedy, quoted in DiLeo, *George Ball, Vietnam, and the Rethinking of Containment*, 69.

80. George W. Ball, "Top Secret: The Prophecy the President Rejected. How Valid Are the Assumptions Underlying Our Vietnam Policy?" *Atlantic Monthly* (July 1972): 43. The memo is dated October 5, 1964.

81. Ellison and Hilsman, *Vietnam*, interview with McGeorge Bundy.

82. Draft Memorandum from the Secretary of State to the President, November 7, 1961, *FRUS, 1961–1963, Vol. I: Vietnam, 1961*, 550–552.

83. Cited in Hunt, *Lyndon Johnson's War*, 77.

84. Hilsman to Rusk, March 14, 1964, *FRUS, 1964–1968, Vol. I: Vietnam, 1964*, 176–179.

85. Memorandum from the Under Secretary of State (Bowles) to President Kennedy, June 13, 1962, *FRUS, 1961–1963, Vol. XXIII: Southeast Asia*, 69–72.

86. Memorandum from the Under Secretary of State (Bowles) to President Kennedy, June 13, 1962, *FRUS, 1961–1963, Vol. XXIII: Southeast Asia*, 69–72.

87. Moyar, *Triumph Forsaken*, 138; R. B. Smith, *An International History of the Vietnam War*, vol. 1 (New York: St. Martin's, 1983). See also Memorandum from the Ambassador to Thailand (Young) to the President's Military Representative (Taylor), October 27, 1961, *FRUS, 1961–1963, Vol. XXIII: Southeast Asia*, 28–31.

88. Memorandum from the Ambassador to Thailand (Young) to the President's Military Representative (Taylor), October 27, 1961, *FRUS, 1961–1963, Vol. XXIII: Southeast Asia*, 28–31.

89. Malayan prime minister Tunku Abdul Rahman, quoted in Moyar, *Triumph Forsaken*, 139–140.

90. Battle to Bundy, July 13, 1961, *FRUS, 1961–1963, Vol. XXIII: Southeast Asia*, 770–774.

91. Lloyd Cox and Berndon O'Conner, "Australia, the US, and the Vietnam and Iraq Wars: 'Hound Dog, not Lapdog,'" *Australia Journal of Political Science* 47, no. 2 (June 2012): 173–179.

92. Memorandum from the Joint Chiefs of Staff to Secretary of Defense McNamara, October 13, 1961, *FRUS, 1961–1963, Vol. XXIII: Southeast Asia*, 443–445; William P. Bundy interview, Princeton, NJ, April 6, 1985, quoted in DiLeo, *George Ball, Vietnam, and the Rethinking of Containment*, 73.

93. Memorandum from Robert W. Komer of the National Security Council Staff to President Kennedy, September 11, 1961, *FRUS, 1961–1963, Vol. XXIII: Southeast Asia*, 426.

94. Memorandum from Robert W. Komer of the National Security Council Staff to the President's Special Assistant for National Security Affairs (Bundy), March 27, 1961, *FRUS, 1961–1963, Vol. XXIII: Southeast Asia*, 333–334; Record of Conversation, March 31, 1961, *FRUS, 1961–1963, Vol. XXIII: Southeast Asia*, 334–336.

95. Memorandum of Conversation, April 24, 1961, *FRUS, 1961–1963, Vol. XXIII: Southeast Asia*, 382–390.

96. Sheldon W. Simon, *The Broken Triangle; Peking, Djakarta, and the PKI* (Baltimore: Johns Hopkins University Press, 1969), 60–72.

97. Michael Lind, *The Necessary War: A Reinterpretation of America's Most Disastrous Military Conflict* (New York: Touchstone, 2002), xv.

98. *The Big Ideas of Lee Kuan Yew*, ed. Shashi Jayakumar and Rahul Sagar (Singapore: Strait Times Press, 2014). Lee Kuan Yew wrote in his memoirs: "Although American intervention failed in Vietnam, it bought time for the rest of Southeast Asia. In 1965, when the US military moved massively into South Vietnam, Thailand, Malaysia, and the Philippines faced internal threats from armed communist insurgencies. . . . America's action enabled non-communist Southeast Asia to put their own houses in order. By 1975, they were in better shape to stand up to the communists. Had there been no US intervention, the will of these countries to resist them would have melted and Southeast Asia would most likely have gone communist. The prosperous emerging market economies of ASEAN were nurtured during the Vietnam War years." See Lee Kuan Yew, *From Third World to First: The Singapore Story: 1965–2000* (Singapore: Times Editions, 2000), 573.

99. Memorandum from the Deputy Assistant Secretary of State for Far Eastern Affairs (Steeves) to Secretary of State-Designate Rusk's Liaison (McGhee), January 18, 1961, *FRUS, 1961–1963, Vol. XXIII: Southeast Asia*, 1–2.

100. Memorandum from the President's Special Assistant for National Security Affairs (Bundy) to the President, January 9, 1964, *FRUS, 1964–1968, Vol. I: Vietnam, 1964*, 8–15.

Reischauer, a personal friend of Bundy's, had warned the Kennedy administration of the danger of fighting a war against Vietnamese nationalism. Reischauer would later recall that Bundy was dangerously ignorant on Japanese issues despite Reischauer's best efforts to educate him and that he never called on Reischauer for advice. Reischauer continued to oppose the war throughout its duration (though he refused to publicly break with the administration while serving as ambassador to Japan) and wrote a caustic memo in May 1965 denouncing the administration's Asia policy. See George R. Packard, *Edwin O. Reischauer and the American Discovery of Japan* (New York: Columbia University Press, 2010), 139, 143, 225.

101. Michael J. Green, *Arming Japan: Defense Production, Alliance Politics, and the Postwar Search for Autonomy* (New York: Columbia University Press, 1995), 31–52.

102. Victor D. Cha, *Alignment Despite Antagonism: The United States-Korea-Japan Security Triangle* (Stanford, CA: Stanford University Press, 1999); Christopher W. Hughes, *Japan's Security Agenda: Military, Economic, and Environmental Dimensions* (Boulder, CO: Lynne Rienner, 2004), 154.

103. Kaname Akamatsu, "A Historical Pattern of Economic Growth in Developing Countries," *Journal of Developing Economies* 1, no. 1 (March–August 1962): 3–25.

104. Edwin O. Reischauer, *Beyond Vietnam: The United States and Asia* (New York: Vintage, 1968), 189–192.

105. Reischauer, *Beyond Vietnam*, 92.

106. Don Oberdorfer, *The Two Koreas: A Contemporary History* (Reading, MA: Addison-Wesley, 1998), 23.

107. Halberstam, *The Best and the Brightest*, 521–522.

108. Robert A. Scalapino, "Vietnam and World Peace," *Vietnam Perspectives* 1, no. 3 (February 1966): 12.

109. B. R. Nanda, ed., *Indian Foreign Policy: The Nehru Years* (Honolulu: University Press of Hawaii, 1976), 12.

110. Evelyn Goh, *Constructing the U.S. Rapprochement with China, 1961–1974: From "Red Menace" to "Tacit Ally"* (Cambridge: Cambridge University Press, 2005), 54–55.

111. Goh, *Constructing the U.S. Rapprochement with China, 1961–1974*, 54–55.

112. Goh, *Constructing the U.S. Rapprochement with China, 1961–1974*, 17–30.

113. "Basic National Security Policy," draft paper prepared by the Policy Planning Council, June 22, 1962, 165–166, http://www.jfklibrary.org/Asset-Viewer/Archives/JFKNSF-294-001.aspx.

114. Gaddis, *Strategies of Containment*, 266.

115. Chen Jian, "China's Involvement with the Vietnam War, 1964–1969," *China Quarterly*, no. 142 (June 1995): 356–387; Kalb and Abel, *Roots of Involvement*, 183.

116. "The Chinese Equation," draft memo, 27 April 1967, Box I, NSF/Jenkins Files, LBJ Library.

117. Goh, *Constructing the U.S. Rapprochement with China, 1961–1974*, 30–34.

118. Chen Jian, *Mao's China and the Cold War* (Chapel Hill: University of North Carolina Press, 2001), 243–245.

119. The troop buildup along the Sino-Soviet border did not begin until 1965. See Chen, *Mao's China and the Cold War*, 240.

120. Memorandum from the Deputy Under Secretary of State for Political Affairs (Johnson) to the Under Secretary of State (Bowles), June 24, 1961, *FRUS, 1961–1963, Vol. XXIII: Southeast Asia,* 9–12; Memorandum from the President's Deputy Special Assistant for National Security Affairs (Rostow) to President Kennedy, July 25, 1961, *FRUS, 1961–1963, Vol. XXIII: Southeast Asia,* 879–882.

121. McGeorge Bundy notes for Tuesday Luncheon Group Agenda, April 17, 1962, Papers of John F. Kennedy, Presidential Papers, National Security Files, 4, http://www .jfklibrary.org/Asset-Viewer/Archives/JFKNSF-294-001.aspx#.

122. Timothy P. Maga, *John F. Kennedy and the New Pacific Community, 1961–1963* (New York: St. Martin's, 1990), x, 48–50.

9. Nixon and Kissinger's Redefinition of Containment in Asia, 1969–1975

1. Alexis de Tocqueville, *Democracy in America* (New York: Vintage, 1945), 240–245, cited in Walter A. MacDougall, "Can the United States Do Grand Strategy?," remarks before the Foreign Policy Research Institute, April 2010.

2. Franz Schurmann, *The Foreign Politics of Richard Nixon: The Grand Design,* 3 vols. (Berkeley: University of California, Institute of International Studies, 1987), 43.

3. White House Background Press Briefing by the President's Assistant for National Security Affairs, December 18, 1969, in U.S. Department of State, *Foreign Relations of the United States,* http://digicoll.library.wisc.edu/FRUS/Browse.html [hereafter cited as *FRUS*], *1969–1976, Vol. I: Foundations of Foreign Policy, 1969–1972,* 153–158.

4. White House Background Press Briefing by the President's Assistant for National Security Affairs.

5. *Public Papers of the Presidents: Richard M. Nixon, 1971* (Washington, DC: Government Printing Office, 1972), 806, quoted in John Lewis Gaddis, "Rescuing Chance from Circumstance," in *The Diplomats,* ed. Craig and Loewenheim, 574. See also Henry A. Kissinger, *White House Years* (New York: Little, Brown, 1979), 56–57.

6. John Lewis Gaddis, *Strategies of Containment* (New York: Oxford University Press, 1982), 282; Joan Hoff, "A Revisionist View of Nixon's Foreign Policy," *Presidential Studies Quarterly* 26, no. 1 (Winter 1996): 111. Kissinger was not hostile to morality in foreign policy, as many of his critics have asserted over the years. As he told an audience in Pakistan earlier in his academic career when explaining why the United States was right to disagree with Europe on former colonies, "one does not oppose one's allies easily, if one is a self-respecting country. We have always supported the attempt of countries to achieve freedom and self-determination." See Henry A. Kissinger, "Some Aspects of American Foreign Policy," *Pakistan Horizon* 15, no. 2 (2nd quarter 1962): 107. If anything, his experience with Europe's trauma and the Holocaust demonstrated that the greatest moral failing would be for a statesman to allow the descent of chaos on the international system.

7. Historian Jeffrey Kimball disputes that Gaddis's argument that Nixon wanted multipolarity is canon. In an overview of the relevant literature, Kimball notes that Nixon and

Kissinger simply prioritized certain goals over others. They sought to achieve an "ensemble" of aims at the expense of "secondary" ones; for example, in 1971, bringing about an "ensemble of a Vietnam settlement and summit meetings in Beijing and Moscow." See Jeffrey P. Kimball, "The Vietnam War," in *A Companion to Richard M. Nixon*, ed. Melvin Small (Malden, MA: Wiley-Blackwell, 2011), 384. Kimball's distinction is useful in terms of explaining Nixon and Kissinger's statecraft but does not change the fact that the Nixon administration embraced pluralism and multipolarity in international relations as being advantageous to U.S. primacy.

8. Ambassador Winston Lord, interview by Charles Stuart Kennedy and Nancy Bernkopf Tucker, April 28, 1998, Foreign Affairs Oral History Collection (Arlington, VA: Association for Diplomatic Studies and Training, 2003) [hereafter Winston Lord ADST Oral History], 102, http://www.adst.org/OH%20TOCs/Lord,%20Winston.pdf.

9. Robert Dallek, *Nixon and Kissinger: Partners in Power* (New York: Harper Perennial, 2007), 438–439, 524.

10. On Kissinger's lead role, see, for example, Marvin Kalb and Bernard Kalb, *Kissinger* (Boston: Little, Brown, 1974), 124, 158; Walter Isaacson, *Kissinger: A Biography* (New York: Simon and Schuster, 1992), 259. Others saw Nixon as the architect and Kissinger as the engineer; see, for example, Schurmann, *The Foreign Politics of Richard Nixon*, 4.

11. Nixon quoted in Stephen E. Ambrose, *Nixon: The Triumph of a Politician, 1962–1972* (New York: Simon and Schuster, 1989), 2:44.

12. William Bundy, *A Tangled Web: The Making of Foreign Policy in the Nixon Presidency* (New York: Hill and Wang, 1998), 3–56; James Mann, *About Face: A History of America's Curious Relationship with China, from Nixon to Clinton* (New York: Knopf, 1999), 17.

13. Richard M. Nixon, "Asia after Viet Nam," *Foreign Affairs* 46, no. 1 (October 1967): 114.

14. Nixon, "Asia after Viet Nam," 119.

15. Nixon, "Asia after Viet Nam," 114.

16. Betty Glad and Michael W. Link, "President Nixon's Inner Circle of Advisers," *Presidential Studies Quarterly* 26, no. 1 (Winter 1996); Hoff, "A Revisionist View of Nixon's Foreign Policy," 111; White House Background Press Briefing by the President's Assistant for National Security Affairs, December 18, 1969, *FRUS, 1969–1976, Vol. I: Foundations of Foreign Policy, 1969–1972*, 153–158.

17. Ambassador Marshall Green, interview by Charles Stuart Kennedy, December 13, 1988, Foreign Affairs Oral History Collection (Arlington, VA: Association for Diplomatic Studies and Training, 2013) [hereafter Marshall Green 1988 ADST Oral History], 22, http://adst.org/wp-content/uploads/2012/09/Green-Marshall.pdf.

18. Marshall Green, *Pacific Encounters: Recollections and Humor* (Bethesda, MD: Dacor, 1997), 100. In fact, Holdridge and others on the NSC used confidential channels to tap expertise from State Department China experts such as Charles Freeman but did so without the knowledge of the State Department leadership.

19. Winston Lord ADST Oral History, 90–95.

20. Lord had particularly close access to Kissinger but was not necessarily the most knowledgeable NSC staff member about the region. John Holdridge and Richard Sneider,

both seconded from State, were leading China and Japan/Korea experts, respectively. Morton Halperin also worked intimately on Okinawa reversion while on the NSC staff.

21. Glad and Link, "President Nixon's Inner Circle of Advisers," 28.

22. Ambrose, *Nixon*, 2:129.

23. Bundy, *A Tangled Web*, 138; Richard M. Nixon, "Address Accepting the Presidential Nomination at the Republican National Convention in Miami Beach, Florida," August 8, 1968, posted online by Gerhard Peters and John T. Woolley, The American Presidency Project, http://www.presidency.ucsb.edu/ws/?pid=25968. The phrase "peace with honor" was used first in 1973. See Richard M. Nixon, "Address to the Nation Announcing Conclusion of an Agreement on Ending the War and Restoring Peace in Vietnam," January 23, 1973, posted online by Gerhard Peters and John T. Woolley, The American Presidency Project, http://www.presidency.ucsb.edu/ws/?pid=3808.

24. Henry A. Kissinger, "The Viet Nam Negotiations," *Foreign Affairs* 47, no. 2 (January 1969): 211–234.

25. Kissinger, "The Viet Nam Negotiations," 230–231.

26. Kissinger, "The Viet Nam Negotiations," 214.

27. This was expressed in "Summary of Responses to NSSM 1," March 22, 1969, *FRUS, 1969–1976, Vol. VI: Vietnam, January 1969–July 1970*, 129–152.

28. The RAND memo was officially rebranded as "National Security Memorandum 1: Situation in Vietnam," January 21, 1969, http://www.fas.org/irp/offdocs/nssm-nixon /nssm_001.pdf. Jeffrey Kimball argues that it had a major influence on the thinking of Nixon and Kissinger. See Jeffrey Kimball, *The Vietnam War Files: Uncovering the Secret History of the Nixon-Era Strategy* (Lawrence: University of Kansas Press, 2004), 11. On the other hand, Kissinger biographer Walter Isaacson contends that the memorandum was used to distract the bureaucracy and test internal government reactions to increased bombing. See Isaacson, *Kissinger*, 164. The reality is that Nixon and Kissinger had largely settled on their approach but used the RAND report and the interagency responses to fine-tune their thinking without ever turning over the decision-making process to the bureaucracy.

29. "National Security Study Memorandum 1: Situation in Vietnam," January 21, 1969. See also Daniel Ellsberg, *Secrets: A Memoir of Vietnam and the Pentagon Papers* (New York: Penguin, 2002), 231–234.

30. Isaacson, *Kissinger*, 163.

31. Nixon and Kissinger assert the former. Kimball concludes that Kissinger sought only an undefined "decent interval." See Jeffrey Kimball, *Nixon's Vietnam War* (Lexington: University of Kentucky Press, 1998); Kimball, "The Vietnam War," 391. Others see a very deliberate effort to push the South's collapse past the 1972 election. See Larry Berman, *No Peace, No Honor: Nixon, Kissinger, and Betrayal in Vietnam* (New York: The Free Press, 2001). The most often-cited military history of the period concludes that military operations were finally succeeding but were undercut by the administration's decision that it had to find a way to withdraw. See Lewis Sorley, *A Better War: The Unexamined Victories and Final Tragedy of America's Last Years in Vietnam* (New York: Harcourt Brace, 1999).

32. William Bundy suspects that the Republicans deliberately sabotaged the talks, but he concedes that it made little difference. See Bundy, *A Tangled Web*, 388. Phil Habib

thought an opportunity to end the war early was lost. See Undersecretary Philip C. Habib, interviewed by Edward Mulcahy, May 24, 1984, Foreign Affairs Oral History Collection (Arlington, VA: Association for Diplomatic Studies and Training, 1998) [hereafter Philip C. Habib ADST Oral History], 51, http://www.adst.org/OH%20TOCs/Habib,%20Philip %20C.toc.pdf. Ken Hughes, *Chasing Shadows: The Nixon Tapes, the Chennault Affair, and the Origins of Watergate* (Charlottesville: University Press of Virginia, 2014), 4–19, makes a strong argument for Nixon's direct involvement in an effort to disrupt peace negotiations—using Anna Chennault as a go-between—for domestic political reasons.

33. Tad Szulc, "How Kissinger Did It: Behind the Vietnam Cease-Fire Agreement," *Foreign Policy*, no. 15 (Summer 1974): 21–69 at 25.

34. Isaacson, *Kissinger*, 166; Jussi M. Hanhimaki, "Foreign Policy Overview," in Small, *A Companion to Richard M. Nixon*, 354. See also "Communist China," circa February 1969, Digital National Security Archive item number CH00042; United States Department of Defense, "Response to National Security Study Memorandum #9," circa February 1969, Digital National Security Archive item number CH00040.

35. Geoffrey Warner, "Nixon, Kissinger and the Rapprochement with China, 1969–1972, Foreign Relations of the United States 1969–1976," *International Affairs (Royal Institute of International Affairs 1944–)* 83, no. 4 (July 2007): 763–781 at 770. Kissinger's special assistant at the time, Winston Lord, noted in a June 18, 2014, interview in New York with the author that the NSC thought Beijing would exert influence in order to remove U.S. troops from Indochina, avoid an ideological embarrassment as their proxy fought the Americans, and redirect American military power toward the Soviets. But he acknowledges that the administration understood only that China made some effort with Hanoi without fully appreciating the context of tense Sino-Vietnamese historic relations. See also Prime Minister Zhou Enlai, as quoted in Memorandum of a Conversation, July 9, 1971, *FRUS, 1969–1976, Vol. XVII: China, 1969–1972*, 359–397.

36. Szulc, "How Kissinger Did It," 25.

37. Isaacson, *Kissinger*, 237–238; Kissinger, *White House Years*, 284, 1480. Nixon and Kissinger made it clear early in their secret negotiations with the Vietnamese that they had not abandoned coercive measures. In preliminary discussions carried out through a French intermediary, it was communicated to the Vietnamese that Nixon was "determined to bring this war to an early conclusion. He totally rejects continued talking and fighting. If this diplomatic approach fails, he will resort to any means necessary." See notes prepared by Jean Sainteny, July 16, 1969.

38. Bundy, *A Tangled Web*, 452.

39. Richard M. Nixon, "Address to the Nation on the Situation in Southeast Asia," April 7, 1971, posted online by Gerhard Peters and John T. Woolley, The American Presidency Project, http://www.presidency.ucsb.edu/ws/index.php?pid=2972.

40. Kissinger to Nixon, undated, *FRUS, 1969–1976, Vol. I: Foundations of Foreign Policy, 1969–1972*, 110–121; Off-the-Record Remarks by President Nixon, September 16, 1970, *FRUS, 1969–1976, Vol. I: Foundations of Foreign Policy, 1969–1972*, 247–257.

41. Isaacson, *Kissinger*, 239. Quotations are taken from notes of a meeting in the Oval Office, October 6, 1969.

42. Szulc, "How Kissinger Did It," 28.

43. Richard M. Nixon, *RN: The Memoirs of Richard Nixon* (New York: Simon and Schuster, 1990), 393.

44. Haiphong handled about 90 percent of North Vietnamese seaborne imports. The port was a vital connection between the North Vietnamese and their communist allies, who provided about $400 million in annual aid. The Office of the CNO recognized that mining Haiphong would be viewed as an "escalation" of the war and could provoke negative responses around the world. See Office of Chief of Naval Operations, "Duck Hook," July 21, 1969.

45. Minutes of Washington Special Actions Group Meeting, March 19, 1970, *FRUS, 1969–1976, Vol. IV: Vietnam, January 1969–July 1970*, 685–694.

46. Bundy, *A Tangled Web*, 71, 520; Ambassador Marshall Green, interview by Charles Stuart Kennedy, March 17, 1995, Foreign Affairs Oral History Collection (Arlington, VA: Association for Diplomatic Studies and Training, 1998), 90 [hereafter Marshall Green 1995 ADST Oral History], http://adst.org/OH%20TOCs/GREEN,%20Marshall.3.17.95.Cambodia .toc.pdf.

47. Seymour M. Hersh, *The Price of Power: Kissinger in the Nixon White House* (New York: Touchstone, 1984), 54–65.

48. See, for example, Wheeler to Laird, March 12, 1970, *FRUS, 1969–1976, Vol. VI: Vietnam, January 1969–July 1970*, 105–107.

49. The Association for Diplomatic Studies and Training Foreign Affairs Oral History Project, Marshall Green 1995 ADST Oral History, 90.

50. Isaacson, *Kissinger*, 264.

51. Nixon told Kissinger that "if while the private talks are going on they are kicking us, we are going to do something." See Editorial Note, *FRUS, 1969–1976, Vol. VI: Vietnam, January 1969–July 1970*, 96–97; Robert A. Pape, Jr., "Coercive Air Power in the Vietnam War," *International Security* 15, no. 2 (Fall 1990): 103–146.

52. Bundy, *A Tangled Web*, 154.

53. Isaacson, *Kissinger*, 275.

54. John H. Holdridge, interviewed by Charles Stuart Kennedy, July 20, 1995, Foreign Affairs Oral History Collection (Arlington, VA: Association for Diplomatic Studies and Training, 1998), 60 [hereafter John H. Holdridge 1995 ADST Oral History], http://www .adst.org/OH%20TOCs/Holdridge,%20John.%201995%20toc.pdf.

55. "Congress, the President, and the Power to Declare War: A Requiem for Vietnam," *University of Pennsylvania Law Review* 121, no. 1 (November 1972): 1–28.

56. Szulc, "How Kissinger Did It," 62–63.

57. H.R. 9055, Public Law 93-50 under the Supplemental Appropriations Act of 1973.

58. S 3394, Public Law 93-559 under the Foreign Assistance Act of 1974.

59. Richard M. Nixon, *No More Vietnams* (New York: Arbor House, 1985), 155–156.

60. Philip C. Habib ADST Oral History, 57.

61. Nixon may have appreciated this fact. As he told Kissinger on February 1, 1972: "Who is more keenly aware than I am, that from a political standpoint, we should have flushed it down the drain three years ago, blamed Johnson and Kennedy. Kennedy got us in, Johnson kept us in. I could have blamed them and been the national hero! As Eisenhower was for ending Korea. . . . But on the other hand, we couldn't do that. Not because of Vietnam, but because of Japan, because of Germany, because of the Mideast." See

David Brinkley and Luke Nichter, eds. and annots., *The Nixon Tapes* (New York: Houghton Mifflin Harcourt, 2014), 360–361.

62. For an assessment of the positive side effects of the Cambodia invasion, see John M. Shaw, *The Cambodian Campaign* (Lawrence: University of Kansas Press, 2005), 158–170.

63. Bundy, *A Tangled Web*, 499.

64. Brian VanDeMark, *Into the Quagmire: Lyndon Johnson and the Escalation of the Vietnam War* (Oxford: Oxford University Press, 1995), 19.

65. Isaacson, *Kissinger*, 247.

66. Jeffrey Kimball, "The Nixon Doctrine: A Saga of Misunderstanding," *Presidential Studies Quarterly* 36, no. 1, Presidential Doctrines (March 2006): 59–74 at 59–60.

67. Hoff, "A Revisionist View of Nixon's Foreign Policy, 112. On Kissinger being surprised, see John H. Holdridge 1995 ADST Oral History, 62.

68. Robert E. Osgood, "Introduction: The Nixon Doctrine and Strategy," in *Retreat from Empire?: The First Nixon Administration* (Baltimore: Johns Hopkins University Press, 1973), 9.

69. Osgood, "Introduction: The Nixon Doctrine and Strategy," 8.

70. NSSM (National Security Study Memorandum) 3, "U.S. Military Posture and the Balance of Power," January 21, 1969, the White House, declassified January 24, 2007; "National Security Decision Memorandum 13," May 28, 1969, 1, https://www.fas.org/irp/offdocs/nsdm-nixon/nsdm-13.pdf.

71. Bundy, *A Tangled Web*, 546; Green, *Pacific Encounters*, 99; Marshall Green 1995 ADST Oral History, 103.

72. Richard Nixon, "Informal Remarks in Guam with Newsmen," July 25, 1969, posted online by Gerhard Peters and John T. Woolley, The American Presidency Project, http://www.presidency.ucsb.edu/ws/?pid=2140.

73. See, for example, "The World of Richard Nixon," *Time*, March 2, 1970.

74. Earl C. Ravenal, *Large-Scale Foreign Policy Change: The Nixon Doctrine as History and Portent* (Berkeley: University of California, Institute of International Studies, 1989), 2.

75. Author's interview with Winston Lord, New York, NY, June 18, 2014. On Kissinger being taken by surprise, see Kissinger, *White House Years*, 222–225; John H. Holdridge 1995 ADST Oral History, 62.

76. Richard Nixon, "Address to the Nation on the War in Vietnam," November 3, 1969, posted online by Gerhard Peters and John T. Woolley, The American Presidency Project, http://www.presidency.ucsb.edu/ws/index.php?pid=2303; Kimball, "The Nixon Doctrine," 70.

77. National Security Council Staff, "The Nixon Doctrine for Asia: Some Hard Issues," undated, received by Kissinger on January 23, 1970, *FRUS, 1969–1976, Vol. I: Foundations of Foreign Policy*, 174–184.

78. Richard Nixon, "First Annual Report to the Congress on United States Foreign Policy for the 1970's," February 18, 1970, posted online by Gerhard Peters and John T. Woolley, The American Presidency Project, http://www.presidency.ucsb.edu/ws/?pid=2835.

79. Earl C. Ravenal, "The Nixon Doctrine and Our Asian Commitments," *Foreign Affairs* 49, no. 2 (January 1971): 207.

80. Gaddis, *Strategies of Containment*, 274.

81. Osgood, "Introduction: The Nixon Doctrine and Strategy," 9.

82. "Joint Strategic Objectives Plan for FY 1973 through FY 1980 (JSOP FY 73–80), Volume II: Analyses and Force Tabulations, Book VII: Free World Forces, Part II: Major Force Objectives for Free World Countries, Section 3: The Pacific/Asia Area," circa May 19, 1971, Digital National Security Archive, United States and the Two Koreas, item number KO00108, 199 pp.

83. "Joint Strategic Objectives Plan for FY 1973 through FY 1980 (JSOP FY 73–80), Volume II: Analyses and Force Tabulations, Book VII: Free World Forces, Part II: Major Force Objectives for Free World Countries, Section 3: The Pacific/Asia Area," circa May 19, 1971, Digital National Security Archive, United States and the Two Koreas, item number KO00108.

84. Telegram from Department of State to the Embassy in Korea, January 29, 1970, *FRUS, 1969–1976, Vol. XIX: Part 1, Korea, 1969–1972*, 121–122.

85. Richard M. Nixon, "[U.S. Troops in South Korea; Includes Follow-Up Memorandum]," November 24, 1969, Digital National Security Archive, United States and the Two Koreas, item number KO00081, 1 p.

86. "Joint Strategic Objectives Plan for FY 1973 through FY 1980 (JSOP FY 73–80), Volume II: Analyses and Force Tabulations, Book VII: Free World Forces, Part II: Major Force Objectives for Free World Countries, Section 3: The Pacific/Asia Area," circa May 19, 1971, Digital National Security Archive, United States and the Two Koreas, item number KO00108.

87. John Lewis Gaddis, *George F. Kennan: An American Life*, reprint ed. (New York: Penguin Books, 2012), 161–617.

88. Walter L. Hixson, *George F. Kennan: Cold War Iconoclast* (New York: Columbia University Press, 1989), 236.

89. Osgood, "Introduction: The Nixon Doctrine and Strategy," 9.

90. Nixon quoted in Ravenal, "The Nixon Doctrine and Our Asian Commitments," 209–210.

91. Osgood, "Introduction: The Nixon Doctrine and Strategy," 18.

92. Kissinger to Nixon, undated, *FRUS, 1969–1976, Vol. I: Foundations of Foreign Policy, 1969–1972*, 110–121; the author's identity remains anonymous.

93. Paper Prepared by the National Security Council Staff, "The Nixon Doctrine for Asia: Some Hard Issues," undated, *FRUS, 1969–1976, Vol. I: Foundations of Foreign Policy, 1969–1972*, 174–184.

94. Nixon quoted in Michael Schaller, *Altered States: The United States and Japan Since the Occupation* (New York: Oxford University Press, 1997), 215.

95. U.S. Department of Defense, Response to NSSM 9: "Review of the International Situation as of January 20, 1969," Volume V: Noncommunist Far East, circa January 23, 1969, Digital National Security Archive, Presidential Directives, item number PR00327, 158 pp.

96. Armin Meyer, "Japanese Reaction on Defense Burden-Sharing," October 23, 1971, Digital National Security Archive, Japan and the U.S., 1960–1976, item number JU01454, 6 pp.

97. U.S. Department of the Treasury, "Treasury Comment on NSSM on Japan," March 24, 1969, *FRUS, 1969–1976, Vol. III: Foreign Economic Policy; International Monetary Policy, 1969–1972*, 44–48.

98. Kissinger later recalled, "When I first came to office, there was no major country I understood less than Japan. . . . I did not grasp Japan's unique character." See Henry Kissinger, *Years of Upheaval* (Boston: Little, Brown, 1982), 735.

99. Francis J. Gavin, *Gold, Dollars, and Power: The Politics of International Monetary Relations, 1958–1971* (Chapel Hill: University of North Carolina Press, 2004), 194.

100. Thomas W. Zeiler, "Nixon Shocks Japan, Inc.," in *Nixon in the World: American Foreign Relations, 1969–1977*, ed. Andrew Preston and Fredrik Logevall (New York: Oxford University Press, 2008), 296.

101. Schaller, *Altered States*, 215–216.

102. Kissinger, *White House Years*, 329; Burke quotation from Marshall Green, *Pacific Encounters, Recollections and Humor* (Washington, DC: Dacor House, 1997), 38.

103. U.S. Department of the Treasury, "Treasury Comment on NSSM on Japan," March 24, 1969, *FRUS, 1969–1976, Vol. III: Foreign Economic Policy; International Monetary Policy, 1969–1972*, 44–48.

104. Wakaizumi Kei and John Swenson-Wright, *The Best Course Available: A Personal Account of the Secret U.S.-Japan Okinawa Reversion Negotiations* (Honolulu: University of Hawaii Press, 2002), 35, 272.

105. "Joint Statement of Japanese Prime Minister Eisaku Sato and U.S. President Richard Nixon" (Washington, DC: Government Printing Office, 1971), *Public Papers of the Presidents of the United States: Richard Nixon, 1969*, 953–957.

106. I. M. Destler, Haruhiro Fukui, and Hideo Sato, *The Textile Wrangle: Conflict in Japanese-American Relations, 1969–1971* (Ithaca, NY: Cornell University Press, 1979).

107. Walter LaFeber, *The Clash: U.S.-Japanese Relations Throughout History* (New York: Norton, 1997), 350; U. Alexis Johnson, *The Right Hand of Power* (New York: Prentice-Hall, 1984), 548–552.

108. Richard Nixon, The President of the United States, to Eisaku Sato, Prime Minister of Japan, Tokyo, March 12, 1971; General Records, Letters Sent, 1971; Historical Documents File No. 2014-2731, SE 1-2-4, "Japan-U.S. Trade/Textile," February 1971–March 1971; Diplomatic Archives of the Ministry of Foreign Affairs of Japan, Tokyo, Japan.

109. Zeiler, "Nixon Shocks Japan, Inc.," 295.

110. Schaller, *Altered States*, 234–235; I. M. Destler, Haruhiro Fukui, and Hideo Sato, *The Textile Wrangle: Conflict in Japanese-American Relations, 1969–1971* (Ithaca, NY: Cornell University Press, 1979), 292–293; Schaller, "The Nixon Shocks and U.S.-Japan Strategic Relations: 1969–1974," Working Paper No. 2, National Security Archives, 1996, http://www2.gwu.edu/~nsarchiv/japan/schallertp.htm.

111. Richard Halloran, "Washington's Harsh Tactics Anger Tokyo Officials, Who 'Won't Forget,'" *New York Times*, October 16, 1971.

112. Michael J. Green, *Arming Japan: Defense Production, Alliance Politics, and the Postwar Search for Autonomy* (New York: Columbia University Press, 1995), 53.

113. Osgood, "Introduction: The Nixon Doctrine and Strategy," 8. A similar point is made in James. E. Dornan, Jr., "The Nixon Doctrine and the Primacy of Detente," *Intercollegiate Review* (Spring 1974): 94.

114. Mann, *About Face*, 34.

115. Ambrose, *Nixon*, 44.

116. Mann, *About Face*, 17.

117. Henry A. Kissinger, *The Necessity of Choice: Prospects for American Foreign Policy* (New York: Anchor, 1962), 209–210.

118. U.S. Department of Defense, Response to National Security Study Memorandum 9: "Review of the International Situation"—as of 20 January 1969—Volume II: Communist China, circa February 1969, Digital National Security Archive, China and the U.S., item number CH0040, 30; U.S. National Security Council, "Communist China," circa February 1969, Digital National Security Archive, China and the U.S., item number CH00042, 26.

119. SNIE 13-69: Communist China and Asia, March 6, 1969, in *Tracking the Dragon: National Intelligence Estimates on China During the Era of Mao, 1948–1976*, ed. John K. Allen, Jr., John Carver, and Tom Elmore (Pittsburgh: National Intelligence Council, 2004), 528.

120. Ambassador Marshall Green, interviewed by self, March 17, 1995, Foreign Affairs Oral History Collection (Arlington, VA: Association for Diplomatic Studies and Training, 1998), 90 [hereafter Marshall Green 1995 Self Interview ADST Oral History], http://adst.org/wp-content/uploads/2012/09/Green-Marshall-China-Policy.pdf.

121. U.S. National Security Council, "Communist China," circa February 1969, Digital National Security Archive, China and the U.S., item number CH00042, 26 pp.

122. John H. Holdridge, interviewed by Marshall Green and Charles Stuart Kennedy, December 14, 1989, Foreign Affairs Oral History Collection (Arlington, VA: Association for Diplomatic Studies and Training, 1998), 27 [hereafter John H. Holdridge 1989 ADST Oral History], http://www.adst.org/OH%20TOCs/Holdridge,%20John.%201989%20toc.pdf.

123. Winston Lord ADST Oral History, 111.

124. Margaret MacMillan, *Nixon and Mao: The Week That Changed the World* (New York: Random House, 2008), 56.

125. Alexander M. Haig, Jr., with Charles McCarry, *Inner Circles: How America Changed the World* (New York: Grand Central, 1994), 257; Marvin Kalb and Bernard Kalb, *Kissinger* (Boston: Little, Brown, 1974), 253.

126. Mann, *About Face*, 19–20.

127. John H. Holdridge 1989 ADST Oral History, 26.

128. Warren Cohen, *America's Response to China*, 5th ed. (New York: Columbia University Press, 2010), 215–217; Association for Diplomatic Studies and Training Foreign Affairs Oral History Project, John H. Holdridge, interviewed by Marshall Green and Charles Stuart Kennedy, July 14, 1989, 28.

129. Marshall Green, "Memorandum for the Record," June 10, 1969, cited in Bundy, *A Tangled Web*, 821.

130. Kissinger, *White House Years*, 192, 712; MacMillan, *Nixon and Mao*, 164.

131. John H. Holdridge 1989 ADST Oral History, 26–27.

132. Chen Jian, *Mao's China and the Cold War* (Chapel Hill: University of North Carolina Press, 2001), 250–251, 364; Cohen, *America's Response to China*, 217; Kissinger, *White House Years*, 687; MacMillan, *Nixon and Mao*, 170.

133. Department of State Memorandum, March 5, 1990 (date may be a typo in Mann and may mean 1970), Warsaw talks file, National Security Archives, cited in Mann, *About Face*, 24.

134. U.S. National Security Council, Interdepartmental Group for East Asia and the Pacific, NSSM 124: "Next Steps Toward the People's Republic of China (PRC) [Includes Study and Issues Paper]," May 27, 1971, Digital National Security Archive, Presidential Directives, Part II, item number PR00721, 80 pp.; U.S. National Security Council, Interdepartmental Group for East Asia and the Pacific Region, "Next Steps Toward the People's Republic of China—NSSM 124," June 1, 1971, Digital National Security Archive, item number CH00211, 88 pp.

135. Mann, *About Face*, 27.

136. As quoted in Chen, *Mao's China and the Cold War*, 249.

137. Cohen, *America's Response to China*, 218; MacMillan, *Nixon and Mao*, 179–180; W. R. Smyser, National Security Council Staff, to Kissinger, "Letter from Your Friend in Paris, and Other Chinese Miscellania," 7 November 1970, Secret/Sensitive/Eyes Only, Box 1032, [Fortune] Cookies II [Chronology of Exchanges with PRC February 1969–April 1971], http://nsarchive.gwu.edu/NSAEBB/NSAEBB66/#doc5; "Memo by Hilaly, Record of a Discussion with Mr. Henry Kissinger on the White House on 16th December 1970," Box 1031, Exchanges Leading Up to HAK Trip to China—December 1969–July 1971 (1), http://nsarchive.gwu.edu/NSAEBB/NSAEBB66/#doc7.

138. MacMillan, *Nixon and Mao*, 183.

139. Mann, *About Face*, 34; Kissinger to Nixon, "My Talks with Chou En-lai," 14 July 1971, Top Secret/Sensitive/Exclusively Eyes Only, Box 1033, Miscellaneous Memoranda Relating to HAK Trip to PRC, July 1971, http://nsarchive.gwu.edu/NSAEBB/NSAEBB66/#40.

140. Richard Nixon, "Remarks to the Nation Announcing Acceptance of an Invitation to Visit the People's Republic of China," July 15, 1971, posted online by Gerhard Peters and John T. Woolley, The American Presidency Project, http://www.presidency.ucsb.edu/ws/?pid=3079.

141. Kissinger had been proposing a Nixon-Brezhnev summit to the Soviet ambassador in Washington right up to his secret trip to Pakistan and had been secretly willing to postpone the China trip if Moscow said yes. The Soviets did not—but then quickly accepted within weeks of the July 15 announcement of Kissinger's secret visit to Beijing. Author's interview with Winston Lord, New York, NY, June 18, 2014.

142. Nancy Bernkopf Tucker, "Taiwan Expendable? Nixon and Kissinger Go to China," *Journal of American History* 92, no. 1 (June 2005): 109–135 at 125; Winston Lord ADST Oral History, 138, 150.

143. Mann, *About Face*, 37.

144. A thorough assessment of regional reactions was presented by Green to the NSC in March 1972. See John H. Holdridge, "Meeting with Mr. Marshall Green, Assistant Secretary of State for East Asia and Pacific Affairs, on Thursday, March 23, 1972, at 4:00 P.M.," March 23, 1972, Digital National Security Archive, Japan and the U.S., 1960–1976, item number JU01518, 3 pp.

145. Mann, *About Face*, 37; Marshall Green 1995 ADST Oral History, 110.

146. NPM, White House Special Files, President's Personal Files, Box 7, Folder "China Notes," cited in MacMillan, *Nixon and Mao*, 234.

147. Evelyn Goh, *Constructing the U.S. Rapprochement with China, 1961–1974: From "Red Menace" to "Tacit Ally"* (Cambridge: Cambridge University Press, 2005), 181.

148. Robert S. Ross, *Negotiating Cooperation: The United States and China, 1969–1989* (Stanford, CA: Stanford University Press, 1995), 41. Nixon further agreed to "Five Principles" that further detailed the U.S. commitment not to support unilateral Taiwanese independence or the stationing of Japanese troops on Taiwan but would support peaceful resolution between Taipei and Beijing and normalization with China, recognizing the centrality of the Taiwan question in that process. Referenced in a (then) classified review of U.S. China policy prepared by James Lilly of the NSC staff for President Reagan. See June 3, 1981, Memo from Allen to VP, Meese, Baker, Deaver, on "First Part of Analysis of US-Chinese Bilateral Relations" (two-page memo with four-page attachment), Folder "China-General 05/27/1981–06/03/1981 CF 0160" in Meese, Edwin: Files, Box 2, Reagan Library.

149. Evelyn Goh, "Nixon, Kissinger, and the 'Soviet Card' in the U.S. Opening to China, 1971–1974," *Diplomatic History* 29, no. 3 (June 2005): 489.

150. Association for Diplomatic Studies and Training Foreign Affairs Oral History Project, Ambassador Winston Lord, interviewed by Charles Stuart Kennedy and Nancy Bernkopf Tucker, April 28, 1998, 167–170; MacMillan, *Nixon and Mao*, 242. Some accounts even suggest that Kissinger shared sensitive intelligence on his first trip. See Mann, *About Face*, 35–36.

151. Memorandum of Conversation, February 22, 1972, 2:10 P.M.–6:00 P.M., NSA, Nixon's Trip to China: Records Now Completely Declassified, Doc. 1, 11–12, cited in MacMillan, *Nixon and Mao*, 236.

152. Interview by the author with Winston Lord, June 18, 2014.

153. Winston Lord ADST Oral History, 144–148.

154. Most significantly, Green pointed out that the draft communiqué listed U.S. defense commitments to South Korea and Japan but did not mention the treaty with Taiwan. Evoking Acheson's 1950 defense perimeter speech and the subsequent North Korean attack on the South, Green enlisted Rogers's help to lobby the president to renegotiate the communiqué. The irate Chinese delegation responded with ideological rants about North Korea and Indochina but finally agreed to smooth over the differences since Beijing now needed the joint communiqué at least as much as the Americans. See Winston Lord ADST Oral History, 167–170; Marshall Green 1995 Self Interview ADST Oral History, 30–33; Mann, *About Face*, 40–52; Joint Communiqué of the United States of America and the People's Republic of China, February 28, 1972, http://www.taiwandocuments.org /communique01.htm.

155. "Joint Statement Following Discussions with Leaders of the People's Republic of China," Shanghai, February 27, 1972, *Public Papers of the Presidents: Richard M. Nixon, 1972* (Washington, DC: Government Printing Office, 1974), 376–379.

156. June 3, 1981, Memo from Allen to VP, Meese, Baker, Deaver, on "First Part of Analysis of US-Chinese Bilateral Relations."

157. "Joint Statement Following Discussions with Leaders of the People's Republic of China," Shanghai, February 27, 1972, Taiwan Documents Project, http://www.taiwan documents.org/communique01.htm.

158. Henry A. Kissinger, "The Moral Foundations of Foreign Policy," Address by Secretary Kissinger at Minneapolis, July 15, 1975, *Department of State Bulletin*, no. 1884 (August 4, 1975), 161–172.

159. U.S. Director of Central Intelligence, "Soviet Foreign Policies and the Outlook for Soviet-American Relations," April 20, 1972, Digital National Security Archive, Soviet Estimate, item number SE00456, 38 pp.

160. Kissinger to Nixon, March 2, 1973, *FRUS, 1969–1976, Vol. XVIII: China, 1973–1976*, 208–223.

161. U.S. Director of Central Intelligence, "Soviet Foreign Policies and the Outlook for Soviet-American Relations," April 20, 1972, Digital National Security Archive, Soviet Estimate, item number SE00456.

162. "Joint Strategic Objectives Plan for FY 1973 through FY 1980 (JSOP FY 73–80), Volume II: Analyses and Force Tabulations, Book VII: Free World Forces, Part II: Major Force Objectives for Free World Countries, Section 3: The Pacific/Asia Area," circa May 19, 1971, Digital National Security Archive, United States and the Two Koreas, item number KO00108.

163. "NSSM 122 Addendum III: U.S.-Japan Relations in the Near Future," circa August 2, 1971, Digital National Security Archive, Japan and the U.S., 1977–1992, item number JA00049, 16 pp.

164. Johnson quoted in Michael Schaller, "The Nixon 'Shocks' and U.S.-Japan Strategic Relations, 1969–1974," National Security Archives Working Paper 2, http://www2.gwu.edu /~nsarchiv/japan/schaller.htm.

165. Marshall Green 1995 ADST Oral History, 108.

166. Conversation Between Nixon and Kissinger, March 12, 1973, *FRUS, 1969–1976, Vol. XXVIII: China, 1973–1976*, 225–227.

167. Conversation Between Nixon and Kissinger, March 12, 1973, *FRUS, 1969–1976, Vol. XXVIII: China, 1973–1976*, 225–227.

168. The speech was Kissinger's "Year of Europe," delivered to the Associated Press Annual Luncheon, New York, April 23, 1973.

169. U.S. Department of State, William P. Rogers to United States Embassy, Philippines, "[United States Policy Interests and Objectives in the Philippines]," November 8, 1971, Digital National Security Archive, Philippines, item number PH00443, 11 pp.

170. Kissinger later explained that ASEAN gave the United States more room to maneuver. See Kissinger to Ford, June 13, 1975, *FRUS, 1969–1976, Vol. E-12, Documents on East and Southeast Asia, 1973–1976*, Document 16.

171. Robert J. McMahon, "The Danger of Geopolitical Fantasies: Nixon, Kissinger, and the South Asia Crisis of 1971," in Preston and Logevall, *Nixon in the World*, 251, 260–261.

172. Kissinger quoted in Goh, "Nixon, Kissinger, and the 'Soviet Card' in the U.S. Opening to China, 1971–1974," 481.

173. Kissinger quoted in Christopher Van Hollen, "The Tilt Policy Revisited: Nixon-Kissinger Geopolitics and South Asia," *Asian Survey* 30, no. 4 (April 1980): 343.

174. U.S. National Security Council, "[Meeting between Alexander M. Haig, Jr. and Huang Hua concerning India-Pakistan War]," December 12, 1971, Digital National Security Archive, China and the U.S., item number CH00236, 4 pp.

175. Goh, "Nixon, Kissinger, and the 'Soviet Card' in the U.S. Opening to China, 1971–1974," 481–482; MacMillan, *Nixon and Mao*, 223.

176. Robert J. McMahon, "The Danger of Geopolitical Fantasies," in Preston and Logevall, *Nixon in the World*, 264–266.

177. Goh, "Nixon, Kissinger, and the 'Soviet Card' in the U.S. Opening to China, 1971–1974," 492–499.

178. Bundy, *A Tangled Web*, 493.

179. Merle L. Pribbenow, "North Vietnam's Final Offensive: Strategic Endgame Nonpareil," *Parameters* (Winter 1999–2000): 58–71.

180. Bruce P. Montgomery, *Richard B. Cheney and the Rise of the Imperial Vice Presidency* (Westport, CT: Praeger, 2009), 30.

181. Andrew J. Gawthorpe, "The Ford Administration and Security Policy in the Asia-Pacific After the Fall of Saigon," *Historical Journal* 52, no. 3 (September 2009): 697–716 at 700.

182. Kissinger quoted in Chris Lamb, "Belief Systems and Decision Making in the Mayaguez Crisis," *Political Science Quarterly* 99, no. 4 (Winter 1984–1985): 684.

183. Yanek Mieczkowski, *Gerald Ford and the Challenges of the 1970s* (Lexington: University of Kentucky Press, 2005), 280–284, described at the Gerald Ford Library at http://www.fordlibrarymuseum.gov/library/exhibits/babylift/babylift.asp.

184. Franklin Odo, ed., *The Columbia Documentary History of the Asian American Experience* (New York: Columbia University Press, 2002), 407–408.

185. Gawthorpe, "The Ford Administration and Security Policy in the Asia-Pacific After the Fall of Saigon," 704.

186. See "Minutes of the Acting Secretary of State's Staff Meeting, June 15, 1975," *FRUS, 1969–1976, Vol. E-12: Documents on East and Southeast Asia, 1973–1976*, Document 15. See also Smyser to Kissinger, July 15, 1975, *FRUS, 1969–1976, Vol. E-12: Documents on East and Southeast Asia, 1973–1976*, Document 17.

187. Gawthorpe, "The Ford Administration and Security Policy," 698.

188. Smyser to Kissinger, May 7, 1975, *FRUS, 1969–1976, Vol. E-12: Documents on East and Southeast Asia, 1973–1976*, Document 14.

189. Address by President Gerald R. Ford at the University of Hawaii, December 7, 1975, http://www.ford.utexas.edu/library/speeches/750716.asp.

10. Jimmy Carter and the Return of the China Card, 1977–1980

1. Jimmy Carter, *Keeping Faith: Memoirs of a President* (Toronto: Bantam, 1982), 142–143.

2. Odd Arne Westad, "The Fall of Détente and the Turning Tides of History," in *The Fall of Détente: Soviet-American Relations During the Carter Years*, ed. Odd Arne Westad (Oslo: Scandinavian University Press, 1997), 10–11; Zbigniew Brzezinski, *Power and Principle: Memoirs of a National Security Advisor, 1977–1981* (New York: Farrar, Straus, and Giroux, 1983), 124.

3. George C. Herring, *From Colony to Superpower: U.S. Foreign Relations Since 1776* (New York: Oxford University Press, 2008), 832.

4. John Lewis Gaddis, *Strategies of Containment* (New York: Oxford University Press, 1982), 320.

5. Public Law 93-365.

6. Public Law 94-329, Section 502(B), quoted in Gaddis Smith, *Morality, Reason, and Power: American Diplomacy in the Carter Years* (New York: Hill and Wang, 1986), 50;

Cyrus Vance, *Hard Choices: Critical Years in America's Foreign Policy* (New York: Simon and Schuster, 1983), 27.

7. Betty Glad, *Outsider in the White House: Jimmy Carter, His Advisors, and the Making of American Foreign Policy* (Ithaca, NY: Cornell University Press, 2009), 1.

8. Peter Rodman, *Presidential Command: Power, Leadership, and the Making of Foreign Policy from Richard Nixon to George W. Bush* (New York: Knopf, 2009), 121.

9. Carter, *Keeping Faith*, 11.

10. Vance, *Hard Choices*, 28; Smith, *Morality, Reason, and Power*, 41.

11. Noted in Roger G. Wiegley, "Reassessing the Security Alliance Between the United States and Japan," *Naval War College Review* 32, no. 1 (February 1979): 18.

12. Vance, *Hard Choices*, 28.

13. Smith, *Morality, Reason, and Power*, 51–52.

14. Jimmy Carter, *White House Diary* (New York: Farrar, Straus, and Giroux, 2010), 425.

15. Smith, *Morality, Reason, and Power*, 36–37.

16. Smith, *Morality, Reason, and Power*, 36–37; Brzezinski, *Power and Principle*, 165.

17. Smith, *Morality, Reason, and Power*, 35.

18. Clark Clifford and Richard Holbrooke, *Counsel to the President: A Memoir* (New York: Random House, 1991), 621.

19. Zbigniew Brzezinski, "The Challenge of Change in the Soviet Bloc," *Foreign Affairs* 39, no. 3 (April 1961): 430–443.

20. Zbigniew Brzezinski, "The Balance of Power Delusion," *Foreign Policy*, no. 7 (Summer 1972): 54–59, cited in Warren I. Cohen and Nancy Bernkopf Tucker, "Beijing's Friend, Moscow's Foe," in *ZBIG: The Strategy and Statecraft of Zbigniew Brzezinski*, ed. Charles Gati (Baltimore: Johns Hopkins University Press, 2013), 88.

21. John B. Hattendorf, *The Evolution of the U.S. Navy's Maritime Strategy, 1977–1986* (Newport, RI: Naval War College Press, Center for Naval Warfare Studies, 2004), 1–15.

22. Association for Diplomatic Studies and Training Foreign Affairs Oral History Project, Ambassador William C. Sherman, interviewed by Thomas Stern, October 27, 1993, 99.

23. Vance is quoting something here, but he does not indicate what (probably Brzezinski's proposal for the creation of the PRC and SCC), in Vance, *Hard Choices*, 36.

24. Oksenberg to Brzezinski, May 25, 1978, in U.S. Department of State, *Foreign Relations of the United States*, http://digicoll.library.wisc.edu/FRUS/Browse.html [hereafter cited as *FRUS*], *1977–1980, Vol. XIII: China*, 462–469.

25. Interview by the author with Zbigniew Brzezinski, November 25, 2014.

26. William H. Gleysteen, Jr., *Massive Entanglement, Marginal Influence: Carter and Korea in Crisis* (Washington, DC: Brookings Institution Press, 1999), 6; Ambassador William H. Gleysteen Jr., interviewed by Thomas Stern, June 10, 1997, Foreign Affairs Oral History Collection (Arlington, VA: Association for Diplomatic Studies and Training, 2000), 119, http://www.adst.org/OH%20TOCs/Gleysteen,%20William%20H.,%20Jr.toc.pdf.

27. Gleysteen, *Massive Entanglement, Marginal Influence*, 32.

28. Jean A. Garrison, "Explaining Change in the Carter Administration's China Policy: Foreign Policy Adviser Manipulation of the Policy Agenda," *Asian Affairs* 29, no. 2 (Summer 2002): 83–98 at 84.

29. Oksenberg to Brzezinski, January 25, 1977, *FRUS, 1977–1980, Vol. XIII: China*, 14–16; Memorandum of Conversation, January 8, 1977, *FRUS, 1977–1980, Vol. XIII*, 2–14; Brown to Brzezinski, February 9, 1977, *FRUS, 1977–1980, Vol. XIII: China*, 26–28.

30. Glad, *Outsider in the White House*, 122.

31. Vance, *Hard Choices*, 32; Smith, *Morality, Reason, and Power*, 91–92.

32. Vance to Carter, April 15, 1977, *FRUS, 1977–1980, Vol. XIII: China*, 76–82.

33. Vance, *Hard Choices*, 78.

34. Brzezinski to Carter, January 25, 1979, *FRUS, 1977–1980, Vol. XIII: China*, 718–725.

35. Brown to Brzezinski, February 9, 1977, *FRUS, 1977–1980, Vol. XIII: China*, 26–28; Brzezinski to Carter, February 14, 1977, *FRUS, 1977–1980, Vol. XIII: China*, 33–38; Carter, *White House Diary*, 38; "annoy the Soviets" from interview by author with Harold Brown, September 22, 2014

36. Author's follow-up interview with Harold Brown by email, June 30, 2015.

37. Quotation is from Brzezinski, *Power and Principle*, 200. See also Smith, *Morality, Reason, and Power*, 86–87.

38. Carter, *White House Diary*, 105.

39. Summary of Conclusions of a Policy Review Committee Meeting, June 27, 1977, *FRUS, 1977–1980, Vol. XIII*, 101–108.

40. Vance quoted in Garrison, "Explaining Change in the Carter Administration's China Policy," 92.

41. James Mann, *About Face: A History of America's Curious Relationship with China, from Nixon to Clinton* (New York: Knopf, 1999), 83; Glad, *Outsider in the White House*, 126.

42. Smith, *Morality, Reason, and Power*, 87–89.

43. Oksenberg to Brzezinski, "China Policy in the Doldrums: Analysis and Measures for Minimizing Risks of Erosion in the Relationship," September 23, 1977, *FRUS, 1977–1980, Vol. XIII*, 231–239.

44. On the "three principles," see Li Xiannian, quoted in Gong Li, "The Difficult Path to Diplomatic Relations: China's U.S. Policy, 1972–1978," in *Normalization of U.S.-China Relations: An International History*, ed. William C. Kirby, Robert S. Ross, and Gong Li (Cambridge, MA: Harvard University Press, 2005), 134.

45. Carter, *White House Diary*, 174.

46. Interview by author with Morton Abramowitz, January 15, 2015.

47. Mann, *About Face*, 89.

48. Cohen and Tucker, "Beijing's Friend, Moscow's Foe," 92; Mann, *About Face*, 86–89.

49. Carter, *White House Diary*, 197.

50. Vance, *Hard Choices*, 101–102; Glad, *Outsider in the White House*, 121; Donna R. Jackson, "The Ogaden War and the Demise of Détente," *Annals of the American Academy of Political and Social Science* 632, Perspectives on Africa and the World (November 2010): 26–40 at 36.

51. Paper prepared by the National Security Council Staff, undated, *FRUS, 1977–1980, Vol. XIII: China*, 302–307.

52. Brzezinski to Carter, October 13, 1978, *FRUS, 1977–1980, Vol. XIII: China*, 569–571.

53. Report quoted in Garrison, "Explaining Change in the Carter Administration's China Policy," 91.

54. Glad, *Outsider in the White House*, 119–120. On the rationale for declaring a deal as soon as possible, see Carter, *Keeping Faith*, 199; Vance, *Hard Choices*, 110. For the First Communiqué, see "Joint Communiqué of the United States of America and People's Republic of China," February 28, 1972, http://beijing.usembassy-china.org.cn/uploads/images /yJIG2IXkWU8gk1uq4Cx1tw/1972_Joint_Communique.pdf. For the Second Communiqué, see "Joint Communiqué of the United States of America and People's Republic of China," January 1, 1979 (released simultaneously in Washington and Beijing on December 15, 1978), http://beijing.usembassy-china.org.cn/uploads/images/9y7T9oJSIFpfgTW6cO2 _5w/1979_Joint_Communique.pdf.

55. The intelligence assessment was NIAM 43-1-77, "The Prospects for Taiwan After Normalization," July 26, 1977, *FRUS, 1977–1980, Vol. XIII: China*, 116–118. For details on Brzezinski's views of Taiwan, see Nancy Bernkopf Tucker, *Strait Talk: United States–Taiwan Relations and the Crisis with China* (Cambridge, MA: Harvard University Press, 2009), 116–126; Smith, *Morality, Reason, and Power*, 86–87.

56. Oksenberg to Brzezinski, December 19, 1978, *FRUS, 1977–1980, Vol. XIII: China*, 658–662.

57. Vance to Carter, December 19, 1979, *FRUS, 1977–1980, Vol. XIII: China*, 1021–1025. See also Summary of a Special Coordination Committee Ad Hoc Group Meeting on China, January 24, 1979, *FRUS, 1977–1980, Vol. XIII: China*, 717.

58. Steven M. Goldstein and Randall Schriver, "An Uncertain Relationship: The United States, Taiwan and the Taiwan Relations Act," *China Quarterly*, no. 165, Taiwan in the 20th Century (March 2001): 147–148.

59. Taiwan Relations Act (Public Law 96-8, 93 Stat. 14, enacted April 10, 1979; H.R. 2479), available at http://www.ait.org.tw/en/taiwan-relations-act.html.

60. Brzezinski to Carter, January 25, 1979, *FRUS, 1977–1980, Vol. XIII: China*, 718–725.

61. Interview by author with Zbigniew Brzezinski, November 25, 2014.

62. Oksenberg to Brzezinski, February 16, 1979, *FRUS, 1977–1980, Vol. XIII: China*, 800–801.

63. Oksenberg to Brzezinski, February 16, 1979, *FRUS, 1977–1980, Vol. XIII: China*, 800–801.

64. Oksenberg to Brzezinski, February 16, 1979, *FRUS, 1977–1980, Vol. XIII: China*, 800–801.

65. Minutes of a Policy Review Committee Meeting, January 8, 1979, *FRUS, 1977–1980, Vol. XIII: China*, 695–701.

66. Brzezinski to Carter, June 14, 1977, *FRUS, 1977–1980, Vol. XIII: China*, 93–99; Paper Prepared in Response to Section III of Presidential Review Memorandum 24, undated (mid-1977), *FRUS, 1977–1980, Vol. XIII: China*, 263–269; Brown to Brzezinski, March 23, 1979, *FRUS, 1977–1980, Vol. XIII: China*, 842–853; Brzezinski to Carter, July 6, 1979, *Foreign Relations of the United States, 1977–1980, Vol. XIII: China*, 894–896; Mondale to Carter, July 11, 1979, *FRUS, 1977–1980, Vol. XIII: China*, 900–903; Garrison, "Explaining Change in the Carter Administration's China Policy," 93. Instead of Brown, Vice President Walter Mondale traveled to China in July 1979. Discussions included possible defense cooperation as part of a larger brief.

67. Harry Harding, *A Fragile Relationship: The United States and China Since 1972* (Washington, DC: Brookings Institution, 1992), 67–77.

68. Oksenberg to Brzezinski, August 1, 1979, *FRUS, 1977–1980, Vol. XIII: China*, 915–916.

69. Vance, *Hard Choices*, 388.

70. Interview by author with Harold Brown, September 22, 2014.

71. Interview by author with Harold Brown, September 22, 2014; Garrison, "Explaining Change in the Carter Administration's China Policy," 88. On arms sales, see Kerry B. Dumbaugh and Richard F. Grimmet, "U.S. Arms Sales to China," Report Number 85-135F, U.S. Congressional Research Service, July 8, 1985, 2.

72. George Crile, *Charlie Wilson's War: The Extraordinary Story of How the Wildest Man in Congress and a Rogue CIA Agent Changed the History of Our Times* (New York: Grove, 2003), 269; interview author with Zbigniew Brzezinski, November 25, 2014.

73. Vance, *Hard Choices*, 122.

74. Brzezinski to Carter, July 7, 1978, *FRUS, 1977–1980, Vol. XIII: China*, 508–509.

75. Vance, *Hard Choices*, 125–127; Derian to Vance, October 2, 1979, *Foreign Relations of the United States, 1977–1980, Vol. II: Human Rights and Humanitarian Affairs*, 602–606.

76. Record of a National Security Council Meeting, February 16, 1979, *FRUS, 1977–1980, Vol. XIII: China*, 795–799; Summary of Conclusions of a Special Coordination Committee Meeting, February 19, 1979, *FRUS, 1977–1980, Vol. XIII: China*, 808–811.

77. Interview by author with Zbigniew Brzezinski, November 25, 2013.

78. Interview by author with Harold Brown, September 22, 2014.

79. Vance to Carter, February 1, 1980, *FRUS, 1977–1980, Vol. XIII: China*, 1086–1087.

80. The U.S. Navy felt particularly abandoned in those years. See, for example, Hattendorf, *Evolution of the U.S. Navy's Maritime Strategy*, 12.

81. Presidential Review Memorandum 10, "Comprehensive Net Assessment and Military Force Posture Review," February 18, 1977, www.fas.org/irp/offdocs/prm/.

82. Don Oberdorfer, *The Two Koreas: A Contemporary History* (Reading, MA: Addison-Wesley, 1998), 84.

83. Smith, *Morality, Reason, and Power*, 85. The foreign policy principals did not object to the objective of withdrawing U.S. troops gradually. See Policy Review Committee Meeting, "Korea," April 21, 1977, in *The Carter Chill: US-ROK-DPRK Trilateral Relations, 1976–1979: A Critical Oral History Project*, ed. Christian F. Ostermann, James Person, and Charles Kraus (Washington, DC: Woodrow Wilson International Center for Scholars, 2013), 98–100; Joe Wood, *Persuading a President: Jimmy Carter and American Troops in Korea*, Case Study C18-96-1319.0 (Cambridge, MA: John F. Kennedy School of Government, Harvard University, 1996), 97–113, http://www2.gwu.edu/~nsarchiv/NSAEBB/NSAEBB431/docs/intell_ebb_002.PDF.

84. Interview by author with Zbigniew Brzezinski, November 25, 2014, Washington, DC.

85. Terence Roehrig, *From Deterrence to Engagement: The U.S. Defense Commitment to South Korea* (Lanham, MD: Lexington Books, 2006), 135. Instructions informing that aid would be conditioned on human rights reforms can be found in "Handwritten Note from Jimmy Carter to Zbigniew Brzezinski and Cyrus Vance," March 5, 1977, in *The Carter Chill*, 77.

86. "Japan: U.S. Defense Secretary Confers with Prime Minister and Director General of Defense Agency," Reuters, July 27, 1977.

87. Smith, *Morality, Reason, and Power*, 104–105.

88. Even Vance, who was deeply hostile toward the Park government in Seoul, worried about the impact on other allies. See Vance, *Hard Choices*, 449. See also Smith, *Morality, Reason, and Power*, 104; Victor D. Cha, *Alignment Despite Antagonism: The United States-Korea-Japan Security Triangle* (Stanford, CA: Stanford University Press, 1999), 154–168.

89. Gleysteen, *Massive Entanglement, Marginal Influence*, 6.

90. Association for Diplomatic Studies and Training Foreign Affairs Oral History Project, John H. Holdridge, interviewed by Charles Stuart Kennedy, July 20, 1995, 152–153; interview by author with Morton Abramowitz, January 15, 2015, Washington, DC.

91. Interview by author with Morton Abramowitz, January 15, 2015, Washington, DC.

92. The JCS presented their own plan to withdraw 7,000 troops over five years. See Cha, *Alignment Despite Antagonism*, 146.

93. Policy Review Committee Meeting, "Korea," April 21, 1977, and Presidential Directive/NSC-12, "U.S. Policy in Korea," May 5, 1977, both in *The Carter Chill*, 98–100 and 100–120, respectively. See also Gleysteen, *Massive Entanglement, Marginal Influence*, 24; Cha, *Alignment Despite Antagonism*, 145. The Pentagon and State Department tried to stanch the crisis in American commitment to the defense of Korea by establishing the Combined Forces Command (CFC) as a U.S.-led headquarters in 1978. The CFC was established under "The Terms of Reference for Military Committee and ROK-US Combined Forces Command" and "Strategic Directive No. 1 (1978)." See also Tae-Hwan Kwak, "U.S.-Korea Security Relations," in *U.S.-Korean Relations, 1882–1982*, ed. Tae-Hwan Kwak, John Chay, Soon Sung Cho, and Shannon McCune (Boulder, CO: Westview, 1982), 223–243; Yong Soon Yim, "U.S. Strategic Doctrine, Arms Transfer Policy, and South Korea," in Kwak et al., *U.S.-Korean Relations*, 317–319.

94. Memorandum for Jimmy Carter from Zbigniew Brzezinski, "Korean Troop Withdrawals: Brown/Habib Testimony," June 10, 1977, in *The Carter Chill*, 167–168; Mike Armacost to Brzezinski, "DOD Transmission to the Congress of JCS Recommendations Concerning Korean Troops Withdrawals," June 29, 1977, in *The Carter Chill*, 169–170. On Brzezinski's earlier position on Korean troop withdrawal, see Wood, *Persuading a President*, 97–113. According to most accounts, Brzezinski remained neutral. He conspicuously fails to mention the episode in his memoir, though he does note his opposition to cutting aid to Seoul. See Gleysteen, *Massive Entanglement, Marginal Influence*, 24; Brzezinski, *Power and Principle*, 127.

95. Statement of the President, April 21, 1978, in *The Carter Chill*, 310. On Carter's persistence, see Oberdorfer, *The Two Koreas*, 85; Douglas Brinkley, *The Unfinished Presidency: Jimmy Carter's Journey Beyond the White House* (New York: Viking Books, 1998), 392.

96. Central Intelligence Agency, "US Ground Forces Withdrawal: Korean Stability and Foreign Reactions," June 7, 1977, in *The Carter Chill*, 159–166.

97. Memorandum for the President from Zbigniew Brzezinski, "Summary of April 11, 1978, Meeting on Korea, and China," April 11, 1978, in *The Carter Chill*, 300–305.

98. Brzezinski to Carter, "Congressional Reaction to Our Korean Policy," July 21, 1977, in *The Carter Chill*, 193–194.

99. Holbrooke, Abramowitz, Armacost, and Oksenberg to Vance, Brown, and Brzezinski, "Issues for Decision on Korea and China," April 4, 1978, *FRUS, 1977–1980, Vol. XIII: China*, 324–337.

100. Brzezinski, through Madeleine Albright, from Nick Platt, "Troop Withdrawals from the ROK—Congressman Stratton and Beard Letter," January 9, 1979, in *The Carter Chill*, 431–433; Wood, *Persuading a President*, 97–113.

101. Oberdorfer, *The Two Koreas*, 103.

102. Brzezinski to Carter, "U.S. Ground Force Withdrawals from the Republic of Korea (S)," July 12, 1979, in *The Carter Chill*, 647–649.

103. Smith, *Morality, Reason, and Power*, 100–102.

104. Morton Abramowitz, interviewed by Thomas Stern, April 10, 2007, Foreign Affairs Oral History Collection (Arlington, VA: Association for Diplomatic Studies and Training, 2009), 65, http://www.adst.org/OH%20TOCs/Abramowitz,%20Morton%20I.toc.pdf.

105. John Lehman, *On Seas of Glory: Heroic Men, Great Ships, and Epic Battles of the American Navy* (New York: The Free Press, 2002), 345–346.

106. George S. Brown (chairman of the Joint Chiefs of Staff), "U.S. Military Posture for FY 1979," January 17, 1978. On Carter's rejection of Ford's naval buildup plans, see Hattendorf, *The Evolution of the U.S. Navy's Maritime Strategy, 1977–1986*, 1–15.

107. John T. Hanley, Jr., "Creating the 1980s Maritime Strategy and Implications for Today," *Naval War College Review* 67, no. 2 (Spring 2014): 11–29 at 16, https://www.usnwc.edu/getattachment/2b962da8-c60f-4916-9a98-86d1dd831b5b/Creating-the-1980s-Maritime-Strategy-and-Implicati.aspx.

108. "Northeast Asia Balance," October 20, 1978, in *The Carter Chill*, 410–412.

109. Wiegley, "Reassessing the Security Alliance Between the United States and Japan," 23.

110. Hideo Tomikawa, "Briefing Memorandum: Regarding the National Defense Program Guideline and the Mid-Term Defense Program," translated from the original Japanese, *National Institute for Defense Studies News*, no. 152 (March 2011): 1–6, http://www.nids.go.jp/english/publication/briefing/pdf/2011/152.pdf.

111. Interview by author with Harold Brown, September 22, 2014, Washington, DC. Brown recalls that neither State nor the NSC showed interest in Japan at the time at senior levels. This was not the last time that the Pentagon would take over management of Japan relations as State or the NSC drifted in other directions—most notably under Clinton in the 1990s.

112. Interview by author with Harold Brown, September 22, 2014, Washington, DC.

113. Michael J. Green and Koji Murata, "The 1978 Guidelines for U.S.-Japan Defense Cooperation: Process and Historical Impact," Working Paper 17, Conference on Power and Prosperity: Linkages Between Security and Economics in U.S.-Japanese Relations Since 1960 (La Jolla, CA, March 14–16, 1997), http://www2.gwu.edu/~nsarchiv/japan/GreenMurataWP.htm.

114. Tatsuro Yoda, "Japan's Host Nation Support Program for the U.S.-Japan Security Alliance," *Asian Survey* 46, no. 6 (2006): 939–940.

115. Smith, *Morality, Reason, and Power*, 107–108.

116. Joseph P. Kedell, Jr., *The Politics of Defense in Japan: Managing Internal and External Pressures* (New York: M. E. Sharpe, 1993), 78–82.

117. Vance, *Hard Choices*, 426–427; Brzezinski, *Power and Principle*, 314.

118. Ambassador William C. Sherman, interviewed by Thomas Stern, October 27, 1993, Foreign Affairs Oral History Collection (Arlington, VA: Association for Diplomatic

Studies and Training, 1998), 114–115, http://www.adst.org/OH%20TOCs/Sherman,%20
William%20C.toc.pdf). See also Roger Buckley, *US-Japan Alliance Diplomacy 1945–1990*
(Cambridge: Cambridge University Press, 1992), 136.

119. The National Intelligence Council convened a group of Japan experts in and out
of government at the end of the Carter administration that concluded, among other
things, that the Japanese forces were drifting and without direction from the United
States and that Japan's future was still open to question. John H. Holdridge, interviewed
by Charles Stuart Kennedy, July 20, 1995, Foreign Affairs Oral History Collection (Arlington, VA: Association for Diplomatic Studies and Training, 1998), 114–115, http://
www.adst.org/OH%20TOCs/Holdridge,%20John.%201995%20toc.pdf.

120. James M. Patton, "Dawn of the Maritime Strategy," (United States Naval Institute)
Proceedings 135, no. 5 (May 2009): 56–60; See also Gregory L. Vistica, *Fall from Glory: The
Men Who Sank the U.S. Navy* (New York: Simon and Schuster, 1995), 31–33, 62.

121. Hattendorf, *The Evolution of the U.S. Navy's Maritime Strategy*, 18–20.

122. Interview with Admiral Thomas Hayward, USN (ret.), conducted by Paul S. Giarra in coordination with the author, July 29, 2014, Mukilteo, WA.

123. Rodman, *Presidential Command*, 136.

124. Deng Xiaoping's speech at a meeting on the Report on Chinese-Vietnamese Border Operations (邓小平在中越边境作战情况报告会上的讲话), March 19, 1979, in *The
Chinese Cultural Revolution Database*, 3rd ed., ed. and comp. Editorial Board of
the Chinese Cultural Revolution Database, editor-in-chief Song Yongyi. CD-ROM
with hard copy indexes in Chinese and English (Hong Kong: Universities' Service Centre
for China Studies, the Chinese University of Hong Kong, 2002), http://ccrd.usc.cuhk.edu
.hk/Default.aspx?msg=%E6%B2%A1%E6%9C%89%E8%AE%A2%E9%98%85%EF%BC%
8C%E6%AC%A2%E8%BF%8E%E8%AE%A2%E9%98%85%EF%BC%81. The author is
grateful to Taylor Fravel for locating this document.

125. Mann, *About Face*, 81.

126. Smith, *Morality, Reason, and Power*, 231.

127. Smith, *Morality, Reason, and Power*, 232–234.

128. For details, see Walter C. Ladwig III, Andrew S. Erickson, and Justin D. Mikolay,
"Diego Garcia and American Security in the Indian Ocean," in *Rebalancing U.S. Forces:
Basing and Forward Presence in the Asia Pacific*, ed. Carnes Lord and Andrew Erickson
(Annapolis, MD: Naval Institute Press, 2014).

129. Gleysteen, *Massive Entanglement, Marginal Influence*, 32; Smith, *Morality, Reason,
and Power*, 51–52.

130. Pat Derian, the assistant secretary of state for humanitarian affairs, confessed as
much in a memo to the secretary in 1979. See Derian to Vance, October 2, 1979, *FRUS,
1977–1980, Vol. II: Human Rights and Humanitarian Affairs*, 602–606.

131. Tuchman to Brzezinski, "PRM-28—Human Rights," July 20, 1977, *FRUS, 1977–1980,
Vol. II: Human Rights and Humanitarian Affairs*, 214–219.

132. Interview with Zbigniew Brzezinski, November 25, 2013.

133. Interview with Zbigniew Brzezinski, November 25, 2013.

134. Carter saw his approach to human rights as an effective political tool to unite different parts of the Democratic Party. See Glad, *Outsider in the White House*, 72.

11. RONALD REAGAN, 1980–1989

1. Reagan quoted in Michael Hausenfleck, "The Reagan Doctrine: A Conceptual Analysis of the Democracy Imperative in U.S. Foreign Policy, 1981–1988" (PhD diss., Brandeis University, 1995), 89.

2. Robert W. Tucker, "Reagan's Foreign Policy," *Foreign Affairs* 68, no. 1 (1988–1989): 8–9, 12, 16.

3. Reagan quoted in Chester Pach, "The Reagan Doctrine: Principle, Pragmatism, and Policy," *Presidential Studies Quarterly* 36, no. 1 (March 2006): 79.

4. National Security Decision Directive 32, "U.S. National Security Strategy," May 20, 1982.

5. U.S. National Security Strategy, quoted in Pach, "The Reagan Doctrine," 80. NSDD 75 spelled out the intention to "take active measures" to support those standing against Soviet expansionism. See NSDD 75, quoted in Pach, "The Reagan Doctrine," 81.

6. John Lewis Gaddis, *Strategies of Containment: A Critical Reappraisal of American National Security Policy During the Cold War*, rev. and exp. edition (New York: Oxford University Press, 1982), 351.

7. Tucker, "Reagan's Foreign Policy," 14. For a negative interpretation of Reagan's handling of foreign policy, see Raymond L. Garthoff, *The Great Transition: American-Soviet Relations and the End of the Cold War* (Washington, DC: Brookings Institution, 1994).

8. Peter Rodman, *Presidential Command: Power, Leadership, and the Making of Foreign Policy from Richard Nixon to George W. Bush* (New York: Knopf, 2009), 149.

9. George C. Herring, *From Colony to Superpower: U.S. Foreign Relations Since 1776* (New York: Oxford University Press, 2008), 865; George J. Church, "The 'Vicar' Takes Charge," *Time*, March 16, 1981.

10. Steven Strasser, Melinda Liu, David C. Martin, and John Walcott, "Arms Across the Sea," *Newsweek*, June 29, 1981.

11. Alexander M. Haig, Jr., *Caveat: Realism, Reagan, and Foreign Policy* (New York: Macmillan, 1984), 194.

12. Interview by author with George P. Shultz in his San Francisco apartment, November 17, 2014.

13. George J. Church, "No Longer Underestimated, George Shultz, Ever Stolid, Continues to Confound His Critics," *Time*, February 3, 1986.

14. George P. Shultz, "New Realities and New Ways of Thinking," *Foreign Affairs* 63, no. 4 (Spring 1985): 720.

15. Shultz quoted in Commitments, Consensus, and U.S. Foreign Policy, Hearings Before the Committee on Foreign Relations, United States Senate, 99th Congress, January 31, 1985 (Washington, DC: Government Printing Office, 1986), 17.

16. George P. Shultz, *Turmoil and Triumph: My Years as Secretary of State* (New York: Charles Scribner's Sons, 1993), 173.

17. Shultz as quoted in Commitments, Consensus, and U.S. Foreign Policy, Hearings Before the Committee on Foreign Relations, United States Senate, 99th Congress, January 31, 1985, 78.

18. Shultz as quoted in Commitments, Consensus, and U.S. Foreign Policy, Hearings Before the Committee on Foreign Relations, United States Senate, 99th Congress, January 31, 1985, 78.

19. Caspar W. Weinberger with Gretchen Roberts, *Into the Arena: A Memoir of the 20th Century* (Washington, DC: Regnery, 2001), 71.

20. Kevin V. Mulcahy, "The Secretary of State and the National Security Adviser: Foreign Policymaking in the Carter and Reagan Administrations," *Presidential Studies Quarterly* 16, no. 2, Congress, the Court, and the Presidency in National Security Policy (Spring 1986): 280–299.

21. David M. Abshire and Richard V. Allen, eds., *National Security: Political, Military, and Economic Strategies in the Decade Ahead* (New York: Praeger for the Hoover Institution on War, Revolution, and Peace, 1963).

22. John H. Holdridge, interviewed by Charles Stuart Kennedy, July 20, 1995, Foreign Affairs Oral History Collection (Arlington, VA: Association for Diplomatic Studies and Training, 1998) [hereafter John H. Holdridge 1995 ADST Oral History], 119, http://www.adst.org/OH%20TOCs/Holdridge,%20John.%201995%20toc.pdf.

23. Jet lag anecdote conveyed by George Shultz in interview with author on November 17, 2014.

24. Gaston J. Sigur, "Normalization and Pacific and Triangular Diplomacy," *International Trade Law Journal* 5, no. 1 (Fall–Winter 1979): 9–17.

25. Paul Kengor and Patricia Clark Doerner, *The Judge: William P. Clark, Ronald Reagan's Top Hand* (San Francisco: Ignatius, 2007), 221.

26. James Mann, *Rise of the Vulcans: The History of Bush's War Cabinet* (New York: Viking, 2001), 46–52.

27. Richard Armitage quoted in Mann, *Rise of the Vulcans*, 35.

28. Interview by the author with Richard Armitage, July 23, 2014.

29. Armitage calculates that 80 percent of difficult policy differences were cleared up in the East Asia Informal Group, preventing the Shultz-Weinberger feud from damaging Asia policy and keeping the NSC principals focused on big strategic decisions. Interview by author with Richard Armitage, July 23, 2014.

30. Kengor and Doerner, *The Judge*, 223; Association for Diplomatic Studies and Training Foreign Affairs Oral History Project, John H. Holdridge, interviewed by Charles Stuart Kennedy, July 20, 1995, 117; "Gov. Reagan in Taipei, Pledges Strengthening of Ties," Associated Press, October 11, 1971; Memorandum of Conversation, October 25, 1971, in U.S. Department of State, *Foreign Relations of the United States, 1969–1976, Vol. E-13: Documents on China, 1969–1972*, http://2001-2009.state.gov/r/pa/ho/frus/nixon/e13/72505.htm.

31. Reagan as quoted in Alan D. Romberg, *Rein in at the Brink of the Precipice: American Policy Toward Taiwan and U.S.-P.R.C. Relations* (Washington, DC: Henry L. Stimson Center, 2003), 111. See also Ronald Reagan, *Reagan, in His Own Hand: The Writings of Ronald Reagan That Reveal His Revolutionary Vision for America*, ed. Kiron K. Skinner, Annelise Anderson, Martin Anderson, and George P. Shultz (New York: Touchstone, 2001), 45–46.

32. Statement by Ronald Reagan upon Ambassador George Bush's Return from Japan and China, August 25, 1980, Los Angeles, California, Folder "China-General 02/08/1981–05/26/1981 CF 0160" in Meese, Edwin: Files, Box 2, Reagan Library.

33. "A Short History of the Department of State: Reagan's Foreign Policy," Office of the Historian, Bureau of Public Affairs, U.S. Department of State, https://history.state.gov/departmenthistory/short-history/reaganforeignpolicy. See also "The Document That Sowed the Seed of Haig's Demise," *Washington Post*, July 11, 1982.

34. February 8, 1981, memo from Allen to President on "Your Policy Toward China," Folder "China-General 02/08/1981–05/26/1981 CF 0160" in Meese, Edwin: Files, Box 2, Reagan Library, p. 5; Walter Taylor, "China Relations Reaffirmed by Reagan Team," *Washington Star*, February 7, 1981.

35. Steve R. Weisman, "Haig Remark on China Puzzles White House Aides," *New York Times*, June 26, 1981.

36. John H. Holdridge 1995 ADST Oral History, 122.

37. John H. Holdridge 1995 ADST Oral History, 119.

38. Haig quoted in Banning N. Garrett and Bonnie S. Glaser, "From Nixon to Reagan: China's Changing Role in American Strategy," in *Eagle Resurgent?: The Reagan Era in American Foreign Policy*, ed. Kenneth A. Oye, Robert J. Lieber, and Donald Rothchild (Boston: Little, Brown, 1987), 276.

39. Alexander M. Haig, "Statement from Secretary Haig," reprinted in *Congressional Record—United States Senate, 97th Congress, July 15, 1981* (Washington, DC: Government Printing Office, 1982), 12724–12725; Memorandum from Secretary of State Alexander M. Haig to the President, "Follow-up Steps on China Policy," July 31, 1981, p. 1, Folder "China-General 06/05/1981–08/23/81 CF 0160" in Meese, Edwin: Files, Box 2, Reagan Library.

40. John H. Holdridge 1995 ADST Oral History, 121–125; interview by the author with Richard Armitage, July 23, 2014.

41. For Haig's assessment, see Alexander M. Haig and Caspar W. Weinberger to the President, "Military Sales to China," August 21, 1981, p. 1, Folder "China-General 08/24/1981–09/30/81 CF 0160" in Meese, Edwin: Files, Box 2, Reagan Library; Romberg, *Rein in at the Brink of the Precipice*, 126. For a contemporary overview of the issue, see A. Doak Barnett, *U.S. Arms Sales: The China-Taiwan Tangle* (Washington, DC: Brookings Institution, 1982).

42. Richard V. Allen to the President on "Secretary Haig's Views on Arms Sales to Taiwan," November 25, 1981 (also contains two-page Haig to POTUS memo on November 13 and two-page November 16 memo of NSC staff response to Haig memo), Folder "Taiwan 07/13/1981–04/30/1982 CF 0219" in Meese, Edwin: Files, Box 3, Reagan Library.

43. March 25, 1982, memo from Alexander M. Haig to President Reagan, "Managing Our China Problem," and one-page "Outline of Alternative Approach to the Chinese," March 25, 1982, both from Folder "China-General 10/01/1981–05/24/1982 CF 0160" in Meese, Edwin: Files, Box 2, Reagan Library.

44. Haig, *Caveat*, 195. Combined with the "I'm in charge" fiasco the day Reagan was shot, Haig was perceived as overreaching and a hothead—which led to his ouster from the government and the end of his political career. See http://adst.org/2014/03/al-haig-and-the-reagan-assassination-attempt-im-in-charge-here/.

45. John H. Holdridge 1995 ADST Oral History, 135–137.

46. "United States–China Joint Communique on United States Arms Sales to Taiwan," August 17, 1982, in *Public Papers of the Presidents of the United States: Ronald Reagan,*

1982, Book 2: July 3 to December 31, 1982 (Washington, DC: Government Printing Office, 1983), 1052–1053.

47. The assurances were:

1.   The United States would not set a date for termination of arms sales to Taiwan.
2.   The United States would not alter the terms of the Taiwan Relations Act.
3.   The United States would not consult with China in advance before making decisions about U.S. arms sales to Taiwan.
4.   The United States would not mediate between Taiwan and China.
5.   The United States would not alter its position about the sovereignty of Taiwan, which was that the question was one to be decided peacefully by the Chinese themselves, and would not pressure Taiwan to enter into negotiations with China.
6.   The United States would not formally recognize Chinese sovereignty over Taiwan.

The "Six Assurances" to Taiwan, July 1982, http://www.taiwandocuments.org/assurances .htm.

48. Alan Romberg cites William Rope, Alexander Haig, and Mark Mohr as proponents of this view. See Romberg, *Rein in at the Brink of the Precipice*, 139.

49. Armitage quoted in United States–Philippines Relations and the New Base and Aid Agreement, Hearings Before the Subcommittee on Asia and Pacific Affairs of the Committee on Foreign Affairs, House of Representatives, 98th Congress, June 17, 1983 (Washington, DC: Government Printing Office, 1983), 72.

50. Interview by author with George Shultz, November 17, 2014.

51. Interview by author with George Shultz, November 17, 2014.

52. See, for example, Nomination Hearings for Paul D. Wolfowitz, of the District of Columbia, to be Assistant Secretary of State, East Asian and Pacific Affairs, Department of State, United States Senate, 97th Congress, December 9, 1982 (Washington, DC: Government Printing Office, 1983), 6–7.

53. Banning N. Garrett and Bonnie S. Glaser, "From Nixon to Reagan: China's Changing Role in American Strategy," in Oye, Lieber, and Rothchild, *Eagle Resurgent?*, 272–273.

54. Talking Points for the President for the September 20 National Security Council Meeting on U.S.-China Relations, attached to William Clark to the President, "NSC Meeting on US-China Relations," Folder "China 1983 CF 0219" in Meese, Edwin: Files; Box 3, Reagan Library.

55. NSDD 76, Peaceful Nuclear Cooperation with China, January 18, 1983, http://www .fas.org/irp/offdocs/nsdd/nsdd-76.pdf.

56. "Reagan and China: Afterglow," *Newsweek*, May 14, 1984.

57. Kerry B. Dumbaugh and Richard F. Grimmet, "U.S. Arms Sales to China," Report Number 85-135F, U.S. Congressional Research Service, July 8, 1985, 41.

58. Interview by author with Richard Armitage, July 23, 2014.

59. Mark Hopkins, "The Two Faces of Deng Xiaoping: China's Last Emperor," *New Leader* 70, no. 15 (October 18, 1987): 7–11.

60. "Deng Xiaoping, Man of the Year," *Time*, January 6, 1986.

61. "A Crackdown Campaign Goes On: Peking Purges Liberals and Slows Economic Reforms," *Time*, February 2, 1987.

62. J. E. D. McDonnell, "China's Move to Rejoin the GATT System: An Epic Transition," *The World Economy* 10, no. 3 (September 1987): 331–350; interview by author with Winston Lord, June 18, 2014, New York.

63. "Shultz in China: Peking Denies Any Return to Past and Confirms Reforms," *The Times* (London), March 4, 1987. See also "No Policy Retreat, China Tells Shultz," *New York Times*, March 3, 1987.

64. Gaston J. Sigur, Jr., "U.S. Policy Priorities for Relations with China," Address Before the National Issues Forum on the Outlook for U.S.-China Trade and Economic Relations at the Brookings Institution on April 22, 1987, *Department of State Bulletin*, no. 2124 (1987): 41–43.

65. Interview by author with George Shultz, November 17, 2014.

66. Sheldon Simon, *The Future of Asian-Pacific Security Collaboration* (Lexington, MA: Lexington Books, 1988), 31.

67. Donald Chipman, "Admiral Gorshkov and the Soviet Navy," *Air University Review*, July–August 1982, http://www.au.af.mil/au/afri/aspj/airchronicles/aureview/1982/jul-aug /chipman.html. Gorshkov was featured on the cover of *Time* in 1968. See "Russia: Power Play on the Oceans," *Time*, February 23, 1968. Gorshkov gained acclaim for his magisterial work on naval strategy, *The Sea Power of the State* (Annapolis, MD: Naval Institute Press, 1979).

68. Kenneth McGruther, *The Evolving Soviet Navy* (Newport, RI: Naval War College Press, 1978), 1–9.

69. Edward A. Olsen, "The Maritime Strategy in the Western Pacific," *Naval War College Review* 40, no. 4 (Autumn 1987): 44–47.

70. John B. Hattendorf, *The Evolution of the U.S. Navy's Maritime Strategy, 1977–1986* (Newport, RI: Naval War College Press, Center for Naval Warfare Studies, 2004), 20–21.

71. Hattendorf, *The Evolution of the U.S. Navy's Maritime Strategy, 1977–1986*, 46.

72. Bill Keller, "The Navy's Brash Leader," *New York Times Magazine*, December 15, 1985, http://www.nytimes.com/1985/12/15/magazine/the-navy-s-brash-leader.html ?pagewanted=1. For an example of one of Lehman's studies at CSIS, see John F. Lehman, Jr., *Aircraft Carriers: The Real Choices* (Washington, DC: The Center for Strategic and International Studies, 1978).

73. Lehman quoted in National Security Policy, Hearings Before the Defense Policy Panel of the Committee on Armed Services, House of Representatives, 100th Congress, March 11, 1987 (Washington, DC: Government Printing Office, 1987), 15–16.

74. Lehman quoted in The 600-Ship Navy and the Maritime Strategy, Hearings Before the Seapower and Strategic and Critical Materials Subcommittee of the Committee on Armed Services, House of Representatives, June 24, 1985 (Washington, DC: Government Printing Office, 1986), 88.

75. National Security Decision Directive (NSDD) 32, May 20, 1982, 4, http://www.fas .org/irp/offdocs/nsdd/nsdd-32.pdf.

76. Admiral James D. Watkins, "*The Maritime Strategy*," and John F. Lehman Jr., "The 600-Ship Navy," United States Naval Institute *Proceedings* 112, no. 1, The Maritime Strategy Supplement (January 1986): 30–40.

77. Linton F. Brooks, "Naval Power and National Security: The Case for the Maritime Strategy," *International Security* 11, no. 2 (Fall 1986): 66.

78. Brooks, "Naval Power and National Security," 70–71.

79. Keller, "The Navy's Brash Leader."

80. A few examples follow. Mike Mansfield, ambassador to Japan from 1977 to 1988, called U.S.-Japan ties "the most important relationship in the world, bar none." See Mike Mansfield, "The U.S. and Japan: Sharing Our Destinies," *Foreign Affairs* 68, no. 2 (Spring 1989): 15. Deputy Secretary of State Stoessel called Japan the "cornerstone" of Asia policy. See Walter J. Stoessel, "Foreign Policy Priorities in Asia," Address Before the Los Angeles World Affairs Council in California on April 24, 1981, *Department of State Bulletin* 81 (June 1981): 33–35. Holdridge declared to Congress in March 1982 that the U.S.-Japan relationship was "the most important bilateral relationship in the world." See Hearings Before the Committee on Foreign Affairs and Its Subcommittees on International Economic Policy and Trade and on Asian and Pacific Affairs, United States House of Representatives, 97th Congress, March 1, 1982 (Washington, DC: Government Printing Office, 1982), 4, and in January 1985, Reagan himself declared that "there's no relationship that is more important to peace and prosperity in the world than that between the United States and Japan." See Ronald Reagan, "Remarks Following Discussions with Prime Minister Yasuhiro Nakasone of Japan in Los Angeles, California," January 2, 1985, http://www.reagan.utexas.edu/archives/speeches/1984/10285b.htm.

81. George P. Shultz, *Turmoil and Triumph: My Years as Secretary of State* (New York: Charles Scribner's Sons, 1993).

82. Richard V. Allen to the President, "Ambassador Mansfield's Cable to You," January 28, 1981, covering a January 26, 1981, cable from Ambassador Mike Mansfield to the President, pp. 3–4, Folder "Japan (1/20/81 (1) Box 8" in Executive Secretariat, NSC: Country File, Asia [Far East] Box 14, Reagan Library.

83. Caspar Weinberger, *Fighting for Peace: Seven Critical Years in the Pentagon* (New York: Grand Central Publishing, 1991), 220.

84. "U.S. National Security Strategy," NSDD 32, May 20, 1982, http://fas.org/irp/offdocs/nsdd/nsdd-32.pdf; John H. Holdridge, "Japan and the United States: A Cooperative Relationship," Statement Before the Subcommittee on Asian and Pacific Affairs of the Committee on Foreign Affairs on March 1, 1982, *Department of State Bulletin*, no. 2061 (April 1982): 52–60.

85. Holdridge, "Japan and the United States."

86. Interview with James E. Auer, conducted by Koji Murata, March 1996, http://www2.gwu.edu/~nsarchiv/japan/auerohinterview.htm. See also Armitage quoted in National Security Policy, Hearings Before the Defense Policy Panel of the Committee on Armed Services, House of Representatives, 100th Congress, March 18, 1987, 355.

87. Michael J. Green, "The Search for an Active Security Partnership: Lessons from the 1980s," in *Partnership: The United States and Japan, 1951–2001*, ed. Akira Iriye and Robert A. Wampler (Tokyo: Kodansha International, 2001), 142.

88. Interview by author with Richard Armitage, July 23, 2014. The intellectual leader of this defense *zoku* (caucus) within Japan was a mid-level representative in the Diet named Motoo Shiina, for whom the author worked from 1987 to 1989.

53. Association for Diplomatic Studies and Training Foreign Affairs Oral History Project, Ambassador Winston Lord, interviewed by Charles Stuart Kennedy and Nancy Bernkopf Tucker, April 28, 1998, 580.

54. Ann Devroy, "Clinton Grants China MFN, Reversing Campaign Pledge," *Washington Post*, May 27, 1994.

55. William J. Clinton, "Remarks to the Korean National Assembly in Seoul," July 10, 1993, http://www.presidency.ucsb.edu/ws/?pid=46829.

56. William J. Clinton, "Remarks to the Korean National Assembly in Seoul," July 10, 1993, http://www.presidency.ucsb.edu/ws/?pid=46829.

57. Sheldon W. Simon, "Alternative Visions of Security in the Asia Pacific," *Pacific Affairs* 69, no. 3 (Autumn 1996): 381–396.

58. Richard H. Solomon, "Asian Architecture: The US in the Asia-Pacific Community," *Harvard International Review* 16, no. 2 (Spring 1994): 26–29, 60; Robert A. Manning and Paula Stern, "The Myth of the Pacific Community," *Foreign Affairs* 73, no. 6 (November–December 1994): 79–93.

59. Henry Kissinger, "America's Role in Asia: Be a 20th-Century Great Britain," *The Los Angeles Times*, June 13, 1993.

60. Dan Williams and Clay Chandler, "U.S. Aide Sees Relations with Asia in Peril," *Washington Post*, May 5, 1994, A38.

61. Solomon, "Asian Architecture."

62. Yōichi Funabashi, "The Asianization of Asia," *Foreign Affairs* 72, no. 5 (November–December 1993): 75–85.

63. Tanaka Akihiko, "The International Context of U.S.-Japan Relations in the 1990s," in Curtis, *New Perspectives on U.S.-Japan Relations*, 267–270.

64. Joel S. Witt, Daniel B. Poneman, and Robert L. Gallucci, *Going Critical: The First North Korean Nuclear Crisis* (Washington, DC: Brookings Institution Press, 2004), 164.

65. Bill Clinton, November 7, 1993, as quoted in Stephen Engelberg and Michael R. Gordon, "Intelligence Study Says North Korea Has Nuclear Bomb," *New York Times*, December 26, 1993.

66. Carter and Perry, *Preventive Defense*, 128–131.

67. Witt, Poneman, and Gallucci, *Going Critical*, 164.

68. Tanaka, "The International Context of U.S.-Japan Relations in the 1990s," 267–270.

69. Hwang Jang-yop met with senior Bush administration officials and testified in front of the Senate Foreign Relations Committee in Washington, DC, in late 2003. See James Brooke, "North Korea Defector Plans Talks in U.S.," *New York Times*, October 27, 2003.

70. Victor Cha, *Impossible State: North Korea, Past and Future* (New York: Harper-Collins, 2012), 400; James Sterngold, "South Korea President Lashes Out at U.S.," *New York Times*, October 7, 1994.

71. Matake Kamiya interviewed members of the commission who said the highlighting of multilateralism was not intended to downgrade the U.S.-Japan alliance. See Kamiya, "Reforming the U.S.-Japan Alliance: What Should Be Done?" in *Reinventing the Alliance: U.S.-Japan Security Partnership in an Era of Change*, ed. G. John Ikenberry and Takashi Inoguchi (New York: Palgrave MacMillan, 2003), 92–93. However, when the report was issued, the author interviewed key members of the panel, who asked that the Pentagon

be told that the order of security modalities, placing multilateralism ahead of the alliance, was a deliberate signal.

72. Interview by author with Joseph Nye, November 2, 2014, Hakone, Japan.

73. Patrick Cronin and Michael Green, "Redefining the U.S.-Japan Alliance: Tokyo's National Defense Program," Institute for National Strategic Studies, McNair Paper 31, National Defense University, November 1994.

74. *United States Security Strategy for the East Asia-Pacific Region* (Washington, DC: U.S. Department of Defense, Office of International Security, 1995), i. Planners' fierce response recalled by then Japan Desk senior director Commander Paul S. Giarra in an interview with the author on June 5, 2015. Giarra was a driving force for the initiative as Nye arrived at the Pentagon.

75. Joseph S. Nye, Jr., "East Asian Security: The Case for Deep Engagement," *Foreign Affairs* 74, no. 4 (July–August 1995): 90–102.

76. *United States Security Strategy for the East Asia-Pacific Region*, 10.

77. Barry Keehn and Chalmers Johnson, "The Pentagon's Ossified Strategy," *Foreign Affairs* 74, no. 4 (July–August 1995). The "dilettantes" line is in Chalmers Johnson, "The Okinawan Rape Incident and the End of the Cold War in East Asia," JPRI Working Paper 16, February 1996.

78. Interview by author with Joseph Nye, November 2, 2014, Hakone, Japan.

79. In interviews with Japanese newspapers in November 1995, Nye cited the North Korean threat as the context for his new initiative, and Perry cited North Korea and—for the first time—China's rise. See *Japan Digest*, November 28, 1995, cited in Johnson, "The Okinawan Rape Incident and the End of the Cold War in East Asia."

80. Tanaka, "The International Context of U.S.-Japan Relations in the 1990s," 276–279.

81. Interview by author with Sandy Berger, February 9, 2015.

82. Association for Diplomatic Studies and Training Foreign Affairs Oral History Project, Ambassador Winston Lord, interviewed by Charles Stuart Kennedy and Nancy Bernkopf Tucker, April 28, 1998, 607.

83. John Lewis Gaddis, *Surprise, Security, and the American Experience* (Cambridge, MA: Harvard University Press, 2004).

84. Joseph Wilson Preuher interview by Bruce A. Elleman, cited in "The Right Skill Sets," in *Nineteen Gun Salutes: Case Studies of Operational, Strategic and Diplomatic Naval Leadership During the 19th and Early 20th Centuries, Issue 62*, ed. Joseph Wilson Preuher, John B. Hattendorf, and Bruce A. Elleman (Newport, RI: Naval War College, 2010), 237.

85. Office of Naval Intelligence, *Chinese Exercise Strait 961: 8–25 March 1996*, n.d. [1996], obtained by National Security Archive.

86. "U.S. Navy Ships to Sail Near Taiwan," CNN, March 10, 1996, http://edition.cnn.com/US/9603/us_china/.

87. Interview by author with former senior director for Japan in the Office of the Secretary of Defense Robin "Sak" Sakoda, June 4, 2015. Sakoda and his immediate predecessor, Commander Paul Giarra (USN), muscled the entire Nye Initiative and Defense Guidelines through the Pentagon for Campbell and Nye.

88. Though Clinton skipped the trip, Ambassador Walter Mondale stepped in to announce a new Special Action Committee on Okinawa (SACO) for reducing bases and

114. Stephen D. Cohen, *The Making of the United States International Economic Policy: Principles, Problems, and Proposals for Reform*, 5th ed. (Westport, CT: Praeger, 2000), 216–219.

115. Henning and Destler, "From Neglect to Activism," 317–333.

116. 19 U.S.C. § 2411(a) (1982 & Supp. III 1985) as quoted in Patricia I. Hansen, "Defining Unreasonableness in International Trade: Section 301 of the Trade Act of 1974," *Yale Law Journal* 96, no. 5 (April 1987): 1122–1146 at 1122–1123. On decision-making, see "How the Big Six Steer the Economy," *New York Times*, November 17, 1985.

117. "Reagan Orders Moves Against Trade Partners," *New York Times*, September 8, 1985; "Clayton K. Yeutter; a Trade War Veteran with Tales to Tell," *New York Times*, February 14, 1987; Douglas A. Irwin, "Trade Policies and the Semiconductor Industry," in *The Political Economy of American Trade Policy*, ed. Anne O. Krueger (Chicago: University of Chicago Press, 1996), 11–72.

118. NSDD 154, "US-Japan Trade Policy Relations," December 31, 1984, 1–2, http://www.fas.org/irp/offdocs/nsdd/nsdd-154.pdf.

119. Michael Mastanduno, "System Maker and Privilege Taker: US Power and the International Political Economy," in *International Relations Theory and the Consequences of Unipolarity*, ed. G. John Ikenberry, Michael Mastanduno, and William Curti Wohlforth (Cambridge: Cambridge University Press, 2011), 162–163; C. Fred Bergsten, "Stabilizing the International Monetary System: The Case for Target Zones," *Exchange Rate Targets: Desirable or Disastrous?*, ed. John H. Malkin, papers presented at an AEI conference on the eve of the 1986 meeting of the International Monetary Fund (Washington, DC: American Enterprise Institute for Public Policy Research, 1986).

120. Marcus Miller, "Target Zones and Monitoring Bands," in *Global Economics in Extraordinary Times: Essays in Honor of John Williamson*, ed. C. Fred Bergsten and C. Randall Henning (Washington, DC: Peterson Institute for International Economics, 2012), 84.

121. Interview by author with George Shultz, November 17, 2014.

122. Cohen, *The Making of the United States International Economic Policy*, 216–219.

123. Nina Hachigan and Mon Sutphen, *The Next American Century: How the U.S. Can Thrive as Other Powers Rise* (New York: Simon and Schuster, 2008), 222.

124. Between 1980 and 1990, the GDPs of Thailand, Malaysia, and Indonesia grew annually, on average, by 7.6, 5.3, and 6.1 percent, respectively. Singapore grew by 6.7 percent, China by 10.1, Korea by 8.9, and Vietnam by 4.6. See K. S. Jomo, "Growth Equity in East Asia?" Department of Economic and Social Affairs (DESA), United Nations, Working Paper 33, September 2006, http://www.un.org/esa/desa/papers/2006/wp33_2006.pdf.

125. On the role of ASEAN from the U.S. perspective, see John H. Holdridge, "U.S. Dialogue with ASEAN and ANZUS," Statement Before the Subcommittee on East Asian and Pacific Affairs of the Senate Foreign Relations Committee, July 15, 1982, *Department of State Bulletin*, no. 2067 (October 1982): 29–32.

126. On the beginnings of Soviet support for peace movements in Europe, see Ingmar Oldberg, "Peace Propaganda and Submarines: Soviet Policy Toward Sweden and Northern Europe," *Annals of the American Academy of Political and Social Science* 481, Soviet Foreign Policy in an Uncertain World (September 1985): 51–60.

127. Mark T. Berger, "APEC and Its Enemies: The Failure of the New Regionalism in the Asia-Pacific," *Third World Quarterly* 20, no. 5, New Regionalisms in the New Millennium

107. David Wessel and Bob Davis, "Limits of Power: Global Crisis Is a Match for Crack U.S. Economists," *Asian Wall Street Journal*, September 25, 1998.

108. Miller Center, "Interview with James Steinberg," University of Virginia, April 1, 2008, http://millercenter.org/president/clinton/oralhistory/james-steinberg.

109. Marc Castelano, "What Happened to APEC? A Decade of Taking Two Steps Forward, One Back," *JEI Report*, Japan Economic Institute, May 7, 1999; Green, *Japan's Reluctant Realism*, 211–215.

110. Eisuke Sakakibara, *Shihonshugi o Koeta Nippon* [*A Japanese Economy That Has Surpassed Capitalism*] (Tokyo: Toyo Keizai, 1990).

111. Eisuke Sakakibara, "Thai Crisis Played a Part in IMF Idea," special to *Yomiuri Shimbun*, November 29, 1999.

112. Anthony Rowley, "The Battle of Hong Kong: Tokyo's Proposal to Establish a Regional Emergency Fund Upsets the IMF, Western Governments," *Nikko Capital Trends* 2, no. 13 (November 1997); Sakakibara, "Thai Crisis Played a Part in IMF Idea"; Green, *Japan's Reluctant Realism*, 244–246.

113. Tanaka, "The International Context of U.S.-Japan Relations in the 1990s," 283–284.

114. Goh, *The Struggle for Order*, 54–57; Green, *Japan's Reluctant Realism*, chap. 8.

115. Harry Harding, "China," *Brookings Review* 15, no. 2 (Spring 1997): 14–15.

116. Nicholas Kristof, "Treaty Commitments; Would You Fight for These Islands?" *New York Times*, October 20, 1996. See also Larry A. Niksch, "Senkaku (Diaouyu) Island Dispute: The U.S. Legal Relationship and Obligations," PACNET, no. 45, Pacific Forum CSIS, November 8, 1996.

117. "Senkaku Shotou wa Anpo Jouyaku no Tekiyou Taishou, Yuuji ni wa Bouei Gimu, Bekokubou Jikanho Dair ga Kenkai" (U.S.-Japan Security Treaty Covers Senkaku Islands: U.S. Deputy Assistant Secretary of Defense Expresses His View), *Yomiuri Shimbun*, November 28, 1996. The State Department continued to refuse to clarify whether the Security Treaty applied. See, for example, Ambassador Foley's Remarks at the Japan Foreign Correspondents Club, April 8, 1998, http://japan2.usembassy.gov/e/p/tp-2647.html.

118. Tucker, "The Clinton Years," 59–60.

119. The President's News Conference with President Jiang Zemin of China in Beijing, June 27, 1998, posted online by Gerhard Peters and John T. Woolley, The American Presidency Project, http://www.presidency.ucsb.edu/ws/?pid=56229.

120. G. John Ikenberry, "Choosing Partners in Asia," *Australian Journal of International Affairs* 52, no. 3 (March 1998): 229–232; "U.S. Signals a Strategic Switch," *Canberra Times*, July 7, 1998, as reprinted in "Clinton to China: 'A Leap Over the Great Wall' in Sino-U.S. Ties," July 8, 1998, http://fas.org/news/china/1998/wwwh8708.html; Richard S. Dunham, "Time for Plain Talk: Is a China-U.S. Alliance at Hand?" *Business Week*, June 22, 1998; Julian Weiss, "A New Asian Agenda," *Washington Quarterly* 23, no. 1 (2000): 21–24. White House surprise given the Clinton attendance at Obuchi's funeral is from the author's interview with Sandy Berger, February 9, 2015.

121. Tanaka, "The International Context of U.S.-Japan Relations in the 1990s," 286. Prominent Blue Team members included William Kristol, Robert Kagan, Bill Gertz, Ross H. Munro, Mark Lagon, and Arthur Waldron, and in the Congress members included Christopher Cox.

Eagle and the Peacock: U.S. Foreign Policy Toward India Since Independence, Contributions in Political Science 345 (Westport, CT: Greenwood, 2003), 159.

141. Jeane J. Kirkpatrick, "Dictatorships and Double Standards," *Commentary* 68, no. 5 (November 1979): 34–45; David Adesnick and Michael McFaul, "Engaging Autocratic Allies to Promote Democracy," *Washington Quarterly* 29, no. 2 (Spring 2006): 9–10.

142. Kirkpatrick, "Dictatorships and Double Standards," 37.

143. Shultz quoted in Hearings Before the Committee on Foreign Relations on the Nomination of George P. Shultz, of California, to Be Secretary of State, United States Senate, 97th Congress, July 13 and 14, 1982 (Washington, DC: Government Printing Office, 1982), 209.

144. John H. Holdridge 1995 ADST Oral History; interview by author with Richard Armitage, July 23, 2014.

145. Hearings Before the Committee on Foreign Relations, United States Senate, 97th Congress, First Session, on the Nomination of Alexander M. Haig, Jr., to Be Secretary of State, January 9, 10, 12, 13, 14, 15, 1981 (Washington, DC: Government Printing Office, 1981), 51.

146. President Reagan, Arrival Ceremony, September 16, 1982, Visit of Philippine President Marcos, September 15–21, 1982, *Department of State Bulletin*, no. 2068 (November 1982): 23. See also Richard J. Kessler, "Marcos and the Americans," *Foreign Policy*, no. 63 (Summer 1986): 40–57.

147. There has been no conclusive inquiry into who ordered the assassination. See "The Unsolved Murder of Ninoy Aquino," *Manila Times*, August 18, 2014.

148. Reagan quoted in Walden Bello, "From Dictatorship to Elite Populism: The United States and the Philippine Crisis," in *Crisis and Confrontation: Ronald Reagan's Foreign Policy*, ed. Morris H. Morley (Totowa, NJ: Rowman and Littlefield, 1988), 235.

149. Quoted in Richard J. Kessler, "Marcos and the Americans," *Foreign Policy*, no. 63 (Summer 1986): 40–57.

150. Bello, "From Dictatorship to Elite Populism," 235; Gary Hawes, "The United States Support for the Marcos Administration and the Pressures That Made for Change," *Contemporary Southeast Asia* 8, no. 1 (June 1986): 18–36.

151. Pach, "The Reagan Doctrine," 75–88.

152. Wolfowitz quoted in Recent Events in the Philippines, Fall 1985, Hearings and Markup Before the Committee on Foreign Affairs and Its Subcommittee on Asia and Pacific Affairs, House of Representatives, 99th Congress, November 12, 1984 (Washington, DC: Government Printing Office, 1985), 6.

153. Armitage quoted in Recent Events in the Philippines, Fall 1985, Hearings and Markup Before the Committee on Foreign Affairs and Its Subcommittee on Asia and Pacific Affairs, House of Representatives, 99th Congress, November 12, 1984 (Washington, DC: Government Printing Office, 1985), 34.

154. Shultz, *Turmoil and Triumph*, 618–619.

155. NSSD, "U.S. Policy Toward the Philippines," November 2, 1984, quoted in Bello, "From Dictatorship to Elite Populism," 236. See also NSDD 163, "U.S. Policy Towards the Philippines," February 20, 1985, 2, http://www.fas.org/irp/offdocs/nsdd/nsdd-163.pdf.

156. Shultz, *Turmoil and Triumph*, 627.

157. James Fowler, "The United States and South Korean Democratization," *Political Science Quarterly* 114, no. 2 (Summer 1999): 270–271.

158. Fowler, "The United States and South Korean Democratization," 285–286.

159. Sigur quoted in Assessing the Prospects for Democratization in Korea, Hearings and Markup Before the Committee on Foreign Affairs and Its Subcommittee on Human Rights and International Organizations and Asian and Pacific Affairs, House of Representatives, 100th Congress, May 6, 1987 (Washington, DC: Government Printing Office, 1988), 187.

160. Neil A. Lewis, "Washington Delivers a Quiet Nudge," *New York Times*, July 5, 1987; Fowler, "The United States and South Korean Democratization," 270–280.

161. Tucker, "Reagan's Foreign Policy," 19.

162. Shultz quoted in Commitments, Consensus, and U.S. Foreign Policy, Hearings Before the Committee on Foreign Relations, United States Senate, 99th Congress, January 31, 1985 (Washington, DC: Government Printing Office, 1986), 17.

PART 4

1. The State Council Information Office of the People's Republic of China, "China's Military Strategy," May 2015, Beijing, http://english.chinamil.com.cn/news-channels/2015 -05/26/content_6507716.htm; "Kaiser Xi's Navy," *Wall Street Journal*, May 29, 2015; Secretary of Defense Ash Carter, "A Regional Security Architecture Where Everyone Rises," May 30, 2015, http://www.defense.gov/Speeches/Speech.aspx?SpeechID=1945; Lee Hsien Long, Keynote Address, May 29, 2015, https://www.iiss.org/en/events/shangri%20la%20 dialogue/archive/shangri-la-dialogue-2015-862b/opening-remarks-and-keynote-address -6729/keynote-address-a51f; Josh Rogin, "Ash Carter Talks Tough on China: But It's Just Talk," Bloomberg, May 29, 2015, http://www.bloombergview.com/articles/2015-05-30/ash -carter-talks-tough-on-china-but-it-s-just-talk; David E. Sanger and Rick Gladstone, "Piling Sand in a Disputed Sea, China Literally Gains Ground," *New York Times*, April 8, 2015.

2. The exception was probably Princeton professor Aaron Friedberg, who argued in a controversial but prescient article in 1993 that Asia was "ripe for rivalry." See Aaron L. Friedberg, "Ripe for Rivalry: Prospects for Peace in a Multipolar Asia," *International Security* 18, no. 3 (Winter 1993–1994): 5–33.

3. Sean O'Keefe, secretary of the navy, ". . . From the Sea: Preparing the Naval Service for the 21st Century, A New Direction for the Naval Service," September 1992.

4. Jeremi Suri, "American Grand Strategy from the Cold War's End to 9/11," *Orbis* 53 (Fall 2009): 611–627.

5. Robert H. Dorff, "A Primer in Strategy Development," in *U.S. Army War College Guide to Strategy*, ed. Joseph R. Cerami and James F. Holcomb (Carlisle, PA: Army War College, 2001), 12–13.

6. Interview with Joe Nye, November 4, 2014. See also Joseph S. Nye, Jr., "The Case for Deep Engagement," *Foreign Affairs* 74, no. 4 (July–August 1995): 90–102.

7. Chicago Council on Global Affairs, "Chicago Council Survey: Americans Shifting Focus to Asia," September 10, 2012, http://www.thechicagocouncil.org/sites/default/files /2012_CCS_AsiaBrief.pdf.

8. In 2007, Walter Russell Mead gave George W. Bush an A– on Asia but was less sanguine on his Mideast and Europe policies. See Walter Russell Mead, interview in Bernard Gwertzman, "Mead: Bush's Foreign Policy Record Around the World," The Council on

Foreign Relations, December 26, 2007; "Clinton's Foreign Policy," *Foreign Policy*, no. 121 (November–December 2000): 18–20, 22, 24, 26, 28–29.

12. George H. W. Bush and the Unipolar Moment, 1989–1992

1. See, for example, Cecil V. Crabb and Kevin V. Mulcahy, "George Bush's Management Style and Operation Desert Storm," *Presidential Studies Quarterly* 25, no. 2, Leadership, Organization, and Security (Spring 1995): 251–265; Wesley B. Borucki, *George H. W. Bush: In Defense of Principle*, First Men, America's Presidents (New York: Nova Science, 2011), preface.

2. Ryan J. Barilleaux and Mark J. Rozell, *Power and Prudence: The Presidency of George H. W. Bush* (College Station: Texas A&M University Press, 2004), 23, 114, 119; David Mervin, *George Bush and the Guardianship Presidency* (London: MacMillan, 1996), 3–37; Michael Duffy and Dan Goodgame, *Marching in Place: The Status Quo Presidency of George Bush* (New York: Simon and Schuster, 1992), 11–12.

3. Philip D. Zelikow and Condoleezza Rice, *Germany Unified and Europe Transformed: A Study in Statecraft* (Cambridge, MA: Harvard University Press, 1995).

4. James Mann, *About Face: A History of America's Curious Relationship with China, from Nixon to Clinton* (New York: Knopf, 1999), 175.

5. Warren I. Cohen, *America's Response to China: A History of Sino-American Relations*, 5th ed. (New York: Columbia University Press, 2010), 232.

6. Cohen, *America's Response to China*, 232–233.

7. Interview by author with Torkel Patterson, September 11, 2014.

8. Michael Oksenberg, "New Challenges and Opportunities in Sino-American Relations," in *US Foreign Policy in the 1990s*, ed. Greg Schmergel, foreword by Derek Bok (London: MacMillan Academic and Professional, in association with the *Harvard International Review*, 1991), 263–273.

9. James A. Baker III with Thomas M. Defrank, *The Politics of Diplomacy: Revolution, War and Peace* (New York: G. P. Putnam's Sons, 1995), 22–27; George Bush and Brent Scowcroft, *A World Transformed* (New York: Knopf, 1998), 25.

10. Jeremi Suri, "American Grand Strategy from the Cold War's End to 9/11," *Orbis* 53 (Fall 2009): 611–627.

11. Baker, *The Politics of Diplomacy*, 99; Walter LaFeber, *The Clash: A History of U.S.-Japan Relations* (New York: Norton, 1977), 385.

12. Baker, *The Politics of Diplomacy*, 100–101.

13. Baker, *The Politics of Diplomacy*, 100–101.

14. Association for Diplomatic Studies and Training Foreign Affairs Oral History Project, Dr. Richard H. Solomon, interviewed by Charles Stuart Kennedy, September 13, 1996, Foreign Affairs Oral History Collection (Arlington, VA: Association for Diplomatic Studies and Training, 2000) [hereafter Richard H. Solomon ADST Oral History], 55–58.

15. Association for Diplomatic Studies and Training Foreign Affairs Oral History Project, Richard H. Solomon ADST Oral History, 55–56; James Lilley with Jeffrey Lilley, *China*

Hands: Nine Decades of Adventure, Espionage, and Diplomacy in Asia (New York: Publi-cAffairs, 2004), 35–46, 169–195.

16. Bush and Scowcroft, *A World Transformed*, 90–91.

17. Interview by author with Richard Solomon, September 1, 2014; Cohen, *America's Response to China*, 232.

18. The White House, *National Security Strategy of the United States*, March 1990.

19. John Lewis Gaddis, "Toward a Post–Cold War World," *Foreign Affairs* 70, no. 2 (Spring 1991): 102–122.

20. G. John Ikenberry, Michael Mastanduno, and William C. Wohlforth, "Introduction: Unipolairty, State Behavior, and Systemic Consequences," in *International Relations Theory and the Consequences of Unipolarity*, ed. G. John Ikenberry, Michael Mastand-uno, and William C. Wohlforth (Cambridge: Cambridge University Press, 2001), 1. See also Nuno P. Monteiro, "Unrest Assured: Why Unipolarity Is Not Peaceful," *International Security* 36, no. 3 (Winter 2011–2012): 9–40.

21. The White House, *National Security Strategy of the United States*, March 1990, 7.

22. The base force would include 1.6 million active-duty personnel (down from the 1989 level of 2.1 million). This would include 12 active army divisions, 16 active air force tactical fighter wings, and 450 warships (including 12 carriers). See Lorna S. Jaffe, *The Develop-ment of the Base Force* (Washington, DC: Joint History Office, Office of the Chairman of the Joint Chiefs of Staff, July 1993), 19; Michael Klare, "The Rise and Fall of the 'Rogue Doctrine': The Pentagon's Quest for a Post–Cold War Military Strategy," *Middle East Report*, no. 208, US Foreign Policy in the Middle East: Critical Assessments (Autumn 1998): 12–15, 47. On congressional intrusion in force posture planning, see Paul Stockton, "Beyond Micromanagement: Congressional Budgeting for a Post–Cold War Military," *Political Science Quarterly* 110, no. 2 (Summer 1995): 233–259.

23. Jaffe, *The Development of the Base Force*, 2–4.

24. Klare, "The Rise and Fall of the 'Rogue Doctrine,'" 12–15, 47.

25. Patrick E. Tyler, "U.S. Strategy Plan Calls for Insuring No Rivals Develop," *New York Times*, March 7, 1992.

26. See, for example, Laura D'Andrea Tyson and John Zysman, "Developmental Strategy and Production Innovation in Japan," in *Politics and Productivity*, ed. Chalmers Johnson, Laura D'Andrea Tyson, and John Zysman (Cambridge: Ballinger, 1989), 59–140. See also Chalmers Johnson, "Their Behavior, Our Policy," *The National Interest*, no. 17 (Fall 1989): 17–25; Chalmers Johnson, *MITI and the Japanese Miracle, 1925–1975* (Stanford, CA: Stanford University Press, 1982); James Fallows, "Containing Japan," *The Atlantic*, May 1989.

27. Chalmers Johnson as quoted in LaFeber, *The Clash*, 384; Paul Tsongas, "Can 'Amer-ica First' Bring Jobs Back?" *Time*, December 23, 1991.

28. Brent Scowcroft, "Eisenhower and a Foreign Policy Agenda," *Presidential Studies Quarterly* 22, no. 3 (Summer 1992): 451–454.

29. Harry Harding, *A Fragile Relationship: The United States and China Since 1972* (Washington, DC: Brookings Institution, 1992), 215; Baker, *The Politics of Diplomacy*, 101.

30. As quoted in Baker, *The Politics of Diplomacy*, 100–101.

31. Bush and Scowcroft, *A World Transformed*, 89–98.

32. "China: Yet Again in Crisis," *Strategic Survey* 90 (May 1990): 126–134. The Soviets agreed to the three conditions for rapprochement with China: the end of support for the

Vietnamese war in Cambodia; a withdrawal from Afghanistan; and removing Soviet forces from the Sino-Soviet border. Cohen sees the rationale for Gorbachev's visit as an effort to reduce the burden of defense on the Soviet economy (his trip came in the wake of announcements of unilateral troop withdrawals from Eastern Europe). See Robert S. Ross, "The Bush Administration: The Origins of Engagement," in *Making China Policy: Lessons from the Bush and Clinton Administrations*, ed. Ramon H. Myers, Michel C. Oksenberg, and David Shambaugh (Lanham, MD: Rowman and Littlefield, 2002), 22; Cohen, *America's Response to China*, 237.

33. Mann, *About Face*, 176–183.

34. Cohen, *America's Response to China*, 243.

35. Baker, *The Politics of Diplomacy*, 104–105.

36. Harding, *A Fragile Relationship*, 229.

37. George Bush, "The President's News Conference," June 5, 1989, *Weekly Compilation of Presidential Documents* 25, no. 23 (June 12, 1989), 839–843, reprinted in *China Cross Talk: The American Debate over China Policy Since Normalization, a Reader*, ed. Scott Kennedy (Lanham, MD: Rowman and Littlefield, 2003), 87–90.

38. Bush and Scowcroft, *A World Transformed*, 89–90.

39. Bush and Scowcroft, *A World Transformed*, 89; Robert G. Sutter, *U.S. Policy Toward China: An Introduction to the Role of Interest Groups* (Lanham, MD: Rowman and Littlefield, 1998), 29.

40. Association for Diplomatic Studies and Training Foreign Affairs Oral History Project, Richard H. Solomon ADST Oral History, 56.

41. Bush and Scowcroft, *A World Transformed*, 111.

42. Henry Kissinger, "The Caricature of Deng as a Tyrant Is Unfair," *Washington Post*, August 1, 1989, A21, reprinted in Kennedy, *China Cross Talk*, 100–104.

43. Stepher J. Solarz, "Kissinger's Kowtow," *Washington Post*, August 6, 1989, B7, reprinted in Kennedy, *China Cross Talk*, 105–107.

44. Sheryl WuDunn, "Kissinger, in Beijing, Seeks to Mend Fences," *New York Times*, November 9, 1989; Richard Nixon as quoted in Harding, *A Fragile Relationship*, 251.

45. Ross, "The Bush Administration," 26–27.

46. Winston Lord, "Misguided Mission," *Washington Post*, December 19, 1989, A23, reprinted in Kennedy, *China Cross Talk*, 109–113.

47. Sutter, *U.S. Policy Toward China*, 30–31.

48. Ross, "The Bush Administration," 26–27.

49. Sutter, *U.S. Policy Toward China*, 33–35.

50. House Foreign Affairs Subcommittee on Human Rights and International Organizations, Asian and Pacific Affairs, and International Economic Policy and Trade, "Most-Favored-Nation Status for the People's Republic of China," 101st Congress, 2nd session, May 24, 1990. Testimony by Nancy Pelosi and Assistant Secretary for East Asia and Pacific Affairs Richard Solomon, reprinted in Kennedy, *China Cross Talk*, 117–121.

51. Cohen, *America's Response to China*, 242–245.

52. Cohen, *America's Response to China*, 242–245.

53. Harry Harding, "The Impact of Tiananmen on China's Foreign Policy," in *China's Foreign Relations After Tiananmen: Challenges for the U.S.* (Washington, DC: National Bureau of Asian and Soviet Research, December 1990), 5.

54. Cohen, *America's Response to China*, 242–245.

55. Sutter, *U.S. Policy Toward China*, 36.

56. Baker, *The Politics of Diplomacy*, 588.

57. Interview by author with Rear Admiral Michael McDevitt, USN (ret.), former acting deputy assistant secretary of state for East Asia and the Pacific, 1991–1992, October 6, 2014, Arlington, VA.

58. Carla Hills, discussant on Christopher C. Meyerson, "Trade Policy Making in the Bush Administration: United States–Japan Trade and the GATT Uruguay Round Negotiations," in *From Cold War to New World Order: The Foreign Policy of George H. W. Bush*, ed. Meena Bose and Rosanna Perotti, Hofstra University Contributions in Political Science 393 (Westport, CT: Greenwood, 2002), 65.

59. Harding, *A Fragile Relationship*, 359–361.

60. Sutter, *U.S. Policy Toward China*, 26–27.

61. Martin Tolchin and Susan Tolchin, *Buying into America: How Foreign Money Is Changing the Face of Our Nation* (New York: Crown, 1988); Stephanie Epstein, *Buying the American Mind: Japan's Quest for U.S. Ideas in Science, Economic Policy and the Schools* (Lanham, MD: University Press of America and The Center for Public Integrity, 1995).

62. The author lived in Japan in 1989–1990 and heard frequent boasts along these lines, including from the vice minister of international trade and industry. See, for instance, Richard J. Samuels, "Japan in 1989: Changing Times," *Asian Survey* 30, no. 1, A Survey of Asia in 1989: Part 1 (January 1990): 42–51; Ronald E. Yates, "Japan May Still Surpass U.S. to Become Leading Economic Power by the Year 2000," *Chicago Tribune*, April 10, 1995.

63. Mike M. Mochizuki, "To Change or Contain: Dilemmas of American Policy Toward Japan," in *Eagle in a New World: American Grand Strategy in the Post–Cold War Era*, ed. Kenneth A. Oye, Robert J. Lieber, and Donald Rothchild (New York: HarperCollins, 1996), 335–360; Michael Crichton, *Rising Sun* (New York: Knopf, 1992).

64. Meyerson, "Trade Policy Making in the Bush Administration," 45–47; Japan policy cell from author's interview with former undersecretary of state for economic affairs, Ambassador Robert McCormack, Washington, DC, October 6, 2014.

65. George H. W. Bush as quoted in Delia B. Conti, "President Bush's Trade Rhetoric: Retaining the Free Trade Paradigm in an Era of Managed Trade," in Bose and Perotti, *From Cold War to New World Order*, 5.

66. Hills, discussant on Meyerson, "Trade Policy Making in the Bush Administration," 63.

67. Hearing Before the Committee on Finance, United States Senate, 101st Congress, 1st session, on the Nomination of Carla Anderson Hills to be U.S. Trade Representative, January 27, 1989; George H. W. Bush, "Statement on United States Action Against Foreign Trade Barriers," May 26, 1989, *Weekly Compilation of Presidential Documents* 25, no. 21 (May 29, 1989): 608.

68. Merit E. Janow, "Trading with an Ally: Progress and Discontent in U.S.-Japan Trade Relations," in *The United States, Japan, and Asia*, ed. Gerald L. Curtis (New York: Norton, 1994), 53–95.

69. Michael H. Armacost, *Friends or Rivals? The Insider's Account of U.S.-Japan Relations* (New York: Columbia University Press, 1996), 60.

70. The White House, Office of the Press Secretary, "Structural Impediments Initiative (SII) Interim Report," April 5, 1990; Michael Mastanduno, "Framing the Japan Problem: The Bush Administration and the Structural Impediments Initiative," *International Journal* 47, no. 2 (Spring 1992): 235–264.

71. Interview by author with Ambassador Robert McCormack, Washington, DC, October 6, 2014. See also Mastanduno, "Framing the Japan Problem," 235–264.

72. Richard T. McCormack, Undersecretary of State for Economic Affairs, Kozo Watanabe, Deputy Foreign Minister, et al., "Structural Impediments Initiative Joint Report," June 1990, http://tcc.export.gov/Trade_Agreements/All_Trade_Agreements/exp_005583.asp.

73. Robert Mosbacher, as quoted in Meyerson, "Trade Policy Making in the Bush Administration," in Bose and Perotti, *From Cold War to New World Order*, 47–48.

74. Author's interview with former NSC Asia director Torkel Patterson, September 11, 2014, Washington, DC.

75. Remarks made by George H. W. Bush, President of the United States, at Kilo 8 Pier (with the USS *Arizona* Memorial in the background) during fiftieth anniversary of Pearl Harbor ceremonies, December 7, 1991.

76. Samuels, "Japan in 1989," 42–51.

77. Michael J. Green, *Arming Japan: Defense Production, Alliance Politics, and the Postwar Search for Autonomy* (New York: Columbia University Press, 1995), 105–106.

78. "Can the Pentagon Keep Shielding Japan?" *Business Week*, March 27, 1989; "Confusion Is Operative Word in U.S. Policy Toward Japan," *New York Times*, March 20, 1989.

79. "Confusion is Operative Word in U.S. Policy Toward Japan," *New York Times*, March 20, 1989.

80. Green, *Arming Japan*, 103–105.

81. Mochizuki, "To Change or Contain," in Oye, Lieber, and Rothchild, *Eagle in a New World*, 335–360.

82. Cited from Memorandum of Telephone Conversation between President George H. W. Bush and Japanese prime minister Toshiki Kaifu, August 13, 1990 (declassified through a Freedom of Information Act request by the National Security Archive and posted June 20, 2012, http://www2.gwu.edu/~nsarchiv/NSAEBB/NSAEBB382/.

83. Iokibe Makoto and Miyagi Taizo, eds., *Hashimoto Ryūtarō Gaikō Kaikoroku [Memoir of Hashimoto Ryūtarō on Foreign Policy]* (Tokyo: Iwanami, 2013), 25.

84. One of Japan's key officials during the crisis, Okamoto Yukio, considered this to be a major factor in the Japanese side's own confusion about how best to respond to the crisis, expressing his views in an interview with the author in Tokyo, July 31, 2013. His American counterpart on the NSC staff, Torkel Patterson, agreed, as he stated in an interview with the author on September 11, 2014, in Washington, DC.

85. Armacost, *Friends or Rivals?*, 99.

86. "How Much Can Bush Bring Home?" *Business Week*, January 12, 1992.

87. Michael Wines, "Bush Collapses at State Dinner with the Japanese," *New York Times*, January 9, 1992.

88. Thomas Omestad, "Why Bush Lost," *Foreign Policy*, no. 89 (Winter 1992–1993): 70–81.

89. Herb Block, *Washington Post* cartoon, January 12, 1992.

90. Richard T. McCormack, discussant on Delia B. Conti, "President Bush's Trade Rhetoric: Retaining the Free Trade Paradigm in an Era of Managed Trade," in Bose and Perotti, *From Cold War to New World Order*, 22–23.

91. John M. Broder, "U.S. Plans 10% Troop Cut in 3 Asian Nations," *Los Angeles Times*, February 14, 1990.

92. Ford had worked in the Senate and deserves the lion's share of credit for creating the East Asia strategic reports requirement in the Defense Act, as stated in author's interview with Rear Admiral Mike McDevitt, USN (ret.), October 7, 2014, in Washington, DC.

93. U.S. Department of Defense, "A Strategic Framework for the Asian Pacific Rim: Report to Congress: Looking Toward the 21st Century," 1990.

94. Admiral Huntington Hardisty, USN, "A Long-Term Game Plan," in *Change, Interdependence and Security in the Pacific Basin: The 1990 Pacific Symposium*, ed. Dora Alves (Washington, DC: National Defense University Press, 1991), 7.

95. U.S. Department of Defense, "A Strategic Framework for the Asian Pacific Rim."

96. Jin-Young Chung, "Cost Sharing for USFK in Transition: Whither the ROK-U.S. Alliance?" in *Recalibrating the US-Republic of Korea Alliance*, ed. Donald W. Boose, Jr. (Carlisle, PA: U.S. Army War College Strategic Studies Institute, 2003), 38.

97. U.S. Department of Defense, "A Strategic Framework for the Asian Pacific Rim: Looking Towards the 21st Century," 1992.

98. U.S. Department of Defense, "A Strategic Framework for the Asian Pacific Rim."

99. Interview by author with Rear Admiral Mike McDevitt, USN (ret.), October 7, 2014, Washington, DC.

100. Lieutenant Colonel Robert C. Pollard, Jr., "Losing the Philippines: Its Impact on Our National Military Strategy for the 90's," U.S. Army War College Study Project (Carlisle, PA: U.S. Army War College, 1992), 1–38.

101. Eric Schmitt, "U.S. Exit from Manila: Making a Hasty Retreat," *New York Times*, January 5, 1992.

102. Formal titles and dates were the December 13, 1991, Agreement on Reconciliation, Non-Aggression and Cooperation and Exchanges between South and North; and the January 20, 1992, Joint Declaration of South and North Korea on Denuclearization of the Korean Peninsula.

103. Don Oberdorfer, *The Two Koreas: A Contemporary History* (Reading, MA: Addison-Wesley, 1998), 256–265.

104. Oberdorfer, *The Two Koreas*, 254–255; Stanley Weeks and Charles Meconis, *The Armed Forces of the USA in the Asia Region* (London: I. B. Tauris, 1999), 3:101–104; Association for Diplomatic Studies and Training Foreign Affairs Oral History Project, Richard H. Solomon ADST Oral History, 61–62.

105. U.S. Department of Defense, *Soviet Military Power, 1989* (Washington, DC: Government Printing Office, 1989), 119, as quoted in Terence Roehrig, *The U.S. Defense Commitment to South Korea* (Lanham, MD: Lexington Books, 2006), 63.

106. IAEA, "Fact Sheet on DPRK Nuclear Safeguards," https://www.iaea.org/newscenter /focus/dprk/fact-sheet-on-dprk-nuclear-safeguards.

107. Warren Christopher, *In the Stream of History: Shaping Foreign Policy for a New Era* (Stanford, CA: Stanford University Press, 1998), 12–13.

108. Richard C. Bush, "Taiwan Policy Making Since Tiananmen: Navigating Through Shifting Waters," in Myers, Oksenberg, and Shambaugh, *Making China Policy*, 179–199.

109. Interview by author with Rear Admiral Mike McDevitt, USN (ret.), October 7, 2014. McDevitt helped to lead the study on the cross-Strait airpower balance that indicated China's introduction of Sukhoi fighters required increased ROCAF capabilities to prevent a dangerous imbalance. Lilley and the Defense Department used the study to overcome State Department objections.

110. Gilbert A. Lewthwaite, "U.S. Asks Asian Nations to Isolate Myanmar," *Baltimore Sun*, July 21, 1991.

111. Richard H. Solomon, *Exiting Indochina: U.S. Leadership of the Cambodia Settlement and Normalization of Relations with Vietnam* (Washington, DC: United States Institute of Peace Press, 2000), 22; also interview by author with Richard Solomon, September 11, 2014, Washington, DC.

112. Solomon, *Exiting Indochina*, 6–22.

113. "Excerpts from Pentagon's Plan: Preventing the Emergence of a New Rival," *New York Times*, March 8, 1992.

114. Arthur Rubinoff, "Incompatible Objectives and Shortsighted Policies: US Strategies Toward India," in *US-Indian Strategic Cooperation into the 21st Century*, ed. Sumit Ganguly, Brian Shoup, and Andrew Scobell (London: Routledge, 2006), 48–49.

115. Association for Diplomatic Studies and Training Foreign Affairs Oral History Project, Ambassador William Clark, Jr., interviewed by Thomas Stern, January 11, 1994, 163. See Dennis Kux, *India and the United States: Estranged Democracies, 1941–1991* (Darby, PA: DIANE, 1992), 130, for more on Dulles and Menon during the Eisenhower administration.

116. Mark T. Berger, "APEC and Its Enemies: The Failure of the New Regionalism in the Asia-Pacific," *Third World Quarterly* 20, no. 5, New Regionalisms in the New Millennium (October 1999): 1013–1030.

117. Baker, *The Politics of Diplomacy*, 610–611.

118. Baker, *The Politics of Diplomacy*, 610–611.

119. Baker, *The Politics of Diplomacy*, 610–611.

120. Berger, "APEC and Its Enemies," 1013–1030.

121. Association for Diplomatic Studies and Training Foreign Affairs Oral History Project, Ambassador William Clark, Jr., interviewed by Thomas Stern, January 11, 1994, 57.

122. James A. Baker III, "America in Asia: Emerging Architecture for a Pacific Community," *Foreign Affairs* 70, no. 5, America and the Pacific, 1941–1991 (Winter 1991): 1–18.

13. BILL CLINTON AND THE UNEXPECTED RETURN OF GREAT-POWER POLITICS

1. "Clinton Enters Race, Urges Citizens to Do More for U.S.," *Los Angeles Times*, October 4, 1991.

2. Thomas Omestad, "Why Bush Lost," *Foreign Policy*, no. 89 (Winter 1992–1993): 70–81.

3. Thomas L. Friedman, "The 1992 Campaign—Issues: Foreign Policy; Clinton's Foreign Policy Agenda Reaches Across Broad Spectrum," *New York Times*, October 4, 1992.

4. William J. Clinton, "Excerpts of Remarks in Milwaukee," October 2, 1992, posted online by Gerhard Peters and John T. Woolley, The American Presidency Project, http://www .presidency.ucsb.edu/ws/index.php?pid=85226. Bob Suettinger points out that the president refrained from calling Chinese leaders the "butchers of Beijing," though it was frequently used by his campaign. See Robert Suettinger, *Beyond Tiananmen: The Politics of U.S.-China Relations, 1989-2000* (Washington, DC: Brookings Institution Press, 2004), 471.

5. Jeremi Suri, "American Grand Strategy from the Cold War's End to 9/11," *Orbis* 53 (Fall 2009): 611–627.

6. Joe Klein, "Bill Clinton: Who Is This Guy?" *New York Magazine*, January 20, 1992. The debate took place on November 1, 1991.

7. Confirmation Hearing, Winston Lord, Assistant Secretary-Designate for East Asian and Pacific Affairs, Statement Before the Senate Foreign Relations Committee, Washington, DC, March 31, 1993, http://www.state.gov/1997-2001-NOPDFS/regions/eap/930331.html.

8. Colin L. Powell with Joseph E. Persico, *My American Journey* (New York: Random House, 1995), 547.

9. Friedman, "The 1992 Campaign—Issues."

10. Interview by author with former national security advisor Sandy Berger, February 9, 2015, Washington, DC.

11. "No Dream Team," *National Review*, December 31, 1996.

12. Hal Brands, *From Berlin to Baghdad: America's Search for Purpose in the Post–Cold War World* (Lexington: University of Kentucky Press, 2008), 106–107.

13. The editors, "Altered State," *New Republic*, December 30, 1996.

14. See, for example, Laura D'Andrea Tyson, *Who's Bashing Whom? Trade Conflict in High Technology Industries* (Washington, DC: The Institute for International Economics, 1993); Peter Behr, "Clinton's CEA Choice Faces Skeptics on Experience, Views," *Washington Post*, January 21, 1993; Peter Behr, "Tyson Willing to Confront Rivals of U.S.," *Washington Post*, December 12, 1992; *Wall Street Journal* editorial writer Kevin Prichett as quoted in Clay Chandler, "Administration's Economic Voice of Reason; Laura Tyson's Straightforward Style Helps Win Over Detractors," *Washington Post*, April 25, 1994.

15. Kenneth Flamm, *Mismanaged Trade? Strategic Policy and the Semiconductor Industry* (Washington, DC: Brookings Institution Press, 1995), 44.

16. W. Bowman Cutter as quoted in Clay Chandler, "Taking On the Japanese Bureaucracy; Clinton Administration Blames Tokyo's Establishment for Thwarting Trade Talks," *Washington Post*, February 12, 1994.

17. As quoted in Brands, *From Berlin to Baghdad*, 111.

18. Bob Woodward, *The Agenda: Inside the Clinton White House* (New York: Simon and Schuster, 1994), 280–281.

19. Paul Kengor, "The Foreign Policy Role of Vice President Al Gore," *Presidential Studies Quarterly* 27, no. 1, Bill Clinton and Al Gore: Retrospect and Prospect (Winter 1997): 14–38.

20. Jacob Heilbrunn, "Lake Inferior: The Pedigree of Anthony Lake," *New Republic*, September 20, 1993.

21. Charles Lane, "Perry's Parry: Reading the Defense Secretary's Mind," *New Republic*, June 27, 1994; "Mr. Perry's Promotion," *Washington Post*, January 25, 1994.

22. Ashton B. Carter and William J. Perry, *Preventive Defense: A New Security Strategy for America* (Washington, DC: Brookings Institution Press, 1999), 92–105.

23. Joseph S. Nye, Jr., *Bound to Lead: The Changing Nature of American Power* (New York: Basic Books, 1990).

24. Warren Christopher, *In the Stream of History: Shaping Foreign Policy for a New Era* (Stanford, CA: Stanford University Press, 1998), 116; Amy Kaslow, "Diverse Group of 'Insiders' Tapped for Cabinet Jobs," *Christian Science Monitor*, December 28, 1992. See also Brands, *From Berlin to Baghdad*, 105.

25. Les Aspin, Secretary of Defense, *Report on the Bottom-Up Review*, Washington, DC, October 1993, http://www.dod.mil/pubs/foi/administration_and_Management /other/515.pdf.

26. Anthony Lake, "From Containment to Enlargement: Remarks of Anthony Lake," as delivered at Johns Hopkins University, School of Advanced International Studies, Washington, DC, September 21, 1993 (Washington, DC: Executive Office of the President, 1993), http://fas.org/news/usa/1993/usa-930921.htm.

27. Aspin, *Report on the Bottom-Up Review*.

28. Aspin, *Report on the Bottom-Up Review*.

29. Aspin, *Report on the Bottom-Up Review*.

30. The White House, *A National Security Strategy of Engagement and Enlargement*, July 1, 1994.

31. Robert L. Galluci, Graduation Ceremony Keynote Address, Monterey Institute of International Studies, May 22, 2010, http://www.macfound.org/press/speeches/president -graduation-ceremony-keynote/.

32. Suri, "American Grand Strategy from the Cold War's End to 9/11," 611–627.

33. Thomas L. Friedman, "Theory vs. Practice: Clinton's Stated Policy Turns Into More Modest 'Self-Containment,'" *New York Times*, October 1, 1993; Susumu Awanohara, "United States: Containing Enlargement," *Far Eastern Economic Review* 156, no. 42 (October 21, 1993): 13; Eric V. Larson, David T. Orletsky, and Kristin J. Leuschner, *Defense Planning in a Decade of Change: Lessons from the Base Force, Bottom-Up Review, and the Quadrennial Defense Review* (Washington, DC: RAND, 2001), 41–80.

34. Interview by author with Sandy Berger, February 9, 2015.

35. See, for example, Laura D'Andrea Tyson and John Zysman, "Developmental Strategy and Production Innovation in Japan," in *Politics and Productivity*, ed. Chalmers Johnson, Laura D'Andrea Tyson, and John Zysman (Cambridge, MA: Ballinger, 1989), 59– 140. See also Chalmers Johnson, "Their Behavior, Our Policy," *The National Interest*, no. 17 (Fall 1989): 17–25; Chalmers Johnson, *MITI and the Japanese Miracle, 1925–1975* (Stanford, CA: Stanford University Press, 1982); James Fallows, "Containing Japan," *The Atlantic* 263, no. 5 (May 1989).

36. Robert M. Uriu, *Clinton and Japan: The Impact of Revisionism on US Trade Policy* (Oxford: Oxford University Press, 2009), 17.

37. Brands, *From Berlin to Baghdad*, 146; United States Census Bureau, *Trade in Goods with Japan*, https://www.census.gov/foreign-trade/balance/c5880.html#1985.

38. The group was composed of Kantor, Laura D'Andrea Tyson, Roger Altman, Bo Cutter, Larry Summers, and Joan Spero. See Uriu, *Clinton and Japan*, 98–99.

39. Robert M. Uriu, "The Impact of Policy Ideas: Revisionism and the Clinton Administration's Trade Policy Toward Japan," in *New Perspectives on U.S.-Japan Relations*, ed. Gerald L. Curtis (Tokyo: Japan Center for International Exchange, 2000), 230–231.

40. Gerald L. Curtis, "U.S. Policy Toward Japan from Nixon to Clinton: An Assessment," in Curtis, *New Perspectives on U.S.-Japan Relations*, 30–31.

41. Michael J. Green, "Balance of Power," in *U.S.-Japan Relations in a Changing World*, ed. Steven K. Vogel (Washington, DC: Brookings Institution Press, 2002), 24–25; 日米ハ イテク摩擦」再燃も 戦略ミサイル防衛構想の行方, 1993/10/14 朝日新聞 朝刊 ["U.S.-Japan 'High-Tech Friction': Missile Defense Concept Heats Up Again," *Asahi Shimbun*, October 14, 1993].

42. Walter LaFeber, *The Clash: A History of U.S.-Japan Relations* (New York: Norton, 1977), 389.

43. Aurelia George Mulgan, "Japan; a Setting Sun?" *Foreign Affairs* 79, no. 4 (July–August 2000): 40–52; Leonard Schoppa, *Bargaining with Japan: What American Pressure Can and Cannot Do* (New York: Columbia University Press, 1997).

44. Amy Searight, "Does Multilateralism Matter? Ideas and Interests Shaping Japan's Behavior in the GATT/WTO Regime," Presentation at Program on U.S.-Japan Relations, Weatherhead Center for International Affairs, Harvard University, March 1999; Uriu, "The Impact of Policy Ideas," 230–235.

45. Michael Mastanduno, "Institutions of Convenience: U.S. Foreign Policy and the Pragmatic Use of International Institutions," in *The Uses of Institutions: The U.S., Japan, and Governance in East Asia*, ed. G. John Ikenberry and Takashi Inoguchi (New York: Palgrave MacMillan, 2007), 41–42.

46. Uriu, *Clinton and Japan*, 3–6. See also Kiesuke Iida, *Legalization and Japan: The Politics of WTO Dispute Settlement* (London: Cameron May, 2006), 87–91.

47. Nancy Tucker, "The Clinton Years: The Problem of Coherence," in *Making China Policy: Lessons from the Bush and Clinton Administrations*, ed. Ramon H. Myers, Michel C. Oksenberg, and David Shambaugh (Lanham, MD: Rowman and Littlefield, 2002), 45.

48. Christopher, *In the Stream of History*, 152–153.

49. Warren I. Cohen, *America's Response to China: A History of Sino-American Relations*, 5th ed. (New York: Columbia University Press, 2010), 253.

50. Association for Diplomatic Studies and Training Foreign Affairs Oral History Project, Ambassador Winston Lord, interviewed by Charles Stuart Kennedy and Nancy Bernkopf Tucker, April 28, 1998, Foreign Affairs Oral History Collection (Arlington, VA: Association for Diplomatic Studies and Training, 2003), 571, http://www.adst.org /OH%20TOCs/Lord,%20Winston.pdf.

51. "Conditions for Renewal of Most-Favored-Nation Status for the People's Republic of China in 1994," Digital National Security Archive, Executive Order, May 28, 1993, China and the U.S., item number CH01589; William J. Clinton, "Statement on Most-Favored-Nation Trade Status for China," May 28, 1993, reprinted in *China Cross Talk: The American Debate over China Policy Since Normalization, a Reader*, ed. Scott Kennedy (Lanham, MD: Rowman and Littlefield, 2003), 135–138.

52. James Mann, *About Face: A History of America's Curious Relationship with China, from Nixon to Clinton* (New York: Knopf, 1999), 290–291; Tucker, "The Clinton Years," 50.

53. Association for Diplomatic Studies and Training Foreign Affairs Oral History Project, Ambassador Winston Lord, interviewed by Charles Stuart Kennedy and Nancy Bernkopf Tucker, April 28, 1998, 580.

54. Ann Devroy, "Clinton Grants China MFN, Reversing Campaign Pledge," *Washington Post*, May 27, 1994.

55. William J. Clinton, "Remarks to the Korean National Assembly in Seoul," July 10, 1993, http://www.presidency.ucsb.edu/ws/?pid=46829.

56. William J. Clinton, "Remarks to the Korean National Assembly in Seoul," July 10, 1993, http://www.presidency.ucsb.edu/ws/?pid=46829.

57. Sheldon W. Simon, "Alternative Visions of Security in the Asia Pacific," *Pacific Affairs* 69, no. 3 (Autumn 1996): 381–396.

58. Richard H. Solomon, "Asian Architecture: The US in the Asia-Pacific Community," *Harvard International Review* 16, no. 2 (Spring 1994): 26–29, 60; Robert A. Manning and Paula Stern, "The Myth of the Pacific Community," *Foreign Affairs* 73, no. 6 (November–December 1994): 79–93.

59. Henry Kissinger, "America's Role in Asia: Be a 20th-Century Great Britain," *The Los Angeles Times*, June 13, 1993.

60. Dan Williams and Clay Chandler, "U.S. Aide Sees Relations with Asia in Peril," *Washington Post*, May 5, 1994, A38.

61. Solomon, "Asian Architecture."

62. Yōichi Funabashi, "The Asianization of Asia," *Foreign Affairs* 72, no. 5 (November–December 1993): 75–85.

63. Tanaka Akihiko, "The International Context of U.S.-Japan Relations in the 1990s," in Curtis, *New Perspectives on U.S.-Japan Relations*, 267–270.

64. Joel S. Witt, Daniel B. Poneman, and Robert L. Gallucci, *Going Critical: The First North Korean Nuclear Crisis* (Washington, DC: Brookings Institution Press, 2004), 164.

65. Bill Clinton, November 7, 1993, as quoted in Stephen Engelberg and Michael R. Gordon, "Intelligence Study Says North Korea Has Nuclear Bomb," *New York Times*, December 26, 1993.

66. Carter and Perry, *Preventive Defense*, 128–131.

67. Witt, Poneman, and Gallucci, *Going Critical*, 164.

68. Tanaka, "The International Context of U.S.-Japan Relations in the 1990s," 267–270.

69. Hwang Jang-yop met with senior Bush administration officials and testified in front of the Senate Foreign Relations Committee in Washington, DC, in late 2003. See James Brooke, "North Korea Defector Plans Talks in U.S.," *New York Times*, October 27, 2003.

70. Victor Cha, *Impossible State: North Korea, Past and Future* (New York: HarperCollins, 2012), 400; James Sterngold, "South Korea President Lashes Out at U.S.," *New York Times*, October 7, 1994.

71. Matake Kamiya interviewed members of the commission who said the highlighting of multilateralism was not intended to downgrade the U.S.-Japan alliance. See Kamiya, "Reforming the U.S.-Japan Alliance: What Should Be Done?" in *Reinventing the Alliance: U.S.-Japan Security Partnership in an Era of Change*, ed. G. John Ikenberry and Takashi Inoguchi (New York: Palgrave MacMillan, 2003), 92–93. However, when the report was issued, the author interviewed key members of the panel, who asked that the Pentagon

be told that the order of security modalities, placing multilateralism ahead of the alliance, was a deliberate signal.

72. Interview by author with Joseph Nye, November 2, 2014, Hakone, Japan.

73. Patrick Cronin and Michael Green, "Redefining the U.S.-Japan Alliance: Tokyo's National Defense Program," Institute for National Strategic Studies, McNair Paper 31, National Defense University, November 1994.

74. *United States Security Strategy for the East Asia-Pacific Region* (Washington, DC: U.S. Department of Defense, Office of International Security, 1995), i. Planners' fierce response recalled by then Japan Desk senior director Commander Paul S. Giarra in an interview with the author on June 5, 2015. Giarra was a driving force for the initiative as Nye arrived at the Pentagon.

75. Joseph S. Nye, Jr., "East Asian Security: The Case for Deep Engagement," *Foreign Affairs* 74, no. 4 (July–August 1995): 90–102.

76. *United States Security Strategy for the East Asia-Pacific Region*, 10.

77. Barry Keehn and Chalmers Johnson, "The Pentagon's Ossified Strategy," *Foreign Affairs* 74, no. 4 (July–August 1995). The "dilettantes" line is in Chalmers Johnson, "The Okinawan Rape Incident and the End of the Cold War in East Asia," JPRI Working Paper 16, February 1996.

78. Interview by author with Joseph Nye, November 2, 2014, Hakone, Japan.

79. In interviews with Japanese newspapers in November 1995, Nye cited the North Korean threat as the context for his new initiative, and Perry cited North Korea and—for the first time—China's rise. See *Japan Digest*, November 28, 1995, cited in Johnson, "The Okinawan Rape Incident and the End of the Cold War in East Asia."

80. Tanaka, "The International Context of U.S.-Japan Relations in the 1990s," 276–279.

81. Interview by author with Sandy Berger, February 9, 2015.

82. Association for Diplomatic Studies and Training Foreign Affairs Oral History Project, Ambassador Winston Lord, interviewed by Charles Stuart Kennedy and Nancy Bernkopf Tucker, April 28, 1998, 607.

83. John Lewis Gaddis, *Surprise, Security, and the American Experience* (Cambridge, MA: Harvard University Press, 2004).

84. Joseph Wilson Preuher interview by Bruce A. Elleman, cited in "The Right Skill Sets," in *Nineteen Gun Salutes: Case Studies of Operational, Strategic and Diplomatic Naval Leadership During the 19th and Early 20th Centuries, Issue 62*, ed. Joseph Wilson Preuher, John B. Hattendorf, and Bruce A. Elleman (Newport, RI: Naval War College, 2010), 237.

85. Office of Naval Intelligence, *Chinese Exercise Strait 961: 8–25 March 1996*, n.d. [1996], obtained by National Security Archive.

86. "U.S. Navy Ships to Sail Near Taiwan," CNN, March 10, 1996, http://edition.cnn.com/US/9603/us_china/.

87. Interview by author with former senior director for Japan in the Office of the Secretary of Defense Robin "Sak" Sakoda, June 4, 2015. Sakoda and his immediate predecessor, Commander Paul Giarra (USN), muscled the entire Nye Initiative and Defense Guidelines through the Pentagon for Campbell and Nye.

88. Though Clinton skipped the trip, Ambassador Walter Mondale stepped in to announce a new Special Action Committee on Okinawa (SACO) for reducing bases and

returning the controversial U.S. Marine Corps Air Station Futenma, which went a significant way toward easing the base crisis sparked by the September rape incident.

89. "Japan-U.S. Joint Declaration on Security—Alliance for the Twenty First Century," April 17, 1996, http://www.mofa.go.jp/region/n-america/us/security/security.html.

90. Ministry of Foreign Affairs, "The Guidelines for Japan-U.S. Defense Cooperation," September 1997.

91. Evelyn Goh, *The Struggle for Order: Hegemony, Hierarchy, and Transition in Post-Cold War East Asia* (Oxford: Oxford University Press, 2013), 44–45.

92. Joseph Nye as quoted in James Mann, "U.S. Starting to View China as Potential Enemy," *Washington Post*, April 16, 1995.

93. "Japan-U.S. Joint Declaration on Security—Alliance for the Twenty First Century," April 17, 1996, http://www.mofa.go.jp/region/n-america/us/security/security.html.

94. Tucker, "The Clinton Years," 66–67; William J. Clinton, "The President's News Conference," May 26, 1994, reprinted in Kennedy, *China Cross Talk*, 143–145.

95. Michaela Eglin, "China's Entry into the WTO with a Little Help from the EU," *International Affairs* 73, no. 3, Globalization and International Relations (July 1997): 489–508.

96. Tucker, "The Clinton Years," 67–68.

97. Association for Diplomatic Studies and Training Foreign Affairs Oral History Project, Ambassador Winston Lord, interviewed by Charles Stuart Kennedy and Nancy Bernkopf Tucker, April 28, 1998, 611.

98. Association for Diplomatic Studies and Training Foreign Affairs Oral History Project, Ambassador Winston Lord, interviewed by Charles Stuart Kennedy and Nancy Bernkopf Tucker, April 28, 1998, 558.

99. This was evident to the author upon joining the NSC Asia office in the beginning of the George W. Bush administration. See also I. M. Destler and Ivo H. Destler, "A New NSC for a New Administration," Brookings Policy Brief Series 68, November 2000.

100. 1993 Leaders' Declaration, "Seattle Declaration—APEC Leaders Economic Vision Statement," Blake Island, Seattle, United States, November 20, 1993, http://www.apec.org/Meeting-Papers/Leaders-Declarations/1993/1993_aelm.aspx.

101. Report of the Eminent Persons Group to APEC Ministers, *A Vision for APEC: Towards an Asia Pacific Economic Community*, APEC Secretariat, October 1993.

102. "Aimless in Seattle," *The Economist*, November 13, 1993, 81.

103. 1994 Leaders' Declaration, "Bogor Declaration—APEC Economic Leaders' Declaration of Common Resolve," Bogor, Indonesia, November 15, 1994, http://www.apec.org/Meeting-Papers/Leaders-Declarations/1994/1994_aelm.aspx.

104. Goh, *The Struggle for Order*, 39–41.

105. For a summary of the conflicting American and Japanese views of the causes of the financial crisis, see Michael J. Green, *Japan's Reluctant Realism: Foreign Policy Challenges in an Era of Uncertain Power* (New York: Palgrave, 2001), 239–242; Morris Goldstein, "The Asian Financial Crisis," International Economics Policy Brief, Institute for International Economics, March 1998; Martin N. Baily, Diana Farrell, and Susan Lund, "The Color of Hot Money," *Foreign Affairs* 79, no. 2 (March–April 2000).

106. Goh, *The Struggle for Order*, 54–55. In fact, the Treasury Department's hands were tied partly because of congressional unhappiness with large U.S.-funded bailouts for Mexico five years earlier.

107. David Wessel and Bob Davis, "Limits of Power: Global Crisis Is a Match for Crack U.S. Economists," *Asian Wall Street Journal*, September 25, 1998.

108. Miller Center, "Interview with James Steinberg," University of Virginia, April 1, 2008, http://millercenter.org/president/clinton/oralhistory/james-steinberg.

109. Marc Castelano, "What Happened to APEC? A Decade of Taking Two Steps Forward, One Back," *JEI Report*, Japan Economic Institute, May 7, 1999; Green, *Japan's Reluctant Realism*, 211–215.

110. Eisuke Sakakibara, *Shihonshugi o Koeta Nippon* [*A Japanese Economy That Has Surpassed Capitalism*] (Tokyo: Toyo Keizai, 1990).

111. Eisuke Sakakibara, "Thai Crisis Played a Part in IMF Idea," special to *Yomiuri Shimbun*, November 29, 1999.

112. Anthony Rowley, "The Battle of Hong Kong: Tokyo's Proposal to Establish a Regional Emergency Fund Upsets the IMF, Western Governments," *Nikko Capital Trends* 2, no. 13 (November 1997); Sakakibara, "Thai Crisis Played a Part in IMF Idea"; Green, *Japan's Reluctant Realism*, 244–246.

113. Tanaka, "The International Context of U.S.-Japan Relations in the 1990s," 283–284.

114. Goh, *The Struggle for Order*, 54–57; Green, *Japan's Reluctant Realism*, chap. 8.

115. Harry Harding, "China," *Brookings Review* 15, no. 2 (Spring 1997): 14–15.

116. Nicholas Kristof, "Treaty Commitments; Would You Fight for These Islands?" *New York Times*, October 20, 1996. See also Larry A. Niksch, "Senkaku (Diaouyu) Island Dispute: The U.S. Legal Relationship and Obligations," PACNET, no. 45, Pacific Forum CSIS, November 8, 1996.

117. "Senkaku Shotou wa Anpo Jouyaku no Tekiyou Taishou, Yuuji ni wa Bouei Gimu, Bekokubou Jikanho Dair ga Kenkai" (U.S.-Japan Security Treaty Covers Senkaku Islands: U.S. Deputy Assistant Secretary of Defense Expresses His View), *Yomiuri Shimbun*, November 28, 1996. The State Department continued to refuse to clarify whether the Security Treaty applied. See, for example, Ambassador Foley's Remarks at the Japan Foreign Correspondents Club, April 8, 1998, http://japan2.usembassy.gov/e/p/tp-2647.html.

118. Tucker, "The Clinton Years," 59–60.

119. The President's News Conference with President Jiang Zemin of China in Beijing, June 27, 1998, posted online by Gerhard Peters and John T. Woolley, The American Presidency Project, http://www.presidency.ucsb.edu/ws/?pid=56229.

120. G. John Ikenberry, "Choosing Partners in Asia," *Australian Journal of International Affairs* 52, no. 3 (March 1998): 229–232; "U.S. Signals a Strategic Switch," *Canberra Times*, July 7, 1998, as reprinted in "Clinton to China: 'A Leap Over the Great Wall' in Sino-U.S. Ties," July 8, 1998, http://fas.org/news/china/1998/wwwh8708.html; Richard S. Dunham, "Time for Plain Talk: Is a China-U.S. Alliance at Hand?" *Business Week*, June 22, 1998; Julian Weiss, "A New Asian Agenda," *Washington Quarterly* 23, no. 1 (2000): 21–24. White House surprise given the Clinton attendance at Obuchi's funeral is from the author's interview with Sandy Berger, February 9, 2015.

121. Tanaka, "The International Context of U.S.-Japan Relations in the 1990s," 286. Prominent Blue Team members included William Kristol, Robert Kagan, Bill Gertz, Ross H. Munro, Mark Lagon, and Arthur Waldron, and in the Congress members included Christopher Cox.

122. "Dangerous Chinese Misperceptions: The Implications for DoD," Digital National Security Archive, Report, circa January 1998, China and the U.S., item number CH02046. Section 1226 of the National Defense Authorization Act for FY 1998 tasked the Department of Defense with the preparation of an annual report on Chinese military organizations and operational concepts, military-technological development, and overall security strategy. In October 2000, Congress created the U.S.-China Economic and Security Review Commission in order to monitor and report on the strategic implications of US trade with China. § 1238 of Title XII of H.R. 5408, the "Floyd D. Spence National Defense Authorization Act for Fiscal Year 2001," enacted by reference to Public Law 106-398, H.R. 4205, 114 Stat. 1654, enacted October 30, 2000, codified at 22 U.S.C. § 7002.

123. CRS Report RL30004, *North Korean Provocative Actions, 1950–2007*, updated April 20, 2007, by Hannah Fischer. See also Kevin Sullivan, "N. Korea Admits Selling Missiles," *Washington Post*, June 17, 1998; David E. Sanger, "North Korea Site an A-Bomb Plant, U.S. Agencies Say: Could Break '94 Accord," *New York Times*, August 17, 1998; Staffdel Kirk Final Report to Benjamin A. Gilman (R-NY), Chairman, International Relations Committee, U.S. House of Representatives: Mission to North Korea and China, August 11–23, 1998.

124. Office of the North Korea Policy Coordinator, United States Department of State, *Review of United States Policy Toward North Korea: Findings and Recommendations*, October 12, 1999.

125. Chronology of U.S.-North Korean Nuclear and Missile Diplomacy, Arms Control Association, updated February 2014, http://www.armscontrol.org/factsheets /dprkchron#1998.

126. "Envoy to North Korea Delivers Clinton Letter," *New York Times*, May 27, 1999.

127. U.S.-D.P.R.K. Joint Communiqué, Released by the Office of the Spokesman, U.S. Department of State, October 12, 2000, http://www.state.gov/1997-2001-NOPDFS/regions /eap/001012_usdprk_jointcom.html; CRS IB98054, *Korea: U.S.-South Korean Relations— Issues for Congress*, updated June 19, 2002, by Larry A. Niksch.

128. Interview: Madeleine Albright, PBS *Frontline*, http://www.pbs.org/wgbh/pages /frontline/shows/kim/interviews/albright.html.

129. "Albright Greeted with a Fanfare by North Korea," *New York Times*, October 24, 2000.

130. National Intelligence Estimate, "Foreign Missile Developments and the Ballistic Missile Threat to the United States through 2015," September 9, 1999, http://www.dni.gov /files/documents/Foreign%20Missile%20Developments_1999.pdf.

131. "Clinton Scraps North Korea Trip, Saying Time's Short for Deal," *New York Times*, December 29, 2000; on Clinton's temptation to go to Pyongyang, see Madeleine Albright, *Madam Secretary: A Memoir* (New York: HarperCollins, 2003), 508.

132. Alka Acharya, "The 'New Deal': China on the Threshold of WTO," *Economic and Political Weekly* 34, no. 51 (December 18–24, 1999): 2565–2568; Kennedy, *China Cross Talk*, 171.

133. Stephen M. Walt, "Two Cheers for Clinton's Foreign Policy," *Foreign Affairs* 9, no. 2 (March–April 2000): 63–79.

134. Richard N. Haas, "The Squandered Presidency: Demanding More from the Commander-in-Chief," *Foreign Affairs* 79, no. 3 (May–June 2000): 136–140.

14. Strategic Surprise and the Asia Policy of George W. Bush

1. James T. Shaplen and James Laney, "Washington's Eastern Sunset: The Decline of U.S. Power in Northeast Asia," *Foreign Affairs* 86, no. 6 (November–December 2007): 82–97; Gerald L. Curtis, "East Asia, Regionalism, and U.S. National Interests," Columbia Business School, APEC Study Center, Discussion Paper Series, Discussion Paper 24, May 2004; Ralph A. Cossa, "East Asia Community-Building: Time for the United States to Get on Board," policy analysis brief, The Stanley Foundation, September 2007.

2. Jeffrey E. Garten, "A Foreign Policy Harmful to Business," *Business Week*, October 13, 2002; Clyde Prestowitz, *Rogue Nation: American Unilateralism and the Failure of Good Intentions* (New York: Basic Books, 2003), 1–17; Richard Higgott, "US Foreign Policy and the 'Securitization' of Economic Globalization," *International Politics* 41 (May 2004): 147–175.

3. T. J. Pempel, "How Bush Bungled Asia: Militarism, Economic Indifference and Unilateralism Have Weakened the United States Across Asia," *Pacific Review* 21, no. 5 (December 2008): 547–581.

4. Barack Obama, Address in Berlin, reprinted in the *Washington Post*, July 24, 2008.

5. Christopher B. Whitney and David Shambaugh, *Soft Power in Asia: Results of a 2008 Multinational Survey of Public Opinion* (Chicago: The Chicago Council on Global Affairs, News Results and Analysis, 2009), 7–11.

6. As director for Asian affairs responsible first for Japan and then Korea, Australia, New Zealand, and the Pacific from April 2001 to December 2003, and then as special assistant to the president and senior director for Asian affairs with responsibility for East Asia and South Asia (excluding Afghanistan).

7. David Rothkopf, *Running the World: The Inside Story of the National Security Council and the Architects of American Power* (New York: PublicAffairs, 2004), 398–401; Ivo H. Daalder and James M. Lindsay, "Bush's Foreign Policy Revolution," in *The George W. Bush Presidency: An Early Assessment*, ed. Fred I. Greenstein (Baltimore: Johns Hopkins University Press, 2003), 102.

8. Jacob Heilbrunn, "Condoleezza Rice: George W.'s Realist," *World Policy Journal* 16, no. 4 (Winter 1999–2000): 49–54; James Mann, *Rise of the Vulcans: The History of Bush's War Cabinet* (New York: Viking, 2004), 249–252; Condoleezza Rice, *No Higher Honor: A Memoir of My Years in Washington* (New York: Crown, 2011), 1–8.

9. Fred I. Greenstein, "The Leadership Style of George W. Bush," in *The George W. Bush Presidency*, 7–9; interview by author with Richard Armitage, December 2, 2014; Eric Schmitt, "A Cadre of Familiar Foreign Policy Experts Is Putting Its Imprint on Bush," *New York Times*, December 23, 1999.

10. Interview by author with Steve Hadley, February 25, 2015.

11. As quoted in Mann, *Rise of the Vulcans*, 256–257; George W. Bush, "A Period of Consequences," The Citadel, September 23, 1999, http://fas.org/spp/starwars/program/news99/92399_defense.htm.

12. Governor George W. Bush, "A Distinctly American Internationalism," Ronald Reagan Presidential Library, Simi Valley, California, November 19, 1999, https://www.mtholyoke.edu/acad/intrel/bush/wspeech.htm.

13. Richard L. Armitage et al., "The United States and Japan: Advancing Toward a Mature Partnership," INSS Special Report, October 11, 2000.

14. Bush, "A Distinctly American Internationalism."

15. Robert Kagan and William Kristol, "Clinton's Sorry Excuse for a China Policy," *The Weekly Standard*, March 22, 1999. See also "Statement of Principles," Project for the New American Century, June 3, 1997; William Kristol and Robert Kagan, "Reject the Global Buddy System," *New York Times*, October 25, 1999. The two expressed similar sentiments in William Kristol and Robert Kagan, "Toward a Neo-Reaganite Foreign Policy," *Foreign Affairs* (July–August 1996): 18–32.

16. Rice quoted in Heilbrunn, "Condoleezza Rice," 49–54.

17. For more discussion on this declaratory policy line, see Evan Medeiros, *China's International Behavior: Activism, Opportunism and Diversification* (Santa Monica, CA: RAND, 2014), 97.

18. Condoleezza Rice, "Promoting the National Interest," *Foreign Affairs* 7, no. 1 (January–February 2000): 56.

19. UN Security Council Resolution 1172.

20. C. Raja Mohan, *Impossible Allies: Nuclear India, United States, and the Global Order* (New Delhi: India Research Press, 2006), 16–17. See also Strobe Talbott, *Engaging India: Diplomacy, Democracy, and the Bomb*, rev. ed. (Washington, DC: Brookings Institution Press, 2006), 1–3, 52–63.

21. Robert D. Blackwill, "The India Imperative: A Conversation with Robert D. Blackwill," *The National Interest*, no. 80 (Summer 2005): 9–17.

22. As Steve Hadley recalls, the president was broadly focused on India, whereas many of the Vulcans approached India in the context of China. The policy prescriptions were the same. Interview by author with Steve Hadley, February 25, 2015.

23. The White House, *The National Security Strategy of the United States of America*, September 2002; Condoleezza Rice, "A Balance of Power That Favors Freedom," The Manhattan Institute's Wriston Lecture, October 1, 2002, http://www.manhattan-institute.org /html/wl2002.htm.

24. A fourth would soon join them—vice chairman and then chairman of the Joint Chiefs, General Peter Pace had served as the deputy commander of U.S. Forces Japan in the 1990s.

25. The White House, National Security Directive-1, Organization of the National Security Council System, February 12, 2001.

26. Remarks of Secretary of Defense Donald Rumsfeld, Town Hall Meeting in Kuwait, December 8, 2004, www.defense.gov/ . . . /transcript.aspx.

27. Terry McCarthy and Jeannie McCabe, "Bitter Passage," *Time*, April 15, 2001; Christopher Marquis, "9 Are Missing Off Pearl Harbor After U.S. Submarine Collides with Japanese Vessel," *New York Times*, February 10, 2001.

28. "Bush Envoy Arrives in Japan with Apology," abcnews.com, February 27, 2001, http://abcnews.go.com/US/story?id=93984; "Japan Adrift," *The Economist*, March 20, 2001.

29. I led the discussion, which included a number of former Mansfield Fellows, Monbusho English Fellows, and other veterans of bilateral programs in the 1980s and 1990s designed to send young American students and officials to Japan at the height of bilateral trade friction.

30. "Partnership for Security and Prosperity," June 30, 2001, http://www.mofa.go.jp /mofaj/area/usa/keizai/eco_tusho/anzen_partner_e.html.

31. Paul D. Wolfowitz, "Clinton's First Year," *Foreign Affairs* 73, no. 1 (January–February 1994): 28–43; Richard Armitage, "A Comprehensive Approach to North Korea," Institute for National Security Strategies, National Defense University, March 1999; "Confirmation Hearing by Secretary-Designate Colin Powell," Washington, DC, January 17, 2001, http://2001-2009.state.gov/secretary/former/powell/remarks/2001/443.htm. For Vulcan views on North Korea, see also Richard Armitage, "A Comprehensive Approach to North Korea," Institute for National Security Strategies, National Defense University, March 1999.

32. Steven Mufson, "Bush to Pick Up Clinton Talks on N. Korean Missiles," *Washington Post*, March 7, 2001; Yōichi Funabashi, *The Peninsula Question: A Chronicle of the Second Korean Nuclear Crisis* (Washington, DC: Brookings Institution Press, 2008), 109.

33. George W. Bush, *Decision Points* (New York: Crown, 2010), 423.

34. The White House, "Remarks by President Bush and President Kim Dae-jung of South Korea," March 7, 2001; George W. Bush, "Statement on Completion of the North Korea Policy Review," June 6, 2001.

35. "High Noon in Hainan," *The Economist*, April 14, 2001; White House, "Statement by the President on American Plane and Crew in China," April 2, 2001; Rice, *No Higher Honor*, 45.

36. Rice, *No Higher Honor*, 48.

37. Interview by author with Richard Armitage, December 2, 2014.

38. Bush, *Decision Points*, 426–427; interview by author with Steve Hadley, February 25, 2015.

39. White House, press briefing, April 24, 2001; interview by author with Richard Armitage, December 2, 2014.

40. David E. Sanger, "U.S. Would Defend Taiwan, Bush Says," *New York Times*, April 26, 2001.

41. Interview by author with Steve Hadley, February 25, 2015.

42. As quoted in Blackwill, "The India Imperative," 9–17.

43. Stephen P. Burgess, "India's Emerging Security Strategy, Missile Defense and Arms Control," U.S. Air Force Institute of National Security Studies Occasional Paper 54, June 2004, 28; Rice, *No Higher Honor*, 129, 168, 696–697.

44. Hendrik Hertzberg, "Manifesto," *The New Yorker*, October 14, 2002. *The Economist* led its weekly roundup of world politics with a direct quotation from the 2002 NSS on the policy of preemption. The blurb read: "The Bush administration published a new National Security Strategy, pledging to work with allies but also emphasising that 'to forestall or prevent . . . hostile acts . . . the United States will, if necessary, act preemptively.'" See *The Economist*, September 28, 2002; Robert Jervis, "Understanding the Bush Doctrine," *Political Science Quarterly* 118, no. 3 (Fall 2003): 365–388. Gaddis argued that the response was steeped in previous American strategies to expand boundaries of defense when attacked, going back to John Quincy Adams and Andrew Jackson. See John Lewis Gaddis, *Surprise, Security, and the American Experience* (Cambridge, MA: Harvard University Press, 2004), 59. On the other hand, Peter Feaver discounts entirely the idea that the administration's preemption statement was either new or a "Bush Doctrine." See Michael Abramowitz, "Many Versions of 'Bush Doctrine,'" *Washington Post*, September 13, 2008.

45. Brad Roberts, "American Primacy and Major Power Concert: A Critique of the 2002 National Security Strategy," Institute for Defense Analyses, IDA Paper P-3751, December 2002.

46. The White House, *The National Security Strategy of the United States of America*, September 17, 2002, 26.

47. The White House, *The National Security Strategy of the United States of America*, September 17, 2002, president's introduction and 29.

48. John Howard, "United States of America: Terrorist Attacks," September 17, 2001.

49. Department of Defense, Office of Public Affairs, "International Contributions to the War Against Terrorism," Fact Sheet, May 22, 2002.

50. The White House, *The National Security Strategy of the United States of America*, September 17, 2002, 26.

51. "Opening Statement by Prime Minister Junichiro Koizumi at the Press Conference," September 19, 2001, http://japan.kantei.go.jp/koizumispeech/2001/0919sourikaiken _e.html.

52. David J. Gerleman and Jennifer E. Stevens, *Operation Enduring Freedom: Foreign Pledges of Military & Intelligence Support*, CRS Report for Congress RL31152, updated October 17, 2001; Stephen A. Carney, *Allied Participation in Operation Iraqi Freedom* (Washington, DC: Government Printing Office, 2012), 71–73.

53. George Bush, "Unity Between the U.S. and Japan," The Diet, Tokyo, Japan, February 18, 2002, as reprinted in *The George W. Bush Foreign Policy Reader*, ed. John W. Dietrich (New York: M. E. Sharpe, 2005), 231–233. See also Kerry Dumbaugh, *President Bush's 2002 State Visits in Asia: Implications*, CRS Report RL31328, March 11, 2002.

54. The author, for example, was in constant real-time coordination with the Prime Minister's Office as the bills were being deliberated, as were Armitage, Wolfowitz, Libby, Kelly, and the remarkably effective U.S. ambassador in Japan, Howard Baker.

55. The Pentagon would not clear a full apology, but Hubbard rightly portrayed it as one. See Don Kirk, "Bush Apologizes to Koreans for Army's Killing of 2 Girls," *New York Times*, November 28, 2002; Koji Murata, "U.S. Military Strategy and East Asia," *Asia-Pacific Review* 10, no. 2 (2003): 52–59.

56. "The First Edition of the National Awareness Poll," *Joong Ang Ilbo*, September 22, 2007, http://article.joins.com/article/article.asp?Total_ID=2892729. (In Korean.)

57. The White House, *The National Security Strategy of the United States of America*, September 17, 2002, 26.

58. Statement on Counter-Terrorism, APEC Leaders' Declarations, October 21, 2001, http://www.apec.org/Meeting-Papers/Leaders-Declarations/2001/2001_aelm/statement _on_counter-terrorism.aspx.

59. Elizabeth Becker, "Bush Rejects Labor's Call to Punish China," *New York Times*, April 29, 2004.

60. Sheryl Gay Stolberg, "Bush to Attend Opening Ceremonies of the Beijing Olympics," *New York Times*, July 4, 2008.

61. The White House, Office of the Press Secretary, President Bush, "President Discusses Unity Between the U.S. and Japan," February 18, 2002.

62. The White House, Office of the Press Secretary, "President Discusses Freedom and Democracy in Kyoto, Japan," November 16, 2005.

63. Embassy of the People's Republic of China in the United States, "Hu, Bush Pledge Developing Constructive Ties," November 21, 2005.

64. See, for instance, The White House, Office of the Press Secretary, "President's Remarks to the Travel Pool in China," November 20, 2005.

65. James Gerstenzang, "Bush Stresses Human Rights in U.N. Talk," *Baltimore Sun*, September 26, 2007; "Bush Rebukes China on Rights," Aljazeera.com, August 8, 2008; Andrew Jacobs, "China Angered by U.S. Lobbying on Rights," *New York Times*, August 1, 2008; "Rebiya Kadeer Meets with President Bush at the White House," The Uyghur American Association, June 30, 2008, uyghuramerican.org; The White House, Office of the Press Secretary, "President Bush Addresses the United Nations General Assembly," September 25, 2007.

66. Bill Gertz, "Guns and Butter," *Washington Times*, December 6, 2002; David Brown, "Strains over Cross-Strait Relations," *Comparative Connections* 5, no. 4 (January 2004).

67. Brown, "Strains over Cross-Strait Relations."

68. Emerson Niou, "The China Factor in Taiwan's Domestic Politics," in *Democratization in Taiwan: Challenges in Transformation*, ed. Philip Paolino and James David Meernik (London: Ashgate, 2008), 173; The PRC's Taiwan Affairs Office and Information Office of the State Council, "The One China Principle and the Taiwan Issue," February 21, 2000, the English version as published by Xinhua [New China News Agency] and translated in FBIS, and the Chinese version as published by *People's Daily Online*.

69. The White House, Office of the Press Secretary, "President Discusses Freedom and Democracy in Kyoto, Japan," November 16, 2005.

70. See also David E. Sanger and William J. Broad, "U.S. Asking China to Increase Pressure on North Korea to End Its Nuclear Program," *New York Times*, February 9, 2005.

71. Robert B. Zoellick, "Whither China: From Membership to Responsibility?" Remarks to National Committee on U.S.-China Relations, New York City, September 21, 2005.

72. Zoellick, "Whither China?"

73. U.S. Department of the Treasury, "Fact Sheet: Creation of the U.S.-China Strategic Economic Dialogue," September 20, 2006, http://www.treasury.gov/press-center/press -releases/pages/hp107.aspx; Henry M. Paulson, Jr., "A Strategic Economic Engagement: Strengthening U.S.-China Ties," *Foreign Affairs* 87, no. 5 (September–October 2008): 59–77; author's interview with former Treasury Department official and senior advisor on China Deborah Lehrer, January 7, 2015. Henry Paulson, who developed many of the key ideas behind the SED, recalls that in July 2006, when he became treasury secretary, "Our dealings with China had become mired in perhaps a hundred diffuse low-level exchanges and needed to be coordinated and prioritized better." See Henry M. Paulson, Jr., *Dealing with China: An Insider Unmasks the New Economic Superpower* (New York: Twelve, 2015), 175; Randall G. Schriver, "Reflections on the Senior Dialogue," Freeman Report, Center for Strategic and International Studies, June 2007; Charles W. Freeman III and Matthew Goodman, "Crafting U.S. Economic Strategy Toward Asia: Lessons Learned from 30 Years of Experience," Freeman Report, Center for Strategic and International Studies, October 2008.

74. James J. Przystup and Phillip C. Saunders, "Visions of Order: Japan and China in U.S. Strategy," *Strategic Forum*, Institute for National Strategic Studies, National Defense University, no. 220 (June 2006), http://www.dtic.mil/cgi-bin/GetTRDoc?AD =ADA450122&Location=U2&doc=GetTRDoc.pdf.

75. Mohan, *Impossible Allies*, 27–28, 34–35.

76. See, for instance, The White House, "Fact Sheet: Promoting Energy Independence and Security," Washington, DC, April 27, 2005, http://georgewbush-whitehouse.archives .gov/news/releases/2005/04/20050427-9.html.

77. Dinshaw Mistry, "Diplomacy, Domestic Politics, and the U.S.-India Nuclear Agreement," *Asian Survey* 46, no. 5 (September–October 2006): 675–698.

78. Rice, *No Higher Honor*, 436–441.

79. Sanjay Baru, *The Accidental Prime Minister: The Making and Unmaking of Manmohan Singh* (New Delhi: Penguin Books India, 2014), 207–209.

80. "India-U.S. Joint Statement," White House, Washington, DC, July 18, 2005, https:// www.indianembassy.org/archives_details.php?nid=568; Ashley J. Tellis, *India as a New Global Power: An Action Agenda for the United States* (Washington, DC: Carnegie Endowment for International Peace, July 2005), 7.

81. U.S. Department of State, Office of the Press Secretary, "Background Briefing by Administration Officials on U.S.-South Asia Relations," March 25, 2005.

82. Interview by author with Richard Armitage, December 2, 2014; "66% Believe That the U.S.-Japanese Alliance Is Effective," *Yomiuri Shimbun*, December 15, 2005, 2 (in Japanese); Horizon Research Consultancy Group, "Horizon Chinese Opinion Poll: Eyes on the World, Future in Hand (P06-19)," December 4, 2006, http://www.mansfieldfdn.org /polls/poll-06-19.htm.

83. Bruce Vaughn et al., *Terrorism in Southeast Asia*, CRS Report RL34194, October 16, 2009, https://www.fas.org/sgp/crs/terror/RL34194.pdf; Sidney Jones, "Indonesia Backgrounder: Jihad in Central Sulawesi," International Crisis Group Report 74, February 3, 2004; Sidney Jones, "Jemaah Islamiyah in South East Asia: Damaged but Still Dangerous," International Crisis Group Report 63, August 26, 2003, 1.

84. Seth Mydans, "Singapore Details Terrorist Plot to Bomb U.S. Ships and Soldiers," *New York Times*, January 11, 2002.

85. Larry Niksch, *Abu Sayyaf: Target of Philippine-U.S. Anti-Terrorism Cooperation*, CRS Report RL31265, updated January 24, 2007.

86. John Gershman, "Is Southeast Asia the Second Front?" *Foreign Affairs*, 81, no. 4 (July–August 2002): 60–74. The administration assessment is from author's interview with Steve Hadley, February 25, 2015.

87. The White House, "Enterprise for ASEAN Initiative," October 26, 2002; Satu P. Limaye, "United States-ASEAN Relations on ASEAN's Fortieth Anniversary: A Glass Half Full," *Contemporary Southeast Asia* 29, no. 3 (December 2007): 447–464; Michael Richardson, "Wave of Trade Deals Seen Bonding U.S. with Asia," *New York Times*, November 4, 2002; Tiziana Bonapace, "Regional Trade and Investment Architecture in Asia-Pacific: Emerging Trends and Imperatives," *Economic and Political Weekly* 40, no. 36 (September 3–9, 2005): 3941–3947.

88. The White House, Joint Vision Statement on the ASEAN-US Enhanced Partnership, November 17, 2005.

89. David E. Sanger, "Aid Summit Talks in Jakarta: U.S. Is Facing a Choice and an Opportunity," *New York Times*, January 2, 2005.

90. Lee Kuan Yew, "Competition in Compassion," *Forbes*, April 18, 2005.

91. Richard Wike, "Does Humanitarian Aid Improve America's Image," Pew Research, Global Attitudes Project, March 6, 2012, http://www.pewglobal.org/2012/03/06/does -humanitarian-aid-improve-americas-image/.

92. Nicholas D. Kristoff, "Hold Your Nose and Negotiate," *New York Times*, December 20, 2002.

93. Some academic and journalistic accounts of the encounter claim Kang left ambiguity about whether there was a program or whether his statement was merely a ploy for negotiations. See, for example, Mike Chinoy, *Meltdown: The Inside Story of the North Korean Nuclear Crisis* (New York: St. Martin's, 2008), 121–123; Leon V. Sigal, "North Korea Is No Iraq: Pyongyang's Negotiating Strategy," *Arms Control Today* 32, no. 10 (December 2002): 8–12. That was not the conclusion of those of us in the room with him. Kang was coy only because we had not said exactly what we know about the HEU program. Moreover, the North Koreans later showed elements of their program to nuclear expert Sig Heckler in November 2010, erasing any doubt. See Siegfried Heckler, "What I Found in North Korea: Plutonium Is No Longer the Only Problem," *Foreign Affairs* (December 9, 2010), http:// www.foreignaffairs.com/articles/67023/siegfried-s-hecker/what-i-found-in-north-korea.

94. Rice, *No Higher Honor*, 162–163.

95. The author was also present. For details, see Larry A. Niksch, *North Korea's Nuclear Weapons Program*, CRS Report IB91141, May 1, 2003.

96. EAP's David Asher pulled together the initiative for State and then an NSC coordination group oversaw implementation, but Treasury's Juan Zarate and Stuart Levy were the real experts at following the North Korean money.

97. Sheena Chestnut, "Illicit Activity and Proliferation: North Korean Smuggling Networks," *International Security* 32, no. 1 (Summer 2007): 80–111.

98. The White House, Executive Order 13382, June 29, 2005.

99. Juan C. Zarate, *Treasury's War: The Unleashing of a New Era of Financial Warfare* (New York: PublicAffairs, 2013), 219–232, 239–242; Joel Brinkley, "U.S. Squeezes North Korea's Money Flow," *New York Times*, March 10, 2006; Chestnut, "Illicit Activity and Proliferation," 80–111. The author cochaired an interagency cell in the NSC that was established to ensure all diplomacy, law enforcement, and counterproliferation efforts toward North Korea were carefully coordinated. Despite the claims of some participants that they opposed the imposition of Banco Delta Asia sanctions, the group in fact agreed unanimously that the sanctions should be imposed consistent with the president's view that legitimate defense and law enforcement issues should not be curtailed in order to ease Pyongyang toward negotiations.

100. *Victor Cha, Impossible State: North Korea, Past and Future* (New York: Harper-Collins, 2012), 266.

101. Joint Statement of the Fourth Round of Six-Party Talks, Beijing, September 19, 2005, http://www.state.gov/p/eap/regional/c15455.htm.

102. Brinkley, "U.S. Squeezes North Korea's Money Flow."

103. Mark Mazzetti, "Preliminary Samples Hint at North Korean Nuclear Test," *New York Times*, October 14, 2006; Cha, *The Impossible State*, 267.

104. "Security Council Condemns Nuclear Test by Democratic People's Republic of Korea," United Nations, October 14, 2006, http://www.un.org/News/Press/docs/2006 /sc8853.doc.htm; Howard Cincotta, "United States Conducting Strategic Consultations in

Asia," IIP Digital, November 4, 2006, http://iipdigital.usembassy.gov/st/english/article /2006/11/20061104123306attocnicho.215069.html#axzz3PfwjeQmq.

105. Christopher R. Hill, Assistant Secretary for East Asian and Pacific Affairs, Briefing in Berlin, Germany, January 17, 2007. See also Christopher R. Hill, *Outpost: A Diplomat at Work* (Simon & Schuster, 2014), 252–254; 256–257; James Yardley, "Private Talks Held in Berlin Spurred Sides to Reach Deal," *New York Times*, February 14, 2007. Holbrooke almost certainly brokered the meeting with the North Koreans.

106. U.S. Department of State, Secretary Condoleezza Rice, "Briefing on the Agreement Reached at the Six-Party Talks in Beijing," February 13, 2007; Glenn Kessler and Edward Cody, "U.S. Flexibility Credited in Nuclear Deal with North Korea," *Washington Post*, February 14, 2007.

107. Rice, *No Higher Honor*, 570–572.

108. Cha, *The Impossible State*, 268.

109. Neil King Jr. and Jay Solomon, "U.S. to Cut Off Macau Bank; Move Follows Probe of North Korean Ties, Could Hinder Nuclear Talks," *Wall Street Journal, Eastern Edition*, March 13, 2007.

110. David Lague, "Korea Talks Break Off over Funds in Macao," *New York Times*, March 22, 2007.

111. Zarate, *Treasury's War*, 255–256.

112. For two views of the significance of al-Kibar, see Hill, *Outpost*, 287; David Sanger, *The Inheritance: The World Obama Confronts and the Challenges to American Power* (New York: Random House, 2009), 269–279.

113. U.S. Department of State, *Patterns of Global Terrorism 2003*, 92; National Association for the Rescue of Japanese Kidnaped by North Korea, Report of Mission to the U.S. from February 25 to March 3, 2001, http://www.state.gov/documents/organization/31912 .pdf.

114. Interview by author with Steve Hadley, February 25, 2015.

115. Special briefing by State Department spokesman Sean McCormack, M2 Presswire, October 11, 2008.

116. In polls in Japan, 80 percent of respondents said the United States and Japan were not on the same page on North Korea, and positive views of the United States dropped to 34 percent—the lowest number since 2000 and a sudden collapse from the strong polling on the alliance only a year before. See Michael Green and Nicholas Szenchenyi, "Traversing a Rough Patch," *Comparative Connections* 10, no. 4 (January 2009). For the decision by the White House to remove North Korea from the list of terrorist countries, see Helene Cooper, "U.S. Declares North Korea Off Terror List," *New York Times*, October 18, 2008.

117. Statement of the Honorable Donald H. Rumsfeld, Prepared for the Confirmation Hearing Before the U.S. Senate Committee on Armed Services, January 11, 2001, http:// www.globalsecurity.org/military/library/congress/2001_hr/010111dr.pdf; Robert D. Kaplan, "What Rumsfeld Got Right," *The Atlantic*, July 1, 2008, http://www.theatlantic.com /magazine/archive/2008/07/what-rumsfeld-got-right/306870/; Paul C. Light, "Rumsfeld's Revolution at Defense," Brookings Policy Brief Series #142, July 2005; U.S. Department of Defense, Donald Rumsfeld, "Positioning America's Forces for the 21st Century," December 1, 2005, http://www.defense.gov/home/articles/2004-09/a092304b.html; U.S. Department

of Defense, *Strengthening U.S. Global Defense Posture*, Report to Congress, September 17, 2004.

118. Kaplan, "What Rumsfeld Got Right."

119. Donald Rumsfeld, Department of Defense News Briefing, interview with *Yonhap News*, November 19, 2003, http://iipdigital.usembassy.gov/st/english/texttrans /2003/11/20031120133612esrom1.665896e-02.html#axzz3NyLLzWyC; Walter T. Ham IV, "Veterans Remember Historic 'Strike Brigade' Deployment," States News Service, May 19, 2014.

120. Chang-hee Nam, "Relocating the U.S. Forces in South Korea: Strained Alliance, Emerging Partnership in the Changing Defense Posture," *Asian Survey* 46, no. 4 (July–August 2006): 615–631.

121. Sunkoon Oh, *The U.S. Strategic Flexibility Policy: Prospects for the U.S.-ROK Alliance*, Naval Postgraduate School, 2006.

122. Nina Silove, "The Pivot before the Pivot: U.S. Strategy to Preserve the Balance of Power in Asia," *International Security* 40, no. 4 (Spring 2016): 45–88.

123. C. Fred Bergsten, "A Competitive Approach to Free Trade," *Financial Times* (London), December 4, 2002.

124. RCEP would include the ten ASEAN states plus Japan, China, Korea, Australia, New Zealand, and India. The East Asian Summit began with the same membership in 2005. For details, see Lowell Dittmer, "Asia in 2006," *Asian Survey* 47, no. 1 (January–February 2007): 1–9.

125. See, for example, Victor D. Cha, "The New Geometry of Asian Architecture: What Works and What Does Not," CSIS, January 2010; interview by author with Steve Hadley, February 25, 2015.

126. Rice, *No Higher Honor*, 486.

127. President George W. Bush, inaugural address, January 20, 2005.

128. Fred Barnes, "Bush's Breakthrough," *The Weekly Standard*, January 20, 2005; Eric Foner, "'Freedom' Belongs to All," *The Nation*, February 14, 2005.

129. The White House, "Accomplishments at the G8 Summit," July 8, 2005.

130. Koizumi's January 2002 proposal for an "Initiative for Development of the Economies of Asia" (IDEA), which highlighted the themes of good governance, rule of law, and economic transparency as new lessons Japan could bring to Southeast Asia's search for sustainable development. See Cabinet Office of the Prime Minister of Japan, "Speech by Prime Minister of Japan Junichiro Koizumi: Japan and ASEAN in East Asia—A Sincere and Open Partnership," Singapore, January 14, 2002, http://www.kantei.go.jp/foreign /koizumispeech/2002/01/14speech_e.html; "The Joint Ministerial Statement of the Initiative for Development of East Asia," Foreign Ministry of Japan, Tokyo, August 12, 2002. India's emerging views were captured by Foreign Secretary Shyam Saran, who said in 2005: "We believe that democracy would provide a more enduring and broad-based foundation for an edifice of peace and cooperation in our subcontinent. [W]hile expediency [by engaging authoritarian regimes] may yield short-term advantage, it also leads to a harmful corrosion of our core values of respect for pluralism and human rights." See Shyam Saran, "India and Its Neighbors," Speech, February 14, 2005, New Delhi, http:// meaindia.nic.in/. India also pledged $10 million to the UN Democracy Fund announced by President Bush in September 2005, and through the Colombo Plan, New Delhi has

budgeted to invite neighbors to send senior officials to study India's own experiences in democracy and good governance.

131. Report of the Eminent Persons Group on the ASEAN Charter, December 2006. See also Michael J. Green, "America's Quiet Victories in Asia," *Washington Post*, February 13, 2007.

132. Wayne Arnold, "Historic ASEAN Charter Reveals Divisions," *New York Times*, November 20, 2007.

133. Bruce Vaughn, *Nepal: Background and U.S. Relations*, CRS Report Order Code RL31599, updated February 2, 2006.

134. "Nepal Government Procuring Military Articles from China, Pakistan," Press Trust of India, January 22, 2006; "A Dangerous Game," *Wall Street Journal*, January 24, 2006.

135. The plan was developed in close coordination with Ambassador for Religious Freedom John Hanford, who understood that progress and momentum were key. Often rebuffed by career diplomats as a zealot, Hanford was in fact a pragmatic and effective diplomat himself. Two successive ambassadors to Hanoi, Ray Burghardt and Mike Meserve, also saw the long game in strategic relations with Hanoi and set the stage with great skill.

136. The JADE Act also called for appointment of a special envoy for Burma. I was eventually nominated for the position, but it was not acted on by Congress after the 2008 election, by which time my strongest supporter (Laura Bush) was gone and the incoming Obama administration was hesitant to use chits with Democratic allies in Congress for a former Bush official, though John Podesta and the Obama transition team could not have been more supportive and collegial. Tom Lantos Block Burmese JADE (Junta's Anti-Democratic Efforts) Act of 2008, Public Law 110-286, July 26, 2008.

137. Walter Russell Mead, interview with Bernard Gwertzman, "Bush's Foreign Policy Record Around the World," Council on Foreign Relations, http://www.cfr.org/world/mead -bushs-foreign-policy-record-around-world/p15080.

138. Bates Gill, Michael Green, Kyoto Tsui, William Watts, *Strategic Views on Asian Regionalism*, CSIS, February 2009.

139. "66% Believe That the U.S.-Japanese Alliance Is Effective"; Horizon Research Consultancy Group, "Horizon Chinese Opinion Poll"; Whitney et al., *Soft Power in Asia*, 7–11.

15. Barack Obama and the Struggle to Rebalance to Asia

1. Interview by author with Jeffrey Bader, June 11, 2015. See also Jeffrey Bader, *Obama and China's Rise: An Insider's Account of America's Asia Strategy* (Washington, DC: Brookings Institution Press, 2012), 1.

2. Barack Obama, Foreign Policy Speech, October 2, 2007, http://www.cfr.org/elections /barack-obamas-foreign-policy-speech/p14356.

3. James Mann, "How Obama's Foreign Policy Relates to Vietnam—or Doesn't," *Washington Post*, June 22, 2012.

4. Barack Obama, Foreign Policy Speech, October 2, 2007, http://www.cfr.org/elections /barack-obamas-foreign-policy-speech/p14356.

5. The White House, *National Security Strategy*, February 2015.

6. Nicholas Lemann, "Worlds Apart," *The New Yorker*, October 13, 2008. See also Anne-Marie Slaughter et al., *Strategic Leadership: Framework for a 21st Century National Security Strategy* (Washington, DC: Center for a New American Security, July 2008).

7. Lemann, "Worlds Apart."

8. See, for example, Richard Danzig, Panel for the Center for Global Engagement, August 28, 2008, http://www.usglc.org/international-affairs-budget-resources/people-to -watch-obamas-top-foreign-policy-advisers/.

9. In *The Audacity of Hope*, Obama offers policy prescriptions for the Middle East and broad platitudes about the need to avoid unilateralism in foreign policy, but Asia is largely conveyed through his experiences with globalization and development in Indonesia. See Barack Obama, *The Audacity of Hope: Thoughts on Reclaiming the American Dream* (New York: Three Rivers, 2006), 271–324.

10. Slaughter et al., *Strategic Leadership*, 31; Bader to the NSC, Steinberg as deputy secretary of state, and Campbell as assistant secretary for East Asia and the Pacific.

11. Slaughter et al., *Strategic Leadership*.

12. Roger Cohen, "Asia's Republican Leanings," *New York Times*, April 10, 2008; Yōichi Funabashi, "Keeping Up with Asia: America and the New Balance of Power," *Foreign Affairs* 87, no. 5 (September–October 2008): 110–125.

13. Henry A. Kissinger, "The Three Revolutions," *Washington Post*, April 7, 2008.

14. Christi Parsons, Kathleen Hennessey, and Paul Richter, "Obama Argues Against Use of Force to Solve Global Conflicts," *Los Angeles Times*, April 28, 2014.

15. The Chicago Council on Global Affairs, Chicago Council Survey, "Americans Shifting Focus to Asia," September 10, 2015, http://www.thechicagocouncil.org/sites /default/files/2012_CCS_AsiaBrief.pdf; German Marshall Fund of the United States, Transatlantic Trends 2011, "Survey: Americans Say Asia More Important than Europe," September 14, 2011, http://trends.gmfus.org/survey-americans-say-asia-more-important -than-europe/.

16. Glenn Kessler, "On Asia Trip, Clinton Shows How She'll Try to Repair the U.S. Image Around the World," *Washington Post*, February 20, 2009; U.S. Department of State, "Secretary Clinton: Travel to Asia, February 15, 2009 to February 22, 2009," The Associated Press, "Hillary Clinton: U.S. 'Is Back' in Asia," *New York Daily News*, July 21, 2009, http:// www.nydailynews.com/news/world/u-s-back-asia-secretary-state-hillary-clinton -declares-article-1.429381.

17. Hillary Clinton, "America's Pacific Century," *Foreign Policy*, no. 189 (November 2011): 56–63.

18. The White House, "Remarks by President Obama to the Australian Parliament," November 17, 2011.

19. The White House, Office of the Press Secretary, Parliament House, Canberra, Australia, "Remarks by President Obama and Prime Minister Gillard of Australia in Joint Press Conference," November 16, 2011, http://www.whitehouse.gov/the-press-office/2011 /11/16/remarks-president-obama-and-prime-minister-gillard-australia-joint-press. For instance, Tom Donilon said, "It was clear [in 2009] that there was an imbalance in the projection and focus of U.S. power. It was the president's judgment that we were over-weighted in some areas and regions, including our military actions in the Middle East. . . . At the

same time, we were underweighted in other regions, such as the Asia-Pacific. Indeed, we believed this was our key geographic imbalance." Quoted in Josh Rogin, "Donilon Defends the Asia 'Pivot,'" foreignpolicy.com, March 11, 2013, http://foreignpolicy.com/2013 /03/11/donilon-defends-the-asia-pivot/. See also Bob Woodward, *Obama's Wars* (New York: Simon and Schuster, 2010).

20. U.S. Department of Defense, *Sustaining U.S. Global Leadership: Priorities for 21st Century Defense*, January 2012, 2.

21. U.S. Department of Defense, *Sustaining U.S. Global Leadership*.

22. U.S. Department of Defense, Secretary of Defense Leon E. Panetta, "Shangri-La Security Dialogue," Shangri-La Hotel, Singapore, June 2, 2012, http://www.defense.gov /speeches/speech.aspx?speechid=1681.

23. The Pew Research Center found that between 2010 and 2012, the percentage of Chinese citizens who believed that U.S.-China relations were defined by cooperation fell from 68 percent to 39 percent, and the percentage who believed the U.S.-China relationship was "one of hostility" rose from 8 percent to 26 percent. See Pew Research Center, "Ratings for the U.S. Decline: Growing Concerns in China about Inequality, Corruption," Pew Global Attitudes Project, October 16, 2012, http://www.pewglobal.org/2012/10/16 /growing-/concerns-/in-/china-/about-/inequality-/corruption. Moreover, a number of articles appearing in periodicals such as *China Daily* and *PLA Daily* suggested that the new strategy was a direct response to China's emergence as a great power and was aimed implicitly at the containment of China. See Michael S. Chase and Benjamin Purser III, "Pivot and Parry: China's Response to America's New Defense Strategy," *China Brief* 12, no. 6 (March 15, 2012).

24. Michael J. Green and Nicholas Szechenyi, "Power and Order in Asia: A Survey of Regional Expectations" (Washington, DC: Center for Strategic and International Studies, June 2014).

25. Green and Szechenyi, "Power and Order in Asia," 12.

26. Stephen J. Hadley et al., *The QDR in Perspective: Meeting America's National Security Needs in the 21st Century: The Final Report of the Quadrennial Defense Review Independent Panel* (Washington, DC: United States Institute of Peace, 2010), 58, http://www .usip.org/sites/default/files/qdr/qdrreport.pdf.

27. Secretary of Defense Leon Panetta, "Letters to Senator John McCain and Senator Lindsey Graham," November 14, 2011, http://armedservices.house.gov/index.cfm/files /serve?File_id=9692f972-eb86-46da-bc8d-ff4d461e6c00.

28. David E. Sanger and Mark Landler, "Obama's Strategic Shift to Asia Is Hobbled by Pressure at Home and Crises Abroad," *New York Times*, April 21, 2014.

29. Karen DeYoung, "Obama's Decision to Turn to Congress on Syria Decision Triggers Debate," *Washington Post*, September 4, 2013.

30. See, for example, Fumiaki Kubo, Yuichi Hosoya, and Satoshi Ikeuchi, "America ga 'sekai no keisatsu' wo yameta hi" [The Day America Quit the World's Police], *Chuo-Koron* 11 (2013). " 久保文明・細谷雄一・池内恵「アメリカが『世界の警察官』をやめた日」(『中央公論』１１月号) The article highlighted that the U.S. presidential deferral to Congress on the intervention into Syria was "Obama-shock" because it was seen that the United States might not respond to the responsibilities to provide deterrence. See "(米国の迷走)「警官」不在、揺らぐ世界: 米世論内向き、政府を縛る" "Beikoku no meisou 'keikan'

no fuzai, yuragu sekai: beiseron uchimuki, seifu wo shibaru" [The U.S. Aimless Wandering—Police Not Present, Shaky World: Inward-Looking U.S. Public Sentiment Restrains the Government]," *Nikkei Shimbun*, December 30, 2013.

31. Lee Kuan Yew, "The United States, Iraq, and the War on Terror: A Singaporean Perspective," *Foreign Affairs* 86, no. 1 (January–February 2007): 2–7.

32. The White House, *National Security Strategy*, May 2010.

33. The author cochaired an independent assessment commissioned by Congress in 2012 and was told this in multiple interviews with administration officials. See David J. Berteau and Michael J. Green, *U.S. Force Posture Strategy in the Asia Pacific: An Independent Assessment* (Washington, DC: Center for Strategy and International Studies, August 2012).

34. Michael J. Green and Zack Cooper, "Revitalizing the Rebalance: How to Keep U.S. Focus on Asia," *Washington Quarterly* 37, no. 3 (Fall 2014): 3.

35. Tom Donilon, "President Obama's Asia Policy & Upcoming Trip to Asia," speech delivered at the Center for Strategic and International Studies in Washington, DC, November 15, 2012, http://www.whitehouse.gov/the-press-office/2012/11/15/remarks-national -security-advisor-tom-donilon-prepared-delivery; Susan Rice, "America's Future in Asia," speech delivered at Georgetown University, November 20, 2013, https://www.whitehouse .gov/the-press-office/2013/11/21/remarks-prepared-delivery-national-security-advisor -susan-e-rice.

36. John Kerry, "Statement of Senator John F. Kerry, Nominee for Secretary of State," Senate Committee on Foreign Relations, January 24, 2013, http://www.state.gov/secretary /remarks/2013/01/203455.htm; Howard LaFranchi, "US 'Pivot to Asia': Is John Kerry Retooling It?" *Christian Science Monitor*, February 20, 2013, http://www.csmonitor.com /USA/Foreign-Policy/2013/0220/US-pivot-to-Asia-Is-John-Kerry-retooling-it; David J. Berteau, Michael J. Green, and Zack Cooper, *Assessing the Asia-Pacific Rebalance* (Washington, DC: Center for Strategy and International Studies, December 2014).

37. See also Hillary Clinton, "Yomiuri Shimbun Interview: The Importance of U.S.-Japan Relations," *Yomiuri Shimbun*, February 17, 2009.

38. Bader, *Obama and China's Rise*, 41.

39. "Clinton: Senkakus Subject to Security Pact," *Kyodo News* via *Japan Times*, September 25, 2010, http://www.japantimes.co.jp/news/2010/09/25/national/clinton-senkakus -subject-to-security-pact/#.VNppmPnF8sJ. The United States takes no position on the question of sovereignty over the islands, but in official documents it lists "Senkaku" (the Japanese name) and holds that Article V (the defense of Japan clause) applies to the islands because they are under the administrative control of Japan.

40. "Trilateral Statement Japan, Republic of Korea, and the United States," Media Note, Office of the Spokesman, Washington, DC, December 6, 2010, http://www.state.gov/r/pa /prs/ps/2010/12/152431.htm.

41. Interview by author with Senior ROK Ministry of Foreign Affairs and Trade Official, December 15, 2010. The collective security statement coincided with a decision by Seoul to renegotiate the KORUS free trade agreement for the third time with Washington, which created extra political vulnerabilities for President Lee at home.

42. James B. Steinberg, "The Administration's Vision of the U.S.-China Relationship," September 24, 2009.

43. See, for example, The White House, *National Security Strategy*, May 2010, 43.

44. The White House, "Remarks by the President at the U.S./China Strategic and Economic Dialogue," July 27, 2009. See also Emma Chanlett-Avery et al., *Japan-U.S. Relations: Issues for Congress*, CRS Report RL33436, September 2, 2009.

45. The White House, Office of the Press Secretary, "U.S.-China Joint Statement," November 17, 2009.

46. "India Rejects Third-Party Role in Pakistan Talks," http://www.cnn.com/2009/WORLD/asiapcf/11/18/india.pakistan.talks/index.html?iref=24hours.

47. In November 2010, U.S. government officials told the *New York Times* that Dai Bingguo had called the South China Sea a "core interest" and had told U.S. officials that one or more Chinese officials had labeled the South China Sea a "core interest." See John Pomfret, "Beijing Claims 'Indisputable Sovereignty' over South China Sea," *Washington Post*, July 31, 2010; Greg Sheridan, "China Actions Meant as Test, Hillary Clinton Says," *The Australian*, November 9, 2010; Edward Wong, "China Hedges over Whether South China Sea Is a 'Core Interest' Worth War," *New York Times*, March 30, 2011. All authoritative Chinese definitions of "core interests" include Chinese territorial integrity and sovereignty, which would include conflicting claims with U.S. allies in the East China and South China Seas. See Information Office of the State Council of the People's Republic of China, "China's Peaceful Development," September 6, 2011; State Councilor Dai Bingguo, "Closing Remarks for U.S.-China Strategic and Economic Dialogue," Washington, DC, July 28, 2009, http://www.state.gov/secretary/rm/2009a/july/126599.htm.

48. Kevin Rudd, "Beyond the Pivot: A New Road Map for U.S.-Chinese Relations," *Foreign Affairs* 92, no. 2 (March–April 2013); Robert S. Ross, "The Problem with the Pivot: Obama's New Asia Policy Is Unnecessary and Counterproductive," *Foreign Affairs* 91, no. 6 (November–December 2012); Daniel W. Drezner, "Does Obama Have a Grand Strategy? Why We Need Doctrines in Uncertain Times," *Foreign Affairs* 90, no. 4 (July–August 2011): 57–60, 61–64, 65–68.

49. The White House, Office of the Press Secretary, "U.S.-China Joint Statement," January 19, 2011.

50. See "How Will John Kerry Deal with China?" xinhuanet.com, February 4, 2013, http://news.xinhuanet.com/english/indepth/2013-02/04/c_132149359.htm.

51. The White House, Office of the Press Secretary, Press Briefing by National Security Advisor Tom Donilon, June 8, 2013, https://www.whitehouse.gov/the-press-office/2013/06/08/press-briefing-national-security-advisor-tom-donilon; John Kerry, "Statement of Senator John F. Kerry, Nominee for Secretary of State," Senate Committee on Foreign Relations, January 24, 2013; The White House, Office of the Press Secretary, "America's Future in Asia," Remarks As Prepared for Delivery by National Security Advisor Susan E. Rice at Georgetown University, November 20, 2013.

52. The White House, Office of the Press Secretary, Remarks by Vice President Joe Biden and President Xi Jinping of the People's Republic of China, December 4, 2013, https://www.whitehouse.gov/the-press-office/2013/12/04/remarks-vice-president-joe-biden-and-president-xi-jinping-peoples-republic.

53. U.S. Department of Defense, Press Operations, Secretary of Defense Speech, IISS Shangri-La Dialogue, As Delivered by Secretary of Defense Chuck Hagel, May 31, 2014.

54. On China, see, for example, Wang Dong and Yin Chengzi, "Territorial Issues in Asia Drivers, Instruments, Ways Forward" (Berlin: German Institute for International and Security Affairs, July 1–2, 2013), http://www.swp-berlin.org/fileadmin/contents /products/projekt_papiere/BCAS2013_Wang_Dong.pdf; Ely Ratner, "Rebalancing to Asia with an Insecure China," *Washington Quarterly*, Center for Strategic and International Studies, April 1, 2013, http://csis.org/files/publication/TWQ_13Spring_Ratner.pdf.

55. Al Kamen, "Among Leaders at Summit, Hu's First," *Washington Post*, April 14, 2010; Bader, *Obama and China's Rise*, chap. 5; Michael J. Green, "The Democratic Party of Japan and the Future of the U.S.-Japan Alliance," *Journal of Japanese Studies* 37, no. 1 (Winter 2011): 91–116.

56. Christopher K. Johnson, *Decoding China's Emerging "Great Power" Strategy in Asia, a Report of the CSIS Freeman Chair in China Studies* (Lanham, MD: Rowman and Little-field, 2014); Michael J. Green, "Japan Is Back: Unbundling Abe's Grand Strategy," Lowy Institute Analysis, December 17, 2013; Vance Serchuk, "Obama Needs to Warm Up to Japan's Abe," *Washington Post*, July 24, 2013.

57. General Herbert Carlisle, as quoted in Sydney J. Freedberg, Jr., "US Won't Fight China over Pacific 'Rock": PACOM Strives for Strategic 'Ambiguity,'" Breakingdefense .com, September 19, 2012, http://breakingdefense.com/2012/09/us-wont-fight-china-over -pacific-rock-pacom-strives-for-stra/; Admiral Samuel J. Locklear III, "The Asia Pacific 'Patchwork Quilt,'" Asia Society speech, Washington, DC, December 6, 2012, http:// asiasociety.org/policy/strategic-challenges/us-asia/admiral-samuel-j-locklear-iii-asia -pacific-patchwork-quilt.

58. Interview by author with senior Japanese political figure involved in the summit negotiations, Tokyo, June 2, 2014.

59. U.S. Department of Defense, "Guidelines for U.S.-Japan Defense Cooperation," April 27, 2015; The White House, Office of the Press Secretary, "U.S.-Japan Joint Vision Statement," April 28, 2015; Japanese Prime Minister Address to Joint Meeting of Congress, April 29, 2015, http://www.c-span.org/video/?325576-2/japanese-prime-minister-shinzo -abe-addresses-joint-meeting-congress; Michael J. Green and Nicholas Szechenyi, "Critical Questions: Abe's Speech to Congress," Asia Maritime Transparency Initiative, April 29, 2015.

60. Aaron Mehta, "Carter: China Isolating Itself in Pacific," DefenseNews.com, May 27, 2015, http://www.defensenews.com/story/breaking-news/2015/05/27/carter-china-warns -isolation-islands-pacific-command-reclamation-pearl-harbor/28025723/; Chris Blake, "ASEAN Leaders Concerned over South China Sea Reclamations," *Bloomberg Business*, April 28, 2015; David Tweed, "China May Gain Control of South China Sea, U.S. Navy Says," *Bloomberg Business*, April 16, 2015; David E. Sanger and Rick Gladstone, "Piling Sand in a Disputed Sea, China Literally Gains Ground," *New York Times*, April 8, 2015; James Hardy and Sean O'Connor, "China Building Airstrip-Capable Island on Fiery Cross Reef," *IHS Jane's*, www.janes.com, November 20, 2014; Jun Osawa, "China's ADIZ over the East China Sea: A 'Great Wall in the Sky'?" *Brookings*, December 17, 2013, http://www .brookings.edu/research/opinions/2013/12/17-china-air-defense-identification-zone -osawa.

61. David A. Shlapak et al., *A Question of Balance: Political Context and Military Aspects of the China-Taiwan Dispute* (Santa Monica, CA: RAND, 2009), 131.

62. Toshi Yoshihara, "Chinese Missile Strategy and the U.S. Naval Presence in Japan: The Operational View from Beijing," *Naval War College Review* 63, no. 3 (Summer 2010): 39–62.

63. Author's interview with PLA experts at the Central Military Academy, 2009. The Pentagon's 2014 report on the PLA noted that in addition to preparing to defeat Taiwan, China was also developing capabilities for conflict in the South China or East China Seas. Evidence of this expansion of possible contingencies that the Peoples Liberation Army Navy (PLAN) had to be prepared to face was given by the MANEUVER-5 in the Philippine Sea, in which all three PLAN fleets participated (North, East, and South Sea Fleets), making it the "largest PLA Navy open-ocean exercise seen to date." See U.S. Department of Defense, *Annual Report to Congress: Military and Security Developments Involving the People's Republic of China*, 2014, i.

64. See U.S. Department of Defense, *Annual Report to Congress: Military and Security Developments Involving the People's Republic of China*, 2011 and 2012.

65. Toshi Yoshihara interviewed by James Rogers, April 6, 2014, http://www .europeangeostrategy.org/2014/04/interview-toshi-yoshihara/.

66. Admiral Jonathan Greenert and General Mark Walsh, "Breaking the Kill Chain," foreignpolicy.com, May 17, 2013, http://foreignpolicy.com/2013/05/17/breaking-the-kill -chain/; U.S. Department of Defense, *Joint Operational Access Concept (JOAC)*, January 12, 2012; U.S. Department of Defense, *Air-Sea Battle Office, Air-Sea Battle: Service Collaboration to Address Anti-Access & Area Denial Challenges*, May 2013.

67. U.S. Department of Defense, *Joint Operational Access Concept (JOAC)*, January 12, 2012.

68. Admiral Jonathan W. Greenert, USN, and General Norton A. Schwartz, USAF, "Air-Sea Battle: Promoting Stability in an Era of Uncertainty," *American Interest*, February 20, 2012; U.S. Navy, "Rear Adm. Foggo Discusses Air-Sea Battle Concept," *Navy Live*, October 10, 2013, http://navylive.dodlive.mil/2013/10/10/rear-adm-foggo-discusses-air -sea-battle-concept/; Toshi Yoshihara and James R. Holmes, "Asymmetric Warfare, American Style," (United States Naval Institute) *Proceedings* 138, no. 4 (April 2012): 24–29.

69. Jan van Tol with Mark Gunzinger, Andrew Krepinevich, and Jim Thomas, *AirSea Battle: A Point-of-Departure Operational Concept* (Washington, DC: Center for Strategic and Budgetary Assessments, May 2010).

70. As quoted in Greg Jaffe, "U.S. Model for a Future War Fans Tensions with China and Inside Pentagon," *Washington Post*, October 3, 2012.

71. T. X. Hammes, "Sorry, AirSea Battle Is No Strategy," *The National Interest*, August 7, 2013; T. X. Hammes, "Offshore Control: A Proposed Strategy for an Unlikely Conflict," *INSS Strategic Forum*, no. 278 (June 2012).

72. Shirley A. Kan, *Guam: U.S. Defense Deployments*, CRS Report RS22570, November 26, 2014.

73. Berteau and Green, *U.S. Force Posture Strategy in the Asia Pacific*, 17.

74. Daniel R. Russel, Assistant Secretary, Bureau of East Asian and Pacific Affairs, "Maritime Disputes in East Asia," Testimony Before the House Committee on Foreign Affairs Subcommittee on Asia and the Pacific, February 5, 2014; The White House, *National Security Strategy*, February 2015, 24; U.S. Department of Defense, Press Operations, Secretary of Defense Speech, IISS Shangri-La Dialogue, As Delivered by Secretary of Defense Chuck Hagel, May 31, 2014.

75. Agreement Between the Government of the Republic of the Philippines and the Government of the United States of America on Enhanced Defense Cooperation, April 29, 2014; U.S. Department of State, Daily Press Briefing, October 2, 2014.

76. Cabinet decision on the Development Cooperation Charter, February 10, 2015, http://www.mofa.go.jp/files/000067701.pdf.

77. See, for example, Chuck Hagel, "Reagan National Defense Forum Keynote," Ronald Reagan Presidential Library, Simi Valley, CA, Saturday, November 15, 2014, http://www.defense.gov/Speeches/Speech.aspx?SpeechID=1903; Robert Work, "The Asia-Pacific Rebalance," Council on Foreign Relations, September 30, 2014, http://www.cfr.org/defense-and-security/deputy-secretary-defense-robert-work-asia-pacific-rebalance/p33538; Robert Work, Speech at the National Defense University, Washington, DC, August 5, 2014, http://www.defense.gov/Speeches/Speech.aspx?SpeechID=1873; Robert Work, "The Third U.S. Offset Strategy and Its Implications for Partners and Allies," Speech to Center for a New American Security, January 28, 2015, http://warontherocks.com/2015/01/video-the-third-u-s-offset-strategy-and-its-implications-for-partners-and-allies/; Robert Martinage, "Toward a New Offset Strategy," Center for Strategic and Budgetary Assessments, October 27, 2014, http://csbaonline.org/publications/2014/10/toward-a-new-offset-strategy-exploiting-u-s-long-term-advantages-to-restore-u-s-global-power-projection-capability/.

78. Chico Harlan, "China Creates New Air Defense Zone in East China Sea amid Dispute with Japan," *Washington Post*, November 23, 2013.

79. Andrew F. Krepinevich, "How to Deter China: The Case for Archipelagic Defense," *Foreign Affairs* 94, no. 2 (March–April 2015): 75–86.

80. Michael J. Green et al., *Asia-Pacific Rebalance 2025: Capabilities, Presence and Partnerships* (Washington, DC: Center for Strategic and International Studies, January 2016), 4–5, 15–19.

81. Barack Obama, "Renewing American Leadership," *Foreign Affairs* 86, no. 4 (July–August 2007); G. John Ikenberry and Anne-Marie Slaughter, *Final Report: Forging a World of Liberty Under Law—U.S. National Security in the 21st Century*, The Princeton Project on National Security, September 27, 2006, http://www.wws.princeton.edu/ppns/repot/FinalReport.pdf.

82. Hillary Clinton, "America's Pacific Century," 56–63.

83. Helene Cooper, "Talking Softly About Democracy Promotion," *New York Times*, January 29, 2009.

84. See, for example, Kurt M. Campbell and Michael E. O'Hanlon, *Hard Power: The New Politics of National Security* (New York: Basic Books, 2006), 6.

85. Douglas E. Schoen, "Obama's Foreign Policy: Abandon Democracy," FoxNews.com, September 1, 2009, http://www.foxnews.com/opinion/2009/09/01/doug-schoen-obama-democracy.html.

86. Fred Hiatt, "Obama's U-turn on Human Rights," *Washington Post*, October 20, 2013. See also The White House, Office of the Press Secretary, "Remarks by President Obama in Address to the United Nations General Assembly," September 24, 2013; Jackson Diehl, "Obama's Myopic Worldview," *Washington Post*, September 23, 2013; The White House, Office of the Press Secretary, "Remarks by the President on the Middle East and North Africa," May 19, 2011.

87. Glenn Kessler, "In China, Clinton Says Human Rights 'Can't Interfere' with Talks," *Washington Post*, February 20, 2009.

88. Hillary Clinton, "America's Pacific Century," 62–63.

89. Anonymous, "No Time for the Dalai Lama," *Wall Street Journal, Eastern Edition*, October 6, 2009.

90. Kadeer argues that the administration's stance on the Uighurs emboldened China's 2009 crackdown on the minority in Xinjiang. See Rebiya Kadeer interviewed by Joseph Hammond, *The Diplomat*, October 25, 2013, http://thediplomat.com/2013/11/rebiya -kadeer/.

91. "White House Mum on Missing Chinese Activist," CBS News, April 29, 2012, http://www.cbsnews.com/news/white-house-mum-on-missing-chinese-activist-chen -guangcheng/.

92. Thomas Carothers, "Why Is the United States Shortchanging Its Commitment to Democracy?," *Washington Post*, December 22, 2014.

93. Kenneth Roth, "Empty Promises? Obama's Hesitant Embrace of Human Rights," *Foreign Affairs* 89, no. 2 (March–April 2010): 10–16.

94. John Garnaut, "Obama Behind Release of Chinese Activists," *The Age*, August 25, 2009.

95. Embassy of the United States, Jakarta, Indonesia, "Deputy Secretary Steinberg's Comments on Burma," EAP Press Guidance, April 2, 2009; Tracy McVeigh, "Aung San Suu Kyi 'Released from House Arrest,'" *The Guardian*, November 13, 2010; Matthew Pennington, "Consensus Cracking on US Policy Toward Myanmar," Associated Press, July 3, 2012.

96. Josh Rogin, "Obama Breaks with Aung San Suu Kyi, Lifts Burmese Investment Ban," foreignpolicy.com, July 11, 2012, http://foreignpolicy.com/2012/07/11/obama-breaks-with -aung-san-suu-kyi-lifts-burmese-investment-ban/; "Suu Kyi Warns Investors Off Myanmar's State Oil and Gas Firm, " Reuters, June 14, 2012, http://uk.reuters.com/article/2012 /06/14/uk-myanmar-suukyi-idUKBRE85D0KA20120614; U.S. Department of State, Background Briefing on Burma, May 17, 2012.

97. Mark Landler, "Obama and Aung San Suu Kyi Meet Again, with Battle Scars," *New York Times*, November 14, 2014; Mark Landler and Thomas Fuller, "Obama Prods Myanmar Back Toward Democracy," *New York Times*, November 13, 2014; Editorial Board, "A Failing Engagement with Burma," *Washington Post*, March 14, 2015; Unocal Myanmar Offshore Co., Ltd. (UMOL), *Submission to U.S. Department of State: Responsible Investment in Myanmar* (San Ramon, CA: Chevron Corporation, Global Issues and Public Policy, 2016), http://photos.state.gov/libraries/burma/895/pdf/Chevron%20Myanmar%20Re-sponsible%20Investment%20Report_24May2016.pdf.

98. See, for example, Chevron, *Responsible Investment in Myanmar: Submission to the Department of State* (Washington: DC, May 2016), http://photos.state.gov/libraries /burma/895/pdf/Chevron%20Myanmar%20Responsible%20Investment%20Report _24May2016.pdf.

99. William A. Galston, "Obama's Moment of Truth on Trade," *Wall Street Journal*, February 4, 2014.

100. Michael Luo, "Despite NAFTA Attacks, Clinton and Obama Haven't Been Free Trade Foes," *New York Times*, February 28, 2008.

101. Nick Timiraos, "Campaign '08: Clinton, Obama Ramp Up Their Rhetoric Against China," *Wall Street Journal, Eastern Edition*, February 27, 2008.

102. World Trade Organization, *World Trade Report*, July 2009.

103. Richard Baldwin and Simon Evenett, "Introduction and Recommendations for the G20," in *The Collapse of Global Trade, Murky Protectionism, and the Crisis: Recommendations for the G20*, ed. Richard Baldwin and Simon Evenett (London: CEPR, 2010), 1–9.

104. Timiraos, "Campaign '08."

105. Andrew F. Cooper, "The G20 as an Improvised Crisis Committee and/or a Contested 'Steering Committee' for the World," *International Affairs* 86, no. 3 (May 2010): 741–757; Geoffrey Garrett, "G2 in G20: China, the United States and the World After the Global Financial Crisis," *Global Policy* 1, no. 1 (January 2010): 29–39; Daniel Drezner, *The System Worked: How the World Stopped Another Great Depression* (Oxford: Oxford University Press, 2014), 8.

106. Office of the United States Trade Representative, "Trans-Pacific Partnership Announcement," December 14, 2009.

107. Office of the United States Trade Representative, Executive Office of the President, "U.S.-Korea Free Trade Agreement," https://ustr.gov/trade-agreements/free-trade-agreements/korus-fta.

108. The White House, Office of the Press Secretary, "Remarks by the President in State of the Union Address," January 27, 2010.

109. "America's Big Bet," *The Economist*, November 15, 2014.

110. William H. Cooper and Mark E. Manyin, *Japan Joins the Trans-Pacific Partnership: What Are the Implications?*, CRS Report R42676, August 13, 2013.

111. Shannon Tiezzi, "Will China Join the Trans-Pacific Partnership?" *The Diplomat*, October 10, 2014; "America's Big Bet," *The Economist*, November 15, 2014; Chen Weihua, "China Warming to US-led Trans-Pacific Partnership," *China Daily*, June 11, 2015, http://www.chinadaily.com.cn/china/2015-06/11/content_20969576.htm.

112. The one exception was an agreement negotiated with Jordan after 9/11. See Scott Miller and Murray Hiebert, "Achieving Trade Promotion Authority Will Require Heavy Lifting from the President," *Southeast Asia from Scott Circle* 5, no. 1 (January 23, 2014).

113. Eric Badner and Manu Raju, "Harry Reid Rejects President Obama's Trade Push," politico.com, January 29, 2014, http://www.politico.com/story/2014/01/harry-reid-barack-obama-trade-deals-102819.

114. Doug Palmer, "White House Wants Trade Promotion Authority," Reuters, February 29, 2012; The White House, Office of the Press Secretary, "President Barack Obama's State of the Union Address," January 28, 2014; Michael B. G. Forman, *2014 Trade Policy Agenda and 2013 Annual Report of the President of the United States on the Trade Agreements Program* (Washington, DC: Office of the United States Trade Representative, March 2014).

115. The White House, "Remarks of President Barack Obama—As Prepared for Delivery in State of the Union Address," January 20, 2015.

116. Paul Kane and David Nakamura, "McConnell Warns That Trade Deal Can't Pass Before 2016 Elections," *Washington Post*, December 10, 2015.

117. "An Asian Infrastructure Bank: Only Connect," *The Economist*, October 4, 2013; The White House, Office of the Press Secretary, "Remarks by President Obama and Presi-

dent Xi Jinping in Joint Press Conference," November 12, 2014; Robert Zoellick, "Shunning Beijing's Infrastructure Bank Was a Mistake for the US," *Financial Times* (London), June 7, 2015; Dan Drezner, "Anatomy of a Whole-of-Government Foreign Policy Failure," *Washington Post*, March 27, 2015.

118. "The Protectionism That Wasn't," *The Economist*, September 10, 2013.

119. International Monetary Fund, *World Economic Outlook*, October 2014; Dhara Ranasainghe, "Goldman Bearish on BRIC Economies," cnbc.com, July 1, 2013, http://www .cnbc.com/id/100858442.

120. See, for example, Jamie Fly and Robert Kagan, quoted in Lois Farrow Parshley, "Grading Obama's Foreign Policy," foreignpolicy.com, January 24, 2012, http://foreignpolicy .com/2012/01/24/grading-obamas-foreign-policy/; Will Inboden, "What Obama's Done Right—and Wrong," foreignpolicy.com, December 28, 2011, http://foreignpolicy.com/2011 /12/28/what-obamas-done-right-and-wrong/. For broader assessments of the Obama legacy, see "53 Historians Weigh in on Barack Obama's Legacy," *New York Magazine*, January 11, 2015.

121. On strategic patience and the nuclear tests, see Emma Chanlett-Avery et al., *North Korea: U.S. Relations, Nuclear Diplomacy and Internal Situation*, CRS Report R41259, January 15, 2016.

CONCLUSION

1. Bates Gill, Michael Green, Kyoto Tsui, and William Watts, "Strategic Views on Asian Regionalism: Survey Results and Analysis," CSIS, February 2009, http://csis.org /files/media/csis/pubs/090217_gill_stratviews_web.pdf.

2. Michael J. Green and Nicholas Szechenyi, "Power and Order in Asia: A Survey of Regional Expectations," CSIS, July 2014, http://csis.org/files/publication/140605_Green _PowerandOrder_WEB.pdf.

3. Richard L. Armitage and Joseph S. Nye, *The U.S.-Japan Alliance: Getting Asia Right Through 2020*, CSIS Report, February 2007.

4. Bates Gill et al., "Strategic Views on Asian Regionalism: Survey Results and Analysis," CSIS, February 2009, http://csis.org/files/media/csis/pubs/090217_gill_stratviews_web .pdf.

5. Jacob Poushter, "Americans Favor TPP, But Less Than Those In Other Countries," PewResearchCenter, Fact Tank, June 23, 2015, http://www.pewresearch.org/fact-tank/2015 /06/23/americans-favor-tpp-but-less-than-other-countries-do/.

INDEX

ABC staff talks, 194, 195

Abe, Shinzo, 508, 527, 528

Abramowitz, Morton, 367, 369, 377–378, 379

Abrams, Creighton, 333

Abrams, Elliott, 514

Acheson, Dean, 142, 249–250, 251, 252, 322; on Asian defense perimeter, 274, 605n134; and China policies, 258, 262, 292; on defense spending, 274; and Dulles, 280; and Japan policies, 226, 264; and Kennan strategies, 274; and Korea policies, 267, 268, 274–276, 278; and San Francisco System, 281; and Southeast Asia policies, 241–242, 270, 310

Adams, Brooks, 75, 82

Adams, John Quincy, 27–31, 33, 51, 71; and China, 30, 31, 33, 36, 37, 44; and Mexican-American War, 34; and Opium War, 44, 55; on Pacific Northwest, 5, 25, 28–30, 53, 54; Seward influenced by, 57, 64

Adams-Onis Treaty (1819), 28

Afghanistan, 6; during Bush (GWB) administration, 492, 493, 501; during Obama administration, 521; Operation Enduring Freedom (OEF) in, 492, 493; Soviet invasion of (1979), 374, 382, 384

Agents of Innovation (Kuehn), 142

Agreed Framework with North Korea, 466–467, 479, 488, 503, 504, 506

Air Defense Identification Zone of China, 531

airpower strategies, 142, 205; island-based, 205; during Nixon administration, 333, 335; during Obama administration, 529–530; in Vietnam War bombing campaigns, 304, 308–312, 331, 333, 335, 336, 341

Air-Sea Battle (ASB) concept during Obama administration, 529–530

Akamatsu, Kaname, 318

Alaska: purchase of, 56, 61, 62, 63, 64, 65, 66, 69, 218, 560n21; in War Plan Orange defense line, 176

Alaska Treaty, 63

Albright, Madeleine, 455, 458, 479, 513, 533

Aleutian Islands, 61–62, 69, 93, 134, 181, 196, 200, 273, 274

Alexander I, 28–29, 53

Alexander III, 64, 65

Alien Exclusion Act (1924), 144

Alien Land Act in California, 124, 126

Allen, Richard, 391–392, 394–397, 403, 416

Allied Advisory Committee, 226

Amau Doctrine, 156, 162, 165, 171

American Asiatic Association, 93

American Banking Group, 120

American Civil War, 54, 56, 59, 63

American Revolution, 9, 21, 22

Americans in Eastern Asia (Dennett), 2, 170

American Volunteer Group (AVG), 210

America's Strategy in World Politics (Spykman), 208–209

Amity, Commerce and Navigation Treaty (1794), 23

Amity and Cooperation Treaty of ASEAN, 512, 513

amphibious operations in War Plan Orange, 142–143, 175

Anglo-American Convention (1818), 28

Anglo–Japanese alliance, 139, 140–141, 155

Anglo-Saxonism, 75–76, 80, 84

Anti-access/area denial (A2/AD) strategy, 529, 531

anti-imperialism, 9, 10, 20, 37, 42, 90–91, 152

Anti-Imperialist League, 90

antitrust laws, 138

ANZUS treaty, 281, 283, 290, 414, 492

APEC. *See* Asia Pacific Economic Cooperation

Aquino, Benigno "Ninoy," 417, 651n147

Aquino, Corazon, 418, 446

Armacost, Michael, 378, 440

Armitage, Richard, 7, 393, 484, 486, 500, 508, 642n29; and China policies, 396, 397; and Japan policies, 405, 406, 485; and Korea policies, 416, 506; and Philippines policies, 418, 446

Armitage–Nye Report, 485, 486–487, 492, 498, 544–545

arms control, 112; Global Disarmament Conference (1932) on, 154; during Hoover administration, 173; during Reagan administration, 389; SALT talks on, 356, 364, 367, 368, 371, 379, 383; Washington Treaty System in, 136–144

arms sales: to China, 395–399; to Taiwan, 395–397, 448–449, 489

Army of the Republic of Vietnam (ARVN), 332, 360

Arnold, Henry H. (Hap), 193, 204

Arrow War (Second Opium War), 38, 45

Arroyo, Gloria Macapagal, 502

Arthur, Chester, 74–75

ASEAN. *See* Association of Southeast Asian Nations

Asia, definitions and concepts of, 14–15

Asian Infrastructure Investment Bank (AIIB), 425, 538

Asian Monetary Fund (AMF), 476

Asia Pacific Community, 464, 473

Asia Pacific Economic Cooperation (APEC), 413, 427, 438, 450, 451; during Bush (GWB) administration, 482, 495, 510–512; during Clinton administration, 454, 463, 464, 471, 472, 473–476; and Early Voluntary Sectoral Liberalization (EVSL), 475–476; during Obama administration, 521, 539

Asia-Pacific Partnership on Clean Climate and Energy, 482, 510

Asiatic Squadron of U.S. Navy, 68, 82, 87, 107, 172, 173

Asō Tarō, 525, 527

Aspin, Les, 457, 459

Assad, Bashar al-, 519

Association of Southeast Asian Nations (ASEAN), 358, 384, 411, 413, 449, 546; Defence Ministers Meeting-Plus (ADMM+), 422; during Bush (GHWB) administration, 449, 451; during Bush (GWB) administration, 490, 502, 512, 513, 514; during Carter administration, 384; during Clinton administration, 464, 476;

during Nixon administration, 358; during Obama administration, 521; during Reagan administration, 411, 413; Regional Forum (ARF) of, 464, 473, 513, 521; Treaty of Amity and Cooperation, 512, 513

Astor, John Jacob, 25, 26–27, 29–30

Astoria (Oregon), 27, 554–555n27

Astoria (USS), 177

Atlantic Charter, 188–189, 192, 206, 221, 228–229, 233, 585n4; Article VII, 235; and Korea policies, 266; and Southeast Asia policies, 268, 269, 271; on trade and economics, 234, 235, 236

atomic bomb, 205, 223, 224, 239, 589n74; first Soviet test of, 258

Auer, James, 404, 405, 407

Augusta (USS), 188–189

Australia: in ANZUS treaty, 281, 283; and Asian regionalism, 412, 413; during Bush (GHWB) administration, 450; during Bush (GWB) administration, 492, 512; during Obama administration, 521; and postwar economic policies, 235, 236; during Reagan administration, 412, 413; response to 9/11 attack, 492; and San Francisco System, 279, 281; in SEATO, 289, 290; in Southeast Asia, 288; and strategic priorities in WWII, 196, 197; and Vietnam War, 316

authoritarianism, 10, 416, 534

Axis Pact, 178, 182

Bader, Jeffrey, 518, 519, 521, 525

Baker, James, 430–431; and China policies, 434, 435–436; and Japan policies, 409–411, 443, 451; and Korea policies, 448, 466

Ball, George, 305, 307, 309, 310, 314

Ballantine, Joseph, 225

Banco Delta Asia, 506, 507

Bandung (Indonesia) meeting (1955), 292–293

banking industry: and China consortium, 120, 121, 131, 146, 147; and Lamont strategies, 145–149

Barshefsky, Charlene, 472, 479

base force concept in Bush (GHWB) administration, 432, 433, 654n22

Bashir, Abu Bakar, 501

Basic National Security Policy (BNSP), 302, 314, 320

Batavia (Jakarta), 30

Battle of Coral Sea, 197, 198

Battle of Manila Bay, 72, 75, 76, 86, 87, 90, 192

Baucus, Max, 438

Bay of Pigs operation, 303, 306

Beaverbrook, Lord (William Maxwell Aitken), 189

Beazley, Kim, 414

Belknap, George, 88

Belknap, Reginald, 135

Benton, Thomas Hart, 28

Berger, Samuel "Sandy," 456

Bergsten, C. Fred, 474

Berlin Wall, fall of (1989), 429, 437

Best and the Brightest, The (Halberstam), 304

Betts, Richard, 2, 4

Biddle, James, 47–48, 54

Biden, Joe, 527

Bismarck, Otto von, 65, 73, 87, 188, 189, 207

Blackwill, Robert, 486, 490

Blaine, James G., 64, 71, 72

Blakeslee, George, 225

Blue versus Orange conflict, 133, 173, 176. *See also* War Plan Orange

Bolshevism, 117, 127–128, 130–131

Bonin islands, 48

Borah, William Edgar, 138, 173

Borton, Hugh, 225, 226

Bowles, Chester, 303, 315–316

Boxer Rebellion, 92, 95, 100, 123, 154

Bracken, Paul, 4

Bradley, Omar, 262, 278, 329

Brandywine (USS), 38

Bretton Woods Conference (1944), 11, 194, 234, 236, 237, 239, 253

Brezhnev, Leonid, 348

Brezhnev Doctrine (1968), 348

Britain: during American Civil War, 54, 59; Astoria sold to, 27, 28; and Atlantic Charter, 188–189, 228–229, 233, 235; in Cairo Conference, 212; in Casablanca

Britain (*cont.*)
Conference, 224; in China, 20, 24, 35, 36–42, 66; in Combined Chiefs of Staff, 192; in Crimean War, 49, 62; Dennett on, 52; in depression era, 149; early commercial presence in Pacific, 17–18, 20; early trade of, 21–22, 23, 35; and Europe first versus Pacific first strategies, 194–198; in First World War, 124; during Hoover administration, 155; and Hornbeck strategies, 162; imperialism of, 229, 230, 231; in India, 231; in Japan, 67; in League of Nations, 129, 137; in left flank approach to Japan, 199–200; in Lend-Lease program, 211; and MacMurray strategies, 167; Mahan on, 84–85; during McKinley administration, 94, 95; during Monroe administration, 28; navy of, 66, 173, 174, 175 (*see also* Royal Navy); Parker on, 46; Perry on, 48, 50, 51, 54; during Polk administration, 34; in post-WWII planning, 228–229, 228–237; and Rainbow Plans, 177; response to Queen Liliuokalani coup attempt, 72, 81; during Roosevelt (FDR) administration, 176–180, 184, 188–189, 228–237; during Roosevelt (TR) administration, 85, 97; in SEATO, 289, 290; in Second Opium War, 38, 45; and Second Revolution, 17–18; and Seward strategies, 61, 65; in Southeast Asia, 268, 269, 288; and Stimson negotiations, 155; surrender to Japanese at Singapore (1942), 196; during Taft administration, 120–121; in Tehran Conference, 212; trade and economic strategies, post-WWII, 235–237; during Tyler administration, 33; in Venezuelan crisis, 85; and Vietnam War, 314; in War of 1812, 27, 54; and War Plan Orange, 176–177; and Washington Treaty System, 138, 139, 140–141, 577n104; during Wilson administration, 124, 125–126, 127, 129, 137; in Yalta Conference, 220–221
British East India Company, 23, 32, 35

Broader Middle East and North African (BMENA) initiative, 514
Brooks, Karen, 490, 502
Brooks, Preston, 60
Brown, George S., 379–380
Brown, Harold, 366, 471; and China policies, 368–369, 374, 375; and Japan policies, 376, 377, 380–381, 383, 639n111; and Korea policies, 377, 378
Brown, Ron, 456
Bryan, William Jennings, 124, 126
Brzezinski, Zbigniew, 7, 365–367; and alliance management in Asia, 376; and China policies, 368, 369–371, 373–375; on human rights issues, 385; and Japan policies, 376, 383; and Korea policies, 377, 378; and Vietnam policies, 375
BUCCANEER, 198
Buchanan, James, 43, 47
Buck, Pearl, 210
Buell, Raymond Leslie, 141
Bullitt, William, 128, 221
Bull Moose Party, 122
Bulwer-Lytton, V. A. G., 155
Bundy, McGeorge, 220–221, 242, 301, 321; and Vietnam policies, 308, 309, 314, 317, 619–620n100
Bundy, William, 304–305, 336
Burke, Arleigh, 343, 391
Burlingame, Anson, 59–60, 66, 77
Burlingame Treaty (1868), 60, 69, 77
Burma: Britain in, 232, 269; during Bush (GHWB) administration, 449; during Bush (GWB) administration, 512, 513, 515–516; independence of, 269; military approach to Japan from, 199, 202; during Obama administration, 535, 539; plans for invasion of, 198, 212; Saffron Revolution in, 512, 515; U.S. and Allied forces in, 228
Burns, Nicholas, 507
Bush, George Herbert Walker, 13, 328, 426, 429–452; as vice-president under Reagan, 392, 394, 397, 415
Bush, George W., 13–14, 427, 482–517
Bush, Laura, 516, 677n136

Bush administration (GHWB), 426, 429–452; base force concept during, 432, 433, 654n22; China policies during, 430–431, 433–439, 448; defense spending during, 445; forward military presence during, 445–447; India policies during, 415, 449–450; Japan policies during, 426, 430, 433–434, 439–445; legacy in Asia strategies, 451–452; National Security Strategy documents during, 430, 432, 433, 439; unipolarity and bipolarity of international relations during, 432, 433

Bush administration (GWB), 427, 482–517; foreign policy advisors in, 484; India policies during, 415, 427, 485–486, 490, 498–500, 514–515; Iraq War during, 482, 483, 486; legacy in Asia strategy, 516–517; September 11, 2001 terrorist attacks during, 483, 486, 491–494, 498, 501; strategic flexibility policy in, 509–510

Bush Doctrine, 491

Buss, Claude, 38

Butterworth, W. William, 249–250, 258

Byrnes, Jimmy, 191, 226, 248, 266

Bywater, Hector, 141

Cairo Conference (1943), 203, 212, 233

California: Asian immigrants in, 100, 124; Oriental schools in, 100; statehood for, 58

California Alien Land Act, 124, 126

Cambodia, 65, 271, 329; during Bush (GHWB) administration, 449; during Nixon administration, 323, 331, 333–335, 336, 359–360; Vietnam invasion of (1978), 375, 384, 414

Campbell, Kurt, 457, 519, 521, 525, 526, 528, 534

Canada, 30, 54, 56, 66

Canning, Charles John, 29

Canterville Ghost, The (Wilde), 74

Canton (Guangzhou), 14; early trade with, 6, 10, 21–25, 30, 34–35, 36

Carbaugh, John, 395

Carl Vinson (USS), 174

Carnegie, Andrew, 91

Caroline Islands, 280; during First World War, 125; in island-hopping strategies, 199, 200, 203; in Rainbow Five Plan, 199; in War Plan Orange, 135, 142, 175

Carter, Ashton, 423–425

Carter, Jimmy, 10, 13, 246, 323, 363–386; North Korea negotiations by, 466

Carter administration, 9, 363–386; alliance management in Asia during, 376–382, 383; China during, 367, 368–377, 379, 383–384, 385, 386, 389, 394; defense spending during, 363, 364, 381, 382; human rights concerns during, 363, 364, 367, 375, 377, 384, 385–386; Korea during, 367, 377–381, 383, 638n93; legacy in Asia strategy, 382–386; policy-making process in, 364; Presidential Review Memorandums during, 376, 378, 379; Reagan on, 387

Carter Doctrine, 365, 382

Casablanca Conference (1943), 197, 198, 208, 224

Castle, William Jr., 152

Catholic Church, 31, 38, 54, 65, 418, 419, 515

Ceausescu, Nicolae, 348

Center for Strategic and International Studies (CSIS), 174, 391; foreign policy survey (2009), 542; foreign policy survey (2014), 522, 542; forward posture strategy report (2012), 530–531

Central Intelligence Agency (CIA): and China policies, 347, 374; establishment of, 248; in Indonesia, 317, 613n243; and Japan policies, 317, 318; and Korea policies, 378, 379; and Soviet policies, 356

Cha, Victor, 285, 506

Cheney, Richard, 431, 445, 446, 484

Chen Guangcheng, 534

Chen Jian, 320

Chennault, Anna Chan, 331, 346, 395

Chennault, Claire, 210, 211, 331

Chen Shui-bian, 496

Chiang Ching-kuo, 377

Chiang Kai-shek, 152, 155, 179, 196, 210–218, 254–260; arms embargo affecting, 255, 260; in Cairo Conference, 212; during

Chiang Kai-shek (*cont.*)
  Eisenhower administration, 286, 295;
  loan request, 214; and Reagan, 394; white
  paper report on (1949), 259, 600n57
Chiang Mai Initiative, 476
Chile, 74
China, 6, 7–8, 10, 542–548, 561n45; and
  Adams, 30, 31, 33, 36, 37, 44; Air Defense
  Identification Zone of, 531; Amau
  Doctrine of Japan on, 156, 162, 165,
  171; arms sales to, 395–399; banking
  consortium in, 120, 121, 131, 146, 147;
  Boxer Rebellion in, 92, 95, 100, 123, 154;
  during Buchanan administration, 43,
  47; Burlingame Treaty (1868), 60, 77;
  during Bush (GHWB) administration,
  430–431, 433–439, 448; during Bush
  (GWB) administration, 427, 484, 485,
  489–490, 494–498, 500, 505–506, 509–510,
  525; in Cairo Conference, 212; during
  Carter administration, 367, 368–377,
  379, 383–384, 385, 386, 389, 394; and
  Chiang Kai-shek (*see* Chiang Kai-
  shek); during Clinton administration,
  426–427, 460, 462–463, 464, 469–473,
  476–478, 479, 481; collision of fishing
  boat with Japanese Coast Guard cutter
  (2010), 525; conclusions on historical
  and future strategies with, 542–548;
  and containment strategy, 259; and
  continental versus maritime strategies,
  7–8, 544–545; core interests of, 526, 544,
  681n47; Cultural Revolution in, 346, 348,
  355; Cushing as envoy to, 37–38; defense
  spending in, 469; Dennett on, 171; dollar
  diplomacy in, 118–122; during Eisenhower
  administration, 284, 285, 292, 295,
  612n234; during Ford administration, 361,
  362; foreign direct investment of Japan
  into, 147–148; during Gilded Age, 93; and
  "good offices" policy, 67–68, 70; Grant on,
  67, 68; Grew on, 164; and Guam Doctrine,
  342; during Hoover administration,
  154–155; Hornbeck on, 160–163;
  immigrants in U.S. from, 100; Japan

in, 69, 72, 112, 126–127, 152, 187; during
  Johnson administration, 317, 319, 320–321;
  joint communiqué with U.S. (1978), 371,
  636n54; during Kennedy administration,
  319–320; in Korean War, 278, 605n136;
  and Lamont economic strategies, 145–148;
  in Lend-Lease program, 210, 211, 254;
  MacMurray on, 166–169; Mahan on, 81,
  82, 92, 93, 107, 548; maritime strategies of,
  424; Marshall as commissioner to, 39–41,
  42; during McKinley administration,
  92–96; military relationship with U.S., 374;
  missile capabilities of, 529; missionaries
  in, 32–33, 43, 93; Morgenthau financial
  assistance plan on, 160, 163; in
  multipolarity strategy of Nixon, 326;
  Near Sea Doctrine (2008), 529; neutrality
  policy of U.S. on, 254, 262; during Nixon
  administration, 13, 42, 246, 323, 326, 329,
  342, 344, 345–359, 365; normalization
  of relations with France, 314;
  normalization of relations with Japan,
  350; normalization of relations with U.S.,
  365, 368, 369–372, 376, 383, 384, 389, 394;
  and North Korean nuclear programs,
  505–506; nuclear weapons of, 291, 469;
  during Obama administration, 423–425,
  521–534, 537, 538–540, 679n23; Open Door
  policy (*see* Open Door policy); Parker
  on, 43–46, 47; Perry on, 47, 50, 55; during
  Pierce administration, 45, 47, 48; and post-
  WWII plans, 208–218, 227; public opinion
  on, 214, 320; Qing Empire in, 34–47
  (*See also* Qing Empire); during Reagan
  administration, 393, 394–400, 420–421; as
  responsible stakeholder, 497; rise of, 1, 5,
  8, 13–14, 423–540; during Roosevelt (TR)
  administration, 96–97, 105–106, 107–108;
  self-determination in, 10, 37, 124, 125,
  167; Seward on, 58, 59, 60–64; Shanghai
  Communiqué (1972), 352–354; in Sino-
  French War, 65; in Sino-Japanese War,
  67, 82; Strategic and Economic Dialogue
  (S&ED) with, 525–526, 534; as strategic
  competitor, 484, 485; Strategic Economic

Dialogue (SED) with, 498, 525, 672n73; as strategic partner, 473, 477–478, 481, 484, 497, 525, 526, 544; strategic reassurance of, 525, 530; Summer Olympics in (2008), 495; table tennis team of U.S. in (1971), 349; during Taft administration, 118–122; Taiping Rebellion in, 38, 40, 41, 46–47, 55, 58; tariff autonomy of, 152, 160, 167, 186; Third Communiqué issued with U.S., 397, 398, 449; Tiananmen Square incident in, 430, 431, 433, 435–436, 438; trade with Japan, 121, 282; Treaty of Shimonoseki, 69–70; Treaty of Tientsin, 47, 60, 66, 67; during Truman administration, 253–263; Twenty-One Demands from Japan, 125, 154; unification plan for, 253, 256, 259; U.S. aircraft and crew held by, 489; Vietnam invasion by (1979), 375; in Vietnam War, 288, 308–309, 311, 320–321, 331–332, 346–347, 351, 624n35; visas for students in U.S. from, 437; war with India (1962), 319; and Washington Treaty System, 137, 140–141, 144; white paper report on (1949), 258–261; during Wilson administration, 116, 123–131, 146, 159, 185; in World Trade Organization, 427, 472, 479; Yalta Conference on, 215–216; Yuan Shikai as provisional president of, 121, 123, 125

China, and Japan policies, 7–8, 55, 544–545; during Bush (GHWB) administration, 430; during Clinton administration, 477–478; Grew on, 164, 225; during Hoover administration, 153–155; Hornbeck on, 160–163; MacMurray on, 165–169; Mahan on, 7, 81–82, 184; during Nixon administration, 345, 348, 350, 357–358, 545; during Obama administration, 524–528; during Reagan administration, 400; during Roosevelt (FDR) administration, 7–8, 156, 209, 225, 238; during Roosevelt (TR) administration, 7, 132, 187; during Taft administration, 102, 121–122; during Truman administration, 251

China, and Soviet Union policies: during Carter administration, 368–376, 383–384; during Nixon administration, 346–352, 353, 356, 358, 359; during Reagan administration, 395, 396, 398–399; during Roosevelt (FDR) administration, 208, 209

China, and trade with U.S., 148, 349, 374, 437–438, 576n85; early strategies in, 19–24, 26, 27, 30, 33, 34–37, 42, 50, 54; exports of U.S. in, 148, 576n85; most favored nation status in, 60, 87, 94. *See also* most favored nation status in China–U.S. relations

China Aid Act (1948), 257

China Air Force (CAF), 211

Chinese Civil War, 117, 144, 254–262; white paper report on (1949), 258–261, 600n57

Chinese Communist Party (CCP), 214–215, 217, 218, 254–262; in Korea, 262; lost opportunity with, 217, 591–592n138; People's Liberation Army of, 286, 295; Soviet support of, 257, 261

Chinese Eastern Railroad, 120

Chinese Exclusion Act (1882), 100

Chinese Nationalists, 214–217, 254–260; arms embargo on, 255, 260; during Clinton administration, 470–471; during Eisenhower administration, 286, 295; in Formosa, 258, 286; during Hoover administration, 152–153; Hornbeck on, 160, 167; MacMurray on, 165, 167; during Reagan administration, 420; during Roosevelt (FDR) administration, 179; on Taiwan (*see* Taiwan)

Cho Man-sik, 266

Christensen, Tom, 498

Christopher, Warren, 448, 456, 457–458, 513, 525; and China policies, 462, 463, 470–471; and Japan policies, 477

"Chrysanthemum Club," 264

Chun Doo-hwan, 416–417, 419

Churchill, Winston, 10; and Atlantic Charter, 188–189, 192, 235; on Britain in India, 231; in Cairo Conference, 212; in Casablanca Conference, 224; Roosevelt meetings with, 188–189, 191, 195, 198, 231, 235; on strategic priorities in WWII, 196,

Churchill (*cont.*)
197; in Tehran Conference, 212; in Yalta Conference, 220–221, 235
civil service reform in Gilded Age, 76
Clark, George Rogers, 25, 26
Clark, William (in Reagan administration), 392, 396, 450
Clark, William (in western exploration with Lewis), 26, 27
Clark Air Base, 270; during Bush (GHWB) administration, 446; during Carter administration, 379; during Reagan administration, 417
Clausewitz, Carl von, 1, 3
Clay, Cassius, 61, 62, 64
Cleveland, Grover, 71–72, 75
Clifford, Clark, 269, 365
climate change, 520, 524, 527
Clinton, Hillary, 303, 528; Asia trip (2009), 520, 524, 533; *Foreign Policy* article (2011), 520–521, 524, 532, 533
Clinton, William Jefferson, 13, 328, 426–427, 453–481
Clinton administration, 426–427, 453–481; Asian financial crisis and strategic focus during, 473–480; Bottom-up-Review (BUR) during, 459; economic nationalism during, 455–456, 460, 468, 469, 535; engagement and enlargement strategy during, 458–464, 469, 471; foreign policy experts in, 455–458; foreign policy objectives during, 454; forward presence strategy during, 468; India policies during, 415; legacy in Asia strategy, 480–481; "malaise" memo during, 465, 468; multilateralism strategy during, 463–464, 465, 468, 663–664n71; National Security Strategy during, 459–460; troop force numbers during, 459, 468; Washington Consensus versus Asian values during, 474–475
coaling stations, 41, 46, 48, 51, 55, 65, 73, 77, 132; Hawaii as, 81, 88; during McKinley administration, 87, 88, 89, 90, 92; Samoa as, 89
Cohen, Warren, 52–53, 162, 249, 438

Cold War era, 13, 189, 222, 223, 228, 245, 246, 247, 252–253; Bush (GHWB) policies after, 433, 439–451, 452; Bush (GWB) policies after, 482; Carter policies during, 364, 376; Clinton policies after, 453, 454, 455, 459, 460, 471, 481; defense perimeter in, 283; definition of Asia during, 15; end of, 425, 429, 432, 433, 442, 444, 453; Europe versus Asia during, 6, 128; forward posture after, 445–447; island stepping stones in, 207; Japan during, 246, 293, 294, 344, 433, 442; Korea during, 233, 246, 274–278, 466, 469; managing new dynamics and unfinished business of, 447–451; Nixon policies during, 339, 344, 359, 421, 469; nuclear weapons during, 295; Philippines during, 361; Reagan policies during, 13, 246, 387, 388, 406, 407; search for strategy after, 425–428; tolerance of authoritarianism during, 10; Vietnam during, 271, 316
Cold Warriors, 264, 324, 519
Columbia River, 25, 26, 27, 30, 33–34
Columbia (USS), 23, 25, 31
Columbus (USS), 48
Combined Chiefs of Staff (CCS), 192, 196, 198, 203, 204
Commerce and Navigation Treaty with Japan (1911), 122, 177, 178
communism, 1, 5, 10, 13, 151; Acheson strategies against, 241, 249; in China, 238, 241, 245, 254–262, 281, 284, 285, 292 (*see also* Chinese Communist Party); domino theory on, 287, 298, 306, 315, 610n210; Eisenhower strategies against, 284, 285, 287, 289, 292; and Europe first strategy, 238; in Greece and Turkey, 256, 257, 260; and Japan policies, 264, 265; Johnson policies against, 321; Kennan strategies against, 270, 276, 277; Kennedy strategies against, 299, 300, 301, 303; Nixon and Kissinger strategies against, 324; Reagan strategies against, 388, 391, 416, 421; Rusk strategies against, 250, 303; San Francisco System in containment of, 281–282;

Truman Doctrine on, 256; in Vietnam, 246, 296, 314

Concert of Europe, 56, 104, 325

concession doctrine, 60

Conger, Edwin, 92

Connally, John, 328, 342

constitutional system of U.S., 2–3

containment strategy, 246, 259; of Carter administration, 384; of Eisenhower administration, 284, 285, 291; Korean War in, 276; of Reagan administration, 407; San Francisco System in, 281–282

Contemporary Politics in the Far East (Hornbeck), 159

continental versus maritime strategies, 7–8, 544–545; of Perry and Marshall, 7, 48, 55; during Roosevelt (FDR) administration, 7–8, 184, 207–210; during Roosevelt (TR) administration, 105, 108, 187; during Truman administration, 251

Cook, James, 21, 25–26

Coolidge, Calvin, 138, 143, 144, 183

Coral Sea, Battle of, 197, 198

Corbett, Julian Stafford, 79

Cornwallis, Charles, 23

Cornwallis (HMS), 35, 38

Corregidor Island, 196; and War Plan Orange, 134, 175, 176

Costin, W.C., 42

cotton trade, 30

Crane, Charles R., 159

Crimean War, 49, 62, 64

Cronin, Patrick, 468, 469

Cuba, 86

Cultural Revolution, 346, 348, 355

culture, strategic, 4, 5, 190

Cunard, Samuel, 30–31

Currie, Laughlin, 230

Curry, Roy Watson, 130

Cushing, Caleb, 36, 37–38, 42, 43, 44, 46, 54, 55, 59, 186

Cutter, W. Bowman, 455

Dai Bing-guo, 497–498

Dalai Lama, 438, 495, 534

Dallek, Robert, 210, 221

Davies, John Paton, 192, 212–214, 218, 233, 251, 252, 598n19; and China policies, 261, 601n68; and Japan policies, 263, 264; in McCarthy era, 320; and Southeast Asia policies, 270

Davis, Cushman, 88

defensive realism, 6, 76

de Gaulle, Charles, 314

Democracy in America (de Tocqueville), 3

Democratic Party, 71, 156

Democratic People's Republic of Korea (DPRK), 267. *See also* North Korea

democratic values, 9–10, 546–547; in Bush (GHWB) administration policies, 435, 436; in Bush (GWB) administration policies, 513–516; in Obama administration policies, 532–535; in Reagan administration policies, 415–421; Shultz on, 390, 391, 416, 420

Deng Xiaoping, 424; during Bush (GHWB) administration, 434–436; during Carter administration, 370, 371, 372, 373, 375, 383; during Reagan administration, 397, 399–400; visit to U.S. (1979), 373, 375

Dennett, Tyler, 2, 24, 42, 48–49, 52, 64, 170–172; *Americans in Eastern Asia*, 2, 170; on Open Door Policy, 52, 170; on Taft-Katsura agreement, 569n86; on Washington Treaty System, 142, 170

depression era, 113, 149, 153, 154, 234

Derian, Patricia, 365

Desai, Morarji, 384

Destler, I. M., 408

Deutch, John, 461

Dewey, George, 75, 131; and Spanish–American War, 86–87, 88, 90

Dewey, Thomas E., 258, 279–280

dictatorships, Reagan administration policies on, 416–421

Diem, Ngo Dinh, 296, 307

Dienbienphu, 288–289

Dieterichs, Otto von, 90

Diplomacy (Kissinger), 96

disarmament, 136–144, 154, 173. *See also* arms control

Discovery (HMS), 25

Dixon, Alan, 445

Dodge, Joseph, 265

Dole, Sanford, 72, 88

dollar diplomacy, 118–124, 146, 183, 185, 186

Dominican Republic, 309

domino theory, 287, 298, 306, 315, 610n210

Donilon, Thomas, 524, 526

Dorff, Robert, 157

Downes, John, 31

Dulles, John Foster, 262, 279–283; and Eisenhower, 284–294; and Kennedy, 299; and Korea strategies, 275–276; Pacific Pact proposal of, 281; in peace negotiations with Japan, 280; and San Francisco system, 279–283

Dulles, John Macy, 279

Dumbarton Oaks Conference (1944), 232

Dutch East Indies, 269, 270

Dwight, Timothy, 32

Eagleburger, Lawrence, 431, 436

East Asian Economic Community (EAEC), 451

East Asia Squadron of U.S. Navy, 31

East Asia Summit (EAS): during Bush (GWB) administration, 511–513, 517; during Obama administration, 521, 539

Easter Offensive (1972), 335, 336

East Indies, 14, 21–25, 30, 269, 270

Eckes, Alfred, 234

Eclipse of American Sea Power, The (Knox), 141

economic strategies, 185; Bretton Woods Conference on, 234, 236, 237; during Bush (GHWB) administration, 439–444; during Bush (GWB) administration, 482–483, 498, 502, 506–507, 510–513; during Clinton administration, 460–464, 473–476; in depression era, 153, 154; dollar diplomacy in, 118–124, 146, 183, 185, 186; embargo of Japan in, 154, 178, 180; in free trade versus protectionism,

10–11, 409, 535–539, 547–548; in Korea, 267, 268; of Lamont, 145–149, 151, 183; with military and ideological strategies, 11–12; of Morgenthau, 160, 163; during Nixon administration, 328, 338, 342–345; during Obama administration, 535–539, 548; in postwar Japan, 263–265; postwar planning on, 194, 226, 234–237; during Reagan administration, 408–411; supporting Chiang, 257

Eden, Anthony, 210, 293

Eisenhower, Dwight D., 245, 246, 284–296; on strategic priorities in WWII, 197

Eisenhower administration, 284–296; alliances during, 285–286, 289–291; China policies during, 284, 285, 292, 295, 612n234; defense spending during, 284, 291; domino theory during, 287, 315, 610n210; Japan policies during, 293–294; and Kennedy administration policies, 300; Korea policies during, 278, 284, 285–286, 287; legacy in Asia strategy, 291–296; New Look concept during, 285, 291, 295–296, 306, 333, 336, 338; Nixon as vice-president in, 286, 325–326, 343, 346; nuclear policies during, 285, 294–296; Solarium Project during, 284–285, 341, 608n191; Southeast Asia during, 287–293, 296, 314, 316, 329, 612–613n243; Soviet Union during, 284–285, 287–288, 292, 612n234

Ellis, Earl H. "Pete," 142–143, 175

Ellsberg, Daniel, 330

embargo: on arms for Chinese Nationalists, 255, 260; on Japan, 154, 178, 180

Embargo Act (1807), 26

Embick, Stanley, 176

Emmerson, John K., 264

Empress of China (merchant ship), 10, 22, 26

Empress of Russia (RMS), 147

Enterprise for ASEAN Initiative (EAI), 502

Enterprise (USS), 202

Essex (USS), 17–18, 27, 31, 47, 55, 199

ethnocentrism, 103

European Union, 511

Europe-first policies, 6–7, 238, 278, 544; and Asia-first policies in Obama administration, 519, 520–524; and Pacific-first policies in Roosevelt (FDR) administration, 194–199

Evarts, William, 64

Everett, Edward, 48

expansionism: of France, 65; of Japan, 68, 82, 117, 132, 146, 164, 171, 183; precursors to (1861–1898), 56–77; in Roosevelt era, 103, 104, 106; of Russia, 64, 65, 85; of Soviet Union, 221

Fairbanks, Richard, 413

Fang Lizhi, 434–435, 438

Far East Squadron of U.S. Navy, 33, 35, 39, 41, 48

Farragut, David Glasgow, 17–18

Fearey, Robert, 263

Feldstein, Martin, 409

financial crisis in Asia, during Clinton administration, 474–476, 477, 501, 511, 665n105

First Great Triumph (Zimmerman), 78

First Island Chain, 207, 297, 322, 424, 545; during Eisenhower administration, 294; and Kennan strategies, 272, 283; military buildup and claims of China in, 8; during Obama administration, 531, 539; during Roosevelt (TR) administration, 92

First World War, 112, 116, 117, 128, 129–130; entry of U.S. into, 126, 146; postwar negotiations, 128–129; and Washington Treaty System, 136, 137, 144

Fish, Hamilton, 60–61, 65

Five Power Treaty, 140, 141, 144, 152

Flamm, Kenneth, 455

Floyd, John, 28

flying geese theory, 318

Flying Tigers, 210

Foote, Andrew, 45

Ford, Carl, 445, 446

Ford, Gerald, 335, 355, 360–362

Ford administration, 360–362; New Pacific Doctrine of, 362; Reagan on, 387

Fordney-McCumber tariff (1922), 149

Formosa, 55, 65, 67, 69; Cairo Conference on, 233; Chinese Nationalists in, 258, 286; coal deposits of, 46, 48; during Eisenhower administration, 286; neutrality policy on, 262; post-WWII plans on, 233

Forrestal, James, 191, 193, 206, 222, 251–252; and China policies, 254; and Japan policies, 225–226, 263–264; and Korea policies, 267; on SWNCC, 193, 225; and Vietnam policies, 307

Forrestal, Michael, 251, 300

Fortis, Abe, 311

forward defense line, 8–9, 184, 190, 427, 545–546; during Adams administration, 30; during Bush (GHWB) administration, 445–447; Hawaii as, 8, 184; during Johnson administration, 321; Kennan on, 272–274; during McKinley administration, 91–92; during Obama administration, 528–532; during Reagan administration, 8, 421; during Roosevelt (TR) administration, 8, 79, 105; in Spykman rimland concept, 209, 225, 277

Foster, John Watson, 279

Four Freedoms, 233

Four Power Treaty, 140–141

Fourteen Points of Wilson, 128, 229, 234

France, 20, 561n43; Catholic missionaries from, 38, 54; in China, 35, 39, 46, 47; in Crimean War, 49, 62; expansionism of, 65; in Franco-Prussian War, 65, 87; in French and Indian War, 24; Germany in, 178, 179; during Hoover administration, 155; in Indochina, 65–66, 111, 179–180, 231–232, 288–289, 306; Louisiana Territory purchased from, 26; in Mexico, 56; naval strength of, 50, 174; normalization of relations with China, 314; in post-revolutionary war era in U.S., 21, 24; and Rainbow Plans, 177; in SEATO, 289, 290; in Second Opium War, 38, 45; Seward concern about, 58, 59, 67; in Southeast Asia, 268, 269–271, 288–289;

France (*cont.*)
    during Taft administration, 120–121; in
    Triple Intervention, 69–70; during Tyler
    administration, 71; and Washington
    Treaty System, 140; during Wilson
    administration, 127
Franco-Prussian War, 65, 87
Freeman, Charles, 457
Free Trade Area of the Pacific (FTAAP), 511
free trade versus protectionism, 10–11, 409,
    535–539, 547–548
French and Indian War, 24
Friedberg, Aaron, 652n2
Friedrich, K. Marlin, 160
Friendship (merchant ship), 31
Fukuyama, Francis, 426
Fulda Gap, 6
Funabashi Yoichi, 465–466, 519
fur trade, 19, 23, 25, 26–27, 30
Fu Ying, 505

G-7 summits, 406, 412, 461
G-20 summits, 511, 536
Gaddis, John Lewis, 5–6, 250, 261, 279, 545;
    on post-Cold War era, 432; on Reagan,
    388; on strategic surprise, 470
Galbraith, John Kenneth, 300, 307
Gallicchio, Marc, 222
Gandhi, Indira, 359, 384, 415
Gandhi, Mohandas, 231
Gardner, Richard, 236
Garfield, James, 71, 79
Gates, Bob, 522
Gelb, Leslie H., 3, 305–306, 312
General Agreement on Tariffs and Trade
    (GATT), 399, 410, 434, 438, 440, 441
General Arbitration Treaty, 139
General Sherman (merchant ship), 62, 68
Gentleman's Agreement (1907), 100, 144
Germany, 6; as Axis power, 178; Bismarck
    in, 65, 73; British-U.S. alliance against,
    179; and Europe first versus Pacific first
    strategies, 194–198; in First World War,
    124–125; in Franco-Prussian War, 65, 87;
    Japan taking territories of, 125; during

McKinley administration, 87, 88, 89,
    90; and Meiji government in Japan,
    67; Pacific acquisitions of, 65, 70; in
    Philippines, 90; postwar planning on, 193,
    194, 226; public opposition to war against,
    180–181; rise in power of, 65; in Samoa,
    73, 89; in Triple Intervention, 69–70;
    unconditional surrender of, 224; during
    Wilson administration, 124–125, 126, 129
Ghent, Treaty of, 27, 554–555n27
Giap, VoNgien, 288, 360
Gilbert Islands, 203
Gilded Age, 56–77; Anglo-Saxonism in,
    75–76; civil service and military reform
    in, 76; "good offices" policy during, 96;
    naval power in, 74–75, 104; strategic
    lessons from, 76–77
ginseng trade, 22
Global Disarmament Conference (1932), 154
Goh, Evelyn, 320, 471
Goldwater, Barry, 308, 329, 372, 388
Good Earth, The (Buck), 210
Goodnow, Frank J., 166
"good offices" policy, 57, 67–68, 70, 73, 77, 96
Gorbachev, Mikhail, 388, 399, 412, 413, 414
Gore, Al, 456, 476
Gore, John, 21
Gorshkov, Sergey, 400
grand strategies, 2–12; China versus Japan
    in, 7–8, 544–545; compared to military
    strategy, 2; continental versus maritime
    strategies in, 7–8, 544–545; definitions
    and concepts of Asia in, 14–15; Europe
    versus Asia in, 6–7, 544; forward defense
    line in, 8–9, 545–546; free trade versus
    protectionism in, 10–11, 547–548; in
    isolationist eras, 3; long-term and
    short-term goals in, 2; realist or idealist
    premises as basis of, 3; self-determination
    versus universal values in, 9–10, 546–547;
    vital and secondary interests in, 2. *See
    also specific strategies*
Grand Strategy of the Byzantine Empire The
    (Luttwak), 3
Grant, Ulysses S., 63, 67, 68, 70

Graves, William S., 127

Gray, Robert, 25, 26

Great Kantō earthquake (1923), 148

Great Leap Forward, 292

"Great White Fleet" of Roosevelt, 101, 112

Greece, anti-communism efforts in, 256, 257, 260

Green, Marshall, 326–327, 333, 338; and China policies, 347, 348, 349, 350, 352, 357; and Japan policies, 342, 350, 357; and Shanghai Communiqué, 352, 631n154

Green, Michael J., 483, 484, 491, 500, 668n6, 669n29, 680n33; on ASEAN Regional Forum, 513; and China policies, 497; at Clinton dinner, 524; on democracy promotion, 514; and India policies, 499–500; and JADE Act, 677n136; and Japan policies, 468, 469, 511; and Korea policies, 494, 503, 504, 674n95, 674n99; on multilateral institution building, 510; and Taiwan policies, 496; and Vietnam policies, 515

Greeneville (USS), 487

Gregg, Don, 392

Grew, Joseph, 158, 163–165, 169, 170, 177; Acheson on, 249; on Amau Doctrine, 156; "green light" cable from (1940), 164, 180; and Hornbeck, 158, 160, 163, 164; on Hurley, 215; and Japan policies, 192, 225, 226, 263; and Soviet Union policies, 221, 222

Griswold, Whitney, 130

group of 7 (G-7) summits, 406, 412, 461

group of 20 (G-20) summits, 511, 536

Guadalcanal, 198, 202

Guadalupe-Hidalgo, Treaty of (1848), 34

Guam, 70; annexation of, 8, 89; during Obama administration, 529, 531; and War Plan Orange, 133, 134, 135

Guam Doctrine, 8, 328, 329, 336–345, 349, 350, 357, 545; during Obama administration, 530, 539

"Guano Law," 62

Guano War, 74

Gulf of Tonkin crisis (1965), 298, 308, 617n49

Gulf War, 432, 433, 438, 443, 492, 493

Gyanendra, King of Nepal, 514–515

Haas, Richard, 481

Habib, Phil, 242, 335

Hadley, Stephen, 489, 499, 522

Hagel, Timothy "Chuck," 527

Hague Peace Conference (1899), 96–97

Haig, Alexander, 328, 333, 347, 359, 389–390, 391; and China policies, 394–397; and Philippines policies, 417; resignation of, 390, 392, 396

Haiphong Harbor, mining of, 333, 625n44

Halberstam, David, 304, 305

Hale, Eugene, 79

Halperin, Morton, 328

Halsey, William "Bull," 202

Hammes, T. X., 530

Hardesty, Huntington, 445

Harding, Harry, 438

Harding, Warren G., 138, 143, 183

Harding administration, 112, 141, 143

Harkins, Paul, 307

Harriman, Averell, 119, 191, 216, 252; in Johnson administration, 304, 314; in Kennedy administration, 304, 306, 307; on Soviet Union strategies, 221, 222, 224

Harriman, E. H., 119–120, 122

Harriman, Mary, 119–120, 122

Harris, Townsend, 49, 54

Harrison, Benjamin, 72, 75, 79

Hart, Thomas C., 177–178

Hasegawa, Tsuyoshi, 202

Hashimoto Ryutaro, 462, 471

Hatoyama Ichirō, 293, 294

Hatoyama Yukio, 294, 527

Hawaii: during Adams administration, 31; annexation of, 5, 8, 62, 71, 72, 88–89, 91, 106, 112; as coaling station, 81, 88; coup attempt against Queen Liliuokalani in, 72, 81; as defensive line, 8, 184; early U.S. assertions of interest in, 53, 54, 57; and island stepping stones, 70–72, 73, 77; Japanese immigrants in, 72, 81; Mahan on, 81, 82, 83, 112; missionaries in, 31, 32,

Hawaii (*cont.*)
65; Monroe Doctrine extended to, 5, 20, 31–32, 53, 70, 87; Pearl Harbor attack in (1941), 4, 6, 142, 149, 158, 195, 196; Perry on, 48; reciprocity treaty with, 83; in Roosevelt era, 82; sandalwood in, 20, 23; Seward on, 58, 62; tariff reduction agreements with, 10; and War Plan Orange, 133, 134, 176, 177

"Hawaii and Our Future Sea Power" (Mahan), 81

Hawke, Bob, 414, 450

Hay, John, 19, 60, 78, 89, 90, 358n11; and Open Door policy, 42, 92, 93–96, 105–106, 121–122, 123, 183

Hayes, Rutherford B., 68, 563n65

Hayward, Thomas Bibb, 381–382, 384, 400–401

Hearst, William Randolph, 86

Heer, Paul, 273

Heinrichs, Waldo, 248

Herbert, Hilary A., 70, 80

Hermit Kingdom, 63, 68, 69. *See also* Korea

Herring, George C., 93, 103–104, 136, 233, 363

Herter, Christian, 277, 294

Hiatt, Fred, 533

Higuchi Commission report, 468

Hill, Christopher, 506, 507, 508

Hills, Carla, 440–441

Hilsman, Roger, 304, 306, 307, 308, 312, 315, 320

Hirohito, Emperor, 226

Hiss, Alger, 325

Hitler, Adolph, 176, 180, 194, 195, 197, 219

Ho Chi Minh, 185, 269–271, 320

Hodge, John R., 266

Hoehn, Andrew, 509

Holbrooke, Richard, 367; and alliance management in Asia, 376, 377, 378; and China policies, 369; and Korea policies, 377–378, 507; and Vietnam policies, 375, 384

Holdridge, John H., 347, 392, 395, 396, 397

Holland, in Southeast Asia, 268, 269, 270

Hoopes, Townsend, 312, 313

Hoover administration, 156; China and Japan policies during, 154–155, 162, 167; defense spending during, 173, 183

Hopkins, Harry, 191, 206

Hornbeck, Stanley, 111, 158, 159–163, 170, 171, 177, 180; on Davies, 213; and Grew, 158, 160, 163, 164; "hands-off approach" of, 163, 171; and MacMurray, 165–167, 169

Hornet (USS), 202

House, Edward, 116, 125–126, 128

Howard, John, 492, 512

Hu, Shizhang, 163

Hua Guofeng, 370

Hubbard, Thomas, 493

Hudson Bay Company, 26

Hughes, Charles Evans, 138–140, 143, 144, 147, 149, 170

Hu Jintao, 495, 496, 497, 525, 526

Hukbalahap insurrection, 270, 288

Hull, Cordell, 156, 158, 177, 191, 192, 193, 195; and post-WWII plans, 225, 230, 232, 235, 236; and Soviet attack on Japan, 219, 220

human rights concerns, 547; during Bush (GHWB) administration, 434–436, 437; during Bush (GWB) administration, 495, 513–516; during Carter administration, 363, 364, 367, 375, 377, 384, 385–386; during Clinton administration, 462–463, 472, 479, 481; during Obama administration, 532–535

Hunt, William, 79

Huntington Wilson, Francis M., 102, 108, 119, 120, 121, 123, 146, 159

Hurley, Patrick, 215–216, 255

Hussein, Saddam, 429, 433, 438, 441, 442–443

Hu Yaobang, 399, 434, 435

Hwang Jang-yop, 467

idealism, 10; of Carter, 364; compared to realism as strategy basis, 3; of Roosevelt (FDR), 191; of Wilson, 185

Ikeda Hayato, 317, 342

immigration: Alien Exclusion Act (1924) on, 144; and antiracism clause of League of Nations, 128–129; of Chinese, 100, 124;

Gentleman's Agreement on, 100, 144; of Japanese, 72, 81, 100, 124

Imperial German Navy, 65, 73

imperialism: British, 229, 230, 231; economic, 2, 6, 76, 103, 234; during McKinley administration, 91

Imperial Japanese Army, 153

Imperial Japanese Navy, 107, 111; and War Plan Orange, 132, 134–135; and Washington Treaty System, 141, 142; during WWII, 201, 204

Independence (USS), 470

India, 15, 30; Britain in, 231, 269; during Bush (GHWB) administration, 415, 449–450; during Bush (GWB) administration, 415, 427, 485–486, 490, 498–500, 514–515; during Carter administration, 384; independence of, 231, 269; left flank approach from, 199–200; in Nixon strategies, 326, 358–359; during Obama administration, 523; postwar policies on, 231, 235; during Reagan administration, 359, 389, 414–415, 421; war with China (1962), 319; war with Pakistan, 358–359

Indianapolis (USS), 156

Indochina: during Eisenhower administration, 287–291; France in, 65–66, 111, 179–180, 231–232, 288–289, 306; during Kennedy administration, 299; during Roosevelt (FDR) administration, 231–232. *See also specific countries*

Indochina Migration and Refugee Assistance Act (1975), 360–361

Indonesia: and Asian regionalism, 413; during Bush (GWB) administration, 490, 501, 502–503; CIA efforts in, 613n243; during Eisenhower administration, 287; independence of, 269; during Johnson administration, 316, 317; during Kennedy administration, 300, 316–317; meeting of nonaligned nations in (1955), 292–293; nationalism in, 300; during Reagan administration, 411, 649n124; Sukarno as President of, 300

industrialization, 57, 318

Influence of Sea Power on History, The (Mahan), 80, 106, 112

Inouye Junosuke, 147, 148, 149, 153

Intermediate Nuclear Forces (INF), 406

International Bank for Reconstruction and Development, 236

International Monetary Fund (IMF), 236, 475, 476

Inukai Tsuyoshi, 155

Iran: during Bush (GHWB) administration, 434; during Carter administration, 381, 418; during Johnson administration, 309; during Obama administration, 519, 521, 523; during Reagan administration, 387

Iran-Contra controversy (1986), 387

Iraq, 6, 415; during Bush (GHWB) administration, 432, 443; during Bush (GWB) administration, 482, 483, 486, 492–494, 500, 501, 503, 505, 506, 509; during Obama administration, 520; Operation Iraqi Freedom (OIF) in, 492, 493

Iriye, Akira, 178–179, 182

Iroquois (USS), 79, 82

Isaacson, Walter, 337

Ishii Kikujirō, 126–127

Ishiwara Kanji, 153

isolationist policies, 3, 6, 181

Italy: as Axis power, 178; British-U.S. alliance against, 179; naval strength of, 174; public opposition to war against, 180–181; and Washington Treaty System, 140

Itō, Masayoshi, 404–405

Iwo Jima, 204, 205

"jackal diplomacy," 23, 53

Jackson, Andrew, 31, 43

Jackson-Vanick Trade Act amendment, 374, 437

JADE Act (2008), 515, 677n136

Japan, 6, 7–8; Amau Doctrine of, 156, 162, 165, 171; anti-imperialism in, 10; antiracism clause proposed by, 116, 128–129, 130; Article 9 in constitution of, 293, 326; and Asian regionalism, 412, 413;

Japan (*cont.*)

as Axis power, 178, 182; Biddle mission to, 47–48, 54; British surrender at Singapore to (1942), 196; Brzezinski interest in, 366; during Bush (GHWB) administration, 426, 430, 433–434, 439–445; during Bush (GWB) administration, 427, 484–485, 486–488, 491–493, 500; during Carter administration, 371, 376, 377, 379, 380–382, 383, 386, 639n111; checkbook diplomacy of, 443; in China, 69, 72, 112, 126–127, 152; during Clinton administration, 426–427, 455–456, 460–462, 463, 464, 467–469, 471–472, 476–478, 480; collision of Chinese fishing boat with Japanese Coast Guard cutter (2010), 525; and continental versus maritime strategies, 7–8, 544–545; defense spending in, 381, 442; Dennett on, 171, 173; development assistance funding by, 442; disarmament and democratization policies on, 263, 264; in East Asia Summit, 511; during Eisenhower administration, 293–294; embargo of, 154, 178, 180; and Europe first versus Pacific first strategies, 195–198; Executive Order freezing assets of, 111, 180; expansionism of, 68, 82, 117, 132, 146, 164, 171, 183; during First World War, 112, 124–125, 126; flying geese theory on industrialization in, 318; during Ford administration, 361, 362; foreign direct investment into China, 147–148; Glynn on, 48; Grant in, 68; Great Kantō earthquake (1923) in, 148; Grew on, 158, 164–165; and Guam Doctrine, 337, 339, 340, 341–345, 350, 357; Guidelines for Defense Cooperation with U.S., 380; Harris negotiations in, 49, 54; during Hoover administration, 152–156, 161–162; Hornbeck strategies on, 160–163; Huntington Wilson and Straight on, 102, 119; immigration from, 72, 100, 124, 144; in Indochina, 111; island defenses of, 199; Kennan strategies on, 273; during Kennedy and Johnson administrations, 317–318; in Korea, 68, 69, 99–100, 119, 120; Lamont economic strategies on, 145–149, 151; in League of Nations, 155–156; long-term U.S. military presence in, 207; MacMurray on, 158, 165, 167–169; Mahan on, 84, 91–92, 105, 184; during McKinley administration, 92–93, 95; Meiji era in, 59, 67, 69; Ministry of International Trade and Industry (MITI) in, 461; naval strength of, 173, 174, 175, 181, 195; during Nixon administration, 326, 337, 339–345, 348–349, 350, 352, 353, 356–358, 361; Nixon shocks to, 344, 358, 361, 380, 383, 410; normalization of relations with China, 350; normalization of relations with Korea, 298, 318; during Obama administration, 524–528; occupation of, 227, 252, 263, 281; Okinawa rape incident in (1995), 469, 487; Operation Matterhorn in, 211, 214; pact with Russia concerning Manchuria, 120, 121; *Panay* bombing by, 171; Pearl Harbor attack by (1941), 158, 195; Perry on, 7, 39, 47, 49, 50–51, 55, 66, 69; during Pierce administration, 48, 49; Plaza Accord with (1985), 410–411; and post-WWII plans, 192, 193, 194, 208–209, 213, 224–234; protectionism versus free trade with, 11; public opinion in U.S. on, 439–440; railroad assets of, 120; during Reagan administration, 246, 358, 389, 393, 399, 403–411, 412, 413, 421, 647n92; repatriation of shipwrecked sailors from, 43, 44; response to 9/11 attack, 491–493; response to Queen Liliuokalani coup attempt, 72, 81; rise of, 13, 111–239; during Roosevelt (FDR) administration, 111, 117, 156, 174–184, 199–205, 208–209, 224–227, 238; during Roosevelt (TR) administration, 82, 97–102, 104, 105, 107, 131–132, 186, 187; routes for military approach to, 199–205; Russia in, 64; in Russo-Japanese War, 78, 97–98, 101, 133, 187; sanctions against (1940), 164; and San Francisco System, 279, 280–283, 298; security treaties with

U.S. (*see* Japan–U.S. security treaties); *Seiyūkai* party in, 152, 155; Self Defense Forces of, 407, 467, 492; Seward on, 58, 59, 62; in Shandong, 125, 126, 128, 129, 130, 134; Shanghai attack (1932), 155, 162; and Shanghai Communiqué (1972), 353; Shufeldt on, 69; in Siberia, 127–128, 130; in Sino-Japanese War, 67; Soviet threat to, 152–153; Soviet Union joining fight against, 219–220; Stimson on, 153–154, 162; surrender of, 208, 224–225, 228, 254; during Taft administration, 102, 112, 118–122, 186; taking German territories, 125; tariff agreements with, 77; technology cooperation with U.S., 406; trade with China, 121, 282; trade with U.S. (*see* Japan–U.S. trade); Treaty of Commerce and Navigation with (1911), 177, 178; and Triple Intervention, 69–70; during Truman administration, 226–227, 252, 253, 263–265; Twenty-One Demands of China, 125, 154; and U.S. submarine incident, 487, 493; and War Plan Orange, 131–136, 173, 174–177, 181; and Washington Treaty System, 136–143, 577n104; during Wilson administration, 116, 123, 124–131

Japan, and China policies. *See* China, and Japan policies

Japan–U.S. security treaties, 607n175; Article V of, 477, 491, 525, 527–528; during Bush (GWB) administration, 491; during Clinton administration, 477; during Eisenhower administration, 293–294, 317; during Johnson administration, 317; during Nixon administration, 342; during Obama administration, 525, 527, 539; during Truman administration, 280–282

Japan–U.S. trade, 121, 138, 148, 152, 154, 177, 576n85; during Bush (GHWB) administration, 439–444, 451; during Clinton administration, 455–456, 460–462, 463; during Nixon administration, 342–344; during Reagan administration, 408–411, 440; during Roosevelt (FDR) administration, 177–178

Jay, John, 22, 24

Jay Treaty, 23

Jefferson, Thomas, 5, 9, 10, 25–27, 51

Jemaah Islamiya (JI), 501

Jiang Zemin, 470, 472, 477, 478, 489–490, 495, 496, 505, 525

Johnson, Andrew, 63

Johnson, Chalmers, 469

Johnson, Louis, 262, 274

Johnson, Lyndon Baines, 241, 246; not seeking reelection, 311. *See also* Johnson administration

Johnson, Nelson T., 152

Johnson, U. Alexis, 327, 357

Johnson administration (LBJ): Harriman in, 304; prestige of U.S. as concern during, 298; Rusk in, 303, 305, 315; Vietnam War during, 241–243, 246–247, 298, 303–322, 331

Joint Chiefs of Staff (JCS), 192, 193; China strategies, 211, 212, 214, 255–256, 272; Europe-first versus Pacific-first strategies, 196, 197–198; and Guam Doctrine, 340; Japan strategies, 265, 280, 343, 380; Korea strategies, 266, 275, 278, 378; on military routes to Japan during WWII, 199, 200, 201, 202, 203, 204; post-WWII strategies, 205–206, 207, 208, 230; Southeast Asia strategies, 289, 291; Soviet Union strategies, 220, 221, 222, 356; strategic plans for the Pacific, 272; Vietnam strategies, 307, 311

Joint Operational Access Concept (JOAC), 529

Joint Strategic Survey Committee (JSSC), 193, 230

Jomini, Henri, 79

Jo Myong-rok, 479

Jones Act (1916), 91, 124

Joseph, Robert, 503, 504, 507

J. P. Morgan Bank, 116, 145, 147, 149

Judd, Walter, 259

Jusserand, Jules, 98

Kadeer, Rebiya, 534

Kagan, Robert, 63

Kaifu Toshiki, 443, 493

Kalb, Bernard, 347

Kalb, Marvin, 347

Kamikaze attack by Japan, 204

Kanagawa Convention, 49

Kang Sok-ju, 503–504, 674n93

Kantor, Mickey, 456, 460, 462, 469; "Saturday Group" sessions of, 460–461

Katsura Tarō, 98, 99, 569n86

Katzenbach, Nicholas, 378

Kellogg, Frank, 144, 152, 165, 167, 186

Kellogg-Briand Treaty, 144, 155

Kelly, Jim, 393, 484, 488, 503, 505

Kennan, George Frost, 169, 213, 218, 250–251, 272–278; and Asian defense perimeter, 272–274; and China policies, 257, 258, 261, 262, 292, 600n57; and Guam Doctrine, 339, 340, 341; and Japan policies, 263, 264; and Korea policies, 267, 268, 273, 274, 275–277; "long telegram" and "Mr. X" article of, 250; maritime strategies of, 272–273, 302; and Solarium Project, 284–285; and Southeast Asia policies, 270, 313

Kennedy, John Fitzgerald, 246; assassination of, 307, 308. See also Kennedy administration

Kennedy, John P., 48

Kennedy, Joseph P., Sr., 300

Kennedy, Robert, 301, 308, 314

Kennedy administration: Basic National Security Policy (BNSP) during, 302, 320; Bay of Pigs operation during, 303, 306; carrot and stick approach during, 302; China during, 319–320; flexible response policy during, 299, 300, 301, 303, 306; Indonesia during, 300, 316–317; Laos during, 306; policy formation approach in, 301, 302; Soviet Union during, 319–320; Vietnam War during, 298–303, 305–307, 308, 312, 316

Kent State University, Vietnam War protest at, 334

Kerry, John, 524, 526

Keynes, John Maynard, 235

Keyson, Carl, 302

Khmer Rouge, 375, 384, 385, 449; *Mayaguez* seized by, 360

Khrushchev, Nikita, 292, 295, 301, 319

Kimball, Jeffrey, 337, 621–622n7

Kim Dae-jung, 416, 418, 479, 488, 503

Kim Il-sung, 223, 266, 267, 274, 276, 448, 466, 605n136; attack on South Korea, 277; death of, 467

Kim Jong-il, 479, 504

Kim Young-sam, 467

King, Ernest, 192–193; on China in WWII, 210; on Europe-first versus Pacific-first strategies, 196–198; on military routes to Japan during WWII, 201, 204; on post-WWII strategies, 206

Kipling, Rudyard, 85

Kirk, Ron, 536

Kirkpatrick, Jeane, 415–416

Kishi Nobusuke, 294, 342

Kissinger, Henry, 3, 7, 78, 96, 252, 520; on Concert of Europe, 325; on morality in foreign policy, 355, 542, 621n6; in Nixon administration, 324–360; opinions on Nixon, 96, 104, 325; on Roosevelt (TR) strategies, 104; on Tiananmen Square incident, 436

Kitty Hawk (USS), 493

KMT (Kuomintang), 216, 217, 295, 420, 470. *See also* Chinese Nationalists

Knox, D. W., 141

Knox, Frank, 178, 193, 195, 206

Knox, Philander Chase, 102, 118, 119, 120, 121

Koch, R. A., 173

Koizumi Junichiro, 487–488, 492–493, 512, 514, 676n130

Kojong (King of Korea), 68, 69

Kokoda Track, 198

Konoe Fumimaro, 180

Korea: authoritarianism in, 10; during Bush (GHWB) administration, 445–446, 447–448; during Bush (GWB) administration, 483, 488–489, 493–494, 503–510; during Carter administration, 367, 377–381, 383, 638n93; Chinese

Civil War affecting, 260; Chinese Communist Party in, 262; during Clinton administration, 466–467, 478–480; demilitarized zone in, 8; democratization in, 419–420; during Eisenhower administration, 278, 284, 285–286, 287; during Ford administration, 362; France in, 65–66, 561n43; *General Sherman* incident, 62, 68; and Guam Doctrine, 340; human rights issues in, 377, 416; independence of, 266; Japan dependence on resources in, 265; Japan in, 68–69, 99–100, 119, 120, 561n45; Kennan strategies on, 267, 268, 273, 274, 275–277; during Kennedy administration, 302; lack of planning of, 228, 233; long-term U.S. military presence in, 207; during Nixon administration, 340, 343, 344, 353; normalization of relations with Japan, 298, 318; occupation of, 266; partitioning of, 228, 233, 250, 266; post-WWII plans on, 233, 266; Potsdam Conference on, 233; proposed withdrawal of U.S. troops from, 377–379, 383; during Reagan administration, 389, 411, 413, 416–417, 418–420; during Roosevelt administration, 99–100, 105; Russia in, 64; Seward strategies on, 62, 66; Shufeldt opening trade with, 68–69, 561n45; Sino-Japanese War concerning, 67; Soviet Union in, 223, 266, 267, 268, 274; during Truman administration, 265–268, 274–278; U.S. Army vehicle accident in (2002), 493; withdrawal of U.S. troops from, 367, 445–446. *See also* North Korea; South Korea

Korean Airlines, 413

Korean War, 249, 250, 251, 275, 280; China in, 278, 605n136; Soviet Union in, 274, 278, 605n136; United Nations forces in, 276, 277, 278

KORUS Free Trade Agreement, 536

Kosygin, Aleksey, 320

Krauthammer, Charles, 388

Krepinevich, Andrew, 312, 532

Kristoff, Nick, 503

Kuehn, John, 142

Kuomintang (KMT), 216, 217, 295, 420, 470. *See also* Chinese Nationalists

Kurile Islands: during Eisenhower administration, 294; during Roosevelt (FDR) administration, 205, 206, 221–222; transfer to Russia, 221–222, 223; during Truman administration, 223

Kuwait, 429, 433, 438, 441, 442–443

Kwantung Army, 152, 153, 220, 223

Kyushū, 184, 204, 205

Lackawanna (USS), 62

Lady Washington, 23

LaFeber, Walter, 64

Laird, Melvin, 328, 332, 333, 336, 341

Lake, Tony: in Clinton administration, 455, 456, 458–459, 471; in Nixon administration, 328, 334, 455; in Obama administration, 519, 533

Lamont, Thomas W., 116, 145–149, 151, 153, 183

Lange, David, 414

Lansing, Robert, 126–127, 129, 131, 164, 279

Lansing-Ishii Agreement (1917), 126–127, 141, 146, 215

Laos, 65, 271, 329; during Kennedy administration, 306; neutralization strategy in, 306, 308; during Nixon administration, 331, 333

Laughton, John Knox, 79

League for Vietnamese Independence, 270

League of Nations, 130, 137, 146; antiracism clause in, 116, 128–129, 130; Japan leaving, 155–156; Manchuria investigation of, 155

Leahy, William D., 174, 176, 192, 205–206, 222, 225, 226

Ledyard, John, 21, 25–26

Lee, Henry, 22

Lee Hsien Loong, 424

Lee Jeong-seok, 494

Lee Kuan Yew, 317, 390, 407, 502–503, 523, 619n98

Lee Myung-bak, 525, 536

Lee Teng-hui, 470

Lehman, John F., 401–402

Lejeune, John, 143

Lend-Lease program, 179, 235, 236, 239; Britain in, 211; China in, 210, 211, 254; India in, 231; Soviet Union in, 211, 221

Levant (USS), 45

Levine, Steven, 259–260

Lewis, Meriwether, 26, 27

Lexington (USS), 142, 202

Libby, Lewis "Scooter," 486, 508

Li Gun, 505, 507, 508

Li Hongzhang, 67, 68

Liliuokalani, Queen, 72, 81

Lilley, James, 392, 416, 419, 431, 448

Lincoln, Abraham, 56, 57, 59

Lind, Michael, 317

Lin Piao, 257

Lippmann, Walter, 3, 140, 144, 155, 181, 296; on Japan, 264; on Soviet Union, 221; *U.S. Foreign Policy: Shield of the Republic*, 191–192, 221

Locke, Edwin Jr., 254, 255

Lodge, Henry Cabot, 78, 79, 91, 98, 101

Lodge, Henry Cabot, Jr., 331

Logevall, Fredrik, 271

London Treaty, 152

Long, Breckenridge, 146

Long, John D., 86

Lord, Bette Bao, 328

Lord, Winston: in Bush (GHWB) administration, 435, 436, 438; in Clinton administration, 455, 456, 462, 463, 465, 472; entering China, 349, 370; "malaise" memo from, 465, 468; in Nixon administration, 328, 338–339, 340, 342, 349

Louisiana Purchase, 26

Lowell, Lawrence A., 162

Luce, Stephen, 79

Lusitania (RMS), 126

Luttwak, Edward, 3–4

Lytton Report, 155

MacArthur, Douglas, 15, 175, 178, 180, 206, 237; on Formosa policy, 262; and Korea strategies, 276, 278; in occupation of Japan, 252, 263; popularity of, 200;

on post-WWII Japan, 227; requesting Soviet attack on Japan, 219; and routes to Japan during WWII, 200–205; strategic priorities in WWII, 196, 198–199

MacArthur, Douglas II, 343

Mackenzie, Alexander, 25

Mackinder, Halford, 7, 208, 209, 221

MacMurray, James Van Antwerp, 158, 159, 165–169, 170, 171, 181, 250

MacMurray, Junius W., 166

MacMurray Memo, 158, 165–169, 171, 250, 545

Madison, James, 22, 27, 32

Mahan, Alfred Thayer, 79–86, 104–106, 107, 151; on China, 81, 82, 92, 93, 107, 548; in Hague Peace Conference, 96–97; *The Influence of Sea Power on History* (Mahan), 80, 106, 112; on Japan, 100, 105; maritime strategies of, 7, 51, 75, 79–88, 97, 106, 112, 184, 204; on moral influence of U.S., 83–84, 234; on Philippines, 89; physical conformation concept of, 80–81; on policy of isolation, 3; *The Problem of Asia*, 97, 104; Roosevelt influenced by, 111–112; on trade, 10–11, 82–83, 85, 237; Zimmerman on, 78

Mahathir bin Mohamad, 412, 451, 476

Maine (USS), sinking of, 86

Malaysia, 269, 316; during Bush (GHWB) administration, 450–451; during Clinton administration, 476; during Johnson administration, 298, 309, 314; during Reagan administration, 411, 412, 649n124

Manchuria, 40, 96; Chinese Civil War in, 255–256, 259–260; economic strategies in, 118, 146, 148; Germany in, 90; Grew on, 164; during Hoover administration, 152–155, 161–162; Hornbeck on, 161–162; Huntington Wilson and Straight on, 102, 119, 121; Kwantung Army in, 152, 153, 220, 223; Mahan on, 93, 97; maritime strategies concerning, 184; Russo-Japanese pact on, 120, 121; Russo-Japanese War concerning, 78, 97–98, 101, 105, 133, 187; Soviet attack on Japanese forces in, 205, 218, 220, 223, 224; Soviet control of, 223, 224; during Taft administration,

102, 112, 119, 186; trade with Japan, 152; Washington Treaty System on, 141; during Wilson administration, 123

Mandated Islands, 206

manifest destiny era, 30–34

Manila Bay, 89; battle of, 72, 75, 76, 86, 87, 90, 192

Manila Pact, 290–291

Mann, Jim, 346, 393

Mansfield, Mike, 318–319, 403, 404, 405, 408, 646n80

Mao Zedong (Mao Tse-tung), 214, 223, 254, 258, 261; during Eisenhower administration, 285, 286, 292, 295; and establishment of PRC, 258; during Johnson administration, 317; during Nixon administration, 344, 347, 349, 351, 352; and Shanghai Communiqué (1972), 352–354; Soviet support of, 254, 255, 319–320; white paper report on (1949), 258

Marco Polo Bridge Incident, 175

Marcos, Ferdinand, 377, 379, 417–418

Marcy, William, 40, 41, 42, 46, 47, 49

Mariana Islands, 125, 203, 280

maritime strategies: during Adams administration, 31–32; during Arthur administration, 74–75; of Britain and Japan, 67; of Britain and U.S., 66; during Bush (GHWB) administration, 446–447; during Carter administration, 379–380, 384–385; of China, 424; during Cleveland administration, 75; during Clinton administration, 470; coaling stations in, 41, 48, 51, 55, 65, 73, 77, 87, 92, 132; versus continental strategies (See continental versus maritime strategies); Europe versus Pacific as priority in, 195, 196; First Island Chain in, 297; forward defense line in, 8; in Gilded Age, 68, 74; of Grew, 164, 173; during Harrison administration, 75; of Hornbeck, 162, 173; island stepping stones in, 70–73, 87–93, 199–207, 227, 238; of Kennan, 272–273, 302; Korea as factor in, 68, 69; of MacMurray, 168; of Mahan, 7, 51, 75, 79–88, 97, 106, 112, 184, 204;

in manifest destiny era, 30–34; during McKinley administration, 92–93; during Monroe administration, 47; during Nixon administration, 340, 341; during Obama administration, 521–522, 529–530; of Perry, 39, 41, 47–51; of Porter, 17–18; during Qing era, 34–35, 39–42, 45–46; during Reagan administration, 8, 246, 382, 393, 400–407, 421; during Roosevelt (FDR) administration, 172–178, 184; during Roosevelt (TR) administration, 101, 105, 106–107; in routes to Japan during WWII, 199–205; of Seward, 57–58, 62–63; of Shultz, 391; swing strategy in, 381, 401, 402; during Truman administration, 253, 274; in War Plan Orange, 116, 131–135, 137, 173, 174–177, 199, 200; and Washington Treaty System, 116, 137–144, 238

Market Oriented Sector Specific (MOSS) talks, 410

Marshall, George C., 42, 192, 193, 204, 211, 248–249; and China policies, 255, 256–257, 258, 259, 597n6, 600n57; and Kennan strategies, 272; on post-WWII Japan, 226; reconstruction plan for Europe, 248, 256–257, 324; and Southeast Asia policies, 269–270; and Soviet attack on Japan, 220, 222, 223

Marshall, Humphrey, 7, 39–42, 48, 52, 53, 55, 59, 60, 94, 108

Marshall Islands, 125, 203, 280

Marshall Plan, 248, 256–257, 324

Matsuoka Yōsuke, 155, 180

Maury, Matthew, 33, 61

Maximilian, Emperor, 56

Mayaguez incident, 360

McCain, John, 333, 445

McCarthy, Joseph, 259

McCarthyism, 252, 259, 300, 320

McCloy, John J., 226

McConnell, Mitch, 538

McCormack, Richard, 444

McCoy, Frank Ross, 155

McDougall, Walter, 3

McFarland, Katrina, 522

McKinley, William, 5; assassination of, 96; protectionism of, 107; and Spanish–American War, 86–87

McKinley Act (1890), 72, 77

McKinley administration, 86–96; Hawaii annexation during, 88–89, 106; Philippines during, 89–92, 93; Spanish–American War during, 86–87, 89–90; trade during, 107

McLane, Robert, 42–43, 44

McNamara, Robert S., 271, 305, 308, 309, 310, 317

Mead, Walter Russell, 516

Meade, Richard W., 72–73

Megawati Sukarnoputri, 501

Meiji era (Japan), 59, 67, 69

Mendès-France, Pierre, 288

Menzies, Robert, 316

mercantilism, 146, 148

metaprocess in U.S. strategy, 4

Mexican–American War, 34

Mexico, 33, 34, 475

Midway, 89, 134, 194, 202, 207; annexation of, 56, 62, 63, 77; Japanese defeat at, 197, 198, 201

Midway (USS), 404

Military Assistance Command in Vietnam (MACV), 307

military strategies: compared to grand strategy, 2; continental versus maritime power in, 7–8; with economic and ideological strategies, 11–12. *See also specific strategies*

Miller, Edward S., 135

Milosevic, Slobodan, 504

missionaries, 31–33, 36, 38, 54, 72; in China, 32–33, 43, 93

Missouri Compromise, 58

Mitchell, John, 342

Mitchell, Kate, 235

Mitter, Rana, 217–218

Miyazawa Kiichi, 380, 441, 444, 461

Mondale, Walter, 366, 370, 374, 417, 664–665n88

Monroe, James, 28, 29, 47

Monroe Doctrine, 5, 29, 83; extended to Hawaii, 5, 20, 31–32, 70, 87

Montojo, Patricio, 87, 88

moral basis of strategies: during Carter administration, 363, 364, 385–386, 415; during Ford administration, 360–361; Kissinger on, 355, 542, 621n6; Mahan on, 83–84, 234; during McKinley administration, 91; during Obama administration, 532–535; during Reagan administration, 415–421

Morgan, John Pierpont, 123, 145

Morgenthau, Hans, 293, 313–314, 325

Morgenthau, Henry, 160, 163, 177, 194, 214; postwar economic plans, 226, 235, 236

Morison, Samuel Eliot, 142, 188, 189

Mori Yoshirō, 487

Morris, Robert, 22

Morrison, Robert, 32

Mosbacher, Robert, 441

most favored nation status: in Japan–U.S. relations, 122, 265; in Korea–U.S. relations, 69; Washington Treaty System on, 141

most favored nation status in China–U.S. relations, 37, 60; during Bush (GHWB) administration, 437–438; during Carter administration, 373, 374; during Clinton administration, 462–463, 472; and Hornbeck strategies, 161; and Lamont strategies, 148; during McKinley administration, 87, 94; and stability in East Asia, 166; during Taft administration, 121; during Wilson administration, 128

Mountbatten, Louis, 15, 269

Moyers, Bill, 311

Murayama Tomiichi, 467, 471

Murphy, Robert, 311

Murray, Williamson, 5

Musharraf, Pervez, 499

Muskie, Edmund, 381

Mutsu Munemitsu, 70

Myanmar Oil and Gas Enterprise
   (MOGE), 535

NAFTA (North American Free Trade
   Agreement), 469, 474, 511, 536
Nakasone Yasuhiro, 344–345, 358, 393,
   405–406, 413
Nanking, Treaty of (1842), 35, 37
Napoleon I, 188
Napoleon III, 65
Napoleonic Wars, 23
National Defense Authorization Act
   (1988), 441
National Economic Council during Clinton
   administration, 454, 473, 475
national interests: Mahan on, 80; secondary,
   2; vital, 2, 9, 187
nationalism in postcolonial Asia, 292–293
National Security Act (1947), 248
National Security Council: during Bush
   (GWB) administration, 484, 486, 487,
   496, 500; during Carter administration,
   374, 375, 381, 385; and China policies,
   258, 260, 262, 347, 381; during Clinton
   administration, 459, 473; during
   Eisenhower administration, 284, 285,
   291; establishment of, 194, 248; and
   Formosa policies, 262; during Johnson
   administration, 320; during Kennedy
   administration, 301, 302, 307, 316; and
   Korea policies, 267, 275, 277, 286; during
   Nixon administration, 327, 328, 333, 334,
   343; NSC 68, 277, 283, 284, 300, 388; during
   Obama administration, 523; during
   Reagan administration, 392, 403, 404, 408,
   412, 413; and Southeast Asia policies, 287,
   289, 290, 291; and Vietnam policies, 307,
   314, 320, 333; on vital interests of U.S., 275
National Security Decision Directives
   (NSDD): NSDD 32, 402, 403, 407; NSDD
   75, 388; NSDD 147, 415
National Security Decision Memorandum
   (NSDM), 327, 395–396
National Security Study Memorandum
   (NSSM), 330, 337, 357

NATO, 246, 278, 283, 546; during Carter
   administration, 381, 382, 383; and
   Guam Doctrine, 340; and Vietnam
   War, 314
naval strategies. See maritime strategies
Naval War College, 79, 401, 529;
   establishment of, 75; Mahan at, 75; during
   McKinley administration, 92; Nimitz at,
   141; and War Plan Orange, 132, 133, 134,
   135, 173, 199, 200, 381
Navarre, Henri, 288
Negroponte, John, 498
Nehru, Jawaharlal, 300, 326
Nepal, 514–515, 516
Netherlands, 179
Neutrality Act (1935), 173
Neutrality Act (1937), 176
New Look concept, 285, 291, 295–296, 306,
   333, 336, 338
New Pacific Community, 321, 412
New Pacific Doctrine of Ford, 362
New Zealand: in ANZUS treaty, 281, 283;
   and postwar economic policies, 235,
   236; during Reagan administration, 414;
   and San Francisco System, 279, 281; in
   SEATO, 289, 290; and strategic priorities
   in WWII, 196, 198
Nicholas II, 96
Nimitz, Chester, 15, 141, 206, 237; and
   military routes to Japan during WWII,
   201–204
Nimitz (USS), 470
Nine Power Treaty, 140, 141, 144, 151, 152;
   and Amau Doctrine, 156; and Hornbeck
   strategies, 161, 162, 163
Ninkovich, Frank, 314
Nitze, Paul H., 251, 276–277, 285
Nixon, Richard, 298; advice to Bush
   (GHWB) administration, 436; advice
   to Carter administration, 372; Carter
   compared to, 363; Foreign Affairs
   essay of (1967), 326, 346, 356, 358, 359,
   415; Kissinger opinion of, 96, 104, 325;
   resignation of, 335, 360; as vice-president
   for Eisenhower, 286, 325–326, 343, 346

Nixon administration, 304, 323–360; China during, 13, 42, 246, 323, 326, 329, 342, 345–359, 365; economic strategies during, 328, 338, 342–345; Ford as vice-president in, 335; Guam Doctrine during, 8, 328, 329, 336–345, 349, 350, 357; Japan during, 326, 337, 339–345, 348–349, 350, 352, 353, 356–358, 361; Kissinger in, 324–360; legacy in Asia strategy, 354–360; military retrenchment during, 337, 339; multipolarity in international relations during, 324–325, 326, 337, 341, 349, 355, 356, 358, 621–622n7; policy-making process in, 327; Reagan on, 387; rebalancing alliances during, 336–345; Shanghai Communiqué during, 352–354, 368; shocks to Japan during, 344, 358, 361, 380, 383, 410; Shultz in, 390; Vietnam War during, 312, 323, 328–336, 339, 341, 360

Nixon Doctrine (Guam Doctrine), 8, 328, 329, 336–345, 349, 350, 357, 545; during Obama administration, 530, 539

Nol, Lon, 333

nonfortification clause in Washington Treaty System, 137, 141, 142, 170, 174, 202, 577n104

nonrecognition doctrine, 158, 187; of Stimson, 155, 162, 170, 171; during Wilson administration, 125

North Africa, 197

North American Free Trade Agreement (NAFTA), 469, 474, 511, 536

North Atlantic Treaty Organization. See NATO

Northeast Asia, 14

North Korea, 6, 8; Agreed Framework with, 466–467, 479, 488, 503, 504, 506; attack on South Korea, 241, 245, 268, 277, 314; during Bush (GHWB) administration, 447–448; during Bush (GWB) administration, 483, 488–489, 492, 493, 494, 500, 503–510; during Carter administration, 378–379, 380; during Clinton administration, 466–467,

478–480; conclusions about historical and future strategies on, 543, 545, 546; during Eisenhower administration, 285–286; financial sanctions against, 506–508; Kim Il-sung election in, 267; missile capabilities of, 467, 479–480, 488; during Obama administration, 521, 523, 525, 531, 534, 539; and Soviet Union, 266, 274; during Truman administration, 266–268, 274–278

North Vietnam, 298; China supporting, 288, 308–309; during Eisenhower administration, 288, 291; in Vietnam War, 242 (See also Vietnam War)

North Vietnamese Army (NVA), 310, 312, 322, 333

Northwest Company, 26

nuclear weapons, 239; during Bush (GHWB) administration, 448; during Bush (GWB) administration, 485–486, 488–489, 499, 503–508; of China, 291, 469; during Clinton administration, 466–467, 479–480; during Eisenhower administration, 285, 291, 294–296; of India, 485–486, 499, 500; during Kennedy administration, 306; during Nixon administration, 338, 339; of North Korea, 466–467, 479–480, 488–489, 503–508, 539, 674n93; during Reagan administration, 398, 402, 406, 414; of Soviet Union, 258; during WWII, 205, 223, 224, 239

Nunn, Sam, 382

Nunn Amendment, 364

Nye, Gerald P., 173

Nye, Joseph, 157, 427, 457; and China strategies, 471–472; and Japan strategies, 468–469, 485; on soft power, 457

Nye Initiative, 473, 485, 525

Obama, Barack, 14, 387, 483, 518–540

Obama administration, 294, 518–540; Advanced Capabilities and Deterrence Panel during, 531; Asia-first policies during, 519, 520–524; China during, 423–425, 521–534, 537, 538–540, 679n23;

defense spending during, 522, 532; Defense Strategic Review during, 521; foreign policy advisors in, 519; forward defense line in Asia during, 528–532; legacy in Asia strategy, 539–540; National Security Strategy during, 519, 523, 540; pivot or rebalance of policies during, 510, 519, 520, 521, 522, 524, 539; policy priorities during, 524, 533; Third Offset strategy during, 530, 684n77; trade policies during, 535–539

Obuchi Keizō, 478

offensive realism, 6, 76

Office of Naval Intelligence, establishment of, 75

Office of Strategic Services (OSS), 230

Okinawa, 204, 205; and Guam Doctrine, 340, 342, 343, 344; Kennan strategies on, 273; rape incident in (1995), 469, 487

Oksenberg, Michael, 367, 383, 430; and alliance management in Asia, 378; and China policies, 367, 368, 369, 370, 372, 374, 375, 376

Oliver, J. H., 133, 134

Olympia (USS), 87, 192

Omestad, Thomas, 444

Omnibus Trade Bill (1988), 440

On Active Service in Peace and War (Stimson and Bundy), 301

Ontario (HMS), 28

Open Door policy, 42, 78, 92, 93–97, 107–108; and Amau Doctrine, 156; and Burlingame Treaty, 60; Dennett on, 52, 170; economic imperialism in, 103; as effort to sustain regional stability, 13, 55; enforcement of, 95, 107, 108; Grew on, 164; Hay notes on, 92, 94–95, 107; and Hornbeck strategies, 158, 159, 161, 162, 163; Huntington Wilson on, 102; Knox on, 119, 120; and MacMurray strategies, 165, 166, 168–169; Mahan on, 97, 107; Roosevelt (TR) on, 96, 105–106, 107, 183, 186; during Taft administration, 119, 120, 121–122, 183; and War Plan Orange, 132, 135, 181; and Washington Treaty System, 139, 140, 141,

151; during Wilson administration, 123, 125, 126, 129–130, 183

Open Door Policy and China, The (Hornbeck), 159

Operation Babylift, 360

Operation Balikatan, 501

Operation Duck Hook, 333

Operation Enduring Freedom (OEF), 492, 493

Operation Iraqi Freedom (OIF), 492, 493

Operation Linebacker II, 335

Operation Matterhorn, 211, 214

Operation Torch, 197

opium trade, 30, 35–36, 38, 43

Opium Wars, 10, 20, 39, 43, 44, 55, 186; Second, 38, 45

Oregon Treaty (1846), 30

Osgood, Robert, 3, 79, 83, 115, 119, 185, 337, 341

Our Country (Strong), 75–76

Paal, Douglas, 431

Pacific Charter, 230

Pacific Economic Cooperation Conference (PECC), 412, 413

Pacific–Far Eastern High Commission, 226

Pacific first strategy, 278; compared to Europe first strategy in WWII, 194–199

Pacific Fur Trading Company, 27

Pacific Pact, 281, 611n228

Pacific Squadron of U.S. Navy, 31, 33, 34, 74

Pago Pago Harbor, 72–73

Paine, Thomas, 9

Pakistan: aligning with China, 319; during Bush (GWB) administration, 498–499, 500; during Carter administration, 384; during Nixon administration, 358–359; in SEATO, 289, 290

Panama Canal: plans for, 81; and War Plan Orange, 133, 134, 176

Panay (USS), 171

Panetta, Leon, 521, 522

Paris, Treaty of (1898), 89, 90

Paris negotiations on Vietnam War, 623–624n32; during Johnson administration, 304, 331; during Nixon administration, 323, 330, 331–332, 334, 335, 336

Paris Pact (1928), 144

Paris Peace Accord (1954), 289, 296, 333

Paris Peace Conference (1919–1920), 128–129, 146, 159, 161

Paris Peace Treaty (1783), 21

Paris Treaty (1898), 89, 90

Park Chung-hee, 340, 377, 379

Parker, Peter, 39, 43–46, 47, 48, 52, 53, 55, 59, 65

Park Geun-hye, 531

Parsons, Levi, 43

Patterson, Torkel, 484, 491

Paulson, Henry (Hank), 498, 525, 672n73

Pax Americana, 144, 151

Peace and Amity Treaty (1854), 49

Pearl Harbor, 72, 101; attack on (1941), 4, 6, 142, 149, 158, 195, 196

Peloponnesian Wars, 1

Pelosi, Nancy, 437

Pentagon Papers, 309, 330

People's Liberation Army (PLA), 286, 295

People's Republic of China, establishment of, 258, 262. *See also* China

Pepper Coast of Sumatra, 23, 31, 53

pepper trade, 23

Perestroika, 399

Perot, Ross, 426, 453

Perry, Matthew Calbraith, 33, 47–51, 52, 53, 55, 59; on Britain, 54; on Japan, 7, 39, 47, 49, 50–51, 55, 66, 69; maritime strategies of, 39, 41, 47–51

Perry, William, 457, 522; and China policies, 470; and Korea policies, 467, 479

Pershing, John, 192

Peru, 74

Phan Van Khai, 515

Philippines, 5; annexation of, 8, 14, 90–92, 103; authoritarianism in, 10; during Bush (GHWB) administration, 446–447; during Carter administration, 377, 379, 385; counterinsurgency in, 91; democratization in, 419–420; Dennett on, 172; during Eisenhower administration, 288; during Ford administration, 361; independence of, 229, 233, 270; Japan in,

185, 199; Jones Act on, 124; MacArthur commanding forces in, 180, 200, 204; MacMurray on, 168–169; during McKinley administration, 89–92, 93; Mutual Defense Treaty with, 281, 283; during Nixon administration, 358; during Obama administration, 531; during Reagan administration, 389, 413, 417–418; during Roosevelt (TR) administration, 105, 106, 107; and San Francisco System, 279, 281, 283; in SEATO, 289, 290, 361; training troops in, 178; during Truman administration, 286–287; and War Plan Orange, 133, 134, 135, 164, 175, 176, 177, 181; during Wilson administration, 124, 185

Phillips, William, 231

Phnom Penh evacuation (1973), 359–360

Phoenix Initiative, 519

physical conformation concept of Mahan, 80–81

Pierce, Franklin, 45, 47, 48, 49–50

Plaza Accord (1985), 410–411, 439

Poland, 178

Polk, James, 34

Porter, David, 17–18, 27, 31, 47, 55, 70, 199

Portman, Rob, 511

Portsmouth, Treaty of (1905), 98, 187

Posen, Barry, 402

Potomac (USS), 31

Potsdam Conference, 227, 233

Potsdam Proclamation (1945), 207, 208

Powell, Colin, 392, 431, 459, 500; base force concept of, 432; and China policies, 489; and Korea policies, 488, 505

Power, Samantha, 533

Power Rules (Gelb), 3

Powers to Lead, The (Nye), 157

Prestowitz, Clyde, 456

Preuher, Joseph W., 470

Prince of Wales (HMS), 189

Problem of Asia, The (Mahan), 97, 104

protectionism, 77, 185; during Bush (GHWB) administration, 437, 441; versus free trade strategies, 10–11, 409, 535–539, 547–548; during McKinley administration,

107; during Obama administration, 520; during Reagan administration, 408–411

Pryzstup, James, 498

Publius (John Jay), 24

Putin, Vladimir, 519, 523

Pye, Lucian, 302

Qingdao-Tian Railway, 125

Qing Empire, 9, 20, 23, 34–47; decline of, 56; defeat of, 37, 69; and Treaty of Tientsin, 60, 66

Quebec Conference (1943), 232

Quezon, Manuel, 180, 201, 229

racism: and antiracism clause in League of Nations proposal, 116, 128–129, 130; in Roosevelt (TR) era, 103

Radford, Arthur, 262, 289

railroads: and dollar diplomacy of Taft, 118, 120, 121, 122, 123; trans-Siberian, 381–382

Rainbow Plans, 177, 179, 181, 194, 199

RAND report on Vietnam, 330, 623n28

Ravenal, Earl, 341

Ravich, Samantha, 504

Read, John, 31

Reagan, Ronald, 8, 10, 13, 246, 298, 323, 328, 361, 386, 387–431

Reagan administration, 387–431; Asian regionalism during, 411–415; Bush as vice-president in, 392, 394, 397, 415; China during, 393, 394–400, 420–421; defense spending during, 388; India during, 359, 389, 414–415, 421; Japan during, 246, 358, 389, 393, 399, 403–411, 412, 413, 421, 647n92; legacy in Asian strategy, 420–421; maritime strategies during, 8, 246, 382, 393, 400–407; National Security Decision Directives (NSDD), 388, 402, 403, 407, 415; offense-oriented military strategies during, 388, 401–402, 407; Strategic Defense Initiative during, 406; trade policies during, 408–411, 420–421, 440

Reagan Doctrine, 388

realism: in Carter administration, 364, 365, 366; compared to idealism as strategy basis, 3; defensive and offensive, 6, 76; of Nixon and Kissinger, 355, 356; of Roosevelt (FDR), 191

Reciprocal Trade Agreements Act (1934), 185

Reed, William B., 47, 66

Regan, Donald, 409, 410

Regional Comprehensive Economic Partnership (RCEP), 511, 512, 537

regionalism: during Bush (GHWB) administration, 450; during Reagan administration, 411–415

Reid, Harry, 537

Reinsch, Paul S., 124, 125, 129, 131, 300; Hornbeck influenced by, 159, 161

Reischauer, Edwin O., 7, 11–12, 300, 318, 619–620n100

Republican Party: antinavalism in, 137–138; Burlingame in, 60, 77; Dulles in, 279–280; Eisenhower in, 284; Harrison in, 72; Hoover in, 154; isolationism of, 146; Lincoln in, 57; Lodge in, 91; McKinley in, 107; Nixon in, 326, 329; and Paris peace negotiations on Vietnam War, 304, 331; post-Civil War, 63; protectionism policy of, 77, 107; Roosevelt (TR) in, 11, 85, 107; Taft in, 117, 118, 122

Republic of China (ROC). See Taiwan

Republic of Korea (ROK), 267. See also South Korea

revisionist histories, 2

Reynolds, David, 180, 186

Reynolds, William, 62

Rhee, Syngman, 266, 267, 286

Rice, Condoleezza, 484, 486, 513; and China policies, 485, 489, 497; and India policies, 485, 499, 500; and Korea policies, 504, 507; on multilateral institution building, 510; and Taiwan policies, 496

Rice, Susan, 519, 526

Ridgway, Matthew B., 313

right to trade, 10, 11

rimland defensive line, 283; Spykman concept of, 209, 225, 277

Roberts, Andrew, 195

Rockhill, William Woodville, 94, 166

Rodgers, John, 68

Rodman, Peter, 328, 382

Rogers, William P., 327, 328, 333, 336, 341, 358

Roh Moo-hyun, 493–494, 509

Roh Tae-woo, 419

Roosevelt, Franklin Delano, 7–8, 10, 111–113, 156–239; anti-colonial policies of, 231; as assistant secretary of navy, 112, 125, 173; and Atlantic Charter, 188–189, 228–229; on Axis powers, 178; at Cairo Conference, 233; in Casablanca Conference, 224; Churchill meetings with, 188–189, 191, 195, 198, 231, 235; command style of, 190–194, 585–586n8; compared to TR, 224; compared to Truman, 248; death of, 194, 222, 226; domestic focus of, 156; inaugural address of (1933), 156; personal advisors of, 191; quarantine speech of, 171; in Tehran Conference, 224; trusteeship plan after WWII, 205–206; in Yalta Conference, 220–221, 224, 232, 235

Roosevelt, Theodore, 18, 134, 186–187, 358n11; compared to FDR, 224; FDR influenced by, 112, 113; grand strategy in era of, 78–108, 116, 122; on Taft policies, 122; on trade tariffs, 11

Roosevelt administration (FDR), 111–113, 156–239; China strategies during, 7–8, 208–218; continental and maritime geopolitics during, 7–8, 184, 207–210; defense spending during, 174, 178; Europe versus Pacific as strategic priority during, 194–199; Executive Order freezing Japanese assets during, 111, 180; Grew strategies during, 158, 163–165; Hornbeck strategies during, 158, 159–163, 171; India policies during, 231; Indochina policies during, 231–232; island strategies during, 199–207; Japan strategies during, 111, 117, 156, 174–184, 199–205, 208–209, 224–227, 238; MacMurray strategies during, 165–169; military routes to Japan considered during, 199–202; policy

inconsistencies during, 238–239; postwar planning during, 207–239; Rainbow Plans during, 177; and Second World War, 188–239; Soviet Union strategies during, 156, 162, 208–209, 218–224, 238; trade and economic strategies during, 234–237; War Plan Orange during, 173, 174–177

Roosevelt era (TR), 13, 18, 78–108; China policies during, 96–97, 105–106, 107–108; expansionism in, 19, 21, 103, 104; forward defense line during, 8; grand strategy in, 78–108, 116, 122; "Great White Fleet" during, 101, 112; Japan policies during, 7, 8, 97–102, 131–132, 186, 187; and Mahan strategies, 79–86, 96–97; Open Door policy during, 93–98, 131, 186; Pacific stepping stones during, 87–93; Russo-Japanese War during, 78, 97–98, 105; and Spanish–American War, 86–87

Root, Elihu, 78, 99–100, 102, 105, 126, 141, 186; and Grew strategies, 164; and Stimson, 153, 225

Root-Takahira agreement, 99–100

Rostow, Walt Whitman, 301–302, 306–307, 310, 314, 320, 321

Roth, Ken, 534

Royal Navy, 6, 21, 23, 24, 27, 28, 29, 66; Mahan on, 84–85; during Roosevelt (FDR) administration, 176; and Washington Treaty System, 141

"Royal Road," 174–175

Rudd, Kevin, 526, 536

Rumsfeld, Donald, 361, 379, 485, 486, 489, 509

Rusk, Dean, 252, 312, 520; in Johnson administration, 242, 303, 305, 309, 310, 315; in Kennedy administration, 303; Korea decision of, 233, 250; in Roosevelt (FDR) administration, 233; in Truman administration, 250, 262, 275–276

Russia, 38, 40, 64–65; during Adams administration, 28–29, 53; during American Civil War, 54, 64, 65; in China, 40, 41, 64; in Crimean War, 49, 64; early trade of, 26–27; expansionism of, 64,

65, 85; Mahan on, 97; during McKinley administration, 94, 95; in Pacific Northwest, 28–29, 53, 54; Perry on, 49, 50; railroad assets of, 120; in Roosevelt (TR) era, 85, 97–98, 100; and Russo-Japanese pact, 120, 121; and Russo-Japanese War, 78, 97–98, 101, 105, 133, 187; sale of Alaska, 62, 64, 65, 218; and Seward strategies, 58, 59, 61, 62, 65; in Siberia, 38; in Treaty of Tientsin, 66; in Triple Intervention, 69–70; during Wilson administration, 123, 127–128, 130–131

Russian-American Company, 26, 27, 28

Russian Civil War, 127

Russo-Japanese War (1904–1905), 78, 97–98, 101, 105, 133, 187

Ryukyu Islands, 48, 49, 55, 67, 274, 280, 287, 294, 605n134

Saffron Revolution, 512, 515

Sainteny, Jean, 331

Saitō Hiroshi, 177

Sakakibara Eisuke, 476, 477

Samoa, 57, 69, 70, 72–73, 77; annexation of, 73; coaling station established on, 89

Samoa Treaty, 563n65

sandalwood, 20, 23, 29, 30

Sandwich Islands, 20, 23, 28, 29, 62, 69. See also Hawaii

San Francisco System, 278–284, 298, 318, 321

Saratoga (USS), 142, 202

Sato Eisaku, 342, 343–344, 350, 380, 471

Saunders, Phillip, 498

Savannah (USS), 34

Scalapino, Robert, 319

Schaller, Michael, 217

Schlesinger, Jim, 361, 379

Schriver, Randy, 496

Schurman, Jacob Gould, 91

Schurz, Carl, 90, 103

Schwab, Susan, 511

Scowcroft, Brent, 430, 431, 433, 436, 437

sea otter fur trade, 19, 23, 26, 30

Sea Power in the Pacific (Bywater), 141

"Sea Strike" concept of Hayward, 382

SEATO. See Southeast Asian Treaty Organization

Second Island Chain, 207, 424, 529, 545

Second Opium War (1856–1860), 38, 45

Second Revolution, 17–18

Second World War, 2, 10, 188–239; command style of Roosevelt during, 190–194; definition of Asia during, 14–15; entry of U.S. into, 179; Europe versus Pacific as strategic priority in, 194–199; island strategies in, 199–207; and postwar planning, 207–239; routes to Japan considered in, 199–205

Section 301 of Trade Act (1974), 410, 411; and Super 301 sanctions, 440, 441, 462

Seiyūkai party in Japan, 152, 155

self-determination, 20, 37; in China, 10, 37, 124, 125, 167; and Johnson administration policies, 319; post-WWII planning on, 229, 230, 233; Roosevelt (FDR) support for, 229; in Southeast Asia, 268, 271, 319; and universality, 9–10, 166–167, 186, 532–535, 546–547; Wilson administration support for, 124, 125, 128, 185, 186, 229

Senkaku Islands, 477, 525, 527, 528, 545, 680n39

September 11, 2001 terrorist attacks, 483, 486, 491–494, 498, 501

Service, John, 214

Seventh Fleet, 201, 202

Seward, William Henry, 7, 29, 56, 57–64, 66, 68, 70, 71, 77, 104; Alaska purchase, 61, 62, 63, 66, 560n21

Shandong, Japan in, 125, 126, 128, 129, 130, 134; Washington Treaties on, 140, 141, 143

Shanghai, Japanese attack on (1932), 155, 162

Shanghai Communiqué (1972), 352–354, 368

Shattuck, John, 463

Shaw, Samuel, 22

Shear, David, 526

Shelton, Hugh, 489

Shidehara Kijuro, 153

Shimonoseki, Treaty of, 69–70

Shufeldt, Robert N., 68–69, 74, 561n45

Shultz, George, 7, 51, 390–391; and China policies, 391, 397, 399–400; on democratic values in policies, 390, 391, 416, 420; and India policies, 415; and Japan policies, 390, 403, 407–408, 409, 410; and Philippines policies, 418; and response to Asian regionalism, 413

Siam, 30, 59

Siberia, 127–128, 130, 294

Sigur, Gaston, 392–393; and China policies, 397, 399; and Japan policies, 405; and response to Asian regionalism, 413

Sihanouk, Norodom, 326, 333, 449

Silver Purchase Act (1934), 160

Simon, John, 155, 162

Singapore, 269; British surrender at (1942), 196; during Bush (GHWB) administration, 447, 450, 451; during Bush (GWB) administration, 482, 490, 501, 502–503, 511; during Carter administration, 423, 424; during Clinton administration, 465; early exploration of, 31, 43, 46; during Johnson administration, 298, 316, 317, 318; Lee Kuan Yew as leader in, 317, 390, 407, 502–503, 523, 619n98; during Obama administration, 521, 523, 527, 536; in Rainbow Five Plan, 199; during Roosevelt (FDR) administration, 179, 196, 199, 219

Singh, Manmohan, 499, 500, 526

Sino-French War, 65

Sino-Japanese War, 67, 82

Sirik Matak, 360

Six Assurances made to Taiwan, 397, 398, 644n47

Six Party Talks, 482, 505–506, 507, 510

Slaughter, Anne-Marie, 533

slavery, 33, 34, 52, 58, 63, 77

Smoot-Hawley Tariff Act, 11, 149, 154, 185, 536

Sneider, Richard, 342

social Darwinism, 75, 80

soft power, 457, 483

Solarium Project, 284–285, 341, 608n191

Solarz, Stephen, 436, 438

Solomon, Richard, 328, 431, 449, 465

Soong May-ling, 214

Southeast Asia, 14; during Bush (GWB) administration, 490; during Carter administration, 375, 384; during Eisenhower administration, 287–293, 296, 314, 316, 329, 612–613n243; during Ford administration, 361, 362; and Guam Doctrine, 340; Japan dependence on resources in, 265; during Nixon administration, 358; during Roosevelt (FDR) administration, 268; during Truman administration, 268–272, 609n205. *See also specific countries*

Southeast Asia Command (SEAC), 232, 269

Southeast Asian Treaty Organization (SEATO): during Eisenhower administration, 246, 289–291, 293, 296; during Ford administration, 361; during Johnson administration, 308, 321; and Vietnam War, 298, 308, 321

Southern Manchurian Railroad, 120

South Korea, 6, 8; during Bush (GHWB) administration, 445–446, 447–448; during Bush (GWB) administration, 493–494, 509; during Carter administration, 377–381; during Clinton administration, 475; during Eisenhower administration, 286, 287; during Nixon administration, 340; North Korea attack on, 241, 245, 268, 277, 314; during Obama administration, 525, 531, 536; during Reagan administration, 389, 416–417, 418–420; Rhee election in, 267; Treaty of Mutual Security with U.S., 286, 287, 609n199; during Truman administration, 266–268, 274–278

South Vietnam, 247, 296; escalation of U.S. presence in, 298; in Vietnam War, 242 (*See also* Vietnam War)

Soviet Union, 8; Afghanistan invasion (1979), 374, 382, 384; atomic bomb testing of, 258; attack on Japanese forces in Manchuria, 205, 218, 220; avoiding

Cairo Conference, 212; Brezhnev Doctrine (1968), 348; Brzezinski on, 365, 366; during Carter administration, 364–376, 377, 379–386; during Eisenhower administration, 284–285, 287–288, 292, 612n234; expansion of, 10, 221; during Ford administration, 361; and Hornbeck strategies, 162; human rights issues in, 385; during Johnson administration, 320–321, 322; joining fight against Japan, 219–220; during Kennedy administration, 319–320, 322; in Korea, 223, 266, 267, 268, 274, 278, 605n136; Korean Air Lines flight shot down by, 413; in Lend-Lease program, 211, 221; and MacMurray strategies, 168; Mao Zedong and CCP supported by, 254, 255, 257, 261; naval strength of, 400; during Nixon administration, 346–352, 353, 356, 358–359; nonaggression pact with Japan (1941), 219; normalization of U.S. relationship with, 219; and post-WWII plans, 208–209, 218–224, 227; public opinion on, 223, 320; during Reagan administration, 387–389, 391, 395, 396, 398–403, 406–407, 412–414, 421; response to Asian regionalism, 412, 413, 414; rise of, 13, 241–421; during Roosevelt (FDR) administration, 156, 162, 208–209, 218–224, 238; SALT talks with, 356, 364, 367, 368, 371, 379, 383; and San Francisco System, 281–282; and strategic priorities in WWII, 195, 197; in Tehran Conference, 212; as threat to Japan, 152–153; trans-Siberian railroad in, 381–382; during Truman administration, 222–224, 253; in Vietnam War, 320; in Yalta Conference, 215–216, 220–221

Soviet Union, and China policies: during Carter administration, 368–376, 383–384; during Nixon administration, 346–352, 353, 356, 358, 359; during Reagan administration, 395, 396, 398–399; during Roosevelt (FDR) administration, 208, 209

Spanish–American War (1898), 78, 79, 86–87, 89, 564n2; Battle of Manila Bay in, 72, 75, 76, 86, 87, 90; peace negotiations, 89–90; Treaty of Paris in, 89, 90

Spector, Ronald, 253

Spender, Percy, 281

Sport and Travel in the Far East (Grew), 164

Spruance, Raymond, 199

Spykman, Nicholas John, 208–209, 221; rimland concept of, 209, 225, 277

Stalin, Joseph, 192, 197; avoiding Cairo Conference, 212; and Chinese Nationalist government of Chiang, 254; invasion of Manchuria, 222, 223, 224; Korea policies, 266; nonaggression pact with Japan (1941), 219; in Potsdam Conference, 223; and Soviet forces fighting Japan, 219–220, 222, 223; in Tehran Conference, 212; and Truman administration, 222–224; in Yalta Conference, 215–216, 221

Stark, Harold R., 180, 195

Star Wars (Strategic Defense Initiative), 406

State Department: in Carter administration, 365, 366, 385, 386; in Nixon administration, 327, 349; in Roosevelt (FDR) administration, 192, 193

State-War-Navy Coordinating Committee (SWNCC), 193–194, 216, 225–226, 227; on Indochina, 232; on Japan, 264; on Korea, 233, 266–267

Steinberg, James, 519, 525

Stettinius, Edward, 193, 216

Stilwell, Joseph, 15, 192, 206, 210, 211; and Chiang Kai-shek, 214; Davies as advisor to, 212, 213

Stimson, Henry L., 153–155, 158; and Grew, 225; and Hornbeck, 158, 160, 161–162; and MacMurray, 167; nonrecognition policy of, 155, 162, 170, 171; on post-WWII Japan, 226; and Roosevelt (FDR), 173, 178, 191, 193, 195; on Soviet expansion, 222; on Yalta Conference, 216

Stoeckl, Eduard de, 62

Stoler, Mark, 193

Straight, Willard, 102, 108, 118, 119–120, 121, 122, 146

Strategic and Economic Dialogue (S&ED) with China, 525–526, 534

Strategic Arms Limitations Talks (SALT), 367, 371, 383; SALT I, 356; SALT II, 364, 368, 379

strategic culture, 4, 5, 190

Strategic Defense Initiative (SDI), 406

Strategic Economic Dialogue (SED) with China, 498, 525, 672n73

Strong, Josiah, 75–76

Structural Impediments Initiative (SII), 440–441

Subic Bay, 89, 101; naval base at, 270, 379, 417, 446

sugar industry, 72

Suharto regime in Indonesia, 317

Sukarno (President of Indonesia), 300, 316–317

Sumatra, Pepper Coast of, 23, 31, 53

Summers, Harry, 312

Summers, Lawrence, 476

Sumner, Charles, 60, 63

Super 301 trade sanctions, 440, 441, 462

Suri, Jeremi, 460

Surprise, Security, and the American Experience (Gaddis), 5–6

Suu Kyi, Aung San, 449, 535

Suzuki Zenkō, 404, 405

swing strategy, 381, 401, 402

Syria, 6, 523

table tennis team of U.S. in China (1971), 349

Taft, William Howard, 91, 96, 102, 112, 117–122; investment strategy of, 116; in negotiations with Katsura, 99, 569n86; as secretary of war, 99, 117, 118; and seventh-inning stretch, 118

Taft administration, 117–122; dollar diplomacy during, 118–122, 183, 185, 186; Open Door policy during, 119, 120, 121–122, 183

Taiping Rebellion, 38, 40, 41, 46–47, 55, 58

Taiwan: arms sales to, 395–397, 448–449, 489; authoritarianism in, 10; during Bush (GHWB) administration, 448–449;

during Bush (GWB) administration, 489, 495–496; during Carter administration, 369, 370, 372–373, 383, 384; during Clinton administration, 470–471; during Eisenhower administration, 286; during Nixon administration, 343–344, 346, 350, 351, 353, 354, 631n148; during Obama administration, 529; during Reagan administration, 389, 394–399, 411, 420; security treaty with U.S., 286, 290, 370, 372, 373; Six Assurances made to, 397, 398, 644n47

Taiwan Relations Act (1979), 372, 395, 397, 398

Taiwan Strait crisis (1958), 295

Takahira Kogorō, 99–100

Takeo Miki, 380

Tanaka Giichi, 152

Tanaka Kakuei, 350

tariffs, 10–11, 21–22, 35, 72, 77; Chinese autonomy in, 152, 160, 167, 186; during Clinton administration, 462; Fordney-McCumber, 149; MacMurray on, 167; Mahan on, 83, 85; Nine Power Treaty on, 144; in Roosevelt (TR) era, 85; Smoot-Hawley act on, 11, 149, 154, 185, 536; on sugar, 72

Tata, Jehangir Ratanji Dadabhoy, 235

Tattnall, Josiah, 66

Taylor, Maxwell, 306–307, 311, 313

tea trade, 21, 22–23, 35

Technology-for-Technology (TfT) Initiative, 455

Tehran Conference, 212, 224

telegraph system, transcontinental, 63

Tentative Manual for Landing Operations, The (Ellis), 175

Terranova, Francis, 35, 54

Tet Offensive (1968), 298, 310–311

textile trade, 343–344, 408, 409, 440

Thailand: during Bush (GWB) administration, 501; during Clinton administration, 474–475; democracy reversed in, 534, 546; during Eisenhower administration, 289, 290; during Ford administration, 361; during Johnson administration, 298, 303, 316, 318, 321; during Kennedy administration, 306, 315, 316; during Nixon administration, 339, 350; during Obama administration, 534; during Reagan administration, 411, 413, 649n124; during Roosevelt (FDR) administration, 211; in SEATO, 289, 290, 298, 361

Than Shwe, 515

Thein Sein, 515–516, 535

Thieu, Nguyen Van, 330, 331, 335, 377

Third Communiqué of China and U.S., 397, 398, 449

Third Offset strategy during Obama administration, 530, 684n77

Thucydides, 1, 3

Thurmond, Strom, 343

Thursfield, James R., 85

Tiananmen Square incident, 430, 431, 433, 435–436, 438; Clinton on, 454, 660n4

Ticonderoga (steamship), 68, 74

Tientsin, Treaty of (1858), 47, 60, 66; "good offices" clause in, 67–68, 73; revision of, 66

Tito, Josip Broz, 260, 261, 269

Tocqueville, Alexis de, 3, 323

Tojo Hideki, 180

Tokugawa Shōgunate, 43, 47, 49

Tonquin (schooner), 27

totalitarian regimes, Reagan administration policies on, 415–416

Tracy, Benjamin, 75, 79

trade, 56, 58, 71, 72, 77, 547–548; Atlantic Charter on, 234, 235; Bretton Woods Conference on, 234, 253; during Bush (GHWB) administration, 437–438, 439–444, 445, 450–451; during Bush (GWB) administration, 482–483, 502, 510–513; of China and Japan, 121, 282; of China and U.S. (*See* China, and trade with U.S.); during Clinton administration, 455–456, 460–462, 463, 465, 473–474; in depression era, 154; dollar standard in, 147, 344, 410–411; early strategies in (1784–1860), 6, 10, 19–55; embargo against Japan in,

154, 178, 180; during Ford administration, 362; gold standard in, 153; of Japan and China, 121, 282; of Japan and U.S. (*See* Japan–U.S. trade); MacMurray on, 169; Mahan on, 10–11, 82–83, 85, 237; during McKinley administration, 107; during Nixon administration, 342–344, 349; during Obama administration, 535–539, 548; Open Door policy on (*See* Open Door policy); postwar planning on, 234–237; protectionism versus free trade, 10–11, 408–411, 547–548; during Reagan administration, 408–411, 420–421, 440; right to, 10, 11; in Roosevelt (TR) era, 82–83, 85, 103, 107; during Taft administration, 121; tariffs in, 10–11 (*See also* tariffs)

Trade Act (1974): Jackson-Vanick amendment to, 374, 437; Section 301 of, 410, 411, 440, 441, 462

Trade Promotion Authority (TPA), 537–538

Trammell, Park, 174

Trans-Pacific Partnership (TPP), 425, 483, 511, 517; during Obama administration, 536, 537–538, 539

Treaty of Amity, Commerce and Navigation (1794), 23

Treaty of Amity and Cooperation of ASEAN, 512, 513

Treaty of Commerce and Navigation (1911), 122, 177, 178

Treaty of General Arbitration, 139

Treaty of Ghent, 27, 554–555n27

Treaty of Guadalupe-Hidalgo (1848), 34

Treaty of Nanking (1842), 35, 37

Treaty of Paris (1898), 89, 90

Treaty of Peace and Amity (1854), 49

Treaty of Portsmouth (1905), 98, 187

Treaty of Shimonoseki, 69–70

Treaty of Tientsin (1858), 47, 60, 66; "good offices" clause in, 67–68, 73; revision of, 66

Treaty of Wanghia (1844), 38, 43, 44–45; renegotiation of, 42, 43, 46

TRIDENT Conference (1943), 198, 201, 202

Trilateral Commission, 366

Trilateral Coordination and Oversight
  Group (TCOG), 479
Trilateral Security Dialogue (U.S.–Japan–
  Australia), 482, 510
Triple Intervention, 69–70
Truman, Harry S., 8, 245, 248–284;
  compared to Roosevelt (FDR), 248; Leahy
  as advisor to, 192; meetings with JCS,
  193; on post-WWII Japan, 226–227; at
  Potsdam Conference, 223, 227
Truman administration, 8, 248–284;
  China policies during, 253–263, 600n57;
  defense spending during, 248, 274, 277;
  Japan policies during, 226–227, 252, 253,
  263–265; and Kennedy administration
  policies, 300; Korea policies during, 265–
  268, 274–278; National Security Council
  established during, 193–194; reduction
  in forces during, 253; risk-management
  strategy in, 260–262; San Francisco
  System during, 278–284; Southeast Asia
  policies during, 268–272, 609n205; Soviet
  Union during, 222–224, 253; white paper
  report on China during, 258–261
Truman Doctrine, 256, 267
trusteeship plans, post-WWII, 205–206,
  230, 232
tsunami relief efforts (2004), 502–503, 510
Tuchman, Barbara, 217
Tuchman, Jessica, 385
Tucker, Nancy, 462, 477–478
Tucker, Robert, 388, 419–420
Tunku Abdul Rahman, 316
Turkey, 256, 257
Turner, Frederick Jackson, 75
Twenty-One Demands from Japan to China,
  125, 154
Tydings-McDuffie Act, 229
Tyler, John, 5, 33–34, 37, 53, 71; expansion of
  Monroe Doctrine to Hawaii, 31–32, 87
Tyson, Laura D'Andrea, 433, 455

United Nations, 189, 208; collective security
  system under, 223, 248, 253; Dumbarton
  Oaks Conference on, 232; in Korean War,
276, 277, 278; Korea resolution proposed
  in, 267; North and South Korea joining,
  447, 448; trusteeship plan after WWII,
  205–206, 232
United States Army: during Carter
  administration, 363, 364; during Hoover
  administration, 173; during Roosevelt
  (FDR) administration, 172–173; and War
  Plan Orange, 175–176
United States Army Air Force, 205, 211, 219
United States Army Observation Group
  (AOG), 214
United States Exploring Expedition, 31, 72
United States Marine Corps, 142, 143;
  amphibious operations, 175; during
  Carter administration, 363; in Gilbert
  Islands assault, 203
United States Navy: during Adams
  administration, 31; Asiatic Squadron,
  68, 82, 87, 107, 172, 173; during Carter
  administration, 364, 379–380; during
  Cleveland administration, 71–72; coaling
  stations needed (See coaling stations);
  during Coolidge administration,
  144; in depression era, 113; East Asia
  Squadron, 31; Europe versus Pacific as
  strategic priority of, 195, 196; Far East
  Squadron, 33, 35, 39, 41, 48; in First
  World War, 112, 125; in Gilded Age,
  74–75, 104; and Grew strategies, 164,
  173; during Harding administration,
  112, 141; during Hoover administration,
  173; and Hornbeck strategies, 162, 173;
  as "long-legged," 202; and MacMurray
  strategies, 168; Mahan on role of, 79–88,
  97, 184; and maritime strategies (See
  maritime strategies); during McKinley
  administration, 86–87, 88, 89–90, 92–93;
  in Midway Atoll annexation, 62, 77;
  during Obama administration, 425,
  521–522; oil-powered ships introduced in,
  135; Pacific Squadron, 31, 33, 34, 74; during
  Pierce administration, 48, 49; during
  Qing era, 34–35, 39–42, 45–47; during
  Reagan administration, 401–402, 407;

during Roosevelt (FDR) administration, 111, 172–178, 179; during Roosevelt (TR) administration, 101, 105, 106–107, 112, 131–132; in Samoa, 72–73; in Spanish-American War, 79, 86–87, 90; during Truman administration, 273–274; Vinson support of, 174; in War of 1812, 85; in War Plan Orange, 116, 131–135, 137, 173, 174–177, 181, 200; and Washington Treaty System, 116, 137–144, 238, 577n104; during Wilson administration, 125, 137

universality and self-determination, 9–10, 166–167, 186, 532–535, 546–547

Uriu, Robert, 462

U.S. Foreign Policy: Shield of the Republic (Lippmann), 191–192, 221

USA Patriot Act, 506

Van Buren, Martin, 43

Vance, Cyrus, 364–365, 366–367; and alliance management in Asia, 376; and China policies, 368–371, 374; and Korea policies, 638n88; resignation of, 381; and Vietnam policies, 375, 384

Vancouver, George, 25

Vandegrift, A. A., 213

Vandenberg, Arthur, 280

Van Fleet, James, 290

Venezuelan crisis, 85, 566n29

Vest, G. G., 90

Vietnam, 65, 269–272, 297–322; Armitage on, 393; during Bush (GWB) administration, 514, 515, 516; Cambodia invasion by (1978), 375, 384, 414; during Carter administration, 375, 383, 384, 385; China invading (1979), 375; Chinese Civil War affecting, 260; division of, 228, 288; during Eisenhower administration, 288–291, 296, 316, 329; during Ford administration, 361; France in, 288–289; Japanese troops in, 181; during Kennedy administration, 298–303, 305–307, 308, 312, 316; lack of planning of, 228, 311, 312; and national interests of U.S., 298, 312, 313, 314, 318; during Nixon administration, 312, 323, 328–336, 337, 341, 351, 360; normalization of relations with U.S., 375, 384, 449; during Obama administration, 531; Operation Babylift (1975) in, 360; during Reagan administration, 414

Vietnamization strategy of Nixon, 328–336, 337, 351

Vietnam War (1955–1975), 3, 7, 8, 13, 241–243, 245, 246–247, 297–322; American POWs in, 332, 335; bombing campaigns in, 304, 308–312, 331, 333, 335, 336, 341; China in, 288, 308–309, 311, 320, 331–332, 346–347, 351, 624n35; Easter Offensive (1972) in, 335, 336; ends of strategy in, 297, 300–301, 311–312, 313; escalation of, 306–311, 314, 317, 320; failure of grand strategy in, 297, 311–312; flexible response policy in, 299; global and regional strategy in, 297, 298, 315–322; ground forces in, 309, 311, 332, 334, 335; Gulf of Tonkin crisis in, 298, 308, 617n49; honorable end to, 329; Mansfield on, 319; mining of Haiphong Harbor in, 333, 625n44; objectives of, 313, 315–316, 329, 618n73; Operation Linebacker II (1972) in, 335; pacification campaigns in, 312, 313; Paris negotiations on, 304, 330, 331–332, 623–624n32; Paris Peace Accords ending, 323; prestige of U.S. as concern in, 298, 305, 313–314, 318, 329, 330, 331; public opinion in U.S. on, 310, 330, 333, 334, 336; RAND report on, 330, 623n28; search-and-destroy tactics in, 310, 312; Soviet Union in, 320; Tet Offensive in, 298, 310–311; Vietnamization strategy of Nixon in, 328–336, 337, 351; withdrawal of troops from, 332, 333, 334, 339, 341, 342

Vincennes (USS), 48, 72

Vincent, John Carter, 216, 249, 252; and China policies, 254, 255, 256, 257, 259; and Japan policies, 263, 264; and Korea policies, 266; and Southeast Asia policies, 270, 271

Vinson, Carl, 113, 174, 181

Vinson Acts, 174, 178

vital interests, 2, 9, 187

Vogel, Ezra, 457, 468

Vulcans, as Bush (GWB) advisors, 484, 492, 500, 508, 509, 517, 669n22; on China, 485, 489; on India, 486, 490; on Japan, 487, 493; on Korea, 488

Wachusett (USS), 62, 68, 79

Wainwright, Jonathan, 196

Wakaizumi Kei, 343, 344

Wake Island, 89

Waldron, Arthur, 160

Walker, Robert, 34

Wallace, Henry A., 191

Walt, Stephen, 480–481

Wanghia, Treaty of (1844), 38, 43, 44–45; renegotiation of, 42, 43, 46

War, Peace, and Change (Dulles), 279

War of 1812, 18, 31, 80, 85

War or Peace (Dulles), 281

War on Terror, 427, 494, 500, 501–502, 503, 509

War Plan Orange, 8, 116, 131–136, 173, 174–177, 181, 204, 545; amphibious operations in, 142–143; island strategies in, 199; and MacArthur, 201; and Rainbow Plans, 177, 181, 199; and Royal Road plan, 174–175; and Washington Treaty System, 137, 142–143

Washington, George, 6, 21, 133

Washington Conference, 138–140

Washington Conference, The (Buell), 141

Washington Treaty System, 13, 116, 136–144, 151–152, 183, 186–187, 238; Dennett on, 142, 170; Grew on, 158; Hornbeck on, 158, 159, 161, 162, 163, 165, 167; legacies of, 149–150; MacMurray on, 158, 165, 167–168; nonfortification clause in, 137, 141, 142, 170, 174, 202, 577n104; Stimson on, 153; Vinson on, 174

Wasp (USS), 202

Watts, Bill, 334

Webster, Daniel, 33, 43, 53

Wedemeyer, Albert C., 257, 270, 271

Wei Jingsheng, 463

Weinberger, Caspar, 391, 403, 404–405

Welles, Sumner, 191, 229

Wen Jiabao, 496

Westmoreland, William, 242, 310, 311, 312

West Pakistan Alawi League, 358

whaling, 17, 18, 20, 23, 30, 48

Wheeler, Earle, 242, 333

white paper on China (1949), 258–261

Whitney, Mary Dorothy, 122

Wilde, Oscar, 74

Wilkes, Charles, 31, 72

Williams, William Appleman, 76

Wilson, Joan Hoff, 145, 148

Wilson, Woodrow, 123–131; Fourteen Points of, 128, 229, 234; idealism of, 185; MacMurray influenced by, 166; Roosevelt advice to, 112

Wilson administration, 116, 123–131; First World War during, 126, 128, 129–130; Hornbeck in, 159; Lamont in, 146; Open Door policy during, 123, 125, 126, 129–130, 183; policy inconsistencies during, 116, 185–186; Siberian intervention during, 127–128

Wisconsin School, 76, 234

Wolfowitz, Paul, 392, 393, 418, 484, 486, 508

Wood, Leonard, 134

Woodcock, Leonard, 370, 376

World Bank Group, 236

World Trade Organization: China in, 427, 472, 479; during Clinton administration, 461–462, 469, 472, 476, 477, 479

World War I. *See* First World War

World War II. *See* Second World War

Xi Jinping, 526–527, 542

Xinjiang, Soviet and Chinese clash in, 348, 349

Yahya Khan, 348

Yalta Conference (1945), 215–216, 220–222, 224, 232, 235, 253, 268

Yamagata Aritomo, 265

Yeh, George, 286

Yeutter, Clayton, 409

Yorktown (USS), 202
Yoshida Shigeru, 185, 281, 282, 290, 293
Young, Andrew, 365
Yuan Shikai, 121, 123, 125
Yugoslavia, 260, 269

Zakaria, Fareed, 76
Zhang Zuolin, 152

Zhao Ziyang, 398, 434
Zhou Enlai, 214, 332, 349–350, 352; and
    Shanghai Communiqué (1972), 352–354
Zhu Rongji, 472, 479
Zia al-Huk, 384
Zimmerman, Warren, 78
Zoellick, Robert, 431, 450, 484, 490, 497–498,
    502, 508, 511

CPSIA information can be obtained
at www.ICGtesting.com
Printed in the USA
LVHW040143100420
652856LV00002B/2

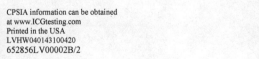

9 780231 180436